FOR REFERENCE

NOT TO BE TAKEN FROM THE ROOM

ENCYCLOPEDIA OF
NEW MEDIA

An Essential Reference to
Communication and Technology

ENCYCLOPEDIA OF
NEW MEDIA

STEVE JONES EDITOR

University of Illinois at Chicago

A Sage Reference Publication

SAGE Publications
International Educational and Professional Publisher
Thousand Oaks ▪ London ▪ New Delhi

Copyright © 2003 by The Moschovitis Group
339 Fifth Avenue; New York, New York 10016
www.mosgroup.com

SAGE REFERENCE

Publisher:	Rolf Janke
Executive Editor:	Margaret H. Seawell
Senior Development Editor:	Vince Burns

MOSCHOVITIS GROUP

Publisher:	Valerie Tomaselli
Executive Editor:	Hilary W. Poole
Associate Editor:	Sonja Matanovic
Editorial Assistant:	Jodi White
Design and Layout:	Annemarie Redmond
Production Assistant:	Rashida Allen
Copyediting:	Tavia Fortt
Proofreading:	Paul Scaramazza
Editorial Interns:	Nicole Cohen, John Lee
Index:	Barber Indexing

For information:
Sage Publications, Inc.
2455 Teller Road
Thousand Oaks, California 91320
Email: order@sagepub.com

Sage Publications Ltd.
6 Bonhill Street
London EC2A 4PU
United Kingdom

Sage Publications India Pvt. Ltd.
M-32 Market
Greater Kailash I
New Delhi 110 048 India

Printed in the United States of America

Library of Congress Cataloging-in-Publication Data

The Encyclopedia of new media / Steve Jones, editor.
    p. cm.
ISBN 0-7619-2382-9
1. Multimedia systems—Encyclopedias. 2. Digital media—Encyclopedias.
3. Communication—Encyclopedias. I. Jones, Steve, 1961–
QA76.575 .E5368 2003
302.23'4'03—dc21
   2002013229

02—03—04—05—06—10—9—8—7—6—5—4—3—2—1

Contents

List of Entries

A Reader's Guide

This list is provided to assist readers in finding articles on related topics. It classifies articles into 12 general thematic categories: Art, Music, and Performance; Business and Commerce; Cyberculture; Hacking; Legal Topics; Networks and Networking; Open-Source Software; Organizations and Labs; People; Social Issues; Technology; and Writing. Some article titles appear in more than one category.

ART, MUSIC, AND PERFORMANCE

Laurie Anderson
ASCII Art
CAVE
Computer Graphics
Computer Music
DeFanti, Thomas
Digital Art and Animation
Digital Audio
Digital Music
Brian Eno
Hypermedia
Interactive Television
Intermedia
Raymond Kurzweil
George Lucas
MIDI
Robert Moog
MP3
MPEG
Multimedia
Napster
Nam June Paik
Daniel Sandin
Streaming Media
Typography

BUSINESS AND COMMERCE

Amazon.com
Jeff Bezos
Business-to-Business
Stephen M. Case
Cookies
Customer Relationship
    Management
Digital Cash
Disintermediation

Peter Drucker
E-Commerce
William H. Gates, III
Harold Innis
Internet Service Providers
Steven P. Jobs
Knowledge Management
Local Area Network
Metrics
MP3.com
Napster
Narrowcasting
Jakob Nielsen
Personalization
Security
Telecommuting
Trademark
Video Conferencing
Margaret Whitman

CYBERCULTURE

Avatar
John Perry Barlow
Blog
CommuniTree
Convergence
Cyberculture
Cyberethics
Cyberfeminism
Cyberpunk
Cyberspace
Cyberwarfare
Esther Dyson
Electronic Civil Disobedience
Electronic Democracy
Electronic Frontier Foundation
Email

Emoticons
Gender and New Media
William Gibson
Habitat
Hacking, Cracking, and Phreaking
Hacktivism
Donna J. Haraway
Instant Messaging
Interactvity
Mitchell Kapor
Killer Application
LambdaMOO
"A Manifesto for Cyborgs"
Marshall McLuhan
Meme
Metrics
Nicholas Negroponte
Neuromancer
The New Hacker's Dictionary
Online Journalism
Peer-to-Peer
Race and Ethnicity and New
    Media
Howard Rheingold
The Soul of a New Machine
Bruce Sterling
Allucquère Rosanne Stone
Sherry Turkle
*Understanding Media: The
    Extensions of Man*
Virtual Community

HACKING

John Perry Barlow
CommuniTree
Computer Emergency Response
    Team

George Lucas
Pattie Maes
Marshall McLuhan
Marvin Minsky
Robert Moog
Hans Moravec
Nicholas Negroponte
Theodor Holm (Ted) Nelson
Jakob Nielsen
Nam June Paik
Seymour Papert
Eric Raymond
Howard Rheingold
Pamela Samuelson
Daniel Sandin
Claude Shannon
Richard Stallman
Bruce Sterling
Allucquère Rosanne Stone
Ivan Sutherland
Edward Tufte
Alan Turing
Sherry Turkle
Hal Varian
John von Neumann
Margaret Whitman

Social Issues

Access
Anonymity
Carnivore
Cyberethics
Cyberfeminism
Cyberwarfare
Digital Divide
Disposal of Computers
Education and Computers
Electronic Civil Disobedience
Electronic Democracy
Encryption and Cryptography
Gender and New Media
Hacking, Cracking, and Phreaking
Hacktivism
Obscenity
Patent
Privacy
Race and Ethnicity and New
    Media

Security
Spam
Technological Determinism
Universal Design
Virtual Community

Technology

ARPANET
Authoring Tools
Bluetooth
Broadband
Browser
Bulletin Board Systems
Carnivore
CAVE
CD-R, CD-ROM, and DVD
Cellular Telphony
Chat
Codec
Compression
Computer-Supported
    Collaborative Work
Content Filtering
Cookies
DeCSS
Desktop Video
Digital Asset Management
Digital Subscriber Line
Digital Television
Distributed Computing
Email
Emulation
Encryption and Cryptography
Expert Systems
Firewall
Flash
Graphical User Interface
Habitat
HyperCard
Hypermedia
Hypertext
Instant Messaging
Interactive Television
Internet
Internet Appliances
Internet Relay Chart
Java
Linux

Local Area Network
Markup Languages
MIDI
Minitel
MP3
MPEG
Object-Oriented Programming
Optical Character Recognition
Optical Computing and Networking
Peer-to-Peer
Personal Digital Assistants
Photoshop
Qube
Robotics
Satellite Networks
Shockwave
Short Messaging System
Sketchpad
Software Agents
Streaming Media
Telecommuting
Telephony
vBNS
Videoconferencing
Videotex
Virus
Wireless Application Protocol
Wireless Networks
World Wide Web

Writing

"As We May Think"
"The Cathedral and the Bazaar"
Cyberpunk
Electronic Publishing
Emoticons
William Gibson
Hypertext
Michael Joyce
"Man-Computer Symbiosis"
"A Manifesto for Cyborgs"
Neuromancer
The New Hacker's Dictionary
The Soul of a New Machine
Bruce Sterling
2600: The Hacker Quarterly
*Understanding Media: The
    Extensions of Man*

Introduction

What is new media? There is no single answer to be given. Even old media were once new, to borrow Carolyn Marvin's observation, and new media are constantly changing and evolving. In truth, the question itself is a shorthand way of asking more than one thing (one might call it "multi-asking"). Those who pose it usually want to know the history of new media, its present outlines, and perhaps most importantly, what it will be like in the future.

The *Encyclopedia of New Media* is the first attempt to comprehensively map the current terrain. Taken together, the encyclopedia's entries constitute an attempt to map the constellation of new media. Particular technologies and artifacts are important; compact discs, the World Wide Web, streaming media, for instance, are of enormous importance to the way new media have developed and have had enormous impacts. At least as important as the "things" of new media is the context in which they are invented and used. A significant portion of the encyclopedia, therefore, examines concepts, contexts, and trends. What is the history of virtual reality? Where did MP3 come from? Who is Douglas Engelbart? Why do these topics matter, what significance do they have in this day and age? Those are the kinds of questions the encyclopedia answers, in clear, jargon-free language.

Taken as a whole, the entries in the *Encyclopedia of New Media* tell us much about where we have been, where we are, and where we are going with new media. The encyclopedia collects information about numerous people, places, ideas, and things that connect to new media. Of course, as is always the case, some information has been left out. The selection criteria were necessarily subjective but deliberately broad, careful but not definitive. The goal was to provide a useful reference source for those interested in specific topics related to new media. One may also view the encyclopedia as a chronicle, in broad strokes, of the past and present state of new media developments. To read it through, cover-to-cover, is to immerse oneself in the world of new media and gain an understanding of its history and significance in everyday life.

THE OLD AND THE NEW

To some degree it may seem odd that the encyclopedia covers a good deal of ground when it comes to the history of new media. After all, one might think, what's new about new forms of media is that they are new. However, history is critically important if we are to understand what makes them new. Simply put, new media do not come to us full-blown from the heads of engineers, marketers, programmers, and artists. They come from media before them, from the experiences we and others have had with old and new media that inform our thinking about the artifacts and relationships we build and, most importantly, imagine building. Marshall McLuhan noted that the content of a medium is usually taken from another medium, and in the case of new media, content typically comes from old media before it. Our understanding of new media comes largely from looking into the "rear-view mirror," as McLuhan observed. We are hard pressed to know new media in any way but by comparing it to the media that preceded it, and therefore our understanding of what we might term "not-so-new" media, of new media's precursors, matters a great deal (hence an entry for ARPANET as well as for Internet).

We will continue to use "old" media as we develop the new, as this encyclopedia itself proves. Handing someone a book when they ask me "What is 'new media'?" seems unlikely to entirely satisfy their curiosity but I believe it is a start. If they open the pages and begin reading it, as you have, it will be immediately clear that the only good answer to the question derives from an understanding of history, technology, and society in combination. To ask, "What is new media?" and to expect a succinct answer is akin to asking, "What is television?" and expecting to be able to read a summary of television's myriad technological and social impacts on the side of a box of cereal. Is new media television, or is it a computer? Is it a telephone line, a fiber-optic cable, or a wireless data link? It is all of these, and more.

The future, to paraphrase William Gibson, is here; it just is not widely distributed yet. As we were completing this encyclopedia, I ran out of shelf space for the ten years' worth of *Wired* magazines I have in my office. It was an astonishing thing—the one periodical that had defined a popular vision of new media had continued its run for ten years, from thin issues to thick ones and back again to skinny, from new media to old. Like the old adage about the ups and downs of Wall Street correlating with hemlines, I suspect we could chart the interest in, and dissemination of, information about new media by looking at the number of pages in each issue of *Wired*.

What we would also find is, in a manner of speaking, the future as we thought it would be. The cover of volume one, issue one of *Wired*, for example, touts as its feature story "Bruce Sterling Has Seen the Future of War." In the story Sterling describes the U.S. military's technological preparations based on its experiences during the Gulf War. Still, Sterling's description is not of the future, it is of the present, of 1992 and the engineering and technology being imagined for the future. What we do not find in the story, or from leafing through back issues of *Wired*, is perspective. While Sterling may have known what types of scenarios were being imagined by the military, he could not have known that the United States would be fighting a war in Afghanistan ten years later and what the outcome of using technology might be—and the U.S. military did not know it either.

In contrast, the *Encyclopedia of New Media* considers the connections between new media developments over a lengthy history, to explain the origins of ideas and technologies. New media may well grow old, but media of the past 200 years have not died, and in a sense have not grown old. They have been recreated, re-engineered, revised and re-mediated. Like artists and musicians who cannot escape some form of influence by those before them, new media perpetuate the old.

Indeed, an encyclopedia is itself not a very new medium. While the ancient Greeks are known to have originated the concept of an encyclopedia, a comprehensive study or "circle of knowledge" (from the Greek *Enkylios-paideia*), it is generally agreed that the first printed encyclopedias appeared in the 16th century (the first possibly being Paul Scalic's *Encyclopaedia: seu orbis disciplinarium, tum sacrarum quam prophanum epistemon*, printed in 1559). Diderot's famed *Encyclopedie* dates to the age of the Enlightenment, and the *Encyclopedia Britannica* came into being in 18th-century Scotland.

However, it was not until the early 1900s that standards—such as alphabetization, bibliographies, indices, cross-referencing, and illustrations—became the norm. Perhaps coincidentally, that is the time that we began to see the spread of media into everyday life in the United States and Europe. It is fitting that we have made another turn in the circle of knowledge with publication of the *Encyclopedia of New Media*, assessing the state of our newest media through use of one of our most venerable and deep-rooted media, the encyclopedia.

In closing, I wish to acknowledge the people whose lives, work, and ideas are represented herein. It is they who keep the circle of knowledge revolving. And I wish to thank the contributors whose effort, knowledge and patience made my task an easy one. What made it easiest was the help of Jodi White who, as assistant editor, kept work on-track and organized. Hilary Poole, Valerie Tomaselli, and Sonja Matanovic at the Moschovitis Group shepherded the encyclopedia and provided guidance and inspiration. Margaret Seawell is a terrific editor and colleague who helped put the encyclopedia into perspective and into motion. Jack Drag and Mick Black provided additional perspective—and respite. Many members of the Association of Internet Researchers have been most generous with their advice, with information, and with their time. Finally, my students and colleagues at the University of Illinois at Chicago, particularly those in the Department of Communication and in the Electronic Visualization Lab, have helped me understand how new media work, where they come from, and how they are developing, for which I am most grateful.

— *Steve Jones*

Access

Access to new-media services is a multifaceted concept. Definitions of access have changed over time as new-media services have developed. The tenets of "universal service" were grounded in U.S. telecommunications policy, and with the advent of networked information and communication technologies (ICTs), these goals are being reconceptualized.

The goal of U.S. telecommunications policy is universal service, which posits that all Americans should have access to affordable telephone service. A commonly used measure of success in achieving universal service is telephone penetration—the percentage of all U.S. households that have a telephone on the premises. In the United States, approximately 94 percent of households have telephone service. Therefore, basic telephone service has not achieved universality, since approximately 6 percent of all Americans lack such service; this represents about 5.6 million households, or 14.8 million people. One of the characteristics of those with low penetration rates is residence in either inner cities or rural areas; they tend to be the young, the transient, and visible minorities.

The universal service concept dates back to 1907, when Theodore Vail, president of AT&T, used the term in reference to his desire to interconnect the fragmented local telephone companies into a unified national system. The Communications Act of 1934 directed the Federal Communications Commission (FCC) to make available an efficient and nationwide wire and radio network. Universal service has been achieved through application of cross-subsidies, made possible through the regulated monopoly scheme of the telephone industry. The Telecommunications Act of 1996 expanded the concept of universal service to consider such advanced services as the Internet. Public policy is thus striving to decrease the digital divide through a variety of funding mechanisms and regulatory schemes.

Access to ICTs implies an extension of the sensibility of POTS (plain old telephone service) in telephony,

which is rooted in the notion that people living in outlying rural areas should get the same basic telephone service as those living in more densely populated locales. In other words, the same level of service will be offered at an equivalent cost, regardless of location. Despite this reliance on geographic markers as a component of access, the implication has been that access to voice telephony is an essential ingredient for stitching together communities and the nation; and that access to basic services such as emergency 911 and operator assistance is a vital social utility that should be available to all citizens.

Access to the networked information infrastructure involves an overlapping mixture of technical, economic, and social infrastructures. Technical factors include carriage facilities (those that store, serve, or carry information, such as telephone, cable, Internet, satellite, and wireless transmission), physical devices (such as telephone terminal equipment, modems, cable modems, personal digital assistants, and Net PCs, and Web TVs), and software tools (including browsers, e-mailers, search engines, authoring and editing tools, groupware). Also key is the content and services that people find useful, such as telephone enhancements, the Web, and email. Content and services need to be affordable, reliable, usable, diverse, secure, and privacy-enhancing.

Social aspects of the infrastructure include services and access provision—the organizations that provide network services and access to users, including employers, educational institutions, Internet Service Providers (ISPs), telephone companies, community networks, and other community organizations. Literacy and social facilitation—the skills people need to take full advantage of ICTs—are crucial. Acquiring these skills is largely a social process, involving a combination of formal and informal methods within the context of supportive learning environments. The means of acquiring network skills need to be affordable, readily available, attuned to the learners' varied life situations, and sensitive to language, cultural, and gender differences. And finally, the central challenge of governance—how decisions are made concerning the development and operation of ICTs—is to foster a democratic system that allows all ICT stakeholders to participate equitably in policymaking.

Various stakeholders and different sectors conceptualize universal access issues differently. Generally, industry representatives define access as elimination of barriers, so that they can deliver services to provide profits and market share. Government representatives see themselves as facilitators, rather than as members of an official body that could and should set universal access goals. Additionally, government is concerned with individual programs (such as various community access grants), which will provide examples to the private sector and perhaps lead to the further commoditization of government services. In contrast, the public-interest sector has been attempting to provide a broader vision of society and democracy, and promotes universal access as a public good.

Achieving consensus on the fundamental values surrounding universal access among the different stakeholders of national and global information infrastructures is a major challenge. Although it is generally agreed that access to networks and services should be equitable, affordable, and ubiquitous, it is also recognized that access will depend on many different physical, technical, and economic factors. In addition, different communities will define access in different ways. For instance, schoolchildren will probably not need the same high bandwidth as that required by researchers in medical imaging. The disabled community will need special features to aid in accessing information that the able-bodied community takes for granted. And, different individuals and groups will demand access to, and the creation of, their own idiosyncratic information content.

Access to ICTs has been found to be inequitable for various communities. Inequities have been found to be based upon different education, class, and income levels, and exist most often among the disabled, visible minorities, and residents of inner-city and rural communities. These various digital divides have been the focus of much recent policy attention.

Public access has been championed by various public interest organizations, particularly in North America, who have been advocating that the information infrastructure maintain a vital public sphere. They contend that universal access to basic network services should be seen as an elemental component of citizen's rights in an information society, where effective citizenship depends on assuring that all citizens can create, and have access to, the content they need for active participation in their local communities and in their more global communities of interest.

Will access to new-media services improve or deteriorate in the near future? Technological developments create a paradox: While computer and Web interfaces may become more user-friendly, such developments may also impose a higher learning curve that could limit new users. And as hardware and software costs decrease, more people will be able to afford new-media services; but will they wish to partake of these services? If access to new-media services and content is a prerequisite for democratic participation in society, then governments should be vigilant about enforcing universal-service mechanisms, particularly for those in society that are at risk of being left behind. Whether this happens will depend on both political forces and citizen initiatives.

Bibliography

Anderson, Robert H.; Bikson, Tora K.; Law, Sally Ann; and Bridger M. Mitchell. *Universal Access to E-Mail: Feasibility and Societal Implications.* Santa Monica, Calif.: Rand Corporation, 1995. <http://www.rand.org/publications/MR/MR650/> (May 10, 2002).

Clement, Andrew, and Leslie Regan Shade. "The Access Rainbow: Conceptualizing Universal Access to the Information/Communication Infrastructure." *Community Informatics: Enabling Communities with Information and Communications Technologies.* Edited by Michael Gurstein, ed. Hershey, Pa.: Idea Group Publishing, 2000; pp. 32–51.

Kahin, Brian, and James Keller, eds. *Public Access to the Internet.* Cambridge, Mass.: MIT Press, 1995.

Further Reading

The Benton Foundation. Communications Policy & Practice. October 2001. <http://www.benton.org/cpphome.html> (May 10, 2002).

Computer Professionals for Social Responsibility; Woodbury, Marsha. The National Information Infrastructure (Internet). "One Planet, One Net: CPSR's 1998–99 Campaign on Internet Governance." July 1998. <http://www.cpsr.org/program/nii/nii.html> (May 10, 2002).

Maxwell, Christine, ed., on behalf of The Internet Society (<http://www.isoc.org>). "Global Trends that Will Impact Universal Access to Information Resources." Submitted to UNESCO, July 15, 2000. <http://www.isoc.org/isoc/unesco-paper.shtml> (May 10, 2002).

Related Topics

Digital Divide; Gender and New Media; Race and Ethnicity and New Media; Universal Design; Usability

— *Leslie Regan Shade*

Agents See Software Agents.

Amazon.com

Amazon.com is one of the most well-known and successful Internet startup companies. Beginning as an online bookstore and expanding into other areas of online retail, Amazon.com pioneered several key features of online shopping, or what is now called e-commerce.

Amazon.com was founded in 1995 by Jeff Bezos. After doing research into the possibilities of Internet commerce, Bezos decided a bookseller was an ideal concept for an online retailer. While other industries had relatively successful mail-order businesses, mail-order books had always been difficult because of the sheer number of titles in print. A mail-order catalogue that even approached the number of books in print would have been about the size of an urban telephone book and too expensive to mail.

Bezos' concept was that an online bookseller could take advantage of the ability of computers and the Internet to process vast amounts of data. Where mail-order and "bricks and mortar" bookstores could provide only a small number of the books in print at any given time, Amazon could provide access to the entire list, online, and without many of the overhead costs of traditional bookselling. For instance, in order to grow significantly, a traditional chain of booksellers needs to open new stores. This involves acquiring the land, building the stores, training and hiring employees, and maintaining additional inventory. An Internet book-store can grow simply by attracting more users to its site and adjusting its inventory accordingly. Amazon offers a searchable list of over 3.1 million books, more than 15 times that of any physical bookstore, and without much of the overhead. Though Amazon incurred high initial costs in editorial staff, software, and hardware, their long-terms costs would, in theory, be lower than those of a traditional bookseller.

Using software developed by programmer Shel Kaphan, Amazon.com went online in July 1995. Its user interface was as important as its business concept. From the beginning, Amazon's Web site loaded quickly and was easy to use. It patented a "1-click" buying option, which meant that customers could buy anything on the site with a single mouse-click once they had provided basic purchasing information such as name, shipping address, and payment method.

Amazon pioneered a number of other strategies for online retailing. In order to make its site more attractive, and to foster repeat business, Amazon hired teams of writers and editors to provide commentary on items the company had for sale, and to create lists of suggested purchases. Amazon also allowed users to provide commentary of their own, resulting in high levels of user participation, then added a Listmania feature that allows users to create public lists of their favorite items by category. Shoppers can also keep a wish list of items they'd like to purchase at a future time, and Amazon automatically recommends new items based on a shopper's previous purchases. Amazon was the first commerce site to use this "collaborative filtering" technology.

By 1997, Amazon was a significant player in the retail book market, pulling in larger revenues per employee than massive and established competitors Barnes and Noble, Borders, and B. Dalton, although still trailing in overall sales. After an initial public offering in 1997, Amazon's stock prices soared during the dot-com stock market boom of the late 1990s. Bezos was named *Time* magazine's Man of the Year in 1999, and Amazon was cast as a model of a successful Internet business.

But as with many other Internet startups, investors gambled on future profitability rather than basing stock prices on actual profits. After the stock plummeted in the spring of 2001, Amazon accepted a $100 million infusion from media conglomerate AOL/Time Warner to continue its expansion, in exchange for licensing some of its e-commerce software to the conglomerate. Amazon turned its first profit—more than $5 million—in the fourth quarter of 2001, after losing over $2.8 billion since its 1995 founding.

Amazon was also a testing ground for labor organizing in the "new economy." Arguing that their wages were too low for the cost of living in Seattle and dissatisfied with their available benefits (which included flagging stock options), a group of employees affiliated with the Communication Workers of America and began organizing a union in the fall of 2000. Because of Amazon's already-high visibility, the union campaign attracted a great deal of attention in the press.

Shortly before there was to be a union election in early 2001, Amazon closed down its 400-person Seattle customer-service facility (where the election was to be held) and moved its operations to India. Citing the need to streamline its operations, Amazon also closed several other facilities, laying off about

1,300 employees. Management initially offered financial incentives to lay off Seattle employees for signing a "nondisparagement" contract, but backed off after the contract became the subject of public controversy. Today, Amazon remains a company without unions.

Amazon's goal is to expand into as many areas of online retailing as possible. Its reasoning is that it will be easier to penetrate markets earlier, rather than waiting to turn a profit in one market before going to the next. In 1998, Amazon began selling compact discs, video tapes, and video games, adding toys and electronic products in 1999. It has since expanded into a wide range of retail areas, including car accessories, cell phones and service agreements, baby goods, cameras and photography equipment, computers, travel services, health and beauty items, and kitchen goods.

Amazon's gamble is that its name recognition will help it garner additional sales in these new areas, but it also faces some challenges. While distribution in the book industry is heavily centralized, this is not the case in many of the other areas where Amazon hopes to grow—many of which also have already-established online retailers. Still, the brand name seems to be effective: In its first quarter of operation, the music division outgrossed established online competitor CDNOW.

Regardless of its ultimate success, Amazon had an almost two-year head-start on software that handles millions of transactions and shapes shoppers' Web experiences to their personal idiosyncrasies. Whether Amazon.com continues to turn a profit in the long run depends on whether it can pull enough money out of already-thin retail profit margins.

Bibliography

"About Amazon.com." Company Information. 1996–2002. <http://www.amazon.com/exec/obidos/subst/misc/company-info.html> (May 24, 2002).

Hansell, Saul. "AOL Invests $100 Million in Amazon." *New York Times,* July 24, 2001, p. C1.

_____. "A Surprise from Amazon: Its First Profit." *New York Times,* January 23, 2002, p. C4.

Helft, Miguel. "Campaign for Unionization at Amazon Intensifies." *InfoWorld,* November 23, 2000. <http://www.infoworld.com/articles/hn/xml/00/11/23/001123hnamazon.xml> (May 24, 2002).

Hof, Robert D., with Ellen Neuborne and Heather Green. "Amazon.com: The Wild World of E-Commerce." *BusinessWeek,* December 14, 1998. <http://www.businessweek.com/1998/50/covstory.htm> (May 24, 2002).

Krantz, Michael. "Inside Amazon's Culture: The Inner Workings and Workers." *Time,* December 27, 1999.
<http://www.time.com/time/poy/amazon.html> (May 24, 2002).

Quittner, Joshua. "The Background and Influences that Made Bezos the Multi-Billion Dollar Champion of E-Tailing." *Time,* December 27, 1999. <http://www.time.com/time/poy/bezos.html> (May 24, 2002).

Further Reading

Saunders, Rebecca. *Business the Amazon.com Way: Secrets of the World's Most Astonishing Web Business.* Dover, N.H.: Capstone, 1999.

Spector, Robert. *Amazon.com—Get Big Fast: Inside the Revolutionary Business Model That Changed the World.* New York: HarperBusiness, 2000.

Williamson, Duncan. "Amazon.com: A Brief History and Analysis." May 2001. <http://duncanwil.co.uk/pdfs/amazoncase.pdf> (May 24, 2002).

Related Topics

Customer Relationship Management; E-Commerce; Interface; Search Engine; World Wide Web

— *Jonathan Sterne*

Anderson, Laurie
1947–

Performance Artist

American performance artist and "techno-storyteller" Laurie Anderson has long been recognized as a pioneer of new media in the arts. Embracing everything from voice-altering Vocoders in the 1970s to CD-ROMs and the Internet in the 1990s, Anderson has consistently been active in groundbreaking creative media. Yet beneath her love of technology lies the profound conviction that it is people who make art, not corporate society or machines.

Born in Chicago on June 5, 1947, Laurie Anderson was a keen violinist as a child, and played with the Chicago Symphony Orchestra for several years. Doubting she could make the grade as a professional, however, she gave up at the age of 16 and began studying library science instead. Majoring in art history, she graduated *magna cum laude* from Barnard in 1969 before earning a master's in sculpture from Columbia University in 1972. Later she taught art history at colleges in New York City, coloring her lectures with improvised fantasy stories, which she now admits "had nothing to do with anything I'd ever read in art history books."

Frequently described as "experimental," "avant-garde," or just plain "quirky," Anderson was interested

Laurie Anderson. (Neal Preston/CORBIS)

in marrying art and technology—however crude—right from the start. Her first performance piece, *Automotive*, which premiered in 1972, was a symphony of car drivers honking their horns and slamming their doors. In her 1973 work *O-Range*, megaphones were used to shout stories across an empty sports stadium. In 1974, she invented her "self-playing violin" (with internal audio speaker). A partnership with audio engineer Bob Bielecki spawned other unusual instruments, including the 1975 Viophonograph (a violin mounted on a record turntable that moves the bow) and the 1976 tape-bow violin (which she plays by passing a prerecorded audio tape, strung across a bow, over a tape player's audio heads, which are mounted in place of the violin strings). Around the same time, Anderson began to experiment with Super-8 film, the inexpensive forerunner of amateur video, for recording her stories and songs. A true multimedia artist long before the term was invented, she was soon producing photography, stories and songs, and installations, as well as the performance pieces for which she

is perhaps still best known, touring widely throughout the United States and Europe.

At the end of the 1970s, Anderson's piece *Americans on the Move*, a 90-minute meditation on transportation, involved her first use of a voice-altering synthesizer called a Vocoder. Along with the Synclavier, the first sound-sampling synthesizer, the Vocoder featured prominently in her later works, including the apocalyptic talking opera *United States*. This work included a haunting, hypnotic, eight-minute song called "O Superman," released in 1981 as a single by Warner Brothers; it became an international hit record and rose to number two in the British pop charts, later appearing on Anderson's *Big Science* album.

Sudden fame gave Anderson the opportunity to develop *United States* into a four-part eight-hour work, which she performed throughout Europe and the United States in 1983. She recorded and toured extensively for the remainder of the decade, and she also collaborated with a number of artists noted for their creative use of technology, including English musicians Peter Gabriel and Brian Eno, with whom she planned to build a theme park in Spain.

During the 1990s, the world of high technology finally caught up with the world of Laurie Anderson. "Multimedia" was the new buzzword; for artists such as Anderson who had been working in multiple media for two decades, it offered both a unified description of a broad body of work and a creative range of new opportunities. Widely reported as a "multimedia extravaganza," Anderson's 1995 tour *The Nerve Bible* was sponsored by a CD-ROM company and involved some 35 tons of equipment, including huge back-projection screens, her trademark violins, and an electronic bodysuit attached to a drum synthesizer that made noises as she danced about. But behind the techno-gadgetry, Anderson's trademark integration of playful storytelling and haunting social observation remained much in evidence; quirky jokes included an observation about the Vatican "being bought out by Microsoft."

The year 1995 also saw the release of Anderson's first CD-ROM, the award-winning *Puppet Motel*, through whose 31 rooms users can roam, exploring various unusual aspects of the performer's mind. Anderson's most recent works include the stage work *Songs and Stories from Moby Dick* (1999) and a musical biography of American aviator Amelia Earhart, which premiered at Carnegie Hall in February 2000. She continues to pioneer technological gadgetry, including the Talking Stick, a wireless sampler shaped like a digeridoo, and a customized cordless violin with MIDI interface designed by renowned electric instrument maker Ned Steinberger.

Laurie Anderson's 30-year career offers one way of putting technology into perspective. In contrast to computer pioneers who repeatedly put the technological cart before the social horse, touting innovations with no thought of social implications, Anderson's work emphasizes technology as a creative tool, which people can use or abuse. But technology *per se* is neither good nor bad: "Obviously you'd never pick up a pencil and say 'This is evil,'" Anderson has observed, "But people say that about technology." Moreover, technology is no substitute for creativity: "I think it's important that artists begin to think along other lines than just expanding techno things." However, she readily concedes that this becomes harder all the time: "The thing that scares me is that every day technology is getting more global, corporate, monolithic and impossible to escape."

Selected Works

Anderson, Laurie. *Big Science*. Burbank, Calif.: Warner Bros, 1982.

———. *Mister Heartbreak*. Burbank, Calif.: Warner Bros., 1984.

———. *Home of the Brave*. Burbank, Calif.: Warner Bros., 1986.

———. *Strange Angels*. Burbank, Calif.: Warner Bros., 1989.

———. *Talk Normal: The Laurie Anderson Anthology*. Wea/ Rhino, 2000.

Bibliography

Goldberg, RoseLee. *Laurie Anderson*. New York: Harry N. Abrams, 2000.

Howell, John. *Laurie Anderson*. New York: Thunder's Mouth Press, 1992; Emeryville, Calif.: distributed by Publishers Group West, 1992.

Further Reading

Anderson, Laurie. *Stories from the Nerve Bible: A Twenty-Year Retrospective*. New York: HarperCollins, 1994.

Related Topics

Digital Music; Eno, Brian; MIDI; Multimedia

— *Chris Woodford*

Andreessen, Marc
1971–

Co-Founder, Netscape

Marc Andreessen is best known for creating the prototype Mosaic, the first graphical browser used for accessing the World Wide Web. Mosaic and its successor, Netscape Navigator, were important innovations in Internet history, and helped popularize the World Wide Web early in its existence.

Andreessen was born in a small town in Wisconsin to parents Pat, a customer-service rep at Lands' End, and Lowell, a sales manager for a seed company. In the fifth grade, Andreessen taught himself computer programming from a book. A year later, he used a computer in his school library to write a calculation program with which to do his math homework; unfortunately, the program was deleted that very night, when the school janitor turned off the power to the building. Soon afterward, his parents bought Andreessen a Commodore 64 computer, and he started programming in earnest.

After high school, Andreessen went on to study computer science at the University of Illinois at Urbana-Champaign, and took a part-time job writing Unix code for the National Center for Supercomputing Applications (NCSA) for $6.85 an hour. There, he and another NCSA programmer, Eric Bina, wrote a program designed to make accessing the World Wide Web easy. Until then, using the Web meant typing in arcane lines of UNIX code and textual commands. Andreessen and Bina's program, which they called Mosaic, allowed users to "point and click" on a graphical user interface (GUI), a process most of us take for granted today. The innovative program utilized the hyperlink, which allowed users to access files and documents by clicking on underlined, colored links rather than typing in reference numbers, and it enabled image files to be incorporated into the Web page itself. The program was a huge success; when NCSA made the free Mosaic browser available in January 1993, it logged two million downloads within its first year.

Mosaic was written in about six weeks, on weekends and at night. However, because Andreessen and Bina were university employees when they wrote the program, Mosaic was the property of the University of Illinois. When Andreessen graduated in 1994 with a B.S. in computer science, he left the Midwest and headed out to Silicon Valley, where a healthy computer culture was in full swing. He was in the area for only a few weeks before he received an email from Silicon Graphics, Inc., founder Jim Clark regarding the possibility of starting a technology company. Clark's original idea was to use the browser as an interface for an inexpensive interactive TV system, but Andreessen convinced Clark that the Internet, with its millions of potential users, was a more lucrative opportunity.

The two recruited Bina and a few other programmers from NSCA, and with Jim Barksdale on board as CEO, they founded Mosaic Communication Corporation in 1994. Their goal was to build a better, more secure version of Mosaic, to be distributed free of charge and thus create a large user base. The program had to be rewritten from the bottom up; no code created at NSCA could be re-used. Even so, the University of Illinois charged them with stealing the product. The company changed its name to Netscape Communications Corporation, and reached a financial settlement with the university.

Netscape's early years were golden. By 1996, 75 percent of all Web users used Netscape Navigator as their browser. The company grew quickly, both in employees and revenues; by 1996, it was generating $100 million annually. However, Microsoft and other software companies began competing for browser users, and Netscape's share of the browser market suffered drastically as a result; by 2001, its user base had dwindled to a mere 13 percent of the browser market. Netscape's downfall was blamed on multiple factors, including its pricing structure, failure to capitalize on traffic to its download pages, poor management, and the power of Microsoft.

In early 1999, America Online acquired Netscape Communications, and Andreessen joined AOL as Chief Technology Officer. Only months later, however, he resigned from AOL, and began putting together a new company called Loudcloud with an impressive group of Internet technology superstars. Andreessen now serves as Loudcloud's chairman. The company automates the process of building and maintaining Web sites, with an emphasis on reducing security flaws, downtime, and cost. Based on its vision and the past accomplishments of its founders, some expect Loudcloud to revolutionize the way in which Web sites are created and maintained.

Bibliography

Griffin, Scott. "Internet Pioneers: Marc Andreessen." Ibiblio.org. <http://www.ibiblio.org/pioneers/andreessen.html> (May 24, 2002).

Massachusetts Institute of Technology. "Internet Browser Technology." January 2001. <http://web.mit.edu/invent/www/inventorsA-H/andreessen=bina.html> (May 24, 2002).

Sheff, David. "Crank It Up." *Wired 8.08*, August 2000. <http://www.wired.com/wired/archive/8.08/loudcloud.html> (May 24, 2002).

Wagner, Douglas, for Jones International. "Marc Andreessen: Co-founder of Netscape." *Jones Telecommunications and Multimedia Encyclopedia*. 2000. <http://www.digitalcentury.com/encyclo/update/andreess.htm> (May 24, 2002).

Further Reading

Allison, David K. "Excerpts from an Oral History Interview with Marc Andreessen." Smithsonian Institution Oral and Video Histories, June 1995. <http://www.americanhistory.si.edu/csr/comphist/ma1.html> (May 24, 2002).

Segaller, Stephen. *Nerds 2.0.1: A Brief History of the Internet*. New York: TV Books, 1998.

Related Topics

Browser; Graphical User Interface; World Wide Web

— *Nicole Ellison*

Anonymity

Anonymity is the quality of being unknown or unacknowledged. In the digital age, primarily among

Internet users, anonymity is perceived as a right, even as a necessity for the preservation of free speech.

There have always been writers and artists who have published anonymously. Scribes using the pseudonym "Publius" wrote and published *The Federalist* papers, on which the U.S. Constitution was patterned. But on the Internet, the first medium to place publishing in the hands of almost any individual, anonymous communication is often motivated by concerns that are far different from those that drove Alexander Hamilton, John Jay, and James Madison to hide their identities while writing in 1787.

People seek online anonymity for many reasons. Perhaps they dabble occasionally in online pornography, and prefer that their neighbors never know of it. Maybe they employ stinging wit to deliver sharp, frequent rebukes of email discussion-list participants. Or they could be whistleblowers who would face the loss of their careers if anyone were to learn that they've posted damning accusations about their companies to an online bulletin board, or emailed such material to a journalist. Or perhaps they are political dissidents in exile, communicating with other exiles under assumed names on Usenet, who would face prosecution or execution at the hands of dictatorial regimes should their names be revealed.

Anonymity and privacy are sometimes confused; though intertwined, they denote different concepts. Privacy is a kind of contract between parties. The online shopper, for instance, may divulge credit-card and other personal information on the condition that the e-retailer won't sell it without permission. Patients searching for information on a medical Web site want assurances that their search queries won't be sold to a health-insurance company. These are privacy concerns.

Those who seek anonymity online however, generally are not seeking the protection of a limited social contract. Rather, they want their identities to remain undisclosed even as they seek to make their feelings, thoughts, schemes, and outrages public.

A number of commercially available technologies have emerged that attempt to protect anonymity online, and they illustrate the types of anonymity that Web users seek. Subscription products like "Anonymizer" guarantee anonymous, secure Web browsing by keeping online activity invisible to site administrators, marketers, Internet service providers, co-workers, or anyone else. Anonymous remailers, meanwhile, are computers connected to the Internet that forward email to other addresses on the network,

stripping away identifying headers from messages to make it nearly impossible to trace a post's origins anywhere except back to the remailer itself. The Onion Routing research project, meanwhile, is building an Internet-based network system that attempts to resist traffic analyses, eavesdropping, and attacks from Internet routers while preventing online users from knowing who is communicating with whom.

There are a number of barriers to anonymity online. Attacks on the network, for instance, can prove insurmountable. A Finnish anonymous remailer called Penet.fi was the longest-running service of its kind as of the mid-1990s. But "mail bombers" (harassers sending quantities of redundant emails) and "spammers" sending bulk email forced administrator Julf Helsingius to close the site down permanently in 1996. A related barrier is the fear felt by system administrators, who often oppose the use of their sites as anonymity servers because they fear being taken to task if acts such as electronic terrorism, defamation, or other crimes are facilitated through anonymous messages passing through their pipelines.

For Ian Clarke, founder of the Freenet online information exchange, anonymity is the only assurance a free society has that speech can ever truly be free. "Freenet is a forum for free speech," Clarke told *Newsbytes* in 2001. "Anonymity is essential for free speech, because if you cannot remain anonymous, then you can be punished for what you say, thus discouraging others from putting forward their opinions. For true freedom of speech, anonymity is absolutely essential."

But author Esther Dyson argues that while Internet anonymity is legitimate and should never be outlawed, it also has a dark, destructive side and should not be openly encouraged by the Internet community. On balance, Dyson writes, it is better for Internet community members to be recognizable and held accountable for their words and deeds, rather than seeking to create a secret society whose inhabitants need not fear identification and can say anything they like—however scurrilous or untrue—without having to face the balancing repercussion of community ostracism.

Anonymity has proven to be one of the thorniest areas of Internet social policy. In the past five years, there has been a blizzard of lawsuits, many brought by people who have been offended by the critical statements of anonymous online writers. In 1997, the Austrian government asked for the disclosure of the identity of an Anonymizer subscriber, who apparently was Austrian, because the writer allegedly had broken

Austrian laws against Nazi propaganda. The head of San Diego-based Anonymizer refused to comply without a U.S. court order mandating it.

But the United States, despite its First Amendment protections, is no safe haven for online anonymity. It took a 1997 federal appeals court decision, for instance, to invalidate a 1996 Georgia statute that criminalized all anonymous and pseudonymous Internet communications. That reversal did not end the debate, though: The number of anti-anonymity lawsuits has been mounting in the United States during the past few years.

Most of these suits (*Erik Hvide vs. John Does, Philip Services Corp. vs. America Online, AnswerThink vs. John Does*) revolve around anonymous postings to bulletin boards or other Web message centers, in which anonymous writers have lambasted companies or individuals in a manner that is considered defamatory. For example, an anonymous poster called Aqua_Cool 2000 had been using Yahoo!'s message boards to criticize the company AnswerThink. Bowing to legal pressure from AnswerThink, Yahoo! gave the company Aqua_Cool 2000's private information; Aqua_Cool 2000 retaliated by filing suit against Yahoo!

While Internet users are free to hide their names in emails, chat rooms, and message boards, court orders almost invariably force ISPs to release anonymity-seeking subscribers' names and personal information. In November 2000, *USA Today* reporter Will Rodger wrote about "a flood of litigation aimed at piercing the anonymity of online critics." America Online reported that it had received some 475 civil subpoenas in 2000 alone asking the company to reveal anonymous users. The flood Rodger described is still waist deep.

Resolutions may be forthcoming. In 2001, the American Civil Liberties Union, with help from the Electronic Frontier Foundation, was working on a pair of cases, one involving a company seeking to force disclosure of an online critic and another in which an online-politics site publisher was being pursued by an appeals court justice who had been criticized by the publication. As part of its defense in both suits, the ACLU asked courts to impose higher standards for accusers seeking to sue anonymous writers for online defamation. The group asked that plaintiffs be forced to prove actual economic harm has been sustained before a suit can proceed. Arguing that online communication has more in common with everyday conversation than formal publication, the ACLU also urged the courts to prosecute online defamation cases under "slander" statutes that regulate spoken mischief,

rather than the more serious "libel" statutes that regulate defamatory printed material.

As the famous *New Yorker* cartoon once remarked, on the Internet no one knows you're a dog. But as things stood in 2002, if you were an Internet dog who offended someone online, chances were a judge would order your ISP to relieve you of your mask.

Bibliography

Arthur, Charles. "Identity Crisis on the Internet." *New Scientist,* March 11, 1995, p. 14.
Bonisteel, Steve. "Lawsuits Shine a Light on Internet Anonymity." *Newsbytes*, October 17, 2000.
Borland, John. "Online Anonymity Gets No Protection in Court." Techweb News, July 13, 1998. <http://www.techweb.com/wire/story/TWB19980713S0020> (March 20, 2002).
Dyson, Esther. *Release 2.0: A Design for Living in the Digital Age.* New York: Broadway Books, 1997.
Rodger, Will. "Online Anonymity Faces Legal Challenges." *USA Today,* November 29, 2000. <http://www.usatoday.com/life/cyber/tech/cti850.htm> (March 20, 2002).

Further Reading

Lessig, Lawrence. *Code and Other Laws of Cyberspace.* New York: Basic Books, 1999.
Rheingold, Howard. *The Virtual Community: Homesteading on the Electronic Frontier.* Reading, Mass.: Addison Wesley, 1993; rev. ed., Cambridge, Mass.: MIT Press, 2000.
Wallace, Jonathan D. "Nameless in Cyberspace: Anonymity on the Internet." Cato Institute, briefing papers, December 8, 1999. <http://www.cato.org/pubs/briefs/bp54.pdf> (March 20, 2002).

Related Topics

Electronic Frontier Foundation; Freenet (File-Sharing Network); Privacy; Spam

— *Kevin Featherly*

ARPANET

The Advanced Research Projects Agency (ARPA), an arm of the U.S. Defense Department, funded the development of an experimental computer network, the ARPANET, in the late 1960s. Its initial purpose was to link computers at Pentagon-funded research institutions over telephone lines. ARPANET was the forerunner of today's Internet.

At the height of the Cold War, military commanders were seeking a computer communications system without a central core, with no headquarters or base of operations that could be attacked and destroyed by enemies, thus blacking out the entire network in one fell swoop. ARPANET's purpose was always more academic than military, but as more academic facilities connected to it, the network did take on the tentacle-like structure military officials had envisioned. Today's Internet essentially retains that form, although on a much larger scale.

ROOTS OF A NETWORK

ARPANET was an end-product of a decade of computer-communications developments spurred by military concerns that the Soviets might use their jet bombers to launch surprise nuclear attacks against the United States. By the 1960s, a system called SAGE (Semi-Automatic Ground Environment) was already built, using computers to track incoming enemy aircraft and to coordinate military response. The system included 23 "direction centers," each with a massive mainframe computer that could track 400 planes, distinguishing friendly aircraft from enemy bombers. The system required six years and $61 billion to implement.

The system's name hints at its importance, as author John Naughton points out. The system was only "semi-automatic," so human interaction was pivotal. For J. C. R. Licklider, the man who would become the first director of ARPA's Information Processing Techniques Office (IPTO), the SAGE network demonstrated above all else the enormous power of interactive computing—or, as he would later refer to it in a seminal 1960 essay, of "man-computer symbiosis." In his essay, one of the most important in the history of computing, Licklider posited the then-radical belief that a marriage of the human mind with the computer would eventually result in better decision-making.

In 1962, Licklider left a post at the Massachusetts Institute of Technology (MIT) to join ARPA. According to Naughton, his brief two-year stint at the organization seeded everything that was to follow. His tenure signaled the demilitarization of ARPA; it was Licklider who changed the name of his office from Command and Control Research to IPTO. "Lick," as he insisted on being called, brought to the project an emphasis on interactive computing, and the prevalent utopian conviction that humans teamed with computers could create a better world.

Perhaps in part because of Cold War fears, by the mid-1960s the Defense Department's ARPA arm had become, in author Ronda Hauben's words, the "sugar

daddy" of computer science. During Licklider's IPTO tenure, it is estimated that 70 percent of all U.S. computer-science research was funded by ARPA. But many of those involved say the agency was far from being a restrictive militaristic environment, giving them free reign to try out radical ideas. As a result, ARPA was the birthplace not only of computer networks and the Internet, but also of computer graphics, parallel processing, computer-flight simulation, and other key achievements.

Ivan Sutherland succeeded Licklider as IPTO director in 1964; two years later Robert Taylor became IPTO director. Taylor would become a key figure in ARPANET's development, partly because of his observational abilities. In the Pentagon's IPTO office, Taylor had access to three teletype terminals, each hooked up to one of three remote, ARPA-supported time-sharing mainframe computers—at Systems Development Corp. in Santa Monica, at UC Berkeley's Genie Project, and at MIT's Compatible Time-Sharing System project (later known as Multics).

In his room at the Pentagon, Taylor's access to time-shared systems led him to a key social observation. He could watch as computers at all three remote facilities came alive with activity, connecting local users. Time-shared computers allowed people to exchange messages and share files. Through the computers, people could learn about each other. Interactive communities formed around the machines.

Taylor also decided that it made no sense to require three teletype machines just to communicate with three incompatible computer systems. It would be much more efficient if the three were merged into one, with a single computer-language protocol that could allow any terminal to communicate with any other terminal. These insights led Taylor to propose and secure funding for ARPANET.

A plan for the network was first made available publicly in October 1967, at an Association for Computing Machinery (ACM) symposium in Gatlinburg, Tennessee. There, plans were announced for building a computer network that would link 16 ARPA-sponsored universities and research centers across the United States. In the summer of 1968, the Defense Department put out a call for competitive bids to build the network, and in January 1969, Bolt, Beranek, and Newman (BBN) of Cambridge, Mass., won the $1 million contract.

According to Charles M. Herzfeld, the former director of ARPA, Taylor and his colleagues wanted to see if they could link computers and researchers together. The project's military role was much less important. But at the time it was launched, Herzfeld noted, no one knew whether it could be done, so the program, initially funded on $1 million diverted from ballistic-missile defense, was risky.

Taylor became ARPA's computer evangelist, picking up Licklider's mantle and preaching the gospel of distributed, interactive computing. In 1968, Taylor and Licklider co-authored a key essay, "The Computer as a Communications Device," which was published in the popular journal *Science and Technology*. It began with a thunderclap: "In a few years, men will be able to communicate more effectively through a machine than face to face." The article went on to predict everything from global online communities to mood-sensing computer interfaces. It was the first inkling the public ever had about the potential of networked digital computing. And it served to attract other researchers to the cause.

A PACKET OF DATA

ARPANET arose from a desire to share information over great distances without the need for dedicated phone connections between each computer on a network. As it turned out, fulfilling this desire would require "packet-switching."

Paul Baran, a researcher at the RAND Corp. think tank, first introduced the idea. Baran was instructed to come up with a plan for a computer communications network that could survive nuclear attack and continue functioning. He came up with a process that he called "hot-potato" routing, which later became known as "packet switching."

"Packets" are small clusters of digital information broken up from larger messages for expediency's sake. To illustrate in today's terms: An e-mail might be split into numerous electronic packets of information and transmitted almost at random across the labyrinth of the nation's telephone lines. They do not all follow the same route, and do not even need to travel in proper sequential order. They are precisely reassembled by a modem at the receiver's end, because each packet contains an identifying "header," revealing which part of the larger message it represents, along with instructions for reconstituting the intended message. As a further safeguard, packets contain mathematical verification schemes that insure data does not get lost in transit. The network on which they travel, meanwhile, consists of computerized switches that automatically forward packets on to their destination.

Data packets make computer communications more workable within existing telephone infrastructure by allowing all those packets to flow following paths of least resistance, thereby preventing logjams of digital data over direct, dedicated telephone lines.

Baran's idea was ignored by the military. A 1964 paper outlining his innovation was published, but it was classified and began to collect dust. Fortunately, one place it was collecting dust was in the offices of ARPA, where it was eventually rediscovered. Baran's idea became the key concept that made ARPANET possible. Packet-switched communication remains perhaps the most important legacy handed down to the Internet by the ARPANET.

RISE AND FALL

In late 1969, a team of UCLA graduate students under the leadership of Professor Leonard Kleinrock sent the first packet-switched message between two computers. A member of Kleinrock's team, Charley Kline, had the distinction of being first to send it, but it was not a rousing start. As Kline at UCLA tried logging into the Stanford Research Institute's computer for the first time, the system crashed just as he was typing the letter "G" in "LOGIN."

The bugs were worked out, and further connections were made flawlessly, but the early network had many limitations. At the time of Kline's first message to Stanford, logging into a remote computer was one of just three tasks possible on ARPANET; the other options were printing to a remote printer and transferring files between computers. Nevertheless, the interest generated by the nascent two-node network was intense. By the end of 1969, academic institutions were scrambling to connect to ARPANET. University of California–Santa Barbara and the University of Utah linked up that year. By April 1971, there were 15 nodes and 23 host terminals in the network. In addition to the four initial schools, contractor BBN had joined, along with MIT, the RAND Corp., and NASA, among others. By January 1973, there were 35 connected nodes; by 1976, there were 63 connected hosts.

During its first 10 years, ARPANET was a testbed for networking innovations. New applications and protocols like telnet, file transfer protocol (FTP), and network control protocol (NCP) were constantly being devised, tested, and deployed on the network. In 1971, BBN's Ray Tomlinson wrote the first e-mail program, and the ARPANET community took to it instantly. "Mailing lists," which eventually became known as "listservs," followed email almost immediately, creating virtual discussion groups. One of the first e-mail discussion lists was SF-LOVERS, which was dedicated to science fiction fans.

What ARPANET could not do was talk to any of the other computing networks that inevitably sprang up in its wake. Its design required too much control and too much standardization among machines and equipment on the network, according to Naughton. So in the spring of 1973, Vinton Cerf and Bob Kahn began considering ways of connecting the ARPANET with two other networks that had emerged, specifically SATNET (satellite networking) and a Hawaii-based packet radio system called ALOHANET. One day, waiting in a hotel lobby, Cerf dreamed up a new computer communications protocol, a gateway between networks, which eventually became known as transmission-control protocol/Internet protocol (TCP/IP). TCP/IP, which was first tested on ARPANET in 1977, was a way that one network could hand off data packets to another, then another and another. Eventually, when the Internet consisted of a network of networks, Cerf's innovation would prove invaluable. It remains the basis of today's Internet.

In 1975, ARPANET was transferred to the Defense Department Communications Agency. By that time, it was no longer experimental, nor was it alone. Numerous new networks had emerged by the late 1970s, including CSNET (Computer Science Research Network), CDnet (Canadian Network), BITnet (Because It's Time network), and NSFnet (National Science Foundation Network); the last of these would eventually replace ARPANET as the backbone of the Internet, before it was itself superceded by commercial networks.

The term "Internet" was adopted in 1983, at about the same time that TCP/IP came into wide use. In 1983, ARPANET was divided into two parts, MILNET, to be used by military and defense agencies, and a civilian version of ARPANET. The word "Internet" was initially coined as an easy way to refer to the combination of these two networks, to their "internetworking."

The end of ARPANET's days arrived in mid-1982, when its communications protocol, NCP, was turned off for a day, allowing only network sites that had switched to Cern's TCP/IP language to communicate. On January 1, 1983, NCP was consigned to history, and TCP/IP began its rise as the universal protocol. The final breakthrough for TCP/IP came in 1985, when it was built into a version of the UNIX operating system. That eventually put it in Sun Microsystems workstations, and, Naughton writes, "into the heart of the operating system which drove most of the computers on which the Internet would eventually run." As Vinton Cerf would observe, "The history of the Net is the history of protocols."

As both free and commercial online services like Prodigy, FidoNet, Usenet, Gopher, and many others rose, and as NSFnet became the Internet's backbone, ARPANET's importance diminished. The system was finally shut down in 1989 and formally decommissioned in 1990, just two years before Tim Berners-Lee would change everything all over again with the introduction of the World Wide Web.

Bibliography

Digital Systems Research Center. "In Memoriam: J. C. R. Licklider, 1915-1990." (Reprints "Man-Computer Symbiosis" and "The Computer as a Communication Device.") <http://www.memex.org/licklider.pdf> (March 19, 2002).

Emigh, Jacqueline. "ARPANET—Standards Established in the '60s." *Newsbytes*, September 15, 1994.

Hauben, Michael, and Ronda Hauben. *Netizens: On the History and Impact of Usenet and the Internet.* Los Alamitos, Calif.: IEEE Computer Society Press, 1997.

Naughton, John. *A Brief History of the Future: From Radio Days to Internet Years in a Lifetime.* Woodstock, N.Y.: Overlook Press, 1999.

Radosevich, Lynda. "The Father of the Internet Predicts His Brain Child's Future." *IDG.net*, October 4, 1999. <http://www.infoworld.com/cgi-bin/displayStory.pl?/features/991004kleinrock.htm> (March 19, 2002).

Further Reading

Detouzos, Michael. *The Unfinished Revolution: Human-Centered Computers and What They Can Do for Us.* New York: HarperCollins, 2001.

Haring, Bruce. "Who Really Invented the Net?" *USA Today,* September 2, 1999. <http://www.usatoday.com/life/cyber/tech/ctg000.htm> (March 19, 2002).

Hiltzik, Michael A. *Dealers of Lightning: Xerox PARC and the Dawn of the Computer Age.* New York: HarperCollins, 1999.

Rheingold, Howard. *The Virtual Community: Homesteading on the Electronic Frontier.* Reading, Mass.: Addison-Wesley, 1993.

Salus, Peter H. *Casting the Net: From ARPANET to Internet and Beyond.* Reading, Mass.: Addison-Wesley, 1995.

Related Topics

BITNET; Cerf, Vinton; Community Networking; Computer-Supported Collaborative Work; Cyberspace; Email; Human-Computer Interaction; Internet Engineering Task Force; Licklider, J. C. R.;

"Man-Computer Symbiosis"; Sutherland, Ivan; USENET; Virtual Community

— *Kevin Featherly*

ASCII Art

ASCII art is text art created with ASCII, a protocol established by the American National Standards Institute (ANSI), which is America's representative to the International Organization for Standardization (IOS). ASCII art uses ASCII text characters to produce images. The emoticon, an element of text messaging and email, is an example of ASCII art at its most popular and functional.

Precursors of ASCII art are techniques such as mosaic, hieroglyphics, and dot art. But ASCII art is most obviously an extension of typewriter art. After E. Remington and Sons began manufacturing typewriters in 1874, they were soon being used not only for writing, but also for creating pictures. Typewriter art competitions were held as early as 1890, and the genre continued to be popular until the 1970s. Text images were later sent via Teletype, which was developed around 1900; drawings transmitted over Teletype are done in capital letters and printed on long paper tapes.

The ASCII code was established by ANSI in the early 1960s, and was standardized between 1968 and 1972. It is a way of presenting and reading the Latin-based alphanumeric keyboard characters used by many language groups. Like other protocols, it was developed as a standard to ensure that the message sent over a network would be similar to the message received.

ASCII art uses the alphanumeric character set to produce images, with characters coming together to mimic pen lines, brush strokes, benday dots, and so on. Its utility in computer-mediated communication (CMC) ranges from the use of such basic emoticons as the "smiley" to the creation of elaborate pieces that emulate classical art. ASCII art is most commonly found in online talk/chat environments, online games, email, ezines, and as "signatures" at the end of email or Usenet messages. (The Usenet newsgroups dealing with ASCII art are alt.ascii-art, where participants post their art, and rec.arts.ascii.) ASCII art is also found on dedicated Web sites, where users exhibit their work and provide links to other exhibitors.

In the past 20 years, ASCII art has become a developed form that includes abstract, cartoon, portrait, realist, and minimalist sub-genres. Much ASCII art relies on line characters, such as _, \, |, /, and –. Other pieces use the whole range of keys, but letters often interrupt the line of the image unless used carefully.

At the level of signature and emoticon, ASCII art continues to be a significant element of text-based communication; as a more complex artistic form, it remains a specialist or niche interest. However, the ease with which it can be developed—and the fact that it does not impact on file size in the same way that

ASCII art by Joan Stark (www.ascii-art.com).

images do—means that it remains both a useful and an entertaining staple of CMC. Despite the multimedia environment of the Web, some users cannot download image files or read HTML. ASCII is the most universally accessible form of CMC, although even this form excludes some language groups.

The Internet was originally a text-based medium, and email is still one of its most frequently employed aspects. Its origin in text helped the Internet to create an environment of experimentation and exploration of the possibilities of text as a primary communications medium. One of the early observations about text-only CMC was that it failed to communicate the complexity of gesture, expression, and emotional nuance that was clearly evident, for example, in verbal exchange. Originating as a way of enriching the text environment and allowing for a greater range of human expression, ASCII art can be viewed as an argument against technological determinism, as it shows that individuals can shape the uses to which technology is put. The continuing popularity of ASCII art is an example of how the older forms of the Internet, such as email and Usenet, undergird the newer forms, such as the Web.

Bibliography

Abbate, Janet. *Inventing the Internet*. Cambridge and London: MIT Press, 1999.
American National Standards Institute. Homepage. <http://www.ansi.org> (March 19, 2002).

Further Reading

Danet, Brenda. *Cyberpl@y: Communicating Online*. Oxford, England: Berg, 2001.
The Great ASCII Art Library, April 1997. <http://www.geocities.com/SouthBeach/Marina/4942/ascii.htm> (March 19, 2002).
Mullen, Allen. ASCII Picture Collections. <http://www.afn.org/~afn39695/collect.htm> (March 19, 2002).
Riddell, Alan, ed. *Typewriter Art: Half a Century of Experiment*. London: Polytechnic of Central London, 1981.

Related Topics

Email; Emoticons; USENET

— *Kate O'Riordan*

Association for Computing Machinery

The first educational and scientific computing society, the Association for Computing Machinery (ACM) was founded in 1947. Today, the ACM has more than 75,000 members worldwide, including students and computing professionals throughout the realms of academia, industry, research, and government. The ACM serves both professional and public interests by providing technical information and promoting high standards in the field of computing.

ACM provides specialized technical information and services through its 33 special-interest groups (SIGs). These SIGs focus on a variety of specialties within the computing discipline, such as computer architecture (SIGARCH), computer-science education (SIGCSE), computer-human interface (SIGCHI), and computer graphics and interactive techniques (ACM SIGGRAPH). Many of these SIGs are highly interdisciplinary, and serve members outside the computing profession. For example, many ACM SIGGRAPH members are artists, and many SIGCHI members are psychologists. The SIGs are sources of significant knowledge in these particular focus areas.

ACM provides service to local and regional communities by supporting more than 700 professional and student chapters worldwide, 20 percent of which are outside the United States. These chapters provide a means for professionals to gather for lectures, seminars, and other events. Some of the SIGs do not allow national chapters (e.g., a U.K. chapter, as opposed to a London chapter) for political reasons, but ACM does charter national chapters. The ACM Lectureship Program, which provides speakers for chapter events, and the ACM International Collegiate Programming Contest are both valuable programs, especially for students.

The primary ACM member publication is the monthly *Communications of the ACM*. It provides articles of general interest and some in-depth discussions, with a different focus each month. The ACM also publishes many journals recognizing research accomplishments in specialized areas such as graphics, programming languages, and Internet technology, and books from the ACM Press cover a wide spectrum of the computing field. In addition, the SIGs produce newsletters and conference proceedings in their specialty areas. The ACM Digital Library contains the full text of all articles published by the association over the past 50 years in journals, transactions, and conference proceedings.

The ACM sponsors eight major awards to recognize technical and professional accomplishments in the field of computing, and most SIGs also have awards for accomplishments in their specialty areas. The highest ACM award, the Turing Award, is often described as "the Nobel Prize of Computing." It was given in 2001 to Andrew Chi-Chih Yao in recognition of his work in computation theory, which included cryptography, the study of techniques for secret writing used in creating codes.

Although the ACM maintains its central goal of providing information and service to computing students and professionals, it has expanded its focus over the years to adapt to changing times. With today's increased focus on theory and people, rather than on machinery per se, the original name, Association for Computing Machinery, is seldom used. Although ACM used to sponsor a large general computing conference each year, major successful conferences are now sponsored by the SIGs. For example, ACM SIGGRAPH sponsors a large general conference on computer graphics and interactive techniques that draws 35,000–45,000 attendees, as well as a dozen smaller, more focused conferences and workshops on topics such as games technology and virtual reality; and SIGARCH co-sponsors the Supercomputing Conference with IEEE (Institute of Electrical and Electronic Engineers, Inc.) Computer Society.

The ACM has expanded its purview into matters of public policy, and has taken a stand on some issues that have an impact on computing or telecommunications, such as computer security, privacy, and intellectual property. The ACM also works to encourage women in the field of computing. There is now a Committee on the Status of Women in Computing that sponsors a mentoring program both for female students interested in computing and for women already in the computing field.

Bibliography

Association for Computing Machinery. Web site. <http://www.acm.org> (May 10, 2002).

Tourelzky, David S. "Free Speech Rights for Programmers." *Communications of the ACM*, August 2001, 23–25.

White, John. "ACM Opens Portal to Computing Literature." *Communications of the ACM*, July 2001, pp. 14–16, 28.

Further Reading

Denning, Peter J., and Bob Metcalfe. "Beyond Calculation: The Next 50 Years of Computing." *Copernicus*, 1997.

Related Topics

Computer Graphics; Digital Art and Animation; Encryption and Cryptography; Human-Computer Interaction; Institute of Electrical and Electronic Engineers

— *Judith R. Brown*

"As We May Think"

Vannevar Bush, science adviser to Franklin Delano Roosevelt, published the influential essay "As We May Think" in *Atlantic Monthly* in July 1945. World War II was still raging, but its outcome was reasonably certain, and Bush looked beyond the war to the science and technology of peace.

Science and technology had enabled increased human control over the material world, improving food, clothing, and shelter; increasing security; reducing labor; improving medicine; increasing life span; and improving communication. The growth of science meant an ever-expanding record of ideas. As human knowledge grew, the ability to transmit and review new knowledge became increasingly difficult. Exchange across disciplines often became superficial, as knowledge increased within ever-more-isolated fields. The first glimmerings of information overload were visible.

Science was extending the boundaries of knowledge. At the same time, research publishing had already exploded far beyond humanity's ability to access and use the knowledge that science was creating, and the ongoing expansion of knowledge meant that the problem would worsen. The knowledge of the atomic age was being managed using the same techniques and media that were used to manage knowledge in the early steam age.

Bush was particularly sensitive to the danger of lost knowledge, not merely through lack of access, but also because of the risk of its burial in a mass of information. For example, he wrote that "Mendel's concept of the laws of genetics was lost to the world for a generation because his publication did not reach the few who were capable of grasping and extending it; and this sort of catastrophe is undoubtedly being repeated all about us, as truly significant attainments become lost in the mass of the inconsequential."

Bush's article focused on one specific challenge: He asked how science and technology could solve the problem of managing human knowledge. His article summarized the technological advances of the time, and demonstrated how they could be applied to the problem.

Bush outlined the concepts of a dozen important inventions. These included the hand-held calculator; the personal computer; and the idea of dry photography that gave birth to the Polaroid camera, the Xerox machine, and electrostatic photocopying. He conceptualized improvements to photography that included universal focus, automatic focus, automatic zoom, automatic exposure and lighting control, and automatic loading and rewind, along with head-mounted cameras for still photography and, by extension, camcorders for live action. He proposed a viewer interface mounted in the lenses of an ordinary pair of eyeglasses, used in some forms of heads-up display. Other technical advances included the telefax (already in partial use), the image scanner, remote imaging, microphotography, video photography, analog data compression, voice-activated text transcription, the text scanner, handwriting storage, document imaging, punch-cards for sophisticated computing, electronic computing, and advanced algorithmic programming. He also explored artificial intelligence, decision-support systems, special computers for local applications, problem-solving systems, educational simulations, distance learning, improved symbolic representation systems for mathematics and logic, logic engines, search engines, digitized search algorithms, associative search algorithms, database programs, credit cards, personal information cards, and electromagnetic code strips.

Improvements in the technology that Bush described meant that the realization of these inventions would use different means than he predicted. Nevertheless, the technology did exist for the applications that Bush proposed in his own time. It was his unique genius to see these opportunities, and to understand how they could be made to work in an integrated series of information-technology devices and knowledge-management systems.

As remarkable as these proposals were, Bush also proposed four remarkable ideas that made him the prophet of Internet and the World Wide Web.

The first of these ideas was the Memex. The Memex was "a device in which an individual stores all his books, records, and communications, and which is mechanized so that it may be consulted with exceeding speed and flexibility." The Memex was a hybrid personal computer, Internet interface, and communications tool. If we consider the personal computer as the front end of the Web, the Memex would have been its gateway. While many features and services of the Web were proposed as stand-alone features of the Memex, its status as a communication device also suggested the linked possibilities that characterize the Internet and the Web as they actually evolved.

The second idea was a universal repository of knowledge. Bush proposed that any Memex owner would be able to acquire books of all sorts, pictures, current periodicals, newspapers, and more. The Memex also provided mechanisms for documenting and storing personal files, whether through records of personal memos and notes or by filing the transcripts generated by the voice-driven transcription system.

The third idea resembled the idea of the desktop metaphor in the graphic user interface (GUI) of most personal computers, and would permit multitasking and multiple document use in windows. It also included personal document annotation features that do not yet exist for most users.

The fourth and most dramatic idea was Bush's unique idea of associative indexing and linking—the idea of hypertext. The inventors of today's hypertext technology acknowledge Bush as the inspiration behind their work. Bush described his other ideas as "conventional, except for the projection forward of present-day mechanisms and gadgetry." The step to associative indexing was the essential feature of the Memex. "The process of tying two items together," wrote Bush, "is the important thing."

The full Memex does not exist, but its partial realization in personal computers, the Internet, database programs, information systems, and most importantly the World Wide Web, has already changed the way that human beings work with what we know. It has increased our ability to learn, to communicate, to cooperate, to work. Entire fields of social science, organization studies, social psychology, and communication theory now focus on the new world taking shape around the applications that Vannevar Bush described in "As We May Think." If there were a Bible of the information age, "As We May Think" would be the book of Genesis.

Bibliography

Brown University Computer Science Department. Memex and Beyond Web Site.
<http://www.cs.brown.edu/memex/home.html> (May 24, 2002).

Bush, Vannevar. "As We May Think." *The Atlantic Monthly*, vol. 176, no. 1 (July 1945), pp. 101–108. <http://www.theatlantic.com/unbound/flashbks/computer/bushf.htm> (May 24, 2002).

Johnson, Steven, ed. "Remembering the Memex. A FEED Document on Vannevar Bush's 'As We May Think'." *FEED*, June 8, 2001.

Simpson, Rosemary; Renear, Allen; Mylonas, Elli; and Andries van Dam. "50 Years After 'As We May Think': The Brown/MIT Vannevar Bush Symposium." *Interactions*, vol. 3, no. 2 (1996).

Further Reading

Engelbart, Douglas C. "A Conceptual Framework for the Augmentation of Man's Intellect." *Vistas in Information Handling*, P.D. Howerton and D.C. Weeks, eds. Washington, D.C.: Spartan Books, 1963.

Nyce, James M., ed. *From Memex to Hypertext: Vannevar Bush and the Mind's Machine.* Boston: Academic Press, 1991.

Zachary, G. Pascal. *Endless Frontier: Vannevar Bush, Engineer of the American Century.* New York: Free Press, 1997.

Related Topics

ARPANET; Berners-Lee, Tim; Bush, Vannevar; Engelbart, Douglas; Graphical User Interface; Hypermedia; Hypertext; Intermedia; Kay, Alan; Kurzweil, Raymond; Multimedia; Nelson, Theodor Holm (Ted); World Wide Web

— *Ken Friedman*

Asynchrony See Synchrony and Asynchrony.

Authoring Tools

In general terms, authoring tools are programs that enable the user to create and publish content over the World Wide Web. The content produced can range from a basic Web page utilizing only HyperText Markup Language (HTML) to complex Web sites that utilize specific authoring tools such as Flash, Director, and Premiere for more user interactivity. Authoring tools are often broken down into three main categories: Web format, editing, and multimedia. These categories are non-exclusive, in the sense that several different authoring tools may be needed to create the desired Web content. The tools themselves sometimes overlap; as more authoring tools offer expanded capabilities, fewer authoring tools may be needed.

Authoring tools must be capable of saving the content so that it can be viewed and/or played over the Internet, as a Web page, a picture, or a multimedia project. The most common forms of saved documents for Web pages are HTML and .pdf files; for pictures, .jpeg and .gif; and for multimedia projects, .avi, .mpeg, and .fla. Any program that is capable of creating one or more of these file extensions can be considered an authoring tool, but the approach the user takes to create these files varies greatly depending on the initial program.

WEB-FORMAT AUTHORING TOOLS

The most basic form of authoring tools involves software programs that were originally designed to produce printable material, but that can expand their function into converting a printable document into a Web-formatted document, mostly in HTML. This doc-

ument can then be uploaded to the Internet. Web-format authoring tools are the simplest for novices, who are probably already familiar with basic programs and therefore do not have to learn new authoring programs. The down side is that using programs designed for other purposes to author a Web site limits what can be done on the created Web page.

Word-processing programs such as Corel's WordPerfect, Lotus' WordPro, and Microsoft's Word originally were used to produce typewritten documents for printing. With the advent of the Internet, the software was expanded to enable Web-formatting features that save documents to an HTML format, and in some cases convert to a .pdf file in addition to the standard file extensions.

Other types of Web-formatting authoring tools are programs that were initially designed for desktop publishing (e.g., PageMaker, QuarkXPress, Publisher, CorelDraw, Photoshop). Documents created using desktop-publishing software can be saved mainly as pictures under a .jpeg or .gif format capable of being viewed on the Internet. However, some desktop-publishing programs, such as Publisher, allow users to save their documents as HTMLs too, and have even included Web-page templates. The files can be uploaded, and they can also be imported and combined with pre-existing Web pages using other Web authoring tools. For example, if a user is working with a word-processing program that allows the importation of a picture, the user can elect to import a project created in Photoshop and saved as a .jpeg. This document will be embedded in the final file, which can be saved as HTML.

A significant drawback to using these types of authoring tools is that the formatting and layout of the Web page may not appear the same on the Web as it appears on the user's screen during the creation of the project. When converting from a written document to HTML code, the programs sometimes add in extra scripting codes; therefore, saved file formats will sometimes become distorted. In order to have more control over the Web page's layout, specific authoring-tool programs created for Web publishing are available; they require users to learn new programs, and to participate in smaller amounts of coding.

EDITING AUTHORING TOOLS

Expanded versions of Web-format authoring tools are programs that are specifically designed to produce content already formatted for the Internet. These programs allow the user to create Web sites through the utilization of HTML, Dynamic HyperText Markup

Language (DHTML) coding, or Extensible Markup Language (XML) coding.

There are two types of editing authoring tools: coding tools and WYSIWYG (What You See Is What You Get) tools. Coding authoring tools are programs that allow users to type out basic HTML-type codes to create a Web site. Once the code is written, the program debugs the code to make sure the user did not forget to close a sequence or miss any punctuation. More recent versions of coding authoring tools have quick reference tags available for the user to help aid in scripting; however, the user still must be knowledgeable about what each of the tags do. Some programs designed as strict coding authoring tools can be downloaded for free, such as the highly rated and popular Evrsoft's 1st Page 2000. (This area of authoring tools does not include programs such as Notepad, as the user cannot run a debugging sequence.) In general, while strict coding authoring tool programs offer users the most control over and provide the least distortion in how the resulting Web page will look, they are not as widely used by novices, as users are expected to have some working knowledge of HTML or its variations.

The most-utilized editing authoring tools are programs that use the WYSIWYG graphical user interface (GUI). Programs such as Microsoft's FrontPage, Macromedia's Dreamweaver, and Netscape's free Composer are among the most popular of these tools. Their users do not need to know HTML codes, although it is helpful to be familiar with them for added control and in order to fix minor formatting problems. WYSIWYG authoring tools allow users to directly type in and manipulate text, import and manipulate pictures on the screen, and easily add in hyperlinks and import multimedia components like audio files. These programs both resemble and utilize the design concepts of standard desktop-publishing programs.

Editing authoring tools support the importation of multimedia content and Web-oriented programming languages (e.g., Java, ASP, CGI, Perl), but most are not capable of creating the kind of sophisticated interactive multimedia displays that are now common to the Internet. (Some programs, such as Dreamweaver, allow for minor multimedia applications.) Therefore, additional programs are available that are geared more toward the advanced user who is knowledgeable in programming.

MULTIMEDIA AUTHORING TOOLS

Multimedia authoring tools incorporate more interactive features than static pictures or simple audio files.

They allow the viewers of the Web site to become actively involved in the content through a combination of sound, sight, and mouse-clicks. Most multimedia authoring tools' finished products need to be imported or linked to an HTML Web page in order to function, so they work in conjunction with editing authoring tools. The desired end result of the content provider will determine which program will be utilized.

If users have pictures or graphics that they wish to animate on their Web site, they can use multimedia authoring tools such as Macromedia's Flash and Adobe's LiveMotion. Conceptually, these programs are similar to creating cartoons for television. A user must either draw or import a graphic, and then manipulate the graphic frame by frame to achieve the desired effect. Some shortcuts are available, such as zoom functions, that allow for the creation of basic movements without making significant changes to the graphic. The resulting animations are placed in a timeline that will keep them sequenced. These animation tools also allow for the importation of sound.

Adobe's Premiere 6.0 and Ulead's VideoStudio allow the integration, editing, and exportation of digital video to the Web in the form of QuickTime, MPEG, or RealVideo files. When using authoring tools involving videos, creators need to have their video footage already digitized, and should be aware of the format they are saving in, as site users may need to download special plug-ins and viewers in order for the video to be playable. It is also important to note that videos may take a long time to load and may have problems streaming. Several formats of video for PCs on the Web are not compatible with Apple computers.

For interactive modules that include quizzes, questionnaires, and games, creators can use Asymetrix's Toolbook II, Macromedia's Director, or Macromedia's Flash. These programs integrate video, sound, and animation along with user input such as mouse-clicks, drag and drop, and quizzes. Authoring tools capable of producing highly interactive content are not for novices.

Many multimedia authoring tools are starting to integrate the basic functions of other authoring tools in their programs' more recent versions. For example, Flash provides its users with a scaled-down version of a graphical program to enable drawing as well as the creation of interactive games, while HTML editors like Dreamweaver have a smaller version of the Flash program built into them.

Before choosing an authoring tool, users should have an idea of what they want their finished product to look like. They should also consider how experienced they are with programming, and how willing they are to learn a new program. Since multimedia authoring-tool capabilities are becoming more integrated, users should familiarize themselves with the limitations and capabilities of different tools; this can help reduce the number of programs needed to create the desired effects.

Bibliography

Breitzer, Frith. "Adobe Flashes Macromedia: LiveMotion May Challenge Web Design Tool." *MacWorld*, May 2000. <http://www.macworld.com/2000/05/news/ adobeflashes.html> (May 10, 2002).

Heng, Christopher. "Free HTML Editors, Web Editors, and Site Builders." March 30, 2002. <http://www.thefreecountry.com/ecentricity/ htmleditors.shtml/> (May 10, 2002).

Strauch, Joel. "Multimedia Authoring: It's Not Just for Experts Anymore." *Smart Computing* vol. 10, no. 2 (February 1999).

Further Reading

Musciano, Chuck, and Bill Kennedy. *HTML & XHTML: The Definitive Guide*. Cambridge, Mass.: O'Reilly, 2000.

Siglar, Jamie. Multimedia Authoring Systems FAQ Version 2.23. *Comp.Multimedia*, April 4, 1999. <http://www.tiac.net/users/jasiglar/ MMASFAQ.HTML#Q.1/> (May 10, 2002).

Related Terms

Desktop Publishing; Graphical User Interface; Interactivity; Plug-Ins

— *Kathy Broneck*

Avatar

An avatar is the graphical representation of a user in an interactive online chat or game environment. Primarily used in virtual chat environments such as ActiveWorlds (ActiveWorlds.com), VZones (Avaterra.com, Inc.), and Black Sun Virtual Worlds (blaxxun interactive), the term originated in Hindu mythology, where it referred to the worldly embodiment of a god.

The first use of the term occurred in an interactive online game called Habitat, created in the late 1980s by Lucasfilm Games in association with Quantum Computer Services, Inc. At a time when almost all online interactive chat (and indeed most online communication) used only text, Habitat pioneered the use of movable cartoon characters to represent people who communicated with each other through the online game. Habitat's creators referred to these cartoon characters as avatars, a term enthusiastically embraced by most subsequent graphical chat systems.

The term captures both the power and the limitations of online interaction. Like gods in a small world, users can manipulate some aspects of online environments in ways not possible in offline environments, changing physical representations with a few simple commands. Yet online communication can be limiting in some ways as well. Graphical representations cannot capture the nuances of expression available to embodied human beings in face-to-face interaction. Thus, the experience of communicating through online avatars provides an experience that could be considered analogous to that of gods submitting themselves to the limitations of corporeal existence.

Neal Stephenson's 1992 novel *Snow Crash* helped perpetuate the use of the term avatar. Stephenson, who had computer-programming experience, depicted an online virtual-reality system that was considered relatively realistic and realizable by many computer engineers. He used the term avatar to refer to representations of people in that system. Stephenson's work has been so influential in the graphical chat community that a speaker at a recent virtual-reality conference jokingly suggested that anyone who had not read *Snow Crash* should leave the room.

When new users connect to a graphical chat system, they usually must download software that allows them to connect to and interact with the virtual world program. Part of this software includes instructions for acquiring an avatar. On some systems, users choose from a set of pre-designed avatars; on others, users can import their own graphics to

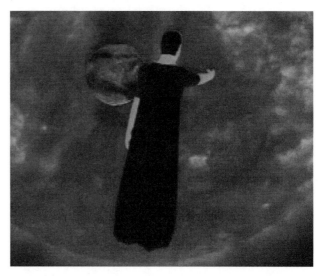

The avatar of a participant flies toward a real-time satellite image of the surface of the sun. From Daniel Sandin's virtual environment, "Looking for Water." (Courtesy of Daniel Sandin)

customize their avatars. Once users select their avatars, they can use a variety of simple keyboard commands to cause their avatars to move, gesture, and "speak." Most graphical chat systems use text to represent avatar speech, although some systems, such as OnLive!, have experimented with audio connections that allow for voice communication.

Avatars range widely in sophistication, flexibility, design style, etc. Creating a fully interactive graphical representation for each user in a game or chat space can require significant computing resources. Designers must make tradeoffs between the advantages and disadvantages of various features. For instance, on one system that provides a flat, two-dimensional view of the environment and the avatars in it, users have discovered that the lack of realistic perspective means that one user can "cover up" another user's avatar, blocking that avatar from view. This is not possible when graphics are rendered with three-dimensional perspective. However, on one three-dimensionally rendered world, the complex graphics involved result in a limitation on the number of avatars that can be seen by any individual user, regardless of how many users are actually present in that virtual location.

Designers must also decide whether to provide a specific set of avatars from which users must choose, or to configure their system to allow users to customize and design their own avatars. Such decisions involve social as well as design and computing issues, since they affect both the amount of control people have over their avatars and the ways those avatars can interact.

From their earliest use online, designers and users have contemplated and debated the meaning of avatars. Some feel that avatars should be accorded the same status and respect as their human operators; others think of avatars as no more than game pieces to be manipulated at will. This debate reflects the uncertain status of online socializing, often held to be less "real" than face-to-face encounters.

Graphical chat systems featuring avatars have had difficulty succeeding commercially, and many have disappeared or changed hands in recent years. Presently, relatively few people use avatars for online interaction. As available bandwidth and computing power increases, graphical online spaces will be able to provide more sophisticated graphics, and will also likely become easier to use. However, these same changes will also result in increased capabilities for applications such as live group audio and video connections. It is therefore unclear whether the use of avatar systems will increase or decrease.

Bibliography

Damer, Bruce. *Avatars!* Berkeley, Calif.: Peachpit Press, 1998.

Morningstar, Chip and F. Randall Farmer. "The Lessons of Lucasfilm's Habitat," in *Cyberspace: First Steps,* ed. by Michael Benedikt. Cambridge, Mass.: The MIT Press, 1991.

Further Reading

Rheingold, Howard. *The Virtual Community: Homesteading on the Electronic Frontier.* Reading, Mass.: Addison-Wesley, 1993.

Stephenson, Neal. *Snow Crash.* New York: Bantam Spectra, 1992.

Taylor, T. L. "Living Digitally: Embodiment in Virtual Worlds," in *The Social Life of Avatars: Human Interaction in Virtual Worlds,* R. Schroeder, ed. London: Springer-Verlag, 2001.

Related Topics

Cyberspace; Habitat; Sandin, Daniel; Virtual Reality

— *Lori Kendall*

b b b b b b B b b b b b

Barlow, John Perry

1947–

Cyberspace Activist

John Perry Barlow is a leading commentator on a vast number of issues relating to cyberspace, including the legal issues of free speech and copyright, privacy, cryptography, and civil liberties, as well as various social and cultural aspects of digital life. As co-founder of the Electronic Frontier Foundation (EFF), he has fought numerous battles on behalf of cybercitizens against governmental and corporate attacks on various freedoms and rights. He is credited with applying the term "cyberspace," taken from William Gibson's science-fiction novels, to digital networks that have become known as the Internet.

Born on October 3, 1947, in Jackson Hole, Wyoming, Barlow was the only child of Norman and Miriam Barlow. He spent his childhood on the family's 20,000-acre cattle ranch, and attended Fountain Valley Military Academy in Colorado Springs after being labeled a "troublemaker." There, he wrote poetry, caused more trouble, and became friends with Bob Weir, future guitarist for the Grateful Dead. After graduation, he studied at Wesleyan University in Connecticut, and graduated with a major in comparative religion in 1969.

After traveling in India, he began writing lyrics for the Grateful Dead. In 1971, he returned to his family ranch to care for his father, who died in 1972. After his father's death, he ran the family cattle ranch for 17 years, while still writing occasional lyrics for the Dead. He briefly followed his father, who had been a Republican state legislator, into politics, serving as Sublette County GOP chairman. In 1988, he sold the ranch and moved to Pinedale, Wyoming, with his wife, Elaine Parker, and three daughters. While living in Pinedale, Barlow began his online life, helping build the cybercommunities that were then emerging.

In July 1990, a series of raids by the U.S. Secret Service, collectively called Operation Sun Devil, caused an uproar in the online community. Most notably, officials charged that the Steve Jackson Games company was the recipient of an illegally copied computer file relating to BellSouth's 911 emergency system; the Secret Service obtained a warrant and seized all of the firm's computers. Delays caused by the seizure crippled Steve Jackson's business, and he was forced to lay off staff. Although the computers were eventually returned, data they contained had been deleted, and Jackson sought the help of civil-liberties groups who might argue the case that his free speech and privacy rights had been violated. When no one stepped forward, Barlow joined with Mitch Kapor, founder of Lotus Development Corporation, and Internet pioneer John Gilmore to form the EFF and represent Steve Jackson Games.

The EFF has won several landmark decisions. In the Jackson case, the court decided in 1993 that electronic mail must be accorded the same protection as telephone calls, and that authorities must have a specific warrant before intercepting them; Jackson was awarded $50,000 in lost profits. The ruling in *Bernstein vs. the U.S. Department of State*, another case taken up by the EFF, decreed that written computer code is constitutionally protected speech (although this precedent has been complicated by subsequent decisions in other cases). More recently, the EFF has been involved with cases dealing with music copyright, trademark law, and anonymity relating to cyberspace.

Barlow writes extensively about the Internet. He was an early contributor to *Wired*, in which he published "The Economy of Ideas," a hugely influential article in which he argued that the nature of digital information and the Internet have made traditional intellectual property and copyright laws obsolete. In 1996, following the passage of the controversial Communications Decency Act, which attempted to place prohibitions on Internet speech in various ways, Barlow wrote "A Declaration of the Independence of Cyberspace." This stirring call to digital arms, which can be found on more than 20,000 Web sites, addresses the "Governments of the Industrial World" and calls for the independence of cyberspace from outdated notions of property, expression, and identity.

More recently, Barlow has been a Fellow at Harvard University's Berkman Center for Internet and Society and the John F. Kennedy School of Government. He also helped found Bridges.org, an organization that attempts to help developing nations to better use technology and the Internet to improve quality of life.

Selected Works

Barlow, John Perry. "A Declaration of the Independence of Cyberspace." February 8, 1996. <http://www.eff.org/~barlow/Declaration-Final.html> (May 10, 2002).

——. "The Economy of Ideas: A Framework for Patents and Copyrights in the Digital Age." *Wired 2.03*, March 1994. <http://www.wired.com/wired/archive/2.03/economy.ideas.html> (May 10, 2002).

Bibliography

Barlow, John Perry. "Barlow Home(stead) Page." <http://www.eff.org/~barlow/> (May 10, 2002).

Electronic Frontier Foundation. "About EFF: General Information About the Electronic Frontier Foundation." <http://www.eff.org/abouteff.html> (May 10, 2002).

Quittner, Joseph. "The Merry Pranksters Go to Washington." *Wired 2.06*, June 1994. <http://www.wired.com/wired/archive/2.06/eff.html> (May 10, 2002).

Further Reading

Gans, David, with Ken Goffman. "Mitch Kapor & John Barlow Interview." August 5, 1990. <http://www.eff.org//Publications/John_Perry_Barlow/HTML/barlow_and_kapor_in_wired_interview.html> (May 10, 2002).

Related Topics

Bernstein vs. the U.S. Department of State; Communications Decency Act; Electronic Frontier Foundation; Encryption and Cryptography; Kapor, Mitchell; Privacy

— *Shawn Miklaucic*

Berners-Lee, Tim

1955 –

World Wide Web Inventor

A quiet, modest Englishman with training in theoretical physics, Tim Berners-Lee brought the Internet to the masses in 1991 after creating the definitive window through which to view cyberspace, then campaigning tirelessly to assure that everyone who wanted to access it could do so for free. Given the scope of the World Wide Web and its potential to transform human communications, the impact of Berners-Lee's invention has been likened to that of Gutenberg's movable-type printing press.

Presumably, Berners-Lee could have become a wealthy man had he leveraged his innovation in a commercial enterprise—the way that Marc Andreessen did, for example, when he devised and marketed an improved Web browser (which itself was another Berners-Lee invention). But Berners-Lee resisted making the Web a proprietary venture like America Online or Compuserve, demanding instead that his creation remain universally accessible to anyone with Internet access. In 1994, he helped to ensure that it would remain a free space by forming the World Wide Web Consortium (W3C), a global body comprising major software makers, hardware manufacturers, academics, and politicians that suggests standardized specifications for Web technologies so that the medium can continue to grow as an "Internet commons." Today, Berners-Lee earns a modest salary as W3C director at the group's Massachusetts Institute of Technology (MIT) headquarters, content to allow others to grow rich from his creation.

"I am convinced that he does so not only from a desire to ensure the Web's future," wrote Michael Dertouzos, the late director of MIT's Laboratory of Computer Science, in a forward written for Berners-Lee's memoir, *Weaving the Web*. Berners-Lee also declined to exploit his invention for material gain, Dertouzos wrote, because of his "wellspring of human decency," which he found "even more impressive than his technical prowess."

BACKGROUND

Berners-Lee was born in London in 1955. His parents, Conway and Mary Berners-Lee, were mathematicians who met while helping to build England's first commercial computer, the Ferranti Mark 1, at Manchester University. Mathematics and computers were common household discussion topics; as a child, Berners-Lee once built a model computer out of cardboard. His parents were enthusiastic about their work, although they also knew well the limitations of machines; namely, computers were incapable of making random associations between objects and concepts the way that humans can. One day after school, Berners-Lee's father discussed this problem with him while preparing a speech for his boss to deliver. According to *Weaving the Web*, Conway Berners-Lee was struggling to think of ways to make computers intuitive. It was an important dilemma that would stick in his son's head.

Berners-Lee excelled in school, and graduated in 1976 with first-class honors in theoretical physics from Queen's College at the University of Oxford. While there, he made his first computer, using a soldering iron, an M6800 processor, and an old television set. After leaving Oxford, he worked for two years with a U.K. telecommunications company on distributed transaction systems and message relays, after which he worked at a company that produced typesetting software for printers. Eventually, he became an independent consultant, and in 1980, he found himself in Geneva, Switzerland, at the European Particle Physics Laboratory (CERN). While there on a six-month contract, Berners-Lee produced for his personal use the precursor to the World Wide Web, a program called Enquire. The name is short for "Enquire Within About Everything," which was the name of a Victorian-era book on manners he'd once read. "I didn't use the book," he told *How the Web Was Born* authors James Gilles and Robert Cailliau, "but that title stuck."

Berners-Lee used Enquire mainly to document programs he was writing for CERN. Enquire, which was constructed to help him find information about the concepts, people, things, and software that went into creating his programs, was capable of arranging information so that random associations could be drawn among the various data. It was not built on a hierarchical menu system, the way most programs were at the time (and as online programs like Gopher were later constructed). Instead, Enquire allowed information to be structured arbitrarily, a feature that Berners-Lee said might make it possible for users to find information they did not even realize they were looking for. This structure became the basis for the World Wide Web.

CREATING THE WEB

Berners-Lee left CERN in 1980, but returned in 1984 to work on information-retrieval systems for the lab. This time he faced a daunting problem: CERN was a huge research installation where many scientists worked on short-term fellowships, with many people using many varieties of computers and storage formats. Researchers frequently produced work on their own terminals, but were unable to share it with colleagues. Even worse, important physics research was often lost, as it was prepared on various outdated computers and stored on outmoded disks, and the data could not be retrieved, or sometimes even located.

Berners-Lee's task was to create a system that would allow all of CERN's computers to share information unencumbered. In 1989, he proposed a decentralized hypertext project that could resolve all those problems—and that, in fact, could also connect CERN's computers with computers outside the lab, or even across the planet. His prospectus outlined the bare bones of the World Wide Web.

Although his proposed project received little attention from his colleagues at the time, Berners-Lee was determined to create it on his own, using CERN's resources and enlisting whomever he could to help him. Berners-Lee had one key ally within CERN; Robert Cailliau, the Belgian-born head of CERN's Proton Synchrotron system software group, became Berners-Lee's lead collaborator, lending the Web project much-needed credibility within the organization.

Credibility was needed because the Web project had become Berners-Lee's sole focus at CERN. He lived in constant fear that a superior might pull the plug on his "universal hypertext system," since it had little direct connection to particle-physics research. (In

Tim Berners-Lee at the Internet Caucus Speakers Series, June 2001. (AFP/CORBIS)

fact, several years later, CERN did bar all non-physics-related projects.) Cailliau played a key role in helping Berners-Lee to promote the wonders of the Web during the first four years of its existence, a period that Berners-Lee calls its "phase of persuasion." Part of his challenge was to keep portraying the system as a way to help CERN to organize and distribute its internal information, even though he was well aware, from the time of his initial proposal, that the Web had global implications, both for text and multimedia applications.

At CERN, the Web was promoted as a way to allow researchers to work together by combining data using a web of hypertext documents. To that end, working on a high-end NeXT computer, Berners-Lee wrote the code for the first Web server, which he called "httpd," beginning in October 1990; it was based on the hypertext transfer protocol that he'd also created. He then wrote code for the first browser, which he called "WorldWideWeb," the name that he eventually bestowed on the whole project. By December 1990, he had submitted the browser to his colleagues at CERN, initially selling it as a telephone-book database. Response within the lab was lukewarm; even with Cailliau's persistent lobbying for more resources, the duo never quite received from CERN what they felt was necessary to make the Web project fly.

GOING PUBLIC

In August 1991, Berners-Lee made a critical move. Realizing that he wasn't going to get what he needed from CERN, he decided to produce what Cailliau referred to in *How the Web Was Born* as a "toolkit," which would allow other developers outside CERN to contribute to the project. He released the World Wide Web browser to the Internet, along with a second, simpler "line-mode" browser developed by student assistant Nicola Pellow, and the Web's first basic server, allowing anyone who wanted to try the system to download it for free, and to modify it to their own liking. Then he announced the release on newsgroups, including alt.hypertext, where hypertext enthusiasts and key members of the academic community congregated.

The public began to take notice of the Web, slowly at first. In July and August 1991, there were between 10 and 100 page views on the info.cern.ch server every day. Between then and 1994, the load on that first Web server rose by a factor of 10 each year. Gradually, developers on the nascent Web began to introduce new browsers that were compatible with systems other than

that of NeXT, which was an expensive computer that was not popular with consumers. By January 1993, there were some 50 servers on the Web, and there were a number of new browsers with names like Erwise, Viola, Cello, and Samba.

In February 1993, a team from the National Center for Supercomputing Applications in Champaign, Illinois, introduced the first version of Mosaic, the precursor to Netscape. It was easy to download and install, had a simple-to-use point-and-click interface, and could display photographs and images along with text on Web pages. To the public, Mosaic was a revelation; it was suddenly clear what the Internet was capable of. The press began to take notice, and the Web took off like a shot; by 1994, there were 100,000 servers on the Web.

Given its core mission, CERN was the wrong place for the Web to be tied to. In 1993, Berners-Lee convinced officials at the lab to release the underlying Web technology to the public domain—which meant that he was also scrapping his idea of having the system licensed under the General Public Licensing scheme. While this idea would have allowed the software to be distributed freely, it would also have attached some proprietary strings. He had already abandoned the idea that he and Cailliau had batted around of starting a company called Websoft to market his invention, because that would probably have caused competitors and incompatible browsers to spring up, fracturing the Web and eliminating its potential as a "universal" hypertext environment. "He thought it better to stay above the fray and try to bring technical harmony," *Time* magazine reported.

After traveling around Europe and the United States gathering input on what was needed to keep the Web stable, Berners-Lee formed the World Wide Web Consortium, with the assistance of MIT's Dertouzos, in October 1994. Among its current 500 members, the W3C.org site says, are technology and product vendors, content providers, corporate Web users, research labs, standards-making bodies, and governments. All work to achieve consensus on the direction that the Web should take. Berners-Lee retains great power over its development, although most members say that he declines to exercise that power; still, according to *Scientific American* magazine, each W3C member must sign a contract giving Berners-Lee the final say in any new Web specifications. Since its inception, the W3C has developed more than 35 new technical specifications for the Web, ranging from the eXtensible

Markup Language (XML) and cascading style sheets to scalable vector graphics (SVG) and the Synchronized Multimedia Integration Language (SMIL) specification.

In recent years, Berners-Lee has turned his attention to Web improvements that he calls "the Semantic Web." A Semantic Web will bring structure, he says, to "the meaningful content of Web pages" by "creating an environment where software agents roaming from page to page can readily carry out sophisticated tasks for users." The new Semantic Web is rooted in notions of human-computer interaction.

"Once the (Semantic Web) dream is reached," Berners-Lee wrote in *Weaving the Web,* "the Web will be a place where the whim of a human being and the reasoning of a machine coexist in an ideal, powerful mixture." As it develops and improves, Berners-Lee has predicted, the Semantic Web could come to resemble a kind of "global brain," with each of its human users and each machine worldwide representing individual neurons.

Berners-Lee created a medium that is used today for everything from buying cars and CDs to getting the daily news—and, in some places, voting for public officials. It has succeeded faster than practically any new-media technology before it. Today, the growth of the Web is synonymous with the growth of the Internet, although they are not in fact the same thing. In April 2002, Nielsen//NetRatings reported that there were more than 428 million people connected to the Internet globally. While many of them use the medium for instant messaging, chats, FTP, and other functions, virtually all of them also use the Web, and there is little argument that the Web has driven the Internet's growth to its current staggering proportions. "The Web and the Internet grew as one, often at exponential rates," Joshua Quittner wrote in *Time* magazine in 1999. "Within five years, the number of Internet users jumped from 600,000 to 40 million. At one point, it was doubling every 53 days."

Berners-Lee readily acknowledges his debt to innovators who came before him—notably Ted Nelson, the inventor of hypertext, and Doug Engelbart, whose 1968 oNLine System (NLS) was the Web's networking ancestor. As Dertouzos noted in his introduction to *Weaving the Web,* Berners-Lee's key epiphany was the realization that the two things that computer scientists had been fixated on for decades—hypertext and networks—belonged together.

What perhaps makes Berners-Lee stand out personally, aside from the overwhelming success of his creation, is his innate humanism, the insistence that his invention belongs not to himself, but to the world. By foregoing personal wealth in the interest of assuring that his invention remain stable, scalable, and available to all Internet-connected human beings, Berners-Lee turned a technical innovation into one of the great acts of philanthropy of the twentieth century.

Selected Works

Berners-Lee, Tim. "Information Management: A Proposal." In *Multimedia: From Wagner to Virtual Reality,* Packer, Randall, and Ken Jordan, eds. New York: W.W. Norton & Co., 2001; pp. 189–205.

Berners-Lee, Tim. "Bio." 1999. <http://www.w3.org/People/Berners-Lee/Longer.html> (April 16, 2002).

Berners-Lee, Tim and Mark Frischetti. *Weaving the Web.* New York: HarperCollins, 1999.

Berners-Lee, Tim, James Hendler, and Ora Lassila. "The Semantic Web." *Scientific American,* May 2001, pp. 35–43.

Bibliography

Gillies, James and Robert Cailliau. *How the Web Was Born.* Oxford, England: Oxford University Press, 2000.

Holloway, Marguerite. "Molding the Web." December 1997. <http://www.sciam.com/1297issue/1297profile.html> (April 16, 2002).

Quittner, Joshua. "TIME 100: Scientists & Thinkers: Tim Berners-Lee." *Time.* 1999. <http://www.time.com/time/time100/scientist/profile/bernerslee.html> (April 16, 2002).

Wright, Robert. "The Man Who Invented the Web." *Time,* May 19, 1997.

Further Reading

Auletta, Ken. *World War 3.0: Microsoft and Its Enemies.* New York: Random House, 2001.

Dertouzos, Michael. *The Unfinished Revolution: Human-Centered Computers and What They Can Do for Us.* New York: HarperCollins, 2001.

Fidler, Roger. *Mediamorphosis: Understanding New Media.* Thousand Oaks, Calif.: Pine Forge Press, 1997.

Naughton, John. *A Brief History of the Future: From Radio Days to Internet Years in a Lifetime.* Woodstock, N.Y.: The Overlook Press, 1999.

Schwartz, Evan I. "The Father of the Web." *Wired.* March 1997. <http://www.wired.com/wired/archive//5.03/ff_father.htm> (April 16, 2001).

Segaller, Stephen. *Nerds: A Brief History of the Internet.* New York: TV Books L.L.C., 1998.

Related Topics

"As We May Think"; Engelbart, Douglas; Hypermedia; Hypertext; Interactivity; Interface; Internet; Linking; Nelson, Theodor Holm (Ted); World Wide Web; World Wide Web Consortium

— *Kevin Featherly*

Bernstein vs. the U.S. Department of State

Bernstein v. the U.S. Department of State is a landmark legal case in the short history of digital technology that set two important precedents. First, it ruled that the U.S. government's export policies that barred the export of encryption software were unconstitutionally restrictive; second, it declared that software source code can be a form of protected free speech.

In the lawsuit, a federal court was asked to rule in a dispute between the U.S. government and University of Illinois–Chicago mathematics professor Daniel Bernstein, to determine if he had the right to distribute encryption software of his own creation over the Internet. The federal government claimed that federal Export Administration Regulations (EAR), which are intended to keep encryption technology out of the hands of rogue states, proscribed Bernstein from freely distributing the code, even if it was his own invention.

Bernstein had devised his encryption program, called Snuffle, in 1990 while he was a graduate student at the University of California–Berkeley. His software converts a one-way "hash function" into private-key encryption system, one that can be decoded only by whoever holds the private "key," or pass code. The functionality of the software depends on two people having exchanged their private keys.

Court documents contended that Bernstein later used Snuffle in his teaching, to convey his ideas about encryption for a course on cryptography. Even the dissenting judge in the Ninth Circuit Appeals Court ruling acknowledged that to teach the course, Bernstein had to actually use his source code "textually." The professor made the software source code available free on the Web site where he placed course-review materials for his classes.

Wanting to disburse the material further to the academic and scientific communities, in the mid-1990s Bernstein asked the U.S. State Department if he would need a license to publish Snuffle. He was told that his creation was tantamount to "munitions" under International Traffic in Arms Regulations (ITAR). Therefore, the government contended, Bernstein would have to obtain export licenses from the State Department for each person outside the United States who wanted to view Snuffle's online source code.

In February 1995, Bernstein sued the government, claiming that the arms regulations were unconstitutional and that his First Amendment rights should permit him the freedom to distribute the material as he wished.

Ninth Circuit District Court Judge Marilyn Hall Patel ruled in the instructor's favor in 1997, citing First Amendment grounds to declare that free-speech rights protected the software's source code. Later, after President Clinton shifted oversight and licensing authority over non-military encryption products to the Commerce Department, Bernstein amended his suit to include the Commerce Department. In August 1997, Patel issued another ruling, identical to her first, reasserting First Amendment protections of encryption source code regardless of which federal agency was in charge of the government's encryption policy.

The U.S. government appealed those decisions, and in May 1999, a three-judge Ninth Circuit Court of Appeals panel voted 2-1, agreeing with Patel. The judges asserted that the government's export rules operated as a kind of pre-publication licensing scheme that obstructed the professor's rights to scientific expression. It also ruled that the Export Administration Regulations gave government officials "boundless discretion" over encryption matters, and that the regulations lacked adequate checks and balances. The panel, with one dissenter, noted that Bernstein's Snuffle software was, in part, a "form of political expression."

Cryptography is not new to the digital age; it probably is almost as old as written language itself. A message is encrypted when it is written in code to keep outsiders from understanding its contents, and among the most famous uses for cryptography were those codes used by the Germans and Japanese during World War II to hide their strategies. Successful efforts by the Allies to break, or decrypt, their codes speeded the end of the conflict.

Encryption is not limited to military use, nor is it all about keeping data secret. In computing, for instance, it can be used to ensure the integrity of data, and it can be used to identify specific messages as coming from specific senders. Nonetheless, encryption in the digital age is an issue of critical concern to military leaders and politicians, because of the implications for cyber-terrorism and other national and international security issues. Even domestically, digital encryption technology is viewed with mistrust; U.S. law enforcement officials have opposed the wide distribution of encryption software, and the FBI even tried to criminalize its sale.

One State Department official cited in the *Bernstein* appeals court ruling said the proliferation of software like Snuffle would make it easier for foreign intelligence sources to keep vital national-security information out of U.S. hands. Encryption software, the official argued, could be used to conceal foreign military communications, or communications between terrorists, drug smugglers, and hackers intent on taking action against U.S. interests. While Snuffle was not designed for those uses, it could have such applications, according to the government.

The Ninth Circuit Appeals Court did not entirely reject the government's argument, but it did rule that cryptographers use source code to express scientific ideas "in much the same way that mathematicians use equations or economists use graphs." Therefore, encryption source code is "expressive," and is protected under the First Amendment. However, the Court cautioned, not all software can be considered expressive, so not all source code is necessarily protected. That caveat was fortified legally in January 2001, when a New York federal judge ruled that the magazine *2600: The Hacker Quarterly* could not use its Web site to link readers to a decryption code called DeCSS, which makes it possible to unscramble the anti-copying technology embedded in digital video discs (DVDs). The magazine filed an appeal of the DeCSS case in late March 2001, but lost when a three-judge panel agreed with first judge's original ruling. In January 2002, the magazine's publisher appealed both rulings to New York's full Second Circuit Court of Appeals.

The *Bernstein* ruling had the effect of forcing the Clinton administration to back down on what had been a tightly restrictive view of encryption software. In September 1999, Attorney General Janet Reno, Commerce Secretary William Daley, and Defense Secretary William Cohen jointly announced that U.S. firms would have more freedom to export encryption products. The new policy allows "the export and re-export of any encryption commodity or software to individuals, commercial firms, and other non-government end-users in all destinations." However, it allows for technical reviews of encryption products in advance of sale, mandates a post-export reporting system, and empowers the government to review "strong encryption" exports to foreign governments.

The administration's reversal in policy stole the momentum from a movement among Republican U.S. legislators to enact the Security and Freedom through Encryption (SAFE) Act, which was designed to allow Americans to use any type of encryption while relaxing export controls over U.S. encryption products. But lawmakers said they would keep their eyes on the future direction of government policy, and vowed to revisit the SAFE Act if necessary.

It remains unclear if the final chapter of *Bernstein* has yet been written. In early 2000, after the modification of the government's encryption-export rules, the full Ninth Circuit Court of Appeals asked the three-member panel to re-examine its Bernstein ruling in light of the relaxed rules. In January 2002 Bernstein's legal team renewed its constitutional challenge to the government's encryption laws, arguing that the government's policy violates the First Amendment and restricts research that Bernstein maintains could help protect computer systems against criminals and terrorists.

Bibliography

Carney, David. "Ninth Circuit Rules Encryption Export Regulations Violate First Amendment." *Tech Law Journal,* May 10, 1999.
<http://www.techlawjournal.com/encrypt/19990510.ht> (March 20, 2002).

Electronic Privacy Information Center. "Revised U.S. Encryption Export Control Regulations." January 2000.
<http://www.epic.org/crypto/export_controls/regs_1_00.html> (March 20, 2002).

FindLaw for Legal Professionals. "U.S. 9th Circuit Court of Appeals, Bernstein v. USDOJ." 1999.
<http://www.laws.lp.findlaw.com/getcase/9th/case/9716686&exact=1> (March 20, 2002).

MacMillan, Robert. "Appeals Court Rules Against DoJ In Crypto Case." *Newsbytes,* May 6, 1999.

McCullagh, Declan. "Crypto Regs Challenged Again." *Wired,* April 4, 2000.
<http://www.wired.com/news/politics/0,1283,35425,00.html> (March 20, 2002).

Further Reading

Barrett, Neil. *The State of the Cybernation: Cultural, Political and Economic Implications of the Internet.* London: Kogan Page, 1996.

Bowman, Lisa. "Free-speech Issues Underlie DVD-code Appeal." *News.com,* January 26, 2001.
<http://news.cnet.com/news/0-1005-201-4616358-0.html> (March 20, 2002).

Freedman, David H. and Charles C. Mann. *At Large: The Strange Case of the World's Biggest Internet Invasion.* New York: Simon & Schuster, 1997.

Lessig, Lawrence. *Code and Other Laws of Cyberspace.* New York: Basic Books, 1999.

McCullagh, Declan. "Don't-Ask-Don't-Tell Encryption." *Wired,* January 14, 2000.
<http://www.wired.com/news/politics/0,1283,33651,00.html> (March 20, 2002).

Wallace, Jonathan and Mark Mangan. *Sex, Laws and Cyberspace.* New York: Henry Holt, 1997.

Related Topics

Carnivore; Electronic Civil Disobedience; Electronic Communications Privacy Act; Encryption and Cryptography; Hacking, Cracking, and Phreaking; Internet; Lessig, Lawrence; Privacy; *2600: The Hacker Quarterly*

— *Kevin Featherly*

Bezos, Jeff

1964–

Internet Entrepreneur

Jeff Bezos launched Internet mega-retailer Amazon.com in 1995. Amazon now has more name-brand recognition than Burger King, Wrigley's, or Barbie, according to *Fortune* magazine, and has customers in 150 countries. The company has made 38-year-old Bezos a multi-billionaire, and had industry-watchers proclaiming him an e-commerce visionary as recently as 1999. However, the rapid economic downturn of 2000 may have taken Bezos's hero status with it.

Bezos was born on January 12, 1964, in Albuquerque, New Mexico. As a child, he had an insatiable curiosity, especially about outer space; before long, he was expressing an interest in space travel—not as an astronaut, but as a colonizing entrepreneur. After his father took a job in Miami as an Exxon engineer, Bezos graduated high school as valedictorian, delivering an address that stressed the importance of outer-space colonization. Later, he attended Princeton University, graduating with majors in electrical engineering and computer science.

Bezos' first job was at a financial-markets networking start-up called Fitel, which had been launched by two Columbia University professors. He left there to join D.E. Shaw & Co., a hedge-fund investment management firm. There he met his future wife Mackenzie, an aspiring novelist who was working at Shaw as a researcher.

While at Shaw, Bezos' job was to discover profit-making opportunities for the company, and it was there that he discovered the opportunity that he would parlay into Amazon. In 1994, while surfing the World Wide Web, he came upon a site that claimed to track the Internet's growth. It showed that the Web was growing by 2,300 percent a year. Bezos had a flash of inspiration, realizing that his own entrepreneurial future lay in building a company on the Internet.

His research indicated that his best chance for success lay in the book business. Books, he discovered, were perhaps the best-catalogued product in any industry; publishers had even put their inventory lists on CD-ROMs, which could easily be transferred to the Web. What's more, due to space constraints, real-world stores were unable to stock most of what was available. An online bookstore, he reasoned, would have no such restrictions, and could radicalize the way that people buy books. It could build a community of book-buyers. Bezos borrowed $300,000 and a used Chevy Blazer from his parents, and he and Mackenzie moved to Seattle, where one of the two biggest book wholesalers was located—and where there was a large community of 'Net-savvy people who could become his employees. Bezos got the Amazon.com site launched in July 1995. In 30 days, it had sold books to customers in all 50 states, and in 45 other countries. By early September, the company was pulling in $20,000 in sales per week.

Growth from that point was prodigious. Bezos quickly began adding product categories—first music and videos, later toys, electronics, software, home-improvement products, auctions, and an "online flea market" called "zShops"—partly to offset competition from other proliferating "e-tail" sites. Amazon, according to Bezos' vision, would compete by becoming the company that sold all things to all people all the time. By April 2001, *Newsweek* magazine was reporting that Amazon.com was raking in nearly $3 billion a year, and ranked it among the 50 top brands in the world.

The world seemed to fall in love with the casually dressed entrepreneur with the cackling laugh who appeared to have spun billions from thin air. The company's stock value sky-rocketed, with Amazon valued at $22 billion in 1999. Influential Wall Street analyst Henry Blodget predicted that the company's stock would one day be worth $400 per share. In its final edition of 1999, *Time* magazine named Bezos its "Person of the Year."

However, in a matter of months, the picture was changing dramatically. The new economy was beginning to follow old rules, such as the one that demands corporate profitability from investment-funded companies, online or otherwise. Despite all its revenue, Amazon's costs, especially those for shipping and distribution, were greater than its income. The notion that, unlike brick-and-mortar firms, a dot-com like Amazon could add sales categories without adding costs turned out to be a fallacy. As they did with almost all dot-com companies beginning around March 2000, investors began losing patience, and analysts downgraded the stock. Some worried that the company would soon run out of cash and go belly up.

Bezos, who had routinely brushed aside questions of Amazon's profitability, had projected that after five years, he'd be netting $5 million in annual profits. But by year six, 2001, the company was still deep in debt and burning its cash reserves. Bezos consequently changed his tune, and began emphasizing to employees and investors alike that profitability was now job one. He laid off workers, hired a former Black & Decker executive to make painful cost-cutting moves, streamlined operations, and helped Amazon to lose just $0.25 cents per share in the third quarter of 2000, beating analysts' expectations of a $0.33-per-share loss. In the first quarter of 2001, losses were a mere $0.22 per share, compared to consensus expectations of a loss of $0.32 cents per share. In April 2001, Bezos predicted for the first time that his company would take in "pro forma" profits by the end of the year. (Pro forma profits are not actual profits; they fail to take into account substantial accounting costs, such as the $125 million in annual interest that Amazon pays on the $2.1 billion worth of debt that the company has racked up over the years. Still, as *Fortune* magazine noted, pro forma profitability is better than nothing.)

Many on Wall Street saw this as good news. Daniel Good, a research analyst with Merrill Lynch, told the *Newsbytes* news service that Amazon would be in the black on earnings per share by the fourth quarter of 2002. By 2003, he said, Amazon would experience its first full year of profitability. However, not everyone viewed things that way. Allan Sloan, Wall Street editor of *Newsweek* magazine, projected a kind of demise for Amazon, predicting that Amazon would survive, but not in its current form. Either it would be bought out, or it would have to switch to some other business model, like developing Web sites for other firms.

Only time will tell who is right, and what will be the ultimate fate of Jeff Bezos' Internet commerce brainstorm. But there can be little doubt that his vision of a new way to shop online made him the very first man capable of lifting all eyes to e-commerce.

Bibliography

Bayers, Chip. "The Inner Bezos." *Wired 7.03*, March 1999. <http://www.wired.com/wired/archive/7.03/bezos.html> (April 5, 2002).

Featherly, Kevin. "Things Look Up Financially for Amazon.com." *Newsbytes*, April 9, 2001.

Levy, Steven, and Brad Stone. "Bedtime for Bezos?" *Newsweek*, April 9, 2001, pp. 36–37.

Quittner, Joshua. "Biography: The Background and Influences that Made Bezos the Multi-Billion-Dollar Champion of E-Tailing." *Time*, December 27, 1999. <http://www.time.com/time/poy/bezos.html> (April 5, 2002).

Further Reading

Hof, Robert D. "Making Money on the Net." *BusinessWeek*, September 23, 1996. <http://www.businessweek.com/1996/39/b34941.htm> (April 5, 2002).

———. "We Want to Be the World's Most Customer-Centric Company." *BusinessWeek*, May 21, 1999. <http://www.businessweek.com/ebiz/9905/521bezos.htm> (April 5, 2002).

Patsuris, Penelope. "Amazon Chief Goes on the Record." *Forbes*. August 24, 2000. <http://www.forbes.com/2000/08/24/mu6.html> (April 5, 2002).

Sloan, Allan. "An Amazonian Survival Strategy." *Newsweek*, April 9, 2001, p. 20.

Related Topics

Copyright; Data Mining; Digital Cash; E-Commerce; Usability; Whitman, Margaret; World Wide Web

— Kevin Featherly

BITNET

BITNET, an acronym that stands for "Because It's Time Network," is a network of universities, colleges, and other academic institutions that was a predecessor to today's Internet—as was ARPANET, a defense and research network. Although crude by today's standards, the purpose of BITNET was to support research and education with a tool for sending email, exchanging files, and generally sharing text-based information between institutions.

BITNET was the product of joint efforts by researchers at the City University of New York (CUNY) and Yale University to create an academic network by linking existing campus mainframe computers. Researchers Ira H. Fuchs of CUNY and Greydon Freeman of Yale are widely credited with recognizing the potential of using existing communications protocols to connect geographically separated scholars and researchers through computer-mediated communication; in fact, the BITNET acronym originally stood for "Because It's *There* Network," in reference to the protocols that were freely available on IBM computers at CUNY. In the spring of 1981, the two universities used leased telephone circuits to allow accounts on their respective mainframe computers to communicate, thus initiating what would eventually become known as BITNET.

It did not take long for the network to grow; within two years, the number of linked BITNET institutions had grown to about 20, and had extended to include institutions in California. BITNET also connected with similar networks internationally, such as AsiaNet in Japan, EARN (European Academic and Research Network), and NetNorth in Canada.

In 1984, the network's development was assisted by two important events. First, funding from IBM helped to develop the BITNET Network Information Center (BITNIC), which provided centralized network support services. This funding continued until 1987, when participating institutions and organizations began paying dues to help support the network. Members also provided a large amount of volunteer support to keep the network operating, in the form of developing software and contributing services to keep operating costs low. Second, representatives from participating institutions and organizations formed the BITNET Executive Committee to establish network policies and procedures, as well as to begin long-term planning.

Several factors contributed to the almost immediate adoption of BITNET by the academic community in the United States. The cost of joining the network was minimal, as the only true expense facing a prospective member was acquiring a leased line to connect to the existing network. Once this was done, the only requirement was to agree to serve as an entry point for at least one other institution wishing to join. It is important to note that since one of the initial goals of the network was to minimize costs to member institutions, this latter point also ensured that no redundant paths existed in the network, and that only one connection would exist between any two points in the network.

Because BITNET was a "point-by-point" network, as described above, it used a "store-and-forward" approach to information distribution. Information, in the form of a complete file traveling through the network from one BITNET location (called a "node") to another, is passed along from one connection point to the next and so forth until reaching its final destination. At each point, the file is forwarded and held until it can be passed along to the next location. When a node is temporarily unavailable, delivery is delayed until the connection is reestablished.

Sending info over BITNET required knowing both the username (or user id) and the node id upon which the account of the recipient resided (e.g., username@node.bitnet). For example, to send a message to Joe Smith at CUNY, one would address the message to Joesmith@CUNY.bitnet; note that the .bitnet tag at the end of the node was a staple of the network.

One of the most unique features of BITNET, however, was the origination of LISTSERV mailing lists. LISTSERV is actually software designed to automate tasks that would typically be done by a person. LISTSERV software automated discussion groups on BITNET, allowing the maintenance and management of mailing lists as well as the distribution of messages to occur without the aid of a human moderator. Most mailing lists also maintained a central archive and index of past messages and discussions, which could be easily searched. LISTSERVs were designed to allow individuals to initiate (or cancel) memberships simply by sending an email to the host computer indicating their wish to "subscribe" (or "unsubscribe") to the list. Since all LISTSERVs were aptly named "listserv," messages were always directed to listserv at a specific node (e.g., listserv@node.bitnet). Although exact numbers are difficult to determine, it is estimated that BITNET hosted approximately 3,000 discussion groups, ranging in size from less than 10 members to several thousand during the early 1990s.

A new set of protocols, named BITNET II, was introduced in late 1987. BITNET II was designed to accommodate problems associated with a network lacking homogeneity among its hosts, each of which had different hardware and software, and to provide better coordination among them. It also suggested ways to make better use of expected increased bandwidth capacities.

By 1987-88, the BITNET Executive Committee formalized network membership by creating a not-for-profit organization of its members. However, two years later, BITNET merged with CSNET, a computer science and engineering academic network connecting government, industry, and university institutions and organizations, although it would be almost five years before the resultant new organization was officially functioning. This new organization, named CREN (Corporation for Research and Educational Networking), was designed to manage the newly formed joint network, with over 600 members in the United States, and to support educational and research organizations by ensuring access to inexpensive networking worldwide.

According to the CREN website (www.CREN.net), the BITNET network reached its peak of popularity in 1991–92, connecting approximately 1,400 members in 49 countries. Shortly thereafter, the migration of academic institutions to the Internet began, reducing the number of BITNET members substantially in less than two years. By 1996, CREN began suggesting to its members that they abandon the use of BITNET in favor of other tools available on the Internet.

Although the original BITNET is now defunct, it remains historically important, and its presence is still felt today. For instance, CREN continues to develop list-management software in the image of LISTSERV. It also concentrates on numerous areas in which networking remains a vital component, such as distance education and the development of collaborative technology. Moreover, many of the discussion groups that originated on BITNET have migrated to the Internet.

Bibliography

Cerf, Vince. "A Brief History of the Internet and Related Networks." June 10, 2001.
    <http://www.skywriting.com/cerf.html> (April 5, 2002).
CREN. "CREN History and Future." 2001.
    <http://www.cren.net/cren/cren-hist-fut.html> (April 5, 2002).
Gedney, Carolyn. "Access to the World Through a Network Known as BITNET." August 20, 1993.
    <http://www.uiuc.edu/uiucnet/2-7-1.html> (April 5, 2002).
Moore, Michael, and Ronald M. Sawey. *User's Guide to BITNET.* Upper Saddle River, N.J.: Prentice Hall, 1992.

Further Reading

Electronic Frontier Foundation. "Big Dummy's Guide to the Internet." 1993.
    <http://www.cruzio.com/cruziolib/bigdummy/chapter5.html> (April 5, 2002).
Gralla, Preston; Ishida, Sarah; Reimer, Mina; and Steph Adams. *How the Internet Works: Millennium Edition.* Indianapolis, Ind.: Que Publishing, 1999.
Grier, David Alan, and Mary Campbell. "Bitnet and Listserv: A Social History of Bitnet and Listserv, 1985-1991." 2000.
    <http://www.computer.org/annals/articles/bitnet.htm> (April 5, 2002).
Indiana University Knowledge Base. "What Was BITNET and What Happened to It?" February 18, 2002.
    <http://kb.indiana.edu/data/aaso.html> (April 5, 2002).

Related Topics

ARPANET; Internet; LISTSERV; USENET; Virtual Community

— *Art Ramirez*

Blog

The earliest blogs (short for "weblogs") were Web pages made up of short, regularly updated posts that usually included hypertext links to Web sites or to online news and information that caught the author's (or "blogger's") interest, attention, or imagination. As the practice of blogging caught on in the late 1990s, the genre expanded to include online journals comprising topical entries about daily events, both public and private. The category has grown broad enough to include sites ranging from personal journals about college dorm life to the Drudge Report, which includes links to a variety of tabloid news and gossip items. Some sites are the product of one or two authors, while others incorporate the contributions of a group of bloggers. Weblogger Jorn Barger is generally credited with coining the term "weblog" to describe the emerging genre.

What unites the various blog formats is the fact that they provide a means of "pre-surfing" the Internet—a necessary function, perhaps, as the number of sites and the amount of information continues to increase. The blog format reflects the time-sensitive nature of the genre, featuring the most recent posts (often dated) at the top, with preceding posts following in reverse chronological order.

Blogs tend to express the interests and personalities of their authors, both through the choice of links and through the short (often sarcastic or witty) observations and summaries that accompany the links. Thus, a blog serves not only as a record of found links, but also as a way for visitors to rely on someone, whose distinctive personality and set of interests may resonate with theirs, to scout online content for them. In this respect, blogs formalize the process through which Internet users swap the URLs (Uniform Resource Locators) for interesting sites. However, rather than merely pointing to Web sites of interest, bloggers generally provide "deep" links to particular items within a site.

The existence of blogs predates the coining of the term. Weblogs first started appearing in the mid-1990s, as Web surfers sought ways to assemble the information they had garnered online. A site called "Links from Underground," authored by college student Justin Hall in 1994, is an early example of a site that shared assembled links with online visitors. An even earlier precursor was the National Center for Supercomputing Applications' "What's New" site, which served as a bulletin board of links on topics ranging from technical developments in networked computing to favorite sites for news, research information, and even culinary tips.

Until recently, it was relatively easy to keep up with the various bloggers and their respective personalities and interests. Rebecca Blood's online history of blogs notes that by 1998, one of the first lists of blogs included only 23 pages. Within a few years, however, the number of blogs had increased to the point where the Blogger Web site, which provides software for blog authors, boasted 150,000 registered users. As the trend continues to expand, readers may well need a meta-level of blogs to pre-surf the booming number of individual blogs. This proliferation reflects not just the broadening of Web literacy and access to the Internet, but also the media attention that blogs have recently received, as well as the development of free, do-it-yourself blog tools, including both Blogger and Pitas. Originally deeply embedded in the Web-surfing culture and limited largely to those immersed in the online world (not least because early bloggers often worked in computer-related fields), blogs have gone mainstream with the advent of sites hosted by newspapers, including the *San Jose Mercury News* and the *Minneapolis Star Tribune*.

The proliferation of non-commercial blogs reflects the ability of the Internet (in its current incarnation) to offer an outlet for self-publishing to almost anyone with online access. Blogs provide a unique forum for self-expression, based not as much on conventional notions of authorship as on the ability to uncover, collect, and cobble together online articles, images, and information. In this respect, blog composition exemplifies Janet Murray's description of online authorship as primarily procedural in nature. Bloggers provide their readers with a series of links to compositions that are usually not their own, but which, by the very nature of their juxtaposition, express the individual or idiosyncratic online "voice" of the blogger. In this respect, they bear a certain resemblance to the practice of journalism, which relies on linking together facts, observations, and quotes that often are not original to the reporter. In both cases, the author's distinctive contribution resides mostly in research and arrangement; the crucial difference lies in the fact that blogs allow a far greater range of interests to be expressed by a far more eclectic group of authors.

Bibliography

Barger, Jorn. "Weblog Resources FAQ." September 1999, <http://www.robotwisdom.com/weblogs/> (April 3, 2001).

Blood, Rebecca. "Weblogs: A History and Perspective." September 7, 2000. <http://www.rebeccablood.net/essays/weblog_history.html> (April 4, 2001).

Frauenfelder, Mark. "Blogging; Weblogs." *Whole Earth*, December 22, 2000, p. 52.

Gallagher, David. "Popular Web Publishing Service to Get Some Help from Helix." *The New York Times*, April 16, 2001, p. C6.

Murray, Janet. *Hamlet on the Holodeck: The Future of Narrative in Cyberspace*. New York: Free Press, 1997.

Further Reading

Barrett, Cameron. "Anatomy of a Weblog." *Camworld*, January 26, 1999. <http://www.camworld.com/journal/rants/99/01/26.html> (April 10, 2001).

Kingston, Matthew. "Weblogs: an Annotated Bibliography." May 1, 2000. <http://www.hit-or-miss.org/bibliography> (April 10, 2001).

Lanham, Richard. *The Electronic Word: Democracy, Technology, and the Arts*. Chicago: University of Chicago Press, 1993.

Rhodes, John. "In the Trenches with a Weblog Pioneer." *Webword.com*, November 29, 1999. <http://www.webword.com/interviews/eaton.html> (April 11, 2001).

Related Topics

Linking; Virtual Community; World Wide Web

— *Mark Andrejevic*

Bluetooth

Bluetooth is a short-range radio technology developed in early 1998 to eliminate the cables that connect electronic devices. Its inventors hoped to create a unified set of rules (in other words, a standardized protocol) of communication between devices, to resolve the problems faced by consumers inundated with incompatible mobile electronic devices. Ideally, smart pagers, cell phones, e-books, personal digital assistants (PDAs), and laptop computers would all be able to "talk" and exchange data, without the need for a separate suitcase just to carry the cables.

Bluetooth is designed to work through tiny short-range FM radio transceivers embedded into mobile devices. These can be installed either directly or through adapters, creating a kind of "virtual cable," an invisible pipeline for electronic data exchanges that would wirelessly link devices within a range of up to 30 feet. Bluetooth's radio signals are robust enough to work through walls.

The technology was devised after Scandinavian telecom company Ericsson launched a 1994 initiative to study a low-power, low-cost radio connection between mobile phones and their accessories. Ericsson approached mobile-device makers about the concept in 1997, to discuss the cooperative development and promotion of the technology. The idea gained momentum, and in April 1998, an industry consortium including Ericsson, IBM, Intel, Nokia, and Toshiba formed the Bluetooth Special Interest Group (SIG) to begin work on uniform specifications. The SIG, which by 2001 included more than 2,000 companies, was still working on bringing Bluetooth-equipped products to market early that year. The companies are working on the technology in tandem, to ensure that Bluetooth works with any device, regardless of the manufacturer.

That concept of unity, in fact, gave the technology its name: The historical Bluetooth (whose real name was Harald Blåtand) was the blueberry-munching Viking leader who united the nations of Denmark and Norway in the tenth century.

The technology was announced publicly in May 1998. Hype intensified in 1999, when the first official technical standard, Bluetooth 1.0, was unveiled. Bluetooth, critics raved, would be a step toward bringing to life some of the wilder fantasies of Nicholas Negroponte's 1995 book *Being Digital*, such as toasters capable of communicating with other appliances.

Bluetooth could not do such things, at least not initially; it was designed only to operate at data speeds of just under one megabyte per second (Mbps), and at a range of just 10 yards. But it could allow a PDA-carrying office worker to use a handheld PC to wirelessly select, order, and pay for a can of soda from a pop machine, debiting the money from the user's wireless online bank account. It could allow a laptop computer to use a cell phone to retrieve email, or make it possible for a notebook PC to send a document wirelessly to a fax machine. It might equip a car radio to play back voicemail messages. In the end, proponents hope that it will connect all cell phones, laptops, etc., with just about any other chip-embedded computing gadget. It could even make possible the much-discussed activity of "sofa-surfing," wirelessly linking a laptop PC to an Internet-connected interactive TV.

Early analysts' projections predicted that the technology would become wildly popular. In October 1999, Cahners In-Stat Group predicted that manufacturers of Bluetooth-equipped devices would produce more than 200 million units by 2003. By 2005, according to that forecast, the Bluetooth market would top $3 billion.

Some have complained that Bluetooth has been slow to hit its stride, however. As of early 2001, the technology had not gained much commercial ground, largely because manufacturers weren't yet making many compatible devices. In January 2001, *Wired News* reported that only one genuine Bluetooth demonstration was presented at the Consumer Electronics Show in Las Vegas: a 3Com Bluetooth PC Card that sent data to a Hewlett-Packard inkjet printer without a cable. Several months later, CNet reported that the technology was just beginning to show up in laptop computers and some expensive cell phones.

Most analysts have not lost their enthusiasm for Bluetooth; if anything, anticipation has been building. In January 2001, analysts at Frost & Sullivan issued a report speculating that 11 million Bluetooth-enabled devices would be sold during the year, generating $2.5 billion in revenues. The company predicted that Bluetooth revenues would soar from $92.3 million in 1999 to $53.12 billion in 2006.

The pace is quickening. On March 9, 2001, ZDNet reported that Bluetooth "is on the verge of maturity." Around that time, the Bluetooth SIG released version 1.1 of its Bluetooth specifications, saying that it soon would boost Bluetooth's transfer speeds from just under 1 Mbps to around 2 Mbps. At some point, it is claimed, Bluetooth speeds could approach 10 Mbps.

While businesses might be faster to adopt Bluetooth, consumer awareness is still virtually non-existent. One analyst has said that the technology would begin making its mark with the public in 2003.

Bibliography

Dennis, Sylvia. "Bluetooth 1.0 Specification Issued At Last." *Newsbytes*, July 28, 1999.

Dennis, Sylvia. "Bluetooth Poised to Take Off—F&S Report." *Newsbytes*, January 13, 2000.

Newton, Harry. *Newton's Telecom Dictionary,* 16th Edition. New York: Telecom, 2000.

Patrizio, Andy. "Bluetooth Shows Off at CES." *Wired*, January 7, 2001. <http://www.wired.com/news/technology/0,1282,41040,00.html> (March 20, 2002).

Telefonaktiebolaget LM Ericsson. "Bluetooth History: Milestones in the Bluetooth Advance." 2001. <http://www.ericsson.com/bluetooth/companyove/history-bl/> (March 20, 2002).

Further Reading

Dertouzos, Michael.*The Unfinished Revolution: Human-Centered Computers and What They Can Do for Us.* New York: HarperCollins, 2001.

Fried, Ian. "Will All Hail Bluetooth?" *News.com*,
December 4, 2000.
<http://news.cnet.com/news/0-1006-200-3958613.html>
(March 20, 2002).

Kolesnikov, Oleg. "Bluetooth Summary—Overview."
March 26, 2001.
<http://triton.cc.gatech.edu/ubicomp/
433> (March 20, 2002).

Negroponte, Nicholas. *Being Digital.* New York: Vintage
Books, 1995.

Related Topics

Broadband; Cellular Telephony; Human-Computer
Interaction; Internet Appliances; Local Area Network;
Personal Digital Assistants; Wireless Networks;
World Wide Web

— *Kevin Featherly*

Borg, Anita

1949–

U.S. Computer Scientist

Anita Borg is president and founding director of the
Institute for Women and Technology, and a member of
the research staff at Xerox's Palo Alto Research Center
(PARC). Borg has been a tireless and passionate advocate in encouraging women to pursue careers in computer science and technology.

Borg, born Anita Borg Naffz in Chicago, grew up
in Illinois, Hawaii, and Washington, and spent her first
two years of college at the University of Washington in
Seattle. After moving to Manhattan, where she learned
the computer language COBOL (Common Business
Language), Borg returned to school at New York
University, where she received a doctorate in computer
science in 1981 for her research in the area of operating systems synchronization efficiency.

After graduation, she worked for several computer companies before spending 12 years with Digital
Equipment. While at Digital, she developed tools for
predicting the performance of future microprocessor
memory systems. In 1992, Borg transferred to Digital's
Network Systems Laboratory, where she developed a
new system for supporting efficient inter-organization-
al communication: Mecca, a fully Web-accessible system that provides security, privacy filtering, and the
ability to get pertinent information to the right people
based on their position, location, or interests.

In 1987, Borg initiated Systers, an electronic community for technical women in computing. Systers
currently has 2,500 members in 38 countries. In 1994,

Borg co-founded the Grace Hopper Celebration of
Women in Computing, a technical conference highlighting talks by women computer scientists. The conference, which was held in 1997 and 2000 as well,
also aims to bring to light the work of women in the
history of computer science, and to advocate for policies to bring more women and minorities into science
and technology.

In December 1997, Borg moved to Xerox PARC
to create the Institute for Women and Technology
(IWT). IWT's mission is to increase the impact of
women in all aspects of technology, and to increase
the positive impact of technology on women. IWT is
a non-profit organization with sponsorship from
Compaq, Hewlett-Packard, Sun Microsystems, and
Xerox, among others. IWT projects include further
developments on Mecca, a workshop on Technology
for Future Families, the Virtual Development Center
(an industry-supported partnership of universities and
communities that brings together universities and
high-school girls to brainstorm on new technological
designs), and the Senior Women's Summit. Held in
2000, the summit focused on the future of women in
computing, public policy, education, and societal challenges. IWT has also focused on increasing young
girls' interest in math and science by engaging in a
pilot project that encourages girls to look critically at
technology in their everyday lives.

Borg has been the recipient of many awards,
including the 1999 Forbes Executive Women's Summit
Award for Outstanding Achievement and the 1999
Melitta Bentz Woman of Innovation Award. In addition, she has been inducted into the 1998 Women in
Technology International Hall of Fame, was made a
1996 Fellow of the Association for Computing
Machinery, and in 1995 received both the Pioneer
Award from the Electronic Frontier Foundation and
the Augusta Ada Lovelace Award from the Association
of Women in Computing.

Borg has fervently argued that women must fight
for technology "citizenship" just as suffragists fought
for the right to vote. Not only is women's participation
in technology an equity concern, Borg contends, but it is
also an issue of quality of life for women around the
world. Future work by IWT will concentrate on policy
issues, particularly with respect to increasing the participation of women and minorities in technological education and the retention of women in technical fields.

Selected Works

Borg, Anita. "What Draws Women to and Keeps Women
in Computing?" *Women in Science and Engineering:*

Choices for Success. The Annals of the New York Academy of Sciences, vol. 869.

———. "Why Systers?" October 19, 2001. <http://www.iwt.org/whatwedo/programs/systers/whysysters.html> (April 5, 2002).

Bibliography

Borg, Anita. Homepage. <http://www.iwt.org/borg.html> (April 5, 2002).

Institute for Women and Technology. Homepage. <http://www.iwt.org> (April 5, 2002).

Jeffries, Robin, et al. "Systers: Contradictions in Community." <http://www.iwt.org/whatwedo/programs/systers/contradictionsincommunity.pdf> (April 5, 2002).

Related Topics

Gender and New Media; Systers

— *Leslie Regan Shade*

Brand, Stewart

1938–

Countercultural Entrepreneur

For the past three decades, Stewart Brand has worn many hats—soldier, lumberjack, photographer, author, editor, publisher, conservationist, corporate consultant—but most of all, he has been a creator of new ideas. Although his interests are expansive and eclectic, one of the strongest threads running through his work is the liberating potential that he sees in technology for individuals and society.

Brand was born on December 14, 1938, in Rockford, Illinois. He completed his undergraduate work at Stanford University, earning a degree in biology in 1960. He then joined the army, returning to the San Francisco Bay area at the end of a two-year stint and blending into the art and hippie scene that was then fermenting. He hooked up with Ken Kesey's Merry Pranksters and toured the California coast, a run that was vividly recorded in Tom Wolfe's 1968 book *The Electric Kool-Aid Acid Test.* During this period, Brand gained experience in organizing festivals and events, skills that he would use in diverse settings throughout his career.

One of Brand's best-known projects is the *Whole Earth Catalog.* Initially published in 1968, it became a bible for counter-cultural groups of that era, offering reviews of books, clothes, stoves, and tools for doing anything from gardening to word processing. The final edition, *The Last Whole Earth Catalog,* received the National Book Award in 1972. The slogan prefacing the volumes reflects the fusion of wit, arrogance, and American pragmatism that Brand had brought together in the project: "We are as Gods, and we might as well get good at it."

In 1975, Brand launched a new magazine, *Co-Evolution Quarterly,* that was modeled on the success story of the *Catalog.* The new publication provided more room for essay-length tracts, and gave greater attention to computers and software. Brand plowed most of the earnings from his *Whole Earth Catalog* into the Point Foundation, which he established to support creative individuals. Over the course of three years, the foundation gave away $1 million. Through these initiatives, Brand was practicing basic business principles combined with the counterculture idealism and ideology prevalent in the United States during the 1960s. He was, in other words, a product and advocate of both American entrepreneurship and alternative culture.

In 1984, Brand organized the first Hacker's Conference, bringing together representatives of the different strains of ideology and technology involved in creating the personal computer: the brilliant former Massachusetts Institute of Technology students who'd developed the first computer game, called Spacewar! back in the 1960s; the pioneers who were

Stewart Brand with the Whole Earth Software Catalog, *1984. (Roger Ressmeyer/CORBIS).*

then working on the development of desktop computers; and the community of software designers populating Silicon Valley in the 1980s.

Brand has repeatedly demonstrated an uncanny knack for envisioning future societal developments. He saw the social potential of computers long before Silicon Valley became what it is today, and was the first to use the term "personal computer" in a publication. In 1984, he also co-founded the very first virtual community, the Whole Earth 'Lectronic Link (the WELL). Then, as now, emphasis was placed on the support the computers could give to human communication. Once the WELL was up and running, Brand spent a year at MIT's Media Lab; his book reflecting on his experiences there, *The Media Lab: Inventing the Future at MIT,* was published in 1987.

Unlike others sharing his countercultural heritage, Brand does not have an innate aversion to corporate power. He established a consultancy operation called Global Business Network (GBN) whose clients include Hewlett-Packard, Xerox, IBM, AT&T, and Royal Dutch Shell, along with the White House and the Pentagon.

Brand continues to initiate innovative and controversial projects. One of the current projects in which he is involved is the Long Now Foundation. Among the core activities of the foundation, which was launched in 1995, are the construction of a clock designed to chime once every century and run for at least 10,000 years, and the construction of a digital library whose purpose is nothing less than the preservation of the knowledge of global civilization, particularly endangered languages.

Brand's most recent endeavor, started in 2001, is the All Species project, which has the daunting goal of recording all known life forms on the planet, from bacteria to Homo sapiens. The scope of this project almost defies the imagination—there may be anywhere from 30 million to 50 million living organisms on the planet—but it is precisely the monumental challenge of the undertaking that attracted Brand to the project. The All Species project allows him to bring his skills in networking, fundraising, and grand gestures to bear, drawing on many of his personal strengths—his optimism, his affinity for organization and technology, his global orientation, and his old-fashioned American pragmatism.

Selected Works

Brand, Stewart. *The Clock of the Long Now: Time and Responsibility—The Ideas Behind the World's Slowest Computer.* New York: Basic Books, 1999.

———. *The Last Whole Earth Catalog.* New York: Random House, 1972.

———. Home page. <http://www.well.com/user/sbb/> (August 30, 2002).

———. *How Buildings Learn: What Happens After They're Built.* New York: Viking Press, 1994.

———. *The Media Lab: Inventing the Future at MIT.* New York: Viking Press, 1987.

Bibliography

Anonymous. Interview with Stewart Brand. *PBS Frontline,* June 15, 1995. <http://www.pbs.org/wgbh/pages/frontline/cyberspace/brand.html> (May 15, 2002).

Betts, Kellyn S. "Conversations: Stewart Brand, Whole Earth Vision for the 21st Century." *Environmental Magazine,* May/June 1996.

Brown, Andrew. "The Guardian Profile: Stewart Brand, Whole Earth Visionary." *The Guardian,* August 4, 2001. <http://www.guardian.co.uk/Archive/Article/0,4273,4233515,00.html> (May 15, 2002).

Collins, Glenn. "Stewart Brand: A New 'Catalog' and All's Well," *New York Times,* November 2, 1984.

Stipp, David. "Stewart Brand: The Electric Kool-Aid Management Consultant." *Fortune Magazine,* October 16, 1995.

Further Reading

Rheingold, Howard. *The Virtual Community: Homesteading on the Electronic Frontier.* Revised edition. Cambridge, Mass.: MIT Press, 2000.

Wolfe, Tom. *The Electric Kool-Aid Acid Test.* New York: Farrar, Straus and Giroux, 1968.

Related Topics

Hillis, W. Daniel; Media Lab, Massachusetts Institute of Technology; Whole Earth 'Lectronic Link

— *Nicholas Jankowski*

Broadband

According to the Federal Communications Commission (FCC), "broadband" describes any Internet connection rate of 200kbps (kilobytes per second) or higher. In common use, however, broadband means connection speeds greater than the "narrowband"—that is, 56kbps. The number of broadband-enabled homes is predicted to rise to more than 90 million worldwide by 2007; Korea and Canada lead broadband saturation globally at 50 percent, with the United States currently at 10 percent. During the late 1990s, the push to affect the "last mile" of broadband connectivity—that is, the final link between a telecommunications service provider and the customer—proceeded at a breakneck pace worldwide, although it has slowed considerably in recent years. According to Nielson NetRatings, more than 21 million Americans used broadband Internet services as of November 2001.

Broadband delivery derives from a wide array of sources. The most well-known of these are cable modems and digital subscriber lines (DSL), but usage of fixed wireless connections and satellite services is currently on the rise, with "fiber to the home" and power line–based broadband predicted for the future. Regardless of how it is transmitted, the benefits of broadband can be summed up in two words: speed and ubiquity. Web surfing, multimedia applications, video conferencing, distance education, and telemedicine are all made easier with broadband, which is highly recommended for accessing high-end proprietary networks such as Internet 2. What's more, unlike dialup connections, broadband connections are always on. A recent Sprint study found that users often move their computer from the study to the kitchen after getting broadband connections, suggesting that access to broadband intensifies the user's relationship to online communications.

History of Broadband: Telephone, Cable, and Beyond

The history of broadband begins with the narrowband Internet. Many people argue that the narrowband Internet flourished as a result of minimal regulation, pointing to the explosion of small, private service providers in the 1980s. The Center for Democracy and Technology (CDT) argues to the contrary, pointing out that telephone lines have always been highly regulated. For example, the 1996 Telecommunications Act has mandated competition among phone providers. This resulted in the creation of "incumbent local exchange carriers" (ILECs) such as Bell Atlantic, and "competitive local exchange carriers (CLECs) such as Covad.

By contrast, cable television has been subject to little or no regulation. During the 1980s, while telephone companies worked to deploy "proto-broadband" technologies such as ISDN, cable companies focused their efforts on wiring American homes for television. Later, they began improving their facilities with two-way lines capable of throughput speeds of 30mbps (megabytes per second) downstream—significantly faster than the FCC's requirement for broadband delivery. ("Downstream" refers to the data coming into the user's computer from the Internet; material that the user uploads to the Internet goes "upstream.")

Today, the cable modem is the most popular form of broadband, and an option for as many as 80 percent of U.S. homes. The massive popularity of cable-based Internet use has prompted many to question earlier decisions to leave that industry unregulated. Proponents of open access argue that cable companies should abide by the same "common carrier" restrictions as telephone companies, and allow multiple ISPs on their systems; as it stands, many cable companies give users a choice of only one provider.

During the 1990s, telephone companies began offering their own low-priced alternative to cable modems: digital subscriber lines (DSL). Asymmetric DSL (ADSL) is the most popular type of DSL service; experts predict that as much as 66 percent of households will be able to receive some form of DSL by 2004. Unlike cable, which is a shared resource, and therefore is subject to lags during busy times, ADSL is a dedicated connection running to individual consumers. Unfortunately, ADSL has some problems. First, although ADSL's downstream speed goes up to 8mbps, its upstream speeds do not yet qualify under the FCC's definition of broadband. In addition, DSL customers must be within three miles of the "local loop" that connects to the telephone company, which prevents 20 percent of U.S. households from receiving service at this time. Finally, many consumers have been left to the mercy of telephone companies who don't want to "play fair" with one another: CLECs routinely accuse ILECs of price-fixing and dragging their heels on common carrier rules.

Some frustrated customers have turned to alternate technologies to receive broadband connections. Fixed wireless broadband, which uses small antennas to receive microwave signals and is especially popular in rural locales, remains plagued by "line of sight" problems, in which trees and buildings can interfere with signal transmission. Satellite broadband does not suffer from line-of-sight issues, but remains costly to deploy. Finally, some broadband technologies have been touted in the press, but aren't yet available on a wide scale. "Fiber to the home" is especially appealing, since fiber optic cables can support extremely high bandwidth—up to 1,000 mbps. Unfortunately, fiber requires costly digging up of existing residential neighborhoods. "Power line–based broadband" proposes to use technology that already exists in everyone's home, but technical problems have hindered implementation.

Broadband's Financial and Legislative Futures

The "broadband push" of the late 1990s saw a tremendous merging of telephone, cable, and wireless companies—so much so that it makes little sense to treat them as discreet entities at this point. Perhaps the most notorious of these mergers was Excite@Home, a $6.7 billion merger between long-distance telephone provider AT&T, cable companies Cox and Comcast, and Excite, a Web portal. In 1999, Excite@Home was touted as a "broadband giant," with stock offered at $99 per share; today, the company is bankrupt. Recently, critics have cited the failure of Excite@Home, along with the fact that several large phone companies have begun cutting back on promised DSL services, to argue that the American demand for broadband is not as high as advertisers would like to believe. Others maintain that if the "Napster phenomenon" is any indication, broadband demand will continue, regardless of market blunders.

Indeed, the next important issue facing broadband consumers—in the United States, at least—may not involve industry mergers, or even redefining the cable industry. A recent white paper from the CDT investigated the dangers of the "content distribution model," in which multiple Web sites with the same materials are established in order to ensure that Web surfers receive multimedia materials quickly. While this practice (which is also called "mirroring") seems benign enough on its face, the CDT warns that "It is quite easy to envision a world in which it is relatively costly to have one's high-bandwidth multimedia-rich broadband content efficiently and smoothly distributed to Internet users, and only the better-funded speakers will be able to afford to have their broadband content 'distributed.'" Were this to happen, the CDT worries, "the rough 'equality of voice' between small and large speakers that is a key characteristic of the narrowband Internet" would be in serious jeopardy.

Bibliography

Berman, Jerry, and John B. Morris, Jr. "The Broadband Internet: The End of the Equal Voice?" *Computers, Freedom & Privacy 2000*, April 2000. <http://www.cfp2000.org/papers/morrisberman.pdf> (May 24, 2002).

Gilbert, Alorie. "Broadband Home Use Jumps." *CNET News*, December 11, 2001.

Kawamoto, Dawn, and Rachel Konrad. "Excite@Home to Shut Down; AT&T Drops Bid." *CNET News*, December 4, 2001.

"New eMarketer Report Projects 90 Million Broadband Households Worldwide by 2004." [Press Release]. <http://Emarketer.com>, April 30, 2001.

Further Reading

DeLong, Stephen E. "E-Biz—Cable: The Tried-and-True Broadband Connection." *UPSIDE Magazine*, October 7, 2000. <http://www.upside.com/texis/mvm/ebiz/story?id=39dbc7fd0> (May 24, 2002).

Fowler, Dennis. "The Last Mile: Making the Broadband Connection." *NetWorker: Publication of the ACM Press* 4, no. 1 (2000), pp. 26–32.

Maxwell, Kim. *Residential Broadband: An Insider's Guide to the Battle for the Last Mile.* New York: Wiley Computer Publishing, 1999.

Miller, Mark. *Analyzing Broadband Networks.* Berkeley, Calif.: McGraw-Hill, 2000.

Morris, John B. "Broadband Backgrounder: Public Policy Issues Raised by Broadband Technology" [Report]. Broadband Access Project, Center for Democracy and Technology, December 2000. <http://www.cdt.org/digi_infra/broadband/backgrounder.shtml> (May 24, 2002).

Munro, Neil. "From Washington: Considering the Broadband Debate." *Communications of the ACM* 44, no. 10 (2001), pp. 17–19.

Spring, Tom. "Broadband from Above: Satellite Services Beam High-Speed Access Anywhere." *PC World*, February 2001, p. 64.

Related Topics

Digital Subscriber Line; Multimedia; Napster; Narrowcasting; Satellite Networks; Streaming Media; Telecommuting; Telemedicine; Videoconferencing; Wireless Networks

— Theresa M. Senft

Brooks, Rodney
1954–
Robotics/Artificial Intelligence Engineer

Rodney Brooks is a professor, innovator, and entrepreneur who has challenged the traditional conception of artificial intelligence. Brooks has established himself as a scholar by introducing "subsumption architecture" or "behavior-based" approaches to robotics design, making his work applicable to both planetary exploration and commercial products.

Brooks was born in Adelaide, Australia, in 1954. As a child, technology and computers fascinated Brooks; a lack of computer availability in his town led him to construct computers from whatever materials he could find. Similarly, a lack of academic programs in computer science at Australian universities directed Brooks to a study in pure mathematics, and he earned his master of science degree from Flinders University in Adelaide, Australia. Utilizing assistantship programs provided by

American schools, Brooks received a Ph.D. in computer science from Stanford University in 1981. Shortly thereafter, he became Fujitsu Professor of Computer Science at the Massachusetts Institute of Technology (MIT), as well as the director of MIT's Artificial Intelligence Laboratory.

At MIT, Brooks envisioned a different way to program robotics. He introduced ideas of behavior-based programming to his robots that differed drastically from the traditional method. Rather than programming a robot with specific actions (e.g., to move forward or backward), he programs with digital interaction behaviors that allow the robot to learn on its own.

Brooks developed insect-like robots at MIT that were small in size and capable of moving in an environment without hitting other objects. These robots became the first products of the lab to be used for experimentation as autonomous planetary explorers. Three generations of robots followed, and the insect-like forms led to more humanoid forms. The artificial intelligence laboratory at MIT became a birthplace for Coco, Cog, and Kismet. Coco, whose body resembles that of a small gorilla, possesses a higher level of self-government than the other robots. Cog's structure looks much like a human body; it has been designed to learn through social interaction, following movement with its two camera eyes and correspondingly moving its appendages. Kismet is a sociable humanoid robot that has been designed to respond to human interaction. For example, waving an object in front of Kismet's eye-like cameras causes it to make a facial expression of interest. If the motion becomes too overwhelming for the robot, its face will express fear.

Brooks believes that his robots can acquire intelligence through social interaction. His MIT Web site describes the foundation of robotics construction as the creation of physical resemblance to humans. If a robot programmed to respond to social interaction is to acquire intelligence or experience, it must have humans to interact with it. Brooks believes that creating robots that look similar to humans will encourage humans to interact with these beings more naturally.

While working at MIT, Brooks co-founded the iRobot Corporation. At iRobot, robots are produced to serve a variety of purposes in businesses and the home. Two of the company's main customers are the Defense Advanced Projects Research Agency (DAPRA) and the Office of Naval Research (ONR). In November 2000, iRobot teamed up with Hasbro, Inc., to commercially release the My Real Baby doll. The doll has similar emotionally responsive traits as Kismet, and uses sensors to react to being rocked, held, or burped by its caregiver.

Brooks has worked to design robots that reduce the problems that stem from traditional programming approaches. These problems include programming mass amounts of instructional code, and the lengthy time needed by a robot to process commands. Brooks contends that intelligence derives from interaction with the environment, which allows the robot to become autonomous and more life-like, rather than from a massive supply of programmed instructions on reacting to the environment.

In addition to his robotics work, Brooks co-founded the *International Journal of Computer Vision*, is a fellow of the American Association for Artificial Intelligence (AAAI), and received the 1991 Computers and Thought Award from the International Joint Conference on Artificial Intelligence (IJACI). He was also interviewed extensively in Errol Morris' 1997 documentary film, *Fast, Cheap & Out of Control*. Brooks' revolutionary and mind-boggling robotics designs have had wide-ranging impact, influencing the programming approaches to robotics construction and reaching the public through commercially available products.

Selected Works

Brooks, Rodney A. *Cambrian Intelligence: The Early History of the New AI*. Cambridge, Mass.: MIT Press, 1999.

———. *Flesh and Machines: How Robots Will Change Us*. New York: Pantheon Books, 2001.

Brooks, Rodney A., and Patty Maes, eds. *Artificial Life IV: Proceedings of the Fourth International Workshop on the Synthesis and Simulation of Living Systems (Complex Adaptive Systems)*. Cambridge, Mass.: MIT Press, 1994.

Bibliography

Coale, Kristi. "Seeding Intelligence." *Wired News*, July 25, 1997. <http://www.wired.com/news/print/0,1294,5433,00.html> (May 10, 2002).

Freedman, David H. "Bringing up RoboBaby." *Wired 2.12*, December 1994. <http://www.wired.com/wired/archive/2.12/cog_pr.html> (May 10, 2002).

MIT Artificial Intelligence Laboratory. Rodney A. Brooks Web Page. 2001. <http://www.ai.mit.edu/people/brooks/index.shtml> (May 10, 2002).

Further Reading

Coale, Kristi. "Seeing His Work in Action, in Space." *Wired News*, July 25, 1997.

<http://www.wired.com/news/print/0,1294,5478,00.html>
(May 10, 2002).
———. "Training Wheels." *Wired News,* July 17, 1997.
<http://www.wired.com/news/print/0,1294,5255,00.html>
(May 10, 2002).
Dibbell, Julian. "The Race to Build Intelligent Machines."
Time, March 25, 1996.
McFarling, Usha Lee. "One Giant Leap for Machinekind?"
Los Angeles Times, August 31, 2000.

Related Topics
Maes, Pattie; Robotics

— *James Pyfer*

Browser

A browser is a program through which pages on the World Wide Web can be viewed. The browser interface in many ways resembles those of word-processing programs, but Web browsers have greater flexibility. Not only can Web users view the text and images on the millions of hypertext pages available on the Web via their browsers, they can also listen to music, watch videos, and play games that are programmed in languages like Flash and Java, among many others. A browser, in essence, is the window to the Web.

THE BEGINNING

Like the Web itself, the first Web browser was invented by Tim Berners-Lee at the Swiss particle-physics lab, the European Center for Nuclear Research (CERN), in 1990. Berners-Lee, long intrigued by the possibilities of hypertext (see entry), realized that he would need a simple way to display pages of information using the hypertext transfer protocol (HTTP) language, which computers now use to communicate over the Web. He needed an interface.

According to his 1999 memoir, *Weaving the Web,* Berners-Lee didn't set out at first to invent a browser. His employers at CERN had a "buy, don't build" credo, he said, which led him to shop around for existing software that could be adjusted to publish hypertext pages on the Internet. Already there were a number of hypertext products on the market, including a point-and-click multimedia manual on repairing automobiles. But to his surprise, Berners-Lee was unable to find anyone who recognized the importance of his browser concept. One product in particular, Owl Ltd.'s hypertext interface known as Guide, looked promising as a Web browser; all it needed was a way to be connected to the Internet. "They were friendly enough," Berners-Lee wrote of company officials at Owl, "but they too were unconvinced." Owl, and another promising company Berners-Lee approached called Dynatext, thus missed opportunities to build the first Web browser. Berners-Lee decided he would have to make it himself.

In October 1990, he set about writing the program that would become the first Web browser while using a $10,000 NeXT computer at the CERN lab. The NeXT PC was built by the company that Steve Jobs formed after his ouster in the mid-1980s from Apple Computer. While it was highly advanced, it was also highly incompatible with other computers, which would later prove to be problematic. But the computer's programming utility, NeXTStep, made it fairly easy for Berners-Lee to create a word-processor-styled program that would serve as the shell of the first Web browser.

He still lacked the ability to turn text into instantly recognizable and click-able hypertext, the key piece of the puzzle. But the NeXT computer made that feasible, too. The computer had a spare 32-bit piece of memory intentionally set aside for tinkerers, and this gave Berners-Lee the computing resource he needed to create HTTP. It also allowed him to create what he called the universal resource indicator (URI)—more popularly known as the universal resource locator (URL)—that indicates Web addresses. He also wrote software that made his NeXT computer the world's first Web server, which made it possible for him to store Web pages on a portion of his computer's hard drive, and for others to access them through the Internet.

In November 1990, Berners-Lee produced a prototype of the first browser, which he called WorldWideWeb (the name later was changed to Nexus). A month later, he had it working with the hypertext markup language (HTML) he had invented to instruct computers on how to display pages. "The browser could decode URIs, and let me read, write or edit Web pages in HTML. It could browse the Web using HTTP, though it could save documents only into the local computer system, not over the Internet." Because the system worked only on the NeXT computing platform in its earliest days, Berners-Lee could exchange Web-based information only with Robert Cailliau, director of CERN's office-computing systems group, because Cailliau also used a NeXT machine.

As a final step, and as a way both to demonstrate his concept of the Web as a universal information space and to quickly tap into an abundance of information that was already available on the Internet, Berners-Lee programmed his browser so that it could follow links to files on servers other than those that relied on his own HTTP platform, including those that were transmitted using file transfer protocol (FTP), the platform on which most newsgroups and articles were stored on the Internet. By Christmas 1990, Berners-Lee and Callilau's browser was communicating through CERN's server over the Internet.

THE PUBLIC DEBUT

The Web was opened to the public on January 15, 1991, and a "line-mode" browser, written by CERN student Nicola Pellow and capable only of displaying text, was distributed by CERN to a limited number of Internet users so they could view the new creation. Those who wished to could dial up CERN using the Telnet protocol to download the line-mode browser and begin viewing the first crude, text-heavy Web sites. The first browser could not display images, or even colors unless they were viewed on the same kind of NeXT workstation that Berners-Lee had used to write his program. Nor was it a "point-and-click" interface that utilized a computer mouse the way browsers do today; unless the users accessing the Web were using a NeXT computer, they had to type instructions on their keyboards.

However, crude as it was, Nexus made real the promise of a global hypertext network. Most importantly, because of its simplicity and ASCII text format, the browser was not limited to just one or two computer operating systems; it could work with and be read on any system. The guiding idea, ingenious for its time, was that new standards would not be imposed on the computer hardware, but instead on the data.

Once the Web was out to the public, other researchers began working to improve Berners-Lee's innovation by introducing improved browsers that could work with Microsoft Windows, Macintosh, and Unix operating systems.

In April 1991, a point-and-click browser called "Erwise" emerged, created by students at Helsinki University; it was built to run on Unix machines that ran X Windows. That was followed a month later by another important early browser created by a University of California–Berkeley student named Pei Wei. This browser was built to demonstrate the capabilities of the interpretive computer language for Unix that Wei had been working on, which he called Viola. The browser, ViolaWWW, was released in a

test version in May 1992, and it was fairly advanced. It could display HTML with graphics, run animations, and download small, embedded applications known as "applets."

Although ViolaWWW was difficult and time-consuming to install, it began to spread the Web among Unix users, and there were many of those at corporations and universities. Later that year, Cailliau, Berners-Lee, and Pellow teamed to create the first browser designed for the Macintosh computer, called Samba. Other browsers, with names like Lynx, Midas, Cello, and Arena, were also invented and distributed. As more browsers and servers were made available, the Web began to grow.

THE ADVENT OF MOSAIC AND NETSCAPE

In January 1993, a browser was unleashed that changed everything, rocketing the Web into the spotlight as the most important new medium since television. Marc Andreessen, an undergraduate student at the University of Illinois at Champaign-Urbana and a part-time staffer at the university's National Center for Supercomputing Applications (NCSA), collaborated with friend and fellow NCSA staffer Eric Bina, working around the clock for three months to create a browser called Mosaic.

Mosaic was the first browser to allow users, regardless of the machinery they were using, to point-and-click their way around the Web. Mosaic made it possible to view hypertext documents with embedded graphics, and—if the client computer had speakers and a sound card—to launch sound files as well as open movie clips and other "rich hypermedia." Aiming to make the browser usable by the maximum number of people on the Internet, Andreessen had spent many hours conversing on newsgroups, seeking input on ways to improve the way that other browsers worked, and he incorporated the many suggestions into Mosaic. The browser ran on simple PC desktops, rather than requiring high-powered Unix machines—although it ran on those too, as well as on Macintoshes.

For a time in the early 1990s, Mosaic was the Web's most popular browser. When it was released in January 1993, there were 50 known Web servers. By October 1993, there were more than 500, and by June 1994, there were 1,500, according to a *Wired* magazine report published at the time. It wasn't that Mosaic was the first or necessarily the best browser, but it was the "most pleasurable" to use at the time, *Wired*'s Gary Wolfe wrote.

Andreessen joined up with venture capitalist Jim Clark to exploit Mosaic's commercial possibilities; when the NCSA protested, Andreessen decided to outdo his own creation by creating and launching an improved, commercial version of Mosaic, which he called Netscape Navigator. The company that Andreessen formed with Clark, Netscape, offered shares to the public in August 1995 in one of the most lucrative and successful initial public offerings (IPOs) of stock in the history of U.S. business; after one day of trading, the company was worth $4.4 billion. Meanwhile, Netscape's share of the browser market skyrocketed in four months from zero percent to 75 percent. The World Wide Web had well and truly arrived.

THE SLEEPING GIANT AWAKES

Netscape's success finally alerted software giant Microsoft to the vast possibilities of the Internet, and Bill Gates did what was almost unthinkable for so large a company. In Netscape's pre-IPO days, Microsoft had approached Clark and Netscape CEO Jim Barksdale about licensing Netscape's browser, buying a slice of the company, and taking a seat on its board of directors. In exchange, Microsoft would devote space to Netscape on the opening screen of its then-forthcoming operating system, Windows '95. When the deal fell through, Gates chose to stop Microsoft in its tracks, spin the company around, and realign it with the forces of the Web and the Internet. One of his first and most substantial moves was to create a competing Web browser, Microsoft Internet Explorer, which was released just two weeks after Netscape's IPO. Although its first version had functionality problems, these were gradually corrected. Microsoft distributed Explorer for free, and its browser quickly whittled away at Netscape's dominance.

In 1996, Netscape released Navigator 2.0, which supported Java's embedded applet files, contained an easy-to-use email program, and incorporated JavaScript, frames, and plug-ins. But in that same year, the popular service provider America Online agreed to include Microsoft's Explorer browser in its service. Very quickly, Microsoft took over about one-third of the browser market.

Then, in the fall of 1997, Microsoft made a key move that would ultimately result in a landmark antitrust lawsuit. The company announced plans to incorporate its Internet Explorer version 4.0 into the latest version of its operating system, Windows '98. It would not be a piece of added-on software, but an integrated part of the operating system itself, one that could not be deleted without affecting the performance of the computer that was being used. The browser and the operating system, in effect, were the same program. The U.S. Justice Department, which had issued a consent decree barring tight integration of software in this manner, sued Microsoft, claiming in part that Microsoft had acted ruthlessly to squash competition. The government eventually won that case, and a judge ruled that Microsoft should be broken up. However, part of that decision was thrown out in early 2001.

In January 1998, Netscape said that its browser, too, would be distributed free. It also said that its source code would be made available for free on the Web, allowing the programmers in the Web community to rewrite and improve its functions. But these moves didn't help the company to stave off Microsoft. Netscape's technological improvements could not keep pace with Microsoft's huge research and development budget, and by the time Internet Explorer 4.0 was out, Microsoft's browser was arguably better, and certainly no worse, than Netscape's. In November 1998, Netscape foundered and was bought by AOL, which nonetheless retained Explorer as the default browser for its online service. It took until November 2000 for Netscape to release version 6.0, the first major upgrade to its browser since 1998.

THE CONTEMPORARY BROWSER ENVIRONMENT

Internet Explorer is now the world's dominant browser, used by 87.7 percent of visitors to Web sites monitored by measurement firm WebSideStory in February 2001. Netscape had just over 12 percent of the market in that same survey. Internet.com's Browserwatch, which logs the browsers that visit its site, indicated in September 2001 that 90.2 percent of the visiting browsers were versions of Internet Explorer; only 5.66 percent were versions of Netscape Navigator. Meanwhile, Opera, an Oslo, Norway-based upstart browser that began making waves in 2001, was the browser in nearly 1 percent of visits to the Browserwatch site, and other browsers continue to be created, albeit sporadically.

Some industry watchers have been building the case for Opera, which is the number-three browser on the market. First developed in 1994, Opera differs from both Netscape Navigator and Internet Explorer in that it was built from scratch, while both Navigator and Explorer are primarily based on the NCSA's Mosaic code. It has some unique functions, such as "page zoom" and a "multi-document interface-browsing environment." But much of the buzz about Opera was the result of its contract with IBM to supply the Opera browser for IBM's Internet appliances. Opera has reached similar deals with Advanced Micro Devices, Ericsson, Psion, and Be as well, a possible signal that major Internet appliance-makers might be looking to Opera as an alternative to Microsoft and AOL Time Warner's browsers. Whether that is the case, and whether it puts a dent in Netscape's dwindling market share, remains to be seen.

Bibliography

Berners-Lee, Tim. "What Were the First WWW Browsers?" Modified December 7, 2001.
<http://www.w3.org/People/Berners-Lee/FAQ.html#browser> (May 10, 2002).

———. "The WorldWideWeb Browser." Modified December 7, 2001.
<http://www.w3.org/People/Berners-Lee/WorldWideWeb.html> (May 10, 2002).

Berners-Lee, Tim, and Mark Frischetti. *Weaving the Web.* San Francisco, Calif.: HarperSanFrancisco, 1999.

Gillies, James, and Robert Cailliau. *How the Web Was Born.* Oxford: Oxford University Press, 2000.

Naughton, John. *A Brief History of the Future: From Radio Days to Internet Years in a Lifetime.* Woodstock, N.Y.: Overlook Press, 2000.

Segaller, Stephen. *Nerds 2.0.1: A Brief History of the Internet.* New York: TV Books, 1998.

Wolfe, Gary. "The (Second Phase of the) Revolution Has Begun." *Wired 2.10,* October 1994.
<http://www.wired.com/wired/archive/2.10/mosaic.html> (May 10, 2002).

Further Reading

Auletta, Ken. *World War 3.0: Microsoft and Its Enemies.* New York: Random House. 2001.

Boutell, Thomas. "Web Browsers OpenFAQ." Boutell.Com, Inc., 1995–2001.
<http://www.boutell.com/openfaq/browsers/1.html> (May 10, 2002).

Fidler, Roger. *Mediamorphosis: Understanding New Media.* Thousand Oaks, Calif.: Pine Forge Press, 1997.

Packer, Randall, and Ken Jordan, eds. *Multimedia: From Wagner to Virtual Reality.* New York: W.W. Norton & Co., 2001.

Related Topics

Andreessen, Marc; Berners-Lee, Tim; Bulletin-Board Systems; Hypermedia; Hypertext; Interactivity; Interface; Linking; Markup Languages; World Wide Web

— *Kevin Featherly*

Bulletin-Board Systems

Predating the World Wide Web by more than 15 years, bulletin-board systems (BBSs) were the first collaborative tools for users of personal computers. Originally unconnected to the Internet, many BBSs today can be accessed via telnet or through specially designed Web interfaces. With their traditions of free speech and self-governance, BBSs have long influenced theorists of virtual community building.

"It's always been hard to describe a BBS to someone who's never heard of one before; part newspaper, part local bar, and maybe even part den of iniquity," notes Jason Scott, who is currently producing a documentary on the history of computer bulletin boards. In large part, BBS culture began with a series of time-sharing experiments in the early 1970s designed to connect ordinary people with mainframe computers. On the PLATO system at the University of Illinois, users gathered to exchange messages with one another and chat, while users of the Community Memory in Berkeley accessed terminals in record stores and community centers. Community Memory, which lasted until 1974, inspired the founders of San Francisco–based Whole Earth 'Lectronic Link (WELL), which still thrives today.

THE BIRTH OF THE BBS

The first "real" BBSs arrived shortly after the 1974 introduction of the first personal modems, which were marketed to the public in 1977. As computing historian Vince Long puts it, this was a time "when names such as Apple, Ohio Scientific, Tandy, and Commodore ruled the landscape," and when modems amounted to little more than two suction cups into which the telephone handset was fitted. BBS enthusiasts "[weren't] interested in ARPA or big laboratories," explains Howard Rheingold. Instead, they "want[ed] to know what they [could] do at home with their own hands and affordable technology."

Ward Christensen and Randy Seuss illustrate Rheingold's point perfectly. January 16, 1978, was a very snowy day in Chicago, where Christensen and Seuss lived. Unable to dig himself out, Christensen called Seuss to talk about a plan he had to hook up their microcomputers to the phone lines. Seuss challenged him: "You do the software, and I'll do the hardware." Christensen, who had already written the first binary-transfer file protocol, MODEM.ASM, envisioned a message system similar to corkboard bulletin boards for his project: "You know, garage for rent, dog grooming, etc."

In two weeks' time, the first bulletin board, CBBS (Computer Bulletin Board System), was functional in Chicago. Afterward, hobbyists bought, borrowed, and tweaked Christensen's original code in order to build systems compatible with their own hardware, and a series of now-familiar BBS names were born: C64 for Commodore 64 machines; MTABBS for TRS-80s; GBB for Apple machines; and Fido, Opus, and Seadog for early IBM 8088s. Whatever software or hardware the various BBSs used, however, they all offered similar services: the ability to send and receive local email, the uploading and downloading of files, and opportunities for online game playing with rudimentary graphics.

SOCIAL ENGINEERING IN CYBERSPACE

Almost from the beginning, BBS users formed their own cultures, complete with interest groups and social strata. Though "hacking for the sake of hacking" has long been a *raison d'être* for BBSs, some services were slightly loftier in their social designs. Communitree, begun in 1981, used tree-like programming that encouraged users to participate in free-wheeling discussions online, while the Citadel BBS software used "rooms," encouraging user "construction crews" to participate in a board's design. The designers of the Habitat BBS, a virtual community that still flourishes in parts of Japan today, learned that contrary to what software engineers might think, "detailed central planning is impossible; don't even try."

In the land of BBSs, system operators, called "sysops," reigned supreme. After sysops, however, notes Jason Scott, "baud was the badge" of distinction among users, because each new type of modem cost hundreds of dollars more than the next-fastest one. In addition, Scott notes, the "Inexpensive Commodore 64 attracted a different family from the relatively expensive Apple II." Once computer hardware dropped in price, BBS users began organizing based on length of time spent online (hence the term "newbie"), level of technical prowess (the highest calling themselves the "elite"), or social power within the BBS itself (with designations like "conference host").

VOLUNTEERS AND CORPORATIONS, LOCAL AND GLOBAL

During the early 1980s, BBSs were primarily volunteer affairs. Two major exceptions were the Source, the first purely consumer online service that was founded in 1978 and later bought by CompuServe, and Quantum Link, which eventually became America Online. For the most part, however, corporations became interested in BBSs only after the arrival of "multinode" service, which allowed multiple phone callers on a single computer. Credit for making multinode BBSing relatively easy and affordable belongs to Tim Stryker, whose company Galacticomm released Major BBS software in 1985. Major's newest iteration, Worldgroup, currently runs on more than 20,000 online systems worldwide, including the National Archive For Law Enforcement project.

In 1984 a programmer named Tom Jennings modified his Fido BBS software to automatically collect and forward messages, which had been sent on other computers using Fido, in the middle of the night when telephone rates were less expensive. By 1985, FidoNet connected over 200 BBSs around the country, and by 1993, it comprised 24,800 "nodes" from all over the world. A decade before the advent of the Web, FidoNet created a true long-distance computer network, maintained entirely through the volunteer efforts of those involved. Today, FidoNet remains popular in areas with extremely low Internet connectivity, such as parts of the former Soviet Union.

ESTABLISHING LIMITS TO FREEDOM ONLINE

Regardless of whether they were run by professionals or hobbyists, BBSs distinguished themselves from other early forms of computer-mediated communications principally by their commitment to free speech, which was often idiosyncratically defined by their membership. Even today, the WELL's slogan is "You own your own words," while the New York City–based ECHO motto warns, "Attack the post, and not the poster." For some, however, offenses on BBSs went too far, even by "free speech" standards. One of the first types of questionable BBS activities, known as "phone phreaking," began when some users felt that they ought to be able to communicate on BBSs beyond their local area codes without paying long-distance charges. Likewise, early software pirates and "crackers" often used phrases like "information wants to be free" to protest the regulations against the copying of proprietary software packages and computer systems.

Beginning with the FBI investigation of the "414 Club" in the early 1980s, and continuing with what researcher Bruce Sterling called "The Hacker Crackdown of 1990," BBSs quite frequently served as terrain on which law-enforcement officials attempted, in Sterling's words, "to break the back of America's electronic Underground." Certainly, software piracy and "trading of wares" has long been the main activity of certain BBSs; one of the biggest software piracy cases ever settled (*Microsoft and Novell vs. the Assassin's Guide BBS*) occurred in 1996.

The issue of pornography distribution via BBS, and in particular the sentencing of the proprietors of the Amateur Action BBS in 1994, had ramifications that are still felt today. First, the Amateur Action case was the first instance of a BBS owner being prosecuted for obscenity based on the standards of a community in a different state; the California-based owners were prosecuted under Tennessee law. Then, researcher Martin Rimm used material from Amateur Action as part of his 1995 study on Internet pornography, even though the BBS wasn't even connected to the Internet at the time. This erroneous study, which was read into the Congressional Record as evidence of the pervasiveness of obscenity online, created what attorney Mike Godwin called "cyberporn panic" in the U.S. Congress.

The Rise of the Web: BBSing, Present and Future

The early 1990s represent for many the "golden years" of BBSing. According to researcher David Carlson, there were more than 60,000 BBSs in the United States alone during that time. Then, suddenly, BBS user interest dropped sharply during 1995–97. This "great migration" happened not as a result of scandal or vice, but because of the technological innovation known as the World Wide Web, which offered wider vistas and more connectivity than BBSing ever could. To compete, some BBSs began offering Internet connectivity and telnet options to their users, while others built Web interfaces to complement their existing BBS systems. Still others steadfastly refused to connect their BBSs to the Internet. Justin Woods likens these BBS denizens to "antique car fanatics, forever waxing a car that will never be driven farther than from the garage to the driveway."

Today, BBSs still thrive wherever Internet connectivity is low, or whenever people desire an "intimate space" online, whether it be to discuss issues of the day with like-minded souls or trade pirated software. BBSs are also successfully used to keep one's sense of physical geography intact, as is the case at the still-functioning CBBS (also known as Chinet), and at the Panix BBS in New York City. And of course, there exists a new generation of message-board systems that have known only the Web as their home, proving that the greatest legacy of BBS culture may well lie not with its outdated technology, but rather with its timeless social structures. Places like Slashdot.org, devoted

to "news for nerds"; message boards like those at Nerve.com, a popular singles site; the "comments" feature of LiveJournal.com, which allows users to create interactive online diaries; and the entries at storytelling site TheFray.com are all examples of what might be called "BBSesque" cultures. A visit to any one of these sites shows people carving out communities, making social adjustments, and defining what constitutes "free speech," just as they did in the earliest days of home computing and BBSs.

Bibliography

Christensen, Ward, and Randy Seuss. "The Birth of the BBS by Ward and Randy." 1989. <http://timeline.textfiles.com/1978/01/16/2/ FILES/cbbs.txt> (April 19, 2002).

Godwin, Mike. *Cyber Rights: Defending Free Speech in the Digital Age*. New York: Times Books, 1998.

Long, Vince. "The BBS: A History and Commentary." *Montana Council for Computers and Technology in Education Newsletter,* December 1996.

Mine, Diamond. "Introduction to Bulletin Board Systems." *Diamond Mine Online,* June 26, 2001. <http://www.thedirectory.org/diamond/about.htm> (April 19, 2002).

Moschovitis, Christos J. P.; Poole, Hilary; Schuyler, Tami; and Theresa M. Senft. *History of the Internet: A Chronology, 1843 to the Present.* Santa Barbara, Calif.: ABC-CLIO, 1999.

NetVillage.com. Galacticomm Technologies Web Site. 2001. <http://www.gcomm.com/> (April 19, 2002).

Rheingold, Howard. *The Virtual Community: Homesteading on the Electronic Frontier.* Revised edition. Cambridge, Mass.: MIT Press, 2000.

Scott, Jason. "The Textfiles.com BBS Timeline: A Collection of Events and Infamy of BBS History." January 16, 2002. <http://timeline.textfiles.com/> (April 19, 2002).

Woods, Justin. Personal communication via email, January 15, 2001.

Further Reading

Barry, Rey. "The Origin of Computer Bulletin Boards." Freeware Hall of Fame, 1993. <http://www.freewarehof.org/ward.html> (April 19, 2002).

Bendtsen, Bo. "FidoNet, the Free Alternative." FidoNet Homepage, Terminate.com. <http://www.terminate.com/fidonet/> (April 19, 2002).

Ford, Steve. "What IS Chinet?" Chinet—Public Access UNIX since 1982. <http://www.chinet.com/> (April 19, 2002).

Hafner, Katie. *The Well: A Story of Love, Death & Real Life in the Seminal Online Community.* New York: Carroll & Graf, 2001.

Horn, Stacy. *Cyberville: Clicks, Culture, and the Creation of an Online Town.* New York: Warner Books, 1998.

Lebens, Tom. "How to BBS." Fanciful Organization, October 13, 2000.
<http://www.fanciful.org/bbs-promotion/> (April 12, 2002).

Powazek, Derek M. *Design for Community: The Art of Connecting Real People in Virtual Places.* Indianapolis, Ind.: New Riders Publishing, 2002.

Schwartz, Jerry. "A FidoNet Primer." 2000.
<http://www.writebynight.com/fidonet.html> (April 12, 2002).

Scott, Jason. "BBS: A Documentary." 2001.
<http://www.bbsdocumentary.com/> (April 12, 2002).

Short, Robert. "BBS? I Was Calling Granny! The Hidden Treasures of Bulletin Board Systems." *Computer Bits Magazine,* March 1998.
<http://iago.computerbits.com/archive/19980300/bbsintro.htm> (April 12, 2002).

Related Topics

Community Networking; CommuniTree; Echo; Habitat; Hacking, Cracking, and Phreaking; PLATO; Rheingold, Howard; Virtual Community; Whole Earth 'Lectronic Link

— *Theresa M. Senft*

Bush, Vannevar

U.S. Scientist

1890–1974

Vannevar Bush, creator of the Differential Analyzer, facilitator of the Manhattan Project, and developer of the National Science Foundation, is best known today for his prophetic anticipation of hypertext in a 1945 *Atlantic Monthly* article entitled "As We May Think."

Bush began his work in engineering with his 1913 master's thesis from Tufts College that culminated in the development of a Profile Tracer, a machine designed to measure distance over uneven terrain. After receiving his Ph.D. in electrical engineering from the Massachusetts Institute of Technology (MIT) in 1916, Bush briefly worked as an assistant professor at Tufts before returning to MIT as an associate professor of electrical engineering in 1919. He contributed to the technological development of the military in World War I, working on the problem of submarine detection for the navy. This military work presaged the major role that he would later play in the negotiations between the military, business, and science during and after World War II.

During the interwar period, Bush made significant advances in analog computing with the creation of the Differential Analyzer, a computer designed to compute differential equations. The first prototype of the Differential Analyzer was developed at the University of Pennsylvania. Later, the Rockefeller Foundation funded advancements on the Differential Analyzer, and with the help of mathematician Warren Weaver, the Rockefeller Differential Analyzer was created. Weighing 100 tons and consisting of 2,000 vacuum tubes and relays, 150 motors, and 200 miles of wire, the Rockefeller Differential Analyzer was rendered obsolete in the 1950s with the emergence of the digital computer.

After the Differential Analyzer, Bush began work on the Rapid Selector, an analog device that could quickly search microfilm for relevant information that could then be read by the user. Along with John H. Howard, Bush built and patented the Rapid Selector in 1938. Although the Rapid Selector attracted the interest of the Navy's Communication Security Group for the purpose of cracking Japanese codes, the machines were unsuccessful in Bush's eyes. In response to the need to break encrypted messages, Bush proposed a new device, the Comparator.

In 1939, Bush proposed to President Roosevelt that a committee be created to encourage military-related scientific exploration; the following year, the National Defense Research Committee (NDRC) was created, with Bush installed as chairman. The NDRC can be credited with such wartime technologies as proximity fuses, designed to detonate explosives close to their target, as well as the application of RADAR (Radio Detection and Ranging) to aircraft detection. In 1941, Bush was appointed director of the Office of Scientific Research and Development (OSRD), a unit that focused scientific and technological resources on weapons development.

During World War II, Bush rose to national prominence as a regular adviser to President Roosevelt. Bush's own technological creations during the war continued with his work on antenna profiles and the calculation of artillery firing tables. However, his inventions took a back seat to his commitment to bring academic and scientific researchers together with the military. The epitome of the interconnectedness of the military and science can be seen in Bush's involvement in the top-secret Manhattan Project, which supervised the development and implementation of the atomic bomb.

Although Bush's work on analog computers has been rendered obsolete in today's digital world, his vision of information organization remains vibrant; in 1945, for example, he prefigured the hypertext used in today's World Wide Web. In July 1945, Bush's extremely influential article entitled "As We

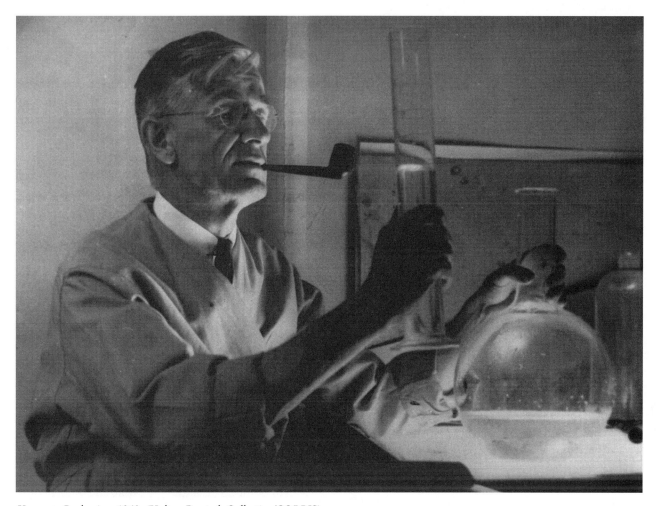

Vannevar Bush, circa 1943. (Hulton-Deutsch Collection/CORBIS)

May Think" was published in the *Atlantic Monthly*. In this article, Bush insisted that too much information existed for researchers to stay current on the latest research. To address this problem, he proposed several hypothetical devices—including, most significantly, the Memex.

The Memex was designed as a supplement to human memory, intended to store all of an individual's books and records. Like Bush's Rapid Selector, the Memex would use microfilm in order to store and rapidly access material. This analog machine, modeled after the workings of the brain, would arrange information by association, rather than in a typical alphabetical index. Bush called this associative indexing "trails of thought."

The Memex addressed the needs of an information-saturated society that demanded new and elegant systems of organization. Bush believed that the answer to an excess of information was to create a machine designed so that individuals could organize and access their own records with the flexibility to continually add new information, and consequently to create new trails.

Bush's rejection of linear, sequential indexing in favor of an interwoven web of references has been a source of inspiration for many computer and Internet researchers. Twenty years after the publication of "As We May Think," hypertext developer Ted Nelson borrowed from Bush's notion of associative trails to create "dynamic footnotes," or hypertext. MIT engineer J. C. R. Licklider cited "As We May Think" as a major influence, and dedicated his 1965 book *Libraries of the Future* to Bush. Similarly, Stanford University senior research engineer Doug Englebart, inventor of the computer mouse and developer of the first functional hypertext system, wrote a letter to Bush in 1962 indicating that "As We May Think" had deeply influenced the direction of Englebart's own research. At the 1987 Hypertext Conference in Chapel Hill, North Carolina, Bush's article was widely cited as being extremely influential on the conceptualization and development of hypertext.

Bush was not only an engineer; he also mobilized the technological and scientific community to contribute to the war effort. He not only created ingenious analog machines such as the Differential

Analyzer and the Rapid Selector, he also fueled the minds of the future with his technological-utopian vision in the groundbreaking "As We May Think." After World War II, Bush directed the establishment of the National Science Foundation in 1950, and in 1957 he became chairman of the MIT Corporation. He is the recipient of nearly 20 honorary degrees, and was made a knight of the British Empire in 1948. Bush left his imprint on the intersections of science, engineering, corporations, and the military—an intertwining that continues to this day.

Selected Works

Bush, Vannevar. "As We May Think." *Atlantic Monthly,* vol. 7 (July 1945), p. 101. Also available on the Web at *The Atlantic Online,* February 17, 2001. <http://www.theatlantic.com/unbound/flashbks/computer/bushf.htm> (March 20, 2002).

———. *Science Is Not Enough.* New York: Morrow, 1967.

———. *Pieces of the Action.* New York: Morrow, 1970.

Bibliography

Campbell-Kelly, Martin and William Aspray. *Computer: A History of the Information Machine.* New York: Basic Books, 1996.

De Landa, Manuel. *War in the Age of Intelligent Machines.* New York: Zone Books, 1991.

Goldstine, Herman H. *The Computer: From Pascal to Von Neumann.* Princeton, N.J.: Princeton University Press, 1972.

Klaphaak, David, Jr. "Events in the Life of Vannevar Bush." February 17, 2001. <http://www.cs.brown.edu/research/graphics/html/info/timeline.html> (March 20, 2002).

Nyce, James M. and Paul Kahn, eds. *From Memex to Hypertext: Vannevar Bush and the Mind's Machine.* Boston: Academic Press, 1991.

Zachary, G. Pascal. *Endless Frontier: Vannevar Bush, Engineer of the American Century.* New York: The Free Press, 1997.

Further Reading

Burke, Colin. *Information and Secrecy: Vannevar Bush, Ultra, and the Other Memex.* Metuchen, N.J.: Scarecrow Press, 1994.

Cooling, Benjamin F., ed. *War, Business, and American Society: Historical Perspectives on the Military Industrial Complex.* Port Washington, N.Y.: Kennikat Press, 1977.

Wildes, Karl L. and Nilo A. Lindgren. *A Century of Electrical Engineering and Computer Science at MIT, 1882–1982.* Cambridge, Mass.: MIT Press, 1985.

Related Topics

"As We May Think"; Engelbart, Douglas; Hypertext; Internet; Licklider, J. C. R.; Nelson, Theodore Holm (Ted); World Wide Web

— *Heidi Marie Brush*

Business-to-Business

The business-to-business (B2B) idea is fairly simple to understand: Businesses use the Internet to sell materials and components to other businesses that need them to produce their own goods. B2B describes doing business with businesses, rather than doing business with the consumers themselves (that model is known as B2C, or "business-to-consumer"). B2B involves the use of complex software that facilitates online communications with other businesses. For instance, components producers can use such software to alert larger businesses about the goods that they have available, or that they can produce on demand, to help the larger companies to build their products.

B2B, Phase One

The integral element involved in the B2B business model is what's known as the supply chain. Consider the example of an auto manufacturer. Cars contain thousands of individual pieces that range in size from the body chassis all the way down to plastic clasps that hold hoses in place. Car manufacturers create some of the largest and most important pieces in their own factories, but they usually do not make radios, or plastic brackets, or any of thousands of other pieces that go into their cars and trucks. Instead, the car companies hire smaller manufacturers—suppliers—to make, ship, and deliver those components instead. It is a complex and expensive process to sort through the many would-be suppliers, take bids on components, and arrange contracts, shipments, and delivery for all of those individual pieces.

That's where the idea of B2B comes in. Instead of poring over numerous catalogues, filling out forms, and faxing them, the manufacturer's purchasing agent can go onto the Web, search a site for a needed component—say, radio antennae—instantly find the best prices among thousands of potential client vendors, and place the order immediately. It has been estimated that if that entire process could be put online, auto manufacturers could charge as much as $2,000 to $3,000 less for a car that now costs $19,000.

The possibilities of B2B do not stop there. The antenna maker, for example, might have bought its aluminum via some B2B exchanges. The company that mined the aluminum ore might have found a source for the metal the same way. Such a potential bonanza was just about enough to make any would-be Internet entrepreneur forget about building the next Amazon.com.

And many of them did. In April 2000, just as the dot-com bubble burst on consumer-oriented Internet retail sites, B2B became the new 'Net buzzword. The composite value of good and services bought and sold between businesses totals about $30 trillion a year, while only $10 trillion worth of consumer goods are sold annually. If the business supply chain could be shifted from the physical realm onto the Internet, the logic went, companies that facilitated those transactions by creating "B2B exchanges," something like electronic middlemen, could grow wealthy beyond their imaginings by taking just the tiniest slice of the overall B2B market.

Soon there was a B2B gold rush not unlike the one that was witnessed during the glory days of the dot-com (or B2C) boom of 1998 and 1999. During 2000, venture capitalists who had shut down the flow to consumer Internet businesses pumped more than $23 billion into more than 1,200 business-to-business companies, according to a May 2001 *Industry Standard* report. Merrill Lynch analyst Henry Blodget told the *Washington Post* that a B2B-fueled Internet could "have as profound an impact on the economy as the Industrial Revolution."

THE COLLAPSE OF PHASE ONE

Such buzz didn't last long. As *Forbes* magazine reported in September 2001, the B2B "space" that had been so hot in May 2000 had cooled to room temperature 16 months later. The U.S. Bancorp Piper Jaffray B2B index showed that B2B stock valuations had tumbled 88 percent during that period, while giant B2B "market makers" like VertcalNet had withered. Of the original 200 B2B firms that the magazine had profiled in its July 2000 issue, 35 had either folded or been bought out by other companies.

There were many reasons for the collapse of B2B, phase one. Many companies had flocked to the Web to build B2B exchanges, frequently spending millions on equipment and infrastructure only to find themselves competing for the same clients with other start-ups. As the *Washington Post*'s Neil Irwin reported, many of the markets for raw materials such as chemicals and metals are saturated beyond hope, with dozens of B2B competitors in each. Because B2Bs don't produce or sell goods themselves and merely take a small cut for matching buyers and sellers, having all that competition and price pressure among suppliers means that B2Bs' profits, if their business is simply to match buyers and sellers, can never rise very high.

Meanwhile, upstarts quickly found themselves challenged by massive competition from industry itself.

One huge B2B, Covisint, was formed by Ford Motor Co., DaimlerChrysler AG, General Motors Corp., Renault SA, and Nissan Motor Co., in cooperation with Oracle Computer and the B2B market-maker Commerce One, in the hope of creating a more efficient form of commerce between automakers and their suppliers. Later, meatpacking companies IBP, Cargill Inc. and its red-meat subsidiary Excel Corp., Smithfield Foods, Tyson Foods, Gold Kist, and Farmland Industries Inc. subsidiaries Farmland National Beef and Farmland Foods, all combined to create a gigantic agri-B2B. There have been many other massive industry-sponsored efforts like these.

Even online retail giant Amazon.com got into the act, forming B2B sales-and-distribution alliances with other retailers like Circuit City, Toys 'R' Us and Borders.com. Some analysts contend that if it continues to add new B2B relationships with such businesses as Target and Wal-Mart, Amazon's B2B profits could exceed those of its retail business.

In this environment, small start-up B2B outfits like Dell Marketplace, Silicon Valley Oil, and FreightWise did not stand much of a chance. It turned out that companies locked in bitter fights over business were much less likely to sign onto a common electronic platform to transact e-business with their suppliers when they were brought together by an unknown outside start-up than they were when they negotiated the B2B's structure and built the conduits themselves.

B2B, PHASE TWO

In the post-hype, phase-two version of B2B that was beginning to take shape in late 2001, businesses had begun to take another look at the model. Efficiency was still prized, but other ideas that were touted when the rush was on faded and died. One of the most important ideas from which phase two retreated was that of eliminating the middleman. According to *Forbes* magazine, it became clear that established businesses were not eager to tear down relationships with established suppliers that had worked so well for so long. Middlemen knew the business; getting rid of them was perhaps not as wise as the promised cost-savings made it sound.

Forbes reported in September 2001 that the new B2B model taking shape is based on a more realistic worldview than that of the Gold Rush model: "Instead of creating disruptive Internet marketplaces, industry-backed and neutral exchanges are now pitching themselves merely as Net channels for distribution." Many B2Bs use software expertise to streamline supply chains, the way that Dell Computer and Cisco Systems do, or mix and match models to fit precise markets. The goal is to help businesses communicate better, organize themselves more effectively, and conduct their own transactions, without the B2Bs taking over transactions themselves.

The market for B2B remains strong despite the shakeout, according to figures from industry analysts at IDC Communications. IDC estimated that the real value of goods and services bought and sold online in 2001 would grow by 83 percent to some $516 billion for the year. *Forbes'* Alberto Vilar projects that during the next decade, more than one-half of all business conducted between companies will take place online. "B2B is where the action will be, creating vast cost savings for businesses," Vilar writes. "Companies that learn how to use the Internet effectively will prosper; those that don't, will fall by the wayside."

Bibliography

Boslet, Mark. "After the B-to-B Revolution." *The Industry Standard,* May 14, 2001.
<http://www.thestandard.com/article/0,1902,24176,00.html> (May 10, 2002).

Irwin, Neil. "This Analyst Still Has A 'B2B' in His Bonnet." *Newsbytes,* August 28, 2001.

Schneider, Greg. "Net Firms Get Down to Business." *Newsbytes,* April 5, 2000.

Vilar, Alberto. "B2B: The Best Is Yet to Be" *Forbes.com,* September 10, 2001.
<http://www.forbes.com/best/2001/0910/028.html> (May 10, 2002).

Vinzant, Carol and Neil Irwin. "To B2B or Not to B2B: Still the Question." *Newsbytes,* June 20, 2001.

Further Reading

Drapkin, Michael; Lawy, Jon; and Daniel Marovitz. *Three Clicks Away: Advice from the Trenches of eCommerce.* New York: John Wiley & Sons, 2001.

Hines, Peter, et al. *Value Stream Management.* Harlow, England: Prentice Hall/Pearson Education Limited, 2000.

Morris, Michael H., Pitt, Leyland F., and Earl D. Honeycutt, Jr. *Business to Business Marketing: A Strategic Approach.* Thousand Oaks, Calif.: Sage Publications, 2001.

Sawhney, Mohan; Paoni, Anthony; and Ranjay Gulati. *Techventure: New Rules on Value and Profit from Silicon Valley.* New York: John Wiley & Sons, 2001.

Related Topics

Broadband; Data Mining; Digital Cash; E-Commerce; Peer-to-Peer

— Kevin Featherly

CCCCCCC C CCCCCCC

Carmack, John

1970–
Game Designer

John Carmack is one of the leading computer-game designers of the late twentieth century. His pioneering work on 3D game design led to the invention of the "first-person shooter" genre, exemplified by such popular games as Doom and Quake. His company, id Software, developed shareware and Internet distribution channels, revolutionizing the ways in which computer games were sold.

Born in 1970, Carmack grew up in Kansas City, Missouri, and knew early on that programming was his calling. After spending a year in a juvenile home following a brush with the law, Carmack attended computer-science classes for a few semesters at the University of Missouri–Kansas City. He dropped out to pursue contract-programming jobs, then accepted a position at Softdisk, a software-publishing firm in Louisiana. There, he met John Romero, Tom Hall, and Adrian Carmack (no relation), and together they created the first Commander Keen game, which was released as shareware in 1990. Following the success of this game, the group left Softdisk to found id Software in 1991.

In May 1992, id released Wolfenstein 3-D, a hit that is considered by many to be the first true first-person shooter. Players navigated a three-dimensional environment of rooms and hallways from a first-person perspective, wielding a weapon that appeared at the bottom of the screen. Game play consisted of finding one's way through various levels while killing Nazi guards and attack dogs. Following this success, on December 10, 1993, id released Doom, a frenetically immersive and violent improvement upon Wolfenstein.

The release of Doom marks a turning point in the history of computer gaming for several reasons. More than 15 million copies of Doom have been downloaded from the Internet, making it one of the most popular games of all time. Doom was short on narrative; players roamed a military base blasting various types of aliens into oblivion. With its realistic floor and ceiling textures, Doom added greatly to the sense of embodied movement that defines the first-person shooter genre. Carmack also released portions of Doom's source code to the public, which allowed its dedicated fan base the opportunity to modify levels and graphics to add their own personal touches. One such modification replaced the sinister-looking aliens with purple dinosaurs like Barney. The practice of making source code available to players has been a key element in the overwhelming popularity of Carmack's games.

In 1996, id released Quake, which further advanced the genre. Along with ever-improving graphic realism, Quake allowed multiplayer gaming over the Internet, so that several people could play with (or against) each other in the same environment. This feature contributed to the immense popularity of online gaming, featuring players going head-to-head in "death matches."

Aside from their pioneering graphic realism and online interactivity, Carmack's games have also been marketed and distributed in revolutionary ways. Both Wolfenstein and Doom were released in free, downloadable shareware versions that contained only the first level; once players were hooked, they could pay for the rest of the game. Dubbed the "crack cocaine model" of distribution, it generated a huge amount of interest and word-of-mouth buzz around a game, boosting sales. When the first episode of Doom was released on University of Wisconsin servers, the rush of downloads crashed the entire system. Similarly, Quake was packaged as a $10 disk that allowed access only to the first level; the disk contained the rest of the game in an encrypted format, the key to which could be purchased by credit card. This allowed Quake to be distributed much more widely in convenience stores, which would not usually have carried $50 computer games.

3D shooters like Quake have not only added to the surge of online gaming, but have also been the catalyst for the growth of the 3D-rendering sector of the computer hardware market. Constantly pushing the boundaries of current technology, Carmack and id Software have made specialized graphics cards standard equipment on computer gaming systems. The Quake engine itself has been licensed for use in numerous other games, most notably the hugely successful Half-Life.

Carmack's games have attracted much negative attention since the Columbine and Heath high school shootings in the late 1990s, and id Software was named as a defendant in the $33 million lawsuit filed by the families of Michael Carneal's victims in Paducah, Kentucky. Carneal and Littleton, Colorado's Eric Harris and Dylan Klebold were all known to be avid fans of Doom and Quake; experts testified that the games served, if nothing else, as excellent training simulations that allowed a 14-year-old like Carneal, who had never fired a weapon before, to shoot eight people with amazing efficiency. The lawsuit was eventually dismissed in U.S. District Court.

Despite the negative coverage, the Doom and Quake series have made Carmack and id Software financial successes. id Software does close to $20 million a year in sales, while employing fewer than 20 people. Despite his wealth, Carmack remains an incredibly hard-working, hands-on figure within id, doing much of the programming work personally. He has refused all buyout offers, preferring to remain independent. Carmack's vision has profoundly affected computer gaming, and his games remain some of the most successful and well known in the industry.

Bibliography

Hall, Justin, with Bob Calayco and Joel Downs. "John Carmack Interview." *Firingsquad*, February 9, 2000. <http://firingsquad.gamers.com/features/carmack/> (April 26, 2002).

id Software. "History." December 1998. <http://www.idsoftware.com/corporate/idhist.html> (April 26, 2002).

Mari, Rich. "Carmack, John." *Current Biography* 61:3, (March 2000), pp. 98–101.

Slashdot. "John Carmack Answers." October 15, 1999. <http://slashdot.org/interviews/99/10/15/1012230.shtml> (April 26, 2002).

Further Reading

id Software. "Archives." September 15, 2001. <http://www.idsoftware.com/archives/index.html> (April 26, 2002).

Poole, Steven. *Trigger Happy: Videogames and the Entertainment Revolution*. New York: Arcade Publishing, 2000.

Sheff, David. *Game Over: Press Start to Continue*. Wilson, Conn.: Gamepress, 1999.

Related Topics

Gaming

— *Shawn Miklaucic*

Carnivore

Carnivore is a controversial surveillance system used by the FBI to search email posts sent by identified criminal suspects during investigations. But the system—which some claim became controversial mainly for its name rather than its capabilities—has come under fire from opponents ranging from the liberal-leaning American Civil Liberties Union to staunchly conservative U.S. senators, all of whom worry that the technology could be used to spy on the public.

FBI officials have said that Carnivore is used rarely, and only after the organization has obtained a court order; in April 2001, the Associated Press reported that it had been used in investigations about 25 times. But it is a vital surveillance tool, the government says, because criminals are using the Internet to communicate and commit crimes in increasing numbers. In March 2001, for example, the FBI estimated that malevolent Russian and Ukrainian hackers had stolen more than one million credit card numbers off the Internet. Terrorist groups and organized-crime syndicates are also said to be relying on Internet technologies.

The FBI gave Carnivore its name because of its ability to get to "the meat" of what would otherwise be a gigantic amount of data passing through ISP channels, *The Wall Street Journal* reported. An earlier, slower version had an even hungrier name: Omnivore. But with controversy swirling around the investigative tool, the government finally was forced to change its name to something more generic: DCS1000.

Carnivore/DCS1000 consists of a personal computer equipped with an array of special surveillance software, which is installed at the network sites of various Internet service providers. It is extremely fast, scanning millions of email posts per second. The system must scan at least a portion of every email that passes through any ISP where Carnivore is installed, in order to detect whether the post might have been sent by a suspect. That aspect of Carnivore creates a massive tangle of unresolved legal and privacy issues, experts have said.

Critics charge that Carnivore creates an unprecedented opportunity for the government to snoop on innocent and unsuspecting citizens. The FBI has defended Carnivore as nothing but a high-tech, more precise version of the telephone wiretapping that the government has engaged in legally during its investigations for much of the past century. It also says that the technology is so advanced that it can be tailored to pluck data coming from a particular suspect's email communications from among all the traffic generated by millions of ISP customers.

Speaking at a cyber-crime discussion panel in March 2001, Orrin Kerr, a U.S. Justice Department trial attorney, accused privacy advocates of smearing the technology's potential based on pure speculation, adding that such efforts run counter to the interests of law-enforcement efforts in cyberspace, where Kerr says that criminals have gained the upper hand. He insisted that there are no documented cases of unwarranted intrusion by investigators using the technology.

The FBI has been mostly mum on the extent of Carnivore's capabilities. The Electronic Privacy Information Center (EPIC) used the Freedom of Information Act to try to force the FBI to release more than 2,000 documents detailing Carnivore, but EPIC received only 800 heavily edited documents. Even from that limited selection, EPIC stated, it learned that Carnivore, contrary to FBI assertions, is capable of capturing and archiving "unfiltered" Internet traffic.

Meanwhile, Lance Brown, founder of the think-tank Future Solutions, has put up a Web site (StopCarnivore.org) detailing what he describes as the system's far-reaching abilities. Brown claims that Carnivore can read all incoming and outgoing emails passing through an ISP's routers; monitor Web surfing and downloading habits; and determine the contents of instant-messaging communication, file transfers, newsgroup posts, or anything else that is routed through an ISP.

Another critic, veteran computer-industry columnist Robert Cringely, has written that Carnivore's most efficient placement at an ISP would be directly after the ISP's incoming routers. He speculated that this might be the reason why some ISPs, notably EarthLink, have resisted Carnivore or even refused to install the system; that position is the most vulnerable part of an ISP's networking chain. According to Cringely, Carnivore could function not only as a monitoring or listening device, but also as a switch. "If we ever hear a proposal from the FBI in which it plans to install Carnivores at all 6,000 ISPs in the U.S.," Cringely wrote, "we'll be giving the government the power to do something it can't do right now: Shut the Internet down."

In September 2000, in response to widespread publicity about the system, then-U.S. attorney general Janet Reno ordered an independent review of Carnivore by a team from the Illinois Institute of Technology (IIT). That review's final draft, released on December 8, 2000, concluded that Carnivore should remain in place, and denied that it has "enough power to spy on almost everyone with an e-mail account." The review did recommend some changes to make Carnivore safer and easier to understand, but it stated that the system's basic safeguards are essentially in place. "When Carnivore is used in accordance with a (court) order," the IIT report says, "it provides investigators with no more information than is permitted by a given court order."

Privacy groups were highly critical of the review, as many of the IIT researchers had close ties to the Justice Department. They noted that several better-known universities had declined to take on the job of reviewing the system because of tight Justice Department restrictions. Meanwhile, the results of an internal Justice Department review have never been made public.

The Pew Internet & American Life Project polled 2,096 Americans on their feelings about Internet crime, discovering that in general, citizens are more worried about child pornography than online surveillance. A majority (54 percent) favored email surveillance if it could help catch criminals, but most of those polled never had heard of Carnivore/DCS1000. Of those who had, opinions about whether it is a good or a bad thing were evenly split: 45 percent said it was good because it furnished law enforcement with another tool for tracking down outlaws; another 45 percent expressed the opposite view, saying it could be used to read emails to and from ordinary citizens. Those results, *The Washington Post* noted, underscored the complex problems facing lawmakers and regulators in dealing with the conflicting demands of computer users, the online industry, and legal authorities.

One of the main sources of controversy is the fact that only the FBI has unrestricted access to Carnivore's software code. Law-enforcement officials argue that it is necessary to keep the code secret in order to block criminals from thwarting the system. Civil libertarians and even some members of Congress think otherwise, saying that there should be more oversight of a system that might be used to secretly spy on regular citizens, in violation of their Fourth Amendment right to be protected from unwarranted search and seizure. EPIC, the ACLU, and others have called for the public release of all FBI records concerning Carnivore, including the software's source code, so that its threat to public privacy can be thoroughly assessed.

Bibliography

Associated Press. "Online Privacy Leaders Meet With Ashcroft." April 20, 2001.

Cringely, Robert X. "Meet Eater: The FBI's Plan for Digital Wiretaps Raises More Questions Than It Answers." July 13, 2000.
<http://www.pbs.org/cringely/pulpit/pulpit20000713.html> (March 20, 2002).

Electronic Privacy Information Center. "Newly Released FBI Documents Show Carnivore Can Swallow Much More Information Than Bureau Claims." November 16, 2000.
<http://www.epic.org/privacy/carnivore/11_16_release.html> (March 20, 2002).

Illinois Institute of Technology. Independent Technical Review of the Carnivore System: Final Report. December 8, 2000.
<http://www.usdoj.gov/jmd/publications/carniv_final.pdf> (March 20, 2002).

McGuire, David. "DOJ Attorney: In Cyberspace, Criminals Have Upper Hand." March 16, 2001.

"Opinion Split on Web Privacy." *Washington Post,* April 3, 2001, E12.

Pew Internet and American Life Project. "Fear of Online Crime: Americans Support FBI Interception of Criminal Suspects' Email and New Laws to Protect Online Privacy." April 2, 2001.
<http://www.pewinternet.org/reports/> (March 20, 2002).

Further Reading

FBI (Statement of Donald M. Kerr, Assistant Director Laboratory Division, Federal Bureau of Investigation, to the U.S. Senate Judiciary Committee). "On Carnivore Diagnostic Tool." September 6, 2000.
<http://www.fbi.gov/congress/congress00/kerr090600.htm> (March 20, 2002).

Garfinkel, Simson. *Database Nation: The Death of Privacy in the 21st Century.* Sebastopol, Calif.: Cambridge O'Reilly, 2000.

Shannon, Elaine. "Ooops! Maybe 'Carnivore' Was Too Meaty . . ." *Time,* July 23, 2000.

Related Topics

Anonymity; Child Online Protection Act and Child Online Privacy Protection Act; Cyberethics; Cyberwarfare; Data Mining; Electronic Communications Privacy Act; Email; Encryption and Cryptography; Hacking, Cracking, and Phreaking; Privacy; Software Agents

— *Kevin Featherly*

Case, Stephen M.

1958–

Co-founder, America Online

Stephen M. Case is chairman of the board of AOL-Time Warner. Before the AOL-Time Warner merger, Case was chairman and CEO of America Online

(AOL). The phenomenal growth of AOL, the first Internet company to be included in the Fortune 500, is the stuff of legend, and much of it is attributed to Case. Since going public, AOL's annual revenues grew from $30 million in 1992 to more than $7.7 billion in 2000.

Born in Honolulu, Hawaii on August 21, 1958, to an elementary school teacher and a lawyer, Steve Case demonstrated his entrepreneurial spirit at a young age. Lore has six-year-old Case, the third of four children, joining up with an older brother to sell limeade; within a couple of years, the two created "Case Enterprises," hawking everything from garden seeds to magazines. Case earned a bachelor's degree in political science from Williams College in Massachusetts, where he met his future wife Joanne Barker, a student at nearby Smith College. Case's entrepreneurial spirit was in evidence at college as well, where he started an airport shuttle business and sold fruit baskets. After graduating in 1980, he pursued a marketing career, working first at Procter & Gamble, then at PepsiCo, where he invented new pizza toppings for the Pizza Hut chain.

In 1983, he joined Control Video Corporation, a video-game specialist, first as a marketing manager and then, after a round of layoffs, as head of marketing. The company was in serious financial trouble, and Case, then 25, became an important player in its desperate attempt to become solvent. Opportunity finally arrived in the form of Commodore, a computer company looking to start an online service for its Commodore 64 users. Control Video offered its services, paid off its creditors, and changed its name to Quantum Computer Services. Quantum's "Q-Link" dial-up network for Commodore Business machines was launched in 1985, and its "PC-Link" network, a joint venture with Tandy, was launched in 1988. In October 1989, Quantum introduced the America Online service for Macintosh and Apple II computers; the DOS version was launched in February 1991.

When Apple pulled out of the deal, Quantum decided to rebrand its remaining online services under one name: Online America, later changed to America Online. The name was chosen when Case held a contest for a new name, and picked his own entry as the winner. In October 1991, Quantum Computer Services officially changed its name to America Online, Inc. The company went public shortly afterward, on March 19, 1992, under the symbol AMER.

In the years that followed, AOL's popularity grew: the company had 10 million subscribers by the end of 1997, 20 million in late 1999, and more than 31 million members by September 2001. The company itself also grew rapidly through a serious of strategic acquisitions, such as its purchase of CompuServe in 1998 and Netscape in March 1999. Today, America Online, Inc., operates a bevy of online services, browsers, and destinations, including America Online, CompuServe, the ICQ instant-messaging service, MapQuest (a resource for maps and directions), the Netscape Netcenter and AOL.COM portals, the Netscape Navigator and Communicator browsers, and AOL MovieFone. AOL acquired Time-Warner for $106 billion in 2001. The resulting company, one of the largest media conglomerates in the world, includes established media companies such as Warner Music, Turner Broadcasting, HBO, Warner Brothers, New Line Cinema, and Time.

By many reports, Case is introverted, awkward, and shy—not the typical personality that one associates with marketing geniuses. Critics contend that AOL's successes have at times been in spite of, rather than due to, the actions of its leadership. For instance, in *AOL.COM*, Kara Swisher recounts several marketing blunders made by Case and his team, such as the time that the company made plans to share customers' telephone numbers with telemarketers. Frequent predictions about AOL's demise have been made since 1985, when the founders tried to get venture capital and were told "It's a dog. You should take it out in back and shoot it."

Despite many dire predictions, AOL has survived and thrived. Case had the instinct and vision to see past the clunky, text-based networking programs that allowed early users to interface with the Internet, to grasp the Internet's commercial potential. Unlike its competitors, AOL eschewed applications such as gaming and focused instead on the networking capabilities of the Internet, creating tools that allowed people to connect with one another online. AOL's success is often attributed to its intuitive design and user-friendly, graphically rich interface, which even technophobic and technically inept users could master. The company's simple installation process and its practice of flooding consumers with ubiquitous installation disks and free trials also helped to popularize it, especially with first-time users.

Although he stumbles at times, Case's expertise with spin is clear. For instance, in late 1997, the company shifted to a bulk-pricing system. The resulting surge in traffic predictably overtaxed the system, preventing many from connecting, but Case was able to position the incident in the media as evidence of consumer obsession with America Online.

Case is an active philanthropist, and has been instrumental in several of AOL's charitable activities. AOL, an early proponent of children's online safety, is one of the founding partners of Network for Good (http://www.networkforgood.org), an online resource that enables the Internet to be used for civic participation and philanthropy, and that helps nonprofit organizations become more effective. AOL is also responsible for the GovernmentGuide site (http://www.governmentguide.com), an online resource to help citizens identify local elected officials and utilize local government services.

Case and his second wife Jean founded the Case Foundation, which supports programs like PowerUp—a partnership of nonprofits, corporations, and federal agencies that gives underserved youth access to technology education and helps them to develop job skills. The Case Foundation's overall strategic mission is to help underserved children and youth through initiatives in technology, education, health care, and community development.

Industry pundits are watching AOL-Time Warner and Steve Case closely. Recent events such as the resignation of chief executive Gerald Levin, a weakened advertising environment for media properties, and the bursting of the technology bubble all make predictions about the future of AOL-Time Warner difficult. Despite these developments, however, it remains clear that Case has become quite an expert at proving the predictions wrong.

Bibliography

AOL Time Warner. "Who We Are: Historical Dates for America Online, Inc." 2002. <http://www.corp.aol.com/whoweare/who_timeline.html> (May 24, 2002).

Munnariz, Rick. "A Look at Steve Case: CEO and Chairman of America Online." *The Motley Fool,* January 14, 1999. <http://www.fool.com/Specials/1999/sp990114ACaseStudy.htm> (May 24, 2002).

Pogue, David. "You've Got Mail." *The New York Times,* August 2, 1998.

Swisher, Kara. *AOL.COM: How Steve Case Beat Bill Gates, Nailed the Netheads, and Made Millions in the War for the Web.* New York: Times Books, 1998.

Further Reading

"Featured Subject: America Online, With Articles From the Archives of The New York Times." *The New York Times,* 1998. <http://www.nytimes.com/books/98/08/02/specials/aol.html> (May 24, 2002).

Stauffer, David. *It's a Wired Wired World: Business the AOL Way*. Milford, Conn.: Capstone, 2000.

Related Topics
Convergence; Internet

— *Nicole Ellison*

Castells, Manuel

1942–

Author and Theorist

Manuel Castells is one of the world's leading thinkers on the social and economic effects of information technology. He was one of the first scholars to recognize the profound changes associated with the information revolution.

After studies in law and economics at the University of Barcelona and the Sorbonne, Castells earned his Ph.D. in sociology from the University of Paris. He holds a second doctorate in human sciences from the Sorbonne, and a third in sociology from the University of Madrid. Since 1979, he has been professor of sociology and professor of city and regional planning at the University of California, Berkeley. In addition to the sociology of information, he works in urban sociology, sociology of development, and technology policy.

Castells has been studying the economic and social transformations of the global information society since 1983. Where most scholars have focused on one nation, society, culture, or social environment in its relations to the larger world, Castells has attempted to map and describe the full global network. Between the early 1980s and the late 1990s, Castells undertook systematic empirical research in North and South America, Europe, and Asia. His approach has been cross-cultural, and the worldwide reception and wide translation of his books demonstrates the value of his work to scholars in the many cultures he has examined.

While Castells' writing depends on broad knowledge and deep scholarship in many fields, reading and understanding his writing does not. Any well-educated citizen with a solid foundation of general knowledge will find Castells an approachable, informative author.

In today's information society, information technology engages and links all other resources. Economic, social, and political power now involve information technology, along with every other aspect of modern society, from military strength to cultural issues, entertainment, and social behavior. The capabilities that information gives to societies and regions and the interactions among information resources have changed the world in many ways. In some cases, information technology diminishes other resources; in some cases, it multiplies them. In some cases, it dissolves social patterns, and in others, it reinforces them.

As the hubs of information networks, cities and city regions have taken on new properties in this reshaped world. In some respects, cities may well become as powerful as nations, while nations may lose power to cities that will be redefined as communities of time and space. While it is impossible to predict all the challenges the future will bring, the fact that they are unavoidable makes Castells' work both interesting and necessary to anyone who hopes to understand the developing global society.

Castells himself believes that information policy is a matter of general concern. His highly popular course on information technology and society reflects the wide range of policy issues that shape his research concerns. The information technology revolution was shaped by historical and geographical circumstance. Industrial actors included microelectronics, computers, telecommunications, and now genetic engineering. The birth of the Internet and the Word Wide Web reinforced and increased earlier trends. Virtual communities and online societies came into existence alongside the physical communities and societies within which they were embedded, and new kinds of social movements, political conflicts, and cultural phenomena were the result.

As the new possibilities inherent in information technology became a common aspect of daily life, the new economy developed. Technology, work habits, and productivity issues shifted in response, and electronic business developed. Globalization in the physical world was a reflection of the information environment, with financial markets, international trade, transnational production networks, and an internationalized labor force being some of the results. These forces were also reflected in a new division of labor; different networks were included in or excluded from a new economy, resulting in a growing digital divide with new kinds of poverty and new kinds of inequality.

At the same time, those who work within the information society are gaining power as knowledge transforms management, work, and employment toward the network enterprise, flexible work, and individualized relationships between capital and labor. The shifting capital ratio toward intellectual capital plays a part in this shift, while changes in gender relations challenge patriarchal cultures in broader ways.

British sociologist Anthony Giddens and others have compared Castells to the German sociologist Max Weber (1864–1920). Many feel that Castells' work will be as fundamental to the social theory of the twenty-first century as Weber's was to the social theory of the twentieth.

Selected Works

Castells, Manuel. *The City and the Grassroots: A Cross-cultural Theory of Urban Social Movements.* Berkeley: University of California Press, 1983.

———. *The Information Age: Economy, Society, and Culture.* Three Volumes: Vol. I: *The Rise of the Network Society;* Vol. II: *The Power of Identity;* Vol. III: *End of Millennium.* Oxford: Blackwell Publishers, 1989.

———. *The Informational City: Information Technology, Economic Restructuring, and the Urban-Regional Process.* Oxford: Blackwell, 1989.

———. *The Internet Galaxy: Reflections on Internet, Business, and Society.* Oxford: Oxford University Press, 2001.

———. *The Urban Question.* Cambridge, Mass.: MIT Press, 1977.

Castells, Manuel, and Peter Hall. *Technopoles of the World: The Making of 21st Century Industrial Complexes.* London: Routledge, 1994.

Bibliography

Barney, Cliff. "Bewildered New World." Interview with Manuel Castells. Upside, 1997. <http://www.upside.com/texis/mvm/story?id=34712c1eb> (April 5, 2002)

Friedman, Ken. "Cities in the Information Age: A Scandinavian Perspective." *The Virtual Workplace.* Magid Igbaria and Margaret Tan, eds. Hershey, Pa.: Idea Group Publishing, 1998; pp. 144–176.

Nye, Joseph S., Jr., and William Owens. "America's Information Edge." *Foreign Affairs,* March-April 1996, pp. 20–36.

Further Reading

Sassen, Saskia. *Cities in the World Economy.* Thousand Oaks, Calif.: Pine Forge/Sage Publications, 1994.

———. *The Global City: New York, London, and Tokyo.* Princeton, N.J.: Princeton University Press, 1991.

Susser, Ida, ed. *A Castells Reader on Cities and Social Theory.* Oxford: Blackwell, 2001.

Related Topics

Access; ARPANET; Business-to-Business; Internet

— *Ken Friedman*

"The Cathedral and the Bazaar"

A key text for those studying the social politics of the open-source software movement, Eric Raymond's "The Cathedral and the Bazaar" inspired Netscape to publish the source code of its Navigator 5.0 Web browser in 1998. Originally released over the Internet as a single essay in 1997, Raymond expanded his material into a book of the same name in 2000.

"What are we to think," a *New York Times* article asked, "when elite programmers . . . donate their precious time to develop software anyone can use without charge?" Eric Raymond set out to answer this question and others in "The Cathedral and the Bazaar," comparing his personal experiences developing an open-source program called sendmail to a more well-known story: the development of the Linux operating system. Linux is a free version of Unix, begun in 1991 when the program's creator, Linus Torvalds, began inviting collaborators all over the Internet to help design an operating system with their volunteer labor. Today, Linux runs one-sixth of the business-server computers in the United States, and is considered by many to be superior to market giant Microsoft's NT.

Before Linux, Raymond confessed, "I believed that the most important software needed to be built like cathedrals, carefully crafted by individual wizards or small bands of mages working in splendid isolation, with not a beta release before its time." By comparison, he points out, the Linux movement resembled not so much a cathedral as a "great babbling bazaar of differing agendas and approaches . . . out of which a coherent and stable system could seemingly emerge only by a succession of miracles." Raymond confessed that he knew Torvald's axioms— "release early and often, delegate everything you can, be open to the point of promiscuity"—worked. He just couldn't figure out *why* they worked. Like many programmers before him, Raymond believed in "Brook's Law," which states (in plain vernacular) that too many software cooks spoil the development stew. However, Raymond realized, "If this were the whole picture, Linux would be impossible."

In 1996, Raymond decided to consciously run the development of the open-source software called fetchmail using the Bazaar style. Invoking psychologist Gerald Weinberg's work in "egoless programming,"

Raymond discovered that people will often provide huge amounts of intellectual labor without thought of profit if they perceive that their reputations within the community will be enhanced as a result.

Raymond, who makes a point of identifying himself in interviews as a Libertarian, argues that the Bazaar philosophy can flourish quite naturally and comfortably within capitalist market economies. Certainly, this argument played a big role in Netscape's 1998 decision to make public the source code for its Web browser, and even Microsoft admitted in its leaked "Halloween" memo that "commercial quality can be achieved/exceeded by [open-source software] projects."

With that said, Raymond's ideas have drawn criticism as well. Jonathan Eunice points out that Raymond too often casts software development as either open-source or commercial, when generally a mix of the two styles is what is needed. For example, although Microsoft is "the company many love to hate," Eunice notes that its Redmond development model actually emphasizes things like quick turnaround, modular construction techniques, a large and active user base, and many entities striving to improve a product in a thousand parallel dimensions—all hallmarks of the Bazaar. Others have pointed to the irony of First World programmers naively celebrating a term strongly associated with the Third World when, for programmers in developing nations, leisure time to participate in the open-source community is possibly the scarcest commodity of all. There are, however, a number of active open-source undertakings in a wide variety of languages that Microsoft currently doesn't address, such as Icelandic.

Raymond has always viewed his essay itself as an open-source document of sorts. Since 1997, he has continually updated his work, pointing to public intersections with his thoughts on the Web, such as Ko Kuwabara's recent work on Linux as an evolvable system. As author Clay Shirky defines them, evolvable systems are "those that proceed not under the sole direction of one centralized design authority but by being adapted and extended in a thousand small ways in a thousand places at once." Shirky argues that programs like Microsoft's Hailstorm will change proprietary questions around computing from "Is this software licensed to run on this machine?" to "Is this software licensed to run for this user?" Ultimately, evolvable systems may prove a more resilient metaphor than either cathedrals or bazaars, if only because they take into consideration just this sort of peer-to-peer software development over the Internet.

Bibliography

Brooks, Frederick P. *The Mythical Man-Month*. New York: Addison-Wesley, 1986.

Eunice, Jonathan. "Beyond the Cathedral, Beyond the Bazaar." illuminata.com, May 11, 1998. <http://www.illuminata.com/public/content/cathedral/intro.htm> (April 26, 2002).

Kuwabara, Ko. "Linux: A Bazaar at the Edge of Chaos." *First Monday* vol. 5, no. 3 (2000). <http://www.firstmonday.org/issues/issue5_3/kuwabara/index.html> (April 26, 2002).

Postrel, Virginia. "The Arrival of Open-Source Software Arouses Researchers' Curiosity on What Motivates Programmers to Work Free." *New York Times*, April 20, 2000, C2.

Raymond, Eric S. *The Cathedral and the Bazaar: Musings on Linux and Open Source by an Accidental Revolutionary*. Cambridge: O'Reilly & Associates, 1999.

———. "The Cathedral and the Bazaar." Tuxedo.org, August 15, 2002. <http://www.tuxedo.org/~esr/writings/cathedral-bazaar/> (April 26, 2002).

Shirky, Clay. *Hailstorm: Open Web Services Controlled by Microsoft*. O'Reilly & Associates, *P2P Newsletter*, May 30, 2001. <http://www.openp2p.com/pub/a/p2p/2001/05/30/hailstorm.html> (April 26, 2002).

———. *In Praise of Evolvable Systems: Why Something as Poorly Designed as the Web Became the Next Big Thing, and What That Means for the Future*. Shirky.com, 1998. <http://www.shirky.com/writings/evolve.html> (April 26, 2002).

Weinberg, Gerald M. *The Psychology of Computer Programming*. New York: Van Nostrand Reinhold, 1971.

Further Reading

DeMarco, Tom, and Timothy Lister. *Peopleware: Productive Projects and Teams*. New York: Dorset House, 1987.

Lerner, Josh, and Jean Tirole. "The Simple Economics of Open Source." December 29, 2000. <http://www.people.hbs.edu/jlerner/simple.pdf> (April 26, 2002).

Roush, Wade. "The Cathedral and the Bazaar, Review." *Technology Review* 103, no. 1 (2000), p. 96.

Schofield, Jack. "Cover Story: Armed, but Not Dangerous, Eric Raymond Is the Gun-Toting Supergeek Who Has the Corporate Moguls in His Sights." *The Guardian*, January 21, 1999, p. 2.

Related Topics

Copyleft; Linux; Open Source; Raymond, Eric; Stallman, Richard

— *Theresa M. Senft*

CAVE

The CAVE (a recursive acronym for CAVE Automatic Virtual Environment) was developed in 1991 by Daniel Sandin and Thomas DeFanti at the University of Illinois at Chicago (UIC). It is an immersive virtual reality display device used for art, scientific visualization, and collaboration.

Sandin, who joined UIC's faculty in 1969, and DeFanti, who was hired there in 1972, were active in merging technology and art in the 1970s and 1980s. Their work initially focused on video art, and later on the use of personal computers for art, education, and scientific visualization. The pair co-founded the Electronic Visualization Lab (EVL) at UIC, and created an environment in which faculty and students from many disciplines (primarily engineering and art, but also mathematics, communication, and psychology, among others) could work together on virtual reality and computer networking projects. In 1991, the pair conceived of a virtual reality "theater"—a room, approximately 10 feet on each side, that people could enter. EVL students Carolina Cruz-Neira, Greg Dawe, Sumit Das, and others helped realize their conception

by building hardware and software components. The CAVE was premiered at the 1992 conference of the Association of Computing Machinery Special Interest Group on Computer Graphics and Interactive Techniques (ACM SIGGRAPH) in Chicago.

The acronym CAVE was chosen in part because of its allusion to Plato's "The Allegory of the Cave." Plato describes a cave occupied by a group of people. They can see only its rear wall and the shadows cast on it from the cave's entrance. The cave's occupants therefore believe that the shadows are reality.

Unlike the users of many virtual reality systems developed in the 1980s and 1990s, CAVE users occupy a room-like space, rather than wearing head-mounted displays or helmets. (However, they do don a pair of glasses similar to the safety goggles used in woodworking shops or chemistry labs.) Since more than one user can be in a CAVE, rather than being individually isolated, as is the case with head-mounted displays or helmets, the CAVE is a multi-person environment.

Using rear-projection, stereo perspective-corrected images can be displayed on all sides of the CAVE. Users' CAVE glasses are synchronized to the images being displayed. The glasses' lenses are made of liquid crystal display shutters that separate the stereo

Electronic Visualization Lab student Marcus Thiébaux demonstrates the CAVE. (Courtesy of National Center for Supercomputing Applications)

images, ensuring that each eye sees only one of the stereo images at a time. As a result, the images appear to the CAVE's occupants to be three-dimensional. They appear to extend into the room, away from and around the viewer. Currently, prototypes exist that make the glasses appear to be little more than classic "Ray-Ban" sunglasses. Research is being undertaken to do away with the glasses altogether.

The CAVE's success at creating 3-D virtual reality is based on Sandin and DeFanti's understanding of optics and perception. They knew that parallax, the different perspectives presented to each eye in binocular vision, depth occlusion, and other visual information are combined in the brain to produce knowledge of the depth of what a person sees. As a result, they were able to create hardware and software that creates a sufficiently information-rich illusion to assist the brain in decoding the CAVE's images as three-dimensional.

Navigation within a CAVE environment is possible using a wand, in effect a 3-D "mouse" that the viewer can use much as one might use a joystick. Additionally, it is possible for a viewer wearing a location sensor, or tracking device, to move around in the areas projected within the CAVE. Most commonly a viewer's head and hands are tracked. Proper perspective, oriented to the viewer, is updated and projected in real time. The images are typically created with high-end computers made by Silicon Graphics, although efforts are under way to create them with PCs. Another Silicon Graphics computer creates audio for the environment, delivered to speakers mounted in each of the CAVE's four corners. Three-dimensional models are typically created in off-the-shelf software like Photoshop, Creator, SoftImage, Alias, and others. Much of the software has been created by EVL students and researchers, including Dave Pape and Jason Leigh.

Aside from its obvious visual qualities, the CAVE has value as a collaborative tool and an interactive visualization device. Concerning the former, it is possible to network CAVE users into a single environment. For instance, a user at UIC can be running a virtual reality environment that looks like a garden; another user, anywhere else in the world, can log in to the same environment. Both users can see one another as computer-drawn avatars), and can hear one another speak. Since each will typically have head and hand tracking enabled, they can nod their heads and wave, direct their gazes and point, and move around the environment. Perspective is drawn accurately for each viewer.

Applications in medicine have also been developed, including virtual "tours" of the body's organs.

CAVE users can also interact with visual images, such as art or data. EVL has developed additional technologies to make the CAVE's advantages for art, interaction, immersion, and visualization accessible in a variety of settings. Most notable is the ImmersaDesk, a drafting table–sized, single-sided CAVE system. Instead of putting a user in a room like the CAVE, the ImmersaDesk fills a viewer's field of vision. A portable system, enclosed in a flight case, the ImmersaDesk and its progeny the ImmersaDesk2 typically are used in museums, schools, and trade shows, where permanent installations are unlikely.

There are more than 100 CAVEs around the world. The goals that drove the CAVE's development continue to move its evolution forward 10 years after it was introduced. The desire for improvements—in the form of the creation of higher-resolution images, faster display of graphics, more and better user tracking, mixing of virtual reality imagery with real objects, better handling of large data sets and visualizations, and the development of methods of teaching and guiding in virtual worlds, among other goals—inspire researchers and students at EVL and other CAVE sites to continue their efforts. The CAVE's contributions to science, art, and entertainment are only beginning to be realized as computer and other technologies used for creating virtual reality catch up to the visions that Sandin, DeFanti, and others uphold.

Bibliography

Cruz-Neira, C.; Sandin, D.; DeFanti, T.; Kenyon, R.; and Hart, J. "The CAVE: Audio Visual Experience Automatic Virtual Environment." *Communications of the ACM,* vol. 35, no. 6 (1992), pp. 65–72.

Cruz-Neira, C.; Sandin, D.; and DeFanti, T. "Virtual Reality: The Design and Implementation of the CAVE." *Proceedings of SIGGRAPH 93 Computer Graphics Conference.* New York: ACM SIGGRAPH, 1993; pp. 135–142.

Cruz-Neira, C.; Leigh, J.; Barnes, C.; Cohen, S. M.; Das, S.; Engelmann, R.; Hudson, R.; Papka, M. E.; Roy, T.; Siegel, L.; Vasilakis, C.; DeFanti, T. A.; and Sandin, D. J. "Scientists in Wonderland: A Report on Visualization Applications in the CAVE Virtual Reality Environment." *Proceedings of IEEE 1993 Symposium on Research Frontiers in Virtual Reality.* Los Alamitos, Calif.: IEEE Computer Society Press, 1993; pp. 59–66.

Further Reading

Burdea, Grigore and Philippe Coiffet. *Virtual Reality Technology.* New York: John Wiley & Sons, 1994.

Ohlsson, S., T. Moher, and A. Johnson. "Deep Learning in Virtual Reality: How to Teach Children that the Earth Is Round." *Proceedings of the 22nd Annual Conference of the Cognitive Science Society*, Philadelphia, Pa., August 13–15, 2000, pp. 364–368.

Stuart, Rory. *The Design of Virtual Environments.* New York: McGraw Hill, 1996.

Vince, John. *Essential Virtual Reality Fast: How to Understand the Techniques and Potential of Virtual Reality.* Berlin/New York: Springer, 1998.

———. *Virtual Reality Systems.* Wokingham, England; Reading, Mass.: Addison-Wesley, 1995.

Related Topics

Avatar; DeFanti, Thomas; Sandin, Daniel; Virtual Reality

— *Steve Jones*

CD-R, CD-ROM, and DVD

CD-R, CD-ROM, and DVD are all acronyms for types of digital optical recording media: CD-R stands for Compact Disc Recordable, CD-ROM is short for Compact Disc Read Only Memory, and DVD is the abbreviation for Digital Versatile (or Video) Disc. Digital optical media have become the most popular tools for the recording, storage, and playback of audio, video, and computer data. Thanks to excellent sound and video quality, and the ability to store massive amounts of data on a small, rugged disc, digital optical media have been adopted rapidly by the public.

Early Development

In the mid-1970s, several corporations began recording video on 12-inch discs read by lasers; the LaserVision format developed by MCA and Philips eventually became the standard. LaserVision players are still around, but were never popular; at their peak, only 1 percent of the U.S. population used them. VHS proved to be a much more popular format for video, despite its inferior quality, because it could record as well as play back.

In contrast to its early failure as a video-recording format, optical disc technology was immediately successful for audio recordings. In 1980, Sony and Philips co-endorsed a standard, called CD-DA (Compact Disc Digital Audio), for audio recording on optical discs. This standard was published in a book with a red binding, which is why today the CD-DA format is often called Red Book audio. In 1982, Sony and Philips introduced the world to the compact disc: a 120 mm diameter, light but rugged, plastic marvel of engineering that could hold 74 minutes of music. The new recording medium wasn't as susceptible to wearing out as vinyl records and magnetic tape, had a much clearer sound thanks to its higher signal-to-noise ratio, and was inexpensive to mass-produce. Even though the players initially cost around $1,000, hundreds of thousands were bought in the first year, and by the end of 1984 more than one million had sold around the world.

It didn't take long for engineers to realize that if compact discs could hold audio data, they could also hold other types of data, including computer programs. However, before CDs could be used for software, the engineers had to design much greater error-correction capabilities into them. After all, missing one bit of data from a song wouldn't be critical, but missing a single number from a computer program could cause it to crash.

Development of Multiple Formats

In 1985, the Yellow Book format, more commonly called CD-ROM (compact disc read-only memory), was introduced. CD-ROMs could hold computer software in a read-only form, which meant that once the software was written on the CD, it could not be altered. Since the drives initially cost $1,000, and their performance was somewhat poor due to the slow speed at which they transferred data, it took some time for them to be widely accepted. But as the cost of drives decreased and their performance improved, CD-ROMs became extremely popular. Thanks to their storage capacity (up to 700 megabytes), one CD-ROM could contain even large software programs, such as word processors.

Between 1986 and 1996, several other types of compact disc were created. CD-i, a.k.a. Green Book, was Philips' interactive multimedia format, and the players could read MPEG (a form of audio/video compression) videos as well as interactive games. CD-i never really caught on, though, and few players currently exist. Kodak's Photo CD has been somewhat more successful. Photographers can shoot a roll of film and get the pictures developed and placed on a Photo CD that can be viewed with a player plugged into a standard television set. Currently, Photo CDs are used primarily in the professional photographic community. Video-CD (White Book) was introduced in 1994, but it was quickly eclipsed by the DVD format.

DVD had its beginnings in the early 1990s, when several companies began to work on increasing the capacity of optical discs. Their goal was to pack a full-length movie on one side of a disc. In 1995, two competing formats were merged into one standard: the Digital Versatile (or Video) Disc, and several companies released the first DVD players in 1996. At this point, the Consumer Electronics Manufacturers Association (CEMA) and the Motion Picture Association of America (MPAA) began pushing for hardware or software that could prevent illegal copying of movies. The resulting conflict between consumer electronics manufacturers and the entertainment industry caused a delay of several years before DVD players reached the market. But by the end of 1999, close to 5,000,000 DVD players had been sold—a phenomenal adoption rate, surpassing even that of the CD player. The storage capacity of DVDs also greatly surpasses CDs; depending on their format, DVDs can hold from 4.7 gigabytes to 17.9 gigabytes, sufficient to record nine hours of audio and video content. DVD players are backward-compatible, meaning they can read audio CDs, CD-ROMs, and most other formats.

Although equipment with which to record DVDs is finding its way into computers (hence DVD-R, or DVD-Recordable; DVD-ROM, or DVD-Read Only Memory; and DVD-RAM, or DVD-Random Access Memory), much as in the early days of the CD, the cost of recording units is high. When CD-R units first appeared on the scene in 1989, they cost more than $1,000. But the price had dropped to under $200 by 2000, and CD recorders became standard equipment on personal computers. Initially, CD-R discs could only been written-to one time; once you had recorded something on the disc, it was there permanently. However, rewritable compact discs (CD-RW), which can be written to around 1,000 times, quickly followed. CD-R and CD-RW units have become popular for one simple reason: the installed base of equipment. CD-R discs can be read by any optical player—including standard audio CD players, if the data is recorded in Red Book format. Because so many people have CD, CD-ROM, or DVD players, users can be confident that nearly everyone will be able to access data that is put on a CD-R.

How They Work

All digital optical media work in essentially the same way: The reflective surface of the compact disc is an alternating pattern of "land" and "pits," or "valleys." A pit or valley is a very slight depression in the polycarbonate material of the CD, while the rest of the surface is the land. Laser light is bounced off this reflective disc, and the resulting signal is converted

into binary data. When the laser light hits the land, most of the light is reflected back to the photodiode detector, but when the laser strikes a pit, no light is reflected back. This is because a light wave is a ripple of high and low points, and if a second light wave is added (through reflection, in this case) a half-wavelength later, the high and low points of the two waves cancel each other out. The pits are positioned a precise distance away from the laser to create a canceling reflection.

The CD drive converts these reflections into a series of 1s and 0s, but not in the way one might expect. The photodiode creates a signal based on transitions between pits and lands, coded as a 1, and the length of time between transitions, coded as a series of 0s. Thus, the pattern on the surface of the disc of up to land, over, down into pit, over, up to land, etc. is transformed into 1, a series of 0s, 1, another series of 0s, 1, and so on.

DVDs operate in basically the same way, but they pack more information onto the disc through four techniques. First, the pits are smaller. Second, the spirals of pits are tighter together. Third, DVDs can use two (and potentially more) layers of data. The first layer is semi-reflective, and the laser can be set to either focus on it or to pass through it and focus on the next layer. Finally, DVDs can be double-sided.

Optical discs are mass-produced by creating a glass master of pits and lands that is used as a mold to create the polycarbonate surface. That surface is coated with aluminum to make it reflective, and sealed with protective layers of lacquer, with a label on the top. CD-Rs, however, are not mass-produced with pits and lands, since the user is the one recording the data. They use gold for the reflective surface, and have a layer of organic dye that is used for recording data. When the laser is set to record, it sends pulses of higher-intensity light that heat the dye, creating mounds that correspond to the pits of a pre-recorded CD.

The Future

The advances in digital optical recording media have led to a fundamental conflict between the recording industry and consumers. For example, it is now possible for individuals to "burn" custom audio CDs with digitally perfect copies of favorite songs. Since these CDs can be listened to with any standard CD player, people can make compilations of music for themselves or their friends. Also, MP3 audio files shared over the Internet through services such as Napster can be burned onto CDs in standard Red Book audio format, often in violation of copyright law. Consumers argue that they ought to be able to create their own custom CDs if they use songs only from CDs they have purchased. However, the recording industry points to people who put together compilations of songs obtained illegally, and lobbies for stricter regulations and more effective copy-protection schemes.

In the coming years, two trends are expected to continue: More and more data will be squeezed onto this remarkable recording medium, and more and more confrontations will be take place between the entertainment industry and consumers. DVDs will soon surpass 18 gigabytes in capacity, as engineers come up with ways to pack information even more densely. DVD-R (Digital Versatile Disc Recordable) player/recorders will decrease in price, allowing more people to burn their own movies on DVD. It is clear that CDs and DVDs will be the storage medium of choice for some time, at least until the next amazing technology arrives.

Bibliography

Boden, Larry. *Mastering CD-ROM Technology*. New York: John Wiley and Sons, 1995.

Purcell, Lee. *CD-R/DVD: Disc Recording Demystified*. New York: McGraw-Hill, 2000.

Further Reading

CNET. "CD-R/CD-RW Beginners Center." April 13, 2001. <http://www.help.com/cat/1/21/602/beginnercenter.html> (March 20, 2002).

DVD Digest. "The PC-DVD Guide." April 13, 2001. <http://www.digital-digest.com/dvd/support/begin.html> (March 20, 2002).

Taylor, Jim. *DVD Demystified*. 2nd ed. New York: McGraw-Hill, 2000.

Related Topics

Compression; Copyright; Desktop Video; Digital Audio; Digital Music; MP3; MPEG; Multimedia; Napster; Peer-to-Peer

— Norman Clark

Cellular Telephony

Cellular telephony is based on the idea of using radio waves (instead of copper wires or fiber-optic cables) to connect mobile telephones to one another and to the ordinary telephone network. Since devices of this kind were first developed in the 1920s, a variety of different systems have arisen using both analog and digital technology. Although cellular phones have revolutionized personal communication, several issues remain unresolved, including the potential health risks of radio transmitters, the interference they cause with other equipment, and the incomplete compatibility of telecommunications standards.

Call Handling

Unlike a landline (a wire-connected telephone fixed in one place), a mobile cellular telephone sends and receives calls using signals carried by radio waves. Different geographical areas are divided into distinct but overlapping areas called cells, each served by a different transmitting and receiving antenna. Cells vary greatly in size, from a few blocks or less in urban centers to entire towns in quieter rural areas.

When a cellular phone user makes a call, the phone sends out a radio signal to the nearest cellular antenna. This transmits the signal to a centralized call-distribution building called a Mobile Telephone Switching Office (MTSO) that can, in turn, send the signal either to the ordinary phone network (the PSTN—Public Switched Telephone Network) or to another cellular phone on the same network. Calls from the PSTN are routed in the opposite direction via the nearest cell to the cellular phone. As cellular phone users move around, the signals they send out may be picked up by more than one antenna in more than one cell. When users cross the boundary from one cell to another, calls they are making or receiving are "handed off" from one cell to the other, usually without any interruption in conversation.

Analog and Digital

Ordinary telephones send signals in analog form (variations in speech are transmitted down a copper wire by a fluctuating electric current). Computerized equipment, by contrast, is more suited to sending information in digital form (continuously varying speech signals are encoded as binary data). The first cellular phones used only analog technology; more recent devices have used a mixture of analog and digital, and the latest systems are entirely digital.

Phone calls are transmitted by radio waves using a mathematical technique called modulation, in which the shape of a radio wave (called the carrier) is changed (modulated) so that it incorporates the speech or data signal. Analog and digital phone systems differ in the type of modulation they use; the number of phone calls a system can handle at once depends on how effectively those calls can be kept separate within the limited band of radio frequencies available to the phone system, which in turn depends on the type of modulation used. The original analog phone network used in the United States was called Analog Mobile

Phone System (AMPS). It used a system of modulation called Frequency Division Multiple Access (FDMA), so that each different phone call was carried by a different frequency of radio waves in a band between 800 and 900 MHz. But such a system rapidly runs out of frequencies as more and more users try to send calls.

An improved system called Digital-AMPS (D-AMPS) used another type of modulation called Time Division Multiple Access (TDMA), in which each caller has a "time-share" of a particular frequency. This gives a threefold increase in capacity over FDMA. The latest, entirely digital cellular phones increase capacity by an additional factor of 10 to 20 with an enhancement called Code Division Multiple Access (CDMA), in which phone calls are identified (and separated) by numeric codes. Another type of digital cellular system called Global System for Mobile (GSM) telecommunications uses a variation on TDMA. Different versions of the latest U.S. digital phone system, Personal Cellular System (PCS), use either TDMA or CDMA, depending on the operating company.

Apart from higher capacity, digital cellular offers numerous advantages over analog. The entirely digital PCS and GSM systems are more secure (calls are encrypted, unlike in analog cellular), are less susceptible to noise interference (so calls are clearer), have better features (offering voice messaging, caller identification, and so on), and use less power (so batteries last longer). By their very nature, digital cellular phones are also more compatible with computer equipment. Yesterday's analog cellular phones were simply a mobile version of analog landlines; today's digital cellular phones combine elements of traditional telephones and radio pagers with elements of modern computers in applications such as Short Message System (SMS—the ability to send text messages from one digital phone to another) and Wireless Application Protocol (WAP—effectively using a mobile phone as a simple Web browser).

Historical Background

Cellular communication dates back at least as far as the 1920s, when emergency services began to experiment with radio telephones. But the first commercial radio telephone system, Mobile Telephone System (MTS), was introduced only in June 1946 by AT&T and Southwestern Bell in St Louis, Missouri. Five antennas around the city linked mobiles in vehicles to a central switching office at Bell's office block. The system was gradually introduced around the country, and later replaced by an Improved Mobile Telephone System (IMTS), but demand always far exceeded

capacity, with thousands of frustrated customers on five- or ten-year waiting lists.

Things improved with the introduction of the Analog Mobile Phone System (AMPS) in 1978; initially introduced in Chicago by Illinois Bell and AT&T, it was later rolled out across the United States, and soon to other countries. But in Europe, the limitations of AMPS were quickly appreciated, and in 1982, the Conference of European Posts and Telecommunications (CEPT), representing 26 European telephone companies, began to define a specification for an improved digital cellular system that could be used to roam not just from cell to cell, but also from country to country. The resulting system, first called Groupe Speciale Mobile and later Global System for Mobile (GSM) telecommunications, was created in 1987, incorporating elements of both analog FDMA and digital TDMA technologies. Data was first successfully transmitted over GSM by the Nokia company in 1994, and the GSM standard was adopted in the United States the following year. By February 2001, GSM had captured over 70 percent of the world market, with over 452 million customers in 162 countries.

Despite its widespread adoption throughout the world, however, GSM is only one of several systems currently used in the United States. Although somewhat outdated, AMPS remains extremely popular throughout North, Central, and South America. PCS has gained in popularity since a massive auction of frequencies by the Federal Communications Commission (FCC) between 1994 and 1997, but it is only partly compatible with GSM.

Issues

The complexity and incomplete compatibility of standards and systems is only one of the issues confronting the cellular telephone industry and its estimated half-billion users worldwide. Other question marks have been raised over the potential health risks of cellular telephones and the antennas that serve them. Although various scientific studies appear to have demonstrated that cellular phone handsets can affect brain activity, the results remain inconclusive, and adverse effects on the brain have yet to be demonstrated. Among those hoping to resolve the issue definitively is the World Health Organization (WHO), which is currently conducting a $6 million epidemiological study into cellular phones and brain tumors.

The human brain is not the only thing affected by cellular phone emissions. Airplanes and hospitals have banned cellular phones due to their interference with

As of this writing, Cerf was serving as chairman of the powerful Internet Corporation for Assigned Names and Numbers, the non-profit company that is responsible for managing the World Wide Web's crucial address-naming function, and the body that some say serves as the Web's de facto government.

Cerf also has done a considerable amount of writing on topics ranging from cryptography to the commercialization of the Web and the Internet's future. In recent years, he has spent much of his packed schedule pushing for the transition to Version 6 of the Internet Protocol (IPv6), which aims to replace the currently used Version 4 by offering enough IP addresses that every computer, cellular phone, and set-top box in the world can be hooked up to the Internet.

In 2000, Cerf wrote that the Internet "is growing beyond my wildest expectations." But he has not been content to let the Internet grow up without him. In fact, he seems to be in the midst of what is potentially the biggest project of his career, working with the Jet Propulsion Laboratory in Pasadena, California, as a distinguished visiting scientist responsible for the architecture and design of an interplanetary Internet. The project involves the creation of a system based on special protocols that would carry transmissions between planets, a communications system that Cerf expects will be needed once humankind begins traversing space in search of usable natural resources. "Commercialization of assets off the planet would mutually reinforce the growth of interplanetary communication," Cerf told *Wired* magazine in January 2000. "Some people argue we should solve all the problems on Earth before going off the planet, but that's like telling Lewis and Clark to stay put until the rest of the East was settled. No way."

Selected Works

Cerf, Vinton. "What Will Replace the Internet?" *Time.com*, June 19, 2000. <http://www.time.com/time/reports/v21/tech/mag_web.html> (May 17, 2002).

Cerf, Vinton G. "Technical Writings: Future Imperfect." *WorldCom.com*, April 1996. <http://www.worldcom.com/generation_d/cerfs_up/technical_writings/futureimperf.phtml> (May 17, 2002).

———. "Suggested Readings and Prose: How the Internet Works (Part I and II)." 1995, 1996. <http://www1.worldcom.com/global/resources/cerfs_up/prose/hownetworks.xml> (May 17, 2002).

Cerf, Vinton G. and Robert E. Kahn. "A Protocol for Packet Network Intercommunication." *IEEE Transactions on Communications*, vol. com-22, no. 5 (May 1974). <http://www1.worldcom.com/global/resources/cerfs_up/technical_writings/protocol_paper/> (May 17, 2002).

Kahn, Robert E., and Vinton G. Cerf. "Internet History: What Is the Internet (And What Makes It Work)." *WorldCom.com*, December 1999. <http://www.worldcom.com/generation_d/cerfs_up/internet_history/whatIs.phtml> (May 17, 2002).

Bibliography

Griffin, Scott. "Internet Pioneers: Vint Cerf." March 1, 2000. <http://www.ibiblio.org/pioneers/cerf.html> (May 10, 2002).

Hafner, Katie. "Ghosts in the Machine." *Wired* 4.07, July 1996. <http://www.wired.com/wired/archive/4.07/ghosts.html> (May 10, 2002).

Hafner, Katie, and Matthew Lyon. *Where Wizards Stay Up Late: The Origins of the Internet.* New York: Simon & Schuster, 1996.

Naughton, John. *A Brief History of the Future: From Radio Days to Internet Years in a Lifetime.* Woodstock, N.Y.: The Overlook Press, 2000.

Segaller, Stephen. *Nerds 2.0.1: A Brief History of the Internet.* New York: TV Books, 1998.

Further Reading

Gillies, James, and Robert Cailliau. *How the Web Was Born.* New York: Oxford University Press, 2000.

Salus, Peter H. *Casting the Net: From ARPANET to Internet and Beyond.* Reading, Mass.: Addison-Wesley Publishing Co., 1995.

Related Topics

ARPANET; Internet; Internet Corporation for Assigned Names and Numbers; Satellite Networks

— *Kevin Featherly*

Chat

In computing parlance, chat refers to a form of communication in which users type text to one another in synchronous or real-time fashion. Enormously popular since its inception, chat recently was ranked first (along with email) by UCLA researchers studying the most used Internet applications. With the recent introduction of "presence management" and mobile connectivity features, chat promises to grow more popular still, becoming what many call "the world's oldest killer app."

Chats take place in a variety of locations, each with their own social culture and history. Today, public chatting occurs on Internet Relay servers, graphical Web spaces like the Palace, in multi-user domains (MUDs), and in commercial chat rooms like those of America Online. Additionally, private chats may occur in spaces like "secret" IRC channels, via closed groupware systems like LotusNotes, or through private two-way instant-messaging systems on computing devices or via telephone. There are currently hundreds of chat spaces set up on the Internet and on private intranets, serving millions of participants worldwide.

THE HISTORIES OF CHAT

Because of simultaneous developments in mainframe-based time-sharing systems and in microcomputer-based bulletin-board services, chat has never followed a singular line of evolution. Thus, the answer to "how electronic chatting began" often changes depending on who is asked, and when. "Even in the days of cards, punches, and dumb printing consoles, chatting was possible," notes programmer Jeff Kell, who remembers rudimentary chats occurring over shared IBM 360s, which were invented in 1964.

For many of the earliest computer users, the story of chatting on shared mainframe computers begins with Talk, Write, and Finger—programs utilized by the UNIX operating system, which was introduced in the 1970s. Talk allowed users running UNIX to speak to one another a sentence at a time, using a split screen. Write, a primitive version of what is now known as instant messaging, allowed users to communicate by copying lines from their terminals to others. Finally, Finger helped UNIX users determine who else was currently online and available for chatting.

As popular as it was, not everyone came to computerized chat through UNIX. In France, for instance, a proprietary system called the Minitel *messageries* permitted teletext chat among users. When offices around America began networking their microcomputers, vendors like Novell began marketing programs similar to, though not identical to, Talk, Write, and Finger. Finally, on microcomputer bulletin board systems (BBSs), chat flourished via specially written programs with names like CompuServe's CB Simulator. Even today, services like America Online still use proprietary software to run their chat rooms.

During the 1970s and 1980s, chats were somewhat local affairs, restricted to users of a specific mainframe, networked together in an office or dialed into a single BBS. There were exceptions, however. National Fido Hour was a one-hour-per-day time slot in which users of the FidoNet BBSs were connected to one another in order to chat without long-distance charges. And Relay was a highly popular service on the BITNET network,

which connected a number of university computers that were not on the ARPANET.

The arrival of wide-scale long-distance online chatting began with a program called—aptly enough—Chat. This program, written by Jarkko Oikarinen in 1988, permitted multiple users on multiple computers to speak to one another using their Internet connections. Though Oikarinen's program wasn't necessarily the first of its kind, it has had the longest lineage, spawning the Internet Relay Chat (IRC) networks. To this day, many Web-based chat rooms use some version of Oikarinen's original program, albeit aided by Java-based interfaces to make the experience easier to navigate for the user.

BECAUSE IT'S FUN

From the earliest experiments in mainframe messaging, users have asserted that one of the main attractions of chat is the fun of speaking to others in real time. Nearly three-quarters of online U.S. youth ages 12 to 17 use instant messaging to chat with friends almost every day, notes a recent Pew Internet report. Many chat room users spend hours online in a "flow experience," in which the activity of typing back and forth to others becomes deeply engaging. Researcher Brenda Dannett has remarked that chat spaces frequently become places of play for regulars, and a recent Pew Internet study bears this out: Fully 56 percent of online teens said that they used more than one screen name in order to compartmentalize different parts of their lives online, or so that they could experiment with different personas.

Psychologist and Internet researcher Sherry Turkle notes that many users employ chat to "try on" identity positions that might not feel permissible in their offline lives. Just as chat allows banter and creative communications conventions (LOL for "laugh[ing] out loud") to flourish, it also seems to promote antisocial behaviors, such as flaming and trolling. Still, points out linguist Susan Herring, although chat spaces may be seen as confusing or hostile to novices, they are often quite successfully navigated by those who stay around long enough to learn their social codes. Eventually, she points out, most people grow to understand that there really are other people on the other side of the computer screen, and that social responsibility exists online as well as off.

BEYOND FUN: THE RISE OF PRESENCE MANAGEMENT

Today, chat is used for more than just fun. Universities use chat to facilitate distance learning, and as an aid to video-conferencing programs. Performance groups use chat programs as part of the dramatic structure of their work. Software developers and political-action groups use IRC chat channels to quickly inform their members of impending changes to their programs. There are even a number of chat experiments that have met with varying degrees of success, such as "inhabited television," an effort to match chatting with group television viewing, all on one screen.

Perhaps the most unexpected growth of interest in chat to date has come from the American business sector. In spite of research indicating that e-chats promote spontaneity and inclusion of voices that might otherwise be silenced in face-to-face meetings, American executives had long resisted chat as frivolous and therefore unimportant to management. This all changed with the introduction of the instant message–based "buddy list." Although the ability to find people online dates back to the Finger program on UNIX, the sheer volume of instant-message users (61 million for AOL's service alone) has made the buddy list an instantly desirable surveillance tool for American business mangers. As Joseph Carusone of StockHouse Media explained to reporter Clive Thompson, "I log on and can immediately see who on my team is available to talk. You can't do that with a phone or email."

This virtual ability to see who's around has been termed "presence management," and it is one of the main reasons that almost all North American corporations today use instant-messaging software, either of their own devising (usually for security reasons) or from vendors like Microsoft or AOL. In fact, many of today's software designers are now beginning to speak about refining presence management to deal not only with who is around, but also with who is unavailable and shouldn't be bothered. Microsoft researcher Mary Czerwinski recently completed a study that proved what most people in offices already know: Sending an instant message while a participant is typing, using buttons or menus, or evaluating search results is harmful to overall task performance.

In Search of Translucence

One answer to increased presence management and decreased interruptions might be an overhaul of chat interfaces themselves. In their essay "Social Translucence," designers Thomas Erickson and Wendy A. Kellogg note that chat as it currently exists has a host of problems, including "managing threads;

bringing other people into the middle of a conversation; keeping a conversation on track; knowing who (or whether) anyone is listening; getting people to respond in a timely manner; finding old messages with crucial information in them; etc." Researchers Murphy and Mauri Collins add that, in the case of distance learning in U.S. classrooms, chat participants must have substantial typing skills to communicate effectively, which sometimes means that conversation may move too quickly for poor typists and non-native speakers of English who have no time to reflect, frame questions, and compose responses.

Ironically, Erickson and Kellogg point out, many problems in computer-mediated chat are often handled with unconscious ease in their face-to-face analogues. "Whether it is wrapping up a talk when the audience starts fidgeting, or deciding to forego the grocery shopping because the parking lot is jammed, social information . . . provides the basis for inferences, planning, and coordination of activity." Taking their cue from the offline world, Erickson and Kellogg argue for chat systems of the future to require "visibility, awareness, and accountability among members." The phrase they use to summarize these goals is "social translucence."

Erickson and Kellogg note that to date, a number of approaches to social translucence in chat have been attempted, with varying degrees of success. The mimetic approach uses representative images to represent social cues from the physical world. The use of emoticons might be said to be one of the oldest mimetic chat approaches, whereby :) is meant to be construed as "I am smiling while I say this." The use of avatars in graphic chat spaces like The Palace also represents a mimetic approach, as does BodyChat, a system developed at MIT that allows users to communicate via text while their avatars automatically animate "attention, salutations, turn taking, back-channel feedback and facial expression, as well as simple body functions such as the blinking of the eyes."

In contrast, Erickson and Kellogg note, the abstract approach to chat uses non-representative graphics and text to communicate relationships to users within an environment. Abstract methods are particularly useful for indicating when a user is trying to get out of a conversation or shouldn't be disturbed. For example, the Babble program portrays chat conversations as large circles, with the participants as colored dots called marbles. Marbles within the circle are involved in the current conversation; marbles outside the circle represent those who are logged on but are in other conversations.

The marbles of those who are active in the current conversation are shown near the circle's center; with inactivity, marbles drift out to the periphery. "Although simple," Erickson and Kellogg point out, "this social proxy gives a sense of the size of the audience, the amount of conversational activity, as well as indicating whether people are gathering or dispersing, and who it is that is coming and going." Another successful abstract experiment has been the Lead Line software, which helps participants in chat sessions by providing them with a "script" of things they are expected to know, or activities they are expected to have undertaken, during a chat session.

To See or Not to See?

Finally, there is the realist approach to chat, which attempts to project users' intentions straight from the physical realm into the digital one. Internet-oriented voice and video technologies, which permit speech rather than keystrokes, and visual images rather than avatars, are examples of realist interventions into chat. To some, realist chat will be the preferred method of communication in the future—provided, of course, that all the participants have the bandwidth necessary to orchestrate such a thing. Realist chat is available right now on services like NetMeeting and ICUII, and Internet portal Yahoo recently announced that it will allow users to swap music and video files on the newest iterations of its instant-messaging service.

Regardless of the push for video and audio, however, text-only chat will always be the preferred experience for some. As psychologist John Suler notes, some people "see beauty in the clean, simple, quiet flow of scrolling words. Sights and sounds are but extraneous noise that clogs the pure expression of mind and soul. To these people, TextTalk is an art that must not die." Perhaps the most telling evidence that text is here to stay is the recent explosion of mobile text messaging in Europe and Asia. In Great Britain, wireless messaging shot from 500,000 messages a month in August 1999 to eight billion in August 2000; and in Japan, NTT DoCoMo recently struck a deal to distribute AOL Messenger services on its hugely successful i-mode mobile service, which already has 17 million teenage members.

Bibliography

Benford, Steve, Chris Greenhalgh, et. al. "Inhabited Television: Broadcasting Interaction from within Collaborative Virtual Environments." *ACM Transactions on Computer-Human Interaction (TOCHI), Special issue on human-computer interaction in the new millennium, Part 1, 7, no. 1 (2000), pp. 510–47.

Czerwinski, Mary; Cutrell, Edward; and Eric Horvitz. "Instant Messaging and Interruption: Influence of Task Type on Performance." Microsoft Research, 2000. <http://research.microsoft.com/users/marycz/ozchi2000.pdf> (April 26, 2002).

Danet , Brenda; Ruedenberg , Lucia; and Yehudit Rosenbaum-Tamari. "Hmmm . . . Where's That Smoke Coming From?" *Network and Netplay.* Cambridge, Mass.: MIT Press, 1998.

Erickson, Thomas, and Wendy A. Kellogg. "Social Translucence: An Approach to Designing Systems That Support Social Processes." *ACM Transactions on Computer-Human Interaction (TOCHI), Special issue on human-computer interaction in the new millennium, Part 1, 7, no. 1 (2000), pp. 59–83.

Herring, Susan. "Interactional Coherence in CMC." *Journal of Computer-Mediated Communication* 4:4 (June 1999). Reprinted with permission from the CD ROM-based "Proceedings of the Thirty-Second Annual Hawaii International Conference on Systems Sciences" (January 5–8, 1999, Maui, Hawaii), Institute of Electrical and Electronics Engineers, 1999. <http://www.ascusc.org/jcmc/vol4/issue4/herring.html> (April 26, 2002).

Kell, Jeff. "Relay: Past, Present, and Future." Paper presented at the NETCON, New Orleans, Louisiana, 1987. NetHistory: An Informal History of BITNET and the Internet. <http://nethistory.dumbentia.com/relayhist.html> (April 26, 2002).

Lebo, Harlan. "The UCLA Internet Report 2001: Surveying the Digital Future." UCLA Center for Communication Policy, 2001. <http://ccp.ucla.edu/pages/internet-report.asp> (April 26, 2002).

Murphy, Karen L, and Mauri P. Collins. "Communication Conventions in Instructional Electronic Chats." *First Monday,* February 11, 1997. <http://www.firstmonday.org/issues/issue2_11/murphy/index.html> (April 26, 2002).

Pew Internet & American Life Project. "Teenage Life Online: The Rise of the Instant-Message Generation and the Internet's Impact on Friendships and Family Relationships." June 20, 2001. <http://www.pewinternet.org/reports/> (April 26, 2002).

Rickard, Wendy, and Coby Green-Rifkin. "Instant Messaging Is a Hit among U.S. Teens." *ISOC Forum* 7, no. 7 (2001).

Smith , Marc; Cadiz , J. J.; and Byron Burkhalter. "Conversation Trees and Threaded Chats." Paper presented at the Proceedings of the ACM 2000 Conference on Computer-Supported Cooperative Work, Philadelphia.

Suler, John. "Psychological Dynamics of Online Synchronous Conversations in Text-Driven Chat Environments." *The Psychology of Cyberspace.*

Lawrenceville, N.J.: Rider University, October 1997. <http://www.rider.edu/users/suler/psycyber/texttalk.html> (April 26, 2002).

Vilhjálmsson, Hannes Högni, and Justine Cassell. "BodyChat: Autonomous Communicative Behaviors in Avatars." MIT Media Laboratory, Gesture and Narrative Language Group. Paper presented at the Proceedings of the Second Annual ACM International Conference on Autonomous Agents, Minneapolis, Minnesota, 1998. <http://gn.www.media.mit.edu/groups/gn/publications/agents98.pdf> (April 26, 2002).

Further Reading

Barnett, James, and Daniel Gray. *Official Palace Tour Guide: Experience Visual Virtual-World Chat on the Internet.* Research Triangle Park, N.C.: Ventana Communications Group Inc., 1997.

Cherny, Lynn. *Conversation and Community: Chat in a Virtual World.* Stanford, Calif.: CSLI Publications, 1999.

Herring, Susan C, ed. *Computer-Mediated Communication: Linguistic, Social and Cross-Cultural Perspectives, Pragmatics & Beyond, New Series, 39.* Amsterdam/Philadelphia: J. Benjamins, 1996.

Meakins, Felicity, and E. Sean Rintel. "Editorial: Chat." *M/C: A Journal of Media and Culture* 3, no. 4 (2000).

Related Topics

Avatar; Bulletin Board Systems; Emoticons; Instant Messaging; Internet Relay Chat; MUDs and MOOs; PLATO; Telephony; Videoconferencing

— *Theresa M. Senft*

Child Online Protection Act and Child Online Privacy Protection Act

The Child Online Protection Act (COPA) is the U.S. Congress' highly controversial 1998 attempt to replace the ill-fated Communications Decency Act (CDA), which was deemed unconstitutional by the U.S. Supreme Court in 1997. The Child Online Privacy Protection Act (COPPA) is a related if somewhat less contested law, aimed at protecting the privacy of minors by preventing commercial Web sites from eliciting information that children might not realize is sensitive, including their street addresses, their phone numbers, and their parents' credit card numbers.

COPA

U.S. Senator Dan Coats (Rep.-Indiana), who had been an original sponsor of the Communications Decency Act (CDA), introduced the Child Online Protection

Act as an amendment to the Communications Act of 1934; the Senate approved COPA on July 22, 1998. According to a *Newsbytes* report that day, Coats called the COPA an attempt to "find a constitutional way to. . . help families protect young minds, hearts and eyes from the rawest, most degrading forms of pornography." The legislation attempted to hold smut peddlers to stringent standards of conduct, albeit while using at least nominally different standards than those of the CDA. The House of Representatives later approved it as well, moving the bill on to the president for his signature. Against the advice of the U.S. Department of Justice, President Bill Clinton signed the measure into law on October 22, 1998, as part of the 1999 federal budget bill.

While critics have condemned the COPA statute as CDA II for its similarities to the previous law, COPA was intended to be a more carefully crafted measure that would apply a standard of "harmful to minors" that has at times held up under judicial scrutiny. The law contains somewhat more narrow language than the CDA, allowing Web sites to distribute pornography, but requiring them to verify that recipients are adults by requiring credit-card numbers, adult access codes, and adult PIN numbers, or by using other technologies not yet developed. In her dissent to the 7-2 decision in the CDA case, Justice Sandra Day O'Connor intimated that such an approach might pass constitutional muster; O'Connor wrote that she felt that only part of the CDA was unconstitutional—the part that seemed to interfere with adults' rights to access "indecent" material. However, she said that the Constitution could protect efforts to create "adult zones" into which children may not stray, but only to the extent that these efforts don't interfere with the adults' First Amendment rights. "Insofar as the . . . provisions prohibit the use of indecent speech in communications between an adult and one or more minors, however, they can and should be sustained," O'Connor wrote.

The COPA law attacks sexually explicit online communication that lacks "serious literary, artistic, political or scientific value." It stipulates that anyone knowingly distributing material "harmful to minors" faces a fine of $50,000, imprisonment for six months, or both. Violators also face additional civil penalties of $50,000 in fines. Each day that someone breaks the law is considered the equivalent of a new and separate offense, the law states.

That same day that President Clinton signed the bill, the American Civil Liberties Union (ACLU) and other groups filed a complaint in preparation for suing the government to challenge COPA's legality. Their concerns were nearly identical to the arguments that had been used against the CDA. Critics charged that COPA too was dangerously vague, and that its prohibitions would apply to sites not peddling pornography. Legal content on topics like safe sex, gynecology, homosexuality, and other issues also could be targeted under the COPA law, they argued.

Again, the courts sided with the opponents. Washington, D.C., federal district court judge Lowell A. Reed Jr. placed a restraining order against the law in November 1998, granting a preliminary injunction against it the following February. Reed wrote in his opinion that opponents had established that there was "a substantial likelihood" that COPA would impose a burden on protected adult speech.

The issue moved on to the federal appeals court, and on August 22, 2000, the appellate court struck down the law. While calling Congress' effort to craft the COPA "laudatory," the court overruled it, saying that current technologies were not sufficient to protect children from harmful material while also protecting adult free speech online. On February 26, 2001, shortly after the new administration of President George W. Bush took power, the U.S. Justice Department filed a petition appealing the appeals court's decision to the U.S. Supreme Court, asking the nation's highest court to overrule the district court's findings and allow the government to enforce the COPA. The Supreme Court agreed to hear the appeal during its October 2001 session, and issued its ruling on May 13, 2002. Instead of deciding any of the legal questions itself, the Court left the injunction in place, barring enforcement of the law, but ordered a lower court to decide the First Amendment issues.

One part of the COPA law that was allowed to remain in force was the creation of a COPA Commission to study the ways that technology could help achieve the legislation's aims. The commission issued a final report in late 2000. It mostly advocated increased support for parental education and the enforcement of existing obscenity laws.

COPPA

Also passed in 1998, the Child Online Privacy Protection Act has not generated the public outcry or the legal challenges that the COPA and the CDA drew, because it does not traverse First Amendment terrain. Its target, instead, is children's privacy, a subject that most Americans feel needs more attention. In early 2001, the Pew Internet and American Life Project found that 62 percent of Americans favor new laws to protect online privacy.

The COPPA stipulates that commercial Web sites and online services that market to children cannot collect, use, or disclose personally identifiable information from children under age 13 without a parent's permission. It also requires that sites post prominent links to notices about how they intend to use what information they do collect, that they refrain from conditioning kids' participation in their sites on providing personal information, and that they allow parents to review and disallow any information collected from children.

While not as controversial as the anti-pornography measures of the COPA and the CDA, the COPPA legislation has encountered some opposition, most of it from Web businesses complaining that it makes it difficult for them to operate. The ZDNet online news service illustrated the problem by describing the plight of Zeeks.com, a children's site. In a September 13, 2000, article, ZDNet reported that Zeeks would have to either shut down entirely or scrub nearly all of its interactive elements in order to remain in compliance with the COPPA. The $200,000 annual cost for employing a dozen employees to monitor chat rooms proved too high, site administrators were quoted as saying, as did the costs of email monitoring software. Another company, Email.com, a service of NBC Internet, was forced to stop email services to kids under age 13 in order to comply with the law, according to *Interactive Week*. There were numerous other examples cited in other reports during that period.

However, despite complaints from merchants and children's sites saying that the law was too strict, others were simultaneously saying that not enough was being done to enforce the COPPA. A report by the non-profit Center for Media Education surveyed Web sites and found that after one year on the books, the COPPA was falling short of its objectives, despite bringing some positive changes into play. The report surveyed 153 commercial Web sites directed at children under age 13 to determine their COPPA compliance. While more sites were beginning to post privacy policies, the majority of those studied did not display these policies in a "prominent" manner, the study said, and most sites that were operating on the condition that they must seek parental consent before collecting children's personal data had not yet begun seeking that consent first.

In April 2002, on the second anniversary of the COPPA, the Federal Trade Commission issued a series of new initiatives to help with the law's enforcement.

These included the release of a compliance survey, a business-education initiative to help children's Web sites comply, and the mailing of warning letters to Web sites alerting them to the COPPA's requirements.

Bibliography

MacMillan, Robert. "Judge Halts Child Protection Act—Update." *Newsbytes.com*, February 1, 1999.

———. "U.S. Supreme Court Will Hear COPA Case." *Newsbytes.com*, May 21, 2001.

Pietrucha, Bill. "Senate Approves Internet Filters, Son of CDA." *Newsbytes.com*, July 22, 1998.

Rothenberg, Matthew. "COPPA Kicks up Controversy." *ZDNet News,* April 24, 2000. <http://www.zdnet.com/zdnn/stories/news/0,4586,2554856,00.html> (May 17, 2002).

Further Reading

COPA Commission. "COPA Commission Executive Summary." October 20, 2000. <http://www.copacommission.org/report/executivesummary.shtml> (May 17, 2002).

Dyson, Esther. *Release 2.0: A Design for Living in the Digital Age.* New York: Broadway Books, 1997.

Lessig, Lawrence. *Code and Other Laws of Cyberspace.* New York: Basic Books, 1999.

Tapscott, Don. *Growing Up Digital.* New York: McGraw-Hill, 1998.

Wallace, Jonathan D., and Mark Mangan. *Sex, Laws, and Cyberspace.* New York: M&T Books, 1996.

Related Topics

Anonymity; Communications Decency Act; Content Filtering; Electronic Communications Privacy Act; Electronic Frontier Foundation; Internet Service Providers; Lessig, Lawrence

— *Kevin Featherly*

Codec

A codec—the term is a shortened combination of the words "compression" and "decompression"—is a standard used for compressing and decompressing digital media, especially audio and video, which have traditionally consumed significant bandwidth. Codecs are used to store files on disk, as well as to transmit media (either as discrete files or as a stream) over computer networks. By rapidly compressing and decompressing this data, the required bandwidth is reduced, resulting in an increase of interactive and multimedia content being accessed and transmitted over networks. Codecs remain of central importance to the success of multimedia applications on the Internet, ranging from Webcasting to teleconferencing.

With the rise and fall of the music-trading site Napster, the term MP3 entered the common parlance, and it is probably still the widest recognized codec. By eliminating sounds not normally heard by the human ear, MP3 (an abbreviation of MPEG-1 Audio Level-3) reduces music files to less than one-tenth of the space that they would normally consume on an audio CD. It allows music to be quickly sent over the Internet for the first time—and it also helped bring questions of copyright on the Internet to a head.

Just as some audio codecs are better at encoding human speech while others are better at encoding instrumental music, different types of video are sometimes better encoded in different formats. The processing power required to compress and decompress data and the flexibility of the compression level also contribute to the effectiveness of a codec. For example, several of the codecs produced by RealNetworks have been lauded for using faster processors to their fullest to increase image quality, while allowing those with slower processors to view a video stream at a diminished quality. An alternative codec, Sorenson Video, which is available as part of the QuickTime architecture, is considered by many to deliver particularly crisp video graphics. Microsoft's AVI (Audio/Video Interleave), Apple's QuickTime, and RealNetworks' G2 are all architectures for delivering encoded video files, and all can carry media that were generated using a variety of codecs.

One video codec in particular, DivX, has attracted a considerable amount of attention, in large part because the efficiency of its compression algorithm threatens to once again allow for the easy exchange of copyrighted goods. For the first time, a full-length motion picture of a quality comparable to broadcast television can be downloaded over a period of several hours using a broadband connection to the Internet. An implementation of the MPEG-4 standard, it allows digital content that is stored on DVDs to be reduced to a size that will fit on a standard data CD. This level of compression is a boon to those who wish to distribute full-motion video over computer networks, and the codec will eventually make high-resolution video available on palmtop computers, televisions, and a variety of other devices.

Both DivX and MP3 are based on standards developed by the Motion Picture Experts Group (MPEG), which has worked since 1988 under the auspices of ISO, an international standards organization, to generate global standards for audio and video codecs. The most recent standard under discussion, MPEG-7, uses a sophisticated combination of algorithms to encode multimedia content of various types. Some have complained that although the standards are open, many of the technologies to implement them are patented, and implementations require a licensing fee to be paid to the owners of these patents. As a result, there are a large number of alternative codecs, both proprietary and open-source. In the former category are dozens of video, audio, and other codecs, including special-use and legacy codecs that are utilized by digital cameras, non-linear video editors, video teleconferencing, and virtual-reality systems, as well as in music production. Free, open-source alternatives have also emerged, including a codec called Ogg Vorbis, which is designed to provide a free equivalent of the MP3 standard.

Codecs have improved significantly over the last decade. Generally, the most efficient codecs also require significant processing power. Distributing multimedia always necessitates a balance of processing power and bandwidth. Given that processing power has continued to grow exponentially while bandwidth bottlenecks remain in many places, the development of more effective codecs has been central to the growth of multimedia on the Internet.

The complexity of these compression schemes continues to increase, moving from simpler signal-processing algorithms to those that decompose an image logically into parts, predict different types of movement, animate virtual faces, and rely on other cutting-edge strategies for achieving the quickest and most significant compression. The new challenge, only beginning to be incorporated as part of the codec itself, will be to encode data about the use of the media being encoded, including indexing data for search engines and libraries as well as controls related to legal copying and distribution.

Bibliography

Conexant Systems. "The (Almost Definitive) FOURCC Definition List."
  <http://www.webartz.com/fourcc/> (May 24, 2002).
Moving Pictures Expert Group. The MPEGHome page.
  <http://mpeg.telecomitalialab.com/> (May 24, 2002).
Fraunhofer Institut Integrierte Schaltungen.
  "MPEG Audio Level-3."
  <http://www.iis.fhg.de/amm/techinf/layer3/>
  (May 24, 2002).
The Xiphophorus Company: Ogg. "The Ogg Vorbis CODEC Project." December 31, 2001.
  <http://www.xiph.org/ogg/vorbis/> (May 24, 2002).
Waggoner, Ben. "A DV WebVideo Guide to Codecs."
  <http://www.dvwebvideo.com/2000/0900/
  waggoner0900.html> (May 24, 2002).

Further Reading

Chang, Shih-fu, T. Sikora, and A. Purl. "Overview of the MPEG-7 Standard." *IEEE Transactions on Circuits and Systems for Video Technology* 11, 6 (June 2001), pp. 688–95.

Related Topics

Broadband; Compression; Digital Audio; Digital Millennium Copyright Act; Digital Music; Interactive Television; MP3; MP3.com; MPEG; Napster; Streaming Media; Videoconferencing

— *Alexander Halavais*

Communications Decency Act

The Communications Decency Act (CDA) is a controversial bill passed by the U.S. Congress and signed into law by President Bill Clinton in 1996. It was an attempt by the federal government to address public concerns about pornographic material on the Internet. The U.S. Supreme Court overturned the law on June 27, 1997, in arguably the first landmark ruling in the history of the Internet.

Senator James Exon, a Nebraska Democrat who had been a two-term governor of Nebraska before his election to the U.S. Senate in 1978, introduced the bill. It was initially brought forward as part of the larger Telecommunications Reform Act of 1994, but Congress adjourned that year before putting it to a vote.

During the next Senate session, alarmed by the apparent anti-free-speech provisions of Exon's amendment, Senator Patrick Leahy, a Vermont Democrat, issued his own amendment to the Telecommunications Reform Act, proposing that Exon's 1994 CDA provisions be tabled to give the U.S Justice Department 150 days to study the best ways to regulate pornographic material on the Internet. Exon reacted by issuing another amendment, this one striking all of Leahy's proposals and reinserting his 1994 CDA provisions. The debate in the Senate from that point focused on which of the amendments the Senate should pass. Eventually, they chose Exon's.

In Senate debate, Leahy questioned the constitutionality of the Exon bill. "I do not think under this amendment a computer user would be able to send a public or private e-mail with the so-called 'seven dirty words,'" he argued. "Who knows when a recipient would feel annoyed by seeing a four-letter word online?"

Exon responded by arguing that the United States did not have 150 days to wait for a government study while America's children became further defiled by online pornography, nearly half of which, Exon claimed, depicted the sexual torture of women. "If nothing is done now, the pornographers might be the primary beneficiary of the information revolution," he said.

Exon's fellow senators agreed, and the CDA passed 84–16 on June 14, 1995. The U.S. House version, known as the Cox-Wyden bill, passed on August 14, 1995, without debate on the CDA issues. However, CDA provisions were resuscitated in the "Hyde amendment," a late change endorsed by Senator Henry Hyde (Rep.) of Illinois. A version of the bill containing Hyde's amendments passed into law, signed by President Clinton on February 8, 1996.

In the 1997 book *Sex, Laws and Cyberspace*, authors Jonathan Wallace and Mark Mangan argue that the CDA, while "innocuous or even incomprehensible" on first blush, was actually "a radical attack" on free speech. First of all, the authors write, the U.S. Supreme Court had already ruled on the applicable issues in a 1957 case, which declared that First Amendment protections forbade a state from restricting adult free speech to a level acceptable to children. Further, the authors maintain, the CDA sought to restore long-discredited "indecency standards." They point to a 1971 case involving a protester convicted of wearing a jacket with a profanity scrawled on it. Justices overturned his conviction, saying that the government "has no right to cleanse public debate to the point where it is grammatically palatable to most squeamish among us."

The decency standard, however, has been applied to broadcast media. The Court upheld sanctions against a radio station that violated FCC rules by broadcasting a George Carlin comedy routine about "the seven dirty words you can't say on the air." The jokes were aired during a mid-afternoon show, at a time when children were likely to be listening. The same standard also was applied to 1-900 sex-chat phone lines, in a law that requires operators to take steps to ensure that minors are not exposed. This law was one of the justifications Exon used in introducing the CDA.

Had the CDA been enforced, violations would have carried a maximum possible penalty of two years in prison or $100,000 in fines. While aimed at pornography, the law also applied to speech. It explicitly forbade knowingly transmitting to minors "any comment, request, suggestion, proposal, image or other communication" that is "obscene or indecent." Further, the CDA made it illegal to use a computer to knowingly make available to children "any

comment, request, suggestion, proposal, image, or other communication" that, "in terms patently offensive," describes or depicts "sexual or excretory activities or organs."

Opponents of the legislation, including the American Civil Liberties Union, the American Library Association, America Online, and the Critical Path AIDS Project, criticized the law as an unconstitutional attempt to regulate free speech online, and the courts agreed. On June 12, 1996, a three-judge federal panel in Philadelphia issued an injunction blocking enforcement of the law. They argued that, "As the most participatory form of mass speech yet developed, the Internet deserves the highest protection from government intrusion." The Internet's strength is chaos, the judges wrote, just as the strength of liberty depends on the "chaos and cacophony of the unfettered speech the First Amendment protects."

At the command of Attorney General Janet Reno, the U.S Justice Department appealed the ruling to the U.S. Supreme Court, which heard oral arguments in *Reno v. ACLU* on March 19, 1997. Three months later, in a landmark 7-2 decision, the Supreme Court affirmed the Philadelphia panel's ruling, declaring that the CDA violated free speech rights under the First Amendment of the U.S. Constitution.

In his majority opinion, Justice John Paul Stevens attacked the law for reaching too far in trying to protect minors. "The level of discourse reaching a mailbox simply cannot be limited to that which would be suitable for a sandbox," Stevens wrote. He also complained that the statute was too vague; in the first of its two parts, it attempts to limit access to "indecent" speech, and in the second part aims at communications that are "patently offensive," without defining either term. Lastly, he objected to the fact that, in the statute, there seemed to be no way to tag and identify "indecent" material without creating extreme burdens on online speech, which would almost certainly dam the free flow of speech and thought on the Internet.

Influential Stanford University law professor and author Lawrence Lessig denounced the CDA in his 1999 book *Code and Other Laws of Cyberspace*. "A law of extraordinary stupidity," Lessig wrote, "it practically impaled itself on the First Amendment."

Not satisfied with this defeat, Congress crafted and passed a similar law in 1998, the Child Online Protection Act (COPA), which opponents call CDA II because of its CDA-like provisions. COPA abandons the concept of indecency, and instead seeks to control online material that is "harmful to minors." The courts thus far have not been impressed. A federal judge issued an injunction barring enforcement of that law in early 1999, and in June 2000 the Third Circuit Court of Appeals struck down the law as unconstitutional. In its October 2001 session, the U.S. Supreme Court heard a Justice Department appeal of the COPA case, ruling in May 2002 to maintain an injunction barring enforcement of the act but to have a lower court decide the first amendment issues.

Bibliography

Congressional Record. Remarks of Senator James Exon. June 9, 1995, <http://www.epic.org/cda/exon_remarks.html> (April 5, 2002).

Featherly, Kevin. "Judges Back Free Speech Online." *Channel 4000*, June 12, 1996. <http://www.channel4000.com/news/stories/news-960612-115755.html> (April 5, 2002).

Lessig, Lawrence. *Code and Other Laws of Cyberspace.* New York: Basic Books, 1999.

U.S. Supreme Court. "Reno v. ACLU Decision." June 26, 1997. <http://www2.epic.org/cda/cda_decision.html> (April 5, 2002).

Wallace, Jonathan, and Mark Mangan. *Sex, Laws and Cyberspace.* New York: Henry Holt and Co., 1997.

Further Reading

Broder, John M. "Clinton Readies New Approach on Smut." *New York Times,* June 27, 1997.

Dyson, Esther. *Release 2.0: A Design for Living in the Digital Age.* New York: Broadway Books, 1997.

Lanier, Jaron. "Unmuzzling the Internet." *The New York Times,* January 2, 1996, p. A15.

Leahy, Sen. Patrick. "A Bill to Amend the Communications Act of 1934 to Repeal the Amendments Relating to Obscene and Harassing Use of Telecommunications Facilities Made by the Communications Decency Act of 1995." Republished at <http://www.epic.org/CDA/repeal.html> (April 5, 2002).

Tapscott, Don. *Growing Up Digital.* New York: McGraw-Hill, 1998.

U.S. Supreme Court. "Reno v. ACLU - Transcript of Supreme Court Oral Argument." March 19, 1997. <http://www.aclu.org/issues/cyber/trial/sctran.html> (April 5, 2002).

Related Topics

Child Online Protection Act and Child Online Privacy Protection Act; Content Filtering; Electronic Communications Privacy Act; Electronic Frontier Foundation; Internet Service Providers; Lessig, Lawrence; Obscenity

— *Kevin Featherly*

CommuniTree

CommuniTree was a San Francisco–based electronic bulletin-board service (BBS) begun in 1978 as a social experiment in free speech and community building. Closed as a result of vandalism by young users in 1982, CommuniTree's destruction is one of the earliest documented examples of deviant user behavior in an online environment.

Before CommuniTree, BBSs were constructed as computerized metaphors for physical bulletin boards: They were places to post information, arranged alphabetically or by date. But as virtual-community expert Howard Rheingold observes, "CommuniTree, starting with its name, was specifically focused on the notion of using BBSs to build community, at a time when most other BBSers were still more interested in the technology itself." In 1978, programmer Jon James designed CommuniTree's software to resemble a tree structure, with each line of conversation functioning as a branch, flourishing or dying based on user interest.

CommuniTree was emblematic of the spirit of "virtual hippiedom" that pervaded the online world of the 1970s and 1980s. As Rheingold recalls it, CommuniTree was a space of freewheeling conversations, held with no censorship or moderation whatsoever. But CommuniTree's "gods" couldn't know that the introduction of the Apple computer to American schools would change the social climate of virtual communities forever. In 1982, students (mostly boys) began getting connected to BBSs using school-contributed computers and modems. They quickly discovered the Tree's telephone number, logged on, and began participating.

CHOPPING DOWN THE TREE

As Internet researcher Allucquère Rosanne (Sandy) Stone reports, the young boys who happened upon CommuniTree "appeared uninspired by the relatively intellectual and spiritual air of the ongoing debates, and they proceeded to express their dissatisfaction in ways appropriate to their age, sex and language abilities." Within a short time, the Tree was covered with obscene and scatological messages. In her analysis of one of the first documented cases of deviant behavior in an online setting, Stone defends the young experimenters, and points out that not all of them necessarily wanted to wreck the conferences on CommuniTree. Rather, she observes, "entering control codes into the Apple's operating system from a remote location was an exploratory operation similar to swinging a crowbar in a darkened pottery factory."

Unfortunately, CommuniTree—which had been designed expressly to allow its users freedom from censorship of any kind—couldn't withstand the onslaught of young users. The BBS had no means of deleting unwelcome messages, and no way to monitor messages as they arrived into the system. After a few months, CommuniTree's hard disk crashed, and the BBS closed permanently. The death of CommuniTree, argues Stone, imparted hard lessons for virtual hippies "about what was and what was not possible in a unstructured and unprotected conference environment." In new observations in the 2000 edition of his 1994 book *Virtual Community*, Howard Rheingold concurs, arguing that "attention-seeking through aggression" has probably destroyed more virtual communities than any other single factor.

New Forms of Self-Protection

Since the fall of CommuniTree, online community architects have included more stringent measures of surveillance and social control in their environments. Some are software-based, such as the controls designed to filter spammers. Others depended on human vigilance, such as the security measures taken to discourage hackers and "script kiddies" in chat forums. Still others, like the numerical post-ranking system used by members the of Web message board Slashdot.org, began as a result of community self-restraint in the face of unrelenting trolls (pointlessly hostile posters). In addition, some cyberspace forums now require users to authenticate their identities online, either by demanding that they use their real names, by telephone verification systems, or (in the most sophisticated forums) via key encryption methods. Forums requiring authentication cite the popular research sentiment that anonymity is the single biggest cause of deviant behavior online.

In spite of (some might say because of) efforts to control aggression among users in cyberspace, the hard lessons begun with the demise of CommuniTree continue. Each time one generation succeeds in developing a system to control its online environment, the next generation works to destabilize those controls, if only to assert its own identity and individuality. "The dilemma is that younger Net users are among the smartest, most technologically-sophisticated people online," researcher Jonathan Katz recently pointed out on Slashdot.org. "If they bring hostility, they also bring creativity and energy. Losing them would be an enormous loss."

Bibliography

Katz, Jonathan. "Rethinking the Virtual Community: Part One." Slashdot.org, December 21–28, 2000. <http://slashdot.org/features/00/12/15/166257.shtml> (April 26, 2002).

Moschovitis, Christos J. P.; Poole, Hilary; Schuyler, Tami; and Theresa M. Senft. "Virtual Hippies: There Goes the Neighborhood." *History of the Internet: A Chronology, 1843 to the Present.* New York: ABC-CLIO, 1999; p.113.

Rheingold, Howard. *The Virtual Community: Homesteading on the Electronic Frontier.* Revised edition. Cambridge, Mass.: MIT Press, 2000.

Stone, Allucquère Rosanne. *The War of Desire and Technology at the Close of the Mechanical Age.* Cambridge, Mass.: MIT Press, 1995.

———. "Will the Real Body Please Stand Up?" *Cyberspace: First Steps.* Michael Benedikt, ed. Cambridge, Mass.: MIT Press, 1991; pp. 81–118. <http://www.rochester.edu/College/FS/Publications/StoneBody.html> (April 26, 2002).

Further Reading

Freeform. "Deviant Behavior." *A Case Study in User Centered Design of a High Traffic World Wide Web Virtual Community.* Master's thesis. University of Illinois at Chicago, 1996. <http://freeform.org/thesis/deviant.html> (April 26, 2002).

Johnson, Deborah. *Computer Ethics.* Upper Saddle River, N.J.: Prentice Hall, 2001.

Reid, Elizabeth, and Beth Kolko. "Dissolution and Fragmentation: Problems in On-Line Communities." *Cybersociety 2.0.* Steven G. Jones, ed. Thousand Oaks, Calif.: Sage, 1998.

Slevin, James. *The Internet and Society.* Oxford: Polity Press, 2000.

Stone, Allucquère Rosanne. "What Vampires Know: Transsubjection and Transgender in Cyberspace." Transcript of a talk given by Stone at "In Control: Mensch-Interface-Maschine," at the Kunstlerhaus, Graz, Austria, May 1993. <http://eserver.org/gender/what-vampires-know.txt> (April 26, 2002).

Related Topics

Bulletin Board Systems; Rheingold, Howard; Stone, Allucquère Rosanne; Virtual Community

— *Theresa M. Senft*

Community Networking

Community networking is the use of computer networks to share information and deepen connections among residents of a local community.

Beginning in the mid-1970s, some people believed that emerging computer networks could be used to serve local community needs. Since that time, the use of computer networks as a community communication medium has taken many forms, and been called by many names: community networks, local bulletin boards, civic networking, telecottages, community information systems, community computing, community telecomputing, Freenets, and more. Whatever form or name community networking takes, it emphasizes several goals: increasing involvement in the life of the community; advancing local issues; providing a space for local news, announcements, and information; empowering residents politically and economically; and (in most cases) connecting members of the community to the Internet at no cost or for a minimal fee.

Community networking is often a joint project between groups concerned with universal access to information, such as public libraries, universities, public access television stations, and local governments, as well as private individuals. While these partnerships sometimes include for-profit businesses such as cable and telephone companies, community networks themselves are typically non-profit organizations.

The first community network, called the Community Memory of Berkeley, California, was created in 1974. It could be accessed only from public terminals in the libraries and laundromats of Berkeley. Terminals were coin operated, charging $0.25 to post a message or $1.00 to start a new discussion group (just reading a message had no charge). The only information on the community network was input by people physically in Berkeley.

As advances in computer and communication technologies began to make larger and larger networks possible, community networking spread. Bulletin board systems (BBSs), which allowed access to a computer over standard telephone lines, first appeared in 1978. Anyone with a computer and a modem could access any community network, but the cost of long-distance phone calls kept many people from calling BBSs outside of their area. The first community BBS was Old Colorado City, which began in 1980. Most of the early community networks started out as telenetworking projects, including St. Silicon's Hospital of Cleveland in 1984 (the precursor to the Cleveland Free-Net), Big Sky Telegraph of Montana in 1988, and the Public Electronic Network (PEN) of Santa Monica in 1989. Still others, like the University of Illinois' PLATO, evolved unexpectedly, while the Whole Earth

'Lectronic Link (WELL), founded by Larry Brilliant and Stewart Brand in 1985, had a far greater impact than anticipated.

In the mid-1990s, with the rapid growth and expansion of the Internet, most community networks moved their information to the World Wide Web. This meant that their services could be accessed easily through graphical browsers, rather than relying on text-only menu systems such as Gopher. At the same time, however, a paradox emerged. Community networks provide low-cost or free access to the Internet so community members can access local information and get involved in local issues. But by moving to the Internet, the community networks made it even easier for residents to look beyond their local communities. They could access information from around the globe, engage in correspondence with people on different continents, or get involved in issues that matter to them personally but are of little or no relevance to their neighbors. Nonetheless, the backers and visionaries driving community networking still insisted that the Internet could help rebuild local communities.

One of the largest backers of the community networking movement was the National Public Telecomputing Network (NPTN). The NPTN was a non-profit group dedicated to developing community networks. By joining the NPTN, community networks received a range of services, including kits to help them select hardware and software; connection to email listservs and access to NPTN staff for technical, legal, and organizational questions; and information on fundraising. However, the NPTN filed for Chapter 7 bankruptcy in 1996. While some organizers worried that this might be the end for community networks, others saw that public interest in (and financial support for) community networks was growing.

One area of increasing support for community networking was in the federal government. The U.S. Commerce Department's National Telecommunications and Information Administration (NTIA) produced a series of reports starting in 1995 titled "Falling Through the Net." These reports noted a growing "digital divide" in the United States, and found that rural residents and members of minority communities were at a serious disadvantage when it came to accessing information online. Starting in 1994, the Telecommunications and Information Infrastructure Assistance Program (TIIAP) awarded grants to projects that were attempting to bring information access to disadvantaged people and communities. Many community networks received a much-needed boost from TIIAP.

While community networking is an international effort, most community networks can be found in the United States. Keeping track of the exact number of community networks is an almost impossible task, but at the beginning of 2001, roughly 120 community networks were operating in the United States, 20 in Canada, and 25 in the rest of the world.

For the past three decades, community networking projects have brought information access and electronic communication tools to thousands of people who could not otherwise afford them. But the future of community networking is uncertain. The declining cost of computers and Internet access has led many to think that these efforts are no longer needed. Michael Powell, appointed as the head of the Federal Communications Commission in 2001, said he prefers the term "'so-called' digital divide." With this shift in public perception and government policy, the outlook for community networking looks grim. However, community networking has been a grassroots, local-level effort since its beginnings, and it has the potential to stay alive without broad support.

Bibliography

Association for Community Networking. "Community Networking's Social Goals." 1998. <http://bcn.boulder.co.us/afcn/cn/goals.html> (March 20, 2002).

Schuler, Douglas. *New Community Networks: Wired for Change.* Reading, Mass.: Addison-Wesley, 1996.

Scott, Peter. "Freenets and Community Networks." March 26, 2001. <http://www.lights.com/freenet/> (March 20, 2002).

Further Reading

Cohill, Andrew, and Andrea Kavanaugh. *Community Networks: Lessons from Blacksburg, Virginia.* Norwood, Mass.: Artech House, 1997.

Rheingold, Howard. *The Virtual Community: Homesteading on the Electronic Frontier.* Reading, Mass.: Addison-Wesley, 1993.

Schmitz, Joseph. "Structural Relations, Electronic Media, and Social Change: The PEN Public Electronic Network and the Homeless." In *Virtual Culture,* Steve Jones, ed. Newbury Park, Calif.: Sage Publications, 1997.

Schuler, Douglas. "Community Networks: Building a New Participatory Medium." *Communication of the ACM,* 37:1 (1994), pp. 39–51.

Tsagarousianou, Roza; Tambini, Damian; and Cathy Bryan. *Cyberdemocracy: Technology, Cities, and Civic Networks.* London: Routledge, 1998.

Werry, Chris, and Miranda Mowbray. *Online Communities: Commerce, Community Action, and the Virtual University.* Upper Saddle River, N.J.: Prentice Hall PTR, 2001.

Related Topics
Bulletin Board Systems; CommuniTree; Digital Divide; Electronic Democracy; Freenet (Community Networks); Rheingold, Howard; Virtual Community; Whole Earth 'Lectronic Link

— *Norman Clark*

Compression

Compression refers to the process of storing information in a manner that uses less space than usual; compressed files provide the same basic amount of data, audio, and/or video information as the original files, but use fewer bits of storage. Current standards of communication, such as the widespread use of 56.6 kbps modems, necessitate the use of compression techniques for experiencing the audio and video content of the Internet.

Two techniques of compression are lossless and lossy. Lossless compression produces files that, upon decompression, are identical to the original file; that is, little to no information is lost during the process. More widely used, however, is lossy compression, which modifies the original file. Lossy compression techniques take advantage of redundancies in the information being stored in order to represent it efficiently. Instead of encoding every piece of information available, as traditional methods of storing audio and video do (e.g., audiotape, videotape), these techniques encode only momentary changes in audio and/or frame-by-frame changes in video in order to produce files that are smaller than the original. This subtle process is done through an initial encoding process that identifies the "static," or redundant, information, and afterwards encodes only data representing changes occurring over time. As these changes accumulate, they produce, for instance, movement or even a change of scenery on video. Although this process removes information from the original file, the difference between the original and compressed files is typically undetectable by human auditory and visual senses. MP3s and digital video based on MPEG standards, for example, use lossy compression.

When compressed media files are opened, the information is streamed, or transmitted, to a media player. Players, such as the Windows Media player and RealPlayer, are software programs capable of playing compressed audio and video files stored in numerous formats (see below). In order for a media file to play over the Internet, portions of it are loaded into a temporary storage area in the memory (buffer) of the user's computer and, without being permanently saved to the hard drive, the file is then streamed.

VIDEO COMPRESSION

Software used to compress and decompress video for viewing is commonly referred to as a codec, a term that originated as a shortened word for "compression/decompression." Although the sound quality of files produced by early codecs was quite poor, more recent versions yield files that are both smaller and of higher quality. Codecs are commonly included in digital-video software programs, most requiring computers with fairly powerful central processing units (CPUs) for compressing video. RealNetworks, for example, includes a codec in its RealPlayer and RealPlayer Plus media players that performs basic encoding tasks.

Codecs generally operate in two different ways, each of which is based on lossy compression techniques, but removes different types of information. Temporal compression identifies and removes non-essential information on a frame-by-frame basis. Each temporal change, or those occurring over time, is encoded while static information is ignored, resulting in smaller files. Spatial compression also removes information that is repetitive in a series of frames within a file, or even within the complete file itself. However, rather than looking for temporal changes, this method essentially monitors spatial areas (hence its name), as identified by coordinates of pixels, for changes. The coordinates help to identify changes in information, which are then encoded to the file. In both cases, the more non-redundant information present in the original file, the larger the compressed file produced will be.

Common formats and tools of compressed video files found on the Internet include (but are not limited to):

MPEG: Named for the Moving Picture Experts Group, MPEG is the standard used for creating DVDs and video CDs, as well as broadcast-quality audio and video.

QT (QuickTime): QuickTime is a cross-platform format that works with both Mac and Windows systems for encoding and viewing video. Versions 4.0 and higher support streaming video and improve compression capabilities.

Wavelet: A growing and relatively new format used by VDOLive, wavelets adjust to the bandwidth available by separating video into layers, which vary in their degree of detail and quality, so that video quality improves when greater bandwidth is available.

AUDIO COMPRESSION

As with video, lossy compression is the most popular audio compression technique. Most audio compression techniques and formats are direct outgrowths of advances in video compression. The MP3 format, for example, is based on the MPEG-1 standard designed by the Moving Picture Experts Group, which also created standards for video and multimedia platforms on the Internet.

Common formats of compressed audio files found on the Internet include (but are not limited to) the following:

AU: Also known as Sun/NeXT audio, the AU is used by UNIX operating systems (OSs).

AIFF (Audio Interchange File Format): A format used by the Mac OS to transmit and store sampled sound. Although many early audio files used this format, AIFF is actually not compressed, so files tend to be larger than those of other formats.

MP3: Based on the MPEG-1 standard, this currently popular audio file format creates small files approximating CD-quality sound.

RealAudio: The first compression format to support live streaming audio over the Internet, RealAudio was initially designed for voice applications over the Internet, and later expanded to multimedia.

RMF (Rich Music Format): Files incorporate both encoded audio and MIDI (Musical Instrument Digital Interface) information; MIDI is a standard that defines how musical synthesizers and instruments connect and interface with computers. The major drawback is the fact that these files require special players (e.g., Beatnik's Player, JavaScript Music Object) to access them.

SWA (Shockwave Audio): SWA compresses files based on the MPEG audio compression standard (as does MP3).

WAV (RIFF WAVE): WAV is one of the earliest audio formats, developed by Microsoft in conjunction with IBM and used by the Windows OS. Files produced by this format remain fairly large in comparison to those of other compression formats used today.

WMA (Windows Media Audio): WMA is a newer compression format created by Microsoft for its Windows Media Player.

COMMON USAGE AND FUTURE DEVELOPMENTS

Until fairly recently, most of the audio files accessible on the Internet were in AU, AIFF, and WAV formats. The growth of MP3 and other newer formats as higher-quality alternatives, however, has changed the landscape, as is evidenced by music sites such as Napster and MP3.com.

It is important to note that media files may be further reduced in size through other methods associated with compression, such as reductions in the video resolution, sample rate, and bit depth of the original file. Unfortunately, these methods also result in poor audio and video quality.

In the future, advancements in the design of codecs will result in greater savings in storage, although a limit must of necessity exist, for it is impossible to reach the theoretical limit of compression—namely, compression of a file to zero bits and subsequent decompression to original size. New codecs will be created, including such open-source alternatives as the MP3-like Ogg Vorbis codec, released to the public in 2001, that seeks to provide an alternative to the proprietary MP3 codec used in most MP3 hardware players and software encoders/decoders.

Bibliography

Adobe Systems Incorporated. "Adding Sound to the Web." 2002. <http://www.adobe.com/support/techguides/webpublishing/audio/page2.html> (May 17, 2002).

Fowler, T. Jay. "Video Compression: A Codec Primer." Lycos, Inc., August 25, 1997. <http://hotwired.lycos.com/webmonkey/html/97/34/index1a.html> (May 17, 2002).

Solari, Stephen J. *Digital Video and Audio Compression.* New York: McGraw Hill, 1997.

Stokas, Panos. "Which Is the Best Low-Bitrate Audio Compression Algorithm? OGG vs. MP3 vs. WMA vs. RA." March 2002. <http://ekei.com/audio/> (May 17, 2002).

Further Reading

Effelsberg, Wolfgang, and Ralf Steinmetz. *Video Compression Techniques: From JPEG to Wavelets.* San Francisco, Calif.: Morgan Kaufmann Publishers, 1998.

Haskell, Barry G., with Atul Puri and Arun Netravali. *Digital Video: An Introduction to MPEG-2.* New York: Chapman & Hall, 1997.

Moving Picture Experts Group. "MPEG Standards." 2000. <http://www.cselt.it/mpeg/standards.htm> (May 17, 2002).

Nelson, Mark. "DataCompression.info." June 24, 2002. <http://datacompression.info/index.shtml> (May 17, 2002).

Related Topics
CD-R, CD-ROM, and DVD; Codec; Digital Audio; MIDI; MP3; MPEG; Napster; QuickTime

— Art Ramirez

Computer Emergency Response Team

The Computer Emergency Response Team (CERT) was formed in 1988 at Carnegie Mellon University's Software Engineering Institute in Pittsburgh, Pennsylvania. CERT issues warnings to governmental agencies and the public at large about viruses and security threats. CERT receives funding from the Department of Defense's Defense Advance Research Projects Agency (DARPA). In 2001, the CERT Coordination Center (CERT/CC) formed an alliance with the private sector as it merged with the Internet Security Alliance (ISA), a group devoted to the improvement of Internet security.

CERT was formed as a response to the Internet Worm incident. In 1988, a Cornell University computer science graduate student named Robert Tappan Morris wrote an experimental program known as a worm; a worm spreads autonomously from one computer to another along a network. Morris released it onto the Internet, and approximately 10 percent of all computers connected to the Internet crashed as a result. According to Richard Power, author of *Tangled Web* (2000), more than 60,000 computers were shut down because of the Morris worm. This incident caused enough concern to prompt a military-funded agency devoted to protecting Internet and computer systems, and to providing 24-hour monitoring, analysis, and response.

The mission of CERT is to manage, control, monitor, and protect the functioning of the Global Information Grid (GIG). CERT has several specialized branches: ACERT (Army CERT), AFCERT (Air Force CERT), NAVCERT (Navy CERT), and DOD-CERT (Department of Defense CERT). CERT/CC is a research facility that studies Internet security vulnerabilities, publishes security alerts, and provides training to other agencies. The tasks of CERT/CC can be divided into four main categories: studies of vulnerabilities, indexes, and fixes; security practices and evaluations; survivability research and analysis; and training and education.

Visitors to the CERT/CC Web site can report such incidents of security violations as attempts to enter a system without permission, denial of service attacks, data storage on remote systems without permission, and changes made on hardware without permission. Incident reports can be submitted to CERT by phone, fax, or email. CERT recommends that all email sent to CERT should be encrypted, preferably with the public key encryption tool PGP (Pretty Good Privacy), which can be found at www.pgp.com.

CERT has also created a number of CSIRTs (Computer Security Incident Response Teams) that are responsible for reporting security breaches on the Internet. CERT/CC Incident Handling Courses provide a curriculum for the CSIRTs. Other governmental agencies are also responsible for reporting security violations. FedCIRC (Federal Computer Incident Response Center) provides an information infrastructure that centralizes security responses from the Department of Defense, law enforcement and intelligence agencies, and academic institutions.

CERT publicizes its security practices and evaluations capabilities in the *CERT Guide to System and Network Security Practices*. CERT security practices consist of five steps. First, CERT advises that secure systems be established by having secure connections. Next, the systems must be prepared for intrusions by practicing detection and response. Third, CERT advises that intrusions must be detected quickly. Fourth, responses should be tailored so as to minimize damage to the system. Finally, security should be improved in order to defend against future attacks.

Under the domain of survivability research and analysis, CERT has developed what is known as the Easel Survivability Simulation, a modeling and simulation computer language. Easel can simulate not only the Internet, but also electronic grids, telephone systems, biological systems, the stock market, and software organizations. In CERT's survivability technical report, entitled "Survivable Network Systems: An Emerging Discipline," the research team emphasizes that the Internet has no central control and no sense of a clear security policy. Instead of traditional security, a distributed system like the Internet requires survivability. Survivable systems must exhibit four essential properties: resistance to attacks, recognition of attacks and ability to assess damage, ability to recover full services, and system evolution in response to any attacks.

In 2001, CERT agreed to support the Internet Security Alliance (ISA), a group devoted to the improvement of Internet security. The alliance between CERT and ISA will provide CERT's resources to the private sector, while CERT itself continues to manage, control, monitor, and protect the Internet, providing up-to-the-minute advisories to governmental agencies. Undoubtedly, CERT's role will become even more valuable as the Internet continues to expand.

Bibliography

Computer Emergency Response Team (CERT), Software Engineering Institute, Carnegie Mellon University. <http://www.cert.org> (April 26, 2002).
Federal Computer Incident Response Center (FedCIRC). <http://www.fedcirc.gov/> (April 26, 2002).
Internet Security Alliance (ISA). <http://www.isalliance.org/> (April 26, 2002).
Power, Richard. *Tangled Web: Tales of Digital Crime from the Shadows of Cyberspace*. Indianapolis, Ind.: Que, 2000.
Survivable Network Technology Team, CERT. "Survivable Network Systems: An Emerging Discipline." Pittsburgh, Pa.: Software Engineering Institute, 1997. Revised May 1999. <http://www.cert.org/archive/pdf/97tr013.pdf> (April 26, 2002).

Further Reading

Computer Incident Advisory Capability (CIAC), U.S. Department of Energy. <http://www.ciac.org/ciac/> (April 26, 2002).
Federal Bureau of Investigation, National Infrastructure Protection Center (NIPC). <http://www.nipc.gov/> (April 26, 2002).
Forum of Incident Response and Security Teams (FIRST). <http://www.first.org/> (April 26, 2002).
President's Commission on Critical Infrastructure Protection (PCCIP). <http://www.info-sec.com/pccip/pccip2/info.html> (April 26, 2002).

Related Topics

Encryption and Cryptography; Hacking, Cracking, and Phreaking; Security; Virus

— Heidi Marie Brush

Computer Graphics

Computer graphics, the use of computers to create and process images, is an essential part of human-computer interaction (HCI) and a central part of contemporary visual culture. Artists have been capturing their imagination on paper in static form for many centuries, but in the space of just a few decades, computer scientists have mastered the art of representing images in a dynamic, digital form that can be continually transformed in any number of imaginative ways. From architecture to choreography and graphic design to typography, it is almost impossible to find a twenty-first-century creative discipline that has not been touched by computer graphics. But the transformation of everyday HCI has been even more fundamental, with green-screen text-only displays now consigned to history by graphical user interfaces (GUIs).

CONCEPTS

The key concept in computer graphics is the representation of an "analog" piece of visual information (a picture made up from a potentially infinite number of brush strokes in any number of colors or gray shades) in a digital format (a table of numbers chosen from a set of fixed values). The advantage to the digital format is that, while a picture drawn on paper is essentially a static item that can be changed only with difficulty, a digital image can be repeatedly transformed by applying various algorithms (predefined mathematical processes) to the stored numbers. For example, an image can be "mirrored" simply by reversing the order of the numbers that represent it, or doubled in size by repeating every number in the table.

Computer-graphic systems have much in common with television displays, in which pictures are built up from thousands of individual dots or squares by electron guns scanning systematically across a phosphor-coated screen. Raster graphics, as this process is called, is very different from an earlier (and much more expensive) form of computer imaging known as vector graphics, in which pictures were built up by plotting successive lines between coordinates a little like the trace on an oscilloscope. Imagine drawing a picture of a house. With raster graphics, the roof might be built up from a collection of red dots that happen to make the shape of a triangle and the main building from a collection of blue dots that happen to make up a square. With vector graphics, the roof would actually be plotted out as a red triangle and the main building as a blue square.

In the crudest computer imaging system, each pixel (the smallest element of a picture) is represented by a single bit (binary digit), with a 1 meaning that the pixel should be lit and a 0 that it should be unlit. As the pixels can only be on or off, this system is good enough only for rendering images in black and white; the resolution of an image (how detailed it can be) is determined by the size of the pixels (the number of pixels in a given area) and thus by the number of bits of memory available. The entire image is effectively a map of bits, or a bitmap. Using 8 bits per pixel, it becomes possible to represent 28 or 256 colors (or gray shades) at each point of the image. With 24 bits per pixel, 16 million colors are possible. For a typical PC screen size of 800 x 600 pixels, that gives a total memory requirement of (800 x 600 x 24)/8 or roughly 1.4 megabytes.

Building up images from individual pixels is slow, time consuming, and often unnecessary. Many images (for example, the characters in a font) can be made from standard shapes such as straight and curved lines, circles, and polygons that are themselves built up from pixels. Algorithms are then used to transform a small number of primitive shapes rather than a large number of pixels; standard transformations include scaling (shrinking or stretching), translation (moving from one place to another), rotation (turning an image about on a point), and shear (distorting an image by scaling it by different amounts in different dimensions).

There is a world of difference between the flat, cartoon-like blocks of color so characteristic of simple computer graphics and the real world of light, shade, and three dimensions. However, two-dimensional computer screens can effectively mimic the three-dimensional world with techniques such as perspective lines, hidden-surface elimination (in which distant objects or lines are hidden behind nearer ones), and the rendering of surfaces to make closer objects brighter and differently textured than more distant ones. Greater realism is achieved using reflection models, which govern how the different objects in a scene reflect light onto one another. These include the popular Phong reflection model, ray tracing (following how light rays reflect off shiny objects), and radiosity (for softly lit scenes containing matte surfaces).

APPLICATIONS

Applications of computer graphics fall into three areas: image synthesis (the creation of entirely new and perhaps completely imaginary images), image processing (in which real-world photographs or video footage are manipulated), and pattern recognition/machine vision (replicating elements of the human visual system in robots and industrial machines). Each of these areas necessarily relates to the others; many of the techniques

Shrek, Princess Diana, and the Donkey in DreamWorks Pictures' Shrek *(2001). (Courtesy of Photofest)*

used in image processing are the reverse of those used in image synthesis, for example.

The now-ubiquitous GUI is the most widespread use of computer graphics, for it forms the cornerstone of HCI in almost every PC, workstation, and hand-held-PC device sold today; even typing ordinary text into a word processing application counts as computer graphics, because the entire screen of a modern PC is processed as a large graphic bitmap rather than rows and columns of letters, as on a microcomputer or electronic typewriter.

More obviously graphical applications can be found in virtually all the creative arts. One of the earliest demonstrations of computer graphics was John Whitney Sr.'s title sequence for Alfred Hitchcock's movie *Vertigo* (1958). Successive generations of graphic software have assisted in the production of groundbreaking movies such as *Tron* (1980) and *Jurassic Park* (1993), which successfully combined computer animation and live-action sequences, and the completely computer-animated *Toy Story* (1995). Movie production involves both image synthesis (in computer animation) and image processing (in special effects); television title sequences and advertising commercials rely more on image processing, and have been revolutionized by computer-graphic equipment such as Quantel Paintbox.

Few fine artists have thoroughly explored the possibilities of computer graphics. Englishman William Latham has been a notable exception, with his swirling, mutating "organic art" creations memorably combining the random inputs and number-crunching ability of a powerful workstation with the selectivity of a creative human being. Design has been revolutionized by computer graphics, through the development of affordable desktop-publishing systems such as QuarkXPress and Aldus (now Adobe) PageMaker, industrial and architectural design packages such as AutoCAD, and typography creation software such as Macromedia's Fontographer.

The sciences have benefited from computer graphics no less than the arts. Like many other technological innovations, image processing has benefited considerably from space research and the use of computers to enhance images gathered by spacecraft. Non-invasive medical imaging has been another obvious beneficiary of graphics research. Image processing also forms an essential first step toward machine vision, for example, in face-recognition programs that automatically identify video footage of criminal suspects from known offenders by matching key features in terms of graphic primitives. Scientific applications have benefited from image synthesis no less than from image processing. Computer models, whose output once consisted of dense reams of fanfold printout, now come to life through full-color computer simulations; day-by-day graphic animations of weather forecasts are a familiar application. The most ambitious form of computer modeling is virtual reality—the development of computer-modeled worlds responsive to living human beings.

HISTORY

Computer graphics is just over half a century old. The first computer to make significant use of graphics is generally considered to be Whirlwind, a 4,500-vacuum-tube mainframe with cathode-ray tube (CRT) output. Developed in 1951 for use in air defense by Jay Forrester and Robert Everett at the Massachusetts Institute of Technology (MIT), Whirlwind produced probably the first ever computer animations, including a bouncing ball, for the *See It Now* TV show. Another MIT machine, the 1955 Semi-Automatic Ground Equipment (SAGE) system, used CRTs with vector graphics (as output) and light pens (as input) to analyze radar displays and provide early warning against missile attacks. By 1959, IBM had developed its first computer-aided design (CAD) system, called Design Augmented by Computers-1 (DAC-1), for General Motors. Publicly unveiled in 1964, it could rotate a 3D graphic model of an automobile.

Modern graphics packages date back to a system called Sketchpad, described by HCI pioneer Ivan Sutherland in 1963. Other notable developments in the 1960s included the development of key graphic techniques, including the Bresenham algorithm for plotting lines on raster displays and the Appel algorithm for removing hidden surfaces; the first exhibition of computer art at New York's Howard Wise Gallery in 1965; and the invention of the cornerstone of virtual reality, the head-mounted display, by Sutherland in 1966. Sutherland went on to co-found Evans and Sutherland, where development of flight simulators became a key stimulus to computer-graphic research. The year 1966 also saw the beginning of image processing from spacecraft at NASA's Jet Propulsion Laboratory (JPL), using an IBM 360 mainframe.

The 1970s was the decade when computers—and therefore computer graphics—moved from the research laboratory to the home and desktop, thanks to computer games such as Atari's Pong (1972) and the affordable, color graphic Apple II microcomputer (1977). More sophisticated graphic algorithms were also developed in the 1970s, including the Phong reflection model (1975), an important technique for rendering surfaces called Gouraud shading (1971), and the Bézier curve (1970), a powerful method of manipulating images with curves that forms the basis of software such as Adobe PostScript (launched in 1985). The early 1970s also saw the development of the GUI at Xerox PARC.

The most important single computing event of the 1980s was IBM's standardization of microcomputers into personal computers (PCs) driven first by DOS and later by Windows, arguably now the world's most important piece of graphic-based software. The 1980s also saw the emergence of powerful graphics-processing workstations, from corporations such as Silicon Graphics (SGI), and the desktop-publishing revolution. Most of today's industry-standard, computer-graphic software packages and systems were launched in the 1980s, including Quantel Paintbox (1981), Autodesk AutoCAD (1982), Aldus PageMaker (1985), and its competitor QuarkXPress (1987). Sophisticated lighting/shading algorithms for ray tracing (1980) and radiosity (1984) were also devised.

If the 1980s was the decade of desktop publishing, the 1990s was the era when desktop multimedia took off, first on CD-ROM and later through the World Wide Web. Web inventor Tim Berners-Lee argued strongly against the design of the groundbreaking Mosaic web browser, developed in 1993 by Marc Andreessen (later of Netscape), which allowed graphics and text to be displayed side-by-side. This design "flaw," which Berners-Lee feared would overload the limited bandwidth of the Internet, has probably been the single most important factor in the explosive growth in Web use, transforming a tool for exchanging text-heavy academic research into a ubiquitous, multimedia, infotainment library almost overnight.

THE IMPORTANCE OF COMPUTER GRAPHICS

To consider computer graphics simply as pictures on computer screens is to underestimate greatly the part it has played in integrating computer science into everyday life. That such a high proportion of the human cerebral cortex is devoted to processing visual information gives an essential clue about how people prefer to interact with machines. GUIs have made computers approachable, meaningful, and intuitively usable; desktop publishing and design packages have revolutionized the creative arts; and the Web has established digital infotainment as a currency accepted worldwide. Thanks to computer graphics, which contributed substantially to all of these innovations, computer science, once the stuff of mainframe computers fed by holes punched in paper tape, is now an integral part of everyday life.

Bibliography

Casti, John L. *Would-Be Worlds: How Simulation Is Changing the Frontiers of Science.* New York: John Wiley & Sons, 1997.

Foley, James; Van Dam, Andries; Feiner, Steven; and John Hughes. *Computer Graphics: Principles and Practice.* Reading, Mass.: Addison-Wesley, 1996.

Pickover, Clifford. *Computers and the Imagination: Visual Adventures Beyond the Edge.* New York: St. Martin's Press, 1991.

Sutherland, Ivan. "Sketchpad: A Man-Machine Graphical Communication System." *Interactive Computer Graphics.* Herbert Freeman, ed. Los Alamitos, Calif.: IEEE Computer Society, 1980.

Todd, Stephen, and William Latham. *Evolutionary Art and Computers.* London/San Diego: Academic Press, 1992.

Vince, John. *Computer Graphics.* London: The Design Council, 1992.

Watt, Alan, and Fabio Policarpo. *The Computer Image.* Harlow, England; Reading, Mass.: Addison-Wesley, 1998.

Further Reading

Cubitt, Sean. *Digital Aesthetics.* London/Thousand Oaks: Sage Publications, 1998.

Henderson, Kathryn. *On Line and on Paper: Visual Representations, Visual Culture, and Computer Graphics in Design Engineering.* Cambridge, Mass.: MIT Press, 1999.

Kyng, Morten, and Lars Mathiassen, eds. *Computers and Design in Context.* Cambridge, Mass.: MIT Press, 1997.

Related Topics

Desktop Publishing; Digital Art and Animation; Graphical User Interface; Sketchpad; Typography; Xerox Palo Alto Research Center

— *Chris Woodford*

Computer Music

Broadly speaking, computer music is music made with the aid of computers. Computer music can refer to the use of computers to compose music, perform compositions, or synthesize sounds. In its earliest incarnations, the mere fact of a computer being involved in the compositional process was significant. Today, computers are widely used in almost all aspects of the composition and performance of music. Where computer music once represented a very specialized form of composition and/or performance, today the fact of computer use is not itself as significant as the ways in which musicians and performers use computers.

By the 1950s, computers were becoming advanced and powerful enough that people could begin to use them for the purposes of creating music. An employee of AT&T's Bell Laboratories named Max Matthews (who would later invent the modular telephone jack) began experimenting with various programming protocols. His first program, MUSIC, was able to play about 17 seconds of a single line of notes on an IBM 704 mainframe computer in 1957. Matthews went through four more versions of his music program, adding multiple parts and more complex functions. As Matthews wrote, the computers on which these early applications ran "were strictly studio machines. They were far too slow to synthesize music in real time." It took about an hour of processing time to generate a minute of music, and the tone was similar to the sounds of a watch or cellular telephone today. "The timbres and notes were not inspiring," wrote Matthews, "but the breakthrough was inspiring."

Also in 1957, University of Illinois scientist and composer Lejaren Hiller began using computers to compose music. His first piece, "Illiac Suite" (named for the kind of computer that it used), was composed for string quartet. This work led to further research in what became known as computer-assisted composition.

Early computer-music facilities were usually housed at universities, and structured around a large mainframe computer. One notable exception to the academic orientation of computer music was the Institut de Recherche et de Coordination Acoustique/Musique (IRCAM), founded in Paris in 1976 by composers Pierre Boulex and Jean Claude Risset with the help of the French government. IRCAM has been an important global center for avant-garde computer music ever since.

By the late 1960s, analog synthesizers had become more widely available to musicians, and Matthews and other programmers created ways to control analog synthesizers with computers. These control devices, which were known as sequencers, could tell a synthesizer what notes to play and in what order, allowing synthesizers to perform "automatically." More elaborate sequencers required more elaborate control circuits, which led sequencer designers to new microprocessor circuits.

When home computers like the Apple II became available in the late 1970s, musicians quickly wrote programs for controlling their synthesizers. As computers moved out of university laboratories and into private homes, computer music moved from an avant-garde academic enterprise to a wider group of performers and listeners who were not affiliated with large research institutions.

As microprocessors caught the interest of musicians attempting to automate their synthesizers, they also caught the attention of John Chowning, a Stanford University researcher who hoped to create a fully digital synthesizer. Chowning used the same principles as FM radio (Frequency Modulation) for computer-generated sound. Stanford actually denied him tenure for this work, and it wasn't until 1976 that a commercial synthesizer manufacturer—Yamaha—became interested in FM synthesis. Seven years later, in 1983, Yamaha released the DX-7, the first fully digital synthesizer. It sold more than 200,00 units, more than any synthesizer before or since, and it can be heard on countless popular recordings from the 1980s. Just before the release of the DX-7, a group of musical instrument manufacturers met to establish the Musical Instrument Digital Interface standard (MIDI), to allow different pieces of digital audio equipment to communication with one another. MIDI is still in use today.

Recent developments in computer music have taken place along various trajectories. Computer music is becoming integrated with live performance, both through sequencing and through other techniques. Meanwhile, as computers become ever more powerful, distinctions erode between synthesizers as physical instruments and synthesizers that are software programs that run on computers. Some of the most important developments in synthesis in the past few years have been in software synthesis. Finally, the composition and performance functions of the computer are merging with its ability to record. Combined sequencer-and-recording programs such as Steinberg Cubase or Mark of the Unicorn's Digital Performer, and loop-based audio programs such as Sonic Foundry's Acid, have merged the computer's ability to record and play back audio with its ability to be used as a compositional tool.

Bibliography

Dorsch, Jim, and Nick Didkovsky. "Discussion on Computer-Generated Music." DoctorNerve.org. <http://www.doctornerve.org/nerve/pages/dorsch.shtml> (May 24, 2002)

Kuehnl, Eric Stephen. "A Brief History of Computer Music." School of Music, California Institute of the Arts. <http://shoko.calarts.edu/~eric/cm.html> (May 24, 2002).

Manning, Peter. *Electronic and Computer Music*. Oxford: Clarendon Press, 1993.

Matthews, Max. "The Father of Computer Music." cSounds.com. <http://www.csounds.com/mathews/> (May 24, 2002).

Further Reading

Born, Georgina. *Rationalizing Culture: IRCAM, Boulez, and the Institutionalization of the Avant-Garde*. Berkeley, Calif.: University of California Press, 1995.

Desain, Peter, and Henkjan Honing. *Music, Mind and Machine: Studies in Computer Music, Music Cognition and Artificial Intelligence*. Amsterdam: Thesis Publishers, 1992.

Roads, Curtis, ed. *Composers and the Computer*. Los Altos, Calif.: W. Kaufman, 1985.

Related Topics

Anderson, Laurie; Compression; Digital Audio; Eno, Brian; Interface; MIDI; Moog, Robert; MP3; MP3.com; Napster

— *Jonathan Sterne*

Computer-Supported Collaborative Work

Computer-supported collaborative work (CSCW) incorporates computer technology into systems that help people work together more effectively. Established in the 1980s, this revolutionary field is closely related to an approach to information-systems development that is based on sociological studies of everyday work practices.

RECONSIDERING PLACE AND TIME

Traditionally, having a meeting has meant gathering people in the same location at the same time. Sometimes that's the case with CSCW, but it does not have to be. With computer technology, the issues of time and place are no longer constraints. If everyone interacts at the same time, the meeting is *synchronous*. *Asynchronous* meetings, in contrast, don't resemble what most people think of when they think of meetings. The interaction among participants do not occur simultaneously; instead, people participate on the task when they can, whether anybody else in the group is currently doing so or not. Just as the time element has become more flexible with CSCW, so too has meeting location. Computer technology can support workers at different locations (*distributed* meetings) as well as the more traditional meetings in which people are in the same location (*collocated* meetings). They can even allow workers to attend multiple meetings simultaneously.

CSCW can be classified along the dimensions of place and time to create four different types of collaborations. Same place/same time (SPST) efforts look most like a traditional face-to-face meeting. Different place/same time (DPST) meetings require participants to coordinate schedules just as with traditional meetings, but they can literally be anywhere in the world. Same place/different time (SPDT) means that people ultimately find themselves in a common location, but not simultaneously. In different place/different time (DPDT) projects, people on opposite sides of the world can interact without having to worry about time zone differences, working outside normal business hours, or how to get to a particular location.

Some analysts take things further and add a fifth type of collaboration: any place, any time (APAT). Wireless technologies let people send and receive messages no matter where they are; equipped with laptops, they are ready to become immersed in a task whenever the need arises.

GROUPWARE: THE ENABLER OF CSCW

Groupware refers to any application/technology supporting multiple users in their quest to collaborate on a task. The groupware concept is the brainchild of Douglas Engelbart—the same man who invented the mouse and pioneered the commercial implementation of hypertext. Though Englebart experimented with groupware technologies in the 1960s, the term *groupware* was not used until the 1980s. Designed to facilitate human-human communication, the best groupware maximizes effective interaction among group members without introducing much technological interference. Many forms of groupware are available; one of the most famous examples is Lotus Notes. Four commonly used types of applications are:

Computer (or Data) Conferencing. Computer conferencing or data communication can take several forms. Some, such as chat rooms, operate in real time and are STDP. Others, including electronic mail (email), and

bulletin-board software, and discussion groups, are asynchronous (DTSP, DTDP, ATAP).

Group Calendaring and Scheduling. These applications help groups organize, prioritize, order, and assign tasks. They can facilitate anything from simple meeting agendas to coordinating the completion of time-sensitive, interdependent, complex, multi-stage processes. They can take any time/place configuration.

Group Document Handling. A variety of applications support collaborative work on traditional text-based documents, databases, and spreadsheets. When the emphasis is on hand-generated content such as drawing and handwriting, electronic whiteboards are preferred. These hardware/software configurations represent in a virtual environment the standard whiteboard found in conference rooms all over the world. Though they utilize the whiteboard metaphor, some can support activities well beyond merely working with manually generated figures. They can take any time/place configuration.

Electronic Meeting Systems. Often referred to as Group Support Systems or Group Decision Support Systems, Electronic Meeting Systems (EMSs) can incorporate any combination of groupware applications.

Like all CSCW applications, EMSs are designed to encourage communication and to improve performance. They are usually STSP or STDP. Most systems include a networked computer terminal for each person. This personal workspace is coupled with a public screen to display material to the entire group. With most EMSs, users can type comments into the system for public display, respond to posted comments, and send private messages to each other. All but the last type of message are anonymous. These communication tools are supplemented with tools designed to help the group manage information, by storing, retrieving, finding, and otherwise processing information. Most systems are designed to provide further task support while the group generates, refines, evaluates, and selects ideas or alternatives. These decision-support functions include, among others, brainstorming and voting. Many systems encourage rational decision-making by providing a logical procedure to structure deliberations.

ADVANTAGES AND DISADVANTAGES OF CSCW

A wide variety of benefits or advantages have been attributed to computer support in collaborative work. Face-to-face meetings can occur less frequently. People can make better decisions, faster, with more complete consensus. Information flow within an organization can be increased.

With an EMS, comments can remain anonymous, which supports a focus on ideas rather than people. It encourages shy—or lower status—group members to participate more fully. EMSs help ensure fuller, more democratic participation; domination of the process by a few members becomes more difficult. In addition, because everyone can use their keyboards simultaneously, they also allow everyone to "talk at once"; people are not as likely to forget what they wanted to say just because they could not say it right away.

A major benefit of groupware is that it relieves time and place constraints. Companies don't incur travel expenses, travel time is not lost, and jet lag and other ill effects are eliminated. International collaboration is facilitated. Even on a local level, avoiding one round trip across town during rush hour could yield several extra productive hours per person.

Additionally, responding to written communication with written communication can allow for a more reflective response. People can think about what they have read and respond when they are prepared, rather than having to make an immediate response in a face-to-face communication situation. Written messages can be more carefully crafted and edited than spoken ones.

Groupware encourages flexibility in organizations; it allows for what have been called dynamic teams—teams that are assembled when required, for only as long as required.

However, there are also disadvantages to groupware. Most people can come right into a new meeting situation ready to get to work. That is not the case with computer-supported collaborative work. By definition, computer-based tools require at least some degree of computer literacy, and some, such as electronic meeting systems, only become understood after several exposures. Because facility with such systems requires multiple uses, the first few meetings may be less satisfying and less productive. Groups using EMSs often take longer than others to accomplish their task, although some studies have shown the opposite result.

While it is nice that most people can read faster than they listen, and hence can process more text more quickly, the fact remains that even very good typists usually can not keep pace with their rate of speech. When people have to key in the content of their mes-

sages, it slows them down. Just as computer-supported collaborations can encourage the more shy group members to fuller participation, those individuals who can not type well or who are not comfortable with the technology may become inhibited.

Further, the more removed that people are from face-to-face interaction, the less "rich" the information is that they receive. When communicating, listeners rely on facial expressions, gestures, pauses, and vocal attributes such as volume, pitch, and rate of speech to understand the full meaning of what the speaker is trying to convey. If these nonverbal cues are not supported by the technology, people have only the words to draw upon. This can make communication more challenging and misunderstandings more likely. People engaged in CSCW need to understand the differences among channels of communication. As valuable and revolutionary as the technology is, there are times when nothing beats an old-fashioned face-to-face conversation.

Bibliography

Jessup, Leonard M., and Joseph S. Valacich, eds. *Group Support Systems: New Perspectives.* New York: Macmillan Publishing Company, 1993.

Lloyd, Peter, ed. *Groupware in the 21st Century: Computer Supported Cooperative Working Toward the Millennium.* Westport, Conn.: Praeger, 1994.

Mittleman, Daniel, and Robert O. Briggs. "Communication Technologies for Traditional and Virtual Teams." *Supporting Work Team Effectiveness: Best Management Practices for Fostering High Performance.* Edited by Eric Sundstrom and Associates. San Francisco: Jossey-Bass Publishers, 1999.

Opper, Susanna, and Henry Fersko-Weiss, eds. *Technology for Teams: Enhancing Productivity in Networked Organizations.* New York: Van Nostrand Reinhold, 1992.

Further Reading

Baecker, Ronald M., ed. *Readings in Groupware and Computer-Supported Work: Assisting Human-Human Collaboration.* San Mateo, Calif.: Morgan Kaufmann Publishers, 1993.

Coleman, David, ed. *Groupware: Collaborative Strategies for Corporate LANs and Intranets.* Upper Saddle River, N.J.: Prentice Hall PTR, 1997.

McGrath, Joseph E., and Andrea B. Hollingshead. *Groups Interacting with Technology.* Thousand Oaks, Calif.: Sage, 1994.

Related Topics

Email; Engelbart, Douglas; Hypertext; Internet; World Wide Web

— *Rebecca Ann Lind*

Content Filtering

From the beginning, the Internet was designed to make information more accessible. We can now obtain incredible amounts of data at any time of day, from almost any place in the world. But open access to all information can be problematic, especially when it comes to obscene or offensive materials. One way to prevent children from accessing objectionable material online is the use of content-filtering devices. These tools, which can be software or hardware-related, can be used to screen and block content that includes particular words or images. Content-filtering devices are a comparatively new development in the history of the Internet, and their use remains complex from a technical perspective, and controversial from a legal one.

Content filters restrict what users may view on their computer or television screen. Programs such as Cybersitter™, NetNanny™, and CyberPatrol™ screen Web pages and email messages for category-specific content. For example, if a parent does not want a child to be able to retrieve pages containing full nudity, they can select the "no full nudity" option in a content filtering program.

Once a user sets up a content-filtering program to restrict access to objectionable material, the program works in two distinct ways when an Internet connection is made. First, it checks to make sure the site is not on the software company's "blocked" site list. Second, it previews incoming pages and email by scanning it against an objectionable "buzzword list." If the site is listed in either of those databases, it will not be displayed on the screen, and instead a page will appear notifying the user that the site or message is blocked.

The blocked and buzzword lists themselves are created in two ways: human review and automated selection. Companies that develop content-filtering software maintain staffs of reviewers who scan the Internet for objectionable sites. The sites are then placed into different categories in the blocked list database. That way, if a user has selected not to view sites related to alcohol or drugs or cults, the software will automatically load the correct category sets from the database.

Such a system is not foolproof. The World Wide Web is growing much faster than the software companies can review it, and it is only logical that the review process relies at least in part on automation. It would be nearly impossible for a team of human reviewers to determine what is and is not objectionable on the Web

in every category. Moreover, today's safe Web site might be tomorrow's top porn website, or vice-versa. As a result, even if there were enough reviewers to catalog the entire Web, the blocked list would be out of date by the time they finished.

Sometimes, acceptable sites get wrongly labeled as objectionable. This results in frustration and anger—especially on the part of the Webmaster of the allegedly objectionable site. Some sites supplying information about breast cancer, for example, might be blocked, if the word "breast" appears on a buzzword list. But the more dangerous problem, according to opponents of content-filtering programs, who often call them "censorware," is that sites are sometimes blocked for apparently political reasons. For example, Peacefire.org, a site that opposes content filters, is often blocked by those same content filters, and select political Web sites are also blocked.

Another option is to use hardware to block content. The V-Chip is an electronic device designed to block content on television. Programs are assigned a rating based on the amount of violent or sexual content, strong language, adult themes, etc. The rating is broadcast along with the show, similar to the way that closed captioning is delivered. Parents can program the television set to block shows above a certain rating level. Proponents of the V-Chip claim that it places control in the hands of parents, but opponents argue that it might glamorize violence and sex, in the same way that "R"-rated movies are often sought out by teenagers; parents might not be able to operate the V-Chip, or teenagers might be able to bypass it; it is difficult to distinguish between different types of violence (e.g., reenactments of battles, cartoons, and gratuitous violence); and it ignores the basic issue that television content is violent and sexual, and that the industry could police itself and create better content.

The governments of several nations, including the United States, have begun to mandate the use of content filters in certain contexts. The Telecommunications Act of 1996 mandated the installation of V-Chips in all new television sets by 2000. The Children's Internet Protection Act (CHIPA), passed by the U.S. Congress in late 2000, requires that all public K-12 schools and libraries install an FCC-approved filtering device on their computers. Failure to comply with the law could make the public school or library ineligible for U.S. "E-rate" subsidies, which are used to purchase new computers, software, and networking equipment. However, the future of the CHIPA is uncertain, since lawsuits to overturn the act were filed in early 2001 by the ACLU and several other groups.

The debate over content filtering raises two key questions: Is it technically feasible, and is it a violation of the First Amendment? At present, the juries (both literal and figurative) are still out on both questions.

Bibliography

Maher, Marcus. "Complexity and Code: The Pitfalls of Regulation in Adaptive Systems." April 17, 1999. <http://cyber.law.harvard.edu/is98/final_papers/Maher.html> (March 20, 2002).

Wagner, R. P. "Filters and the First Amendment." *Minnesota Law Review* 83 (1999), p. 755.

Further Reading

American Library Association. *ALA's CIPA Website.* November 19, 2001. <http://www.ala.org/cipa/> (March 20, 2002).

Lawson, J. *The Complete Internet Handbook for Lawyers.* Chicago: American Bar Association, 1999.

Price, Monroe. *The V-Chip Debate: Content Filtering from Television to the Internet.* Mahwah, N.J.: Lawrence Erlbaum Associates, 1998.

Related Topics

Carnivore; Child Online Protection Act and Child Online Privacy Protection Act; Communications Decency Act; Obscenity

— *Norman Clark*

Convergence

Before the information revolution of the late twentieth century, telecommunications, television, and computers were usually considered to be different technologies, produced by different industries, and studied by different academic fields. Convergence refers to the growing interdependency among these technologies, and indeed among all communication media. The term has come to be associated not only with technology, but also with industrial and institutional structures, as well as social and cultural norms that shape and are shaped by converging media. More recently, it has had some influence on the potential successors of the personal computer, including television set-top boxes, multimedia cellular telephones, and Internet appliances.

Ithiel de Sola Pool is usually credited with first describing convergence in his 1983 book, *Technologies of Freedom,* which examined how media were becoming interdependent, and the implications of this interdependency for public policy. Pool suggested that, increasingly, a given physical network could provide any sort of media service, and that conversely, a media service that had once been constrained to one physical technology could now be carried on any number of physical distribution networks. Advances in electronic communication were allowing for a complex merging of hitherto separate media systems. While he focused on what have come to be seen as the emblematic technologies—telephone, television, and personal computers—he also provided earlier examples, discussing the use of the telephone system to send text messages ("telegraphs"), as well as the interesting intersections of telephone and radio.

While Pool recognized that codes and conventions were an important part of electronic media, he failed to clearly indicate the role of digitization in this process—what author Nicholas Negroponte has famously labeled as the transformation from "atoms to bits." As the production and transmission of information becomes increasingly digital, the walls between media become more porous. New motion pictures (which can no longer accurately be called "films") have begun to be recorded digitally, and often ultimately end up as DVDs to be viewed on televisions or personal computers. While there still remains a significant amount of media in non-digital form, the adoption of digital equivalents has been accelerating over the last decade.

Mergers among media owners have accompanied this convergence in technology, either reflecting or driving the technological change. More subtly, the expectations of users of communication technologies, and the nature of the content these technologies record and carry, have also shifted. Many argue that these economic, social, and cultural shifts are as much a part of convergence as the technological changes. Pool, and many of those who have followed, recognized the vital part that economic and cultural structures have in the process of convergence. Deregulation in the United States has placed media and telecommunications companies in the same competitive arena, each hoping to provide telephony, broadband Internet access, cable television, cellular telephone, and a wide range of other media services to the customer.

Commentators agree that the word convergence is more often the object of hype than a clear analytical category. However, there are certainly key milestones of the convergence of media. Some of the most striking examples may be found in the interactive television experiments that began in the 1980s.

Warner's Qube project, a first attempt at cable television-on-demand and interactive programming, failed to produce a long-term profit, although it served as a template for the current trends in digital set-top boxes. WebTV, an effort to provide access to the World Wide Web via a set-top box, has met with moderate success. Intel has made a number of efforts over the last few years to unite broadcast television and the PC, and the recent emergence of Personal Video Recorders (PVRs) will likely spur further development in this area.

Convergence appears to be leading to the ideal of accessing all media through a single device, although the nature of this device remains an open question. For some time, the major contenders were the television (through a set-top box) or the PC. The latter has given way to a number of other possibilities, including what has come to be called the Internet appliance, a scaled-down computer reminiscent of the "smart terminals" of the 1980s. Many are heralding the latest home-gaming console system offerings from Sony, Microsoft, and Nintendo as clear examples of convergence; they are able to play DVDs and provide email and Web access in addition to supporting game play. Most recently, the promise of mobile and wireless devices has been added to this list, providing the potential for near-invisible and ubiquitous access to information and communication. Personal Area Networks (PANs) may provide high-speed access to a global library of information in the not-distant future, using wireless protocols (such as Bluetooth) or even transmitting information through the human body itself.

Bibliography

Jenkins, Henry. "Digital Renaissance: Convergence? I Diverge." *Technology Review.* June 2001. <http://www.techreview.com/articles/jenkins0601.asp> (April 26, 2002).

Negroponte, Nicholas. *Being Digital.* New York: Knopf, 1995.

Pool, Ithiel de Sola. *Technologies of Freedom.* Cambridge, Mass.: Belknap Press, 1983.

Zimmerman, Thomas G. "Personal Area Networks: Near-Field Intrabody Communication." *IBM Systems Journal,* vol. 35, no. 3/4 (1996).

Further Reading

Dodd, Annabel Z. *The Essential Guide to Telecommunications.* Second edition. Upper Saddle River, N.J.: Prentice Hall, 2000.

Green, John. *The New Age of Communications.* New York: Henry Holt & Co., 1997.

Lubar, Steven. *InfoCulture.* Boston, Mass.: Houghton Mifflin, 1993.

Related Topics

Bluetooth; Broadband; Digital Subscriber Line; Disintermediation; Internet Appliances; Multimedia; Narrowcasting; Qube; Technological Determinism; vBNS; Wireless Networks

— *Alexander Halavais*

Cookies

Cookies are bits of encrypted information deposited by some Web sites on a computer's hard drive after a person has accessed a particular site.

Cookies were originally created as a tool to save time and allow for the personalization of sites, by enabling users to be treated differently from one another and according to specific preferences chosen by the users, rather than by programmers. The Web site stores cookies, so that when the same site is accessed again from the same computer, the site can recognize the computer and provide the same set of personalized settings and information—layout, shopping cart, search information, or user's name—each time the site is visited. Unless a computer is specifically told not to accept a cookie, when the site is accessed again, the Web browser automatically sends the cookie back to the Web site from which it came.

When a surfer visits a Web site, a few key broad identification points about the surfer are immediately available. The site can identify the URL from which the surfer came, the Internet domain name or IP address of the computer the surfer used, and which browser the surfer used. Cookies build on this initial knowledge, permitting sites to gather more details, not just about the computer accessing the site, but also about the person using the computer.

The cookie as we know it today was created by Netscape in 1994 as a special feature of the Netscape browser, for the purpose of maintaining site information on a computer even after the computer has been shut down. The original intention of the cookie was to make life easier for the person browsing the Web. The concept is somewhat similar to that of a computer's preferences file; it keeps track of how the user wants a site to look or function, and once the preferences are set, the user does not have to re-input routine information upon each visit. No one took much notice of cookies until Netscape released its second version: Netscape Navigator 2.0 featured a new option that could turn off cookies completely.

Conflicting stories exist about the origin of the term *cookie*. According to Chris Sherman of About.com, many computer users believe *cookie* comes from the fairy tale of Hansel and Gretel, who leave a trail of cookies to find their way out of the forest. Although Sherman acknowledges that in the story the children supposedly dropped rocks along their path to mark their way, the idea of cookies to mark a path stuck with the Web usage. Access Vanguard's Web site argues that *cookie* seems to apply because of the Internet programming tendency to name functions after food, as in the case of spam or Java. Netscape has claimed the bits of encrypted information are called cookies "for no compelling reason."

Web browsers limit the number of cookies that a user's computer can store at any given time. Default browser settings allow about 300 cookies, or 20 per server or domain. When these limits are reached, the least used or oldest cookies are deleted. Cookies are also kept to a 4 Kb limit of space used on the computer's hard drive.

While cookies have enabled Web site developers to create many new tricks and tools to benefit the user, there are still many things that cookies cannot do. Author Simon St. Laurent points out that cookies cannot perform tasks most feared by Internet users, like stealing money from bank accounts, spreading viruses, or reading hard drives. What cookies *can* do, however, is track users as they move from site to site.

Web surfers can refuse to accept cookies on their computers and still surf the Web. St. Laurent advises that perhaps a better strategy for protecting oneself on the Web might be to lie about one's identity, or about any other information of a personal nature that some sites request, rather than by turning off cookies. For users who prefer to refuse cookies, there are several options for doing so. One way to refuse cookies is to set a browser to automatically reject every cookie offered. A few sites will not be accessible, others will look different than they do to cookie-enabling users, and some searching mechanisms and shopping carts will not be usable. Another option is to set a browser to give a warning before accepting a cookie. This allows the user to selectively accept or reject cookies. This might be a good temporary solution for new users who would like to see how many cookies they are actually receiving per surfing session.

Cookies themselves are not inherently bad, or necessarily invasive to Web user privacy. What has become a growing concern, however, is the manipulation of cookies to track user data in ways that raise fears about user privacy, and in a way that was not an original purpose of the cookie.

One privacy concern related to cookies is a practice known as profiling. In late 1999, DoubleClick, Inc., the Internet's largest advertising company, purchased the direct-marketing database company Abacus, and was able to correlate cookies left by their clients' Web sites with information about individuals in the Abacus database. More than 11,500 sites belonging to the DoubleClick network could be paired with Abacus' existing database of more than two billion consumer catalog transactions. The practice allowed DoubleClick to build profiles of individuals' activities at client Web sites.

Another privacy issue relating to cookies arose in February 2000, when a class action lawsuit was filed in Dallas County District Court against Yahoo! Inc. and Broadcast.com, primarily for violations of the state's anti-stalking laws. Dallas lawyer Lawrence J. Friedman claimed that Yahoo's use of cookies was a "surveillance-like" device, monitoring users' actions without their knowledge or consent.

With advances in data mining and knowledge management, the use of cookies must be considered in relation to privacy. Web users should be aware of the existence and purpose of cookies in order to make informed decisions regarding their surfing. Maintaining complete privacy by turning off the cookie function in a browser must be weighed against the convenience that cookies provide, in terms of enabling access to previous grocery lists from online grocers, book or gift purchases from online retailers, or favorite newspaper columns or specific city weather updates on Web portals.

Bibliography

Access Vanguard. "Ask Vanguard: Internet Cookies." 2000. <http://www.vanguard.com/cgi-bin/NewsPrint/926533852> (March 20, 2002).

Macavinta, Courtney. "Privacy Fears Raised by DoubleClick Database Plans." *Cnet.com*. January 25, 2000. <http://news.cnet.com/news/0-1005-202-1531929.html> (March 20, 2002).

Netscape Communications Corporation. "Persistent Client State HTTP Cookies." 1999. <http://home.netscape.com/newsref/std/cookie_spec.html> (March 20, 2002).

St. Laurent, Simon. *Cookies.* New York: McGraw-Hill, 1998.

Further Reading

Berners-Lee, Tim. *Weaving the Web: The Original Design and Ultimate Destiny of the World Wide Web by Its*

Inventor. San Francisco, Calif.: HarperCollins Publishers, Inc., 1999.

Flanagan, David. *JavaScript: The Definitive Guide.* Sebastopol, Calif.: O'Reilly & Associates, 1998.

Hansen, Evan. "Rights Groups Urge Government to Protect Privacy." *Cnet.com.* November 5, 1999. <http://news.cnet.com/news/0-1005-202-1431252.html> (March 20, 2002).

Related Topics

Berners-Lee, Tim; Browser; Communications Decency Act; Content Filtering; Data Mining; Electronic Communications Privacy Act; Knowledge Management; Security; World Wide Web

— *Jodi White*

Copyleft

Copyleft is a license granting general permission to copy and reproduce intellectual property—most commonly software, but also writings or other creative content. The term "copyleft" was coined by computer scientist Richard Stallman to reverse the idea of copyright.

Understanding copyleft requires an understanding of the basic aspects of copyright. Copyright reserves exclusive control of copyrighted property to its creator. The creator decides what rights to grant others, and each grant of rights is established under a specific agreement. The creator of a copyrighted work may elect to transfer copyright ownership to another individual, or to a business; in this case, the new copyright owner takes over all rights of copyright control, and decides how to manage those rights.

Copyleft is a general license agreement granted by a copyright owner permitting anyone to freely use copyrighted property, but under specific terms. Common terms of a copyleft license state that a copylefted work is freely available to all potential users. Copylefted software allows users to run, modify, copy, and distribute software on the condition that the source code remains open and publicly available. Copyleft usually states that copylefted software must be passed on with a copyleft license requiring successive users to accept and transmit copyleft. The license further requires that modifications or improvements to copylefted software be transmitted under copyleft. Copylefted content is transmitted in much the same way as software, and under similar agreements.

Interpretations of copyleft's scope vary somewhat. Some argue that copyleft involves placing copyrightable material in the public domain. Others argue that copyleft is a specific license granted under copyright law, and they argue that the international statutes governing copyright law are the mechanisms that establish and protect copyleft.

Copyleft can be considered a return to the earliest ideas of intellectual property. Copyleft embodies three traditional principles that governed intellectual property before the industrial revolution, when intellectual property was considered a common good:

- Knowledge builds on prior knowledge. Innovation embodies prior art, and even revolutionary ideas build on the knowledge that successful revolutions overturn.

- No one can truly own knowledge. Knowledge grows with use as a common property that increases through circulation while shrinking with disuse. This view asserts that we can own knowledge only by sharing it; knowledge as private property is a contradiction in terms.

- Knowledge requires the support of tradition. Traditional knowledge grows incrementally, and new knowledge must incorporate earlier knowledge to be acceptable. Traditions of knowledge build on precedent, including law, theology, philosophy, and mathematics. Modern science and scholarship also build on precedent by incorporating or refuting earlier knowledge.

Many cultures respect the traditional view of knowledge, giving rise to different views on intellectual property. Japanese and Chinese scholars, for example, often treat scholarly ideas as a shared heritage that demands respectful incorporation into their writing. While Western property law allowed for the growth of personal property rights for all forms of property, some cultures that accept personal property for physical goods follow traditional law for intellectual property.

The development of capitalism and banking in fifteenth-century Venice led to the first patent law of 1474. In 1710, England enacted the first copyright law. Intellectual property law has grown from those roots to its current state. In recent years, however, several ideas have challenged the idea of applying private property rights to mental creations.

First, knowledge develops in a complex sequence of interactions in communities of practice and learning, and in larger societies and economies. Intellectual property is inevitably predicated on prior work. Individuals contribute to the whole, shaping variations and giving specific form to the statements that constitute intellectual property. The philosophical position of copyleft is that communities have rights in knowledge along with individuals. Moreover, copyleft asserts that copyright itself is often used against individuals by a legal system that favors powerful interests over individual creators.

One of the important predecessors of copyleft was architect and theorist Buckminster Fuller. Fuller copyrighted and patented his work, both to document his creations and to preserve the work for humankind while protecting it against monopoly control by the legal system.

Soon, artists began to experiment with notions of general copyright and anti-copyright. In the early 1960s, Fluxus publisher and impresario George Maciunas promulgated a publishing and performance strategy similar to the concept of the general public license that would emerge later. Other Fluxus artists began to circulate event scores and program-like project notes with specific permissions for use and reprint on condition of transmitting the copyright conditions. In the early 1970s, British Fluxus artist David Mayor developed an anti-copyright philosophy, complete with an anti-copyright mark in the form of a tiny x in a circle.

Copyleft itself probably began in the work of MIT computer expert Richard Stallman. In 1983, Stallman started an open-source programming project called GNU (a reflexive acronym for "GNU's Not Unix"). He created the first general public license to govern the use of GNU, keeping it and its derivatives open and freely available. Today, the concept of copyleft is central to many programming projects. Many creators in the information society use it, from software programmers and digital artists to content providers, composers, and designers.

Where copyright protects society's interests in invention and creativity by providing individual incentives through copyright control, copyleft protects social interests in knowledge creation by vesting copyright control in a large, general community. In one sense, it extends the benevolent hacker knowledge ethos that asserts that "Information wants to be free." In another, it returns to the traditional concept of knowledge, which treats general ideas and their specific forms as a common heritage. Mental creations build on what has come before, and they shape the platform of what comes next. Copyleft is a bridging mechanism developed to encourage the growth of social knowledge and common good.

Bibliography

Lillington, Karlin. "In Defense of Copyleft." Wired Digital, 8:35 A.M. February 7, 2001. <http://www.wired.com/news/politics/0,1283,41679,00.html> (April 5, 2002).

Stallman, Richard. "The Right to Read." *Communications of the ACM,* vol. 40, no. 2 (February 1997), pp. 85–87.

———. "Copyright and the Globalization of Computer Networks." Speech given at the Massachusetts Institute of Technology, April 19, 2001. <http://www.gnu.org/philosophy/copyright-and-globalization.html> (April 5, 2002).

Stutz, Michael. "Copyleft and the Information Renaissance." <http://www.dsl.org/copyleft/> (April 5, 2002).

Further Reading

Anderson, Judy. *Plagiarism, Copyright Violation, and Other Thefts of Intellectual Property: An Annotated Bibliography with a Lengthy Introduction.* Jefferson, N.C.: McFarland and Company, 1998.

Buranen, Lisa, and Alice M. Roy. *Perspectives on Plagiarism and Intellectual Property in a Postmodern World.* Albany, N.Y.: State University of New York Press, 1999.

Copyright and Copyleft. [Online resource collection.] <http://www.edu-cyberpg.com/Internet/copyrightleft.html> (April 5, 2002).

Eisenstein, Elizabeth. *The Printing Press as an Agent of Change: Communications and Cultural Transformation in Early Modern Europe.* Cambridge: Cambridge University Press, 1979.

Goldstein, Paul. *Copyright's Highway: From Gutenberg to the Celestial Jukebox.* New York: Hill and Wang, 1995.

Schwartz, Hillel. *The Culture of the Copy.* New York: Zone Books, 1996.

Williams, Sam. *Free as in Freedom: Richard Stallman's Crusade for Free Software.* Cambridge, Mass./Sebastopol, Calif.: O'Reilly & Associates, 2002. <http://www.oreilly.com/openbook/freedom/> (April 5, 2002).

Related Topics

"The Cathedral and the Bazaar"; Copyright; Linux; Patent; Raymond, Eric; Stallman, Richard

— *Ken Friedman*

Copyright

Copyright is law that regulates the copying of creative works. Under U.S. law, it is a right granted to authors and artists (and in some cases to the companies for which they work). Its goal is to ensure that creative works will be produced in exchange for limited guarantees that rights of compensation will be preserved when works such as books, articles, photographs, and music recordings are published and sold to the public.

Copyright, as initially envisioned, was not a one-way street. Its protections extended to those who purchased creative works too, and it limited the power artists have over their works. Traditional notions of copyright have been sorely tested by new media such as MP3 files and the Web.

THE EVOLUTION OF COPYRIGHT LAW

Modern copyright law was established in England in 1710, when the British Parliament enacted the Statute of Anne. This law codified legal protection of consumers by limiting copyright's duration, preventing publishing monopolies among booksellers. The statute instituted the concept of "public domain," which among other things limits copyrights' terms and prohibits copyright holders from controlling the use of works after they have been sold. Finally, the Statute of Anne initiated an author's copyright, but that benefit was limited since most authors could not be paid unless they contracted with booksellers or publishers to put works out to market.

U.S. copyright law derives from the Statute of Anne and from common law, and the framers of the Constitution included federal copyright provisions that give Congress the power "to promote the progress of science and useful arts . . . by securing for limited times to authors and inventors the exclusive rights to their respective writings and discoveries." Congress enacted the Copyright Act of 1790, and several major revisions followed in 1831, 1870, 1909, 1976, and 1998.

Copyright laws were intended to protect creators' rights to reap rewards from their works, and to ensure that the public would reap rewards from publication. But the idea was to reasonably limit rights so that creative works—or, distilled to their essence, ideas—would eventually be exchanged freely. Creative works could be used in any way after copyrights expired. In 1790, copyrights expired after 14 years, with an option for one renewal that extended protection to a maximum of 28 years.

The duration of U.S. copyrights and the scope of their protections gradually changed. Its rules no longer apply only to maps, charts, and books, as they did in 1790, but to anything "fixed in a tangible medium of expression." Copyright law no longer regulates only publishers; its dictates now can apply to anyone who makes a "copy" of a creative work. Copyright is not even limited to copying. Even a derivative version of a work can also be subjected to copyright restrictions.

The 1909 revision expanded the scope of creative works under protection to include all forms of authorship, and it extended copyright protections to a total 56 years, including renewals. This legislation directed the focus of copyrights away from marketplace regulation to the proprietary rights of authors and publishers.

The 1976 U.S. copyrights revision was a response to changing technologies. Under the 1976 rewrite, which superceded all previous laws, technologies like tape recording and photocopying were addressed for the first time. The most important new rules codified into law the rights of "fair use" and "first sale." Fair use means, as one example, that an author cannot sue a critical reviewer for using portions of the author's own text in a critique of the work; small portions of copyrighted materials may be used without permission without worry of infringement. Another instance of fair use is the right that one has, after having legally purchased a copyrighted work, to use it in private for any purpose. For example, one can make a copy of a CD on tape so it can be played in the car. First-sale rights mean that, once an author or publisher sells a work once, their control over what happens to that work thereafter is lost. This means you can take your used books to a shop and resell them—or sell them yourself—without hiring an attorney.

The concepts of fair use and first sale would take on immense weight as the Internet came of age. Digital technology makes it easy to copy and redistribute creative works without quality degradation (previous copying technologies like photocopiers and tape recorders invariably diluted the quality of each copy). Napster, the peer-to-peer online music-swapping service that made available copies of virtually any popular music recordings for free, is a key example. It has been under legal attack by the recording industry for copyright infringements, and has been held up as justification for the further strengthening of copyright protections in the digital age.

On October 28, 1998, the Digital Millennium Copyright Act (DMCA) was enacted into law. It was designed to comply with two 1996 World Intellectual Property Organization (WIPO) treaties that strengthened protections for copyrighted works produced in electronic formats, and it was a direct response to the Internet. Among its provisions, the DMCA prohibits "code cracking," or circumventing technologies that control access to and use of copyrighted works. It also forbids the manufacture and sale of technologies that intentionally circumvent copyright-protecting technologies. At the same time, Congress extended copyright protections to the life of an artist plus 75 years; for corporations, the term is 95 years (for example, Microsoft's Windows 95 copyrights expire in 2090). Some observers, like *San Jose Mercury News* technology columnist Dan Gilmore, think the changes gave rights holders "almost total control over information created or converted into digital form."

SHOULD INFORMATION BE FREE?

The proper role of copyright (and its sister concept, intellectual property) in the Internet age is hotly debated. There are those who argue that the Internet is a kind of anarchic space where creative works enjoy virtually no protection. Some believe that information will wind up being free—both free of charge for access and free for unrestrained public use—and that no anti-piracy software will ever effectively stop that trend. To make a living under such circumstances, artists and authors would have to resort to collecting money from "peripherals," such as paid concert performances, speaking engagements, even T-shirt sales.

This is the view represented by former Internet Corporation for Assigned Names and Numbers (ICANN) chair Esther Dyson, who believes that ease of content copying and distribution over the Internet will force creators to work strictly for hire, simply because they will lose all control over their creations once they are made public. So, if a freelance writer is assigned to write an article for a magazine, that writer gets paid upon publication for the job and receives nothing further. There would be no royalties or residual payments for further online distribution, just that initial paycheck. Similar conditions would apply to musical artists, novelists, photographers, and other intellectual property holders.

On the other hand, there are many who fear that digital technologies could render copyright protections absolute, carrying copyright laws far beyond what the framers intended, allowing rights holders to maintain complete control of every aspect of a work's use. Imagine buying from the Internet enough downloaded songs to fill a compact disc, only to find that the tracks expired and became useless after 100 plays. Imagine buying a book that you could read only three times, and that you could never sell afterward. Such things could happen, activists charge, if digital copyrights are not reigned in.

Ian Clarke, founder of the Web-like file-sharing interface Freenet, believes that copyrights are not simply unenforceable in the Internet age; he argues that they have outlived their usefulness. Clarke's Freenet project, an anonymous and untraceable peer-to-peer file-sharing network, can facilitate the trading of any kind of electronic media, from music to books to video, without regard for copyright restrictions. Clarke defends Freenet as a necessary step to protect the rights of free speech. Where copyrights exist, he insists, the free flow of information is impeded, and Clarke thinks that all information ought to be freely available.

WHO NEEDS COPYRIGHT?

Lawrence Lessig, a noted Stanford University law professor who has been called "the James Madison of our time," counters Clarke's view. Lessig's book, *Code and Other Laws of Cyberspace* (1999), is in part an argument in favor of some government regulation of the Internet, not to restrict liberties online, but to ensure that certain freedoms are not sacrificed to corporate interests.

As Lessig has written, it is not just pirates who have to worry about violating copyrights in the digital age. Software code can give rights holders almost unfettered control over content. It can direct, for example, how often a book can be read and who reads it. Software code can determine if a work, or certain parts of it, can be copied. It can dictate what machine can read or play back a creative work. And with the DMCA's restrictions on circumventing anti-piracy technology, that software code has the force of law. Or, to use Lessig's phrase, the code becomes the law. Whether the code is infringing on the consumers' right to "fair use" of copyrighted material does not enter the equation.

The Recording Industry Association of America (RIAA), for one, takes an extremely conservative view of what constitutes fair use. The group has lobbied for an interpretation of copyright law that would enforce restrictions on random access memory buffers that are used whenever a multimedia signal is streamed to a PC across the Internet. A PC collects and temporarily stores several seconds of a performance before it begins to play it back, in order to assure that the stream will execute without interruption. The RIAA has backed up its stance with arguments like this one, taken from its Web site: "Generally speaking, you are not allowed to take the 'value' of a song without permission," RIAA says, "and sometimes that value is found even in a three-second clip."

Lessig argues that through technology, copyright laws become, in effect, privatized laws—laws that act like contractual agreements. But there is a key difference: Contracts generally are the result of negotiations between parties, while copyright-protecting code is dictated to the consumer without negotiations of terms. And privatized copyright law, Lessig argues, will have none of the balance that the framers of the Constitution built into copyrights.

THE FUTURE OF COPYRIGHT

The debates about online copyright protections are nowhere near resolution. Corporate interests like the RIAA, along with some recording artists, have battled effectively to build the sort of privatized copyright laws that Lessig rails against. But as of early 2001, lawmakers were beginning to take a fresh look at the issue.

One such legislator, Senator Orrin Hatch (Rep.-Utah), himself a musician, expressed such irritation at the Ninth Circuit Court ruling against Napster in March 2001 that he threatened to rewrite copyright laws to legalize file-swapping over services like Napster. Another lawmaker, U.S. Representative Rick Boucher (Dem.-Virginia), said he planned to introduce legislation to rework the DMCA, to better balance the interests of artists and corporations that create and distribute intellectual property with the interests of consumers. Boucher's legislation will likely attract the support of public libraries and electronics manufacturers, whose products could be greatly restricted in their functionality if the DMCA is not altered.

From the outset, copyright laws were a response to new technology; at the time of the Statute of Anne, the new medium was the printing press. As things currently stand, copyrights will continue to be affected, perhaps radically, by the emerging digital technologies.

Bibliography

Association of Research Libraries. "A History of Copyright in the U.S." August 16, 2001.
<http://arl.cni.org/info/frn/copy/timeline.html> (March 21, 2002).
Digital Media Association. "Report to Congress Pursuant: Comments of the Digital Media Association." August 4, 2000.
<http://www.ntia.doc.gov/ntiahome/occ/dmca2000/DiMA.html> (March 21, 2002).
Featherly, Kevin. "Freenet: Will It Smash Copyright Law?" Newsbytes, March 20, 2001.
——. Telephone interview with Ian Clarke. March 19, 2001.
King, Brad. "Copyright or Copy Wrong?" Wired online, February 16, 2001.
<http://www.wired.com/news/business/0,1367,41845,00.html> (March 21, 2002).
Lessig, Lawrence. "The Limits of Copyright." The Industry Standard, June 19, 2000.
<http://www.thestandard.com/article/display/0,1151,16071,00.html> (March 21, 2002).
Mann, Charles. C. "Who Will Own Your Next Good Idea?" The Atlantic Online. September 1998.
<http://www.theatlantic.com/issues/98sep/copy.htm#mann> (March 21, 2002).

Further Reading

Dyson, Esther. Release 2.0: A Design for Living in the Digital Age. New York: Broadway Books, 1997.
Lessig, Lawrence. Code and Other Laws of Cyberspace. New York: Basic Books, 1999.
Negroponte, Nicholas. Being Digital. New York: Vintage Books, 1995.
Recording Industry Association of America. "Copyright Basics." 1996–2001.
<http://www.riaa.org/Copyright-Laws-2.cfm> (March 21, 2002).
St. Pierre, Nicole. "Musicians to Congress: What About Us?" BusinessWeek Online, April 4, 2001.
<http://www.businessweek.com/bwdaily/dnflash/apr2001/nf2001044_327.htm> (March 21, 2002).
Stallman, Richard. "Why Software Should Not Have Owners." 1994.
<http://www.gnu.org/philosophy/why-free.html> (March 21, 2002).
Stern, Christopher. "Freelance Writers Fight for Share of Online Profit." Washington Post, March 28, 2001, E01.

Related Topics

Barlow, John Perry; Copyleft; Digital Millennium Copyright Act; Digital Music; Freenet (File-Sharing Network); Lessig, Lawrence; MP3; Peer-to-Peer; Stallman, Richard; Streaming Media

— Kevin Featherly

Customer Relationship Management

Customer relationship management (CRM) is an organizational approach to business where the most important asset is the consumer. This organizational method, driven by technology, uses software applications to create an intricate system of data, automation, and evaluation to aid companies by improving productivity and enhancing efficiency.

CRM is a term that describes any software application that manages information on a customer for many different uses. The data being managed by CRM systems is entered as customer contact information; it then becomes available for use by sales representatives and by customer service and marketing departments within a company.

Companies use CRM in order to improve business functionality and remain competitive. CRM software helps companies to understand and know their existing customers, as well as find new ones. The systems use a database to store information ranging from customer addresses and telephone numbers to their purchasing behaviors.

CRM systems range from simple to complex, varying with the amount of features employed by the software. They are able to track and record customer complaints and pinpoint problems with untimely sales. They are also able to determine the lifecycle of particular products and track individual consumer purchases. For example, CRM can measure the success or failure rates of direct-mail marketing techniques. CRM systems are capable of delivering valuable information that would otherwise be stored in the minds of company employees: For example, software can "remember" who buys what, and can offer that information to the entire staff via computer networks.

Depending on the CRM vendor and software, automation can also be implemented in service, sales, and marketing relations across computer networks and telephone systems. The software can automatically analyze data and provide managers with feedback on services and relationships with customers. For instance, CRM systems can send out mass mailings from a database that surveys consumers on purchasing interests. When consumers reveal what they are interested in through the questionnaire, the company can then prepare to meet the demand for a certain product for an upcoming holiday season.

Many CRM applications work to store information on customers in order for companies to be able to treat their clientele on a personal level. For example, a service representative can type a customer's name into a database to retrieve data on any previously filed complaints; while on the phone with the consumer, the representative can use this information to answer questions about the service. The many features of CRM software can help companies to simplify relationships with their customers, and offer an easier means of obtaining the necessary information for contacting them. The information managed by CRM software can also be used to organize, analyze, and predict the best match-up of resources to customers.

The technology still faces a few problems, however. First, the storage of personal information on CRM systems has sparked privacy concerns; in particular, the collection of credit-card numbers and contact information raises trepidation among consumers. A second problem deals with the many versions and vendors of CRM software. Since CRM retailers offer different features within different versions of their software, companies find it difficult to purchase CRM software packages that meet all of their needs. Even though the development of CRM software continues to advance into multifaceted suites, companies still need to work with different vendors to resolve all of their issues.

In the future, the capabilities of CRM will become more crucial to competition among industry players. The next step in CRM software development will include a tie to business-intelligent software, which remembers advanced information on the behavior of Web site visitors. Coupled with CRM, the business-intelligent software will allow companies to provide better customer service to online shoppers.

Bibliography

Black, Jane. "Tracking Customers While Preserving Their Anonymity." *BusinessWeek,* April 26, 2000. <http://www.businessweek.com/bwdaily/dnflash/ apr2001/nf20010426_926.htm> (May 17, 2002).

Singh, Arvind. "Customer Relationship Management: New Horizons for Institutional Banking." *US Banker* 109:10, (October 1999), pp. 79–82.

Songini, Marc. "Users: CRM Systems Require a Mixed Bag of Apps." *Computerworld*, April 20, 2001. <http://www.computerworld.com/softwaretopics/crm /story/0,10801,59857,00.html> (May 17, 2002).

Sweat, Jeff. "CRM Under Scrutiny." *Information Week* 804 (September 18, 2000), pp. 42–52.

Whiting, Rick. "Customers Come into Focus with Combination Software." *Information Week* 824 (February 12, 2001), p. 30.

Further Reading

Apicella, Mario. "A Rich Dollop of CRM." *InfoWorld.com*, August 10, 2001. <http://iwsun4.infoworld.com/articles/tc/xml/01/08/13/ 010813tcsforce.xml> (May 17, 2002).

Electronic Commerce Institute. "Leadership Montreal: When Memory Fails . . . CRM Systems Come to the Rescue!" Leadership Montreal. December 2000. <http://www.institut.qc.ca/english/articles/ leader_dec2000_en.html> (May 17, 2002).

Groenfeldt, Tom. "Customer Data, Right Here, Right Now." *US Banker* 110:5, (May 2000), pp. 73–7.

Lynch, Ian. "Banks Must Adopt CRM Systems or Die." *Vnunet.com*, April 17, 2001. <http://www.vnunet.com/Print/1120570> (May 17, 2002).

Related Topics
Data Mining; Digital Asset Management; E-Commerce; Knowledge Management

— *James Pyfer*

Cyberculture

As with many similar new words coined to deal with the expanding use and influence of computers, the exact definition of cyberculture varies. In some accounts, nearly any social phenomenon that somehow combines computers and culture might be referred to as cyberculture. Most frequently, however, cyberculture refers to cultures formed in or associated with online social spaces.

ORIGINS OF THE WORD

The prefix "cyber" comes from the word cybernetics. Norman Weiner created the modern definition of cybernetics in 1948 as "the science of control and communication in the animal and the machine." While Weiner is often credited with coining the term, the word cybernetics (from a similar Greek term meaning "steersmanship," or to steer or govern) appeared prior to his usage, and most notably was used by the French physicist André-Marie Ampère in the 1830s to describe the science of government. Modern cybernetic theory has been particularly concerned with artificial intelligence (computer programs that think and are self-aware), and with communication and control interfaces between humans and computers.

Interest in the relationship between humans and computers has led to the creation of various other words derived from cybernetics. The most familiar of these is probably cyborg, from *cybernetic organism*, which refers to an animal/computer hybrid. Examples of cyborgs in popular culture include Robocop and the Borg characters from *Star Trek*. Other words have been formed by combining the root "cyber" with commonplace words to add a computerized context. The resulting neologisms essentially drop the "steer," "govern," and "control" meanings contained in the word cybernetics, and refer merely to various types of computer-mediated social relationships.

The first of these words to enter popular usage, cyberspace, probably influenced the creation of the others. Cyberspace refers to the Internet and the World Wide Web, or to any similar shared interactive computer-mediated environment. The term was coined by science-fiction writer William Gibson, in his depictions of a future world in which people can immerse themselves in graphical representations of information. The use of the term cyberspace to refer to the Internet has led to a whole host of "cyber-" words to refer to activities that people engage in on the Internet, including cybersex, cyberdemocracy, etc. In this sense, cyberculture refers to the culture of cyberspace.

INTERNET CULTURE

There are so many different people from different countries, cultures, and subcultures who interact on the Internet that it doesn't really make sense to say that there is one single Internet culture. However, there are many cultural elements that originated online, and that continue to be widely known and used both online and offline. These include specialized terminology, patterns of language use, and standards of etiquette.

Terminology. In addition to words with a "cyber-" prefix, use of the Internet has generated a host of terms with an "e-" prefix. The "e" stands for electronic, and first appeared in the term email. In recent years, other words have followed, especially those referring to online transactions, such as e-commerce, e-business, and e-cash. As indicated by these examples, "e-" words tend to refer to the commercial end of the Internet, while "cyber-" words tend to refer to more social and cultural aspects.

While the proliferation of "e-" words was driven to some extent by the dot-com boom of the 1990s, when investment in and excitement about online businesses increased to a fever pitch, other cyberculture terms have arisen out of specifically online practices and experiences. Some examples include: spam, the Internet's equivalent of junk mail; newbie, referring to inexperienced Internet users; and flaming, the practice of posting or emailing a message that includes hostile language or is deliberately intended to provoke hostility.

Language Practice. In addition to specific new words coined by people interacting online, various practices of language use have emerged as well. Two of these have received considerable media attention: the use of emoticons and of online acronyms. Emoticons consist of simple ASCII characters arranged to approximate various facial expressions. One of the most basic consists of a colon for eyes, a hyphen for a nose, and a close parenthesis for a mouth—:-). This emoticon, the smiley, indicates humor or happiness.

Numerous Web pages, chapters in guidebooks, and a few entire books explain and define these symbols, and many humorous versions circulate widely online. Emoticons have been in use since the earliest days of networking, as a concise form for adding emotional nuance to the bare text of email and newsgroup posts. Many guides for the Internet suggest using emoticons to add clarity to email and group posts. However, among many long-term Internet users, the use of too many emoticons is considered frivolous, and marks one as a newbie.

Online acronyms have also been in use since the earliest computer networks, and were particularly popular among local BBS (bulletin board system) users prior to the wider availability of the Internet. Like emoticons, acronyms use a few keystrokes to convey as much meaning as possible. Some well-known examples include LOL (Laugh[ing] Out Loud), IMHO (In My Humble Opinion), YMMV (Your Mileage May Vary), and IRL (In Real Life). Among the earliest users of computer networks (including ARPANET, the Internet's precursor) were members of two subcultural groups notoriously fond of inventing acronyms: the military and computer programmers. The use of chat acronyms by these early online subcultures began a cultural practice that spread as other groups arrived on the Internet.

Netiquette. Netiquette (a contraction of "net" and "etiquette") consists of understood rules of online behavior. Many online forums such as newsgroups or listservs post specific rules, and many Web sites provide general online netiquette guidance. While standards differ from forum to forum, some practices have become widespread enough to be commonly accepted. For instance, writing in all capital letters is understood to indicate shouting, and should therefore usually be avoided. Other accepted rules include: Participants on a particular forum are expected to familiarize themselves with the conventions of that forum before posting messages; messages should be kept relatively short and to the point; posts responding to a previous post should include some of that post for context, but should not merely reproduce the entire earlier message; and people should not send "flame bait" messages, which seek to deliberately anger others.

CYBERCULTURAL INFLUENCES: HACKERS, CYBERPUNK, AND OTHER COMPUTER CULTURES

Like other cultures, the Internet has a history that continues to influence its present culture. While Internet demographics have been changing rapidly, the earliest users were predominantly white, middle-class males, often connected with academic computer-science departments. This group shaped many of the cultural conventions of and set a particular tone for the Internet. In particular, Internet culture has been influenced by hacker and other computer-related cultures. The disproportionately large number of libertarian political viewpoints expressed online reflects this, as do many of the language conventions discussed above. In addition, hackers place a high value on the free exchange of information, and often view this as the most important function of the Internet. This view has affected the direction of Internet development, and is evidenced by the conflicts that occur whenever any governmental entity attempts to limit Internet communications.

The influx of new and more diverse groups to the Internet has sometimes caused conflict with earlier users. One example is the infamous invasion of the USENET newsgroup rec.pets.cats. USENET is an online BBS, or electronic message center, which started in the earliest days of the Internet. Users could post messages to specific "newsgroups" based on topics of interest for thousands of others to read. One such group was devoted to information about caring for cats. In 1993, the participants in this group tended to differ demographically from those on many other USENET groups: They tended to be female, older, and newer to the Internet. Several participants on some USENET humor groups, primarily young males, began posting insulting and disgusting messages to rec.pets.cats implying harm to cats, eventually causing so much disruption that it became almost impossible to use the newsgroup for its original purpose. This incident, written up in *Wired* magazine and discussed extensively online, demonstrated, among other things, the vulnerability of online groups and the struggle to define cyberculture in the face of rapidly changing Internet demographics.

Tensions between newer and older users were also heightened when the online service provider America Online (AOL) enabled its users to connect to the Internet. Prior to that, a large proportion of Internet users connected from academic, government, or computer industry–related accounts. Although AOL was not the first online service provider to connect to the Internet, it had so many users that the influx of new people, particularly to USENET newsgroups, was immediately felt. In addition, because AOL had made a point of increasing its client base by being easy to use, the opinion of some of the more savvy computer users already on USENET was that AOL users were not as competent with computers and did not share the values then prevalent on the Internet. As a result, email addresses, which show up when a user posts a message to a USENET newsgroup, became a status marker. Users with an address ending in aol.com were more likely to be subjected to flames, or to other forms of dismissive or rude behavior.

Another important, historic Internet cultural event occurred after the 1996 passage of the Telecommunications Reform Act in the United States. Many Internet participants felt that this legislation threatened the continuance of the Internet as a venue for free speech, and violated the Internet's status as an emerging culture without a central governing authority. The act generated significant discussion online. In addition to lawsuits and lobbying campaigns offline, many people used their Web pages to display markers of protest against the act.

A significant literary influence on cyberculture has been the science fiction subgenre known as cyberpunk. This loosely defined subgenre includes works such as William Gibson's 1984 novel *Neuromancer*, which introduced the term cyberspace. Cyberpunk works tend to emphasize the role of computer technology in future society, and often depict human/computer couplings such as cyborgs or brain/computer interfaces. Even when depicted as potentially dangerous, these technological enhancements appear more desirable than the unenhanced human body, which tends to be denigrated as mere "meat." The term meatspace, sometimes used in online chat to designate face-to-face encounters, derives from this cyberpunk usage. Cyberpunk tends to be dark, dystopic, and graphically violent. Many computer programmers read and are influenced by cyberpunk, while developments in Internet technology and social practices also influence cyberpunk authors.

CYBERCULTURE'S INFLUENCE AND FUTURE

Just as offline cultures have influenced the development of the Internet, aspects of cyberculture have influenced offline culture as well. Offline media such as newspapers and magazines frequently publish articles about the Internet, disseminating information about Internet cultural practices. Numerous books provide guidance, information, commentary, and research results concerning online life. A few magazines not only report on the Internet, but also seek to embody its values and become part of cyberculture.

The most well-known of these magazines is *Wired*, which has greatly influenced the wider cultural understanding of cyberculture.

Changes in the Internet, especially in its demographics, continue to be rapid and significant. A "digital divide" still appears to exist between relatively wealthy Internet users and the economically disadvantaged who lack online access; but other online demographic gaps seem to be closing. Currently, women nearly equal men online, and the number of African-American users is rising dramatically. In addition, the United States no longer completely dominates the Internet, with more people around the world gaining access and bringing new influences to cyberculture.

Meanwhile, the increasing proliferation of hand-held wireless devices is creating at least a small subsection of more mobile online users. Use of "instant messaging" services is also increasing, especially among the young and in Scandinavian countries. As accessing cyberculture ceases to require sitting in front of a desktop computer, cyberculture may begin blending more rapidly with other cultures.

Bibliography

The Cyberpunk Project. <http://www.cyberpunkproject.org> (April 5, 2002).

Gibson, William. *Neuromancer.* New York: Ace Books, 1984.

Quittner, Josh. "The War between alt.tasteless and rec.pets.cats," *Wired*, May 1994. <http://www.wired.com/wired/archive/2.05/alt.tasteless_pr.html> (April 5, 2002).

Weiner, Norbert. *Cybernetics, or Control and Communication in the Animal and the Machine.* Cambridge, Mass.: MIT Press, 1948.

Further Reading

Cherny, Lynn, and Elizabeth Reba Weise, eds. *wired_women: Gender and New Realities in Cyberspace.* Seattle: Seal Press, 1996.

Coupland, Douglas. *Microserfs.* New York: ReganBooks, 1995.

Jones, Steven G., ed. *Cybersociety: Computer-Mediated Communication and Community.* Thousand Oaks, Calif.: Sage Publications, 1995.

Porter, David. *Internet Culture.* New York: Routledge, 1997.

Raymond, Eric. *The New Hacker's Dictionary.* Third ed. Cambridge, Mass.: MIT Press, 1996.

Sanderson, David, and Dale Dougherty. *Smileys.* Sebastopol, Calif.: O'Reilly & Associates, 1993.

Shea, Virginia. *Netiquette.* San Francisco: Albion Books, 1994.

Related Topics

Avatar; Chat; Cyberpunk; Cyberspace; Email; MUDs and MOOs; Netiquette; Spam; USENET; Virtual Community

— Lori Kendall

Cyberethics

Ethics is a set of moral principals that guide decision-making among people in a society, in a profession, or in a business; it is the thought process that helps people to determine what is right and wrong when they are forced to make a choice. In the digital age, computing has made certain kinds of moral decision-making more difficult than ever, precipitating a desire for the formation of new "computer ethics" or "cyberethics," and for the creation of a corresponding new field of academic study and research. Cyberethics is a complex discipline; its questions outdistance the moral problems and solutions outlined by ancient ethicists like Aristotle, and even those of more modern thinkers like David Hume or Immanuel Kant, because of its unique thinking man/thinking machine dynamic.

The topic of cyberethics is broad. Dartmouth College philosophy professor James H. Moor describes it as "the analysis of the nature and social impact of computer technology and the corresponding formulation and justification of policies for the ethical use of such technology." In other words, it means studying the right ways and the wrong ways for people to make choices when using computers. For Moor, targets of examination include not just computers themselves, but also the associated peripheral hardware and software. It includes the personal behavior of individuals and the behaviors of a computer-reliant society. He notes the truth behind the cliché that technology often outstrips the ability of ethics to keep pace, and describes a "policy vacuum" at the level of laws and social mores that could help determine how computing technologies should best be used. This social deficit, he says, is exacerbated by a "conceptual vacuum." What he means is that there is a serious problem with muddled thinking caused by the sheer complexities and sophistication of digital technology, complexities that even the most brilliant human minds cannot fully understand.

Deborah G. Johnson, professor of public policy at the Georgia Institute of Technology, gives a concrete example of such muddled thinking and its impact on computer ethics in her discussion of computer "hackers," those who use their computing skills to gain unauthorized access to computer systems and networks. Early in computing history, the popular attitude was that hacking was almost a humorous pursuit, a kind of practical joke. But in reality, Johnson asks,

how is hacking different than breaking the locks off an office door and rifling through someone's file cabinet?

Perhaps a better analogy would be setting fire to a mall after hours to demonstrate presumed flaws in its automatic sprinkler system. Would this also be acceptable? No one would be physically hurt in either case, although one might assume that the monetary and property damage would be greater in the case of the burned mall building. But that may be a false assumption, considering the costs of the massive denial-of-service attacks of early 2000, or of the destructive Internet "worms" like Code Red from the summer of 2001, which probably caused greater financial losses worldwide than the destruction of any brick-and-mortar store. Yet even today, Johnson notes, much of the technology press continues to treat hacking as more mischievous than criminal. Meanwhile, corporations hungry for computer security offer huge salaries to talented hackers who make their mark through high-profile public hacking incidents. Ethical standards seem indistinct.

Such is the nature of many of the ethical questions raised by technology—and not just in terms of the Internet. Technologies have also made it possible for humans to donate organs for transplant, to create human babies outside the body using new medical practices, and to subject human DNA to criminal investigations. Instantaneous global communication using fax machines, email, and telephones can be good, or they can increase human stress, according to Johnson. So where do we pin our values? "The possibilities created by new technologies need to be evaluated," Johnson writes. "Will they make life better or worse? Are the benefits to be gained worth the negative effects or risk of negative effects? Can we do something to ensure that a new technology develops with a minimum of negative effects?" These all are fundamental questions of cyberethics.

Computers take such questions to new levels of difficulty compared to traditional, philosophical ethics. For all the good that computers have caused—enabling space travel, building new online communities, simplifying personal records keeping—it is also possible to point out ways in which they have created or increased moral lapses. Computers mean that authorities can track and monitor citizens without their knowledge on a scale never before imagined, and it is sometimes questionable whether authorities should have so much latitude. Also, computers can help create ever more heinous weapons. They can eliminate the need for human contact. They can lead to new forms of theft, some of which may take place deep in arcane bank databases and be all but undetectable. Other forms of stealing, as in the case of music-swapping Internet services like Napster, Grokster, and AudioGalaxy, may or may not even be genuine forms of theft. At the very least, many of those engaged in swapping copyrighted music, software, and movies for free on such peer-to-peer Internet systems do not consider their own behavior unethical.

Beyond these issues, computers can lead companies to sell information about the online keyword-search activities of Web surfers; the search patterns of medical site visitors, for instance, might be sold to insurance companies or prospective employers who might want to weed sick people from their rolls. Perhaps most troubling is the fact that computers often make what Moor calls "invisible calculations." For instance, computers are largely in control of national missile-defense systems, and through their invisible calculations, they have the capacity to make "decisions" about whether a nuclear attack should be launched against national enemies, based on various internally processed data with minimal or no human input.

Such situations call for a solid code of conduct to set specific boundaries for behavior among computer programmers and the professionals who utilize computing technologies, attorney Joel Rothstein Wolfson noted in his white paper, "A Conduct Code: An Ethics Code With Bite." Published in *The Journal of Computing and Society* in 1991, his paper provided a model for one such code of conduct, and others have followed. Perhaps most notable among them is the Code of Ethics of the Association of Computing Machinery (ACM), adopted in 1992. It takes foremost into account human well-being, and the potential for computing technology to cause people harm. "Computing professionals who design and develop systems must be alert to, and make others aware of, any potential damage to the local or global environment," the ACM code states. This means that steps must be taken to mitigate problems even when well-intended actions have harmful side effects. Computing professionals must minimize malfunctions by following generally accepted standards for system design and testing, the code says.

Many writers have made the point that machines, even computers, do not independently think, do not make moral judgments, and therefore are themselves value-neutral. In the case of computers, it is often argued that without a human at the helm making underlying judgments for them, there is no subjective morality, no

ethics in play. However, whether morally neutral or not, there are serious ethical implications to much computer technology. "As our society changes," wrote Oregon State University philosophy professor Michael Scanlan in 1995, "the face of ethical decision making changes."

Scanlan argues that large computer systems are here to stay, and that it is up to the societies using them to tackle ethical questions on a case-by-case basis. Some massive computing systems, like those that have the sole function of protecting airline safety, do not pose serious ethical challenges. Others, like computerized criminal-records databases, need to be examined, and consensus on how they can be used must be achieved. In any case, the ethical problems posed are in the hands of those who design and use the systems; they are issues of human ethics, not of "computer ethics."

The ethical problems inherent in widespread computer use have led some academics—Moor for instance—to visualize a moratorium on all further advances in computing technology until we catch up in our ethical thinking. Others, like author David Brin, suggest that we should just get used to the idea that, owing to computers, such luxuries as privacy are relics of the past; we simply must learn to live with the notion that all computerized data is part of the fiber of public life, whether it is personal or impersonal data. At the same time, he calls on society to demand what he calls "reciprocal transparency," giving all citizens the right to know who is watching them and for what purpose—in effect, to allow them to "watch the watchers."

In recent years, a primary response to computer ethics issues has been to initiate educational programs aimed at guiding young people—those who currently are most prone to "mischievous" use of computer technology, and who will one day control the computer ethics of the future. The idea is to teach kids now about moral standards of interacting with people and computers, on the Internet and on private networks. In 1999, for instance, the U.S. Department of Justice, in association with the Information Technology Association of America, launched the Cyber Citizen Partnership Web site, which is meant to outline ethical guidelines for online behavior for parents, teachers, and kids. Similarly, Marymount University assembled a conference in Arlington, Virginia, in October 2000, aimed at coaching parents and teachers to pass on ethical values to kids regarding the use of the Internet.

But new and even greater cyberethics issues may be just around the corner, centering on emerging artificial intelligence (AI) technologies. Some scientists have warned (or, depending on their viewpoint, have promised) that AI will one day exceed human intelligence. Artificially intelligent robots—in essence, walking computers with brains—will no longer be the stuff of pure science fiction. When they emerge, how will they be dealt with ethically? Will they be accorded the same, similar, or none of the rights of humans?

A framework may already be in place, provided by the science-fiction writer Isaac Asimov in his 1950 short-story collection *I Robot*. In that work, fictional robots were programmed to function under three primary laws—in effect, their own code of ethics: "1. A robot may not injure a human being, or, through inaction, allow a human being to come to harm. 2. A robot must obey the orders given it by human beings except where such orders would conflict with the First Law. 3. A robot must protect its own existence as long as such protection does not conflict with the First or Second Law."

While they may not stem specifically from Asimov, much of the debate about AI focuses on whether artificially intelligent, sentient machines would in fact find it in their best interest to obey the first two laws, or to factor in humans when obeying the third law. Marvin Minsky, the father of AI, helped filmmaker Stanley Kubrick fashion an AI computer that found it necessary to break the first two in the landmark film *2001: A Space Odyssey*. And Sun Microsystems chief scientist Bill Joy has raised many questions with his assertions that AI technology, along with robotics and microscopic nanotechnology, promises to cause tremendous, if not fatal, harm to mankind: "I think it is no exaggeration to say we are on the cusp of the further perfection of extreme evil," Joy wrote in his April 2000 *Wired* magazine essay, "Why the Future Doesn't Need Us." "[It's] an evil whose possibility spreads well beyond that which weapons of mass destruction bequeathed to the nation-states, on to a surprising and terrible empowerment of extreme individuals."

New technologies often raise moral concerns, and it is clear that the ethical implications of any new technologies need to be examined with tremendous care. The introduction of computers in society has created possibilities for questionable behavior by individuals and institutions that were impossible in the past. Computers, like other technologies, create potentially undesirable as well as desirable possibilities, and must be evaluated morally and ethically.

Bibliography

Brin, David. *The Transparent Society*. Reading, Mass.: Addison-Wesley, 1998.

Johnson, Deborah G. *Computer Ethics*. Second edition. Englewood Cliffs, N.J.: Prentice Hall, 1994.

Joy, Bill. "Why the Future Doesn't Need Us." *Wired* 8.04, April 2000. <http://www.wired.com/wired/archive/8.04/joy.html> (May 17, 2002).

Keegan, Daniel. "Should Cyber Ethics Be Taught At School?" *CNN.com*, May 9, 2000. <http://www.cnn.com/2000/TECH/computing/05/09/cyber.ethic.conference.idg/index.html> (May 17, 2002).

Marymount University, Arlington, Va. "National Conference on Cyber Ethics: Teaching Responsible Use of Technology." October 6–8, 2000. <http://www.marymount.edu/ethics/cyberethics/cyberethics2.html#2> (May 17, 2002).

Moor, James H. "If Aristotle Were a Computing Professional." *Computers and Society*, September 1998, pp. 13–26. Republished in *Cyberethics: Social and Moral Issues in the Computer Age*. Robert M. Baird, Reagan Ramsower, and Stuart E. Rosenbaum, eds. Amherst, N.Y.: Prometheus Books, 2000.

———. "What Is Computer Ethics?" *Metaphilosophy*, vol. 16, no. 4 (1985), pp. 23–33. Republished in *Cyberethics: Social and Moral Issues in the Computer Age*. Robert M. Baird, Reagan Ramsower, and Stuart E. Rosenbaum, eds. Amherst, N.Y.: Prometheus Books, 2000.

Saunders, Laverna M., University of Nevada, Las Vegas. "Ethics in Cyberspace." CPSR.org, May 22, 1994. <http://www.cpsr.org/program/ethics/ethics.cyberspace.saunders> (May 17, 2002).

Scanlan, Michael. "Does Computer Ethics Compute?" *Reflections: The Newsletter for the Program for Ethics Science and the Environment*, vol. 2, no. 1 (1995). Reprinted in *Cyberethics: Social and Moral Issues in the Computer Age*. Robert M. Baird, Reagan Ramsower, and Stuart E. Rosenbaum, eds. Amherst, N.Y.: Prometheus Books, 2000.

Further Reading

Kahn, Jeremy, and Feliciano Garcia. "Presto Chango! Sales are Huge!" *Fortune*, March 20, 2000.

Lehman, DeWayne, Computerworld Online. "Consortium Pushes Net Ethics." *PCWorld.com*, April 5, 2000. <http://www.pcworld.com/news/article/0,aid,16056,00.asp> (May 17, 2002).

Mason, Richard O. "Four Ethical Issues for the Information Age." *Management Information Systems Quarterly*, vol. 10, no. 1 (March 1986), pp. 5–12.

Spinello, Richard A. *Cyberethics: Morality and Law in Cyperspace*. Boston: Jones and Bartlett, 2000.

Useem, Jerry. "New Ethics or No Ethics?" *Fortune*, March 20, 2000.

Zetter, Kim. "Freeze! Drop That Download!" *PCWorld.com*, November 16, 2000.

<http://www.pcworld.com/features/article/0,aid,34406,pg,1,00.asp> (May 17, 2002).

Related Topics

Anonymity; Child Online Protection Act and Child Online Privacy Protection Act; Communications Decency Act; Content Filtering; Copyright; Cyberculture; Cyberwarfare; Digital Millennium Copyright Act; Electronic Civil Disobedience; Electronic Communications Privacy Act; Hacking, Cracking, and Phreaking; Joy, Bill; Minsky, Marvin; Technological Determinism; *2600: The Hacker Quarterly*

— *Kevin Featherly*

Cyberfeminism

Cyberfeminism is a term coined in 1994 by Sadie Plant, director of the Cybernetic Culture Research Unit at the University of Warwick in Britain, to describe the work of feminists interested in theorizing, critiquing, and exploiting the Internet, cyberspace, and new-media technologies in general. The term and movement grew out of "third-wave" feminism, the contemporary feminist movement that follows the "second-wave" feminism of the 1970s, which focused on equal rights for women, and which itself followed the "first-wave" feminism of the early 20th century, which concentrated on woman suffrage. Cyberfeminism has tended to include mostly younger, technologically savvy women, and those from Western, white, middle-class backgrounds. The ranks of cyberfeminists are growing, however, and along with this increase is a growing divergence of ideas about what constitutes cyberfeminist thought and action.

Prior to the advent of cyberfeminism, feminist study of technology tended to examine technological developments as socially and culturally constructed. One major argument was that technology has been positioned as part of masculine culture—something that men are interested in, good at, and therefore engage in more than women. Even though women throughout history have been active in developing new technologies, feminists have argued that technology has still been looked upon as a masculine creation. For example, although women had been involved in the creation and development of the computer, their contributions were largely marginalized, and their participation often ignored or written out of history. Therefore, feminists such as Judy Wacjman, a professor of sociology at the Australian National University in Canberra, and Cynthia Cockburn, an independent scholar and activist in London, argued that technology needed to be continually interrogated and re-conceptualized, and that women needed to become more active in technological areas as well.

Also pointing the way for cyberfeminism was the work of Donna Haraway, a professor in the History of Consciousness program at the University of California at Santa Cruz. In her groundbreaking essay "A Manifesto for Cyborgs," she argues for a socialist, feminist cyborg that challenges the singular identities and "grids of control" that work to contain women and other marginalized groups. Haraway agreed that women needed to become more technologically proficient, better able to engage with the "informatics of domination" and challenge these systems. But Haraway also and importantly argued that women would need to be savvy and politically aware users of these technological systems; simply using them was not enough.

From these beginnings, cyberfeminism began to develop. Plant, an important early proponent, has argued that women are naturally suited to using the Internet, because women and the Internet are similar in nature—both, according to Plant, are non-linear, self-replicating systems concerned with making connections. She has argued that although previous feminists have believed computers to be essentially male, we should instead see computers and the Internet as places for women to engage in new forms of work and play—where women are freed from traditional constraints and are able to experiment with identity and gain new avenues for claiming power and authority. Her view of cyberspace is as a welcoming, familiar space for women, where they can and must seize opportunities to advance themselves and to challenge male authority.

Some younger feminists active on the Internet, while they do not identify with theoretical arguments about masculinity or the similarities between women and computers, also see the Internet as a vital space for women to "claim their territory," and use the technology to gain power and authority in contemporary society. Some women in this group would reject the label "feminist" altogether, but would still see the Internet as a vital tool or space for women to learn about and engage with. To advance these ends, individuals and groups have created Web sites, discussion groups, and other online resources for women interested in learning more about Internet technologies, and also for women already employed in information technology areas. These groups believe that empowerment for women can be achieved through women's greater knowledge of new-media technologies, and through the creation of more opportunities to advance in these lines of work.

Another branch of cyberfeminism argues that the idea of women gaining power and authority merely through greater use of new-media technologies is overly simplistic or reductive. Australian feminist scholars, such as Susan Luckman of the University of Queensland and Anna Munster of the University of New South Wales, believe that this approach reduces complex technological systems into mere tools and ignores their historical contexts of production and use. They believe that technologies are embedded in structures of power, which are not always positive. In their opinion, calls for women and girls to uncritically take up and advance the use of these new technologies does nothing to critically assess technology's larger role in culture, and how we wish to see technology develop—or not. Women must be part of this future, not by simply advocating for more women to engage in using technology, but by becoming more critically aware of the perils as well as promises that new technologies offer.

Other critiques of earlier cyberfeminist work suggest that the call for more women to engage with new technologies is based on mistaken assumptions about real living conditions. Simply put, all women do not have access to computers and the Internet, and likely will not in the foreseeable future; cyberfeminists who make the simple declaration that "all girls need modems" are ignoring the conditions of those who do not share their privileged middle-class, Western (and often white) background. Women's material conditions must be taken into account when considering how best to advance feminist ideas, online or otherwise.

Beyond the root idea that gender equity, particularly in new-media technologies, is a desired goal, cyberfeminism itself, a growing area of thought and study, is not a unified set of ideas concerning women and new technologies. Cyberfeminists explore many areas of theory: that women are naturally suited to using the Internet, as both share important commonalities; that women can best empower themselves by becoming fluent in online communication and acquiring technological expertise; and that women would do best to study how power and knowledge are constructed in technological systems, and how and where feminists can disrupt and change these practices for the betterment of all members of society.

Bibliography

Haraway, Donna. *Modest_Witness@Second_Millennium. FemaleMan©_Meets_OncoMouse™: Feminism and Technoscience.* New York: Routledge, 1997.

Luckman, Susan. "(En) gendering the Digital Body: Feminism and the Internet." *Hecate*, 25:2 (1999), pp. 36–48.

Munster, Anna. "Is There Postlife After Postfeminism? Tropes of Technics and Life in Cyberfeminism." *Australian Feminist Studies,* 14:29 (April 1999), pp. 119–131.

Plant, Sadie. "Babes in the Net." *New Statesman & Society,* January 27, 1997, p. 28.

Spender, Dale. *Nattering on the Net: Women, Power and Cyberspace.* North Melbourne, Victoria: Spinifex Press, 1995.

Further Reading

Haraway, Donna. *Modest_Witness@Second_Millennium. FemaleMan©_Meets_OncoMouse™: Feminism and Technoscience.* New York: Routledge, 1997.

Millar, Melanie Stewart. *Cracking the Gender Code: Who Rules the Wired World?* Toronto: Second Story Press, 1998.

Plant, Sadie. *Zeros + Ones: Digital Women + the New Technoculture.* London: Fourth Estate, 1997.

Related Topics

Cyborg; Gender and New Media; Haraway, Donna J.; Laurel, Brenda; World Wide Web

— *Mia Consalvo*

Cyberpunk

The literary genre called *cyberpunk*, which is most closely aligned with science fiction, arose in the early 1980s. It was popularized by what remains its defining work, William Gibson's 1984 novel *Neuromancer*, although it was also given a visual reference point in the 1985 film *Blade Runner,* which in turn influenced the genre's novelists. The word also has come to be associated with a "hacker/phreak" subculture whose participants related their own lives to those of the literary genre's characters, and who appropriated its trappings and anarcho-tech attitude. But the term remains most closely associated with the literary form.

Cyberpunk's name contains the germ of its definition. The "cyber-" prefix derives from cybernetics, the science of communication and control in animal and machine, and reveals the literary movement's permeating technological underpinnings. The "-punk" suffix—

borrowed from the radical, do-it-yourself rock-music movement of the late 1970s—describes the anarchistic alienation of most of the genre's main characters, usually outcasts populating a decadent, technology-dominated society.

However, unlike the characters of previous works like Aldous Huxley's *Brave New World* or George Orwell's *1984*, or even Arthur C. Clarke's more tech-tolerant *2001: A Space Odyssey*, cyberpunk characterizations do not involve cautionary tales to illuminate the modern reader. In the near future of cyberpunk, a world of virtual sex and smart drugs and the bodiless "matrix," it's simply too late to moralize; permeating technology has already been accepted permanently as part of everyday life, even if it's often a dreadful part of it. Cyberpunk characters accept the technology on its own terms, and are simply "going along for the ride," as one author put it. To use Gibson's famous phrase, "The street has its own uses for technology."

Gibson, while providing the genre's foundation in *Neuromancer*, was not its founder. The term cyberpunk was actually coined by writer Bruce Bethke, who used it as the title of a short story that appeared in the pulp publication *Amazing Science Fiction Stories* in November 1983. The story itself dealt with a group of teen-age hacker-crackers (as would a 1991 non-fiction work titled *Cyberpunk* by Katie Hafner and John Markoff). Bethke says he coined the term in the spring of 1980 to describe the "bizarre, hard-edged, high-tech" science fiction that was emerging in the early 1980s.

William Gibson was one of the first writers of that kind of new fiction. In 1981, three years before *Neuromancer*, he published a seminal short story called "The Gernsback Continuum." It ridicules the utopian visions of much past science fiction, and incites future writers to begin addressing the ambivalent feelings of a society where technology is both intimate and invasive, where the haves and have-nots must battle for control of a new, digital world. Even more than *Neuromancer*, some critics consider this short story to be the real blueprint for cyberpunk to come.

Meanwhile, in Houston, Texas, writer Bruce Sterling began publishing a one-page fanzine called *Cheap Truth,* published between 1983 and 1986. In essence, it was the voice of the cyberpunk critic—although, tellingly, the word *cyberpunk* rarely appears in its pages, and even when it did, it was usually an insult; some of its critics denied cyberpunk

even existed. According to a cyberpunk history by author Tom Maddox (himself a former *Cheap Truth* contributor), all the fanzine's articles were written under pseudonyms; in the aggregate, he wrote, they all "amounted to guerilla raids" on standard science fiction. The publication, which intentionally was never copyrighted, also served to make cyberpunk's writers aware of one another and of each other's works, thus helping to congeal a community of cyberpunk authors. *Neuromancer* appeared a year after the first issue of the fanzine.

In *Neuromancer*, and in subsequent works like *Count Zero* and *Mona Lisa Overdrive*, Gibson's gritty, Raymond Chandler-like narrative helped set the tone of all cyberpunk. It established the device of a near-future world where data cowboys "jack into" cyberspace (a term Gibson coined in *Neuromancer*). They exist in a world where a ruined environment is all but irrelevant, and where human bodies are considered mere "meat" compared with the hallucinatory experience of exploring the data-fattened "matrix." Protagonists are rockers, hackers, rebels clinging to their individuality in the face of an increasingly conformist and corporation-dominated culture. They excel at using the high-tech tools of control to satisfy their own ends, and they can fire back with their own forms of resistance at vast corporations, using the same technologies relied on by the corporations themselves to maintain their societal command—for example, by tapping into vast wells of shielded corporate data.

Also, in most cyberpunk fiction, the main characters are in some ways a rebellious update on the "rugged individualist" theme of 1950s John Wayne movies; conversely, however, the form also is often characterized by a breakdown of individual identity in the face of pervasive, powerful, personal digital media. As critic H.J. notes, that loss can take the form of self-stylings like the "glo worms" in James Patrick Kelly's *Solstice* who inject luminous paint into their skin. Or it can be represented in the military-industrial takeover of workers' bodies, as in Tom Maddox's "Snake Eyes." In *Neuromancer*, consciousness can be uploaded and digitally stored, allowing a mind to live on without its body, possibly forever. Other writers of importance who emerged to follow these patterns included Bruce Sterling, Rudy Rucker, John Shirley, Lewis Shiner, and Neal Stephenson.

A key moment in the history of cyberpunk took place when Bruce Sterling published *Mirrorshades: The Cyberpunk Anthology* in 1986, a book that helped to crystallize the genre and define its boundaries. In his introduction to the book, Sterling argued that cyberpunk described new cultural perspectives on technology among consumers as much as sci-fi writers. In fact, as Sterling wrote, the genre imagined an "overlapping of worlds that were formally separate: the realm of high tech and the modern pop underground."

That might also have been the movement's high-water mark. According to one claim, there were never more than 100 "pure" cyberpunks writing at any one time before the term achieved mainstream status after the success of *Neuromancer* and the arrival of the Ridley Scott film *Blade Runner*. While cyberpunk writers continued to produce important works, one of the last being Stephenson's 1992 *Snow Crash*, mass-media status invited others to co-opt the form. Even mainstream writers like Michael Crichton began to cautiously introduce elements of cyberpunk to their books. Much like the punk-rock music movement before it, relative success in cyberpunk literature resulted in a dilution of the real thing. Writers like Sterling and Gibson continued to release new novels, some with pronounced cyberpunk stylings, but none would have the impact of their 1980s work.

By September 1993, *Wired* magazine was pronouncing "pure" cyberpunk dead. But in writing its obituary, Paul Saffo, then a research fellow at the Institute for the Future in Menlo Park, California, compared the cyberpunk authors' impact to that of the 1950s "beat generation" writers like William Burroughs, Jack Kerouac, and others, casting them as harbingers of a mass movement waiting in the wings. Just as the hippy movement followed the closing of the beatnik era by about 10 years, Saffo projected that some form of underground mass movement—he guessed they might be called "tekkies"—is likely to emerge at some point in the future. Eight years after his prediction, there is little indication that Saffo is correct on the cultural side. But cyberpunk style continues to have a distinct influence on futuristic fiction.

Long after the height of the cyberpunk movement, the genre retains continuing power, mostly because the intimate, personal technology it forecast in the near-future of the 1980s has begun to arrive in the form of Internet-connected personal digital assistants, Net-enabled wireless phones, and the continuous tracking of personal data by Internet firms like DoubleClick. While these devices are being adopted without regret by the masses a little more each day, the uneasiness remains in many quarters. Bill Joy's monumental 2000 *Wired* magazine article, "Why the Future Doesn't Need Us," is not a work of fiction; it is intended to be a genuine warning about the impact of biotechnology, nanotechnology, and other developments that were the subjects of cyberpunk fiction 15 years earlier. Had it not been intended as a real-life red flag, Joy's article could have served as an outline for the next great cyberpunk novel.

Bibliography

Bonner, Patrick A. "The Style that Defines Cyberpunk." September 30, 1995. <http://www.cwrl.utexas.edu/~tonya/cyberpunk/papers/bonner1.html> (April 5, 2002).

Jones, Steve. "Hyper-punk: Cyberpunk and Information Technology." *Journal of Popular Culture*, 28:2 (Fall 1994), pp. 81–92.

Möttönen, Sari. "About a Science Fiction Movement Called Cyberpunk." *Nettiset Webzine,* February 1997. <http://www.cc.jyu.fi/jyucomm/nettiset/ns001/juttu010.html> (April 5, 2002).

Sterling, Bruce. "Cyberpunk in the Nineties." 1998. <http://www.streettech.com/bcp/BCPtext/Manifestos/CPInThe90s.html> (April 5, 2002).

Further Reading

Gibson, William. *Count Zero*. New York: Ace Books, 1986.
———. "The Gernsback Continuum." *Mirrorshades: The Cyberpunk Anthology*. Bruce Sterling, ed. New York: Arbor House, 1986; pp. 1–11.
———. *Mona Lisa Overdrive*. New York: Bantam Books, 1988.
———. *Neuromancer*. New York: Ace Books, 1984.
Maddox, Tom. "Snake Eyes." *Mirrorshades: The Cyberpunk Anthology*. Bruce Sterling, ed. New York: Arbor House, 1986; pp. 12–33.
Rucker, Rudy. *Software*. New York: Avon Books, 1982.
Shirley, John. "Freezone." *Mirrorshades: The Cyberpunk Anthology*. Bruce Sterling, ed. New York: Arbor House, 1986; pp. 139–177.
Stephenson, Neal. *Snow Crash*. New York: Bantam Books, 1992.
Sterling, Bruce, ed. *Cheap Truth*. 1983–86. Republished at <http://bush.cs.tamu.edu/~erich/cheaptruth/> (April 5, 2002).
———. *Crystal Express*. New York: Ace Books, 1989.
———. *Islands in the Net*. New York: Ace Books, 1989.
———. *Schismatrix*. New York: Ace Books, 1985.

Related Topics

Cyberculture; Cyberspace; Cyberwarfare; Hacking, Cracking, and Phreaking; Joy, Bill; *Neuromancer; The New Hacker's Dictionary;* Sterling, Bruce; *2600: The Hacker Quarterly;* Virtual Reality

— *Kevin Featherly*

Cyberspace

In its most common current usage, cyberspace refers to the Internet and the World Wide Web, or to any similar shared, interactive, computer-mediated environment. The term was coined by science-fiction writer William Gibson in his fictional depictions of a future world in which people could immerse themselves in graphical representations of information contained in computers. The prefix "cyber" comes from the word cybernetics, a term that since the 1940s has referred to, among other things, interconnections and similarities between humans and computers.

HISTORY OF THE TERM

Early uses of the term cyberspace referred primarily to immersive, multi-person, three-dimensional virtual-reality systems. In such systems, complex technological interfaces enable the computer to create feedback for the user, creating the illusion that the user is moving through and interacting with an artificial environment. For instance, in virtual-reality games—one of the more common applications of virtual-reality technology—users don interface equipment, usually consisting of a helmet and a glove. The helmet projects three-dimensional visuals, while the glove enables the user to navigate (flying by pointing, for instance) and to pick up and manipulate virtual objects. Cyberspace was originally envisioned as a virtual reality similar to this, in which many people could simultaneously interact with the system and with each other.

More recently, however, the term has become so broadly used within popular culture that it now applies to nearly any form of computer-mediated communication. Cyberspace refers metaphorically to social and informational connections created by computers. People are said to be "in cyberspace" when they engage in such activities as browsing the World Wide Web, writing email, chatting with others through text online, etc. (Some have suggested that we are also in cyberspace when we talk on the phone, since a computer-mediated connection enables a conversation occurring in a non-physical "space.")

The prefix "cyber," as mentioned earlier, comes from the word cybernetics. Norman Weiner created the modern definition of cybernetics in 1948 as "the science of control and communication in the animal and the machine." While Weiner is often credited with coining the term, the word cybernetics (from a similar Greek term meaning "steersmanship," or to steer or govern) appeared prior to his usage, and most notably was used in the 1830s by the French physicist André-Marie Ampère to describe the science of government. Modern cybernetic theory has been particularly concerned with artificial intelligence (computer programs that think and are self-aware) and with communication and control interfaces between humans and computers.

William Gibson coined the term cyberspace in his 1984 novel *Neuromancer*. (The term actually appears briefly in his earlier short story *Burning Chrome,* but in that story Gibson mainly uses the term "matrix" to refer to what he eventually calls cyberspace in the trilogy of novels that begins with *Neuromancer*.) Gibson envisioned a virtual realm, accessed through direct brain-to-computer connections, in which users could navigate among quasi-physical graphical representations of computer data. Gibson's cyberspace was generated through some unspecified interaction between multiple overlapping and interconnected computer programs and the many computer users connecting to them. One significant difference between Gibson's cyberspace and existing virtual reality and similar programs is that in a virtual reality program, every graphical representation must be programmed and projected to the human user. Gibson's cyberspace was spontaneously generated through the direct brain connections to the computers. At one point, Gibson describes it as "a consensual hallucination."

Gibson's cyberspace was populated by legitimate business users utilizing futuristic three-dimensional versions of spreadsheet programs; students engaged in educational activities; sophisticated computer intelligences (called AIs, or Artificial Intelligences) with mysterious agendas of their own; and outlaw "cyberspace cowboys" who used computer programs in cyberspace to steal others' data or make illegal fund transfers. Gibson's protagonists fall in the latter group, and the ability of these "cybernetic second-story men" (as they are referred to in *Burning Chrome*) to manipulate cyberspace to their own ends drives much of the plot in these stories.

THE MEANING OF CYBERSPACE

While Gibson's vision, both of cyberspace and of the future in general, was decidedly dystopic and dangerous, the concept of cyberspace represented a positive vision for most computer and virtual-reality designers who initially adopted the term. Along with Vernor Vinge's 1987 science-fiction short-story collection *True Names . . . and Other Dangers* and Neal Stephenson's 1992 *Snow Crash*, Gibson's work greatly influenced designers of virtual-reality systems, computer games, and online graphical chat spaces, and has also affected many other areas of computer and media design. Many in the computer industry feel that such interactive and immersive uses of computers represent the ultimate realization of the potential of computer technology in society.

Discussions of cyberspace in mainstream media have been mixed. Popular press accounts have included on the one hand tremendously overblown hype concerning a utopian disembodied future lived in ideal virtual environments, and on the other hand dire warnings about the increasing dehumanization and isolation of computer-addicted human beings.

As depicted in popular media, the best-case scenario of cyberspace represents a step forward in human evolution. Because it theoretically enables human beings to leave their bodies behind while interacting with each other, some feel that we would also be able to leave behind such social problems as sexism and racism. A few have even predicted that people will eventually be able to "download" their minds into computers prior to death, achieving a kind of immortality. Other accounts have suggested that the environment will benefit as commerce and business are increasingly conducted online, as fewer people commute to work or drive to the shopping mall.

While some early media accounts thus viewed cyberspace as an unmitigated technological advance, others depicted it as a dangerous place that could change people for the worse. Some stories focused on accounts of actual Internet activities, such as harassment of women online or the sexual predation of children. Others suggested that the more people used computers, especially for social contact, the more isolated and solipsistic they would become.

These polarized accounts also fueled considerable debate online concerning both the future of computers and the Internet and the usefulness of the term cyberspace itself. Some of the earliest online participants envisioned the Internet and virtual reality as a new frontier, a new kind of place to be inhabited, with new rules and ways of being. One example of this view is contained in John Perry Barlow's well-known document *A Cyberspace Independence Declaration*. Barlow wrote this diatribe in response to the 1996 U.S. Telecommunications Reform Act legislation, which, in part, attempted to regulate and suppress certain types of online communication. In his *Declaration*, Barlow characterized cyberspace as a domain separate from previously existing governments, populated by people with no bodies, creating a "civilization of the mind." Barlow's depiction thus echoed the utopian views of cyberspace as a new and potentially better kind of human society.

However, some people, especially those who were users of the Internet (and its predecessor, the ARPANET) before the word cyberspace existed, felt that the term misrepresented what occurs online. They disagreed with the idea of cyberspace as a separate realm of disembodied people, and were more likely to see the Internet as a communications or computational tool. Some long-term Internet users also reacted to the increase in media attention—and the subsequent influx of newbies, or new Internet users—with the suspicion of those whose elite subculture has just gone mainstream. For them, the word cyberculture represented misguided and misinformed hype promoted by people who did not really understand computers and their possibilities and limitations.

As researchers began studying people's online behavior, a more nuanced and less technologically determinist view of cyberspace emerged. Researchers have found that social problems such as sexism and racism do not disappear online. Furthermore, potential environmental benefits of the Internet are mitigated by the environmental costs involved in the extremely toxic manufacture of computer equipment, as well as by the mass disposal of that equipment as technological advances rapidly render computers obsolete. On the other hand, the Internet does enable real social connections between people. Although some well-publicized research suggests that increasing Internet use can cause isolation and depression, other research shows that use of the Internet enhances and even increases other forms of social contact.

THE FUTURE OF CYBERSPACE

We are a long way from realizing anything like the cyberspace Gibson envisioned. That cyberspace would include a three-dimensional graphical representation of space, including objects and people, as well as the ability for individual users to "move" through this space, interacting with the objects and other people using all of their physical senses. Activities in such a cyberspace might resemble many of the things people do on the Internet today, but in a more immersive and sensual form. For instance, theorists have envisioned a cyberspace where people could visit a virtual art gallery, walking through halls and discussing the art with other people they encounter; or perhaps they could take a class in organic chemistry, in which three-dimensional models of molecules could be manipulated and discussed by class members.

Some limited versions of these environments exist. For instance, some virtual-reality gaming systems allow more than one person to play, and enable multiple players to communicate with each other. There have also been virtual walk-throughs of architectural models, which allow an architect and a client to jointly survey a planned building. However, a fully realized multi-person cyberspace would require immense computational and telecommunications resources to calculate and transmit the necessary graphics, tactile feedback, information, and communications. It would also require an extremely sophisticated and sensitive human/computer interface, allowing for audio-visual transmission and reception as well as tactile feedback. Immense amounts of programming would also be necessary to render the graphics and enable interactions between objects and people.

Programmers, engineers, and designers are working on technologies that might become components of such a system. Computers continue to increase in power, a necessary requirement to handle the computations involved in creating interactive graphical representations of data and people. Improvements in data transmission are also increasing the bandwidth (or rate of data transmitted per second) available, and increasingly fast Internet connections are becoming available to more and more people. While the popularity of virtual-reality gaming systems has waned, designers continue to work on scientific, military, and medical applications for virtual reality, although most such systems involve only one person and cannot be accessed over the Internet.

Online, people continue to build social connections and find new ways to enhance their lives using computers. Most online socializing still occurs through text, sometimes augmented by still photos or graphics (as on personal Web pages). However, various graphical chat spaces currently provide a limited form of interactive cyberspace (avatars).

Most people still interface with their computers through keyboards, mice, and screen icons. However, designers continue to experiment, and have had some success with voice-command interfaces. Recently, medical engineers have even developed direct brain/computer interfaces, in one case to enable communications and computer-use capabilities in a stroke victim, and in another to provide a visual prosthesis for a blind person, using a video camera and a computer.

These components may never come together to create a fully networked virtual world. But in the meantime, the word cyberspace continues to describe existing computer-mediated interactions. While other terms are in use to refer to the Internet—matrix, information highway, the 'Net—for the moment, cyberspace appears to be the most popular. The ability of the word to metaphorically evoke visions of potential new worlds and connections continues to appeal both to people using computers and the Internet and to those developing new technologies for such use.

Bibliography

Barlow, John Perry. *A Cyberspace Independence Declaration.*
<http://www.eff.org/pub/Misc/Publications/John_Perry_ Barlow/barlow_0296.declaration> (April 5, 2002).

Gibson, William. *Burning Chrome.* New York: Ace Books, 1986.

———. *Neuromancer.* New York: Ace Books, 1984.

Stephenson, Neal. *Snow Crash.* New York: Bantam Books, 1992.

Vinge, Vernor. *True Names . . . and Other Dangers.* New York: Baen Books, 1987.

Weiner, Norbert. *Cybernetics, or Control and Communication in the Animal and the Machine.* Cambridge, Mass.: MIT Press, 1948.

Further Reading

Benedikt, Michael, ed. *Cyberspace: First Steps.* Cambridge, Mass.: MIT Press, 1992.

Gray, Chris Hables, ed. *The Cyborg Handbook.* New York: Routledge, 1995.

Jones, Steven G., ed. *Cybersociety: Computer-Mediated Communication and Community.* Thousand Oaks, Calif.: Sage Publications, 1995.

Related Topics

Avatar; Barlow, John Perry; Cyberculture; Cyberpunk; Gibson, William; Hacking, Cracking, and Phreaking; Virtual Community; Virtual Reality; World Wide Web

— *Lori Kendall*

Cyberwarfare

At the most general level, cyberwarfare refers to a new type of war that relies on computers and other digital technologies as primary weapons. The term cyberwar does not have a single definition; the inflection of the term changes depending on whether it appears in a military report, a newspaper story, or an activist manifesto. Cyberwarfare emerged as a term during the late twentieth century in an attempt to create a label for the shift in warfare toward increased computerization and automation. Other terms that are used interchangeably with cyberwar include: hypermodern war, permanent war, technology war, postmodern war, netwar, and pure war.

Cyberwarfare falls under the more general category of infowar, which refers to warfare that emphasizes communications, intelligence, real-time data about the battlefield, networked communications systems, and simulations. Cyberwar specifically refers to reliance on computers and computerized networks. The arena of cyberwar takes place not in the air, on the land, or on the sea, but rather in the electromagnetic realm of cyberspace.

The reliance of the United States on computers as a primary weapon and technology began during World War II, when developments in computer science were a response to the need to calculate gunning tables with more accuracy. Computers such as the Colossus were also used during the war in attempts to decrypt encoded enemy messages, while the ENIAC was designed to calculate artillery-range tables. After World War II, computers became increasingly central to governmental and military institutions; they were used to wage the Cold War, and played a strong role in the U.S. invasion of Vietnam. Computers were also used by think tanks and military strategists in order to create simulations of possible war scenarios throughout the 1980s.

Most accounts describe the Persian Gulf War as the first instance of cyberwar; it featured extensive reliance on computers for battle simulations and for controlling technologically sophisticated weaponry. Furthermore, the Gulf War aimed to use fewer troops in land battle, attempting to substitute computers for human operators. This removal or reduction of the human element can be seen as the culmination of cybernetics and robotics projects dating back to World War II. Italian theorist Paul Virilio notes in *Desert Screen* that the Gulf War marked a new stage in conflict, in which the speed of electromagnetic exchanges came to prevail over the spatial battlefields of land, air, and sea. Virilio called it a "remote control war," a "virtual war," and a "cyberwar." The U.S. actions in Kosovo have also been classified as a cyberwar.

The characteristics of a cyberwar have been defined by RAND Corporation analysts John Arquilla and David Ronfeldt, in their reports entitled *Cyberwar Is Coming!* and *The Advent of Netwar*. Arquilla and Ronfeldt define cyberwar as the use of computers and computer networks by the military for high- to medium-intensity conflicts. They use the term netwar to indicate low-intensity conflicts waged through a network by non-military actors. Both cyberwar and netwar use information technologies as primary weapons, and target information in attacks. Although Arquilla and Ronfeldt identify a clear difference between cyberwar and netwar, many commentators use the term cyberwar loosely to mean cyberwar, netwar, or even cyberterrorism.

Netwar involves using computer and information technology networks for political, rather than military, ends. Arquilla and Ronfeldt describe netwar as a form of asymmetrical warfare: Non-hierarchical non-state actors can use communications and information technologies in order to disable a hierarchical organization, such as a military operation. After the demise of the Cold War, rogue states and terrorist cells became the new threat to U.S. and Group of 8 (G8) national and economic security. The Center for Strategic and International Studies (CSIS) released a 1998 report entitled "Cybercrime, Cyberterrorism, Cyberwarfare," which frequently invoked the names of Osama bin Laden and Saddam Hussein as possible and suspected netwar enemies. Muslim fundamentalist groups are frequently cited as having the capability of waging a netwar against the United States. The Pakistani Hackerz Club uses the techniques of hacking to achieve their political purposes of protest against Israeli aggression. Activists have described this behavior as hacktivism, but it also falls under the rubric of netwar.

The Zapatista political movement in Chiapas, Mexico, is an example of a non-state actor capable of waging a netwar. Noted for their non-hierarchical arrangement, the Zapatistas are also credited with prioritizing communication and information technologies, such as laptop computers, to organize and to spread their political message. Although security experts call the Zapatistas' actions an act of netwar, political activists have described them as electronic civil disobedience, or peaceful electronic protest.

Since it relies most heavily on computers and computer networks, the United States is the nation most vulnerable to cyberwar or netwar. Most discussion about cyberwar and netwar focuses on how to maintain the security of computer networks;

indeed, much of the literature concerning cyberwar stresses the need for defense of and security for vulnerable computer networks, especially the World Wide Web. Therefore, much of the literature regarding a new type of computerized warfare stresses the need for security and defense against acts of netwar by political insurgencies. The U.S. military and governmental agencies pursue the development of cyberwar techniques in the name of defense against possible outbreaks of netwar. Computerized and digitized networks have become a new battleground, a new virtual territory through which many competing parties are struggling to assert their military or political agendas.

Bibliography

Arquilla, John, and David Ronfeldt. *The Advent of Netwar*. Santa Monica, Calif.: RAND, 1996.

De Landa, Manuel. *War in the Age of Intelligent Machines*. New York: Zone Books, 1991.

Edwards, Paul N. *The Closed World: Computers and the Politics of Discourse in Cold War America*. Cambridge, Mass.: MIT Press, 1996.

Global Organized Crime Project. *Cybercrime, Cyberterrorism, Cyberwarfare*. Washington, D.C.: The Center for Strategic and International Studies Press, 1998.

Gray, Chris Hables. *Postmodern War: The New Politics of Conflict*. New York: The Guilford Press, 1997.

Virilio, Paul. *The Virilio Reader*. James Der Derian, ed. Malden, Mass.: Blackwell Publishers, 1998.

Further Reading

Adams, James. *The Next World War: Computers Are the Weapons and the Front Line Is Everywhere*. New York: Simon & Schuster, 1998.

Bey, Hakim. *The Temporary Autonomous Zone*. Brooklyn, N.Y.: Autonomedia, 1991.

Der Derian, James. *Virtuous War: Mapping the Military-Industrial-Media-Entertainment Network*. Boulder, Colo.: Westview Press, 2001.

Hundley, Richard; Anderson, Robert; and John Arquilla, eds. *Security in Cyberspace: Challenges for Society; Proceedings of an International Conference*. Santa Monica, Calif.: RAND, 1996.

Power, Richard. *Tangled Web: Tales of Digital Crime from the Shadows of Cyberspace*. Indianapolis, Ind.: Que, 2000.

Stocker, Gerfried, and Christine Schopf, eds. *Infowar*. New York: Springer, 1998.

Related Topics

Electronic Civil Disobedience; Encryption and Cryptography; Hacking, Cracking, and Phreaking

— *Heidi Marie Brush*

Cyborg

Traditionally, the word cyborg describes a body that is part organic and part mechanical. In recent years, however, the descriptor "mechanical" has expanded to include things like chemical enhancements and communication technologies. Cyborgs are the stuff of science fiction and of everyday fact: Robocop and the Terminator are cyborgs, as is wheelchair-bound physicist Stephen J. Hawking. People wearing contact lenses are considered cyborgs by some, as are those who contact their friends in communities over the Internet. Cyborgs don't even have to be human. "Cyborgologist" Chris Hables Gray argues that "Biocomputers, artificial life programs, genetically manipulated mice, are all cyborgs in different ways." In recent years, theorists have begun rapidly expanding their definition of what constitutes a cyborg, speaking of things like cyborg gender, cyborg writing, and cyborg politics.

HISTORY OF THE CYBORG

The history of the cyborg begins with the field of cybernetics in the 1940s. During his research with automatic range finders for antiaircraft guns, MIT mathematics professor Norbert Wiener found himself increasingly struck by the seemingly "intelligent" behavior of some machines he was dealing with, and by the "diseases" that could affect them. Wiener coined the term cybernetics (based on the Greek for "steersman") to describe how humans and machines both use information, control, and communication in order to regulate themselves.

Historian of science N. Katherine Hayles points out that during the 1950s and 1960s, cybernetics ushered in an "unprecedented synthesis of the organic and the mechanical" in scientific circles. One of the places where this synthesis was most obvious was at NASA, where the issue of how to put a man safely on the moon was a topic of great interest. In 1960, NASA scientists Manfred Clynes (a computer theorist) and Nathan Kline (a psychiatrist) delivered a paper in which they suggested that existence in space without space suits might be possible if a human being were modified with implants and drugs. "It is not as crazy as it sounds," argues Chris Hables Gray. "But even Clynes would admit today that you'd need genetic modifications as well to make such a transition possible." To frame their paper, Clynes and Kline combined the words cybernetics and organism to form a new term: cyborg.

Cyborg Fiction and Cyborg Fact

Since its introduction, scientists shied away from Clynes' terminology, favoring more specific labels such as human augmentation and human-machine interface to describe their work. But science-fiction writers took to the word cyborg almost immediately, incorporating it into what later came to be called cyberpunk fiction. William Gibson's *Neuromancer* (1984) and Neal Stephenson's *Snow Crash* (1993) are two seminal science-fiction works filled with cyborg characters traversing the space between humanity and machinery. What's more, as real-world scientists move their conceptualizations of life from biological to informational metaphors (for instance, in the areas of DNA research), science-fiction writers have speculated about cyborg bodies traveling freely from one substrate to another. As Hayles notes, "It is not for nothing that 'Beam me up Scotty' has become a cultural icon for the global information society."

Nevertheless, it is important to remember that cyborgs aren't just the stuff of science fiction. Ten percent of humans in the current U.S. population are what Hayles terms "cyborgs in the technical sense." These include people with pacemakers, artificial limbs and joints, drug implants, implanted corneal lenses and artificial skin, and others. A still higher percentage Hayles calls "metaphoric cyborgs." These include surgeons guided by fiberoptics during operations, game players in local video arcades, and anyone regarding themselves as netizens online. While their bodies may not be mechanically or chemically enhanced, Hayles argues, they nonetheless demonstrate what cyberspace ethnographer Sherry Turkle has called "life on the screen."

Sometimes, Hayles' distinction between real cyborgs and metaphoric ones becomes blurry. For example, Hables Gray cites current emergency medical techniques to point out how "working doctors and medical technologists no longer speak of death plain and simple." Instead, he points out, patients are referred to as single-dead, double-dead, or triple-dead, "depending on what machines they are hooked to, what their heart and brain are doing, and whether or not their organs can be harvested." Even in less dire situations, the lines are not always clear. In 1995, when MIT scientist Steve Mann decided to Webcast images he viewed through two tiny TV screens that he wore as glasses, he became a cyborg in both the literal and the metaphoric sense, traversing the space between the life of the body and life on the computer screen.

According to *The Cyborg Handbook* (1995), someone with an organ transplant might be referred to as a "restorative" cyborg, while a person who undergoes cosmetic surgery after an accident might be called a "normalizing" cyborg. Humans who have to undergo modifications to live in space, or individuals who think of themselves as residents of cyberspace communities, are called "reconfiguring cyborgs." Those receiving specialized vaccinations, drugs, and mechanical devices designed to improve peak performance (as occurred with soldiers during the Gulf War, and as happens with many professional athletes) are referred to as "enhanced cyborgs."

Perhaps the most well-known enhanced cyborg today is Kevin Warwick, a cybernetics researcher who had a silicon chip implanted in his arm for 10 days in 1998, and is planning another implant soon. Warwick maintains that his desire for scientific advancement far outweighs his concern for his health, exulting that in the future, "Anything a computer link can help operate or interface with could be controllable via [body] implants." There are also people who choose to become enhanced cyborgs not for science, but for art. In 1990, the French artist Orlan initiated a series of "plastic surgeries as performance" designed to progressively sculpt her face into a combination of the Mona Lisa, Diana, and Botticelli's Venus. Her goal was to critique conventional ideas about "natural" feminine beauty, using her own face as a cyborg canvas. Unfortunately, notes art theorist Tanya Augsburg, Orlan's critique is all too often lost on her viewers, who ask not "Is this art?" but rather, "Is she mad?"

Manifesto for Cyborgs

As the case of Orlan demonstrates, the ethics of cyborg bodies can be complex, particularly when they are created without a citizenry's knowledge or consent (for example, in the development of biological weaponry). One of the first political treatises for living in a cyborg world was written in 1985 by Donna J. Haraway, a biologist and a feminist historian of science. In her essay "A Manifesto for Cyborgs," Haraway reminded technophiliacs that the cyborg was born of the military-industrial complex of the post-World War II United States, with a legacy of death and destruction behind it. On the other hand, cyborg research has enabled the creation of life-saving prosthetics, agricultural products, and communications technologies, none of which the world could do without.

Whether we like it or not, Haraway pointed out, "we are all cyborgs." She felt that women especially needed to recognize that they were "the information economy workers of choice" worldwide, serving as microchip producers, telemarketers, word processors, and secretaries, as well as the bodies on which many reproductive-technologies and population-control experiments are carried out. Haraway argued that advances in genetics, medicine, virtual entertainments, and communications networks have changed the world from a place of stable bodies, communities, and identities into what she termed a "problem of coding." As she put it, "The cyborg is our ontology; it gives us our politics."

THE RISE OF CYBORGOLOGY

Haraway's "Manifesto" inspired the rise of the field now known as cyborgology, and today, it is common to see the prefix attached to many sorts of discussions about living in a technological world. Sherry Turkle and Claudia Springer have argued that the cyborg identity one finds in cyberspace role-play is emblematic of postmodern subjectivity in general. Anne Balsamo and Allucquère Rosanne (Sandy) Stone use the notion of cyborg gender to describe advances in transsexual hormone therapies, as well as the demand for female breast-enhancement surgery. George Landow and Julie Allbright have theorized that the prosthetic qualities of hypertext qualify it as cyborg writing. And Chela Sandoval writes about cyborg political strategies, emphasizing how one is made a member of (rather than born into) affinity groups such as "women of color."

Indeed, one of the major criticisms of cyborgology is that it has now moved so far from its roots in cybernetic theory as to be unrecognizable. Chris Hables Gray agrees with that assessment, noting that today, "the cyborg is as specific, as general, as powerful and as useless a term as tool or machine." Nonetheless, he maintains, as long as cyborgs continue to proliferate, they will continue "redefining many of the most basic concepts of human existence." The fact that Hables Gray himself has recently written up a Cyborg Bill of Rights attests to as much.

Bibliography

Augsburg, Tanya. "Orlan's Performative Transformations of Subjectivity." *The Ends of Performance*. Peggy Phelan and Jill Lane, eds. New York: New York University Press, 1998.

Balsamo, Anne M. *Technologies of the Gendered Body: Reading Cyborg Women*. Durham, N.C.: Duke University Press, 1996.

Gray, Chris Hables, et al., eds. *The Cyborg Handbook*. New York: Routledge, 1995.

Gray, Chris Hables; Mentor, Steven; and Jennifer Figueroa-Sarriera. "Cyborgology: Constructing the Knowledge of Cybernetic Organisms." *The Cyborg Handbook*. Chris Hables Gray, ed. New York: Routledge, 1995.

Greco, Diane. "Cyborgs among Us: Bodies and Hypertext." *Hypertext '96: The Seventh ACM Conference on Hypertext*. New York: ACM, 1996; pp. 87–88.

Haraway, Donna J. "A Cyborg Manifesto: Science, Technology, and Socialist-Feminism in the Late Twentieth Century." *Simians, Cyborgs, and Women: The Reinvention of Nature*. New York: Routledge, 1991; pp. 149–81.

Hayles, N. Katherine. *How We Became Posthuman: Virtual Bodies in Cybernetics, Literature, and Informatics*. Chicago, Ill.: University of Chicago Press, 1999.

Landow, George P. *Hypertext 2.0*. Baltimore, Md.: Johns Hopkins University Press, 1997.

Sandoval, Chela. "New Sciences: Cyborg Feminism and the Methodology of the Oppressed." *The Cyborg Handbook*. Chris Hables Gray, ed. New York: Routledge, 1995.

Springer, Claudia. *Electronic Eros: Bodies and Desire in the Postindustrial Age*. Austin, Tx.: University of Texas Press, 1996.

Stephenson, Neal. *Snow Crash*. New York: Bantam Books, 1993.

Stone, Allucquère Rosanne. "Split Subjects, Not Atoms; or, How I Fell in Love with My Prosthesis." *The Cyborg Handbook*. Chris Hables Gray, ed. New York: Routledge, 1995.

Sützl, Wolfgang. "Cyborg Society: An Interview with Chris Hables Gray." World-Information.org, Cultural Intelligence, May 7, 2001. <http://world-information.org/wio/news/992003309/994352905> (April 26, 2002).

Turkle, Sherry. *Life on the Screen: Identity in the Age of the Internet*. New York: Simon & Schuster, 1997.

Warwick, Kevin. "Cyborg 1.0." *Wired* 8.02, February 2000. <http://wired.lycos.com/wired/archive/8.02/warwick_pr.html> (April 26, 2002).

Further Reading

Davis-Floyd, Robbie, and Joseph Dumit, eds. *Cyborg Babies: From Techno-Sex to Techno-Tots*. New York: Routledge, 1998.

Gray, Chris Hables. *Cyborg Citizen: Politics in the Posthuman Age*. New York: Routledge, 2001.

Haraway, Donna. *Modest_Witness@Second_Millennium. FemaleMan©_Meets_OncoMouse™: Feminism and Technoscience.* New York: Routledge, 1997.

Kunzru, Hari. "You Are Cyborg: For Donna Haraway, We Are Already Assimilated." *Wired* 5.02, February 1997. <http://www.wired.com/wired/archive/5.02/ffharaway_pr.html> (April 26, 2002).

Senft, Theresa, and Stacy Horn, eds. *Sexuality and Cyberspace: Performing the Digital Body.* New York: Women and Performance Press, 1997. <http://www.echonyc.com/~women/Issue17/index.html> (April 26, 2002).

Related Topics

Cyberpunk; Cyberspace; Cyberwarfare; Gender and New Media; Gibson, William; Haraway, Donna J.; "A Manifesto for Cyborgs; *Neuromancer*; Robotics; Stone, Allucquère Rosanne; Turkle, Sherry; Virtual Community

— *Theresa M. Senft*

Data Mining

Data mining is an emerging technology that extracts useful information, patterns, and trends from various data sources. Computerization has resulted in the availability and accumulation of a large amount of data. As the amount of data increases, it becomes more and more difficult to access and understand the meaning of both historical and current data from multiple sources. Data mining fulfills the need to access data efficiently, share data, and extract information from existing data, in order to assist decision-making in organizations.

Often called knowledge discovery or pattern discovery, data mining represents efforts to integrate various data sources that may be scattered across several sites, and to extract information from these data sources by locating patterns and trends that were previously unknown. Data may be in computer files, relational databases, or other types of databases such as multimedia files. Some data are structured (e.g., relational databases), while others are unstructured (e.g., text, voice, images, and video).

Data mining provides information to improve marketing capabilities, detect abnormal patterns, and predict future developments based on existing trends. A supermarket could analyze the purchase record of its customers and, based on patterns the analysis shows, arrange items on shelves to improve sales. A credit bureau could analyze the credit history of its current or potential clients and find out which are at risk. Physicians could analyze patient histories and current medical conditions and predict potential problems that might arise.

TECHNOLOGIES FOR DATA MINING

Data mining is an integration of multiple technologies, including database systems, data warehousing, statistics, machine learning, decision support, visualization, and parallel processing.

When data mining is performed, a large quantity of information is analyzed. Therefore, it is important to utilize various data-management technologies to prepare data for mining in order to obtain meaningful results. Data management systems, which include database systems technology and data warehousing, are designed to organize, structure, and manage data.

A database system includes the database management system (DBMS) and the database itself; the DBMS manages the database, which contains the permanent data. A data warehouse is needed in light of the heterogeneous data sources used. Several processing modules may have to cooperate with one another to process a query using heterogeneous sources; a data warehouse brings together essential data from heterogeneous databases to allow one-stop data access. Many organizations build their own data warehouses, while some go for help to companies that specialize in developing and maintaining data warehouses.

Key components in data mining also include machine learning and statistical methods. Machine learning allows a computer to learn various rules and patterns from the data, and then apply these rules to solve problems. Statistical methods that are used to compute sums, averages, and distributions are integrated with databases for mining. Recently, statistical analysis has been integrated with machine-learning techniques to develop sophisticated statistical techniques for data mining. As a result, various statistical analysis packages are being marketed as data-mining tools. Although data mining encompasses the use of more than just sophisticated statistical techniques, statistics do play an important role.

Other technologies used in data mining include visualization, parallel processing, and decision support. Visualization techniques help graph the data to facilitate interpretation. Parallel processing techniques improve the performance of data mining. Decision support systems are a set of tools to prune the results, assist in decision-making, and provide guidance in management.

DATA-MINING PROCEDURES

A series of procedures are involved in data mining: preparing and organizing data for mining, determining the desired outcomes, selecting tools, carrying out the mining itself, pruning the results so that useful ones are considered further, taking actions based on the results, and evaluating the actions to determine benefits.

Once data is obtained, it has to be prepared for mining; this is one of the most difficult tasks in data mining. Preparation may include putting the data in the right database format, building a data warehouse, or establishing a database management system. Once the data is prepared, efforts must be made to clean the data, eliminating unnecessary items and keeping only essential data. Based on the expected outcomes, different tools are selected to carry out the mining. Expected outcomes include classification, clustering, estimation, prediction, and association. Mining can produce abundant information; it is up to the users to prune the results.

Once useful results are obtained, they need to be examined, and potential courses of action identified. After the actions have been implemented, users need to evaluate the benefits and costs of the actions. The outcome of this evaluation will then be incorporated into the next round of data mining. In the new cycle, new mining tools may have to be used, because the data may have changed.

Challenges in data mining are manifold. Data may be incomplete, with many missing values. Also, users may not be certain how accurate the data is. Other challenges include determining which technique to use, what type of data mining to do in light of large volumes of data, and who will administer the mining itself—in-house personnel or outside contractors.

TRENDS IN DATA MINING

Trends in data mining include mining distributed, heterogeneous, and legacy data sources; mining multimedia data, such as text, images, and video; and mining data on the World Wide Web.

In some cases, a single database or warehouse is mined. However, in most cases, mined databases are distributed and heterogeneous in nature. A distributed database is one in which data is found in multiple databases, and heterogeneous data are data from divergent sources. The trend is toward providing interoperability between heterogeneous databases in order to provide transparent access.

Legacy databases are those systems that were developed 20 to 30 years ago using older hardware and software, and that are becoming obsolete. Efforts are being made to migrate legacy databases to easier and faster applications, which will also be less costly to upgrade and less difficult to support.

Multimedia data, which include audio, video, texts, and images, is heterogeneous due to the various forms of media used. Multimedia mining means that the combinations of two or more data types—text and video, or text, video, and audio—are mined. Currently, only one data type is mined at a time; efforts are being made to develop tools to operate on multimedia directly.

As one considers information overload on the World Wide Web, mining data and extracting patterns and relevant information from the Web is a logical thing to do to assist the users. There has been much interest in mining the Web to make browsing much easier for users. Mining the databases on the Web as well as Web usage patterns to gain useful information are also areas of interest in Web mining.

Digital libraries are an emerging technology in Web mining, providing digitized information distributed across several sites. Efforts are being made to allow users to access this information in a transparent and timely fashion. Issues associated with digital libraries include security and privacy, as well as copyright protection and data ownership. Initiatives have been undertaken to address these issues.

Despite its many uses, data mining poses a potential threat to the security and privacy of individuals. For example, one controversial issue in data mining is inference, the process by which users pose queries and deduce unauthorized information from the legitimate responses they receive. Users with sophisticated tools can now access data and deduce patterns that could be sensitive. In addition, Web mining could potentially compromise the privacy of individuals, whose personal information can be obtained and analyzed as they browse the Web.

Data mining is still a relatively new technology. Although data management, statistical reasoning, and machine learning are not new, it is only recently that these technologies are being integrated to mine data effectively. Data mining is something like an art form at present; however, as various technologies mature, progressive developments will eventually make data mining a more precise scientific practice.

Bibliography

Berry, Michael, and Gordon Linoff. *Data Mining Techniques: For Marketing, Sales, and Customer Support*. New York: Wiley, 1997.

Han, Jiawei, and Micheline Kamber. *Data Mining: Concepts and Techniques*. San Francisco: Morgan Kaufmann Publishers, 2001.

Thuraisingham, Bhavani. *Data Mining: Technologies, Techniques, Tools, and Trends*. Boca Raton, Fla.: CRC Press, 1999.

Further Reading

Cabena, Peter. Discovering *Data Mining: From Concept to Implementation.* Upper Saddle River, N.J.: Prentice Hall PTR, 1998.

Berry, Michael, and Gordon Linoff. *Mastering Data Mining: The Art and Science of Customer Relationship Management.* New York: Wiley, 2000.

Johnson, R. Colin. "Protocol Aimed at Data Mining." *Electronic Engineering Times,* September 18, 2000, p. 72.

Related Topics

Digital Asset Management; E-Commerce; Knowledge Management; Multimedia

— *Shing-Ling Sarina Chen*

DeCSS

DeCSS is a small computer program that allows a user to override the copy-protection system employed by most commercial digital versatile disk (DVD) producers. The name of the program refers to its ability to decrypt the most common form of DVD copy protection, the Content Scrambling System (CSS). In addition to ensuring that DVDs cannot be copied, CSS provides other restrictions on use, including regional controls and required viewing of previews on some DVDs. DeCSS has become a test case for the application of new copyright law to multimedia, and a rallying point for those concerned with the fair use of copyrighted material.

CSS uses a system of encryption that requires a DVD player to provide a 40-bit key to temporarily decrypt and display the video. This key is provided by the hardware itself in the case of a stand-alone DVD player, or by the software that displays the video on a computer screen. In the latter case, the required software and keys are licensed to makers of commercial software by a trade group called the DVD Copy Control Association (DVD-CCA). A number of DVD players for computers have been made available, including WinDVD, ATI DVD, XingDVD, and many others.

Several groups attempted to "reverse-engineer" the CSS system and discover its encryption process soon after its introduction. Although it is not entirely clear who was the first, as many as three groups managed to successfully uncover the workings of CSS. The process was made far easier when the makers of one such program, XingDVD, failed to adequately protect their key. As part of a larger project to provide video playback for the Linux operating system (the "Livid" project), a group of young Norwegian programmers led by 16-year-old Jon Johansen, used this information to write DeCSS. DeCSS would allow those using the Linux operating system to view legally purchased DVDs, and (either coincidentally or centrally, depending upon your perspective) put no barriers on copying these DVDs.

At the end of October 1999, Johansen placed a copy of DeCSS on his father's Web site, and the program spread over much of the Web soon afterward. Though it was argued that DeCSS was part of a multimedia system for the Linux operating system, the program, in fact, ran on Windows. Other portions of the system would have to be implemented before it could be used on Linux systems directly. Attorneys for the DVD-CCA demanded that the program be taken down; in late January 2000, Johansen and his father were detained and interrogated, and computers and cellular phones were seized from their home. The coverage of this event set the stage for court battles over the following years.

DeCSS was not the first piece of software to enable DVD copying. For example, one could create an exact copy from one DVD to another using a DVD burner found in commercial replication (and pirating) operations. However, DeCSS was the first widespread and effective system for easily "ripping" the content of a DVD—that is, for being able to store that content on a hard drive and manipulate it.

Soon after the release of DeCSS, many suggested that the process of ripping DVDs was too difficult to become widespread, and that the storage space required would limit its diffusion. When the video content of a DVD was copied to a hard drive, it took up around nine gigabytes of storage. Even with large disk drives, storing or trading these movies over the Internet seemed very unlikely. However, these movies could also be converted to a new video-encoding system called DivX, which preserved most of the clarity of the original video in less than one-tenth of the required space. Once converted to the DivX format, films could often be burned onto a standard CD and could, with patience, be downloaded over the Internet. The combination of DeCSS and DivX made for the real possibility of widespread piracy and file trading on a scale similar to that of MP3s.

COURT CASES

Under the provisions of the 1998 Digital Millennium Copyright Act, it is illegal to distribute technology that is used to "circumvent a technological measure that effectively controls access to a work." As such, the reverse-engineering of the system and creation of a tool that evaded the CSS licensing scheme was, to use the metaphor provided by the DMCA, the equivalent of creating a method of gaining entry to a locked building.

In November 1999, the DVD-CCA, joined by the Motion Picture Association of America (MPAA), brought action against dozens of individuals and organizations who had posted the DeCSS code or who had linked to it in separate cases in California and New York. Among the defendants were *2600: The Hacker Quarterly,* a magazine dedicated to cracking computer systems, and Slashdot, a widely read technology Web site. In the New York case, the MPAA argued that DeCSS violated the DMCA, while in the California case, they argued that the defendants stole trade secrets owned by the DVD-CCA. A preliminary injunction was issued in both cases, and those named as defendants were forced to take down any copies of DeCSS. Though *2600* refrained from providing the program directly, as required by the injunction, they provided links to hundreds of other sites from which DeCSS could be downloaded, and encouraged readers "all throughout the world" to "take a stand and mirror these files."

In the New York case, defendants presented two arguments. First, they claimed that CSS impeded their fair use of the digital videos they had purchased. Early copyright law in the United States recognized that while copyright may foster innovation by protecting the rights of authors, there are times when the public good requires that copyrighted materials be allowed to be copied and used. For example, a scholar may want to quote the work of another to illustrate an idea or to criticize that work, or those who have legally purchased music albums might want to create a tape compilation of music for their own use. The defendants argued that DeCSS enabled the use of DVDs in a way that did not infringe upon the movie studios' copyrights. Judge Lewis Kaplan dismissed this argument, suggesting that the balance between protecting against piracy and restricting fair use had already been struck by the Congress in creating the DMCA, and that there was "no serious question" that DeCSS violated the DMCA.

The second argument in favor of the distribution of DeCSS was that it was not a "device," but rather a fragment of speech, and as such deserved the full protection of the First Amendment. Kaplan recognized that code could be expressive, but that it was not purely expressive "any more than the assassination of a political figure is purely a political statement." Kaplan indicated that anything less than "pure speech" was at best partially protected by the First Amendment. Earlier court cases related to the dissemination of encryption code had established that computer code was a form of speech, and that source code could receive protection as such under certain circumstances.

DeCSS as Illegal Speech

By July 2000, both the New York and California cases had been decided in favor of the motion picture industry, much to the consternation of the Electronic Frontier Foundation (EFF), which continued to provide legal defense for those involved. Especially surprising was the decision that not only were the sites prohibited from providing DeCSS, but also defendants could not provide hyperlinks to any such site. Hyperlinks were found by Kaplan to be a form of "trafficking" in illegal goods, and therefore illegal according to the DMCA. Given the importance of hyperlinks to the structure of the World Wide Web, such a decision came as a shock to many. At present, the case is going through the appeals process. For now, those who continue to support the distribution of DeCSS have little to worry about in practice. A search on Google for "DeCSS" yields thousands of sites from which it can be downloaded, and links have appeared on sites like Download.com and CNN.com.

The principles argued in the DeCSS case remain at issue, and this has spurred some interesting cultural and artistic responses. To further press the question of where code ends and expression begins, many have recast the DeCSS code in artistic contexts. The first attempts at this were transcriptions of the DeCSS code onto T-shirts, a tactic used in earlier conflicts over encryption as speech. (The organization that produces the T-shirts [copyleft.net] was added to the California lawsuit.) DeCSS has been made into pieces of music, hidden within graphics, cast as a haiku, and represented as a single prime number that can be decompressed to the DeCSS program, all of which are available at David Touretzky's "Gallery of CSS Descramblers" Web site.

It may seem odd that such a simple program could have caused, and continues to cause, such a furor. Both sides argue that the legal status of DeCSS has significant repercussions. Those involved in writing open source software—software that provides the alterable code with the program, often free of charge—argue that if DeCSS is found to be illegal, it will have a chilling effect on the software community, stifling creativity and the exchange of ideas. The motion picture industry claims that if DeCSS is widely distributed, it will establish a precedent that will make protecting intellectual property impossible, and that as a result the DVD standard will go unused and studios will not release versions of their work in digital form. Two things are certain: The DeCSS controversy will continue to be of importance as broadband Internet access becomes more prevalent, and this issue will serve as a prototype for future skirmishes over intellectual property.

Bibliography

Post, Robert. "Encryption Source Code and the First Amendment." *Berkeley Technology Law Journal* 15 (Spring 2000), p. 713.

Touretzky, David. "Gallery of CSS Descramblers." <http://www.cs.cmu.edu/~dst/DeCSS/Gallery/index.html> (April 5, 2002).

Universal vs. Reimerdes, Final Judgment. <http://eon.law.harvard.edu/openlaw/DVD/NY/trial/finaljudgment.pdf> (April 5, 2002).

Further Reading

Electronic Frontiers Foundation. "Campaign for Audio Visual Freedom of Expression (CAFÉ)." <http://www.eff.org/cafe/> (April 5, 2002).

Lemos, Robert. "DeCSS 2? DVD Code Broken Again." *ZDNet News,* March 7, 2001. <http://www.zdnet.com/zdnn/stories/news/0,4586,2693768,00.html> (April 5, 2002).

Lessig, Lawrence. *Code and Other Laws of Cyberspace.* New York: Basic Books, 1999.

Litman, Jessica. *Digital Copyright.* New York: Prometheus, 2001.

Open Law DVD/DeCSS Forum. "DVD/DeCSS Frequently Asked Questions." May 2000. <http://eon.law.harvard.edu/openlaw/DVD/dvd-discuss-faq.html> (April 5, 2002).

Related Topics

Copyright; Digital Millennium Copyright Act; Electronic Frontier Foundation; Encryption and Cryptography; Hacking, Cracking, and Phreaking; Linking; Open Source; *2600: The Hacker Quarterly*

— *Alexander Halavais*

DeFanti, Thomas

1948–

Virtual Reality and Networking Technologies Specialist

Thomas DeFanti is an important figure in the fields of virtual reality (VR), computer graphics, and high-speed broadband networks, and is co-inventor of the "virtual-reality theater" known as the CAVE at the University of Illinois at Chicago (UIC). A professor whose research contributions span the concepts of technology and art, DeFanti is also co-director of the Electronic Visualization Lab (EVL) at UIC, along with fellow CAVE inventor Dan Sandin.

DeFanti was born on September 18, 1948, and grew up in Queens, New York. He was the second child of Charles L. and Madeline K. DeFanti, both civil servants who worked for the New York City Department of Sanitation. He graduated from Stuyvesant High School in Manhattan and, like his brother Charles, became a professor. While his passion was (and is) for photography, his skill in math, science, and languages led him to a career in computer science.

DeFanti recalls that he was "extraordinarily dumbstruck" when, as a graduate student at Ohio State, he discovered Charles Csuri's Computer Graphics Research Group lab and studio. It was there that DeFanti realized that he could combine his interest in image production with his abilities in computing. DeFanti earned his master's degree in computer and information science from Ohio State in 1970, and his Ph.D. from the same school in 1973. After four years as a university fellow and research assistant at Ohio State, DeFanti took a job in 1973 as an assistant professor at UIC, and he has remained there ever since, taking on the title of full professor in 1988.

DeFanti hooked up with media artist Sandin at UIC's EVL, combining their abilities in computer graphics and video imaging. Maxine Brown, a UIC colleague since 1977, joined EVL in 1986, and proceeded to market the lab to potential benefactors. Prior to that, DeFanti recalls, he and Sandin had paid for work at the lab with "very small grants" and through their own personal consulting fees.

In 1986, DeFanti and Sandin connected with Larry Smarr, founder of the National Center for Supercomputing Applications (NCSA) at the University of Illinois at Urbana-Champaign. Recognizing the potential of the DeFanti-Sandin-Brown team, Smarr funded their work; he also introduced the group to key people at the National Science Foundation and the Defense Advanced Research Projects Agency (DARPA), the agency that created the Internet's predecessor, the ARPANET. DeFanti recalls that Rick Stevens of the U.S. Energy Department's Argonne National Lab, also impressed by EVL's work, provided both funds and important network engineering support for their research. The lab now brings in about $5 million a year.

With assistance from a variety of students and programmers, DeFanti and Sandin's work over the years culminated in 1991, with the design and construction of the virtual-reality laboratory, CAVE. The recursive acronym CAVE stands for "CAVE Automatic Virtual Environment," but it doubly references Plato's allegory, "The Simile of the Cave." The lab unites video, audio, and database technologies to create collaborative virtual environments aimed at facilitating everything from new designs in architecture to new forms of distance medicine and new vistas for interactive art. Formed in the early 1990s, the CAVE remains at the forefront of virtual-reality experimentation.

Walking into the CAVE is something like walking into a cube-shaped closet, or a small bedroom of about three cubic meters that has no furnishings. There are only walls, a floor, and a ceiling; each serves as a view screen onto which video presentations that correspond with each other in a three-dimensional way are projected. The visitor to this space has no need for the bulky, claustrophobic headgear normally associated with virtual reality, and instead needs only to wear a pair of stereoscopic glasses with automatic head-tracking gear. The visitor also carries a "magic wand" that is used to manipulate the imagery with subtle wrist movements.

DeFanti recalls that he and Sandin conceived of the CAVE as a way to provide an immersive experience without the burdens of head-mounted displays, with science, engineering, and fine art converging in the content. DeFanti named this effect "tele-immersion."

In 1995, Steve Goldstein of the National Science Foundation urged DeFanti and his team to propose a way to connect the world's emerging high-performance Internet research networks, a project that led to STAR TAP (Science, Technology and Research Transit Access Point). EVL's ongoing international networking efforts have resulted in the building of CAVE-like interfaces around the world, attracting great interest from science and engineering sponsors.

It is within these realms of science and engineering that the CAVE shows its most immediate promise. With its large bandwidth and graphical flexibility, the CAVE can allow two people in different locations, even in different nations, to communicate as though they were standing in the same space. Animations are used to create "avatars," cartoonish representations of the people involved in the communication, and the great processing speeds and high bandwidth available over the STAR TAP network allow the avatars to stand in for the people involved.

The CAVE can thus be used by architects working together on a large-scale project to try out design ideas virtually. If one of the partners doesn't like the location of a support column or stairwell, they can simply move it to another part of the virtual design. And both can "walk" through the entire structure, reassembling and redesigning its components as they work. The same kind of communication can take place between instructors and medical students, who might take animated tours of the internal organs of the human body, substituting healthy organs for diseased ones for instructional purposes. The possibilities, in fact, are endless.

Selected Works

Johnson, Andrew E.; Leigh, Jason; DeFanti, Thomas A.; Brown, Maxine D.; and Daniel J. Sandin. "CAVERN: The CAVE Research Network." Paper presented at the First International Symposium on Multimedia Virtual Laboratory, Tokyo, Japan, March 25, 1998.

Leigh, Jason; Johnson, Andrew E.; Brown, Maxine; Sandin Daniel J.; and Thomas A. DeFanti. "Visualization in Teleimmersive Environments." *IEEE Computer,* December 1999, pp. 66–73. <http://www.startap.net/images/PDF/Leigh_IEEEComputer.pdf> (April 26, 2002).

Bibliography

Featherly, Kevin. Email Interview with Thomas DeFanti. August 30, 2001.

Leigh, Jason; DeFanti, Thomas A.; Johnson, Andrew E.; Brown, Maxine D.; and Daniel J. Sandin. "Global Tele-Immersion: Better than Being There." *Proceedings of the 7th International Conference on Artificial Reality and Tele-Existence,* Tokyo, Japan, December 3–5, 1997, pp. 10–17. <http://www.evl.uic.edu/cavern/cavernpapers/icat.pdf> (April 26, 2002).

Sandin, Daniel; DeFanti, Thomas; and Carolina Cruz-Neira. "A Room with a View." *Multimedia: From Wagner to Virtual Reality.* Randall Packer and Ken Jordan, eds. New York: W.W. Norton & Co., 2001; pp. 266–72.

University of Illinois at Chicago. STAR TAP Web page. 1997. <http://www.startap.net/> (April 26, 2002).

University of Illinois at Chicago. "Thomas A. DeFanti." <http://www.cs.uic.edu/~tom/> (April 26, 2002).

Further Reading

Aukstakalnis, Steve, and David Blatner. *Silicon Mirage: The Art and Science of Virtual Reality.* Berkeley, Calif.: Peachpit Press, 1992.

Brand, Stewart. *The Media Lab: Inventing the Future at MIT.* New York: Penguin Books, 1988.

Laurel, Brenda. *Computers as Theatre.* Reading, Mass.: Addison-Wesley, 1991.

Rheingold, Howard. *Virtual Reality.* New York: Summit Books, 1991.

Related Topics

— *Kevin Featherly*

Desktop Publishing

Desktop publishing (DTP) is the practice of using personal computers and specialized software to create professional-looking documents for public distribution. These can include everything from professionally published newspapers and magazines to self-designed greeting cards created by amateurs. Once viewed as a revolutionary development in the application of computers, DTP has become so ingrained in routine computer use that the once-ubiquitous term has begun to fade from the popular lexicon. Some critics argue that the desktop-publishing trend has been supplanted by Web publishing, or even that desktop publishing today, in large measure, is Web publishing.

Nevertheless, the practice of creating polished-looking printed documents using desktop computers remains alive and well. Today, the majority of magazine, newspaper, and book publishers routinely use DTP software suites such as QuarkXPress, CorelDraw, and PageMaker, often with Macintosh computers, to compose pages. Meanwhile, many amateurs use Windows-powered PCs and less expensive DTP software products such as Microsoft Publisher, or even word-processing programs like Microsoft Word and Corel Corp.'s WordPerfect.

Publishing Before PCs

Before desktop technologies arrived on the scene in the mid-1980s, publishing documents involved a great deal of time and expense. Most were prepared for publication through cutting and pasting—a familiar enough term in the computer age, but one with a much more literal meaning in decades past. Text intended for publication was input into machines called photocomposition typesetters, which used cathode-ray tubes in the 1960s, later switching to laser and computer technologies and employing special photography to create page "galleys." These were long strips of glossy paper onto which sentences intended for publication were printed. Galleys had to be physically cut, with scissors or razor blades, and pasted with hot wax onto layout boards. Images to be published also were affixed to these boards. When the boards were completed, they were turned over to the composing room as "camera-ready art"—ready to be photographed for conversion into printing plates by the printer. Beyond that, several other steps also had to be performed before a page was ready for publication, depending on the type of printing process that was chosen for a given job.

In the mid-1980s, however, desktop computers and software types offered people a chance to create documents without manual cutting and pasting—in fact, without even getting up from their seats. At the same time, new laser printers arrived in the marketplace that printed finished documents that looked nearly as good as those produced in professional printing plants. Suddenly, anyone with the means to purchase a computer and laser printer could conceivably become a publisher, without having to invest in massive pieces of equipment or pay the salaries of the skilled workers needed to operate them. The DTP revolution was under way.

"What made this little 'revolution' so exciting to some," *Cyberia* columnist Paul Bissex wrote in 1996, "was not that a better technology had come along . . . but that it had come along in such a seemingly democratic form. Coupled with the cheap reproduction offered by the photocopier, (desktop publishing) looked like a big break for the 'little guy.'"

Xerox PARC

DTP has its roots in word processing. Indeed, decades after the first word-processing system was created, new text-editing programs were developed that integrated advanced functions such as ready-made page templates, tables and borders, and variable column-widths, blurring many of the distinctions between word processing and DTP.

Like much in the history of personal computing, DTP was first conceived in the early and mid-1970s in the Xerox Palo Alto Research Center labs in California. Author Michael A. Hiltzik details the story in his 1999 book *Dealers of Lightning: Xerox PARC and the Dawn of the Computer Age.* According to Hiltzik, the first word-processing program code was written by Butler Lampson, a research fellow at Xerox PARC. It was written for the Alto, the first personal computer, which Lampson had helped create at Xerox PARC in 1973.

Initially, the Alto could perform few functions; moving an image of *Sesame Street*'s Cookie Monster around on its display monitor was about the extent of its bag of tricks. Lampson knew that to keep Xerox's corporate masters interested in marketing the Alto, better software was needed. So he drew up the first word-processing system schematics by hand, on three sheets of lined yellow paper. It caught the eye of an ace Xerox PARC programmer, Charles Simonyi, who immediately understood the importance of the idea; soon, a team was assembled, including Simonyi and Lampson, to create the first "what-you-see-is-what-you-get" (WYSIWYG) text-editing program. Code-named Project Bravo, the software application was completed in October 1974.

Although Bravo didn't have the advanced desktop processing functions that later, sturdier programs like Aldus PageMaker would have, Simonyi told Hiltzik that he saw the future of DTP immediately upon viewing the arcane lines of code that Lampson had scribbled on that yellow legal pad. "I could see books in their entirety flowing there in front of you, virtual books and everything," he said. "In retrospect, it seems obvious. Uh-uh, it wasn't obvious to anyone."

Bravo served as the basis of a later Xerox PARC project, code-named Gypsy, which began the same month that Bravo was completed, and which moved text editing closer to the realm of modern DTP. Gypsy was created by a team that included Tim Mott, a computer scientist at the Ginn & Co. publishing house, who was sent to Xerox PARC to determine if the lab's emergent computer systems could adapt to the rigors of book publishing. Gypsy was developed with Ginn editors serving as a focus group, and their input was key to creating a number of editing functions—including cut-and-paste and page scrolling—that remain standard in DTP and word-processing systems.

Gypsy was finished in 1975. It included the first use of the computer mouse as a point-and-click interface tool; it allowed editors to retain multiple versions of a document and display them as a list; and it allowed editors to manipulate large blocks of text on the computer screen and store documents on magnetic disks, rather than having to physically cut, paste, and mark up typewritten manuscripts. Editors who had a chance to use Gypsy were reluctant at first, but later said that the system actually improved the quality of their work. However, decisions at the Xerox corporate headquarters held back both Gypsy and Bravo, preventing them from being fully developed and integrated as software to be bundled with commercial desktop

computers. Xerox failed to capitalize on these and a number of other ideas—including a chance to market the first personal computer—and others, like Apple Computer's Steve Jobs, took these ideas and ran with them. Despite Xerox PARC's innovations, the term "desktop publishing" is rarely associated with it.

PAGEMAKER AND THE MACINTOSH

Instead, the desktop publishing boom usually is credited to Paul Brainerd, who created Aldus Corp.'s PageMaker program. PageMaker, the first fully functional DTP software product, was designed for use with the Apple Macintosh computer. In fact, many observers credit PageMaker with making Apple a computer-industry powerhouse of the 1980s by making Apple computers the de facto DTP standard, a stature that it retains among many professional publishers to this day.

The Macintosh, itself patterned after computing advances by Xerox PARC programmers, featured a graphical user interface (GUI); coupled with PageMaker's, it allowed editors to see their edited documents on the computer screen precisely as they would appear in print. Computers powered by Microsoft, which was still reliant on its DOS interface well into the late 1980s, had no such WYSIWYG display. (That situation has been rectified, and Windows-based DTP systems today are considered by some to be the equal of Apple's.)

There were already several other programs available for the Mac that could edit text and/or handle images in the mid-1980s, but PageMaker was the first to successfully integrate both functions in a way that editors found universally easy and convenient. PageMaker also provided the needed interface for printing out documents using Apple's new LaserWriter printer, which produced documents far superior to the dot-matrix printers of the day, and which even rivaled the quality of professionally printed documents. For documents too large or complex to be handled by the user's own LaserWriter, PageMaker made it possible to store material for publication on magnetic disks, to be delivered to professional printing houses. Printers had less work to do with these saved documents than they did when working with page galleys. Mostly, they only had to load up the paper, set up the plates, and run the presses; PageMaker dealt with all other so-called "pre-press" operations. At a minimum, the software cut a number of specialized workers out of the process, greatly reducing publishing costs.

By the late 1980s and early 1990s, columnist Bissex writes, DTP was so "hot" that it spawned an industry. The impact radiated throughout the publishing world. It forced laborers who had spent their lives working with scissors and gluepots to learn new technologies or face losing their jobs. Its low cost allowed for the launch of numerous small-niche magazines that would not otherwise have existed. But big publishers did not roll over and die, Bissex noted, even though some predicted that the democratization of publishing would, for example, kill off newspapers. Instead, Bissex said, DTP was absorbed into the print-world mainstream, became "normal," and actually helped many publications survive into the new millennium.

DTP TODAY

Today, QuarkXPress and PageMaker (now an Adobe Systems product) are the preeminent DTP software suites used by professionals at newspapers and magazines; Adobe has recently tried, unsuccessfully, to supercede both with its advanced InDesign program. Amateurs and small-business owners, meanwhile, tend to use less expensive programs like Broderbund's PrintShop Deluxe and Microsoft's Publisher to render private documents or reports intended for business clients. Image-rendering software packages like Adobe Photoshop, or the less advanced, less expensive JASC PaintShop Pro, often augment DTP systems by working in tandem with page-editing programs. Some basic word-processing programs also allow image importation.

Dorothy Stonely of the *Silicon Valley/San Jose Business Journal* identifies three general categories of desktop publishers: those who publish for others, those who publish for themselves, and those who do both. A desktop publisher might be the city desk editor at *El Cajon Daily Californian* or the volunteer editor of a cancer support-group newsletter. A desktop publisher might be a small-town motel proprietor who sends out self-designed Christmas cards to frequent customers, produced on a home computer. Or a desktop publisher might be an out-of-work Web site producer polishing up a resume. The equalizer is the software.

Among the most important characteristics of DTP software are the programs' ability to allow editors to choose among a variety of type sizes and fonts; allow users to import text, illustrations, and photographs; create text columns of varying widths; and save documents and images in multiple formats. Upper-end packages like QuarkXPress allow editors to flow text around oddly shaped images on a page, or to create color separations for the printer. Many also provide pre-designed document templates that eliminate much of the effort needed to create slick-looking documents, and allow for "kerning," the adjusting of spaces between letters in a sentence. They usually also include spellcheckers, thesauruses, and other handy features.

Much of DTP has shifted from print to the World Wide Web. The Web is an even less expensive method of publishing documents than print-based DTP, and makes documents instantly available around the world to anyone with an Internet connection who wants to see them. The Web's hypertext structure also allows for new media possibilities not feasible in print, including the importation of sound and video clips on published "pages." While producing such audio and video on the Web may not be as easy as importing a graphic with QuarkXPress, it is getting easier, especially as faster processing speeds and improved computer hardware make audio and video easier to utilize, and as newer software products such as Macromedia's Flash, MGI's VideoWave, and RealNetworks' RealProducer bring animation, video, and audio elements within the grasp of everyday Web publishers.

"The one-person Web page is looking more and more like the typewritten newsletter," Bissex writes. "But while this second, electronic, 'desktop publishing' revolution won't do an end-run around Big Media any more than the paper one did, it will, like the paper one, bring out a few more voices that haven't been heard before. And that's what publishing, whether on paper or in cyberspace, is really about."

Bibliography

Bissex, Paul. "The Web: Desktop Publishing Redux." *The WELL,* February 19, 1996. <http://www.well.com/user/pb/cyb/arc/Cy.96.02.19.html> (May 24, 2002).

Hiltzik, Michael A. *Dealers of Lightning: Xerox PARC and the Dawn of the Computer Age.* New York: HarperCollins Publishers, 1999.

Holmes, Dave. "The State of Desktop Publishing Today." *The Computer Paper,* April 1997. <http://www.geocities.com/SiliconValley/Office/6224/davedtpstate.html> (May 24, 2002).

Jones Digital Century. "Desktop Publishing (DTP)." 1994–99. <http://www.digitalcentury.com/encyclo/update/desktop.html> (May 24, 2002).

Kennedy, Roger. "Next Generation of Publishers." *Business First,* January 29, 1999. <http://louisville.bcentral.com/louisville/stories/1999/02/01/focus2.html> (May 24, 2002).

Kvern, Olav Martin. "Still Waiting for the Revolution." *Creativepro.com,* October 26, 1999. <http://www.creativepro.com/story/feature/2502.html> (May 24, 2002).

Ott, Christopher. "The Desktop Publishing War Heats Up." *Denver Business Journal,* March 26, 1999. <http://denver.bcentral.com/denver/stories/1999/03/29/smallb7.html> (May 24, 2002).

Ryburn, Paul. "Desktop Publishing." Department of Mathematical Sciences, The University of Memphis, Tennessee, January 1997. <http://www.msci.memphis.edu/~ryburnp/cl/wp/dtp.html> (May 24, 2002).

Tennyson Graphics. "History of Desktop Publishing." 1995–96. <http://www.tennysongraphics.com/desk1b.htm> (May 24, 2002).

Webopaedia. "Desktop Publishing." March 1, 2002. <http://www.pcwebopaedia.com/TERM/d/desktop_publishing.html> (May 24, 2002).

Further Reading

Lumgair, Christopher. *Desktop Publishing.* New York: McGraw-Hill Professional, 2001.

Mello, Adrian. "The Next Killer App: The Search Continues." *Macworld*, September 1994. <http://www.macworld.com/1994/09/opinion/1320.html> (May 24, 2002).

Stonely, Dorothy. "Desktop Publishing Industry Evolves with Demand." *Silicon Valley/San Jose Business Journal,* March 14, 1997. <http://sanjose.bcentral.com/sanjose/stories/1997/03/17/focus2.html> (May 24, 2002).

Related Topics

Authoring Tools; Graphical User Interface; Information Design; Jobs, Steven P.; World Wide Web; Xerox Palo Alto Research Center

— *Kevin Featherly*

Desktop Video

The term desktop video (DTV) refers to any pre-recorded or real-time video that is capable of being played or edited on a desktop computer. Examples of playable desktop DTVs can range from converted video camera footage to computer video conferencing.

Before DTVs could be introduced to the public, hardware capable of handling both the editing and playback of DTVs needed to be designed. In the mid-1980s, Amiga introduced the Amiga 1000, which was capable of handling the necessary graphic and sound requirements for DTV. In 1990, a company named NewTek, credited as the first makers of a DTV system, introduced the first desktop video-editing device for the Amiga, called the Video Toaster. Unfortunately, NewTek's hardware and software were still too expensive for the average computer user.

During this time, Apple Computer's "Project Warhol" had begun creating a more affordable DTV system. In 1991, Apple introduced QuickTime 1.0, which was capable of showing a short movie in a postage stamp–sized window and allowing users to engage in basic video editing. Soon thereafter, Apple introduced QuickTime for Windows, thus making QuickTime movies multi-platformed. Microsoft quickly introduced its own movie player called Video for Windows, but was unable to produce a desktop movie of equal quality.

In October 1993, Apple expanded the computer's DTV capabilities to the playing of real-time television broadcasts. Macintosh TV (MacTV) outfitted computers with a specialized video card capable of linking to cable television outputs. While this proved that real-time television could be shown using a computer, they discontinued it six months after its introduction, only to reintroduce it a few years later. MacTV and TV video cards for IBM clones, while currently available, are still not very popular.

Most current versions of DTV player programs (e.g., RealVideo, QuickTime) show videos on a 640x480 pixel screen, and can stream more frames per second than pervious versions, allowing the picture's movement to appear smoother.

Initially, computer users could play only DVD movies, because a digital encryption disabled the copying of movies to the hard drive. By 2000, the code used to encrypt DVDs was broken by a program called DeCSS, which allows for DVD movies to be copied, and therefore pirated. DivX;-), a new compression format and software for DVDs, is able to save movies as smaller files than MPEG-4 compressions, which then can speedily be sent over the Internet.

DTV also comprises real-time motion videos, such as video conferencing and video chatting via the Internet. Using "Eyeball" cameras in conjunction with conferencing software, users can chat with one another over a network in real time. These videos need high amounts of memory and streaming in order to work, and their quality of movement is mostly jumpy.

DTV users can also create, manipulate, and publish movies by using hardware and software programs to add special effects, graphics, and sound overlays. In order to begin desktop-video publishing, several different hardware and software components are needed, in addition to a minimum of a Pentium I 100 MHz chip, 64 MB of RAM, a 32-bit sound card, and a 4-gigabyte hard drive. Any video footage to be manipulated on the computer must first be captured using either an analog or digital camcorder. If an analog camcorder is used, the video will need to be digitized through a video capture card, which converts the analog signal to a digital signal, thereby making it playable on the computer. Once the video is converted, a number of software packages (e.g., Premiere) can be used to edit them. These programs vary in difficulty level as well as capabilities.

People interested in DTV editing need to be aware that the process of capturing, converting, and editing a video is time consuming, and requires a good deal of equipment (e.g., camcorder, video capture card, specialized software) in addition to a standard computer. Users should also be aware that different compression levels may be necessary, depending on the make of the recipient's computer, as well as on download times and streaming rates.

DTV is not without its philosophical complications. As DTV becomes easier and more affordable to play, produce, and manipulate, it becomes harder to distinguish factual videos from created videos. Sometimes videos distributed over the Internet, while appearing real, may be spoofs involving voice dubovers of prominent people. In combination with the Internet's ability to disseminate information freely, DTV also allows materials such as pornographic movies and pirated VHS or DVD movies to be shared and viewed from home. On the positive side, advancements in DTV make it possible for video conferencing and home videos to be shared as email attachments, on CDs, on VHS tape, or over the web.

Bibliography

Apple Computers. "Systems Requirements." 2002. <http://www.apple.com/quicktime/download/requirements.html> (April 5, 2002).

"Desktop Video." *About.com.* <http://desktopvideo.about.com> (April 5, 2002).

Dodd, Jeff. "PC Tips: Video." *Smart Computing*, 7:1, (January 2000), pp. 83–84.

RealPlayer. "RealPlayer 8 Basic Minimum System Requirements." 2001. <http://www.realplayer.com> (April 5, 2002).

Further Reading

College of Education, University of Missouri–Columbia. "Desktop Video Conferencing." 1998. <http://www.coe.missouri.edu/~cjw/video/index.htm> (May 5, 2002).

Holzberg, Carol. "Video-Editing Packages: Software Puts You in the Director's Chair." *Smart Computing*, 7:1, (January 2001), pp. 64–65.

Related Topics
DeCSS; QuickTime

— *Kathy Broneck*

Digital Art and Animation

Digital art and animation refers to the use of computer-generated visual imaging techniques, which are used most prominently in the film and computer game industries. It also refers to the use of simulated graphics, rendering, and image manipulation in art installations, software, and interface design.

Companies involved in the development and production of these techniques include Industrial Light and Magic, Dreamworks, Klasky Csupo, Pixar, and Disney. Films noted as leading examples in the use of computer-generated animation include *Jurassic Park* (1993), *Titanic* (1997), *A Bug's Life* (1998), *Antz* (1998), and *The Matrix* (1999). Types of films such as these fall into two major categories: films that use digitally animated characters and effects alongside, or integrated with, traditional techniques (e.g., *Titanic*); and those that use these effects to produce an entire film (e.g., *A Bug's Life*).

The development of digital art and animation techniques can be traced through several intersecting fields. The art of special effects in the film industry has developed from analog effects and animation to computer-generated images. Fine art animation and photography have also had direct input. These developments can be seen through the evolution of cartoon and animated forms, which have developed from the use of models and drawings, which are then filmed to create movement, to the use of simulation, where three-dimensional modeling and computer animation can be rendered directly through the software. Aesthetic influences from print forms such as graphic novels and Japanese anime are also relevant, as are animated film and science fiction.

The development of the field of digital art and animation also owes much to the computer-gaming industry, research into avatars and multi-user environments, and techniques such as motion capture and rendering. Sound and voice synthesis is also an important aspect of this field. It is via computer games that cutting-edge digital art and animation are distributed to the widest consumer groups. The game Quake is often cited as an

Psychedelic image of a sunset, in which the colors are controlled by the viewer. From Daniel Sandin's installation, "From Death's Door to the Garden Penninsula." (Courtesy of Daniel Sandin)

example of the popular consumption of leading digital-imaging techniques. Also important is the intersection of these techniques with scientific and medical imaging processes, such as endoscopy and magnetic resonance imaging (MRI). The application of digital art and animation techniques thus extends beyond the entertainment industry to other business arenas, the arts, science, medicine, and the military.

The history of digital art and animation is also part of the history of visual culture. The emergence of film and photography as influential and widespread media forms occurred at the end of the nineteenth and beginning of the twentieth centuries. From their inception, these technologies were used to create illusion and spectacle as well as for the purposes of realism. Early cinema was effects-oriented, and the dramatic use of light helped make black-and-white images compelling.

The history of special effects is more properly the history of cinema, but digital art and animation represent the convergence of computing and film. The use of digital effects in film emerged in the 1970s and saw exponential growth in the 1980s and 1990s, growth that can be related to a wider convergence in the media industries more generally. An example of this convergence is the development of Dreamworks SKG, which was formed in 1994 by Steven Spielberg, David Geffen, and Jeffrey Katzenberg. Industrial Light and Magic, an effects company, is one of the forerunners of the field of digital special effects, founded by George Lucas and awarded more than 14 Academy Awards for best visual effects.

There are also many independent and smaller-profile companies and practitioners that have developed

digital art and animation as a form. While graphic design and fine art are fields that input directly into the production of digital multimedia, computer-game development is the single most important contributor; computer game companies currently lead graphic research. Research into techniques such as image-based rendering, visibility processing, and voice synthesis have been largely driven by the need for realistic, real-time graphics in gaming.

In the 1980s, the Commodore 64 and Atari were the platforms for computer games. These types of platforms had an eight-bit capacity, game design was programming-driven, and graphics were realized through a two-dimensional vector grid, with block figures and heavy use of color to compensate for lack of depth. Home computing's limited processing capacity presented a challenge to programmers, and it has been argued that game-play design was more innovative during this period. Contemporary computer graphics are supported by three-dimensional raster-grid technology, which enables filmic realization. With the development of dedicated game consoles and personal computing on the kind of scale that occurred in the 1990s, games have become similar to the experience of film, and it is in this context that the two forms have converged. As entertainment formats, film, television, and computer games (which can also be played on the television) have become competing products.

The ability to incorporate any media element into the computer has placed the consumption of computing technologies and visual media in the same paradigm. A current example of this convergence is the Sony PlayStation, now into its second model. The PlayStation is a dedicated game console, with all of its processing power directed to this end. It is played using a handset to control a game environment, which appears on the television screen and is stored on CD. The graphics capacity of the PlayStation is filmic, and the pre-programmed sequences of current console games have the same graphic resonance as film. The digitally animated film *A Bug's Life* has spawned a computer game of the same name, and the pre-programmed sequences that frame each section of the game are scenes from the film. In order to make such a convergence successful, the graphics in the game must match those of the film. It is this necessity that drives digital animation, because although pre-programmed sequences have filmic quality, the episodes of the game that are driven by the player do not have the same level of graphic quality. The current aim of commercial digital art and animation research is to produce games that look like films, and films that are aesthetically indistinguishable from games.

Contemporary directions in digital art and animation can be characterized by a preoccupation with realism. The simulation of realism is a contemporary generic style, and the pursuit of a realization of the human form drives much contemporary research. The application of human realism has already been applied to film to simulate actors; examples include the animated film *Final Fantasy: the Spirits Within* (2001) or the crowd scenes generated for *Gladiator* (2000). The sophisticated technologies required to synthesize voice and motion, and the level of rendering detail required for such simulation to work in close-up, involve prohibitive costs and time considerations at present. However, the application of digital animation in military and scientific projects, the experiences of computer gaming, and the popularity of animation in general indicate that this field will continue to attract investment and research.

An organizing body in the field of digital art and animation is SIGGRAPH—The Special Interest Group on Computer Graphics and Interactive Techniques. This organization has been active since the 1960s, and has held annual conferences since 1974 that have become a showcase for new industry developments. Another important center for development is ZKM (The Centre for Art and Media/Zentrum für Kunst und Medientechnologie), which was set up in 1997; like SIGGRAPH, ZKM promotes production, research, exhibition, and the dissemination of information in the field.

Bibliography
Darley, Andrew. *Visual Digital Culture: Surface Play and Spectacle in New Media Genres*. London: Routledge, 2000.

Hourvitz, Leo. "About ACM SIGGRAPH." <http://www.siggraph.org/> (April 5, 2002).

O'Riordan, Kate. "Playing With Lara in Virtual Space." *Technospaces: Inside the New Media*. Munt, S. R., ed. London: Continuum, 2001.

Further Reading
Holtzman, Steven R. *Digital Mantras: The Languages of Abstract and Virtual Worlds*. Cambridge: MIT Press, 1994.

Laurel, Brenda. *The Art of Human-Computer Interface Design*. Reading/Wokingham: Addison-Wesley, 1990.

Penny, Simon. *Critical Issues in Electronic Media*. New York: State University of New York Press, 1995.

Related Topics
Carmack, John; CAVE; Computer Graphics; Gaming; Krause, Kai; Lucas, George; SIGGRAPH

— *Kate O'Riordan*

Digital Asset Management

Digital is a term used to describe binary data; an asset is anything considered valuable; and management is the process of controlling. Taken collectively, digital asset management (DAM) is the organization, manipulation, and control of media files in a database. The advent of the computer has changed the standards for creating documents, artwork, and multimedia. Many forms of media can be created and manipulated through computer programs. Internet growth, too, has emphasized the importance of using images to sell items or attract visitors to Web sites. Increasing use of digital media has made it important for organizations and individuals to find the means by which to manage it.

DAM systems were created as a method for labeling, tracking, sharing, and inventorying important data of various digital types. The functionality of DAM is found in its ability to organize information and make it accessible to many different sectors of business while reducing expenses, time, and effort. Possessing a combination of a searchable database and Internet/Intranet connectivity, DAM enables companies to use Web browsers and networking to access items from remote offices or computer terminals. Web pages created by DAM systems present an easy way for digital items to be shared, browsed, and searched from remote computers with access to the Internet. The application itself acts as a tool for storage and retrieval. Finding a fit between management objectives and the application software functionality becomes important when selecting a DAM system.

Synonymous with media assets, digital assets encompass text, images, audio, video, and almost anything capable of being created with or captured through the use of a digital camera, scanner, or computer. Once a piece of media is produced, DAM systems can save money and time by automating handling procedures. Due to the functionality of the software, there is a reduction in the amount of labor required to locate specific assets. By typing asset identification words into the DAM system, an actual image, or a thumbnail image that is smaller in size, returns to the client station, completely removing the physical task of finding items. The digital nature of the media allows for easy re-purposing, ultimately saving time and increasing workflow efficiency. A copy of the digital media can be utilized for a project or development, then used again. And, if anything were to happen to the actual assets, an image could be presented to insurance companies for reimbursement.

According to Teri Ross, owner and president of Imagine That! Consulting Group, there are five category types of DAM systems, ranging from the simplest to the most complex. As the asset management objectives increase, DAM software features also increase, enabling almost any task to be handled. A desktop system, the simplest of the DAM application categories, is appropriate for smaller objectives. Such systems are capable of organizing smaller compilations of data, and often provide only a thumbnail image with reference information for the actual asset. Advancements in the second category of DAM applications, called a collaborative solution, include features that support communication within the management process and allow media files to be shared across a network.

Process-oriented solutions, the third category, further add to the application's management abilities. By focusing its functionality on the project itself, this application permits a manager to monitor the development of assets within a firm. Communication capabilities continue to expand and include the sharing of information with distributors and service providers in an industry-centric application, the fourth category. Using this software, a retail store could notify a clothing company of a decline in its stock and a need for re-supply. The final DAM software category connects different department functions within a firm to one system. Known as merchant-centric applications, this software is capable of delivering automated processes to a firm by accounting for the ordering, reporting, and billing of sold assets.

WebAspire, a digital assets developer, credits the DAM technology as an effective method for organizing digital assets, in addition to the software's ability to increase an asset's usability. For example, online clothing retailers can keep track of original shirt designs, colors, and sizes using DAM software applications. Through different working versions of the asset-management technology, retailers can sell articles of clothing on their Web sites, as well as keep track of their inventory.

Libraries are often faced with the problems of meeting book demand, as well as of maintaining the physical integrity of their collections—book covers and pages tend to degrade over time. Through digitizing, or capturing the cover and pages into an image, books can be represented through a series of images that will not fall apart; in addition, accessibility will increase through computer streamlining. Digitized texts can then be accounted for, stored, and distributed through a DAM system. Escalating an asset's longevity became an important project for Cornell during the 1990s. According to Anne R. Kenny and Oya Y. Rieger of Cornell's Department of Preservation, studies were conducted to find a way to preserve texts and increase their accessibility to students. For a library system, it would be more effective to generate digital images of books, preserving their physical state and multiplying their access. The digital images would then be considered assets, and finding a way to manage them becomes important.

Whether a company is trying to make sales on the World Wide Web or a library is trying to safeguard its brittle books, the future of DAM looks strong. Developments in computer peripherals such as the digital camera and scanner are making it easy for almost anything to be rendered in digital form by almost anyone. The creation of a digital object can permit greater accessibility and preserve an object's physical state by making it virtual (in the sense that the object in the image is intangible, but viewable). For these reasons, a digital object becomes a valuable asset. Ultimately, asset organization becomes essential, and DAM software applications make it easier.

Bibliography

Kenny, Anne R., and Oya Y. Rieger. "Preserving Digital Assets: Cornell's Digital Image Collection Project." *First Monday* 5, no. 6 (June 2000).

Iverson, Hans Christian. "Digital Assets Management." *International Broadcast Engineer* no. 314 (February 2001).

Ross, Terri. "Digital Asset Management: The Art of Archiving." September 1999. <http://www.techexchange.com/thelibrary/DAM.html> (April 5, 2002).

Further Reading

Asbury, Eve. "The DAM Revolution Heats Up." *Publishing & Production Executive* 99, no. 13 (August 1999).

Garone, Liz. "Technology Overview: Digital Asset Management." <http://www.garone.com/writing/dam.html> (April 5, 2002).

Leland, Liza. "Can You Profit with DAM?" *American Printer* 223, no. 2 (May 1999).

Shrake, Scott. "Finding an Asset Management Solution That's Right for You." *Target Marketing* 23, no. 6 (June 2000).

Related Topics
Customer Relationship Management; Data Mining;
Internet; Knowledge Management; World Wide Web

— *James Pyfer*

Digital Audio

While digital audio has become a core component of modern music and telecommunications, digital audio technology is still very much in flux.

When sound is recorded on tape or transmitted via telephone, it is converted into an electrical signal. This is called "analog" audio, because the electrical signal is an analogue of the sound that created it. Upon playback, the electrical signal is converted back into sound. In digital audio, another step is added in which the electrical signal is converted into digital data—a series of zeros and ones—for the purposes of storage or transmission. There are several ways to do this, but the most common system in use, which was developed by Sony, is called Pulse Code Modulation (PCM).

Two variables are important for converting analog audio to digital data: bit depth and sampling rate. Bit depth determines the possible distance between maximum and minimum volume in a sound. For instance, in a one-bit system, the possible values are zero and one, so a sound is either off or on at full volume. With additional bits, possible levels double, so a 16-bit system (the standard for CDs) has over 65,000 possible levels, and a 24-bit system (the DVD standard) has over 16 million possible levels. Higher bit resolution is usually thought to correspond with higher sound quality. However, higher resolutions require more space to store and more bandwidth to transmit; a 24-bit file is 1.5 times as large as a 16-bit file. Specifications for digital audio formats reflect a compromise between audio quality and available storage space.

Sampling rate denotes how many thousands of times per second (kilohertz, or kHz) a digital audio system takes a "snapshot" of the analog signal. Think of sampling rate like the frames of a movie: By itself, each frame appears as a still image, but by projecting a series of still images, we create the illusion of motion. The same is true for digital audio. By playing back 44,100 samples a second, CDs provide the illusion of continuous sound. As with bit depth, higher sampling rates tend to sound better than lower rates, just as a higher number of frames per second provide a smoother image of motion. But the same tradeoffs are at issue with bandwidth and storage space; a 96 kHz file (the standard for DVD) is more than twice as large as a 44.1 kHz file.

Because digital audio converts sound into data, it has brought with it an unprecedented level of flexibility and portability in the production and consumption of music. Although much analog equipment is still used to record music, a whole new breed of microprocessor-based technologies has made recording cheaper and more powerful. Since digital audio is simply a series of digital data streams, it can be manipulated through computer software via a graphical user interface (GUI). This allows musicians and audio engineers to manipulate and edit any aspect of a sound, often through the creation and manipulation of images of sounds. Perhaps the most musically important innovation in this area is a device called the sampler (although sampling can also be done with a computer and software), which records a sound and can play it back in original or modified form. By stringing together a group of modified samples, it is possible to create an entirely new piece of music from other audio recordings.

Digital audio has also impacted the design and use of musical instruments. Keyboard instruments and synthesizers were the first to make use of digital technology in both synthesizing sound and synchronization. One important development here was the Musical Instrument Digital Interface (MIDI), which allowed for the exchange of information between electronic music devices such as keyboards and synthesizers. More recent developments in digital audio have involved modeling acoustic properties and applying those properties to a sound. Digital reverberation algorithms can now model a wide variety of different spaces. Other digital modeling devices aim to replicate expensive or rare analog audio equipment, such as guitar amplifiers, synthesizers, and signal-processing devices.

Digital recording has significantly reduced the cost of entry for digital audio while greatly increasing the complexity of some equipment (although this increase may in part be a result of poor interface design). It is true that a relatively powerful personal computer can accomplish recording and editing feats that required tens of thousands of dollars to accomplish in the analog realm, but digital technology is not a panacea for audio recording.

For musicians and engineers, instruments and recording technologies are now subject to the relatively rapid product cycles of computers. Whereas a microphone or guitar can continue to be viable 50 or more years after its initial purchase, digital audio equipment that is even 10 years old is often considered out of date and unsuitable for professional use, although some pieces of equipment have had a little more staying power. Musicians and recording engineers no longer simply use technology; they also have to manage it.

Today, most new music is released on CD. For consumers, digital audio has become the de facto standard. Digital audio has also facilitated the trading of audio files over the Internet, causing much concern for the recording industry. But it remains to be seen if digital distribution, without other fundamental changes, poses a real threat to the music industry. The widespread availability of cheap cassette technology in the 1970s and 1980s, for example, fostered a marked increase in piracy in many countries around the world, but despite the proliferation of recordings, the record industry did not collapse.

Although standards continue to change, digital audio has become a staple of the production and consumption of music. In the process, music has become more mobile, and more easily managed and manipulated.

Bibliography

Goodwin, Andrew. "Sample and Hold: Pop Music in the Age of Digital Production." *On Record: Rock, Pop, and the Written Word*. Simon Frith and Andrew Goodwin, eds. London: Routledge, 1990; pp. 258–73.

Negativland. "Shiny, Aluminum, Plastic, and Digital." <http://www.negativland.com/minidis.html> (April 5, 2002).

Théberge, Paul. *Any Sound You Can Imagine: Making Music/Consuming Technology*. Hanover, N.H.: Wesleyan University Press, 1997.

Further Reading

Pohlmann, Ken. *Principles of Digital Audio*. 4th Edition. New York: McGraw-Hill, 2000.

"The Recording FAQ." <http://go.to/recordingfaq> (April 5, 2002).

Wallis, Roger, and Krister Malm. *Big Sounds from Small Peoples: The Music Industry in Small Countries*. New York: Pendragon Press, 1984.

Related Topics

Compression; Desktop Video; Electronic Publishing; Graphical User Interface; Interface; MIDI; Moog, Robert; MPEG

— *Jonathan Sterne*

Digital Cash

Digital cash, also known as digital money or e-cash, is the electronic currency used to make purchases for merchandise and services, mostly through online transactions. Users pre-purchase cash credits from a digital cash provider, then transfer these credits to vendors in lieu of using a credit card, bank account number, or check. When users pay for purchases using digital cash, clearance for the purchase is done automatically online, and neither a bank nor credit-card vendor need to be contacted for approval.

David Chaum, creator of DigiCash, Inc., the first digital cash-transfer company, is credited with being the father of digital cash. The primary motivators for the invention of digital cash were to enable consumers to shop and purchase from any online store without waiting for their checks to be mailed and cleared; to allow them to shop from any store without worrying if the store accepted specific credit cards; and, more importantly, to transcend real-world currency exchange rates to create a globally accepted, universal currency.

To begin using digital cash, users need to set up an account with a digital-cash service provider. Money is transferred from users' real-world bank accounts or credit cards and stored as digital money either in their online accounts, on their computer's hard drive, or in electronic "wallets" as pieces of encrypted information.

Once an account is started, users of digital cash are given public keys. The concept of a key in cryptography references a very large string of random numbers that encrypt coded information and help to make it indistinguishable from a stream of other random bits. Such keys are generated in pairs—a public key and a private key.

The public key is a string of numbers that is available to anyone using a system, and can be freely given to anyone by the user. The private key is one to which only the user has access, and it is kept secret. Both keys are needed to encode and decode the message or transaction. If you sent a transaction request that was encoded using your private key, the recipient would need your public key in order to read the information, and vice versa. Current users of digital cash do not need to worry about learning their code numbers, as the digital-cash providers automatically retrieve the appropriate codes.

There are two kinds of digital cash currently available for consumers to use: identified digital cash (IDC) and anonymous digital cash (ADC). Using IDC is similar to making purchases using credit cards and checks. IDC leaves transaction trails, as personal information about the purchaser is contained with the IDC. This information enables banks, stores, and other recipients of IDC to trace where the money originally came from. In order to obtain an IDC account, a user must identify an account from which the money was transferred, as well as enable a non-blind signature. By contrast, ADC does not contain any personal information, nor can a transaction trail be created; in this sense, it works in the same manner as do cash purchases.

In its early stages, digital-cash companies such as DigiCash utilized only bank accounts; users specified amounts of money that were then taken from their accounts and converted to digital money. However, one of the latest trends in digital cash is for users to supply an online-payment service company, such as the popular PayPal service, with a credit card or bank account number from which money can be taken.

In addition, companies such as Cybermoola and Western Union allow people to purchase digital cash credits, similar to gift cards, from real stores. Users type the number on the card into their online account to activate the digital cash credit. Cybermoola also allows its users to send checks through the mail that they then credit to users' accounts. Echarge Phone works in conjunction with telephone billing agents, and allows users to purchase items that are then billed directly to their telephone bills.

Recently, technology has advanced to the point where consumers now have the ability to transfer their digital cash from the PC to a smart card if they should decide to use the money offline. The smart card stores the information in a special computer chip, and is used just like a debit card in real-world stores. However, users and retailers alike must purchase smart card readers for their personal computers in order to take advantage of this option.

Most people think of digital cash in relation to large online purchases, but micropayment, the ability to charge and pay for smaller online services, has been available since the early 1990s. Before digital cash, the cost of charging for small purchases (e.g., small excerpts of information, one song, or pay-per-play games) was too high for businesses, as they paid credit-card companies a fee per transaction. When digital cash started becoming more prevalent, companies such as CyberCash's CyberCoin started offering software that would enable a business to charge for small services without incurring the large transaction fees associated with credit cards. CyberCoin was discontinued in the United States, as it was not proving popular; other prototypes, such as Carnegie Mellon's NetBill, never made it into the consumer mainstream. Developments in the entertainment industry, most notably on the part of companies such as Napster, have created a renewed interest in micropayments. Compaq's Millicent, Pay2see, and IBM's NewGenPay already have software that companies interested in using micropayments can download. Still, micropayments, while projected to be lucrative, are not commonplace; users do not want to carry multiple accounts, and businesses do not want to utilize the software if the micropayment providers do not have many active users.

While digital cash affords consumers more freedom and ease of purchase, e-commerce companies are still concerned about fraud, money laundering, duplication, and security. Because digital cash is essentially an electronic string of numbers, many consumers and businesses alike are worried that these strings can be duplicated, thereby increasing the amount of digital money on a person's hard drive or smart card. These concerns took on new urgency with the increased use of Digital Gold, whose users buy grams of gold that are held by a Web company and exchanged virtually in online transactions. This allows for the avoidance of currency exchange rates, and in effect creates an international currency independent of government control.

Even though the use of digital cash is increasing every year, consumers must still remember that they need Internet and computer access, plus money up front, in order to obtain digital cash. Users also should be aware that not all Internet companies accept digital cash payments, and that, as with credit cards, a company that does accept digital cash payments may utilize only specific providers.

Bibliography

Askt, Daniel. "In CyberSpace, Nobody Can Hear You Write a Check." *Los Angeles Times Magazine*, February 4, 1996, p. 20.

Associated Press, "PayPal Leads the Digital Cash Movement." *USA Today*, October 30, 2000. <http://www.usatoday.com/life/cyber/bonus/qa/ans045.htm> (March 22, 2002)

Bannan, Karen. "No Credit? No Problem! Digital Cash Made Easy." *PC World*, February 2001.

Denton, Chad. "Online Payment Systems: Parting with Cash Is Never Sweet, but It's Getting Easier." *Smart Computing* 12:4, (April 2001), pp. 88–91.

Soper, Mark. "E-money! Digital & Spendable. Is It Curtains for Cash?" *How Computers Work*, 3:4 (November 1999).

Further Reading

Chaum, David. "Achieving Electronic Privacy." *Scientific American*, August 1992, pp. 96–101.

Schneier, Bruce. *Applied Cryptography: Protocols, Algorithms, and Source Code.* New York: Wiley, 1995.

Related Topics

E-Commerce; Encryption and Cryptography; Napster; Privacy

— *Kathy Broneck*

Digital Divide

Digital divide refers to the gap between those who have access to the Internet (the "haves") and those who do not have access (the "have-nots"). There are several dimensions to the digital divide: the social divide, the gap between the information-rich and information-poor within nations; the global divide, the gap between industrialized and developing countries; and the democratic divide, the gap between those who use the Internet for civic participation and those who are passive consumers of Internet resources.

The term digital divide, which became widely popular in the mid-1990s, initially had a fairly simplistic definition, with access defined solely as technical access—access to computers and telecommunication services. Later, definitions of the digital divide began to encompass more complex measures of access—not just access to the technical infrastructure, but also access to the social infrastructure. The social infrastructure includes access to education and content, the ability to produce as well as consume information. A variety of socio-demographic characteristics were also recognized as increasing or inhibiting access, including income, education, gender, race, ethnicity, age, linguistic background, and location (e.g., rural vs. urban).

In the North American context, efforts to ameliorate the digital divide have concentrated on setting up community access points for public spaces, such as schools and libraries. International organizations are also making efforts to decrease the digital gap in developing countries. Thus, the digital divide encompasses three main trajectories: access to information and communication technologies, access to the appropriate content, and geopolitical aspects.

Various studies, by governments, industry groups, and non-governmental organizations (NGOs), have attempted to measure the digital divide. The U.S. National Telecommunications and Information Administration (NTIA) produced the first high-profile study in 1995, with the release of *Falling Through the Net: A Survey of the "Have Nots" in Urban and Rural America*. Measuring household telephone, computer, and Internet penetration rates to determine who owned telephones and personal computers and who accessed the Internet at home, the study revealed that access was related to socioeconomic and geographic factors, with the information have-nots disproportionately found in rural areas and central cities.

The NTIA's 1999 version of *Falling Through the Net*, subtitled *Defining the Digital Divide*, revealed that while more Americans are accessing the Internet, significant discrepancies in access still existed, and in some instances had widened considerably. Race is a factor, as blacks and Hispanics are less likely to be connected anywhere compared to whites at home. Education is a factor, as those with a college degree are more than 16 times more likely to have home Internet access as those with an elementary school degree. Income is a factor, as high-income urban households are more than 20 times as likely as rural, low-income households to have Internet access. Marital status is also a factor, as children in dual-parent white households are nearly twice as likely to have the Internet at home as children in white single-parent households.

The NTIA's 2000 *Falling Through the Net* report, *Toward Digital Inclusion*, looked at individual access, household access to high-speed services (such as digital subscriber lines, or DSL), and access for people with disabilities. Overall, the NTIA concluded, digital inclusion is advancing rapidly among most groups of Americans, regardless of income, education, race/ethnicity, location, age, or gender. Furthermore, those who were previously not connected are now making significant gains, particularly across education and gender lines. However, even though computer ownership and Internet access are rising rapidly for most groups, in some cases the digital divide remains the same, or has expanded slightly. This is especially the case for people with disabilities, single-parent households, and for blacks and Hispanics.

Although digital-divide studies were initially conducted in the North American context, the international promotion of electronic commerce and a liberalized telecommunication sector has led to the recognition that the digital divide also exists between and among countries. So, although the 1990s witnessed a fantastic penetration rate of the Internet in most regions of the world, other countries, such as Central and South America, have lagged behind. According to the Organization for Economic Cooperation and Development (OECD), Internet growth in Africa has been negligible, with 0.25 percent of Internet hosts being located there, compared to 88 percent in North America and Europe.

According to the OECD, the fundamental barrier in this case is access to basic telecommunications services, and trade liberalization and increased market competition for telecommunications services are the mechanisms to overcome this digital divide. Trade liberalization has increased the demand for communication services, and has led to an increase in the growth of access lines (fixed and mobile), alternative access technologies, and Internet access and use, as well as to lower bandwidth prices.

Bridging the global digital divide between industrialized and developing countries is another trend. The Okinawa Charter on the Global Information Society was unveiled with much fanfare at the annual G8 summit held in Japan in the summer of 2000. There, the G8 leaders formed the Digital Opportunities Task (DOT) Force, and extended the invitation to 32 members of organizations, private industry, and non-profits to join the DOT Force in an international effort to bridge the "international information and knowledge divide."

A variety of public-sector and non-profit policy initiatives have been generated to close the digital divide, through technology acquisition, education, training, and lifelong learning. In the United States, the Telecommunications Act of 1996 directs the Federal Communications Commission (FCC) to implement a funding mechanism—the E-rate—to bring Internet technology to public schools and libraries. Canada has several funding programs to create Internet access in public spaces, such as schools and libraries, and community access points, particularly in rural and remote areas. Corporations (including Microsoft, AT&T, Intel, Hewlett-Packard, and AOL/Time-Warner) have established foundations that help provide Internet access to local communities, typically through donations of used equipment and training.

The question of whether or not these policy fixes will eliminate the digital divide will be the basis of future research. Will the digital divide be transitory or persistent? Some contend that as the cost of computers and online access decreases, and as more schools and public institutions become wired, concerns about a digital divide will become moot. After all, there will always be areas of social stratification that no amount of public subsidy can fix. But others contend that if the assumption remains that basic computer skills are essential for economic success, and if the Internet is essential for participation in civic and cultural life, then we need to be concerned

and diligent so that the information-poor will not become further marginalized.

Bibliography

Compaine, Benjamin M. *The Digital Divide: Facing a Crisis or Creating a Myth?* Cambridge, Mass.: MIT Press, 2001.

Digital Opportunity Task Force. <http://www.dotforce.org/> (May 5, 2002).

Norris, Pippa. *Digital Divide? Civic Engagement, Information Poverty and the Internet Worldwide.* Cambridge: Cambridge University Press, 2001.

Organization for Economic Cooperation and Development (OECD). *Understanding the Digital Divide.* 2001. <http://www.oecd.org/dsti/sti/prod/Digital_divide.pdf> (May 5, 2002).

U.S. Department of Commerce. "A NATION ONLINE: How Americans Are Expanding Their Use of the Internet." February 2002. <http://www.ntia.doc.gov/ntiahome/dn/index.html> (May 5, 2002).

Further Reading

Benton Foundation Digital Divide Resources. <http://www.benton.org/Divide/> (April 5, 2002).

Children's Partnership. "Online Content for Low-Income and Underserved Americans: Digital Divide's New Frontier." <http://www.childrenspartnership.org/pub/low_income/> (April 5, 2002).

Digital Divide Network. <http://www.digitaldividenetwork.org/> (April 5, 2002).

Hoffman, Donna L.; Novak, Thomas P.; and Ann E. Schlosser. "The Evolution of the Digital Divide: How Gaps in Internet Access May Impact Electronic Commerce." *Journal of Computer-Mediated Studies* (JCMS) 5:3 (March 2000). <http://www.ascusc.org/jcmc/vol5/issue3/hoffman.html> (April 5, 2002).

Internet Society (ISOC) Divide Links. March 20, 2002. <http://www.isoc.org/internet/issues/divide/> (April 5, 2002).

World Economic Forum—Global Digital Divide Initiative. <http://www.weforum.org/digitaldivide> (April 5, 2002).

Related Topics

Access; Gender and New Media; Race and Ethnicity and New Media

— *Leslie Regan Shade*

Digital Millennium Copyright Act

The Digital Millennium Copyright Act (DMCA), signed into law by President Bill Clinton on October 28, 1998, was an attempt by the U.S. government to vault analog-media copyright protections into the digital age. The law extends legal protections for software and content authors and for media businesses, in an era when it is possible for almost anyone to make unlimited, perfect copies of digital music, books, software, and movies and to sell them or redistribute them free over the Internet. The most recent prior update to U.S. copyright laws in 1976 addressed none of those issues, because digital media barely existed at that time.

The DMCA was hatched just as it was becoming clear that copyrights were being battered on all sides by the piracy-inducing qualities of digital media. The law initially was formulated to make it possible for the U.S. government to abide by treaties it had signed at the December 1996 convention of the World Intellectual Property Organization (WIPO) in Geneva, Switzerland. However, as passed, the DMCA contains provisions that were not part of the WIPO discussions.

DMCA Overview

The DMCA makes it a crime to circumvent anti-piracy tools in commercial software, or to sell code-cracking devices or programs. It does, however, allow some copyright-protection protocols to be cracked in the name of encryption research, or of assessing product interoperability, or of testing computer security systems. It has other provisions that, like the existing copyright laws, prevent unauthorized copying of a copyrighted digital work. Making or selling devices or services that are capable of either copying or circumventing the protections of copyrighted works is also a crime under the law, in certain circumstances. The law provides some exemptions for non-profit libraries, archival database keepers, and educational institutions.

The DMCA limits the culpability of Internet service providers (ISPs), so they can't be punished if someone uses their routers and servers to illegally transmit copyrighted content over the Internet; however, ISPs are supposed to remove such infringed material when they find it. Universities and colleges are also protected under the DMCA; they can't be punished if students or staff using the schools' Internet channels put up Web sites that infringe copyrights.

Other parts of the law require that Webcasters pay licensing fees to record labels when playing their recordings online, while mandating that the U.S. Copyright Office submit recommendations to the U.S. Congress on "maintaining an appropriate balance between the rights of copyright owners and the needs of users."

Violators of the DMCA may be punished by fines of up to $500,000 and five years in prison for a first offense, and by fines of up to $1 million and 10 years in prison for any subsequent offenses.

Fair Use

Whatever its intentions, the DMCA has sparked great public controversy among civil liberties groups, free-speech advocates, digital-device manufacturers, and content users, who complain that the law does not merely extend copyrights to digital media, it supercedes old copyright protections, and in some cases cancels out the public's traditionally guaranteed limited rights to fair use of copyrighted material. Fair use is a legal doctrine that allows individuals to duplicate copyrighted material without compensating the copyright holder if the copied material is used for education, research, criticism, or certain other purposes. The fair-use doctrine suggests that such commonplace behaviors as making copies of software programs to use on a second household computer, or "ripping" tracks from CDs to make "mix" compilations for personal listening, would be protected. But the legality of such behavior is in fact in dispute under the DMCA.

In particular, critics say the threat of jail time and fines against anyone circumventing built-in anti-piracy programs in e-books, computer programs, MP3 files, and other digital media is disconcerting, because embedded security systems sometimes seem to erase the public's fair use rights.

The writers of the DMCA made attempts to balance the rights of copyright holders with those of the public. For instance, the law states explicitly that its provisions "shall (not) affect rights, remedies, limitations or defenses to copyright infringement, including fair use." However, to Stanford University law school professor Lawrence Lessig, who frequently is cited as an expert in digital-media law, it is a protection without muscle. Lessig points out that the DMCA protects fair-use rights only when copyright-protecting software codes permit those rights to be exercised. In other words, the question of whether someone may exercise their fair-use rights on digitized, copyrighted works is up to the rights holder to decide—and rights holders are likely to find it more profitable to maintain a monopoly on their copyrighted works than to allow people to use them without paying, regardless of whether the consumer has legal rights to do so. Importantly, the law makes it explicitly illegal to circumvent security software like the Content Scrambling System (CSS) encryption codes embedded in digital-video disks (DVDs), even if the code is cracked for the legitimate purpose of legally guaranteed fair-use rights.

In a July 21, 2000, opinion piece in the *New York Times,* however, Motion Picture Association of America (MPAA) chairman Jack Valenti defended the use of such technologies, arguing that it is important to maintain locks on digital content in order to keep creative people in business in the computer age. "If copyrights can no longer protect the distribution of the work they produce, who will invest immense sums to create films or any other creative material of the kind we now take for granted?" Valenti wrote. "Do the thieves really expect new music and movies to continue pouring forth if the artists and companies behind them are not paid for their work?"

TEST CASES EMERGE

Since its passage, the DMCA has been used in a series of controversial prosecutions and civil suits that promise to help define the DMCA's future.

The first major legal test of the DMCA was launched in December 1999, when the five major recording conglomerates (Sony Music Group, Vivendi Universal, EMI Recorded Entertainment, Warner Music, and BMG Entertainment) sued the MP3 file-swapping service Napster. The online music-swapping service had generated an audience of millions almost overnight, and record companies, later to be joined by a number of individual artists and music publishers, accused Napster of contributory copyright infringement by allowing its users to swap music for free over the Internet without paying for it.

At the service's peak in February 2001, virtually every song ever recorded was available through Napster. It didn't directly distribute the songs, but instead allowed users to link directly to each other's computer hard drives to share whatever MP3 song files they had stored there. Although an appeals court twice overruled U.S. District Court Judge Marilyn Hall Patel's orders to shut Napster down, the recording industry has won virtually every other court skirmish associated with the case, which seems destined for a legal rout. In July 2001, Napster voluntarily shut down while it prepared to switch over to a fee-based music subscription service. Bertelsman Music Group purchased Napster in May of 2002. (Other, more difficult-to-trace programs like Bearshare, Limewire, and AudioGalaxy have emerged and begun attracting Napster's fan base, however, promising more legal wrangling in this area of case law.)

Another important DMCA case also began in late 1999. It involved software developed by Norwegian teenager Jon Johansen called DeCSS, which is designed to defeat CSS encryptions embedded in DVDs. Johansen has indicated that DeCSS code was written to help create a DVD player that would work in computers running the Linux operating system (OS). At the time he created the program, the movie industry had yet to license a DVD player with CSS technology that was compatible with the Linux OS, rendering DVDs useless in Linux users' computers. However, the MPAA rejected that argument, saying that the real motivation behind DeCSS was to make it possible to copy movies and transmit them over the Internet using Napster-like online distribution services.

The legal fight over DeCSS began when Eric Corley, publisher of *2600: The Hacker Quarterly,* published the DVD-cracking code on his magazine's Web site. Corley was sued by the movie industry, and a Manhattan federal district court judge, Lewis Kaplan, ruled in August 2000 that publishing the DVD-cracking code was a violation of the DMCA. What's more, he barred *2600* from creating hyperlinks to other sites on the Internet that were publishing the code, thereby making this case not just a battle over the nature of copyrights, but also a fight over First Amendment rights. Lawyers for the Electronic Frontier Foundation, which helped defend Corley in the case, put it this way: "The dissemination of DeCSS, here by a member of the media covering an issue of public concern, is pure speech." Nevertheless, on July 3, 2002, *2600* announced that it would not pursue any further appeals.

The DMCA's First Amendment implications came even more sharply into focus in the third major DMCA case to reach U.S. courts. In that case, Princeton computer-science professor Edward W. Felten was threatened with a lawsuit for DMCA violations when he proposed to publish findings of research he had conducted seeking a way to crack the music industry's much-touted Secure Digital Music Initiative (SDMI). Ironically, the Recording Industry Association of America (RIAA) had spurred the research, issuing a public challenge to the Internet community to try to crack the SDMI's copyright protections.

When Felten and other researchers from Rice University and Xerox succeeded and announced plans to unveil a paper based on their research at a conference, the RIAA threatened to sue, saying that discussing the results could be prosecuted under the DMCA. Felten immediately withdrew his plans to discuss the findings, out of fear of being sued by the well-funded recording industry. Hours later, the

RIAA issued a press release saying that it had never intended to sue. Felten eventually published his research without incident, but a cadre of groups led by the Electronic Frontier Foundation (EFF) filed a lawsuit, asking a federal judge to rule that the DMCA cannot be used to chill the release of scientific research.

That question was prompted by the most recent, and possibly the most pivotal DMCA case. It involves Russian programmer and cryptography researcher Dmitry Sklyarov, who helped his Russian company ElcomSoft create a program called "Advanced eBook Processor," which allows users to override the security code written into Adobe Systems Inc.'s eBooks and to make digital copies of them. Sklyarov was arrested on July 17, 2001, at his hotel in Las Vegas after speaking at a conference about the eBook's security shortcomings. In August 2001, a grand jury indicted the programmer on copyright-circumvention charges under the DMCA; it also accused him of trafficking conspiracy charges, alleging that he helped his company sell and distribute the illegal software. The Russian pleaded not guilty to the charges, and has vowed not to enter into a plea bargain in the case, laying the groundwork for what promises to be a key test of the DMCA.

Interestingly, the victim of Sklyarov's alleged crime, Adobe Systems Inc., has withdrawn its support of the case, possibly due to the intense public protest that followed the programmer's arrest. The EFF, which has thrown its support behind Sklyarov, calls the Russian a victim of an unjust U.S. law that muffles the free speech of computer programmers while stripping everyone of their right to use e-books they've purchased in whatever ways they choose. The Sklyarov case is being watched particularly closely by the international Internet community, both to gauge how well the DMCA's provisions will hold up in court, and to test the extent to which U.S. Internet-related laws will hold up internationally.

VARYING LEVELS OF CONCERN

Not everyone is worried that cases like these pose serious threats to civil liberties. GartnerG2 senior analyst P.J. McNeely, for instance, has suggested that a free market will eventually sort out the DMCA's controversies. If copyright-protection schemes and legal sanctions are stretched beyond the public's tolerance, McNeely told *Newsbytes.com*, people will simply refuse to buy new digital-media products and continue buying older products—opting to own paperbacks

instead of e-books, for example. They will, in short, "vote with their wallets," McNeely says.

Another organization that seems relatively unconcerned about the DMCA is the U.S. Copyright Office, which issued its required DMCA recommendations to Congress on August 29, 2001. The Copyright Office's judgment, for the most part, was that Congress does not need to act immediately to change the law's provisions since most of the concerns expressed in the public comments collected by the office addressed "speculative concerns."

The 166-page report focuses in large measure on the "first sale doctrine," a traditional copyright-infringement defense that allows people who purchase books, records, and software to pass them on to family members, friends, or public libraries, or to sell them to second-hand retailers like used-book shops. As the *Washington Post* reported at the time of the report's release, book publishers and others have said that the first-sale privilege shouldn't extend to electronic media, because lending a copy of a digital work often requires duplicating the work. Others, however—especially librarians—said that this interpretation makes it difficult to share electronic materials, and they pushed the Copyright Office to recommend that Congress change the law to clarify those points.

The Copyright Office did suggest several minor revisions to the DMCA. It recommended that Congress allow consumers to make backup copies of their software and digital media, so long as it is clear that the copies may not be passed on to anyone else. The office's report also asks Congress to clarify the issue of temporary "buffer" recordings, which typically reside in a computer's random-access memory (RAM) as media is being streamed off the Internet. The music industry has pushed Congress to allow extra royalties to be collected on those temporary copies, even though they cannot be played or stored separately, and are used only to keep the streaming media from being interrupted during the transfer from the Internet to a user's PC.

However, the most contentious aspects of the DMCA remain to be sorted out. As was noted earlier, several court cases are still pending at the time of this writing, and their outcomes may go a long way toward determining the fate of such issues as fair use, first-sale rights, and the power of media companies to squelch free speech in the digital age.

Bibliography

Cha, Ariana Eunjung. "Keep Digital Copyright Law Intact, Agency Says." *Washington Post*, August 30, 2001.

Lessig, Lawrence. *Code and Other Laws of Cyberspace.* New York: Basic Books. 1999.

McGuire, David. "Scientists Publish Digital Music Security Research." *Newsbytes.com*, August 15, 2001.

The 105th Congress of the United States of America. "Final Joint Version of H.R. 2281, (The Digital Millennium Copyright Act)." October 28, 1998. <http://www.eff.org/IP/DMCA/hr2281_dmca_law_19981020_pl105-304.html> (May 17, 2002).

U.S. Copyright Office. "The Digital Millennium Copyright Act of 1998: U.S. Copyright Office Summary." December 1998. <http://www.loc.gov/copyright/legislation/dmca.pdf> (May 17, 2002).

———. "A Report of the Register of Copyrights Pursuant to §104 of the Digital Millennium Copyright Act." August 2001. <http://www.loc.gov/copyright/reports/studies/dmca/sec-104-report-vol-1.pdf> (May 17, 2002).

The UCLA Online Institute for Cyberspace Law and Policy. "The Digital Millennium Copyright Act." UCLA Graduate School of Education & Information Studies, February 8, 2001. <http://www.gseis.ucla.edu/iclp/dmca1.htm> (May 17, 2002).

Valenti, Jack. "There's No Free Hollywood." *New York Times,* June 21, 2000. <http://www.eff.org/IP/Video/20000621_valenti_oped.html> (May 17, 2002).

Further Reading

Allis, Sam. "Battle Brews on Right to Web Content." *Boston Globe,* March 26, 2000, p. A1.

Gillmore, Dan. "Arrest of Russian Programmer Shows Threat to Fair-Use Rights." *San Jose Mercury News,* July 18, 2001, p. 1C.

Jesdanun, Anick. "Case Tests Copyright Law: Decryption Software Raises First Amendment Question." *San Jose Mercury News,* May 2, 2001, p. 5C.

Lessig, Lawrence. "Copyright Thugs." *The Industry Standard*, May 7, 2001. <http://www.thestandard.com/article/0,1902,24208,00.html> (May 17, 2002).

———. "Copyrights Rule." *The Industry Standard,* October 2, 2000. <http://www.thestandard.com/article/0,1902,18964-1,00.html> (May 17, 2002).

Samuels, Edward. *The Illustrated Story of Copyright.* New York: Thomas Dunne Books, 2000.

Related Topics

Copyright; DeCSS; Desktop Publishing; Digital Music, Electronic Frontier Foundation; Lessig, Lawrence; Linking; MP3; Napster; Peer-to-Peer

— *Kevin Featherly*

Digital Music

Digital music is music that has been converted from sound into binary digital code. It represents the single biggest innovation in the music industry since Thomas Edison first scratched his own voice reciting "Mary Had a Little Lamb" into a piece of tinfoil in 1876. It has proved to be both boon and bane to the recording industry.

In 1981, two electronics manufacturers (Philips and Sony) perfected the compact disc (CD), the first mass-marketed digital-music format. CD sales rapidly overtook those of vinyl long-playing records, first surpassing them in 1988. However, the same digital technology that helped to pull the recording industry out of an extended recession in the 1980s later shook record companies to their foundations.

In the mid-1990s, a combination of new consumer-electronics products, improved software, and enhanced digital-compression algorithms made it suddenly easy for music listeners to make digital copies of CDs at home. Coupled with the Internet, digital home copying led to music piracy, as fans began downloading the near-perfect digital clones of their favorite tunes that were offered in abundance online. The record industry had been slow to react to the Internet gold rush, and initially ignored the download trend. But by early 2000, with "pirates"—especially users of the online service Napster—numbering in the millions, labels launched numerous court battles on many fronts to stem the digital-music tide. Belatedly, in late 2001, they also launched their own online music initiatives.

BACKGROUND

The history of digital music parallels the history of computing. Harry Nyquist's 1929 publication of what is known as Nyquist's Theorem was a key initial development; it proved that periodic "snapshots" or "samples" of a sound could be taken, and that the sounds could be reconstructed later using those snapshots. Nyquist further demonstrated that if sounds are sampled at a rate at least twice as fast as their original frequency, no sound quality is lost upon reconstruction. Nyquist's Theorem, published before the invention of digital computers, is now the foundation for all digital-audio processing. In 1937, an International Telephone and Telegraph electrical engineer, Alec H. Reeves, advanced Nyquist's idea by devising pulse code modulation (PCM), a technology that digitizes sounds by sampling them 8,000 times a second. PCM still is used in most forms of digital recording.

Two decades would pass before Max Mathews, head of behavioral sciences research at Bell Labs and an amateur violinist, generated the first digital music from a computer in 1957. Mathews' work with digital signal processing (DSP) helped push analog telecommunications into the digital realm, while also helping to inaugurate modern digital music.

In 1979, the Royal Philips Electronics firm developed a prototype for the CD, a five-inch-diameter plastic disk with many tiny pockets pressed into it. A song's digital code is "burned" into these dimples on the disk's surface using laser technology, storing the song for later playback. At the end of the 1970s, Philips and Sony of Japan entered an agreement to jointly produce a commercially viable version of the CD, and by 1980 they arrived at a standard that gave CDs 650 MB (megabytes) of data storage, about 74 minutes of music. By 1983, electronics companies began rolling out CD players, and by 1988, Philips alone was manufacturing three million players a year. Record stores around the world began tearing out their album racks to give CDs more retail space.

In his 2001 book *Sonic Boom,* John Alderman noted that during the CD's early days, some music industry insiders argued that all disks should be stamped with protective encryption, or "watermarks," that would hinder the digital copying of music pressed on CDs. However, they were vetoed; companies determined that watermarking wasn't worth the trouble or expense. It's a decision, Alderman writes, that still haunts the music industry.

Digital home recording became possible in the late 1980s and early 1990s, with the 1987 introduction of digital audiotape (DAT) and the 1992 release of digital mini-discs. While neither format was very successful—DATs are bulky, and record labels chose to release few titles on mini-disc—another device, the portable MP3 player, which allowed copying of digital files into a small Walkman-like device, did become popular with the public in 2000. (The manufacturer of one early MP3 player, the Diamond Multimedia Rio, was unsuccessfully sued by the record industry in 1998 for facilitating copyright infringements. This was the first in a long line of MP3-related industry lawsuits.)

THE MP3 CRAZE

Work on what became known as the MP3 was first conducted in Germany in 1987. Engineer Karl-Heinz Brandenburg of the Fraunhofer Institute devised a digital audio compression-decompression (codec) technique that reduced file sizes enough for songs to be transmitted as digital files over phone lines with little loss of quality. Fraunhofer's idea was to shrink massive digital video and audio files to a size that would make them usable in low-bandwidth applications, such as multimedia programs on personal computers. At the time, computers still suffered from critically slow processing speeds and lack of file storage space.

In May 1988, the *Moving Picture Experts Group* (MPEG), a committee of the International Organization for Standardization (ISO), met for the first time to talk about digital video and audio multimedia standards. At MPEG, a group led by Italian engineer Leonardo Chiariglione incorporated Brandenburg's work into the first audiovisual standard, known as MPEG-1. There were several "layers" of the standard developed. MPEG-1 Layer 1 and Layer 2 were devised for high-performance applications, but a third layer, Layer 3, was scaled down for use in slower applications. MPEG-1 Layer 3 squashed song files down to about one-twelfth of their original size by deleting digital data that the human ear cannot hear or distinguish. Layer 3, which became famous under its abbreviated name, MP3, would soon turn the recording industry on its ear.

Atlantic Monthly reporter Charles C. Mann writes that the MP3 codec was not intended to go public. To give interested businesses a demonstration of MP3, a sample "player" was created, and its source code stored on a computer at the University of Erlangen in Germany. But a Dutch hacker calling himself SoloH gained access to the computer and nabbed the player's source code, revamping it so that it not only played music, but also could convert CD tracks into decent-quality MP3 files. "This single unexpected act undid the music industry," Mann wrote. It was able to have such huge impact thanks to the Internet.

Music went online in 1993 in Santa Cruz, California, thanks to two friends named Jeff Patterson and Rob Lord. Both were frustrated by the narrow range of musical selections available at local record stories, and by the lack of opportunities for budding musicians to make it in the record business. Their answer was the Internet Underground Music Archive (IUMA), a Web site and FTP download location that charged musicians $240 a year to post one MP3-formatted song online and to make their merchandise available for sale online. The site attracted intense media interest in the early 1990s, but the music labels appeared mostly unconcerned, because most IUMA bands had no recording contracts.

In 1995, there was another important development: a former Microsoft executive, Rob Glaser, formed Progressive Networks and debuted "streaming" media software called RealAudio. The program compressed music and voice recordings and even live radio events to the maximum extent, leaving only the bare bones of audio quality, but it was enough to allow near-real-time broadcasts on computers, even using the 14.4 kbps (kilobits per second) modems then in vogue. Streaming media thus became the chief alternative to MP3 downloads; where MP3s are stored on a computer's hard drive, streaming media comes and goes, playing in full but without being stored. Microsoft issued its competitor format, Windows Media, shortly after RealAudio's launch.

These formats allowed radio stations around the world to begin Webcasting online, and led to the creation of thousands of online-only radio stations. When plans for music subscription services began surfacing during 2000, streaming audio was the automatic preference. One of the first digital-music subscription services, Musicmatch's Radio MX, signed up nearly 100,000 customers at $4.95 a month after its launch in May 2001, offering only streaming music.

The MP3 revolution began picking up steam with the 1997 launch of MP3.com. The name of the site alone was a draw for MP3-savvy music fans all over the Internet. Like IUMA, MP3.com made music by unknown bands available online, but unlike IUMA, it did not charge them for the privilege. MP3.com became the rallying point for online music downloads, at least until the Napster phenomenon erupted in 1999.

Napster and File Sharing

Napster was a free peer-to-peer file-sharing service that allowed users to tap into each other's computers to swap MP3 files; Napster's 100 or so servers made the connections and routed the requests, and the files requested were sent to whoever sought them. Napster was stunningly easy to use, and it quickly became a monstrous success. But a judge found the company guilty of facilitating copyright infringements, and a federal judicial panel eventually upheld a court injunction against Napster in March 2001. Just one month prior to that, Napster users swapped 2.79 billion songs, according to the Webnoize research firm. By mid-2000, Mann wrote, unauthorized MP3 files

circulating online numbered somewhere between 100 million and 1 billion songs. By February 2001, the consumer-behavior research firm Ipsos-Reid was estimating that more than 50 million Americans had downloaded music off the Internet in some form.

Shocked record labels represented by the Recording Industry Association of America (RIAA), along with several musicians, a number of songwriters and publishers, and several independent record companies, all served Napster with massive copyright-infringement suits beginning in late 1999. These suits were combined, and eventually they forced Napster to shut down in the summer of 2001.

MP3.com, perhaps tarnished by its inadvertent association with Napster, also was hit with a copyright suit, and eventually was forced to pay millions of dollars to settle the litigation. MP3.com then sold out to Vivendi Universal, one of the record labels that had sued it.

The recording industry already had legislation in place to prohibit digital-music piracy. The 1998 Digital Millennium Copyright Act banned, among other things, any attempts to circumvent technological copyright protections. The DMCA was used against Napster, MP3.com, Scour Exchange, and other companies that allegedly infringed copyrights.

However, undaunted by threat of legal action, numerous peer-to-peer file-sharing services have arisen in the wake of Napster's demise. Replacement clients like KaZaA, Morpheus, Grokster, and a raft of others have surfaced, many of them designed without Napster-style central servers, making them more difficult legal targets. Nonetheless, on October 3, 2001, the RIAA sued several of them.

Copyright Protection and Subscriptions

The recording industry sought finally to install automatic copyright protection schemes in its recordings—either on physical CDs or distributed online—so that they could not be copied or further distributed except under tightly controlled circumstances. Record labels began working with a large consortium of retailers, electronics firms, trade associations, and even Napster company officials on a project known as the Secure Digital Music Initiative. It has not gone well. SDMI members include record labels, offline retailers, e-commerce Web sites, hardware manufacturers, and such legal antagonists as Napster and the RIAA, with many disparate motivations and philosophies. *Atlantic Monthly*'s Mann noted, "The initiative has been plagued by feuding and foot-dragging."

Meanwhile, the first CD released with SDMI-style copy protection was riddled with problems. In May 2001, Music City Records released "A Tribute to Jim Reeves" by country singer Charley Pride, which was encoded with SunnComm MediaCloQ technology to keep fans from making digital copies of its songs. However, consumers complained bitterly that the CD could not be played in computer CD drives or in many car stereos. The effectiveness of the technology itself came into question when eight of the 15 songs on the album showed up as MP3 files on a private Yahoo Web site. In late November 2001, however, reports surfaced that Universal Music Group planned to try again by copy-protecting a movie soundtrack CD.

The latest push in digital music has been for the creation of online subscription services. Even Napster has promised to become a legitimate subscription service, charging monthly fees to allow users to swap copy-protected songs. The five major record labels divided into two camps around two online subscription services known as MusicNet and Pressplay, both of which finally emerged in December 2001. Set up like cable TV services, MusicNet and Pressplay charge monthly fees to distribute copy-protected digital music to listeners. Both allow users to stream a fixed number of songs, or to download an even more limited number of tunes each month.

Initial reactions to the services were tepid at best, especially because the major labels have said that they have no plans to make digitally delivered music portable, so that songs downloaded off MusicNet or Pressplay could be uploaded onto portable MP3 players. Some analysts have said that this limitation will prevent many users from subscribing to the services at all. Unlike MusicNet, however, Pressplay does allow users to burn a small number of songs per month to CD.

In early 2002, other competing subscription services—including FullAudio, Listen.com, and Rioport—had begun licensing music from the major labels, and either had recently launched or had near-term plans to launch, promising to drive more flexible digital-music offerings though increased competition. Nonetheless, many analysts and scholars remain skeptical that subscription services can ever effectively compete with rogue digital music-swapping services.

In August 2002 the Bush Administration announced an intensification of efforts to stop music piracy and said they would be invoking the NET Act (signed into law in 1997) which enables criminal prosecution in cases of illegal file-sharing. A Justice Department spokesman told reporters that the prosecutions would protect creators of intellectual property and prevent the Internet from becoming "the world's largest copy machine."

Bibliography

Alderman, John. *Sonic Boom: Napster, MP3, and the New Pioneers of Music.* Cambridge, Mass.: Perseus Publishing, 2001.

Davenport, Dexter. "I Want My MP3! The Battle for the Digital Living Room." *Net4TV*, August 1, 1999. <http://net4tv.com/voice/Story.cfm?storyID=1135> (April 26, 2002).

Kelsey, Dick. "50 Million in U.S. Have Downloaded Music—Survey." The Washington Post Company, February 1, 2002. <http://www.newsbytes.com/news/02/174156.html> (April 26, 2002).

Ketchum, Bob. "A Timeline of Audio/Video Technology." Robin's Video Web Site, ca. 1997. <http://penny100.home.mindspring.com/info/timeline.htm> (April 26, 2002).

Mann, Charles C. "The Heavenly Jukebox." *The Atlantic Monthly,* vol. 286, no. 3 (September 2000), pp. 39–59. <http://www.theatlantic.com/issues/2000/09/mann.htm> (April 26, 2002).

Mariano, Gwendolyn. "Label Releases Copy-protected CD With Pride." *CNET News.com,* May 14, 2001. <http://news.cnet.com/news/0-1005-200-5924584.html> (April 26, 2002).

Schoenherr, Steven E. "The Digital Revolution—Digital Audio Recording Formats Compared." 1999–2001. <http://history.acusd.edu/gen/recording/digital.html> (April 26, 2002).

Further Reading

Carey, Dermot Martin. "MP3, Now Portable." Electrical Engineering and Computer Science Department, Lehigh University, December 8, 2000. <http://www.eecs.lehigh.edu/~dmc6/MP3/MP3Overview.html> (April 26, 2002).

Featherly, Kevin, and Steve Jones. "Who Will Hear You When You Stream?" *San Francisco Chronicle,* February 22, 2001. <http://sfgate.com/cgi-bin/article.cgi?file=/chronicle/archive/2001/02/22/ED115722.DTL> (April 26, 2002).

Fraunhofer Gesellschaft. "MPEG Audio Layer-3." 1998–2001. <http://www.iis.fhg.de/amm/techinf/layer3/index.html> (April 26, 2002).

Lessig, Lawrence. *Code and Other Laws of Cyberspace.* New York: Basic Books, 1999.

———. *The Future of Ideas: The Fate of the Commons in the Connected World.* New York: Random House, 2001.

Mewton, Conrad. *All You Need to Know About Music & the Internet Revolution.* London: Sanctuary Publishing Limited, 2001.

Packer, Randall, and Ken Jordan, eds. *Multimedia: From Wagner to Virtual Reality.* New York: W.W. Norton & Co., 2001.

Pizzi, Skip, and Steve Church. "Audio Webcasting Demystified." *New Architect* (CMP Media), August 1997. <http://webtechniques.com/archives/1997/08/pizzi/> (April 26, 2002).

Ridgley, Mitch. "The History of MP3 and How Did It All Begin?" 1999–2000. <http://www.mp3-mac.com/Pages/History_of_MP3.html> (April 26, 2002).

Samuels, Edward. *The Illustrated Story of Copyright.* New York: Thomas Dunne Books, 2000.

Related Topics

Codec; Compression; Copyright; DeCSS; Digital Millennium Copyright Act; Freenet (File-Sharing Network); Internet Appliances; Lessig, Lawrence; MIDI; MP3; MPEG; Multimedia; Napster; Peer-to-Peer; Streaming Media

— *Kevin Featherly*

Digital Subscriber Line

The copper-wire-based digital subscriber line (DSL) service is one of the two main competing forms of broadband Internet connectivity, the other being cable. (Wireless and satellite broadband services are not commercially available, although both show some promise.) DSL differs significantly from cable in its technology, which is based on copper twisted-pair wires, not fiber-based coaxial cables. It also differs in its data speeds, which are slower than cable's, at least theoretically. DSL differs greatly from cable in its point of origin as well—usually telephone companies rather than cable-TV system centers.

But despite cable's apparent advantages, DSL is emerging as a serious challenger to cable broadband, especially among small businesses and home offices, largely because DSL's one-to-one connection between customer and provider is more secure; cable services are shared in a network among users, meaning that the more customers there are online at once, the slower the overall cable Internet service flows. Also, cables' shared customer network has prompted fears that cable-service hackers could break into other cable customers' computers. Although it offers slower peak data speeds than cable, DSL service nonetheless is up to 50 times faster than 28.8 kbps (kilobits per second) dial-up modem Internet connections.

DSL was first developed in 1989, primarily for use with video. At the time, video-on-demand was considered a high priority among telephone company executives, who saw it as a way to compete against cable TV providers. But the video-on-demand market never

flourished, and DSL foundered. Then, in the mid-1990s, as online music and video, large documents and images, and other multimedia content were gaining in popularity, the technology reemerged as a perfect way to provide broadband Internet service to businesses and residences. DSL was also a way for telephone companies to get involved in the broadband Internet business, after it became clear that the costs of upgrading the entire phone network with fiber-optic cable would be prohibitively high.

DSL service requires no special telephone wires to provide high-speed Internet access at potential speeds of up to 1.1 mbps (megabytes per second); standard phone lines already in place are sufficient. Also, because DSL services utilize the unused high-frequency end of the spectrum on the same wires that deliver voice telephone service to homes and businesses, it is possible for both voice and data to run simultaneously over the phone line without having to install new phone lines or maintain separate Internet services. In other words, unlike dial-up connections, the phone will still ring if a DSL customer is surfing the Web, and the customer can take the call while remaining online. In fact, DSL service is "always on," whether the user is currently on the Internet or not.

However, DSL has some serious drawbacks. It is often very difficult for the user to set up and install the service without the help of visiting technicians. Also, DSL is not available at all in many areas. Customers hoping to gain DSL access, for instance, must be located within certain short distances from a telephone company's central offices; the most common consumer form of DSL service, ADSL, requires that customers be located within 12,000 feet of the telephone company hub.

According to a Federal Communications Commission (FCC) DSL fact sheet published online, DSL works through the use of a digital modem, or router, which connects to a user's phone lines. The router, which may be purchased or rented from the DSL provider, accesses the local telephone company's central offices, where a DSL access multiplexer is located. This device translates the user's DSL signal and transmits it from the copper phone line onto the network backbone, directing the signal to the user's Internet service provider (ISP). The ISP then verifies the user, and allows access to the Internet. Often, the customer must maintain relationships with both a DSL phone service provider and an outside ISP.

There are several different varieties of DSL service on the market, which is the reason that DSL services are often referred to generically as "xDSL." The most common form is asymmetrical DSL (ADSL). This technology assumes that most people require more data speed for downloading files than for uploading information—for instance, that the music files a user pulls off of Morpheus are likely to be much bigger and require more bandwidth than the email a user uploads onto the Internet to send to friends. ADSL is "asymmetric" because it devotes much greater bandwidth to "downstream" use, or downloading, than it dedicates to "upstream" use for outbound messages. Using ADSL, downstream speeds of up to 6.1 mbps are possible, although speeds of about 780 kbps are more common; maximum upstream speed is about 640 kbps, while actual speeds are generally much slower. ADSL providers generally require that users install splitters on their telephone lines to separate voice traffic on the low end of the frequency spectrum from data, which employs the middle and high ends of the spectrum.

There is a slower-speed version of ADSL that does not require the use of line splitters. This variation, or "flavor," of DSL is known as "Universal ADSL" or "G.Lite." Offering maximum downstream speeds of only 384 kbps, this version of ADSL is meant to operate in the same market as the faster version, but aims at reducing the complexity of the service and the costs of implementation.

Yet another common form of DSL is "symmetrical DSL" (SDSL). Upstream and downstream speeds for SDSL service are identical, making it better for businesses, such as companies maintaining busy Web sites, that must both receive and respond to requests for data from Internet users. Data speeds of 192 kbps to 1.1 mbps are possible. SDSL service is available up to 18,000 feet from a telephone company hub, a greater distance than ADSL.

Another form of DSL branches off of Integrated Services Digital Network (ISDN) service, which was a slower-speed precursor to DSL. IDSL, or ISDN-DSL, essentially aims to provide DSL service to customers who otherwise do not qualify for SDSL or ADSL because of their distance from phone company offices. IDSL can reach customers up to 36,000 feet away from a telephone company's local central hub, and it operates at symmetrical speeds of about 128 kbps. IDSL is meant mainly for customers who already have the ISDN circuit in place, but want to convert to DSL.

Finally, there is HDSL, or high-bit-rate DSL. According to DSL provider New Edge Network, this variation was developed as "a faster cousin" to ISDN.

It allowed companies to offer the equivalent of T-1 line speeds (1.544 mbps) over regular copper wires. But HDSL requires two sets of twisted-pair copper lines, making it an expensive alternative to new versions such as ADSL. HDSL is the oldest version of DSL, and has traditionally been the most heavily deployed.

Bibliography

Computer Solutions, Inc. "History of DSL." New Edge Networks, 2000. <http://www.csolutions.net/newedgehistory.html> (May 24, 2002).

DSL Prime. "Short Sketch of the History of DSL." 1999. <http://www.dslprime.com/Technology/DSL_s_History/dsl_s_history.html> (May 24, 2002).

DSL World Forum, Voice Over Digital Subscriber Line (VoDSL). "DSL Primer." International Engineering Consortium, 2002. <http://www.iec.org/online/tutorials/voice_dsl/topic01.html> (May 24, 2002).

The DSL Zone. "DSL Information—Digital Subscriber Line (DSL): What Is It?" 2000. <http://thedslzone.com/DSLinfo.html#DSL> (May 24, 2002).

Glasner, Joanna. "Slowdown on High-Speed Express." Wired News, August 22, 2001. <http://www.wired.com/news/business/0,1367,46219,00.html> (May 24, 2002).

Konsynski, Benn. "What Is DSL??" Emory University, 2001. <http://www.emory.edu/BUSINESS/et/P98/dsl/whatis.htm> (May 24, 2002).

Nelson, Lynn A. "DSL: The Fast Track to the Internet." Rural Telecommunications, vol. 18, no. 2 (March-April 1999). <http://www.ntca.org/pubs/rtonline/rt_mar99/story4.html> (May 24, 2002).

Further Reading

Federal Communications Commission. "FCC Consumer Facts: Broadband Access for Consumers." February 12, 2002. <http://www.fcc.gov/cib/consumerfacts/dsl2.html> (May 24, 2002).

Gilder, George. Telecosm: How Infinite Bandwidth Will Revolutionize Our World. New York: The Free Press, 2000.

Related Topics

Access; Bluetooth; Broadband; Peer-to-Peer; Privacy; Streaming Media; Telephony; Wireless Networks

— *Kevin Featherly*

Digital Television

Digital Television (DTV) refers to the transmission of digital signals to a digital TV set for display.

Similar to analog television signals, these digital signals can be broadcast over the air or sent through a cable or satellite system. With its brilliant, high-definition images, CD-quality audio, and the possibility of transmitting multiple programs and information simultaneously, the quality of digital television is a vast improvement over the analog television that most of us experience today.

With DTV, more visual information can be sent without increasing the broadcast frequency spectrum because the data is compressed, making the DTV picture noticeably clearer. Most analog television broadcast stations transmit a picture that contains 480 vertical interlaced lines with about 340 horizontal pixels per line, whereas DTV's pictures can be 1,080 vertical interlaced lines with 1,920 horizontal pixels per line.

DTV allows transmission of television programming in new wide-screen, high-definition television (HDTV) formats. HDTV sets take full advantage of the digital signal, and use the highest DTV image resolution combined with Dolby Digital surround sound. In addition to the higher-resolution picture, HDTV can display images in a 16:9 ratio, which is wider than the 4:3 ratio of traditional, analog televisions. The standard for the traditional ratio was set in 1889 in Thomas Edison's laboratories; in the 1950s, filmmakers adopted the wider ratio to give viewers a more realistic, immersive experience. HDTV viewers will be able to see films in their original ratio, as well as television programming (such as football games) that will benefit from the wider screen. HDTV requires expensive new production and transmission equipment, but some broadcasters are already airing programs in HDTV. CBS, ABC, and many cable channels have announced plans to air programs such as college football, movies, and primetime comedy and drama series in HDTV.

Eventually, all television programming will be transmitted digitally, and analog programming will cease to exist. Until then, television programmers will operate two channels: one digital and one analog. The Federal Communications Commission (FCC), which oversees the television industry and allocates portions of the airwaves to broadcasters, is directing the slow transition to DTV, which has been hampered by standardization issues and by the massive expense of the effort (estimated at $1.6 billion system-wide). In 1997, the FCC gave broadcasters $70 billion worth of broadcasting spectrum so they could broadcast digital programming alongside their traditional

analog programming, and set 2006 as the date by which the transition to digital would be complete, at which point the broadcasters would have to give up their analog signals. However, broadcasters have asked for a delay, citing the tremendous cost involved in switching over to digital, the fact that relatively few stations have made the switch, and the low rate of consumer adoption.

Consumer adoption of DTV has been hindered by the fact that televisions capable of displaying the digital signal correctly are expensive ($1,500 and up). Currently, less than one percent of TV owners have digital TV sets. Another issue is affecting adoption: Hollywood studios were reluctant to release high-resolution, digital versions of their products until a method was in place to combat piracy, because digital signals are far more susceptible to piracy than are analog. With analog media such as videotapes, the quality of the image degrades each time the product is copied, providing a built-in disincentive to create multiple copies of a product; but with digital media, each copy is exactly the same.

Considering these facts alongside the potential for the Internet to be used to distribute digital copies quickly and inexpensively, the studios balked at releasing digital versions of their valuable films to broadcasters. However, the studios have agreed on an anti-piracy technology called Digital Transmission Content Protection (DTCP), which encrypts the digital signal as it is transmitted from a digital receiver to a monitor or recorder and prevents it from being copied. Unfortunately, the early HDTV sets purchased by eager consumers are not DTCP-compliant, and therefore may not be able to display certain types of programming.

The expense of new broadcasting and production equipment, the threat of piracy, and lackluster consumer reception are significant hurdles for the DTV industry to overcome, but many are confident that the vastly superior quality of DTV and HDTV will ensure their success.

Bibliography

Brown, Gary. "How HDTV Works." *Marshall Brain's How Stuff Works.* <http://www.howstuffworks.com/hdtv1.htm> (May 24, 2002).

FCC Office of Engineering and Technology. "Digital Television Consumer Information." November 1998. <http://www.fcc.gov/Bureaus/Engineering_Technology/Factsheets/dtv9811.html> (May 24, 2002).

Shiver, Jube, Jr. "Broadcasters Seek to Delay Digital TV." *Los Angeles Times*, July 30, 2001.

Further Reading

Cringely, Robert X. "Digital TV: A Cringely Crash Course." *PBS Online*, 1999.
<http://www.pbs.org/opb/crashcourse/>
(May 24, 2002).
Federal Communications Commission. "Digital Television (DTV)." May 13, 2002.
<http://www.fcc.gov/dtv/> (May 24, 2002).

Related Topics

Compression; Digital Audio

— *Nicole Ellison*

Disintermediation

Disintermediation describes the removal of intermediaries—people or companies we commonly refer to as "middlemen." When disintermediation occurs, consumers deal directly with manufacturers, audiences are in direct contact with authors or artists, and citizens hear directly from people who have something to say. The retail outlet, the publishing company or record label, and the news media no longer come between providers and consumers of ideas, goods, or services.

When best-selling author Stephen King made his short story *Riding the Bullet* available exclusively online, that was disintermediation. If we wanted to read the story, we went right to King's website, rather than to any other source such as a magazine or bookstore. King estimated he'd earn $450,000 for those 66 pages of fiction, rather than the $10,000 he'd probably have been paid if he'd published the story in a magazine.

The music-sharing system Napster, which created such an uproar in the recording industry that the Recording Industry Association of America sued its creator, is another example of disintermediation. Napster is a file transfer system that allows users to swap songs that have been encoded into the MP3 format. Developed by college student Shawn Fanning, Napster gave rise to a new type of application—peer-to-peer software—that allows individual computer users to exchange files among themselves. Now that the courts have spoken, the prospects for the revolutionary application are uncertain. Still, Napster has had such an impact on our popular culture that our vocabulary now includes the word Napsterize, which means, essentially, to disintermediate.

Because disintermediation means that people who have information and ideas make the material available for us to access at our convenience, we can be more certain that we're getting what people actually wanted to give us—that material hasn't been screened, evaluated, or censored by editors or other so-called gatekeepers. Gatekeepers are intermediaries who determine what will or will not be disseminated via the mass media. They influence almost every medium—what films will be produced, what bands will get contracts and what songs they'll record, what authors will be allowed to publish what books, what television shows will be programmed and when they'll be scheduled, and even what news stories will be covered and in how much detail.

The Internet has begun to reduce the power of gatekeepers. If *The New York Times*, for example, doesn't want to write a story about a certain product that an activist group thinks is harmful, people in that group can simply prepare information about the product and post it on the Web. Disintermediation means that gatekeepers have not come between us and the people with something to say.

There are positive and negative aspects to the process of disintermediation. A democracy is stronger when a wide variety of ideas and viewpoints—even those that challenge the status quo—are considered and debated. But with no gatekeepers, how can we know that the information we obtain online is accurate? Most people feel fairly confident that the journalistic integrity and standards of media outlets such as *The New York Times* result in the publication of the truth. But when we search the Web more broadly, exactly who is providing the content? It could be literally anyone with a computer and Internet access. What are the content providers' qualifications, biases, and backgrounds? Often, we do not know. Consumers must always be critical of information obtained online; just because something has been posted on the Web doesn't mean that it is true.

Although disintermediation has gained quite a bit of attention with the rise of the Internet, it is actually a fairly old term. Bankers used it in the 1970s to describe changes in corporate and retail banking, although the concept of disintermediation had begun taking hold in the financial services industry in the early 1960s. Even the Sears & Roebuck catalogue, when it was introduced in the 1800s, represented disintermediation, allowing people to make purchases without visiting local stores. Some say that disintermediation's history extends all the way back to the Middle Ages. It is also a widely applied concept; besides the retail, cultural, financial, and information industries already mentioned, disintermediation is of concern to many other industries, including insurance, travel, and managed health care.

Some observers argue that the disintermediation encouraged by the Internet hasn't actually happened; we do, after all, still have grocery stores, stockbrokers, and newspapers. Others, such as Nicholas G. Carr, a senior editor at the *Harvard Business Review*, say that not only has the "middleman" not vanished, but also that a whole new intermediary industry is being born. Carr calls this "hypermediation," and says that Web transactions involve numerous intermediaries both familiar and unfamiliar, such as search engines, portals, Internet service providers, content providers, affiliate sites, software makers, and others. But still others indicate that things will never be the same for certain industries, in which people who have served as intermediaries in the past will need to redefine their roles and bring some added value to the transaction, rather than merely "handle" it.

Bibliography

Adams, Stephen. "The Disintermediation Fallacies." *Information World Review,* December 1999, p. 26.

Carr, Nicholas G. "Hypermediation: Commerce as Clickstream." *Harvard Business Review,* January/February 2000, p. 46.

Evans, Bob. "Shades of Gray." *Informationweek,* October 23, 2000, p. 254.

Gillespie, Nick. "Cutting Out the Middlemen." *Reason,* August/September 2000, p. 4.

Greenfeld, Karl Taro. "Meet the Napster." *Time,* October 2, 2000, pp. 60–66, 68.

Ratnesar, Ramesh, and Joel Stein. "everyone'sastar.com." *Time,* March 27, 2000, pp. 70–75.

Further Reading

Gilbert, Alorie, and Beth Bacheldor. "The Big Squeeze." *Informationweek,* March 27, 2000, pp. 46–56.

Tapscott, Don. *The Digital Economy: Promise and Peril in the Age of Networked Intelligence.* New York: McGraw-Hill, 1996.

Wildemuth, Scott. "A Simple Case of Supply and Demand." *Datamation,* November 1997, p. 99.

Related Topics

Freenet (File-Sharing Network); Internet; Napster; Peer-to-Peer; World Wide Web

— *Rebecca Ann Lind*

Disposal of Computers

Computing is often thought of as a "clean" industry, but the disposal of computers has become a significant environmental and economic problem. Obsolescence remains the primary reason for computer disposal. Rapid increases in processor speed and continual changes in computer architecture have resulted in an ever-increasing rate of computer obsolescence. The Environmental Protection Agency projects that by 2005, for every new computer manufactured, another one will become outdated.

In the United States alone, more than twenty-four million computers became obsolete in 1999. Of those, only four million were properly recycled or donated; the remaining twenty million were dumped into landfills, incinerated, shipped as waste exports (and probably dumped or incinerated upon arriving at their destination), or stored. Because users are often unaware of options for disposal, computers are usually placed in storage once they are deemed obsolete. While a computer's condition is generally known before it is put in storage, those that have been stored for some time have to be tested before they can be put to any sort of use. A company would pay a technician to do such testing; this expense adds to the financial liability of computer recycling.

When thrown into landfills or incinerated, computers and computer monitors can release hazardous materials and heavy metals into the environment, such as lead, mercury, and hexavalent chromium. Each of these substances poses unique dangers to human beings. The assorted plastics in computers contain brominated flame retardants, which can act as endocrine disruptors. Lead, which is used to protect computer users from radiation, can have negative effects on the nervous system, the endocrine system, the liver, the blood, and the kidneys. Mercury can cause brain damage, and hexavalent chromium can cause DNA damage in human cells.

In landfills, these substances will eventually leak into the drinking water supply and enter the human food chain. Incineration releases toxic chemicals into the air, where they can be breathed in; it also creates ash and slag containing toxic substances, which require specialized disposal. Additionally, some pollutants released through computer disposal, such as lead, do not disappear over time. As a result, many places have declared computers, or at least computer monitors, to be hazardous waste. This means that they require special means of disposal, and cannot be dumped into landfills or processed with other garbage.

Most states have some way to deal with obsolete electronics. The Electronic Industries Alliance (EIA)—

a group that promotes electronics manufacturing—has links to information about disposal on its Web site (<http//www.eiae.org>). Several industry and environmental groups are working together to test various models of computer recycling, such as municipal collection, funding retailers to collect old machines, and providing consumer drop-off sites. The U.S. Department of Education and several non-governmental organizations have also been working to get used but functional computers into public schools.

The disposal of computers has become an issue worldwide. In Canada, Toronto and other cities have established public disposal depots for recycling computers. Elsewhere, governments are exploring the idea of Extended Product Responsibility (EPR). Germany, the Netherlands, Norway, Switzerland, and Denmark have all enacted EPR-related laws, and other European countries are following suit. In EPR, producers are held responsible for the physical management of their products, for the costs of the waste created by their products, and for informing consumers about the possible environmental effects of a product at different times in its life cycle. They are also liable for environmental damage caused by their products. Some companies are beginning to implement EPR measures on their own, but it is not yet a pervasive practice in computer manufacturing.

The environmental cost of computer disposal is a major challenge facing manufacturers and consumers. While environmentally safe disposal efforts are underway, computer manufacturers are beginning to explore building computers that are safer to throw away. Fujitsu, for instance, already advertises a more "environmentally friendly" computer, though it remains to be seen whether significant changes can be made in the materials used to manufacture computers and monitors. In the meantime, if you have a computer to dispose of, you can find resources for computer reuse or recycling on the World Wide Web.

Bibliography

"Disposal of Computers Goes Slowly." *Taipei Times Online Edition*, May 24, 2001. <http://www.taipeitimes.com/news/2001/05/24/story/0000087159> (April 5, 2002).

"Manufacture and Disposal of Computers an Environmental Nightmare." *Earth Crash Earth Spirit* (eces.org), November 23, 2000. <http://www.eces.org/articles/static/97495920099756.shtml> (April 5, 2002).

Goldberg, Carey. 1998 (March 12). "Where Do Computers Go When They Die?" *The New York Times*, March 12, 1998.

<http://www.ce.cmu.edu/GreenDesign/comprec/nytimes98/12die.html> (August 30, 2002).

U.S. Environmental Protection Agency. 2001. "Life Cycle of Old Computers." http://www.epa.gov/Region2/r3/problem.htm> (April 5, 2002).

Further Reading

Computer Professionals for Social Responsibility. "Position Paper on the European Union Directive on Waste Electrical and Electronic Equipment (WEEE)."2001. <http://www.cpsr.org/program/environment/WEEEPositionPaper.html> (April 5, 2002).

Related Topics

Digital Divide; Education and Computers; Universal Design

— *Jonathan Sterne*

Distance Learning

Distance learning is teaching that utilizes a variety of telecommunication technologies (video, voice, and data), sometimes in combination with print materials, to send and receive instructional material. Students and teachers can be separated in space and time. Distance learning is a revolutionary concept; people can take courses, even earn a college or advanced degree, without ever setting foot in a traditional classroom.

Distance learning (sometimes called distributed learning) had its humble beginnings in what were called correspondence courses, which used "snail mail," or the postal service, to deliver materials. By the 1950s, such efforts had expanded into an era in which radio and television stations broadcast educational programs, which usually just featured a lecturer dispensing information. Now technology has developed to the point where effective two-way communication between teacher and student can take place remotely, using computers as a channel. The potential of distance learning to offer education to people who otherwise would not have the opportunity is immense.

Traditional mail-based delivery, as well as broadcast radio and television programs, can still be a part of distance learning. Now, however, there are many other delivery systems available, both analog and digital. Distance learning can utilize audio- or video-conferencing, video- and audiotapes, interactive videodisk, satellite-delivered content, computer networks, closed-circuit or low-power broadcasting, the Internet, and audiographic teleconferencing (audio signals supplemented by relatively low-quality video and fax). Many of these newer delivery systems, unlike the older systems, allow participants to hear and/or see each other in real time.

When computers are incorporated into distance learning, however, most interaction takes written form. Email, bulletin board systems (BBSs) or newsgroups, online discussion groups, and chat rooms all allow students to "talk with" each other and their teachers.

Some interactions occur when people are "together" at the same time, even though they may be in different places. This is synchronous distance learning, and it occurs in most of the systems using audio- and video-conferencing, and in traditional broadcast distance-education contexts. Chat rooms and some online discussion groups also provide synchronous learning environments, although some discussion groups are asynchronous. Asynchronous distance learning occurs when students are not only in different locations, but are also "attending class" (accessing the material) at different times. This occurs in traditional print-based correspondence courses, as well as when students and teachers use email, BBSs, and newsgroups to communicate with each other.

Distance learning can revolutionize education, because it opens classroom doors to people who previously couldn't afford school, or whose work and family commitments make it otherwise impossible to attend. It brings educational opportunities to people in remote locations who don't have access to qualified teachers or a vast array of courses. And distance learning is already relatively common. According to a report by the Web-based Education Commission (sponsored by the U.S. Congress), more than 6,000 accredited courses were already available on the Web in 1998; by 2002, nearly 84 percent of U.S. four-year colleges will offer distance learning courses, in which 2.2 million students are expected to enroll.

Traditionally, distance learners have been adults, with courses offered by colleges and universities. Some universities, such as the Open University in the U.K., are dedicated to distance education, while others offer both traditional and distance-learning courses. However, distance learning is also conducted at the elementary-, middle-, and secondary-school levels, as well in organizational settings. Businesses often find it easier and cheaper to arrange a video-conferenced seminar with an expert rather than to invest the money and time in employees' travel to a distant seminar location. Elementary and middle schools often use distance education to enrich the traditional curriculum, with projects such as the National Geographic Kids Network. Distance learning in secondary schools is often used by small rural and underserved urban school districts; some schools offer required courses that they otherwise couldn't provide, others present advanced placement or other specialized courses, and still others use the technology to meet the needs of disabled or gifted students.

Although the possibilities of distance learning are vast, it is not for everyone. Just because it is easy to access the course, that does not mean that the course itself will be easy—and not only because of the subject matter. Individual characteristics and skills play a large part in a student's success with distance learning. The successful distance learner must be disciplined, and have the motivation to keep up with assignments and follow through on projects without encouragement. Solid organizational and time-management skills are required; without the constant reminder and reinforcement provided by attending class twice a week, it is all too easy to let assignments pile up until the experience becomes anything but successful.

Furthermore, good writing skills are essential. Students using computer-assisted forms of communication (email, chat rooms, discussion groups, and so on) quickly discover that all of their "conversations," both inside and outside of "class," take the form of written communication, and those who are lacking in writing skills can find themselves at a significant disadvantage. Finally, students enrolled in distance-learning courses should be familiar with the technology used in the course, know how to use a computer and the Internet, and try not to become frustrated by technical difficulties when they occur.

Bibliography

Byron, I., and R. Gagliardi. "Communities and the Information Society: The Role of Information and Communication Technologies in Education." *The Acacia Initiative*, 1998.
<http://www.idrc.ca/acacia/studies/ir-unes1.htm> (April 5, 2002).

Rees, Jennifer. "Understanding Distance Learning Consortia?" *Petersons*. 2001.
<http://iiswinprd03.petersons.com/distancelearning/code/articles/understanding.asp> (April 5, 2002).

Sherry, L. "Issues in Distance Learning." *International Journal of Educational Telecommunications*, 1996.

Further Reading

Lane, Carla. "Our Library: DLKRN's Technology Resource Guide." *Distance Learning Resource Network*.
<http://www.dlrn.org/text/library/dl/guide.html> (April 5, 2002).

United States Department of Education. "e-Learning: Putting a World-Class Education at the Fingertips of All Children: The National Educational Technology Plan." 2000. <http://www.ed.gov/Technology/elearning> (April 5, 2002).

Related Topics

Bulletin Board Systems; Chat; Email; Interactivity; Internet; Newsgroups; World Wide Web

— *Rebecca Ann Lind*

Distributed Computing

While the term distributed computing has been used for many years to describe the design and operation of local and wide area networks, more recently it has come to refer to the use of these networked computers in concert to solve problems. A growing number of tasks performed by computers are well suited to parallel processing, and the use of distributed networks of desktop computers to economically perform such operations has established an important niche. The Internet allows for many millions of machines to be networked together to solve problems in a piecemeal fashion, often during times when the computers would not otherwise be utilized.

The Beginnings of Distributed Computing

The idea of distributed computing was first hatched in the 1930s, when AT&T attempted to perform parallel computations on Monroe mechanical calculators to perform what is known as "switching mathematics." But the descendant of distributed computing as it is known today didn't come along until the early 1970s.

Installation of the first Ethernet network on the 100 or so computers at Xerox's Palo Alto Research Center (PARC) in 1973 created an in-house network of computers that could share data. PARC scientist John F. Shoch took advantage of the setup, devising a program he called a "worm," through which one Ethernet-connected computer could gain access to another computer, using its own resources to convince the remote computer to accept and download a program, after which it commanded it to reboot. Shoch was able to access every machine on the Ethernet that way, getting each to download his program.

Soon, Shoch and his partner, fellow PARC scientist Jon Hupp, began changing focus. Instead of one computer commanding other computers individually, why not get it to talk with a number of other computers at once, and get them all to perform related computing tasks in tandem? And why not have each of those computers talk to still more computers, and so on, and get a great many more involved in a gargantuan parallel-processing project?

Richard Crandall, then chief scientist at NeXT Software, refined this idea by inventing the first "community supercomputer" in 1991. He created software known as Zilla, and installed it in a group of networked NeXT computers. Zilla allowed the PCs to respond to commands from a control computer, and to perform computations while they otherwise would have been sitting idle. Zilla-equipped computers combining their processing power were able to calculate and identify the largest known prime number. The grouped computers were later used in tandem to test ultra-complex encryption codes.

Crandall's invention roughly coincided with the beginning of the Internet's widespread popularity. After his innovation, it became a simple thing to involve millions of computers around the world in distributed computing. Each terminal on the network simply had to download and run the appropriate software.

Distributed Computing Today

Supercomputers generally use more than a single processor. In the case of a machine called Janus, for example, a total of 9,216 processors are used together within one machine. These machines are extremely expensive to construct, and are used primarily within research institutions and by national security agencies. Parallel processing machines are useful in solving only problems that can be broken down into many small parts, elements that have a minimum of reliance on one another. These problems run from simulations of nuclear blasts and climate change to breaking codes and searching the Web. The same sort of computing power is useful in rendering three-dimensional images for film or television. Many studios that generate computer graphics make use of "render farms," networks of relatively small computers working together to render a scene.

This practice can be used with more widely distributed computers, as well. In 1993, Arjen Lenstra and Mark Manesse of DEC Systems Research Center, along with a group of 600 volunteers, won a challenge issued by RSA Security to factor a 129-digit number. Finding primes and factors is a necessary part of many cryptographic systems. Over the next few years, more experience was gained with distributed computing, and in 1997, two organizations were created: distributed.net and Entropia. Distributed.net helped to develop a large group of users who donated their extra processor "cycles" (those times the computer was on but not being used) to help work on cryptography challenges.

Commercial projects like those of Entropia and a similar company called ProcessTree were established in the hope of selling unused processor cycles to businesses at a profit. The idea is tempting to an individual user: You are paid for work that your computer does in its spare time. The viability of the plan is still unclear, though. Problems remain with optimization and security that must be solved before wide acceptance will be achieved among corporate clients.

Although the cryptographic successes of distributed.net certainly captured the attention of many in the computing community, the SETI@home (http://setiathome.ssl.berkeley.edu/) project has carried the idea of distributed computing to a much larger audience. The project, which was begun in 1999, analyzes the massive radio spectrum data collected by the Search for Extra-Terrestrial Intelligence (SETI) project. When going unused, or when not being used to its full capacity, each computer searches through a portion of the data collected by the project, and informs SETI if there are any patterns that might be of interest. More than two million people have used SETI@home; the computing power donated by these volunteers has allowed the SETI project to perform an analysis that would otherwise be impossible at any cost. SETI has shown that distributed computing can be both successful and relatively inexpensive.

In the meantime, distributed computing has come full circle. In the 1970s, "worms" moved through the networks at Xerox PARC and duplicated themselves in the memory of each computer, treating the network for the first time as a kind of unified machine. The concepts that drive distributed computing today, especially programs (sometimes called "distributed agents") that can move easily from computer to computer and share data seamlessly, are seen as central to the future development of the Internet. Microsoft's .NET initiative, the diffusion of the XML standard, and what the inventor of the World Wide Web, Tim Berners-Lee, has called the "semantic web," all rely upon the closer integration of distributed machines. What now seems to be a novelty may soon become commonplace.

Bibliography

Hayes, Brian. "Collective Wisdom." *American Scientist.* Mar./Apr. 1998, pp. 118–122.

Rheingold, Howard. "You Got the Power." *Wired.* August 8, 2000. <http://www.wired.com/wired/archive/8.08/comcomp.html> (April 5, 2002).

Vizard, Michael. "Above the Noise: The Second Wave of the Internet." *InfoWorld.* June 4, 2001, p. 8.

Further Reading

Berst, Jesse. "No Alien Idea: How Distributed Computing Will Change the Web." *ZDNet Anchor Desk.* December 27, 2000. <http://www.zdnet.com/anchordesk/stories/story/0,10738,2667710,00.html> (April 5, 2002).

Coulouris, George, Jean Dollimore, and Tim Kindberg. *Distributed Systems: Concepts and Design.* 2nd ed. Reading, Mass.: Addison-Wesley, 1994.

Geist, Al, et al. *PVM: Parallel Virtual Machine.* Cambridge, Mass.: MIT Press, 1994.

Related Topics

Berners-Lee, Tim; Encryption and Cryptography; Software Agents; Virus; World Wide Web

— Alexander Halavais and Kevin Featherly

Drucker, Peter F.

1909–

Management Theorist

Peter Drucker is the most influential management and business writer of the twentieth century. His 1946 book, *The Concept of the Corporation,* was a classic in the true sense of the word: It established a new class of book while redefining business administration as one aspect of a larger framework.

Born in Austria in 1909, Drucker earned a doctorate in public law and international relations at Frankfurt University while working full-time as financial writer and senior editor of Frankfurt's largest daily newspaper. He moved to London to spend five years in merchant banking while writing for European and American periodicals. In the late 1930s, he moved to America to begin a long career as a writer, consultant, and teacher. Still active in his nineties, he has published more than 30 books with over six million copies sold. Most are still in print.

Drucker revolutionized the management field, which he defined as "the organized, systematic study of the structure, the policies, and the social and human concerns of the modern organization," with a series of powerful distinctions resting on two central insights. The first was that management is more than just administration. A social innovation of the twentieth century, management is a specific kind of work, a practice enabling groups to become effective, purposeful, and productive. Management has two specific tasks. The first task is creating wholes that are larger than the sum of their parts—that is, helping organizations produce more than the sum of the resources fed into them. The second task is balancing the immediate and long-term future of the organization in actions that manage the organization, its managers, its workers, and their work. Drucker's second insight was that ours is a society of organizations, public and private. Managers form a professional class serving social needs.

Drucker developed these insights while studying General Motors in preparation for *The Concept of the Corporation*. When he started the book, he was launched on a promising academic career in economics and political science; when he finished, he was warned that his view of the modern organization would offend both economists and political scientists—and it did, at least initially.

Since 1946, Drucker has examined all the major aspects of social life in the industrial world. His work links a broad knowledge of history to a focused sense of time and circumstance. He examines the social effects and vital linkages of current trends, bringing historical, political, and economic facts together with an encyclopedic knowledge of current events and technology. Drucker's ability to understand emerging developments rests on a deep understanding of the ways that technology affects society.

Drucker has consistently been among the first to identify and articulate important trends. In the 1950s, he coined the term "knowledge workers," in one of the first books to report on the idea of a post-modern world. By the 1970s, he identified such central trends of our time as globalization, post-industrial society, the knowledge economy, the knowledge society, and many others. While many see the phenomena that Drucker describes, he draws profound conclusions by analyzing the consequences to which they lead.

Drucker's most creative insights involve ideas that are as dramatic as they are current. One discovers with astonishment that many first appeared in his writings 30 and 40 years ago. For example, he predicted in the 1950s how—and why—telecommunication would kill *Life* magazine, and also predicted the ways in which emerging media would shape a phenomenon much like today's Internet. His ability to bring social theory together with technological understanding reveals a scientific mind of the first order.

Despite Drucker's reputation as a business guru, his current focus is on social-sector organization. "The more economy, money, and information become global," he writes, "the more community will matter. And only the social sector nonprofit organization performs in the community, exploits its opportunities, mobilizes its local resources, solves its problems."

Drucker's great contribution has been to serve society by focusing attention on the broad challenges of leadership, and his current focus places him at the forefront of community service in the global village. In 2002 he was awarded the Presidential Medal of Freedom, the highest civilian honor in the United States.

Selected Works

Drucker, Peter F. *Adventures of a Bystander*. New York: John Wiley and Sons, 1998.

———. *The Age of Discontinuity: Guidelines to Our Changing Society*. New York: Harper Torchbooks, 1973.

———. *The Concept of the Corporation*. Rutgers, N.J.: Transaction Publishers, 1993.

———. *The Ecological Vision*. Rutgers, N.J.: Transaction Publishers, 1993.

———. *Innovation and Entrepreneurship: Practices and Principles*. New York: Harper and Row, 1985.

———. *Landmarks of Tomorrow: A Report on the New "Post Modern" World*. With a new introduction by the author. Rutgers, N.J.: Transaction Publishers, 1996.

———. *Management Challenges for the 21st Century*. New York: HarperBusiness, 1999.

———. *The New Realities*. London: Mandarin, 1990.

———. *Post-Capitalist Society*. Oxford: Butterworth-Heinemann, 1993.

Bibliography

Beatty, Jack. *The World According to Peter Drucker*. New York: Broadway Books, 1999.

Further Reading

Gabor, Andrea. *The Capitalist Philosophers: The Geniuses of Modern Business—Their Lives, Times, and Ideas*. New York: Crown Business, 2000.

Heller, Robert. *Business Masterminds: Peter Drucker*. New York: DK Publishing, 2000.

The Peter F. Drucker Foundation for Nonprofit Management. <http://www.pfdf.org/> (April 5, 2002).

Related Topics

Knowledge Management

— *Ken Friedman*

DSL See Digital Subscriber Line.

Dyson, Esther

1951–

Computer Industry Analyst, Entrepreneur

Esther Dyson was referred to in a 1993 *Wired* magazine article as the most powerful female in the computer industry, even though she does not own and is not an executive at any of the major computer or Internet companies. Instead, her influence has stemmed largely (though not entirely) from her powerful intelligence and her writings, which date back to a four-year stint as a fact-checker and reporter at *Forbes* magazine beginning in 1974. She has continued writing in her monthly newsletter, *Release 1.0,* an industry forecast that has at times had the ear of virtually every important Silicon Valley industry executive. Her uncanny ability to detect trends—she foresaw the emergence of the personal digital assistant (PDA) a decade in advance, for example—led "Digerati" author John Brockman to label Dyson "the pattern recognizer."

In the 1990s, Dyson shifted her interests from her one-time obsession, the software industry, to focus on the Internet. She exerted considerable influence on the medium's development, both as a board member of the Electronic Frontier Foundation, and as a founding board member and one-time president of the powerful Internet Corporation for Assigned Names and Numbers (ICANN), the international agency charged with setting policy for the Internet's core infrastructure—and which serves, as some observe, as a kind of de facto government over the Internet. Today, she is president of her own firm, EDventures, an information-services company that also is involved in venture funding. But she has continued, through her newsletter, articles, and her 1997 book *Release 2.0* (and its 1998 sequel, *Release 2.1*) to use her writing skills to help shape the public discourse on the Internet, commenting on such Internet-related topics as online communities, intellectual property, governance, and privacy. "If anyone's been in charge of the Internet, it's Esther Dyson," *Crain's New York Business* once said. "She acts as the moderator of (the) global conversation about technology and the future."

Although Dyson grew up in a home with no TV set, her origins are anything but humble. Her father, Freeman Dyson, was a well-known scientist and writer whose interests ranged from space travel to global diplomacy. Her mother, Verena, held a Ph.D. in mathematics, earned from the same Swiss institution where Albert Einstein once studied. Esther's brother, George B. Dyson, is among the world's foremost authorities on kayak building, and is author of the 1997 bestseller *Darwin Among the Machines.*

By age 16, Esther Dyson was a student at Harvard University. However, she wrote in *Release 2.1,* she spent much less time attending classes than hanging out in the offices of the school newspaper, the *Harvard Crimson.* She tried out as a reporter, got the job, and wrote for the paper all through school. In fact, she had started writing at age eight, compiling her own *Dyson Gazette* using ballpoint pens and carbon paper. She liked to write so much, she said, that she assumed she would grow up to be a novelist.

Instead, after leaving Harvard, Dyson went to work at *Forbes* magazine. There, direct exposure to the business world began to modify her Harvard liberalism, reshaping it into a firm free-market ethos. Meanwhile, her ability to scope out the future began to form. She wrote a seminal article for *Forbes* that predicted—ten years before anyone else—that Japan would pose an immense threat to the U.S. computer industry, and that the main threat would be hardware,

Esther Dyson. (Reuters NewMedia Inc./CORBIS)

not software. This article, *Wired* magazine said, "presaged her future as the self-propelled prophet of the computer industry."

In 1977, Dyson left Forbes to become a Wall Street analyst, eventually joining up with Morgan Stanley's Ben Rosen, who had launched the *Rosen Electronics Newsletter*. Eventually, he sold the venture to Dyson, who refashioned it as *Release 1.0,* changing its editorial mission to publish longish think pieces about coming trends. However, Dyson continued the annual PC Forum conference that Rosen had started, a convention that was open only to *Release 1.0* subscribers, and operated it throughout the 1980s. It was at that time a premier computer-industry gathering—a place, Dyson wrote in her book *Release 2.1*, where Lotus Corp.'s Mitch Kapor could clash with Microsoft's Bill Gates, where "people met by pools to do deals."

As the 1980s ended, however, she began to look to Eastern Europe, a region that needed help establishing new high-tech markets. There was by that time much competition in the newsletter and convention business, and she needed to differentiate herself. "The U.S. market was fine on its own," she wrote, "but Central and Eastern Europe needed me." She began consulting with entrepreneurs in the Eastern bloc, attempting—often in vain, she later wrote—to get them to understand concepts such as investment for the long haul, marketing, and competition. She started a second newsletter, *Rel-EAST*, and a second conference, the East-West High-Tech Forum. In a 1993 article, *Wired* magazine fretted that by dabbling in hopeless Eastern European ventures, Dyson was expending the coin of her influence at home.

Wired need not have worried; in 1989, Dyson discovered email and the Internet. In 1991, old friend Mitch Kapor called on her to join his newly formed online civil liberties group, the Electronic Frontier Foundation. Her relationship with the EFF quickly made Dyson a Washington Beltway insider. In 1994, Vice President Al Gore convened the National Information Infrastructure Advisory Council, with Dyson as a member and co-chair of the group's intellectual property, privacy, and security subcommittee. There, Dyson wrote, she found herself at loggerheads with fellow members like her co-chair, a senior Disney executive, over issues of intellectual property. "I was more concerned with users' needs—and with the notion that intellectual property will lose much of its value anyway as content proliferates on the Net," Dyson wrote. "That isn't 'should,' but 'will.'"

Her Washington insider status made her a natural selection when the U.S. government devised ICANN, an agency meant to end monopoly control of the government over Internet policy and the stranglehold that Network Systems Inc. held over the assigning of domain names (the Web addresses that end in .com, .org, and .net). Dyson became ICANN's first chair, serving two years until leaving the post and the ICANN board in November 2000.

Her tenure at ICANN was stormy; the group was accused of holding meetings and making key decisions over domain-name policies in secret while discouraging public input. It was also accused of stacking its membership with industry leaders who had a powerful motivation to dislodge the Internet's libertarian underpinnings, in order for companies to exert more control over a commercialized Internet. Dyson herself was accused of arbitrarily stifling public testimony during policy input sessions. Complaints about the Dyson-era ICANN board gained credence when several original members declined to step down at the end of their nominal terms in office.

"This 'first lady' of Internet governance *could* have gone down in history as the George Washington of our day," Jay Fenello, president of domain registrar Iperdome Inc. wrote in a widely circulated newsgroup posting. "Instead," Fenello wrote, "she'll be remembered as the leader that botched the ICANN experiment."

Indeed, after stepping down as ICANN president, Dyson said the agency rests in the hands of "arbitrary interest groups." The group's at-large membership, elected by all Internet users who register with ICANN for the right to vote, is the initial step toward an open and fairly regulated Internet, Dyson has said. But even they represent stilted interests in the present structure, she added. All the Germans tended to vote for a German candidate in elections for an ICANN at-large membership seat, for instance.

Giving new meaning to the phrase "New World Order," Dyson has advocated that Netizens assemble worldwide political parties that represent the interests of the Internet, presumably as part of a latter-day ICANN governance authority. "I would like to see parties emerge," she told the openDemocracy.net Web site in July 2001. "A 'More New TLDs Party,' or an 'IP is Sacred' party. They would represent an interest rather than a nationality or a region. Voting for individuals doesn't mean much on its own."

Despite some lost confidence owing to her tenure at ICANN, Dyson remains very much an Internet icon. Reviewing her first book, *Release 2.0,* in 1999, *USA Today* writer Kevin Maney summed up the Dyson mystique. "Dyson is a force of brainpower, not of the physical," he wrote. "She is elfin in size. She is to public speaking what Leonard Nimoy is to singing. But she is revered for her ideas and because she can attract other people who have interesting ideas. She is beloved because her motives are pure. Dyson wants to spread technology to make life better."

Selected Works

Dyson, Esther. "E-Government Will Be a Reality." EDventure.com, August 23, 2000. <http://www.edventure.com/conversation/ article.cfm?Counter=9950162> (June 7, 2002).

———. "Esther Dyson's Response to Questions (Letter to Ralph Nader and James Love)." June 15, 1999. <http://www.icann.org/chairman-response.htm> (June 7, 2002).

———. "Identity and Security." EDventure.com, October 18, 2001. <http://www.edventure.com/conversation/ article.cfm?Counter=7911978> (June 7, 2002).

———. "Intellectual Value." *Wired* 3.07, July 1995. <http://www.wired.com/wired/archive//3.07/dyson> (June 7, 2002).

———. *Release 2.1: A Design for Living in the Digital Age.* New York: Broadway Books, 1998.

———. "What Is in a Name?" EDventure.com, July 26, 2000. <http://www.edventure.com/conversation/ article.cfm?Counter=6817604> (June 7, 2002).

Bibliography

Borsook, Paulina. "Release." *Wired* 1.05, November 1993. <http://www.wired.com/wired/archive//1.05/dyson> (May 24, 2002).

Brockman, John. "The Pattern-Recognizer." *Edge.org,* 1996. <http://www.edge.org/digerati/dyson/> (May 24, 2002).

The Internet Corporation for Assigned Names and Numbers (ICANN). "ICANN Board of Directors Biographies: Esther Dyson." June 30, 2001. <http://www.icann.org/biog/dyson.htm> (May 24, 2002).

Maney, Kevin. "Computer Maven Dispenses Wisdom." *USA Today* Tech Report, January 26, 1999. <http://www.usatoday.com/life/cyber/tech/ctb453.htm> (May 24, 2002).

openDemocracy.net. "Governing Freedom: An Interview with Esther Dyson by openDemocracy." July 4, 2001. <http://www.opendemocracy.net> (August 30, 2002).

Further Reading

Gelman, Robert B.; McCandlish, Stanton; and members of the Electronic Frontier Foundation. *Protecting Yourself Online: The Definitive Resource on Safety, Freedom, and Privacy in Cyberspace.* New York: HarperCollins, 1998.

Related Topics

Anonymity; Barlow, John Perry; Cyberculture; Electronic Frontier Foundation; Internet Corporation for Assigned Names and Numbers; Kapor, Mitchell; Personal Digital Assistants; Privacy; Rheingold, Howard; Virtual Community

— *Kevin Featherly*

eeeeeeeEeeeeeee

Echo

Echo (which stands for "East Coast Hang Out") is an electronic bulletin-board system (BBS) based in New York City. Founded in 1990, it claims more than 2,000 members. In its early days, Echo was a rarity among computer forums, boasting a user base that was 40 percent female.

Echo is the brainchild of writer Stacy Horn. While a graduate student in the Department of Interactive Telecommunications at New York University, Horn was given an assignment to visit the Whole Earth 'Lectronic Link (WELL), the famous California-based BBS. Intrigued at first, Horn was ultimately disappointed in the experience. "There were almost no women there," she recalled, "and their humor was either non-existent or very different than mine."

By 1990, Horn was ready to begin building a BBS that would reflect the culture of her New York City hometown. "Everyone on the WELL thought that I just didn't 'get it,'" Horn recalls. At the time, most Internet enthusiasts were lauding the fact that cyberspace was "geography free," yet Horn was interested in creating a digital environment chiefly tied to the experience of being a New Yorker. "I wanted to get together in-person with the people I was getting to know online," she insists. In a recent poll, 83 percent of the people who responded said they met with other people on Echo "face to face" on a regular basis.

When Horn began her bulletin board, women made up roughly 10 percent of the entire population of cyberspace, yet almost from the beginning, Echo boasted an exceptionally large female user base. When asked how she did it, Horn answered, "First, I have the home team advantage, I am a woman. When I asked the women of Echo what they didn't like about being online I was really listening and they told me the truth." Still, Horn objects to the idea that Echo was a "safe space" for women on the Net. "I wanted to get more women on Echo to make it better," she insists. "And safety is not an effective lure.

'Come to Echo, we're safe.' That would be like hanging out a sign that said: BORING."

A BBS FOR THE FUTURE?

In 2000, the anticipated sale of Echo to a large conglomerate was abruptly cancelled, causing some to speculate that its days were numbered. The *Silicon Alley Reporter* observed that Echo's existing command-line software was "no longer retro-chic, but technologically behind the times." Horn ruefully concurs, understanding that the advent of services like America Online has profoundly changed BBS culture. "These days, you gotta give people point and click," she admits. As soon as she finds an interface that can incorporate Echo's earlier online material and is also affordable, she'll make the leap to the Web, says Horn.

In the meantime, economic insecurities in the technology sector have convinced Horn of the necessity to "downsize" Echo somewhat. Recently, she abandoned her corporate office and moved her equipment to neighbor ISP Panix. Now Horn runs Echo as she did in 1990—simply, and out of her apartment. "It didn't seem like it at the time, but really, it was the best thing that could have happened to me," she recently confessed. Today, she splits her time between Echo and her successful writing career.

As for people's predictions about the future of her BBS, Horn is sanguine. "You either like the people on Echo and find it worth it to stay, or you don't," she remarks. Her long-range plan is to "still be here, perhaps slightly larger," in the coming years. "Remember, I found users when most people didn't have modems," she likes to say, "and I'm happily back there again."

Bibliography

Horn, Stacy. *Cyberville: Clicks, Culture, and the Creation of an Online Town.* New York: Warner Books, 1998.

Moschovitis, Christos J. P., Poole, Hilary; Schulyer, Tami; and Theresa M. Senft. "These Boots Are Made for Echo." *History of the Internet: A Chronology, 1843 to the Present.* Santa Barbara, Calif.: ABC-CLIO, 1999; p. 129.

Senft, Theresa M. Personal telephone communication with Stacy Horn, November 24, 2001.

Further Reading

Davis, Kaley, and Theresa M. Senft. "Modem
Butterfly, Reconsidered." *Sexuality & Cyberspace:
Performing the Digital Body* (*Women &
Performance Special Issue*, no. 17). New York:
Women & Performance Press, 1997.
<http://www.echonyc.com/~women/Issue17/
senftmodem.html> (April 26, 2002).
Echo Communications Group. Echo Home Page.
1998–2001.
<http://www.echonyc.com> (April 26, 2002).
Hafner, Katie. "The Epic Saga of the WELL."
Wired 5.05, May 1997.
<http://www.wired.com/collections/
virtual_communities/5.05_well_pr.html> (April 26, 2002).
Williams, Mary Elizabeth. "The Mayor of Cyberville."
Salon, January 1998.
<http://www.salon.com/21st/books/1998/01/
cov_21books.html> (April 26, 2002).

Related Topics

Bulletin-Board Systems; Gender and New Media;
Virtual Community

— *Theresa M. Senft*

E-Commerce

E-Commerce (electronic commerce) involves buying
and selling goods and services across the Internet,
rather than through traditional outlets such as retail
stores. Electronic forms of trade date back to the
1960s, but it was the introduction of the World Wide
Web in the early 1990s that made global trading by
Internet possible and brought about the rise of the so-
called "dot-com" enterprise. Although e-commerce
sales currently represent only 1 percent of total commerce, they are growing at a rapid rate. Recent failures
of dot-com ventures have shaken investor confidence,
but industry analysts remain confident that e-commerce represents an unstoppable force for business
transformation in the coming decade.

TYPES OF E-COMMERCE

For thousands of years, commerce has involved a
buyer and a seller exchanging goods or services, usually for money, in what is known as a transaction.
Buyer, seller, funds, and goods still feature in e-commerce, but the transaction is carried out over the
Internet, the buyer and seller may be on opposite
sides of the planet, and the buyer probably gets to see
the goods for the first time only when they are finally delivered. The basis of e-commerce is therefore

transaction processing, a computerized method of
handling the purchase of goods and the exchange of
funds from buyer to seller.

Commercial Web sites vary greatly in sophistication. For example, in Internet retailing, or "e-tailing,"
the least sophisticated approach is simply to use a
Web site as a catalogue, providing photographs of
products and addresses of stores and perhaps a tele-
phone-order hotline through which products can be
bought directly. A more committed form of e-tailing
involves setting up a site as a virtual store, completely
separate from and in addition to an existing store network. Online orders may be processed by one of the
existing stores and shipped using an existing mail-
order network. The ultimate form of e-tailing is based
on Web sites that act as virtual stores, make no use of
an existing store network, and run according to
entirely different business models. E-tail transactions
are conducted online, and warehouses and transportation systems are set up specifically to cope with
them. E-tailing is an example of business-to-consumer
(B2C) e-commerce. The other main type of e-
commerce, which is expected to be much more valuable overall, is business-to-business (B2B).

Selling goods is only one type of e-commerce.
Another popular type involves selling information
("content") over the Web; many online newspapers,
for example, sell back issues of their articles this
way. Perhaps the best-established business model for
e-commerce involves giving things away for free to
attract customers to a Web site that pays its way
through advertising or by selling other products.
Yahoo! was the pioneer of this approach, currently
giving free access to its Web directory, news, email,
chat rooms, photograph albums, and many more
services and subsidising them through a combination
of advertising and paid services such as domain-
name sales.

It was widely predicted that e-commerce would
revolutionize the commercial world by putting buyers
directly in touch with sellers, thus cutting out intermediaries (middlemen) in a shake-up sometimes
known as disintermediation. But it has also spurred
entirely new business models, including the rise of the
"infomediary," who uses the geographical reach of the
Web to link people together in a way that has never
previously been possible. Examples include National
Transportation Exchange, which uses the Internet to
link haulage companies together so they can pool
resources and eliminate wasted journeys (such as
trucks traveling empty on their back hauls), and

Lastminute.com, which offers products such as late-availability flights at significant discounts.

INFRASTRUCTURE

Setting up an e-commerce enterprise requires more than just a Web site, although this is its most visible component. Industry experts also stress the importance of meaningful domain names, even though many successful dot-coms have been founded with meaningless names (Amazon.com and Yahoo! for example) and some of the best-named dot-coms (including Garden.com and Pets.com) have already folded.

Apart from Web site and domain name, another important element is a server that is powerful enough to process hundreds or thousands of transactions at the same time, reliable enough to offer around-the-clock availability, fast enough to process each transaction in a time acceptable to users, and secure enough to protect both buyers and sellers from various forms of electronic crime. Typically, security means using a type of encryption called SSL (Secure Sockets Layer) to scramble credit-card information as it passes from the buyer's browser to the seller's server; however, this does not protect information on the server from hacking or viruses once it has been unscrambled. Greater security is offered by Secure Electronic Transaction (SET), a worldwide standard for e-commerce in which digital certificates are used to verify the identity of all participants at all stages of a transaction.

Where it was once possible to throw together an e-commerce site in an afternoon with a few simple pages of HTML and a server capable of processing transactions, general wisdom now suggests that an investment of several million dollars is required to launch a typical e-commerce dot-com. That price hike represents a corresponding hike in customer expectations, the increased general sophistication of e-commerce sites, and the generally greater difficulty of establishing a distinctive new business venture after the dot-com world has already arrived on the scene.

STATISTICS

According to the U.S. Department of Commerce, total U.S. retail e-commerce sales for the fourth quarter of 2000 were $8.6 billion, an increase of 67 percent over the previous year. Although e-commerce still represents only around 1 percent of total retail sales, it must be kept in mind how rapidly the industry has grown; the Web is little more than a decade old, and e-commerce is younger still. Total e-commerce sales in the United States for 2000 were $25.8 billion. Forrester Research predicts that by 2004, total worldwide revenue from e-commerce will reach $68.6 billion.

The relatively small value of e-commerce conceals a vast amount of transaction activity. The market research group Keenan Vision predicts the total number of Web transactions will increase from 50 billion (30 billion of them B2B) in 1998 to 1.4 trillion (1.1 trillion of them B2B) by 2004. The growth in the number of transactions is being accompanied (and partly prompted) by a decrease in the value of each transaction as e-commerce becomes a more pervasive method of trade; a recent survey by ActivMedia shows that the average value of e-commerce transactions fell from around $388 in 1995 (and before) to just $187 in 1998–99.

If e-commerce is revolutionizing retailing, statistics suggest that it has already had a much more dramatic effect on banking. International Data Corporation estimates that some 61 percent of U.S. banks now offer online services, compared to just 6 percent in 1998. Electronic banking is eliminating bank branches and reducing the use of checks; Telecheck estimates that some 24 billion fewer checks will be processed in 2003 than in 1998, with a potential cost saving of around $8 billion. There is a simultaneous growth in wireless financial services (for example, banking using WAP phones), and Meridien Research estimates that some 40 million people worldwide will bank this way by 2003.

HISTORY OF E-COMMERCE

E-commerce arguably predates even the invention of computers; its beginnings lie in the early twentieth century, when IBM pioneered the use of mechanical calculators in business accounting. The electronic equipment that replaced these machines from the 1950s onward made possible "on-line" transaction processing (OLTP) by airlines, banks, and stores during the 1960s; for the first time, transactions (such as cash withdrawals from ATMs) could be processed immediately, rather than batched up and processed overnight. American Airlines was one of the first corporations to exploit OLTP, using large mainframe computers to process its ticket-handling transactions.

True e-commerce is a much more recent phenomenon, born shortly after the invention of the Web in 1989. Early pioneers of the virtual store included Amazon.com and the Peapod.com grocery store. A key development was the release of the first Netscape Navigator browser in October 1994, later versions of which incorporated built-in SSL encryption to make secure transactions possible. Toward the end of 1995, Netscape's success was one of the main reasons for a 7 percent drop in the value of Microsoft stock, prompting Bill Gates to announce that his company would put the Internet at the heart of its business. Microsoft's commitment was echoed elsewhere in the computer industry, notably at IBM, which reinvented itself as an e-commerce specialist in the late 1990s, repositioning its unfashionable, monolithic mainframes as "enterprise servers" capable of industrial-strength transaction processing for blue-chip e-commerce.

With the technology in place and corporations such as Netscape, Microsoft, and IBM determined to make money from it, the commercial world was soon sold on the idea of going e-commercial. A period of dot-com hype and investor speculation rapidly followed, with e-commerce businesses launching and speeding toward multimillion-dollar initial public offerings (IPOs) even before they had shown a profit.

The widely predicted burst of the dot-com bubble began in earnest shortly after e-stocks reached an all-time high in March 2000; notable casualties included the fashion e-tailer Boo.com, Garden.com (which had traded since 1995), Pets.com, and E-Toys.com. Studies by industry analysts Webmergers.com suggest that at least 109 e-commerce firms collapsed during 2000, with Internet company failures totaling more than 200. Around 15,000 jobs and $1.5 billion of investment capital were estimated to have been lost. By 2001, the collapse of dot-coms and the loss of investor capital and confidence were having a more profound effect on the world's stock markets, with the Dow Jones reporting its worst week for 11 years on March 16, 2001, and technology stocks attracting much of the blame.

FUTURE OF E-COMMERCE

Skeptical financial analysts have wasted no time filling media columns with "told-you-so" obituaries for the dot-com phenomenon. According to them, the industry was over-hyped and overstaffed with people ill-qualified to build businesses around ill-defined business models. But rumors of the death of the dot-com are greatly exaggerated. For every dot-com that folds, more start up. For every high-profile B2C dot-com that crashes in a blaze of publicity, there is a low-profile B2B dot-com quietly selling mundane goods or services and quietly turning a profit. As IBM CEO Lou Gerstner commented in a speech to Wall Street analysts in 1999, the frenzy of dot-coms was like "fireflies

before the storm—all stirred up, throwing off sparks." The "storm" then marks the more gradual, more measured entry of blue-chip corporations such as Sears into e-commerce, and the progressive reinvention of their entire business and supplier relationships around electronic forms of trading.

Hype aside, the economics of e-commerce make its global adoption a virtual inevitability. Internet banking illustrates this well: A single Internet transaction costs a bank around $0.13 to process—one quarter the cost of a typical $0.54 telephone banking transaction, and around 1 percent of the typical $1.08 cost of a face-to-face branch transaction. No business can ignore such basic economics, and every business so persuaded necessarily requires the same commitment from its suppliers, who demand it in turn from their own suppliers. All told, dot-com failures seem to be a relatively minor setback in the transformation of commerce into e-commerce.

Bibliography

"Dot-com crash." *Fortune*, October 30, 2000.

Epaynews. "E-commerce Statistics." March 22, 2002. <http://www.epaynews.com/statistics/index.html> (March 22, 2002).

Internetstats.com "Internet Statistics & Online Survey Information." <http://www.internetstats.com/> (March 22, 2002).

"Survey: Business and the Internet: The Real Revolution." *The Economist*, June 26, 1999.

"Survey: Electronic Commerce: Tremble Everyone." *The Economist*, May 10, 1997.

U.S. Government Department of Commerce. "Measuring the Electronic Economy." E-stats home page, April 5, 2001. <http://www.census.gov/econ/www/ebusiness614.htm> (March 22, 2002).

Further Reading

Cataudella, Joe; Sawyer, Ben; and Dave Greely. *Creating Stores on the Web*. Berkeley, Calif.: Peachpit Press, 1998.

"Dot-com is Dead; Long Live Dot-com." Numerous articles in a special report from TheStreet.com, November 3, 2000. <http://www.thestreet.com/funds/investing/1151550.html> (March 22, 2002)

Henning, Kay. *The Digital Enterprise: How Digitisation Is Redefining Business*. New York: Random House, 1998.

Leebaert, Derek, ed. *The Future of the Electronic Marketplace*. Cambridge, Mass.: MIT Press, 1998.

Seybold, Patricia. *Customers.com: How to Create a Profitable Business Strategy for the Internet and Beyond*. New York: Times Business/Random House, 1998.

Related Topics

Business-to-Business; Disintermediation

— *Chris Woodford*

Education and Computers

Computers have proven to be immensely useful tools for educators and students, and they are now considered to be an essential component of primary and secondary education in the United States. However, the computerization of schools has raised a number of pressing issues: unequal access to machines and resources, the commercialization of school curricula, teachers' responses to computing, and a whole host of other pedagogical issues.

Although computers had made occasional appearances in American schools during the 1970s, it was in the 1980s that they became a major issue in education. In 1980, for instance, an elite private high school made headlines in *Fortune* magazine by requiring its students to purchase and use computers. By 1982, the use of computers in schools was a more widespread phenomenon in upper-middle-class and upper-class school districts.

From the beginning, many forces conspired to get computers into schools and classrooms. The computer industry made students and education a priority, in part because they knew that they could get lifelong customers if they caught them young. Education was also conceived as a major computer market early on. By 1984, *Forbes* magazine was estimating the educational computing market to be worth billions of dollars in revenue. Some computer manufacturers, like Apple and Hewlett-Packard, ran educational promotions.

For the most part, higher-income school districts were the first to be equipped with computers. But income was not the only significant factor. An *American Demographics* survey showed that even low-income families were disposed toward buying computers if their children used them in school. Since American schools were heavily segregated by race, the inequalities of neighborhood were reproduced in cyberspace. Now called the digital divide, this unequal access to and interest in computing was a side effect of the ways in which computers were marketed to educators. Even where districts found the money for computers, there were still important resource issues. Computer budgets were often placed in competition with allocations for other resources like library books or textbooks—and, in some cases, even teacher salaries.

A major thrust of computer education has been computer literacy, the idea that students needed to have a basic set of competencies in computing. While basic reading and writing skills are generally agreed upon as standards for traditional literacy, there is a much wider range of opinion on the question of computer literacy. Some educators believe that it is enough to teach students how to run and use basic programs for word processing, Internet use, spreadsheets, and so forth. Others believe that computer literacy requires some basic knowledge of programming as well.

Regardless of one's definition of computer literacy, a number of other factors will influence students' facilities with computers. Students who excel at reading, writing, and math will tend to excel at computing as well; students who have access to a keyboard outside the classroom will learn to type more quickly. There is also a debate among educators as to the proper age for introducing computers into the curriculum. Some argue that students should start very young on computers—at kindergarten age or earlier. Others argue that students should pass through a few years of schooling before computers are significantly integrated into the curriculum.

A variety of pedagogical issues remain with computer use in schools today. Even if a school has the resources to supply a meaningful number of computers for its students and teachers, the use of those computers varies widely. Many educational computing programs come with a fairly restricted range of curricular options, forcing teachers to, in essence, design their curricula around the program. In the process of designing an easy-to-use interface, many educational programs also wind up making curricular decisions for teachers, especially concerning how and what students should learn. Although this has been an issue since the introduction of standardized, mass-produced textbooks, it takes on a new urgency when software designers have to balance ease of use against curricular flexibility. The more options a teacher has with a program, the more difficult it may be to use.

Teachers' computer literacy is an issue as well. In order to be able to teach with computers, teachers need to have mastered a basic level of computer literacy, and they need to develop pedagogical techniques for integrating computers into the curriculum. If a school is wired for the Internet, but teachers are not knowledgeable about the Internet and how to use it in teaching, Internet connections are not likely to see much use. So in conjunction with the installation of computers, teachers must be trained to use them.

Integration of computers into classroom design (and the design of computer labs as classrooms) is another important issue. Where the non-computerized classroom might have independent desks that could be rearranged to suit the project at hand, many computer-centered classrooms are modeled after lecture halls, with rows of students facing the front of the classroom and a teacher station facing the students. This arrangement emphasizes the teacher and the computers while deemphasizing physical interaction among students in the classroom itself.

Computer usage outside the classroom raises still more issues. Because students have differing economic and social backgrounds, teachers cannot assume or depend upon students' access to computers outside the classroom. Schools' efforts to use computers for distance learning are also conflicted. While they make educational resources available to people who would otherwise not have them, interactions between teacher and student have to be rethought.

Today, the value of computers in education has been established as U.S. federal policy. The Department of Education, for instance, has published material arguing for the importance of computers in schools, and advises districts on installing computers. Created by the Telecommunications Act of 1996, the E-rate program provides discounted telecommunications services for schools and libraries serving underprivileged students. The Department of Education's Computers for Learning (CFL) program transfers used government computers to educational and nonprofit institutions.

Similarly, a wide variety of volunteer efforts are underway to get computers into schools, and to wire schools for Internet service. Groups like CYFERnet, EDUcom, and the Educational Resources Information Clearinghouse (ERIC) advocate for the use of computers in education, advise parents and educators on implementation, and connect organizations and resources.

While computers have become an important part of American education and "computerization" has become a major cornerstone of educational policy, many curricular and practical issues remain unresolved. Even if the government's goal of universal Internet service is met, important questions will linger about how schools will use computers and Internet connections to educate their students.

Bibliography

Hargittai, Eszter. "The Pros and Cons of Implementing the Internet in the Classroom: Making Sense of the Hype." 2001. <http://www.princeton.edu/~eszter/edu/toc.html> (April 5, 2002).

U.S. Department of Education. "Getting Technology and Computers into the Classroom." *America Goes Back to School—August 1995.* <http://www.ed.gov/Family/BTS/pt7.html> (April 5, 2002).

U.S. Department of Education. 2001. "Reasons for Bringing Technology into Schools." <http://www.ed.gov/pubs/EdReformStudies/EdTech/reasons.html> (April 5, 2002).

U.S. General Services Administration. "Computers for Learning Website." <http://www.computers.fed.gov/School/user.asp> (April 5, 2002).

Further Reading

Robins, Kevin, and Frank Webster. *The Technical Fix: Education, Computers and Industry.* New York: St. Martin's Press, 1989.

Sterne, Jonathan. "The Computer Race Goes to Class: How Computers in Schools Helped Shape the Racial Topography of the Internet." *Race in Cyberspace.* Beth Kolko, Lisa Nakamura, and Gilbert Rodman, eds. New York: Routledge, 2000; pp. 191–212.

Related Topics

Digital Divide; Distance Learning; Gender and New Media; Jobs, Steven P.; Race and Ethnicity and New Media

— *Jonathan Sterne*

Electronic Civil Disobedience

Electronic Civil Disobedience (ECD) is a political strategy that uses electronic techniques for the purpose of blocking information access and/or disrupting the functioning of an institution. Examples include triggering denial-of-service attacks, posting electronic graffiti, and staging virtual sit-ins. ECD adapts the traditional practices of civil disobedience, such as non-violent demonstrations focusing on economic disruption and symbolic protest, and relocates the forum of resistance from the streets to the Internet.

A group of artists and theorists known as the Critical Art Ensemble first coined the term in their 1995 book, *Electronic Civil Disobedience and Other Unpopular Ideas.* The Critical Art Ensemble argues that traditional civil-disobedience techniques of street resistance are now outdated and ineffective, except at local levels. Street resistance was useful during the 1960s when capital was concentrated in cities, and when buildings themselves were literal sites of power. Today, however, capital has become decentralized and transnational, so that power no longer has a stable physical location. The Critical Art Ensemble argues that capital and power now flow in cyberspace; therefore, resistance must become electronic.

The Critical Art Ensemble believes that cyberspace is insecure, so online resistance is still possible. Of course, hackers have frequently exploited the weaknesses of the online security of corporations and governmental agencies. However, hacking has frequently been considered the work of apolitical and immature actors. ECD embraces the techniques of the hacker and adds the convictions and agendas of a political activist, a fusion that has come to be known as hacktivism.

HACKTIVISM AND ELECTRONIC CIVIL DISOBEDIENCE

Hacktivism, a central technique of ECD, first emerged as a term and practice in 1995, when many hackers became politicized over the jailing of hacker Kevin Mitnick. One example of hacktivism occurred when hackers attacked the *New York Times* Web site and replaced the news with a plea to release Mitnick from prison. Hacktivism relies on such techniques as jamming or blocking an electronic flow and placing electronic graffiti on Web sites.

During the conflict in the Balkans, politicized anti-war hacktivism was prevalent on all sides, making Kosovo the first known hacking war. According to Amy Harmon of the *New York Times,* a Serb hacker group known as the Black Hand attacked the Web site of Croatian newspaper *Vjesnik.* Croatian hackers responded by hacking onto the Web site of the Serbian National Library and leaving electronic graffiti messages. Similar graffiti populate the Web, with hacktivists urging readers to "Save Kashmir" or "Free East Timor."

Hacktivism has been employed in the name of many political causes around the globe, and undoubtedly will continue into the future. Unfettered by geographical constraints, hackers and activists can organize and demonstrate solely through electronic means, enabling large groups to assemble and operate quickly, effectively, and non-violently. In 1999, for example, hacktivists organized a demonstration against the National Security Agency (NSA), which was accused of conducting a project known as Echelon. According to a 1997 report by the European Parliament, this project featured the routine monitoring of all emails, faxes, and telephone messages in Europe, looking for key words that may indicate terrorist or other threats. Responding to Echelon's

eavesdropping, hacktivists declared "Jam Echelon Day," exclaiming "Give the NSA their key words!" as they flooded the NSA with emails featuring such key words as "bomb" or "hijack."

This technique not only was designed to overwhelm the NSA's surveillance systems, it also effectively focused media attention and public awareness on the ethical implications of Echelon technologies and practices. Furthermore, it engaged an electronic political issue using electronic means. Duncan Campbell of Edinburgh, Scotland, who wrote the Echelon report for the European Union, said that "Jam Echelon Day" would not affect the NSA. Although the NSA's operations may have remained unaffected, the political message was spread, raising awareness through electronic means.

Activists concerned with more earthly matters also find ECD to be a useful technique for promoting environmental and animal-welfare issues. For example, radical animal-rights group Animal Liberation Front has an online division called the Tactical Internet Response Network, assembled for ECD. Attacking the Web sites of fur dealers and vivisection laboratories, animal-interest hacktivists can effectively protest inhumane practices. On January 15, 1999, more than 800 people from 15 countries staged a "virtual sit-in" of denial-of-service attacks, effectively halting the operation of a Swedish vivisection laboratory. The Animal Liberation Front's Tactical Internet Response Network described the action as a digital blockade that allowed people to protest in the tradition of non-violent direct action and civil disobedience.

ZAPATISTAS AND THE ELECTRONIC DISTURBANCE THEATRE

Perhaps the most well publicized acts of ECD have been performed in the name of the Zapatista Army of National Liberation (EZLN), the radical Mexican group commonly known as the Zapatistas. The EZLN represents the interests of the indigenous Mayans in Chiapas, Mexico. The Zapatistas' leader, known as Subcommandante Marcos, was frequently said to use his Internet connection to spread the Zapatistas' political messages. More and more rebel groups are discovering the Internet as an effective way of spreading their messages and organizing actions without the risk of state intervention. In most nations, the content of Web sites is not subject to governmental regulation or penalty, so resistant or guerrilla groups find that the Internet is the safest way to reach the widest audience with their political messages. Marcos allegedly uses a laptop computer powered by the battery of a truck to type his communiqués; others then post his messages online. Through raising awareness on the Internet, Marcos and the Zapatistas became known as guerrilla "net-warriors," taking on the status of media celebrities.

Mere political messages on the Internet alone do not constitute ECD, however. Exploiting the technological specificity of the medium in the form of denial-of-service attacks would come later in the Zapatista struggle, as U.S. hacktivists came to support the Zapatistas.

New York activists Ricardo Dominguez and Stefan Wray co-founded the Electronic Disturbance Theatre in support of the Zapatistas. The organization gained popular attention when it was featured in a 1998 *New York Times* cover story on hacktivism by Amy Harmon called "'Hacktivists' of all Persuasions Take Their Struggle to the Web." Wray told the *Times* that the Electronic Disturbance Theatre is "transferring the social-movement tactics of trespass and blockade to the Internet." Wray noted that although the Electronic Disturbance Theatre aims to disrupt Internet traffic, no data is destroyed. In the spirit of traditional civil disobedience, online participants are encouraged to use their real names.

FloodNet

In order to create an electronic blockage, the Electronic Disturbance Theatre and other groups use a computer program known as FloodNet, which was created by software engineer Carmin Karasic as an act of "conceptual art." FloodNet works as a denial-of-service attack, requesting a Web page at a rate of 10 times per minute, thereby overwhelming the server into refusing service. In addition to the denial-of-service attack, FloodNet also provides what author Brett Stalbaum calls the "conceptual-artistic spamming of targeted server error logs." For example, after choosing to attack a particular symbol of Mexican neo-liberalism, a hacktivist would request "bad" URLs, such as "human_rights." The server error message would read, "human_rights not found on this server."

FloodNet attacks—indeed, the techniques of ECD in general—are themselves vulnerable to counterattack from governmental agencies, or perhaps even corporations. When the Electronic Disturbance Theatre attacked the Pentagon's Web site as a protest against U.S. support of the Mexican government, the Pentagon launched a formidable counterattack. According to

information security expert Winn Schwartau, requests from the hackers' browsers were redirected to a Java applet called "hostileapplet."

In response to hacktivism, then-attorney-general Janet Reno created a new federal agency in 1998 called the National Information Protection Center, which was designed to investigate groups that hack for political causes. However, regulating non-violent electronic political protest at present remains ambiguous.

Blending the technical expertise of hacking with the political agendas of activism, hacktivists effectively transform the techniques of civil disobedience, updating peaceful protest for the Information Age. In the name of a variety of political causes, from defending hacker Kevin Mitnick to protesting inhumane acts by vivisection laboratories, ECD has emerged as an effective means of non-violent electronically mediated protest.

Bibliography

Bridis, Ted. "Spy Network Eavesdrops on Emails." *Pittsburgh Post-Gazette*, October 22, 1999, p. A6.

Bronskill, Jim. "RCMP Fears Escalation of Cyber Sabotage by Extremists." *The Ottawa Citizen*, December 7, 1999, p. A8.

Harmon, Amy. "'Hacktivists' of All Persuasions Take Their Struggle to the Web." *The New York Times*, October 31, 1998, p. A1.

Schwartau, Winn. "Cyber-Civil Disobedience: Political Dissent in the 90's." <http://www.infowar.com/class_3/cybciv.html-ssi> (May 17, 2002).

Stalbaum, Brett. "The Zapatista Tactical FloodNet." <http://www.nyu.edu/projects/wray/ZapTactFlood.html> (May 17, 2002).

Further Reading

Bey, Hakim. *The Temporary Autonomous Zone, Ontological Anarchy, Poetic Terrorism.* Brooklyn, N.Y.: Autonomedia, 1991.

Critical Art Ensemble. *The Electronic Disturbance.* Brooklyn, N.Y.: Autonomedia, 1994.

Electronic Civil Disobedience at thing.net. Web site. <http://www.thing.net/~rdom/ecd/ecd.html> (May 17, 2002).

Ludlow, Peter, ed. *Crypto Anarchy, Cyberstates, and Pirate Utopias.* Cambridge, Mass.: MIT Press, 2001.

Schwartau, Winn. *Cybershock: Surviving Hackers, Phreakers, Identity Thieves, Internet Terrorists, and Weapons of Mass Disruption.* New York: Thunder's Mouth Press, 2000.

Related Topics

Cyberwarfare; Hacking, Cracking, and Phreaking; Hacktivism

— *Heidi Marie Brush*

Electronic Communications Privacy Act

The U.S. Electronic Communications Privacy Act (ECPA) of 1986 was created in order to address privacy issues surrounding the pervasiveness of computers and databases in the government and the workplace. Its major provisions include extending privacy protection to email, voice mail, and remote computing services. It has been criticized for allowing law-enforcement agencies easier access to consumer records, and for allowing a certain amount of employer surveillance. Debates have more recently focused on whether its extension of law-enforcement monitoring of private communications could undermine the constitutional right to privacy.

Before the ECPA was enacted in 1986, electronic surveillance was covered by Title III of the Omnibus Crime Control and Safe Streets Act of 1968, also known as the Federal Wiretap Act. Because the wiretap law did not consider electronic technologies, both industry and civil-liberty groups urged Congress to update the law. It was believed that strengthening privacy through ECPA would create a principle that privacy is beneficial for both consumers and businesses. Signed into law by President Reagan on October 21, 1986, and effective January 20, 1987, the ECPA expanded privacy protection to radio pagers, electronic mail, cellular telephones, private-communication carriers, and computer transmissions.

Under the ECPA, privacy protection was extended to all carriers, private and branch telephone exchanges, and local area networks. Under the Stored Communications provisions of the ECPA, the contents of stored email, voicemail, and remote computing services are protected. These provisions protect email from unauthorized access, alteration, and disruption, as well as from unauthorized disclosure without the lawful consent of the originator of the communication. The ECPA also restricts government access to customer and subscriber records, and requires government entities to acquire a search warrant, court order, or subpoena to access any service-provider records without the prior notification of the customer or subscriber.

Criticism of the ECPA has focused on its potential threats to civil liberties. In particular, critics are worried that more and varied law-enforcement agencies have easier access to customer and subscriber information

records, that the federal infringement of privacy under the guise of electronic surveillance has increased, and that there could be a possible increase in the surveillance of citizens who have been targeted as members of particular political groups.

Workplace privacy has also been a concern, as the ECPA, although not allowing employers to monitor employee email or telephone calls, does allow employers to eavesdrop on their employees if they are notified in advance, or if there is reason to suspect that the employers' interests are being jeopardized.

One of the first major decisions under the ECPA was the 1993 ruling in *Steve Jackson Games Incorporated, et al., vs. United States Secret Service, United States of America, et al.* In this case, the court ruled that the U.S. Secret Service had violated the ECPA when it seized computer equipment belonging to Steve Jackson, believing that he was involved in software theft from BellSouth. Of particular interest in this case is the judge's ruling that the ECPA was violated when agents seized a computer containing private, stored emails.

After the Oklahoma City bombing in 1995, proposals were made to reinforce the wiretap laws so that law enforcement would have easier access to electronic records. Two recent court cases demonstrate the increasing complexity of email privacy.

In *McVeigh v. Cohen* (1998), the D.C. District Court's ruling suggested that amendments should be made to the ECPA that require a legal process for any disclosure of user information to subscribers of commercial online services. Highlighted here was Section 2703(c) of the ECPA, which allows Internet Service Providers (ISPs) to disclose information, without legal authorization, about their subscribers to non-governmental entities. This section prohibits the disclosure of such information to governmental organizations without a subpoena or court order. However, in this instance, a naval investigator collected information about Timothy McVeigh (no relation to the Oklahoma City bomber) from America Online, and failed to identify himself as a government agent. McVeigh had described himself as gay in his online profile; armed with this information, the U.S. Navy initiated discharge proceedings against him. The federal court's decision suggested that the ECPA might have been violated, and ordered the navy to discontinue its discharge proceedings against McVeigh.

In *Konop vs. Hawaiian Airlines* (2001), the Ninth Circuit Court held that Title 1 of the ECPA protects stored Internet communications, not merely those in transit. The court ruled that the contents of secure Web sites are "electronic communications" in intermediate storage, and are protected from unauthorized interception under the Wiretap Act. The case came about when Robert Konop, a pilot for Hawaiian Airlines, set up a password-protected Web site for his fellow pilots to discuss the airline during pilots' union negotiations. A member of Hawaiian Airlines management persuaded a pilot to let him into the site; after he discovered negative statements about management on this private Web site, Hawaiian Airlines threatened to sue Konop for libel and suspended him from his job. The ruling in this case should set a precedent for secure Web sites to be covered under the ECPA. Although employers can monitor employee Web-surfing habits, email, and other information on workplace computer screens, they are not allowed to break into secure sites maintained outside of the work environment.

The September 11, 2001, attacks inspired new calls to strengthen the ability of law enforcement to monitor electronic messages. In 2002 the FBI was granted vastly expanded access to electronic communications. Alongside the current war against terrorism, the development and spread of Internet communication will undoubtedly create new challenges to the ECPA provisions.

Bibliography

Corn, Robert. "Tapping New Technologies: New Law Offers Easy Listening." *The Nation,* vol. 243 (December 20, 1986), p. 696.

99th Congress. Electronic Communications Privacy Act (ECPA); Public Law 99-508—October 21, 1986. <http://www.cpsr.org/cpsr/privacy/communications/wiretap/electronic_commun_privacy_act.txt> (May 24, 2002).

Regan, Priscilla M. "Ideas or Interests: Privacy in Electronic Communications." *Policy Studies Journal* vol. 21 (Autumn 1993), p. 450.

Samoriski, Jan J.; Huffman, John L.; and Denise M. Trauth. "Electronic Mail, Privacy, and the Electronic Communications Privacy Act of 1986: Technology in Search of Law." *Journal of Broadcasting & Electronic Media,* vol. 40 (Winter 1996), p. 60.

United States District Court Western District of Texas, Austin Division. *Steve Jackson Games Incorporated et al., vs. United States Secret Service, United States of America, et al.,* No A91 CA 246 SS, 1993.

Unites States Court of Appeals for the Ninth Circuit. *Konop vs. Hawaiian Airlines.* January 8, 2001. Appeal decision. <http://www.ca9.uscourts.gov> (May 24, 2002).

Unites States District Court for the District of Columbia. *Timothy R. McVeigh, Plaintiff, v. William Cohen, et al., Defendants.* Civil Action No. 98-116. (Electronic Privacy Information Center Alert.) <http://www.epic.org/privacy/internet/aol/navy_decision.html> (May 24, 2002).

Further Reading

Burnside, Russell S. "The Electronic Communications Privacy Act of 1986: The Challenge of Applying Ambiguous Statutory Language to Intricate Telecommunication Technology." *Rutgers Computer & Technology Law Journal,* vol. 13 (Winter 1987), pp. 451–517.

O'Neil, Michael. "Cybercrime Dilemma." *Brookings Review,* vol. 19, Winter 2001, p. 28.

Rosen, Jeffrey. *The Unwanted Gaze: The Destruction of Privacy in America.* New York: Random House, 2000.

Solove, Daniel J. "Privacy and Power: Computer Databases and Metaphors for Information Privacy." *Stanford Law Review,* vol. 53 (July 2001), p. 1,393.

Related Topics

Anonymity; Electronic Frontier Foundation; Email; Privacy

— *Leslie Regan Shade*

Electronic Democracy

Electronic democracy refers to the use of information and communication technologies (ICTs) to extend, strengthen, and promote effective and efficient democratic practices between and among governments and citizens. The inherent nature of ICTs lends itself to electronic democracy. ICTs are interactive, global in scope, and increasingly ubiquitous. As more stakeholders (including diverse civil liberties groups) want a say in governance, and as access to ICTs becomes more pervasive, electronic democracy has taken on a new vitality and viability. Electronic democracy is practiced by governments, and through new forms of citizen engagement whereby diverse stakeholders use the Internet for mobilization, consultation, and public education and awareness campaigns.The benefits of electronic democracy are many. It can allow for communitarian democracy, where citizens can participate regardless of socioeconomic status or geographic location. It supports simultaneous, interactive communications among many people, with low set-up costs. Email allows for the forwarding and redistribution of information, and email and the Web also support action alerts and online petitions. Political decision-making becomes more transparent, as citizens can ascertain which industry associations, political-activist groups, lobbyists, and consumer and public-interest groups are active in various causes.

There are also disadvantages to electronic democracy, however. Access issues loom large; not everyone has access to ICTs, and various digital divides exist. Even when people have access to ICTs, attention needs to be paid to adequate training and support for the fostering of digital literacy. Many politicians resist electronic democracy; for instance, their traditional practice has been to respond primarily to requests from the people whom they represent, and with email, one often cannot determine where messages are coming from. The organizational culture of politics is also impacted; more work is created for staff when email is added to the deluge of regular mail.

E-government initiatives are flourishing in the United States, Canada, Australia, the U.K., and parts of Europe. These programs support citizen access to government information, personal benefits, and procurement (including bidding, purchasing, and payment); the facilitation of general compliance; and government-to-government information and service integration. A new trend is to create government portals, allowing for one-stop shopping for government services.

Some early examples of electronic democracy in the United States led many to believe in its inevitability. In 1989, one of the earliest community networks, the Public Electronic Network (PEN) in Santa Monica, California, developed an online proposal for the homeless known as SWASHLOCK (showers, washers, and lockers). What was interesting here was the involvement of local politicians, community activists, and the homeless themselves, who were able to talk among themselves on terminals set up in community locations. In 1984, the Minnesota Electronic Democracy Project hosted the first-ever online debate between candidates for the U.S. Senate. The controversy over the Communications Decency Act (CDA) inspired an estimated 65,000 to 100,000 Internet users to read legislative updates about the bill within three to four days of each update's posting. The May 1998 Federal Communications Commission (FCC) Hearing on Universal Access included live audio feed, live photos, interactive chat, background information, and a mechanism for citizens to submit their own questions to the FCC.

THE FUTURE OF ELECTRONIC DEMOCRACY

Recent trends in e-democracy include the electronic delivery of political communication through Web sites for governments, political parties, candidates, and elected representatives, all in order to communicate directly and constantly with voters. An example of this is the U.K. Citizens On-line Democracy Group (UKCOD) whose objective is to bring politicians together with the public around a "virtual table." Citizen participation in public planning on policy issues can be supported by ICTs, which allow for the provision of information on a problem and background issues; the support of communication processes, including debates; and the support of decision-making processes through electronic voting.

Electronic democracy faces many challenging questions, particularly regarding the ways that the Internet is most likely to affect citizens' participation by changing their awareness of political events and their knowledge of the political process. How can one measure the effect of the Internet on political participation, given the rapidly changing demographics of the Internet itself? How can one distinguish between Internet use and non-use as factors influencing political activity? How can one regulate Internet-based mischief, like security breaches, sexism, poor etiquette, and flaming? In terms of design, what will be electronic democracy's "killer app"?

Although ICTs can broaden and extend democratic practices, there are still significant barriers for widespread citizen engagement. If democracy includes three essential elements—equality, participation, and a healthy public sphere—then electronic democracy has not yet lived up to its potential. Participation in the public sphere via the Internet is not yet universal, and even if it was, would citizens participate more in online political processes, given the paucity of participation in general elections?

Despite these questions, it is clear that electronic-democracy practices have allowed a diverse range of groups to educate and organize online. In many instances, these groups have been able to successfully influence both public opinion and government policy-making. Electronic democracy is becoming both more sophisticated and increasingly widespread, and governments that ignore online activism do so at their own peril. In fact, many governments are now adapting the same tactics in order to influence their citizenry. As the new century unfolds, electronic democracy practices will continue to expand and evolve.

Bibliography

Alexander, Cynthia, and Leslie A. Pal, eds. *Digital Democracy: Policy and Politics in the Wired World.* Toronto: Oxford University Press, 1998.

Barney, Darin. *Prometheus Wired: The Hope for Democracy in the Age of Network Technology.* Vancouver: UBC Press, 2000.

Friedland, Lewis. "Electronic Democracy and the New Citizenship." *Media, Culture & Society,* 18:2 (1996), pp. 185–213.

Hague, Barry N., and Brian Loader. *Digital Democracy: Discourse and Decision Making in the Information Age.* New York: Routledge, 1999.

Wilhelm, Anthony G. *Democracy in the Digital Age: Challenges to Political Life in Cyberspace.* New York: Routledge, 2000.

Further Reading

Clift, Steven. *The E-Democracy E-Book: Democracy Is Online 2.0.* 1998. <http://www.e-democracy.org/do/article.html> or <http://publicus.net/ebook/> (May 17, 2002).

Dahlgren, Peter. "The Internet and the Democratization of Civic Culture." *Political Communication,* 17:4 (2000).

Hacker, Kenneth L., and Jan van Dijk, eds. *Digital Democracy: Issues of Theory and Practice.* Thousand Oaks, Calif.: Sage Publications, 2000.

Tambini, D. "New Media and Democracy: The Civic Networking Movement." *New Media & Society,* 1:3 (1999), pp. 305–29.

Related Topics

Access; Community Networking; Digital Divide; Electronic Civil Disobedience; Hacktivism

— *Leslie Regan Shade*

Electronic Frontier Foundation

John Perry Barlow and Mitch Kapor founded the Electronic Frontier Foundation (EFF) in 1990, with additional support from John Gilmore and Steve Wozniak. The purpose of the EFF was to raise funds for lobbying, litigation, and education about civil liberties on the Internet. The EFF's Web site also currently serves as an archive for a broad spectrum of information about the Internet.

The formation of the EFF was prompted primarily by the reaction of Barlow and Kapor to efforts by the Secret Service and the FBI to crack down on hackers during early 1990. Both Kapor and Barlow were questioned by law-enforcement authorities about suspected connections to hackers. Both reached the conclusion that law-enforcement agencies were dangerously uninformed about the new forms of communication occurring through computers and the Internet. They felt that there was a need to increase civil-liberties protections for online communication.

Barlow, previously a Wyoming cattle rancher and lyricist for the Grateful Dead, and Kapor, the founder of Lotus Development Corporation, were participants on the Whole Earth 'Lectronic Link (WELL) bulletin board service (BBS). Barlow and Kapor had met through their participation on the WELL, and when Barlow posted an account of his encounter with the FBI, the two got together, exchanged information about their experiences, and decided to form the EFF.

The EFF's first important battle related directly to the investigations that had sparked its formation. In its attempt to track down various hackers thought to be in possession of an illegally obtained telephone-company document, the Secret Service raided a small role-playing-game company called Steve Jackson Games, confiscating computer equipment and other materials, without which the business was unable to function. Unable to find any copies of the document in question, the Secret Service eventually returned the equipment and did not press charges. However, they had deleted unrelated personal email contained on BBS files. The EFF brought suit against the government on behalf of Steve Jackson Games, charging that the search warrant used during the raid had been insufficient, and that the privacy rights of the BBS users had been violated by the erasure of their personal email. The suit was successful on most points, and received a significant amount of press coverage. The EFF's involvement with this and other hacker-related cases provided the organization with considerable early publicity. It quickly gained respect among many computer-related and Internet subcultures, and became a force to contend with in legal and political battles relating to computer-mediated communication and commerce.

Since that initial case, the EFF has been involved in litigation relating to a wide range of online and computer-related civil-liberty issues. In general, it has sought to extend free speech and privacy rights to online communications, including such forms of "speech" as encryption and other computer programs. It was particularly active in opposing the Communications Decency Act (CDA) of 1995, instigating the "Blue Ribbon Campaign," in which hundreds of Web sites displayed a blue ribbon graphic in protest of the passing of the CDA.

In 1991, the EFF moved its offices from Cambridge to Washington, D.C., in order to engage more directly in attempts to influence governmental policy and legislation regarding computers and the

Internet. The somewhat controversial move was seen by some of the EFF's online supporters as "selling out" to political interests in the government. While in Washington, in affiliation with the Digital Privacy and Security Working Group (DPSWG), a coalition of more than 50 communications and computer companies and civil-liberty groups, the EFF successfully lobbied to stop the Digital Telephony bill, which would have greatly increased the scope of the FBI's powers to perform wiretaps on digital communications. When a similar act was proposed during the Clinton administration in 1994, the EFF got involved in drafting a weaker alternative that eventually passed. However, as it considered even the weakened version to be an unnecessary intrusion on privacy, the EFF did not fully support the legislation it had helped draft.

The EFF's experiment in Washington-insider politics highlighted some of the tensions within the organization. Some of these tensions stem from the strong and often flamboyant personalities of many members of both the board of directors and the staff. The organization has also had to clarify the relationship between its mission and its funding structure. Most of the EFF's ideological support comes from a wide-ranging and strongly libertarian online grassroots community, while much of its funding during its Washington sojourn came from corporate sources (including, somewhat ironically, telephone companies). These two groups do not always share objectives and viewpoints, and the EFF found it difficult to satisfy both constituencies. Its treatment by *Wired* magazine forms an illustrative example of the disillusionment of some of its supporters: A 1994 feature article describes the EFF in glowing, utopian terms, while a 1996 article portrays it as ineffectual, naive, and ultimately corrupted by Washington politics.

Because of these tensions, the EFF has undergone a variety of reorganizations over the years. Disagreements over the experiences in Washington caused a major shake-up in 1995, during which then-executive-director Jerry Berman was fired and co-founder Mitch Kapor left the organization. The EFF then moved its offices to San Francisco, greatly in debt and with a significantly reduced staff. Another reorganization occurred in early 2000, sparked by internal disagreements over whether to take on a case relating to corporate copyright protection.

The EFF's fortunes appear to be on the upswing again. Of the original co-founders, Barlow remains as vice-chairman, and John Gilmore, whose involvement

with the organization has generally increased over the years, remains on the board of directors. Shari Steele, who served for several years as the EFF's legal director, took the executive director post in 2000 after a brief absence from the organization, and has overseen the EFF's move to new, larger offices in San Francisco. Recent news articles represent the EFF as rediscovering its original purpose and drive. The organization also continues to attract well-respected and high-profile board members. While the EFF continues to fight against legislation it deems to have negative implications for online civil liberties, it currently focuses most of its energies on court cases and educational campaigns.

Bibliography

Barlow, John Perry. "Crime and Puzzlement." Electronic Frontier Foundation, June 8, 1990. <http://www.eff.org/Misc/Publications/John_Perry_Barlow/HTML/crime_and_puzzlement_1.html> (April 26, 2002).

Electronic Frontier Foundation. *EFFector* Online Newsletter archives. <http://www.eff.org/effector> (April 26, 2002).

Kirby, Carrie. "Online Freedom Fighters Free-Speech Group Returns to Its Roots, Battles Studios over DVD Program." *San Francisco Chronicle,* May 27, 2001.

Youman, Mark. "The Electronic Frontier Foundation: A Sojourn in Washington." *LBJ Journal of Public Affairs,* vol. 8, no. 1 (Spring 1996).

Further Reading

Borsook, Paulina. *Cyberselfish: A Critical Romp Through the Terribly Libertarian Culture of High Tech.* New York: Public Affairs, 2000.

Electronic Frontier Foundation. "About EFF." <http://www.eff.org/abouteff.html> (April 26, 2002).

Sterling Bruce. *The Hacker Crackdown.* New York: Bantam Books, 1993.

Related Topics

Barlow, John Perry; Hacking, Cracking, and Phreaking; Kapor, Mitchell; Privacy; Whole Earth 'Lectronic Link

— Lori Kendall

Electronic Publishing

Electronic publishing is a central feature of the information age. It can involve converting the content of paper media to electronic form and/or inventing new forms of publishing.

Electronic publishing emerged when print media began migrating to electronic digital formats. While some formats were parallel versions of earlier forms, such as books going onto CD-ROM, or motion pictures transferring to video and later to DVD, added features led to a "paper-plus" version of earlier media, when printed newspapers and magazines grew Web sites. With the birth of the World Wide Web, electronic publishing soon came to encompass more than just individual works. Huge collections of artifacts became available in the form of archives, electronic libraries, and other resources. Some are now worldwide resources, available on the Web to any connected computer, while others are local or private repositories comparable to closed research libraries.

The migration to digital media had an astonishing effect on the scale of publishing, for the addition of digital variants means a vast multiplication of accessible information. Another effect is a new manipulability of information. Searches across wide ranges of information have become possible in more comprehensive ways than ever before. The cost of accessing and searching this increasing pool of information resources shrinks continually, and the time required for any search has also decreased, despite the growth of available information.

A third effect was partially predictable, but few people fully understood its power: the fact that all information in electronic digital media is carried in the same form—digital code. While media outputs and transmission methods vary dramatically in operation and look and feel, all electronic publishing is done using the same basic medium: coded software. For the first time in human history, Marshall McLuhan's observation that "the medium is the message" is literally true. The power of this third effect lies in its bestowal of any number of forms and outputs on any kind of content.

One simple fact makes the protean and changeable nature of electronic publishing clear: The computer is not a medium in the original sense of the word. The computer is a device that uses software to emulate the performance and characteristics of many kinds of media. Any computer is, in theory and practice, a multitude of machines that can be used for any purpose that can be programmed.

Hidden behind the visible and powerful face of electronic publishing is a less visible and more powerful phenomenon. Three factors give it meaning, and point to a form of publishing never before possible. The first factor is media convergence. The second is the use of information technology to control an increasing number of the world's important operating systems. The third factor is the connection of the planet's computing systems to an invisible datasphere far larger and more powerful than the visible interface of the Web.

Electronic publishing can, in theory, involve any content distributed by electronic media or any program that electronic media can execute. The nature and variety of digital electronic media give astonishing power and diversity to the meaning of what it is to publish, and change the nature of what can be published. In a world increasingly powered by converging technologies, this means that electronic publishing encompasses a wide range of possibilities.

Different kinds of publications are released every day, each with dramatic effects in cyberspace and in the physical world. Ill-conceived email messages multiplied by millions of copies have shifted the course of government and ended business careers. Automated financial transactions executed by computer programs have triggered major financial disruption. Worms have seized control of millions of computers to replicate and publish themselves further while executing instructions on the computers that they corrupt. The union of digital code, computer networks, media convergence, and automated control systems makes electronic publishing inconceivably powerful. The mutable and open-ended nature of electronic publishing in an era of converging technologies raises important questions: What are the many possibilities for future forms of electronic publishing? Which possibilities are most likely? What ought to happen? What will happen?

The future effects of electronic publishing may be quite dramatic. While e-books and hypertext give us a glimpse of electronic publishing's future, they do so from the perspective of a print culture, and are rooted in traditional media forms. Although these may be electronic publishing's near future, its long-term development may lie in entirely unpredictable realms.

Bibliography

Friedman, Ken. "Information, Place, and Policy." *Built Environment,* vol. 24, no. 2/3 (1998), pp. 83–103.

———. "Multiple Views on Multimedia and the World Wide Web: A European Perspective." INFO2000 Project Proposal. Contextual Information for Biological Conservation. Brussels: Union of International Associations, 1997.

Kahin, Bryan, and Hal R. Varian, eds. *Internet Publishing and Beyond.* Cambridge, Mass.: MIT Press, 2000.

Lyman, Peter, and Hal R. Varian. "How Much Information?" School of Information Management and

Systems, University of California at Berkeley, 2000.
<http://www.sims.berkeley.edu/research/projects/
how-much-info/summary.html> (April 26, 2002).

Further Reading

Bot, Marjolein; Burgemeester, Johan; and Hans Roes.
"The Cost of Publishing an Electronic Journal.
A General Model and a Case Study." *D-Lib Magazine*,
November 1998.
<http://www.dlib.org/dlib/november98/11roes.html>
(April 26, 2002).

ebrary—a Leading Provider of Information Distribution &
Retrieval Services. Web site.
<http://www.ebrary.com> (April 26, 2002).

Electronic Society for Social Scientists (ELSSS). "A New
Challenge to Journal Publishers." *The Chronicle of
Higher Education* (online edition colloquy),
March 7, 2001.
<http://chronicle.com/colloquylive/2001/03/journal/>
(April 26, 2002).

Fialkoff, Francine. "Publishing Partners: The Press, the
Library, and Academic Computing." *Library Journal*,
September 1998.

Givler, Peter. "Scholarly Publishing in an Electronic Age:
8 Views of the Future. Scholarship Waits to Be
Reinvented." *Chronicle of Higher Education*,
June 25, 1999, B7.

Hunter, Karen. "Electronic Journal Publishing. Observations
from Inside." *D-Lib Magazine,* July/August 1998.
<http://www.dlib.org/dlib/july98/07hunter.html>
(April 26, 2002).

Nielsen, Jakob. "End of Web Design." Jakob Nielsen's
Alertbox, July 23, 2000.
<http://www.useit.com/alertbox/20000723.html>
(April 26, 2002).

Related Topics

Data Mining; Desktop Publishing; McLuhan, Marshall;
Multimedia; World Wide Web

— *Ken Friedman*

Email

Email is a shortened version of the phrase "electronic
mail," and refers to messages exchanged through networked computers. These messages primarily comprise
text, although advances in mail programs have made it
easier to include graphics, sound, and more.

HISTORY OF EMAIL

Email was introduced in the 1960s, when people began
sending messages to others working on the same mainframe computer. In the late 1960s, Ray Tomlinson set
out to create a program that would send messages
from one computer to another on the same network.
He combined the mailing program used on mainframes
with a file-transfer system. To send an email message,
the sender had to know the recipient's identification
and the address of the computer on which they
received email. The ID was separated from the address
by the symbol @. Tomlinson's first email message to a
remote computer read: "QWERTYUIOP" (the top
row of characters on a computer keyboard).

Tomlinson released two programs in 1972 that
worked in tandem: READMAIL and SNDMSG. The
applications were quickly adopted by early users of
ARPANET (the precursor to the Internet), even
though they were primitive. The most significant limitation was the fact that people had to use two different programs to communicate through email:
READMAIL to check their mail, and SNDMSG to
send mail to others. Throughout the early 1970s,
ARPANET developers made email more user-friendly
and functional, adding the ability to delete messages
and to access help files. But even though the program
used to read email was improved, it remained separate from SNDMSG.

An all-in-one email utility clearly was needed, and
in 1975 John Vittal wrote it, named it MSG, and
added features such as automatic addressing for email
replies and email forwarding. MSG was the first fully
functional, all-in-one email utility. Since the release of
MSG, relatively few major functional changes have
been made to email utilities. Most of the changes since
1975 have been matters of style and access.

One stylistic change to how people accessed
email came with the creation of Pine. Pine (which
stands for Program for Internet News & Email) is an
email utility that was created at the University of
Washington in 1989. Pine was specifically developed
to be used by people who were not familiar with the
detailed ins and outs of networked computers, and
was designed to be simple, user-friendly, and nearly
mistake-proof. The main advantage of Pine over
other mail programs was its combination of a simple
but tightly connected editor with an easy-to-navigate
menu system. For most users of email in the early
1990s, and for many people today, Pine was the program of choice.

The rise of commercial network services had significant impacts on the popularity of email and on its
commercial viability. Two of the first companies to
provide email service to the public, Compuserve and
MCI Mail, emerged in 1989. Their early successes

sparked the imagination of Steve Case, the cofounder of America Online (AOL). AOL's simple graphical interface helped to further popularize email after the service connected its internal email system to the rest of the Internet in 1993. Commercial services such as AOL opened the door to email for people who did not have university or employer accounts.

The doors were blown wide open in the second half of the 1990s, thanks to one key development: free email. Beginning in 1996, companies began offering Web-based email accounts. Users could access their email from anywhere by simply logging onto a Web page that could be pulled up in any browser. Best of all, there was no up-front charge for these email accounts, since the companies made their money by selling advertising space on the Web pages where people viewed their mail. In many cases, these free email accounts were part of an overall portal strategy. Portals were intended to be one-stop Web sites, where people would go first to get customized news, weather reports, and stock quotes, as well as check their calendar and email. Netscape and Yahoo, for example, both offered free email as part of the package of services available on their "My Netscape" and "My Yahoo" pages.

With the coming of advertising-supported accounts, the use of email grew phenomenally. Many people who already had email accounts through either work or their school started another account on services such as Hotmail. People who could not afford a commercial network service such as AOL were more than happy to put up with on-screen advertising, and even with advertisements attached to their own email messages, in exchange for a free account. Today, email addresses show up everywhere: in advertisements, on business cards, and even as tattoos. Multiple email addresses have become quite common, as people use one for business and another for personal communication.

Basics of Messages and Programs

All email messages share a basic structure, starting with the header. The header is a block of information at the start of an email message that tells you who sent it, what it's about, and other technical information. The "subject," "date," "from," and "to" lines are self-explanatory; sometimes the header includes a "cc" line, which lists any other people who received carbon copies of the message. After the header, a message normally has a body of text. With the earliest email programs, such as Pine, the message had to be composed in plain text. This limitation was an inspiration for some users, who came up with creative ways to combine standard keyboard

characters into images, a practice known as ASCII art. Most current programs, however, can use HTML codes to format the text and insert images.

Sometimes email may come with an attachment, a file that is sent along with a message. The file might be a graphic image, a word-processing file, or a program. When you receive an attachment that your mail program knows how to handle, such as most graphic images, it will simply show up in the text area of the message window. If it is a type of file that your mail program cannot open, like a word-processing file, then it typically shows up as an icon that, when clicked, gives you the option of opening or saving the file.

Current email programs—Eudora and Microsoft Outlook are among the most popular—all share the same basic commands and tools. They allow users to compose new messages, reply to received messages, or forward a received message to someone else. Address books allow users to store email addresses and associate them with a nickname, making it unnecessary to remember or type in a long and often complicated string of characters. Messages can be stored in folders, making it easier to keep mail organized. Finally, many different filters can be applied to incoming email, sorting it into folders, changing the priority of the message, or even automatically deleting it.

Cultural Impacts of Email

Email is one of the oldest means of online communication, and it has had numerous effects on online culture. Since email was a new medium for interpersonal communication, new standards for behavior had to be developed. The name for these new standards was formed by collapsing the words "net" and "etiquette" into "netiquette." Because nonverbal communication was not possible with this new medium, much of the emotional nuance of ordinary face-to-face exchanges was lost. To make up for this, standard keyboard characters were combined into small icons, such as the ubiquitous :-), called "emoticons."

In addition to being used for interpersonal communication, email was quickly turned into a medium for communication between groups. It was a relatively easy matter to send an email message to more than one person, and eventually programs such as ListServ were created to automatically send email to a list of addresses. Mailing lists were created about every imaginable topic, making it easy for people who shared an interest or hobby to interact. The people in these groups often formed strong relational bonds. This led researchers to speculate that new "virtual communities" were being formed through the use of email. A considerable amount of research has been done on how computer-mediated communication can be used to foster relationships and communities.

Not everything about email has been positive, however. Computer viruses can be spread through email attachments. Even more frequently, fake virus warnings (as well as fraudulent charitable solicitations, urban legends, and so on) are forwarded over and over again, no matter how often they are exposed as hoaxes. In addition, just as junk mail is sent through the postal service, so too are unwanted messages known as "spam" mass-distributed to email accounts. The practice of spamming has grown so prevalent and so despised that several legislative bodies have begun formulating laws to ban it.

In 2000, 536 billion email messages were sent in the United States alone. Clearly, email has become a new medium of widespread use and impact. As other technologies such as cellular phones, personal digital assistants, and pagers make it possible to access email anywhere, its use will no doubt continue to grow.

Bibliography

Baron, Naomi. *Alphabet to Email: How Written Language Evolved and Where It's Heading.* New York: Routledge, 2000.

Pine Information Center. "A Pine Project History." November 9, 1998. <http://www.washington.edu/pine/overview/project-history.html> (March 22, 2002).

Stewart, William. "The Living Internet: How Email Was Invented." May 6, 2000. <http://www.livinginternet.com> (March 22, 2002).

Further Reading

Chesebro, James, and Donald Bonsall. *Computer-Mediated Communication: Human Relationships in a Computerized World.* Tuscaloosa, Ala.: University of Alabama Press, 1989.

Civin, Michael. *Male, Female, Email: The Struggle for Relatedness in a Paranoid Society.* New York: Other Press, 2000.

Jones, Steven G., ed. *Cybersociety 2.0: Revisiting Computer-Mediated Communication and Community.* Thousand Oaks, Calif.: Sage Publications, 1998.

Kehoe, Brendan P. *Zen and the Art of the Internet: A Beginner's Guide.* Englewood Cliffs, N.J.: PTR Prentice Hall, 1996.

Palme, J. *Electronic Mail.* Norwood, Mass.: Artech House, 1995.

Related Topics

ARPANET; ASCII Art; Case, Stephen M.; Emoticons; LISTSERV; Netiquette; Newsgroups; Spam; USENET; Virtual Community; Virus

— *Norman Clark*

Emoticons

Emoticons (a contraction of the words "emotional icons") are glyphs used in computer-mediated communications, meant to represent facial expressions. When the Internet was entirely text-based, emoticons were rendered in ASCII, and read by tilting one's head to the left, as the "smiley" indicates :-). While more sophisticated methods to display emoticons exist today, their purpose has remained the same: They are used to communicate the emotional state of the author.

HISTORY AND CONTROVERSIES

The history of the emoticon begins in 1979, with Kevin MacKenzie. As Internet lore has it, MacKenzie was troubled by the flame wars (online fighting) on one of the original mailing lists of the ARPANET, called MsgGroup. MacKenzie, who was apparently a "rank newbie" to MsgGroup, wrote a note suggesting a way to help list users with what he saw as the loss of emotional nuances in cyberspace. Using an idea he'd found in *Readers Digest,* MacKenzie proposed that if someone meant sarcasm in a post, they use the symbol -) to indicate "tongue in cheek." The first emoticon was born.

From MacKenzie's first missive, the use of emoticons has caused controversy online. Original critics of the idea argued that emoticons would further erode the ability of people to communicate clearly and use language creatively in cyberspace. Today's critics maintain that the rise of corporate culture on the Internet has made the use of emoticons even more pernicious. For instance, America Online's Instant Messaging software contains built-in defaults that turn users' typed emoticons into AOL proprietary icons, so that :-) is now automatically rendered as a smiley face unless a user deliberately overrides the decision. Purists charge that by rendering emoticons as icons, corporations are eroding one of the earliest forms of ASCII art on the Internet.

Still, most 'Net popularizers insist that emoticons in any form help online communication more than they hurt it. At their most basic level, emoticons are perhaps the crudest attempts to address the issue of emotion and feelings among users in computer environments, in the absence of the "high bandwidth" capacities of live, face-to-face contact. "I'm worried about what may need to be called 'stunted emotions' [online]," said computer scientist Rosalind Picard of MIT, in a 1998 interview with *First Monday*. Picard defined stunted emotions as "the misinterpretation of the mood of your e-mail, or when conversations take ten times longer than necessary because the writers weren't skilled enough to convert vocal intonation into text, and the danger of what will happen to people if they spend all their waking hours interacting with and through a device that constantly ignores their emotions."

EMOTIONAL COMPUTING PRESENT AND FUTURE

To address these issues, the Affective Computing Lab at MIT has been established to address "computing that relates to, arises from, or deliberately influences emotions." Picard's group has already developed a number of affective computing protoypes, including eyeglasses with the ability to sense if the wearer is furrowing his brow in confusion or raising it in interest. Another approach can be found in the Conversational Agents division of MIT, headed by linguistics expert Justine Cassell. Embodied conversational agents are computer-generated cartoon-like characters that can emulate humans in face-to-face conversation. For example, Rea is a life-sized animated humanoid figure on a screen developed by Cassell's group. Rea not only understands the conversational behaviors of people in front of her, she also responds herself with appropriate speech, animated hand gestures, body movements, and facial expressions.

Interest in emotional computing solutions is particularly high in areas like distance learning, in which teachers often struggle to deliver the most effective communication they can to their students, often without any face-to-face contact whatsoever. Recently, poet and digital theorist Norman Weinstein urged manufacturers to design software to engage the full emotional range of students. "Think of a 'Freshman Composition' software program," he suggests, "tapping various student feelings about self image, language structures, rhetorical styles, various academic subjects, and computer technology itself, all at once."

In spite of the progress being made in the area of emotional computing, it is important to remember that no matter how effectively represented, one person's emotional state can never be entirely understandable by another. Even in live, face-to-face environments, the words of psychoanalyst Jacques Lacan apply: "Language always intends more and less than it conveys." Indeed, there is a good chance that even in a future boasting the most technologically advanced videoconferencing systems and the latest in emotional computing gadgetry, emoticons will still exist in one form or another.

Bibliography

First Monday. "FM Interviews: Rosalind Picard." *First Monday,* Issue 3.4 (1998).
<http://www.firstmonday.org/issues/issue3_4/picard/index.html> (April 26, 2002).

Moschovitis, Christos J. P.; Poole, Hilary; Schuyler, Tami; and Theresa M. Senft. "In Cyberspace, No One Can Hear Your Sarcasm." *History of the Internet: A Chronology, 1843 to the Present.* Santa Barbara, Calif.: ABC-CLIO, 1999.

Rivera, Krisela; Cooke, Nancy J.; and Jeff A. Bauhs. "The Effects of Emotional Icons on Remote Communication." From the proceedings of the Association of Computing Machinery's Computer Human Interaction Conference, 1996. <http://www.acm.org/sigs/sigchi/chi96/proceedings/intpost/Rivera/rk_txt.htm> (April 26, 2002).

Weinstein, Norman. "Socrates at the Terminal: Emotion's Neglected Role in High-Tech Education." *Educause Review,* vol. 32, no. 6 (November/December 1997). <http://www.educause.edu/pub/er/review/reviewarticles/32652.html> (April 26, 2002).

Further Reading

Cassell, Justine; Sullivan, Joseph; Prevost, Scott; and Elizabeth Churchill, eds. *Embodied Conversational Agents.* Cambridge: MIT Press: 2000.

Cassell, J., and H. Vilhjálmsson. "Fully Embodied Conversational Avatars: Making Communicative Behaviors Autonomous." *Autonomous Agents and Multi-Agent Systems,* 2:1 (1999), pp. 45–64. <http://gn.www.media.mit.edu/groups/gn/publications/agents_journal99.pdf> (April 26, 2002).

ComputerUser.com. "High Tech Dictionary: Emoticons." <http://www.computeruser.com/resources/dictionary/emoticons.html> (April 26, 2002).

Media Laboratory, Massachusetts Institute of Technology. Affective Computing Home Page. <http://www.media.mit.edu/affect/> (April 26, 2002).

Media Laboratory, Massachusetts Institute of Technology. Gesture and Narrative Language Group Home Page. March 3, 2001. <http://gn.www.media.mit.edu/groups/gn/> (April 26, 2002).

Nelson-Kilger, Max. "CFP'93—The Digital Individual." Meeting of the Computer Professionals for Social Responsibility, Burlingame, California, March 9–12, 1993. <http://www.cpsr.org/conferences/cfp93/nelson-kilger.html> (April 26, 2002).

Picard, Rosalind W. *Affective Computing.* Cambridge, Mass.: MIT Press, 1997.

Related Topics

ASCII Art; Avatar; Chat; Distance Learning; Internet Relay Chat; USENET; Videoconferencing

— *Theresa M. Senft*

Emulation

Emulation refers to the ability of software and/or hardware to imitate another program or piece of equipment. Emulation is particularly useful for running programs originally designed for another operating system, computer, printer, or even video-game console.

The basic emulation process is simple to understand. Assume that you are interested in using a program written for an Apple IIc, a very early computer. In order for your current computer to run the program, it must somehow trick the program into believing that it is an Apple IIc. The Apple IIc and your current computer use different chips and different instructions to tell the computer how to process information; an emulator converts the Apple IIc instructions into a set that your current computer can understand. The result is that the computer's processor and memory simulate the environment that was originally used to run the program.

In general, two types of emulators exist: interpretive and dynamic. Interpretive emulators interpret information as they access it, but once the instructions are executed, they are not stored. Since the information is not stored, it slows the emulation process, as every piece of information must be freshly converted. Dynamic emulators follow the same basic process as the interpretive ones; however, they also store information that is interpreted (if needed) for future use. This speeds the emulation process, although it places more of a strain on a system's memory capacity.

Although almost any type of hardware or software can be emulated, one of the best-known computer emulations was made by Apple, whose 1994 introduction of the PowerPC was hailed as a major advance in computing. It used emulation to simulate an Intel-based PC, allowing it to run Microsoft Windows and Windows-based software. Until the PowerPC's introduction, Mac users were unable to use PC-based programs, and cross-platform programs were just starting to be introduced to the mass market. The PowerPC introduced emulation to a new audience, and demonstrated its potential.

Emulation is also commonly used to take advantage of software written in specific formats, or with specific pieces of equipment in mind. For instance, it is common for most laser-jet printers to be able to emulate those created by Hewlett Packard (HP), due to the abundance of software available for the latter.

One of the most popular uses for emulators involves classic video games. The use of emulators to recreate the operating environments of early video-game consoles and machines on a PC has allowed long-time enthusiasts to reacquaint themselves with games from their past. Most of these games can now be located and downloaded quite easily on the Internet as Read-Only Memory (ROM) files, which contain the same information found on the original game cartridges, and which are translated by emulators to recreate the games. The Multiple Arcade Machine Emulator (MAME) is among the most popular and powerful video-game emulators available. MAME can emulate over 1,500 video games, including classics such as Asteroids, Defender, and Pac-Man.

Emulators such as MAME also bring to light various legal issues. For example, emulating a video game on a computer is legal only if you own a copy of that game, or if it has become part of the public domain. Since the games that MAME and other similar programs help to simulate are quite old, most companies do not threaten legal action over the downloading of their ROM files. Proprietors of newer games and consoles have been less lenient, however, and have pursued legal means to protect their games. Companies such as Sony have recently brought legal action against individuals and companies marketing PlayStation emulators, which could impact company sales profits.

Although emulators are sometimes thought of as being synonymous with virtual machines (VMs), they are not the same. VMs such as Java VM are independent operating systems that exist apart from a computer's own operating system. VMs do not affect the computer's operations, and can operate irrespective of the operating system—almost as an extra layer of software. In the case of Java VM, it can operate applets on any desktop regardless of whether it is an Intel-based PC or a Mac.

The future may see the increased use of emulation to run legacy software and access legacy data. In addition, the high-tech world is watching the progress of Transmeta Corp., a company that builds microprocessors that emulate other company's chips but consume less power. Should Transmeta prove successful, emulation may increasingly become a feature of hardware as well as of software.

Bibliography

Anderson, Heidi V. "Windows NT Emulation." *Smart Computing in Plain English,* vol. 5, no. 1 (January 1999).

Baker, Tracy. "Emulators & Virtual Machines: Run More than One Computer on Your PC." *Smart Computing in Plain English,* vol. 11, no. 11 (November 2000), pp. 78–80.

————. "Past to Present: The History of Electronic Entertainment." *Smart Computing in Plain English,* vol. 11, no. 10 (October 2000), pp. 6–9.

Hoffman, Marc. "The OS Emulation HomePage!" December 21, 2001. <http://www.kearney.net/~mhoffman/> (May 17, 2002).

Further Reading

Holzberg, Carol S. "PowerPC: A 'RISC'y Business?" *Smart Computing in Plain English,* vol. 5, no. 6 (June 1994).

Sems, Marty. "Laser Printers." *PC Today,* vol. 13, no. 6 (June 1999).

Related Topics

Gaming; Java

— *Art Ramirez*

Encryption and Cryptography

Encryption is as old as communication. Early written languages were a form of encryption: Only those who knew the language could read the messages. Throughout history, encryption has taken a wide variety of forms; for example, the Navajo language was used as a form of encryption during World War II. Cryptography is the science of digital security, and a branch of mathematics. Historically, it has been limited to encryption—the creation of secret messages—but since the mid-1970s it has been expanded to include other security-related techniques, such as digital signatures.

The increasing usage of electronic-data communications systems in banking and business has generated a need to ensure data security, as it is fairly easy to intercept communication traffic between two computers. Consumers who use credit cards, electronic mail, electronic cash, electronic purses, and home banking in transmitting electronic information demand advanced applications that provide enhanced security for the data sent. For instance, a customer of home banking can use a home computer to instruct the bank to pay bills by transferring funds from her account to another (i.e., to the payee). Security concerns include ensuring that the electronic message sent was not intercepted by a third party, who then might change the identity of the payee, and/or that the message was not recorded by the third party and sent again and again. Cryptographic systems operate with an encryption algorithm and key, which convert an original message (plain text) into a coded message (cipher text). In turn, in order to decode the cipher text, a decryption algorithm and key are needed.

An encryption program scrambles a file, using a user-selected password. When encrypted, the file turns into a hodgepodge of unreadable letters, numbers, or symbols. The text is restored using the decryption program with the same password. There are several methods used to scramble data. Some techniques involve simply substituting one character with another, while others employ several stages of encryption, with a different character each time.

Cryptography provides safety measures to address common security threats to electronic data transmission. According to Antony Watts, most common security threats include:

- Interception, which resembles passive eavesdropping;
- Replay, in which genuine messages are recorded and repeatedly resent;
- Masquerade, the receipt of a message from a source other than the source indicated in the message;
- Repudiation, the receipt of a message that the sender denies sending;
- Manipulation, the interception and modification of messages for fraud or sabotage.

Watts also notes the following safety features, which are provided by most cryptographic systems to protect against the above-mentioned threats:

- Secrecy, which protects message privacy from anyone without an appropriate key;
- Integrity, which allows for the detection of alterations made to a message;
- Signature, which establishes sender identity, proving that an individual sent the message.

SECRET-KEY SYSTEMS

Cryptographic schemes can be secret-key or public-key systems. The secret-key system is fully reversible and symmetric—that is, decrypting the cipher text yields the original plain text. The most commonly used secret-key scheme is the Data Encryption Standard (DES). The DES breaks plain text into 64-bit blocks and encrypts each block using a 56-bit secret key to generate a 64-bit block of cipher text. The user must use the same key in decoding in order to recover the original text.

Secret-key systems, although providing enhanced data security, do have their drawbacks. First of all, employing the key system is time-consuming; complex encryption methods such as the DES require a large amount of calculation time. Secondly, anyone who knows the key can decode the data, and there is no measure to check whether the decoder is a person with authorized access. Thirdly, data-error sensitivity is a concern; an error in a block of encrypted text can cause error rates of up to 50 percent when decryption is performed. Errors in an encrypted file may prevent the file from ever being successfully decrypted.

Also, some cryptographic programs are designed to be user-friendly to the point of compromising the protection offered. Many applications prompt users for a password when a file is to be decrypted. When an inaccurate password is entered, most would beep and ask the user to try again until the correct password is entered, without limiting the number of unsuccessful tries. Therefore, the protection of the program is weakened, as it invites a guessing attack from unauthorized users.

PUBLIC-KEY SYSTEMS

The public-key system is asymmetric, meaning that passing the cipher text through the encryption stage again would not yield the original message. To use public-key systems, users need one key to encrypt, and another to decrypt. Public-key systems allow the encryption keys to be distributed in public directories. When sending a message using a public-key system, the sender can look up the recipient's public encryption key in a directory, and use the key found to encrypt the message. Upon receiving the encrypted message, the recipient would then use her secret decryption key to decode. Public-key systems provide an enhanced safety measure; only the user knows and remembers her own secret decryption key, unlike secret-key systems, where the key is shared between the sender and the receiver.

An additional safety measure, providing electronic signatures, is an important feature for home banking and electronic mail that protects against masquerade and repudiation. Using public-key systems, users can employ a two-step encryption procedure to produce an electronic signature for the message sent. First, a sender uses her secret key to generate an intermediate cipher text. Then the sender uses the receiver's public key to further encrypt the text. In this way, the sender produces a signed message by encoding it with her secret key.

When receiving the cipher text, the receiver uses her secret key to decrypt the message. Upon the first decryption, the receiver gets the intermediate cipher text. The receiver then further decrypts the message using the public key. After this second decryption, the receiver has both the original message and the sender's signature.

Public-key systems provide other safety features to counteract various threats to electronic-data transmission. First of all, public-key systems provide ways to verify the identity of the sender in order to repel the threat of repudiation. The use of a secret key to encode and decode ensures that no third party will be able to send a message purporting to be from the sender, or perform an unauthorized decoding. Therefore, one can not deny having sent an encoded message, since a message that is successfully decoded using one's public key must have been encoded by one's secret key.

Another safety measure provided by public-key systems, designed to address the threats of replay and manipulation, is the users' ability to add date and time information to messages before encrypting. This allows the receiver to verify if duplicate messages have been received.

Thanks to these safety measures, public-key systems have gained acceptance in many organizations. However, even with the significant safety advantages offered by public-key systems, secret-key systems are still more widely used. Public-key systems require more computational resources to carry out the encryption and decryption, which adds to the cost of the systems; many organizations shy away from public-key systems due to the high costs of these system requirements.

POLICY ISSUES

Cryptography became an important political issue in the late 1990s, when the FBI, the CIA, and the National Security Agency (NSA) appealed to Congress to limit the production and export of sophisticated encryption techniques. Encryption posed problems for intelligence gathering; the proposal was designed to prevent hostile nations and criminals from plotting nefarious activities via transmissions that would be unreadable by U.S. law-enforcement agencies. Software manufacturers lobbied heavily against this proposal, realizing that their products would be more valuable if they remained inviolate. The software industry claimed that encryption was the technical backbone for the Internet's commercial revolution, and that confidentiality and the need to transfer funds worldwide demand strong and exportable encryption programming. In the end, the government's appeal was unsuccessful, and unregulated exportation was permitted.

In the wake of the September 11 terrorist attacks in the United States, there have been renewed calls among U.S. lawmakers for restrictions on the use, availability, and export of strong encryption products. Members of Congress are now suggesting a ban on encryption that cannot be broken or accessed by law enforcement through a secret "back door," or key-escrow system. Some support legislation to require the establishment of mandatory key-escrow systems to be installed in encryption products. Key-escrow systems provide "back doors" for encrypted data, to be used by government agencies for law enforcement and intelligence purposes; they are similar to master keys, and would allow agents to unlock any secured file.

This reconsideration of strong encryption technology is backed by the testimonies of U.S. officials, who say that encryption technologies have stymied law-enforcement efforts to detect, prevent, and investigate illegal activities. They argue that uncrackable encryption is allowing terrorists to communicate about their criminal intentions without fear of intrusion.

Records also show that terrorist plots were developed covertly over the Internet because of widely available encryption technologies. Encryption was used by Khalil Deek, an alleged terrorist arrested in Pakistan in 1999, to plot bombings in Jordan. Authorities seized Deek's computer at his home in Peshawar, Pakistan, for file decoding, and were able to thwart his attempt. Encryption was also used by Ramzi Yousef, the convicted coordinator of the 1993 World Trade Center bombing, to hide plans to destroy 11 U.S. airliners. Philippine officials found Yousef's computer, and U.S. technicians broke the encryption and prevented the incident.

The software industry strongly opposes legislative proposals to revive government controls on strong encryption, insisting that imposing weakened encryption would endanger the public and damage the economy. It is argued that key-escrow systems are inherently less secure, more costly, and more difficult to use than similar systems without such features. In addition, industry experts say that this approach would be counter-productive, since potential criminals or terrorists are unlikely to use a system that they know to be escrowed by law enforcement.

Bibliography

Hankerson, Darrel. *Coding Theory and Cryptography: The Essentials.* New York: Marcel Dekker, 2000.

Miller, Stanley. "Coded Data May Have Helped; Encryption Can Be Used to Keep Plans Secret." *Milwaukee Journal Sentinel,* September 16, 2001, p. 23A.

Watts, Antony. "Cryptography Is Key to Securing Proprietary Information." *EDN,* vol. 40, no. 4 (July 1995), pp. 99–102.

Further Reading

Dam, Kenneth, and Herbert Lin, eds. *Cryptography's Role in Securing the Information Society.* Washington, D.C.: National Academy Press, 1996.

Loshin, Peter. *Personal Encryption Clearly Explained.* San Diego, Calif.: AP Professional, 1998.

Schneier, Bruce. *Secrets and Lies: Digital Security in a Networked World.* New York: Wiley, 2000.

Singh, Simon. *The Code Book: The Evolution of Secrecy From Mary, Queen of Scots to Quantum Cryptography.* New York: Doubleday, 1999.

Stallings, William. *Cryptography and Network Security: Principles and Practice.* Upper Saddle River, N.J.: Prentice Hall, 1999.

Related Topics

Anonymity; *Bernstein vs. U.S. Department of State*; Carnivore; Cyberwarfare; E-Commerce; Electronic Communications Privacy Act; Privacy; Security

— *Shing-Ling Sarina Chen*

Engelbart, Douglas
1925–
U.S. Inventor, Theorist

Doug Engelbart is a pioneer in the area of human-computer communications, and is one of the early visionaries of both the personal computer and the Internet. His theories on using computers and software to augment the human intellect led to the development of the graphical user interface (GUI) and the computer mouse. Believing that the complexity of the problems facing the world are growing faster than our ability to solve them, Engelbart has dedicated himself to the notion of using computers to augment the collective human intelligence.

Engelbart was born in Portland, Oregon, in 1925. After spending two years at Oregon State University in Corvallis, where he learned radar technology, he was drafted into the U.S. Navy, where he served from 1944 to 1946. After the war, he returned to Oregon State and received his B.S. in electrical engineering. Upon his graduation in 1948, he took a job at the Ames Navy Research Center in Mountain View, California, where he worked as an electrical engineer. While there, he began to work on his personal crusade to improve human capability–what he called the "augmentation of the human intellect."

Influenced by cybernetics (the science of communication and control), Engelbart proposed a technical solution to the development of human intellect—using the computer. He enrolled at the University of California at Berkeley, receiving his Ph.D. in electrical engineering in 1956. That year, Engelbart also joined Stanford Research Institute (SRI) in Menlo Park, California, a center for sponsored industrial research. His interest as an engineer was not in the technical side of things, but in the social and human aspects of technology, and particularly in how the computer could be used as a tool to serve the desires of the user. He was influenced by Vannevar Bush (who wrote "As We May Think," an early precursor to hypertext's development) and by J. C. R. Licklider's "Man-Computer Symbiosis," which conceptualized interactive computing. In 1962, Engelbart published "A Conceptual Framework for the Augmentation of Man's Intellect," in which he made an argument for the development of online libraries, and for storing and retrieving documents electronically.

In the late 1950s, the U.S. federal government developed the Advanced Research Projects Agency (ARPA), whose objective was to fund new research projects to boost technological innovation. In 1963, ARPA funded Engelbart's research at SRI on a process designed to move computer technology into a new realm. Engelbart dubbed this process "bootstrapping," derived from the metaphor of pulling yourself up by your bootstraps. Bootstrapping, which refers to an iterative and co-adaptive learning environment, did not focus on a specific product, but on a process that involved the coevolution of the user along with the computer. Engelbart's laboratory was called the Augmentation Research Center (ARC), and the research program the Framework for the Augmentation of Human Intellect. Engelbart's premise was that computers should serve as a powerful auxiliary to human communication. Augmentation would allow for the development of greater human intellect by allowing machines to perform the mechanical part of thinking and idea sharing.

At the ARC, Engelbart and his colleagues developed the On-Line System (NLS), described as an integrated environment for idea processing. NLS featured a number of tools that computer users now use on a daily basis: an outline editor for idea development, a mouse/pointing device for on-screen selection, shared-screen teleconferencing, hypertext linking, word processing, email, on-line help systems, and a full windowing software environment. The NLS system was demonstrated in December 1968. Dubbed "the mother of all demos," the demonstration galvanized the audience and ushered in a new reign of interactive computing.

In the spring of 1967, it was announced that all the ARPA-sponsored computer research labs, including ARC, would be networked to promote resource sharing. Engelbart saw this as an excellent mechanism for extending the NLS for wide-area collaboration, and therefore proposed to host a Network Information Center (NIC). The NIC provided basic library services (indexing, referencing, and basic information retrieval) and online services using the Journal (which allowed for permanent indexing and storage of mail submissions) and Mail programs.

ARPA cancelled ARC's funding in the early 1970s, and the center closed in 1977. Many ARC members went on to work at the Palo Alto Research Center (PARC), a new research center that Xerox Corporation had built. At PARC, many of Engelbart's creations were refined, added to, and used as the basis for the first personal computer, the Altair.

Engelbart joined Tymshare Inc. (which had bought the teleconferencing system he demonstrated at the Joint Computer Conference in San Francisco) as a senior scientist, departing in 1989 when McDonnell Douglas Corporation purchased the company and shut his program down. Engelbart founded the Bootstrap Institute in 1989 to further pursue his concepts of bootstrapping human-computer systems in order to promote collaboration and raise the human collective IQ. Among the institute's goals are plans to: "promote awareness of the scale, urgency, and complexity of the challenges we face, catalyze, launch, and shepherd an active, strategic pursuit of boosting the collective IQ on a scale commensurate with the rate, scale, and pervasiveness of change, create an exploratory environment where participants can collaborate, experiment, and set in motion advanced pilot outposts in diverse application areas, enable a whole new way of thinking about the way we work, learn, and live together, promote development of a collective IQ among, within, and by networked improvement communities and cultivate a knowledge environment that includes a shared dynamic knowledge repository (DKR)."

A current project at the Bootstrap Institute, the Open Hyperdocument System (OHS) Project, is developing open-source tools for collaborative knowledge management, building on XML and other open standards as well as on NLS. Its goal is to manage and create knowledge across the Internet, allowing users to package and share information for collaborative work. Designed as a scalable system for international use, the OHS allows all groups and nationalities to build on top of its architecture. It uses Hyperscope, a browser plug-in accessing the architecture and databases of the OHS. Features will be designed so that users can control email, package information, and annotate documents, as well as manage broken links and lost Web pages.

Engelbart has authored more than 25 publications, and has generated 20 patents, including the patent for the mouse. His accomplishments in the areas of personal computing and networking have been nothing short of revolutionary. Early on, he conceived of the computer as a prosthesis to extend or augment the individual's capacity, as a coevolutionary tool that would enable new forms of creative thought, communication, and collaboration for people in both workplace and domestic contexts. His On-Line System—NLS—is now seen as the precursor to hypertext, and was one of the earliest innovative systems to promote computer-supported collaborative work (CSCW). Hypertext took ordinary documents and allowed authors to embed associative "links" within them, allowing for related information to be electronically organized on a vaster scale.

NLS also created a new GUI that used a window environment, allowing users to utilize email, word processing, and video teleconferencing. Engelbart's invention of the mouse (although the tool was not widely used until Apple Computers introduced it in the early 1980s) involved a design process that focused on ergonomic and cognitive factors, and this in turn led to the conception of the computer user as socially constructed and socially situated in the processes by which technology is developed and diffused. And finally, Engelbart foresaw the rise of the knowledge worker—workers who create, manipulate, and diffuse information, and who work collaboratively and asynchronously.

Engelbart has received numerous awards and honors, including the 1990 ACM Software System Award, the 1991 Coors American Ingenuity Award, the 1992 Electronic Frontier Foundation Pioneer Award, the 1993 IEEE Computer Pioneer Award, the 1994 Price Waterhouse Lifetime Achievement Award, a 1994 honorary doctorate from Oregon State University, the 2000 National Medal of Technology, the 2001 British Computer Society's Lovelace Medal, and a 2001 honorary doctorate from Santa Clara University.

Selected Works

Engelbart, Douglas C. "A Conceptual Framework for the Augmentation of Human Intellect." *Vistas in Information Handling*, vol. 1. P. W. Howerton and D. C. Weeks, eds. Washington, D.C.: Spartan Books, 1963; pp. 1–29.
Engelbart, Douglas C., and Kristina Hooper. "The Augmentation System Framework." *Interactive Multimedia*. Sueann Ambron and Kristina Hooper, eds. Redmond, Wash.: Microsoft Press, 1988; pp. 14–31.
Engelbart, Douglas C., and William K. English. "A Research Center for Augmenting Human Intellect." AFIPS Conference Proceedings of the 1968 Fall Joint Computer Conference, San Francisco, December 1968, vol. 33, pp. 395–410 (AUGMENT, 3954). <http://sloan.stanford.edu/mousesite/Archive/Research Center1968/ResearchCenter1968.html> (April 5, 2002).

Bibliography

Bardini, Thierry. *Bootstrapping: Douglas Engelbart, Coevolution, and the Origins of Personal Computing.* Stanford, Calif.: Stanford University Press, 2000.
Bootstrap Institute. Web site. <http://www.bootstrap.org> (April 5, 2002).
Engelbart Collection, Special Collections, Stanford University. Demo of NLS Online system, Fall Joint Computer Conference, Convention Center, San Francisco, December 9, 1968. Streaming video. <http://sloan.stanford.edu/MouseSite/1968Demo.html> (April 5, 2002).
Rheingold, Howard. *Tools for Thought.* New York: Simon and Schuster, 1985.
Stanford Center for Professional Development. "Engelbart's Unfinished Revolution: A Symposium at Stanford University, December 9, 1998." <http://stanford-online.stanford.edu/engelbart/> (April 5, 2002).

Further Reading

Barnes, Susan B. "Douglas Carl Engelbart: Developing the Underlying Concepts for Contemporary Computing," *Annals of the History of Computing*, vol. 19, no. 3 (1997), pp. 16–26.
Bush, Vannevar. "As We May Think." In *From Memex to Hypertext.* Edited by J. M. Nyce and P. Kahn. Boston: Academic Press, 1991.
Goldberg, Adele. *A History of the Personal Workstation.* New York: ACM Press, 1988.

Related Topics

Bush, Vannevar; Computer-Supported Collaborative Work; Distributed Computing; Graphical User Interface; Human-Computer Interaction; Hypertext; Interactivity;

Interface; Knowledge Management; Licklider, J. C. R.; "Man-Computer Symbiosis"; Multimedia; Nelson, Theodor Holm (Ted); Xerox Palo Alto Research Center

— *Leslie Regan Shade*

Eno, Brian

1948–

Musician, Multimedia Artist

Brian Eno is a music innovator whose career has spanned 30 years, during which he pioneered the use of electronics in the recording studio while leaving an indelible stamp on the techno, punk, glam, electronica, and ambient music sub-genres. He is also among the world's most successful recording producers, collaborating at various times with David Bowie, U2, Laurie Anderson, John Cale, Talking Heads, and others to generate some of their greatest works. In the mid-1990s, Eno was a founder of the computer-driven "generative music" scene, which utilizes digital technology to create music pieces that recreate themselves continuously upon playback, so that a particular piece of music never sounds exactly the same way twice. Even within the confines of his music career, his connection to cyberculture is direct: Eno created the 3.5-second arpeggio that sounds when Microsoft Windows and Office programs are booted up.

While his many achievements have garnered Eno respect and fame worldwide, it's likely that none of them would have earned him space in this book had he not also acquired a reputation as one of the most salient cultural thinkers of the digital age—an influential cyber-critic whose sometimes paradoxical theories landed him on the cover of *Wired* magazine's third issue. Cyberpunk godfather William Gibson has said that Eno's song "King's Lead Hat" has been a pivotal influence on his work, providing a "benchmark of peculiarity" for him. Today, Eno occupies a place of honor among the cyber-age intelligentsia. Interestingly, Eno insists that he hates computers; they reduce the illogical and intuitive things that artists do, and as such they represent perhaps equal parts threat and promise to the world's cultural vibrancy.

Brian Peter George St. Baptiste de la Salle Eno was born in Woodbridge, Suffolk, England, on May 15, 1948. He was the son of an English postman father and a Belgian immigrant mother, who met in Germany during World War II. Various accounts credit both a grandfather, who habitually tinkered

Brian Eno, 1974. (Neal Preston/CORBIS)

with mechanical musical instruments, and a "peculiar and eccentric" uncle, also a tinkerer, as the family catalysts for Eno's creative talents. Eno attended the Winchester School of Art, now part of the University of Southampton, in the 1960s. There, he learned about conceptual painting and sound sculpture, and first began experimenting with what he calls his first musical instrument, the tape recorder; he earned a Diploma in Fine Art from the school. Afterward, in 1969, Eno moved to London, where he joined Roxy Music, playing synthesizer for Bryan Ferry's famed glam-rock band.

After making two acclaimed albums with Roxy Music, Eno went solo, although his first move, in 1973, was to collaborate with avant-garde guitarist Robert Fripp on a record called *No Pussyfooting*. During those sessions, Eno invented a tape-manipulation technique, which he dubbed "Frippertronics," that relied on looped delays, pioneering the use of studio technologies to actually compose music on the spot, as opposed to recording fully finished musical pieces. As such, Eno paved the way for later digital sampling in pop music forms like techno, electronica, and rap.

His musical innovations and accomplishments are legion, yet Eno regards himself as a non-musician. Perhaps because of this, he has felt free to engage in other pursuits, such as experimenting with make-up and costume design (his feather-and-boa ensembles while a Roxy Music member are the stuff of legend) and writing soundtrack material for films and movies—not to mention two soundtrack albums to accompany *imaginary* movies. He has also developed interactive media presentations—although, again somewhat paradoxically, he dislikes CD-ROMs and even the concept of "interactivity," because he believes that the media user is not sufficiently involved in what interactive presentations attempt to achieve. In fact, Eno thinks that the digital-media benchmark should not be "interactive" media, but "permanently unfinished" media, which both the artist and the user would have to engage in creatively, and which could be modified continuously.

A simple example of permanently unfinished media, according to Eno, is hypertext. Although he says that it is unpleasant to use (because it is on a computer screen, and again, Eno hates computers), he also says that hypertext represents a radical reconfiguration of the way people think. "The transition from the idea of text as a line to the idea of text as a web is just about as big a change of consciousness as we are capable of,"

he told *Wired*'s Kevin Kelly. "I can imagine the hypertext consciousness spreading to things we take in, not only things we read. I am very keen on this unfinished idea because it co-opts things like screen savers and games and models and even archives, which are basically unfinished pieces of work."

Among his other art projects, Eno has constructed "video installations" at museums around Europe and in the United States, combining sights and sounds to create "alternative environments." In 1995, he established with Laurie Anderson a presentation called "Self-Storage," a honeycomb-like structure containing 650 interactive time capsules and featuring visuals, whispers of sound, and displays of everyday objects from everyday lives, erected in Acorn Storage Centres in Wembley, England.

Equally important are Eno's theories on remaining human while embracing cyber-culture. For instance, he provided the namesake and some of the intellectual impetus for the Long Now Foundation, a group of artists, scholars, and scientists that plans to establish a long-term cultural library and build a self-correcting, 32-bit digital-mechanical clock that will keep perfect time for the next 10,000 years. The Long Now Foundation's aim is to encourage people to slow down their "pathologically short attention span" by developing a new way to perceive time, such that the "long term" is understood in terms of centuries, not just months, or election cycles, or decades. That way, people might begin to take a longer view of their social responsibilities toward their own and subsequent generations. The Long Now Project has the cooperation of a number of other important cyber-figures, including former Internet Corporation for Assigned Names and Numbers president Esther Dyson, new-media writer Stewart Brand, and parallel-computing pioneer Danny Hillis.

"I suppose ideas are what I really think of as my job," Eno told *GQ* magazine in 1996, relating that he hopes to accomplish for culture what Darwin achieved for natural science. "He established a frame in which it was possible to look at all life, ask serious questions about it and organize it in some way. I've been wanting to do the same thing for culture for a long time. By culture I mean everything from fashion, to fine art, to cake decoration to you know—the whole thing, all the things that humans do."

While he may not like computers because of the way they are currently designed, Eno does not fear them. And unlike many artists, he has embraced the possibilities that artificial intelligence provides for the artist and musician. In the mid-1990s, he became a proponent of Koan Pro software, a tool that helps composers to create "generative music." It allows the composer to feed in the kernels of an idea—a snippet of melody here, a harmonic variation there—without creating a fully fledged, finished piece. The software reads the input, manipulates the ideas without the intervention of the user, and in effect writes variations on the music that the composer might have written, had the composer thought of them. Although generative technology remains somewhat primitive, Eno thinks that it may well hold the germ of the future of music. It is a way to make every musical recording function the way an improvisational jazz combo performs, changing the structure, feeling, and meaning of each piece each time it is played.

"I really think it is possible," Eno once said, "that our grandchildren will look at us in wonder and say, 'You mean you used to listen to exactly the same thing over and over again?'"

Selected Works

Eno, Brian. "The Big Here and Long Now." digitalsouls.com, 2001. <http://www.digitalsouls.com/ BrianEnothebighereandlongnow.html> (May 24, 2002).

———. "The Revenge of the Intuitive." *Wired* 7.01, January 1999. <http://www.wired.com/wired/archive/7.01/eno.html> (May 24, 2002).

———. *A Year with Swollen Appendices.* London, England: Faber & Faber, 1996.

Bibliography

Brockman, John. "A Big Theory of Culture: A Talk with Brian Eno." *Edge.org*, 2002. <http://www.edge.org/3rd_culture/eno/eno_p1.html> (May 24, 2002).

Edwards, Mark. "Brian Eno Biography." *In Motion Magazine*, June 8, 1996. <http://www.inmotionmagazine.com/eno2.html> (May 24, 2002).

"GQ&A: Lenny Henry and Brian Eno." *GQ Magazine* (U.K. edition), no. 87 (September 1996). <http://music.hyperreal.org/artists/brian_eno/interviews/ gqa96.html> (May 24, 2002).

Kelly, Kevin. "Gossip Is Philosophy." *Wired* 3.05, May 1995. <http://www.wired.com/wired/archive/3.05/eno.html> (May 24, 2002).

Rubinstein, Geoffrey. "Brian Eno: Musician and Digital Philosopher." *Jones Telecommunications & Multimedia Encyclopedia*, 1994–99. <http://www.digitalcentury.com/encyclo/update/ enobrian.html> (May 24, 2002).

Shachtman, Noah. "New Eno Music Gets 'Generative.'" *Wired News*, October 27, 2001. <http://www.wired.com/news/culture/0,1284,47670,00.html> (May 24, 2002).

Further Reading

Boulware, Jack. "Mondo1995." *SF Weekly*, vol. 14, no. 35 (October 11, 1995). <http://www.scrappi.com/deceit/mondosfw/mondosfd.html> (May 24, 2002).

McLennan, Jim. "This Is the Future." *The Observer Preview*, May 12–18, 1996. <http://music.hyperreal.org/artists/brian_eno/interviews/ obser96b.html> (May 24, 2002).

Selvin, Joel. "Q and A with Brian Eno." *San Francisco Chronicle*, June 2, 1996. <http://www.sfgate.com/cgi-bin/chronicle/ article.cgi?PK70006.DTL:/chronicle/archive/1996/06/02> (May 24, 2002).

Related Topics

Anderson, Laurie; Digital Art and Animation; Digital Music; Hillis, W. Daniel; Human-Computer Interaction; Interactivity; Multimedia

— *Kevin Featherly*

Expert Systems

An expert system is a computer program that aims at capturing and using a human expert's knowledge, making it available to non-experts. The focus of the program is usually decision-making, diagnosis, or prediction. The significance of expert systems lies in their application to domains where expertise is at risk of getting lost (e.g., old-fashioned machinery) or is scarce (e.g., mineral prospecting), or to situations in which experts are distant (e.g., medical aid on an oil platform).

The computing power of an expert system derives from artificial intelligence (AI). The first generation of expert systems relied upon so-called "production rules," rules for actions to take when certain conditions were met. Alan Newell and Herbert Simon were the first to use production systems in the intelligent solving of logic problems (1956) and in simulating human intelligence (1972). Their developments were based on the idea that human beings use heuristics—something like rules of thumb—to solve problems, rather than deterministic rules. In the early 1970s, Edward A. Feigenbaum started a project called "Heuristic Programming," which aimed at the practical application of heuristic ideas in the realm of AI.

Two main issues related to the development and use of expert systems are knowledge acquisition and knowledge engineering. Knowledge acquisition refers to the process by which a non-expert in the domain, a knowledge engineer, works in order to capture knowledge from the expert(s). This process includes collecting documents and interviewing experts, as well as observing them during their work. The knowledge-acquisition process can be time-consuming, and has to be intertwined with the work of actually getting the system to function in a similar way as the expert.

Knowledge engineering is the process by which the acquired knowledge is formulated in terms that a computer system can understand. Nowadays, there are several support systems available (so-called "expert system shells") to help the knowledge engineer to model the expert's knowledge.

Designing the user interface is an important issue in the development of an expert system. The system has to ask the user questions about a given problem, use the answers to work out a problem solution, and present this solution to the user. Early in the development of expert systems, it was found that the presentation of a solution was often insufficient; the user also needed an explanation as to why the presented solution was reasonable. Deriving explanations from a rule-based system was found to be very difficult. A model-based system, by contrast, enabled its user to get explanations, constructed on the basis of the model.

However the knowledge is represented, the dialogue with the user has to be understandable. Therefore, a great deal of work is invested in the creation of natural language interfaces, which may achieve a "natural" dialogue with the user.

Expert systems have been viewed optimistically as well as critically. Optimists have been validated by the multitude of problems that have been found to lend themselves to AI solutions, from process planning in industry to individual health planning. At the same time, the fear of expert systems abounds. Can we really trust expert-system solutions? Who should be blamed should the system be wrong? These questions led to the requirement that expert-system performance be evaluated against the performance of human experts.

The role of the expert-system user, particularly in a work context, has also been questioned. Users might risk becoming mindless robots, answering only the system's questions. How would they be able to judge the system's solutions, if a system uses knowledge foreign to their own? One answer to this question has been offered by systems that support learning, either by offering explanations to arrived-at solutions or through intelligent tutoring systems,

which would give users the opportunity to compare their solutions to those of an expert. Another opportunity lies in building expandable systems, to which users can add their own expertise. These kinds of systems have passed the periods of exaggerated claims and of corresponding criticisms. Recent developments in the field include using expert systems in weather prediction, and Web inventor Tim Berners-Lee's proposal to use expert systems to prepare semantic indices of Web pages.

Bibliography

Berners-Lee, Tim; Hendler, James; and Ora Lassila. "On the Semantic Web." *Scientific American,* May 1, 2001. <http://www.sciam.com/2001/0501issue/0501berners-lee.html> (May 17, 2002).

Feigenbaum, E.A. *Knowledge Engineering: The Applied Side of Artificial Intelligence.* Stanford, Calif.: Stanford University, Heuristic Programming Project, 1980.

Hart, Anna. *Knowledge Acquisition for Expert Systems.* London: Kogan Page, 1986.

Jackson, Peter. *Introduction to Expert Systems.* Third edition. Harlow, England: Addison-Wesley, 1999.

Newell, A., and H.A. Simon. "The Logic Theory Machine: A Complex Information Processing System." *IRE Transactions on Information Theory,* IT-2, 1956, pp. 61–79.

Newell, Allen, and Simon Herbert. *Human Problem Solving.* Englewood Cliffs, N.J.: Prentice-Hall, 1972.

Further Reading

"Machining Chip Prediction Expert System." Computer Aided Manufacturing Laboratory, Worcester Polytechnic Institute. <http://www.me.wpi.edu/Research/CAMLab/chipctrl/exprtsys.htm> (May 17, 2002).

Moralee, D.S., ed. *Research and Development in Expert Systems IV.* Cambridge: Cambridge University Press on behalf of the British Computer Society, 1988; pp. 146–52.

Smith, Peter. *An Introduction to Knowledge Engineering.* London: International Thomson Computer Press, 1996.

Somaini, Bertino. "Evaluation of an Expert System for Smoking (ERES Project)." Universität Zürich, February 5, 2000. <http://www.research-projects.unizh.ch/med/unit43900/area245/p2008.htm> (May 17, 2002).

Wærn, Y., and S. Hägglund. "User Aspects of Knowledge Base Systems." *Handbook of Human-Computer Interaction.* Second edition. M.G. Helander, T.K. Landauer, and P. Prabhu, eds. Amsterdam, Netherlands: Elsevier Science, 1997.

Zeide, J.S., and J. Leibowitz. "Using Expert Systems: The Legal Perspective." *IEEE Expert* 2 (1987), pp. 19–22.

Related Topics

Berners-Lee, Tim; Interface; Knowledge Management; World Wide Web

— Yvonne Wærn

Firewall

The term firewall refers to a group of security tools used to secure network connections from unauthorized access. In general, a firewall is hardware or software, or some combination of the two, that acts as a gatekeeper by controlling who can access a network, as well as what information can enter and leave it, according to preset criteria. Information is allowed to pass through the protected Internet connection or network as long as it meets these criteria; otherwise, it is stopped. While a firewall can effectively protect both commercial and private network connections, it should be considered only one part of an overall security plan.

Firewalls are commonly recommended for any computer connected to a network. Although all connections are at risk, broadband Internet connections (those using a cable modem or DSL) are particularly vulnerable to intrusions. Because these connections have static Internet addresses and are always connected to the Internet, they are especially attractive targets to intruders, who use special programs to randomly scan computers for openings; once located, open ports on a computer can be used to gain access to its operating system and infiltrate a network. Intrusions of this type have the potential to compromise sensitive information on a computer's hard drive, and therefore constitute security threats.

Firewalls come in different forms, focusing on protection at different levels of a network. Common types of firewalls are packet filters, application gateways, and circuit-level gateways; in addition, information logs and proxy servers increase the effectiveness of firewalls.

Packet filters: When information is sent over the Internet, it is broken into packets, small bits of data that are reassembled at their final destination to recreate the original file. A packet filter inspects each incoming and outgoing packet according to the criteria set by the user to determine if it is allowed access to a network.

Application gateways: These provide a different level of security by determining rules or settings for specific programs that require Internet access. For instance, many newer software programs have built-in features that inform users of the availability of updates and/or additions. These programs use network connections to access the Internet for this information. Application gateways determine what programs can access the network, what ports they may use, and how to best secure the connection.

Circuit-level gateways: Similar to application gateways, this form of firewall focuses on specific programs; however, it provides a faster monitoring process. When a remote PC is accessed from a network connection, a circuit-level gateway monitors the connection process and examines packets being exchanged to ensure authenticity (e.g., make sure packets meet preset specifications). Once the examination is complete and the connection is secured, packets are exchanged between the computers without the need for further filtering.

Proxy servers: These are used as intermediaries between a network and, for example, the Internet, to hide the network and make a computer's address more difficult to identify; together with a firewall, however, proxy servers provide more effective security. A proxy eliminates the direct connection to the Internet, and funnels all incoming and outgoing requests through a central location; when an intruder attempts to access the network, the Internet address the intruder finds is that of the proxy server, and not of any of the network connections and computers.

Information logs: Most firewalls also include information logs, which can add another level of security. Logs record useful information, and can serve as an early alert mechanism to upcoming attacks. Suspicious activity such as repeated unsuccessful logins, probes of ports, and rejected IP addresses can be signals that a connection or network is being targeted.

Most firewalls currently available on the market are software-based, including those offered by well-known companies such as Symantec, Zone Labs, and McAfee, and incorporate one or more layers of security. Unlike their hardware-based counterparts, software-based firewalls must be matched to the specific operating system in which they will operate (e.g., Windows, Mac OS). Hardware-based firewalls are commonly used in businesses; they offer flexibility and adaptability far beyond what a private user would require, but tend to be more expensive as well.

Firewalls have the potential to create problems, improper installation being the most common. Firewalls need to be properly configured and tailored to the needs of the individual using it; improper configuration can block access to sites known to be secure. Individuals must also remember to keep the firewall enabled all the time, and not only when they are working online. Fortunately, most software-based firewalls operate in the background, and can be activated automatically whenever the computer is on.

It should be kept in mind that firewalls are not substitutes for safe Internet behavior. Even with a firewall, downloading suspicious emails or failing to routinely scan attachments can import viruses into a network. Similarly, using older versions of firewall software leaves a network connection vulnerable to newer invasion tactics that might be recognized by the more recent version.

Bibliography

Graven, Matthew P. "Personal Firewalls." *PC Magazine*, January 3, 2001.
Raikow, David. "Do I Need a Home Firewall?" *ZDNet*, December 15, 2001.
<http://www.zdnet.com/zdhelp/stories/main/0,5594,2610905,00.html> (April 5, 2002).
Taylor, Laura. "Read Your Firewall Logs!" *ZDNet*, Business & Technology Today, July 10, 2001.
<http://techupdate.zdnet.com/techupdate/stories/main/0,14179,2782699,00.html> (April 5, 2002).
Vicomsoft. "Vicomsoft Firewall FAQ." 2001.
<http://www.vicomsoft.com/index.html> (April 5, 2002).
Vamosi, Robert. "What Is a Firewall?" *ZDNet*, November 15, 2001.
<http://www.zdnet.com/zdhelp/stories/main/0,5594,2460298,00.html> (April 5, 2002).

Further Reading

Baker, Tracy. "Personal Firewalls Block Out Bad Guys: Protect Your Data from the World." *How the Internet Works, Part I*, vol. 5, no. 1 (February 2001), pp. 177–180.
Denton, Chad. "Put Your PC Behind a Firewall: Simple Tools for Controlling Incoming & Outgoing Traffic," *Smart Computing in Plain English,* vol. 12, no. 2 (February 2001), pp. 49–51.
Zwicky, Elizabeth D.; Chapman, D. Brent; and Simon Cooper. *Building Internet Firewalls*. Second edition. Cambridge, Mass.: O'Reilly & Associates, 2000.

Related Topics
Cookies; Hacking, Cracking, and Phreaking; Privacy; Security

— Art Ramirez

Flash

Flash, an animation software product from Macromedia Inc., has emerged as the leading tool for creating interactive animations on the Web because of its ability to produce low-bandwidth, interactive animated images. Flash animations have grown tremendously popular in recent years, becoming the default standard after both Netscape and Microsoft agreed to include the Flash Player as a browser plug-in. The program uses the SWF (Shockwave Flash) file format to deliver graphics, animations, and accompanying sound.

Flash debuted in 1995 under its original name, FutureSplash Animator, and was purchased the following year from its producer, FutureWave, by computer-multimedia pioneer Macromedia. Renamed Flash, the product has outperformed even Macromedia's own animation format Shockwave in terms of popularity.

Flash is a vector-based Web animation format. Unlike bitmap graphics, which are produced pixel by pixel on the computer screen, vector graphics manipulate coordinates and mathematical formulas, defining images using lines and curves (or vectors) that describe the positions of various parts of an image as well as their color properties.

There are numerous advantages to using vector graphics rather than bitmaps. For example, an image can be moved, resized, and reshaped—and hence, animated—and its colors can be changed, all without losing any of the image's original quality. Vector images also are resolution-independent, which means that they can be displayed on computer monitors of varying display resolutions without loss of quality. It is not easy to edit bitmaps (although Flash does allow the importation of bitmaps into its animations), because they are resolution-dependent, and are drawn by modifying pixels instead of vectors. They also are fixed to a grid, the total size of which is predetermined by the artist. Bitmaps become compromised when they are resized, because pixels are redistributed around the grid.

Perhaps the greatest advantage of vector-based graphic formats like Flash is the fact that they produce images that use just one-tenth the bandwidth of bitmaps, and so can be transmitted to the Internet and received by standard dial-up modems without any particular loss of quality.

By now, Flash is all but ubiquitous on the Web. The program's inventor, Jonathan Gay, wrote in a January 2001 TechTV.com article that the format is present on the computers of 95 percent of Web users, somewhere between 250 million and 300 million people. It is frequently used by companies to build "first-screen" Web pages, with animated graphics that fall into place over the span of several seconds. Companies ranging from Disney to Microsoft and Pepsi have used Flash to add zip to their Web sites.

Flash is also among the most popular tools being adopted by a growing culture of Web animators, giving them the ability—without having to purchase many thousands of dollars of animation-rendering machinery—to turn their drawings into animated cartoons using only their computers and the appropriate Flash software. Some recognized filmmakers have even turned to the format to produce short subjects that they otherwise would probably never attempt. Director Tim Burton is a prime example, having produced a series of quirky Flash cartoons called *Stainboy*, which are available on the Web site of Macromedia spin-off Shockwave.com.

In fact, a do-it-yourself subculture of animators has sprung up as Flash has grown in popularity, although an early batch of commercial Web sites such as Icebox.com—host of such edgy, popular Flash series as "Mr. Wong" and "Queer Duck"—failed to make enough money taking advantage of the format's popularity, and were forced to stop buying new content. Nonetheless, in July 2000, the *San Jose Mercury News* reported that some 300,000 animators were using Flash to create "Web-bound cartoons."

THE FLASH DEBATE

Flash is so flexible that it can be used to create Web sites made up entirely of rich multimedia content, and some designers have called on their peers to use it in place of HTML (hypertext markup language) as the standard for Web site design. However, others argue that overuse of Flash is little more than an annoyance to Web surfers, and that it should be used as a design element sparingly, if at all. This debate has continued since the program was first introduced.

The notion that Flash would overtake HTML evoked shudders from some critics. Web-usability guru Jakob Nielsen was notably outspoken; his October 29, 2000, Alertbox column denounced the program, proclaiming that Flash is "99 percent bad." Nielsen, who frequently focuses on the usability of e-commerce sites, complained that Flash encourages "design abuse," breaks with "the Web's fundamental interaction principles," and distracts users' attention away from a site's real mission. He wrote, "About 99 percent of the time, the presence of Flash on a Web site constitutes a usability disease. Although there are rare occurrences of good Flash design . . . the use of Flash typically lowers usability. In most cases, we would be better off if these multimedia objects were removed."

Other critics, like Chris Rourke of the British Web-usability consultancy User Vision, have taken a middle ground. In recommendations published on the company's Web site, Rourke mostly agrees with Nielsen's analysis, insisting that designers using Flash as a design element of their Web sites should remember the sites' goals and what the user is looking for, avoid gratuitous animated site introductions, and provide logical and consistent navigation. One of Nielsen's biggest complaints, for instance, is that Flash renders the "back" button on a Web site inoperable, thus interfering with users' ability to navigate. "Animations should help, not distract users who are trying to achieve goals such as finding items on a web site," Rourke wrote. "Too much motion is usually unwelcome, especially on e-commerce sites where supporting the user's goals is critical for commercial success."

Perhaps noticing that its product is to some degree being utilized to excess, Macromedia has itself established a Flash usability initiative, aimed at helping designers to understand and adhere to some basic principles of usability in their designs.

Bibliography

Gay, Jonathan. "Good Software Design and the Evolution of Flash." Techtv.com, March 20, 2001. <http://www.techtv.com/screensavers/showtell/story/0,24 330,3317749,00.html> (May 24, 2002).

Mardesich, Jodi. "Navigator to Get Flash for Browser Animations." *San Jose Mercury News*, June 9, 1998, p. 4C.

Netscape Communications. "What Is Flash?" 2000. <http://home.netscape.com/computing/webbuilding/ flashcontent.html> (May 24, 2002).

Nielsen, Jakob. "Flash: 99% Bad." Jakob Nielsen's Alertbox, October 29, 2000. <http://www.useit.com/alertbox/20001029.html> (May 24, 2002).

Rourke, Chris. "A Usable Future for Flash?" *User Vision*, 2000–2001. <http://www.uservision.co.uk/Articles/FlashArticle.html> (May 24, 2002).

Further Reading

CNet Builder. "Best Animation Tool: Macromedia Flash." 1998. <http://builder.cnet.com/webbuilding/pages/Business/1998Awards/ss04.html> (May 24, 2002).

Healey, Jon. "The Regeneration of Animation." *San Jose Mercury News*, July 30, 2000, p 1F.

Silverman, Jason. "Animators Overrun Sundance Online." *Wired News*, December 20, 2001. <http://www.wired.com/news/digiwood/0,1412,49258,00.html> (May 24, 2002).

Related Topics

Authoring Tools; Broadband; Compression; Desktop Publishing; Desktop Video; Digital Art and Animation; Hypermedia; Nielsen, Jakob; Multimedia; Shockwave; Streaming Media; Usability

— *Kevin Featherly*

Freenet (Community Networks)

The freenet movement comprised dozens of community-based bulletin board systems (BBSs), often based in a public library and accessible through the Telnet protocol, which made online public information available to local citizens. They usually were accessible through local phone dial-ups, and often were either free or nearly so to users (some asked for $25 annual donations). As the *Christian Science Monitor* noted in February 1996, freenets were, for many citizens, the first connection they had ever had to the broader Internet.

In the late 1980s, the heyday of the freenet movement, municipalities often built local electronic networks using government funds, supplemented by private donations. The people who posted information to freenets—for example, a boat-repair expert handing out free advice on boat care—were almost never paid, and neither were network administrators or content overseers. The systems invariably relied on volunteers, which resulted in a certain amateurish quality. Nevertheless, for many thousands of pre-Web online users, freenets offered their first access to e-mail, as well as their first encounter with coordinated and organized online information posted by governments, schools, libraries, and specific cultural and interest groups.

The movement remained strong into the late 1990s, until commercial Internet services and the World Wide Web became more popular, more ubiquitous, and more reliable substitutes. However, some freenets, notably the Minneapolis-based Twin Cities Freenet, moved their resources onto the Web and continue to thrive.

The freenet model was created at Case Western Reserve University in Cleveland, Ohio. Dr. Tom Grundner became interested in creating an online network at Case Western that could be accessed by people in the community seeking health information from public-health experts. In 1984, Grundner launched the "St. Silicon's Hospital and Information Dispensary," a medical bulletin board that proved so successful that it attracted early funding from AT&T and Bell Ohio.

This encouraged Grundner to devise a wider network. The Cleveland Free-Net, the first of the true freenet systems, opened to the public in 1986. It too proved successful, attracting 7,000 registered users and handling more than 500 phone accesses a day during its first year. In addition to serving as a place to collect information, the BBS allowed people to post messages online and form discussion threads that could be read and responded to by anyone on the network. It was one of the very earliest examples of people who were not part of the computer-industry elite being able to discuss and debate issues of community interest using computer technology.

Over time, the Cleveland Free-Net developed many sections of topical interest where citizens could discuss issues of importance to their communities, while also gathering such information as city-council meeting agendas and county-board meeting minutes. Cleveland Free-Net section titles eventually included areas labeled "The Administration Building," "The Post Office," "Public Square," "The Courthouse and Government Center," and "The Arts Building," among numerous others. This labeling format became common among subsequent freenets.

The Cleveland Free-Net allowed people to dial in from cities outside the Cleveland area, but it limited those connecting to the discussion of topics of interest in Cleveland. Inevitably, other cities began picking up on the idea of generating community conversation using computer technologies. As the movement spread, other cities generally based their local freenets at public libraries, largely because most people in the community did not yet have personal computers at home, and public libraries generally made computer terminals accessible to the public. The Heartland FreeNet, launched in Peoria, Illinois, in 1990, was apparently the first such library-based freenet system.

Encouraged by the success of his efforts in Cleveland and the spread of his idea elsewhere,

Grundner decided to organize existing freenets and to foster the creation of more local networks across the United States. The National Public Telecomputing Network (NPTN) was formed in 1989 to assist in spreading the freenet gospel. Existing freenets were encouraged to join NPTN; they could either pay $2,000 a year for membership or release names of their local users for fundraising purposes. By 1996, there were 70 freenets around the country, and NPTN had plans to help bring another 115 online in the United States and in 10 other countries. "This is real grass-rootsy, '60s stuff," Gail Featheringham, an NPTN representative, told the *Christian Science Monitor* in February 1996. "It's really accelerating."

The brakes were about to be applied. Freenets had serious problems that rather quickly contributed to their demise. They relied on volunteers, which meant that staffing and service could be haphazard and unprofessional. Despite successes in large cities like Cleveland, Minneapolis, and Tallahassee, Florida, freenets came to appeal largely to smaller communities that were still underserved by then-emerging local dial-up Internet access; this situation changed as Internet service providers (ISPs) began to sell Internet service over local phone exchanges around the country.

Further, many freenets were small operations that could not afford to offer the glitzy amenities of commercial providers like America Online and CompuServe, or provide access to the World Wide Web. (However, like the commercial services, NPTN did offer daily content from *USA Today* for a time.) Worst of all, freenets had fewer telephone lines and modems, and often used aging equipment. It could be frustratingly difficult for callers to get through, especially during periods of intensive use, such as during the evening.

In December 1996, NPTN filed for bankruptcy; three years later, Cleveland Free-Net, the original service, was unplugged. The movement essentially ground to a halt.

At its peak, the freenet movement had lofty ambitions, aiming at "rebuilding civil society" by providing online information access to the physically, technologically, and economically disadvantaged. Providing a platform for minority and alternative voices, improving civic communication, and boosting literacy were also stated goals. In some ways, the movement seems to have fallen prey to its own success; as commercial ISPs came to understand the demand for freenets and their services, they were able to justify the expense of extending their own networks to lure users away from the freenets.

Bibliography

Belsie, Laurent. "Communities Put Local Residents On-Line for Free." *Christian Science Monitor*, February 13, 1996, p. 15.

Brown, Joel D. "Free-Netting." *Wired*, July 2, 1994. <http://www.wired.com/wired/archive/2.07/net_surf.html> (April 5, 2002).

Hauben, Michael, and Ronda Hauben. *Netizens*. Los Alamitos, Calif.: IEEE Computer Society Press, 1997.

Grundner, T. M. "The National Public Telecomputing Network: Mission Statement." Coalition for Networked Information, August 4, 1991. <http://www.cni.org/docs/infopols/NPTN.html> (April 5, 2002).

Further Reading

Gamboa, Glenn. "Free-Netting into the 21st Century." *Akron Beacon Journal*, November 29, 1993, D1.

———. "Like Putting the World at Your Fingertips." *Akron Beacon Journal*, November 29, 1993, D1.

Gray, Miranda. "Frequently Asked Questions: Community Networks and Free-Nets." *National Capital FreeNet*. March 24, 1996. <http://www.ncf.carleton.ca/help/alt.fan.freenet.faq> (April 5, 2002).

Rheingold, Howard. *The Virtual Community: Homesteading on the Electronic Frontier.* Reading, Mass.: Addison-Wesley Publishing Co., 1993.

Stallings, Ben. "A Critical Study of Three Free-Net Community Networks." [In Fulfillment of Intel's Robert N. Noyce Technology Summer Internship.] 1996. <http://ofcn.org/whois/ben/Free-Nets/FN_background.html> (April 5, 2002).

Related Topics

Access; BITNET; Brand, Stewart; Bulletin-Board Systems; Community Networking; Cyberculture; Electronic Democracy; Internet Service Providers; Virtual Community

— *Kevin Featherly*

Freenet (File-Sharing Network)

Freenet is an application for sharing computer files of all kinds (music, text, video, and so on) over the Internet while protecting the confidentiality of the data source and its recipient. The goal is to develop the potential of computer networks to render any centralized regulation or censorship of information unfeasible. This goal, explicitly stated by Freenet's creator Ian Clarke, is a controversial one that has triggered an ongoing discussion of ethical and legal issues surrounding copyright protection online.

According to *The Economist* magazine, Clarke dreamed up Freenet because he feared that the Internet could become an instrument of such authoritarian control as to make dystopian author George Orwell appear unimaginative. Clarke wanted an information system to exist that not only had no centralized administration, but also provided complete anonymity to each user on its network, whether they were creators or users of information. His University of Edinburgh paper, "A Distributed Decentralized Information Storage and Retrieval System," outlined Clarke's vision in 1999; shortly thereafter, Clarke and a team of volunteers began building the system.

While Clarke helped to force the issue of online censorship and copyright protection, he also aspired to build a community of users who would continue to develop and expand the application. In keeping with this hope, Freenet's source code is open to the public, so users can continue to develop and improve the application. During the project's early months, Clarke estimated that more than 100,000 copies of the application were downloaded, but it is part of the nature of the project that it is impossible to determine the exact number of users.

Freenet makes regulation difficult by relying on a decentralized computer network that allows computer files to be distributed so that users don't know which files are being stored on their computers. Rather than sharing information in a top-down, server-to-client model, wherein files are centrally stored and distributed to individual users, Freenet relies on a peer-to-peer model, in which information is passed from computer to computer on the network until it reaches its destination. When a file, such as a music track, is entered into one computer in the network (called a node), it is encrypted and copied onto several other nodes with which the computer is in contact. Each node keeps track of the files that it is storing, and of the files stored on a few other nodes. Thus, each node of the network can "see" only a fraction of the information available, and there is no centralized record of the location of all the available data.

To retrieve a file from the network, a user needs to determine the name, or key, with which the data was entered by learning it from another user or from an online index. The request to retrieve the file is passed along the network from node to node, until it encounters a node that "knows" where the file is. Once the file is located, it is handed back along the same path, leaving a trail of copies. The duplication process has a dual function: It increases the availability of frequently requested files, and it makes it more difficult to trace the file's source. In addition, this process ensures that any attempt to trace a file in order to eliminate it results only in its further duplication.

Offered as a truly decentralized form of file sharing, Freenet remains more complicated and cumbersome to use than more centralized applications like Napster, the application for sharing music files online that gained notoriety in 2000 when it was sued by the Recording Industry Association of America. There is no easy way to search a network or even the names of available files, and until Freenet programmers develop such a system, users must rely on Web sites with partial and often out-of-date key indexes.

The limitations of Freenet in its current form inhibit its potential to render copyright protection and censorship obsolete. However, Clarke's vision raises the issue of the desirability—or, as some might argue, the inevitability—of pursuing such a course. Clarke argues that since copyright allows "middlemen" to monopolize control of the creative process, the system should be replaced by one in which audiences provide voluntary contributions to content creators or invest in them.

As for objectionable content, Clarke argues that the importance of unregulated speech in a democratic society outweighs the regulatory interest in protecting users from banned content. "I really think this is an extremely moral position," he said. "It might be black and white. It might be a very uncompromising position. But I think it needs to be, because if you create the means to censor information, even if your intentions are initially good, you will also have created the machine to censor information that probably deserves not to be censored." The willingness of users to share this version of free-speech absolutism by transforming their computers into conduits for information that could include anything from child porn to alternative news may help decide the viability of Clarke's vision.

Bibliography

Cohen, Adam. "The Infoanarchist." *Time*, June 26, 2000, pp. 46–47.

The Economist. "Here, There and Everywhere." June 22, 2000. <http://www.economist.com/ displayStory.cfm?Story_ID=81436> (March 22, 2002).

Featherly, Kevin. "Freenet: Will It Smash Copyright Law?" March 20, 2001. <http://www.newsbytes.com/news/01/163395.html> (March 22, 2002).

————. Telephone Interview with Ian Clarke. March 19, 2001.

The Free Network Project: Rewiring the Internet. "FAQ."
May 10, 2001.
<http://freenetproject.org/cgi-bin/twiki/view/Main/
FAQ> (March 22, 2002).

Further Reading

Kleiner, Kurt. "Free Speech, Liberty, Pornography."
Reed Business Information New Scientist, March 10,
2001, p. 32.
Koman, Richard. "Free Radical: Ian Clarke has Big Plans
for the Internet." *O'Reilly Open P2P.com,* November
14, 2000.
<http://www.openp2p.com/pub/a/p2p/2000/11/14/
ian.html> (March 22, 2002).
Oram, Andy, ed. *Peer-to-Peer: Harnessing the Power
of Disruptive Technologies.* Beijing/Cambridge:
O'Reilly, 2001.

Related Topics

Digital Millennium Copyright Act; Encryption and
Cryptography; Napster; Open Source Movement;
Peer-to-Peer

— Mark Andrejevic and Kevin Featherly

Fuzzy Logic

Fuzzy logic is a form of logic created to address the
distinctions of empirical reality and natural language. It is used to program computers that can imitate human reasoning.

Understanding fuzzy logic requires understanding
classical logic and the problems it sometimes entails.
Classical logic sharply divides propositions into two
possible states, true or false. In contrast, fuzzy logic
distinguishes and articulates a continuum of states,
permitting partial truth-values located between complete truth and complete falsehood.

Classical logic is an axiomatic field of mathematics using the principles of excluded middle and double
negation. It is bivalent, either-or logic; true or false, off
or on. The excluded middle means that a proposition
must either be true (p) or false (not-p). The excluded
middle generates sets of members that are strictly
excluded or included. Double negation means that a
second negation cancels the first negation of any
proposition; therefore, (not-not-p) equals (p).

Logic began as a branch of philosophy. Aristotle
codified and developed logic into a program of valid
reasoning using the formal theory of deduction.
Aristotelian logic is independent of truth-value. False
premises lead to logically valid arguments, while
invalid logic disqualifies arguments reasoned from true
premises. Therefore, while it is necessary to rational
discourse, scientific discovery, and technological control, logic alone is insufficient.

Information technology and cybernetic systems
now manage activities once controlled only by human
operators. Some of these systems are therefore required
to simulate aspects of human judgment. Some systems
can be controlled by simple mechanical rules, which
are suitable to thermostatic controls or governors for
engine speed.

While control by classical logic works in many linear and mechanical systems, it is inadequate to the
ambiguous or inexact situations implicit in other systems, especially those arising in advanced control of
systems formerly governed by human control. Such
systems often require the kinds of decisions known as
"judgment calls." Rather than decisions based on
mechanical rules, such situations require finesse and
decisions based on experience.

The advanced control systems of the information
society involve a paradox. It was the binary logic of
computer technology that gave rise to these systems,
and yet these systems now address ambiguous, non-
binary problems. Fuzzy logic was created to meet the
challenges of ambiguous problems.

Fuzzy logic and the theory of fuzzy sets began in
the 1960s with the work of Lotfi Zadeh, professor of
electrical engineering at the University of California,
Berkeley. According to Zadeh, classical logic was
unsuited to describing a world where many entities
belong to several sets. Strict principles of inclusion or
exclusion oversimplify the concept of set membership,
and fail to address reality. In contrast, fuzzy logic can
be used to describe the extent or degree to which any
individual is related to a set.

Fuzzy logic emulates human judgment and the
ability of natural language to recognize more than simple true-false values. It permits propositions to represent degrees of truthfulness and falsehood. The
mathematical expression of fuzzy logic builds on the
concept of fuzzy sets. Membership in fuzzy sets is
expressed in probabilities or degrees using a continuum of numerical values from 0 to 1. For example, the
statement "it is rainy today" might be 1.0 if rain is
pouring down, between .3 and .8 if rainstorms are broken by intermittent clear skies, another number for
drizzling showers, and 0.0 if skies are clear.

Fuzzy systems can also be used to predict probabilities. A fuzzy system might, for example, predict
that something will happen, will probably happen,
might happen, might not happen, will not happen, and

so on. Probability statements predict the outcome of events. The values assigned to different probabilities can be adjusted as fuzzy systems gather data, which gives fuzzy systems the appearance of learning. Since fuzzy systems appear to mimic human thought, some people consider them a form of artificial intelligence.

Fuzzy systems, which were an experimental technology until the late twentieth century, began to achieve commercial application in the early 1990s. Today, fuzzy logic and fuzzy systems are the scientific basis of the field known as soft computing. Fuzzy logic is applicable to systems that require judgment. Soft computing methods are used in expert systems, artificial intelligence, industrial control systems, pattern recognition, data mining, data compression, human-reasoning modeling, decision making, statistics, and robotics, as well as in such programs as those that computerize speech, recognize handwriting, or suggest probable words to replace misspelled words in spell checkers.

Linguistic modeling is one of the most significant uses of fuzzy logic. Fuzzy systems can be used to apply linguistic or imprecise values and reasoning to problems. These can imitate the attributes of human reasoning. This often means that a small number of language-based rules can replace complicated mathematical formulas and models. Systems based on classical logic cannot manage this type of linguistic modeling. Linguistic modeling is suited to cognitive maps, examining and simulating dynamic systems and human reasoning.

Fuzzy logic plays an essential role in soft computing. Hard computing is mechanistic and precise, governed by complex sets of mathematical rules; soft computing is designed to cope with problems of imprecision, uncertainty, and learning. The goal of soft computing is the creation of simple, fast, user-friendly systems. From the programming standpoint, language-based rules also permit rapid, effective programming.

Even though philosophers debate the epistemology and ontology of fuzzy logic, engineers and designers are employing fuzzification in an ever-increasing number of useful applications—for example, in the design of more sophisticated search engines for the World Wide Web.

Bibliography

Berkeley Initiative in Soft Computing (BISC), University of California, Berkeley. Web site. <http://www-bisc.cs.berkeley.edu/> (April 5, 2002).

Bezdek, James C. "Fuzzy Models—What Are They, and Why?" *IEEE Transactions on Fuzzy Systems*, 1:1 (1993), pp. 1–6.

Kosko, Bart. *Fuzzy Engineering*. Englewood Cliffs, N.J.: Prentice-Hall, 1996.

———. *Heaven in a Chip: Fuzzy Visions of Society and Science in the Digital Age*. New York: Three Rivers Press, 2000.

McNeil, Daniel, and Paul Freiberger. *Fuzzy Logic: The Revolutionary Computer Technology that Is Changing Our World*. New York: Touchstone, 1994.

Nguyen, Hung T., and Elbert A. Walker. *A First Course in Fuzzy Logic*. Boca Raton, Fla.: CRC Press, 1999.

Ortech Engineering Inc. Fuzzy Logic Reservoir. Web site. <http://www.ortech-engr.com/fuzzy/reservoir.html> (April 5, 2002).

Zadeh, Lotfi A. "Fuzzy Sets." *Information and Control* 8 (1965), pp. 338–53.

———. "Outline of a New Approach to the Analysis of Complex Systems." *IEEE Transactions on Systems, Man, and Cybernetics* 3 (1973).

———. "The Calculus of Fuzzy Restrictions." *Fuzzy Sets and Applications to Cognitive and Decision Making Processes*. Lotfi A. Zadeh et al., eds. New York: Academic Press, 1975; pp. 1–39.

Further Reading

Bandler, W., and L.J. Kohout. "Fuzzy Power Sets and Fuzzy Implication Operators." *Fuzzy Sets and Systems* 4 (1980), pp. 13–30.

The Center for Fuzzy Logic, Robotics, and Intelligent Systems (CFL). Texas A&M University. Web site. <http://www.cs.tamu.edu/research/CFL/> (April 5, 2002).

Hakel, Milton D. "How Often Is Often?" *American Psychologist*, vol. 23 (1968), p. 534.

John, Robert. "Fuzzy Logic Sources of Information." De Montfort University. <http://www.cms.dmu.ac.uk/~rij/fuzzy.html> (April 5, 2002)

Lakoff, George. "Hedges: A Study in Meaning Criteria and the Logic of Fuzzy Concepts." *Journal of Philosophical Logic*, vol. 2 (1973), pp. 458–508.

North American Fuzzy Information Processing Society (NAFIPS). December 2001.Web site. <http://morden.csee.usf.edu/Nafipsf/> (April 5, 2002)

Simpson, Ray. "The Specific Meanings of Certain Terms Indicating Differing Degrees of Frequency." *The Quarterly Journal of Speech*, vol. 30 (1944), pp. 328–30.

Related Topics

Data Mining; Expert Systems; Knowledge Management; Search Engine; Shannon, Claude

— *Ken Friedman*

g g g g g g **G** g g g g g g

Gaming

Computer and video games have been key arenas for the development and proliferation of new media forms and technologies. The three main platforms for electronic gaming are stand-alone arcade games, consoles that connect to televisions, and computer-game software. Video and computer-game software sales exceeded $6 billion in 2000, with more than 200 million units sold. Including hardware such as consoles and control devices, sales approached $9 billion. (By comparison, in 2000 the Nevada casino gambling industry produced $9.6 billion in revenues, domestic DVD and videocassette sales were $10.8 billion, and U.S. movie ticket sales reached $7.7 billion.) Gaming industry growth averaged 15 percent annually from 1997 to 2000, and electronic gaming is expected to grow by 50 to 75 percent between 2001 and 2005.

THE BIRTH OF COMPUTER GAMES

There are two competing stories about the birth of computer games. The first credits William A. Higinbotham, an engineer at the Brookhaven National Laboratory, a U.S. government nuclear facility, with developing a simple, ping pong-like game in 1958 on the facility's computer as an exhibition piece for visitors. However, Higinbotham never patented the idea, and the program never left the site.

Four years later, a group of programmers at MIT wrote the computer code for a game called Spacewar! It involved two space ships that players could navigate around a screen, firing torpedoes at each other, while avoiding the gravitational pull of a star in the center of the screen. Steve Russell and his co-programmers distributed the software source code for free, and as years passed, the game could be found on mainframe computers throughout the world.

During the 1960s, other programmers developed similar games, including Lunar Landing, a space-flight simulation; Hammurabi, a text-based strategy game involving planting crops and levying taxes; and

ADVENT, short for adventure, an interactive narrative that allowed players to explore a virtual environment using rudimentary textual commands like "go north" or "use key." These games defined distinct computer-game genres (simulation, strategy, and adventure games) that have shaped electronic gaming over the past three decades.

In 1966, Ralph Baer, working for a military defense contractor, developed a console machine that worked with a television to play a Pong-like hockey game. He applied for a patent in 1968, and the company he worked for sold the rights to the machine to Magnavox, which marketed the first home-gaming console, the Odyssey, in 1972. The console, which sold for about $100, hooked up to a television and included a version of the tennis game Pong.

In 1971, Nolan Bushnell, working for the pinball company Nutting Associates, marketed the first mass-market video game, Computer Space, which was based on Spacewar! and sold 1,500 units. Bushnell left Nutting and designed his own version of Pong as an arcade game. Its success led him to found Atari in 1972, which also marketed a home console version of Pong. Since Magnavox had introduced the Odyssey six months earlier with essentially the same game, Atari was forced to pay royalties to Magnavox. From 1972 to 1977, so many different console games were released featuring Pong-style games that the budding industry declined as rival versions drove down prices.

GAMING GOES MASS MARKET

In 1978, Space Invaders was released in Japan to huge success, ushering in a new phase of arcade video-game popularity. From 1978 to 1983, numerous now-classic arcade games were released, including Asteroids, Defender, Missile Command, Pac-Man, Donkey Kong, Tempest, Frogger, and Tron (which was based on the 1982 Disney film of the same name, which itself was about arcade games). In 1981, $5 billion in quarters was spent on arcade games alone.

During the same period, several game consoles were marketed, which in some cases were essentially early forms of personal computers. These included Atari's VCS 2600, which played games from interchangeable cartridges, and the Atari 400 and 800, which were basically primitive PCs with keyboards. The VCS 2600 allowed the software for games to be developed independently of the hardware, leading to the founding of the first software-development company, Activision, in 1979. It produced game content for the 2600 and other consoles.

A second crash struck the console-gaming industry in 1983, as numerous second-party software developers flooded the market with cheap, low-quality games. The industry, which had taken in $3 billion in 1982, generated only $100 million in 1985.

GAMING 1983–1993

While the arcade-game segment of the industry leveled off during the late 1980s, the wide-scale introduction of personal computers into homes combined with the success of the Nintendo NES and Sega Genesis consoles to revitalize the electronic gaming industry. By 1989, Nintendo consoles were in 21 percent of American homes, and 50 million games for the system were sold. In 1990, 22 percent of American homes had a personal computer, and computer- and console-game sales combined to reach $2.2 billion.

During the 1980s, numerous technological advances had significant impacts on gaming. The text-adventure game Zork, originally played on mainframe computers in the late 1970s, was released in several software formats in the early 1980s. By the end of the decade, it had spawned numerous sequels that sold more than a million copies. Text-based games were soon superceded by graphics-based games, thanks to PC and console technology advances. The graphical user interface (GUI) allowed point-and-click interaction with onscreen graphics, and became a central element in games.

The adventure-game genre, defined in its infancy by a text-only interface, began using graphics to allow players to explore virtual landscapes. Ken and Roberta Williams developed the first text-and-graphics adventure game, Mystery House, for the Apple II in 1980. Founding Sierra On-Line, the Williamses were commissioned by IBM to develop a graphics-based game, and King's Quest was released in 1984; it became one of the best-selling computer-game series. In 1983, the fledgling company Electronic Arts, currently the largest independent gaming-software developer in the United States, marketed Dr. J and Larry Bird Go One

on One, which allowed players to control virtual opponents based on real-world athletes.

Will Wright created a unique game genre with the release of SimCity in 1989. Innovative in its open-endedness, the game involves managing the economy and infrastructure of a virtual city. It generated a host of sequels and other Sim (short for simulation) games (e.g., SimEarth, SimAnt) over the next decade. SimCity inspired Sid Meier to create Civilization, another seminal game that defined the strategic-simulation genre, which also flourished throughout the 1990s with games like Civilization II, Age of Empires, and Starcraft. The latter game has sold more than two million copies in the United States alone since its release in 1997.

In 1989, Nintendo launched the Game Boy, a handheld computer-gaming system costing just over $100. The success of the Game Boy, which sold 3.2 million units in 1990, defined a new segment of the industry targeting younger children, who can link devices together to play games with each other at school, on buses, and elsewhere.

In 1990, Capcom released the arcade game Street Fighter II, whose popularity established the fighting-game genre. Players choose from 10 different warriors, each possessing unique fighting moves and skills, who face off in one-on-one matches. By 1992, Acclaim launched the game Mortal Kombat on four different computer platforms. It allows "fatality moves" that involve one player graphically tearing the heart out of an opponent, for example, or tearing a head off and brandishing it over the fallen victim. Despite concerns voiced in some quarters about the game's violent content, Mortal Kombat sold over six million copies. The following year, Sega and Nintendo released versions of the game on their console systems, and Senator Joseph Lieberman (D-Conn.) launched Senate hearings to look into the possibility of banning ultra-violent games. Those hearings lead to the creation of the Entertainment Software Adoption Board (ESRB) and of a video-game ratings system similar to that used for movies.

DOOM AND THE 3D REVOLUTION

The release of Id Software's Doom in 1993 marked a key turning point in the history of computer gaming. Using what has become known as "the drug-dealer business model," Id's John Carmack and John Romero released free versions of the innovative 3D game on the Internet. Five million were downloaded, which led to more than 150,000 full copies of the game being sold.

Doom redefined gaming, virtually overnight. Characterized by fast-paced graphics that give the player the visceral feeling of running through detailed environments, firing weapons at and avoiding enemies, Doom spawned an entire subculture of FPS (first-person shooter) and a host of similar games. The popularity of 3D-rendered environments created a booming desire for specialized 3D computer video cards, which are now a standard feature in the PC market.

At the turn of the century, FPS games such as Doom and Quake themselves came under fire in the wake of the killings at Columbine High School and elsewhere, as examples of the propensity of games to cultivate violent behavior.

Screen-shot from Lara Croft Tomb Raider: Angel of Darkness. *(Tomb Raider and Lara Croft are copyright to Core Design. All Rights Reserved.)*

ONLINE GAMING

While online games were first conceived of and developed in the early 1980s, it was not until the mid-1990s, with widespread Internet access, that online gaming flourished. FPS titles like Quake and Half-Life began incorporating online gaming features, and eventually were marketed as "arena" games in which online players competed as teams or dueled head-to-head in "death matches." Role-playing games (RPGs) also flourished online, with Everquest and Ultima Online boasting more than half a million subscribers between them who are willing to pay $10 a month to maintain virtual characters in persistent virtual game worlds. Online game sites for casual gamers, which offer card games like bridge or board-based games such as Monopoly, have also become popular in recent years.

All three gaming consoles released in 2000–01 (Sony's Playstation 2, Microsoft's X-Box, and Sega's Dreamcast) have some level of Internet connectivity. Meanwhile, popular gaming franchises such as The Sims and Star Wars demonstrated online versions in 2002. Internet gaming, although still in its infancy, is expected to grow into a $2.8 billion industry in the United States by 2004.

SYNERGY AND CONVERGENCE

Two elements characterize the success of electronic gaming: synergy and convergence. A relatively insulated industry in the 1970s and 1980s, electronic gaming entered the synergy-driven media market of the late 1990s with explosive growth and great effect. Cross-promotion and brand licensing allowed gaming to become a significant aspect of popular culture. Nintendo's Pokémon game spawned animated TV shows, movies, comic books, action figures, and trading cards, in addition to sales of 75 million Pokémon-related games worldwide, netting the company more than $14 billion. Lara Croft, Tomb Raider's virtual heroine, has become a media celebrity; she has appeared on countless magazine covers and in several commercials, and was featured in a live-action movie in 2001.

Technologically, electronic gaming spurred numerous advances, most notably in 3D graphics-rendering hardware and software; online gaming servers that allow for real-time interaction among players; and numerous peripheral devices, including high-quality sound cards and computer speakers, force-feedback controllers, and voice-activated controls. Gaming has been a huge impetus for linking the personal computer, the television, and the Internet.

With Web-surfing and DVD-playing capabilities, the inclusion of hard-drive memory, and eventual connectivity to printers and other PC peripherals, the newest gaming consoles are being envisioned and marketed as full-scale "entertainment systems." Relatively cheap compared to PCs, they combine computer and video gaming, online gaming, movie-viewing capability, and access to online information and shopping, blurring the previous distinction between the PC and console platforms. These advances have resulted in gaming going mainstream, as women, girls, and older adults join young males to widen the demographics of the gaming market.

Bibliography

Au, Wagner James. "Showdown in Cyberspace: Star Wars vs. The Sims." *Salon.com*, July 9, 2002. <http://www.salon.com/tech/feature/2002/07/09/mmorpg/index.html> (July 16, 2002).

Herz, J. C. *Joystick Nation*. Boston: Little, Brown and Company, 1996.

Hunter, William. "The Dot Eaters Videogame History 101." EmuUnlim.com, June 12, 2001. <http://www.emuunlim.com/doteaters/> (April 5, 2002).

Poole, Steven. *Trigger Happy: Videogames and the Entertainment Revolution*. New York: Arcade Publishing, 2000.

Thomas, Jr., Donald A. "The Whens of the Integrated Circuit: A Chronological History of Computers, Video Games and Related Technologies." January 12, 2001. <http://www.icwhen.com/index.html> (April 5, 2002).

Wilson, Johnny L. "What a Long, Strange Blip It's Been: The Untold Story of the History of Interactive Entertainment, From Mainframes to Mainstream." *Computer Gaming World* 200 (2001).

Further Reading

Laplante, Alice, and Rich Seidner. *Playing for Profit: How Digital Entertainment Is Making Big Business out of Child's Play*. New York: Wiley, 1999.

Sheff, David. *Game Over: Press Start to Continue*. Wilson, Conn.: Gamepress, 1999.

Silverman, Barry; Silverman, Brian; and Vadim Gerasinov. "Spacewar!" The Epistemology and Learning Group. <http://lcs.www.media.mit.edu/groups/el/projects/spacewar/> (April 5, 2002).

Turkle, Sherry. *Life on the Screen: Identity in the Age of the Internet*. New York: Simon & Schuster, 1995.

Related Topics

Carmack, John; Computer Graphics; Digital Art and Animation; Graphical User Interface; Laurel, Brenda

— *Shawn Miklaucic*

Gates, William H., III

1955–

U.S. Industrialist

In the process of building the Microsoft empire, Bill Gates has become one of the richest men in the world, and is considered by many to be a living symbol of the best and worst aspects of U.S. capitalism. Gates has written two books explaining his vision of the future of technology, and his views have helped to shape the computer industry in the United States.

Born to a prominent family, Gates grew up in Seattle and attended the private Lakeside School, where he discovered his interest in computer software and began programming at the age of 13. Gates and friend Paul Allen wrote a scheduling program for the school. While in high school, Gates and Allen founded a company, Traf-O-Data, to analyze and graph traffic data for the city.

In 1973, Gates entered Harvard University. While there, he and Paul Allen developed the first BASIC interpreter for the Intel 8080 microprocessor, as well as a version of the programming language BASIC for Altair, the first microcomputer from Micro Instrumentation and Telemetry Systems (M.I.T.S.). MBASIC was later used by M.I.T.S. to accompany its Altair 8800 kit; by 1977, 10,000 Altairs had been sold. His success in software programming led Gates to leave Harvard in his junior year and turn his focus to Micro-Soft, a company he had co-founded with Allen in 1975 (the hyphen was later dropped).

Microsoft established its leadership in microcomputer programming languages, first by fitting IBM PCs with its Disk Operating System (DOS) in 1981, and later by equipping non-IBM PCs with MS-DOS. In 1987, Microsoft introduced its first version of the Windows operating system (OS). By 1993, Microsoft was selling a million copies of Windows a month. The popularity of Windows 3.0, and later Windows 95, established Microsoft's leadership role in the computer-software industry worldwide; Windows currently runs on 85 percent of the world's computers. Microsoft became the world's leading supplier of OSs and applications, with a market capitalization that exceeded half a trillion dollars. Its success with Windows also contributes to the immense growth of the computer industry. Microsoft's Windows OS is the de facto desktop standard, as well as a leader in the server arena, and Microsoft Office is a highly successful application suite.

Microsoft is also successful in other software categories. It has a strong presence in the Internet industry; its Internet Explorer, which was later integrated into its Windows 98 OS, is currently a leading Web browser. In addition to its operating systems and a spectrum of software products that ranges from programming tools to end-user applications, Microsoft has also ventured into different types of media; it has entered into the development and production of CD-ROMs, and collaborated with the NBC television network to create MSNBC.

Gates himself is known not only for Microsoft's success, but also for its legal battles over alleged antitrust violations. Taking advantage of its leading role in the OS arena, Microsoft induced PC makers who relied heavily on Windows to adopt other Microsoft products as well, such as its Office applications and Web browser. By doing so, Microsoft protected its place as the standard OS for PCs.

Netscape Communications, America Online, Sun Microsystems, and other competitors would like to end Microsoft's monopolistic control of the corporate desktop. Some advocate the adoption by PC makers of a new model of computing, in which a PC runs small Java applets locally, with most of the OS functionality provided by Internet servers. In 1998, the U.S. government and 19 states filed an antitrust lawsuit against Microsoft. A 2000 court order that Microsoft be broken into two companies—one for software mainstays like Microsoft Office and Internet Explorer and the other for the Windows OS—was remanded in summer 2001.

Gates demonstrated foresight with a decision not to abandon the IBM PC in light of the immense success and popularity of the Macintosh in the late 1980s. Rather, Microsoft developed Windows software to give the PC an Apple-like interface, which helped the PC to survive. However, critics have often charged that Microsoft, instead of capitalizing on designs of its own, tended to react to competitors' ideas—the graphical interface of Apple, or the Web browser of Netscape are two famous examples. In addition, many criticized Gates' shrewd business attitude as he thrashed competitors in desktop operating systems and the software industry. Critics see a pattern of unfair and relentless use of Microsoft power to retard competitors. Despite the criticism, Gates aims at putting Microsoft software on every computing device.

Gates has authored two books. In 1995, he wrote *The Road Ahead*, which dealt with the impact of computer technology and the software industry, as well as with their future development. In 1999's *Business @ the Speed of Thought*, Gates discussed the application of computer technology in business sectors. A tireless advocate of computer technology, Gates wrote enthusiastically about the positive contributions of the use of computers in social life and in business.

Selected Works

Gates, Bill. *Business @ the Speed of Thought: Using a Digital Nervous System.* New York: Warner Books, 1999.
Gates, Bill, with Nathan Myhrvold and Peter Rinearson. *The Road Ahead.* New York: Viking, 1995.
Lowe, Janet. *Bill Gates Speaks: Insight from the World's Greatest Entrepreneur.* New York: John Wiley, 1998.

Bibliography

Edstrom, Jennifer, and Martin Eller. *Barbarians Led by Bill Gates: Microsoft from the Inside, How the World's Richest Corporation Wields Its Power.* New York: Holt, 1998.
Isaacson, Walter. "In Search of the Real Bill Gates." *Time.* January 3, 1997, pp. 44–56.

Microsoft. Company profile.
<http://www.microsoft.com/presspass/exec/billg/default.asp>
Wallace, James. *Overdrive: Bill Gates and the Race to Control Cyberspace.* New York: John Wiley, 1997.

Further Reading

Dearlove, Des. *Business the Bill Gates Way: 10 Secrets of the World's Richest Business Leader.* New York: AMACOM, 1999.
Gatlin, Jonathan. *Bill Gates: The Path to the Future.* New York: Avon Books, 1999.
Manes, Stephen, and Paul Andrews. *Gates: How Microsoft's Mogul Reinvented an Industry and Made Himself the Richest Man in America.* New York: Doubleday, 1993.
Rohm, Wendy Goldman. *The Microsoft File: The Secret Case Against Bill Gates.* New York: Times Business, 1998.

Related Topics

Browser; Interface; Internet; World Wide Web

— *Shing-Ling Sarina Chen*

Gender and New Media

"Gender" describes the social construction of people as male and female, apart from biological considerations. Gender theorists argue that most notions regarding what it means to "act as a man" or "seem like a woman" stem from culturally inherited ideas about gender, rather than from physiological differences between the sexes. When people speak of gender in a new-media context, they are usually referring to the gender gap in digital production and consumption, or to the notion of "gender performativity," usually as it occurs over the Internet.

THE NEW-MEDIA GENDER GAP

One of the clearest examples of the gender gap in new media today is the paucity of women computer scientists in the United States. According to the U.S. Department of Labor, nearly 75 percent of tomorrow's jobs will require the use of computers, yet fewer than 33 percent of participants in today's computer courses and related activities are girls. Ironically, the notion that computing is "men's work" isn't at all historically accurate. From Ada Lovelace to Patti Maes, history abounds with examples of gifted women computer programmers and software engineers. Indeed, the Grace Hopper Celebration of Women in Computing Conference is held each year to honor such pioneers.

Recently, educators and government agencies have attempted to launch a full-out attack on the stereotype of women as computer illiterates. As a recent American Association of University Women Education report put it, "As violent electronic games and dull programming classes turn off more and more girls to the computer culture, schools need to change the way information technology is used, applied, and taught in the nation's classrooms." One such new approach, "summer technology camps," is used by the Women in Technology Program to encourage young girls.

Another can be found in the work of Brenda Laurel, who "simply wanted to find out what it would take to motivate a little girl to put her hands on the computer and become comfortable with it." To do this, she conducted extensive interviews with young girls regarding their likes and dislikes in video games, striving to create interactive experiences that girls could enjoy.

In addition to the gender gap in computer-science classrooms, a serious scarcity of women existed on the Internet until the mid-1990s. As late as 1994, CompuServe estimated that females made up only 12 percent of their cyberspace population. In a 1993 study, Leslie Regan Shade discovered that even in "women's spaces" online, male posts outnumbered female in frequency and length. And in 1994, linguist Susan Herring found that men were more verbose and "adversarial" than women online. Herring, who studied eight separate online mailing lists, argued that the Internet often reproduced, and sometimes exaggerated, long-standing communication inequities faced by women in the real world every day.

These discoveries alarmed a number of feminist activists, who feared that women might be left behind in the "Internet revolution" in the 1990s. As early as 1987, Anita Borg began the Systers mailing list with a singular goal: Get more women using the Internet. Feminist magazines and book publishers followed suit, offering "female-friendly" instructions for getting online. And efforts were made by people like Stacy Horn, who began the New York City–based bulletin-board system ECHO with the express purpose of actively recruiting women's perspectives. Internationally, groups like the Electronic Witches made an effort to get women online in places like the former Yugoslavia.

CLOSING THE GENDER GAP ONLINE

The efforts of activists paid off, at least in the United States, Canada, and other countries with relatively high teledensity. Today, Nielsen/NetRatings reports that women are on the Internet at a rate of 51.7 percent in the United States, a gender breakdown that exactly mirrors the general population. In the United States at least, education, age, and income level have surpassed gender as significant factors affecting Internet access. Unfortunately, this fact is somewhat misleading, as gender often overlaps with these other categories; for instance, single mothers, who are often among the poorest people, are significantly underrepresented in computer and Internet usage.

Still, women around the world continue to join the Internet in record numbers. In Australia, New Zealand, Finland, South Korea, Sweden, Ireland, and Mexico, women's Internet usage is fast approaching 50 percent. In the U.K., Denmark, Norway, Austria, Switzerland, Japan, Hong Kong, Singapore, Taiwan, Russia, and Israel, women's 'Net usage is currently over 40 percent. Unfortunately, in areas where teledensity is low, such as South Asia and Africa, the number of women online remains negligible. And in countries where women remain politically repressed, female participation on the Internet exists only at token levels. In 1999, women in Saudi Arabia were finally granted permission to go online in an Internet café in Jeddah, but a year later, the government shut down an all-women Internet café in Mecca for "reasons of public morality."

As the number of female Internet users begins to climb worldwide, a number of critics have argued that earlier observations regarding the online gender gap ought to be reconsidered. Laura Miller, for example, has criticized what she sees as Herring's urge to "protect the women and children" in public discourse online, linking it to older practices of chivalry and imperialism. In a similar vein, Amy Bruckman argues that asking such questions as "Are women comfortable on the Net?" is analogous to asking "Are women comfortable in bars?" For Bruckman, the better question is "Which woman? Which bar?"

In spite of these much-needed caveats, older worries regarding the quality of life for women on the Internet remain. Sexual harassment and stalking, for example, are still serious concerns, regardless of the increased presence of women online. A recent Ipsos-Reid study, conducted in 16 countries, found that girls were twice as likely as boys to have received unwanted comments of a sexual nature or repeated requests for face-to-face meetings during their time online.

GENDER PERFORMATIVITY ONLINE

Early proponents of cyberspace used to laud its potential as a gender-free environment. As a now-famous

New Yorker cartoon once joked, "On the Internet, nobody knows you're a dog" (the cartoon featured a picture of a dog surfing the 'Net). But feminist theorist of science N. Katherine Hayles argues that gender has always been a touchstone used to evaluate "what's real" in computer-mediated communication. In her 1999 book *How We Became Posthuman*, Hayles describes the genesis of the famous Turing Test, developed in the 1950s to distinguish between human and artificial intelligence. Professor Alan Turing's test required users to pose questions to an unseen recipient through a computer terminal. Based solely on text of the answers received, users were to determine whether they were talking with another human or with a computer simulation. Hayles points out that the earliest versions required users to guess at the gender of the entity on the other side of the screen, as well as its humanity. While Turing eliminated gender in later formulations of his test, Hayles points out, his early preoccupation with the question of gender in mediated environments anticipated discussions of online performativity that persist to this day.

In linguistics, the concept of performativity begins in the 1960s with the work of J.L. Austin, who was interested in moments in language when "saying something makes it so." Austin's famous example of performativity is the marriage ceremony, which requires a couple to say "I do" in order for their marriage to exist under the law. During the late 1980s, feminist theorist Judith Butler expanded on Austin's ideas to argue that gender is an example of performativity. Indeed, one only need consider the doctor's first pronouncement of "It's a boy" or a driver's license marked "female" to understand how, from the time we are born, authority's "saying" makes gender "so." In universities around the country, Butler's observations caused a great deal of consternation, especially among those who argued that gender was primarily a force of biology. However, Butler's notions influenced a great number of younger Americans, many of whom were beginning to gravitate toward the Internet.

During the early 1990s, Internet sociologists began charting a phenomenon they termed "virtual sexuality," including online role-playing (including gender-bending), the relationship of cybersex to cyberrape, and the role of computer-generated robots as members of Internet communities. In her 1995 book *Life on the Screen,* psychologist Sherry Turkle expressly linked linguistic performativity to

virtual sexuality, arguing that on the Internet especially, words held an exceptional power to "make things so." It wasn't that people were deluded about the differences between their online and offline lives, Turkle maintained; in her exhaustive interviews, she found that people knew full well that their online gender-swapping was not equivalent to living as a different gender offline. She also found that many users didn't care that they were flirting with robots online, rather than with real humans. Rather, Turkle hypothesized, some people (though not all) were exploring different identity choices in the "safe space" of cyberspace, as a way of psychologically "working through" and challenging their preconceived notions of gender. Perhaps, Turkle reasoned, their online sophistication might ultimately manifest itself offline as well.

Not every researcher agreed. As Internet ethnographer Lisa Nakamura observed, "This desire to escape from fixed identity roles is more than a passing fancy—it is a fancy for passing, a desire to try out different identity positions." Nakamura, who studied users who adopted "exotic" racial stereotypes online, argued that "far from sensitizing users to the often painful experience of Otherness, [in online 'passing'], Otherness itself becomes commodified."

It is important to remember that Turkle, Nakamura, and others formed their opinions about virtual sexuality during a period when text-based online environments were the norm. Since the adoption of the image-intensive Web in the 1990s, activities like gender swapping have grown significantly more difficult to execute successfully. Nevertheless, gender performativity is still alive and well in today's age of instantaneous visual exchange. In fact, one interesting byproduct of surveillance cameras on the Web has been an increased interest in documenting the performative aspects of one's "natural" gender for the world to watch. How else to explain the appeal of Web cameras like Jennicam.org, which purport to show "the real life of a real woman, online?"

FROM CYBORGS TO CYBERFEMINISM

The appeal of the "real life" Webcam echoes feminist theorist Donna J. Haraway's 1984 essay, "A Manifesto for Cyborgs," in which she argued that "we are all cyborgs"—that is, bodies composed partly of organic matter, and partly of machines. "Why should our bodies end at the skin?" asks Haraway, who urged women to engage technology from the "belly of the beast," lest they become its victims.

On the Internet, cyborg feminism manifested itself as the movement called cyberfeminism. Internet theorist Radhika Gajjala points out that even though there are many approaches to cyberfeminism, all agree that "women should take control of and appropriate the use of Internet technologies in an attempt to empower themselves." One such approach is outlined by Rosi Braidotti, who advocates "Riot Grrl feminism" and its propensity for do-it-yourself aesthetics online.

Internet ethnographer Krista Scott concurs with Braidotti, arguing that e-zines, personal home pages, Webcasts, and more are serving to redefine what it means to be called a "woman" in cyberspace. Today, these efforts seem to be paying off somewhat, at least according to a recent Pew Internet Study, which noted that far from finding the Internet alienating, many women have found it to be a way to forge connections with one another.

Still, it is important to remember that these Internet-generated connections between women still remain largely the privilege of those who can afford them. Perhaps the biggest challenge of the next decade will be how to expand cyberfeminism to include the poorest women in the world in a way that doesn't further alienate them. "By all means let [poor women] have access to the Internet, just as all of us have it—like chocolate cake or AIDS," writes activist Annapurna Mamidipudi. "Just let it not be pushed down their throats as 'empowering.' Otherwise this too will go the way of all imposed technology and achieve the exact opposite of what it purports to do."

Bibliography

American Association of University Women. "Tech Savvy: Educating Girls in the New Computer Age." April 5, 2000. <http://www.aauw.org/2000/techsavvy.html> (April 26, 2002).

Artamonova, Anna. "4.2m Russians accessed the net in the last 6 months." Europemedia.net, July 8, 2001. <http://www.europemedia.net/shownews.asp?ArticleID=4951&Print=true> (April 26, 2002).

Austin, J. L. *How to Do Things with Words*. Cambridge: Harvard University Press, 1975.

Braidotti, Rosi. "Cyberfeminism with a Difference." <http://www.let.ruu.nl/womens_studies/rosi/cyberfem.htm> (April 26, 2002).

Bruckman, Amy. "Finding One's Own in Cyberspace." *Technological Review,* January 1996. <http://llk.media.mit.edu/papers/1996/Bruckman.html> (April 26, 2002).

Butler, Judith. *Gender Trouble: Feminism and the Subversion of Identity*. New York: Routledge, 1990.

Gajjala Radhika, and Annapurna Mamidipudi. "Cyberfeminism and Development." *Gender and Development,* vol. 17, no. 2 (1999), pp. 8–16. <http://www.cyberdiva.org/erniestuff/cybergad.html> (April 26, 2002).

Haraway, Donna J. *Simians, Cyborgs, and Women.* New York: Routledge, 1991.

Hayles, N. Katherine. *How We Became Posthuman: Virtual Bodies in Cybernetics, Literature, and Informatics.* Chicago: University of Chicago Press, 1999.

Herring, Susan. "Posting in a Different Voice." *Philosophical Perspectives on Computer-Mediated-Communication.* Charles Ess, ed. Albany: State University of New York Press, 1996.

Ipsos-Reid. " Internet Youth Chat Sessions Lead to Correspondence and In-Person Encounters—Ipsos-Reid Study." Press release, January 31, 2001. <http://www.ipsos-reid.com/media/content/displaypr.cfm?id_to_view=1142&refer=main> (April 26, 2002).

Laurel, Brenda. "Technological Humanism and Values-Driven Design." Keynote address, CHI-98, Los Angeles, California, April 1998. <http://www.tauzero.com/Brenda_Laurel/Recent_Talks/Technological_Humanism.html> (April 26, 2002)

Nakamura, Lisa. "Passing Fancies: Identity Tourism on the Internet." Abstract for talk delivered at the Annual Meeting of the Pacific Ancient & Modern Language Association (PAMLA), University of California, Irvine, November 8–10, 1996. <http://www.humanities.uci.edu/English/ETC/nakamura.html> (April 26, 2002).

Miller, Laura. "Women and Children First: Gender and the Settling of the Electronic Frontier." *Resisting the Virtual Life.* James Brook and Iain A. Boal, eds. San Francisco, Calif.: City Lights, 1995.

Nielsen/NetRatings. "German Internet Audience World's Most Heavily Male, According to Nielsen/NetRatings Global Internet Index." Press release, July 25, 2001. <http://www.nielsen-netratings.com/pr/pr_010725_eratings.pdf> (April 26, 2002).

Pew Internet & American Life Project. "Tracking Online Life: How Women Use the Internet to Cultivate Relationships with Family and Friends." May 10, 2000. <http://www.pewinternet.org/reports/toc.asp?Report=11> (April 26, 2002).

Scott, Krista. "Girls Need Modems! Cyberculture and Women's Ezines." Master's research paper, York University, January 30, 1998. <http://www.stumptuous.com/mrp.html> (April 26, 2002).

Shade, Leslie Regan. "Gender Issues in Computer Networking." Unpublished manuscript; address given at Community Networking: The International FreeNet Conference, Carleton University, Ottawa, August 17–19, 1993.

Stone, Allucquère Rosanne. *The War of Desire and Technology at the Close of the Mechanical Age.* Cambridge, Mass.: MIT Press, 1995.

Turing, Alan M. "Computing Machinery and Intelligence." *Mind* 54 (1950), pp. 433–57.

Turkle, Sherry. *Life on the Screen: Identity in the Age of the Internet.* New York: Simon & Schuster, 1995.

Further Reading

The Ada Project. Homepage. <http://tap.mills.edu/> (April 26, 2002).

Association for Women in Computing. Web site. <http://www.awc-hq.org/> (April 26, 2002).

Cyberfeminism.net. Homepage. <http://www.artswire.org/subrosa/> (May 10, 2002).

Dyke Action Machine. Web site. <http://www.dykeactionmachine.com/> (April 26, 2002).

Supercomputer Center, University of California at San Diego. The Grace Hopper Celebration of Women in Computing (Conference), September 14–16, 2000. <http://www.sdsc.edu/Hopper/GHC_INFO/index.html> (April 26, 2002).

Harcourt, Wendy, ed. *Women@Internet: Creating New Cultures in Cyberspace.* London: Zed Books, 1999.

Institute for Women and Technology. Web site. <http://www.iwt.org/> (May 10, 2002).

National Science Foundation. "Women, Minorities, and Persons with Disabilities in Science and Engineering: 2000." March 25, 2002. <http://www.nsf.gov/sbe/srs/nsf00327/start.htm> (May 10, 2002).

Senft, Theresa, and Stacy Horn, eds. *Sexuality & Cyberspace: Performing the Digital Body* (*Women & Performance Special Issue,* no. 17). New York: Women & Performance Press, 1997. <http://www.echonyc.com/~women/Issue17/introduction.html> (May 10, 2002).

Systers. Web site. <http://www.systers.org/> (May 10, 2002).

Related Topics

Borg, Anita; Cyberfeminism; Cyborg; Echo; Haraway, Donna J.; Laurel, Brenda; "A Manifesto for Cyborgs"; Stone, Allucqu'ere Rosanne; Systers; Turkle, Sherry

— *Theresa M. Senft*

Gibson, William

1948–

Science-Fiction Author

In his 1984 book *Neuromancer,* novelist William Gibson coined the term "cyberspace," which, like "information superhighway," has been adopted as a universal euphemism for the Internet. That book and his subsequent novels have made Gibson the leader of a new school of science fiction called cyberpunk—a gritty, cynical rendering of the future that combines the punk attitude from rock 'n' roll culture, the cynical cadences of mystery writer Raymond Chandler, and an often hellish vision of a technocentric near future.

Gibson was born in Conway, South Carolina, the son of a civilian contractor who helped build the Oak Ridge plant that manufactured the first atomic bomb. After his father's death, Gibson moved with his mother to a small mountain town in southwestern Virginia, later moving on to attend boarding school in southern Arizona. He avoided the Vietnam War draft at age 19 by fleeing the United States for Canada, and has lived in Vancouver, British Columbia, since 1972.

Gibson wrote his first fiction when he was a student at the University of British Columbia, where he earned a bachelor's degree in English literature. In 1981, three years before he published his first novel, Gibson published the seminal short story "The Gernsback Continuum," which skewers the utopian techno-visions of past science-fiction writers, and goads emerging writers to address the ambivalence of a society where technology is both intimate and invasive, where the haves and have-nots must battle for control of a new, digital landscape. Some critics consider this short story to be the real blueprint for all cyberpunk to come.

Nonetheless, it is 1984's *Neuromancer,* Gibson's first novel, that remains the work with which his name and reputation are most often linked. *Neuromancer* concerns the exploits of an "interface cowboy" named Case whose stomping ground is "the matrix," a digital place where he performs virtual highway robbery (not unlike the online credit-card thefts that sometimes happen today) on behalf of a black-market data-crime syndicate. What Case really desires, though, is "the bodiless exaltation of cyberspace." Caught stealing from his employers, he is punished by having his nervous system and brain subtly damaged with a mycotoxin, rendering him unable to use his talents effectively as a cowboy in the Matrix. He is left with a body, nothing but "meat," imprisoned in his flesh, his reality miserably lacking in virtuality—until he finds a new way to "jack in" and ride the electronic range once again.

The theme of bodilessness is an important one in *Neuromancer,* and in Gibson's other books. "People hate to be reminded sometimes that they have bodies, they find it very slow and tedious," he told interviewer Dan Josefsson in 1994. "But I've never presented that as a desirable state, always as something almost pathological growing out of this technology."

For Gibson, cyberspace is a fascinating and crucial new development in the history of mankind. It can go so far as to level the economic playing field between classes, he has said, but it is not preferable to the experience of being physically and mortally human. He has related that he doesn't like the "highway" metaphor for the Internet that has emerged in recent years. A highway implies two-way traffic, but as the Internet becomes commercialized, Gibson believes, what is left is a kind of virtual shopping mall. "They want to give you an infomall where you pay for every bit of information you download, and you'll download from a menu that some corporation has assembled," he told Josefsson.

Gibson's subsequent works, many of which have been critically acclaimed and influential, have nonetheless failed to achieve the impact of *Neuromancer*, a book that won the Hugo Award, the Philip K. Dick Memorial Award, and the Nebula Award, all key honors for science-fiction writers. He wrote two *Neuromancer* sequels (*Count Zero*, 1986, and *Mona Lisa Overdrive*, 1988), and then turned to other themes. The 1992 "steampunk" fantasy *The Difference Engine*, co-written with Bruce Sterling, imagines a Victorian Age in which massive, steam-powered computers were developed. *Johnny Mnemonic*, a movie based on Gibson's ideas about cyberspace, was made in 1995. In 1993, Gibson's novel *Virtual Light* was a return to cyberpunk literature, but in a future much closer to our present. A sequel, *Idoru* (1996), returned his fiction to a favorite setting, Japan, for a meditation on the role of celebrity in a techno-centric age. Gibson finished up the trilogy with his most recent novel, *All Tomorrow's Parties* (2000), set in California, in which he takes his theme of bodiless virtual immersion to new extremes.

Most recently, Gibson has been featured in Mark Neale's independent film, *No Maps for These Territories* (2000), in which the laconic southerner's personality comes sharply into focus. The film in some sense brings Gibson full circle: It follows him and Neale as they travel across the country in a limousine, observing and commenting on the state of change as the world rushes deeper into a new computer-driven future. The real Gibson, as seen in the film, displays none of the frantic nervousness of his prose, but instead proves to be a rail-thin, quiet, slow-talking South Carolinian in his forties, a writer who admits to some embarrassment about the juvenile overtones of his earliest novels. But he also remains a thinker, still focused on his career's guiding themes.

Gibson will long be hailed as cyberpunk's prophet for laying the foundation of the genre by entrenching the character of the punk as hero in a society where people blend into machinery. Gibson's vision has served to spur on much of what has followed, not just in science fiction but in journalism (*Mondo 2000*, *Wired*), in movies (*The Matrix*), and even in serious discussions of the future of humanity (Bill Joy's influential essay "Why the Future Doesn't Need Us"). As such, William Gibson may be remembered as one of the late twentieth century's most pivotal literary figures.

Selected Works

Gibson, William. *All Tomorrow's Parties*. New York: Ace Books, 2000.

———. *Burning Chrome*. New York: Ace Books, 1987.

———. *Count Zero*. New York: Ace Books, 1986.

———. "The Gernsback Continuum." *Mirrorshades: The Cyberpunk Anthology*. Bruce Sterling, ed. New York: Ace Books, 1988; pp. 1–11.

———. *Idoru*. New York: G.B. Putnam and Sons, 1996.

———. *Mona Lisa Overdrive*. New York: Bantam Books, 1988.

———. *Neuromancer*. New York: Ace Books, 1984.

———. *Virtual Light*. New York: Bantam Spectra, 1993.

Bibliography

Doctorow, Cory. "No Maps for These Territories." *Wired* 9.08, August 2001. <http://www.wired.com/wired/archive/9.08/streetcred.html?pg=13>

Josefsson, Dan. "I Don't Even Have a Modem" (interview). Sevriges Television AB, 1995. <http://www.josefsson.net/gibson/> (May 10, 2002).

O'Hara, R. Andrew. "William Gibson" (interview). October 1996. <http://members.tripod.com/~rem_ind/visual/gibsonint.htm> (May 10, 2002).

"The Salon Interview: William Gibson." Salon, August 27, 1996. <http://www.salon.com/weekly/gibson961014.html> (May 10, 2002).

Further Reading

Cyberpunk Project. "Cyberpunk Literary Style." April 3, 2000. <http://www.cyberpunkproject.org/idb/cyberpunk_literary_style.html> (May 10, 2002).

Möttönen, Sari. "About a Science Fiction Movement Called Cyberpunk." *Nettiset Webzine*, February 1997. <http://www.cc.jyu.fi/jyucomm/nettiset/ns001/juttu010.html>

Leonard, Andrew. "Gibson Hits Overdrive." *Wired* 4.10, October 1996. <http://www.wired.com/wired/archive//4.10/streetcred.html> (May 10, 2002).

Sterling, Bruce, ed. *Mirrorshades: The Cyberpunk Anthology.* New York: Ace Books, 1988.

Related Topics

Cyberpunk; Cyberspace; Joy, Bill; *Neuromancer*; Sterling, Bruce

— Kevin Featherly

Graphical User Interface

Graphical user interfaces (GUI, pronounced "gooey") are visual displays of software and information presented on a computer monitor. The most common GUIs in personal computing are the Apple Macintosh OS and Microsoft Windows. GUIs consist of the desktop icons, program windows, toolbars, and menus that users first encounter on their operating system desktops, as well as in most any program they use. Thanks to GUIs, it is no longer necessary to learn complicated programming and text commands and shortcuts to accomplish tasks when using a program, allowing the user to focus instead on the work at hand. Through the use of GUIs, users communicate with their computers and perform a variety of functions, like starting programs, emptying the trash, moving windows, and so on.

GUI Origins

When computers were first introduced to the general public, they had to be operated via complex punch-card systems. Eventually, users were able to abandon the punch-card system in favor of a text-only operating system. Users would see a command prompt on a blank screen, and would have to input textual command codes (e.g., "run" and "copy"), similar to those found in MS-DOS personal computer systems. Knowledge of programming languages allowed users to write their own programs to handle simple tasks. The extent of a computer's use was defined, and often restricted, by what the user could get the system to do through programming or text commands.

Between 1972 and 1974, researchers at the Xerox Palo Alto Research Center (PARC), created a computer called the Alto that featured a mouse, a network card, the first GUI, and Smalltalk, a computer language. These components helped aid users to communicate more easily with their computers. During these years, Xerox PARC researchers like Jef Raskin, Bruce Horn, and Alan Kay were trying to create an easier-to-use interface for computers. Prototypes for Xerox's computer named Star drew the attention of Steve Jobs, head of Apple Computer. After visiting Xerox PARC, Jobs later hired many of these same researchers to work on his two lines of Apple computers, Lisa and Macintosh.

There is disagreement among computer aficionados as to whether or not Apple "stole" Xerox's ideas and interfaces. Some records say that Jobs saw only the Alto and not the Star; some say he saw a working model of the Star; and some claim that Apple computers already had its own ideas being put into production, and that all Jobs really did was share ideas. Regardless of which version of the story a person believes, the fact is that Xerox's Star, released in 1981, was the first computer to have a GUI operating system available to commercial businesses, while Apple Computer's Lisa, released in 1983, was the first computer sold to the public that had a working GUI. Because Apple used stronger marketing techniques and targeted the general public, Apple became known as the first computer with a GUI.

Even with the new GUI concept, Lisa was not a commercial success, and was ultimately pulled off the market, to be succeeded by the Macintosh (Mac) and an improved GUI, with features that would become standards of a working Macintosh desktop, and later the IBM PC-clone Windows desktop. Users could double-click on folders, drag unwanted files to a trashcan, choose various options from pull-down menus, and even customize what they wanted to see on their desktop when the computer booted up.

Around this time, Microsoft Corporation was involved with producing computer languages for operating systems. Bill Gates met with Jobs, and saw the Mac prototype and its GUI. Gates decided to hire some of the Mac GUI researchers; eventually, Microsoft created a GUI for IBM clones called Windows 1.0. Apple later sued Microsoft, since the Windows GUI looked strikingly similar to the Mac interface, but lost due to vagueness in the wording of its licensing technologies agreements. Credit for the appearance of the more common GUIs for operating systems can be traced back to the Macintosh computer, which helped to create the GUI standard.

GUIs consist of three main components. The first is a windowing system, which allows for windows and menus to appear on the screen. With the windowing system, multiple tasks can be run simultaneously in a single screen space; the capability of minimizing, maximizing, and overlapping windows became an important feature of GUIs. The second component is an imaging model that standardizes displayed graphics, colors, and fonts. Consistency within the programs' GUIs is necessary in order to curb user confusion, and also to begin to standardize the layout that a user can expect. An application program interface (API), the third component, allows programmers to specify what windows and graphics they would like to appear on the screen at any given time. The majority of computer operating systems and software programs utilize these three components when designing GUIs.

The first real GUIs commercially marketed were originally designed for computer operating systems. Both the Mac and Windows GUIs followed what was initially called the WIMP model (windows, icons, menus, and push-buttons/point-and-click/pull-and-drag). Icons, small pictures on the desktop, corresponded to program-executable files, which could be opened by pointing and clicking on a given icon. Windows containing bits of information, groups of icons, or programs became a standard, as did the ability to run commands by pulling down a menu and choosing the desired function—all via mouse instead of code or keyboard shortcuts (e.g., using the mouse to move the cursor to select File\Save versus keying the Ctrl+S command). By using WIMP, people were able to issue commands to a computer without having to worry about textual codes and programming. Since the acronym WIMP held negative connotations, the name was changed to graphical user interface, or GUI.

GUIs in the Consumer Market

GUIs have become an integral part of any commercial program being distributed to consumers. Thanks to the integration of graphics, text, and mouse clicks into an application's GUI instead of employing codes, programs become easier to learn, and users are better able to focus on the task at hand rather than on the complex programming that would otherwise be involved in running the system. Accordingly, the commercial products for task-related events that become the most widely used and integrated by consumers impact the GUI standards on all other parallel commercial products. By keeping GUIs similar, programmers and manufacturers decrease the learning curve for new software and applications.

Microsoft is the leader in software applications for task-related events such as word processing and spreadsheet creation. The software application packages that it produces have standardized GUIs so that the "look" of one Microsoft program is similar to others. GUIs are kept constant, so that users who are

familiar with the basic layout and look of Microsoft GUIs will find it easier to use its other products, and would be more willing to remain product-loyal when searching for other programs for different tasks. If a competing program wants to gain market entry, companies designing the software find that their products need to look like already-established software programs. For example, Corel WordPerfect's interface was initially structured via hotkey commands, and was not point-and-click driven. Over time, with the increase in use of Microsoft Word, WordPerfect's GUI began to employ the pull-down menu features of Word, and now generally has the same overall layout.

Mosaic was the first Web browser that utilized a GUI to make it easier for people to search the Internet. Some members of the same team who created Mosaic's GUI created the GUIs for Netscape; therefore, while Netscape added to browser design, its appearance was similar to that of Mosaic. However, Netscape was able to corner the market for Internet Web browsers, and thus became the industry standard—so much so that even Microsoft's Internet Explorer uses the same GUI layout techniques, while adding some new components. Internet Web browsers' GUIs have impacted users so powerfully that GUIs designed for Windows '98 and later versions have modeled their windows and push-buttons to look like those found on the browsers.

A great many users have become familiar with the WIMP-model GUI, thus dictating the features that need to be built into new programs being introduced into the market. As with the QWERTY keyboard, however, many feel that even though the WIMP model is the "standard" and most widely used GUI, it may not be the best. Nevertheless, due to its popularity, it seems very likely that the WIMP model will remain at the forefront of GUI designs.

Bibliography

Crow, D., and B. J. Jansen. "Seminal Works in Computer Human Interaction." *SIGCHI Bulletin*, 30:3 (1998), pp. 24–28.

Every, David K. "Microsoft, Apple, and Xerox: The History of the Graphical User Interface." July 16, 1998. <http://www.mackido.com/Interface/ui_history.html/> (March 22, 2002)

Hayes, Frank, and Nick Baran. "A Guide to GUIs." *Byte Magazine*, vol. 4 (July 1989), pp. 250–57.

Smith, D. C.; Irby, C.; Kimball, R.; Verplank, B.; and E. Harslem. "Designing the Star User Interface." *Byte Magazine*, April 1982, pp. 242–82.

Further Reading

Cooper, Alan. *About Face: The Essentials of User Interface Design.* Foster City, Calif.: IDG Books Worldwide, 1995.

Mandel, Theo. *The Elements of User Interface Design.* New York: John Wiley & Sons, 1997.

Related Topics

Interface; Jobs, Steven P.; Object-Oriented Programming; Xerox Palo Alto Research Center

— *Kathy Broneck*

Graphics See Computer Graphics.

Grids

The term grid refers to a new infrastructure that builds on the Internet and the World Wide Web to enable and exploit the large-scale sharing of resources within distributed, often loosely coordinated groups—what are sometimes called virtual organizations. Grid infrastructure provides scalable, secure, high-performance mechanisms for discovering and negotiating access to remote resources. The availability of grid infrastructure, when combined with ubiquitous Internet connectivity and exponentially faster networks (performance per unit cost doubles every nine months), enables entirely new, often communication-intensive grid applications.

Grid concepts and technologies emerged first within the scientific-computing community, as a means of pooling computers; streaming large amounts of data from databases or instruments to remote computers; linking sensors with each other and with computers and archives; and connecting people, computing, and storage in collaborative environments that reduce the need for travel. However, interest within corporate industry is also growing rapidly, as companies realize that the needs of advanced e-business have much in common with those of e-science: Both require systems that span multiple institutions and that execute reliably, delivering consistent performance despite heterogeneous hardware, software, and policies.

The central motivation for grid computing is the fact that in a world where communication is nearly free, we need not be restricted, when solving problems, to local resources. For example, users can run interesting computer programs (games, scientific simulations, and so on) remotely, rather than installing them locally. When analyzing data, users can have the remote software access relevant datasets directly.

Computations can be repeated hundreds of times, on different datasets, by calling upon the collective computing power of a company or research collaboration—or by purchasing cycles from a cycle provider. Users can then review output with remote colleagues in rich collaborative environments.

While high-speed networks are often necessary to implement such scenarios as these, they are far from sufficient. Remote resources are typically owned by others, exist within different administrative domains, run different software, and are subject to different security and access-control policies. These issues have historically made distributed computing difficult. In order to access remote resources, users must first discover that they exist, then negotiate (and perhaps pay for) access, then configure their computation to use them effectively—and they must do all these things without compromising their own security, or the security of the resources on which they are calling.

Today's Internet and Web technologies address basic communication requirements, but do not provide uniform mechanisms for such critical tasks as creating and managing services on remote computers; supporting "single sign-on" to distributed resources; transferring large datasets at high speeds; or forming large, distributed virtual communities and maintaining information about the existence, state, and usage policies of community resources. Grid technologies address these and other related needs, providing simple infrastructure elements that can be broadly deployed and then used to develop advanced computing applications, much as today's Internet and Web protocols provide the substrate for communication applications.

Grid concepts date back to the earliest days of computing: Discussions of the ARPANET in 1969 talked about grid scenarios. However, the event that moved grid concepts out of the network laboratory was the I-WAY experiment led by Tom DeFanti and Rick Stevens, an ambitious effort that linked 11 experimental networks to create, for a week in November 1995, a national high-speed network infrastructure that connected resources at 17 sites across the United States and Canada. Some 60 application demonstrations, running the gamut from distributed computing to virtual-reality collaboration, showed the potential of high-speed networks. The I-WAY experiment also presented the first unified grid software system, I-Soft, which provided single sign-on, unified scheduling, and other services.

Research and development has produced considerable consensus on grid architecture principles and technologies; in particular, the community-based, open-source Globus Toolkit is being applied by most major grid projects, and is seeing significant industrial adoption. Numerous government-funded research and development projects are developing core technologies, deploying production grids, and/or applying grid technologies to challenging applications. (See http://www.mcs.anl.gov/~foster/grid-projects for a list of major projects.) Industrial interest is growing; for example, a dozen companies announced support for the Globus Toolkit in late 2001. Progress has also been made on organizational fronts: The Global Grid Forum is a significant force for standard-setting and community development.

Grid computing is a compelling example of how sustained, exponential technology evolution can have revolutionary impacts on the practice of computing. With high-speed networks becoming ubiquitous, and with e-business and e-science concepts achieving broad adoption, we can expect grid technologies and applications to become a major part of the computing landscape.

Bibliography

Catlett, C. "In Search of Gigabit Applications." *IEEE Communications Magazine,* vol. 30, no. 4 (April 1992), pp. 42–51.

Foster, Ian, and Carl Kesselman, eds. *The Grid: Blueprint for a New Computing Infrastructure.* San Francisco, Calif.: Morgan Kaufmann, 1999.

Foster, Ian; Kesselman, Carl; and Steven Tuecke. "The Anatomy of the Grid: Enabling Scalable Virtual Organizations." *International Journal of High Performance Computing Applications,* vol. 15, no. 3 (2001), pp. 200–22. <http://www.globus.org/research/papers/anatomy.pdf> (May 10, 2002).

Global Grid Forum. Web Site. <http://www.gridforum.org> (May 10, 2002).

Kleinrock, L. "The Latency/Bandwidth Tradeoff in Gigabit Networks; Gigabit Networks Are Really Different!" *IEEE Communications Magazine,* vol. 30, no. 4 (April 1992), pp. 36–40.

Further Reading

Committee on a National Collaboratory Establishing the User-Developer Partnership. *National Collaboratories: Applying Information Technology for Scientific Research.* Washington, D.C.: National Academy Press, 1993.

Leiner, Barry M.; Cerf, Vinton G.; Clark, David D.; Kahn, Robert E.; Kleinrock, Leonard; Lynch, Daniel C.; Postel, Jon; Roberts, Larry G.; and Stephen Wolff. "A Brief History of the Internet." August 2000. <http://www.isoc.org/internet-history/brief.html> (May 10, 2002).

Licklider, J.C.R., and R.W. Taylor. "In Memoriam: J. C. R. Licklider (1915–1990). The Computer as a Communication Device." *Science and Technology,* April 1968. <http://memex.org/licklider.pdf> (May 10, 2002).

Teasley, S., and S. Wolinsky. "Scientific Collaborations at a Distance." *Science* 292 (2001), pp. 2,254–55.

Related Topics

Broadband; Business-to-Business; Data Mining; DeFanti, Thomas; Distributed Computing; Peer-to-Peer; Security; Software Agents

— *Ian Foster*

Habitat

The first online chat system with a graphical rather than a text-based interface, Habitat greatly influenced the development of future systems. Both the design decisions made for Habitat and the social lessons that emerged from it continue to shape the online graphical-chat industry. Created in 1988–89 by Chip Morningstar and F. Randall Farmer, Habitat ran for several years in the United States before moving to Japan, where Fujitsu still operates a version called Habitat II. In the United States, Habitat's direct descendant, WorldsAway, later became VZones, operated by Avaterra.com, Inc.

Habitat was originally developed for LucasFilms through the online service QuantumLink. The use of Commodore 64 computers by QuantumLink's subscribers confined Habitat's designers to the capabilities of what even then was an outdated and very limited machine. Given the fact that almost all online communication occurred through text at that time, Habitat's creators accomplished a great deal with a very small amount of computing power, and pioneered the use of graphical representations for online chat users.

Habitat started at about the same time that MUDs (Multi-User Dungeons or Dimensions) were becoming popular online, and it resembled many of the social MUDs, but with the addition of graphics. MUDs are online text-based systems; users, sometimes numbering in the hundreds, connect to a single computer and communicate with each other through text. MUDs are set up to textually represent a virtual world and allow people to chat, explore the virtual environment, and play games with each other or with the computer. Habitat most closely resembled TinyMUDs, which also got started in 1989. TinyMUDs differed from the previous, more game-oriented MUDs in that they did not include a scoring system and allowed users greater freedom to create their own virtual environments. Similarly Habitat had an open-ended virtual economy rather than a scoring system, and allowed users considerable freedom of choice with regard to activities and use of its virtual world.

Habitat looked like an animated cartoon. Houses, trees, and other landscape features were represented by simple, blocky graphics, and people were represented by avatars, which looked like cartoon characters. Avatars—the term is derived from a Hindu word referring to the worldly incarnation of a god—represented individual users in Habitat, serving as their virtual selves in the graphical environment. The avatars were usually human in appearance, and users could customize them somewhat by choosing from a variety of different heads. In keeping with the cartoon style, even speech in Habitat appeared as text-filled balloons over the avatars' heads.

Avatars could also acquire and interact with various objects in the virtual environment. "Vending machines" allowed users to purchase objects, using tokens. A certain number of tokens were given to each avatar each day as the user logged on, so the longer a user participated, the more control he could have over the environment. Since objects could be sold as well as bought, users could exchange objects and create a simple virtual economy. In one instance, a few savvy users discovered that one vending machine was buying certain objects for a higher price than another machine was charging for them. Overnight, these users engaged in the tedious task of repeatedly buying from one machine and selling to the other over and over again, until they had amassed a considerable fortune in tokens.

Many of Habitat's initial participants considered themselves to be building an online community. Some created analogues to offline social practices and institutions; users created an online church, a newsletter, and a sheriff's office (to deal with such crimes as theft and the "murder" of one avatar by another), and held social events such as treasure hunts, parties, and online avatar weddings. Habitat's designers gave users a great deal of freedom in organizing these online institutions and activities, and felt that such latitude was important to the appeal and viability of the system. Essentially, this amounted to applying user-centered principles to the design of online graphical systems, and letting the users determine to some extent the direction of design decisions.

A variety of companies continue to expand upon Habitat's legacy. In addition to the existing graphical-chat systems, developers are attempting to expand graphical virtual worlds for other uses. Habitat creators Morningstar and Farmer, along with their associate Douglas Crockford, formed Electric Communities (later Communities.com) in 1993, and hoped through the company to expand the application of online graphical spaces to consumer and other business uses. However, graphical-chat spaces have been slow to catch on in the business community, and Electric Communities filed for bankruptcy in early 2001.

Bibliography

Morningstar, Chip, and F. Randall Farmer. "The Lessons of Lucasfilm's Habitat." *Cyberspace: First Steps.* Michael Benedikt, ed. Cambridge, Mass.: MIT Press, 1991.

Further Reading

Damer, Bruce. *Avatars!* Berkeley, Calif.: Peachpit Press, 1998.
Rheingold, Howard. *The Virtual Community: Homesteading on the Electronic Frontier.* Reading, Mass.: Addison-Wesley, 1993.

Related Topics

Avatar; Cyberspace; Lucas, George; MUDs and MOOs; TinyMUD; Virtual Community

— *Lori Kendall*

Hacking, Cracking, and Phreaking

Hacking, cracking, and phreaking are all ways of gaining access to protected or classified channels of information by an unconventional use of communications and information technologies. Phreaking manipulates telephone signaling in order to make free phone calls, while hacking typically involves using a computer and a modem to break into protected systems and networks. Hackers can be classified as white hat (good) or black hat (nefarious). They use a wide variety of programs and technologies, including but not limited to: logic bombs, denial-of-service attacks, password crackers, demon dialers, and sniffers. The term cracking is sometimes used to describe the act of hacking solely for the intention of making a profit or to destroy a system. Typically, only those familiar with hacking and hacker culture will employ the term cracking, whereas mainstream journalism and popular discourse simply uses the term hacking to refer to a wide variety of practices, including cracking.

PHONE PHREAKING

Phreaking is a way of emulating the 2,600 MHz (megahertz) tones that allows one to make free telephone calls. According to Paul Mungo and Brian Clough, authors of a 1992 book about hackers called *Approaching Zero,* the term "phreak" comes from a combination of the words phone, free, and freak.

Phone phreaking first began in the 1960s and continued until 1983, when the techniques of phreaking had been made obsolete by new developments in the telephone companies. Some people could whistle in a perfect 2,600 MHz pitch, most notably a blind man named Joe Engressia, who became known as the whistling phreaker. Also, a man named John Draper discovered that a whistle distributed as a prize in Captain Crunch cereal emitted a perfect 2,600 pitch. Draper, who became a very popular phreaker, came to be known as Captain Crunch. However, the most typical way of phreaking involved the use of what was known as a blue box or Mfer, a multifrequency transmitter that allowed the user the same access as a Bell operator. Blue boxes were constructed by phreakers using the 12 tones described in the *Bell System Technical System Journal* (1954 and 1960). Both Engressia and Draper, who were friends, distributed blue boxes to many blind children so that they could make free phone calls.

Phreaking entered the popular imagination in October 1971, when *Esquire* featured a story about phreaking entitled "The Secrets of the Little Blue Box." Phreaking became popular on university campuses, prompting future Apple Computer founders Steve Jobs and Steve Wozniak to make blue boxes long before they built their first Macintosh.

During the 1970s, phreaking had become associated with political radicalism. Abbie Hoffman, leader of the Youth International Party Line (YIPL), became interested in phreaking as a means of resisting telephone monopoly. Hoffman described phreaking as a way of liberating Ma Bell. In 1971, Hoffman and a phreaker known as "Al Bell" began publishing a newsletter called *Party Line,* which described ways of subverting telephone lines for their own uses. In 1973, *Party Line* became known as *TAP,* standing for "technological assistance program." Hoffman advocated liberating the telephone lines because he believed that taking control of communications systems would be a crucial action for mass revolt. In order to democratize telephony, *TAP* published many articles from AT&T's technical journals. In the spirit of freedom of information, *TAP* also published phone numbers for the White House and Buckingham Palace. By the mid-1970s, AT&T revealed that it lost approximately $30 million per year to telephone fraud, including phreaking.

Techniques of phreaking also included a technique called "social engineering"—using interpersonal persuasion skills to gain information, a method that hackers continue to employ. "Shoulder surfing" was also employed by phreakers, meaning that they might look over people's shoulders as they entered passwords or credit-card numbers. Phreakers also examined dumpsters outside of phone company offices and other locations in order to find discarded manuals or equipment.

Phreaking as such ended in 1983, when telephone lines were upgraded to Common Channel Interoffice Signaling (CCIS), which separated signaling from the voice line. The year 1983, which also marked the end of TAP, was when Bell's monopoly was shattered, splintering the company into the regionals (Bell South, Bell Atlantic, Bell Pacific) as competitors such as Sprint and MCI emerged. As phreaking became obsolete, the personal computer became widely accessible, inaugurating the era of the hacker.

Although phreaking largely died out, the spirit of phreaking infuses hackers and hacking even to the present day. In fact, many phreakers became hackers when personal computers and modems became available during the early 1980s. The hackers of the 1980s emerged from the same tradition as phreakers, with their anti-bureaucratic sentiments and belief that lines of communication should be free.

From Phreakers to Hackers: A History of Hacking

Hacking emerged as a term during the 1960s at MIT, used to describe a particularly elegant program written by a programming expert known as a hacker. By the early 1980s, hacking had come to indicate the ability to break into computer systems in order to acquire protected information and materials, and also to gain an understanding of how those systems work. Pranks also form a central feature of hacking culture; witness the time when hackers broke into the CIA site and changed the title to the "Central Stupidity Agency." The successful completion of what hackers call a "prestige hack," such as breaking into the Pentagon or the National Security Agency (NSA), will usually be followed by

the hackers posting evidence of their success, thereby gaining prestige within the hacking community.

By 1984, hacking had become popular (or notorious) enough to warrant a book devoted to it: Steven Levy's *Hackers*. Along with Levy's book, John Markoff and Katie Hafner's 1991 book *Cyberpunk* contributed to the cliché of the hacker that still circulates today. The profile of the hacker has come to be that of an adolescent white male who is generally anti-social and maladapted, but who uses his virtuosity with computers to break into computer systems and feel a sense of power. The prototype of the hacker was Kevin Mitnick, known in the media as the "superhacker." In 1981, the 17-year-old Mitnick was convicted of stealing computer manuals from Pacific Bell. The next year, he broke into the American Air Defense Command Computer. Mitnick eventually spent time in jail for hacking, becoming a cause célèbre in the hacking community.

A more recent book, Paul A. Taylor's *Hackers* (1999), also describes the hacker as anarchic, secretive, and strongly anti-bureaucracy and anti-government. The popular stereotype also relies on the notion that the hacker is apolitical, breaking into such systems as the FBI or CIA only for the sake of personal curiosity or prestige, rather than for political or economic reasons.

Hackers have often tried to define for themselves and in their own words what hacking means and who hackers are. At the 1989 "Galactic Hacker Party," an international hacker's convention, speakers insisted on two principles that are central to a hacker's belief system: Information should be free, and computer technologies should not be used by government and corporate institutions to control and oppress people. Hackers tend to share a belief in the absolute openness of information, regardless of any perceived harm that such free access might precipitate.

To this end, early hackers in the 1980s based their operations on bulletin-board systems (BBSs). Here, hackers could exchange information not readily found elsewhere, such as credit-card numbers, copies of software, and instructions on making bombs. Needing only access to a computer with a modem, the hacker now was able to acquire and disseminate both practical and controversial materials. On the BBSs, hackers formed alternate identities, such as Phiber Optik, Knightmare, and the Marauder. They could join or fight hacker groups such as the German Chaos Computer Club, the NASA Elites, or the notorious Legion of Doom.

Breaking into a system depends on operating in secrecy and under the shroud of invisibility. The invisibility of hacker's identities, locations, and practices precipitated a crisis for law enforcement. Furthermore, the popular press has sensationalized hackers and hacking, and often relies on fictionalized or anecdotal information in news coverage.

One particularly notorious hacking incident involving law enforcement, computer scientists, top-secret CIA and NSA information, and journalism was popularized by Clifford Stoll in his 1989 book, *The Cuckoo's Egg: Tracking a Spy Through the Maze of Computer Espionage*. Stoll recounts a 1989 case in which German hackers paid by the KGB had been breaking into military systems, including Milnet, the military network, in order to view weapons specifications and other classified information. The Cuckoo's Egg incident linked hacking with international espionage. No longer simply maladjusted teens, hackers came to be viewed in some quarters as an international threat to security. Financial institutions became more vigilant about network security, and the stock of Internet security corporations soared.

HACKING IN THE 1990S AND TO THE PRESENT

Hacking has come under serious investigation by a number of governmental agencies, including the Secret Service. In July 1990, the Secret Service raided a number of locations thought to hold copies of detailed technical information from Bell South regarding the Emergency 911 system. As cyberpunk science-fiction author Bruce Sterling mentions in his 1992 book *The Hacker Crackdown*, the Secret Service claimed that hackers' possession of knowledge about the Emergency 911 system would constitute a threat to national security.

One of the raids targeted a company called Steve Jackson Games for allegedly possessing this Emergency 911 information. Although no such information was found on the premises, the computing capacity of the company was severely crippled as a result of the raid. The Electronic Frontier Foundation (EFF) was established to provide the legal defense for Steve Jackson Games. The EFF was founded by Grateful Dead lyricist John Perry Barlow, former president of Lotus Development Corporation Mitch Kapor, and early member of Sun Microsystems John Gilmore. The EFF has continued to protect speech against governmental regulation; one of its recent cases has involved the hacker subculture magazine *2600: The Hacker Quarterly*, a publication that emerged in 1984 as a journal for hackers, by hackers.

During the late 1990s, hacking was regularly discussed in the mainstream news by security experts.

In 1999 supporters of hacker Kevin Mitnick protest outside the federal courthouse in Philadelphia. (AP Photo/Rusty Kennedy)

Reports of viruses, worms, and Trojan horses proliferated, and the shadow of the hacker seemed to lurk behind every unusual occurrence on the Internet. The Pentagon estimates that its computer networks are hacked around 250,000 times per year. Hacking became linked with the threat of online wars waged by online terrorists, prompting Rand prognosticators John Arquilla and David Ronfeldt to predict a cyberwar in the near future. Security experts frequently pointed out the vulnerability of the Internet, indicating that its decentralized design makes regulation and security very difficult.

Concerns grew over hackers being paid by unfriendly governments to wage cyberterrorism, or by corporations to conduct corporate espionage. Rand Corporation's Roger Molander notes that cyberattacks are a growing security concern at an early stage of evolution. In 1997, the NSA hired 35 hackers to stage simulated attacks on the United States and its information infrastructure. The hackers quickly reached the deepest level of access, known as root access, in 36 of the Department of Defense's networks, and were also able to easily shut down the power grid and all 911 systems. Such concern over Internet vulnerability led the FBI to create a new unit, the National Infrastructure Protection Center, in 1998.

Today, many hackers have applied their technical skills toward the goal of online political activism, also known as hacktivism. During the 1990s, hackers—many of whom no longer conform to the stereotype of the antisocial, apolitical teenaged male—became politicized. Hackers have played major roles in wars and political conflicts, including the war in Kosovo, which is known as the first hacking war, or cyberwar. Furthermore, some geopolitical conflicts have expanded to cyberspace, as Indian and Pakistani hackers battle online and Israeli and Palestinian hackers attack each other's Web sites. Hackers will undoubtedly continue to use their skills in the name of religious and political goals, prompting calls for greater security and regulation from governments and corporations.

Bibliography

CSIS Task Force. *Cybercrime Cyberterrorism Cyberwarfare: Averting an Electronic Waterloo.* Washington, D.C.: CSIS Press, 1998.

Hafner, Katie, and John Markoff. *Cyberpunk: Outlaws and Hackers on the Computer Frontier.* New York: Simon & Schuster, 1991.

Levy, Steven. *Hackers: Heroes of the Computer Revolution.* New York: Anchor Press/Doubleday, 1984.

Mungo, Paul, and Bryan Clough. *Approaching Zero: The Extraordinary Underworld of Hackers, Phreakers, Virus Writers, and Keyboard Criminals.* New York: Random House, 1992.

Sterling, Bruce. *The Hacker Crackdown: Law and Disorder on the Electronic Frontier.* New York: Bantam, 1992.

Stoll, Clifford. *The Cuckoo's Egg: Tracking a Spy through the Maze of Computer Espionage.* New York: Doubleday, 1989.

Taylor, Paul A. *Hackers: Crime in the Digital Sublime.* New York: Routledge, 1999.

Further Reading

2600: The Hacker Quarterly. Web site. <http://www.2600.com/> (May 17, 2002).

Computer Underground Digest. Homepage. Updated December 1, 2000. <http://www.soci.niu.edu/~cudigest> (May 17, 2002).

Cult of the Dead Cow. Web site. <http://www.cultdeadcow.com/> (May 17, 2002).

Guisnel, Jean. *Cyberwars: Espionage on the Internet.* New York: Plenum Trade, 1997.

Ludlow, Peter, ed. *Crypto Anarchy, Cyberstates, and Pirate Utopias.* Cambridge, Mass.: MIT Press, 2001.

Power, Richard. *Tangled Web: Tales of Digital Crime from the Shadows of Cyberspace.* Indianapolis, Ind.: Que, 2000.

Schwartau, Winn. *Cybershock: Surviving Hackers, Phreakers, Identity Thieves, Internet Terrorists, and Weapons of Mass Disruption.* New York: Thunder's Mouth Press, 2000.

Related Topics

Barlow, John Perry; Computer Emergency Response Team; Cyberwarfare; Electronic Civil Disobedience; Electronic Frontier Foundation; Hacktivism; Kapor, Mitchell; Security; *2600: The Hacker Quarterly*

— *Heidi Marie Brush*

Hacktivism

Hacktivism uses the usual tools and strategies of hackers for explicit political ends. Hacktivists may target the Web sites of the organizations whose behavior, politics, or symbols they dislike. They can try to disrupt an organization's internal information networks, search for private information that will help a protest movement plan strategy or expose wrongdoing, or damage an organization by defacing or debilitating Web sites. Hacktivist goals can range from trying to spread the message of a social movement to trying to destroy a target organization's computing facility.

Some hacktivists use different kinds of viruses for political ends, constructing programs that copy themselves either independent of or related to a damaging instruction. For example, a hacker might write a quine virus program that generates complete copies of itself as part of its output, a worm virus program that reproduces itself across a network, or a wabbit virus program designed to perpetually duplicate itself, at least until the system crashes. In contrast to the wabbit's slow growth, a fork bomb quickly generates multiple copies itself. Other hacktivists might use a Trojan horse that carries a virus on as an infected program engages with other programs.

Whereas a hacker might use these kinds of viruses to propagate silently for some time before shutting down systems and generating cute messages, a hacktivist deliberately times viral activity to coincide with other staged political events, often making his or her political critiques clear through an overt message in the hack.

Hackers often target specific organizations—from firms to state agencies, the military, and non-profit charities—but hacktivists have an explicit ideological program that helps them justify their selection of targets. Unlike most hackers, they rarely work alone, and are by definition part of a broader ideological project. Just as an activist can come from any part of the political spectrum, hacktivists and their projects cover a wide range of political objectives.

Most hacktivists share the conviction that information is a public good, and feel that they have a political responsibility to use their skills to force the information they feel should be out of organizations and into the public sphere. In this sense, hacktivists are often described as informational Robin Hoods, who believe that governments and corporations control people by controlling the flow of information. Hacktivists believe that they have a responsibility to expose abuses of power and to redistribute informational resources.

For example, a frequent hacktivist objective is to protect the Internet from over-regulation. Hacktivists were involved with the battle over the Communications Decency Act of 1996, and more recently have played a role in international politics. Wars between pro-Israeli and pro-Palestinian hackers erupt through attacks on each other's Web sites and information infrastructures. When a Chinese fighter jet collided with an American spy plane in 2001, Chinese and American hacktivists defaced and aggressively attacked each other's Web sites. To protest globalization, hacktivists have stolen and broadcast the credit-card numbers and private financial information of world political leaders attending international conferences. In Mexico, a group called x-ploit hacked a government Web site and put up pictures of Emiliano Zapata, hero of the Zapatista rebels in the southern state of Chiapas. They threatened to continue their hacktivism by using their skills to expose government corruption, make the world aware of human-rights abuses within the justice system, and protest the treatment of Zapatistas in particular.

Hacktivism, like hacking, is illegal, but hacktivists claim to work for a higher moral authority. They want their hacks to change behavior and attitudes. Like hackers, hacktivists have an informal organization based on meritocracy and high-profile hacks, but their personal affiliation is with an issue-specific group. Depending on the cause, the news media will label some hacktivists as cyberterrorists. Because they take greater risks by targeting powerful political actors, hacktivists tend to be even more secretive than hackers, who are often willing to share technical tricks, software, and even computer resources. They marry their enthusiasm for programming with political agendas, and go beyond the usual hacker ethic to actively press their political commitments.

Bibliography

Critical Art Ensemble. *The Electronic Disturbance.* Brooklyn, N.Y.: Autonomedia, 1994.

Harmon, Amy. "'Hacktivists' of All Persuasions Take Their Struggle to the Web." *The New York Times*, October 31, 1998, p. A1.

Ludlow, Peter, ed. *Crypto Anarchy, Cyberstates, and Pirate Utopias.* Cambridge, Mass.: MIT Press, 2001.

Schwartau, Winn. "Cyber-Civil Disobedience: Political Dissent in the 90's." <http://www.infowar.com/class_3/cybciv.html-ssi> (May 10, 2002).

Further Reading

Hacktivism. Web site. <http://hacktivism.openflows.org/> (May 10, 2002).

The Hacktivist. Web site. <http://thehacktivist.com/> (May 10, 2002).

Stalbaum, Brett. "The Zapatista Tactical FloodNet: A collaborative, activist and conceptual art work of the net." <http://www.nyu.edu/projects/wray/ZapTactFlood.html> (May 10, 2002).

Related Topics

Communications Decency Act; Cyberwarfare; Electronic Civil Disobedience; Hacking, Cracking, and Phreaking; Security

— *Philip E. N. Howard*

Haraway, Donna J.

1944–

U.S. Academic

Donna J. Haraway is a feminist historian of science and technology, perhaps best known for her "invention" of cyborg studies in the 1990s. She is currently a professor in the History of Consciousness Program at the University of California, Santa Cruz.

Donna Haraway was born in Denver, Colorado. Her mother was a Colorado native, and her father moved there as a boy from Tennessee to be treated for childhood tuberculosis. In spite of life-long physical disabilities associated with illness, Haraway's father was an avid sports fan, working as a sports writer for the *Denver Post* throughout her childhood. Her mother, a devout Irish Catholic, died in 1960, when Haraway was 16. As a young girl, Haraway attended Catholic schools, and after high school she enrolled at Colorado College, a small liberal arts school where she received a full scholarship, and where she became active in the civil rights movement occurring across college campuses at the time. She graduated with a major in zoology and minors in philosophy and English literature.

In 1966, Haraway was awarded a Fulbright to study the history and philosophy of science in Paris. When she returned to the United States, she was accepted for graduate school in biology at Yale University. While at Yale, Haraway lived in an academic commune and was active in the anti-Vietnam War movement. Her dissertation, which concerned the use of metaphor in the history and philosophy of biology, was accepted in 1972, and later published in 1976 as the book *Crystals, Fabrics, and Fields*.

In 1970, Haraway married Jaye Miller, a graduate student in history at Yale, and the two moved to the University of Hawaii in Honolulu. In 1974, Haraway left Hawaii and moved to Baltimore, Maryland, where she was hired as an assistant professor in the Department of the History of Science at Johns Hopkins University. Then in 1980, she moved again, this time to teach feminist studies and science studies in the History of Consciousness Program at the University of California, Santa Cruz. She has remained on faculty at Santa Cruz for more than 20 years, developing her long-range academic focus— the relationship between feminism, anthropology, and the history of science.

Haraway's personal politics have long fueled her writing. In 1973, she and her husband Jaye Miller separated, as Miller, openly gay since 1968, grew more involved with gay rights and activism. Still, the two remained close friends. In 1974, she met Rusten Hogness, a graduate student in the History of Science at Johns Hopkins, with whom she has lived ever since. In 1977, Haraway, Miller, and Hogness bought land together in Healdsburg, California, where they shared a house with Miller's lover Robert Filomeno until Filomeno's death from AIDS in 1986; Miller succumbed to the same disease in 1991.

As Haraway explained to interviewer Thyrza Nichols Goodeve, "From the beginning and to the present, my interest has been in what gets to count as nature and who gets to inhabit natural categories." *Primate Visions* (1989), Haraway's first book after her dissertation, investigated the field of primatology, a discipline that she argued was as much about "the origin and nature of 'man'" as it was about the world of monkeys. At the same time, Haraway was writing the essays for *Simians, Cyborgs, and Women: The Reinvention of Nature*, published in 1991. In them, she coupled her discussions about the breakdowns between animals and humans (for example, baboon heart transplants in humans) with analyses regarding the raging "border wars" between humans and machines (for example, the increased use of prosthetic body parts, the labor of women in the microprocessing industries, and the rise of telecommunications networks).

Simians, Cyborgs and Women worked to create an "ironic mythology" for feminists who were encountering technoculture for the first time. It contained a reprint of Haraway's 1985 paper called "A Manifesto for Cyborgs," which she wrote when the editors of *Socialist Review* asked her to describe "what socialist-feminist priorities are in the Reagan years." In this paper, she argued that feminists needed to engage the "cyborg" body, which in her reading had a very specific history: It was only made possible after World War II; it came about through specific scientific and military developments; and it is tied to communications, psychiatry, behavioral, and psychopharmacological theories of information-processing. Advocating neither technophobia nor technophilia, Haraway instead argued that the contradictory militaristic/life-saving histories of the cyborg mandated that women take responsibility for their participation in the technological world. According to Haraway, "we are all cyborgs" in part, because we live in a political moment when our bodies and the bodies of those around us are constantly being read and interpreted as "information machines."

Modest_Witness@Second_Millennium.FemaleMan© _Meets_OncoMouse™: Feminism and Technoscience (1997) continues Haraway's themes of "body as information machine" and personal responsibility in a technocultural age, dealing with such topics as patent and copyright laws, the Human Genome Project, and fetal imaging. In addition to the primate and the cyborg, Haraway's ever-expanding "metaphorical menagerie" now includes Onco-Mouse, a transgenic mouse that develops tumors to aid in breast-cancer research. Haraway argues that whether or not women may approve of the creation of transgenics (which traverse the boundary between nature and labor the way that the cyborg traversed the boundary between human and machine), they will nonetheless "someday owe a huge debt" to the contributions of transgenics to scientific research.

Haraway's future research plans will cross even more borders between the "hard" and "social" sciences. One of her newest projects is an inquiry into the teaching of biology, in a transnational context; another is an investigation of forest-conservation struggles, focusing on indigenous versus scientific knowledge of forestry. She is also exploring the belief systems that people hold regarding the breeding, behavior, and genetics of dogs. Whatever she tackles next, Haraway plans to continue her practice of "modest witnessing." She defines that act as a "collective, limited practice that depends on the constructed and never finished credibility of those who do it, all of whom are mortal, fallible, and fraught with the consequences of unconscious and disowned fears and desires."

Selected Works

Haraway, Donna J. "The Biopolitics of Postmodern Bodies: Determinations of Self in Immune System Discourse." *Differences: A Journal of Feminist Cultural Studies* 1:1 (1989).

———. "enlightenment@science_wars.com: A Personal Reflection on Love and War." *Social Text*, no. 50 (Spring 1997).

———. *How Like a Leaf: An Interview with Thyrza Nichols Goodeve*. New York: Routledge: 2000.

———. "A Manifesto for Cyborgs: Science, Technology and Socialist Feminism in the 1980s." *Socialist Review*, no. 80, 1985.

———. "Mice into Wormholes: A Technoscience Fugue in Two Parts." *Cyborgs and Citadels: Interventions in the Anthropology of Technohumanism*. Gary Downey and Josephy Dumit, eds. Santa Fe, N.M.: School of American Research, 1998.

———. *Modest_Witness@Second_Millennium. FemaleMan©_Meets_OncoMouse™: Feminism and Technoscience*. New York: Routledge, 1997.

———. *Primate Visions: Gender, Race, and Nature in the World of Modern Science*. New York and London: Routledge, 1989.

———. "The Promises of Monsters: A Regenerative Politics for Inappropriate/d Others." *Cultural Studies*. Lawrence Grossberg, Cary Nelson, Paula A. Treichler, eds. New York; Routledge, 1992; pp. 295–337. <http://www.stanford.edu/dept/HPS/Haraway/monsters.html> (May 10, 2002).

———. *Simians, Cyborgs and Women: The Reinvention of Nature*. New York and London: Routledge, 1991.

———. "Situated Knowledges: The Science Question in Feminism as a Site of Discourse on the Privilege of Partial Perspective." *Feminist Studies* 14, no. 3 (1988).

———. "Teddy Bear Patriarchy: Taxidermy in the Garden of Eden, 1908–36." *Social Text*, no. 11, (Winter 1984/85).

Bibliography

Haraway, Donna J. *How Like a Leaf: An Interview with Thyrza Nichols Goodeve*. New York: Routledge, 2000.

Kunzru, Hari. "You Are Cyborg." *Wired* 5.02, February 1997. <http://www.wired.com/wired/archive/5.02/ffharaway_pr.html> (May 10, 2002).

Further Reading

Christie, R. R. John. "A Tragedy for Cyborgs." *Configurations* 1:1, 1993, pp. 171–96.

Erratic Impact's Philosophy Research Base. "Donna J. Haraway Resources." <http://www.erraticimpact.com/~feminism/html/women_haraway.htm> (May 10, 2002).

Mercer, Trudy. "Donna Haraway." Feminist Science Fiction Speculative Fiction and Fantasy (FSFSFF) Resources for the Serious Fan. <http://www.drizzle.com/~tmercer/fsfsff/resources/haraway.shtml> (May 10, 2002).

Scott, Krista. "Notes on Donna Haraway." Stumptuous.com. <http://www.stumptuous.com/comps/haraway1.html> (May 10, 2002).

———. "The Cyborg, the Scientist, the Feminist and Her Critic." Stumptuous.com, 1997. <http://www.stumptuous.com/cyborg.html> (May 10, 2002).

Sells, Laura. "Donna Haraway: A Permanently Incomplete and Always Partial Annotated Bibliography." <http://www.svdltd.com/sells/voxygen/donna.htm> (May 10, 2002).

Tonella, Karla. "Border Crossings: Cyborgs." Department of Communication Studies—Cultural Studies Resources, University of Iowa, January 20, 2000.

<http://www.uiowa.edu/~commstud/resources/ bordercrossings/cyborgs.html> (May 10, 2002).

Zupko, Sarah J. "Theorists and Critics: Donna Haraway." Popcultures.com, June 1, 1996. <http://www.popcultures.com/theorists/haraway.html> (May 10, 2002).

Related Topics

Cyberfeminism; Cyborg; Gender and New Media; "A Manifesto for Cyborgs"

— Theresa M. Senft

Hillis, W. Daniel

1956–

Technology Innovator and Entrepreneur

W. Daniel Hillis, an inventor, scientist, engineer, consultant, visionary, and author—among other things—is known for his futuristic thinking, revolutionary designs, and wild imagination. Renowned for creating massive parallel supercomputers, Hillis aspires to change the way that people think about technology.

Hillis was born in Baltimore, Maryland, in 1956, and spent the majority of his youth living in a variety of developing countries; his father, a scientist, explored the occurrence of hepatitis among children throughout the world. As an undergraduate in mathematics at the Massachusetts Institute of Technology (MIT), he developed computer hardware and software for children at MIT's Logo Laboratory, as well as toys and games for the Milton Bradley Co. Before receiving his bachelor of science degree in 1978, Hillis co-founded Terrapin, Incorporated, where he designed computer software for elementary-school students. By 1981, Hillis received a masters of science in robotics at MIT while studying artificial intelligence. There, he was credited with producing tendon-controlled robotic arms, and built a tic-tac-toe computer from fishing line and 10,000 Tinkertoy parts. (The tic-tac-toe computer can currently be viewed at the Boston Computer Museum.)

After receiving a Ph.D. in computer science from MIT in 1988, he developed and marketed a new technology known as the massive parallel supercomputer, which forever changed the standard of supercomputing—the process of calculating, computing, and processing vast amounts of information. Hillis co-founded Thinking Machines Corporation in Cambridge, Massachusetts, to market the supercomputer; his dissertation, *The Connection Machine,* became a very successful book.

Hillis' Connection Machine was sold to such establishments as Harvard University, American Express, and NASA. The massive parallel-supercomputing power of the Connection Machine transformed the standard of supercomputing through a change in processing that utilizes Hillis' design concepts of parallelism. In contrast to sequential computing, where one computer processor attacks one computing objective quickly, parallel computing used anywhere from 32 to 64,000 computer processors simultaneously to accomplish many tasks at once. Sequential computer processing can be compared to one ant digging a tunnel quickly; parallel computing is 64,000 isolated ants digging many smaller tunnels, in synchronization, to form one big one very quickly.

By 1985, Hillis had created by far the fastest computer in the industry. The Connection Machine enabled visualization of simulated events—for example, the result of two galaxies colliding—that were inconceivable by other means. Upon leaving Thinking Machines in 1995, he formed a consulting company called DHSH. In 1996, Hillis left DHSH to work full-time for one of the company's clients—the Walt Disney Company.

While with Disney, Hillis became vice president of research and development, as well as fellow, and developed business strategies and new technologies. His efforts contributed to the design of theme-park rides, and to a full-sized robot dinosaur. As Hillis explained in an article that he wrote for *Forbes* magazine in 1997, his job entailed teaching Disney to utilize technology.

Thriving on his ability to imagine what the future will be like, Hillis contemplates the future many decades from now, rather than a few years from now. He believes that the problem with technology has been the way it hindered people, and that this phenomenon has been responsible for stunting thinking to a short-term standpoint. *Wired* magazine freelance writer Po Bronson described the meaning of a "Hillisesque" object: If something is "Hillisesque" it represents Hillis' goal of changing the way that one thinks about technology. For instance, why should one believe that a computer could function only on electricity when Hillis considers it possible to construct a computer that derives its power from water that runs through copper plumbing?

Hillis co-founded the Long Now Foundation in 1996, which dedicated its efforts to creating a 10,000-year clock. The clock is Hillis' brainchild, and is being designed to run accurately through the year 12,000. It is expected to bear one of the world's largest pendulums, as well as three-ton sandstone dials. Hillis' design embraces technology that is capable of self-adjusting itself to the noon sun while ticking only once a day. The clock's construction, it is hoped, will inspire its viewers. According to the Long Now Foundation, the goal of the 10,000-year clock is to encourage thinking that is slower and better. In addition, the designers of this "Hillisesque" object wish its presence to encourage collective thought about the next 10,000 years.

Hillis also serves as co-chairman and chief technology officer of Applied Minds, a research and development company he co-founded that creates products and services for the technology industry. He consults and develops software applications, mechanical devices, and electronics.

Hillis' technological contributions are plentiful and overwhelming, earning him award-winning recognition. He has received acknowledgment for his inventions through the Spirit of America Creativity Award (1991), and through the Hopper Award (1989) for contributions to computer science; he has also received the Ramanujan Award (1988) for his studies in applied mathematics. Hillis also served on President Bill Clinton's Information Technology Advisory Committee. He holds more than 40 patents that cover his 10,000-year clock, parallel computers, forgery prevention methods, and disk arrays among other inventions.

In an interview with *Omni Magazine,* Dr. Hillis spoke of his most recent projects, including an idea known as "computer evolution by computer." Similar to the way that genetics works for humans, computer evolution by computer would create machines able to solve problems themselves. The concept presents many interesting opportunities for ethical debate on the subjects of human and mechanical evolution; with his strong imagination, his creative ability to visualize the future, and his numerous inventions, Hillis has been, and will continue to be, at the forefront of these debates.

Selected Works

Hillis, W. Daniel. *The Connection Machine.* Cambridge, Mass.: MIT Press, 1985.

———. "Working at Child's Play." *Forbes,* December 1, 1997. <http://www.forbes.com/asap/1997/1201/113_print.html>

———. "The Big Picture." *Wired,* January 1998. <http://www.wired.com/wired/archive//6.01/hillis_pr.html>

———. *The Pattern on the Stone: The Simple Ideas that Make Computers Work.* New York: Basic Books, 1998.

Bibliography

Bronson, Po. "The Long Now: Time-Traveling with Danny Hillis." *Wired,* May 6, 1998. <http://www.wired.com/wired/archive//6.05/hillis_pr.html> (April 5, 2002).

Mitchell, Dan. "Clinton Puts High-Tech Honchos on Panel." *Wired,* February 13, 1997. <http://www.wired.com/news/print/0,1294,2043,00.html> (April 5, 2002).

Further Reading

Garreau, Joel. "Thinking Outside the Box." *Washington Post,* March 19, 2001. <http://washingtonpost.com/ac2/wp-dyn/A23937-2001Mar18?language=printer> (April 5, 2002).

Shasha, Dennis, and Cathy Lazere. *Out of Their Minds: The Lives and Discoveries of 15 Great Computer Scientists.* New York: Copernicus, 1995.

Related Topics

Media Lab, Massachusetts Institute of Technology

— *James Pyfer*

Hoffman, Donna

19??–

E-Commerce Researcher and Analyst

Donna Hoffman is a psychologist and management professor at Vanderbilt University's Owen Graduate School of Management. A leading authority on e-commerce and a pioneer in Web research, Hoffman has been hailed by *Newsweek* as one of the 50 "people who matter most on the Internet."

After receiving a Ph.D. in quantitative psychology at the University of North Carolina-Chapel Hill, Hoffman made important contributions to psychometric research methods for modeling customer perception. Her work with George R. Franke on correspondence analysis and the graphical representation of categorical data earned the prestigious William O'Dell Award in 1991 for the most significant long-term contribution to the marketing discipline.

In the early 1990s, Hoffman began research on consumer behavior in hypermedia computer-mediated environments (CMEs) such as the World Wide Web. She studied online customer behavior and developed standardized measurement methodologies for relating online visits and network navigation patterns to consumer response. By 1994, Hoffman was doing advanced work on the implications of CMEs for consumer behavior.

In 1994, Hoffman and Thomas Novak founded eLab, the renowned e-commerce research laboratory. *The New York Times* called eLab one of the "premiere research centers in the world for the study of electronic commerce." Hoffman and Novak apply advanced research methods and fundamental principles of business and economics to create a framework for understanding the strategic marketing implications of CMEs. Along with models for marketing and advertising, they study the policy implications of new media, including privacy, anonymity, consumer rights, and ethics.

Hoffman proposes a vision of the Internet as an open, democratic marketplace. The many-to-many network properties of the Web permit both consumer choice and corporate efficiency; the immediacy and transparency of the Web shifts the power balance toward individual consumers in their relationships with the large organizations that have dominated markets in recent years.

In an attention economy, companies must establish trust. The results of any transaction are felt quickly. The immediate, aggregated behavioral feedback of customers and potential customers through the online medium is even swifter than the effect of reputation in older forms of business. The relationship between a firm and its customers changes rapidly in an environment where alternatives are within immediate reach. All forms of commerce constitute an information and service package, as well as a possible product or service purchase.

According to Hoffman, information providers must be honest and up-front in order to stay in business in this environment. Collapsing time-scales bring short-term tactics and long-term strategy close together; this inevitably affects marketing strategies so that ethics becomes a necessity rather than a preference in the CME environment. This explains Hoffman's optimism and her faith in the democratic possibilities of the electronic marketplace.

Since the flow of information is linked to social interaction and the exchange of products and services in CMEs, the medium itself acquires vast new importance. Hoffman states that the Internet is the most important cultural innovation since the development of the printing press. CMEs offer an operating environment as well as an information medium. They become a forum for human behavior and interaction. It is the possibility of community in an all-at-once, many-to-many network that makes CMEs radically different than any communication medium that came before. Where most media shape changes in society and in the world, the printing press and CMEs have demonstrated a far higher gearing ratio than most technologies exert. This ratio is visible in the many differences in the world before and after printing and CMEs were introduced; both have radically transformed cultures in many ways over a short period.

Hoffman's large-scale vision of the Internet as a public forum also leads her to an active role in public policy. One of her most famous contributions to the larger public debate on Internet issues was her critique of a deeply flawed study on Internet pornography in the mid-1990s. Hoffman and Novak's sensible, articulate critique of the study reshaped public opinion by creating a climate for reasoned debate. Later, she served as an expert witness on the Communications Decency Act (CDA) portion of the Telecommunications Bill of 1996.

Donna Hoffman's work demonstrates how rigorous scholarship contributes to public good anchored in public markets. Hoffman herself is a model of the public intellectual, and a pioneering visionary in cyberspace.

Selected Works

DeSarbo, Wayne, and Donna L. Hoffman. "Simple and Weighted Multidimensional Unfolding Threshold Models for the Spatial Representation of Binary Choice Data." *Applied Psychological Measurement* 10:3 (1986), pp. 247–64.

Hoffman, Donna L. "An Argument for Qualitative Ratings." *Television Quarterly* 21:4 (1985), pp. 39–44.

Hoffman, Donna L.; Kalsbeek, William D.; and Thomas P. Novak. "Internet and Web Use in the United States: Baselines for Commercial Development." *Communications of the ACM* 39 (December 1996) (special section on Internet in the Home), pp. 36–46.

Hoffman, Donna L., and Thomas P. Novak. "Bridging the Racial Divide on the Internet." *SCIENCE*, April 17, 1998.

———. "Marketing in Hypermedia Computer-Mediated Environments: Conceptual Foundations." *Journal of Marketing* 60 (July 1996), pp. 50–68.

———. "A New Marketing Paradigm for Electronic Commerce," *The Information Society* 13 (special issue on Electronic Commerce, January–March 1996), pp. 43–54.

Hoffman, Donna L.; Novak, Thomas P.; and Marcos A. Paralta. "Information Privacy in the Marketspace: Implications for the Commercial Uses of Anonymity on the Web." *The Information Society* 15:2 (April–June 1999), pp. 129–40.

Hoffman, Donna L.; Novak, Thomas P.; and Patrali Chatterjee. "Commercial Scenarios for the Web: Opportunities and Challenges." *Journal of Computer-Mediated Communication* 1:3 (special issue on Electronic Commerce, 1995).

Novak, Thomas P., and Donna L. Hoffman. "Residual Scaling: An Alternative to Correspondence Analysis for the Graphical Representation of Residuals from Log-Linear Models." *Multivariate Behavioral Research* 25 (July 1990), pp. 351–70.

Novak, Thomas P. and Donna L. Hoffman. "New Metrics for New Media: Toward the Development of Web Measurement Standards." *World Wide Web Journal* 2:1 (Winter 1997), pp. 213–46.

Bibliography

Rheingold, Howard. "Mind to Mind with Donna Hoffman: The Medium Is the Market."(Interview.) <http://www.well.com/user/hlr/texts/mindtomind/hoffman.html> (April 5, 2002).

Further Reading

Boisot, Max H. *Information Space: A Framework for Learning in Organizations, Institutions, and Culture.* London: Routledge, 1995.

Flichy, Patrice. *Dynamics of Modern Communication: The Shaping and Impact of New Communication Technologies.* London: Sage Publications, 1995.

Friedman, Ken. "Information, Place and Policy." *Built Environment,* 24:2/3 (1998), pp. 83–103.

Jones, Steven G., ed. *Cybersociety 2.0. Revisiting Computer-Mediated Communication and Community.* Thousand Oaks, Calif.: Sage Publications, 1998.

Related Topics

Digital Divide; E-Commerce; Hypermedia; Internet; Lessig, Lawrence; Varian, Hal; World Wide Web

— *Ken Friedman*

Human-Computer Interaction

Human-computer interaction (HCI) is the study of how people use computer hardware and software, and the application of that knowledge to the design and development process in order to make computers easier to use. At its broadest, HCI can legitimately take in such disciplines as organizational psychology (how the deployment of computers affects a corporation), cognitive psychology (how human brains process information somewhat like a computer), communication (how humans communicate via computers), and sociology (how social factors affect people's behavior); however, it is essentially an applied science that is most concerned with improving the usability of computers and the productivity of users.

HUMANS AND COMPUTERS

The three essential elements of HCI are the human, the computer, and the interface between the two.

Humans are thinking, reasoning beings that behave according to theories and models of the world that are based on past experience. They have limited memories and attention spans. Their ability to concentrate and perform tasks varies, for reasons as unpredictable and arbitrary as the time of day or whom they might be meeting for lunch. Most importantly, they learn and are intelligent, so their learning for one task can be generalized to help with other tasks.

Computers share some of these characteristics. They are better at storing and retrieving information consistently, and better at processing information quickly, but worse at recognizing patterns, and almost completely incapable of generalizing their learning to other tasks; they are not, so far, intelligent. The problems that HCI seeks to investigate and address stem essentially from the differences between humans and computers at the place where they meet: the so-called user interface, which includes everything from a laptop's on-off switch to the choice of icons on its screen, from the angle at which users sit to the shape of the mouse they use.

Although HCI has always been important, it became a crucial issue with the proliferation of personal computers during the early 1980s. In the mainframe-dominated world of the 1960s and 1970s, trained computer operators, locked away with their behemoths in high-security vaults, were a physical embodiment of human-computer interaction, skilled interpreters fluent in both human and machine who kept computers quite separate from the scientists and engineers who typically made use of (but seldom actually used) them. Today, many people use computers or computer-based devices, and the quality of the user interface can make the difference between the success and the failure of a technically excellent product.

APPROACHES TO HCI

Arguably, there is no more justification for a subject called human-computer interaction than for those called human-building interaction, human-automobile interaction, or human-book interaction; HCI is simply the application of age-old design principles—such as architect Mies van der Rohe's famous statement that "less is more"—to computer technology. The approach known as user-centered design involves users at all stages of the computer-design process, from initial market-research to final prototype testing. User-centered design implies that the user interface must be developed before other elements of the product, and that usability professionals must be properly integrated into the development team. Apart from prioritizing the quality of a product's usability over the quantity of its features, user-centered design stresses other values, such as making the user interface consistent (all panels look the same), intuitive (activating the icon of a trash can will delete the files it contains), predictable (there will always be a way to save work in draft form), reversible (users must confirm that they want to delete files), and customizable (expert users can program their own shortcuts).

Although HCI is an academic and sometimes theoretical discipline, its cutting edge is often to be found in product-design laboratories run by hardware and software manufacturers around the world; the collaboration between academia and industry has been crucial to the success of HCI. The product-focused, market-driven approach to HCI is typically known as usability or human factors (the terms often used interchangeably), and concentrates either on designing new products around their users or making existing products easier to use. The usability approach involves understanding the users of a product (user analysis) and the jobs they are likely to do with it (task analysis). Prototype products undergo usability testing, typically in a laboratory equipped with video cameras that record typical users carrying out typical tasks.

The difference between usability and HCI is sometimes confusing; industrial HCI specialists usually devote most of their time to usability concerns, for example. But it may be convenient to think of usability as that part of HCI concerned with individual products and the tasks they enable users to perform, whereas HCI overall has a broader remit that can extend to how groups of people use computers in general, or to the organizational or wider social impact of computer technology.

Where usability specialists are sometimes employed only as advisers, and their expertise may be called on only at relatively late stages of the product-development cycle (when a prototype is ready to test), user-interface designers tend to be involved at the earliest stages of product design (when the technical specifications are first written). The difference between usability and user-interface design may simply reflect organizational culture—and the difference between a company that designs technically innovative or feature-packed products

before "prettifying" them with a usable interface, and one that starts from the user interface to begin with. User-interface designers are responsible for all aspects of the human-machine interface, including writing manuals and online hypertext help—or better still, making the product so intuitively easy to use that no manual is required (see entry for Information Design).

The concerns of HCI extend beyond usability and user-interface design. Other key areas include the development of interfaces for users such as the elderly and the disabled, for whom standard interfaces are inadequate. This requires even greater focus on the "human" part of HCI—for example, accounting for differences in short-term memory or speed of response due to the aging process, or developing input/output devices tailored to accommodate particular disabilities.

Another key aspect of HCI is the development of entirely new interfaces that bring computers closer to people, such as voice, handwriting, and gesture recognition, and software that can understand natural language (ordinary language as spoken by humans). Future developments along these lines may include eye-guided pointers to replace the mouse, and computer "screens" projected directly onto the user's retina. Today's window-based graphical user interfaces (GUIs) are also being developed into more sophisticated forms of interaction. These include a 3D interface called Task Gallery, currently under development at Microsoft Research, which expands the traditional two-dimensional desktop interface into a complete 3D office.

HISTORICAL DEVELOPMENT

HCI can trace its origins back to the industrial psychology and ergonomics movements that became popular in the early decades of the twentieth century, particularly during World War II, when different nations battled for tactical advantage (for example, with airplanes that would be more responsive than others during a dogfight). But the field really began to develop in the 1960s, with work by such pioneers as Ivan Sutherland and Douglas Engelbart. Sutherland's Sketchpad graphics-drawing system, outlined in a paper in 1963, pioneered the kinds of "direct-manipulation" interfaces (in which an external input device such as a mouse moves objects on the screen) that are used in every PC sold today. The mouse itself was first demonstrated by Engelbart in 1968, in a text-editing system called NLS.

The GUI is now popularly associated with Microsoft Windows, based on the user interface of the Apple Macintosh (1984) and its forerunner, the Apple Lisa (1983). But Apple borrowed ideas substantially from the Alto workstation designed in the 1970s at Xerox Palo Alto Research Center (PARC), which in turn owed a debt to work on the use of a tiled-window interface in Engelbart's NLS.

The human-computer interface includes information that helps users to accomplish their tasks as well as the hardware and software with which they accomplish them. The user interface to online information has been revolutionized by hypertext, a method of designing information as a set of relatively small, highly interlinked modular chunks that can be read in whichever order the user wishes. A child of many "fathers," hypertext was outlined by U.S. government scientist Dr. Vannevar Bush in 1945, named by Ted Nelson for his never-realized system Xanadu, and refined by such pioneers as Andries van Dam and Ben Shneiderman. Hypertext has been most extensively (but perhaps least perfectly) realized in the design of the World Wide Web by Tim Berners-Lee.

The Importance of HCI

Although computers became affordable with the arrival of microcomputers (early, non-standard PCs) in the mid-1970s, they became truly ubiquitous only in the 1980s, with the standardization of their internal design, built around the IBM PC, and their external user interface, built around the windows-icon-mouse-pointer (WIMP) or GUI interface. HCI can take much of the credit for this, transforming microcomputers popular with hobbyists into PCs popular with the general public. Where every computer application program once seemed to work differently, applications today are standardized around a windowed interface that looks and behaves in a consistent and predictable way, whether it runs on a Windows PC, a Macintosh, a UNIX workstation, or even a personal digital assistant (PDA) or a wireless application protocol (WAP) phone.

Despite this general gain in usability and the continuing advance in computer performance, human productivity has gained little from the massive deployment of computer technology, if HCI expert Thomas Landauer is to be believed. Observing that "Productivity growth in the United States and other developmentally advanced nations went into a long, hard-to-explain slide from the early 1970s on, coinciding with the period of large-scale deployment of business computing," he blames this lack of progress on a continuing lack of commitment to "usefulness and usability." The problem is often that the developers of a product are seldom its typical users, and if they are not on the receiving end of its design drawbacks, they have no immediate incentive to worry about them.

The World Wide Web brought another problem to light: What it originally gained in usability through the standardization of HTML and the basic browser interface, it has now partly lost through the proliferation of different approaches to Web-page design and functionality. Search engines, for example, have deceptively similar interfaces (keywords are usually typed into a box), but are hampered by subtle differences (multiple keywords are often processed in different ways by different search engines). The commercialization of the Web requires Web sites to make themselves distinctive at a time when usability requires increasing standardization. On commercial Web sites, usability takes on crucial importance since, as HCI guru Jakob Nielsen states, "E-commerce sites are eminently easier to leave than a physical store."

All told, HCI has been tremendously beneficial to the usability of computer technology, helping to make its deployment much more widespread and requiring, in turn, an even greater commitment to usability. Despite unique problems raised by computer technology, usability is really part of a wider design aesthetic. Architects and industrial designers have always had to reconcile the problem of standardizing their designs around human expectations with the need to simultaneously exceed those expectations and delight their users; user-interface designers must learn to do the same.

Bibliography

Landauer, Thomas. *The Trouble with Computers.* Cambridge, Mass.: MIT Press, 1995.

Meister, David. *The History of Human Factors and Ergonomics.* Mahwah, N.J.: Lawrence Erlbaum Associates, 1999.

Myers, Brad A. "A Brief History of Human Computer Interaction Technology." *ACM Interactions,* vol. 5, no. 2 (March 1998), pp. 44–54. <http://www.cs.cmu.edu/~amulet/papers/uihistory.tr.html> (March 22, 2002).

Nielsen, Jakob. *Designing Web Usability: The Practice of Simplicity.* Indianapolis, Ind.: New Rivers, 1999.

Further Reading

Bardini, Thierry. *Bootstrapping: Douglas Engelbart, Coevolution, and the Origins of Personal Computing.* Stanford, Calif.: Stanford University Press, 2000.

Dix, Alan; Finlay, Janet; Abowd, Gregory; and Russell Beale. *Human-Computer Interaction.* Hemel Hempstead, England: Prentice-Hall, 1998.

Helander, Martin, ed. *Handbook of Human-Computer Interaction.* Amsterdam: North Holland/Elsevier, 1997.

Nielsen, Jakob. *Usability Engineering.* San Francisco: Morgan Kaufmann Publishers, 1993.

Shneiderman, Ben. *Designing the User Interface: Strategies for Effective Human-Computer Interaction.* Reading, Mass.: Addison-Wesley, 1997.

Related Topics

Engelbart, Douglas; Graphical User Interface; Hypertext; Information Design; Kurzweil, Raymond; Nelson, Theodor Holm (Ted); Nielsen, Jakob; Responsive Environments; Sutherland, Ivan; Usability

— *Chris Woodford*

Hypermedia

The term hypermedia refers to a nonlinear way of organizing and presenting information in multiple media. The design of hypermedia offers challenges to technical developers, and hypermedia applications have aroused great interest among educational and information designers, as well as artists of various kinds.

Hypermedia are often introduced as more "interactive" ways of engaging media than the more "passive" methods such as reading books or watching television. The consumer of hypermedia material may decide what to read or watch by following links, or may cause things to happen by interacting with programs. Hypermedia also offer the opportunity for people to write parts of stories, then leave an open ending for others to fill in. This kind of interaction is not easily performed in media that are more "static" and difficult (or impossible) to change or that demand greater-than-average technical skills. Most people can write a piece of text, or select pictures among a database of clip-art; thus, hypermedia offer the opportunity to interact with the material given, and to create new material that may be used by other people.

THE EVOLUTION OF HYPERMEDIA

The "father" of hypermedia, at least on a technical level, is usually thought to be Vannevar Bush (1890–1974). In 1932, he started developing ideas for a system later called the Memex (memory extender). Two important concepts were involved: the recording of individual, independent pieces of information, and the linking of these pieces that would make it possible to retrieve records very quickly by going from one to the next. For scientists, this storage and linkage system would solve the problem of keeping track of and retrieving an exponentially increasing amount of information.

The idea of linking information to a text is very old, and is most notably employed through use of footnotes and indexes in books and other printed materials. In addition, dictionary and encyclopedia readers have learned to read short pieces of information independent of other items, and to find relevant references within these short pieces.

The idea of "hypertext" can extend beyond footnotes, indices, and dictionaries, enabling readers to read and follow a story in a non-sequential manner. This idea was realized in books written with forking paths, which allow readers to decide which path to follow, and thereby decide what will happen next in the narrative. This type of hypernovel required a lot of turning of pages, and did not become particularly popular. However, when computers enabled readers to read books via computers, it became easier to "turn the pages," and alternate paths began to be designed for computers rather than for books. The idea of links between parts is also an essential concept for the design of computer games; a quick transition between images is needed to maintain the illusion of changes in a stable world.

The first computer applications prioritized text over pictures. Word processors as well as databases and administration systems primarily needed text and numbers. The ASCII (American Standard Code for Information Interchange) code provided a means by which computers could translate binary symbols into letters and numbers, but there was no way of easily working with graphics in the early days of computing. Creative visual artists found ways to generate graphical representations using ASCII, creating a genre known as ASCII art.

In 2002, multimedia is commonplace in computer applications, and encompasses everything from a simple combination of text and pictures to complex movies and Web sites. The term multimedia is also used in various computer and non-computer contexts: in information provision, educational demonstrations and simulations; in entertainment; and in advertising and other business applications. The most far-reaching place for multi- and hypermedia nowadays is the World Wide Web.

OPPORTUNITIES AND DIFFICULTIES WITH HYPERMEDIA

Artists using new media, as well as computer programmers and other technologists, tend to see hypermedia as a great advance compared to sequential text and ordinary databases. This may be the case when a fairly constricted set of information is concerned. However, as soon as a wide range of information is covered, difficulties arise with both constructing (authoring) and navigating the hypermedia. Tools have been developed to support both authoring and navigating (e.g., browsers or search engines) but both tasks still present hurdles.

For authoring, it is difficult to imagine pieces of information that are independent of one another. No criminal novel would be interesting if you could, without any limit, discover the clues of the story or find the criminal, nor would a love story be interesting if you examined the problems last and the happy ending first. Where presentation systems are concerned, we have seen a change from support systems that allow total freedom of sequencing (such as the Macintosh HyperCard system) to systems that support a sequential presentation (such as the Microsoft Powerpoint system). Nowadays, most custom-made presentations are sequential, or at best incorporate very few forking paths.

When navigating a hypertext such as might be found on the Web, difficulties may arise. Without a proper map, readers tend to get lost. Of course, it is impossible to create a map of the Web itself, where people all over the world freely input and remove information every minute without any (or at least very little) consideration of already existing information.

As for multimedia, it is often considered by nature to be better than any single medium; "the more, the better." Some designers also seem to think that the closer a piece of information gets to reality, the better human beings understand that information. However, it is quite easy to see that a "smart" rendering of information for some purposes is far better than a mirroring of reality. It is easier to understand anatomy from a model of a human body, for instance, than from a dissection. Most researchers aim at presenting their information in condensed visual overviews. There is at present a great stress on "information visualization," where various ways of presenting information in smart ways are tested.

The future of hypermedia is bright. Creators are starting to understand what restrictions must be placed upon their creation, both in terms of the structure and the presentation of information. Increasingly, new applications are being developed. Still, the entangled nature of the "hyper" portion of hypermedia may be the greatest hurdle to any further development.

Currently, hypermedia applications are becoming more specialized to fit the different needs of cultural development, entertainment, and information provision; a flood of new applications that aim at providing a sensory experience is being created. In the future, hypermedia will not be confined to the computer screen; applications embedded in our ordinary environment, in clothes as well as furniture, are already being developed.

Bibliography

Conklin, J. "Hypertext: A Survey and Introduction." *IEEE Computer,* vol. 20, no. 9, pp. 17–41.

Hutchings, G. A.; Hall, W.; and C. J. Colbourn. "Patterns of Students' Interactions with a Hypermedia System." *Interacting with Computers,* 1993, pp. 295–313.

Mayer, R. E., and V. K. Sims. "For Whom Is a Picture Worth a Thousand Words? Extensions of a Dual-Coding Theory of Multimedia Learning." *Journal of Educational Psychology* 86 (1994), pp. 389–401.

McKnight, C.; Dillon, A.; and J. Richardson, eds. *Hypertext: A Psychological Perspective.* New York: Ellis Horwood Ltd., 1993.

Waterworth, John A. *Multimedia Interaction with Computers: Human Factors Issues.* New York/London: Ellis Horwood, 1992.

Willows, Dale M., and Harvey A. Houghton, eds. *The Psychology of Illustration.* Volume 1: *Basic Research.* New York: Springer-Verlag, 1987.

———. *The Psychology of Illustration.* Volume 2: *Instructional Issues.* New York: Springer-Verlag, 1987.

Winn, W. "Learning from Maps and Diagrams." *Educational Psychology Review* 3 (1991), pp. 211–47.

Further Reading

Andrews, Keith. "Applying Hypermedia Research to the World Wide Web." <http://www2.iicm.edu/apphrweb> (May 17, 2002).

Card, Stuart K.; Mackinlay, Jock D.; and Ben Shneiderman, eds. *Readings in Information Visualization: Using Vision to Think.* San Francisco, Calif.: Morgan Kaufmann, 1999.

Edwards, D. M., and L. Hardman. "Lost in Hyperspace: Cognitive Mapping and Navigation in a Hypertext Environment." *Hypertext: Theory into Practice.* Ray McAleese, ed. Oxford: Intellect, 1989; pp. 105–25.

Landow, G. P. "Hypertext in Literary Education, Criticism, and Scholarship." *Computers and the Humanities* 23 (1989), pp. 173–98.

McManus, Bill. "Hypermedia in Construction Education." University of Oklahoma, Construction Science Division, 1991. <http://www.cns.ou.edu/bill/research/hypermedia.htm> (May 17, 2002).

Nelson, T. "Replacing the Printed Word: A Complete Literary System." *Proc. IFIP Congress 1980.* S. H. Lavington, ed. Amsterdam: North-Holland, 1980; pp. 1,013–23.

Nielsen, Jakob. *Multimedia and Hypertext: The Internet and Beyond.* Boston, Mass.: AP Professional, 1995.

UCLA Research Hyper-Media Interactive Studio. Web site. <http://hypermedia.ucla.edu/project/main.html> (May 17, 2002).

Related Topics

ASCII Art; Authoring Tools; Education and Computers; Hypertext; Interactivity; Multimedia; Virtual Reality

— *Yvonne Waern*

Hypertext

Hypertext is a form of electronic writing that allows writers to link paragraphs or pages of text using computer-mediated connections that, in essence, enable computer users to draw relationships and make connections between discrete ideas. In the words of hypertext inventor Ted Nelson, however, the definition is much simpler. In his influential 1974 treatise, *Computer Lib/Dream Machines,* Nelson described hypertext simply as "non-sequential writing."

However, hypertext does not involve simply scrambling the words in sentences to create inscrutable babble. Hypertext, which Nelson devised and named in the early 1960s, was initially his attempt to align the processes of writing and reading more closely with the processes that he believed are evident in human thinking. Although it was not exactly Nelson's intention that it should be so, the underlying engine of today's World Wide Web is a universal computer language called hypertext transfer protocol (HTTP), and hypertext is the Web's primary driver. The Web uses highlighted hypertext words and phrases, often underlined, that can be clicked on with a computer mouse to allow users to leap from Web page to Web page, skipping passages or pages that are not of interest to explore ideas that are interesting. These hypertext links, or hyperlinks, allow users to engage in informational flights of fancy based entirely on their unique interests, assuming only the presence of hyperlinks on the page.

NELSON DISCOVERS HYPERTEXT

In shaping hypertext, Nelson's fundamental insight was the notion that human thinking is non-linear. Take a fictitious example: A man named Mark is at work. Around noon, he realizes that he is hungry, and the image of a hot dog forms in his mind. From there, his thoughts flip to his pet terrier Jack, who, Mark suddenly remembers, was never let out for his morning toilet run. From there, of course, Mark's thinking moves to the idea that he will probably have a big, disgusting mess to clean up in his apartment that evening. Mark has forgotten all about his appetite; now he is thinking about cleaning solvents.

In strictly logical terms, there is no clear linear connection between the idea of a hot dog and the idea of cleaning solvents (at least none that we know of). But strictly logical links are not necessary for thoughts to emerge. Mark's mind followed his own internal mental links, a trail of thought unique to his own perspective, life situation, and interests. His mind followed that path from one concept to the other fluidly, in the span of seconds. Non-linear links like these are the basis of much of, if not most of, human thought.

However, as Nelson noted in *Computer Lib/ Dream Machines,* this is not how writing usually works. Writing traditionally has been bound inflexibly to the printed page, in linear structures that can be broken only by flipping through a book or following footnotes away from the main text, and these are not particularly efficient or convenient methods. "Ordinary writing is sequential for two reasons," Nelson wrote. "First, it grew out of speech and speech making, which have to be sequential; and second, because books are not convenient to read except in a sequence. But *the structures of ideas* are not sequential."

This is especially true of the infamously disorganized Ted Nelson. According to Roger Fidler's 1997 book *Mediamorphosis: Understanding New Media,* Nelson's breakthrough with hypertext was the direct product of his frustration with his own inability to stay organized or to keep track of his written notes on standard 3 x 5 index cards. "For him," Fidler wrote, "all methods of paper to manage information seemed inadequate and imposed restrictions that masked the true structure of his ideas."

Nelson has had little formal computer-science training, but nonetheless has achieved prominence in the pantheon of computer scientists because of his discovery, which he first arrived at in 1960, at age 23, while a student at Harvard; the innovation was part of a term project intended to create a "writing system," which featured the ability to use computers to compare alternate versions of texts side-by-side, backing up sequentially through earlier versions of documents, and revising by outline.

To describe his idea, Nelson coined the terms "hypertext" and "hypermedia" (the latter of which extends the concept to digital sound, pictures, and video). The terms were first used in a paper that Nelson delivered at an Association for Computing Machinery (ACM) conference in 1965, wherein he described a nearly Utopian dream of a global "docuverse" that he called Xanadu.

Xanadu, a conceptual precursor to the World Wide Web, reflected Nelson's dream "for everything to be in the hypertext," but it never got off the ground. What's more, Nelson was slow in showing how hypertext could function practically. Hypertext was not actually demonstrated until Andries and Nelson van Dam showed the IBM-funded Hypertext Editing System at Brown University in 1967. Nevertheless, there is no serious dispute that hypertext is Nelson's discovery.

"As We May Think"

Nelson does, however, acknowledge being inspired by the influential 1945 *Atlantic Monthly* article "As We May Think" by Vannevar Bush, a key science adviser to President Franklin Delano Roosevelt during World War II. The article, which was written just as the war was ending and just prior to the advent of digital computers, foreshadows with astonishing clarity the underlying hypertext concept.

Bush's "Memex" (memory extender), as he called it in his article, was a mechanical machine, not a digital one, and it was based on technologies that were either in existence or just emerging in 1945. Rather than discussing the highlighted point-and-click techniques that came to characterize hyperlinks, Bush's Memex involved a special desk affixed with view screens capable of selecting from vast stores of miniaturized microfiche documents and instantly zooming in on the one that was wanted. The Memex would use a system of "dry photography," allowing its owner to input new records at will. It employed a typewriter-styled keyboard, through which special codes (recorded in an easily used index) could be inputted, telling the machine which document to display. A lever on the desk would then be pushed, instantly drawing up the desired document. Through a kind of mechanical memory, Memex users could traverse a unique path of information according to their interests of the moment, and the lever could be used as the equivalent of the "Back" and "Forward" buttons on the modern Web browser, allowing users to retrace their idea paths. What's more, Bush proposed, that document trail could itself be stored and shared.

The similarities of this system to Nelson's hypertext concept are obvious, despite its mechanical foundation and its comparative limitations. A researcher could not cut and paste material from a microfiche into a written document as easily as today's Web surfer can when drafting a paper using Microsoft Word, for example.

Bush had high hopes for the Memex. He wrote that it could allow users to store ideas confidently, and to know exactly where and how they could be retrieved if they proved useful later. Meanwhile, the mind's faculties could be freed up from the task of trying to remember where old documentation was stored and how to get at it. This, in turn, would free the human intellect to focus on what it does best—generating new ideas.

The Vision of Douglas Engelbart

Computer-science engineer Douglas Engelbart, head of the Augmentation Research Center in San Francisco, was fascinated by the ways that computing technology could be used to augment and increase human intelligence, and as a result his work brought the concept of hypertext and hypermedia, indeed virtually of all personal computing and community networking, into sharp focus. Engelbart staged a 1968 demonstration at the Fall Joint Computer Conference in San Francisco that Paul Saffo, director of the Institute for the Future, would later say was no less remarkable than if Engelbart had landed a UFO on the White House lawn.

At that conference, Engelbart demonstrated his "oNLine System" (NLS) in a 90-minute multimedia computer presentation. The demo introduced the tool that is synonymous with the now ubiquitous point-and-click hypertext-selection method, the computer mouse. The NLS contained a "shared journal," storing more than 100,000 papers, reports, memos, and cross-references, all of which were accessible through hypertext links. His presentation also included a live videoconference with staff members who were in a lab 30 miles away.

The demonstration in many ways represented the first time that computer technology was shown to be interactive. However, Engelbart's ambitions were far removed from simply creating an interactive tool for human productivity and play. His insights about how the human mind works—relying on paths, branches, and webs of thought rather than operating on a strictly linear plane—played a key role, and were very much in keeping with Nelson's ideas. If anything, Engelbart's ambition was even greater than Nelson's. Using networked computing in a hypertext environment, he theorized, would make people more intellectually effective by fostering a collaborative method of sharing their knowledge. The title of his 1962 white paper, in which he laid the groundwork for his NLS, defines Engelbart's vision fully: It was called "Augmenting Human Intellect: A Conceptual Framework." But Engelbart's ideas were perhaps too far ahead of their time, and even today his contributions are not popularly known.

MAKING HYPERTEXT A REALITY

The use of hypertext grew rather slowly over the next decade and a half. The ZOG Project, founded in 1972 by researchers at the Computer Science Department of Carnegie Mellon University, was intended to create a front-end application for use in a summer workshop on artificial-intelligence research, and was one of the first pure hypertext systems. ZOG (the initials apparently don't stand for anything) was first made available as a commercial application in 1983 as the Knowledge Management System (KSM), a publishing-software package that allowed the creation of well-formatted paper documents from hypertext elements.

In 1978, Andy Lippman of the MIT Architecture Machine Group (later known as the MIT Media Lab), helped push the hypertext concept into multimedia by creating the Aspen Movie Map, a virtual tour of Aspen, Colorado. Regarded as the first hypermedia videodisk, it contained video images from four cameras, pointing in different directions, that had been mounted on a truck as it was driven through the streets of Aspen. The resulting pictures were compiled onto videodisk and linked to allow the user to start anywhere in the city and move forward, backward, left, or right.

Beginning in 1985, with the introduction of the Intermedia program, hypertext authoring systems capable of producing interactive documents began appearing in computers. Janet Walker's Symbolics Document Examiner, a hypertext manual for Symbolics computers that was distributed as an alternative to the 8,000-page printed manual, became the first widely used hypertext-based application. Other hypertext editing systems followed, including Guide, Linkway, Writing Space, and HyperCard, the last of which was distributed free on Macintosh computers and arguably contributed the most to hypertext's popularity. The first major hypertext convention, Hypertext '87, was organized by the Association for Computing Machinery in 1987.

THE WORLD WIDE WEB

Unbeknownst to anyone outside of CERN (Centre Européen pour la Recherche Nucléaire), the Swiss nuclear-physics lab, around this time a young computer programmer was independently reinventing hypertext. Tim Berners-Lee, an Englishman who eventually created the World Wide Web, has written in his book *Weaving the Web* that he was at best dimly aware of Nelson's work, and had not been exposed to Bush or Engelbart when he set to work in 1980 on a program that he called Enquire (short for Enquire Within Upon Everything).

Enquire's mission was to solve CERN's massive data-retrieval problems. The lab had immense amounts of research stored on a variety of computer operating systems, in a number of data formats. Enquire was Berners-Lee's way of solving this problem. It worked somewhat in the style of HyperCard; pages in the system resembled index cards, and the only way to create new pages was to link to old ones. Enquire had two kinds of hyperlinks: "internal" links connected data from one page in a single file to another page, while "external" links could connect unrelated files. This is not unlike Berners-Lee's later design for the Web.

Berners-Lee left CERN in the early 1980s, taking jobs as a networking consultant before returning to CERN in 1989 to follow up on the problem of incompatible computer systems and data at the research lab. In March 1989, he submitted to his supervisors a simple paper titled "Information Management: A Proposal," which laid the groundwork for the World Wide Web. By this time, Berners-Lee was aware of Nelson's work, and made reference to it in his paper, referring to what later became known as hyperlinks as "hot spots," and acknowledging Nelson's belief that these hot spots could work not only to connect widely dispersed text, but also to trigger multimedia applications in computers. While he had to approach his project from the limited vantage point of CERN's immediate needs, it is clear from the paper that Berners-Lee was keenly aware of the global possibilities of his proposed networked hypermedia system.

At the time that Berners-Lee started his work, hypertext was used mostly within programs and databases, allowing readers to access, for instance, one part of a database by connecting to it from information stored in another part. Berners-Lee's innovation, gleaned from his experience as a computer-networking administrator, was to use hypertext to connect computers in the outside world. This was important at CERN, where computers in different buildings and in some remote locations had to communicate. The important trick was not to make those incompatible machines conform to a single standard, but to make the data itself conform. Berners-Lee accomplished this by creating HTTP, the computer language that made it possible for hypertext connections to work over wide networks like the Internet.

Through HTTP, a computer could be linked not only to information stored within its own internal database, but also to information stored on a computer far away. HTTP is the language that established the Web address format (e.g., http://www.cnn.com), and it made it possible for pages to be requested and retrieved through the Web. Of course, to make the Web truly work, Berners-Lee also had to create the first Web browser, write the program for the first Web-server computer, and create the hypertext markup language (HTML) that makes it possible for simple documents to be displayed in readable form on a Web browser once a successful document request has been fulfilled.

When the World Wide Web went public in 1992, Nelson's concept of linking everything to everything through hypertext began to be realized—although Nelson has long complained that the Web is something of a "stupid" version of Xanadu, which he imagined would make all the world's literature available online permanently in a single unified system. After the Mosaic browser was released to the public in early 1993, hypertext became popularized as the most revolutionary new form of communication technology since the advent of television—and arguably the most significant since the invention of Gutenberg's printing press, which democratized both reading and writing. The Web, obviously, has only continued to grow since its inception. Meanwhile, hypertext has continued to flourish in other interactive media, such as CD-ROMs, e-books, video games, and interactive television.

THE IMPORTANCE OF HYPERTEXT

Like Nelson and Engelbart, a number of critics and researchers have suggested that profound changes in human comprehension may result from the use of hypertext. Professors George Landow and Paul Delaney, in their 1991 essay "Hypertext, Hypermedia and Literary Studies: The State of the Art," predict vast changes in the relationships between readers and writers, audiences and creators. Whereas the writer traditionally has been completely in charge, telling the reader exactly what to read and all but dictating the exact order in which it should be read, hypertext places more control in the hands of the reader, who no longer has to plow through pages of uninteresting detail to get to the meat of a work. If there is a link to a concluding paragraph on page one, the reader can jump directly to it, skipping everything else, or start in the middle and fan out in either direction.

These new possibilities have been explored by a number of experimental authors, notably Michael Joyce, whose *afternoon, a story*, is an early and famous experiment in hypertext fiction. In it, Joyce presents the blocks of text that make up a story, but allows readers to select hyperlinks to connect the prose in any order that they choose. The end result is that the reader is nearly as responsible for the outcome of the story as is the writer; the writer creates the story's framework, and the reader is set loose to explore its many possibilities.

Hypertext "changes our sense of authorship, authorial property and creativity . . . by moving it away from the constrictions of page-bound technology," Landow and Delaney write. "In so doing, it promises to have an effect on cultural and intellectual disciplines as important as those produced by earlier shifts in the technology of cultural memory that followed the invention of writing and printing."

Bibliography

Berners-Lee, Tim. "Information Management: A Proposal." *Multimedia: From Wagner to Virtual Reality.* Randall Packer and Ken Jordan, eds. New York: Norton, 2001; pp. 189–205.

——. "What Influenced the Design of The Web?" October 15, 2001. <http://www.w3.org/People/Berners-Lee/FAQ.html#Influences> (May 24, 2002).

Berners-Lee, Tim. *Weaving the Web.* New York: HarperCollins, 2000.

Bush, Vannevar. "As We May Think." *The Atlantic Monthly,* vol. 176, no. 1 (July 1945), pp. 101–08.

Landow, George, and Paul Delaney. "Hypertext, Hypermedia and Literary Studies: The State of the Art." *Multimedia: From Wagner to Virtual Reality.* Randall Packer and Ken Jordan, eds. New York: Norton, 2001; pp. 206–16.

Nelson, Theodor H. *Computer Lib/Dream Machines.* Revised edition. Redmond, Wash.: Tempest Books of Microsoft Press, 1987.

Nielsen, Jakob. "Short History of Hypertext." Useit.com, June 1995. <http://www.useit.com/alertbox/history.html> (May 24, 2002).

Segaller, Stephen. *Nerds 2.0.1: A Brief History of the Internet.* New York: TV Books, 1998.

Further Reading

Berners-Lee, Tim; Hendler, James; and Ora Lassila. "The Semantic Web." *Scientific American,* May 2001, pp. 35-43.

Gillies, James, and Robert Cailliau. *How the Web Was Born.* Oxford, England: Oxford University Press, 2000.

Naughton, John. *A Brief History of the Future: From Radio Days to Internet Years in a Lifetime.* Woodstock, N.Y.: The Overlook Press, 2000.

Nelson, Theodor H. *Literary Machines.* Sausalito, Calif.: Mindful Press, 1992.

Nielsen, Jakob. *Multimedia and Hypertext: The Internet and Beyond.* Boston, Mass.: Academic Press Professional, 1995.

Pavlik, John V. *New Media Technology: Cultural and Commercial Perspectives.* Boston, Mass.: Allyn and Bacon, 1996.

Related Topics

"As We May Think"; Berners-Lee, Tim; Cyberspace; E-Commerce; Engelbart, Douglas; Hypermedia; Interactivity; Interface; Internet; Joyce, Michael; Linking; Markup Languages; Nelson, Theodor Holm (Ted); World Wide Web

— Kevin Featherly

Information Design

Information design is a general approach to arranging the content and presentation of information so that ideas are communicated clearly and effectively. Originally developed to improve the usefulness of printed textbooks and manuals, it is now just as likely to be found in the production of online information for CD-ROMs and Web sites. But the general principles of information design apply to any situation where words or pictures are used to communicate information, from highway signs and computer manuals to AIDS-education leaflets intended for people who are unable to read.

PRINCIPLES OF INFORMATION DESIGN: WHO, WHAT, AND HOW

Poetry, sculpture, music, and other art forms communicate ideas and emotions in a variety of unpredictable and open-ended ways. Such indirect communication is of little use in everyday situations, where information must be communicated quickly, directly, and unambiguously; imagine the confusion that would ensue if highway signs were replaced by abstract sculptures, or if fire-exit instructions were delivered by mimes. Information design is a more focused form of communication that can be thought of in stages called "who," "what," and "how."

The goal of information design—effective communication—is realized through an absolute focus on the user of the information, often known as the audience or target audience. The starting point for information design is often a user analysis, which may include interviewing typical users and classifying them according to demographic and socioeconomic background. This focus on users is evident not only at the start of information design; if the information is something like a product manual, for example, draft versions may also be tested with typical users under typical conditions, just as the product's user interface is subject to "usability" testing.

Having arrived at a clear picture of who the users are, the next step is to work out what needs to be communicated. This depends substantially on what job the information will do. If a manual is being prepared for a complex computer product, a key (and substantial) part of information design involves the designer sitting down with product developers and translating often very technical information into a form that users can understand. Here, information designers and product developers may diverge substantially; whereas developers often want to detail how their product works (that is, their focus is on the product), designers concentrate on what tasks users want to do (their focus is on the user). Often this raises one of the most crucial issues of information design: Knowing what information to take out is just as important as knowing what to leave in.

The next step is to work out how information will be communicated, which reflects the research that designers have done on what they need to communicate and to whom. If a museum exhibit is being designed for children rather than adults, it might be best to present information in the form of cartoons, or to use short paragraphs and large type. If statistical data needs to be presented so that trends are obvious, it makes more sense to use graphs than tables or text. The "how" stage also involves important decisions about the medium in which the information will be delivered, which may include a choice between books, leaflets, CD-ROMs, Web sites, and a variety of other formats.

Overall, information designers strive for effective communication through a set of guiding principles. Putting the user first leads to an emphasis on information that is properly structured, so the logic of the subject matter is clear to readers. Making information retrievable is also very important; for example, reference books may put articles in alphabetical or chronological order, and online information will typically include some form of keyword search. Structure and retrievability are also related to the concept of navigation, the way users work their way through an overall structure to reach the particular information they need. In well-designed information structures, the focus is on ensuring that users generally get only the information they need, as quickly and effectively as possible.

VISUAL INFORMATION

A picture may be worth a thousand words, but a thousand words rarely communicate as quickly and effectively as a well-chosen picture. Designing information means thinking carefully about the balance between words and pictures (and perhaps also sound, video, animation, and other media), and about which one conveys a particular piece of information most effectively. Tables, graphs, photographs, and drawn artworks all have their place, but they are not interchangeable; photographs may contain many unnecessary visual details, for example, while a drawn artwork, although less realistic, may focus the reader's attention only on the parts of an image that are actually relevant. Factors such as the cost of reproduction rights (for photographs) or the use of a professional illustrator (for artwork) inevitably lead to design compromises.

Information design draws a clear distinction between using decorative pictures simply to break up text and using well-chosen visual examples to explain text. In information design, colors, typography, and page layout all work together to communicate, not to decorate, although visual attractiveness is a byproduct of good design. Consider the choice of colors in public information signs, for instance, where one dominant color is typically used to communicate a clear message that can be understood by an international audience. The value of using graphics to communicate scientific and technical data has been most notably demonstrated by Yale University statistics professor Edward Tufte, whose seminal books on visual information design illustrate his maxim that good design is "clear thinking made visible."

DEVELOPING TECHNOLOGIES

Different media are suited for conveying different types of information. Cellular phones are shipped with reference cards small enough to be carried around in a wallet. Computer software has contextual help (e.g., small text files that pop up to tell you how to fill in particular fields of a form). Museums and galleries have audio-cassette guides of their collections. Some children's books are printed with "scratch 'n' sniff" panels to convey basic smells, or with touch-sensitive electronic panels that play sound effects. Information design means choosing the medium that communicates information best.

The strengths and weaknesses of printed and online information present designers with some of their greatest challenges. Explosive growth in Web use has led to a great deal of information designed for print being made available online with relatively little thought given, in many cases, to how clearly that information communicates when viewed on a small computer screen. Generally, online media such as CD-ROMs, help files, and Web sites favor modular packets of information, thoughtfully hypertext-linked together in a logical and clearly navigable structure.

Sometimes the same information must be delivered in more than one medium. In the 1990s, IBM shifted away from its policy of shipping vast quantities of printed manuals, and began to supply information simultaneously as books and as CD-ROMs. Although this approach made it possible to ship hundreds of manuals to customers on a single inexpensive CD-ROM, IBM's digital books could not display artworks and text on the screen at the same time. Meanwhile, some customers still preferred paper books that they could leave open on their desks.

Developing technologies play a crucial role in information design. When Tim Berners-Lee first conceived the Web, it was a text-only information library. In the early- and mid-1990s, most HTML Web pages were "marked up" by hand, using only a relatively small set of tags; early versions of HTML did not include tables, for example, or more sophisticated forms of presentation such as style sheets. That the Web has evolved into multimedia is partly a reflection of user expectations, and partly a reflection of WYSIWYG ("what you see is what you get") Web authoring tools, which make it easy for people to design Web pages even when they have no knowledge of the underlying mark-up language. Thus, the design of Web sites reflects not just the principles of information design, but also the limitations of Web browsers and authoring software, as well as the expectations of users.

THE IMPORTANCE OF INFORMATION DESIGN

In the early 1970s, journalist Alvin Toffler speculated that society would soon be overwhelmed by "information overload"; with information arriving through ever more channels every day, some people believe that his prediction has already been borne out. As it becomes increasingly difficult to filter the useful information from the useless, information design can only become more important.

A relatively obscure field as recently as 10 years ago, information design is central today to the success or failure of commercial Web sites, not simply because it makes them more attractive or easier to use, but also because it gives them a competitive advantage. The growing demand for "information architects," who apply information-design principles to Web-site structure and content, is perhaps the clearest indication of this centrality.

Bibliography

Rosenfeld, Louis, and Peter Morville. *Information Architecture for the World Wide Web.* Cambridge, Mass./Sebastopol, Calif.: O'Reilly, 1998.

Toffler, Alvin. *Future Shock.* New York: Random House, 1970.

Tufte, Edward. *Envisioning Information.* Cheshire, Conn.: Graphics Press, 1990.

———. *The Visual Display of Quantitative Information.* Cheshire, Conn.: Graphics Press, 1999.

———. *Visual Explanation.* Cheshire, Conn.: Graphics Press, 1996.

Further Reading

Hartley, James. *Designing Instructional Text.* London: Kogan Page/East Brunswick, N.J.: Nichols, 1994.

Jacobson, Robert, ed. *Information Design.* Cambridge, Mass.: MIT Press, 1999.

Wurman, Richard Saul. *Information Anxiety.* New York: Doubleday, 1989.

Related Topics

Human-Computer Interaction; Hypertext; Markup Languages; Tufte, Edward; Usability

— *Chris Woodford*

Innis, Harold
1894–1952

Canadian Media Theorist

Harold Adams Innis pioneered the study of media by writing an economic history of communication. He enunciated the first systematic medium theories about how media can bias the quality and quantity of information—how a living society communicates, who controls information in the living society, and what we remember of the society after it collapses. He provided the intellectual foundation for the Toronto School of Communication, influencing Marshall McLuhan, James Carey, and others, and generating some of the first ideas about how a medium of communication can affect the dissemination of ideas over time and through space.

Innis was born near Hamilton, Ontario, and graduated from McMaster University shortly before World War I. After fighting on the front lines in France, Innis studied political economy at the University of Chicago, writing a dissertation that, like many of his early works, explored the economic history of Canada. After World War II, he began to investigate the history of communication, producing two important manuscripts—*Empire and Communications* (1950) and *The Bias of Communication* (1951)—that describe how knowledge and power were stored and projected as civilizations rose and fell.

Innis made three important contributions through his excruciatingly detailed accounts of how communication tools can shape culture. First, he argued that the use of a particular communication tool would define the quality and quantity of knowledge communicated and preserved. Second, since new media always seemed to help new forms of social organization to emerge, he thought that a civilization would be constrained by its dependence on a single dominant medium, growing culturally stagnant and inflexible. Third, he illustrated how our knowledge of dead or culturally distant societies depended largely on the character of their media.

MONOPOLIES OF KNOWLEDGE

According to Innis, civilizations survive and evolve by developing new media. Modernization creates a pressure to retain and preserve more and more information, and this pressure has been responsible for the decay and succession of communication traditions. For example, he traced many different kinds of communication traditions, from the oral tradition in Homeric poems to the minstrel tradition triggered by Hesiod's poetry and the codification of laws that began when Athens adopted the ionic alphabet in 403–02 B.C.

He retold the history of early civilizations by charting the circulation of papyrus supplies, the construction of libraries, and the means of codifying law and keeping records. He argued that the bias of this early print medium lay in allowing bureaucracies to monopolize knowledge within larger and larger empires in and around the Mediterranean, because papyrus was easily transportable. However, papyrus was not durable, limiting the development of early societies until the durable parchment codex was invented. When this print technology developed, it was used primarily to translate and transcribe Hebrew scripture and Christian writing, which, Innis said, helped raise these cultures to historical prominence. Ultimately, a significant amount of knowledge was deemed heretical by St. Augustine, and therefore was not preserved by the improved technology. Again, changes in print technology helped break down the monopoly of knowledge held by monasteries in rural districts, in favor of new copyist guilds in centralized cities, cathedrals, and universities.

For Innis, media created bias in the popular construction of reality by transforming information and organizing knowledge in patterns consistent with the structure of powerful social institutions. He argued that one of the most important social challenges lay in preserving information over time and making it transportable through space. For most of human history, communication media have achieved one goal at the expense of another, being either durable or transportable. But in the first half of the twentieth century, Innis observed new electronic media, like motion pictures, loudspeakers, and radio and television technologies, that seemed to achieve both goals. As a distinguishing feature of modernity, the radio helped overcome both space and time, letting politicians appeal to people over vast areas, bypassing class divisions in education and literacy, bringing science into popular culture, and empowering centralized bureaucracy.

However, Innis sometimes made very broad claims about the effect of technology on culture. For example, he argued that the new printing presses and photographic sciences gave rise to a visual tradition. Since the printing industries fought for freedom of the press, they advanced the cause of an individualistic, visual communication medium that preserved individual memories over wider spaces, displacing the oral tradition that better preserved collective memory through time. In his opinion, these new printing technologies grounded the Enlightenment ideas of individualism and national self-determination that later sparked such significant social upheavals as the fall of the Austro-Hungarian Empire. He even argued that catchwords like democracy, freedom of the press, and freedom of speech appeared in the popular imagination only because new printing-press technology devolved the power to communicate.

Innis' thinking was not as technologically determined as some charge, as he was also careful to catalogue the social conditions for innovation in communication technology. For example, whereas printing houses in Europe were not always protected from governments, in the United States the Bill of Rights supported the development of journalism, and created the right environment for the social ingenuity that led to the fast press, the stereotype, and the linotype.

In 1969, the University of Toronto created Innis College, now one of Canada's most prestigious undergraduate educational institutions, in recognition of the scholarship he inspired around the world. Innis wrote at a time when radio and television were the new media, but his comparative work in the history of media spelled out some of the basic propositions about the relationship between technology and culture that we still work with today. As a scholar of old media and the early forms of electronic media, Innis' invaluable studies laid the foundation for our understanding of "new media," showing how communication technology provides both the capacity and the constraints for social development.

Selected Works

Innis, Harold. *The Bias of Communication*. Toronto: University of Toronto Press, 1951.
———. *Empire and Communications*. Oxford: University of Oxford Press, 1950.
———. *Staples, Markets and Cultural Change: Selected Essays of Harold Innis*. Montreal: McGill–Queen's University Press, 1995.

Bibliography

Acland, Charles, and William Buxton. *Harold Innis in the New Century: Reflections and Refractions*. Montreal: McGill–Queen's University Press, 2000.
Diebert, Ronald. *Parchment, Printing and Hypermedia: Communication in World Order Transformation*. New York: Columbia University Press, 1997.

Related Topics

McLuhan, Marshall; Technological Determinism

— *Philip E. N. Howard*

Instant Messaging

In its simplest form, Instant Messaging (IM) seeks to accomplish two goals: monitoring presence and messaging. The software relies on a central server or servers to monitor presence. When a user logs on to an IM system, the login is recognized and other online users who have that address listed as a "buddy" or friend are notified of the user's presence. The software establishes a direct connection between users so they can talk to each other synchronously, in real time. IM has a long history, but it has only been in the late 1990s that IM applications have come to the forefront, due to ongoing battles between commercial ventures engaged in its development.

IM was invented in 1971 as a chat function on a government computer network. Murray Turoff created it as part of the Emergency Management Information Systems and Reference Index (EMISARI) for the Office of Emergency Preparedness. Its original purpose was to help exchange information on opinion surveys between people in geographically distributed locations. EMISARI users accessed the system through Teletype terminals linked to a central computer. EMISARI continued to be used by the U.S. government for management of emergency situations until 1986.

"Chat" is a way to talk in real time with multiple users on a network channel, where everyone on the channel sees everything being said by all other users. IM, on the other hand, is a one-to-one real-time conversation between two users. The EMISARI chat function was called the Party Line, and was originally developed to replace telephone conferences. Party Line users all had to log on to the same computer over phone lines and read the text of the chats on Teletype units.

The first public chat software was called "Talk," and again, users had to be logged on to the same computer to use the program. This was truly the forerunner of IM systems, since users could send a message to anyone else on the system and a note would pop up on the user's terminal.

The first large-scale rollout of IM came from America Online (AOL). IM had been a part of the AOL browser as early as 1988, in the form of "buddy lists" that let AOL customers know when their friends who also use AOL were online. AOL Instant Messenger (AIM) flourished, and as the popularity of the Internet grew, so did the demand for software systems that allowed real-time conversation. The early-to-mid 1990s saw the introduction of Internet Relay Chat (IRC) software for group conversations, as well as IM software such as ICQ (or "I Seek You") for non-AOL Internet users. An Israeli company, Mirabilis, launched ICQ in the mid-1990s as a free messaging program. AOL later bought out ICQ but kept the ICQ interface intact, even though it competed with AOL's own IM system. In 2000, at least five IM systems were in use on the Internet, with multiple versions for different computer platforms (Windows, MacOS, Linux). The diversity of this "client" software for messaging created a problem for users; there has been no standardized set of protocols among different systems. For example, an ICQ user cannot message an AIM user, because the programs are not compatible.

In late 1997, Microsoft submitted a proposal to the Internet Engineering Task Force (IETF), seeking to establish a standard for interoperability between different IM clients. The proposal was backed by 40 other vendors, with the notable exception of AOL. Since AOL controls the two largest IM systems (AIM and ICQ, with a reported combined user base of over 100 million people worldwide), the proposal would have little impact if adopted. Many industry observers feel that this battle between AOL/Time Warner/Netscape and Microsoft will have repercussions that will be felt for a long time to come.

Bibliography

Clark, Dan. "Web's Next Battle: Instant Messaging." *ZDNet News,* July 1999. <http://www.zdnet.com/zdnn/stories/news/ 0,4586,2301773,0,0.html> (March 26, 2002).

Hu, Jim. "AOL Rivals Put Instant Messaging Wars on FCC Radar." *CNet News,* September 2000. <http://news.cnet.com/news/0-1005-200-2768596.html> (March 26, 2002).

Internet Engineering Task Force. "Instant Messaging and Presence Protocol (IMPP)." 2002. <http://www.ietf.org/html.charters/impp-charter.html> (March 26, 2002).

Marsan, Carolyn Duffy. "IETF Split on Instant Messaging Standard." CNN.com, December 20, 2000. <http://fyi.cnn.com/2000/TECH/computing/12/20/ instant.messaging.idg/> (March 26, 2002).

Microsoft Corporation. "Chapter 11: Instant Messaging and Presence Monitoring." Microsoft TechNet, September 2000. <http://www.microsoft.com/technet/exchange/manuals/ planning/c11inst.asp> (March 26, 2002).

Further Reading

Herring, Susan C., ed. *Computer-Mediated Communication: Linguistic, Social and Cross-Cultural Perspectives.* Amsterdam/Philadelphia: John Benjamins, 1996.

Rheingold, Howard. *The Virtual Community: Homesteading on the Electronic Frontier.* Reading, Mass.: Addison-Wesley, 1993.

Related Topics

Chat; Emoticons; Peer-to-Peer; Virtual Community

— Gary W. Larson

Institute of Electrical and Electronic Engineers

The Institute of Electrical and Electronic Engineers (IEEE) is a professional organization of engineers, scientists, and associated professionals whose interests are in the fields of electrical and computer science, engineering, and allied fields. The organization is anchored in 10 geographic regions; includes 36 professional societies and four technical councils; and coordinates 298 IEEE sections, 1,188 chapters, and 1,032 student branches as part of its outreach mission. IEEE was formed in 1963 from a merger of the American Institute of Electrical Engineers (AIEE) and the Institute of Radio Engineers (IRE). It is the world's largest professional organization, with more than 350,000 members in 150 countries.

The initials IEEE are probably best known to computer and technology enthusiasts due to the fact that the association is responsible for producing and documenting standards for hardware such as the IEEE 1394 designation (commonly called "Firewire"), which allows users to directly connect digital camcorders to, and edit video on, their computers. The standard is used for other equipment as well (e.g., digital cameras). The IEEE has also been instrumental in the development of other standards, such as those used by Bluetooth technology, which allows cellular phones, computers, and other technologies to communicate wirelessly.

The AIEE was formed in 1884 in New York, when several prominent figures in the development of electrical technology recognized the need for a professional organization in the rapidly expanding field. At the first general meeting of the AIEE, held on May 13, 1884, an official organizational structure and accompanying rules were adopted, and officers to lead the new organization were elected. The president of Western Union Telegraph Company, Norvin Green, was elected the first president, while other well-known figures including Alexander Graham Bell and Thomas Edison served as the six initial vice presidents.

The first professional meeting occurred later that year at the International Electrical Exhibition in Philadelphia, and served as the impetus for the creation of the predecessor to one of IEEE's signature publications, *Transactions of the AIEE,* which published the papers presented at the meeting.

One of the earliest functions of the AIEE was to develop standards for engineers and the electrical industry. Early efforts focused on defining and refining relevant language and definitions and, by the 1890s, on creating and formalizing technical standards and protocols designed to create consistency across the industry. These efforts led to the creation of the Committee on Standardization in 1898. By the end of the century, the AIEE had grown into a respected professional organization; its first international section was created in Toronto, Canada, in 1903.

The IRE, on the other hand, was actually a splinter organization, created by the departure of radio engineers from the AIEE—who perceived themselves as too specialized for the organization—and the merger between two faltering organizations, the Society of Wireless Telegraph Engineers (SWTE) and the Wireless Institute. The resulting international organization was patterned after the AIEE. Officially created in 1912, the IRE would take only three years to expand into 11 other countries. Like the AIEE, it quickly took on responsibility for standardizing the radio industry and published a professional journal, *Proceedings of the Institute of Radio Engineers.*

Several factors lead to the merger of the AIEE and the IRE, not the least of which was World War II. The war brought to the forefront the importance of radio and related technologies (e.g., radar), which created a demand for education in the areas of electronics and an increase in the number of students entering the field of study. The membership of IRE grew significantly because of earlier efforts to attract students into the organization, something that the AIEE had failed to do. The IRE had also been responsive to the changing landscape of its field, and diligently tried to include new areas in its organizational structure.

By the late 1950s and early 1960s, movement toward a merger had begun. Both societies acknowledged that neither could adequately represent the entire field alone, and in 1962, 87 percent of voting members accepted the merger to form IEEE, which officially came into existence on January 1, 1963.

According to the organization, its goal is to "advance global prosperity by promoting the engineering process of creating, developing, integrating, sharing, and applying knowledge about electrical and information technologies and sciences for the benefit of humanity and the profession." The IEEE produces a vast number of publications and technical journals focused on various specialties, including computer graphics, intelligent systems, multimedia, robotics, semiconductors, and speech processing.

Bibliography

Institute of Electrical and Electronics Engineers. "About the IEEE." IEEE.org, 2001.
<http://www.ieee.org/about/> (April 5, 2002).
———. "IEEE History Center." IEEE.org, 2001.
<http://www.ieee.org/organizations/history_center/> (April 5, 2002).

———. "IEEE History Center: Historical Articles."
IEEE.org, 2001.
<http://www.ieee.org/organizations/history_center/
historical_articles_menu.html> (April 5, 2002).

Further Reading

Anderson, Don. *Firewire System Architecture: IEEE 1394.*
Boston, Mass.: Addison Wesley Longman, 1998.

Institute of Electrical and Electronics Engineers. "IEEE
History Center: IEEE Institutional History." IEEE.org,
2001.
<http://www.ieee.org/organizations/history_center/
related_sites/ieee.html> (April 5, 2002).

Related Topics

Bluetooth; Wireless Application Protocol

— *Art Ramirez*

Interactive Television

Interactive television (iTV) is a broadcasting innovation that promises to bring TV, the power of computing, and broadband Internet access together in ways that range far beyond the TV viewers' traditional choices of selecting channels, adjusting volume, and deciding whether to watch a broadcast, a videotape, or a DVD. ITV is a broad category of real and potential television applications in which the TV set can be used for exchanging email or chat messages, ordering pizzas or CDs, or accessing the World Wide Web, much in the same ways that people use computers. ITV also holds the promise of allowing viewers greater control over what they watch, how they choose to watch it, and when they choose to tune in.

ITV applications are accessed using a TV remote pointed at a special digital set-top box—a specialized computer containing both memory and microprocessors—that connects the TV to the Internet and processes and decodes digital television signals. More sophisticated set-top boxes contain hard drives that can store recorded TV shows, download software, and work with other digital TV services. There are also separate and less expensive services like TiVo and ReplayTV that can record, pause, and zap through unwanted TV commercials, even during live broadcasts.

However, while iTV holds tremendous promise, some perceive it as a serious threat to individual privacy. Set-top boxes can record and transmit back to the cable operator detailed records about TV viewing habits, demographics, and other personal information. Critics contend that this information could be sold to marketers and used to target viewers uniquely, or for other purposes, and some have suggested that laws may need to be changed in order to restrict the ways that media companies and marketers can exploit the information that they collect.

ITV has been fairly slow to take off in the United States, but it has been much more successful in the U.K. and in Western Europe. There are, however, numerous predictions holding that iTV applications will become tremendously popular in the United States by 2006—the year by which the U.S. television industry is required to switch to all-digital transmissions—and that as a result, set-top boxes could soon become the hub of all home networking, supplanting personal computers.

BACKGROUND

The history of iTV can be traced to a 1953 CBS-TV children's show, *Winky Dink and You.* Interaction with the show was quite primitive; children were encouraged to buy plastic sheets that they could attach to their TV screens, and on which they could draw. By sketching such objects as bridges and roads on the sheet, kids could help the program's ever-troubled cartoon hero to escape his latest jam—at least in their own imaginations. Obviously, children could not participate if they didn't have the plastic sheets. The show was cancelled in 1957.

Later, AT&T began experimenting with video-over-telephone-line services, a technique that became known as the "Picturephone." It was first publicly demonstrated in 1964 at the World's Fair in New York, and was publicly marketed afterward. The system allowed callers to see each other as they spoke, but its usefulness was limited because so few people had Picturephones. In addition, the video quality was poor, and the service was expensive. The Picturephone never caught on.

In 1977, an iTV experiment in Columbus, Ohio, known as Qube became the first two-way commercial cable TV service. Operated jointly by Warner Communications and Amex Cable, Qube allowed cable TV subscribers to select pay-per view movies for the first time. They could also participate in simple polls, offer the cable company direct feedback, and attend broadcast "town meetings"; in one infamous event, they were even allowed to make the play calls during a live football game. Still, audience interest never ignited, and Qube was scrubbed in 1985. Other U.S. experiments followed, including Cox Cable's two-way Indax cable service; Time Inc.'s Teletext project in Orlando, Florida, and San Diego, California; and

Knight Ridder's Viewtron, a "videotext" service. Each showed intriguing promise, but none was successful.

Broadcasters kept trying to perfect iTV well into the mid-1990s, the most famous attempt of the period being Time Warner's Full Service Network (FSN), an Orlando, Florida, service featuring interactive games, shopping, news, and video on demand. But it too closed down, in 1997. In all cases up to the late 1990s, despite huge corporate investments, customers either consistently expressed dissatisfaction with iTV services or simply failed to use them if they had them.

By the turn of the century, the confluence of the Internet's spiraling popularity and the arrival of digital TV services made iTV services more viable. Cable operators, driven by competition from satellite TV providers, began switching to digital systems and rapidly implementing the new services, pushing digital set-top boxes into homes.

The Future of ITV

Some marketing campaigns have attempted to convince buyers to use television as a kind of interactive Web browser, with services such as Microsoft's WebTV. But these have not succeeded, largely because a TV screen's resolution lines make it hard to read text. Nonetheless, the broadband Internet holds much promise for iTV, particularly considering the set-top box's ability to download and run applications off the Internet. Further, the promise of broadband-enabled video-game players such as Playstation has some analysts predicting that the game player could one day rival the set-top box as the hub of home networking.

Jens F. Jensen, a communications-department researcher at Denmark's Aalborg University, concluded in a 1999 Danish National Center for IT-Research white paper that iTV seems now to have a destiny, despite a history littered with failures. "Considering the success of interactive technologies in general, such as computers, automatic teller machines, credit cards, consumer electronics, etc.," Jensen wrote, "and considering the huge amounts of money that have been and will be spent on interactive home entertainment, there is no doubt that interactive television will, in some form or another, succeed in the future."

Some success already has been found in Europe. In a 2000 report, journalist Ken Freed cited numbers indicating that set-top box manufacturer Pace Micro Technology had deployed 2.6 million set-top boxes for the News Corp.'s U.K.-based BSkyB cable service. Cable & Wireless, meanwhile, had deployed about

60,000 Pace boxes for interactive cable services over the Liberate iTV system, while another 552,000 Pace set-top boxes were deployed in Great Britain, using the Canal+ MediaHighway and Media GuardCA systems. By comparison, between 1998 and 2000, only around 200,000 digital TV products, including set-top boxes and integrated digital receivers, were sold in the United States, according to the Consumer Electronics Manufacturers Association.

Andrew Wallace, vice president of marketing for Pace Micro, told Freed in April 2000 that he expects iTV to reach near-ubiquity in the U.K. and Western Europe by 2005, while showing solid growth in the United States. "I see the evolution of the set-top box into a home gateway for high-bandwidth video, data and voice services," Wallace said. "Within the household, I see the emergence of the set-top box as the central node for home networking."

Despite such optimism, iTV faces a number of challenges. First, there is the issue of privacy. The non-profit Center for Digital Democracy, for one, has warned that a raft of companies are interested in collecting vast amounts of data on iTV viewers, so that they can target advertisements at them and personalize their programming. But the industry has not put needed privacy safeguards in place, Center for Digital Democracy representatives have complained. Meanwhile, in a December 2001 CNet article, Gartner Inc. analyst Adam Sarner suggested that targeted ads probably won't win over U.S. consumers' hearts or make giving up their personal information seem worthwhile. However, "targeted viewing" might do the trick. "For example," Sarner wrote, "if ITV could tell dedicated watchers of 'Buffy the Vampire Slayer' when their favorite episode will be on next, they will likely feel they have a stake in profiling."

In the United States there has been reluctance among consumers—even among those who have the service available in their home—to use iTV. In an August 2001 study, media-research company Statistical Research Inc. (SRI) found that 72 percent of poll respondents said that they had no interest in interacting with TV programs. Even where iTV was present, most respondents said that they almost never use interactive links within TV shows, and never plug their TV into the Internet or use it for email.

Instead of those Internet-like features, consumers in the SRI study indicated that their interest lies in features that allow them a measure of control over programming and content. ITV features that place such power in the hands of the viewers include interactive program guides, video on demand, and personal digital video recording. Although it is still early in the iTV game on American shores, the SRI results could be an early indication as to the types of iTV features that could become prominent in the United States when digital interactive television finally takes root, as many analysts expect it will during the next several years.

Bibliography

Bartlett, Michael. "Consumers Think Interactive TV Is Too Much Work—Update." *Newsbytes.com*, August 31, 2001.

———. "Convergence 2001: Interactive TV Must Poll the Viewers." *Newsbytes.com*, September 11, 2001.

Freed, Ken. "Interactive TV for Newbies." *Media Visions Journal*, 2000. <http://www.media-visions.com/itv-newbies.html>

———. "2001 Pace Report Shows Digital Television Trends." *Multichannel News International*, February 2001. <http://www.media-visions.com/itv-pacereport.html> (May 24, 2002).

———. "UK & Europe Leading Interactive TV Drive." *EXTRA EXTRA*, 2000. <http://www.media-visions.com/itv-europe.html> (May 24, 2002).

———. "When Cable Went Qubist." 2000. <http://www.media-visions.com/itv-qube.html> (May 24, 2002).

Olsen, Stefanie. "Interactive TV: It's Watching You." *CNET News,* June 26, 2001. <http://news.cnet.com/news/0-1005-200-6386456.html> (May 24, 2002).

Rose, Michael; Dormann, Claire; Olesen, Henning; Beute, Berco; and Jens F. Jensen. "White Paper on Interactive TV." Danmarks Tekniske Universitet, December 1999. <http://www.cti.dtu.dk/~berco/html/cti/research/ITV%20white%20paper.html> (May 24, 2002).

Stenzler, Michael K., and Richard R. Eckert. "Interactive Video." *SIGCHI Bulletin*, vol. 28, no. 2 (April 1996). <http://www.acm.org/sigchi/bulletin/1996.2/eckert.html> (May 24, 2002).

Further Reading

Fidler, Roger. *Mediamorphosis: Understanding New Media*. Thousand Oaks, Calif.: Pine Forge Press, 1997.

Freed, Ken. "Hospitality Industry Leading in iTV." *Broadband Week*, March 2001. <http://www.media-visions.com/itv-hoteltv.html> (May 24, 2002).

Kishore, Adi. "TV Portals: Opening the Door to Interactive Television." *Media & Entertainment Strategies Report*, vol. 5, no. 17 (November 2001).

Pindoria, Keval, and G. C. Wong Ping Hung. "The Parents the Kids and THE INTERACTIVE TV!!!!" Department of Computing, Imperial College of Science, Technology and Medicine, University of London, 1996.

<http://www.doc.ic.ac.uk/~nd/surprise_96/journal/vol4/khp1/report.html> (May 24, 2002).

Related Topics

Data Mining; Gaming; Interactivity; Interface; McLuhan, Marshall; Multimedia; Narrowcasting; Privacy; Videotex; Virtual Reality

— Kevin Featherly

Interactivity

Interactivity is usually thought of as a characteristic of the World Wide Web, and of forms of digital media like CD-ROMs. Two characteristics are central to interactivity: Communications are multidirectional between senders and receivers, and participating individuals have control over the communication experience.

Face-to-face communication between people typically is interactive. Conversations require two-way communication, and people who are conversing can often control the direction of the conversation by adding a related comment, contradicting, changing the topic, and so on. However, as Michael Schudson pointed out, face-to-face communication is not always interactive. For example, an employee may talk to her employer, but the employer may be reading the newspaper, not really listening to what she says, and may reply with words that are not responsive.

Interactivity can occur without face-to-face conversation. Telephone calls are interactive; radio talk shows can be interactive. Even letters to the editor can be interactive.

FEATURES OF INTERACTIVE MEDIA

Author John Carey has suggested that the modern era in interactive media began in 1964, when AT&T demonstrated a picture telephone at the New York World's Fair. But it was with the advent of personal computing that the term interactivity came to be widely used.

In the late 1980s, several researchers began to work on defining interactivity. Sheizaf Rafaeli defined it as the relatedness of messages, and Carrie Heeter suggested that interactive media offer complex choices, require some user effort, are responsive to users, monitor information use, make it easy to add information, and facilitate interpersonal communication.

Louisa Ha and Lincoln James developed an early set of criteria to measure the interactivity of corporate Web sites. They looked for features such as chat rooms and newsgroups, email links, and search engines. Similar measures have been used to examine newspaper Web sites, and to measure interactivity at health-related Web sites. All these studies found relatively limited interactivity at many Web sites.

To understand interactivity, it may be more important to look at what people think about new media, rather than at the characteristics of those media. People might perceive that a Web site gives them opportunities to interact, even if it doesn't have some of the features that seem to be associated with interactivity. User interest in the subject of a Web site is one of the best predictors of how interactive they would believe the site to be. Other factors that might influence perceived interactivity in media such as the Web include experiences that people have while at a Web site, their attitudes toward both the content and design of the site, and the ways in which they use the site's navigational tools.

INTERACTING WITH WHOM?

Whether interactivity is examined in terms of features or perceptions, there are different types of interactivity.

There are two basic types of computer-mediated interactivity. First, interactivity may occur between individuals who are communicating with each other and simply using the computer as a tool. This can be described as user-to-user interactivity. Second, individuals can actually interact with the computer itself. This can be described as user-to-system interactivity.

Janet H. Murray, in her 1997 work on interactive fiction, *Hamlet on the Holodeck*, writes about a third kind of interactivity: interacting with the text or message. This can be described as user-to-documents interactivity.

Two characteristics have been identified as central to interactivity: direction of communication and control over the communications process. These characteristics can be adapted and applied to help explain different levels of interactivity in user-to-user, user-to-system, and user-to documents interactivity.

USER-TO-USER INTERACTIVITY

When individuals communicate with each other through the computer, high levels of interactivity might be best described as mutual discourse. During two-way communication, participants have control over the communication. Sender and receiver roles are almost indistinguishable. Chat rooms and instant messaging (see entries) often facilitate mutual discourse.

At the opposite extreme is monologue: communication is one-way, and receivers have little control. Many corporate Web sites present a monologue, as the company "tells its story" to site visitors. Sometimes, two-way communication might exist while the message creator retains primary control. This may be called responsive dialogue, and might be observed at Web sites that offer customer service or e-commerce.

In other cases, communication might be primarily one-way, but the receiver might be in control. This form of interactivity can be called feedback. Visitors to a Web site might click on a hyperlink that allows them to sign a guest book or send a message to the Webmaster. However, the interactivity remains limited unless someone who received the feedback replies, thus opening up (at least) responsive dialogue.

USER-TO-SYSTEM INTERACTIVITY

In user-to-system interactivity, it is useful to view the two primary characteristics of interactivity as how transparent or apparent the computer interface is to the user, and whether control over communication is centered in the computer or the human using it.

The most interactive form of user-to-system communication is sometimes called "flow." When individuals achieve flow, they are controlling the computer, and the computer becomes transparent. They often forget not only that they are interacting with a computer, but also about things like the time of day and the need to eat. People who play computer games often report that they achieve this kind of flow. Providing an opportunity for flow is also the goal of many virtual-reality systems.

At the other extreme is computer-controlled interaction, during which users are very aware that they are sitting in front of a computer. They often respond to prompts or cues the computer gives them. Much computer-based instruction uses this kind of interactivity; filling in Web-based forms is another example.

However, it is possible for the computer to remain very apparent while control shifts to the user. This can be called human-controlled interaction. In this form of interactivity, individuals use tools such as databases, spreadsheets, and word processors to manipulate and organize data to make it is more useful to them and their colleagues.

A final form of user-to-system interaction is adaptive interaction. The computer remains in command of the interaction, but it is more responsive to users' individual needs, and users are less aware of the computer. For example, advanced gaming and educational systems are able to adapt to changes in the individual user's skill level.

USER-TO-DOCUMENTS INTERACTIVITY

In user-to-documents interactivity, the audience can be either active or passive. Additionally, individuals who examine the documents (the receivers) may have either high or low levels of control over messages.

The most interactive form of user-to-document communication can be called co-created content. All participants actively share in the creation of content. Group decision support systems (GDSSs) are designed to create this kind of environment. Interactive fiction and multi-user environments such as MUDs and MOOs are other examples.

By contrast, relatively little interactivity is found when a content creator (often a professional communicator) packages messages and delivers them to a passive audience. This form of user-to-documents interactivity can be called packaged content. It can be found at many online newspapers and magazines.

Many content creators have come to realize that, in interactive environments such as the Web, they must give their audience more control over what they will view. Audience members remain relatively passive, but they provide input and/or control over the delivery of messages. This form of interactivity can be thought of as content-on-demand. Examples include online newspapers that allow users to customize their "front page," and services that deliver daily email messages with weather information for selected cities.

Sometimes the audience can be active while the sender of messages retains primary control over the communication process. This form of interactivity can be thought of as information exchange. An example might be a computer bulletin board system or ListServ. Message senders have control over what they post, and people who visit the bulletin board or receive messages form the ListServ can actively choose which messages they wish to read.

Interactivity is evolving. As new media systems become more sophisticated, users are likely to expect more two-way communication and more control. But there will probably always be a place for less interactive forms of communication such as monologue, computer-controlled interaction, and packaged content. Sometimes it's easier to be entertained than to interact.

Bibliography

Carey, John. "Interactive Media." *International Encyclopedia of Communications.* Erik Barnouw, ed. New York and Oxford: Oxford University Press, 1989; pp. 328–30.

Ha, Louisa, and Lincoln James. "Interactivity Re-Examined: A Baseline Analysis of Early Business Web Sites." *Journal of Broadcasting & Electronic Media* 42, no. 4 (1998), pp. 457–74.

Heeter, Carrie. "Implications of New Interactive Technologies for Conceptualizing Communication." *Media Use in the Information Age: Emerging Patterns of Adoption and Computer Use.* Jerry L. Salvaggio and Jennings Bryant, eds. Hillsdale, N.J.: Lawrence Erlbaum Associates, 1989; pp. 217–35.

Lee, Jae-Shin. "Interactivity: A New Approach." Paper presented at the Association for Education in Journalism and Mass Communication, Phoenix, Ariz., 2000.

Massey, Brian L., and Mark R. Levy. "Interactivity, Online Journalism, and English-Language Web Newspapers in Asia." *Journalism & Mass Communication Quarterly* 76, no. 1 (1999), pp. 138–51.

McMillan, Sally J. "Interactivity Is in the Eye of the Beholder: Function, Perception, Involvement, and Attitude toward the Web Site." *Proceedings of the 2000 Conference of the American Academy of Advertising.* Mary Alice Shaver, ed. East Lansing, Mich.: Michigan State University, 2000; pp. 71–78.

———. "Who Pays for Content? Funding in Interactive Media." *Journal of Computer Mediated Communication* 4, no. 1 (1998). <http://www.ascusc.org/jcmc/vol4/issue1/mcmillan.html> (March 26, 2002).

McMillan, Sally J., and Edward J. Downes. "Defining Interactivity: A Qualitative Identification of Key Dimensions." *New Media and Society* 2, no. 2 (2000), pp. 157–79.

Morrison, Margaret. "A Look at Interactivity from a Consumer Perspective." *Developments in Marketing Science.* J. B. Ford and E. J. D. Honeycutt, Jr., eds. Norfolk, Va.: Academy of Marketing Science, 1998; pp. 149–54.

Murray, Janet H. *Hamlet on the Holodeck: The Future of Narrative in Cyberspace.* New York: Free Press, 1997.

Rafaeli, Sheizaf. "Interactivity: From New Media to Communication." *Advancing Communication Science: Merging Mass and Interpersonal Process.* Robert P. Hawkins, John M. Wiemann, and Suzanne Pingree, eds. Newbury Park, Calif.: Sage, 1988; pp. 110–34.

Schudson, Michael. "The Ideal of Conversation in the Study of Mass Media." *Communication Research* 5, no. 3 (1978), pp. 320–29.

Further Reading

Bezjian-Avery, Alexa; Calder, Bobby; and Dawn Iacobucci. "New Media Interactive Advertising vs. Traditional

Advertising." *Journal of Advertising Research* 38, no. 4 (1998), pp. 23–32.

Csikszentmihalyi, Mihaly. *Beyond Boredom and Anxiety.* San Francisco: Jossey-Bass, 2000.

Heeter, Carrie. "Interactivity in the Context of Designed Experiences." *Journal of Interactive Advertising* 1, no. 1 (2000). <http://www.jiad.org> (March 26, 2002).

Jensen, Jens F. "Interactivity: Tracing a New Concept in Media and Communication Studies." *Nordicom Review* 19, no. 1 (1998), pp. 185–204.

Kirsh, David. "Interactivity and Multimedia Interfaces." *Instructional Science,* 25 (1997), pp. 79–96.

Rafaeli, Sheizaf, and Fay Sudweeks. "Networked Interactivity." *Journal of Computer Mediated Communication* 2, no. 4 (1997). <http://www.usc.edu/dept/annenberg/vol2/issue4/rafaeli.sudweeks.html> (March 26, 2002).

Schultz, Tanjev. "Mass Media and the Concept of Interactivity: An Exploratory Study of Online Forums and Reader E-Mail." *Media, Culture & Society* 22, no. 2 (2000), pp. 205–21.

Simms, R. "Interactivity: A Forgotten Art?" *Computers in Human Behavior* 13 (1997), pp. 157–80.

Walther, Joseph B. "Computer-Mediated Communication: Impersonal, Interpersonal, and Hyperpersonal Interaction." *Communication Research* 23, no. 1 (1996), pp. 3–43.

Walther, Joseph B.; Anderson, Jeffrey F.; and David W. Park. "Interpersonal Effects in Computer-Mediated Interaction: A Meta-Analysis of Social and Antisocial Communication." *Communication Research* 21, no. 4 (1994), pp. 460–87.

Related Topics

Bulletin-Board Systems; E-Commerce; Email; Human-Computer Interaction; Hypertext; LISTSERV; Man-Computer Symbiosis; MUDs and MOOs; Online Journalism; Responsive Environments; Search Engine; Virtual Community; Virtual Reality; World Wide Web

— *Sally McMillan*

Interface

Technically, an interface is any means by which a device communicates with something else. Cables, plugs, sockets, and various software protocols are used to create an interface between a computer and an external device, such as a printer. But most often, the term interface is used to define the way the computer communicates with its human user—the user interface. A computer's user interface is a combination of hardware and software that shapes the interaction between the computer and its human user. The most common hardware components of the interface on computers today are the screen, the keyboard, and the mouse.

At its core, the computer is a machine that manipulates electric signals that can only be on or off. These signals are used to represent the mathematical numbers one and zero. Programmers have agreed on standard codes, in which combinations of ones and zeros are used to represent certain commands, letters of the alphabet, and other symbols. Various software programs translate these basic coded sets of ones and zeros into symbols that are meaningful to humans, so that humans can "interface" with the computer. Usually, the interface encourages the user to think of what the computer is doing in terms of some commonly understood metaphor. For example, the Macintosh operating system uses the metaphor of the desktop, with images on the screen representing objects commonly found on or near a desk, such as folders, files, and a trashcan.

The earliest computers used rows of lights and switches as the only interface hardware. The user had to do a great deal of interpretation to understand the meaning of certain lights being on, representing ones, and other lights being off, representing zeros. In order to allow them to be utilized for practical applications, early computers added a keyboard in place of switches, and a printer in place of flashing lights. These computers had a command-line interface, in which the user would type in a command word, such as "run," followed by the name of a program, and the computer would then run the program, printing out the results. The entire system was text based, and users had to remember long lists of commands. Shortly thereafter, a television screen replaced the printer.

In the 1970s, engineers at the Xerox Palo Alto Research Center (PARC) in California began to experiment with a graphical user interface (GUI; pronounced "GOO-ee"). The system involved attaching a pointing device, called a mouse, to the computer. The position of the mouse was represented on the computer display screen, and various programs or operations were represented on the screen by small pictures, called icons. The main advantage of the GUI system was that it made it unnecessary to memorize long lists of commands. The system also took advantage of the fact that humans' visual memory is much more accurate than their memory for words; we may forget a person's name, but we remember the face. Similarly, we may not recall the name of a computer file, but will recall the location on the screen where its icon normally appears.

The GUI system was popularized by the introduction of the Apple Macintosh computer in 1984, and then with the first version of Microsoft Windows in late 1985. These products not only provided a graphical interface to the computer's own operating system, but also standardized many attributes of the user interfaces of the programs that were designed for them. This further simplified computer use.

The Internet also began with a text-based interface, requiring the user to remember many command words. The GUI principle was applied to the Internet around 1990 by Tim Berners-Lee, a computer scientist working for the European Organization for Nuclear Research (CERN) in Switzerland. His work allowed text, graphics, and photos to be presented together over the Internet. It also applied the idea of embedding links to other Internet sites into a text, allowing the user to follow a number of different paths to access information, rather than looking at pages in a pre-arranged sequence from start to finish. Today, we call this GUI-based interface the World Wide Web.

The current trend in interface design is toward user customization of programs and operating systems. "Skins" or "themes" are the terms designating the visual styles that users can choose (or create themselves) to customize the appearance of their computer screen. A single program may offer one set of functions, but users may attach dozens of different skins, each of which provides a different look and feel—that is, a different visual metaphor for the program's operation by the user. Current developments in interface design also incorporate speech recognition and playback.

Bibliography

Edwards, Alistair D. N. "The Rise of the Graphical User Interface." Department of Computer Science, University of York, England. <http://www.rit.edu/~easi/itd/itdv02n4/article3.html> (April 12, 2002).

Johnson, Steven. *Interface Culture: How New Technology Transforms the Way We Create and Communicate.* San Francisco: Harper San Francisco, 1997.

Further Reading

Hix, Debra, and H. Rex Hartson. *Developing User Interfaces: Ensuring Usability Through Product and Process.* New York: Wiley, 1993.

Jansen, Bernard J. "The Graphical User Interface: An Introduction." Computer Science Program, University of Maryland (Asian Division), Seoul, Korea. <http://jimjansen.tripod.com/academic/pubs/chi.html> (April 12, 2002).

Lineback, Nathan. "Graphical User Interface Timeline." Nathan's Toasty Technology Page. <http://toastytech.com/guis/guitimeline.html> (April 12, 2002).

Liu, Y. "Software-User Interface Design." In *Handbook of Human Factors and Ergonomics.* Edited by Gavriel Salvendy. Second edition. New York: Wiley, 1997.

Related Topics

Berners-Lee, Tim; Graphical User Interface; Universal Design; World Wide Web

— *Shing-Ling Sarina Chen*

Intermedia

Intermedia is a term used to describe art forms that draw on several media and grow into new hybrids. Intermedia works cross the boundaries of recognized media, and often fuse the boundaries of art with media that had not previously been considered art forms.

Artist and composer Dick Higgins coined the word intermedia in a 1966 essay. Higgins, a former student and then-colleague of composer John Cage, described an art form appropriate to artists who felt that there are no boundaries between art and life. For a philosophy that denied the boundary between art and life, there could be no boundaries between art form and art form.

Higgins was a founding member of the influential circle of artists, architects, and composers known as Fluxus. Many of the artists active in intermedia art forms in the 1960s took part in Fluxus, including Korean Nam June Paik; Germans Wolf Vostell and Joseph Beuys; Japanese Takehisa Kosugi and Shigeko Kubota; Lithuanian-born Americans George Maciunas and Jonas Mekas; French Jean Dupuy, Robert Filliou, and Ben Vautier; and others. The interpretations that these artists gave to intermedia ran from the simple and primitive to the technically sophisticated. At one end of the spectrum, there were the folklore-based projects of Sweden's Bengt af Klintberg and the poetry performances of American Emmett Williams. At the other, there were Nam June Paik's technologically dazzling video proposals, the sophisticated book-print-installation works of American Alison Knowles, or Higgins' innovative radio plays and computer-generated art works.

The first intermedia courses entered the university curriculum in 1967, with Ken Friedman's projects at San Francisco State University and in 1968 with Hans Breder's courses at the University of Iowa. By the late 1960s, the term was in wide use in Europe and around the world; one of the hallmark projects in its diffusion was a book published in Germany titled *Intermedia 1969*. By the 1970s, artists of many kinds had begun to adopt the term.

The intermedia concept was discernible in three artistic directions of the late 1950s and early 1960s. One direction emphasized engagement with technology. In an era when multimedia often meant separate and disparate art forms being presented at the same time, however, this was often a fruitless approach. In contrast, those artists who were exploring the boundaries of technology and art and examining the larger social meaning of information technology in a post-industrial society often made good use of intermedia theory. In a powerful sense, these artists began to explore the generally unrealized dimensions of a world in which digital computer code and information flows would begin to render all media fluid, as digital control began to break down boundaries between separate forms of input, transmission, and output. Early examples include the electronic music of John Cage and Richard Maxfield and the early television experiments of Paik and Vostell. This direction blossomed in the art and technology programs of the 1960s and in the video art of the 1970s.

The second direction emphasized simplicity, a tradition of conceptual exploration. Often anchored in Zen Buddhism or philosophy, this stream was typified by the event structures of George Brecht, the early concept art of Henry Flynt, and the neo-haiku theater of Mieko Shiomi and Yoko Ono. In the 1960s, this second direction entered another phase with George Maciunas' publishing program for Fluxus, the radical reductive films of Paul Sharits, and the expanded use of events and scores for objects, installations, and performances by Higgins, Vautier, Robert Watts, Knizak, Filliou, Friedman, and others.

The third direction emerged from the ambiguous and often-boisterous tradition of happenings pioneered by Allan Kaprow, Al Hansen, Claes Oldenburg, Milan Knizak, and others.

These streams were never as separate as some maintained, and they never constituted the single forum that others described. Rather, in overlapping and informing each other, they led to the flowering of new art forms that typified the 1960s and 1970s. Conceptual art, artists' books, performance art,

installation, video, and many other artistic media and traditions emerged from them.

While it remained possible to separate art forms for scholarship, historical reflection, or theoretical distinction, Higgins' vision of intermedia posited that our time often calls for art forms that draw on the roots of several media, growing into new hybrids.

The conceptual importance of intermedia is its profound yet often paradoxical relationship to new media. Intermedia is important because it emphasizes conceptual clarity and categorical ambiguity; the intermedia concept is powerful because it stretches across the boundaries of all media, many of them old. Intermedia provide impetus to new media while offering a balance to the overly technological bent that new media can sometimes engender.

Intermedia links many forms of media conceptually, and requires us to consider them in terms of human effects. This creates a sympathetic yet challenging position from which to interrogate and conceptualize new media. It strengthens the development of new media by encouraging us to think in large, cultural terms. Intermedia are not arts of technical applications, but arts of subtle ideas.

Intermedia forms were often spawned when several individual media hybridized and grew into forms that became effective and convincing media in their own right. Film and opera were once intermedia; today, they are media moving into multimedia. Today's electronic digital media open new technical policies, and the intermedia concept enriches them by challenging the reduction of media to digital form. The intermedia idea becomes clear through a consideration of the world of the 1950s and 1960s, a time when today's technology was possible only in science fiction. It also becomes clear in thought experiments to develop intermedia that do not exist, and that may never exist outside the mind.

Imagine an intermedia form made up of 10 percent music, 25 percent architecture, 12 percent drawing, 18 percent shoemaking, 30 percent painting, and 5 percent smell. What would it be like? How would it work? How would specific works appear? How would they function? How would the elements interact? Thoughts like this have given rise to some of the most interesting art works of our time.

Bibliography

Di Felice, Attanasio. "From Bernini to Beuys: Historical Sources of Performance and Time-Space Art." *The Art of Performance*. Gregory Battcock and Robert Nickas, eds. New York: E. P. Dutton, 1984.

Friedman, Ken, ed. *The Fluxus Reader.* Chichester, England: Academy Editions, 1998.

Higgins, Dick. "Intermedia." *Something Else Newsletter,* vol. 1, no. 1 (1966), pp. 1–6.

Paik, Nam June, and Kenworth W. Moffett, eds. *The Electronic Superhighway.* New York, Seoul, and Fort Lauderdale: Holly Solomon Gallery, Hyundai Gallery, and the Fort Lauderdale Museum of Art, 1995.

Further Reading

Cage, John, ed. *Notations.* New York: Something Else Press, 1969.

Friedman, Ken. *The Aesthetics.* Cullompton, England: Beau Geste Press, 1973.

Hendricks, Jon. *Fluxus Codex.* New York: Harry N. Abrams, 1988.

Higgins, Dick. *Horizons: The Poetics and Theory of the Intermedia.* Carbondale, Ill.: Southern Illinois University Press, 1984.

———. *Modernism Since Postmodernism: Essays on Intermedia.* San Diego, Calif.: San Diego State University Press, 1997.

Kahn, Douglas. *Noise, Water, Meat: A History of Sound in the Arts.* Cambridge, Mass.: MIT Press, 1999.

Packer, Randall, and Ken Jordan, eds. *Multimedia: From Wagner to Virtual Reality.* New York: Norton, 2001.

Staeck, Klaus, ed. *Intermedia 1969.* Düsseldorf: Editions Tangente, 1969.

Related Topics

Digital Music; Multimedia; Paik, Nam June; Sandin, Daniel

— *Ken Friedman*

Internet

The Internet is the global, interconnected network of computer networks that has in the past decade spawned radical changes in the way people communicate, retrieve and publish information, work, shop, and live. Because of the way that the Internet connects powerful computers, PCs have ceased to exist as stand-alone boxes of information-processing tools, and have instead become perhaps the most complete communications appliances ever devised. In recent years, the Internet has slowly spread to other devices such as cell phones, handheld personal digital assistants (PDAs), and laptop PCs, bringing about the promise of a constant connection to a universe of information.

ARPANET

The Internet has its roots in the ARPANET, a small network of unwieldy mainframe computers that,

beginning on October 29, 1969, connected two computers—one at the University of California–Los Angeles, the other at the Stanford Research Institute in San Francisco, hundreds of miles away. Other mainframe computers, or "nodes," were added later at various universities, corporations, and U.S. government installations, so that by 1972 there were some 31 nodes, or host computers, connected to the ARPANET.

The ARPANET was funded by the U.S. government's Advanced Research Projects Agency (ARPA), a small agency under the umbrella of the U.S. Department of Defense that was formed by President Dwight D. Eisenhower in the wake of the Soviet Union's launch of Sputnik, the first telecommunications satellite. The agency was given wide latitude, and the funding to concentrate on whatever projects it wanted. By the early 1960s, under the guidance of the agency's visionary director J. C. R. Licklider, ARPA had changed focus from outer space to unmasking the potential of computer technology as an aid in human problem-solving, even on the grandest of scales. As part of his vision, Licklider foresaw what he called an "intergalactic network" of computers that could communicate and share information all over the planet.

Subsequent ARPA directors, most importantly Robert Taylor, picked up on Licklider's ideals. With one 20-minute conversation, Taylor procured $1 million from his supervisors to build and launch the first long-distance, computerized network to connect ARPA with the various research agencies that it was funding. In 1966, Taylor recruited Larry Roberts away from Lincoln Laboratories, where he had been working on computer graphics, to head up the team that would design, build, and implement the ARPANET. Roberts in turn put the project up for competitive bids, and selected a small Cambridge, Massachusetts, consulting firm, Bolt Beranek and Newman (BBN), to bring the ARPANET project to fruition.

The ARPANET was built on an innovation that would also serve as the basis for the wider Internet. In 1961, an engineer named Paul Baran had devised a system for the transmission of information through phone lines that involved breaking messages up into "blocks"; British researcher Donald Watts Davies independently came up with an almost identical breakthrough, but he referred to divided message bits as "packets," the name that would stick. Baran's idea was built on the notion that, in order to create a computerized system that would survive a nuclear

In 1999 Professor Leonard Kleinrock poses with the first network switch, or IMP, created in 1969. Kleinrock is gesturing to his watch to point out that the watch has a more powerful microprocessor than the IMP. (AP Photo/Mark J. Terrill)

attack, decentralization was needed. He devised a way to split up information so that it would flow over the phone lines according to the route the served as the shortest and least congested path. A computer on the other end would reassemble the blocks, and present the message to the receiver in a way that could be properly read.

Roberts adopted the Baran/Davies packet idea for ARPANET, as well as Baran's notion of decentralization. A problem, however, was that computers at the time were universes unto themselves—most were built with unique operating systems, and even computers made by the same individual manufacturers were often completely incompatible. BBN's solution was to insert computers, interface message processors (IMPs), at various points on the nascent network that had no other function but to intercept message packets, determine where they were to go, check for errors, and then forward the packets onto the receiving machine. To do this, a computer program, or "protocol," needed to be devised to determine how these

IMPs would communicate with the computers on either end. This protocol, in turn, made it possible for even incompatible computers to communicate with one another, using the IMP as a kind of silent interpreter. BBN's IMPs, then, were the basis for what eventually became the modern networking router.

The ARPANET went through many changes in the early 1970s, as more host facilities joined the network. One of the most important was the rise of email as the "killer app" (most popular application) of the network; a 1973 study indicated that 75 percent of all ARPANET traffic was made up of email posts.

However, despite its revolutionary traits, ARPANET was limited in important ways. For most, it represented more a sealed fence than an open gateway. Firstly, it had been designed for a maximum of about 19 host sites, and there was a threat of potentially fatal traffic congestion bringing the system down if too many people came onboard at once. Also, the ARPANET was open mainly to research facilities and companies that performed U.S.-government-funded research, most of it for the Department of Defense. One response to these limitations was to begin forming new networks, separate from the ARPANET.

ARPA (now known as "DARPA" for Defense Advanced Research Projects Agency) funded the first new networks, including the radio-based ALOHANET and the satellite-based SATNET; both of them, like ARPANET, relied on the Baran/Davies packet scheme. But neither of the new networks was capable of communicating with the other; each functioned under its own protocols. History seemed to be repeating itself, except that the inability to communicate now impacted entire networks of computers, rather than individual machines.

NETWORKING THE NETWORKS

Vinton Cerf, who once had been a graduate student on the original ARPANET project, provided a solution to the new communication difficulty; Robert Kahn, a former member of the BBN team who had moved over to ARPA, helped him. Based on Cerf's initial idea, the duo designed a new networking protocol in 1974 that would allow incompatible networks to communicate with other networks around the world. It was based on two innovations. First, networks would communicate through "gateway" computer interfaces that would understand what each of the networks was saying, and would seamlessly forward information from one network to the next; the end user would never know that the gateway was there.

Second, Cerf and Kahn refined the packet concept, devising a system in which host computers would send packets in "electronic envelopes" that were specially addressed to reach their destinations. The gateway would read only the envelope, not the content of the message, greatly speeding up transference from one host computer to another. This eliminated the step of re-transmitting data, which had been used by APRANET's IMPs. What Cerf and Kahn were creating was simply a forward-and-store system. If it worked, Cerf and Kahn both knew, the protocol that they dubbed "Transmission Content Protocol" (TCP) could open the world to an unprecedented, interconnected universe of information.

TCP was first demonstrated in July 1977, linking ARPANET, ALOHANET, and SATNET in an experiment that sent messages through all the networks, far overseas and back to the United States, without losing a single packet of information. Later, in 1978, Cerf, researcher Jon Postel, and several others revised TCP by separating out all the pieces of the protocol that dealt with routing packets and combining them into a simplified twin protocol, Internet Protocol (IP). With the rise of TCP/IP, the foundation was laid for today's Internet.

Parallel to Cerf and Kahn's work with what became TCP/IP, a Harvard doctoral candidate named Bob Metcalfe discovered a way to create high-speed networks of computers within a single building, agency, or company. This was Ethernet, which borrowed part of its design from ALOHANET, but which differed in that it was completely "hardwired," meaning that all of the computers in the facility would be tethered to high-speed data cables. Metcalfe was allowed to test his concept in 1973 on computers at the Xerox Palo Alto Research Center (PARC) in California. The first Ethernet network, then known as the "Alto Aloha System," was formed there.

Ethernet eventually became one of the key reasons for the Internet's growth; rather than connecting one mainframe computer at a time to networks like the ARPANET, Ethernet connected all computers in a building together, allowing them to share all the information they contained with one another. In turn, a router pointed outward to a larger computer network, vastly increasing the number of host computers capable of communicating with the world. Xerox began selling Ethernet as a commercial product in 1980, and Bob Metcalfe became a rich man.

Gradually, more networks formed. In 1977 at the University of Wisconsin, Larry Landweber created the THEORYNET, which provided email to more than 100 computer-science researchers. In 1979, the online news network USENET launched, connecting Duke University and the University of North Carolina through the Unix-to-Unix Copy (UUCP) protocol. The Packet Radio Network (PRNET) followed that same year. Also in 1979, Landweber organized a conference of computer scientists who were tired of being shut out of the ARPANET, and who wanted to form their own research network. The conference was attended by representatives of DARPA and of the National Science Foundation (NSF); CSNET formed in 1981 as a result, funded by the NSF. While the CSNET itself would be relatively short-lived, it demonstrated for the NSF's board the importance of computer networking, and the role that NSF could play.

Many more networks formed, often firmly relying on the TCP/IP protocol. Among these were the BITNET (Because It's Time Network), the EUNet, the Fidonet, the JUNET, and the JANET. Even within the U.S. government and separate from the ARPANET, NASA had its own network, the Space Physics Analysis Network. Private research institutions and corporations began building networks as well.

The year 1983 was the turning point: In that year, it was decided that every computer on the ARPANET would have to switch from the network's original transmission protocol (Network Control Protocol, or NCP) to Cerf and Kahn's TCP/IP. The ARPANET was no longer the closed, impenetrable network it had been; now, to borrow Cerf's phrase, "it could go where no network had gone before." It also became so big as a result of the switch that the ARPANET was split into two pieces in 1983, one for unclassified military information (MILNET), the other retaining the ARPANET name. However, the two could still communicate with one another, making the ARPANET itself a genuine "internet."

With network communications restrictions erased, the number of networks began to proliferate rapidly. By 1996, Cerf would later write, there were some 100,000 separate networks, almost all using TCP/IP, and almost all capable of communicating easily with all the others.

There was one final development in the 1980s that helped to permanently shape the Internet. After five supercomputer centers opened in 1985, the NSF agreed to build a "backbone network" connecting them. In addition, it allowed regional academic networks to form that could tap into this backbone,

NSFNet, for free. Taking advantage of a spine that employed lines that were 25 times faster than the old ARPANET, anyone on a college campus with a computer could connect to the Internet. Researchers now had a choice to make between the ARPANET and NSFNet; not surprisingly, most chose the latter.

There had been no single point at which the Internet had been created, but it was clear by the end of the 1980s that the Internet existed. So robust was this network of networks by the end of the decade that, unable to compete with NSFNet, ARPANET was mothballed. Its unplugging, while unsettling to some of the pioneers who had built it, had no measurable effect on the rest of the Internet, which only continued to grow.

GLOBAL INTERNET

By 1990, the network of networks was a global affair, and to some it appeared that all its important innovations were behind it. Now, it seemed, it was just a matter of getting computers in people's hands so they could take advantage of all that the Internet had to offer—everything from the file-transfer protocol (FTP), which allowed users to shift files from computer to computer, to the Telnet, which allowed users to open sessions on other computers on the network, in effect using other computers through one's own keyboard. There was also Internet Relay Chat (IRC), the first widely used chat program, as well as the thousands of newsgroups on the USENET.

However, the greatest Internet innovation, the one that would spark the Internet revolution, was still to come, in the form of Tim Berners-Lee's World Wide Web, coupled with the Mosaic browser that made viewing the Web and taking advantage of the Internet's full multimedia capabilities a snap—assuming the user had access to sufficient bandwidth. With the evolution of the Web in the early 1990s, the public finally "got it." Concurrently, in 1993, the NSF, at the urging of the Clinton administration, relaxed its ban on commercial activity on the Internet. The medium exploded.

By the turn of the century, the Internet had spent 10 years morphing from a phenomenon and media sensation into something so popular and universal as to resemble a common household utility, like water or telephone service. Untold millions of people now use the medium to create private Web pages, read news, chat, send instant messages, distribute email, research purchases, buy Christmas presents. It has brought incredible benefits to society, while also adding to its problems.

At the same time that it has brought the Library of Congress to the fingertips of every computer-savvy child, it also has made pornography, anarchic sloganeering, and racial hatred easier to access as well. The Internet has made music available directly to audiences via download, but has also disrupted the music industry, which has seen many songs swapped online by people who aren't paying for the privilege. It has made security and privacy keen issues, and it has created new forms of crime and terrorism. Still, given the Internet's vast and rising popularity, society seems willing to make the tradeoffs to remain online.

The Nielsen/NetRatings firm estimated that the Internet population had risen from a mere 2,000 or so privileged researchers in 1973 to 428 million people worldwide by April 2002. That number can be expected to continue growing in the coming decade, especially as newer, more inexpensive technologies emerge that allow people to carry the Internet with them wherever they go, using cell phones, pagers, Internet appliances, laptops, and PDAs. One of the most profound media innovations of any century, the Internet shows no signs of being the fad that some critics once accused it of being. The Internet, it now seems clear, is here to stay.

Bibliography

Berners-Lee, Tim, and Mark Frischetti. *Weaving the Web: The Original Design and Ultimate Destiny of the World Wide Web.* San Francisco: HarperSanFrancisco, 1999.

Crocker, Steve. "Initiating the ARPANET." *Matrix News,* vol. 10, no. 3 (March 2000). <http://www.mids.org/pay/mn/1003/crocker.html> (May 24, 2002).

Digital Systems Research Center. "In Memorium: J. C. R. Licklider, 1915–1990." (Reprints "Man-Computer Symbiosis," 1962, and "The Computer as a Communication Device," 1968.) Memex.org. <http://www.memex.org/licklider.pdf> (May 24, 2002).

Featherly, Kevin. "Half a Billion People Online—Survey." *Newsbytes.com,* August 27, 2001.

Hauben, Michael, and Ronda Hauben. *Netizens: On the History and Impact of Usenet and the Internet.* Los Alamitos, Calif.: IEEE Computer Society Press, 1997. <http://www.columbia.edu/~hauben/netbook/> (May 24, 2002).

Leiner, Barry M.; Cerf, Vinton G.; Clark, David D.; Kahn, Robert E.; Kleinrock, Leonard; Lynch, Daniel C.; Postel, Jon; Roberts, Larry G.; and Stephen Wolff. "A Brief History of the Internet." *Internet Society,* August 4, 2000. <http://www.isoc.org/internet-history/brief.html> (May 24, 2002).

Naughton, John. *A Brief History of the Future: From Radio Days to Internet Years in a Lifetime.* Woodstock, N.Y.: Overlook Press, 2000.

Radosevich, Lynda. "The Father of the Internet Predicts His Brain Child's Future." *InfoWorld News,* October 4, 1999. <http://www.infoworld.com/cgi-bin/displayStory.pl?/features/991004kleinrock.htm> (May 24, 2002).

Salus, Peter H. *Casting the Net: From ARPANET to Internet and Beyond.* Reading, Mass.: Addison-Wesley Publishing, 1995.

Segaller, Stephen. *Nerds 2.0.1: A Brief History of the Internet.* New York: TV Books, 1998.

Zakon, Robert H. "Hobbes' Internet Timeline v5.6." Zakon.org, 1993–2002. <http://www.zakon.org/robert/internet/timeline/> (May 24, 2002).

Further Reading

Berners-Lee, Tim. "Information Management: A Proposal." *Multimedia: From Wagner to Virtual Reality.* Randall Packer and Ken Jordan, eds. New York: Norton, 2001; pp. 189–205.

Dertouzos, Michael. *The Unfinished Revolution: Human-Centered Computers and What They Can Do for Us.* New York: HarperCollins, 2001.

Gillies, James, and Robert Cailliau. *How the Web Was Born.* Oxford, England: Oxford University Press, 2000.

Griffiths, Richard T. "History of the Internet, Internet for Historians (and just about everyone else)." Universiteit Leiden, October 4, 2001. <http://www.let.leidenuniv.nl/history/ivh/frame_theorie.html> (May 24, 2002).

Hiltzik, Michael A. *Dealers of Lightning: Xerox PARC and the Dawn of the Computer Age.* New York: HarperBusiness, 1999.

Rheingold, Howard. *The Virtual Community: Homesteading on the Electronic Frontier.* Reading, Mass.: Addison-Wesley, 1993.

Related Topics

Berners-Lee, Tim; BITNET; Browser; Cerf, Vinton; Cyberspace; Email; Human-Computer Interaction; Hypertext; Interactivity; Interface; Internet Engineering Task Force; Licklider, J. C. R.; Peer-to-Peer; Rheingold, Howard; Satellite Networks; USENET; Virtual Community; World Wide Web

— *Kevin Featherly*

Internet Appliances

Internet appliances are electronic devices used to perform tasks (e.g., write letters and send emails) that do not necessarily require the processing power and all the functionality that a personal computer (PC) affords. Internet appliances are also referred to as Web appliances, information appliances, Internet toasters, and Internet terminals. Arguments persist about what type of technology an Internet appliance actually is. However, the majority agree that the appliance needs to meet two criteria: It connects directly to the Internet through an Internet service provider (ISP) in order to connect with an application service provider (ASP) to download necessary software; and its primary use is to connect to the Internet. Internet appliances are becoming more numerous, so much so that Cahners In-Stat Group predicts the sales of Internet appliances may outstrip those of the PC by 2004.

The trend among many computer users is to use PCs for tasks like surfing the Internet, emailing friends, and writing letters. Such tasks require little computer processing power, but consumers often buy expensive PCs to perform these mundane tasks; hence the need for a smaller device that is more specifically tailored to accomplishing such simple tasks with minimal cost and equipment.

Internet appliances are less powerful than PCs. They have minimal memory, smaller hard drive space, less local software, and less processing power. The size of an Internet appliance can vary, from a desktop model that looks like a regular PC to a handheld device no bigger than a portable cassette player. Most Internet appliances utilize an internal modem to connect with an ISP and ASP, although the trend is to use wireless networks, which allows some of the smaller Internet appliances to be portable.

Small Internet appliances such as two-way pagers, Web cellular phones, and WebTV, can already be found in homes. WebTV, one of the first commercially available Internet appliances, adds Internet surfing and email capabilities to a television. Some consumers observed that while WebTV is relatively cheap compared to a PC, the fact that other household members could not watch TV if one person was using the TV to search the Internet was a distinct drawback. This difficulty led companies to begin creating stand-alone desktop Internet appliances.

Desktop Internet appliances like Qubit's Atom and iPac's IA-2 looked like a standard PC. However, these eventually gave way to portable handheld devices such as 3Com's Ergo Audrey, Gateway's Gateway Connected Touch Pad, and Compaq's iPac IA-1, with flat-panel LCD screens, and miniaturized keyboards or stylus for inputting. Recent Internet appliances also have the ability to link with other hardware devices, such as digital cameras and printers.

Each Internet appliance is built specifically to execute a small number of tasks, and the uses to which it can be put vary greatly. For this reason, some critics initially believed that the industry had taken a step backward; instead of utilizing one computer for thousands of tasks, a person would need several Internet appliances to accomplish different tasks.

With the advent of more capabilities for Internet appliances, consumers should be aware that other drawbacks exist over and above their lack of standard PC computing power. Internet appliances are sometimes tied to specific ISPs and ASPs, thus restricting what software is available. Fees still must be paid for Internet connections to the ISP and, in addition, different ASP providers ask for fees for users to utilize their programs. Different fees may be charged on a regular basis, even after the Internet appliance is bought, although some free programs are being made available. With the market for Internet appliances expanding, users can expect them to tackle a broader range of tasks and feature more refined programs in the future.

Bibliography

Anderson, Heidi. "Skip the PC & Go Online Via Web Terminals." *Smart Computing,* vol. 6, no. 12 (December 2000), pp. 26–28.

"How the Internet Works, Part I." *Smart Computing,* vol. 5, no. 1 (February 2001), pp. 140–145.

Moschovitis, Christos; Poole, Hilary; Schuyler, Tami; and Theresa M. Senft. *History of the Internet: A Chronology, 1843 to the Present.* Santa Barbara, Calif.: ABC-CLIO, 1999.

Further Reading

Cole, Bernard Conrad. *The Emergence of Net-Centric Computing: Network Computers, Internet Appliances, and Connected PCs.* Upper Saddle River, N.J.: Prentice Hall, 1999.

Related Topics

Graphical User Interface; Internet; Internet Service Providers; Java; Wireless Networks

— *Kathy Broneck*

Internet Corporation for Assigned Names and Numbers

Controversial from its inception, the Internet Corporation for Assigned Names and Numbers (ICANN) is a private, nonprofit, non-governmental policymaking body chartered by the U.S. Commerce Department in 1998 to take over much of the U.S. government's formal oversight of the Internet's Domain Name System (DNS). Through its Defense Department, the federal government funded and par-

ticipated in most of the work that created the Internet, and when the Internet was still relatively small, it was also saddled with the network's address administration. But the Internet exploded in the late 1990s, and ICANN was created to free the government from the burden of overseeing the monumental task of dispensing World Wide Web addresses to businesses and individuals. ICANN also helped deflect growing criticism, especially among European Union states, that the U.S. government held too much power over the global Internet. Nevertheless, ICANN itself has been the object of almost constant criticism since its formation.

While the Internet is usually thought of as ungovernable, some form of central authority over the DNS is essential to make sure that all Web addresses are unique. The DNS is what allows Web surfers to type easily remembered names (like "Amazon.com") into their browsers instead of arcane server numbers when they want to view a Web site. For instance, we can type in http://www.congress.gov rather than having to recall the more difficult server number for the same site, which is http://140.147.248.209. The DNS is the reason that Web addresses end in "top-level domains" (TLDs) like ".com," ".edu," ".gov," ".mil," ".net," and ".org." Without some form of central oversight, it would not be possible to prevent a situation in which, for example, two or more sites called "Ebay.com" fight for audience share on the Web.

INITIAL STRUCTURING, INITIAL CRITICISM

Based in California, ICANN comprises 19 volunteer, voting board members and a staff of 14 employees. It was instituted as a "technical coordinating body" by Jon Postel, the affable former leader of the Internet Society and one of the original builders of the Internet.

Postel began assembling ICANN in 1998, several years after the National Science Foundation handed over the tremendous responsibility of domain-name management duties to the U.S. Department of Commerce. ICANN was to be a "global consensus-building setting" forum, and would succeed the Internet Assigned Numbers Authority (IANA), a body that had answered directly to the Department of Commerce; Postel had been IANA's head. In fact, as World Wide Web founder Tim Berners-Lee wrote in *Weaving the Web* (1999), Postel in effect *was* the IANA, guiding it firmly but neutrally as a public trust. Much of the Web's growth in those years actually depended on Postel's personal credibility and authority, and Postel was successful in seeing that the distribution of domain names was for the most part fair and impartial. However, just before the creation of ICANN was complete, Postel died of complications from heart surgery at age 55.

Some critics complain that the Clinton administration's policy of Internet privatization really was just an effort to give businesses power over the Internet's future, an approach that many said ran contrary to the egalitarian interests of the Internet. With ICANN in place, they claimed, the best domain names would eventually wind up in the hands of the people with the most money.

ICANN says that to "run the Internet" is not its mandate. Rather, the organization says on its Web site, it is to oversee management "of only those specific technical managerial and policy development tasks that require central coordination: the assignment of the Internet's unique name and number identifiers."

PRACTICES AND DECISIONS

Still, ICANN has often been criticized for such practices as holding its early board meetings in secret. But it has proven to be greatly influential over public Internet policy. The United States and other governments generally recognize its DNS decisions, and rely on ICANN's judgments on issues such as how to allocate Internet protocol addresses, how to manage the crucial root-server system, and how to assign such technical parameters as transmission control protocol (TCP) port numbers and address resolution protocol (ARP) hardware types. ICANN also decides what TLD names the public should have at its disposal.

Via a very controversial process, ICANN created seven new TLDs: .aero, .biz, .coop, .info, .museum, .name, and .pro. (Numerous other possibilities, like .kids, .shop, and .web were rejected, although they might be reconsidered later.) The new TLDs were the first to be created since the advent of .com more than a decade ago, and are aimed at alleviating the lack of available .com addresses; the first two additions, .biz and .info, went live in 2001.

Within its first two years of existence, ICANN made a series of decisions that could have far-reaching ramifications for future control of the Internet. First, it pressured the commercial domain-name registry Network Solutions Inc. (NSI) to surrender its monopoly over the sale of domain names and allow other registrars to compete. That decision has proven mostly popular, although NSI has vigorously resisted it.

Next, ICANN set a policy of mandatory arbitration in "cybersquatting" disputes, which typically occur after someone intentionally buys a commercial-sounding domain name (McDonalds.com, for instance) in the hope of reselling it to a company at a huge profit. Initially, domain-name rights spelled out in ICANN's Uniform Domain-Name Dispute Resolution Policy (UDRP) focused strictly on such disputed trademarks. But within eight months, a series of decisions quickly expanded protections to informal trade names—and to the names of famous people like movie star Julia Roberts, who was awarded the use of Juliaroberts.com even though she had never registered her name as a trademark. Many complain that this process is unfair. One study, conducted in August 2001 by University of Ottawa Law School professor Michael Geist, concluded that the World Intellectual Property Organization (WIPO), whose Arbitration and Mediation Center has handled 58 percent of ICANN's cybersquatting arbitration cases, rules in favor of trademark holders 82.2 percent of the time. Critics complain that this imbalance is a direct result of "privatizing" Internet governance, which was a specific goal of the Clinton administration in the formation of ICANN.

In another important decision, ICANN's board decided that only five of its 19 board members, rather than the promised nine, would be elected from the Internet community at large instead of appointed by ICANN members. This restriction would seem to ensure that the "Internet community" that ICANN ostensibly represents will remain firmly in the minority when voting on important DNS decisions. ICANN board chairman Vinton Cerf, inventor of the TCP protocol and normally regarded as something of a hero in Internet circles, rankled some when he said that he couldn't see how electing board members from the public would help ICANN get its work done. Further aggravating the situation, in November 2000, four of the board's original members—Frank Fitzsimmons, Hans Kraaijenbrink, Jun Murai, and Linda Wilson—said they would stay on as board members until late 2002, rather than step down after a year or two, as was the original plan. While five other members, including former board chair Esther Dyson, did agree to step down on November 16, 2000, having four "board squatters" change their minds about leaving made policy over board members' terms in office unclear.

It also is unclear how much authority ICANN actually possesses in the end, or where its dominion ends. As critic Steven Hill writes, ICANN "is either an innocuous nonprofit with a narrow technical mandate or the first step in corralling the Internet for commercial and other purposes." David Holtzman, former chief technology officer at NSI, puts his concerns more bluntly: "If we're going to have a world government," he wrote, "then I want a revolution first."

ROOT-SERVER CONTROL AND OTHER ISSUES

Another view holds that ICANN may be a tool used by the U.S. to maintain a hold on the Internet, the development of which was mostly funded by the federal government. University of Miami Law School professor Michael Froomkin is among those who suggest that the U.S. Department of Commerce is "laundering its policymaking" through ICANN. Froomkin points out that the National Telecommunications and Information Administration (NTIA) within the Department of Commerce is still under a contract with ICANN that grants the NTIA the right to approve any additions to the main root file—the document contained in the "root server" that determines which new generic TLDs may be visible to most Internet users.

ICANN's control over the root server is perhaps the key issue. The root server is a single, high-powered computer that contains the root file. All requests to view Web pages are routed through this one supermachine, which, together with the various domain servers that it points to, form the very heart of the Internet. Despite talk that the Internet is decentralized and ungovernable, if anyone wanted to control it, they could do no better than to begin with the root server.

"Since ICANN controls the root server," Hill writes, "it is technically feasible for this nearly anonymous organization to exercise a kind of life-or-death power over the global network. Eliminate the entry for Xyz.com from the .com domain server, and Xyz.com vanishes entirely from cyberspace."

There are other issues as well. ICANN could, for example, determine that operators of the racist MartinLutherKing.org hate site have no right to free speech on the Web, and pull its plug. ICANN could determine which warring faction in a strife-torn nation has the right to that nation's country-code domain (aside from the .com and .org and other TLDs, nations have their own TLDs, such as .us and .uk). ICANN has already raised eyebrows, in fact, by dispensing a country-code TLD to the Palestinian authority, although that right is generally granted only to legally recognized nation-states. Critics contend that ICANN's potentially unfettered ability to make such decisions makes it perhaps the first global regulatory body, complete with an alternative world

court that dispenses key legal determinations in trademark disputes. ICANN continues to disavow any such ambitions, insisting that it leads through consensus, not through centralized command.

Bibliography

Berners-Lee, Tim, and Mark Fischetti. *Weaving the Web: The Original Design and Ultimate Destiny of the World Wide Web.* San Francisco: HarperSanFrancisco, 1999.

France, Mike. "Behave—or Lose Your Domain Name." *BusinessWeek* e.biz, August 23. 1999. <http://www.businessweek.com/cgibin/ebiz/ebiz_frame.pl?url=/ebiz/9908/ep0823.htm> (May 24, 2002).

Froomkin, Michael. "Wrong Turn in Cyberspace: Using ICANN to Route Around the APA and the Constitution." University of Miami School of Law, 2000. <http://personal.law.miami.edu/~froomkin/articles/icann-main.htm> (May 24, 2002).

Hill, Steven. "ICANN: Secret Government of the Internet?" *In These Times*, vol. 24, no. 12 (May 15, 2000). <http://www.inthesetimes.com/issue/24/12/hill2412.html> (May 24, 2002).

Holtzman, David. "If We're Going to Have a World Government, I Want a Revolution First." *ICANNWatch.org*, April 9, 2001. <http://www.icannwatch.org/article.php?sid=98> (May 24, 2002).

ICANNWatch.org. "ICANN for Beginners." 2001. <http://www.icannwatch.org/icann4beginners.php> (May 24, 2002).

Internet Corporation for Assigned Names and Numbers (ICANN). "ICANN: A Structural Overview." March 24, 2002. <http://www.icann.org/general/structure.htm> (May 24, 2002).

Internet Corporation for Assigned Names and Numbers (ICANN). "Background." July 1999. <http://www.icann.org/general/background.htm> (May 24, 2002).

Newton, Harry. *Newton's Telecom Dictionary*. New York: CMP Books, 2001.

Further Reading

Barrett, Neil. *The State of the Cybernation: Cultural, Political and Economic Implications of the Internet.* London: Kogan Page, 1996.

Dyson, Esther. *Release 2.0: A Design for Living in the Digital Age.* New York: Broadway Books, 1997.

Koppell, Jonathan G.S. "Analysis: Internet Body Seen As Future of Government." *CNN.com*, August 24, 2000. <http://www.cnn.com/2000/TECH/computing/08/24/icann.future.gov.idg/> (May 24, 2002).

Mueller, Milton. "ICANN and Internet Governance: Sorting Through the Debris of 'Self-egulation.'" *The Journal of Policy, Regulation and Strategy for Telecommunications Information and Media*, vol. 1,

no.6 (December 1999), pp. 497–520.
<http://www.icannwatch.org/archive/muell.pdf>
(May 24, 2002).

Perine, Keith. "Throwing Rocks at ICANN."
The Industry Standard, April 3, 2000.
<http://www.thestandard.com/article/0,1902,13205,00.html>
(May 24, 2002).

Related Topics
ARPANET; Dyson, Esther; Internet; Internet Engineering
Task Force; Wireless Networks

— Kevin Featherly

Internet Engineering Task Force

The Internet Engineering Task Force (IETF) is the main
organization engaged in the development of new
Internet standard specifications. These standards specify procedures for operating the Internet system, and
are developed using an open-systems manner. The
IETF is composed of an international community of
Internet network designers, operators, vendors, and
researchers who are concerned with the evolution and
development of Internet architecture.

The IETF has a number of goals. Perhaps most
importantly, its members work to identify Internet
operational and technical problems, and propose
solutions to solve these problems, specifying the development or usage of protocols and architecture. The
IETF makes recommendations to the Internet
Engineering Steering Group (IESG) concerning the
standardization of Internet protocols and protocol
usage. It also facilitates technology transfer from the
Internet Research Task Force (IRTF) to the wider
Internet community, and provides a forum for the
exchange of information within that community,
which includes vendors, users, researchers, agency
contractors, and network managers.

The IETF is sub-divided into working groups
managed by area directors, who are members of the
IESG. Architectural oversight is provided by the
Internet Architecture Board (IAB), which also adju-
dicates appeals when there are complaints against
the IESG. The IETF and the IAB are organized bodies of the Internet Society (ISOC), which charters the
IAB and IESG.

Although the IETF meets three times a year in
various venues, much of the actual work is done
online through various mailing lists. The IETF is open
to any interested individual, and there are no formal

membership criteria. All IETF members are considered volunteers. Most members have full-time jobs,
and many participate with the sponsorship of
employers to conduct IETF business and attend the
various meetings.

The first IETF meeting was held in San Diego in
1986. Since then, IETF membership has grown exponentially. Members often do not attend the physical
meetings, but convene and discuss issues online. The
IETF Secretariat provides daily logistical support,
coordinates meetings, makes sure that the official
Internet Drafts directory is timely and orderly, and
assists the IESG with its work.

The IETF has expanded to more than 100 working groups (WGs), which include those covering the
following areas:

- Applications Area—protocols seen by user pro-
  grams, such as email and the Web;
- Internet Area—different ways of moving IP pack-
  ets and DNS information;
- Operations and Management Area—administra-
  tion and monitoring;
- Routing Area—making sure packets reach their
  destinations;
- Security Area—authentication and privacy;
- Transport Area—special services for special packets;
- User Services Area—support for end users and
  user support organizations;
- General Area—groups that don't fit in anywhere else.

WG activities are conducted through mailing lists
that are open to anyone. Criteria for posting depends
on the WG; some WG mailing lists let only list subscribers post to the mailing list, while others let anyone
post. Each WG has a charter, which states the scope of
the discussion and the goals of the WG. WGs have one
or two chairs who organize meeting agendas and facilitate consensus.

In terms of reaching consensus by WG members
on drafts, the IETF concurs by "rough consensus,"
meaning that a large majority of those that care
about an issue must agree. There is no formal voting
structure. Face-to-face WG meetings are certainly
not as important in the IETF as they are in other
organizations, as any decision made at a face-to-face
meeting must also gain consensus on the WG mailing
list. A WG will, within the terms of its charter,
decide which Internet Drafts get published as "official" WG documents.

IETF standards are published as a "request for
comments" (RFC). RFCs consist of proposed standards, draft standards, Internet standards (sometimes

referred to as "full standards"), experimental protocols, informational documents, and historic standards. Every RFC starts out as an Internet Draft. Steps for getting IETF standards published include:

- publishing the document as an Internet Draft;
- receiving comments on the draft;
- editing the draft based on the comments (this could happen multiple times);
- asking an area director to take the draft to the IESG;
- making any changes deemed necessary by the IESG;
- waiting for the final draft to be published by the RFC editor.

With the growth in IETF membership and the economic imperative of the Internet, the IETF has had to create several membership protocols, including a Code of Conduct, Guidelines and Procedures for Working Groups, and a delineation of the process by which the IETF appoints representatives to ICANN's (Internet Corporation for Assigned Names and Numbers) Protocol Support Organization's Protocol Council (PSO-PC).

The relationship between the IETF and the ICANN is, at this time, sensitive and confusing. The ISOC supports various Internet administrative infrastructures, including the IETF and the Internet Assigned Numbers Authority (IANA, the technical team making and publishing the assignments of Internet protocol technical parameters). IANA protocol assignments were done in cooperation with the IETF, but the IANA technical team is now part of ICANN. In March 2000, a memorandum of understanding (MOU) concerning the technical work of the IANA was signed between the IETF and the ICANN. This MOU defines the technical work to be carried out by the IANA on behalf of the IETF and the IRTF. Specifically, the MOU states that the IANA will assign and register Internet protocol parameters as per the criteria and procedures specified in IETF RFCs. IANA will also work with the IETF to develop any missing criteria and procedures over time.

The IETF has remained a durable and effective organization in delineating and creating Internet standards. Remarkably, this loosely organized group has helped nurture the growth of the Internet while remaining politically independent.

Bibliography

The Internet Engineering Task Force (IETF). Web site. <www.ietf.org> (May 24, 2002).

———. "The Tao of the IETF: A Novice's Guide to the Internet Engineering Task Force." August 2001. <http://www.ietf.org/tao.html> (May 24, 2002).

Carpenter, B.; Baker, F.; and Roberts, M. "Memorandum of Understanding Concerning the Technical Work of the Internet Assigned Numbers Authority." Globecom.net, June 2000. <http://globecom.net/ietf/rfc/rfc2860.html> (May 24, 2002).

Further Reading

Abbate, Janet. *Inventing the Internet*. Cambridge, Mass.: MIT Press, 1999.

Related Topics

Internet; Internet Corporation for Assigned Names and Numbers

— *Leslie Regan Shade*

Internet Relay Chat

Often called "the Net's equivalent of CB radio," Internet Relay Chat (IRC) is a real-time chat program accessible via the Internet. People in over 120 countries and territories have used IRC, and one can easily find conversations flourishing in English, German, Japanese, French, Finnish, and other languages there.

FROM SERVERS TO NETWORKS

According to its creator, Jarkko Oikarinen, "the birthday of IRC was August 1988." Oikarinen, a network administrator at the University of Oulu, Finland, wanted to expand some of the school's bulletin-board system (BBS) software to include real-time discussions among members. At the time, a program called Talk was already in existence; it enabled two remote computer users to carry on a sentence-by-sentence conversation with one another. Oikarinen's contribution was made when he modified Talk to Chat, which permitted multiple users to join in the conversation.

Although IRC was not the first real-time chat system to be implemented on a large scale (the U.S. military had been using one for some time), it was the first to be available to ordinary users. Oikarinen had intended to implement his chat program only on his own server, tolsun.oulu.fi. Soon, however, friends at Helsinki University and Tampere University began running chat servers connected to Oikarinen's over the Internet. IRC was entirely a Finnish affair until servers at the University of Denver and Oregon State University connected as well. By the middle of 1989, IRC had spread across the Internet, with 40 servers worldwide.

In the beginning of IRC's popularity, all servers were connected to one another. But in August 1990, IRC users began complaining about one specific server, eris.berkeley.edu, which had particularly lax security. In protest, a group of servers formed the first IRC "Net," EFNet, which stood for "Eris Free network." Today, there are hundreds of independent IRC networks, but the "Big Four" are EFNet, UnderNet, DALnet, and IRCnet. Researcher Daniel Stenberg has discovered what he calls an "increasing regionalization" of the global networks. For example, IRCnet users are generally European, he notes, whereas EFNet users are generally from the Americas and Australia. In addition, there exist a number of regional IRC networks, such as BrasNet for Brazilian users.

RELAYS AND CHANNELS

As IRC expert Alexander Charalabidis explains, "The keyword in IRC is 'relay.'" In its simplest form, IRC consists of two programs: a server program that accepts connections, and a client program that connects to a server. The most popular client for connecting to IRC these days is MIRC freeware for Windows, although Java-based interfaces now permit users to join IRC chats via the Web as well. Once connected to an IRC server, users join conversation spaces called channels, whose names are designated by the # sign. Channels can be public or private, moderated or unmoderated, and conversational topics generally range from the profound to the banal to the "wild and wooly." It is not uncommon for one IRC server to have dozens, hundreds, or even thousands of chat channels open simultaneously, and experienced users often find themselves juggling multiple channels at a time.

Perhaps the most famous IRC channel is known as #report, devoted to breaking news stories. Particularly in crises, #report provides real-time communication among people worldwide, without the filters of mass media. The #report channel gained its reputation during the 1991 Gulf War, and then again during the coup attempt against Boris Yeltsin, when IRC users in Moscow typed in live reports of what they were witnessing. On September 11, 2001, IRC was used once again by those trying to get information regarding the state of New York City and Washington, D.C., after the terrorist attacks.

Oikarinen's original Chat program required multiple users to type their responses to one another a line at a time, with no built-in mechanism for turn-taking or other conversational niceties. As a result, the average IRC channel reads as conversational chaos to novices. Although programmers are currently working on different software solutions to make IRC chats clearer, linguist Susan Herring notes that some people enjoy "exploit[ing] the potential of loosened coherence"

that IRC affords over face-to-face conversations. Experienced users report that they generally ignore the presence of other users who aren't discussing the same thing as they are, and use shared conventions (such as the belief that typing in all capital letters constitutes "shouting") to facilitate communication.

ANONYMITY AND ATTACKS

Far more serious than the issue of conversational coherence on IRC is the matter of anonymity and server attacks. On IRC, users remain anonymous until they choose to disclose their identities. Recently, media attention has been focused on certain IRC channels that function as "anonymous town squares" for hackers to brag about their abilities. As a recent *Wall Street Journal* report noted, "People familiar with the hacker IRC channels describe them as a subculture complete with a social hierarchy, vocabulary and codes of conduct—as well as its own version of warfare."

One of the most pernicious sorts of social warfare on IRC has been the recent rise of distributed denial-of-service (DOS) attacks, deliberate acts of vandalism in which anonymous users overload servers with so much data that legitimate users are effectively locked out. As DALnet founder Sven Nielsen noted, "The hacker will run a denial-of-service attack proving 'I'm bigger than you because I can run this tool against you.'" Recently, DOS attacks have become so virulent that several hosting companies have decided to unhook their servers from a number of IRC networks; several chat services have had to shut down as a result.

THE FUTURE OF IRC

Between its security woes and the rise of visual-based chat systems, some have said that IRC's days are numbered. Others disagree, pointing out that security problems are rectifiable, and that while IRC will never appeal to those who find it necessary to be in visual contact during conversation, it still has a place on the 'Net. Indeed, there are a few prototypes on the horizon that may cause a renaissance within the IRC movement. One of these is Butterfly, an intelligent agent designed by scientists at MIT that allows users to search channels for conversations most interesting to them. Butterfly is destined to excite those for whom, as Charalabidis notes, IRC is "more than just a chat system or a meeting place—it can become a way of life."

Bibliography

Cha, Ariana Eunjung. "Hackers' Web Weapons Test-Fired on Chat Sites; Internet Communities Ravaged Daily by E-Vandals." *Washington Post*, February 19, 2000, p. E1.

Charalabidis, Alexander. *The Book of IRC: The Ultimate Guide to Internet Relay Chat.* San Francisco, Calif.: No Starch Press, 2000.

Danet, Brenda; Ruedenberg, Lucia; and Yehudit Rosenbaum-Tamari. "Hmmm . . . Where's That Smoke Coming From?" *Network and Netplay: Virtual Groups on the Internet.* Fay Sudweeks, Margaret McLaughlin, and Sheizaf Rafaeli, eds. Cambridge, Mass.: MIT Press, 1998.

Danet, Brenda; Wachenhauser, T.; Bechar-Israeli, H.; Cividalli, A.; and Y. Rosenbaum-Tamari. "Curtain Time 20:00 GMT: Experiments with Virtual Theater on Internet Relay." *Journal of Computer-Mediated Communication* 1, no. 2 (1995).

Gomes, Lee. "Internet Relay Chat Is Suspected Launch Pad of Web Hackers." *Wall Street Journal,* February 14, 2000, p. B6.

Herring, Susan. "Interactional Coherence in CMC." *Journal of Computer-Mediated Communication,* vol. 4, issue 4 (June 1999). <http://www.ascusc.org/jcmc/vol4/issue4/herring.html> (May 10, 2002).

Markoff, John, and Sara Robinson. "Chat Systems Yield Clues in Web Attacks by Hackers." *The New York Times,* February 15, 2000, p. C2.

Oikarinen, Jarkko. "Early IRC History." December 10, 1993. <http://www.the-project.org/history.html> (May 10, 2002).

Stenberg, Daniel. "History of IRC (Internet Relay Chat)." January 8, 2002. <http://daniel.haxx.se/irchistoryhtml> (May 10, 2002).

Suler, John. "Psychological Dynamics of Online Synchronous Conversations in Text-Driven Chat Environments." *Psychology of Cyberspace,* October 1997. <http://www.rider.edu/users/suler/psycyber/texttalk.html> (May 10, 2002).

Van Dyke, Neil W.; Lieberman, Henry; and Pattie Maes. "Butterfly: A Conversation-Finding Agent for Internet Relay Chat." Paper presented at the International Conference on Intelligent User Interfaces, Los Angeles, California, 1999.

Further Reading

Cherny, Lynn. *Conversation and Community: Chat in a Virtual World.* Stanford, Calif.: CSLI Publications, 1999.

Farnham, Shelly; Chesley, Harry R.; McGhee, Debbie E.; Kawal, Reena; and Jennifer Landau. "Structured Online Interactions: Improving the Decision-Making of Small Discussion Groups." Paper presented at the Proceedings of the ACM 2000 Conference on Computer Supported Cooperative Work, Philadelphia, Pennsylvania, December 2000.

Herring, Susan C., ed. *Computer-Mediated Communication: Linguistic, Social and Cross-Cultural Perspectives, Pragmatics & Beyond.* Amsterdam/Philadelphia: J. Benjamins, 1996.

Hinner, Kajetan. "Statistics of Major IRC Networks: Methods and Summary of User Count." *M/C: A Journal of Media and Culture* 3, no. 4 (2000). <http://www.media-culture.org.au/0008/count.txt> (May 10, 2002).

Liu, Geoffrey Z. "Virtual Community Presence in Internet Relay Chatting." *JCMC* 5, no. 1 (1999).

Simpson, Carol. "Internet Relay Chat." *Teacher Librarian* 28, no. 1 (2000), pp. 18–20.

Suler, John. *Psychological Dynamics of Online Synchronous Conversations in Text-Driven Chat Environments* 1 (October 1997). <http://www.rider.edu/users/suler/psycyber/texttalk.html> (May 10, 2002).

Toyer, Kathryn. *Learn Advanced Internet Relay Chat.* Plano, Texas: Wordware Pub., 1998.

Vronay, David; Smith, Marc; and Steven Drucker. "Alternative Interfaces for Chat." Paper presented at the 12th annual ACM Symposium on User Interface Software and Technology, Asheville, North Carolina, 1999.

Related Topics

Bulletin-Board Systems; Chat; Security; Virtual Community

— *Theresa M. Senft*

Internet Service Providers

An Internet Service Provider (ISP) is a company that provides access to the Internet. The majority of ISPs supply users with software, dial-up numbers, Internet Protocol (IP) addresses, login names, and passwords in exchange for a monthly fee, which can range from $10 to more than $100 depending on the company, the type of connection, the number of access hours, and the availability of additional packages for Web building. ISPs are also in charge of maintaining hardware such as servers, routers, and multiple phone lines, which are necessary in order for information to be exchanged between the users and the Internet. The general public tends to use the terms ISP and Internet Access Provider (IAP) interchangeably, but there is a small distinction between the two. IAPs often offer only modem or PPP (point-to-point protocol) connections; ISPs offer the same access, but can also provide direct connections (e.g., T1, DSL, satellite service) and additional services such as Web development and Web hosting.

EARLY INTERNET CONNECTIVITY AND THE RISE OF THE FIRST ISPs

From the 1960s to the 1980s, the Internet was primarily used by the government and the academic community; therefore, there were only small groups of networks throughout the nation, with limited accessibility. It was not until the late 1970s and early 1980s that the National Science Foundation (NSF) initiated the idea to expand access to include more users. ISPs such as Performance Systems International (PSI), Advanced Network and Systems (ANS), and Sprint's Sprintlink were made available, but were restricted to specific groups of users, such as those in academia and military branches. It was not until around 1989 that the first commercial ISP, The World, allowed the general public to connect to the Internet. Companies such as CompuServe and Prodigy, while providing online services, did not become ISPs until after The World debuted. America Online (AOL), which entered the ISP market in 1989, accumulated a million users by 1994, thus becoming the biggest national ISP.

Initially, in order to promote their services, ISPs mailed installation software on CDs or disks to the general public, offering them free trial memberships that ran in tens or even hundreds of hours. ISPs had alliances with Web browser companies at that time, and would include that browser on their installation CDs. In late 1998, AOL proposed a merger with Netscape, thereby cornering a significant share of the ISP and Web browser business. This alarmed Microsoft, as AOL's default browser was Internet Explorer (IE) and Microsoft promoted AOL's dial-up service icon on its Windows desktop. During Microsoft's anti-trust lawsuit, AOL alleged that Microsoft planned to include the Microsoft Network (MSN) icon, and exclude AOL's, in the event of the AOL/Netscape merger. AOL claimed that it would not drop IE as its preferred Web browser and merged with Netscape in 1999. The majority of ISPs, including AOL, carry both browser manufacturers' software on their installation CDs, and the user can decide which to install.

ALLIANCES AND COMPETITION

The latest trend in ISPs is to form alliances with companies other than browser providers, in order to gain and sustain users. ISPs team up with local companies that already have an established customer reputation; the recent alliance between America Online and retailer CompUSA is one example of this trend. Local companies, called Virtual Internet Service Providers (VISPs; in this instance, CompUSA) promote and sell the Internet connection in their stores, while the ISP (in this instance, AOL) provides the VISP and its

customers with the actual service (e.g., dial-up numbers, servers), and also promote the VISP's stores within its service. Other ISPs like MSN have started forming alliances with computer companies such as Dell. Consumers who buy new computers receive such promotions as rebates on computers or one year of free access if they sign up with the partner ISP.

The Telecommunications Act of 1996 also brought changes to ISPs. One of the act's intentions was to promote competition among telecommunication companies. Still, mergers between large ISPs to increase their user base are becoming more common, and may be negating the act's hoped-for impact. A recent merger between AOL, CompuServe (which had been the number two ISP in the United States), and Time Warner has contributed to AOL's current status as the nation's largest ISP provider. Other mergers between Gateway, EarthLink, and MindSpring have made them collectively the new number two ISP. AOL, with its combined user base of more than 19 million in the United States, is still far ahead of the other ISPs in the top 20, such as Prodigy, MSN, and AT&T's WorldNet.

Several years ago, free ISPs were gaining a footing in the business. Companies such as Juno and NetZero offered limited free Internet access in exchange for its users completing surveys and questionnaires. In 2001 Juno and NetZero merged to become United Online; each company has kept its own service and brand. Juno eventually started charging a fee for its service, but has extended the service to unlimited hours, while NetZero still offers a free 40-hour-a-month limited Internet connection. However, NetZero has also started charging a fee—albeit a minor one in comparison to its competitors—for unlimited access.

ISP SIZE AND TRAFFIC LEVELS

Most of the larger, more recognizable ISPs are national, with users numbering in the millions. Many users of large ISPs complain about slow connection times, an inability to connect due to heavy usage, getting dropped if the system becomes too busy, and increasing fees. Many ISPs offer their services via phone lines, and it is important to note that the telephone companies that supply the phone lines can affect the connection, as can slower modems (24.4 bps vs. 56 kbps). Some companies, like AT&T and Sprint, offer broadband connections at speeds of 256 kbps or more, affording users continual access without phone-line connections, but use has been limited thus far since special cables need to be installed. In June 2001, ISPs such as AOL and EarthLink joined with Cox

Communications to pioneer Internet access through pre-existing television cable lines, thus expanding the reach of ISPs to the home.

ISPs play a crucial role in the life of the Internet, providing the gateway for general public access. Consumers should be aware, though, that as mergers of ISPs continue, public usage increases, and computer equipment ages, their ability to connect to the Internet will be impacted. Additionally, while Internet-ready computers with an ISP's software already pre-loaded may offer a consumer discounts and rebates, that particular ISP may not be the best one for the consumer. Depending on their usage times and the services and connection speeds they need, users may be financially better off with other ISPs.

Consumers are likely to see more VISPs as the need for more localized customer service by national ISPs increases and mergers and joint efforts between telecommunication companies become more commonplace. The Federal Communications Commission (FCC) also predicts that the created competition between the varying bandwidth technologies will mean an increase in available broadband access, as well as more competitive prices.

Bibliography

Aboba, Bernard. *The Online User's Encyclopedia*. Reading, Mass.: Addison-Wesley, 1993.

Olavsrud, Thor. "NetZero Migrates Free Users to Premium Service." *InternetNews—ISP News Archive*, May 3, 2001. <http://www.internetnews.com/isp-news/article/0,,8_758651,00.html/> (March 26, 2002).

Scalet, Sarah D. "Internet Service Providers: Companies Marked by New Alliances & Free Services." *Smart Computing: Computing Winners and Losers* (Learning Series), vol. 6, no. 3 (March 2000).

W3. "The History of the World Wide Web." 2001. <http://www.w3history.org/> (March 26, 2002).

Further Reading

Henry, Hannah. "Internet Service Providers & Phone Lines: Ways to Improve Your Connection and Its Speed." *Smart Computing: Troubleshooting Edition* (Reference Series), vol. 4, no. 1 (February 2000).

Moschovitis, Christos; Poole, Hilary; Schuyler, Tami; and Theresa Senft. *History of the Internet: A Chronology, 1843 to the Present*. Santa Barbara, Calif.: ABC-CLIO, 1999.

The List. "The Definitive ISP Buyer's Guide." 2001. <http://thelist.internet.com/> (March 26, 2002).

Related Topics

ARPANET; Broadband; Browser; Internet; Telephony

— Kathy Broneck

Java

Java is an object-oriented, cross-platform programming language that is used to create stand-alone applications, mostly used by Web sites, that have the capacity to run animations and promote interactivity. Unlike other object-oriented languages, Java code can run across varying equipment designs, and unlike C++, it is multithreaded, able to execute multiple processes simultaneously.

Java is considered to be the first programming language that is independent from both the operating system and the microprocessor. Most computer languages translate their programs into binary code, zeros and ones, using a complier; the resulting program can be run only by a specific operating system. Java's executable code does not require constant contact with a server to execute its script, and does not need to be translated by separate compilers. Java programs do not need to be rewritten when operating systems are updated or new hardware is installed, because their actions are contained within their scripts, not tied to the hardware or software being used. This makes Java virtually universal across Web browsers and platforms. Java is therefore used to create Java Applets that give Web browsers the capability of displaying interactive programs as well as animations.

JAVA'S ORIGINS

In 1990, Sun Microsystems initiated the Green Project, whose goal was to create a new language that would be easier to program and run across a vast array of household appliances such as toasters, TV cable boxes, and lamps. This language would enable all of the appliances to communicate with each other as well as be controlled by a single remote device. The result was the 1991 creation of a language called Oak, named for the tree that grew outside programmer James Gosling's window. By 1992, a prototype system was built called *7 (pronounced "star seven"), using the Oak language. *7 was a handheld device that operated via touch screen, and was able to share information with other devices. The successful use of the Oak language within this prototype allowed for the continuation of the project and its integration into a commercial team called FirstPerson, Incorporated.

FirstPerson tried to market its new Oak programming language to Time-Warner for its set-top cable television boxes in 1993, but lost the bid. It continued to pursue selling its language in an effort to advance interactive television, but gave up in 1994—around the time that Marc Andreessen's Netscape Web browser was becoming a major phenomenon.

The World Wide Web was the perfect medium for Oak, because the language could run on multiple platforms, and could safely run Oak-based programs on users' computers from a Web page that contained the Oak script rather than from the server. Using Oak code, Sun Microsystems developed its own Internet browser called WebRunner. However, before the Oak language or WebRunner could be marketed in 1995, Sun changed Oak's name to Java—a move credited to Sun project manager Kim Polese—and WebRunner's name to HotJava, because the original names conflicted with already-established trademarks. Netscape quickly bought licensing rights to Java in 1995, and included Java beta support in its Navigator 2.0. The company showcased Java's capabilities to the general public on its own homepage by writing Java programs that brought animation and interactivity to the site. Microsoft's Internet Explorer was not so quick to allow Java onto its systems; Sun had to sue before Microsoft would allow its browser to run Java.

Before Java, the Web was seen mostly as a one-way communication medium. Users would go to a static Web site, view the page, go to another site, view it, and so forth. The introduction of Java to Internet browsers added interaction and animation within the Web site through small, self-contained programs written using Java, called Java Applets. These small programs run over the Web, allowing stock tickers and countdown clocks to continue to receive updated information while the user is on the site. Interactive programs such as forms used to collect data and user feedback, and online entertainment such as crossword puzzles, video games, and sounds, have all benefited from the Java programming language.

JAVA PROGRAMMING

When a user goes to a Web page that calls for a Java Applet, the appropriate applet is loaded directly onto the user's computer from the centralized network server where they are stored. These applets run automatically, using memory from the user's computer and not the server, and also allowing multithreading to occur. The user does not actually give permission for the program to download onto the computer; in light of the number of viruses that are spread through downloading programs onto desktop computers, Java Applets must pass through several levels of security.

First, Java programs are written and compiled into several bytecodes, instructions for running the program on different machines. A Java Virtual Machine (JVM), which is located on a user's machine within major Web browser software, processes these bytecodes. The JVM checks the Java code for any violation of user security before allowing the code to be downloaded. If security is breeched, the Java Applet will not be deployed.

The Java code used to write applets is not capable of reading or writing information to a local file system, nor can it be used to list directory contents, or to create or rename files. While this limitation is beneficial for user security, programmers that wish to read or write files, store data, process it, and return it cannot do so using just a Java Applet. Users are also at a disadvantage if they are using 16-bit computers rather than 32-bit, and are unable to print any outputs done by Java Applets.

However, the advantages of using Java code to write executable mini-programs outweigh its disadvantages. More than one applet can run at once, and other Internet features such as file transfers, downloading, and scrolling through Web pages can be utilized without upsetting a running Java Applet.

Java continues to be revised and updated by Sun, and integrated into a variety of applications. With an increase of Java users and programmers, Sun has decided to return to Oak's original goal and integrate Java into household electrical products such as telephones. It is also applying Java to speech recognition and speech synthesis projects, and to creating picoJava, a tiny chip that can deploy Java programs that will not require the aid of a central processing unit. Furthermore, handheld Internet appliances, cellular phones, and PalmPilots are now using Java Applets

through Internet connections that expand their capabilities from surfing the Internet and email access to include word processing, database manipulation, and checkbook balancing.

Bibliography

Barr, Christopher. "Wait Till You See the Net on Java." *CNET.com*, 1995.

Gosling, James. "A Brief History of the Green Project." 2001. <http://java.sun.com/people/jag/green/> (March 29, 2002).

Gosling, James; Steele, Guy; and Bill Joy. *The Java Language Specification*. Reading, Mass.: Addison-Wesley, 1996.

IT Toolbox. Homepage. <http://java.ittoolbox.com> (March 29, 2002).

O'Connell, Michael. "Java: The Inside Story." *SunWorld Online*, July 1995. <http://www.sunworld.com/swol-07-1995/swol-07-java.html> (March 29, 2002).

Further Reading

Arnold, Ken, and James Gosling. *The Java Programming Language* (Java Series) 2nd Edition. Reading, Mass.: Addison-Wesley, 1998.

Sun Microsystems, Inc. "What Is the Java Platform?" 2001. <http://java.sun.com/nav/whatis/index.html> (March 29, 2002).

Related Topics

Internet Appliances; Object-Oriented Programming

— *Kathy Broneck*

Jobs, Steven P.

1955–

Entrepreneur

Co-founder of the companies Apple and NeXT, Steve Jobs did not invent any of the radical computing technologies that he has promoted; rather, his role has been that of an evangelist, driving the world toward things it never knew it needed. In the 1970s, the Apple II pioneered the world of user-friendly personal computing. The Apple Macintosh, although borrowing heavily from previous innovations at Xerox PARC, influenced the "look and feel" of almost every desktop computer produced in the 1980s and 1990s.

Jobs' career in Silicon Valley began in 1974, when he took a job designing video games for Nolan Bushnell's company, Atari. He was soon attending meetings of the Homebrew Computer Club in Menlo Park, California. Jobs' old friend and fellow club member Steve Wozniak produced a machine called the Apple I. Jobs persuaded Wozniak to give up his job as an engineer at Hewlett-Packard so they could go into business together selling the machine. Apple Computer was formed on April 1, 1976, and soon produced the classic microcomputer called the Apple II. With sound and color graphics, and a price of $1,298, it became the most widely used computer in homes and schools; it was used by businesses primarily for its VisiCalc spreadsheet software. By 1979, the sales of the Apple II computer totaled $139 million, which represented a phenomenal 700 percent growth. One can fully grasp the pioneering role of Apple by noting that it was not until four years later that IBM sold its first personal computer.

Technically innovative though the Apple II was, what made it remarkable was its design and usability; it was not a machine for electronics enthusiasts, but a mass-market consumer product. Jobs' revolutionary influence was even more evident in his next projects, the Apple Lisa and Macintosh computers. Featuring an interface that was substantially influenced by a visit that Jobs and his engineers paid to the Xerox Palo Alto Research Center (PARC) in late 1979, these computers were supremely easy to use; it was Jobs who referred to the Macintosh as "the computer for the rest of us."

In an effort to find a killer application for the Macintosh, Jobs also helped to pioneer the field of desktop publishing. While the Mac was favored for its graphic capacities and ease of use, its slow speed, small monochrome screen, and closed architecture limited its use in the business sector. Nevertheless, the Lisa and the Macintosh were considered milestone achievements, as many components of the Macintosh graphical user interface (GUI) later became de facto standards, and were adopted by other operating systems such as Microsoft Windows.

For all his visionary thinking, and his ability to inspire devotion in Apple's customers and employees, popular accounts of Jobs the revolutionary paint him as an arrogant, intolerant workaholic who drove his engineers into the ground, then berated them for not working harder. In May 1985, Jobs became the casualty of a boardroom fight with Apple chief executive officer (CEO) John Sculley. Sculley stripped Jobs of all his official duties and banished him to a one-person office on the Apple campus.

By the fall of 1985, Jobs decided to leave the company; he started a new business called NeXT to concentrate on the profitable education market. NeXT attracted a great deal of media attention, as well as huge financial support from Japanese electronics

Apple Computer CEO Steve Jobs delivers the keynote speech at MacWorld Expo, January 2002. (AFP/Corbis)

company Canon and Texas billionaire H. Ross Perot. But critics believed that Jobs had misread what the market really wanted. The powerful $10,000 NeXT workstation announced in 1989 sold poorly, and NeXT stopped making the machine four years later. Nevertheless, NeXT continued to produce a technically innovative operating system called NeXTStep, which allowed programmers to write object-oriented programs made up of standard building blocks of code, making the programs quicker and cheaper to code and to maintain.

NeXT did not occupy all of Jobs' time, however. In 1986, he bought for around $60 million a majority stake in a computer-graphics company called Pixar, part of the Lucasfilm company run by *Star Wars* producer George Lucas. The company remained largely unknown outside Hollywood until 1995, when a film called *Toy Story,* which Pixar had produced for the Disney company, became a massive international success. Pixar's later successes included the animated feature *A Bug's Life* (1998), which became one of the most profitable animated films of all time, and *Monsters Inc.* (2001), which won the first-ever Academy Award in the newly created best animated film category.

Meanwhile, Apple had fallen on troubled times since Jobs' departure. In need of a new operating system, Apple bought NeXTStep in 1996 for $430 million. As part of the deal, Steve Jobs rejoined Apple as an unpaid adviser to then-CEO Gilbert Amelio. Amelio was removed by the Apple board in July 1997, and Jobs was promptly installed as "interim CEO."

Jobs was eventually confirmed as Apple's CEO, and rapidly restored profit and confidence. In 1998, Apple introduced the iMac; a low-priced, Internet-ready Mac with a colorful and stylish look, it was also the first personal computer without a floppy disk drive. The iMac quickly gained its popularity among users, with 800,000 units sold in 1998, and Apple was again on solid technological and financial footing. A redesigned iMac was introduced in Spring 2002, and a powerful update to the Mac operating system, OS X, continued to keep Apple profitable and in the limelight.

Jobs' name has become synonymous with innovation in personal computing. Many regard him as legendary, citing his artistic, idealistic, and creative impulses. Jobs is characterized as the defining personality of Silicon Valley, as his career development resembles the rise and fall of the computer industry there. In the 1970s and early 1980s, Jobs enjoyed great success with Apple Computer as Silicon Valley surged to the forefront of the computer industry. In the late 1980s, as Jobs' career took a downturn, so too did Silicon Valley experience setbacks. And in the late 1990s, the resurgence of Apple Computer with Jobs again at its helm paralleled the reviving of Silicon Valley as a center of computer innovations. Jobs will continue to be watched by industry analysts, and his career will continue to be an indicator of emerging trends in computer design and marketing.

Bibliography

Carlton, Jim. *Apple: The Inside Story of Intrigue, Egomania, and Business Blunders.* New York: Times Business/Random House, 1998.

Cringely, Robert X. *Accidental Empires: How the Boys of Silicon Valley Make Their Millions, Battle Foreign Competition, and Still Can't Get a Date.* New York: Harper Business, 1996.

Levy, Stephen. *Insanely Great: The Life and Times of Macintosh, the Computer That Changed Everything.* New York: Viking, 1994.

Kirkpatrick, David. "The Second Coming of Apple." *Fortune,* November 9, 1998, p. 42.

Stross, Randall. *Steve Jobs and the NeXT Big Thing.* New York: Atheneum, 1993.

Further Reading

Deutschman, Alan. *The Second Coming of Steve Jobs.* New York: Broadway Books, 2000.

Schlender, Brent. "Steve Jobs: Apple Gets Way Cooler." *Fortune,* January 24, 2000, p. 36.

Young, Jeffrey. *Steve Jobs: The Journey Is the Reward.* Glenview, Ill.: Scott, Foresman, 1988.

Related Topics

Computer Graphics; Education and Computers; Graphical User Interface; Xerox Palo Alto Research Center

— *Shing-Ling Sarina Chen and Chris Woodford*

Joy, Bill
1954–
Software Developer, Entrepreneur

As a creative mind bulldozing new pathways into the digital age, Bill Joy arguably ranks second in importance only to Microsoft's Bill Gates—and may in fact rank second to no one. Joy is one of the originators behind the open-source movement. As a student in his twenties, he devised a version of the Unix operating system (Berkeley Unix) that utilized the TCP/IP networking language, helping to place Unix servers at the forefront of the Internet revolution. He helped found Sun Microsystems, and helped invent both the Java programming language and the Jini networking system that he hopes one day will link everything from living-room lights to toasters and thermostats to the Internet and to each other.

Bill Joy was the eldest of three children growing up in Farmington Hills, Michigan. Early on, he wanted to be a ham radio operator, but his mother disapproved, worried about what she feared were her son's antisocial tendencies. His father, a business professor and stockbroker, felt the same concern, but his parents could not fail to notice the obvious gifts of a boy capable of memorizing the periodic table in a single evening at age 13.

Joy excelled in mathematics, and graduated from high school at age 15. He enrolled as an engineering undergraduate at the University of Michigan, where he worked on one of the earliest parallel-processing supercomputers. After graduating, he went to the University of California–Berkeley in 1975; he said that he made the choice to attend Berkeley because its relatively poor computer systems would force him to "be more ingenious." Once at Berkeley, Joy quickly gained notice in the computing community for helping to spruce up the Unix operating systems that were running the school's Digital Equipment computers. He compiled the improvements on computer tape, and sold copies for $50. The next year, he performed more advanced fixes to newer Digital Equipment VAX computers, this time selling his work for $300. Soon, hundreds of orders for his "Berkeley Unix" began rolling in. He responded in 1977 by creating Berkeley Software Distribution (BSD). BSD distributed Berkeley Unix's source code for free, allowing other programmers to learn and improve on the software. It was a pioneering moment in what is now called the open-source movement.

In 1978, Joy went to work for the federal government. His Unix team, which had beaten out Digital Equipment's own programmers in a bid to work for the Pentagon's Defense Advanced Research Projects Agency (DARPA), was assigned the task of devising software for the VAX computer that would allow it to link to the fledgling Internet, then still known as ARPANET.

In 1982, a team led by entrepreneur Scott McNealy recruited Joy for a new start-up company that proposed to create a high-powered version of Unix for a small, cheap, desktop-computer workstation that a member of McNealy's team had created. The computer was called the Stanford University Network workstation, or S.U.N. for short. The company built on it eventually became Sun Microsystems.

Joy led Sun's technical strategy, spearheading its open systems philosophy. He designed Sun's Network File System (NFS) and co-designed the SPARC microprocessor at a time when most software programmers barely understood what microprocessors did. In 1991, he designed the basic pipeline of the UltraSparc-I and its multimedia processing features. He drove the initial strategy for Java, co-designed Java processor architectures, and co-authored its programming-language specifications, helping to create an important, simplified new object-oriented programming language. Upon its 1995 release, Java was almost immediately integrated into early versions of the Netscape Navigator Web browser.

In 1997, President Bill Clinton appointed Joy co-chairman of the Presidential Information Technology Advisory Committee. The following year, Joy was appointed Sun's chief technologist, and went to work on new forms of distributed computing using Java and a related technology called Jini. According to *The Economist,* Jini works by embedding slivers of tiny Java applications into chips in devices like printers, TV set-top boxes, personal digital assistants, and cell phones, allowing them to remain constantly connected to the Internet and to constantly communicate among themselves. Joy has described the concept with two words: "simply connect."

In February 2001, Joy announced the launch of Juxtapose, or JXTA, which Sun says will provide a basis for future peer-to-peer content exchanges, although it is likely to have better controls and copyright protections than the renegade Napster program. Sun expects the technology to make it easier to access certain kinds of digital content while working in a peer-to-peer computing environment.

Joy is sometimes described as the Thomas Edison of the Internet. Given those credentials, it is little wonder that Joy sent shockwaves through the wired world when he became the first important new-media technologist to raise the alarm about the potential of computing technology to run amok, and possibly even to destroy humanity: In April 2000, *Wired* magazine published Joy's nightmarish, groundbreaking essay, "Why the Future Doesn't Need Us."

Influenced by Raymond Kurzweil's 1999 book called *The Age of Spiritual Machines: When Computers Exceed Human Intelligence,* Joy became convinced that Moore's Law of Progress, the computing theorem stating that computer processing speed will double every 18 months, will not run out of gas in 2010, as many scientists have believed. Instead, processing speed will follow Moore's Law until about 2030, Joy predicts. This means that ultrapowerful computing with molecule-sized processors is distinctly possible. While Kurzweil predicts good things from such a development—an era in which humans gain near-immortality by becoming one with robotic technology—the implications were for Joy profound and frightening.

Joy wrote that "robotics, genetic engineering, and nanotechnology pose a different threat than the technologies that have come before. Specifically, robots, engineered organisms, and nanobots share a dangerous amplifying factor: They can self-replicate. A bomb is blown up only once—but one bot can become many, and quickly get out of control." If such wonders as molecular electronics, genetic engineering, and robotics are permitted to develop unchecked, the future will be one that "doesn't need us."

The essay was met with a blast of media attention, but there was near-silence from Silicon Valley; Joy later joked that his peers must have been too busy starting up new companies. But some writers, virtual-reality inventor Jaron Lanier among them, criticized Joy's essay as a panicky reaction to technological breakthroughs that humanity likely will not allow to slip out of control.

Writing for *The Industry Standard*, John Seely Brown, director of Xerox Palo Alto Research Center, and Paul Duguid, a UC–Berkeley researcher, likewise criticized Joy's fears as premature. After all, if processors never shrink to the molecular size, there is little to fear in Joy's hypothesis. However, the authors also warn that such words of caution from the likes of Bill Joy must be heeded. They compared Joy to doom-saying eighteenth-century sociologist Thomas Malthus, who predicted that populations would grow so fast that agriculture would be unable to keep pace. They also referred to novelist H.G. Wells, who often wrote of technology wresting control from humanity. Malthus and Wells knew when and how to sound the alarm, Brown and Duguid wrote, and each, by their actions, probably helped prevent the very future they were so afraid of. Perhaps, they suggest, by writing "Why the Future Doesn't Need Us," Bill Joy has done the same thing.

Selected Works

Joy, Bill. "Design for the Digital Revolution." *Fortune*, March 6, 2000.
———. "Fears of a Tech Pioneer." *Time*, October 2, 2000.
———. "Why the Future Doesn't Need Us." *Wired* 8.04, April 2000. <http://www.wired.com/wired/archive/8.04/joy.html> (September 10, 2002).
Joy, Bill, and Ken Kennedy, eds. *Information Technology Research: Investing in Our Future*. Collingdale, Pa.: DIANE Publishing Co., 2000.

Bibliography

Brown, John Seely, and Paul Duguid. "Ideas to Feed Your Business: Re-Engineering the Future." *The Industry Standard*, April 24, 2000. <http://www.thestandard.com/article/0,1902,14013,00.html> (May 17, 2002).
Lanier, Jaron. "One-Half of a Manifesto." *Wired* 8.12, December 2000. <http://www.wired.com/wired/archive/8.12/lanier_pr.html> (May 17, 2002).
Schlendler, Brent. "The Edison of the Internet." *Fortune*, February 1999. <http://www.ecompany.com/articles/mag/1,1640,4658,00.html> (May 17, 2002).
Sun Microsystems. "Executive Bios: Bill Joy—Chief Scientist and Corporate Executive Officer." 1994–2002. <http://www.sun.com/aboutsun/media/ceo/mgt_joy.html> (May 17, 2002).

Further Reading

Auletta, Ken. *World War 3.0: Microsoft and Its Enemies*. New York: Random House, 2001.
Naughton, John. *A Brief History of the Future: From Radio Days to Internet Years in a Lifetime*. Woodstock, N.Y.: Overlook Press, 2000.
Kelly, Kevin, and Spencer R. "Creating One Huge Computer." *Wired News*, July 15, 1998. <http://www.wired.com/news/technology/0,1282,13744,00.html> (May 17, 2002).
O'Reilly, Tim. "A Conversation with Bill Joy." O'Reilly OpenP2P.com, February 13, 2001. <http://www.openp2p.com/pub/a/p2p/2001/02/13/joy.html> (May 17, 2002).
Segaller, Stephen. *Nerds 2.0.1: A Brief History of the Internet*. New York: TV Books, 1998.
Williams, Kathleen. "Bill Joy, Realist." *UPSIDE Magazine*, May 16, 2000. <http://www.upside.com/texis/mvm/story?id=3921cac40> (May 17, 2002).

Related Topics

Cyberspace; Cyborg; Java; Kurzweil, Raymond; Lanier, Jaron; Open Source; Stallman, Richard; Technological Determinism

— *Kevin Featherly*

Joyce, Michael

1945–

Hyperfiction Novelist

Michael Joyce is an author whose *afternoon: a story* was named "the granddaddy of hyperfiction" in a 1992 *New York Times* review. Hyperfiction, or hypertext fiction, is a form of writing, developed by Joyce and several others in the late 1980s, that relies on hyperlinks to connect readers to various story passages in the order of their choosing. In fact, the reader *must* choose, or else the novel ends on the first page, making the reader's role in the story's ultimate outcome, in theory, at least as important as the author's. There are so many possible avenues, in fact—so many possibilities for a story to go either forward or backward in time, for the prominence of one or all characters to change with each reading— that a work of hyperfiction can never truly be read the same way twice. It can even be said that a work of hyperfiction has no end (or beginning) at all. For Joyce, whose other hyperfiction works include *Twilight: A Symphony* (1996), *Twelve Blue* (1996), and *Sister Stories* (2000), hypertext fiction's radically new qualities make it a far more accurate reflection than traditional novels of the role of rote chance and the absolute arbitrariness of events in "post-modern" life.

Joyce was born in Lackawanna, New York, on November 9, 1945, and grew up in South Buffalo, New York. He was one of eight children of a steel-worker father (Thomas) and homemaker mother (Joyce) in an Irish-American family. Joyce graduated from Canisius High School in Buffalo, later studying English and philosophy at Buffalo's Canisius College. He graduated with a bachelor of arts degree from Canisius in 1972, later receiving his master of fine arts degree in 1974 from the University of Iowa Writers Workshop for Fiction. At various times in his life, Joyce has worked as a professor, a consultant, a carpenter, and a New York City community organizer; he gained what he calls in his curriculum vitae "a life-time's experience, during one day as a taxi driver."

Joyce published his first novel, *The War Outside Ireland,* in 1982; he won the Great Lakes New Writers Award in fiction for this effort, beating out *Shoeless Joe,* the W.P. Kinsella book that was the basis of the movie *Field of Dreams.* Joyce writes in the introduction of his 1995 book of essays, *Of Two Minds: Hypertext Pedagogy and Poetics,* that 1982 was also the year that he bought a personal computer, an event that he indicates began to change him almost immediately. Suddenly, he writes, he understood that he was possessed of "two minds," his own and the silicon brain contained in his computer. "Slowly I came to recognize myself veering toward becoming something of a cyborg," Joyce writes. "Previously stable horizons across my psychic landscape gave way to dizzying patterns of successive contours, each of which was most assuredly real, each of which did not last." Such new technology-laced perceptions formed the basis of the hyperfiction he would pioneer during the late 1980s.

Probably the first serious attempt at a hyperfiction novel, *afternoon: a story* was written during a single week in 1987, using the Storyspace hypertext computer authoring system that Joyce himself invented, with the assistance of computer-communications researcher and fellow author Jay Bolter. Influenced by such 1980s hypertext writing systems as the HyperCard system created for Apple's Macintosh computer, both Storyspace and *afternoon* predate the hypertext-driven World Wide Web by several years. Like the works of several other hyperfiction authors, *afternoon* was initially distributed on diskette by publisher Eastgate Systems. Joyce continues to write all his hypertexts in Storyspace, often moving them to the Web later.

Joyce, a self-professed postmodern author, is also an associate professor of English at Vassar College. His *afternoon: a story* and J. Yellowlees Douglas' 1993 hyperfiction novella *I Have Said Nothing* were chosen as the first two hyperfictions ever to be published by academic publishing house W.W. Norton & Co. The two works also spurred the staid Norton Anthology, for the first time, to publish a companion Web site so that the two works could be read as genuine hyperfiction works, instead of merely publishing them on paper as linear samples of disconnected snippets. Norton's inclusion of the two works was perhaps the most serious indication from the literary community that hyperfiction had gained acceptance as a major new literary form.

In a famous 1992 essay, author and Brown University professor Robert Coover declared the novel dead, killed by the irresistible force of hyperfiction, with Joyce's *afternoon* the first to strike a blow. "For all its passing charm," Coover wrote, "the traditional novel . . . is perceived by its would-be executioners as the virulent carrier of the patriarchal, colonial, canonical, proprietary, hierarchical and authoritarian values of a past that is no longer with us." Hypertext writers and readers, quite conversely, are considered both "co-writers and co-learners," according to Coover, and "its network of alternative routes" favors a variety of discourses emerging from one work of literature. In short, hyperfiction frees "the reader from domination by the author."

Many critics, however, have tended to dismiss hyperfiction as formless, confusing, frustrating and pointless. A 1997 *Salon* essay by Scott Rosenberg noted that there is only a "miniscule" audience for serious hyperfiction, and declared the form "unavoidably academic—lab experiments produced by grad schools for grad schools."

In March 1998, *New York Times* book critic Laura Miller aimed a dart at the heart of hyperfiction, contending that the form and its theoreticians have proved nothing so much as their inability to understand what real readers need and want. Wild proclamations that hypertext had killed off the modern novel still had the power to raise eyebrows, Miller wrote, but in the end, after hyperfiction's decade in existence, such claims about its new dominance had "proved to be little more than empty, apocalyptic showboating." Had not the Civil War novel *Cold Mountain* just sold a million copies? "I've yet to encounter anyone who reads hypertext fiction," Miller wrote. "No one, that is, who isn't also a hypertext author or a journalist reporting on the trend." Others, the critic sneered, simply shudder at the thought of reading a hyperfiction piece. "It's the very concept of hypertext fiction that strikes readers as dreary and pointless," Miller wrote. Still other critics have lumped hyperfiction together with narrative computer games such as *Myst*, and even Joyce has acknowledged "a common heritage with them."

For his part, Joyce has never wavered in his support of the literary form that he helped establish, although he once lamented in *The Atlantic Monthly* that he is dedicating himself to writing in what may be "a passing form in an uncertain medium."

Selected Works

Joyce, Michael. *afternoon: a story*. Watertown, Mass.: Eastgate Systems, 1987.

———. *Of Two Minds: Hypertext Pedagogy and Poetics*. Ann Arbor, Mich.: University of Michigan Press, 1995.

———. *Othermindedness: The Emergence of Network Culture*. Ann Arbor, Mich.: University of Michigan Press, 2001.

———. *Twilight, a Symphony*. Watertown, Mass.: Eastgate Systems, 1996.

Bibliography

Bakker, Jan-Hendrik. "Hypertext and the Human Factor. Narrativity After Modernism." Erasmus Universiteit Rotterdam, Centrum voor Filosofie & Kunst, 2001. <http://www.eur.nl/fw/cfk/kunsten/hypertext.shtml> (May 31, 2002).

Coover, Robert. "The End of Books." *The New York Times,* June 21, 1992. <http://www.nytimes.com/books/98/09/27/specials/coover-end.html> (May 31, 2002).

Kakutani, Michiko. "Culture Zone: Never-Ending Saga." *The New York Times,* September 28, 1997, p. 40.

Lapham, Chris. "Hypertext Illuminated: An Interview with Michael Joyce." *Computer-Mediated Communication Magazine,* June 1997. <http://www.december.com/cmc/mag/1997/jun/joyce.html> (May 31, 2002).

Lombreglia, Ralph. "The End of the Story: Excerpts from a recent e-mail exchange with Michael Joyce." *The Atlantic Monthly,* November 13, 1996. <http://www.theatlantic.com/unbound/digicult/dc9611/joyce.htm> (May 31, 2002).

Miller, Laura. "Bookend: www.claptrap.com." *The New York Times,* March 15, 1998, p. 43.

Mirapaul, Matthew. "A Vote of Confidence for Hypertext Fiction." *The New York Times,* September 11, 1997. <http://www.nytimes.com/library/cyber/mirapaul/091197mirapaul.html> (May 31, 2002).

Rosenberg, Scott. "Clicking for Godot." *Salon,* October 2, 1997. <http://www.salon.com/21st/feature/1997/10/02godot.html> (May 31, 2002).

Further Reading

Lombreglia, Ralph. "So Many Links, So Little Time." *The Atlantic Monthly,* November 20, 1996. <http://www.theatlantic.com/unbound/digicult/dc9611/dc9611.htm> (May 31, 2002).

Snyder, Ilana, ed. *Page to Screen: Taking Literacy into the Electronic Era*. London: Routledge, 1998.

SUNY Press. "An Interview with Michael Joyce." SUNY Press, September 2001. <http://www.sunypress.edu/joyce/interview.html> (May 31, 2002).

Related Topics

Authoring Tools; Cyberculture; Gibson, William; Hypertext; Interactivity

— *Kevin Featherly*

Kapor, Mitchell

1950–

Software Entrepreneur, Activist

Mitchell Kapor is the founder of Lotus Development Corporation and the designer of Lotus 1-2-3, a pioneering spreadsheet and database-management software system that was one of the most successful commercial computer products of the 1980s. He has gone on to use his wealth both as co-founder of the civil-rights organization Electronic Frontier Foundation and as an early investor in companies like UUNet and Real Networks. After spending much of the 1990s espousing a belief in the Internet as the nexus of a decentralized society, Kapor began decrying the Internet's blatant commercialization.

Kapor was born in Brooklyn, New York, in 1950 to Jesse and Phoebe Kapor, owners of Corrugated Paper Products, Inc. As a child, he attended public schools in Freeport, Long Island, graduating in 1967, and attended Yale University to study psychology, linguistics, and computer science as part of a multi-disciplinary cybernetics major. While at Yale, Kapor served as the program director at the college radio station; this led to a short career as a progressive-radio disc jockey in Hartford, Connecticut, in the 1970s. Later, after jumping into teaching transcendental meditation in Cambridge, Massachusetts, and Fairfield, Iowa, he returned to working with computers as an entry-level programmer. In 1978, he earned a master's degree in counseling psychology at New England Memorial Hospital, before attending the Massachusetts Institute of Technology's Sloan School of Management. He dropped out of MIT one term short of graduation, and bought an Apple II personal computer after scrounging up enough money to cover the $1,500 price tag.

It was around this time that he met the authors of VisiCalc, the first computer spreadsheet program, who inspired him to develop a similar application that would graph the results of a spreadsheet's calculation. He called it VisiPlot, and later developed another related product called VisiTrend. Very quickly, $100,000

monthly royalty checks began arriving. Along with a partner in his nascent business, Kapor was bought out for $1.2 million.

In 1982, Kapor founded Lotus Development Corp., the company that would seal his reputation. Along with Jonathan Sachs, the new company's chief technical architect, Kapor created Lotus 1-2-3, an elegant, popular business-software tool that helped make desktop computers ubiquitous in the office environment of the 1980s. Lotus 1-2-3 placed Kapor among the ranks of 1980s computer barons like Microsoft's Bill Gates and Apple's Steve Jobs. By 1984, Lotus' revenues reached $156 million a year, and the company had more than 1,200 workers by 1986.

True to his earlier form, Kapor again dropped out in 1986, resigning as CEO of Lotus and leaving the company altogether a year later. In many eyes, that act of abandonment cemented Kapor's hero status. As *The New Republic*'s Robert Wright put it: "Kapor, in short, seemed the more authentic embodiment of Silicon Valley's hacker ideals: anti-corporate, nonconformist, vaguely whole-earthish, creative."

His first job after Lotus was as a visiting scientist at MIT's Center for Cognitive Science and at the school's Artificial Intelligence Laboratory. He left academia in 1987 to serve as chairman and CEO of another start-up, ON Technology, until 1990, achieving only modest success compared to Lotus.

In 1990, Kapor joined up with John Perry Barlow, an early Netizen and a one-time lyricist for the Grateful Dead. Together, they launched what was probably the second most important phase of Kapor's career to date. FBI agents had interviewed both Kapor and Barlow regarding the activities of an "info-terrorist" group, the NuPrometheus League, that was illegally distributing copies of Macintosh computer read-only memory (ROM) code. Barlow has written that he received a visit in Wyoming from a confused FBI agent (who actually suspected Barlow of being involved in the NuPrometheus League), and he quickly realized that computer technology had raced far ahead of law enforcement's ability to react. Kapor, having received his own FBI visit, agreed with Barlow that civil rights were at risk as a result of law enforcement's ignorance of computer technology. This agreement inspired the formation of the Electronic Frontier Foundation (EFF).

The EFF is a non-profit group whose goal is the protection of privacy, free expression, and online public-information access. Kapor served as its chairman during its first four years. Though its initial mission was to fund the defense of several hackers under federal indictment, the EFF gradually began to modify its mission, and to fall out of favor with a staunchly libertarian computer culture. By 1993, the EFF had moved from Cambridge, Massachusetts, to Washington, D.C. By then, the organization was underwritten by huge corporations—IBM, Apple, AT&T, MCI, Bell Atlantic, and even Microsoft—and its mission had expanded from protecting civil liberties to helping the Clinton administration oversee the expansion of the information superhighway. Kapor became, in Wright's words, "a Washington player."

Kapor gave up his EFF chairmanship in 1994. But before doing that, he laid out in writing the Jeffersonian underpinnings of the EFF, and of his overall approach to cyberspace, in an August 1993 *Wired* magazine essay. In it, Kapor described cyber-life as a kind of primitive frontier existence, and cyberspace as a place that was not elitist, but rather egalitarian in its values. Above all, life in cyberspace was decentralized, he wrote, serving individuals and communities, not mass audiences. "In fact," Kapor wrote, "life in cyberspace seems to be shaping up exactly like Thomas Jefferson would have wanted: founded on the primacy of individual liberty and a commitment to pluralism, diversity, and community."

Seven years later, however, Kapor had essentially changed his mind; he no longer talks of using the Internet to reconfigure society. In a January 14, 2000, *Boston Globe* article, Kapor admitted that he had grown disenchanted with the corporatization of the Internet. In an email interview for this encyclopedia, he reiterated that stance. "The rampant and ugly commercialization is disappointing," he wrote. However, he added, his Jeffersonian ideals have not been completely lost; one just has to think smaller to find them. "There are lots of terrific people-to-people uses which are Jeffersonian in their character," he wrote.

Kapor took some personal advantage of the Internet's commercial qualities in recent years, serving as a venture capitalist throughout the 1990s. Kapor Enterprises, Inc., was started in the mid-1980s as a high-tech investor in start-up companies, and it funded several successful online start-ups. Kapor has also served as a director of Real Networks, Allaire Corporation, and Groove Networks. In 1997, he started and endowed the Mitchell Kapor Foundation, which is dedicated to improving human health and the environment. In January 1999, he joined the venture-capital firm Accel Partners.

By summer 2001, however, Kapor had pulled out of venture capitalism altogether. In the email interview for this encyclopedia, he did provide at least a hint of what would come. "I haven't announced publicly what I'm doing next and don't have a time frame for doing so," he said. "I can tell you it will have to do with making open-source application programs."

Selected Works

Kapor, Mitchell. "High Tech Hypocrisy About Government." *The New York Times* Op-Ed, May 26, 1998. <http://www.kapor.com/homepages/mkapor/newyorktimes.980526.html> (June 7, 2002).

———. "Where Is the Digital Highway Really Heading? The Case for a Jeffersonian Information Policy." *Wired* 1.03, July/August 1993. <http://www.wired.com/wired/archive/1.03/kapor.on.nii.html> (June 7, 2002).

Kapor, Mitchell, and John Perry Barlow. "Across the Electronic Frontier." Electronic Frontier Foundation, July 10, 1990. <http://www.eff.org/EFF/electronic_frontier.eff> (June 7, 2002).

Bibliography

Featherly, Kevin. Email interview with Mitchell Kapor. June 24, 2001.

Kapor, Mitchell. "Biographical Sketch." Kapor.com, February 1999. <http://www.kapor.com/homepages/mkapor/Bio299.html> (May 31, 2002).

Quittner, Joshua. "The Merry Pranksters Go to Washington." *Wired* 2.06, June 1994. <http://www.wired.com/wired/archive/2.06/eff.html> (May 31, 2002).

Syre, Steven, and Charles Stein. "Where Once He Led, Now He Ventures." *Boston Globe*, January 14, 2000, p. C1.

Wright, Robert. "The New Democrat from Cyberspace." *The New Republic*, May 24, 1993, pp. 18-27.

Further Reading

Howe, Peter J. "Internet Boosters Singing the Blues: Web Leaders Gather to Lament the Past, Shape the Future." *Boston Globe*, June 1, 2000, p. C1.

Impoco, Jim. "The Digital Democrat." *U.S. News and World Report*, November 29, 1993, pp. 88–89.

"Mitchell Kapor on Maharishi, Levitation, and Freedom." *Tricycle: The Buddhist Review*, Summer 1994. <http://www.trancenet.org/personal/kapor.html> (May 31, 2002).

Barlow, John Perry; Cyberculture; Electronic Democracy; Electronic Frontier Foundation; Interface; Open Source

— *Kevin Featherly*

Kay, Alan

1940–

Computer Scientist

Alan Kay is considered a creative visionary in the area of interactive computing, or "dynamic media" as he has called it. He has influenced the nature of personal computing while working as a researcher at Xerox, Atari, Apple, and most recently Disney. His principal contributions have been in the fields of human-computer interaction and object-oriented programming.

Born in Springfield, Massachusetts, in 1940, Kay spent his early childhood in Australia, returning to the United States before the end of World War II. His father, a physiologist and researcher, and his mother, a musician, fed Kay's early inquisitiveness; by the time he had reached first grade, he was already well read. The young Kay had difficulties with the rigidity of school, and found himself at odds with school administrators from elementary school through college. He eventually made his way to Denver, Colorado, where he decided to enlist in the air force. After he took a programming aptitude test on a lark, the air force sent him to a two-week training program with IBM, which sparked his lifelong interest in how computers are used. He also finished an undergraduate degree in mathematics and molecular biology at the University of Colorado.

Kay attended graduate school at the University of Utah, and worked under David Evans on an ARPA-funded research project on computer graphics. In his dissertation, Kay described what a "personal computer" might consist of, an idea that would serve in some ways as a model for the Xerox Alto computer. The manifestation of this idea, the FLEX, was a 350-pound machine that reflected some of his ideas about both personal computing and object-oriented programming. Influenced by a visit to Utah by Doug Engelbart in 1967, a demonstration of one of the first flat-panel displays in 1968, and Seymour Papert's work with children and the programming environment called LOGO, Kay began thinking about how the FLEX might be incorporated in a laptop device, a device that he called the Dynabook.

After receiving a Ph.D. in computer science in 1969, Kay worked at the renowned Stanford Artificial Intelligence Laboratory before being recruited by Xerox's Palo Alto Research Center (PARC), where he formed the Learning Research Group. With some effort, Kay convinced other PARC researchers to explore his vision of a personal computer. The result of a marathon design and construction effort, the Alto can fairly be considered to be the first personal computer, at least as we think of them today. For Kay, the Alto was the beginning, and not the end.

In the years following the first Alto, Kay's group made significant inroads into interactive programming and multimedia. With others at PARC, Kay helped to create the first graphical user interfaces (GUIs); GUIs are now central features of most operating systems. He and his group also created some of the first interactive documents and markup languages, as well as tools for creating music with computers.

Kay might have been content to work in relative obscurity but for a 1972 article in *Rolling Stone* magazine reporting on the first computer game, called Spacewar! The article provided a view of the personal computer that aligned nicely with Kay's own views, and quoted his prognostications and aphorisms liberally. The notoriety provided by the article would shape the public view of PARC for years to come, and would arguably make Kay the first superstar of computer science.

Kay recognized that his temperament was not well suited to programming, but that his gift lay in thinking about how people could use computers. Most of the programming languages of the time were procedural: A program would indicate what data was being used, and what to do with it. Kay thought that the units of a program should be flexible and able to act in some way on their own, and believed that the division between program and data was not useful. A computer program, he thought, could instead be made up of "objects," pieces of code that acted like small machines.

Kay thought that a programming language should be simple enough to be described on a single sheet of paper, and colleagues at PARC challenged him to create such a language. This language, called Smalltalk, was based on his ideas of object-oriented programming, and Kay drew from earlier object-oriented systems like his FLEX and the Simula programming language, as well as from programming languages like Lisp. In turn, Smalltalk has influenced the creation of computer languages like C++ and Java.

After working briefly for Atari, in 1984 Kay became a research fellow at Apple Computer, the company that owed much of its inspiration to his work on the Alto a decade earlier. At Apple, Kay became more heavily involved in the educational possibilities of computers. The Vivarium Project, which began in 1987, provided a Macintosh computer for every two elementary students at the Los Angeles Open School. The objective of the project was to see how computers and computer literacy could be integrated within a school environment. In addition, Kay's vision of the Dynabook would again be reflected, this time in the Apple Newton, a device that some have called the first personal digital assistant (PDA).

Since 1997, Kay has worked with Walt Disney Imagineering as a Disney Fellow and the vice president of research and development. He remains interested in ways that computers can be used by children and adults to learn, and is a frequent speaker on computers, education, and the human intellect.

Selected Works

Kay, Alan. "The Computer 'Revolution' Hasn't Happened Yet!" EDUCOM '98.
<http://www.educause.edu/conference/e98/webcast98.html> (June 7, 2002).
———. "The Early History of SmallTalk." *History of Programming Languages—II.* Thomas J. Bergin, Jr., Richard G. Gibson, and Peter S. Gordon, eds. New York: ACM Press, 1996; pp. 511–78.

Bibliography

Brand, Stewart. "Spacewar: Fanatic Life and Symbolic Death Among the Computer Bums." *Rolling Stone,* December 7, 1972, p 58.
Hiltzik, Michael. *Dealers of Lightning: Xerox PARC and the Dawn of the Computer Age.* New York: HarperBusiness, 1999.
Shasha, Dennis, and Cathy Lazere. *Out of Their Minds: The Lives and Discoveries of 15 Great Computer Scientists.* New York: Copernicus, 1995.

Further Reading

Kelly, Kevin, with Steven Levy. "Kay + Hillis." *Wired* 2.01, January 1994.
<http://www.wired.com/wired/archive/2.01/kay.hillis_pr.html> (May 31, 2002).
Rheingold, Howard. *Tools for Thought: The History and Future of Mind-Expanding Technology.* Cambridge, Mass.: MIT Press, 2000.
Waldrop, M. Mitchell. *The Dream Machine: J. C. R. Licklider and the Revolution that Made Computing Personal.* New York: Viking, 2001.

Related Topics

Computer Graphics; Education and Computers; Graphical User Interface; Human-Computer Interaction; Information Design; Interactivity; "Man-Computer Symbiosis"; Markup Languages; Multimedia; Xerox Palo Alto Research Center

— *Alexander Halavais*

Killer Application

A computer application is a software program that performs a specific function, such as a word-processing or spreadsheet program. The earliest usage of the phrase killer application, or killer app, denoted a computer application so useful and popular that it would provide potential users with the motivation to purchase the hardware needed to run it. The software program would then be known as the killer application of the particular hardware. For example, spreadsheet programs were once identified as the killer application of personal computers, because people would buy PCs specifically to use spread sheet programs.

Later, the term killer application came to be used more generally to refer to any extremely successful computer program. In this sense, rather than being the killer application of a particular type of hardware, a program might be the killer application for a particular business, organization, or industry. In this sense, a computer start-up company seeks to find the killer application that will enable it to survive. The term has also found a use outside the computer industry, and has been used to describe the successful application of other types of technology.

The term killer application was first used to refer to electronic spreadsheet programs. By some accounts, it was first applied to the VisiCalc spreadsheet program, which is credited with helping sell the Apple II computer to business users; previously, computers were primarily of interest to programmers, computer enthusiasts, and other electronic hobbyists. Other accounts indicate that the term was first used in the mid-1980s to refer to Lotus 1-2-3, another spreadsheet program that similarly helped foster the personal-computer revolution, during which PCs were sold in large numbers both to individual businesspeople and to home users. Accounts that identify Lotus 1-2-3 as the first designated killer application indicate that the term was then retroactively applied to VisiCalc, in recognition of VisiCalc's similar role with regard to Apple computers.

Spreadsheet programs were the killer application for PCs, because they gave a new set of people a reason to buy a personal computer. Both email and the World Wide Web have similarly been described as the killer application for the Internet—email because it is arguably the largest single application in use on the Internet, and the Web because it made the Internet more accessible and easier to use. Web browsers have also been described as the killer application both for the Internet and for PCs, now that the Internet is recognized by many as a valuable resource.

The difference between the earlier, narrower definition and the later, looser one recently figured in an important legal case. In the well-known battle of *U.S. vs. Microsoft,* a key issue concerned whether or not Microsoft had violated anti-trust statutes by including its Web browser as part of its more popular operating system. Bill Gates, the head of Microsoft Corporation, was specifically questioned in deposition about his definition of killer application. Gates had purportedly written an essay that referred to word processors and spreadsheets as the killer apps for PCs in the 1980s, and that identified Web browsers as the latest killer app.

Questioned about his definition of the term, Gates indicated that it referred to a very popular application. Gates was then read two definitions from the 1997 edition of the *Microsoft Computer Dictionary.* The first defined killer application as referring to an application that "fuels sales of the hardware platform or operating system for which it was written," and the second defined it as merely "an application that supplants its competition." In response, Gates reiterated his own definition.

While this line of questioning can hardly be seen as a key element of the case against Microsoft, it certainly demonstrates the ubiquity of the phrase killer application in the computer industry. It also provides insight into the difference between various uses of the term: If killer application refers to an application that sells something else, this suggests a very different business strategy than if the term merely refers to a program that is better than other programs of the same type.

Bibliography

Excerpts from Bill Gates' Deposition, as Contained in the December 15, 1998, Transcript of Proceedings Before the Honorable Thomas P. Jackson, *U.S. vs. Microsoft.* <http://www.microsoft.com/presspass/trial/transcripts/dec98/12-15-am.asp> (May 31, 2002).

Microsoft Press Computer Dictionary. Fourth edition. Redmond, Wash.: Microsoft Press, 1998.

Power, Daniel J. "A Brief History of Spreadsheets." DSSResources.com. <http://dssresources.com/history/sshistory.html.> (May 31, 2002).

Further Reading

Cringely, Robert X. *Accidental Empires: How the Boys of Silicon Valley Make Their Millions, Battle Foreign Competition, and Still Can't Get a Date.* New York: HarperBusiness, 1996.

Raymond, Eric. *The New Hacker's Dictionary.* Third edition. Cambridge, Mass.: MIT Press, 1996.

Related Topics

Email; Gates, William H., III; Internet; World Wide Web

— *Lori Kendall*

Knowledge Management

Human knowledge is a central factor in the production of goods and services. Knowledge management, which is now a distinct field with a philosophical perspective and an applied focus, began with work in many fields, including management studies, organization theory, communication, philosophy, sociology, and information science. Knowledge management is multifaceted; it involves a research field, a professional practice, and the social and technical systems that support them.

Working with knowledge implies understanding organizations as systems. Effective work demands the creation, sharing, and distribution of information as the raw material that individuals and organizations process into knowledge. Using knowledge requires individual and organizational learning and interaction. As actors in a system, human participants enable an organization to learn. Individuals share, improve, and effectively recycle existing knowledge.

Knowledge management develops systematic policies, programs, and practices to create, share, and apply knowledge in organizations. Social and technical systems support knowledge management by helping organizations to identify, select, acquire, store, organize, present, and use information for problem-solving, learning, innovation, strategic planning, and decision-making.

Knowledge management involves two parallel streams. The first stream is social. Philosophical, interpersonal, and organizational in perspective, it involves human dynamics, dialogue, and organizational learning. Such concepts as storytelling, communities of practice, reflective practice, and behavioral modeling characterize what is sometimes called a "person-to-person" approach to knowledge management. This approach employs both tacit and explicit knowledge.

The second stream is technological. Based on information technology and data processing, it uses information systems to harvest, gather, codify, and represent knowledge. Such concepts as data warehousing, data mining, knowledge mapping, and electronic libraries characterize what may be termed a "people-to-documents" approach. Because it is mediated through information systems, it is almost exclusively explicit.

Knowledge management is a consequence of the information society. In 1940, Australian economist Colin Clark classified economies as primary, secondary, and tertiary: Primary economies extract wealth from nature, secondary economies transform extracted material through manufacturing, and tertiary economies engage in service. In 1967, Daniel Bell built on this classification to describe three kinds of societies: pre-industrial society extracts, industrial society fabricates, and post-industrial society processes information. Bell argued that a significant change in the character of knowledge was taking place, with a professional knowledge elite developing to manage it.

Knowledge has always been a key factor in productivity. The earliest manufacturing took place millions of years ago, when *homo habilis* made the first weapons and tools. The search for productivity focused on scarce material resources and the challenges of understanding the physical world. All manufacturing was handicraft until the industrial revolution gave rise to mass manufacturing in the nineteenth century.

By the 1940s, a focus on knowledge became inevitable. The ideas of knowledge management have been emerging for several decades; for example, W. Edwards Deming's work in postwar Japan reflects the principles of knowledge management and organizational learning. Economists such as Harold Innis and Fritz Machlup have gained increasing importance, along with psychologists such as Abraham Maslow and sociologists such as Daniel Bell and Manuel Castells. The shift to knowledge management emerged in many places during the 1990s. Central figures include Ikujiro Nonaka and Hirotaka Takeuchi in Japan, Mats Alvesson and Bo Hedberg in Sweden, George von Krogh and Johan Roos in Switzerland, Max Boisot in England, and Lawrence Prusak, Peter Senge, and Karl Wiig in North America.

Effective work demands creating, sharing, and distributing information as the raw material that individual and organizations process into knowledge. The administrative principles of turn-of-the-century theorists Henri Fayol and Frederick W. Taylor restricted the flow of information and power in vertically stratified organizations. The management principles of a knowledge economy encourage the flow of information and knowledge within dynamic networks.

The earliest example of knowledge-management philosophy is found in a book written circa 1,000 B.C.E. by an Egyptian public administrator named Amenemopet. From that time to our own, thinkers have articulated knowledge-management issues in such fields as philosophy, economics, and management. For example, a 1776 description of a pin factory by Adam Smith is now used as a case study on intellectual capital.

Three thousand years separate Amenemopet and Deming, but the philosophical themes of knowledge management have been remarkably durable. Theoretical reflection and behavioral action form the substance of knowledge management. This was true before knowledge management emerged as a specific field, and it remains true for any endeavor where human beings add value to goods and services.

Bibliography

Boisot, Max. *Knowledge Assets.* New York: Oxford University Press, 1998.

Brown, John Seely, and Paul Duguid. "Organizational Learning and Communities-of-practice: Toward a Unified View of Working, Learning, and Innovation." The Institute of Management Sciences (now INFORMS), 1991. <http://www.parc.xerox.com/ops/members/brown/papers/orglearning.html> (April 12, 2002).

Friedman, Ken, and Johan Olaisen, eds. *Knowledge Management in Scandinavia: Research in Theory and Practice.* Hershey, Pa.: Idea Group Publishing, 2002.

Fruin, W. Mark. *Knowledge Works: Managing Intellectual Capital at Toshiba.* New York: Oxford University Press, 1997.

Graduate School of Business, University of Texas at Austin. Knowledge Management Server. <http://www.bus.utexas.edu/kman/> (April 12, 2002).

Knowledge Board. The Portal for the European KM Community. <http://www.knowledgeboard.com> (April 12, 2002).

Nonaka, Ikujiro, and Hirotaka Takeuchi. *The Knowledge-Creating Company: How Japanese Companies Create the Dynamics of Innovation.* New York: Oxford University Press, 1995.

Further Reading

Alvesson, Mats. *Management of Knowledge-Intensive Companies.* Hawthorne, N.Y.: Walter De Gruyter, 1995.

Bell, Daniel. *The Coming of Post-Industrial Society: A Venture in Social Forecasting.* New York: Basic Books, 1999.

Clark, Colin. *Conditions of Economic Progress.* London: Macmillan and Co., 1940.

Deming, W. Edwards. *The New Economics for Industry, Government, Education.* Cambridge, Mass.: Massachusetts Institute of Technology, Center for Advanced Engineering Study, 1993.

Drucker, Peter F. *The New Realities.* New York: Harper & Row, 1989.

Halal, William E., and Raymond Smith, eds. *The Infinite Resource: Creating and Leading the Knowledge Enterprise.* San Francisco: Jossey-Bass, 1998.

Mahbubani, Kishore. "The Pacific Way." *Foreign Affairs,* vol. 74, no. 1 (1995), pp. 100–11.

McGregor, Eugene B. *Strategic Management of Human Knowledge, Skills, and Abilities: Workforce Decision-Making in the Postindustrial Era.* San Francisco: Jossey-Bass, 1991.

Savage, Charles M. *Fifth Generation Management: Co-Creating Through Virtual Enterprising, Dynamic Teaming, and Knowledge Networking.* Boston: Butterworth-Heinemann, 1996.

Stewart, Thomas A. *Intellectual Capital: The New Wealth of Organizations.* New York: Doubleday/Currency, 1997.

Sveiby, Karl Erik. Sveiby Knowledge Associates. Web site. <http://www.sveiby.com.au> (April 12, 2002).

Related Topics

Castells, Manuel; Data Mining; Distance Learning; Drucker, Peter F.; Expert Systems; Information Design; Innis, Harold

— *Ken Friedman*

Krause, Kai

1957–

Imaging Software Innovator

Kai Krause is a software programmer and visionary who has greatly influenced digital graphics manipulation, and whose successful graphics software has provided a remarkable canvas for the imagination. His image-manipulation add-ins convey a sense of novelty and uniqueness in a world saturated with commonplace graphical design.

Krause was born in Germany in 1957. He was educated in Essen, West Germany, where he studied several languages, including French and English. He also had an interest in music, and studied classical piano. Krause was also skilled in mathematics, which later fueled his software-programming approach that allowed for quicker image processing. He received a master's degree in image processing, and earned a Ph.D. in philosophy. Krause moved to California and during the late 1970s he became an independent special-effects consultant in the entertainment industry, working in the Disney sound-effects library and on television shows and record albums.

Krause's talent for art and his ability to program a computer led to his developing the first of a series of imaging-effects software programs: Power Tools, the product of a company that he founded called MetaTools. Originally designed as a third-party plug-in for Adobe's Photoshop, an image-processing application, Power Tools is a software-utility program that is used to manipulate images with visual effects. For example, a photograph of a sphere can be given a shadow, an edge, or a glowing effect.

Introduced in 1992, Krause's Power Tools was impressive, creating distinctive effects that would free the user from the long and tedious task of creating the same effects manually. The software interface was also noteworthy due to its appearance, which lacked conformity with the industry standards set by Microsoft and Apple. Krause aims for his software interfaces to encourage users to have fun and experiment—an approach that has drawn adults, as well as children, to his software.

In addition to Power Tools, MetaTools has released different forms and generations of graphics-altering software applications. Each application is distinguishable by the type of effects it can produce, and by the area of image processing in which it works. For instance, Kai's Power Goo contains special effects for drastically altering or morphing an image; an image of a person's face can be stretched as if reflected in a fun house mirror. Another type of image-effects software designed by Krause, called Bryce, works in specific areas of graphical design. It can generate natural and paranormal landscapes that can also be manipulated. Bryce allows image objects, such as weather, to be added into graphic scenes; a landscape of stretching knolls can have fog, rain, or snow coming in from various angles and directions. An additional feature of the professional version of Bryce is the ability to add animation to the graphics.

MetaTools merged with Fractal Design and became MetaCreations in May 1997. The new company had broader horizons, creating more products and adding more employees. In May 1999, Krause left MetaCreations, resigning his position as chief design officer. Shortly thereafter, he returned to Germany to begin building a research facility that he hopes will match the likes of the Massachusetts Institute of Technology's (MIT) Media Laboratory. Krause's research lab, named the Byteburg, is housed in a castle along the Rhine River.

Included among the various awards and recognition that Krause has earned for his work is a Clio for his contributions to the first *Star Trek* movie. In addition, the Royal British Photographical Society has honored Krause with its David Medal. Krause's software has also been used by the Academy of Motion Picture Arts and Sciences for the Oscars, by Issey Miyake for clothing design, and even by NASA for the Mars mission.

Krause has brought new life to otherwise ordinary images through his design concepts, unique interfaces, and mind-boggling effects. His software has helped individuals conceive fresh graphic ideas that can be found in print, multimedia, Web sites, television broadcasts, and nearly all aspects of graphic design. The extraordinary effects that Krause fashions continue to revolutionize the way that graphics can be created and transformed.

Selected Works

Alspach, Ted, and Steven Frank. *Official Kai's Power Tools Studio Secrets.* Afterword by Kai Krause. Boston, Mass.: IDG Books, 1996.

Greenberg, Adele Droblas, and Greenberg, Seth. *Digital Images: A Practical Guide.* Foreword by Kai Krause. Berkeley, Calif.: Osborne McGraw-Hill, 1995.

Bibliography

Auckerman, William. "So Many Pixels, So Little Time: An Interview with Kai Krause" *Computing Japan,* September 1994.
<http://www.cjmag.co.jp/magazine/issues/1994/sep94/09kai.html> (May 17, 2002).

Harrison, David. "Kai's Power Goo." *Computer User.* 01 October 1996.

Pell, Mike. "Hey—Where Did Kai Go?" *Futuristic Design,* September 1, 2000.
<http://www.futuristic.com/straightface/09012000.htm> (May 17, 2002).

Further Reading

Clarke, Nick. *Kai's Power Tools 3: An Illustrated Guide.* 2nd ed. Berkeley, Calif.: Peachpit Press, 1997.

Frauenfelder, Mark. "Kai's Corporate Goo." *Wired* 6.10, October 1998.
<http://www.wired.com/wired/archive/6.10/newmedia.html> (May 17, 2002).

Lombreglia, Ralph. "Artist at Play." *The Atlantic,* April 16, 1997.
<http://www.theatlantic.com/unbound/digicult/dc9704/krause.htm> (May 17, 2002).

MacCentral Online. "Kai Krause Leaves MetaCreations." *MacCentral Online.* April 21, 1999.
<http://maccentral.macworld.com/news/9904/21.kai.shtml> (May 17, 2002).

Related Topics

Computer Graphics; Digital Art and Animation

— *James Pyfer*

Kurzweil, Raymond

1952–

Computer Scientist and Futurist

Raymond Kurzweil is a scientist whose innovations in human-computer interaction have made him particularly well-qualified as a commentator on how the computers of today will evolve into what he calls the "spiritual" and "intelligent" machines of tomorrow. But his vision of a future in which minds merge with machines has proved controversial, prompting equally controversial calls for high-tech research to be carefully controlled.

Although he has been many things in his life—child prodigy, high-tech entrepreneur, champion of the disabled—Ray Kurzweil might best be described as a pragmatic pioneer of human-computer interaction. While academics and theorists were speculating about the psychological Berlin Wall between humans and machines, he had already discovered the loose bricks.

In 1974, shortly after graduating from the Massachusetts Institute of Technology (MIT) with degrees in computer science and creative writing, Kurzweil developed the process of optical-character recognition (OCR), the technique by which a computer can "read" text printed in almost any font. The following year, he developed the first speech synthesizer, which could read text aloud, and the first flatbed optical scanner using charge-coupled display (CCD) video technology. These technologies were put to good use in his best-known product, the award-winning Kurzweil Reading Machine (KRM). Arguably the most important development in the education and empowerment of the blind since the invention of Braille, this photocopier-like device could scan and recognize printed documents, then read them aloud. Kurzweil's OCR technology was later bought by Xerox, and is now used in its TextBridge products.

Kurzweil was no less innovative in the 1980s and 1990s. One of the KRM's most enthusiastic users was musician Stevie Wonder, who describes Kurzweil as "truly among the sunshines of my life." Together, they developed the revolutionary Kurzweil Music Synthesizer (KMS), which could successfully copy the sounds of grand pianos and other acoustic instruments using advanced sound-modeling techniques. Around the same time, Kurzweil began to pioneer voice-recognition products, ultimately launching the first voice-dictation system for Windows (1994) as well as the first continuous-speech, natural-language voice control system (1997), which allowed users to operate their PC applications using voice commands alone. Later, he sold these technologies to Lernout and Hauspie.

Although Kurzweil continues to develop innovative technologies that break down the barriers between humans and machines, most recently experimenting with expert systems to play the financial markets, he is now equally well known as a futurist. He has long been in demand as a keynote speaker and journalist, and his speeches and writings are characterized by an enthusiastic vision of how computer technology and human minds will eventually overcome one another's limitations. This theme was developed at length in Kurzweil's two best-selling books, *The Age of Intelligent Machines* (1990) and *The Age of Spiritual Machines: When Computers Exceed Human Intelligence* (1999). Among the ideas explored in these books was "reinstantiation," Kurzweil's prediction that human personalities will eventually be "downloaded" into computers that will "claim to be people, and to have the full range of emotional and spiritual experiences that people claim to have." In November 2000, in a speech to the Foresight Institute's Conference on Nanotechnology, Kurzweil predicted: "By the end of this century, I don't think there will be a clear distinction between human and machine."

Not surprisingly, predictions such as these have proved immensely controversial, notably provoking alarm from Sun Microsystems co-founder Bill Joy, whose long essay about the downside of technological advance was called "Why the Future Doesn't Need Us." Joy, who says he can "date the onset of my unease to the day I met Ray Kurzweil," spoke of his mounting concern as he read a draft of *The Age of Spiritual Machines*. What alarmed him most was that, unlike legions of science-fiction writers who had made similar predictions, brilliant innovators like Kurzweil might actually realize some of their visions, notably the gradual replacement of the human body and mind with robotic and computer technology. According to Joy, Kurzweil and others like him do not give sufficient thought to the deep philosophical and ethical implications of what they propose—in particular, to the ultimate question of whether obsolete humans have any role in a world of smart machines: "As Thoreau said, 'We do not ride on the railroad; it rides upon us'; and this is what we must fight, in our time. The question is, indeed, Which is to be master? Will we survive our technologies?"

Non-technologists might instinctively side with Joy. After Kurzweil's speech to the Foresight Institute, a graduate student stood up and declared that his vision was "the most hideous message that has been proposed in human history." But criticisms of this kind, it might be argued, are less about Kurzweil and computers than about human anxiety over progress and change in general—restatements of the "apocalypse myth," a recurring human nightmare of the future which, according to some authors, runs through much of human thought, from ancient Christianity to modern environmentalism. Others, doubtless, would agree with Kurzweil, who responded that Joy's neo-Luddite view is "unfeasible, undesirable, and basically totalitarian." Criticisms that Kurzweil's vision is dehumanizing seem to be undermined by his own track record; the success of the KRM in empowering blind people, and of the KMS in extending the creative power of musicians, suggest that humans could be the most profound beneficiaries of any marriage of mind and machine in the future. On the question of whether Kurzweil or Joy is correct, however, the jury may be out indefinitely.

Selected Works

Kurzweil, Raymond. *The Age of Spiritual Machines: When Computers Exceed Human Intelligence*. New York: Viking/Penguin, 1999.
———. *The Age of Intelligent Machines*. Cambridge, Mass.: MIT Press, 1990.
———. "When Will HAL Understand What We Are Saying? Computer Speech Recognition and Understanding." *HAL's Legacy: 2001's Computer as Dream and Reality*. David G. Stork, ed. Cambridge, Mass.: MIT Press, 1996.
———. "The Coming Merging of Mind and Machine." *Scientific American*, September 1999. <http://www.sciam.com/1999/0999bionic/0999kurzweil.html> (March 29, 2002).

Bibliography

Joy, Bill. "Why the Future Doesn't Need Us." *Wired* 8.04, April 2000. <http://www.wired.com/wired/archive/8.04/joy.html> March 29, 2002.
McCullagh, Declan. "Kurzweil: Rooting for the Machine," *Wired News*, November 3, 2000. <http://www.wired.com/news/technology/0,1282,39967,00.html> March 29, 2002.

Further Reading

Proudfoot, Diane. "How Human Can They Get?" *Science*, vol. 284 (April 30, 1999), p. 745.
Shaffer, Richard. "Pundit Forecasts Portable Praying PCs in *The Age of Spiritual Machines*." *Fortune*, February 1, 1999, p. 74.

Related Topics

Digital Audio; Digital Music; Human-Computer Interaction; Joy, Bill; Lanier, Jaron; "Man-Computer Symbiosis"; Moog, Robert; Optical Character Recognition

— *Chris Woodford*

LambdaMOO

One of the oldest and most famous still-running MUDs on the Internet, LambdaMOO went online in late 1990. MUDs (multi-user dungeon) and MOOs (MUD, object oriented) are computer programs that allow multiple users to connect from remote locations and to both interact with the program and communicate with each other. Once connected to a MUD, participants must log on as a "character" on that MUD. They then type text to the program and receive responses from the program and from other users.

Pavel Curtis, who in 1990 was a programmer at Xerox Palo Alto Research Center (PARC), used a heavily revised version of the original MOO code developed earlier that year by Stephen White to create the LambdaMOO environment. (The program itself is also called LambdaMOO, and many other MOOs use some version of this program.) The opening of LambdaMOO was announced in early 1991 on the Usenet newsgroup rec.games.muds, and LambdaMOO quickly became extremely popular. It currently runs on a computer located at Stanford University, sponsored by the Web conferencing company PlaceWare.

LambdaMOO was initially maintained and operated by its "wizards," a group that included founder Pavel Curtis. In a 1993 post to an internal LambdaMOO bulletin board entitled "LambdaMOO Takes a New Direction," Curtis, citing time constraints as well as philosophical considerations, turned over such functions as dispute resolution and aesthetic planning to the growing LambdaMOO community, reserving only technical programming functions for the wizards.

Since the wizards' abdication, a variety of social events on LambdaMOO have influenced the direction of participants' self-government strategies. One of the most infamous of these events, known as "the Bungle Affair," occurred in 1993, and involved one participant's use of MOO programming capabilities to sexually harass other players via the "virtual rapes" of their characters. In the aftermath of this disturbing incident, LambdaMOO participants developed several formal ways for dealing with conflicts and disputes, including a petition system, dispute arbitration, and an "Architectural Review Board."

Petitions may be put forth by any member of the community, and all participants are encouraged to vote on open petitions; reminders appear on users' screens when they log on. Wizards implement any program changes necessary to effect approved petitions. Petitions have addressed virtually every aspect of LambdaMOO life, including such issues as the content of official LambdaMOO texts, the operation of the petition process itself, technical strategies for dealing with disruptive participants, and rules for creating new characters. Dispute arbitrators intervene in interpersonal conflicts, and impose sanctions against offending participants. The Architectural Review Board makes decisions about additions to the LambdaMOO database, in an attempt to ensure the continued integrity of the whole and to protect the database from malfunctions. The exact procedures for each of these three systems have evolved over time, and remain sources of conflict and controversy.

When detailed descriptions of social life on LambdaMOO appeared in a *Wired* magazine article in 1994, LambdaMOO experienced a tremendous surge of new participants. Many of these newcomers were new not only to LambdaMOO but also to MUDs in general, and often disrupted the activities of long-term LambdaMOO participants through their lack of knowledge and failure to adhere to community social norms. In addition, the sudden increase in population taxed the program itself, resulting in increased lag (the gap in time between input of a command and the program's processing of that command, primarily experienced by participants as awkward pauses) as well as higher incidences of the program crashing, or going offline due to program errors. Numerous petitions have attempted to address the difficulties caused by LambdaMOO population growth, and several have resulted in changes in the ways that characters are created and deleted.

LambdaMOO's status as a well-known, highly populated, and long-running MUD has made it a favorite among researchers. Academics from various fields—including communications, sociology, and computer science—and from undergraduates to professors have conducted research on LambdaMOO. Topics have included computer-mediated communication, virtual community-building, visualization and navigation of online geography, and the use of artificial-intelligence agents for interpersonal connections. In addition, numerous journalists have visited and reported on LambdaMOO. Concerns about the community's hyper-observed status prompted participants to include language in the initial login message asking journalists and researchers to acquire permission from participants before quoting them.

Pavel Curtis' experience with LambdaMOO influenced his later work, which has included numerous projects geared toward providing online support for computer-supported cooperative work, business and professional conferencing, and virtual community-building. Among his projects at Xerox PARC were Astro-VR, which served as a virtual meeting site for astronomy researchers, and Jupiter, which performed a similar function for Xerox PARC researchers. PlaceWare, a company founded in 1996 by Curtis and two other Xerox PARC veterans, has taken the idea of MOOs into a Web-based format, creating multimedia software for online conferencing.

Bibliography

Dibbell, Julian. "A Rape in Cyberspace: How an Evil Clown, a Haitian Trickster Spirit, Two Wizards, and a Cast of Dozens Turned a Database Into a Society." *The Village Voice*, December 23, 1993.
<http://www.levity.com/julian/bungle_vv.html> (March 29, 2002).
Mnookin, Jennifer. "Virtual(ly) Law: The Emergence of Law in LambdaMOO." *Journal of Computer-Mediated Communication*, vol. 2, no. 1 (1996).
<http://www.ascusc.org/jcmc/vol2/issue1/lambda.html> (March 29, 2002).

Further Reading

Curtis, Pavel. "Mudding: Social Phenomena in Text-Based Virtual Realities." *Intertek* 3 (1993), pp. 26–34.
<http://ftp.game.org/pub/mud/text/research/DIAC92.txt> (March 29, 2002).
Dibbell, Julian. *My Tiny Life: Crime and Passion in a Virtual World*. New York: Henry Holt, 1998.
Quittner, Josh. "Johnny Manhattan Meets the Furry Muckers." *Wired* 2.03, March 1994.
<http://www.wired.com/wired/archive/2.03/muds.html> (March 29, 2002).

Related Topics

Computer-Supported Collaborative Work; MUDs and MOOs; USENET; Virtual Community; Xerox Palo Alto Research Center

— *Lori Kendall*

Lanier, Jaron

1960–

Virtual-Reality Pioneer, Artist

Jaron Lanier has been described as a Renaissance man of the Digital Age. Though he considers himself to be primarily a musician, to the world he is the pioneer of virtual reality (VR). But he also is a cyberspace theorist, a mathematician, a programmer, a painter, a composer of classical music, a writer, and a recent pioneer in the burgeoning field of tele-immersion technology, a kind of VR writ large.

Lanier grew up in a small New Mexico town. He was raised by his father, who was a science writer, after his mother, a concert pianist, died while Lanier was still a child. It was this background that made him unique: a loner and social misfit who immersed himself in his music and an endless stream of science projects. Bored, he dropped out of high school very early, but at age 14, he charmed New Mexico State University officials into allowing him to take classes there. He received a grant from the National Science Foundation (NSF) commissioning him to study whether mathematical notation is truly needed. (Lanier believes that the symbols of mathematics obscure its meaning and keep its "beauty" inaccessible to normal people.) In order to perform the math study, Lanier needed to learn computer programming. As he learned, he began to see that the problems of programming were similar to those of mathematics—both are languages that rely on symbols that may not be their best manifestation. This idea propelled him onto the possibility of designing "a post-symbolic 'visual' programming language," which would allow people to program computers by interacting with graphical icons in various shapes, such as kangaroos, melting ice cubes, and chirping birds. This new programming language would be called Mandala.

In addition to working on Mandala and his musical projects, Lanier also did freelance ideo-game programming for Atari, and created the first successful "art" videogame, Moondust, in 1983. Lanier took his money from Moondust and started his own company, VPL (Visual Programming Language) Research, the first commercial VR company.

VPL made VR an industry. The company introduced the first interface gloves, or "data gloves," in 1984; these programmable gloves served, in part, as the interface through which interaction with Mandala programs was conducted. In 1987, VPL invented the head-mounted displays that have since become, for many people, synonymous with VR. VPL also introduced "eye phones," as well as a networked "virtual world" system. Meanwhile, Lanier's company helped develop the first popular software platform architecture for immersive VR applications. By 1991, the company had sales of $6 million, and Lanier himself was a millionaire.

Lanier had many dreams for the role of technology in humanity's future. His oldest abiding dream was the idea that computers could allow people to exchange simulations in the form of images, sounds, and dynamic models, just as they normally exchange written and spoken words. This is the essence of VR. Lanier has held onto that dream, and many of his other ideas have come alive over the years, even as his role at VPL ended rather ignominiously when Thomson CSF, a French company with interest in VPL, seized the firm's patents and ousted Lanier as part of the settlement of $1.6 million in debts.

In 2000, Lanier published a long online essay titled "One Half of a Manifesto," which served as a kind of tonic to Bill Joy's *Wired* magazine essay, "Why the Future Doesn't Need Us," published that same year. Joy projected a day when artificial intelligence and self-replicating robots, engineered organisms, and nanobots would come to compete with human beings for precious resources, a fight Joy feared that humanity would lose. In "One Half of a Manifesto," Lanier doubted the feasibility of the argument, not because Joy's nightmare scenario is not conceivable, but because laxity among software programmers over the last decade has left the art of programming in a shambles, with little thought given to its continued improvement. The kind of future that Joy sketched, Lanier said, would require much less fallible software than is now being produced. "Just as some newborn race of superintelligent robots are about to consume all humanity, our dear old species will likely be saved by a Windows crash," he ribbed.

Furthermore, Lanier thinks that where humanity remains in touch with the power of computing and its responsibility for it, it will remain in control of technology, as long as people hold up their end of the high-tech bargain. "I think that treating technology as if it were autonomous is the ultimate self-fulfilling

prophecy," Lanier wrote in the article. "There is no difference between machine autonomy and the abdication of human responsibility."

Not all of Lanier's predictions have turned out as he expected. For example, he expected VR gear to be commonplace in American homes by the turn of the decade, which has not happened. Nonetheless, he remains at the forefront of VR developments. He is currently the lead scientist for the National Tele-Immersion Initiative (NTII), a coalition of research universities studying advanced applications for Internet 2. The initiative seeks to use a VR interface to put people, separated by great distances, in the same virtual room together. Similar work is being done independently at places like the University of Illinois–Chicago's Electronic Visualization Labs. Under Lanier's lead, NTII aims to build VR into the core of the Internet.

Lanier works in a wide variety of fields to fuse artistry with technology. He continues to compose classical music; he is expert in a number of Asian wind and string instruments, creates music on virtual instruments that don't really exist, and has worked on reconstructing the music of ancient Egypt under a commission from the BBC and the Discovery Channel. His paintings and sketches have been exhibited in the United States and Europe, he directed a film called *Muzork* (1994), and he has pioneered the use of virtual instruments in live concert performances with a band called Chromatophoria. Meanwhile, Lanier has written extensively on many high-tech topics, as well as on business, the social impact of technology, the philosophy of information, Internet politics, and the future of humanity. His book, *Confessions of a Closet Human,* is forthcoming.

Selected Works

Lanier, Jaron. "How Music Will Save the Soul of Technology." Well.com, 1996. <http://www.well.com/user/jaron/knittalk.html> (July 12, 2002).
———. "One-Half of a Manifesto." *Wired* 8.12, December 2000. <http://www.wired.com/wired/archive/8.12/lanier_pr.html> (July 12, 2002).
———. "Taking Stock." *Wired* 6.01, January 1998. <http://www.wired.com/wired/archive//6.01/lanier.html> (July 12, 2002).
———. "A Tale of Two Terrors." *CIO Magazine,* July 1, 2000. <http://www.cio.com/archive/070100_diff.html> (July 12, 2002).
———. "Virtually There: Three-Dimensional Tele-Immersion May Eventually Bring the World to Your Desk." *Scientific American,* April 2001.

Bibliography

"Brief Biography of Jaron Lanier." The Well, April 2000.
<http://www.well.com/user/jaron/general.html>
(May 17, 2002).

Perkins, Michael C. "Jaron Lanier Gets Real."
Red Herring Magazine, June 1993.
<http://www.redherring.com/mag/issue01/guru.html>
(May 17, 2002).

Snider, Burr. "Jaron." *Wired* 1.02, May/June 1993.
<http://www.wired.com/wired/archive//1.02/jaron.html>
(May 17, 2002).

Further Reading

Aukstakalnis, Steve, and David Blatner. *Silicon Mirage:
The Art and Science of Virtual Reality.* Berkeley, Calif.:
Peachpit Press, 1992.

Ditlea, Steve. "Father of Virtual Reality Embraces Virtual
Music." *The New York Times,* July 10, 1996.
<http://www.nytimes.com/library/cyber/week/
0710lanier.html> (May 17, 2002).

Powell, Corey S. "Jaron Lanier: A Cyberspace Renaissance
Man Reveals His Current Thoughts on the World Wide
Web, Virtual Reality, and Other Silicon Dreams."
Scientific American, September 15, 1996.

Rheingold, Howard. *Virtual Reality.* New York: Summit
Books, 1991.

Williams, Sam. "Why Software Still Sucks." Upside.com,
December 13, 2000.
<http://www.upside.com/Open_Season/3a3661271.html>
(May 17, 2002).

Related Topics

Avatar; Computer-Supported Collaborative Work; Digital
Music; Human-Computer Interaction; Interactivity;
Interface; Joy, Bill; "Man-Computer Symbiosis";
Responsive Environments; Rheingold, Howard; Software
Agents; Technological Determinism

— *Kevin Featherly*

Laurel, Brenda

1950–

*Interactive Media Pioneer, Entrepreneur,
Social Theorist*

Brenda Laurel is a software designer, researcher, and writer who has been described as everything from a "visionary" to a "humanist," but whose primary interest throughout her career has been human-computer interaction. In 1993, *Wired* magazine writer Susan McCarthy called Laurel "a woman whose thoughts are shaping the way people think about the design of cyberspace." Laurel's work has long focused on interactive narrative, and on the cultural ramifications of technology.

Laurel was among the early video game designers. She worked at the company that manufactured the CyberVision home computer in the late 1970s, and created an interactive fantasy version of the story of Goldilocks, as well as the first lip-synched animation for a microcomputer game called Hangman, in which an executioner delivered menacing lines in a Transylvanian accent. By 1980, she was designing video games for Atari. Her approach to interactive media—including her pioneering work in virtual reality—has always tended to reflect her early work in and obsession with the theater.

Her doctoral dissertation was composed at Ohio State University after several years away from academic training, during which time she worked on educational software and interface theory at Atari under the direction of Alan Kay. Her dissertation reputedly presented the first outline of a comprehensive architecture for combining interactive fantasy and fiction. Again, this line of interest was based on her experiences in drama. Like theater, Laurel said, games and educational software focus on characters and action. Therefore, she theorized, computers are inherently a theatrical medium, and people can use them to participate in events that have dramatic impact and emotional resonance. Such observations led her in the mid-1980s directly into the field of virtual reality (VR).

As author Howard Rheingold described it, Laurel and other ex-Atari programmers left the company wanting to redefine the computer interface, changing it from a medium in which user and computer are separated by a glass window—to build a new interface in which people could walk into and experience a virtual life, to construct environments where rocks in the soil would be difficult to loosen, places populated with heroes and villains like any good fantasy.

Laurel joined ActiVision Inc. in 1985 as director of product development, learning, and creativity. During the next two years, she was responsible for strategic planning and product-line management, producing and designing more interactive games. She also worked with Lucasfilm Games and Tom Snyder Productions as a creative consultant. In 1990, Laurel and NASA émigré Scott Fisher co-founded a company called Telepresence Research, which experimented with VR environments, building prototypes and creating designs for custom VR installations.

Her first book was 1991's *Computers as Theatre,* which borrowed heavily from Aristotle's ancient analysis of the form and structure of drama, and which built a case that computers should not be designed with a focus on the interface *between* machine and user, but strictly on the user's very personal experiences using the machine. As such, Laurel's work has long focused on interactive narrative and on the cultural ramifications of technology. Also in 1991, Laurel joined the research staff at Interval Research Corp., a VR company founded in 1992 by Microsoft co-founder Paul Allen. In 1993, she and fellow Interval researcher Rachel Strickland designed a large VR installation called Placeholder. According to *Wired* magazine, Placeholder emerged after Laurel observed that kindergarten children habitually created make-believe roles for themselves and switched them with other children almost at random. The VR space allowed two people to participate; users wore white helmets and stood on carpeted circles with wires running upward from their headgear to allow for mostly free movement. *Wired* reported that Placeholder was a "virtual world," one "populated by whimsical creatures such as a snake, a spider and a crow." Users could "inhabit" the creatures by pushing into the virtual space that they occupied.

While at Interval, Laurel began concentrating further on ways that technology and culture intersect, particularly with respect to the way that technology—especially video games—tended to ignore little girls. She began four years or research into the relationships between gender, the way that kids play and learn, and the ways that technology design responds to and incorporates children's behavior. In particular, Laurel wanted to know why girls tended to lose interest in technology. Her research led her to form another company, Purple Moon, a spin-off of Interval, in 1996. The company, though small, rose to prominence for several years as the first software maker to focus specifically on girls.

Purple Moon developed what it called "friendship adventures," games aimed at girls aged 8 to 12 that emphasized the "formation of self" while ignoring the violence and mayhem endemic in most video games. "I think I got into doing games for girls" Laurel said in a 1999 speech, "because I was so tired of seeing things explode." Purple Moon created and marketed a bright, resourceful pre-teen female cartoon character, Rockett Movado, who recognized that different situations presented her with various choices. Purple Moon also became a dot-com venture, creating a girls-only Web community where children could go to "get to know" Rockett and other Purple Moon characters while exchanging messages among themselves.

Despite Rockett's popularity, the business failed, and was acquired in 1999 by Mattel. Laurel later chronicled that business experience in *Utopian Entrepreneur* (2001). The book is something of a manifesto, in which Laurel defined her career as "culture work," and in which she explained why she chose that pursuit. "Culture work," Laurel wrote, "is a potent way of working for peace. Changing minds is ultimately more powerful than blowing things up."

Today, Laurel is on the faculty of the Art Center College of Design in Pasadena, California. She also continues to work as a consultant for such clients as Citibank, Oregon Public Broadcasting, and the Children's Television Workshop. Brenda Laurel is a rare example, perhaps the sole example, of a Silicon Valley veteran who has played roles in all four of the crucial computer tech movements of the past three decades—games, multimedia, virtual reality, and the World Wide Web—all the while injecting a strong dose of humanism into what can otherwise be a dehumanizing medium.

Selected Works

Laurel, Brenda. "Activism for a New World." Commencement Address, California State University at Monterey Bay, May 19, 2000. <http://www.tauzero.com/Brenda_Laurel/Recent_Talks/CSUMBCommencmentSpeech.html> (May 31, 2002).

———. "Commentary: Virtual Reality." *Scientific American*, vol. 273, no. 3 (September 1995).

———. *Computers as Theatre.* Reading, Mass.: Addison-Wesley, 1991.

———. "Making Better Media for Kids." Speech given at UCLA, June 1999. <http://www.tauzero.com/Brenda_Laurel/Recent_Talks/MakingBetterMediaForKids.html> (May 31, 2002).

———. *Severed Heads: Notes on Technology, Art, and Nature.* TauZero.com, 1992-98. <http://www.tauzero.com/Brenda_Laurel> (May 31, 2002).

———. "Technological Humanism and Values-Driven Design." Keynote Address, CHI-98, Los Angeles, Calif., April 1998. <http://www.tauzero.com/Brenda_Laurel/Recent_Talks/Technological_Humanism.html> (May 31, 2002).

———. *Utopian Entrepreneur.* Cambridge, Mass.: MIT Press, 2001.

Laurel, Brenda; Strickland, Rachel; and Rob Tow. "Placeholder: Landscape and Narrative in Virtual Environments." *Computer Graphics*, vol. 28, no. 2 (May 1994), pp. 118–26.

Bibliography

Helft, Miguel. "Maker of Girls' Software Is Broke: Purple Moon Pioneer Can't Compete with Barbie." *San Jose Mercury News*, February 19 1999, p. 1C.

McCarthy, Susan. "Techno Soaps and Virtual Theatre." *Wired* 1.02, May/June 1993. <http://www.wired.com/wired/archive//1.02/brenda.html> (May 31, 2002).

Rheingold, Howard. *Virtual Reality*. New York: Summit Books, 1991.

Further Reading

Aukstakalnis, Steve, and David Blatner. *Silicon Mirage: The Art and Science of Virtual Reality*. Berkeley, Calif.: Peachpit Press, 1992.

Beato, G. "Girl Games." *Wired* 5.04, April 1997. <http://www.wired.com/wired/archive/5.04/es_girlgames.html> (May 31, 2002).

Lanier, Jaron. "One-Half of a Manifesto." *Wired* 8.12, December 2000. <http://www.wired.com/wired/archive/8.12/lanier_pr.html> (May 31, 2002).

Montfort, Nick. "Spawn of Atari." *Wired* 4.10, October 1996. <http://www.wired.com/wired/archive//4.10/atari.html> (May 31, 2002).

San Jose Mercury News Staff. "Visions of a World Where the Net Is Everywhere." *San Jose Mercury News*, March 5, 1997, p. 11A.

Related Topics

Digital Art and Animation; Gaming; Human-Computer Interaction; Interactivity; Interface; Kay, Alan; Multimedia; Responsive Environments; Rheingold, Howard; Virtual Reality

— *Theresa M. Senft*

Lessig, Lawrence

1961–

Cyberlaw Expert, Author

Lawrence Lessig is an important figure in defining the scope of cyberspace law as an author, legal adviser, and law professor, and has been at or near the center of most of the key cyberlaw cases of the young Digital Age. He has been dubbed both "a James Madison of our time" and "the Paul Revere of the Web." His singular analysis and understanding of cyberspace's legal complications (and hence of cyberspace governance), and the warnings that he has issued as a result, earned him both labels. *BusinessWeek* magazine, for one, has dubbed Lessig "the most original thinker in the new field of cyberlaw."

Lessig was born on June 3, 1961, in Rapid City, South Dakota. Lessig's father, Lester L. "Jack" Lessig, owned a steel-fabrication firm in Williamsport, Pennsylvania, the city where Lessig grew up. His mother, Patricia, sold real estate for a time as a hobby.

In an email interview for this encyclopedia, Lessig said that his early interests were stamp collecting, music, and politics. "A right-wing loon I was," he says now. "Only music has survived."

Loony or otherwise, Lessig nearly made a career of conservative politics. As a teenager, he was president of the Pennsylvania Teenage Republicans, and seemed destined to be a conservative's darling. While still a sophomore at the University of Pennsylvania in 1980, he was hired to manage a key U.S. Senate race. However, despite that year's Reagan landslide, his candidate lost, pushing him away from politics.

Lessig earned a bachelor's degree in economics from the University of Pennsylvania in 1983, then a master's degree in philosophy from Cambridge University in 1986. He got his law degree from Yale University in 1989. He served as a clerk for Judge Richard Posner, an influential, conservative Illinois federal circuit-court judge, and later for U.S. Supreme Court justice Antonin Scalia. Eventually he abandoned Republican politics. By the time of his graduation from Yale, he began questioning the prevailing anti-government sentiments of conservative political leaders and the courts.

The fall of communism also played a role in his transformation; touring Eastern Europe during a college break in 1982, he saw firsthand the extremes to which bureaucracies could resort in attempting to maintain authority in the face of revolutionary change. By the mid-1990s, the Internet had begun to radically transform parts of American society, and Lessig saw the government and the corporations clinging in similar ways to their power bases, attempting to thwart these changes. Lessig has said that his goal in the face of this struggle is to identify the basic rules that society should adopt in preventing capitalistic interests from grinding digital progress to a halt.

Lessig rejects the Internet culture's usual libertarianism, in which the free will of the individual is prized above all, and in which government involvement is perceived as something akin to leprosy. He disagrees with the common wisdom that says that the Internet cannot be regulated. Indeed, while Lessig says that he remains skeptical of government intervention, he strongly favors regulation and judicial activism on Internet issues when there is no other way to protect the individual's rights. He calls himself "a constitutionalist," but he argues that constitutional interpretations need to be periodically updated to protect against new threats to freedom that were not conceived of by the Constitution's framers in the late eighteenth century.

His ideas have illuminated much of the debate over cyberlaw during the past decade. U.S. Supreme Court justice Sandra Day O'Connor cited Lessig's writings in overturning 1996's anti-pornography Communications Decency Act. Federal district court judge Thomas Penfield Jackson appointed him a special master in the *U.S. vs. Microsoft* case, although he lost that job when Microsoft alleged conflict of interest after releasing private emails showing that Lessig supported Netscape Communications, the government's key witness in the case. However, Lessig did write a crucial *amicus* (friend-of-the-court) brief siding with the government's case that Microsoft violated antitrust laws by tying products together in an effort to kill competition. Finally, Lessig was instrumental in pushing the federal government to require that America Online and Time Warner Communications open up Time Warner Cable's network to competitors as a condition of the AOL/Time Warner merger. As detailed in Ken Auletta's 2001 book on the Microsoft trial, *World War 3.0*, Lessig explains that it would be folly to insist that government or the courts take no role in such issues. To do that, he says, would be "to allow commerce to restructure the Net in a certain way" that runs contrary to the public good.

Lessig's philosophies have not always put him on the winning side of cyberlaw debates. He argued in favor of MP3 file-swapping service Napster in its suit against five major record labels and a raft of music publishers; Napster lost badly in court. A backer of the open-source software movement, he also took the side of hackers who posted DVD-cracking code on the Web, a move that might have allowed people to make unauthorized private copies of movies; that was a losing battle, too. And he backed an effort to repeal the so-called "Sonny Bono Law" that extended copyright monopolies on artistic and creative works to 95 years. Lessig and others argued that the law violates the spirit of the United States' founding fathers, who intended that copyrights should be of limited duration, and that inventive materials (including, for instance, the Microsoft Windows operating system) should revert sooner rather than later to the public domain, where the underlying ideas could be recycled and possibly improved upon. According to Lessig's cyberlaw theory, this limitation of copyright is crucial to continuing innovation, and an important way to minimize the overweening power of corporations to turn cyberlaw to their advantage. But the copyright-limitation effort has thus far been unsuccessful.

Lawrence Lessig, 2001. (AP Wideworld Photos)

Nearly as important as his involvement in legal disputes are Lessig's writings, which may eventually frame his legacy. His 1999 book *Code and Other Laws of Cyberspace* has been highly influential, and has helped define for a wider segment of the public the most pressing issues of cyberlaw. *The New York Times* partly panned the book for its occasionally arcane writing style, which might prohibit people from reading and comprehending the complex issues involved in cyberlaw. Lessig's monthly column in *The Industry Standard* seems to have taken that criticism to heart; they are generally readable, and continue, somewhat in the fashion of the pro-Constitution *Federalist Papers* two centuries ago, to define and shape the issues involved. Another book, *The Future of Ideas: The Fate of the Commons in a Connected World*, was published in late 2001.

The chief warning of *Code and Other Laws of Cyberspace* is that unchecked capitalism can kill the free Internet, and can do so without involving government or the courts. According to Lessig's argument, code—meaning the underlying programming languages used to construct the applications and protocols used in online commerce and communications—can be constructed to control the way the Internet is used, and can do so without the need of new laws or supportive rulings from the courts. In effect, Lessig says, "Code is law."

"This code presents the greatest threat to liberal or libertarian ideals, as well as the greatest promise," Lessig writes in the book. "We can build, or architect, or code cyberspace to protect values that we believe are fundamental, or we can build, or architect, or code cyberspace to allow those values to disappear. There is no middle ground."

He cites digital-rights management as an example. This technology can be used to track when and where a product—an e-book, for instance—is purchased. It can report back to the seller (and whoever the seller markets his user-information databases to) about whether the book has been read, how much of the book has been read, and whether there has been an attempt to sell or delete the book once it was purchased. This information can be used to create a database of the kinds of books that a person reads and identify the flavor of the passages that they tend to home in on. To Lessig, these are fundamental violations of everything from the Fair Use provisions of the U.S. Copyright Act to basic privacy protections. (Yet, in Real Networks' announcement of the kind of technology it would employ in its forthcoming MusicNet service, these kinds of digital-rights management technologies appeared very much in evidence.)

As one possible antidote, Lessig backs the open-source software movement that hopes to open software code to public scrutiny, and to authorize private programmers to alter and improve whatever is there. Open code, Lessig argues, could serve as an important check on both governmental authority and corporate power. "Anyone can take (code) and use it as he wishes," Lessig writes. "Anyone can take it and come to see how it works."

The standard cliché is that cyberspace changes everything. But for Lessig, the Internet cannot be allowed to change everything, especially when it comes to the rights of the individual. Lessig's importance as a cyberspace theoretician lies in his identification, description, and proposal of solutions to a number of genuine civil-liberties threats that are inherent in corporate rights-management tools, in closed networking protocols, and in governmental regulation of underlying code. His former conservatism has not disappeared; if anything, it has simply transformed itself into an effort to preserve the best things about the law's past, without simply diving headlong into a new, digital age and ignoring the toll. "We can choose to architect cyberspace with a commons, or not," he wrote in *Code*. "We should choose to architect it with a commons."

Selected Works

Lessig, Lawrence. "Artful Dodges." *The Industry Standard,* June 11, 2001. <http://www.thestandard.com/article/0,1902,26946,00.html> (June 7, 2002).

———. *Code and Other Laws of Cyberspace.* New York: Basic Books, 1999.

———. "The Code in Law, and the Law in Code (Draft)." Stanford Law School, March 15, 2000. <http://cyberlaw.stanford.edu/lessig/content/works/pcforum.pdf> (June 7, 2002).

———. "Copyright Thugs." *The Industry Standard,* May 7, 2001. <http://www.thestandard.com/article/0,1902,24208,00.html> (June 7, 2002).

———. *The Future of Ideas: The Fate of the Commons in a Connected World.* New York: Random House, 2001.

———. "In Search of Skeptics." *The Industry Standard,* April 24, 2000. <http://www.thestandard.com/article/0,1902,14103-1,00.html> (June 7, 2002).

———. "Innovation, Regulation, and the Internet." *The American Prospect,* vol. 11, issue 10 (March 27, 2000). <http://www.prospect.org/print/V11/10/lessig-l.html> (June 7, 2002).

———. "The Limits in Open Code: Regulatory Standards and the Future of the Net." *Berkeley Technology Law Journal,* vol.14, issue 2 (Spring 1999). <http://www.law.berkeley.edu/journals/btlj/articles/14_2/Lessig/html/text.html> (June 7, 2002).

Bibliography

Auletta, Ken. *World War 3.0: Microsoft and Its Enemies.* New York: Random House, 2001.

Featherly, Kevin. Email interview with Lawrence Lessig. June 30, 2001.

Mullaney, Timothy J. "The E-Biz 25: Larry Lessig." *BusinessWeek,* May 15, 2000. <http://www.businessweek.com/2000/00_20/b3681066.htm> (May 31, 2002).

Mullaney, Timothy J., and Jay Green. "The Paul Revere of the Web." *BusinessWeek,* March 6, 2000. <http://www.businessweek.com/2000/00_10/b3671138.htm> (May 31, 2002).

Schmidt, Robert. "Battle Royal." *Brill's Content,* April 2001.

Further Reading

Mann, Charles. C. "Roundtable: Life, Liberty, and . . . the Pursuit of Copyright?" *The Atlantic Monthly,* September 10, 1998. <http://www.theatlantic.com/unbound/forum/copyright/intro.htm> (May 31, 2002).

———. "Who Will Own Your Next Good Idea?" *The Atlantic Monthly,* September 1998.

<http://www.theatlantic.com/issues/98sep/copy.htm#mann>
(May 31, 2002).

Wasserman, Elizabeth. "Microsoft to the Feds: We Like
These Judges." *The Industry Standard*, June 28, 1998.
<http://www.thestandard.com/article/0,1902,824,00.html>
(May 31, 2002).

Related Topics

Copyright; Electronic Frontier Foundation; Napster;
Open Source; Privacy; Trademark

— *Kevin Featherly*

Licklider, J. C. R.

1915–1990

Computer Scientist, Internet Pioneer

There has long been a war of semantics, revolving
around which of the early computing pioneers can
justly be described as "the father of the Internet," but
the reality is that no one person invented it. However,
it can safely be said that no one anywhere in the world
dreamt of it before J. C. R. Licklider.

Licklider's contribution to the development of
what became the Internet, indeed to the field of
computer science as a whole, can hardly be overes-
timated. But his was not just a visionary role. As the
first director of the Information Processing
Techniques Office (IPTO) at the U.S. Department of
Defense's Advanced Research Projects Agency
(ARPA), Licklider oversaw one of the most fertile
periods of creativity in the history of computer science, recruiting the key people and securing the government funding that would lay the groundwork for
the creation in 1969 of the ARPANET, the direct
precursor to today's Internet. His legendarily infec-
tious enthusiasm for his idea—which he jovially
called the "intergalactic computer network," over-
came staunch opposition from some in key positions
who considered "on-line" computing to be a farce
and a waste of government dollars—probably was
just as great a contribution.

Licklider, or "Lick" as he insisted on being called,
was born Joseph Carl Robnett Licklider on March 11,
1915, in St. Louis, Missouri, the only son of Baptist
minister Joseph Parron Licklider and Margaret
Robnett Licklider. In 1937, Licklider graduated from
St. Louis' Washington University with majors in psychology, mathematics, and physics. He received his
master's degree the following year, and continued graduate studies in psychology at the University of
Rochester, receiving a Ph.D. in 1942.

Licklider's Ph.D. research investigated theories
about perception and loudness, measuring the brain's
responses to tone impulses. Later, as a Harvard
University behavioral scientist, he worked throughout
the 1940s and 1950s on "psychoacoustics" (a field in
which Licklider's contributions are also historically
significant), trying to model the way the brain works in
connection with hearing. This work led to his shift into
computing: It was while trying to create such a model
on an already-archaic early 1950s–vintage analog
computer that Licklider decided that he had better
learn digital computing if he ever hoped to complete
the work. By 1960, Licklider had left academia,
including a mid-1950s tenure at the Massachusetts
Institute of Technology (MIT), to become a vice president at Bolt, Beranek, and Newman, Inc. (BBN), where
he served as head of the psychoacoustics, engineering
psychology, and information-systems research departments. BBN procured a digital computer for Licklider,
on which he began to learn programming. It was a por-
tentous moment.

In his memorable 1960 paper titled "Man-
Computer Symbiosis," Licklider leapt far ahead of any
computer's current capabilities to tell of a day when it
would be possible to "bring computing machines effectively into processes of thinking . . . in real time." His
background in psychology had everything to do with
this cheerfully naïve approach. As a specialist in engineering psychology, Licklider simply thought that
computers could and should function more like the
human brain, and even serve as an indispensable partner and machine extension of the mind.

At a time when computers could do little more
than crunch numbers—and even then, only after a programmer had written out programming instructions by
hand and given them to a lab technician to implement
on punch cards—Licklider imagined computers as
interactive, capable of taking on rote, time-consuming
tasks of data processing, record keeping, and remote
information access that were drudgery for humans.
Licklider estimated that such tedious work had consumed 85 percent of his working life. By performing
routine tasks on demand, computers could help
humans to think harder, achieve new insights, and
make more important, more complex decisions.

"Man-Computer Symbiosis" also managed to
anticipate such far-in-the-future developments as the
handwriting recognition systems that now can be found
in Palm Pilots, and the voice-recognition systems that
even today are not yet fully developed. As writer John
Naughton has noted, Licklider's guiding insight was

that a symbiotic human-computer relationship would create a whole that would be greater than the sum of its parts. As such, it could have tremendous impact on improving the human condition.

From BBN, Licklider moved on to ARPA in 1962. He quickly began to make the agency over, changing it from one that emphasized esoteric military projects, such as an air force initiative to detect patterns in the behavior of Soviet leaders, into one that focused on his personal vision of the "intergalactic network" (an idea that he sketched out in a series of memos between 1962 and 1963). Thanks to his enthusiastic leadership, Licklider managed to procure immense sums of money for his pet project.

As writer David Bennahum noted in *Slate* magazine in 1996, an entire generation of computer scientists—some of whom would invent video games, the mouse, graphical computer displays, the "windows" interface, and "icons"—would be influenced by Licklider. The Internet would also be devised by people who were hired by Licklider at ARPA—notably, his successor at IPTO, Robert Taylor. As one writer put it, Licklider fashioned in ARPA a management culture where graduate students were left to run a multimillion-dollar research project. His agency also funded research at the first four universities that ever offered computer science degrees. During Licklider's two-year term at ARPA, an astonishing 70 percent of all computer science funding was procured by his agency.

Bennahum notes that Licklider's prescience about computer networking was born from his pioneering work in "time-sharing," a method of computer use that differed from batch processing, then the norm, which involved stacks of paper punch cards and tightly controlled lab conditions. With batch processing, technicians acted as computing "priests," deciding who would be allowed to use the apartment-sized mainframes of the day, and who would have to wait to test their programs out. For most users, time-sharing was the first opportunity they had to predictably rely on computer availability, and for many, the process introduced keyboards, terminals, and video displays to the computing equation for the first time. Time-sharing allowed multiple users to log on to a single mainframe computer simultaneously, something that had only recently been impossible. Not only were users now able to accomplish work through computers, they also could communicate with one another via the machines. Although very localized in comparison with Licklider's vision of a global computer-communications network, time-sharing was a baby step in that direction.

Licklider left his ARPA post in 1964 to return to MIT. But his "intergalactic network" concept left a lingering impression on others he had worked with, most notably Robert Taylor and Larry Roberts, who continued working on his ideas.

Away from ARPA, Licklider did not drop out of the picture. In the early 1960s at BBN, he had done some work on formulating plans for computer-driven libraries. After returning to MIT, he published a book called *Libraries of the Future* (1965), which fellow computer scientist Robert M. Fano has described as being based on the same visions as those of "Man-Computer Symbiosis." In the first half of the book, Licklider discussed how documents could be stored in digital form without losing their value. Then he presented a detailed analysis of the intellectual processes involved in the acquiring, organizing, and using of knowledge. He described "procognitive systems" that would be capable of allowing users to search documents. Finally, he outlined a research program that could help develop his ideas. When Fano published his Licklider biography for the National Academy of Sciences in 1998, he noted that libraries were only just beginning to catch up with Licklider's ideas.

In 1968, Licklider co-authored "The Computer as a Communication Device" with Robert Taylor, a paper that was perhaps in its way even more important than "Man-Computer Symbiosis." In "The Computer as a Communication Device," Licklider and Taylor discussed the development of "on-line" communities. A global computer network could make human communication more efficient, the paper said, and it left little room for doubt as to just how much more efficient: "In a few years, men will be able to communicate more effectively through a machine than face to face."

Licklider and Taylor established several principals regarding the crucial role that computers can play in human communications. First, they described communication as a two-way interactive process—two tape recorders playing at one another while simultaneously recording the noise are not communicating, they wrote. Second, they articulated the need for a relatively short response time in order to foster real-time information exchanges. Third, based on their own observations at ARPA, they wrote that larger computer networks would tend to form out of small regional ones. Lastly, they anticipated that large communities would form, organized not by geography, but by shared interests, spurred on by the interactivity of computer communications. "When minds interact," they wrote, "new ideas emerge."

There was also a political dimension to the message of "The Computer as a Communication Device." The paper anticipated today's concerns about a "digital divide," worrying that people with scant resources would be at a major communications disadvantage compared to the wealthy. But it also presciently guessed that by 2000, millions of people would be online using computer networks to communicate with one another around the world. Not coincidentally, the first connections on the ARPANET, the primitive computer-network ancestor of the Internet, were completed one year after the paper's publication, in 1969.

"The Computer as a Communication Device" would be Licklider's last major contribution to the development of the Internet, although he did return to his old post at ARPA for one unsatisfying year in 1974. After that, he focused on smaller research projects, and often worked as an in-demand speaker and lecturer.

Licklider died in 1990, at the age of 75 from complications following an asthma attack, while serving as professor emeritus in MIT's Department of Electrical Engineering and Computer Science. Department Chair Paul Penfield Jr. eulogized Licklider by telling his faculty members that, "In a very real way, computer science in America today owes its strength to him."

Selected Works

Licklider, J. C. R. "Man-Computer Symbiosis." *Transcriptions on Human Factors in Intelligence,* March 1960, pp. 4–11. Republished in *Multimedia: From Wagner to Virtual Reality.* Randall Packer and Ken Jordan, eds. New York: Norton, 2001.

———. "Memorandum For: Members and Affiliates of the Intergalactic Computer Network." Advanced Research Projects Agency, April 23, 1963. <http://www.olografix.org/gubi/estate/libri/wizards/memo.html> (June 7, 2002).

———. *Libraries of the Future.* Cambridge, Mass.: MIT Press, 1965.

Licklider, J. C. R., and Robert W. Taylor, "The Computer as a Communication Device." *Science and Technology,* April 1968, pp. 21–31.

Bibliography

Fano, Robert M. "Biographical Memoirs: Joseph Carl Robnett Licklider; March 11, 1915–June 26, 1990." *National Academy of Sciences,* 1998. <http://www.nap.edu/readingroom/books/biomems/jlicklider.html> (May 31, 2002).

Hafner, Katie, and Matthew Lyon. *Where Wizards Stay Up Late: The Origins of the Internet.* New York: Simon & Schuster, 1996.

Hauben, Michael, and Ronda Hauben. *Netizens: On the History and Impact of Usenet and the Internet.* Los Alamitos, Calif.: IEEE Computer Society Press, 1997.

Lardner, James. "The World's First Nethead." *U.S. News & World Report,* December 27, 1999. <http://www.usnews.com/usnews/news/991227/makers.htm> (May 31, 2002).

MIT News Office. "Dr. J. C. R. Licklider Dies at 75." July 18, 1990. <http://web.mit.edu/newsoffice/tt/1990/jul18/23439.html> (May 31, 2002).

Naughton, John. *A Brief History of the Future: From Radio Days to Internet Years in a Lifetime.* Woodstock, N.Y.: Overlook Press, 2001.

Further Reading

Dertouzos, Michael. *The Unfinished Revolution: Human-Centered Computers and What They Can Do for Us.* New York: HarperCollins, 2001.

Dertouzos, Michael, and Joel Moses, eds. *The Computer Age: A Twenty-Year View.* Cambridge, Mass.: MIT Press, 1979.

Hacker, Kenneth L. "A Tribute to J. Licklider." Department of Communication Studies, New Mexico State University, May 7, 1997. <http://web.nmsu.edu/~comstudy/licklider.html> (May 31, 2002).

Mayer, Paul, ed. *Computer Media and Communication: A Reader.* New York: Oxford University Press, 1999.

Packer, Randall, and Ken Jordan, eds. *Multimedia: From Wagner to Virtual Reality.* New York: W. W. Norton, 2001.

Segaller, Stephen. *Nerds 2.0.1: A Brief History of the Internet.* New York: TV Books, 1998.

Related Topics

Computer-Supported Collaborative Work; Cyberspace; Graphical User Interface; Human-Computer Interaction; Interactivity; Interface; "Man-Computer Symbiosis"; Peer-to-Peer; Virtual Community

— Kevin Featherly

Linking

Linking, or hyperlinking, is a way to connect information, words, ideas, or pictures to blocks of text or to images within a document, or between multiple sites on the Internet. Users may click on a phrase, word, or image within a Web page or Internet document to move to a new location or source of information.

Through the use of linking, paths are established that can lead to additional knowledge or information on subjects related to the original point of interest. The links may activate a Web site, a Web page, an audio clip, or a video clip. Active text links can be identified in most cases by their appearance in a contrasting color with underlining, and links leading to a different Web site altogether often begin with the prefix "http://." The text of a previously clicked link generally changes color, allowing the user to identify what links have already been selected.

Linking within documents encourages users to read and write in a nonlinear fashion. This differs from the traditional path of consuming information in the exact order in which it appears or is presented. The linking process makes for a more dynamic, fluid relationship between the reader, the writer, and the information. The author or designer of a Web site may choose to refer to related ideas by linking to other information elsewhere on the Web page, or by linking to other ideas and works on other Web pages. Within one document, an author may choose to insert links to different sections of the document, allowing the reader to skip to the conclusion, for instance, by clicking on a word, phrase, or URL address within the text. In order to present outside ideas, the author may wait until the end of a document and link to information in the footnotes, or may allow the reader to go to other people's written comments through links to other sites at any point while reading through the original text.

The establishment of linking has also lead to new ways of measuring the use and popularity of Web sites. Linking Popularity measures how popular a site is by determining and analyzing other sites linked to it. Search engines, which allow Web users to locate specific information or sites on the Web, use Linking Popularity to review and rank the relevancy of a Web site presented as a result of a search. Although search engines have complex algorithms for determining the order in which searched information is presented, location and frequency of links to a site remain a dominant factor.

PROBLEMS WITH LINKING

One problem associated with linking occurs when a link becomes inactive, or "dead." In this case, the link no longer connects to another location. Dead links can occur as a result of technical difficulties on the part of the linked-to site or page, or when linked content is moved to another location or removed from the Web altogether.

The excessive placement of links in a document is another issue. Readers can become confused and lose track of the location of their starting point. Linking is most commonly unidirectional, in which case the user goes forward by clicking on the link itself, but can go

back only by using the Web browser's "back" button, clicking within the history of the links, or by clicking on the saved bookmark of the previous site.

As innocuous as linking might seem at first, in fact it has led to a complex set of legal issues that must be thoughtfully considered by anyone implementing or using a link on the Web. Some of the most frequently recurring issues associated with linking include copyright infringement, defamation, unfair competition, misappropriation, and the right of publicity.

Copyright infringement on the Web can potentially occur by means of linking. Although the link itself only points a user in the direction of a source of content, an unauthorized link may position the linked content in an unintended way. For example, a newspaper Web site could maintain its own home page with links to stories from another Web-based newspaper. In what is called "passing off," the first newspaper "passes off" the other newspaper's articles as its own. The reader might never know that the actual stories came from a different source, because the link bypasses the other home page and goes directly to a deeper portion of the site, where the linked document resides.

In a lawsuit involving the Microsoft Corporation, Ticketmaster alleged that a Microsoft Web site used an unauthorized link to a Ticketmaster ticket-order Web page. The link bypassed the Ticketmaster home page, which provided Web users with information, advertisements, and policies. Ticketmaster alleged that by linking to a page within its Web site other than its home page, Microsoft benefited from Ticketmaster's name and services.

Another example of copyright infringement comes from the use of derivative works on a Web site. If a pre-existing image or a derivative of that image is linked on a Web site without the permission of the image's owner, it could be considered copyright infringement. The ease of linking can also lead to misappropriation, or trademark infringement. This can occur when a link is used to suggest an affiliation or sponsorship that does not exist.

Defamation can also occur by means of linking. Although a document might not overtly name an individual being defamed, a link within the document might provide a way in which the individual could be identified, and thus defamed. Bitlaw.com provides an example: "This <u>man</u> killed my cat, stole my invention, and threatened to destroy the Internet." The word "<u>man</u>" is not in itself defamatory, but it appears as a link in the document. When clicked, it leads to the identification and resulting defamation of that person.

In the early days of the Web, authors encouraged others to link to their pages, counting "hits" to indicate the traffic level, thereby gauging the popularity of their pages. Later, however, copyright problems arose from commercial and scholarly interests.

Lawsuits have prevented people from copying well-known brands and logos and linking to them, even for satirical purposes. Creators of sites dependent upon the advertising revenue gained from banners frown upon links that bypass their front pages to avoid these ads. On the other hand, academics who post articles appreciate being linked to, preferring it to the wholesale copying of their articles.

Netiquette, the informal set of societal rules that govern Internet use and action, suggests that consent be obtained from the source to which a link may connect before that link is activated. It is also advisable to get permission for any linked images used within a site, and to link directly to another site's home page rather than bypassing it to link directly to a deeper location within the site. Many sites also include link disclaimers; in a "terms and conditions" portion of the disclaimer, the policy on links may be explained as it relates to copyrighted content and images, as well as to issues of linking to and from other Web pages.

Linking has provided users of the World Wide Web with a tool that allows for a non-linear journey into its contents. As valuable as the function of a search engine on the Web, linking creates an easy and useful way to navigate through large quantities of information. However, linking cannot be taken lightly, or employed without thought. Legal issues continue to arise as more and more content becomes available online. More devices to track individual clusters of interests may develop in the future, as links to more databases or other sources of information pervade text, images, and sounds on the Internet. Simultaneous linking to several sources related to the link of origin could also occur. Linking has become a pervasive Web tool; therefore, the rules that govern current copyright and commercial transactions are applicable to Web content, and must be considered when creating a Web site.

Bibliography

Berners-Lee, Tim, and Mark Fischetti. *Weaving the Web: The Original Design and Ultimate Destiny of the World Wide Web by Its Inventor.* San Francisco: HarperCollins, 1999.

Esau, Gregory. Private communications with the author, June 2001.

Gaggi, Silvio. *From Text to Hypertext: Decentering the Subject in Fiction, Film, the Visual Arts, and Electronic Media.* Philadelphia: University of Pennsylvania Press, 1997.

Levinson, Paul. *The Soft Edge: A Natural History and Future of the Information Revolution.* London: Routledge, 1997.

Pemberton, Lyn, and Simon Shurville, eds. *Words on the Web: Computer Mediated Communication.* Exeter, England: Intellect Books, 2000.

Reinking, David; McKenna, Michael; Labbo, Linda; and Ronald Kiefer, eds. *Handbook of Literacy and Technology: Transformations in a Post-Typographic World.* Mahwah, N.J.: L. Erlbaum Associates, 1998.

Rich, Lloyd L. "Internet Legal Issues: Linking." Publaw.com, 1999. <http://www.publaw.com/linking.html> (May 31, 2002).

Swiss, Thomas, ed. *Unspun: Key Concepts for Understanding the World Wide Web.* New York: New York University Press, 2000.

Tysver, Daniel. "Linking and Liability." BitLaw, 2000. <http://www.bitlaw.com/internet/linking.html> (May 31, 2002).

Further Reading

Landow, George, P. *Hypertext: The Convergence of Contemporary Critical Theory and Technology.* Baltimore, Md.: Johns Hopkins University Press, 1992.

O'Donnell, James J. *Avatars of the Word: From Papyrus to Cyberspace.* Cambridge, Mass.: Harvard University Press, 1998.

Rheingold, Howard. *Tools for Thought: The History and Future of Mind-Expanding Technology.* Cambridge, Mass.: MIT Press, 2000.

Related Topics

Copyright; Hypertext; Internet; World Wide Web

— *Andrea Baker*

Linux

Linux is a computer operating system (OS) that is open source, which is a development model in which software is written collectively and the source code is freely available. Linux originated in 1991 in Finland as a project of University of Helsinki student Linus Torvalds, who was attempting to produce a Unix-like kernel (the essential, central part of an OS) for his Intel 386–based computer. Linux comprises the Linux kernel, the GNU utilities from the Free Software Foundation, and other utilities that are usually found in a variety of Unix environments, such as user environment tools, text interfaces, and graphical user interfaces (GUIs).

In the early 1990s, an online community of developers and experts, self-identified as hackers, responded to Torvalds' initial post in a Usenet newsgroup, in which he outlined his project and requested feedback. Building even a rudimentary kernel for a processor is no small feat, and Torvalds' kernel was slightly past rudimentary when he announced it. He posted the kernel to the FTP server in Finland, licensed under the GNU Public License; the FTP site's administrator renamed the development kernel Linux. Then hackers started to download it, and to "play" with it.

Thanks to the hackers' interest in the project and their abilities in general, in addition to Torvalds' ability to work with people, Linux entered a new mode of development, which, to use a description coined by Eric Raymond, resembled a bazaar. This model of development occurs when enough people are brought together on a project, and each person contributes his or her skills to its development, forming a fluid and organic self-organizing group with little central control.

On a technical level, Linux is an aberration from the predominant OS design style that was taught in colleges in the 1980s and early 1990s. It was a monolithic kernel, being developed when microkernels were the style of the day. Monolithic kernels include all of the memory systems, all of the driver systems, and every system that interacts with the core machine into one program, the kernel. The opposing school called for smaller programs called daemons to manage most of the secondary services involved in actually operating the computer. Over its years of development since its initial announcement, the Linux kernel has evolved more and more toward an open and adaptable design focused on user needs; the kernel can be built either in modular or monolithic formats, which makes Linux highly customizable.

It is this ability to customize the system that allows the Linux kernel to work in diverse operating environments, from a wristwatch based on embedded Linux to the world's most massive and powerful supercomputing environments. This configurability is also what makes Linux interesting for the developers and companies, which are using it for everything from teaching the development of embedded systems and the creation of wearable computers to implementations of mission-critical systems for corporate uses.

In Linux, one is presented with many choices of interface, most commonly either a window interface or a text-based one. While the window interface is more usable in certain respects, the text interface is immensely more powerful, backed as it is by a diverse toolkit of utilities and languages. It provides the architectural backbone of all Linux systems. The text interface, the muse of all Unix-like systems, allows administrators to optimize and automate the system. It also provides the rapid prototyping and problem-solving that are common in Unix-based computing. It is these tools' familiarity and usefulness that have helped Linux gain its initial foothold in the competitive OS market.

The reliance on a textual interface is the biggest burden for Linux in terms of its future. Some people argue that the key to the future of Linux is its popularization, and as such, its use as a desktop-oriented OS. While it is likely that Linux will be on the majority of the world's desktops due to its inexpensive nature, it is not likely that it will invade the same corporate high-cost, low-risk market space as other popular desktop environments. Instead, it will most probably find a home on desktops in Brazil, India, China, and similar markets, where its features make it significantly better than comparable systems.

Due to the number of applications built upon open standards in networking environments, Linux has been adopted as strategically central to the server market, and therefore to the development of the Internet. Linux, because of its Unix-like nature, has access to a wide variety of protocols through independently developed projects that provide applications and daemons for managing all aspects of network-enabled computing, such as file sharing, network management, and network protection. Linux has become a corporate system multi-tool in many respects. Due to its adaptability, configurability, relative ease of use for experts, and low cost, it can be used to rapidly respond to the needs of networked users.

The significance of the arrival of Linux into the OS market is immense. Linux has changed the field significantly, and has opened up new methods and arenas for software and OS development. It has also changed the face of software, bringing the source code back to the user, and thereby empowering its users to join the broader community of developers and supporters of the OS. It has also made huge contributions to the publicly available code that can now be used freely and without hindrance from a proprietary owner. Linux has lowered the cost of computing by removing the financial barriers included in the use of a proprietary OS, and continues to revolutionize all levels and types of computing.

Bibliography

Gancarz, Mike. *The UNIX Philosophy*. Boston, Mass.: Digital Press, 1995.

Hasan, Ragib. "History of Linux, Version 2.1." Ragib Hasan's Page of Dreams.
<http://ragib.hypermart.net/linux/> (May 31, 2002).

Raymond, Eric S. *The Cathedral and the Bazaar: Musings on Linux and Open Source by an Accidental Revolutionary.* Cambridge, Mass.: O'Reilly & Associates, 1999.

Stallman, Richard. "Linux and the GNU Project." Gnu.org.
<http://www.gnu.org/gnu/linux-and-gnu.html> (May 31, 2002).

Torvalds, Linus. *Just for Fun: The Story of an Accidental Revolutionary.* New York: HarperBusiness, 2001.

Further Reading

DiBona, Chris; Ockman, Sam; and Mark Stone, eds. *Open Sources: Voices from the Open Source Revolution.* Sebastopol, Calif.: O'Reilly, 1999.

Free Software Foundation. "GNU's Not Unix!—The GNU Project and the Free Software Foundation." 1996–2001.
<http://www.fsf.org/> (May 31, 2002).

Linux International. "Linux History." 1994-2001.
<http://www.li.org/linuxhistory.php> (May 31, 2002).

Related Topics

"The Cathedral and the Bazaar"; *The New Hacker's Dictionary*; Open Source; Raymond, Eric; Stallman, Richard

— *Jeremy Hunsinger*

LISTSERV

LISTSERV is a commercial mailing-list manager that allows anyone on the Internet to set up an email discussion forum to which similarly interested people can subscribe. The software, initially distributed for free, is perhaps the most important remnant of the old BITNET ("Because It's There Network"), an early online network that was prevalent in the early 1980s, before the advent of today's Internet.

The email service, originally developed for BITNET mailing networks, works when a LISTSERV participant sends an email message to a server containing the correct software, which automatically forwards that message to the email addresses of all other list subscribers. The system was a tremendous boon to advancing online discussion forums, rendering unnecessary such onerous tasks as keeping track of all the email addresses of list participants, and carbon-copying any messages intended for the group to each recipient. When the Internet became the de facto standard for online networking in the early 1990s, BITNET fell by the wayside. Nevertheless, many thousands of LISTSERV email lists continue to thrive online.

Eric Thomas, a computer science student at France's Ecole Central de Paris, developed LISTSERV in 1986, at a time when BITNET had grown so crowded with new computer users that managing the lists of email addresses by hand had become extremely cumbersome. In a May 2001 interview with the ChannelSeven.com Web site, Thomas said that he came up with the idea for what he initially called "Revised Listserv" after judging it "silly" that people were attempting to manage such a repetitive and error-prone process manually, when a computer could obviously do it better and more efficiently.

More importantly, Thomas said, existing manual email lists were generating thousands of messages every day, many of which traveled overseas on saturated telephone lines over 9,600 bps (baud per second) modem connections. "Every time someone posted a message, hundreds of copies of the message added to the thousands of messages that were already waiting to cross the Atlantic," Thomas said. "In fact, the traffic from the mailing lists alone was threatening to make private email totally unusable, with delivery delays approaching a week."

Realizing that no one else had considered writing an automated mailing-list management program, Thomas wrote one himself. He set a distributed-computing model for the system, allowing several machines, particularly servers separated by the Atlantic Ocean, to share the email traffic load and to better manage its flow. Revised Listserv, later shortened and capitalized as LISTSERV, was distributed free to BITNET members in July 1986; this was the first time that a software program had ever managed a mailing list. With LISTSERV in place, a single email post was automatically distributed to an entire discussion list, vastly simplifying the use of email forums by subscribing group members. The system was soon improved to allow the creation of LISTSERV databases for each mailing list, resulting in searchable online archives of discussion threads.

In 1994, Thomas formed L-Soft International Inc., based jointly in Landover, Maryland, and Stockholm, Sweden, where Thomas resides. The company now markets LISTSERV as a commercial product. Initially, the software ran only on IBM mainframes that ran the VM operating system, but Thomas has since reconfigured the software to allow it to run on Unix, OpenVMS, Microsoft Windows, and Windows 95/98 operating systems. Of course, it can also run on the Internet, now that BITNET has disappeared.

Imitators sprang up soon after LISTSERV's invention, including several software versions written for Unix called Listproc, SmartList, and Majordomo. Of these, Majordomo has probably grown most in popularity over the years as a freeware service, used primarily by those who wish to join or administer private email lists but who cannot afford to purchase a LISTSERV license.

By September 1998, LISTSERV was delivering more than 35 million messages on an average weekday to subscribers on more than 100,000 managed lists worldwide. As it has become commercialized, LISTSERV has gravitated away from its initial scope of facilitating private email discussions. Today, for instance, Merriam-Webster uses L-Soft's LISTSERV software to mail out its "Word of the Day" message to thousands of recipients. Corporations pay anywhere from a penny to a dime for each message, or some roughly equivalent monthly fee, to have their messages sent out from L-Soft servers using LISTSERV. L-Soft adds and drops users as needed, ensures that lists are not plagued by unsolicited email (or "spam"), and eliminates outdated or dead email addresses. Commercial competitors like InfoBeat, Critical Path, and the Electric Mall have arisen to challenge L-Soft's primacy.

Bibliography

Buckman, John. "A History of List Servers." White Paper, Lyris Technologies Inc., 1998.
<http://www.lyris.com/about/company/whitepapers/listserver_history.html> (May 17, 2002).

L-Soft International. "The History of LISTSERV."
<http://www.lsoft.com/products/listserv-history.asp> (May 17, 2002).

Parker, Pamela. "Featuring Eric Thomas: Chief Executive Officer of L-Soft." ChannelSeven.com, May 18, 2001.
<http://www.channelseven.com/newsbeat/2001features/seven20010518.shtml> (May 17, 2002).

Further Reading

Hauben, Michael, and Ronda Hauben. *Netizens: On the History and Impact of Usenet and the Internet.* Los Alamitos, Calif.: IEEE Computer Society Press, 1997.

Rheingold, Howard. *The Virtual Community: Homesteading on the Electronic Frontier.* Reading, Mass.: Addison-Wesley, 1993.

Related Topics

BITNET; Bulletin-Board Systems; Community Networking; Cyberculture; Cyberspace; Internet Service Providers; Virtual Community

— *Kevin Featherly*

Local Area Network

A local area network (LAN) is a group of computers linked together over a relatively small area, generally within a business, institution, or residence; essentially, a LAN connects computers at high data speeds within one building or among a group of adjacent buildings. Users on a LAN can share files from computer to computer, tap into shared databases, and share expensive peripheral resources such as laser printers. LANs also allow users on the network to form private email groups and chat lists. Copper wires, coaxial cables, fiberoptic lines, or wireless radio-based technologies such as Bluetooth can be used to connect devices on a LAN.

A LAN can also be connected to other LANs outside its own small area, forming what is known as a wide area network, or WAN. This ability to interconnect made LANs one of the primary drivers in the growth of the early Internet. One could argue that the Internet itself is the world's ultimate WAN, comprising innumerable LANs that span the globe.

The history of the LAN runs parallel to the history of the Internet in some important ways, although the LAN's inventor, Bob Metcalfe, was trying to connect computers in different rooms, not different cities. In 1973, as a graduate student, Metcalfe was already a networking expert, and he was trying to earn his Ph.D. from Harvard University with a thesis examining the Internet's precursor, the ARPANET. He had some expertise in this area, having worked at the Massachusetts Institute of Technology (MIT), and built the interface between MIT's PDP-10 mainframe computer and the interface message processor (IMP, an early router) that connected MIT to the ARPANET. (According to Katie Hafner and Matthew Lyon in their 1996 book, *Where Wizards Stay Up Late: The Origins of the Internet,* Metcalfe offered to do the same thing for Harvard's PDP-10 but was denied the job on the premise that a mere graduate student could not possibly handle such a large and important task.) Metcalfe's thesis was rejected because it contained too much engineering and not enough theoretical science. The rejection was embarrassing, since Metcalfe had already accepted work at the Xerox Palo Alto Research Center (Xerox PARC), on the other side of the country.

Metcalfe stumbled upon a white paper by Norm Abramson, the architect of the radio-powered ALOHANET in Hawaii, which utilized APRANET's packet-switching technologies to connect computers wirelessly over relatively long distances. Abramson's paper, Metcalfe would later say, was "infuriating" because he thought it showed that ALOHANET was modeled on inaccurate math, manipulated to fulfill the designer's desired model. Then and there, Metcalfe determined to build a new and better network model based on ALOHANET. He traveled to the University of Hawaii, staying a month to study the radio system. Upon his return, he had the theoretical material that he needed to complete his Harvard thesis, and he had also taken the first steps toward inventing the LAN.

At the time, Xerox PARC was busy building the first personal computer, the Alto, and the company believed that people would want to connect these machines together. They assigned Metcalfe to the task of figuring out how this connecting could be done. He immediately faced two huge challenges: His network had to be fast enough to work with Xerox PARC's new laser printer, and it had to successfully bind together hundreds of computers within the same building, something that had never been done before.

To accomplish these tasks, he borrowed concepts directly from ALOHANET (in fact, he initially called his creation the "Alto Aloha Network"). The possibility existed that small data packets traveling over the local network during computer communication might not get distributed to their destinations quickly enough and log-jam the system. Rather than worrying about this potential problem, Metcalfe decided that it was fine to allow the packets to collide, but that they would "listen" to the system until it was quiet, then try to pass through again; if the system was particularly busy, packets would retransmit at random intervals to avoid further collisions, and they would still arrive at the desired destination.

Unlike ALOHA's radio-powered wireless connection, however, Metcalfe's entire network was hardwired together via thousands of feet of cable that connected all the computers from room to room, and from building to building. With the help of Xerox PARC researchers Butch Lampson, David Boggs, and Chuck Thacker, Metcalfe completed the system in May 1973. Shortly after successfully testing the first LAN, Metcalfe renamed his creation, recalling the word that nineteenth-century scientists had coined to explain how light passes through empty space: It was now known as Ethernet.

Metcalfe's initial LAN allowed for the transmission of data down coaxial cables at a rate of 2.67 million bits per second—fast enough to transmit a page of text from workstation to printer in 12 seconds. Before the development of the LAN, this transmission had typically taken 15 minutes.

"There is no central intelligence which manages access to the (Ethernet) loop," wrote Robert W. Lucky, executive research director at Bell Laboratories' communications sciences division, in a 1991 essay. "(There is) merely an agreement about how the passive cable loop is to be used by all. In fact, Ethernet is very much like a human conversation around a large table. If you want to speak, you wait until there is a lull in the ongoing conversation; then you speak."

Xerox began selling the system commercially in 1980, and Metcalfe eventually left PARC to start his own company, 3Com, to peddle his creation. He also successfully lobbied Digital Equipment, Intel Corp., and Xerox Corp. to team up on promoting his Ethernet as a standard LAN platform, a move that assured Ethernet's success in the wider world of computing.

If there's a downside to Ethernet, it is that there are limits to the number of machines that can be on a single LAN, and to the distance that computers can be separated and still be a part of the system. Traditionally, the setup of a LAN has consisted of workstations connected by cables to servers through network hubs. These hubs work in a way that's similar to the way that television transmission repeaters work, taking information sent from one workstation or server and retransmitting it to the other computers on the network. The workstation or server that the information was intended for then responds appropriately. The concept is actually simpler than the implementation, which can be complicated by many factors, not the least of which is incompatible protocols between machines.

By the early 1980s, Ethernets were very much in vogue. Universities everywhere wanted to connect all their many computers together, and they wanted to connect their entire networks to the ARPANET backbone, rather than be limited to one machine accessing the ARPANET per university, the model that had grown up around the Internet's ancestor. By routing local traffic outbound to the wider public network through so-called "gateways," Ethernet and other LANs made connecting to the ARPANET possible. Soon those schools and research institutions not privileged enough to be connected to the ARPANET scrambled to connect their LANs to the National Science Foundation–funded alternative, CSNET, which in turn connected them to the ARPANET.

In a 1991 essay, authors Al McBride and Scott Brown, both consultants for a company called Tandem Computers, described data speeds over LANs of between four million and ten million bits per second (mbps), over cables that might reach thousands of feet in length. While slower than the internal processing speeds of computers of that time, this speed was much greater than maximum T-1 Internet data speeds of 1.544mbps. Fiberoptic LANs, McBride and Brown said, could transmit at up to 100mbps, much more even than T-3 telephone systems that reached speeds of up to 43mbps. Of course, once a LAN's data is dumped onto the Internet, data speeds reflect the wider network's speeds.

LANs have proved a powerful boon to corporations and academic institutions alike, allowing easy access to computing peripherals and common databases, as well as easy communications between employees and managers. As John Naughton, author of *A Brief History of the Future: From Radio Days to Internet Years in a Lifetime* (2001), expressed it, the development of the LAN led some people to the epiphany that "the network *is* the computer."

With the success of the Internet, email, and electronic commerce, LANs have become increasingly sophisticated; businesses in particular have come to rely on them to keep workers and executives connected, and they have incorporated many sophisticated technologies in the process.

However, there are many who predict that the concept of the LAN is about to undergo a fundamental shift, given the advent of new radio-based wireless technologies such as Bluetooth and the high-speed IEEE 802.11b standard (also known as "Wi-Fi"). By 2001, wireless LANs were already popping up in corporate campuses and in hotels, airports, coffee shops, and residences, connecting people traveling on business to their in-house computer network at work.

Writer Matt Foster, in an article published on the Tom's Hardware Guide Web site, notes that the wireless LAN adds new layers of convenience to networking; for instance, wireless LANs can reduce the cost of creating and maintaining a network. However, they also raise the potential for compromised security—unprotected wireless data signals, like those of unencrypted cell phones, can easily be tapped. The benefits, especially for smaller and medium-sized companies, may be too good to pass up, Foster writes, but further improvements are needed.

"As wireless technology matures, there could be a point at which wireless has a great chance of overtaking wired networking as the mainstream networking media, as long as the security and privacy implementations are corrected," Foster writes. "As handheld devices, mobile computers, and smart appliances proliferate, the convenience of having a wireless network starts to make better sense."

Bibliography

Foster, Matt. "Wireless Area Networking: An Introduction." Tom's Hardware Guide, August 22, 2001. <http://www4.tomshardware.com/network/01q3/010822/> (May 31, 2002).

Hafner, Katie, and Matthew Lyon. *Where Wizards Stay Up Late: The Origins of the Internet.* New York: Simon & Schuster, 1996.

Hiltzik, Michael A. *Dealers of Lightning: Xerox PARC and the Dawn of the Computer Age.* London: Orion Business, 2000.

INT Media Group, Inc. "Local-Area Network." Webopedia.com. <http://www.webopedia.com/TERM/L/local_area_network_LAN.html> (May 31, 2002).

Luckey, Robert W. "In a Very Short Time: What Is Coming Next in Telecommunications." *Technology 2001: The Future of Computing and Communications.* Derek Leebaert, ed. Cambridge, Mass.: MIT Press, 1991.

McBride, Al, and Scott Brown. "A Multi-Dimensional Look at the Future of On-line Technology." *Technology 2001: The Future of Computing and Communications.* Derek Leebaert, ed. Cambridge, Mass.: MIT Press, 1991.

Newton, Harry. *Newton's Telecom Dictionary.* Sixteenth edition. Gilroy, Calif.: CMP Books, 2000.

Further Reading

Bellis, Mary. "Inventors of the Modern Computer: The Invention of the Ethernet—Local Area Networks." About.com, November 15, 1998. <http://inventors.about.com/library/weekly/aa111598.htm> (May 31, 2002).

Brand, Stewart. *The Media Lab: Inventing the Future at M.I.T.* New York: Viking, 1987.

Dertouzos, Michael. *The Unfinished Revolution: Human-Centered Computers and What They Can Do for Us.* New York: HarperCollins, 2001.

Gilder, George. *Telecosm: How Infinite Bandwidth Will Revolutionize Our World.* New York: Free Press, 2000.

Negroponte, Nicholas. *Being Digital.* New York: Knopf, 1995.

Related Topics

Bluetooth; Broadband; Cellular Telephony; Internet; Narrowcasting; Privacy; Wireless Networks; Xerox Palo Alto Research Center

— *Kevin Featherly*

Lucas, George

1940–

Film Producer, Director

George Lucas is a screenwriter, producer, and director who has worked in the film industry since 1970. Regarded as a founding figure in the history of digital animation and effects, he is a leading figure in the use of digital technologies and computer-generated special effects for film. He is also considered a pioneer of cyberculture, due to his involvement with the networked computer-game environment Habitat, one of the earliest online gaming communities.

Lucas' name is synonymous with both the *Star Wars* films and his effects company, Industrial Light and Magic. He was screenwriter, producer and director of *Star Wars* (1977), and executive producer of the two sequels, *The Empire Strikes Back* (1980) and *Return of the Jedi* (1983); he also wrote, directed, and produced two prequels, *The Phantom Menace* (1999) and *Attack of the Clones* (2002). He has also been involved with Disney, and with the Indiana Jones film series directed by Steven Spielberg (e.g., *Raiders of the Lost Ark* [1980]).

George Walton Lucas Jr. was born in 1944 in Modesto, California, and studied film at the University of Southern California. He founded Lucasfilm Limited in 1971, and also has holdings in LucasArts Entertainment Company, Lucas Digital Limited, Lucas Licensing Limited, and Lucas Learning Limited. This diverse set of business holdings represents his interests in various digital effects, including sound, filmmaking, and distribution, as well as in interactive entertainment, software, and multimedia educational resources. Aside from *Star Wars*, Lucas is probably best known for his filmic digital effects and interactive software. His collaborations with other leading film directors, particularly Francis Ford Coppola and Spielberg, have also contributed to his high profile.

Industrial Light and Magic (ILM), a Lucas Digital holding, is one of the major visual effects companies in the world, and produces computer-generated effects for the film industry. The company has produced some of the most high-profile special effects to date, such as those of *Jurassic Park* (1993), *Titanic* (1997), and *The Perfect Storm* (2000). The Lucas Digital company has received more than 26 Academy Awards for both sound and visual effects. ILM has been a major contributor to the transformation of the status of digital effects from an experimental and novel aspect of filmmaking to a central feature of contemporary cinema.

Its contribution has also been a significant catalyst of the convergence between analog entertainment technologies and digital media. Lucas is a central figure in this convergence, because he is also viewed as a founding figure in discourses of cyberculture.

LucasArts developed the game environment Habitat in 1986 for the Commodore 64 computer. Chip Morningstar and F. Randall Farmer wrote up the project as a research paper, which was published in one of the primary cybercultural texts, *Cyberspace: First Steps* (1990). Habitat is a multi-user gaming environment that deploys computer-generated graphic characters, known as avatars, to represent the players onscreen. There are many such environments in contemporary cyberculture, for which Habitat arguably provided a template. An example of an online or networked gaming environment, Habitat is an early attempt at accessible modes of virtual reality, as well as the expression of early notions of online community. It has also become significant in the histories of computing and cyberculture, because it continues a tradition of discursive interrelation between the artifacts of computing and the science-fiction genre of cyberpunk.

Lucas has displayed an ability to innovate and diversify across both the form and the content of new technological production. This makes him an important figure in the history of cyberculture and of visual digital culture, as well as in the current production of digital entertainment and educational materials.

Bibliography

Benedikt, Michael, ed. *Cyberspace: First Steps*. Cambridge, Mass.: MIT Press, 1991.

Darley, Andrew. *Visual Digital Culture: Surface Play and Spectacle in New Media Genres*. London: Routledge, 2000.

Lucas Arts Entertainment Company. Web site. <http://www.lucasarts.com> (May 31, 2002).

Maltin, Leonard; Green, Spencer; and Luke Sader, eds. *Leonard Maltin's Movie Encyclopedia*. New York: Dutton, 1994.

Stephenson, Neal. *Snow Crash*. New York: Bantam Books, 1993.

Vinge, Vernor. *True Names and Other Dangers*. New York: Baen Books, 1987.

Further Reading

Baxter, John. *George Lucas: A Biography*. Hammersmith, London: HarperCollinsEntertainment, 1999.

Von Gunden, Kenneth. *Postmodern Auteurs: Coppola, Lucas, De Palma, Spielberg, and Scorsese*. Jefferson, N.C.: McFarland, 1991.

Related Topics

Avatar; Cyberspace; Digital Art and Animation; Habitat; MUDs and MOOs

— *Kate O'Riordan*

m m m m **M** m m m m

Maes, Pattie

1961–

Software Engineer and Entrepreneur

Pattie Maes, a scholar, innovator, and entrepreneur, changed the interactive relationship between the computer and its user. Her software creations have fundamentally influenced the way that e-commerce companies compete, as well as provided a simple means for individuals to accomplish complex and tedious digital tasks.

Maes was born in Brussels in 1961. Growing up, she was fascinated with architecture and biology; however, technology was beginning to evolve quickly, and the demand for work led her to study computer science. Maes received a bachelor's degree in computer science in 1983, and a doctorate in 1987, from the Vrije Universiteit Brussel in Belgium. During her undergraduate and graduate studies, Maes was a research fellow for the Belgian National Science Foundation, eventually becoming a research scientist from 1987 to 1990. In 1989, Maes left Belgium to study artificial intelligence (AI) with Rodney Brooks at the Massachusetts Institute of Technology (MIT). Influenced by Brooks' radical approach to AI design, Maes joined MIT's Media Laboratory as an assistant professor in 1990, becoming an associate professor in 1995.

Maes has been involved in several projects at MIT. In 1990, she founded the Software Agents Group of the MIT Media Lab; the group creates and tests prototype agent systems. She also founded the MIT Media Lab's e-markets special interest group, which works to promote collaboration between sponsors and Media Lab members.

Maes' work at the Media Lab focused on the development of software applications called intelligent agents. This software gets its name from its ability to "learn" from its user. For example, an intelligent agent can be programmed to monitor scheduling tendencies, and then perform scheduling tasks automatically. If meetings are never scheduled before a certain time of day, the software recognizes this trend and will automatically schedule appointments accordingly. The

software becomes artificially intelligent by learning through repetitive monitoring.

Maes' work with software agents has played a considerable role in the growth and personalization of e-commerce. Her software-agent services have been used by Barnes & Noble, among others, to provide a Web presence that supplies a form of personalization to online shopping. The Web site is capable of "remembering" the topic, author, and genre preferences of the individual consumer, and offers recommendations for similar and upcoming books.

Maes' intelligent-agent applications are employed in many different areas. One such application became commercialized in 1995 as a collaborative filter when Maes founded a Web-based service called Firefly. Firefly offered a way for individuals to develop an online community through shared interests. Users informed the Web site of what they enjoyed, and Firefly would learn individual preferences, then foster communication between users with similar interests. In 1998, Microsoft bought the company to use its technology in Microsoft's "passport" services.

With agent applications changing the ways that people gather and organize information in the digital age, Maes helped to develop a method for handling information overload. Earlier in her research, she had developed a browser for the Web that tracks and records Web pages visited by the user. The application uses key words to remember the desired information, and searches for additional pages that offer related information.

Software agents are employed by commercial entities, but they can also be effective tools for individuals. Consider a reader who would like to find the latest news stories online. Rather than virtually sift through dozens of online services, agents can be used to find and retrieve articles whose topics dovetail with the interests of the reader. Rather than programming agents with rules, Maes uses an AI method: Algorithms are used to produce successful agents that are able to retain user preferences, and unsuccessful agents are discarded.

In 1999, Maes founded a company called Open Ratings, which offers technology that can track and identify performance patterns of suppliers, then use simulations to make predictions and improve the decision-making process. In addition, the company incorporates rating systems that try to establish trust between consumers and vendors. For example, an online auction site will provide ratings for sellers and buyers to help establish credibility for the virtual correspondents. Ratings are supplied through the feedback of previous purchasers or vendors.

Maes has forever influenced the relationships between individuals and the Internet through the designs of her intelligent agents. Her efforts help to promote easy use, automation, and trust within the faceless virtual world of the Web.

Selected Works

Brooks, Rodney A., and Pattie Maes, eds. *Artificial Life IV: Proceedings of the Fourth International Workshop on the Synthesis and Simulation of Living Systems.* Cambridge, Mass.: MIT Press, 1994.

Maes, Pattie, ed. *Designing Autonomous Agents: Theory and Practice from Biology to Engineering and Back.* Cambridge, Mass.: MIT Press, 1990.

Bibliography

Germain, Ellen. "Software's Special Agents." *New Scientist,* April 9, 1994.
<http://www.newscientist.com> (May 10, 2002).

Holloway, Marguerite. "Pattie." *Wired* 5.12, December 1997.
<http://www.wired.com/wired/archive/5.12/maes.html> (May 10, 2002).

Williams, Mark. "Firefly's Pattie Maes is still an agent of change." *Red Herring.* March 1, 2000.
<http://www.redherring.com/mag/issue76/mag-firefly-76.html> (May 10, 2002).

Further Reading

Lawrence, Andy. "Agents of the Net." *New Scientist,* July 15, 1995.
<http://www.newscientist.com> (May 10, 2002).

Oakes, Chris. "Firefly's Dim Light Snuffed Out." *Wired,* August 12, 1999.
<http://www.wired.com/news/culture/0,1284,21243,00.html> (May 10, 2002).

Related Topics

Brooks, Rodney; Interface; Personalization; Robotics; Search Engine; Software Agents

— *James Pyfer*

"Man-Computer Symbiosis"

"Man-Computer Symbiosis" is the title of a paper published in 1960 by American psychologist J. C. R. Licklider (1915–90). It outlines the author's personal vision of what in the following years became known as interactive computing. Licklider envisioned that "human brains and computing machines will be coupled together very tightly, and that the resulting partnership will think as no human brain has ever thought and process data in a way not approached by the information-handling machines we know today." His vision has guided the development of artificial intelligence, hypertext, and other advances in computing.

The central idea of Licklider's paper is based on the fact that computers and humans have very different capabilities. Computers operate sequentially and quickly on narrowly defined tasks; humans can easily handle a much wider range of tasks, some even in parallel, but are considerably slower. When combined, the capabilities of humans and computers would complement each other, with the effect of dramatically increasing the intellectual capabilities of the computer user.

In order to accomplish this combination, according to Licklider, computer science would have to move beyond what had by then already been accomplished—namely, the partial automation of tasks formerly carried out by humans. Automation had been identified as an increasingly desirable technology during World War II, as mechanized battle systems gradually outpaced the reaction time and motor skills of the human operator. With the establishment of the SAGE (Semi-Automatic Ground Environment) early warning system of the 1950s, this kind of man-machine integration had become reality. SAGE used radar (Radio Detection and Ranging) and computers equipped with cathode-ray tube (CRT) screens and lightpens to help operators detect incoming airplanes.

Even though it served as an inspiration to Licklider, the SAGE system was not what he had in mind. His use of the word "symbiosis," which literally means "living together," points toward a much more active role for the machine component of the equation. Licklider's example of symbiosis, which involved a kind of larvae living in trees, is characterized by a mutual interdependence where both parties play an active role. In order to become more active, the machine would have to be able to contribute to the formation of conceptual models, and to acquire the kind of problem-solving skills envisioned by such artificial-intelligence researchers as Allen Newell and Herbert Simon. At the time of Licklider's writing, it was thought that true artificial intelligence was only a few years from realization. However, present-day computers still do not have such capabilities.

In addition to a more active participation by computers, the interchange between man and machine would have to proceed uninterrupted, or in real time. The cost of computers in 1960 dictated that they be shared by multiple users. The predominant mode of computer use was batch processing, which used punched cards or tape for data input and output, as well as printed paper for output. Users were allocated computer time based on the priority of their jobs, and frequently had to wait for hours or days before receiving results. In contrast, real-time computing required sub-second response times for which other input/output devices were clearly needed, such as the screen, keyboard, and mouse of present-day personal computers. Users of real-time systems still had to share the computer between them, but it switched so rapidly between users as it served them that each user had the illusion of being the only one using the computer. This process, referred to as time-sharing, was used extensively in the 1960s and 1970s but has mostly been replaced by the use of personal computers.

Licklider's vision as stated in his paper was to guide not only his own career as a computer scientist, but also the use of computers in general. From 1962 to 1964, Licklider served as director of (D)ARPA, the U.S. (Defense) Advanced Research Projects Agency. During this brief period, he managed to change the general direction of the agency away from command, communication, control, and intelligence (C3I) systems and toward making computers more usable by humans. Under the direction of Licklider and his successors, the DARPA office funded research that led to the construction of the Internet, and to the creation of essential ingredients of the personal computer revolution.

Bibliography

Licklider, J. C. R. "Man-Computer Symbiosis." *Computer Media and Communication: A Reader*, P. A. Mayer, ed. New York and Oxford: Oxford University Press, 1999.

Further Reading

Dreyfus, Hubert L. *What Computers Still Can't Do: A Critique of Artificial Reason.* Cambridge, Mass.: MIT Press, 1992.

Edwards, Paul N. *The Closed World: Computers and the Politics of Discourse in Cold War America.* Cambridge, Mass.: MIT Press, 1996.

Hafner, Katie, and Matthew Lyon. *Where Wizards Stay Up Late: The Origins of the Internet.* New York: Touchstone, 1998.

Rheingold, Howard. *The Virtual Community: Homesteading on the Electronic Frontier.* Revised edition. Cambridge, Mass.: MIT Press, 2000.

Related Topics

Bush, Vannevar; Engelbart, Douglas; Human–Computer Interaction; Internet; Licklider, J. C. R.

— *Charlie Breindahl*

"A Manifesto for Cyborgs"

Written in 1985, Donna J. Haraway's "A Manifesto for Cyborgs: Science, Technology, and Socialist Feminism in the 1980s" is a key text for those studying the politics of technoculture. Haraway, a feminist biologist and historian of science, later updated and revised the "Manifesto" (renaming it "Cyborg Manifesto") for her 1991 book, *Simians, Cyborgs, and Women: The Reinvention of Nature.*

In an interview, Haraway described the genesis of her essay: "In 1982," she relates, "I was asked by the editors of the journal *Social Text* [to] describe what socialist-feminist priorities [would be] in the Reagan years." Among the many issues in the news at the time was the so-called "Star Wars" defense system, an $84 billion item in the U.S. defense budget. Meanwhile, many women at that time were advocating what became known as goddess feminism, which advocated, among other things, a celebration of the "essentially feminine body," and which exhorted women to "return to nature."

Although she was no fan of the military-industrial complex, Haraway was troubled by the notion of opting out of technological life entirely. As she explained it, at least three "contemporary border crossings" mixed nature and technology to such a degree that it was impossible to tell where one began and the other ended. The first border crossing was the breakdown between humans and animals, occurring as a result of things like pollution, tourism, and medical experimentation. The second boundary transgression was between humans and machines. Without ever citing the Internet or virtual-reality technologies, Haraway described our machines as being "disturbingly lively," while we are "frighteningly inert." The third boundary crossing was the erosion of space between "the physical and the non-physical," caused by the ubiquity of microprocessors in contemporary life. "Small is not so much beautiful," observed Haraway, "as pre-eminently dangerous."

LIFE AS A CYBORG

Coupling her training as a scientist with a stringent political critique, Haraway argued that the feminist fantasy of "returning to nature" was not only impossible, but was also rooted in cultural privilege. Women (particularly women of color) are the "home-workers" of the new high-tech sectors of the world economy, and any socially responsible feminism needed to address this issue. Rather than resurrecting pre-technological ideas about the natural body, feminists needed to think of themselves in terms of the cyborg, a body both organic and mechanical. Haraway defined the cyborg in four different ways: a cybernetic organism, a hybrid of machine and organism, a creature of lived social reality, and a creature of fiction.

Haraway pointed out that cyborgs are the stuff of both science fiction and reality. Modern medicine is full of them, as is modern agriculture, genetic reproduction, manufacturing, and warfare. In short, writes Haraway, "we are cyborgs," whether we know it or not, if only because it is the cyborg that "is our ontology; it gives us our politics." Using examples from molecular genetics, ecology, sociobiological evolutionary theory, and immunobiology to support her claim, Haraway points out that in the cyborg era, communications technologies and biology are of a piece. This is why she calls writing the "pre-eminent technology of cyborgs," and lauds science fiction as a "new kind of political theory."

THE FUTURE OF CYBORG POLITICS

In spite of her warnings about cyborg life, Haraway does not see the picture as entirely bleak. This is because she believes that cyborgs also have the potential to organize politically with one another, at times transgressing older party lines of race, gender, and nationality that hindered them before. By practicing "affinity politics," she notes, "high-tech cowboys" who do not want to produce industrial products might form alliances with women of color on high-tech assembly lines. This is just one example of what Haraway alludes to as the "monstrous and illegitimate" promise of cyborg politics for socialist feminism.

Haraway's "Manifesto" was intended as an "ironic political myth," a middle ground of sorts, placing the future of feminism somewhere between technophilia and technophobia. Haraway emphasizes that the political struggle of the cyborg (and by extension, the feminist) lies neither in the wholesale adoption nor in the wholesale rejection of technoculture, but rather in the capacity to understand both perspectives at once. She would "rather be a cyborg than a goddess," Haraway admits, but she admits this ironically.

Although she has gone on to publish extensively, Haraway's "A Manifesto for Cyborgs" remains her most well-known essay, and has been responsible in large part for inspiring the fields of both "cyborgology" and cyberfeminism. Asked by Thyrza Nichols-Goodeve in a recent interview about the potential overuse of her cyborg metaphor, Haraway noted that, "Part of how I work is not to walk away when a term gets dirty and is used in all these appropriate and inappropriate ways because of its celebrity." As she puts it, "Instead of giving [the cyborg] up because it has become too famous, let's keep pushing it and filling it."

Bibliography

Haraway, Donna J. *How Like a Leaf: An Interview with Thyrza Nichols Goodeve.* New York; London: Routledge: 2000.

———. "A Manifesto for Cyborgs: Science, Technology and Socialist Feminism in the 1980s." *Socialist Review,* no. 80 (1985).

———. "A Cyborg Manifesto: Science, Technology, and Socialist-Feminism in the Late Twentieth Century." Stanford University Department of History and Philosophy of Science. Web site. <http://www.stanford.edu/dept/HPS/Haraway/CyborgManifesto.html> (September 16, 2002).

———. *Modest_Witness@Second_Millennium.FemaleMan© _Meets_OncoMouse™: Feminism and Technoscience.* New York: Routledge, 1997.

———. *Simians, Cyborgs, and Women: The Reinvention of Nature.* London: Free Association, 1991.

———. "Situated Knowledges: The Science Question in Feminism as a Site of Discourse on the Privilege of Partial Perspective." *Feminist Studies* 14, no. 3 (1988).

Further Reading

Balsamo, Anne. *Technologies of the Gendered Body: Reading Cyborg Women.* Durham: Duke University Press, 1996.

Downey, Gary, and Joseph Dumit, eds. *Cyborgs & Citadels: Interventions in the Anthropology of Technohumanism.* Santa Fe, N.M.: School of American Research, 1998.

Gray, Chris Hables; Figueroa-Sarriera, Heidi J.; and Steven Mentor, eds. *The Cyborg Handbook.* New York: London: Routledge, 1995.

Hayles, N. Katherine. *How We Became Posthuman: Virtual Bodies in Cybernetics, Literature, and Informatics.* Chicago: University of Chicago Press, 1999.

Kunzru, Hari. "You Are Cyborg." *Wired* 5.02, February 1997. <http://www.wired.com/wired/archive/5.02/ffharaway> (May 10, 2002).

Stone, Allucquère Rosanne. *The War of Desire and Technology at the Close of the Mechanical Age.* Cambridge, Mass.: MIT Press, 1995.

Related Topics

Cyberfeminism; Cyborg; Gender and New Media; Haraway, Donna J.

— Theresa M. Senft

Markup Languages

Originally developed to produce large volumes of printed documentation, markup languages are now used to author a variety of different media, the best-known of which are Hypertext Markup Language (HTML) Web pages. Markup languages are a method of structuring a text or multimedia file (a process called "marking up" or "tagging") without defining how that structure will ultimately be formatted.

CONCEPTS

Word processors such as Microsoft Word are based on the principle of "what you see is what you get" (WYSIWYG): What the author creates is essentially what the reader sees. Unlike an unformatted ASCII text file, a document produced in Word can be instantly and attractively formatted with different fonts and effects. Word processors achieve this by embedding control characters (strings of normally invisible characters that control formatting effects) in and around the main text. WYSIWYG word processing became possible only in the 1980s, with the invention of graphical user interfaces (GUIs) and high-resolution, bitmapped computer screens that could display a range of different fonts. Before then, word processing meant text editing—text was simply typed into and moved around in ASCII files before being printed out, often on a crude dot-matrix printer. That was fine for utility bills and simple letters, but not for more sophisticated documents that needed a range of different formatting effects.

Markup language offers a way of embedding structural codes called tags into a basic ASCII text file. To mark the start of a paragraph, one might use <P>. To make text into a main heading, one might put <H1> (meaning start a heading 1) in front of it and </H1> (end heading 1) after it. The crucial difference between a word processor and a markup language is that, while the former involves specifying exactly how different bits of text will appear, and not what they are, the latter involves using tags to specify exactly what elements of text are, and not how they will appear.

This difference is clearly illustrated by HTML Web pages, whose various elements are identified with tags such as <UL> for a bulleted (unordered) list, <P> for paragraphs, and so on. Using basic HTML, it is impossible to control exactly how a Web page will ultimately appear, because that depends on how the user's Web browser is configured to process the tags. While on one browser, <H1> might produce a large, bold Times font, on another it might produce a medium-sized, italic Courier font. The HTML conveys no formatting information of this kind.

To someone accustomed to Microsoft Word, markup initially seems confusing and perverse. What is the logic in using a text-processing system that does not allow its authors to control the ultimate appearance of their documents? Isn't markup an extraordinary waste of time? Why type hundreds of extra control characters when one can simply click on the appropriate words and immediately make them into a heading in 14-point, boldface Times?

ADVANTAGES AND DISADVANTAGES

The huge advantage that markup offers over word processing is the way it separates the process of authoring text (adding markup) from the process of formatting text (turning the markup into a printed or online document). This can bring tremendous benefits to publishers. IBM's policy of using markup languages rather than desktop publishing to produce its reams of documentation—the company is reputedly the world's second-largest publisher—reaped huge dividends in the mid-1990s. Thousands of computer manuals tagged in IBM's internal markup language BookMaster, and originally designed for printed output, were almost instantly converted for publication on CD-ROM, not by changing the markup, but by formatting the markup in a different way to produce online hypertext files instead of printed output. With the same markup, IBM could simultaneously produce output for different printers, numerous different electronic book systems on CD-ROM, and HTML files for the Web. Had the original files been prepared with a word-processing program, it would have been necessary to convert them laboriously for each different type of output.

This flexibility is markup's main advantage. Another advantage is the compactness of marked-up files. As these are essentially ASCII files with tags inserted here and there, they occupy not much more disk space than plain text files—a fraction of the size occupied by word-processed files. This has been important for the growth of the Web, where the size of files determines how quickly they are transmitted from server to browser, the overall speed of a Web site, and user satisfaction.

Markup has its drawbacks, too. By definition, it is impossible to produce precise formatting effects, so markup tends to be used for "industrial-strength," text-intensive reference publishing rather than for the production of glossy flyers. Marked-up documents may ultimately appear very differently than the author intended—a problem for Web site designers, particularly because different browsers display the same HTML markup in different ways. Depending on the number of tags involved, markup can be difficult to learn and master, because users sometimes have to know and key in the tags themselves. The emergence of programs that look like word processors but automatically produce tagged HTML files (such as the popular Web-authoring programs Microsoft Front Page, Claris Home Page, and Netscape Composer) has gone some way toward solving this problem, although the WYSIWYG impression that they convey is highly misleading. The usefulness of a markup language is a compromise between a tag set that is extensive but simultaneously easy to use. A markup language such as HTML, with relatively few tags, may be easy to learn but inadequate for the needs of publishers who want to produce sophisticated documents; but feature-laden languages such as IBM's BookMaster are much harder to master.

Historical Development

Markup's origins can be traced to RUNOFF, developed in the 1960s by Jerome Saltzer at the Massachusetts Institute of Technology (MIT). A formatting language rather than a markup language, RUNOFF used control words preceded by a period to achieve particular formatting effects, such as .sp2 to leave two blank lines (spaces) and .ctr to center text. Similar formatting programs included TeX (and LaTeX), popular with the academic and technical publishing communities, and IBM's Document Control Facility (DCF), also known as SCRIPT/VS.

During the late 1960s, members of the Composition Committee of the Graphic Communications Association (GCA) had realized the importance of separating the structure of documents from their appearance, crystallizing the idea in a concept known as generic coding (or GenCode). This inspired the invention of the first markup language, GML (Generalized Markup Language), whose name also credits its IBM inventors Charles Goldfarb, Ed Mosher, and Ray Lorie. Based on tags preceded by a colon and ended by a period, such as :p. for a paragraph and :ul. for a bulleted list, GML evolved in two different directions. IBM vastly extended its tag set to make a feature-laden, proprietary document-production system called BookMaster, for which its legions of technical writers were the main customers.

Meanwhile, during the late 1970s and early 1980s, Goldfarb (who coined the term "markup language") took GML in a different direction, evolving an international standard for markup languages called SGML (Standard Generalized Markup Language).

Arguably misnamed, SGML is not a standard markup language, but a set of rules around which new markup languages can be developed, allowing publishers to write their own tag sets and define them in a central reference document called a Document Type Description (DTD). One of the first applications of SGML was CALS (Computer-Aided Acquisition and Logistic Support), developed in 1987 by the U.S. Department of Defense for its own documentation. More recent and better-known applications include the development of multimedia CD-ROMs by publishers such as Dorling Kindersley, as well as of HTML, VRML (Virtual Reality Markup Language), and XML (Extensible Markup Language). Unlike HTML, which restricts Web site developers to a small set of standard tags, XML allows developers to design their own tag sets. For example, an e-commerce site might include tables of information listing clothing for sale, described by tags such as <SIZE>, <PRICE>, <FABRIC>, and so on.

During the desktop-publishing revolution of the mid-1980s, a common view was that markup was simply an anachronism, an irrelevant relic from pre-WYSIWYG days, best confined to computer history. But one person's anachronism is another person's idea whose time will come again. The value of markup has since been repeatedly demonstrated, both by the use of SGML in large-scale reference publishing and by HTML and XML in Web authoring. There is a philosophical canyon between the purist's approach to desktop publishing (in which every aspect of the design communicates information and in which, say, choices of type are a crucial part of the authoring process) and the purist's approach to markup (where, to the author, the ultimate formatting of a document's structure is arbitrary). The important thing is to recognize the difference; these two complementary approaches have much to contribute to different aspects of the publishing process.

Combining as it does the power of SGML with the ubiquity of HTML, XML represents for many people the future of markup languages. As a streamlined, simplified SGML-to-go for the Web, XML will not supplant SGML in industrial-strength publishing. Although HTML is likely to survive in personal Web pages and other simple applications, industry pundits believe that XML will gradually replace HTML in more sophisticated Web applications. Indeed, HTML has itself been redesigned by the World Wide Web Consortium as an XML application called XHTML. Because XML lends itself to representing data, its main applications are expected to involve sharing data between Web applications and transforming databases and spreadsheets into a form that can be easily presented over the Web—in other words, acting as a kind of universal data-sharing language.

Bibliography

Charles F. Goldfarb's SGML Source Home Page. Web site. 2002. <http://www.sgmlsource.com/> (March 29, 2002).

Goldfarb, Charles F. *The SGML Handbook*. Oxford: Clarendon Press, 1990.

Goldfarb, Charles F., and Paul Prescod. *The XML Handbook*. Second edition. Upper Saddle River, N.J.: Prentice Hall, 2000.

Knuth, Donald. *The TeXbook*. Reading, Mass.: Addison-Wesley, 1986.

Further Reading

Berners-Lee, Tim, with Mark Fischetti. *Weaving the Web: The Original Design and Ultimate Destiny of the World Wide Web by Its Inventor*. San Francisco: Harper SanFrancisco, 1999.

Bryan, Martin. *SGML and HTML Explained*. Harlow, England/Reading, Mass.: Addison Wesley Longman, 1997.

Romano, Frank J. *Digital Media: Publishing Technologies for the 21st Century*. Torrance, Calif.: Micro Publishing Press, 1996.

Related Topics

Authoring Tools; Browser; Desktop Publishing; Electronic Publishing

— *Chris Woodford*

McLuhan, Marshall

1911–1980

Media Theorist

Canadian intellectual Marshall McLuhan remains one of the most influential new media theorists. He evaluated the social construction of technology and the technological construction of society with rich, detailed studies of the history of communication, skillfully reduced to evocative turns of phrase that are still embedded in the popular imagination. He believed that new media could be socially debilitating if used improperly. However, he did not want humankind to be bound by new media, but to be freed by it, and

through his investigations, McLuhan sought to chart a course of social development that would avoid the risks of oppressive technologies.

Marshall McLuhan was born in Edmonton, Alberta, Canada, on July 21, 1911. His interest in literature took him from the University of Manitoba to Cambridge University, where he earned a Ph.D. in 1943. A devout Catholic, he was happy to take a post at St. Michael's College at the University of Toronto in 1944, and he remained based there for most of his career. McLuhan was made a full professor in 1952, a year after publishing his first book, *The Mechanical Bride: Folklore of Industrial Man*. Subsequently, he headed up some of the first large projects in communication studies. Between 1953 and 1955, he was chairman of the Ford Foundation Seminar on Culture and Communication, and between 1959 and 1960 was the director of the Understanding New-Media Project of the National Association of Educational Broadcasters. At the University of Toronto, he helped found the Centre for Culture and Technology in 1963, mandated to study the psychic and social consequences of media technologies, and he remained its director until shortly before his death in 1980.

McLuhan's Catholicism and his studies of contemporary literature, especially James Joyce, would help him assemble rich metaphors and referents for his cultural criticism. From the end of the Great Depression to the close of World War II, he taught in the United States, and later wrote that his initial teaching experiences at the Universities of Wisconsin and St. Louis introduced him to a cultural and media environment that he did not always understand. Along with Harold Innis and other scholars, McLuhan developed ideas that became known as the Toronto School of medium theory.

CULTURE AS BUSINESS

During his lifetime, McLuhan's most frequent role as a public intellectual was as a critic of advertising, popular culture, and the commercial applications of information technology. He believed that Hollywood and the industry of advertisers and marketing specialists provided the content for collective hallucinations. Many media were deliberately used to manufacture demand by saturating popular culture with commercial messages. The resulting polluted mental environment was the most dangerous consequence of many new media.

Of course, McLuhan himself contributed to the business of pop culture in the late 1960s with the release of *The Medium is the Massage,* in which he made the basic argument that the study of communication patterns must emphasize media context over particular media content. The technologies themselves, he argued, have subliminal effects on users because they transmit and transform the user's experience of reality. This book was a bestseller, combining words and images in a way that challenged the reader's notions of how ideas could be communicated in print. He described himself as a metaphysician, skilled in the art of generating cultural insights and recognizing large patterns in media ecology and human history

COMMUNICATION AND HISTORY

For McLuhan, the key turning points in human history were the result of the invention and diffusion of new communication technologies. His studies of history and culture contrast the villages of small tribal cultures, where oratory was dominant, with the writing and print communication patterns that enabled industrial-age towns and cities. In this sense, McLuhan taught us to be conscious of media environments and information ecologies—the context in which human artifacts exist, and the context that human artifacts produce. Darwin's laws of biological evolution no longer apply in McLuhan's history of the world; instead, the laws of communication needed to be elucidated in order for us to understand human development.

Communication technologies are used to transmit power, McLuhan argued, and printing an alphabet on papyrus weakened the authority of priests who monopolized knowledge, transferring political and economic power from the stationary temple bureaucracies to more mobile, military bureaucracies. Whereas complex hieroglyphics were difficult to learn and required craftsmanship to inscribe on brick and stone, alphabets could be mastered more quickly, and papyrus made ideas transportable.

McLuhan described four important stages in history, each marked by innovations in communication: the period of oral communication habits used by tribal societies; the construction of an alphabet that required visual acuity; the development of movable type, which made mass communication possible; and the invention of the telegraph in 1844, and of other electronic tools that greatly accelerated mass communication. McLuhan believed that portable alphabetic scripts revolutionized the ancient world, and that new electronic technology would similarly revolutionize the way we communicate and perceive reality.

THE ELECTRONIC REVOLUTION

Whereas fragmented mechanical technologies allowed people to extend the reach, strength, and accuracy of their bodies, the electronic revolution allows people to connect with a social nervous system. This global simulation of consciousness collectively and corporately embraces humankind, extending all of our senses and the creative process of generating knowledge. The electronic revolution decentralizes, integrates, and accelerates social interaction, but it does so by combining and building on technologies, not by replacing inferior technologies. For example, during the print revolution, alphabets replaced hieroglyphics, and papyrus replaced stone as the medium of choice. During the electronic revolution, new media like the Internet adopt mail, television, and radio functions.

McLuhan tried to reveal the different ways that new media exploited our senses. New electronic media did not replace old print media, but did reveal aspects of reality by privileging certain senses over others. In other words, our perspective of a story will change as we read a story, listen to the story on the radio, or watch the story unfold via video. Each medium reveals different dimensions of the storyline, and each taxes our senses in different ways. Each medium has its own bias, introducing peculiar distortions into the story, and taking all the different versions together can give us the most complete experience of the story. Moreover, understanding the cultural impact of this electronic revolution, according to McLuhan, required that we think differently about learning and perceiving culture.

At one time, scholars could write and think in linear, sequential, and logical propositions, and the earliest mechanical media clumsily extended single sensory skills. By contrast, today we must be aware of large, complex information ecologies that evade easy understanding. Special skills must be developed to interpret informational patterns and appreciate broad, dynamic, electric systems. Understanding these informational ecologies was crucial for McLuhan, because one of his founding premises was that they structured our very perception of reality.

He contrasted the Western propensity to perceive reality as a visual space using sequential, quantitative reasoning skills with the Eastern propensity to perceive reality as an acoustic space using holistic, qualitative reasoning skills. The skills suitable for static print media and visual space, McLuhan argued, would be unworkable in a dynamic media environment. For this reason, he often experimented with teaching techniques and developed a style of mosaic argumentation that can be difficult to follow; it was often tantalizing for generalists, and sometimes infuriating for specialists. He surrendered narrative argument, and preferred to generate ideas about the construction of cultural communication with infectiously poetic turns of phrase that propelled his ideas deep into the popular zeitgeist.

ASSESSMENT

Many of the tropes and ideas that made McLuhan famous during his lifetime were either infamously wrong or magnificently right. The metaphors he supplied have fed many dreams about the potential of new media—particularly the Internet. If Harold Innis was the founder of contemporary communication studies and medium theory through his research in economic history, McLuhan was the first to popularize communication studies through what he called tropes, probes, and memes. He termed his short, challenging investigative statements probes, because they were designed to trigger an avalanche of critical questions rather than address a specific problem. He would heighten the intellectual tension by using religious or literary tropes that embellished, interpolated, or connected familiar cultural phenomena with unusual connotations or word plays. Most powerful were the memes that McLuhan generated—short, potent ideas in cellular sentences that still circulate in popular dialogue.

For example, McLuhan penned the idea of the "global village" to describe the way in which the electronic revolution seemed to make Earth a smaller planet by recreating the kinds of tribal social interactions that were possible in small communities. Since he felt that we were ill-equipped to critically evaluate our global media environment, he developed the concept of "feedforward" to describe the trajectory of social processes triggered by the use of new media.

McLuhan was also famous for distinguishing between "hot" media, like radio, photography, and films, which irradiate a single sense with intense, high-definition information, and "cool" media, like the telephone, cartoons, or television, which provide limited information, demanding sensory concentration and interpretive involvement. "Sense-ratios" describe the relationship between a particular media technology

and the amount of information about reality that survives when that technology is used to communicate. Most communication technologies feed particular senses, but he expected that new media would help restore balance by supplying all of our senses with information simultaneously.

Since his thinking developed well before the Internet and other new-media technologies were invented, much less widely marketed, McLuhan's writings are especially prescient, provocative, and controversial. His writings were frequently criticized for suggesting that technology determined social outcomes, but he was optimistic that new media would benefit society if we managed the tools well. Linear, sequestered information was too easily monopolized by social elites, and by restructuring information so that it could be shared anywhere at anytime, humankind could begin new, collectively beneficial projects.

McLuhan studied cultural communication not to illustrate how humankind was constrained by technology, but because he felt that we are constrained only when we are not critical of the tools that we build for ourselves. The strain and anomie that we experience today, he would say, are a function of our uncritical use of new media. McLuhan left us a vast toolkit—some tools better than others—for thinking more critically about new media.

Selected Works

McLuhan, Marshall. *The Gutenberg Galaxy: The Making of Typographic Man.* Toronto: University of Toronto Press, 1962.

———. *The Mechanical Bride: Folklore of Industrial Man.* New York: Vanguard Press, 1951.

———. *Understanding Media: The Extensions of Man.* Cambridge, Mass.: MIT Press, 1994.

McLuhan, Marshall, and Quentin Fiore. *The Medium is the Massage: An Inventory of Effects.* New York: Random House, 1967.

Bibliography

Marchand, Philip, and Neil Postman. *Marshall McLuhan: The Medium and the Messenger: A Biography.* Cambridge, Mass.: MIT Press, 1998.

McLuhan, Eric, and Frank Zingrone, eds. *The Essential McLuhan.* New York: Basic Books, 1995.

Further Reading

Diebert, Ronald J. *Parchment, Printing, and Hypermedia: Communication in World Order Transformation.* New York: Columbia University Press, 1997.

Klein, Naomi. *No Logo: Taking Aim at the Brand Bullies.* Toronto: Knopf Canada, 2000.

Related Topics

Hypertext; Innis, Harold; Meme; Multimedia; Technological Determinism; *Understanding Media*; Virtual Community; World Wide Web

— *Philip E. N. Howard*

Media Lab, Massachusetts Institute of Technology

The Media Laboratory at the Massachusetts Institute of Technology (MIT) was conceived in 1980, and formally established in 1985, by MIT professors Nicholas Negroponte and Jerome Wiesner. The Media Lab has become the prototype for media-oriented research laboratories at technical universities around the world.

The Media Lab was founded at a point in time when the traditionally distinct divisions of the communications industry were fusing as a result of what has become known as convergence. The momentum of this transformation, along with the rapid development of computers, created a situation ripe for this interdisciplinary initiative. Specialists in artificial intelligence (AI), graphic design, holography, and cognition came to share working space at the Media Lab with musicians and other artists, all bent on exploring how digital technologies can be adapted for personal use. Within the span of slightly more than 15 years, the Media Lab has made extensive and substantial contributions to a variety of technologies that we take now for granted, from holograms on credit cards to interactive forms of television. The Lab has experienced two-figure growth almost every year, and at the turn of the century, it laid the groundwork for similar initiatives in Europe and Asia. In the words of Stewart Brand, author of a 1987 book on the Media Lab, it is engaged in nothing less than inventing the future.

LEADING THE LAB

It is difficult to pinpoint exactly which factors have contributed most to the success of the Media Lab. It is probably fair to say that the vision shared by Negroponte and Wiesner is central to the configuration. Part of that vision involved developing a genuinely interdisciplinary environment and establishing a strong association with the arts; another involved distancing the Lab from the product orientation of most engineering and applied-science laboratories. Christopher M. Schmandt, head of the Media Lab Speech Interface Group, expressed the difference succinctly: "We're not making a product, we're making an idea."

Wiesner had plenty of time and experience to develop a vision for the Lab. As the senior member of the duo, Wiesner can be credited with wanting something like the Media Lab long before it became a reality. In the late 1950s, he proposed establishing a Communications Sciences Center, but the idea was shelved for lack of funds. He then took a leave of absence from MIT and served as a presidential science adviser during the administrations of John F. Kennedy and Lyndon B. Johnson. On returning to MIT in 1964, Wiesner accepted various administrative positions, including spending nearly a decade as president of the institution. Since 1980, Wiesner devoted much of his time to collaborating with Negroponte in promoting and planning the Media Lab. It was clearly one of his most favorite enterprises; he once called it "the most challenging intellectual activity I've seen in 30 years."

The Lab is also the product of the personality and élan of its first director, Negroponte. Shortly after completing a degree at MIT, he joined the faculty in 1966, and founded the Architecture Machine Group in 1967, some of whose early work contributed to development of computer-aided design (CAD). Other projects and demos were also developed then, like the Aspen Movie Map produced in 1978, which laid the groundwork for subsequent Media Lab innovations in human-computer interactions. Reflecting on the first ten years of the Lab, Negroponte says that the main thrust of the work was creating multimedia—adding sound, color, and motion to computing, "all of those things we tend to take for granted in computing which ten years ago more or less didn't exist." Another important area of Lab research was the personalization of traditional media. The early projects designed to develop electronic newspapers—typically named the *Daily Me*, where content reflects the interests of individual readers—are illustrative of this feature of much Media Lab research.

After some 15 years of directing the Lab, Negroponte resigned in 2000. He remains on the board of directors, but has been replaced by Walter Bender as executive director. Bender joined MIT's Architecture Machine Group after graduation from Harvard in 1978, and he has stayed ever since. At the Media Lab, he took charge of what is known as the Terminal Garden, an expansive work area where demonstrations of projects are developed and run. In the early years of the Lab, Bender would often give demos to visitors, in part because his projects on electronic publishing and personalized forms of mass media could be intuitively understood and appreciated by outsiders.

THEORY AND APPLICATION

More is involved in the equation of success than charismatic and insightful leaders. Another important factor is the basic notion of what constitutes science at the Media Lab. Most university-based research distinguishes theoretical from applied endeavor, with status being awarded to the former. At the Media Lab, this distinction is considered irrelevant; both theory and application are deemed equally important features of science. For this reason, giving demonstrations of works in progress is an important aspect of Media Lab projects.

Some of the demos from past projects have taken on mythic proportions. One frequently told tale concerns a demo of a hologram of a new car design for Media Lab sponsor General Motors. For the first time, automobile designers could see three-dimensional images without having to go through the time-consuming and expensive procedure of carving out a clay model. This demo illustrated how research could achieve major advances of a practical nature, while simultaneously contributing to the theoretical understanding of holograms.

The Media Lab distinguishes itself from major corporation-based laboratories through the broader intellectual climate provided by an institution of higher education like MIT and, as Negroponte says, by "the excitement of young students." This position is supported by co-founder Wiesner: "The new interdisciplinary

Two members of the wearable-computer research group in the lobby of the Media Lab building, 1998. (AP Photo/Victoria Arocho)

things are done by students, not by faculty." One Media Lab professor went a step further, and claimed that MIT's secret of success is, quite simply, that "We have the best students in the country. What we teachers do, or how, seems almost irrelevant."

MIT's research laboratories distinguish themselves from many other university labs in that, since 1960, proprietary research—for example, on behalf of corporations—is not contracted. Negroponte qualifies this position somewhat with regard to the Media Lab: "We do write reports for sponsors that only they see, but when we write papers for publication, everybody gets them."

This position has not seriously hampered sponsor recruitment. Media Lab sponsors include, as would be expected, the major computer and information technology companies in the world—IBM, Toshiba, Intel, BT, Motorola, and many others. As may not be expected, research funders also include companies like Swatch, MasterCard, McDonald's Merrill Lynch, LEGO, and J.C. Penney. All told, there are presently some 150 companies that "buy into" the Lab's research. Sponsors do not generally contract a specific project, but instead support a broad line of research. Such support provides the opportunity for sponsors to benefit from all of the projects undertaken by the Lab. Although there are various forms of sponsorship, the basic arrangement involves an annual commitment of $200,000 for a three-year period. Some 95 percent of the Media Lab budget is derived from such corporate sponsorship; the remaining 5 percent represents investments from U.S. government agencies and non-profit organizations. About half of the corporate sponsors are based in the Americas, a quarter in Europe, and the remaining quarter in Japan.

The roughly 300 projects underway at the Media Lab as of 2002 are clustered into five research consortia, carrying the following cryptic titles: Changing Places, Digital Life, Digital Nations, information: organized, and Things That Think. In addition, the Lab has special interest groups dealing with particular subject areas. Some of these include: Broadercasting, Counter Intelligence, Gray Matters, E-markets, and Toys of Tomorrow. Finally, to complicate matters further, each of the 34 Media Lab faculty members and senior scientists leads a research group involving graduate students.

One of the five research consortia, called information: organized, was formerly known as News in the Future. The name was changed as interest expanded from exploring the nature of news, particularly newsworthiness, and news technologies to a more general interest in information-seeking behavior. Projects in

the consortium are concerned with understanding how digital content can enhance human experience. Three core areas of research in this consortium are concerned with description (exploring "smart" machinery for describing and analyzing digital content), design (developing new expressive modes of presentation of digital content), and debate (developing tools for involving media users in public discourse).

One of the Media Lab special interest groups, Broadercasting, examines broadcasting—as the name suggests—more broadly, from production to dissemination within a digital environment. Four themes are represented in the work of this group: developing new production methods, creating program materials with responsive behaviors, broadcasting to devices other than traditional radio and TV receivers, and developing equipment that allows anyone to produce and broadcast video and audio programs.

FUTURE PLANS

The personnel and facilities of the Media Lab have been expanding almost continually since the first building was opened in 1985. By 2000, the number of faculty, senior research staff, and visiting scientists had risen to 40, supported by another 100 personnel for administration and laboratory functions. The annual budget of the Lab hovers between $30 million and $40 million. The economic recession associated with information-technology industries in 2001 had an impact on the acquisition of sponsors, but only a relatively small percentage of supportive personnel were dismissed during this period.

In 2004, the second Media Lab building will be opened on the MIT campus adjacent to the Wiesner Building, and will double the current workspace. Presently, almost 200 students are enrolled for university degrees at the Lab, 40 percent as Ph.D. candidates, and the rest as master's degree students. Another 200 MIT undergraduates participate in a special program designed to introduce especially talented students to the research enterprise.

The Media Lab is also undertaking major initiatives abroad. In 2000, it launched a ten-year period of collaboration with the Republic of Ireland, opening Media Lab Europe (MLE) in Dublin. Like the Media Lab in Cambridge, MLE is to develop into an independent, university-level educational facility. Eventually, some 20 faculty and 35 research staff are to be employed, and 200 students enrolled. There will not, however, be formal classes; as Negroponte once suggested, instruction "will be like a 17th century painter's atelier, where a student will work with a master." As at the Media Lab in the United States, funding for MLE is to come primarily from corporate sponsorship, and projects will initially focus on the arts and education.

Shortly after completing arrangements in Dublin, the Media Lab announced plans to explore the establishment of a unit in India; in 2001, MIT and India agreed to consider the development of Media Lab Asia (MLA). Dependent on the results of this exploration, the intention is to initiate a ten-year plan for implementing projects in the areas of rural development and education.

The MIT Media Lab is, in other words, going global, exporting its mission of inventing the future to Europe and Asia. Although it is difficult not to be awed by the enormity of the research enterprise and the brilliance of those involved, engineers generally have a poor track record when it comes to predicting how their communication technologies will eventually be adopted and transformed by users. The ultimate inventing of the future, it could be argued, will take place in the laboratory of everyday life, far from the terrain of the MIT Media Lab.

Bibliography

Brand, Stewart. *The Media Lab: Inventing the Future at MIT.* New York: Viking, 1987.

Joseph, Manu. "Who Owns What at Media Lab Asia?" *Wired News,* July 2, 2001. <http://www.wired.com/news/technology/0,1282,44823,00.html> (May 31, 2002).

Lillington, Karlin. "Ireland's 'Mad' New Media Lab." *Wired News,* July 26, 2000. <http://www.wired.com/news/culture/0,1284,37794,00.html> (May 31, 2002).

———. "Media Lab's New Guy in Europe." *Wired News,* January 24, 2001. <http://www.wired.com/news/culture/0,1284,41358,00.html> (May 31, 2002).

Further Reading

Media Laboratory, Massachusetts Institute of Technology. Home page. <http://www.media.mit.edu/about>

Related Topics

Brand, Stewart; Human–Computer Interaction; Interface; Negroponte, Nicholas; Virtual Reality

— *Nicholas Jankowski*

Meme

Memes are contagious ideas that compete with each other for attention and longevity. Just as genes are the basic building blocks of life, memes are the smallest components of culture. Like viruses or genes, they replicate themselves through communication networks or face-to-face contact, and they alter human behavior in such a way as to propagate themselves. Memes can be melodies, icons, slogans and old sayings, inventions, tunes, ideas, catchphrases, or clothing fashions. Memes can also be habits, norms, rules, and patterns of behavior that we inherit or pass on. In the age of new media, memes circulate with increasing alacrity.

A meme is a piece of information that survives long enough to become a component of culture, passing from mind to mind across communities and generations. Thus, memetics is the study of the components and patterns of cultural evolution, and a meme complex is an organization of self-referential ideas that form a belief system, like a religion or an ideology. Oxford zoologist Richard Dawkins is credited with defining the meme and its socio-biological roles in his 1989 book *The Selfish Gene.* One of his controversial proofs was that God really does exist, at the very least as a common pattern shared by the brain structures of billions of people around the world. But it was Marshall McLuhan who in the 1960s began writing about culture and technology by manifesting his ideas in short, self-promulgating cellular sentences.

For example, this entry in an encyclopedia of new media is a meme that propagates the larger meme complex that there is a meaningful category called new media with important social implications. The opening melody of Beethoven's Fifth Symphony, McLuhan's quip that "the medium is the message," and Nike's "swoosh" logo are examples of melodic, textual, and graphic memes. In each case, readers are likely to know something of the history of the meme, and are likely to have other ideas come to mind—the rest of Beethoven's melody, McLuhan's full explanation of what his statement meant, or some Nike product. Moreover, these ideas will come to the readers' minds even if they have never attended the symphonic performance or listened to the full recording, met McLuhan or read his original writings, or bought Nike products. More importantly, we may not be fully aware of how we know this melody, where we heard the expression, or when we first encountered the Nike logo, but they are all eminently recognizable. Each is a meme that has propagated itself in human minds since Beethoven first conducted the symphony in 1808, McLuhan published *The Medium is the Massage* in 1967, or the swoosh appeared in 1971.

With new media, the same meme can take different forms, as each can be described orally, recorded as information about acoustic or light frequencies, and printed as musical notations, text, or image. Moreover, digitally constituted memes have longer lives and are given more opportunities to evolve, because they are more easily copied, altered, and transmitted.

For better or worse, memes are often defined with biological descriptors, as a kind of self-replicating, parasitic idea that people cannot help but propagate and share with others. Good memes self-propagate, bad memes are self-destructive. Astrology and Freeware are examples of self-propagating memes; Nazism, suicide cults, and the idea that it is cool to smoke are examples of self-defeating memes. Historically, memes and meme complexes can be traced from a period of seeding, through periods of plague-like growth, to periods in which the size of the meme complex collapses to reside among small numbers of people. However, the term is often used with the assumption that humans and cultures learn and evolve by an autonomous process of natural selection among ideas. Ideas adapt and succeed one another, while retaining both hereditary features and characteristics that make them perniciously memorable.

For example, scientists who make useful discoveries pass their ideas on to colleagues and students. Through articles, lectures, and word of mouth, the idea catches on, and human brains themselves become the vehicle for the meme and the means for its propagation, the same way that a virus or parasite lives off a host. Like a virus or parasite, the meme has a biochemical structure that can be found in the nervous systems of everyone who has caught the idea. Some memes, like clothing fashions, replicate quickly but have short lives. Others, like world religions, are slow to replicate but live longer than any particular human host.

Whether metaphors of biology can be usefully applied to the evolution of culture is highly debatable. How is it that an individual thinker can create an idea that both constrains and empowers another person's actions? Is the story of World War II really the story of the rise and collapse of the Nazi meme complex? If everything from "fire" to language is a propagating meme that alters human behavior, then the term is too all-encompassing, because every piece of transmitted knowledge can be described as mimetic. In other words, it is not clear that an idea can have agency.

With the advent of new media, memes have proliferated, circulating with greater speed, over greater distances, among more people in diverse cultures. The different meme forms of text, sound, and graphic can be digitized and transmitted with new media.

Bibliography

Blackmore, Susan J. *The Meme Machine.* Oxford, England: Oxford University Press, 1999.

Brodie, Richard. *Virus of the Mind: The New Science of the Meme.* Seattle, Wash.: Integral Press, 1995.

Dawkins, Richard. *The Selfish Gene.* Oxford, England: Oxford University Press, 1989.

Further Reading

McLuhan, Marshall, and Quentin Fiore. *The Medium is the Massage.* New York: Random House, 1967.

Related Topics

McLuhan, Marshall

— *Philip E. N. Howard*

Metrics

Web metrics—methods of tracing who uses a Web site and how the site is used—have evolved considerably over the short life of the World Wide Web. Although the ways of collecting information have changed little, analysis and integration of this data is now far more intensive than it was in the early days, driven largely by the needs of commerce. Metrics are now used as part of a wider "Web analytics" that extends beyond the Web site itself to business processes and performance.

The grandfather of all Internet metrics is the hit, or the request made for an individual Web page. Many Web sites have hit counters indicating how many visitors have come to the site. There are several ways to generate counts of individual hits, but most often they are assembled from information recorded in server logs, which note the time of each server request and some information about the computer making the request.

While tracking Web-page hits provides some indication of the change in popularity of a page, very little else can be inferred from such a simple measure. Someone who reloaded a page, or crossed over it more than once, would be counted each time. If an individual or organization cached (or saved) a copy of the page, however, only a single hit would be recorded. For example, if many hundreds of AOL users visit a site, the site owner might see only a single hit, since AOL retains a copy of each page for later visitors. Previously, this inaccuracy was inconsequential, but with the expansion of commerce on the Web, accurate measurements became a necessity.

ADVERTISING

Vital to a growing advertising market was a set of standards that would accurately reflect the value of online advertisements. While some of these standards related to the way that advertisements were handled (standard sizes for banner ads, for example), others related directly to the measurement of how effective those advertisements were. The number of hits an advertisement received was clearly an inadequate way of determining its value.

The first systems of measurement, which might be called passive systems, evolved from analyzing server logs. For example, by examining the referring Web page and the location of a given client, a path that the user followed through the site could be inferred. A number of products have been developed to assist in this process, and are in wide use.

Generally, advertisements, online and off, are sold by impressions—that is, the number of times that a particular advertisement will be viewed by an audience member. This method of pricing is sometimes called "pay per view." While this has remained the standard for many years, some advertisers prefer to pay instead for clicks on their banners, a practice called "pay per click." (Note that the terms click and clickthrough are now generally used interchangeably in Web advertising.) Even if an advertiser does not pay directly for clicks, it will be concerned with the click rate, which is the percentage of impressions that lead to a click.

Advertisers have turned to a number of other metrics that attempt to place a value on an advertisement's effectiveness. Cost per thousand impressions (CPM) is a standard measure taken from advertising in other media. The CPM for Web advertising tends to be closer to that of magazines than to that of television, because Web advertising, like magazine advertising, provides access to a much narrower demographic. Since CPM tends to paint costs and benefits with too broad a brush, other measures have emerged, including cost per thousand targeted (CPTM), which accounts for a particular demographic; cost per action (CPA), which measures the number of actions generated by an advertisement (requesting further information, for example); cost per click (CPC); and cost per sale (CPS).

Because the way the Web is used differs from the way other media are used, these measures alone do not provide enough information. Advertisers want to know how many unique visitors a site receives, that is, how many different individuals (or at least different client computers) request a page during a 24-hour period. This need necessitated a move beyond the passive server log to a more active practice of tagging users, using cookies. Cookies are tiny programs that allow users to be identified upon their return to a site, so that use can be tracked by user instead of by request. A popular site might receive many visits from the same individual during a single day, but the user will be counted only once as a unique visitor. If some measure of multiple visits is desired, the number of sessions, continuous clicks through a site during a given visit, might be measured instead.

As advertising online became a sizable industry, it was able to support metrics that spanned the Web as a whole rather than detailing single sites. The standardization of metrics led to companies that provided ratings to advertisers. Media Metrix and Nielsen/NetRatings, for example, provide both demographic information for the Web at large and ratings for individual sites on the Web. They do this by examining the behavior of users, capturing information about how they move through the Web, what sites they visit, and how much time they spend at these sites. This approach provides a starting point for companies involved in e-commerce that are looking for more extensive metrics that can improve their profitability.

E-COMMERCE

E-commerce creates new needs as well as new sources of information. The simple act of ordering something online and having it delivered requires interactions between a number of business processes and organizations. While these interactions normally remain hidden to the user, companies that engage in e-commerce have attempted to develop ways of measuring and improving performance within this complex environment.

Just as advertisers were interested in tracking the behavior of users on other sites, those engaged in e-commerce want to better map what is and is not working on their own commerce-based sites. The improvements on CPM listed above are not fine-grained enough to allow for small adjustments to content. A more complete picture of users' behavior is needed, including how consumers make particular decisions about purchases, what pages seem to help or hurt sales, what makes customers return to the site, and other difficult questions.

The basic data can still be extracted from server logs and cookies, tracking the clickstream of individual users. By examining each hyperlink clicked in turn, different patterns or paths that lead through a site can be determined, such as the differences between the paths of those searching for something specific and those just browsing. Those pages that are most central to the buying experience can be identified, and pages that seem to encourage users to abandon the site can be identified and improved. The difficult analysis of these data has spawned a new industry of both professionals and specialized software. Some companies have chosen to implement user panels by asking individuals to place software on their PCs that tracks not only Internet use but also PC use, providing such additional information as which programs are used, how long and when the computer is on, and the amount and type of data flowing between the PC and network.

The sort of user-based tracking done by Nielsen/NetRatings can also be done on a smaller scale when users can be tracked from one site to another. This is possible when sites are owned by the same company, have affiliate agreements, or use a service like DoubleClick that can track behavior over the sites of multiple clients. The value of these data is multiplied considerably when they can be integrated with other sources of information. When the patterns of usage can be matched against demographic information supplied by user questionnaires or past purchasing records, for example, Web designers can target the most profitable demographic groups, or make inferences about how to best present products to different groups. Increasingly, metrics provide information that seamlessly extends to other parts of the business, from the performance of delivery companies to the maintenance of long-term customer relationships.

As with any combination of data about individuals, modeling user behavior raises serious questions about privacy. DoubleClick has already been the target of (unsuccessful) lawsuits related to invasion of privacy, and it is likely that such issues will only increase in importance as metrics become more accurate.

The increased use of servers that create dynamic content for the Web provides a new challenge for those hoping to measure such interactions. In particular, e-commerce sites are often driven by applications that generate active pages rather than deliver pre-designed and stored pages. There will continue to be new sources of information on user behavior online, ranging from user- or agent-provided data to information from eye-tracking, but the most important advances will continue to be in finding ways to make sense of this information and act upon it.

Bibliography

CustomerCentric Solutions. "E-Metrics: Measuring Success in the New Economy." <http://www.customercentricsolutions.com/content/solutions/e-metrics.cfm> (May 31, 2002).

Gomory, Stephen; Hoch, Robert; Lee, Juhnyoung; Podlaseck, Mark; and Edith Schonberg. "E-Commerce Intelligence: Measuring, Analyzing, and Reporting on Merchandising Effectiveness of Online Stores." IBM Research, IBM T.J. Watson Research Center. <http://www.research.ibm.com/iac/papers/eabs3.pdf> (May 31, 2002).

Further Reading

"Advanced Eye Interpretation Project." Stanford University, December 1, 1999. <http://eyetracking.stanford.edu> (May 31, 2002).

Menascé, Daniel A., and Virgilio A.F. Almeida. *Capacity Planning for Web Services: Metrics, Models, and Methods.* Revised edition. Upper Saddle River, N.J.: Prentice Hall PTR, 2002.

Sterne, Jim. *World Wide Web Marketing: Integrating the Web into Your Marketing Strategy.* New York: Wiley Computer, 2001.

Related Topics

Cookies; Customer Relationship Management; E-Commerce; World Wide Web

— Alexander Halavais

MIDI

MIDI is an acronym for "Musical Instrument Digital Interface," a standard that defines how musical synthesizers and instruments connect and interface with computers and with one another. The standard defines both the hardware, such as the input and output ports used to connect equipment, and the manner in which information is stored and used to control the equipment.

Although the MIDI acronym was originated by Roland Corporation, a company best known for making electronic keyboards, the actual protocol was a product of the joint efforts of musicians and musical manufacturers interested in synchronizing keyboards and synthesizers. During the early 1980s, no standard had yet been defined to allow instruments created by different manufacturers to communicate with each other. Existing protocols were manufacturer-specific, so they did not allow an instrument from one maker to interface with one from another.

The movement toward a MIDI standard began with the efforts of Roland to produce instruments that could be connected to computers. At the time, the Commodore 64 home computer—equipped with a crude analog synthesizer chip—had been introduced, as had the first IBM PC, which lacked a sound chip of any kind. Concentrating on the latter, Roland worked to develop a digital sequencer that would be compatible with its entire line of musical equipment. The result was a PC card that could be inserted into an available expansion slot; the card, known as the MPU-401 (Musical Processing Unit, model 401), was the first MIDI interface created exclusively for a computer. More importantly, accompanying the card was a digital language designed to allow computers to communicate with instruments; this language became known as MIDI, and was eventually adopted by other companies as the standard for the industry.

The widespread adoption of the MIDI standard led to the creation of the MIDI Manufacturer's Association (MMA), an organization composed of musical-instrument manufacturers that would be responsible for documenting and circulating existing and new standards.

In its most basic form, the MIDI standard determines when a synthesizer, for example, should begin or stop playing a note or sequence of notes. MIDI files do not contain actual sounds; rather, they contain information about how to create the sounds. MIDI files store data in the form of electronic information transmitted to and used by instruments to control, for example, which, when, and how notes are played, as well as any adjustments that need to be made to the instrument (e.g., volume). The data is in binary form, a series of codes composed of different sequences of 1s and 0s.

MIDI files are general files that follow a standard format used to describe how to create whatever music is encoded; they are decoded by sequencers, which use the directions stored in binary to play back or recreate the musical performance. In everyday language, MIDI files contain a series of messages. When MIDI files are created, each message receives a timestamp indicating when it was created. These timestamps are then used by the sequencer to determine when to "play" each message and in what sequence (hence the name "sequencer") relative to the other messages.

In general, three types of MIDI files exist:

- Type 0 files, which use only one track to store all of the information associated with a performance, irrespective of how many different channels or musical parts are encoded.
- Type 1 files, which use separate tracks to store information for each musical part, and include only a single song or performance.
- Type 2 files, which (like Type 0) use only one track, but encode multiple patterns and songs. These files

are the equivalent of taking a group of Type 0 files and collectively encoding them into one file.

MIDI files store musical information differently from other formats such as .WAV or MP3. .WAV files store digital audio in a manner that requires the encoding of all of the sounds (e.g., music, vocals, etc.), as they are being compiled into a single large file, making it difficult to edit data associated with individual instruments. This process is analogous to dubbing music from one source to another. As a result, the better the source sounds, the better the file sounds.

The MIDI standard has remained fairly consistent since its introduction in the early 1980s, with a few exceptions. Specification of the MIDI File Format, for example, lead to the mass production of MIDI sequencer software that allowed data files to be written and read universally, irrespective of the manufacturer. Another change occurred with the introduction of a MIDI Time Code standard, which allowed the synchronization of playback from different sequencers.

Recent technological developments, however, will require some re-specification of the standard, as these developments were not envisioned when the standard was introduced. The standard serial baud rate of 32K needs to be updated to today's faster data-transfer standards. Similarly, changes are needed to compensate for the increased number of channels of information over which MIDI information can be sent and received (currently limited to 16), in order to accommodate newer synthesizers.

Bibliography

The MIDI Farm. Web site.
<http://www.midifarm.com/support/> (April 12, 2002).
The MIDI-Store. "MIDI Basics." 2001.
<http://www.midiworld.com/basics.htm#intro> (April 12, 2002).
Ultimate MIDI Page. "What Is MIDI?: A Beginner's Guide." 2001.
<http://www.ultimatemidi.com/midiinfo.html> (April 12, 2002).
White, Paul, ed. *Basic MIDI*. London: Sanctuary Publishing, 2000.

Further Reading

Huber, David Miles. *The MIDI Manual: A Practical Guide to MIDI in the Project Studio*. Second edition. Boston: Focal Press, 1999.
Rona, Jeffrey. *The MIDI Companion*. Ronny S. Schiff, ed. Milwaukee, Wis.: Hal Leonard Publishing, 1994.

Related Topics

Digital Audio; MP3; MPEG; Napster

— *Art Ramirez*

Minitel

Minitel is the name of a videotext system instituted in France in 1981. In most areas of the world, videotext, which uses telephone lines to send text and graphics from central computers to terminals, has been surpassed in popularity by the World Wide Web. In France, however, many users remain happily "behind the times," arguing that Minitel's security and ubiquity serve them just as well (and sometimes better) than the Web.

FROM TELEMATIQUE TO MINITEL

The creation of Minitel began in 1975, after it was determined that only 60 percent of French homes had telephones, a situation that critic Howard Rheingold called "nearly a third world state of telecommunications." To remedy this, President Giscard d'Estaing commissioned Simon Nora and Alain Minc to issue a report on how to bring France into the technology age. The visionary Nora-Minc study recommended a program called Telematique, which would merge computers and communications technologies for France. The Telematique program

involved supplying volunteers with free computer terminals, keyboards, and jacks that fit into telephone wiring slots, to be placed in their homes and businesses. To fund this effort, the researchers recommended that paper telephone directories be abandoned, and instead published on the free computer system.

By 1981, the government was ready to implement Minitel, a teletext system that ran on the donated terminals. As part of its promotional campaign, the first three minutes of a directory search on Minitel were free of charge, and for years the French press ran stories of estranged families reunited through the magic of the new technology. Directories weren't the only thing to be found on Minitel; the service quickly expanded to include (for a fee) weather reports, bank statements, stock-exchange information, and clothes shopping. A decade before the arrival of the Web, universities began to use Minitel to coordinate student registration, course delivery, and examination results.

Out of all of Minitel's 20,000 different services, its *messageries*, the system's chat services, are the most popular. Minitel chats differ from other sorts of online chats in important ways, notes linguistics

A Minitel terminal from 1989. (Owen Franken/CORBIS)

expert Anna Livia. Because the average per-minute cost of the *messagerie* is about $0.38 U.S., brevity becomes an important consideration. In addition, because Minitel exchanges typically take place under conditions of pseudonymity (users are not allowed to list phone numbers or addresses in their bylines), users often wind up inventing masquerade-like identities for themselves. Pseudonymity is certainly important to users of the *messageries roses,* the name given to Minitel's adult-sex chat lines. Although conservatives have called them "electronic urinals," a 1991 Harris poll showed that 89 percent of French citizens had no problems with the *messageries roses,* and thought they should remain on Minitel.

THE PRICE OF SUCCESS

Minitel was not the first teletext system to find its way to Europe (the British had launched their Prestel system years prior), but as a method for getting shopkeepers, students, farmers, and housewives "wired," it was certainly the most successful. Some would say that is was too successful. By the late 1990s, Minitel claimed 15 million users, compared to only 12 million French users on the Web. Many French people prefer Minitel to the Web because the former requires no software to load and no hardware to configure. As Rheingold puts it, "It's no mystery why modem dial-up services for PC users in Paris did not grow explosively, when the government was handing out free terminals (with built-in modems) by the millions."

For all its strengths, though, even the French concede that Minitel has significant drawbacks. Older Minitel terminals, many of which are still in service 20 years later, run with a connection speed of only 1,200bps (bits per second), making the transmission of complex graphics all but impossible. The primary language of Minitel is French, a feature that makes people in France quite comfortable, but that has also contributed to Minitel's insularity from the world community—and led to a dearth of French-language sites on the Web. Most troubling is the fact that, for many years, Minitel had absolutely no Internet connectivity whatsoever.

By 1997, Prime Minister Lionel Jospin worried aloud that Minitel was holding back France's entry into the information age. In order to get in step with the times, France Télécom began developing a line of "Et-Hop" services to connect Minitel users to the Internet. Approaching the problem from the opposite side, the "I-Minitel" allows Minitel services to be accessed on PCs, personal digital assistants (PDAs), and mobile phones.

THE MINITEL LEGACY

Not everyone thinks that the upgrade is worth the effort. When France Télécom launched its most expensive promotional campaign ever to promote the "new Minitel," *Wired* magazine wondered whether the company had lost its collective mind. "Minitel is a creature of the 80s and now seems as dated as mullet hairdos and Bananarama," the Manchester, U.K., *Guardian* complained in 2000. Yet Francophiles counter that Minitel has much to teach the world about computing, noting that the newest "Internet appliances" on the world market these days resemble nothing so much as sophisticated Minitel terminals.

Certainly, Minitel's security and pricing systems are exemplary, and experts note that Minitel may be the most self-supporting of all free online services. According to *The Wall Street Journal,* $700 million in connection fees were collected in 2000; $280 million went to France Télécom, the rest to the companies providing listed services. In addition, *The Wall Street Journal* praised Minitel's simple and secure billing structure. Unlike the Web, which requires a credit card, Minitel allows users to pay for online services via their telephone bills. Because Minitel operates on a closed network, it has remained free from hackers and credit-card fraud. For this reason alone, nearly four million French people bank through Minitel, compared with fewer than two million on the Internet. As *The Industry Standard* recently observed, "Minitel may use outdated technology, but it's an online service with a solid business model. That's more than most Internet companies can say."

Perhaps the most interesting Minitel-related development in recent years has occurred not in France, but in Japan, where the uptake of the Internet has been poor compared to other parts of Eastern Asia. Recently, NTT Japan gained government approval to move forward on the L-mode, a proprietary data service that uses an HTML-like interface and a screen phone with email capability and telephony tied in. According to communications expert Charles Dodgson, the L stands for lady, local, or living, and the system specifically targets women in their homes who are seeking to quickly access community-based information online. "Twenty years after France launched its Minitel experiment,"

Dodgson points out, "NTT's new L-mode service looks remarkably similar in concept."

Bibliography

Borzo, Jeanette. "Aging Gracefully: France's Minitel Is Hanging On, Much to the Surprise of Its Critics." *The Wall Street Journal*, October 15, 2001, p. R22.

Dodgson, Charles. "Is There Life in the Screen Phone?" *Communications International*, June 2001, pp. 60–63.

Giussani, Brund. "A Mini Yahoo." *The Industry Standard*, November 27, 2000.

Jeffries, Stuart. "Vive le Minitel." *The Guardian*, October 17, 2000 p. 2.16.

Livia, Anna. "Doing Sociolinguistic Research on the French Minitel." *The American Behavioral Scientist*, vol. 43, no. 3, (November/December 1999), pp. 422–35.

McGrath, Dermot. "Minitel: The Old New Thing." *Wired News*, April 18, 2001. <http://www.wired.com/news/technology/0,1282,42943,00.html> (May 10, 2002).

Moschovitis, Christos J.P.; Poole, Hilary; Schuyler, Tami; and Theresa M. Senft. "Vive le Minitel." *History of the Internet: A Chronology, 1843 to the Present*. Santa Barbara, Calif.: ABC Clio, 1999; p. 106.

Rheingold, Howard. "From Telematique to Pink Messages: The Surprises of Minitel." *The Virtual Community: Homesteading on the Electronic Frontier*. Reading, Mass.: Addison-Wesley, 1993.

Further Reading

Adminet. "Information on the French Minitel." <http://www.adminet.com/minitel/> (May 10, 2002).

Delaney, Kevin J. "AOL Devices Get You Online Without PCs." *Wall Street Journal*, April 16, 1999, p. B6.

France Télécom. LesKiosques.com. Web site. <http://www.minitel.com/> (May 10, 2002).

Hill, Richard. "Electronic Commerce, the World-Wide Web, Minitel, and EDI." *The Information Society*, vol. 13, no. 1 (January–March 1997). <http://www.batnet.com/oikoumene/arbecom.html> (May 10, 2002).

Project Foresight. "Videotex System." Project of the Hong Kong University of Science and Technology, August 16, 1995. <http://www.ust.hk/~webiway/content/France/index.html> (May 10, 2002).

Sutherland, Ewan. "Minitel: The Resistible Rise of French Videotex." *International Journal for Information Resource Management*, vol. 1, no. 4 (1990), pp. 4–14. <http://www.sutherla.dircon.co.uk/minitel/> (May 10, 2002).

Related Topics

Chat; Videotex; Virtual Community

— *Theresa M. Senft*

Minsky, Marvin

1927–

Artificial Intelligence Pioneer, Scientist, Author

Marvin Minsky is considered by most to be the father of artificial intelligence (AI). He is credited with coining the term in the late 1950s, when he was participating in much of the field's founding research, including the creation of the first mechanical neural network. In 1959, he and fellow Massachusetts Institute of Technology (MIT) professor John McCarthy formed the MIT Artificial Intelligence Laboratory, where even today the most important research in the field is conducted. Since then, Minsky has made crucial contributions to all spheres of AI theory, in addition to making important contributions to a wide array of other fields like robotics, mathematics, virtual reality (VR), and even space exploration. His work has led to both theoretical and practical breakthroughs in AI, cognitive psychology, neural networks, VR telepresence, and the theory of Turing Machines. He has long been a forceful presence at MIT's famed Media Lab as well, and even co-wrote a science fiction novel with genre stalwart Harry Harrison, called *The Turing Option* (1992), that integrates his AI theories.

Minsky was born in New York, the son of an ophthalmologist. He was raised in a home that was "full of lenses, prisms and diaphragms," as he would write in 1988, in an essay detailing his invention of the confocal scanning microscope. "I took all his instruments apart," he wrote, referring to his father, "and he quietly put them together again." After attending the Bronx High School of Science in New York and the Phillips Academy in Andover, Massachusetts, Minsky served in the navy from 1944 to 1945. Then, in 1946, Minsky attended Harvard, where the 19-year-old took up undergraduate studies in mathematics, neurophysiology, neuroanatomy, psychology, and classical mechanics.

In 1951, he went to graduate school at Princeton, where he wrote a theoretical thesis on "connectionistic" learning machines, based on early nerve-cell science, and built the SNARC (Stochastic Neural-Analog Reinforcement Computer), the world's first artificial neural network, which simulated the learning process that a mouse goes through as it walks through a maze. It was all simply a way for Minsky to build on a lifelong fascination that would come to define a career that began when he became an assistant professor of mathematics at MIT in 1957, and which has continued there ever since.

"As long as I can remember," Minsky would write, "I was entranced by all kinds of machinery—and, early in my college years, tried to find out how the great machines that we call brains managed to feel and learn and think." However, he soon learned that brain science was mostly uncharted territory, and if he really wanted to learn, he would have to blaze most of the trails himself.

Author Stewart Brand has described Minsky as resembling a bald eagle, "complete with predator's gaze," albeit one with a personal devilish style and a "fearless, amused intellect creating the new by teasing taboos." No idea was so taboo as the idea that humans should build thinking machines that might one day outstrip our own talents, intellects, and abilities, but Minsky was never deterred from this task.

The professor's career is littered with groundbreaking research papers and books demonstrating his abilities as a scientific trailblazer, and as a writer of clarity, vision, and wit. In 1961, he wrote what is perhaps his most seminal work, "Steps Toward Artificial Intelligence," which would come to define the parameters of the AI field. In it, one finds the Minsky manifesto: "I believe . . . we are on the threshold of an era that will be strongly influenced, and quite possibly dominated, by intelligent problem-solving machines. But our purpose is not to guess about what the future may bring; it is only to try to describe and explain what seem now to be our first steps toward the construction of 'artificial intelligence.'"

A number of other works were also highly influential. In 1963, Minsky produced the paper "Matter, Mind, and Models," which proposed a general direction for AI research and addressed the problems involved in creating "self-aware" machines. In 1969's *Perceptrons*, written with Seymour Papert, Minsky helped outline the capabilities and limitations of "loop-free" learning and pattern recognition in machines; the book is also considered to be the first systematic study of parallel computing. In his 1974 essay, "A Framework for Representing Knowledge," Minsky begins to tackle the huge problem of bringing to AI the "common sense" knowledge that is required to understand even the simplest natural texts; this essay also outlines a systematic way to represent knowledge, using what Minsky calls "frames." Today, those ideas are viewed as an early prototype for object-oriented programming languages such as C++ and Java.

In 1985, Minsky collected a series of his short essays that he'd been compiling since the 1970s, and published them in a book called *The Society of Mind*, perhaps his most popular and influential work. It argues that intelligence is not the product of any singular mechanisms within the brain, but results from interactions among many diverse "agents," or minineural networks, within the brain. The book is designed as a series of 270 interconnected, one-page ideas to depict graphically the structure of the theory. Among other ramifications, the book challenges basic psychological, and even philosophical principles. In a class syllabus on the subject, which Minsky still teaches, he writes: "These issues have never been understood because of our traditional image of the mind as controlled by a single, central Self. The folly of this becomes obvious when you think about how to build systems to do things that might help answer questions like . . . why does red look red? . . . what use are emotions? . . . why do we like jokes? . . . "

Minsky's most recent work has expanded on his earlier ideas and attempts to define a need for machines to develop "common sense" thinking skills, and even emotions, in order to become truly perceptive and intelligent. His next book, *The Emotion Machine*, will address the idea that emotions are simply different ways of thinking, and that effective machines need a variety of ways of thinking about problems in order to solve them efficiently; most computers now have only one or two ways of approaching any problem. Minsky explained this at length in an interview with ZDNet: "The emotion machine is about how to make a machine that's resourceful," he said. "There is no particular reason to make it angry, but you certainly would want to make it impatient internally so that if it's not making progress, it will switch to some other way of thinking."

There are some, such as MIT science sociologist Sherry Turkle, who are pessimistic about the ways that emergent AI technologies attempt to integrate feeling into their models. In her 1995 book *Life on the Screen: Identity in the Age of the Internet*, Turkle criticizes Minsky's discussion of the Oedipus complex in *The Society of Mind*. The Oedipus complex is a psychoanalytical precept coined from ancient Greek literature, in which a male patient experiences powerful feelings of affection for the mother figure while wanting to kill the father figure. According to Turkle, Minsky sees this idea in an AI context as simply "an adaptive mechanism that facilitates the construction of an unconfused agent by removing (quoting Minsky) 'one [of the models] from the scene.'" She denounces Minsky for turning passionate, sexually jealous thoughts and murderous emotions "into an engineering fix for a purely cognitive problem."

Despite such critiques, Minsky has soldiered on with his efforts. "There are deconstructionists and strange humanists, but they don't have influence on the technical community," he told *Newsbytes* in August 2001.

In recent times, though, Minsky has lamented the slow progress of AI, which started out so promisingly more than 40 years ago. He has projected that true AI will take anywhere from 100 to 300 years (or possibly never) to realize, since, as he has commented, there are only six people really involved in the field now, and the public seems generally disinterested in funding the research. (Interestingly, in *The Turing Option*, Minsky places the birth of genuine AI technology in the year 2030.) However, he remains an unflinching champion of the science, and has written an article for *Scientific American* magazine, "Will Robots Inherit the Earth?" in which he answers his own question with an enthusiastic yes. If we as humans are reaching our intellectual limits as sentient beings, what would be wrong, he suggests, with plugging into the technology of our own creation to drive human intelligence ever onward, perhaps even to immortality? "Will robots inherit the earth?" Minsky writes. "Yes, but they will be our children. We owe our minds to the deaths and lives of all the creatures that were ever engaged in the struggle called evolution. Our job is to see that all this work shall not end up in meaningless waste."

Selected Works

Harrison, Harry, and Marvin Minsky. *The Turing Option.* New York: Warner Books, 1992.

Minsky, Marvin. *Computation: Finite and Infinite Machines.* Englewood Cliffs, N.J.: Prentice-Hall, 1967.

———. "Matter, Mind, and Models." *Semantic Information Processing.* Marvin Minsky, ed. Cambridge, Mass.: MIT Press, 1968. Simplifications made 1995. <ftp://ftp.ai.mit.edu/pub/minsky/MatterMind&Models.txt> (July 3, 2002).

———. *The Society of Mind.* New York: Simon & Schuster, 1988.

———. "Steps Toward Artificial Intelligence." *Computers and Thought.* Edward A. Feigenbaum and Julian Feldman, eds. New York: McGraw-Hill, 1963; pp. 406–50. <http://www.ai.mit.edu/people/minsky/papers/steps.html> (July 3, 2002).

———. "Why People Think Computers Can't." *AI Magazine,* vol. 3 no. 4 (Fall 1982). Reprinted in

Technology Review, Nov./Dec. 1983, and in *The Computer Culture,* Donnelly, ed. (Cranbury, N.J.: Associated Univ. Presses, 1985). <ftp://ftp.ai.mit.edu/pub/minsky/CausalDiversityMatrix.txt> (July 3, 2002).

———. "Will Robots Inherit the Earth?" *Scientific American,* October 1994. Republished online with "minor revisions." <ftp://ftp.ai.mit.edu/pub/minsky/sciam.inherit.txt> (July 3, 2002).

Minsky, Marvin L., and Seymour A. Papert. *Perceptrons: An Introduction to Computational Geometry.* Cambridge, Mass.: MIT Press, 1969.

Bibliography

Brand, Stewart. *The Media Lab: Inventing the Future at MIT.* New York: Viking, 1987.

Featherly, Kevin. "Artificial Intelligence: Help Wanted—AI Pioneer Minsky." *Newsbytes.com,* August 31, 2001.

———. Interview with Marvin Minsky. August 29, 2001.

Media Laboratory, Massachusetts Institute of Technology. "Brief Academic Biography of Marvin Minsky." 2001. <http://www.media.mit.edu/people/minsky/minskybiog.html> (May 31, 2002).

Turkle, Sherry. *Life on the Screen: Identity in the Age of the Internet.* New York: Simon & Schuster, 1995.

Further Reading

Flint, Anthony. "Artificial Intelligence Evolves." *Boston Globe,* March 18, 1995 p. 1.

Garfinkel, Simson L. "'Artificial Intelligence' Solves a Mystery." *Christian Science Monitor,* January 16, 1991.

Hafner, Katie, and Matthew Lyon. *Where Wizards Stay Up Late: The Origins of the Internet.* New York: Simon & Schuster, 1996.

Knox, Andrea. "Man and Machine Are Not of One Mind." *Philadelphia Inquirer,* June 19, 1987, p. D14.

Negroponte, Nicholas. *Being Digital.* New York: Knopf, 1995.

Rheingold, Howard. *Virtual Reality.* New York: Summit Books, 1991.

Rosenberg, Ronald. "Intelligence Alley—Where There's Nothing Artificial About the Future." *Boston Globe,* August 6, 1985, p. 35.

Sabbatini, Renato M. E. "The Mind, Artificial Intelligence and Emotions: Interview with Marvin Minsky." Universidade Estadual de Campinas, 1998. <http://www.epub.org.br/cm/n07/opiniao/minsky/minsky_i.htm> (May 31, 2002).

Related Topics

Cyberculture; Cyborg; Human-Computer Interaction; Kurzweil, Raymond; Media Lab, Massachusetts Institute of Technology; Responsive Environments; Robotics; Turing, Alan; Turkle, Sherry; Virtual Reality

— *Kevin Featherly*

Moog, Robert

1934–

Inventor of the Moog Synthesizer

Robert Moog, a musician, electrical engineer, and physicist, invented the Moog Synthesizer in 1964 to aid in the production of new musical sounds. Using electricity, Moog's synthesizer can imitate the sounds made by any musical instrument, as well as generate new ones. Moog's invention permanently changed the world of music.

Moog was born in New York City in 1934. His association with music became pronounced as a child through the influence of his mother, who introduced him to the piano; his father, an amateur radio operator, introduced him to engineering. After reading an article describing how to build Theremins—small wooden boxes with antennas that emitted the first form of electronic music—Moog began constructing his own as a hobby at the age of 15. By age 19, he had published an article instructing readers on how to build their own Theremin kits.

The foundational design used in Moog's unique synthesizer came from applied concepts in physics, electrical engineering, and music. His education generously supported such designs. He received a bachelor of science degree in physics from Queens College, and also received a bachelor's degree in electrical engineering from Columbia University. In 1965, Moog received a doctorate in engineering physics from Cornell University. By the time he had finished his education, he had already started his own company.

In 1954, Moog began the first of a series of companies when he founded the R. A. Moog Company, which filled orders for custom-built Theremins and other innovative instruments. In 1964, he introduced the Moog Synthesizer, which attracted the attention of musicians from a wide variety of musical genres. When it was introduced to the general public in 1968, after it was used on Walter Carlos' "Switched on Bach" recording, the instrument became an instant hit.

Moog's Synthesizer captured the attention of the music world due to its revolutionary design. Journalist Frank Houston described the revolutionary instrument as being the first to offer a process called attack-decay-sustain-release (ADSR) envelope shaping, where each envelope corresponds to a physical characteristic of sound. The concept of attack represents the rate at which sound achieves its highest volume. Decay corresponds to the volume level of sound heard after a note reaches its maximum value. Sustain represents the volume and continuation of sound heard after a note is released. Finally, release corresponds to a rate that defines the length of time before a sound falls silent. Taken collectively, these factors made the Moog Synthesizer adjustable and able to copy any instrument, as well as to create entirely new sounds.

In 1971, Bill Waytena bought the R.A. Moog Company, merged it with his own company, Musonics, and changed its name to Moog Music. Waytena's interest in the company came from a desire to improve productivity by building and marketing an even newer electronic synthesizer that appealed to the ordinary consumers. The lucrative company was sold to Norlin Music, Incorporated in 1973. Moog remained in the newly appointed division of Norlin Music, Inc. until 1978, when he moved to North Carolina and started his present company, Big Briar. Big Briar produces various types of Theremins and musical instrument digital interfaces (MIDIs).

Moog's founding of Big Briar allowed the musical entrepreneur an opportunity to design and construct more instrumental equipment. The company offers a wide range of innovative electrical equipment, as well as new types of performance-control devices. Big Briar's work to advance the MIDI has helped to improve the compatibility of computers and synthesizers. From 1984 to 1988, Moog was also vice president of new product research for Kurzweil Music Systems.

The Moog Synthesizer's success derives from its ability to let musicians invent their own distinctive music. With an appreciation for music and a knack for electrical design, Moog has altered the musical landscape, and his designs and work have caught the attention of scientists, musicians, inventors, and fans. The future of music and instruments may lie in the hands and mind of Moog and Big Briar.

Selected Works

Glinsky, Albert. *Theremin: Ether Music and Espionage.* Foreword by Robert Moog. Urbana: University of Illinois Press, 2000.

Bibliography

Hargus, Billy Bob. *Robert Moog.* March 1997. <http://www.furious.com/perfect/moog.html> (May 31, 2002).

Houston, Frank. "Brilliant Careers: Robert Moog." *Salon*, April 25, 2000. <http://www.salon.com/people/bc/2000/04/25/moog/> (May 31, 2002).

Vail, Mark. *Keyboard Magazine Presents Vintage Synthesizers: Pioneering Designers, Groundbreaking*

Instruments, Collecting Tips, Mutants of Technology. San Francisco, Calif.: Miller Freeman Books, 2000.

Woodford, Chris. "Music Synthesizers." *The Cutting Edge: An Encyclopedia of Advanced Technologies.* New York: Oxford University Press, 2000.

Further Reading

Chadabe, Joel. *Electric Sound: The Past and Promise of Electronic Music.* Upper Saddle River, N.J.: Prentice Hall, 1997.

Crawford, Franklin. "Synthesizer Inventor Robert Moog, Ph.D. '65, to be Honored at Smithsonian." *Cornell Chronicle,* April 13, 2000.

Munnshe, J. "Interview: Robert Moog." *Amazing Sounds,* 2001. <http://www.amazings.com/articles/article0036.html> (May 31, 2002).

Who2. "Who2 Profile: Robert Moog." 2002. <http://www.who2.com/robertmoog.html> (May 31, 2002).

Related Topics

Computer Music; Digital Audio; Digital Music; Kurzweil, Raymond; MIDI

— *James Pyfer*

Moravec, Hans

1948–

Robotics Innovator

A researcher in robotics at Carnegie Mellon University for the last two decades, Hans Moravec has advanced the state of the art in mobile robotics, especially with regard to providing robots with better spatial information via computer vision and other sensors. He is perhaps best known for his outspoken views on the future co-evolution of human beings and robots, and the eventual superiority of the latter.

Moravec was born in Kautzen, Austria, but lived in Canada from age five. He earned a bachelor's degree in mathematics from Acadia University in 1969, and a master's degree in computer science from the University of Western Ontario in 1971. He completed a Ph.D. in computer science at Stanford University in 1980 before moving to Carnegie Mellon, where he continues to work as the director of the Robotics Institute.

Moravec argues that what seem like the more mundane problems that must be solved before robots can interact within a real-world environment are actually among the most intractable problems of artificial intelligence (AI). Examining the evolutionary progress of biological systems, he notes that the higher functions of the human brain took very little time to

develop on an evolutionary scale, while the perceptual apparatus took much longer. While we may be more impressed by a chess-playing computer, the more difficult tasks are ones that we as humans take for granted, like creating a cognitive map of the area around us or being able to quickly and safely grasp an object.

His dissertation treated the problem of moving a robot through a crowded environment, using a television picture to help guide it from one side of the room to another. This robot, called the Stanford Cart, was developed between 1973 and 1980. Although it could make it safely through the room about 75 percent of the time, it took several hours to complete the task, and it was remote-controlled by a large computer. More recent work using binocular television cameras and an approach that Moravec calls "3D occupancy grids" allows a robot to determine the layout of a real-world environment in several seconds.

Moravec is probably better known for his opinion that robots will overtake humans in the near future. In two books, *Mind Children: The Future of Robot and Human Intelligence* (1988) and *Robot: Mere Machine to Transcendent Mind* (1999), he has suggested that when robots do become superior, the most reasonable response will be for humans, at least in their current biological form, to gracefully bow out of the evolutionary process. Once these robots begin reproducing, their improvement will be exponential from generation to generation.

Based on an approximation of the relationship of neurons to computer processors, and on the exponential growth rate of processing power, Moravec estimates that we will have developed computers with processing power equivalent to humans by 2040, and that machines will far surpass human intellect in the years thereafter. This is a fairly inevitable process, he argues. Only through robots will human culture be able to thrive and spread itself across the universe.

His work spans from the near future, in which he expects robots to require procedural programming; to a middle term, when humans can co-exist with intelligent robots; to a more distant future in which biological humans are rendered extinct. He concedes that there are ways for our minds to continue on in this future, but our bodies will no longer be competitive from an evolutionary perspective. They will be replaced by robots that are able to thrive in harsh environments—possibly those that are structured like robot "bushes" with molecular-level fingers attached to increasingly larger branches.

Moravec has his critics. By his own admission, his position tends to be more extreme than that of other researchers. He has engaged in an extended public dialogue with eminent mathematician Roger Penrose, who argues that machines can never be truly intelligent. Others have also criticized Moravec's views, criticisms that he answers by noting that progress over the next few decades will provide the ultimate proof of his predictions.

Selected Works

Moravec, Hans. Home page.
   <http://cart.frc.ri.cmu.edu/users/hpm/> (April 12, 2002).
———. *Mind Children: The Future of Robot and Human Intelligence.* Cambridge, Mass.: Harvard University Press, 1988.
———. *Robot: Mere Machine to Transcendent Mind.* Oxford: Oxford University Press, 1999.
———. "Robots, Re-Evolving Mind." Robotics Institute, Carnegie Mellon University, December 2000.
   <http://cart.frc.ri.cmu.edu/users/hpm/project.archive/robot.papers/2000/Cerebrum.html> (April 12, 2002).

Bibliography

Bringsjord, Selmer. *What Robots Can and Can't Be, Studies in Cognitive Systems,* vol. 12. Dordrecht, Netherlands: Kluwer Academic Publishers, 1992.
Penrose, Roger. *Shadows of the Mind: A Search for the Missing Science of Consciousness.* Oxford: Oxford University Press, 1994.
Platt, Charles. "Superhumanism." *Wired* 3.10, October 1995.
   <http://www.wired.com/wired/archive/3.10/moravec.html> (April 12, 2002).

Further Reading

Joy, Bill. "Why the Future Doesn't Need Us." *Wired,* 8.04, April 2000.
   <http://www.wired.com/wired/archive/8.04> (April 12, 2002).
Nilsson, Nils J. *Artificial Intelligence: A New Synthesis.* Orlando, Fla.: Morgan Kaufmann, 1998.

Related Topics

Brooks, Rodney; Kurzweil, Raymond; Robotics

— *Alexander Halavais*

MP3

MP3 is a digital music-compression format that squeezes song files down to about one-tenth of their normal size. Smaller file sizes mean that MP3 users can download music from the Internet quickly, and there is almost no loss of sound quality. It also means that less storage space is needed for songs downloaded to a computer's hard drive.

Research into what would become MP3 dates back to 1987, when experiments were conducted at the Fraunhofer Institut Integrierte Schaltungen (Fraunhofer IIS-A) in Erlangen, West Germany, with assistance from University of Erlangen professor Dieter Seitzer. Work focused on creating a high-quality, low-bandwidth music format that capitalized on flaws in human hearing. Since the human ear is insufficient to detect the full range of sound, researchers guessed that certain elements in digitally truncated sound files would never be missed. MPEG encoders could read digital audio files to determine which bits contained audible data. Then, before the files were encoded, inaudible elements were eliminated, rendering sound files much smaller.

That research led, in 1989, to a German patent for Fraunhofer IIS-A. The International Standards Organizations (ISO) accepted the format three years later, as did the Motion Picture Experts Group (MPEG), a subcommittee of the ISO that formed in 1988 to create digital formats and standards for multimedia producers. MP3 is a direct descendant of MPEG-1, a low-bandwidth video format used in online video, and of MPEG-2, a high-bandwidth audio and video format that is the basis for current DVD technology. MP3 technology, formally known as MPEG Layer III, has become an international digital music standard.

According to a September 8, 2000, ZDNet.com article, a key to MP3's eventual success was the early decision by Fraunhofer IIS-A not to exercise its patent on the technology; that allowed the format to be widely adopted, and to be tweaked at will by developers around the world. As a result, in 1997, Tomislav Uzelac of Advanced Multimedia Products invented the first MP3 player, which he called AMP. AMP eventually morphed into versions for Windows (WinAmp) and Macintosh (MacAmp). Innumerable MP3 players followed, including compatible versions of RealPlayer and Windows Media; many are available for free on the Internet. Also, the first portable MP3 player, Diamond Multimedia's Rio, was introduced in November 1998, with many others following its lead, such as the iPod from Apple Computer.

The other factor crucial to MP3's success was its tight compression. A five-minute music track copied directly from a CD to a computer hard drive takes up approximately 50MB (megabytes) of space. Converted to an MP3 file, however, the same song takes up about 5MB of space, delivering roughly equal sound clarity. Commercial MP3-encoding software that allowed people to copy, or "rip" songs from CDs onto their computer hard drives began emerging in the late 1990s from companies like Magix, Orion Studios, and Adaptec.

By the end of the 1990s, the MP3 format was immensely popular on the Internet. Because of the small file sizes, music listeners with a high-speed Internet connection can download songs in minutes. Even over dial-up connections, most songs can be transmitted in less than half an hour, a significant improvement over older, bulkier formats like .WAV or .AIFF. One online service, MP3.com, even took its name from the format, enabling unknown bands to use the Internet medium to their advantage by distributing their music to fans who otherwise would' never encounter it. MP3s also lend themselves to peer-to-peer file sharing, the direct swapping of songs between users' hard drives over the Internet. This propensity led to the creation of Napster, a service that enabled the direct sharing of MP3 files between music listeners.

Despite the immense popularity it currently enjoys, the MP3 format faces a murky future, partly because, thanks to Napster and other file-swapping services, its name is now synonymous with online music piracy. But there is another, probably more important factor at work: Like many successful technologies, MP3 may have sown the seeds of its own demise, as other, better standards are being worked on. Dolby Labs, for example, announced the development of one possible usurper, Advanced Audio Coding (AAC), in December 2000. AAC reputedly produces even smaller and more easily transmitted files that retain higher sound quality than MP3s, and it is being developed in partnership with AT&T, Sony, and Fraunhofer IIS-A, the same German labs where MP3 was invented. In the summer of 2001, Fraunhofer announced MP3Pro, a collaborative effort with Thomson Multimedia that had achieved AAC's goals. Meanwhile, Vorbis, an independent group of software developers, announced its Ogg Vorbis music format, which challenges MP3's audio quality and is free for public use.

Bibliography

Fraunhofer Institut Integrierte Schaltungen (Fraunhofer IIS-A). "MPEG Audio Layer-3." 1998–2001. <http://www.iis.fhg.de/amm/techinf/layer3/index.html> (April 1, 2002).

Ridgley, Mitch. "The History of MP3 and How Did It All Begin." 1999–2000. <http://www.mp3-mac.com/Pages/History_of_MP3.html> (April 1, 2002).

Snider, Mike. "Ray Dolby: Audio Innovator." *USA Today*, December 28, 2000.

<http://www.usatoday.com/life/cyber/tech/cti952.htm> (April 1, 2002).

Further Reading

Auletta, Ken. *World War 3.0: Microsoft and Its Enemies.* New York: Random House, 2001.

Carey, Dermot Martin. "MP3, Now Portable." December 8, 2000. <http://www.eecs.lehigh.edu/~dmc6/MP3/MP3Overview.html> (April 1, 2002).

Tapscott, Don. *Growing Up Digital: The Rise of the Net Generation.* New York: McGraw-Hill. 1998.

Related Topics:

Compression; DeCSS; Digital Millennium Copyright Act; Digital Music; MPEG; Multimedia; Napster; Peer-to-Peer; Streaming Media

— *Kevin Featherly*

MP3.com

The Web site MP3.com played a principal role in popularizing the MP3 music file format among both music fans and musicians who wanted to use the format to distribute their music. The site's outspoken founder, Michael Robertson, also helped to galvanize many in the online music community to rally against the standard practices of the major record companies. MP3.com eventually cooperated with the music industry to create a service allowing users to listen to their CD collections from any computer with an Internet connection.

Robertson launched MP3.com in November 1997, after noticing the growing frequency with which users of his Filez search engine were including "MP3" in their searches. With MP3.com, he created a site that served as a central hub where users could obtain MP3 software, news, and music. Artists were invited to post MP3s of their music on the site free of charge. By early 2001, nearly 145,000 artists offered almost one million songs for free download. While it initially made money through advertising, MP3.com later sold online CDs by its member artists, and broke sharply with music industry standards by splitting profits 50-50 with the artist. The company also sold music programs for retail outlets to play as background music in stores.

Within a year of its launch, both its popularity among Internet users and Robertson's evangelism established MP3.com as a key player in the quickly developing online music world. The major music labels, however, regarded Robertson as an adversary. Because there is no copy-protection mechanism in

MP3 technology, a song from a CD could be converted into an MP3 and sent endlessly, for free, across the Internet without the permission of the copyright owner—which is typically a music label. By contrast, secure formats such as Liquid Audio contained technology to prevent files from being copied. Most music companies, therefore, viewed the MP3 format in general as a vehicle that promoted piracy and robbed them of royalties. For example, when singer-songwriter Tom Petty posted his song "Free Girl Now" on MP3.com in March 1999, Warner Bros. Records demanded that it be taken down two days later. The song was downloaded 157,000 times before it was pulled, which supporters cited as evidence that MP3 files could serve as useful promotional tools.

MP3.com's battle with the music industry came to a head with the January 2000 launch of the My.MP3.com service, which allows a user to insert a CD into a computer and have an MP3 version of the disc transferred immediately from a database to an online account with MP3.com. The user can then listen to the music from any computer connected to the Internet. Songs are streamed, which means that they cannot be downloaded and saved. The database contained music from tens of thousands of CDs. Because MP3.com did not obtain a license from copyright holders (music companies and publishers) to create that database, the major music companies—Sony, BMG, EMI, Time Warner, and Universal Music Group—sued MP3.com.

After a U.S. District Court sided with the recording industry, MP3.com settled, agreeing to pay undisclosed damages and licensing fees. In November 2000, Universal Music Group carried its suit to the final phase, and was awarded $53.4 million in damages and attorney fees. Although the service tried to re-launch with licensed content from all the major music companies, Universal acquired MP3.com in May 2001 and Robertson stepped down as chief operating officer. While MP3.com continues to operate as an independent website, Universal has used its technology to develop a music subscription service.

Since MP3.com's inception, Robertson has touted the site as a pioneering business in the digital-music arena. The Web site was indeed instrumental, not only in winning converts to the opinion that MP3 is a more viable format than its copy-protected rivals, but also in demonstrating the feasibility of artists distributing their music worldwide outside the structure of the major music industry. With My.MP3.com, Robertson bolstered the notion, likely to gain credence in the wireless age, that music should be seen not as a product, but as a service.

Bibliography

Alderman, John. *Sonic Boom: Napster, MP3, and the New Pioneers of Music.* New York: Perseus Publishing, 2001.

Haring, Bruce. *Beyond the Charts: MP3 and the Digital Music Revolution.* Los Angeles, Calif.: JM Northern Media, 2000.

Robertson, Michael, and Ron Simpson. *The Official MP3.com Guide to MP3.* San Diego, Calif.: MP3.com, 1999.

Further Reading

Wired News. "MP3 Rocks the Web: A Month-By-Month Wired News Collection." <http://www.wired.com/news/mp3/> (April 1, 2002).

Sonicnet.com. "Digital Music News." <http://www.sonicnet.com/news/digital/> (April 1, 2002).

Related Topics

Compression; Digital Music; MPEG; Napster

— *Chris Nelson*

MPEG

MPEG refers to a group of digital video and audio compression standards and file formats commonly used to store and play back movies, video clips, and audio—a universal means of efficiently and compactly coding digital video and audio signals for consumer use.

MPEG takes its name from its creators, the Moving Picture Experts Group, who developed the original set of standards under the direction of Leonardo Chiariglione (CSELT) and Hiroshi Yasuda (JVC Corporation). Originally convened in 1988 under the direction of the International Standards Organization (ISO) and the International Electro-Technical Commission (IEC), the group sought to address the concern of "interoperatability" for audio and video playback—the ability to operate across software or hardware produced by different manufacturers. The result was a set of universal standards, proposed in 1991, defining the encoding and decoding of full-motion video and associated audio, commonly referred to as MPEG. It is noteworthy that about the same time that the Moving Picture Experts Group convened, another compression method, Digital Video Interactive (DVI), was being developed by a research group at Princeton University. It was eventually bought by Intel, where it continues to be developed.

The first phase of the MPEG standard, named MPEG-1, is what is typically thought of when full-motion digital video is discussed as an MPEG file or format. MPEG-1 consisted of four sets of standards, including those related to the synchronization of video and audio, video compression, audio compression, and the compliance testing of each. The goal of the MPEG-1 standard was to introduce guidelines that would be independent of a particular application, allowing the user to determine how it is used. The standard determines an encoding procedure, and by default a decoding procedure, and the user decides how to apply it. Common applications of the MPEG-1 standard include products such as video CDs and MP3s.

MP3, a popular format for storing digital audio that is increasingly used to distribute music online, gets its name from MPEG-1 Layer 3, which outlines audio compression standards. MP3 files are commonly downloaded from a site and require a special player to be heard. As with any compressed file, the MP3 player decompresses and decodes the file, resulting in sound.

MPEG-1 encoding takes advantage of redundancies in the information being stored in order to represent it efficiently; as a rough estimate of its efficiency, an hour of video encoded in this format uses approximately one gigabyte of storage space. The encoding process used by MPEG-1 is somewhat analogous to the individual frames found on film, except for one major difference. A high video compression rate is produced not by encoding all of the information for each frame as traditional film does; rather, it encodes only the changes from frame-to-frame, through a technique called DCT. Although this process inevitably results in a loss of information, it is hardly noticeable to the naked eye, and the video quality that it produces approximates that of the typical home VCR.

MPEG-1 specifications also determine how full-motion video is decoded. MPEG-1 video viewing on, for instance, a personal computer requires an MPEG decoder, which can be in the form of hardware, software, or a combination of the two. The decoder communicates with the software programs used to view the video through its drivers, which determine the procedures needed to translate the information into what is seen on the monitor as full-motion video.

Other MPEG standards that have been created include MPEG-2, which defines a standard for digital television with CD-quality audio. It uses a similar encoding scheme to that of MPEG-1, but is further refined to deal with more complex or interlaced information; MPEG-1 was designed to work with only two channels of audio. DVDs are based on the MPEG-2 standard, and can work with multiple audio channels.

MPEG-4 defines standards for multimedia applications for the Internet. This standard addresses the need for universal standards in unstable environments, or in those susceptible to high error rates, such as those found in computing networks. It codes content objects, and allows them to be manipulated either one at a time or as a group in audiovisual environments.

MPEG-7 defines a standard for describing features of multimedia environments for the purposes of conducting information searches. This standard will allow, for example, search engines to extend their current capabilities from text-based searches to those including visual and/or audio information.

MPEG-21, when completed, will define standards for multimedia frameworks designed to support the creation, production, and retrieval of content over networks characterized by different hardware and network architecture. In other words, the MPEG-21 standard will describe how the various parts of this type of multimedia environment relate to each other.

It is worth noting that an MPEG-3 standard was originally discussed to target High Definition Television (HDTV) applications. However, both MPEG-1 and MPEG-2 standards were later adjusted to work better with HDTV-rate video, eliminating the need for an MPEG-3 standard.

Alternatives to MPEG include QuickTime, which was used as the basis for MPEG-4, and Video for Windows.

Bibliography

Haskell, Barry; Puri, Atul; and Arun Netravali. *Digital Video: An Introduction to MPEG-2.* New York: Chapman & Hall, 1997.

———. *Digital Video Compression Standard.* New York: Chapman & Hall, 1996.

LeGall, Didier. "MPEG: A Video Compression Standard for Multimedia Applications." *Communications of the ACM,* vol. 34, no. 4 (April 1991), pp. 47–58.

Moving Picture Experts Group. "MPEG Standards." 2000. <http://www.cselt.it/mpeg/standards.htm> (April 1, 2002).

MPEG.org. "MPEG Pointers and Resources." 2001. <http://www.mpeg.org/MPEG/index.html> (April 1, 2002).

Further Reading

Chiariglione, Leonardo. "MPEG and Multimedia Communications." *IEEE Trans. CSVT,* vol. 7, no. 1 (February 1997).

Mitchell, Joan; Pennebaker, William; Fogg, Chad; and Didier LeGall. *MPEG Video Compression Standard.* New York: Chapman & Hall, 1997.

Related Topics

Compression; Digital Audio; MP3; Multimedia; QuickTime

— *Art Ramirez*

MUDs and MOOs

MUDs and MOOs are computer programs that allow multiple users from remote locations to interact with the program and communicate with each other. The acronym MUD originally stood for Multi-User Dungeon, and is also sometimes translated as Multi-User Dimension or Multi-User Domain. The acronym MOO stands for MUD, Object-Oriented, and refers to a particular type of MUD program.

Although there have been some recent experiments in adding graphics to MUDs, most MUDs are text-based. People using a MUD send typed text to the program, and in return see text from the program and from other users on their computer screens. Like other chat systems available online, MUDs allow people to communicate in real time, and many MUDs are used primarily for conversation and socializing.

How MUDs Work

MUDs are primarily accessed through Telnet, a program that enables people to connect to and enter commands on remote computers on the Internet. However, most MUD participants, or "mudders," use "client programs," which create easier-to-read and more user-friendly interfaces to the MUD. Most client programs also enable mudders to connect to more than one MUD at a time. Because MUDs generally appear as a window of text on a user's computer screen, the user might play an adventure game on one MUD, for instance, while simultaneously engaging in conversation on a different MUD. Many mudders pride themselves on being good at engaging in other activities, computer-related or not, while mudding.

Once connected to the MUD, participants must log on as a "character" on that MUD. Each character has a unique name (or names), and most MUDs require a password to reserve that name and character for a particular participant. Characters also include a text description (which can be viewed by other participants using a "look" command) and a range of other information, depending on the MUD. At a minimum, most characters include a gender designation, although these are rarely limited to male and female; many MOOs, for instance, have up to 13 different gender designations. Some MUDs allow users to create characters on the spot, or to use a generic "guest" character, while others require users to contact the person who runs the MUD program (usually through email) to acquire a character.

Each MUD consists of different virtual "rooms." A large MUD may have as many as 200 or more characters logged on at once, but these characters are scattered throughout a variety of different rooms, with perhaps no more than 20 in any given room. Users move their characters through the different rooms by typing simple commands such as "up," "down," "north," "south," and so on. For the sake of speed and ease of typing, most of these commands can also be abbreviated by typing only the first letter of the word. MUD commands also allow people to determine who is connected to the MUD, and who is in the same room. Participants can easily communicate with all people located in the same room. In addition, MUDs include commands that allow users to "page" people in other rooms, or to "whisper" to only one other person in the room with them.

On most MUDs, a single person or a small group of people—called "wizards" on some MUDs, "gods" on others—are responsible for the maintenance of the MUD program, implementation of new features, and in some cases, arbitration of disputes among participants.

The most significant difference between MUDs and other chat software (as well as most other gaming programs) is that most MUDs allow any participant to add to the program itself through the creation of virtual objects. These objects range from very simple objects consisting of a simple description ("you see a small round ball on the floor"), to more complex objects that can react to several commands. A more complex "ball" object might, for instance, allow the user to type in "pick up ball," resulting in text from the MUD program stating, "You pick up the ball." A further command of "throw ball" might result in "You throw the ball, which bounces wildly around the room." Other participants would see the text, "Lori throws the ball, which bounces wildly around the room." Virtual objects and the commands associated with them create the feel of a virtual environment, adding to the richness of MUD interactions.

Uses of MUDs

Many MUDs are primarily for socializing; however, MUDs began life as online interactive textual games, and some, called combat MUDs, are still primarily used for gaming. Combat MUDs do allow players to communicate with each other, and some combat MUDs have developed complex and long-standing social communities. Another popular use of MUDs, especially in TinyMUDs and MOOs, is role-playing.

Role-playing MUDs adopt a theme, often based on science fiction or fantasy literature, and all participants assume fictional roles within the interactive, mutually developed story line. Role-players differentiate between "in-character" (IC) and "out-of-character" (OOC) interactions, with most public interactions on a role-playing MUD being IC interactions. (Groups of participants on a role-playing MUD will sometimes set up a separate social MUD for the purpose of OOC discussions.) Participants have described role-playing MUDs as a form of interactive storytelling with the added element of improvisational drama. Popular themes for role-playing MUDs include the TV show *Star Trek*, Anne McCaffrey's "Pern" books, Roger Zelazny's "Amber" books, and the White Wolf role-playing games.

The ability to program objects enables people to import and jointly view and discuss documents, making MUDs of interest to educators and other professionals. Among educational MUDs, some—like Cyberion City—are available to the public, while others function as private classrooms or extensions of college classes. Professional groups also use MUDs for Computer-Supported Cooperative Work (CSCW). For instance, BioMOO and MediaMOO are meeting spaces for biologists and media researchers, respectively.

A Brief History of MUDs

The first MUD, called MUD1, was developed in 1979 and 1980 by Roy Trubshaw and Richard Bartle, both then students at Essex University in the U.K. MUD1 was a multi-player online game, similar to computer games such as Zork and Advent—Dungeons and Dragons–inspired games that had been available since the early 1970s. These earlier games, which were also text-based, allowed players to explore virtual terrain, search for treasures, and solve puzzles, but could be played by only one person at a time. MUD1 immediately attracted outside attention, primarily from computer-science students in several countries. Many of the original players began developing their own MUD programs, making continual technical improvements.

During their first decade of development, MUDs were still primarily gaming programs. Two particularly influential programs still in use today are AberMUD, developed in 1987 by Alan Cox, then a student at the University of Aberystwyth, Wales; and LP MUD, developed in 1989 by Lars Pensjö, a student at the Chalmers University in Gothenburg, Sweden.

In 1988, James Aspnes of Carnegie Mellon University developed a type of MUD program called TinyMUD. TinyMUD differed from most previous MUD programs in that it had no specific game-related hierarchy of players, did not assign points for solving puzzles or succeeding in combat, and allowed all users to create extensions to the database, programming objects and rooms that other users could explore and interact with. This enabled users both to socialize more easily and to experiment with the creation of virtual environments. TinyMUD became extremely popular for these purposes.

In early 1990, Stephen White developed the first MOO program. MOO programs make it easier for users to create and develop rooms and objects. Later that year, Pavel Curtis, a programmer at Xerox Palo Alto Research Center (PARC), significantly added to White's program and opened the first publicly available MOO, called LambdaMOO. No longer based at Xerox PARC, LambdaMOO is one of the longest-running and most famous MUDs.

While the type of program does not dictate its use, AberMUDs and LP MUDs tend to be used as combat MUDs. TinyMUDs and MOOs are more likely to be used for socializing, chat, and role-playing. Most educational and professional MUDs use MOO programs.

MUDs were primarily developed and used by college computer-science students; the growing MUD subculture cooperated in continuously improving and developing new MUD programs. Richard Bartle went on to develop commercial gaming MUDs, but most MUDs have been available free of charge to users. College students still make up a large proportion of MUD participants; however, in addition to the increase in older populations using MUDs for professional and educational purposes, as MUDs have aged, to some extent, their user population has aged along with them. Many people who started mudding in 1989 are still participating, balancing their online activities with the increasing demands of their careers and family lives.

Some have predicted the demise of MUDs as the availability of greater bandwidth allows for easier use of real-time video and other graphics capabilities. However, others have suggested that text allows for greater user creativity than graphics programs. (Pavel Curtis, for instance, frequently uses the example that most people can describe a tree more effectively than they can draw one.) In addition, the ability of participants to mask their identities and represent themselves in ways that differ from their offline appearance may contribute to MUDs' continued popularity. Currently, MUDs are a relatively small but vibrant online subculture.

Bibliography

Burka, Lauren P. "The MUDdex." 1993. <http://www.apocalypse.org/pub/u/lpb/muddex> (March 29, 2002).

Kendall, Lori. *Hanging Out in the Virtual Pub: Identity, Masculinities, and Relationships Online.* Berkeley, Calif.: University of California Press, 2002.

Reid, Elizabeth. "Cultural Formations in Text-Based Virtual Realities." Master's thesis, University of Melbourne, 1994. <http://www.aluluei.com> (March 29, 2002).

Further Reading

Cherny, Lynn. *Conversation and Community: Chat in a Virtual World.* Stanford, Calif.: CSLI Publications, 1999.

Curtis, Pavel. "Mudding: Social Phenomena in Text-Based Virtual Realities." *Intertek* 3, 1993, pp. 26–34. <http://ftp.game.org/pub/mud/text/research/DIAC92.txt> (March 29, 2002).

Dibbell, Julian. *My Tiny Life: Crime and Passion in a Virtual World.* New York: Henry Holt, 1998.

Fanderclai, Tari. "MUDs in Education: New Environments, New Pedagogies." *Computer-Mediated Communication Magazine,* vol. 2, no. 1 (January 1995). <http://www.ibiblio.org/cmc/mag/1995/jan/fanderclai.html> (March 29, 2002).

Rheingold, Howard. *The Virtual Community: Homesteading on the Electronic Frontier.* Reading, Mass.: Addison-Wesley, 1993.

Turkle, Sherry. *Life on the Screen: Identity in the Age of the Internet.* New York: Simon & Schuster, 1995.

Related Topics:
Computer-Supported Collaborative Work; Chat; Internet Relay Chat; LambdaMOO; TinyMUD; Virtual Community; Xerox Palo Alto Research Center

— Lori Kendall

Multimedia

Multimedia refers to the integration of multiple media forms, including text, music, spoken words, video, illustrated graphics, and still photographs, to communicate unified messages that, ideally at least, are also interactive. Optical data storage made multimedia a watchword in the computer industry in the mid-1980s, and after the release of the multimedia-rich Mosaic Web browser in 1993, combined-media forms have been increasingly apparent on the Internet. When presented using hypertext links, digital multimedia becomes "hypermedia."

Some of the most powerful and popular forms of modern multimedia are found in CD-ROM video games running on specialized computer consoles like Sony's Playstation, Microsoft's Xbox, and Nintendo's GameCube, all of which contain potent multimedia-rendering processors. Multimedia elements also are present on many Web sites, especially those that use Macromedia Flash software to generate low-bandwidth animation, video, and sound along with explanatory text. PC-bound CD-ROMs like the *Guinness Encyclopedia* are also crowded with multimedia elements.

Even traditional TV, already a multimedia platform (although not an interactive one), has recently tried to up its multimedia ante. In 2001, CNN's Headline News service changed format, splitting the TV screen four ways in an apparent effort to mimic the look of a busy multimedia Web site, crowding the news anchor's image into one corner of the screen while flashing two separate textual news stories below and running graphics or video in a fourth segmented space beside the anchor.

Meanwhile, virtual reality (VR) developers, such as those at the University of Illinois at Chicago's Electronic Visualization Lab, are focused on making multimedia an immersive sensory experience that a person can walk into and interact with, rather than something read, heard, and viewed from a desktop computer or television screen.

THE BEGINNINGS OF MULTIMEDIA

The history of multimedia arguably ranges back to 3,000 B.C.E., when Chinese entertainers used firelight to project silhouetted puppets on a screen, presumably combining their visual presentations with vocal sounds. In fact, those ancient displays are not that far removed from the definition of "multimedia" that was popular in the 1960s, when rock bands such as the Grateful Dead and Pink Floyd used movies, slides, strobe lights, black lights, and overhead projectors filled with colored oils to accompany their onstage performances, creating a kind of sensory overload. Perhaps the most famous of the rock-music multimedia presentations was artist Andy Warhol's "Plastic Exploding Inevitable," created in 1966 to showcase the Velvet Underground, the group that Warhol managed at the time. Those presentations used Warhol's movies, distortedly projected through colored gelatin plates, along with various colored spotlights and strobes flashing on the musicians; dancers and various props such as bullwhips, barbells, and wooden crosses rounded out the visual imagery.

In their 2001 book *Multimedia: From Wagner to Virtual Reality,* editors Randall Packer and Ken Jordan argue that the modern history of multimedia has roots in an 1849 essay by German composer Richard Wagner, titled "The Artwork of the Future," which introduced the concept of "total artwork." According to Packer and Jordan, Wagner was the first modern artist to systematically attempt to integrate all arts.

"It would be difficult to overstate the power of this idea and its influence," the editors assert. "(Wagner's) drive to embrace the full range of human experience, and to reflect it in his operas, led him to give equal attention to every aspect of its production. He was convinced that only through this integration could he attain the expressive powers he desired to transform music drama into a vehicle capable of affecting German culture." Wagner's ideas remained among the underlying tenets in the development of multimedia well into the computer age.

The multimedia concept continued to evolve after Wagner. Photography developed, as did the first telegraph lines—both important steps along the way to modern multimedia. The end of the nineteenth century witnessed the creation of sound recordings and motion pictures, although the two were not integrated successfully until the late 1920s. In a 1916 essay, Italian Futurist poet and writer F. T. Marinetti declared that film was the ultimate art form, because it integrated all art forms. (Since movies at first were silent, early theaters integrated sound by hiring a piano player to provide musical accompaniment, and the films commonly used onscreen text panels to display dialogue.) Cutting-edge, mid-century artists like John Cage worked to break down the boundaries between audience and art by pioneering collaborative performances that encouraged, even demanded, participation from the audience—an early form of interactivity.

Digital Multimedia

Early computers were calculating machines, not powerful multimedia devices. But some pioneers like hypertext inventor Ted Nelson and psychologist/computer scientist J. C. R. Licklider described rough multimedia computing in the early and mid-1960s. Inventor and theorist Douglas Engelbart exhibited the first genuine digital multimedia in 1968, when he demonstrated his NLS (oNLine System), which offered pioneering displays of computer-based video-conferencing and hypermedia, and showed off such innovations as the first computer mouse, operating system "windows," email, word processing, and one of the earliest examples of successful hypertext. Although Engelbart would receive little public recognition for his achievement, the demonstration proved crucially influential to many later computer developers, notably Alan Kay—inventor of a prototype personal computer (the Dynabook), the Smalltalk programming language, and the graphical user interface—and Tim Berners-Lee, the founder of the World Wide Web. With the NLS, Engelbart established the groundwork for all digital multimedia to follow.

In fact, the accomplishments of many people contributed to the development of digital multimedia as we know it today, but in terms of putting multimedia in the hands of artists and designers, the achievements of Marc Canter during the mid-to-late 1980s have proved to be among the most crucial. Canter, founder of Macromind Inc. (later Macromedia), was himself a musician, a music-video producer, a software programmer, and an entrepreneur, who was impressed by the graphical user interface (GUI) displays being mass-marketed by Apple Computer in the early 1980s. (The Commodore Amiga, released in 1985, combined advanced graphics, sound, and video capabilities, and was actually the first real multimedia PC.) Using his unusual set of skills, Canter produced the first multimedia authoring systems for desktop computers, SoundWorks and VideoWorks.

Authoring systems, as Canter has described them, are hardware and software tools that allow for the design of interactive programs; the hardware—the computer—converts information to machine-readable formats, and the software makes it possible for non-programmers, especially artists and musicians, to build complex multimedia programs. Canter handed creative people with little or no grounding in arcane computer programming languages a way to transfer their art into the digital realm, and to merge artistic endeavors in ways that Wagner never imagined. Canter's design became the standard for all future new-media development.

Multimedia programs at first were sold as CD-ROMs, the only format in those still-early days of personal computing that could hold the immense amounts of data that multimedia programs use; old-fashioned floppy disks could not compete. In a 1991 essay, Sony Computer Peripheral Products Co. vice president Olaf Olafsson noted that there were already 1,000 CD-ROMs being marketed at the beginning of the 1990s. In that article, he praised multimedia as representing "a technique that will eventually make interactions between humans and computers more interactive than ever." The new optically stored multimedia format was seen, by Olaf and others, as representing a future boon not only to entertainment through games, but also to education through interactive CD-ROM versions of encyclopedias and specialized education software. But in 1991, another major innovation was on its way.

Multimedia and the World Wide Web

At about the same time that Olafsson was publishing his essay, Tim Berners-Lee was busy perfecting and selling his peers on his new invention, the World Wide Web. While multimedia was not specifically a part of the proposal that Berners-Lee made to his employers at the CERN nuclear physics lab in Switzerland while pitching the project, he did mention in his prospectus that multimedia elements could eventually be integrated into his global content-distribution scheme. Two years later, with the introduction of the Mosaic browser by developers at the University of Illinois at Urbana-Champaign, it became clear just how effective the Web could be as a conduit for multimedia programs. The browser was easy to download and install, had a simple-to-use point-and-click interface, and was capable of displaying color images, launching video and sound clips, and running animations, all at the same time. To many in the general public, Mosaic was a revelation, and with its release the World Wide Web phenomenon was born.

The early Web was constrained by lack of network bandwidth, which prevented such "rich" and data-heavy media elements as audio and video from being transmitted efficiently. One response was the invention of the low-bandwidth authoring software that was purchased in 1995 by Macromedia and marketed as Flash. Flash made multimedia elements usable even over the then-standard 28.8kbps (kilobits per second) dial-up connections most computer users had access to through their Internet service providers (ISPs). Flash, which relies on fairly clunky animations (which can nonetheless be used to terrific effect by talented artists), remains popular, and the problem of low bandwidth remains an issue for most Web users. Consumers connected to the Internet through broadband cable connections and digital subscriber lines (DSL) remain very much in the minority, keeping the richest forms of multimedia out of many Web users' reach.

One of the most important developments in Internet multimedia during the past five years has been the arrival of "streaming" media, first introduced and popularized by Real Networks' groundbreaking RealAudio software—which was quickly followed by a RealVideo cousin, and later by Microsoft's competing platform, Windows Media Player, among other upstarts. Streaming media plays in near-real-time by feeding part of an audio or video signal into a computer and launching the file even as later portions of the signal are still incoming from the Internet. This play-on-the-fly feature saves a great deal of time and bandwidth, since the user does not have to wait for the entire file to download before viewing it. Streaming media has allowed many more Web developers to integrate hypermedia elements into their Web pages, and many more Web users to take advantage of at least some "lo-fi" forms of multimedia.

Nicholas Negroponte—whose Media Lab at the Massachusetts Institute of Technology (MIT) opened in 1985, in part, to further multimedia applications research—said in a 1994 *Wired* magazine essay that developments in multimedia would democratize the arts, eventually creating an adult population that would be much more "visually literate" and entirely more artistic than at present. "Ten years from now," Negroponte wrote, "teenagers are likely to enjoy a much richer panorama of options because the pursuit of intellectual achievement will not be tilted in favor of bookworms, but cater to a range of expressive tastes."

Debates About Multimedia

Not everyone is enamored of the tendency of Web and computer developers to focus on multimedia, or "rich media" elements, in their offerings. While video games are among the most significantly interactive multimedia platforms, very little text—and therefore, very little reading—is involved, and so their ability to help children learn has been questioned.

On the Web, which started as a text-based medium and remains heavily textual, some critics charge that too much multimedia serves as little more than a distraction to the Web user. Web usability guru Jakob Nielsen, for example, warned about this problem in 1995, saying that an animated object moving on a computer screen at the periphery of a reader's vision makes it hard to concentrate on the essential text. He also warned against bandwidth-clogging video segments, and said that audio is best used to establish a mood or atmosphere of a site, as is done so effectively in the video game Myst.

Michael Dertouzos, director of the MIT Computer Science Lab, wrote in his 1997 book, *What Will Be: How the New World of Information Will Change Our Lives,* that multimedia's promise "includes a lot of wishful thinking." Computers, even by the late 1990s, were incapable of processing video as well as text, he wrote, making it difficult for the two media truly to work in tandem, which is the entire point. Dertouzos preferred a new approach that he called "multi-modal," which would make several methods of conveying a message work together in a way that is easy to understand. An example, he wrote, would be a word-processing text editor that allows a writer to draw a line through text on a screen with a stylus. The computer would then respond appropriately to the user's voice command, "Delete." Such methods, Dertouzos wrote, could make multiple media work in concert for users.

Writer, analyst, and new-media critic Esther Dyson, in her book *Release 2.0: A Design for Living in the Digital Age,* openly worries that the ability to throw multimedia elements together—for instance, a video segment of oneself accompanying an email—might tend in the long run to be harmful to education and to human knowledge. Dyson fears that over-reliance on multimedia could cause humans to "lose the power of mere words," which she notes are inexpensive to create and distribute, unlike the "jumps and flashes" of digitized multimedia. "I don't want to sound like a Luddite," Dyson wrote in her book, "but I think it's bad for our minds. Images may sell, but they don't enlighten. We're in danger of getting a society where people don't bother to think or assess consequences."

Such concerns notwithstanding, multimedia's development and use continue unabated. Marketers for companies such as BMW, for example, have taken to using the Web's multimedia capabilities, giving potential customers informational material to read about its cars on the same Web site that allows them to watch specially created Web movies starring the likes of singer Madonna, which use a more emotionally appealing approach to get people interested in their product. And VR scientists like Thomas DeFanti and Jaron Lanier continue to push multimedia's possibilities by creating virtual spaces that people can enter while wearing special head gear and earphones to experience what amounts to separate "worlds," a process that DeFanti calls "tele-immersion." There

have even been efforts to make such spaces portable, or to transport them onto desktop machines. Says DeFanti, "Tele-immersion, in one form or another, is catching on."

"It might be fair to say that the medium's only defining element is its mutability," write *Multimedia* editors Packer and Jordan. "We can't possibly predict the variety of its various manifestations. Perhaps multimedia's most consistent quality will be its relentlessly changing nature."

Bibliography

Alderman, John. *Sonic Boom: Napster, MP3, and the New Pioneers of Music.* Cambridge, Mass.: Perseus Publishing, 2001.

Atomic Rom Productions. "Great Moments in Multimedia History." 1996, 2001. <http://home.earthlink.net/~atomic_rom/moments.htm> (May 31, 2002).

Dertouzos, Michael. *What Will Be: How the New World of Information Will Change Our Lives.* San Francisco, Calif.: HarperEdge, 1997.

Dyson, Esther. *Release 2.1: A Design for Living in the Digital Age.* New York: Broadway Books, 1998.

Nielsen, Jakob. "Guidelines for Multimedia on the Web." Useit.com Alertbox, December 1995. <http://www.useit.com/alertbox/9512.html> (May 31, 2002)

Olafsson, Olaf. "The Multiplier: Future Productivity in Light of Optical Storage." *Technology 2001: The Future of Computing and Communications.* Derek Leebaert, ed. Cambridge, Mass.: MIT Press, 1991.

Packer, Randall, and Ken Jordan, eds. *Multimedia: From Wagner to Virtual Reality.* New York: W. W. Norton, 2001.

Stranahan, Paul. "Cable TV: Advanced Technologies." Jones Telecommunications & Multimedia Encyclopedia, 1994–99. <http://www.jonesencyclo.com/encyclo/update/catvtech.html> (May 31, 2002).

Further Reading

Ketchum, Bob. "A Timeline of Audio/Video Technology." Robin's Video Web Site, 1997. <http://penny100.home.mindspring.com/info/timeline.htm> (May 31, 2002).

McBride, Al, and Scott Brown. "A Multi-Dimensional Look at the Future of On-line Technology." *Technology 2001: The Future of Computing and Communications.* Derek Leebaert, ed. Cambridge, Mass.: MIT Press, 1991.

Mewton, Conrad. *All You Need to Know About Music & the Internet Revolution.* London: Sanctuary, 2001.

Negroponte, Nicholas. "Digital Expression." Media Lab, Massachusetts Institute of Technology, December 1, 1994. <http://nicholas.www.media.mit.edu/people/nicholas/Wired/WIRED2-12.html> (May 31, 2002).

Pidgeon, Billy; Hertzberg, Robert; Sinnreich, Aram; and Seamus McAteer. "Streaming Video: Effective Deployment Necessitates Contextual Integration." *Jupiter Vision Report,* October 18, 2000.

Poon, Theresa V. "What's Next for Streaming Media?" *The Industry Standard,* February 14, 2001. <http://www.thestandard.com/article/0,1902,22225,00.html> (May 31, 2002).

Samuels, Edward. *The Illustrated Story of Copyright.* New York: Thomas Dunne Books/St. Martin's Press, 2000.

Related Topics

Anderson, Laurie; Broadband; CD-R, CD-ROM, and DVD; DeFanti, Thomas; Digital Music; Dyson, Esther; Eno, Brian; Flash; Lanier, Jaron; Moog, Robert; MP3; MPEG; QuickTime; World Wide Web

— Kevin Featherly

n n n n n **N** n n n n n

Napster

While the final verdict on Napster's impact has yet to be rendered, the music file-sharing service is universally recognized for launching peer-to-peer networking into the mainstream. While its foes in the music industry claim that Napster facilitated Internet piracy on a monumental scale, supporters call it a bellwether program that revolutionized music distribution.

College freshman Shawn Fanning began work on what would become the Napster program in his Northeastern University dorm room in January 1999. His roommates, music fans who collected songs in the MP3 computer file format, had complained that Web sites offering MP3s for free download were often clogged by too many users, that they listed files that were no longer available, or that they had been shut down entirely for offering copyrighted music without permission. Fanning set about creating a system that would allow users to swap files directly from one another, without having to go to a Web site. He named the software Napster in tribute to his own nappy hair. When he finished the first version of the program, he shared it with some friends, and it quickly became apparent to Fanning that his software had tremendous potential. He dropped out of college, formed Napster, Inc., and with the help of others released an early version of the software in the summer of 1999.

Users who launched the program while connected to the Internet were plugged into Napster's central computer system, and the MP3 files they had designated to share were added to Napster's continuously updated index of files available at that moment. Napster, it should be noted, did not store MP3s, but only indexed files that were stored on its users' own computers. If users turned off their computers or otherwise disconnected from Napster, their files were no longer available, and were removed from the index. A user searching for a particular song typed the song title or artist's name into Napster's search engine, and a list of results would be returned from the index showing matching files held by other Napster users. By selecting one of the files, the user would begin downloading it directly from another user's computer.

Word-of-mouth endorsements and media coverage helped ensure Napster's quick adoption in the online music community, particularly on college campuses with speedy Internet connections. Many industry observers heralded the program as the most important Internet development since the Web browser.

The music industry, which had been steadily losing ground in its fight to halt unauthorized MP3 trading, saw Napster as a formidable threat. A Web site that offered MP3s to millions of downloaders without the permission of the artist or the music label could still potentially be tracked and closed through court action; stopping individual users from swapping single files among themselves was a much more difficult task. In December 1999, the Recording Industry Association of America (RIAA), a trade group representing the major music companies, sued Napster, Inc., charging that the company facilitated piracy.

Napster's ease of use, coupled with its outlaw status as a source of free music under fire, captured the popular imagination. An estimated 50 million people had signed up to use the program 18 months after its release. Artists chose sides in the debate: Hard-rock band Metallica and rapper Dr. Dre filed their own piracy suits against the company, while rapper Chuck D defended Napster and rap-metal band Limp Bizkit embraced the company as a sponsor.

With Napster facing potential fines that could put the company out of business, computer programmers began developing other peer-to-peer networks, such as Gnutella and Freenet. Unlike Napster, these systems are not owned by anyone, nor do they route files through a central server, which makes them nearly impossible to shut down. However, the systems are also less stable than Napster, and require more computer experience from their users.

From the beginning, Napster and its supporters positioned the service as a new business model for a music industry undergoing transformation in the digital era. The company could theoretically charge a monthly subscription fee for the ability to swap major

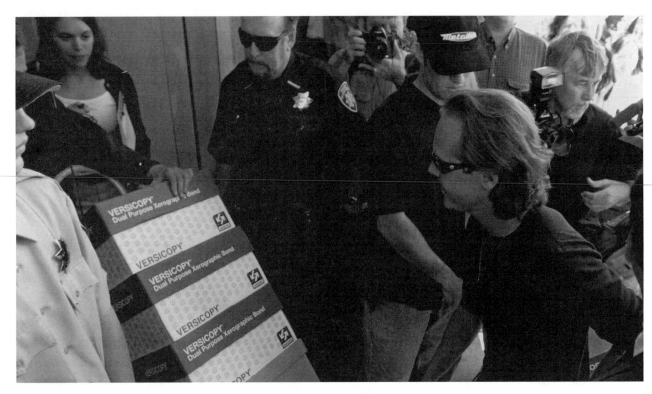

In May 2000, Metallica drummer Lars Ullrich (right) delivers the names of more than 317,000 Napster users who the band claims have illegally traded Metallica songs. (AP Photo/Ben Margot)

labels' copyrighted songs with permission. In October 2000, Bertelsmann—parent company to the BMG family of labels, which had released million-selling albums by Dave Matthews Band and Santana—announced a subscription alliance with Napster, if Napster could first develop a new version of its software that would track file trading for royalty payments to artists, labels, and publishers. Five months later, two of the other five major music companies, Sony and Universal, announced that they would develop a Napster competitor program called Duet.

In July 2000, a federal judge issued a preliminary ruling siding with the music industry in its piracy case. The judge's injunction against Napster was upheld by the Ninth Circuit Court of Appeals in February 2001, and Napster began attempts to filter from its system copyrighted songs that major labels wanted blocked. By July 2001, the company was officially shut down. Throughout 2002 Bertelsmann attempted to purchase Napster while simultaneously keeping it afloat; Napster finally accepted a buyout offer in May but the deal was rejected by the bankruptcy judge presiding over the case. In fall 2002 a trustee was appointed to oversee the bankruptcy reorganization.

Despite its short lifespan, Napster's overwhelming popularity with users seems to indicate that file-sharing will play a large role in the future of digital music.

Successor programs such as Gnutela and KaZaA continue to provide music-swapping opportunities. If subscription models are embraced as a new avenue for music distribution, Napster will rightly be seen as a pioneer in this revolution for the music industry.

Bibliography

Alderman, John. *Sonic Boom: Napster, MP3, and the New Pioneers of Music.* Cambridge, Mass.: Perseus Pub., 2001.

Electronic Frontier Foundation Archive. "Intellectual Property/ Peer-to-Peer Network Filesharing Archive." March 2002. <http://www.eff.org/intellectual_property/P2P/> (April 1, 2002).

Sonicnet.com. The Napster Watch. 1999–2001. <http://www.sonicnet.com/news/special_coverage/ napster_watch/index.jhtml> (April 1, 2002).

Further Reading

Haring, Bruce. *Beyond the Charts: MP3 and the Digital Music Revolution.* Los Angeles, Calif.: JM Northern Media, 2000.

Heilemann, John. "David Boies: The Wired Interview." *Wired* 8.10, October 2000. <http://www.wired.com/wired/archive/8.10/boies.html> (April 1, 2002).

Tapscott, Don. *Growing Up Digital: The Rise of the Net Generation.* New York: McGraw-Hill, 1998.

Related Topics

Compression; Digital Music; Freenet (File-Sharing Network); Lessig, Lawrence; MPEG; MP3; MP3.com; Peer-to-Peer

— *Chris Nelson*

Narrowcasting

Narrowcasting refers to a customized version of broadcasting that targets information to a specific, narrowly defined group of recipients—or, at the extreme, to a specific individual—at a particular time and place. Since Internet-based media offer the ability to customize information delivery on an unprecedented scale, these media potentially facilitate the extension of narrowcasting to an increasing variety of informational services and products.

In a documentary on the origins of broadcasting, Mike Adams notes that the term narrowcasting is as old as broadcasting itself, and was invoked by radio pioneer Charles Herrold in the early 1900s to refer to point-to-point wireless transmissions. (The term broadcasting was adapted from the description of agricultural machinery that distributed seed across a wide area.) Narrowcasting later came to characterize the fragmentation of the broadcast audience. It has been used, for example, to describe the increasing reliance of radio upon niche markets as television gained ascendancy during the 1950s. Later, the term was adapted to describe network television's response to competition from cable stations that fragmented the television market and fostered programming tailored to specific demographic and interest groups (women, sports fans, and so on). In this context, narrowcasting represents a market response to a multi-channel environment, in which it is difficult for any one channel to consistently monopolize the majority (or a significant minority) of the viewing audience. As media scholars Sut Jhally and Bill Livant argue, segmenting the audience has the added commercial benefit of allowing advertisers to target viewers more efficiently.

Although narrowcasting relies heavily on some form of interactivity (since narrowcasters need to know enough about their audience to customize content), it no longer refers to two-way, point-to-point transmission. Rather, it most frequently describes a one-to-many model of distribution, wherein audience members receive personalized or niche content. Customized "push" technologies that allow users to specify what type of information they are interested in and then to receive, for example, a customized electronic newspaper tailored to their interests, represent one way in which digital media facilitate narrowcasting as a means of allowing users to filter the rapidly proliferating quantity of available information.

Digital narrowcasting relies heavily on interactive technology, as well as on computer-based techniques for processing consumer data and customizing content. Whereas developing individualized radio or television content may once have been prohibitively expensive, digitization makes it increasingly easy. Bill Gates, for example, anticipates that one day television programming and advertising will be readily customizable to provide viewers with the cast members of their choice. Michael Lewis, writing for *The New York Times*, describes the way in which digital television anticipates the autonomization of this process: "Intelligent" TVs will learn viewer preferences and seek out relevant programming. Eventually, information about preferences can be used to create custom-tailored programming.

One possible result of such developments is that the anticipated convergence of electronic media on the Internet may be accompanied by the fragmentation of the mass audience into narrower and more specifically defined categories. Digital-television services already facilitate the ability of audience members to customize their viewing menus and to continue the process of time-shifting enabled by VCRs. In an era of narrowcasting, content providers would no longer assume a mass audience that consumes the same programming at the same time. Rather, content could be customized not just according to the audience members' tastes, but also according to their location in time and space. Digital radio, for example, might be able to provide a tourist driving through a foreign city with information about restaurants or movies playing in the vicinity. This information could be further customized to fit the user's profile of culinary and cinematic tastes.

The tastes, behaviors, and even location of consumers will become an increasingly important resource for narrowcasters, and perhaps an increasingly important site for the struggle over privacy protection. Moreover, the fragmentation of content delivery raises the question of the fate of shared culture in a digitized society. For example, some people worry that narrowcasting may undermine the basis for shared public discussion and debate. Others argue that narrowcasting, in conjunction with the interactive potential of the Internet, may help facilitate the social mobilization of disparate and far-flung users around shared sets of interests and concerns. The question raised by these differing views is whether the result of customized information delivery will be a more informed collectivity or an increasingly fragmented and alienated audience.

Bibliography

Adams, Mike. "Broadcasting's Forgotten Father: The Charles Herrold Story." PBS, 1994. <http://www.oldradio.com/archives/jurassic/Doc_Herrold_TV_Show.htm> (April 1, 2002).

Carter, Meg. "Technology Alarm Call." *Campaign*, November 10, 2000, p. 41.

Gates, Bill. *The Road Ahead*. New York: Penguin, 1996.

Jhally, Sut, and Bill Livant. "Watching as Working: The Valorization of Audience Consciousness." *Journal of Communication*, vol. 36, no. 3 (1986), pp. 124–43.

Lewis, Michael. "Boombox." *The New York Times Magazine*, August 13, 2000. <http://www.nytimes.com/library/magazine/home/20000813mag-boombox.html> (April 1, 2002).

Further Reading

Albarran, Alan B., and David H. Goff. *Understanding the Web: Social, Political, and Economic Dimensions of the Internet*. Ames: Iowa State University Press, 2000.

Massey, Kimberly. "Narrowcasting." Museum of Broadcasting. <http://www.mbcnet.org/ETV/N/htmlN/narrowcasting/narrowcasting.htm> (April 1, 2002).

Owen, Bruce M. *The Internet Challenge to Television*. Cambridge, Mass.: Harvard University Press, 1999.

Vane, Edwin T., and Lynn S. Gross. *Programming for TV, Radio, and Cable*. Boston, Mass.: Focal Press, 1994.

Related Topics

Data Mining; Digital Television; Privacy

— *Mark Andrejevic*

Negroponte, Nicholas

1944–

Founder and Director, Media Laboratory, Massachusetts Institute of Technology

Nicholas Negroponte is a professor of media technology at the Massachusetts Institute of Technology (MIT) and the founding director of the MIT Media Laboratory, an institution that he helped establish, he said, "to invent the future." He gained fame with his best-selling book, *Being Digital* (1995), which stunned readers with wild predictions about a digital future in which technology becomes an intimate part of everyday life.

Negroponte was born in 1944 into a wealthy Greek shipping family, growing up in Switzerland, London, and New York. However, despite a privileged childhood, Negroponte and his three brothers were forced to pave their own way in the world as adults. "My father gave all of us infinite education and nothing after that," he told *The Boston Globe*. "When I turned 30, he sent me $500 as a present, nothing since."

Part of his "infinite education" took him to MIT in 1961, where he studied architecture. The discipline directed him toward the use of computers as a tool in architectural design. In 1966, the crisply dressed and persuasive 22-year-old Negroponte joined the MIT faculty, working as a visiting professor at Yale University, the University of Michigan, and the University of California at Berkeley at about the same time. In 1968, he founded the MIT Architecture Machine Group, an institution that performed some of the first human-computer interface research. Negroponte wrote a book in 1970, *Architecture Machine: Toward a More Human Environment*, detailing his work. In 1980, he was the founding chairman of the International Federation of Information Processing Societies' Computers in Everyday Life program, founded in Amsterdam.

At the beginning of the 1980s, personal computers were just beginning to hint at the profound role that digital multimedia might play in everyday lives, and Negroponte conceived the MIT Media Lab in response. With the strong patronage of MIT president Jerome Wiesner, the lab launched in 1985 with a mandate to raise funds and to find creative ways to develop new digital-media technologies. It was a controversial move; the lab grew out of MIT's School of Architecture rather than out of its School of Electrical Engineering, which housed the computer-science department. The lab's plans had little to do with architecture, either, even if the building it was housed in was a state-of-the-art facility designed by I. M. Pei. In a *Boston Globe* article published at the time of the lab's launch, Negroponte said its mission was "to couple people primarily interested in advanced new technology . . . with the 'community of users' who would apply it in a variety of fields, such as education, music, medicine and the graphic arts."

With Negroponte serving as its tireless cheerleader and motivator, the lab's successes were immediate. By 1987, it had an annual budget of $7 million and was engaged in developing speech recognition, advanced television, "movies of the future," electronic publishing, and computer games, among other things. The lab attracted such high-tech luminaries as Alan Kay, Marvin Minsky, and Seymour Papert to conduct its research. It adopted an unusual "demo or die" credo, demanding that students and faculty not simply publish their technical research, but also demonstrate innovations to the lab's corporate sponsors.

The Media Lab has never suffered for lack of publicity. A leading technology writer, Stewart Brand, took up a residency there and chronicled his experience in *The Media Lab: Inventing the Future at MIT* (1987)— a book that proved, if nothing else, that Brand was a Negroponte convert. But some in the journalism and research communities, notably MIT's Computer Science Lab chairman Michael Dertouzos, were not as enamored of Negroponte and his corporation-courting research institute, complaining that he was great at generating new ideas, but not so great at following through. "The achievement—the accomplishment—is where he is weak," Dertouzos appraised. "True progress happens when people combine vision with the can-do aspect and think through the social, political and technological implications."

In many ways, that criticism has lingered, with critics pointing out that the Lab's serious innovations seem to be limited to programmable LEGOs and electronic ink. But the lab has continued to attract large amounts of seed funding from some 160 corporations and non-profits ($32 million in 2000, according to *The New York Times*), and it has continued to expand its research mandate. In 1999, for instance, it launched the "Counter Intelligence" initiative aimed at making kitchens smarter by embedding processing chips in various devices.

In addition to his Media Lab work, Negroponte has funded a number of start-up businesses. One of the most successful was *Wired* magazine, to which Negroponte contributed $75,000 of his own money, giving him 10 percent ownership in what became one of the hottest new magazines in decades. In exchange for his money, Negroponte was given regular space to write an opinion column on the digital culture for each edition, heightening the professor's profile. In 1995, he refashioned some of his columns to produce *Being Digital,* the book that made him a minor celebrity. The book received a massive initial printing of 100,000 copies, and has been reprinted many times and translated into more than 40 languages. Reportedly, *Being Digital* made Negroponte something of a superstar in China, where he and his wife once found themselves mobbed by his adoring fans. Elsewhere, the book was more calmly received, but it solidified his reputation as a kind of new-media preacher, spreading the gospel of a coming digital age.

Negroponte's most enduring contribution to public discourse about high technology has been to draw a line separating an anticipated future, composed of digital bits, from an archaic analog world, comprising objects, or "atoms." The world of atoms, which still exists but is under metamorphosis, is a world of newspapers, books, films, cars, and airplanes. These things largely will continue to exist, but bits, in the form of new media innovations, can be substituted for all of them. For Negroponte, bits—the basic units of information in the binary system of computing—are the new technology's DNA, the underlying particles of a coming digital world.

In Negroponte's eyes, bits promise a future right out of the cartoon TV show *The Jetsons.* He suggests that your computer—indeed, your entire networked home—will one day sense your mood and adjust the lighting, play appropriately calming or energizing music, even speak to you in soothing tones. Your wired household will decide whether it's a good day for you to take phone calls, or whether your doorbell should be allowed to ring. (And if it does, it will automatically turn down your stereo so you don't fail to hear it.) Your digital newspaper interface might take on Larry King's personality, if you care for that—or perhaps it will adopt Dan Rather's persona. Children will be able to surf the 'Net with Dr. Seuss as their kindly, colorful, rhyming guide. The Internet will be available everywhere, from your toaster to your wallet, and it will transform much more than your relationship to media. It will render even the nation-state obsolete.

In recent years, Negroponte's role in the Media Lab has diminished somewhat. Although he continues to trot the globe raising money, the day-to-day operations of the lab have been handed over to Walter Bender, a founding member. Negroponte has also become an advocate for the 2B1 Foundation, which is premised on the idea that the future is in the hands of children, and which attempts to connect all the world's children to the Internet.

Most in the digital community agree that Negroponte has been on target with his central insight— the notion that bits will transform video, text, audio, and photography into a single unified medium. Personalized Web interfaces such as My Yahoo! suggest that Negroponte may also be right about the creation of man-machine interfaces that are completely geared to the tastes, needs, and preferences of the individual user—that even the prosaic newspaper will one day become, in effect, the *Daily Me* for each member of its audience.

If Negroponte's visions are plausible (if not inevitable), they remain simultaneously fantastic: "You'll find that your left cuff link will be in communication with your right cuff link via satellite," Negroponte told an audience in 1987. "With flat-panel technologies, every license plate, wine label or price tag will be a 'display.' . . . There will be many more MIPS (millions of instructions per second) in the nation's appliances than in its computers." Fourteen years later, while few of his most concrete predictions have come true, a number of them appear to be on the verge of realization.

Selected Works

Negroponte, Nicholas. "000 000 111—Double Agents." *Wired* 3.03, March 1995. <http://www.media.mit.edu/people/nicholas/Wired/WIRED3-03.html> (July 3, 2002).

———. "Affective Computing." *Wired* 4.04, April 1996. <http://www.media.mit.edu/~nicholas/Wired/WIRED4-04.html> (July 3, 2002).

———. *Architecture Machine: Toward a More Human Environment.* Cambridge, Mass.: MIT Press, 1970.

———. *Being Digital.* New York: Knopf, 1995.

———. "Being Digital—A Book (P)review" *Wired* 3.02, February 1995. <http://www.media.mit.edu/~nicholas/Wired/WIRED3-02.html> (July 3, 2002).

———. "Beyond Digital." *Wired* 6.12, December 1998. <http://www.media.mit.edu/~nicholas/Wired/WIRED6-12.html> (July 3, 2002).

———. "Pricing the Future." *Wired* 6.11, November 1998. <http://www.media.mit.edu/~nicholas/Wired/WIRED6-11.html> (July 3, 2002).

Bibliography

Brand, Stewart. *The Media Lab: Inventing the Future at M.I.T.* New York: Penguin Books, 1988.

Guernsey, Lisa. "M.I.T. Media Lab At 15: Big Ideas, Big Money." *The New York Times,* November 9, 2000, p. G1.

Hamilton, William L. "M.I.T. Media Lab: Let Them Eat Cache." *The New York Times,* February 18, 1999, p. F1.

Higgins, Richard. "MIT Dedicates Center Aimed at Combining Arts, New Technology." *The Boston Globe,* October 3, 1985, p.38.

Mehegan, David. "Multimedia Animal Wired Visionary Nicholas Negroponte Is MIT's Loud Voice of the Future." *The Boston Globe,* March 1, 1995, p. 52.

Further Reading

Garfinkel, Simson L. "Life Is About More Than 'Being Digital.'" *Christian Science Monitor,* March 15, 1995.

Lasica, J.D. "Nicholas Negroponte: The Revolution Will Be Digitized." *The WELL,* March 21, 1995. <http://www.well.com/~jd/nicholas.html> (May 31, 2002).

Rheingold, Howard. *Virtual Reality.* New York: Summit, 1991.

Rosenberg, Ronald. "Intelligence Alley—Where There's Nothing Artificial About the Future." *The Boston Globe,* August 6, 1985, p. 35.

Warsh, David. "Economic Principals: Rebuilding Futureland." *The Boston Globe,* January 31, 1999.

<http://www.media.mit.edu/physics/publications/books/ba/press/99.01.warsh.html> (May 31, 2002).

Related Topics

Cyberculture; Cyborg; Human-Computer Interaction; Media Lab, Massachusetts Institute of Technology; Personalization; Responsive Environments; Robotics

— *Kevin Featherly*

Nelson, Theodor Holm (Ted)

1937–

Software Developer, Author, Hypertext Pioneer

Of all the pioneering figures of the Internet age, perhaps none is quite as fascinating as the iconoclastic Ted Nelson. Variously described as a visionary, a "discombobulated genius," and a misanthropic crank, Nelson's place in the history of computing would have been secure even if he had never done anything but discover and describe the concept of hypertext. In fact, his reputation is forever secure, some might argue, precisely because during the past four decades since identifying hypertext, Nelson has accomplished very little and has spent a lifetime's worth of 16-hour working days doing it. This would be a very uncharitable view; Nelson has written at least three highly influential books in the interim. But mostly, he has spent the last 41 years perfecting the grandly elusive, World Wide Web–like Xanadu project.

Nelson grew up in New York's Greenwich Village, the son of a movie-director father and actress mother; he was raised by his elderly grandparents. His heroes, according to a 1995 *Wired* article, were nonconformists and businessmen like Buckminster Fuller, Orson Welles, and Walt Disney. Never ashamed of his own genius, Nelson described himself as having been "a brilliant child."

He earned a bachelor's degree in philosophy from Swarthmore College; during his years there, he also spent time in show business as an actor and as a record producer. At age 23, in 1960, Nelson became a graduate student at Harvard University. One of his projects there was to create a "writing system" inspired by Vannevar Bush's seminal *Atlantic Monthly* article, "As We May Think." Some of Nelson's design features involved the use of computers to compare alternate versions of texts side-by-side, backing up sequentially through earlier versions of documents, and revising by outline. "I was furious at the process of writing and how long it took, the organizational problems and the arbitrariness of writing," Nelson told an interviewer in

1996. "The process that fascinated me most was cut and paste." While working on this project, Nelson invented (he prefers to say "discovered") hypertext.

Hypertext is a method of using computers to prepare and publish text, allowing readers to pave their own unique paths through written material. Its chief characteristic is the hyperlink, simple lines of code that are used today to create links among Web pages, Word documents, and other electronic files; hypertext transfer protocol (HTTP) is the basic point-and-click language of the World Wide Web. The idea was entirely Nelson's, and it evolved during that graduate-school term project at Harvard. However, he did not finish the project's source code, and received a grade of "incomplete" for the assignment.

Nelson coined the words "hypertext" and "hypermedia" in a paper delivered at an Association for Computing Machinery conference in 1965. But it wasn't until 1967 that hypertext was demonstrated for the first time (Nelson was not the one who demonstrated it).

Also at the 1965 conference, he added to his hypertext concept an idea he called "zippered lists," which would create texts that could be linked to related elements from other writings. These lists could link up large sections of books, small sections of academic papers, entire newspaper pages, or single paragraphs from a diary; any linked combination of writing was possible. It would even be possible to compose entirely new works by fusing material from others' writings and zipping them together via Nelson's favored "cut-and-paste" method.

These ideas became two essential ingredients for the design of Xanadu, which Nelson described in his 1982 book *Literary Machines* as a "magic place of literary memory." That magic memory was tied to Nelson's insistence that no document placed on Xanadu could ever be erased. Mistakes could be corrected with add-on documents, but the original would always exist and be accessible. The other major element was what Nelson called "transclusion," the ability of any writer to quote from another writer's text. The catch would be that the original source material would always be "virtually included" with the new version through links back to the original. This would be framed by a legal principle that Nelson called "transcopyright," which necessitated another new idea, "transpayments," which would allow users to buy and assemble documents in Xanadu from any electronic publishing source whatsoever, automatically debiting their bank accounts. This is perhaps Xanadu's core principle: Anyone ought to be able to use any source to create new literature, but if they do, the source material's original creator needs to get paid.

For the first ten years, Nelson worked alone on Xanadu's design as programmer. In the early 1970s, the project languished, but Nelson managed to establish powerful counter-cultural computing credentials with the 1974 publication of *Computer Lib/Dream Machines*. This publication was actually two books, printed facing one another, one upside down in relation to the other. According to *Wired*, *Computer Lib* was a portrait of Nelson's boiling passions and rages that dealt in a scattered way with everything from hacking culture to population statistics to the evils of IBM. The book unleashed on the hacker culture the four maxims that Nelson has lived by since childhood: "most people are fools, most authority is malignant, God does not exist and everything is wrong." *Computer Lib*'s flip side dealt with the transformation of the arts though the use of computers, and it contained a brief description of Xanadu. The book was enormously influential on the hacker culture that followed, especially after it was republished in 1987.

Between 1970 and 1978, Nelson brought in various teams to help work on Xanadu before he settled in with a group that included Roger Gregory and Mark Miller at Swarthmore College in 1979. The two would continue to work with Nelson on the design of Xanadu for the next 13 years. In 1988, a company called Autodesk invested in XOC, Inc., the name under which Xanadu had been incorporated in 1983. The project was slated for a 1989 release, but delays followed delays. When the similar but vastly simplified World Wide Web emerged in 1992, Xanadu instantly seemed like that most rarified of relics: a genuine historical monument that, in truth, never existed. Autodesk dropped out of the project in 1992.

Nelson has never given up. In 1999, whatever Xanadu source code existed was released to the public as an open-source project, one in which any programmer interested in adding to its design could try to help achieve its completion. In San Francisco, Roger Gregory continues to work on the project, while Nelson works on it separately in Japan, where he also works as a research fellow at the Sapporo HyperLab and at Hokkaido University.

Nelson has completed a side project, a software system called ZigZag that seems to be an update on spreadsheet software, comprising "a multidimensional system of unconstrained rows, columns, and interactions," according to an article on the TechTV Web site.

Nelson considers it "the kernel of a new approach to computing," the article says.

With his very concrete innovation of hypertext and his important theoretical innovation of Xanadu, Ted Nelson was a direct predecessor of and inspiration for the World Wide Web. Nelson views the Web somewhat spitefully, calling it a "brilliant simplification," but also labeling it a dumb-down of the actual Xanadu concept: "The World Wide Web," he said, "was what we were trying to avoid." Tim Berners-Lee, the Englishman who invented the World Wide Web, holds a more charitable view toward Nelson. In his book *Weaving the Web*, Berners-Lee posits the idea that Nelson simply overreached, particularly in his insistence on a pricing mechanism for all information, something that posed an enormously complex and difficult—if not impossible—programming and engineering challenge. "I was not keen on the idea of having only one business model for paying for information," Berners-Lee wrote, immediately before paying tribute to the innovator: "But I was keen on meeting Ted."

Selected Works

Nelson, Theodor H. *Computer Lib/Dream Machines*. Redmond, Wash.: Tempus Books of Microsoft Press, 1987.

———. *Literary Machines*. Sausalito, Calif.: Mindful Press. 1992.

———. "Hyperformance in the Hyperfuture." Presented at the John Moores University Multimedia Conference, Liverpool, May 1994. <http://www.aus.xanadu.com/archive/hyperformance.html>

———. Home Page: "Starting Over." 2001. <http://ted.hyperland.com/> (May 17, 2002).

Bibliography

Keep, Christopher; McLaughlin, Tim; and Robin Parmar. "Ted Nelson and Xanadu." *The Electronic Labyrinth*, Institute for Advanced Technology in the Humanities, University of Virginia. <http://jefferson.village.virginia.edu/elab/hfl0155.html> (May 17, 2002).

Naughton, John. *A Brief History of the Future: From Radio Days to Internet Years in a Lifetime*. Woodstock, N.Y.: Overlook Press, 2000.

Sampson, Shauna, and Iolande Bloxsom. "Father of Hypertext: Visionary Ted Nelson Takes a Dim View of the Web, Microsoft, and the Millennium." Techtv.com, August 17, 1998. <http://www.techtv.com/print/story/ 0,23102,2128796,00.html> (May 17, 2002).

TechTV.com. "Ted Nelson, Hypertext Pioneer." August 12, 1998. <http://www.techtv.com/screensavers/showtell/ story/0,24330,2127396,00.html> (May 17, 2002).

Wolf, Gary. "The Curse of Xanadu." *Wired* 3.06, June 1995. <http://www.wired.com/wired/archive//3.06/xanadu.html ?pg=2&topic=(none)&topic_set=wiredpeople> (May 17, 2002).

Further Reading

Almaden Research Center, IBM. "Generalized Links, Micropayment and Transcopyright." 1996. <http://www.almaden.ibm.com/almaden/npuc97/1996/ tnelson.htm> (May 17, 2002).

Barlow, John Perry. "An Interview with Xanadu Founder Ted Nelson." *Mondo 2000*, August 1991, pp. 136–141.

Bush, Vannevar. "As We May Think." *The Atlantic Monthly,* July 1945, pp. 106–107.

Gillies, James, and Robert Cailliau. *How the Web Was Born*. New York: Oxford University Press, 2000.

Rheingold, Howard. *Tools for Thought: The People and Ideas Behind the Next Computer Revolution*. New York: Simon and Schuster, 1985.

Segaller, Stephen. *Nerds 2.0.1: A Brief History of the Internet*. New York: TV Books, 1998.

Xanadu.net. "Project Xanadu History." August 20, 1999. <http://www.xanadu.net/HISTORY/> (May 17, 2002).

Related Topics

"As We May Think"; Berners-Lee, Tim; Copyright; Cyberculture; Cyberspace; Engelbart, Douglas; Hacking, Cracking, and Phreaking; Human-Computer Interaction; Hypertext; World Wide Web

— Kevin Featherly

Netiquette

Netiquette is the contraction of "Internet etiquette," or of "network etiquette." Much like traditional etiquette, which provides rules of conduct in social situations, netiquette provides guidelines for courteous communication in the online environment. It includes proper manners for sending email, posting on USENET newsgroups, conversing on online chats, and so on. The purpose of netiquette is to help construct and maintain a pleasant, comfortable, and efficient environment for online communication, as well as to avoid placing strain on the system and generating conflict among users.

The need for netiquette has grown in parallel with the expansion of the Internet itself. One of the first published netiquette guides was Chuq von Rospach's "A Primer on How to Work with the Usenet Community." It, like many other netiquette guides, was published on the Internet rather than in printed form, and is still updated periodically.

Netiquette includes rules that provide guidance for appropriate social interaction and technical performance online. What constitutes good netiquette varies among the many subcultures of the Internet; and, of course, netiquette issues change with time and technology. But some general principles of proper online manners can be outlined. They include:

Lurking. Lurking means that one reads the posts of a group without participating in the conversation—that is, one assumes the role of a silent reader/observer. Proper netiquette requires some knowledge of the culture of a group in which one chooses to participate; therefore, preliminary knowledge of the group, gained from lurking, is beneficial.

Reading the FAQs. FAQ stands for Frequently Asked Questions; FAQs also provide answers to these questions. A FAQ is a list of questions that are commonly asked among newcomers. Reading a FAQ before posting helps a new group member to avoid committing the faux pas of asking questions that have already been answered, an act that often generates negative responses from other users.

Remember the Human. Communicating via computers tends to lead people to lose sight of the feelings of, or to be insensitive to, the people on the network; consequently, users tend to be more blunt in stating their views than they probably would be in a face-to-face situation. Users need to be reminded that although communication online is a form of virtual communication, they are nevertheless dealing with real people who have real emotions.

Avoid Flames. A flame is a message that contains strong personal criticism or attack. Users are advised not to engage in flaming or participate in flame wars. One should treat others the same way that one would like to be treated, and profanity is not good netiquette. A rational tone and a polite manner are preferred.

Avoid Shouting. Typing in ALL UPPER CASE is considered shouting, which is not good netiquette. To emphasize a point, instead of typing in all upper case, one can use _underlining_ or *asterisks* around the text needing emphasis.

Not a Homework Center. Online groups are resourceful arenas; however, users should not use the groups as a first resort for information-gathering, or as a "quick" source for homework or class assignments. Before going online to ask questions, users should have completed preliminary research by visiting the library or doing a Web search.

Composition Protocols. Users should observe correct grammar and be careful about punctuation and spelling when composing their messages. Online messages should be clear, concise, and organized; an articulate and thoughtful message generates more responses.

Considerations of proper online technical performance include:

Cross-Post Carefully. Cross-posting is the posting of an article to more than one group. Users are advised to post their articles to only one group; but if it is necessary to post an article to more than one group, it is suggested that it be posted to the smallest possible number of groups. The names of all the groups to which the article is sent should be included in the message, along with an apology for the inconvenience caused by the cross-posting.

Do Not Spam. Posting off-topic messages or a single article to many different groups is called spamming. It is definitely not good netiquette, and often results in angry responses from recipients. Spam, which most often takes the form of commercial advertisements, is frowned upon partly because it clogs the system and slows down the communication between users.

Format Simply. In order to ensure the consistency of textual presentation, in light of the wide variety of computers and formats used around the world, users should use plain text and avoid using special control characters or the tab key. In addition, text lines should be kept under 72 characters wide to avoid distortion of presentation. Also, articles should not be right-justified; right-justified texts are difficult to read.

Netiquette is enforced by the community at large, as the Internet does not have a policing entity. Users may openly object to breaches of netiquette with email flames; if the breach is severe, they may even contact a perpetrator's Internet service provider for recourse.

Bibliography

Kehoe, Brendan. "Zen and the Art of the Internet." January 1992. <http://www.ele.auckland.ac.nz/info/doc/zen/zen-1.0_toc.html> (April 1, 2002).

Shea, Virginia. "Netiquette Home Page." 1994. <http://www.albion.com/netiquette/index.html> (April 1, 2002).

Usenet Info Center Launch Pad. <http://www.ibiblio.org/usenet-i/> (September 17, 2002).

Von Rospach, Chuq. "A Primer on How to Work With the Usenet Community." 1999. <http://www.faqs.org/faqs/usenet/primer> (October 3, 2000).

Further Reading

Rinaldi, Arlene. "The Net: User Guidelines and Netiquette." 1998. <http://www.fau.edu/netiquette/net> (April 1, 2002).

Shea, Virginia. *Netiquette.* San Francisco: Albion Books, 1994.

Related Topics
Chat; Email; Newsgroups; Spam; USENET

— *Shing-Ling Sarina Chen*

Neuromancer

It seems impossible to overstate the cultural and literary impact of *Neuromancer*, William Gibson's 1984, original paperback novel that, in the mid-1990s, exploded into the mainstream. The novel, a fast-paced, gritty, Raymond Chandler-like meditation on a computing-fueled dystopia of the near future, had an impact on many of its readers much like that of Jack Kerouac's *On the Road* on the hipster-bohemian counter-culture of the 1950s and 1960s. If anything, Gibson's debut novel has had even broader cultural significance.

Just as Kerouac did not invent "beat" writing, Gibson did not create cyberpunk, a sub-genre of science fiction. Known simply as "the Movement," cyberpunk had been bubbling for perhaps five years prior to *Neuromancer*'s publication, and in fact Gibson had made several important previous contributions to the sub-genre with such short stories as "Johnny Mnemonic" and "The Gernsback Continuum." However, *Neuromancer* established the movement's enduring face, and provided its true founding text. The book established the filthy setting of an environmentally damaged, alienated dystopian society, dominated by global computer networks in which characters battle "artificial intelligences, monopoly capitalism and a world culture as ethnically eclectic as it is politically apathetic and alienated," in the words of *Webster's New World Dictionary of Computer Terms*. Gibson's characters, like Kerouac's, are fringe lowlifes, drug-ingesting anti-heroes, and outlaws. They are also innately brilliant hackers who undertake insane adventures in the virtual reality of "cyberspace"—a word that Gibson coined for *Neuromancer*, and that has since become a mainstream pseudonym for the World Wide Web and the Internet.

In the first years after *Neuromancer*'s publication, its ripples spread, lending the hacking culture an enduring psychedelic outlaw-in-the-Matrix self-image (many hackers actually call themselves "cyberpunks"). Meanwhile, like previous science-fiction works by Arthur C. Clarke and Robert Heinlein, Gibson's book also provided inspiration for several scientific advancements, particularly in virtual-reality programming.

Science-fiction writing as a whole seems to have drifted away from cyberpunk, although mainstream writers like Michael Crichton have incorporated some of its elements in books like *Timeline* (1999). Nonetheless, *Neuromancer* pressed a firm stamp into the popular culture, first by inspiring and shaping underground hacker-culture magazines like *Mondo 2000, RayGun,* and *bOING bOING,* and later by providing the writing voice and audience milieu necessary for the existence of the popular magazine *Wired,* and of movies like *Hackers* (1995), *Strange Days* (1995), *The Net* (1995), *Johnny Mnemonic* (1995; based on Gibson's story), and *The Matrix* (1999). To a lesser degree, television programs such as *The X-Files* and *Dark Angel* also are permeated by Gibson's vision. All these developments occurred, first and foremost, because *Neuromancer* established the cyberpunk movement as an important under-the-radar cultural force of the mid- to late 1980s, providing a direction for fellow cyberpunk writers like Bruce Sterling, Rudy Rucker, and Neal Stephenson, and further stirring the increasingly computerized popular mentality of the 1980s and 1990s.

Gibson wrote *Neuromancer* at a time when the personal computer was just beginning to make inroads in private homes; famously, he wrote the book on an antiquated 1937 Hermes manual portable typewriter, and bought a computer only after the royalties from *Neuromancer* began rolling in. In 1984, the Internet had only recently acquired its name as a generic pseudonym for the recently divided ARPANET system, and it had healthy competition from other computing networks like BITNET and USENET. Most people were blissfully unaware of the potential of networked computing. For 1984, Gibson's book was ambitiously prophetic, leapfrogging beyond any notion of a text-and-image-based World Wide Web and directly into a computerized virtual reality, into which hackers could "jack" themselves using body implants and cables, injecting their brains directly into the Matrix.

Cultural critic Paul T. Riddell even gives Gibson credit for "most of the development of the Web," saying that after the trailblazing innovations of the scientist Tim Berners-Lee, later improvements to the Web were the result of "impressionable students reading (Gibson's) stories and novels; instead of whining and complaining after reading Robert Anton Wilson, they read Gibson and thought, 'You know, we can do this.'"

Why? What is the quality of *Neuromancer* that has caused so many people to embrace its cybernetic vision? It may be that Gibson's most alluring quality as a writer, aside from his surprising prescience, is his decision to populate his books with characters that are not products of some remote, high-tech future. They are not the products of Tolkien-like fantasy worlds, and they do not sound the foghorn warning blasts that the characters of old-school writers like Jack Williamson and George Orwell did while the authors tried to compel readers to reject an unthinkable, robot-dominated future. Gibson made what was then a radical literary choice, creating in *Neuromancer* a near-future world permeated internally and externally by technologies that were already in existence in 1984, even if many were not fully developed then (or today). Gibson did not bother to warn his readers to avoid the terrifying place that we may be heading as a society, but instead showed the far side of cultural space that we already inhabit. In an interview with 1960s acid-guru Timothy Leary in a 1989 issue of *Mondo 2000*, Gibson explained his approach:

"What's most important to me," he said, "is that it's about the present. It's not really about an imagined future. It's a way of trying to come to terms with the awe and terror inspired in me by the world in which we live." Considering that many movers and shakers in the computer-science, telecommunications, and new-media industries as well as in policy circles were fans of *Neuromancer*, the book's impact on the way that the imagined future has been realized may well be greater than that of most other twentieth-century fiction.

Bibliography

Blair, Dike. "Leading into the Light While Playing in the Dark: An Interview with Mondo 2000's Editor-in-Chief, R.U.Sirius . . ." 1995–1998. <http://adaweb.walkerart.org/~purple/mondo.html> (May 17, 2002).

Boulware, Jack. *SF Weekly*, vol. 14, no. 35 (October 11, 1995). <http://www.scrappi.com/deceit/mondosfw/mondosfd.html> (May 17, 2002).

Brin, David. *The Transparent Society: Will Technology Force Us to Choose Between Privacy and Freedom?* Reading, Mass.: Addison-Wesley, 1998.

Chesher, Chris. "Colonizing Virtual Reality: Construction of the Discourse of Virtual Reality, 1984–1992." *Cultronix*. <http://eserver.org/cultronix/chesher/> (May 17, 2002).

Gibson, William. *Neuromancer*. New York: Ace Books, 1984.

Hayward, Philip. "Situating Cyberspace: The Popularization of Virtual Reality." *Future Visions: New Technologies of the Screen*. Philip Hayward and Tana Wollen, eds. London: BFI Publishing, 1993; pp. 180–204.

<http://www.rochester.edu/College/FS/Publications/HaywardCyberspace.html> (May 17, 2002).

Riddell, Paul T. "Thoughts and Observations on William Gibson." July 1996. (Originally published in the Readercon 8 program guide.) <http://www.hpoo.com/errata/gibson.html> (May 17, 2002).

Further Reading

Rheingold, Howard. *The Virtual Community: Homesteading on the Electronic Frontier*. Reading, Mass.: Addison-Wesley, 1993.

Sterling, Bruce. "Preface." *Mirrorshades: The Cyberpunk Anthology*. New York: Ace Books, 1988; pp. ix–xvi.

Related Topics

Cyberculture; Cyberspace; Cyberwarfare; Hacking, Cracking, and Phreaking; Human-Computer Interaction; Sterling, Bruce; *2600: The Hacker Quarterly*; Virtual Reality

— *Kevin Featherly*

The New Hacker's Dictionary

The New Hacker's Dictionary, available online as well as in book form, provides a guide to the hacker subculture. Currently compiled and maintained by Eric Raymond, it originated as an online document called the Jargon File, and is still found online under that name. In addition to its status as a definitive collection of computer-related slang, *The New Hacker's Dictionary* provides a compendium of hacker lore and history.

The Jargon File was begun by Raphael Finkel at Stanford University in 1975. Until the early 1980s, it circulated within a relatively small community of computer programmers, primarily at universities such as Stanford, Massachusetts Institute of Technology, and Carnegie Mellon. Many of these programmers were involved in the early operation of ARPANET, the precursor to the Internet. The shared slang contained in the Jargon File reflected the fact that many of these programmers used similar operating systems and hardware. It also reflected shared norms and attitudes among this growing new subculture.

In 1981, a portion of the Jargon File was published in *CoEvolution Quarterly*, edited by Stewart Brand, who also later founded The WELL (Whole Earth 'Lectronic Link). Meanwhile, the Jargon File continued to be updated, maintained, and circulated through ARPANET, and later through the Internet. Guy L. Steele, Jr., who with Mark Crispin was responsible for many of the early revisions to the Jargon File, compiled the first book version, published in 1983 as *The Hacker's Dictionary*.

The online version continued to circulate but was not updated again until Eric Raymond took over maintenance of it in 1990. Raymond took the original file, which primarily reflected the earlier 1970s hacker culture (which focused in particular around programming strategies for the PDP-10, a computer in use at that time), and added slang from other hacker and computer subcultures, such as USENET newsgroups. USENET is a bulletin board system (BBS) that began on ARPANET. It allows people to post messages in topically divided "newsgroups," which can then be read and responded to by others via the Internet. Raymond's revision also included slang from MOOs and MUDs, computer programs that allow multiple users to connect from remote locations and to interact with the program and communicate with each other through text-based "chat." Both USENET and MUDs began in 1979, and by the time that Raymond began revising the Jargon File, both had generated rich subcultures. Raymond compiled and published *The New Hacker's Dictionary* in 1991, with subsequent updated editions coming out in 1993 and 1996.

The Hacker's Dictionary and *The New Hacker's Dictionary* sought to celebrate hacker culture, provide a repository of hacker history for younger and future hackers, and perhaps most importantly, to represent hacker culture in a positive light to the general public. In the early 1990s in particular, many news stories emerged portraying hackers as law-breakers with no respect for the personal privacy or property of others. Raymond wanted to show some of the positive values of hacker culture, particularly the hacker sense of humor. Because love of humorous wordplay is a strong element of hacker culture, a slang dictionary works quite well for such purposes.

Because of these additional aims, *The New Hacker's Dictionary* includes several sections in addition to the word definitions; the introductions provide some background and history of the Jargon File itself, while the appendices provide further insight into hacker culture. Appendix A provides several examples of "hacker folklore," while Appendix B supplies a description of a generic hacker. The word-definition entries also include more than simple definitions, often explaining the cultural significance of particular terms, and sometimes including historical notes. Even the revision history, especially in the online version, demonstrates hacker values; the online Jargon File versions are numbered like computer program revisions (Version 2.9.12, Version 3.3.3, etc.). Each version also lists the exact numbers of entries, lines, words, and characters it contains, providing a level of detail only a hacker could love.

Bibliography

Raymond, Eric. *The New Hacker's Dictionary*. Third edition. Cambridge, Mass.: MIT Press, 1996.

Steele, Guy L., Jr., et al. *The Hacker's Dictionary: A Guide to the World of Computer Wizards*. New York: Harper & Row, 1983.

Further Reading

Himanen, Pekka. *The Hacker Ethic and the Spirit of the Information Age*. New York: Random House, 2001.

Levy, Steven. *Hackers: Heroes of the Computer Revolution*. Updated edition. New York: Penguin Books, 2001.

Sterling, Bruce. *The Hacker Crackdown: Law and Disorder on the Electronic Frontier*. New York: Bantam Books, 1992.

Related Topics

Brand, Stewart; Cyberculture; Hacking, Cracking, and Phreaking; MUDs and MOOs; Raymond, Eric; USENET; Whole Earth 'Lectronic Link

— *Lori Kendall*

Newsgroups

Newsgroups are worldwide public discussion forums, hosted on USENET. Users can post to newsgroups, respond to posts, and create new newsgroups. By the end of 1997, there were more than 50,000 newsgroups on a wide variety of topics, all distributed via USENET, and hundreds are added each month.

In terms of online discussion groups, newsgroups are different from "chat rooms" in that they are not "real-time" conversations; rather, they present delayed correspondence between users. Newsgroups also differ from mailing lists, another type of online forum. Newsgroups are free and indiscriminate, while membership to mailing lists requires subscription, which may involve an application process or even a small fee. Also, mailing lists distribute new articles (or messages) to each subscriber's private email address, whereas newsgroups function as public bulletin boards to which members go in order to read and post messages.

USENET newsgroups are organized hierarchically by subject. The first few letters of the newsgroup name indicate the major subject category, and sub-categories are represented by a subtopic name. Groups generally have multiple levels of subtopics, such as rec.games.video.nintendo. USENET has a number of "official" subject hierarchies: biz, comp, misc, news, rec, soc, sci, talk, and humanities. "Alternative" subject hierarchies include alt, national, and local.

When one starts a topic with a posting on a newsgroup and someone else replies, this initial post and the response constitute a "thread" on the topic. A thread may grow to involve dozens or even hundreds of users responding to the initial post, or to any posting that came after it. Users may also start threads of their own as offshoots of the original discussion.

Postings on newsgroups generally expire after a few days or a few weeks; expired messages are deleted from the newsgroups to make room for new ones. The "expiration time" differs from one server to another, and may also vary from one newsgroup to another. It is possible that when an article expires on one server, it is still visible on other servers. In 1995, Deja News (www.dejanews.com), a search engine, provided an interface to USENET to archive and index messages so they can be searched and sorted. In 2001, Google Inc. acquired the Usenet Discussion Service from Deja News, which included the entire USENET archive of more than 500 million messages.

The best way to learn about USENET newsgroups is by observing how other users use them. Therefore, after locating a group of interest, users should lurk in the group for a couple of weeks. Lurking means reading the posts in the group without posting any messages of one's own—being a silent reader/observer. Lurking helps new users to learn about the rules and conventions of a group. It is believed that only after gaining lurking experience can a user effectively participate in online conversations. For new users, posting without lurking first would likely generate negative responses from others.

Another way to learn about the functioning of a particular group is to study its list of Frequently Asked Questions—its FAQ. FAQs are usually lists of questions, with answers, that have been asked over and over again by new users. New users are advised to search for the FAQ of a group, and read them to minimize their likelihood of asking questions for which answers are already available. Posting a question for which answers already have been provided in FAQs can result in negative feedback from other users. However, posting is appropriate for questions that remain after reading the FAQs.

Many newsgroups post their FAQs periodically, from once a week to once every two months. Whenever one is unsure if a group has or posts its FAQ, one can post the question "Where can I find a copy of the FAQ for this newsgroup?" and wait for replies. In addition, many of the more traditional FAQs are usually cross-posted to news.answers. To find a FAQ for a particular newsgroup, one can search for that newsgroup using the headers of the postings in news.answers. Also, one can search the FAQs via the World Wide Web at http://www.faqs.org/faqs/, which is searchable by newsgroup or keywords.

Much as people observe etiquette when interacting offline, users are advised to observe netiquette for civil communication online. Netiquette is a set of guidelines constructed to help maintain a courteous and efficient environment for communication, as well as to avoid placing strain on the system and generating conflict among users. Ground rules include avoiding the use of ALL CAPS when typing a sentence, as it represents shouting; avoiding sending copies of a post to multiple groups, which constitutes spamming (if there is a need to post in multiple groups, one should observe the guidelines for proper cross-posting); and avoiding participating in flame wars, which are hostile exchanges among users engaging in personal attacks.

The indiscriminate and participatory nature of newsgroups makes them a valuable forum for public

---

TOP-LEVEL SUBJECT HIERARCHIES OF NEWSGROUPS

alt: Alternative newsgroups about any conceivable topic.

biz: Business newsgroups about business products, services, reviews, and so on.

comp: Computer newsgroups about computer hardware, software, consumer information, and so on.

humanities: Newsgroups about fine art, literature, philosophy, and so on.

misc: Miscellaneous newsgroups.

news: USENET news carrying information about the USENET.

rec: Recreational newsgroups about games, hobbies, sports, and so on.

sci: Newsgroups about applied science, social science, and so on.

soc: Newsgroups about social issues, culture, and so on.

talk: Newsgroups about current issues and debates, and so on.

discussion. However, without a central policing agency to regulate the traffic on USENET and to control the quality of exchanges, chaos is inherent and evident. The self-governing system of newsgroups is essentially like that of a cocktail party; it becomes the user's responsibility to evaluate the environment and to validate the truthfulness of the information gathered.

Bibliography

McGuire, Mary; Stilborne, Linda; McAdams, Melinda; and Laurel Hyatt. *The Internet Handbook for Writers, Researchers, and Journalists.* New York: Guilford Press, 1997.

Moraes, Mark. "A Guide to Social Newsgroups and Mailing Lists." May 12, 1998. <news.announce.newusers.> (October 29, 2002).

———. "A Primer on How to Work With the Usenet Community." May 12, 1998. <news.announce.newusers.> (October 29, 2002).

Further Reading

Harrison, Mark. *The Usenet Handbook: A User's Guide to Netnews.* Sebastopol, Calif.: O'Reilly & Associates, 1995.

Hauben, Michael, and Rhonda Hauben. *Netizens: On the History and Impact of Usenet and the Internet.* Los Alamitos, Calif.: IEEE Computer Society Press, 1997.

Spencer, Henry, and David Lawrence. *Managing Usenet.* Sebastopol, Calif.: O'Reilly & Associates, 1998.

Related Topics

Bulletin-Board Systems; Netiquette; USENET; Virtual Community

— *Shing-Ling Sarina Chen*

Nielsen, Jakob

1957–
Web Usability Guru

Jakob Nielsen is a computer-interface engineer, an author, and a researcher in human-computer interaction, and is the best-known expert on Web-site usability. Usability is determined by "how well a Web site allows its users to navigate and transact business efficiently, and with a minimum of swearing, scowling and confusion," as he once told *BusinessWeek* magazine. For Nielsen, that invariably means keeping Web design simple.

Nielsen is credited with forming the "discount usability engineering" movement, which aims to create fast and cheap improvements in user interfaces. He has invented several such methods, including one known as "heuristic evaluation," the goal of which is to find usability problems within Web-page design so that they can be fixed in subsequent redesigns. He holds some 71 patents, mostly for technologies and methods intended to make the Internet easier to use.

As he has gained experience in the field of Web usability, Nielsen has grown ever more convinced that the strongest key to a usable Web site lies in its ability to convey content to users effectively and quickly. For Nielsen, issues such as effective site navigation and underlying interface technologies take a back seat to good content, a commodity he still considers hard to find.

The son of a Danish TV network executive and a psychologist, Nielsen was born in Copenhagen, Denmark, in 1957, one day after the Sputnik satellite launched. While attending high school in 1974, he had his first computer experience with an already outdated Dutch GIER mainframe manufactured in 1961, which took up an entire room, had 5KB (kilobytes) of random-access memory, relied on punch-tape storage, and had no integrated circuits. However, it was a simple computer, and easy to use. Later, as a college student, he switched to his first "modern" time-shared mainframe. "It was a horrible computer and one of the reasons I work in usability," he told the U.K.'s *Guardian* newspaper. "Personally speaking, that experience gave me the feeling that modern computers are alienating," he told an interviewer for Webreference.com, "because when I made the switch, my computer didn't feel like my machine anymore. It felt like the computer was dominating me, as opposed to me dominating the computer."

During those early years, Nielsen fell under the influence of hacker hero Ted Nelson and his 1974 book *Computer Lib/Literary Machines,* which discussed improving the ways that computers were designed and used, with the aim of bettering the human condition. Nielsen earned his undergraduate and master's degrees at Aarhus University in Denmark, and as early as 1983, he began to research usability issues relating to everything from the ergonomics of software to Videotex systems and the Macintosh interface. He was first exposed to hypertext in 1984, and first encountered the Internet the following year. He earned his Ph.D. in user-interface design and computer science from the Technical University of Denmark in 1988, and worked there as an assistant professor from 1986 to 1990. He began working on computer usability studies as an undergraduate student in the early 1980s.

In the early 1990s, Nielsen served on the research staff at Bell Communications Research (Bellcore), and was also affiliated with the IBM User Interface Institute at the T.J. Watson Research Center. During that period, he published his first book, *Hypertext and Hypermedia* (1990), although he had edited several others in previous years; he has since written eight more. He first encountered the early World Wide Web during this period, in 1991, using one of the earliest line-mode browsers.

In 1994, Nielsen went to work for Sun Microsystems as a Distinguished Engineer. His concentration on Web usability stems partly from his years at Sun, where he led the computer-interface design team that created Sun's Web site. He also worked on next-generation, object-oriented user interfaces, and on enhanced usability engineering methods while at Sun. Also during this period, Nielsen began publishing the Alertbox column for which he is perhaps best known, which runs on his Useit.com Web site. Topics run the usability gamut, with titles like "Ten Good Deeds in Web Design," "Flash: 99% Bad," and "Are Users Stupid?"

One column in particular, titled "Top Ten Mistakes In Web Design," proved widely influential. That column, published in May 1996, laid down the law of Web design, insisting that readers should not have to scroll when reading Web pages, and that the use of frames to divide sections of Web pages is a horrible practice. In subsequent years, Nielsen has toned down these particular complaints. But other points argued in the column—that page designers should never include elements that move incessantly, that they should design pages for minimum download times, and that outdated information should be habitually pruned—remain Nielsen dogma.

His online writings have garnered Nielsen a considerable audience. In 2000, he stated on his Web site that his Alertbox column collects 9 million page views per year.

Nielsen today makes his living as a consultant and speaker for his own Mountain View, California–based company, the Nielsen Norman Group, which he founded in 1998 with former Apple and Hewlett-Packard executive Donald Norman. As part of his work, Nielsen has spent thousands of hours studying people's experiences and behavior while surfing various Web sites. This user feedback, he has said, has changed his thinking about usability in general, moving him away from a desire to improve Web technology to simply improving the ways that content—

words, graphics, video, sound—is designed, arranged, and presented. "Whenever I had users in the lab for usability tests," he told the online publication *Contentious*, "I found they were highly focused on the articles or other content in the site. Users were very concerned with whether the content was something they liked, something they thought was useful. *That* was what they kept commenting on—not the design, layout, or navigation. (In other words, all the things we were trying to test!)"

Nielsen insists that this emphasis on content should extend beyond Web publications to e-commerce sites. He argues that the biggest sites, such as Amazon.com and Yahoo! are always the simplest. A key rule, he says, is that one should use only 50 percent of the words on the Web that one would use to convey the same message in print.

With his background and increasing reputation, Nielsen's Web-site usability reviews can garner him up to $30,000 each, and his keynote speeches have been known to fetch $25,000, according to one biographical sketch. His clients have included start-up Web operations such as Epinions.com and the Motley Fool, and major companies like General Electric and Hallmark Cards, Inc.

Author Daniel Drew Turner suggests that it is possible to boil down Jakob Nielsen's usability theory to a couple of key principles. First, content is king, and a snazzy site may draw visitors, but it will not keep customers. Second, poor usability means that there will be no customers to worry about losing. "People come to your site in order to accomplish something specific," Nielsen echoes in *Designing Web Usability* (2000). "If they are frustrated, they'll leave without spending one cent."

Selected Works

Nielsen, Jakob. "About Jakob Nielsen." Useit.com, 2000.
<http://www.useit.com/jakob/> (May 31, 2002).
———. "Are Users Stupid?" Useit.com—Alertbox,
February 4, 2001.
<http://useit.com/alertbox/20010204.html> (July 3, 2002).
———. *Designing Web Usability*. Indianapolis, Ind.: New
Riders Publishing, 2000.
———. *Hypertext and Hypermedia*. Boston, Mass.:
Academic Press, 1990.
———. *Multimedia and Hypertext: The Internet and
Beyond*. Boston, Mass.: AP Professional, 1995.
———. "Top Ten Mistakes in Web Design." Useit.com—
Alertbox, May 1996.
<http://www.useit.com/alertbox/9605.html> (May 31, 2002).
———. *Usability Engineering*. Boston, Mass.: AP
Professional, 1994.

———. "Usability Metrics?" Useit.com—Alertbox, January 21, 2001. <http://useit.com/alertbox/20010121.html> (July 3, 2002).

Nielsen, Jakob, and Marie Tahir. *Homepage Usability: 50 Websites Deconstructed.* Indianapolis, Ind.: New Riders Publishing, 2001.

Bibliography

Barger, Jorn. "Infamous Villain: Jakob Nielsen (Impersonating a Scientist)." RobotWisdom.com, October 2000. <http://www.robotwisdom.com/issues/nielsen.html> (May 31, 2002).

Gahran, Amy. "Interview—Jakob Nielsen, Part 1: Content is a Service." *Contentious,* August 5, 1998. <http://www.contentious.com/articles/1-5/qa1-5a.html> (May 31, 2002).

Hamilton, Joan. "Diss My Web Site, Please: Jakob Nielsen Believes the Best Design Critics Are Users." *Business Week,* November 20, 2000. <http://www.businessweek.com/2000/00_47/b3708076.htm> (May 31, 2002).

Keegan, Victor. "Usability Guru." *Guardian Newspapers,* August 16, 2001. <http://www.guardian.co.uk/online/story/0,3605,537243,00.html> (May 31, 2002).

Miller, Robin. "Jakob Nielsen Answers Usability Questions." Slashdot, March 3, 2000. <http://slashdot.org/interviews/00/03/03/096223.shtml> (May 31, 2002).

Solomon, Karen. "The Purist." *On—The New World of Communication,* May 2000, pp. 43–45. <http://on.magazine.se/stories/story.asp?articleID=263> (May 31, 2002).

Webreference.com. "Making the World a Happier Place, One Web Site at a Time." Revised October 11, 2001. <http://www.webreference.com/authoring/design/usability/interview/> (May 31, 2002).

Further Reading

Catapano, Peter. "Web Guru: It's the User, Stupid!" *Wired News,* November 15, 2000. <http://www.wired.com/news/print/0,1294,40155,00.html> (May 31, 2002).

Plotnikoff, David. "The Future of Web Design from One Who Knows It." *San Jose Mercury News,* March 30, 2001, p. 3C.

Related Topics

E-Commerce; Human-Computer Interaction; Interactivity; Interface; Usability; World Wide Web

— Kevin Featherly

Object-Oriented Programming

Object-oriented programming (OOP) is an approach to writing computer code that uses "objects" created by programmers to trigger specific functions in software. Objects in the programming sense are not physical, palpable things like desks or cars; they are software modules, or self-contained mini-programs, that stand on their own. Existing objects can be copied into new programs as they are created. This is a principal distinction between OOP and older, "procedural" programming languages like BASIC and Pascal, in which the programmer must always spell out each distinct procedure for a computer to follow to accomplish a task.

With OOP, developers can combine objects into structured networks, eventually creating complete programs. Michael Hiltzik, in his 1999 book *Dealers of Lightning: Xerox PARC and the Dawn of the Computer Age,* likens objects to TV sets. When using a remote control to tell a TV to power up, turn off, or change channels, one doesn't have to reprogram the channel-changing mechanism to change a channel; one can just punch a button. The TV "understands" what the viewer is doing, because the remote conveys a message in a way that both viewer and the television understand. Within objects, data and the procedures that work on the data are combined, and are manipulated when someone sends them a "message." Objects are portable. What OOP means for programmers is that a lot of code, once written, can be reused; the same function can be used again and again whenever it comes in handy.

The history of OOP dates back to Norway in the early 1960s, where Ole-Johan Dahl and Kristen Nygaard created the Simula language in 1962, at the Norwegian Computing Center in Oslo. They introduced most of the key concepts that are still at work in OOP today. *Newton's Telecom Dictionary* indicates that observations of the way that children learn (i.e., object + action = result) served as the inspiration for Simula's methodology. In 2001, Dahl and Nygaard

won the Turing Award, the highest prize in the computer-science field, for their contributions to OOP.

However, neither Simula nor its successor, Simula 67, were truly the first OOP languages. That distinction belongs to SmallTalk, invented by Alan Kay in 1971 at the Xerox Palo Alto Research Center (PARC). According to L. Peter Deutsch and Adele Goldberg, former Xerox PARC engineers, Kay discovered that object-oriented design "could produce an appealing, intuitive, and direct mapping between objects in the real world and objects in a software implementation." This was "a radical breakthrough" in one of the most problematic steps in software development—trying to translate terms and relationships that humans understand into those that a computer also understands.

Many later programming languages evolved that borrowed from this idea of man-machine symbiosis, but two OOP languages followed the lead of SmallTalk (which itself is still a force in programming) to rise above all others: C++ and Java.

C++ evolved from the earlier C language, which was written in 1972 by Dennis Ritchie of Bell Laboratories. C was developed for the UNIX operating system, but was not tied to any particular hardware, making it possible to write programs for nearly any computer. For years, C was the primary language for writing professional applications. Most of Microsoft's Windows operating system, for example, was written in C.

C++ followed in 1979, designed by Bjarne Stoustrup of AT&T's Bell Laboratories as an upgrade to C. It retained all the power of the original, but added object-orientation. It quickly became the standard programming language of several major software vendors, including Apple Computer. However, many programmers struggled with C++. While it had flexible OOP possibilities, it was still bound to C's tether. It was fast but inconsistent; its programs could break down. Sun Microsystems founder Bill Joy was among those who saw C++ as too complicated for its own good. In 1990, work began on a simpler, more powerful language: Java. In 1995, *Wired* magazine stated its view plainly: "In time," David Bank wrote, "a distributed object-oriented language like Java will probably establish itself as the foundation of the Net." Whatever shape its successors may take, OOP will continue to serve as the primary paradigm for computer programming.

Bibliography

Bank, David. "The Java Saga." *Wired* 3.12, December 1995. <http://www.wired.com/wired/archive/3.12/java.saga.html?topic=&topic_set> (July 12, 2002).

Carpenter, Vinit. "The Origins of C and C++." 1993–99. <http://cyberdiem.com/vin/learn.html> (July 12, 2002).

Dahl, Ole-Johan, and Kristen Nygaard. "How Object-Oriented Programming Started." *Universitetet I Oslo*, 1990. <http://www.ifi.uio.no/~kristen/FORSKNINGSDOK_MAPPE/F_OO_start.html> (July 12, 2002).

Hiltzik, Michael A. *Dealers of Lightning: Xerox PARC and the Dawn of the Computer Age.* New York: HarperBusiness, 1999.

Newton, Harry. *Newton's Telecom Dictionary: The Authoritative Resource for Telecommunications, Networking, the Internet and Information Technology.* 18th updated and expanded edition. New York: CMP Books, 2002.

Pfaffenberger, Bryan. W*ebster's New World Dictionary of Computing Terms.* Foster City, Calif.: IDG Books Worldwide, 2000.

Further Reading

Oman, Paul W., and Ted G. Lewis, eds. *Milestones in Software Evolution.* Los Alamitos, Calif.: IEEE Computer Society Press, 1990.

Schmucker, Kurt J. "Object-Oriented Languages for the Macintosh." *Byte*, August 1986.

Tesler, Larry. "The Smalltalk Environment." *Byte*, August 1981.

Wirfs-Brock, Rebecca; Wilkerson, Brian; and Lauren Wiener. *Designing Object-Oriented Software.* Englewood Cliffs, N.J.: Prentice Hall, 1990.

Related Topics

Graphical User Interface; Human-Computer Interaction; Information Design; Java; Joy, Bill; Xerox Palo Alto Research Center

— *Kevin Featherly*

Obscenity

In the United States, obscenity is considered an illegal subset of pornography. Pornography is often defined as "words, sounds or images that present sexual content, intended to sexually arouse the viewer." Pornography is legally protected in the United States under the free-speech portion of the First Amendment, with two exceptions: child pornography and obscenity. Today, the Supreme Court determines obscenity using the three-pronged "Miller Test." First, the material must violate a state law that describes the particular sex acts being labeled as "obscene." Second, the material must be "patently offensive" and "appeal to prurient interest," as judged by a reasonable person applying the standards of the community. Third, the obscene material must lack "serious" literary, artistic, scientific, political, or other social value.

The rise of new-media technologies has sparked energetic debates between religious groups, legislators, and civil libertarians about the definition of obscenity online. But according to attorney Mike Godwin, "the Internet and the Web don't pose any new community standards problems—just a digital version of a very old one that we've been coping with for a long time."

HISTORY OF OBSCENITY LAW

The history of obscenity law in the United States begins as early as 1815, when a Pennsylvania court declared it an offense to exhibit for profit a picture of a nude couple. By the 1860s, reformer Anthony Comstock had successfully campaigned for the passage of obscenity laws in nearly every state. Prior to 1973, the Supreme Court set the national standard for obscenity law, deciding whether particular content was "obscene" on a case-by-case basis. After 1973, the Supreme Court began incorporating state obscenity standards into its federal analyses.

Contemporary legal definitions of obscenity have their roots in three Supreme Court cases that were decided in 1957. In *Butler vs. State of Michigan*, the court reversed the "Hicklin Test," a directive from the 1860s that had defined obscene material as anything that might offend children or the "weak-spirited" in a community. In *Roth vs. United States* and *Alberts vs. California*, the Court ruled that obscenity was to be determined by "the average person," and that the material in question must be considered in its entirety, rather than excerpted. In Justice William Brennan's words, for obscenity not to have First Amendment protection, it had to be "utterly without redeeming social importance."

Unfortunately, the 1957 laws raised as many questions as they answered. For example, who was an "average person"? How was "utterly without redeeming social importance" to be established? And what was the dividing line between communities' attempts to prosecute obscenity and the nationwide guarantee under the Constitution of free speech for all? From

1967 to 1973, the Supreme Court attempted to answer these questions during "movie days," screening films previously ruled as obscene in lower courts. Ultimately, it turned out that each of the justices had his own personal standard for what constituted obscenity, the most infamous being Justice Potter Stewart's claim, " I know it when I see it."

MILLER AND ITS AFTERMATH

By 1973, the Supreme Court seemed prepared to codify its film-watching experience into legal guidelines for obscenity. The Court's view, articulated in *Miller vs. California*, remains the standard used to this day. In *Miller*, the Court synthesized and refined its 1957 decisions, ruling that obscenity must be determined by a "reasonable person" using the "standards of the community." It provided a check on community standards by stating that any jury decision in an obscenity case must be subject to an independent constitutional review. Finally, the Court provided important defenses against obscenity, ruling that if a work was found to have serious "literary, artistic, scientific, political or other social value," it was protected under the Constitution as free speech.

After the *Miller* decision, much of the debate about obscenity moved from the courts to other political arenas. To some degree, this was understandable, as the notion of "serious literary, artistic, scientific, political or other social value" (also known as SLAP) has always been more social than legal. During the 1980s, for example, the National Endowment for the Arts came under heavy criticism for "sponsoring obscenity," not in a legal sense (the work of the artists easily met the SLAP provisions), but in a social sense, as a waste of taxpayer dollars. Likewise, when a Florida state prosecutor charged the owner of a record store with criminal obscenity for selling an album by the rap group 2 Live Crew, the case was eventually dismissed, but a public clamor for music censorship persisted in Congress.

OBSCENITY AND THE INTERNET

During the 1980s and early 1990s, Internet enthusiasts argued that community standards for obscenity ought to work differently online than off, in part because the Internet was "only words." This view held until 1994, when the FBI arrested University of Michigan student Jake Baker after he used the name of a real female classmate in a fictional "snuff" story posted on the USENET group alt.sex.stories. Feminist attorney Catherine MacKinnon argued that Baker's

story was indefensible under *Miller*, and that his "mere words" held real danger. The American Civil Liberties Union (ACLU) argued to the contrary, stating that "the notion of thought-crimes is not consistent with that of a free society." The courts agreed with the ACLU, dismissing the case.

Robert and Carleen Thomas were not quite so lucky, in part because their case went well beyond "just words." The Thomases ran a private, commercial bulletin-board system (BBS) called Amateur Action, in Milpitas, California. When a postal inspector in Memphis, Tennessee, downloaded sexually explicit pictures and ordered videotapes from their BBS, the Thomases were charged with violating local community standards in Memphis. In 1996, their conviction was upheld by the Sixth Circuit Court of Appeals, in effect making geography apply to cyberspace.

Amateur Action was a private BBS, unconnected to the Internet. Yet when researcher Martin Rimm undertook a Carnegie Mellon University study on Internet pornography in 1995, he chose to focus on Amateur Action to argue that a high portion of Internet content is pornographic. Later that year, *Time* magazine ran an article on "cyberporn" that featured Rimm's findings. The article, which was effectively retracted by *Time* later that year, was nonetheless read into the *Congressional Record* as evidence that Internet images needed legislative control, and began what attorney Mike Godwin has called "cyberporn panic" in Congress.

THE CDA AND CENSORWARE

In recent years, Congress has attempted to pass a series of laws regarding content on the Internet, particularly content that currently passes the Miller Test but still seems to some to be harmful to children. In 1996, the framers of the Communications Decency Act (CDA) argued that the Internet should be regulated in the same way that broadcast media, like radio and television, are regulated. The ACLU argued to the contrary, calling droves of witnesses who testified about their free-speech experiences on the Internet. The Supreme Court eventually struck the indecency portions of the CDA as being inconsistent with the First Amendment right to free speech. Congress responded by passing the Child Online Protection Act of 1998 (COPA), which avoided the CDA's language of indecency, instead expanding current definitions of obscenity online by adding an "as to minors" focus. In other words, an otherwise non-obscene work may be found "obscene as to minors" if it appeals to minors' prurient interests, violates community standards for minors, and so on. The Supreme Court issued a ruling on COPA on May 13, 2002. Instead of deciding any of the legal questions itself, the Court barred enforcement of the law and ordered a lower court to decide the First Amendment issues.

Recently, parents have turned to content-filtering software to help protect their children from exposure to obscenity online. Unfortunately, parents are too often uninformed as to what such software is blocking, and in their urge to protect, they may be cutting off their children's access to important information that would not be judged in any American court to be "obscene as to minors." Nevertheless, Congress recently passed the Children's Internet Protection Act (CIPA), which will force public and private libraries (and schools) to install Internet blocking software, or else be denied a variety of federal funds. CIPA was ruled unconstitutional by a Pennsylvania district court in June 2002, and the case is being appealed to the Supreme Court.

CONTROLLING THE INTERNET OF THE FUTURE

The reversal of the VoyeurDorm.com case, which involved the shutdown of a Web site broadcasting the lives of college-age women, may serve as the standard by which future decisions are made by the courts. In its September 2001 decision, the Eleventh Circuit Court of Appeals ruled that lower courts had incorrectly applied the community standards of Tampa, Florida (where the VoyeurDorm house is located) to the "environment" of the Web site, which is viewable only via the Internet. "The public does not, indeed cannot, physically attend" activities at the dorm, wrote Circuit Judge Joel Dubina, making VoyeurDorm exempt from Tampa's zoning ordinance. The city of Tampa appealed the case further, but its appeal was rejected by the Supreme Court.

Today, there is still no clear definition of what constitutes obscenity online. Webmasters are told by their attorneys to work within the guidelines of *Miller*, screening for minors via credit-card or age-verification systems before showing their more risqué images online. Attorney Jonathan Wallace has argued that thus far, all approaches to dealing with obscenity on the Internet have been analogous to "kludges" in computer programming—inelegant solutions to an as-yet-undefined problem.

Case Law Citations

Regina vs. Hicklin, L.R. 3 Q.B. 360 (1868).
Butler vs. State of Michigan, 352 U.S. 380 (1957).

Roth vs. United States and *Alberts vs. California*, 354 U.S. 476 (1957).
Miller vs. California, 413 U.S. 15 (1973).
United States vs. Baker, 890 F. Supp. 1375 (E. D. Mich. June 21, 1995), aff'd. sub. nom., *U.S. v. Alkhabaz*, 104 F 3d. 1492 6th Cir. 1997.
United States vs. Thomas, 74 F.3d 701 (6th Cir. 1996), cert.denied, 117 S.Ct. 74 (1996).
ACLU vs. Ashcroft, No. 00-1293.
VoyeurDorm vs. City of Tampa, No. 00-16346 (11 Cir. 2001) D. C. Docket No. 99-02180-CV-T-24F.

Bibliography

Finkelstein, Seth, and Lee Tien. "Censorware White Paper #1: Blacklisting Bytes." Electronic Frontier Foundation, March 6, 2001.
<http://www.eff.org/Censorship/Ratings_filters_labelling/20010306_eff_nrc_paper1.html> (May 10, 2002).

Godwin, Mike. " The Supreme Court, 'Community Standards,' and the Internet." *Reason Online,* October 2001.
<http://www.reason.com/0110/cr.mg.standards.html> (May 10, 2002).

Morris, Stan "A Review of the Law of Obscenity for Webmasters and Others." Gigalaw.com, July 2000.
<http://www.gigalaw.com/articles/2000-all/morris-2000-07-all.html> (May 10, 2002).

Shachtman, Noah. "VoyeurDorm: Address Unknown." *Wired News,* September 26, 2001.
<http://www.wired.com/news/politics/0,1283,47104,00.html> (May 10, 2002).

Wallace, Jonathan. "Threats to the Net: Amateur Action." *The Ethical Spectacle,* July 1995.
<http://www.spectacle.org/795/amateur.html> (May 10, 2002).

———. "The Free Speech Museum: Obscenity." *The Ethical Spectacle.*
<http://www.spectacle.org/freespch/musm/obsne.html> (May 10, 2002).

———. "Freedom of Speech: There Is No Such Thing as Obscenity." *The Ethical Spectacle,* February 1996.
<http://www.spectacle.org/296/obscene.html> (May 10, 2002).

Wallace, Jonathan, and Mark Mangan. "The Internet Censorship FAQ."
<http://www.spectacle.org/freespch/faq.html> (May 10, 2002).

Further Reading

American Civil Liberties Union. "Briefing Paper Number 14: Freedom of Expression in the Arts and eEntertainment."
<http://www.aclu.org/library/pbp14.html> (May 10, 2002).

———. "Cyber-Liberties." 2002.
<http://www.aclu.org/issues/cyber/hmcl.html> (May 10, 2002).

Center for Democracy and Technology. "Free Speech." <http://www.cdt.org/speech/> (May 10, 2002).

Edwards, Lilian, and Charlotte Waelde, eds. *Law and the Internet: Regulating Cyberspace*. Evanston, Ill.: Northwestern University Press, 1997.

Electronic Frontier Foundation. "Active EFF Legal Cases and Efforts." <http://www.eff.org/Legal/active_legal.html> (May 10, 2002).

Godwin, Mike. *Cyber Rights: Defending Free Speech in the Digital Age*. New York: Times Books, 1998.

Saunders, Kevin W. *Violence as Obscenity: Limiting the Media's First Amendment Protection*. Durham, N.C.: Duke University Press, 1996.

Sugarman, Rogers, Barshak & Cohen, P.C. "Net Litigation: First Amendment and the Internet, Background Notes." <http://www.netlitigation.com/netlitigation/backgrnd/firstamendback.htm> (May 10, 2002).

Wallace, Jonathan, and Mark Mangan. *Sex, Laws, and Cyberspace: Freedom and Censorship on the Frontiers of the Online Revolution*. New York: Henry Holt, 1997.

Related Topics

Child Online Protection Act and Child Online Privacy Protection Act; Content Filtering

— *Theresa M. Senft*

Online Journalism

Online journalism has combined the best, and in some cases the worst, aspects of all previous traditional news media. It offers a level of interactivity—direct communication between news organizations and audiences—never before known, made possible by online news forums. However, although it has brought text, audio, video, and graphics together in a single presentation, the practice of journalism on the Internet has not as yet broken any serious new journalistic ground.

The most common form of online journalism is the news Web site, such as CNN.com, Washingtonpost.com, and CNET.com. Some are partnered with or belong to traditional news outlets, and others stand alone on the Web. Email news services, which usually provide fragments of information and hyperlink pointers back to a Web site, are also important. Online bulletin board systems (BBSs), which are sometimes a haven for amateur journalists, and intranets, where financial news is often distributed to corporate employees and executives, are two other examples of online journalism.

What each of these adds to the pre-existing journalistic mix is interactivity. In online news, interactivity is most obviously represented by hyperlinks, which are the beginning of a new form of journalistic communication. They make news stories "non-linear," meaning that readers or viewers don't have to rely on the judgment of editors or producers to decide which story deserves the greatest emphasis or should be looked at first; readers can choose what is most interesting to them. Online news agencies have responded in some cases by "pushing" personalized news to readers, often in customized emails, that are stocked with stories according to a pre-selected set of topics in which the reader has expressed interest. Many sites embed hyperlinks to background stories, audio and video clips, or other ancillary information directly within their news pages. In some cases, readers may choose not to view what is presented to them as "news" at all, but instead may seek out historical information on related topics instead. Or they may choose to visit another site altogether, by means of the hyperlinks that many news sites provide to other Web sites of interest. These are levels of choice and opportunity that have never before been present in any medium at any time in the history of news.

Interactivity's journalistic impact doesn't stop at hyperlinks. News organizations also can set up chats, email forums, and message boards, and they can conduct online polls. These tools enable news bureaus to trade ideas and information with their audiences, learn of news story ideas, and listen and respond to direct public criticism and praise.

At a forum sponsored by the University of Minnesota's Institute for New Media Studies in October 2000, former *Wired* magazine and Slashdot.org writer Jonathan Katz described how his reporting has been directly affected by the inclusion of an email link in his author's byline. Katz said that he once wound up writing five different versions of the same column, which initially was a condemnation of the rap artist Tupac Shakur. When he first blasted the murdered rapper's violent and misogynistic lyrics, African Americans in the audience complained that he didn't understand Shakur's true artistic intent. When Katz admitted that they were right, he wrote another column saying so, sparking waves of protest from those who'd agreed in the first place, which in turn prompted a third column. Later, he produced two others, as further and more refined communication continued between columnist and audience. Katz said that by the time he was done, he had an understanding of rap culture that he could never have gained any other way, and his final column was the one that he would have written in the first place had he better understood his subject.

If these are the best aspects of online journalism, its worst sides have arguably had even greater impact. These have, on occasion, fed a news-culture frenzy that has involved not just online journalism, but also by association all journalism organizations. Venerable TV journalist Marvin Kalb said as much in a blistering paper, "The Rise of the New News," published in 1998 by Harvard University's Joan Shorenstein Center on the Press, Politics and Public Policy. To some degree, Kalb blames Matt Drudge for the hair-trigger mentality that today characterizes much of journalism.

THE DRUDGE REPORT

Depending on who is talking, gossipmonger/journalist Matt Drudge either represents the impending death of legitimate journalism, or is (in his own words) a John Peter Zenger for the modern age, fighting a one-man war to wrest a free press from the clutches of a journalistically tepid and self-interested corporate culture. The truth may contain elements of both views.

As a teen and young adult, Drudge worked menial jobs, daydreaming all the while of working at the local news bastion, *The Washington Post.* But before he took the news business by storm as a 31-year-old in 1997, the closest he came to a newsroom job was managing a CBS-TV gift shop in Los Angeles.

In 1995, Drudge's father bought him a computer. Two months later, Drudge launched himself into the gossip business by posting discarded media tidbits and daily TV ratings purloined from CBS wastebaskets. He began emailing his *Drudge Report* to a small group of subscribers, and published it on a Web site. By August 1997, around the time he was sued for $30 million for falsely writing that an aide to President Clinton had once been charged with spousal abuse, Drudge had some 85,000 email subscribers and tens of thousands of site visitors.

In January 1998, Drudge hit the apex of his influence. It was Drudge who first linked the names of Bill Clinton and Monica Lewinsky, launching one of the most controversial episodes ever in American politics. One Saturday night, on January 17, 1998, Drudge's subscribers received a post that would rattle the Washington establishment: "*Newsweek* Kills Story On White House Intern," the headline said.

The dispatch quoted unnamed sources saying that *Newsweek* had a story detailing a presidential peccadillo in the White House at a time when Clinton was already under investigation for sexual harassment in the case involving Paula Jones. *Newsweek* had cancelled the intern story at the last minute. Drudge's

report turned out to be essentially true, although it later emerged that *Newsweek* had merely delayed the story to double-check its explosive facts. Drudge did not name Lewinsky in his first emailed dispatch, but he did identify her the following night. By the middle of the next week, every major news organization in the United States began running the story.

Meanwhile, Drudge had set in motion a feeding frenzy among news organizations, each clamoring to find any new nugget of the Clinton-Lewinsky story. Suddenly, *The New York Times, The Washington Post,* ABC News, and everyone else was in a losing competition battle with the lowly *Drudge Report,* which still was being produced on a cheap computer with an inexpensive modem in a run-down Hollywood apartment. "Now, with a modem, anyone can follow the world and report on the world; no middle man, no big brother," Drudge told the National Press Club in 1998. "And I guess this changes everything."

THE 24-HOUR NEWS CYCLE

As Kalb sees it, Drudge's lack of reliance on credible sources and his willingness to go public with sketchy rumors is what led to an explosion of what Kalb calls the "24-hour news cycle." It is a phenomenon already familiar from cable-TV news, but one that gained propulsive momentum in the Internet age.

One incident during those shark-tank times of "Monicagate" is illustrative. On January 26, 1998, the Web site of *The Dallas Morning News* stated that a Secret Service agent was "reportedly" ready to testify that he saw President Clinton with Lewinsky in "a compromising position." The newspaper quoted "an unidentified lawyer familiar with the negotiations" between the agent and Special Prosecutor Ken Starr. Ninety minutes after it was published online, the story was pulled because the paper's source called to say that the newspaper had gotten it wrong. The story never appeared in *The Dallas Morning News* in print, and the newspaper retracted the online version.

But the Associated Press already had picked up the story. Larry King, broadcasting live on CNN, read the AP dispatch live on the air that night, as did Geraldo Rivera on CNBC. The story was loose in the world, driven by fiercely competitive news organizations that publicized the story without waiting for verification. With every news organization's Web site transforming it suddenly into a 24-hour news operation, directly competing with every other news division in every other medium, the drive for a scoop pushed *The Dallas Morning News* to publish a story that, according to

Brill's Content, turned out to be "a one-source story from a fifth-hand source."

As Kalb writes, in a previous age, such lapses in judgment at an organization as respected as *The Dallas Morning News* would have been far less likely. In the past, newspaper exclusives had to wait for the morning edition. While it might have been tempting to publish a hot piece early, there simply was nowhere to do it. But the Internet allows editors and reporters to publish instantly, before bothering to check and double-check their facts.

The fallout has been extensive. In February 1999, the Pew Research Center did a nationwide telephone survey of 1,203 adults and detected a striking decline in the public's regard for news-media values since the mid-1980s. The number of Americans who saw news organizations as immoral tripled, with the public split evenly on whether the press was immoral or not. And the two-to-one margin of people who believed that the press protects democracy had evaporated since 1985. In 1999, 45 percent of those polled said that news media protect democracy, while 38 percent said that the media hurt it. Online news is not the single-handed cause of this drop, but its ability to create a constant deadline situation has contributed significantly to the decline.

THE IMPACT OF ONLINE JOURNALISM

Journalists themselves are ambivalent about the Internet's role in the news media. The 2000 Middleberg/Ross survey of journalists found that while most who use the Internet to research or develop stories feel that the medium lacks credibility, 60 percent of them would still be willing to disseminate rumors picked up online, if they got confirmation elsewhere. Concerns about a Web-fed "Wild West" mentality sparked the formation in 1999 of the Online News Association, a group of high-profile journalists headed by *Wall Street Journal* interactive managing editor Rich Jaroslovsky. The group's mission, according to its Web site, is "to encourage the best journalism possible in this new medium."

Online news, despite its flaws, is not going away. From an audience perspective, there are so many advantages to online news that there is an open question as to whether some other media forms, especially printed newspapers and magazines, can survive long with the Internet as competition. Doug Millison, in his Online Journalism FAQ, says that some Web publications will do a better job of profiting from relationships with customers than print publications, especially if those sites are good at identifying their specific audiences. Print publications, Millison asserts, may lose customers to the Web if they fail to find ways of delivering their product effectively to Web-savvy customers, both in print as well as online.

But if online journalism has the capacity to destroy old news mainstays, it may also have the ability to create radically new ones. John Pavlik, director for the Center for New Media at Columbia University, is among those testing a technology package that he calls the "mobile journalism workstation," which combines wireless Internet access, a satellite-based global positioning system (GPS), digital photography and sound recording, a personal digital assistant (PDA), and a miniaturized wearable computer. "It's all about finding new ways to tell stories," Pavlik says. The technology could one day turn every reporter into a roving newsroom capable of conducting every conceivable journalistic chore, from writing a newspaper-style story to taping and editing a video segment, and transmitting the whole package wirelessly to the Internet almost instantly.

Bibliography

Brill, Steven. "Pressgate." *Brill's Content,* August 1998.

Featherly, Kevin. "Columbia Prof Foresees Next Best Thing to Time Travel." *Newsbytes,* March 7, 2001.

Kalb, Marvin. *The Rise of the New News: A Case Study of Two Root Causes of the Modern Scandal Coverage.* Cambridge, Mass.: The Joan Shorenstein Center on the Press, Politics and Public Policy, John F. Kennedy School of Government, Harvard University, 1998.

Middleberg, Don, and Steve Ross. "The Middleberg/Ross Print Media in Cyberspace Study." March 2, 2000. <http://www.middleberg.com/studies/print/fulloverview.cfm> (July 12, 2002).

Millison, Doug. "Online Journalism FAQ." 1999. <http://www.online-journalist.com/faq.html> (July 12, 2002).

The Pew Research Center for the People and the Press. "Big Doubts About News Media's Values: Public Votes for Continuity and Change in 2000." February 1999. <http://people-press.org/dataarchive/signup.php3?DocID=53> (July 12, 2002).

Further Reading

Fidler, Roger. *Mediamorphosis: Understanding New Media.* Thousand Oaks, Calif.: Pine Forge Press, 1997.

Pavlik, John V. *New Media Technology: Cultural and Commercial Perspectives.* Boston, Mass.: Allyn & Bacon, 1996.

———. "Understanding the Impact of New Media on Journalism." Columbia University, 1998. <http://www.columbia.edu/~jp35/lectures/lect_intro.html> (July 12, 2002).

Woolner, Ann. "Just Doing Their Jobs." *Brill's Content*, April 2000.

Zollman, Peter. *Interactive News: State of the Art.* Washington, D.C.: Radio and Television News Directors Foundation, 1997.

Related Topics

Content Filtering; Desktop Publishing; Digital Millennium Copyright Act; Electronic Democracy; Multimedia; Narrowcasting; Personalization; Streaming Media

— Kevin Featherly

Open Source

Open source refers to the software-industry tradition of developing and sharing source code and standards, and of encouraging collaborative development. Often aligned with hacker culture, open-source software has contributed to many important developments in Internet infrastructure, including BIND, the Berkeley Internet Name Daemon servers that run the Domain Name System; in software, including Linux and the Apache Web server; and in software languages, including Perl, Tcl, and Python. Open source also epitomizes the philosophy of the "gift culture" within the Internet community, wherein people collaborate and exchange information freely in a climate of mutual respect.

Open-source software refers to programs whose source code (the human-readable instructions that make up software) has been openly distributed on the Internet so that others can use, test, develop, and improve them independently. This is in contrast to proprietary software products, where the source code is secret and closely guarded through patents and intellectual-property protection. An example of proprietary software is Microsoft Corporation's Windows operating system (OS); many of the current open-source creations by commercial entities are being generated in reaction to the Microsoft monopoly.

The ethos of open-source software is guided by the hacker ethic, which emphasizes creativity and the sharing of resources for the public, or common, good. Open-source software code is studied and improved upon by other programmers, with such improvements publicly revealed and, under most licenses, distributed freely in a process that encourages constant, continual innovation.

Open-source programs were particularly key in the early development of the Internet, when ARPANET moved to open-architecture networking. Much of what drives the Internet, such as Sendmail and the World Wide Web, is derived from open-source principles.

The Free Software Movement presaged what we now know as the Open Source Movement. In 1983, dismayed by the increasing commercialization of OSs, Richard Stallman, then at MIT's Artificial Intelligence Laboratory, began the GNU ("GNU's not Unix") project, which distributed a free version of the UNIX OS. Stallman believed strongly that innovation in computer science could be achieved only if source code was made freely available. Therefore, his Free Software Foundation developed a suite of tools for a robust OS, including Emacs, an editor favored by many hackers, and GCC, a C compiler that would later become very important to the development of Linux OS.

To ensure that GNU software would not evolve into proprietary software, the Free Software Foundation adopted the method of "copyleft," which keeps software free instead of privatizing it. A software author uses his or her own copyright to guarantee those rights to all users by affixing a standard licensing notice, such as the General Public License (GPL), to the code.

In 1991, Linus Torvalds, a student at the University of Helsinki, developed a free and freely modifiable version of UNIX. He released his code on the Internet, and through collaboration with a global retinue of Internet programmers, Linux, as the version came to be called, has become the fastest-expanding OS in the world. The Linux OS can be downloaded for free over the Internet, and is also available packaged with documentation and technical support by commercial companies Red Hat and Caldera. Not only is Linux popular in North America and Europe, it is also extremely popular in developing nations like South Africa, Mexico, Cuba, India, and the Philippines.

In 1997, a group of free-software leaders, including Eric Raymond and Tim O'Reilly, became concerned that the more anti-business sensibility of the Free Software Foundation distracted a wider audience from adopting open-source software. They therefore devised an Open Source Definition, which stipulates nine criteria that the distribution license of software must meet in order for that software to be considered to be open source. These criteria include the ability to distribute the software freely, the availability of the source code, the right to create derived works through modification, and licensing that does not discriminate against persons or groups in a specific field of work.

Other popular open-source projects include Apache and Perl. Apache Open-Source Software is used on Web-server computers, which host Web pages and provide appropriate content as requested by Internet browsers. Perl is a popular software language that has been modified and improved through a global network of collaborators.

The repository SourceForge lists more than 10,000 projects utilizing open source. Open source is also entering the mainstream to an increasing degree, as major players in the computer industry adopt it. In 1998, Netscape decided to make the next version of its Web browser (then dubbed Mozilla) an open-source product. Soon thereafter, IBM adopted the Apache Web server as the core of its product line. Corporate support for Linux and other open-source software has become increasingly popular, with Corel (maker of WordPerfect) developing a suite of office applications for Linux, IBM supporting the Apache Web server, and Hewlett-Packard, Compaq, IBM, and Silicon Graphics installing and supporting Linux for their hardware customers.

Many see open source as more than just a software movement, but as a business ethos. The hacker ethic looked upon the development of the Internet as a public good, created with the collaboration of many volunteers. This development in turn created innovation and growth in the network, which in turn became a more valuable resource because of its ability to connect people, resources, and knowledge. Open-source software projects have led to innovation, development, and unique communities run completely by and for their users.

Bibliography

DiBona, Chris; Ockman, Sam; and Mark Stone. *Open Sources: Voices from the Open Source Revolution.* Sebastopol, Calif.: O'Reilly & Associates, 1999. <http://www.oreilly.com/catalog/opensources/book/toc.html> (May 31, 2002).

Himanen, Pekka. *The Hacker Ethic and the Spirit of the Information Age.* New York: Random House, 2001.

Moody, Glyn. *The Rebel Code: The Inside Story of Linux and the Open Source Revolution.* Cambridge, Mass.: Perseus Publishing, 2001.

Roberts, Alan. "Open Source: The New, New Economy." *Arena Magazine,* February 2001, p. 21.

Starr, Paul. "The Electronic Commons." *The American Prospect,* vol. 11, no. 10 (March 27, 2000–April 10, 2000). <http://www.prospect.org/print/V11/10/starr-p.html> (May 31, 2002).

Further Reading

Castells, Manuel. "The Culture of the Internet." *The Internet Galaxy: Reflections on the Internet, Business, and Society.* Oxford/New York: Oxford University Press, 2001; pp. 36–63.

The Free Software Foundation. "GNU's Not Unix!" <http://www.fsf.org/> (May 31, 2002).

Kogut, Bruce, and Anca Metiu. "Open-Source Software Development and Distributed Innovation." *Oxford Review of Economic Policy,* vol. 17 (Summer 2001), p. 248.

Newman, Nathan. "The Origins and Future of Open Source Software: A NetAction White Paper." 1999. <http://www.netaction.org/opensrc/future/> (May 31, 2002).

Raymond, Eric S. *The Cathedral and the Bazaar: Musings on Linux and Open Source by an Accidental Revolutionary.* Sebastopol, Calif./Cambridge, Mass.: O'Reilly & Associates, 2001. <http://www.tuxedo.org/~esr/writings/cathedral-bazaar/> (May 31, 2002).

von Hippel, Eric. "Innovation by User Communities: Learning from Open-Source Software." *MIT Sloan Management Review,* vol. 42 (Summer 2001), p. 82.

Williams, Sam. *Free as in Freedom: Richard Stallman's Crusade for Free Software.* Sebastopol, Calif.: O'Reilly & Associates, 2002. <http://www.oreilly.com/openbook/freedom/> (May 31, 2002).

Related Topics

Berners-Lee, Tim; "The Cathedral and the Bazaar"; Copyleft; Hacking, Cracking, and Phreaking; Linux; *The New Hacker's Dictionary*; Raymond, Eric; Stallman, Richard

— *Leslie Regan Shade*

Optical Character Recognition

Optical character recognition (OCR) uses machines—computers and sometimes other peripherals such as scanners—and software to recognize printed text characters. OCR enables users to digitally "read" and store printed text, thereby reducing the amount of typing required for inputting text. Scanning and interpreting text may seem simple, but the technologies required are complex; the potential uses are broad, important, and may be scaled toward increasingly general and difficult recognition problems.

The first general-use OCR system was created by futurist Ray Kurzweil in 1976. His company, Computer Products, Inc., released a commercial version two years later.

OCR is an analog-to-digital process; it begins with analog materials, and converts them to digital data. In order to scan printed words (typically, black text printed on a white page), a computer must utilize a charged coupled device (CCD)—a scanner. The CCD is charged by light, and successively codes and records the reflections at each point on the image. Scanning a text document turns it into a bitmap. The OCR software then analyzes the light and dark areas of the bitmap, and translates the results to a computer for storage and output. The success of the process depends in large part on the quality of the source material (clarity of the image being scanned), the effectiveness of the hardware (for example, the resolution ability of the scanner being used), and the quality of the software (its level of sophistication and accuracy).

The most difficult part of the process is the translation from light/dark images to words, a procedure that requires sophisticated pattern recognition. The OCR software must match shapes to character definitions. Since there is an abundance of fonts (letter and number character-shape sets) and languages (many using a wide variety of letter and number character-shape sets), there are many complexities and ambiguities that must be recognized, interpreted, and translated. Introducing non-regularized characters, like those produced by handwriting, further complicates the process.

OCR software must first find and note the boundary and region of a pattern; it must then match the object to items with which the object is conceptually related. The context in which the item is used informs the machine's ability to make choices about its identity. For example, one does not often find two instances of the letter "y" together in English words, so if there are two adjacent shapes that both look like "y," at least one of them is probably something else. The software must then select the proper representation pattern. Since pattern recognition is a sort of under-constrained problem—one in which there isn't enough information to know that the arrived-at solution is uniquely correct—the system must also include other means of evaluating the accuracy of the solution.

The algorithms in OCR and other character-recognition software work using complex trial-and-error functions that model and simplify human cognitive systems. Using fuzzy logic and concepts of neural networking, computers (and programs) can be "taught" to recognize ambiguous or previously unknown characters (via repetitive trial and error using complex algorithms), thereby enabling scanners and OCR software to recognize handwriting or exotic languages, and/or to respond to idiosyncratic written input.

A large number of industries use scanning and character recognition for important everyday functions. Banks process checks using bar codes and signature recognition, stores process sales by scanning bar codes, and the post office scans addresses on envelopes. An additional range of computerized activities is related to OCR. For instance, writing recognition, used in personal digital assistants (PDAs), is strongly associated with the procedures used to scan printed text. OCR will likely continue to gain in importance as interaction between humans and computers increases.

Bibliography

Anzai, Yuichiro. *Pattern Recognition and Machine Learning.* Boston: Academic Press, 1992.

Kovalevsky, V. A., ed. *Character Readers and Pattern Recognition.* Translated by A.M. Karpovich and A.M. Leavitt. New York: Spartan Books, 1968.

Peters, Liliane, and Ashutosh Malaviya. "Off-line Handwritten Character Recognition: READ." Fraunhofer AiS, updated January 1999. <http://set.gmd.de/EIA/read.html> (July 12, 2002).

Further Reading

Tannenbaum, Robert S. *Theoretical Foundations of Multimedia.* New York: Computer Science Press, 1998.

Tiscione, Jason. "OCHRE—Optical Character Recognition Using Neural Networks in Java." <http://www.geocities.com/SiliconValley/2548/ochre.html> (July 12, 2002).

Related Topics

Fuzzy Logic; Kurzweil, Raymond

— *Edward Lee Lamoureux*

Optical Computing and Networking

Optical computing and networking denotes the use of light in computer processing and communication. The physical properties of natural light, introduced with discoveries as early as the nineteenth century, now allow scientists to understand and utilize light as a technique for computing and a method for networking. Light acts as a substitute for electricity in computer processing and information channeling.

In 1870, physicist John Tyndall established the physical properties of light during a demonstration of how light reacts in water. When water was poured from an illuminated pitcher, Tyndall revealed that light from the sun bent with the shape of the pouring water. This later led to research on photons, particles of light, and the ways in which they could be transmitted and controlled. Optical computing—hereinafter referred to as optics—became a heavily investigated field of research in the 1980s, in the hope of speeding up computer processing.

Optics uses photons instead of electrons to establish on-and-off switches within the microchips of computer technology. These switches regulate the flow of information, power, and instructions within the computer.

Optics offers a way to overcome some of the limitations of electronics in areas such as miniaturizing computer processors, increasing the flow of data traffic, and supporting greater bandwidth. Since light moves at extremely high speeds when compared to electricity, computers that process light can function at rates much faster than the technology of today. Furthermore, beams of light can be crossed without problems, reducing the chance of short circuits. With the innumerable possibilities that optics offer to computer technology, dedicated researchers found a new way to address the problems set forth by optics, and designed optoelectronics.

Optoelectronics merges optical networking with electrical computing to form a hybrid. It is a process by which electrons can interact with photons to achieve a working relationship between the speed capabilities possessed by optics and the already-established methods of electrical computer processing. For instance, when a file is sent between computers, optoelectronics can translate it into a photonic form and send it through fiberoptic cables; then the receiving computer can translate the file back into an electronic form.

The significance of optical networking lies in its ability to channel massive amounts of information quickly. As Internet use grows, bandwidth becomes an essential commodity; each Internet user needs a portion of the available bandwidth to receive data. Fiberoptics can be used as medium for information transmission to solve such dilemmas. Philip Ball, a writer for *Nature News Service,* describes the unique size and ability of fiberoptics. As Ball explains, fiberoptics are made up of strands of glass or plastic that can transmit far more information than normal copper wires can. Using optical carrier technology that passes and controls the flow of light, gigabits of information, at data transmission rates in excess of 1,000,000,000 bits per second, can travel much faster than the 4,500,000 bits per second permitted through copper wires. In addition, light will travel great distances through fiberoptics, and unlike electronic transmissions, the fiberoptic signals do not need to be recharged.

Fiberoptics are the underlying vehicle for information transmission, and are essential components to optical networking. However, they provide only a carrying method for light. A laser, similar to the component that reads information from a CD-ROM, must first generate the light. Light-emitting diodes (LEDs), or miniature lasers, send instructions and information in the form of binary data through fiberoptic cables. The pulses of light generated by the LED are then received by a photodiode on the alternate end, which transforms the light into electronic current that can be understood by the corresponding computer.

Currently, scientists at the Massachusetts Institute of Technology (MIT) are addressing the problems associated with optical computing. Researchers at MIT who are trying to create computer systems that run solely on optics, instead of electricity, have produced deigns for a photonic processing chip. Since photons cannot successfully operate on microchips, the new design replaces the silicon chip with clusters of atoms. Once optical computing is perfected and then coupled with optical networking, it is predicted that light will be able to offer computers with unimaginable speeds, and networks with abundant information capacity and ultra-fast transmission rates.

Bibliography

Ball, Philip. "Rosy Glow on Information Horizon." *Nature News Service,* January 26, 2001. <http://www.nature.com/nsu/010201/010201-2.html> (May 31, 2002).
Kelly, Kevin. "George Gilder: When Bandwidth Is Free." *Wired* 1.04, September/October 1993. <http://www.wired.com/wired/archive/1.04/gilder_pr.html> (May 31, 2002).
"Ten Technologies: Optical Computing." *Business Week,* 2001. <http://www.businessweek.com/bw50/2001/tech_optical.htm> (May 31, 2002).
Woodford, Chris. "Fiber Optics." *The Cutting Edge: An Encyclopedia of Advanced Technologies.* New York: Oxford University Press, 2000; pp. 97–100.

Further Reading

Crease, Robert P. "Can Optical Computing Bounce Back?" *The Scientist,* vol. 3, no. 4 (February 20, 1989).
Passmore, David. "Optical Optimism." *Business Communications Review,* vol. 30, no. 12 (December 2000).
Platt, Charles. "Bright Switch." *Wired* 8.09, September 2000. <http://www.wired.com/wired/archive/8.09/optical.html> (May 31, 2002).
Steinert-Threlkeld, Tom, and Charles Babcock. "After the PC: A World 'Bathed' in the Net." *Inter@ctive Week,* vol. 6, no. 16 (April 19, 1999).

Related Topics
Broadband; Internet

— *James Pyfer*

p p p p p P p p p p p

Paik, Nam June

1932–
Multimedia Artist

Nam June Paik is a Korean-born artist and composer who lives in New York and Düsseldorf. He was the first artist to work with television and video, and his career includes many contributions to intermedia and multimedia. Paik's 1964 manifesto, "Utopian Laser Television," conceptualized a world in which television meant thousands of channels broadcasting at any time, day or night, each channel programmed by its owner-director for an audience as small or as large as any concept might attract. In a 1974 study for the Rockefeller Foundation, Paik coined the term "electronic superhighway," which evolved into the ideas of the information superhighway and the Infobahn.

In the late 1950s and early 1960s, Paik lived and worked in Germany, where he had gone to study music. He conceptualized music as an extended frame of action and philosophy linked to the ideas of John Cage. Paik's ideas involved a Buddhist vision of universal and anti-elitist approaches to music, art, and social philosophy. He shared these with the international community of experimental artists, architects, composers, and designers known as Fluxus.

The Fluxus ideas included the unity of art and life; an experimental approach to the arts; and the use of chance, playfulness, and simplicity. Another central idea is the concept that artist and composer Dick Higgins labeled intermedia.

The intermedia idea erased the boundaries between art forms in a fluid, experimental approach to the arts—including music. New forms emerged across the boundaries of existing media, and entirely new arts media were born.

During his stay in Germany, Paik began to imagine new ways of understanding and working with television. Unable to gain access to expensive studio equipment and costly broadcast time, Paik's first television experiments used magnets directly on the cabinets of early television sets to distort the broadcast images shown on screen.

By 1964, Paik had moved to New York. There, he purchased the first available Sony portable video camera. Within moments of the purchase, he shot about ten minutes of raw, grainy footage and made history that evening with a presentation of the world's first video art at New York City's Café a Go-Go. Paik essentially invented the medium of video art as an experimental extension of his search for new music.

Later, as a professor at the Düsseldorf Art Academy and the California Institute for the Arts, Paik began to experiment with ever-more-sophisticated video techniques. Among other things, he invented the world's first video synthesizer together with Japanese inventor Shuya Abe, and taught a generation of artists who were later to emerge as the first video artists. Paik's students had also become the first generation of producer-directors on MTV, closing the circle in two decades from experimental art to commercial entertainment.

Many of Paik's Fluxus colleagues were important to the birth of video art, multimedia, and intermedia. These included the Germans Wolf Vostell and Joseph Beuys, Japanese artists Takehisa Kosugi and Shigeko Kubota, Lithuanian-born Americans George Maciunas and Jonas Mekas, and French artists Jean Dupuy, Robert Filliou, and Ben Vautier, among others. The interpretations that these artists gave to multimedia and intermedia ran from the simplest and most primitive possibilities, typified by the folklore-based projects of Sweden's Bengt af Klintberg and the poetry performances of American Emmett Williams, to Paik's own technologically dazzling installations and the sophisticated book/print/installation works of American Alison Knowles.

Paik's philosophical rigor and unorthodox approach to the arts placed him at the center of several artistic innovations. His nearly single-handed invention of video as an art form shaped a field to which many others would later contribute. With Vostell, Paik pioneered artist television. He was active in the experimental film of the 1960s, and he helped to pioneer mail art through his eclectic

Journal of the University of Avant-Garde Hinduism. He helped to shape the field of video installation, and played an important role in the development of installation as an art form. With George Brecht, Vautier, and Yoko Ono, he co-invented the event structure. With his Fluxus colleagues, he played a central role in early performance art.

For many, Nam June Paik ranks with John Cage as one of the most extraordinary and influential composer-philosophers of the twentieth century, as interesting for the music he did not make as for the music he did. He is equally important for the intellectual and artistic territory that he opened in encouraging others to explore new media.

Selected Works

Paik, Nam June. *Nam June Paik: Video Works 1963–88.* London: Hayward Gallery, 1988.
———. *Nam June Paik: Werke 1946-1976 Musik, Fluxus, Video.* Cologne, Germany: Kölnischer Kunstverein, 1977.
———. *Nam June Paik: Eine Data Base.* La Biennale di Venezia, XLV esposizione internazionale d'arte. Padiglione tedesco. Klaus Bussmann, Florian Matzner, and Nam June Paik, eds. Stuttgart: Edition Cantz, 1993.
———. "Utopian Laser Television." *Manifestoes.* New York: Something Else Press, 1964.
Paik, Nam June, and Kenworth W. Moffett, eds. *The Electronic Superhighway.* New York/Seoul/ Fort Lauderdale: Holly Solomon Gallery, Hyundai Gallery, and the Museum of Art, Fort Lauderdale, 1995.

Bibliography

Friedman, Ken, ed. *The Fluxus Reader.* Chichester, West Sussex/New York: Academy Editions, 1998.
Hanhardt, John G. *The Worlds of Nam June Paik.* New York: Guggenheim Museum; distributed by Harry N. Abrams, 2000.
Higgins, Dick. "Intermedia." *Something Else* Newsletter, vol. 1, no. 1 (1966), pp. 1–6.

Further Reading

Art in Context Center for Communications. "Nam June Paik Reference Page." 1995–2002. <http://www.artincontext.org/artist/p/nam_june_paik/> (April 12, 2002).
Artcyclopedia—The Fine Art Search Engine. "Nam June Paik, Korean/American Video Artist, Born 1932." 1999–2002. <http://www.artcyclopedia.com/artists/paik_nam_june.html> (April 12, 2002).

Related Topics

Multimedia; Sandin, Daniel

— *Ken Friedman*

Papert, Seymour
1928–
Mathematician and Computer Scientist

Seymour Papert is best known for his contributions to our understanding of children's learning processes, and to the ways in which technology can support learning. He invented the Logo computer language, a valuable educational tool used by children and their teachers throughout the world. He is also one of the pioneers of Artificial Intelligence (AI) and an acclaimed mathematician.

Papert was born and educated in South Africa, where he participated in the anti-apartheid movement. He did mathematical research at Cambridge University from 1954 to 1958, then worked with the well-known psychologist Jean Piaget at the University of Geneva until 1963. Famous for his work on the cognitive development of young children, Piaget was an extremely influential figure in Papert's thinking about children and learning. In the early 1960s, Papert became a professor of mathematics at the Massachusetts Institute of Technology (MIT). There he co-authored the seminal work *Perceptrons: An Introduction to Computational Geometry* (1970) with Marvin Minsky, and worked with Minsky on the theory of the Society of Mind (which Minsky continued to explore while Papert turned his attention to education). At MIT, Papert also helped found the Media Lab, and co-founded the Artificial Intelligence Lab. Papert currently lives in Maine, where he has founded a small laboratory for learning research called the Learning Barn.

Although Papert is highly regarded and influential in the fields of AI research and mathematics, his best-known work concerns children's learning styles and technology. Papert is highly critical of traditional educational thought, in which children are cast in the role of passive recipients of knowledge, rather than active participants in activity-based, creative, non-structured learning exchanges.

Papert refers to his educational philosophy as constructionism, in that it focuses on the idea of mental construction. In his 1993 book, *The Children's Machine: Rethinking School in the Age of the Computer,* he explains: "The principal other necessary change parallels an African proverb: If a man is hungry you can give him a fish, but it is better to give him a line and teach him to catch fish himself. Traditional education codifies what it thinks citizens need to know and sets out to feed children this 'fish.'

Constructionism is built on the assumption that children will do best by finding ('fishing') for themselves the specific knowledge they need."

Papert is highly critical of schools for their hierarchical organization, dependence on testing and learning by rote, commitment to uniformity, and valuing of information over knowledge. Children learn best, he believes, through tinkering ("bricolage"), unstructured activities that resemble play, and research based on partial knowledge—by solving problems that are interesting to them, much as they do in non-school situations. An example would be learning about measurement while baking a cake, as opposed to passively observing abstract lessons about cups and gallons. Rather than attempt to change the schooling system incrementally by including technology in the curriculum, he calls for a fundamental shift in our epistemology of learning—how we understand the goals of education and the ways in which children learn best.

Papert believes that computers have the potential to revolutionize learning, but that schools will not allow this type of shift to occur. Claims that the computer will revolutionize schools are misguided, he believes, because schools will assimilate computers into their rote way of educating students, like an organism defending itself against a foreign body, rather than allowing the computer to cut across subject boundaries and permitting active, playful, exploratory learning. As Papert explains in an interview published in the online journal MEME: "Instead of becoming something that undermines all these antiquated teachings of school, computers became assimilated. . . . So school turned what could be a revolutionary instrument into essentially a conservative one. School does not want to radically change itself. The power of computers is not to improve school but to replace it with a different kind of structure."

Papert's best-known contribution may be his invention of Logo, which was created in his laboratory. Logo is a programming language that children can use to draw pictures, direct robot-like creatures, or engage in other learning activities. In one of its more interesting applications, Logo can be used in combination with special LEGO components. Embedded into these LEGO pieces are tiny computers that can process information from sensors and act accordingly, so children can create objects out of the LEGO pieces—animals, buildings, vehicles—and then program behaviors into them. One example Papert discusses is that of an eight-year-old girl who programmed a "mother cat" and its "kitten." Both

would move about the room until the "kitten" beeped and flashed a light mounted on its head, at which point the "mother cat" would move toward it. This type of playful learning allows children to interact with and understand new concepts—in this case, the concept of feedback—in a way that stresses activity, creativity, and qualitative knowledge.

In his 1996 book, *The Connected Family: Bridging the Digital Generation Gap,* Papert's focus is the home. He argues that the introduction of personal computers into the home has opened new doors for children's learning, moving the locus of learning from the school into the home and giving parents new opportunities to participate in their children's learning experiences. In order to further this development, he is involved in current industry initiatives aimed at encouraging children's learning and creativity through technology and play. For instance, he serves on the advisory boards for MaMaMedia Inc. (a children's Web site) and of LEGO Mindstorms (a line of programmable robots).

Selected Works

Minsky, Marvin, and Seymour Papert. *Perceptrons: An Introduction to Computational Geometry.* Cambridge, Mass.: MIT Press, 1969; expanded edition, 1988.

Papert, Seymour. *The Children's Machine: Rethinking School in the Age of the Computer.* New York: BasicBooks, 1993.

———. *The Connected Family: Bridging the Digital Generation Gap.* Atlanta: Longstreet Publishing, 1996.

———. *Mindstorms: Children, Computers, and Powerful Ideas.* New York: Basic Books, 1980; second edition, 1993.

Bibliography

Abelson, Harold, and Andrea diSessa. *Turtle Geometry: The Computer as a Medium for Exploring Mathematics.* Cambridge, Mass.: MIT Press, 1981.

Bennahum, David S. "School's Out? A Conversation with Seymour Papert." *MEME* 2.13, October 15, 1996. <http://www.memex.org/meme2-13.html> (May 31, 2002).

Further Reading

Papert, Seymour. "Technology in Schools: Local Fix or Global Transformation?: Remarks by Seymour Papert for a House of Representatives Panel on Technology and Education." MIT Media Lab, October 12, 1995. <http://kids.www.media.mit.edu/projects/kids/sp-talk.html> (May 31, 2002).

Related Topics

Distance Learning; Education and Computers; Minsky, Marvin

— *Nicole Ellison*

Patent

A patent is a government grant giving an inventor the right to exclude others from making, selling, or using an invention for a fixed period of time. Despite the centuries-long history of patents, the evolution of new forms of media raises challenges to the framework of patents. Although patent law has always had to adapt to new technologies, the issues surrounding computer-software patents have created considerable stresses on the system.

Patents are one of a constellation of legal devices for protecting intellectual property. Other protections include copyright and trademark. Copyright protects an "original work of authorship": a novel, for instance, or a recipe, a song, a painting, or a photograph. Trademark protects a name or mark used to identify the source of a product and differentiate it from similar products. There are some interesting exceptions to these categories, resulting from historical accidents. Ships' hulls and architectural designs, for example, can be protected by copyright, although they seem quite dissimilar from other types of copyrightable work.

Patents protect the creation of a particular device or process. For an invention to be patentable, the inventor must demonstrate that the invention is original (that it has not been thought of before), that it is useful, and that it is "non-obvious." In the United States, patents protect a device or process for a period of twenty years from the date of application.

Patents are an important part of any technology corporation's property, and this is especially true of software companies. While software creation requires a significant investment of programming time and talent, it does not require the infrastructure needed by, for example, an automobile manufacturer. New software producers have relatively few barriers to entering the market and producing software applications. Therefore, the industry has attempted to find ways of enforcing its ownership over certain software processes.

Copyright seems like a viable alternative for protecting software. Indeed, protection for source code (computer programs in a form that can be easily read by humans) and object code (computer programs in a form that can be directly executed by machines) has met with fairly strong success. There has been a great deal of difficulty, however, in interpreting what has come to be called the "look and feel" of a program's interface—the graphics used or organization of menus, for instance. Recently, software companies have turned to patents for further protection of the underlying processes and ideas embodied in a software application.

Early on, it seemed as though patents would offer little protection to computer programmers. A Supreme Court decision in 1972, *Gottschalk vs. Benson,* determined that a computer algorithm was not subject to patent protection. Computer algorithms are procedures a programmer creates to perform particular tasks. A method for more quickly sorting a list of names into alphabetic order, for example, would be considered an algorithm. The court determined that algorithms are more like mathematical formulae, abstract ideas, or natural laws: They are discovered rather than invented.

While *Gottschalk* effectively made software unpatentable, the Supreme Court opened up the possibility of software patents a bit almost a decade later, in *Diamond vs. Diehr.* The Court still maintained that many kinds of software were not patentable, but stated at the same time that the mere inclusion of a mathematical formula or an algorithm did not mean that an invention could not be patented. This position was cemented for the case of software in *Whelan vs. Jaslow* in 1986. This warming to software patents was further reinforced in the 1998 *State Street vs. Signature* case, whose ruling did away with the exclusion of "business process" patents, allowing for patents on processes for services and sales techniques, which had become increasingly important on the Internet.

Especially since the *State Street* case, a number of software patents have come under harsh criticism. In a few cases, the patents have even been reexamined and overturned. Some of these patents, if enforced, would make the World Wide Web impossible. British Telecommunications, for example, has attempted to enforce an older patent that appears to give it ownership over the idea of hyperlinking, and Unisys has recently begun to enforce its patent on the GIF picture-file format. Amazon.com's patents for "one-click" shopping (that is, ordering and paying for a product with a single mouse click on a hyperlink) and for affiliate advertising have been criticized by many in the software industry. Some, like those who make up MIT's League for Programming Freedom, free-software pioneer Richard Stallman, and Harvard University Law School professor Lawrence Lessig, see software patents as impeding innovation in software design, when patents, by design, are actually meant to encourage innovation. According to those who argue against software patents, many patents are used as leverage between large corporations, which force one another to share the use of a collection of patents to mutual benefit. As a result, individual programmers or small companies are unable to compete without worrying about infringing on one of the thousands of existing software patents.

On the other hand, there are those who believe that companies that invest in the research to create new software should be able to reap the benefits of that research. A number of potential solutions have been offered. In the wake of criticism of Amazon's aggressive patent strategy, CEO Jeff Bezos suggested that the number of years that software patents are in effect be significantly reduced from the current 20. Others, critical of the Patent and Trademark Office patent examiners, who are responsible for making sure that only suitable inventions are granted a patent, suggest that a more careful examination of applications would reduce later difficulties. To aid in this process, many software engineers have recently tried to establish a database of "prior art"—techniques already known to the programming community—to help the patent office determine whether an application is original and not obvious. As legal scholar Anne Branscomb points out, information societies are based on stable intellectual property. While the problems of determining originality in computer programming are very complex, the need for a functioning system for determining ownership is urgent.

Bibliography

Branscomb, Anne Wells. *Who Owns Information? From Privacy to Public Access.* New York: BasicBooks, 1994.

Lessig, Lawrence. "Patent Problems." *Industry Standard,* January 2000.

Massachusetts Institute of Technology. "League for Programming Freedom." <http://lpf.ai.mit.edu/index.html> (April 12, 2002).

Schulman, Seth. "Software Patents Tangle the Web." *Technology Review,* March/April 2000.

Further Reading

IP Watchdog.com. Patent Law Page. <http://www.ipwatchdog.com/patent.html> (April 12, 2002).

Kirsch, Gregory J. "The Changing Roles of Patent and Copyright Protection for Software." Gigalaw.com, April 2000. <http://www.gigalaw.com/articles/2000/kirsch-2000-04.html> (April 12, 2002).

Shulman, Seth. *Owning the Future.* Boston: Houghton Mifflin, 1999.

U.S. Patent and Trademark Office. "Patents." <http://www.uspto.gov/main/patents.htm> (April 12, 2002).

Related Topics

Copyright; Lessig, Lawrence; Open Source; Stallman, Richard; Trademark

— *Alexander Halavais*

Peer-to-Peer

Peer-to-peer (P2P) interaction refers to the ability of any two information appliances, such as computers, to connect directly with one another without going through any central intermediary.

The notion of P2P interaction is not unique to the Internet. Consider the following scenario. Someone who is interested in obtaining a recipe for strawberry rhubarb pie can pursue a couple of strategies: go to a library (or log onto the Web) and search a central repository of documents for a recipe, or ask one or more friends if they have a recipe. A person who followed the first strategy would be a "client" obtaining information from a "server" that stored all of the information at one location—the library or Web site. A person who followed the second strategy would be engaging in P2P interaction, bypassing any intermediary central collection of recipes. For any given purpose, it may be far more effective to pursue one type of strategy or the other.

The same two strategies are in effect on the Internet. The advent of the Web made it possible for some large Web sites to "serve" information to millions of "clients" who used Web browsers. Users can find recipes, buy books, and read the news on many well-known Web sites, such as Amazon.com, Yahoo! and AOL. More recently, there have been many applications on the Internet that also make it possible for users to pursue P2P strategies. These applications fall into three broad categories: file sharing, computer-resource sharing, and communication and collaboration.

First, there are applications that allow peers to share information (audio, text, video, and graphics files) directly with one another without going to a Web site. Perhaps the most popular such application was Napster, which allowed individuals to share music files on their computers with millions of their peers anywhere in the world. Some have argued that Napster is not a "true" P2P application, because it had an intermediary "server" that provided a directory of which peers had what songs on their computers. There are other applications, such as Gnutella and Freenet, that dispense with the intermediary directory server and are therefore indisputably P2P. With these applications, a user would send his request for information (a song or any other digital document) to a small subset of peers who were connected to the application; they in turn relayed the request to a further subset of their peers. Soon, the user would have a list of peers from around the world that had the information that she requested.

Second, there are applications aimed at sharing computing resources among peers' computers, rather than sharing files. Clay Shirky, an expert on Internet applications, observes that "At a conservative estimate . . . the world's Net-connected PCs presently host an aggregate of 10 billion megahertz of processing power and 10 thousand terabytes of storage." In many cases, these Internet-connected PCs have spare storage space on their hard drives. In addition, these PCs are not being used much of the time. In 1995, scientists at University of California–Berkeley proposed using the computing power of these PCs to help in the search for extraterrestrial civilizations.

The SETI (Search for Extraterrestrial Intelligence) Project was collecting massive amounts of radio signals from the skies using radio telescopes; unfortunately, it did not have the vast computing resources required to analyze these signals to detect extraterrestrial life. To solve this problem, a program called SETI@home was designed. It worked as a screensaver that a user could download. Whenever the user's computer was idle, this screensaver would be launched, and would connect with the SETI@home data distribution server. It would download a small portion of the data, analyze it on the user's computer, then send the results to the server. As of October 2000, the project had received more than 200 million results from users, making up the largest computation ever performed in the world. Inspired by SETI's success, others are launching similar applications to help with computational challenges in genetic research, fighting AIDS, and financial data mining. While users volunteer their computing resources for the SETI@home project, companies such as Popular Power and Distributed Net offer to compensate users for the donation of their idle computing resources.

Third, some applications help peers to communicate and collaborate directly with one another. In 1996, a young Israeli firm called Mirabilis launched the first such application, called ICQ ("I seek you"). It allowed users to instantly send messages between PCs connected to the Internet without going through any central server (such as an email server). American Online's Instant Messenger (AIM) program is a similar P2P application (AOL acquired ICQ in 1998), allowing users to communicate on a P2P basis with "buddies." More recently, Ray Ozzie, who created Lotus Notes, developed Groove, a P2P collaboration environment that allows groups of individuals to create a shared space without the presence of a central network server. These environments allow not only for the sharing of files, but also for more intensive collaboration such as simultaneous editing and automatic updating of files, even when users are not all connected at the same time.

Some applications incorporate more than one of the three P2P categories described above. For instance, programs such as Aimster allow AIM users to share files only with others on their "buddy" lists. Mojo Nation allows users to pay for downloading files with a digital "currency" called Mojo, which they can earn by sharing their computer's resources.

The use of P2P applications may increase with the advent of millions of Internet-enabled information appliances, such as mobile phones and personal digital assistants (PDAs). Technologies such as Bluetooth and Jini will greatly facilitate the participation of these appliances in P2P applications. However, many of the stand-alone P2P applications have not yet developed successful business models. In addition, users need to contend with issues such as trust, accountability, security, intellectual property, and privacy, which are raised by P2P environments that bypass the central, reliable, and well-established Web "servers" that have been embraced over the past decade.

Bibliography

Cave, Damien. "Come Together, Right Now, Over P2P." *Salon*, December 14, 2000. <http://www.salon.com/tech/feature/2000/12/14/popular_power/index.html> (May 31, 2002).

"Computing Power on Tap." *The Economist*, June 21, 2001.

Grimes, Brad. "Enterprise Technology: Peer-to-Peer Gets Down to Business." *PC World*, May 2001, pp. 150–54. <http://www.pcworld.com/features/article/0,aid,44862,00.asp> (May 31, 2002).

Heingartner, Douglas. "The Grid: The Next-Gen Internet?" *Wired News*, March 8, 2001. <http://www.wired.com/news/technology/0,1282,42230,00.html> (May 31, 2002).

Minar, Nelson, and Marc Hedlund. "A Network of Peers: Peer-to-peer Models through the History of the INTERNET." *Peer-to-Peer: Harnessing the Benefits of a Disruptive Technology*. Andy Oram, ed. Sebastopol, Calif.: O'Reilly, 2001; pp. 3–20.

Oleck, Joan. "PCs of the World, Unite!" *Business Week*, March 9, 2001.

<http://www.businessweek.com/bwdaily/dnflash/ mar2001/nf2001039_707.htm> (May 31, 2002).

O'Reilly, Tim. "Remaking the Peer-to-Peer Meme." *Peer-to-Peer: Harnessing the Benefits of a Disruptive Technology.* Andy Oram, ed. Sebastopol, Calif.: O'Reilly, 2001; pp. 38–58.

"Profit from Peer-to-Peer." *The Economist,* June 21, 2001.

Shirky, Clay. "Listening to Napster." *Peer-to-Peer: Harnessing the Benefits of a Disruptive Technology.* Andy Oram, ed. Sebastopol, Calif.: O'Reilly, 2001; pp. 21–37.

Further Reading

Oram, Andy. ed. *Peer-to-Peer: Harnessing the Power of Disruptive Technologies.* Sebastopol, Calif.: O'Reilly, 2001.

Smarr, Larry. "Towards the 21st Century." *Communications of the ACM,* vol. 40, no. 11 (November 1997), pp. 29–32.

Stevens, Rick; Woodward, Paul; DeFanti, Tom; and Charles Catlett. "From the I-way to the National Grid." *Communications of the ACM,* vol. 40, no. 11 (November 1997), pp. 51–60.

Related Topics

Bluetooth; Computer-Supported Collaborative Work; Data Mining; Distributed Computing; Freenet (File-Sharing Network); Grids; Instant Messaging; Napster

— *Noshir Contractor*

Personal Digital Assistants

Personal digital assistants (PDAs) are handheld computers, initially marketed as electronic replacements for paper pocket organizers like the Filofax. In many cases, PDAs have evolved to include important utilities with functions far beyond simply scheduling appointments, storing phone numbers, and making shopping lists; today, many PDAs are wireless Internet devices capable of receiving email and downloading information off the Internet. Some even double as cellular phones or digital music players. They are expected to be important tools for mobile communications and e-commerce within the next few years, as people buy products aimed at keeping them connected to their information wherever they go.

In essence, PDAs are smaller, handheld versions of personal computers, reduced in size to make them even more portable than laptop PCs. Like any standard desktop PC or laptop, PDAs are powered by microprocessors that coordinate their utilities. Like computers, they have operating system (OS) software; in fact, Microsoft adapted its Windows OS for use in handhelds, calling the PDA version Windows CE. The most popular PDAs are small enough to fit comfortably in a shirt pocket, functioning as a kind of carry-along personal database.

There are two types of PDAs. "Hand-held computers," the larger of the two, have a larger liquid crystal display (LCD) interface, and often employ a small keyboard with optional touch-screen software for data entry. These often are Windows CE, or as they were later known, Pocket PC-styled devices, and contain complex computer programs, making them literally palm-sized personal computers. On the other hand, "palm-sized computers," the Palm Pilot-styled devices, are smaller and lighter, with less screen-display space, and usually with less complex computing power. These usually rely on a pen-shaped stylus used to tap virtual keys or to scrawl along the surface of the LCD screen, to write data into the device.

In both PDA types, handwriting recognition programs can be used to input data. Both also are battery-powered, whether by AAA alkaline batteries or by rechargeable lithium, nickel-cadmium, or nickel-metal hydride cells. Battery life usually depends on how many and what kinds of programs the device runs. Some PDA batteries can last several weeks with regular usage, others just a couple of hours if the PDA is running complex software like music players.

Since PDAs have no hard drives, they store their core programs on solid-state, read-only memory (ROM) chips, which hold data even if a device is not powered up—but not if the batteries die. Any data or additional programs uploaded after purchase are stored in the device's random-access memory (RAM). PDAs usually contain no less than 2MB (megabytes) of memory, enough to store 4,000 address entries and 100 email messages, but some have much more. Microsoft's revamped Pocket PC has a complex Windows-styled OS that operates such programs as Word and Excel, so it contains up to 32MB of memory. The Palm operating system is far simpler, taking up less than 100KB (kilobits) of total memory—about 1 percent the space eaten up by Windows 98. Therefore, the Palm OS needs less preinstalled memory. The memory on many PDAs can be upgraded, however.

One of the most important benefits of PDAs is their ability to synchronize their data with desktop or laptop computers. The ability to have a PDA backup its data is key, because their batteries frequently run out, and if a device remains without its power supply long enough, it loses all its data. But after installing the appropriate software in the desktop PC, placing the device in a special cradle connected to a computer, and punching a button, the desktop and PDA exchange, or "synch," data. This means that if information intended for the PDA has recently been added to the desktop, it will show up on the PDA after synching. Likewise, information added to the PDA will be sent to a designated folder on the desktop's hard drive. Many PDAs also have a special communications port that uses infrared (IR) light to beam information from one PDA to another, or between a PDA and a PC. In June 2001, Palm Inc. also added a radio-based Bluetooth wireless plug-in that allows its newer PDAs to communicate with other Bluetooth-compatible devices.

HISTORY OF THE PDA

PDAs have been available commercially for nearly 20 years. But despite great promise, they achieved only modest popularity during most of their existence. In the late 1990s, however, the PDA market exploded.

The first PDA was the Psion Organiser 1, a calculator-styled device introduced by the British-based technology company Psion in 1984, only three years after IBM's first desktop PC emerged. Marketed as "the world's first practical pocket computer," the Psion 1 was a simple device: It had a 16-character alphanumeric display, and was capable of scrolling down to about 200 characters; it could store addresses and phone numbers, and keep calendar appointments. It also included a clock and a calculator, and retailed for $199 Canadian. The device was slightly bigger than a large pack of cigarettes.

The Psion 1's functions were limited compared to the PDAs that followed, but improved versions of the product were gradually introduced. The Psion II arrived in the late 1980s, followed by the Series 3a in 1993, which was shaped more like a typewriter. The latter introduced a crucial function mimicked by all subsequent PDA manufacturers: the ability to synchronize data with a PC. Psion's 32-bit Series 5 devices emerged in 1997, featuring the largest screen among all PDAs at 640 x 240 pixels, along with the largest input keyboard. But these enhancements did little to help Psion retain its industry lead, which at one time seemed insurmountable.

Over the years, Psion generated a lot of competition, none of it particularly successful at first. Apple Computer's Newton MessagePad, for example, proved too expensive, too big, and too complicated for consumers, and its pioneering handwriting-recognition software never improved sufficiently for consumers to adopt it. In the end, the Newton proved a costly blunder for Apple at a time when the company was trying to redefine itself. (This failure was given as one reason

that previously ousted founder Steve Jobs was brought back to run the company.) Although the Newton OS demonstrated the possibilities of handheld computers, it was so unsuccessful that it was discontinued in 1998. Many other companies also made attempts to conquer the market, including Motorola, Sony, Hewlett-Packard, and Sharp, but none met with great success. Then, in 1996, Palm Computing Inc., a U.S. Robotics subsidiary, introduced the Palm Pilot.

The Palm Pilot was the first PDA to achieve popular success, largely on the strength of its simplicity. The Palm Pilot initially did a relatively small number of things, like keeping lists and appointments. Even its handwriting software, Graffiti, proved useful to Palm owners, despite the fact that it required them to learn a new way to write the alphabet.

To ensure its simplicity, Palm Pilot creator Jeff Hawkins served as a one-man focus group for his invention. Hawkins had created an early, unsuccessful PDA in the late 1980s called the GriDPAD; it had failed, he claimed, because it was too big. His prototype for the Palm Pilot was cut from a block of wood the size, shape, and weight of his ideal PDA. It had to be small and light enough to sit comfortably in his shirt pocket, he reasoned; Hawkins carried the block around in his shirt pocket for months, pretending it was a PDA, even going so far as to take it out and tap on it whenever he was asked to make an appointment. According to *Time* magazine, he tried various interface designs by drawing them up on a workstation, printing them out, and gluing them to the woodblock. In the end, *Time* reported, the device Hawkins created was surprisingly similar to the fake wooden version he had toted around. Later, Hawkins also created the Graffiti handwriting-recognition software, which requires that any letter written on the screen pad must be drawn in a continuous motion, without lifting the stylus. (The letter "A" in Graffiti resembles an upside-down "V"; a "T" looks like an inverted "L.") Users easily adapted.

Within 18 months, more than a million Palm Pilots had shipped. By the end of 1997, Palm could claim ownership of two-thirds of the handheld-device market, according to *Time* magazine. After unleashing the Palm V with its built-in serial port and TCP/IP Internet software in 1999, new corporate parent 3Com introduced the Palm VII, the first handheld device with the ability to wirelessly access the Internet. That same year, Handspring's Visor debuted using Palm's OS, validating the device's simpler-is-better model; however, the Visor also came with a port into which attachments could be fitted for more complex operations. According to

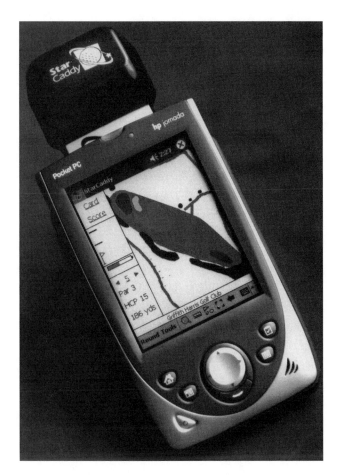

In July 2002, Hewlett-Packard displayed its golf-course navigator with Global Positioning System, which plugs into most PDAs. (AP Photo/Bebeto Matthews)

International Data Corp., Palm's OS controlled 83.5 percent of the PDA market in 1999, while Windows CE ran on just 9.7 percent of the devices purchased that year.

However, as the millennium turned, the PDA market was not sitting still. After early disappointments with its Windows CE OS, Microsoft renamed its OS and debuted Windows for Pocket PC, which many reviewers viewed as an improvement. The Pocket PC platform debuted in Hewlett-Packard's Jornada 545, with an OS that included less memory-intensive versions of Microsoft Outlook, Word, Excel, Money, Media Player, and Internet Explorer.

The two systems continue to vie for dominance. Palm's OS still takes up less memory, runs faster, and is easier to use. Windows Pocket PCs, meanwhile, support color graphics and can play both MP3 song files and movies, while running programs like Excel. But the complexity of Windows for Pocket PC continues to make it function more slowly and use more memory, and keeps it more difficult to use, according to some critics.

Nonetheless, since PDAs are really about providing information to users on the move, Aberdeen Group research in August 2001 concluded that Microsoft's

Pocket PC would overtake Palm as the most popular handheld OS by 2005. Aberdeen analysts said that overall handheld sales would grow by 30 percent a year though 2005, bringing total sales to 39 million units, compared to 8.9 million PDAs sold in 2000.

Strategy Analytics, however, disagreed with Aberdeen's analysis, saying in a study at about the same time that the consumer market would drive PDA shipments in 2006, with the Palm OS retaining its global dominance by 2006, even while losing market share to the Pocket PC.

With mobile communications with PDAs and other devices like Internet-enabled cellular phones promising to transform the way that people communicate and receive information, Craig C. Freudenrich of the How Stuff Works Web site has identified several PDA trends. First, he writes, there will be more add-ons and multifunctional devices; for instance, PDAs will be combined with global positioning system (GPS) devices. Second, he says, built-in audio capability will become the norm, as will wireless connectivity to the Internet and to other devices, through add-on technologies like Bluetooth. Finally, PDAs will get both smaller and larger, and will acquire more add-on hardware attachments.

Michael Dertouzos, former director of the MIT Computer Science Lab, outlined how wireless-enabled, network-connected devices, including PDAs, promise to transform human life. "If machines can help us reach the humans and things we care about, wherever we and they may be, we can do even more by doing less," he wrote. "This change has already begun with laptops, PDAs and cellular phones. But the rapidly advancing wireless terrain will extend it further, with the result that roving humans will get increasingly closer to the computer and communications power they now have at their desks."

Bibliography

Bonisteel, Steven. "Palm's Bluetooth Add-On Cheers Wireless Industry." *Newsbytes*, June 7, 2001.

Freudenrich, Craig C. "How Personal Digital Assistants (PDAs) Work: Cool Stuff." Howstuffworks.com, 1998–2002. <http://www.howstuffworks.com/pda9.htm> (May 31, 2002).

Jackson, David S. "Palm-To-Palm Combat." *Time*, March 16, 1998. <http://www.time.com/time/magazine/1998/dom/980316/ business.palmtopalm_comb7.html> (May 31, 2002).

Pastore, Michael. "Competition Heats Up in Immature PDA Market." *INT Media Group*, August 3, 2001. <http://cyberatlas.internet.com/big_picture/hardware/ article/0,,5921_859691,00.html> (May 31, 2002).

PCTechGuide. "Components/Mobile Computing: PDAs."
Updated May 1, 2002.
<http://www.pctechguide.com/25mob3.htm> (May 31, 2002).

Further Reading
Dertouzos, Michael. *The Unfinished Revolution: Human-Centered Computers and What They Can Do for Us.* New York: HarperCollins, 2001.
Kounalakis, Markos. *Defying Gravity: The Making of Newton.* Hillsboro, Ore.: Beydon Words Publishing, 1993.

Related Topics

Access; Bluetooth; Broadband; Browser; Gates, William H., III; Interface; Internet; Internet Appliances; Jobs, Steven P.; Local Area Network; Wireless Networks

— Kevin Featherly

Personalization

Personalization software collects consumer information for e-commerce companies so that the businesses can tailor communications with their individual customers. Interactions between company and customer are altered, or personalized, to fit consumer preferences, which the customer either offers voluntarily or which businesses silently collect as they record and analyze the behavior of visitors to their Web sites. According to the industry-backed Personalization Consortium, personalized technology has three aims: to better serve customers by anticipating their needs; to make business interactions with customers "efficient and satisfying"; and to build relationships that encourage customers to keep conducting business with e-commerce sites. However, despite their promise for merchants, there are serious privacy concerns connected to the growing use of personalization technologies.

Personalization has become increasingly popular among businesses as a competitive tool in a glutted e-commerce market. *BusinessWeek*, for one, has said that personalization is the one thing that can distinguish business conducted online from more traditional means of commerce: "Personalization may represent the best chance for survival by online merchandisers in the ongoing Internet shakeout," the magazine said in an August 4, 2000, report. Forrester Research, meanwhile, issued a May 1997 report titled "Personalize or Perish?"

According to an August 28, 2000, *New York Times* article, dot-com executives tend to equate Web personalization with the old-fashioned proprietor who knew how much money a particular customer could spend, what size shoes his kids wore, and what kinds of shirts he liked. As practiced on the Internet, personalization means tailoring Web pages in ways meant to appeal directly to an individual customer's tastes, as opposed to indiscriminately displaying the same basic page to everyone who visits the site. The concept is closely related to "one-to-one marketing," which has also gained prominence in the digital age.

In his 1995 book *Being Digital*, MIT Media Lab director Nicholas Negroponte was among the first to describe the potential benefits of personalization. He used the example of how newspapers could use digital technologies—he dubbed them "personal filters"—to attract readers. According to Negroponte, personalizing a newspaper would be a simple matter of refashioning it to match the way that readers already use them, by emphasizing news items that are of great interest to individual readers while relegating less-interesting material to secondary status. Someone might be willing to pay a newspaper like the *Boston Globe* more money for less information, Negroponte guessed, if personalization software made it possible for the reader to receive only the news desired, while eliminating the clutter. Meanwhile, thanks to its reader's stated preferences, a personalized digital newspaper might be aware that a business trip to London is being planned, so it would serve up relevant U.K. hotel and car-rental information. Negroponte called this scheme for a personalized newspaper *The Daily Me*.

Web sites like My.Yahoo.com and Excite.com have offered something similar to Negroponte's model for several years. These portal sites often allow users to receive quotes from their stock portfolios, local weather reports, regional sports news, and other news items that are listed according to reader preferences. However, in the industry vernacular, this kind of personalization has come to be known instead as "customization," because it usually involves options or preferences selected by the users from a pre-set list.

As *New York Times* writer Susan Stellin described it in August 2000, personalization involves information that companies have "discreetly gathered about consumers, like their purchase history or the Web pages they have viewed." Unlike customization, which requires companies to wait for customers to tell them what they want, companies employing personalization techniques attempt to anticipate what customers will want. Users' preferences are determined based on data profiles built up through data mining, which sifts through customers' data using sophisticated algorithms to discover correlating patterns in Web usage and purchase patterns. Such data is often collected when Web sites implant information-gathering "cookies" into visitors' Web browsers, or by detecting and identifying the unique Internet protocol address of a user's computer.

There are various ways that personalization manifests itself. The simplest are email and newsletter updates about a company's products. More sophisticated personalized services include the recommendations that Amazon.com automatically dishes up whenever a past customer returns to browse the site. (For example, a typical Amazon.com greeting is: "Hello, Jimmy Jones. We have recommendations for you.") Or there might be a sophisticated history of previous transactions listed on the site, or a fulfillment-status record of current orders. Amazon.com has led the way in developing such technologies, based on algorithms that compute such factors as past purchasing patterns and critical ratings that site visitors have contributed to sites reviewing products like books, CDs, and gaming software. Such data is often mathematically compared to similar data elements collected from like-minded customers to develop trends, comparisons, and correlations that help to further improve personalized services.

Personalized technologies were relatively slow in developing, largely because the software that was used to mine such data has often been unreliable in the past. It is also expensive; the necessary software and hardware usually costs a company anywhere from several hundred thousand to several million dollars. But competitive pressures have pushed personalization ahead, and personalization techniques have begun to gain a foothold in the e-marketplace. In-Stat researchers reported in May 2001 that 43 percent of businesses with 100 or more employees planned to utilize personalization technology by 2002, nearly double the 2001 levels. The same report said that 9 percent of smaller Internet-accessing companies already used personalization technologies.

As companies use the technologies to create user databases and learn ever more about their customers, privacy concerns have mounted. Many doubts were raised in 1999, when online ad company DoubleClick acquired direct-marketer Abacus Direct Corp., making it possible for the first time for DoubleClick to link browser cookies to the names of people and their street addresses, which were present in Abacus' database. Many privacy advocates were outraged when they discovered that the DoubleClick information was usually used without the consumer's knowledge. In-Stat indicates that many companies, perhaps because of the DoubleClick fiasco, have been reluctant to adopt personalization technologies out of fear of violating their customers' privacy.

In response to these concerns, 26 companies involved in e-commerce formed the Personalization Consortium in April 2000 to tackle consumer privacy issues. Members included American Airlines, PricewaterhouseCoopers, and DoubleClick; the latter was being investigated for its data-collection practices at the time that the group formed. At the time of this writing, a message on the consortium's Web site indicated that a planned ethical practices standard was still in the works: "Our goal," the site said in November 2001, "is to create a clear process that enables our customers to use personalization technology in a way that enhances continued public confidence and trust in the Internet."

There is one final issue facing the personalization trend: In the final analysis, personalization does not always work that well, or at best, it may still be too new as a technology. In July 2000, Internet research firm Jupiter Communications issued a report that put the brakes on some of its early enthusiasm for the technology. It noted that many companies were finding it difficult to integrate personalization features with their other site-analysis tools, while many personalization systems were scaling poorly as companies grew. Jupiter predicted that personalization techniques would therefore "creep forward" in the marketplace, rather than taking the world by storm.

Bibliography

CRM Advisor Zone. "Market Research: Despite Benefits of Personalized Web Sites, Privacy Still an Issue." May 16, 2001. <http://www.advisor.com/Articles.nsf/aid/OLSEE189> (May 31, 2002).

Eads, Stefani. "The Web's Still-Unfulfilled Personalization Promise." *BusinessWeek Online*, August 4, 2000. <http://www.businessweek.com/bwdaily/dnflash/aug2000/nf2000084_506.htm> (May 31, 2002).

Lehman, DeWayne. "Consortium Pushes Net Ethics." PCWorld.com, April 5, 2000. <http://www.pcworld.com/news/article/0,aid,16056,00.asp> (May 31, 2002).

Personalization Consortium. "Personalization Information." 2000–2001. <http://www.personalization.org/personalization.html> (May 31, 2002).

Pew Internet & American Life Project. "Trust and Privacy Online: Why Americans Want to Rewrite the Rules." August 20, 2000. <http://www.pewinternet.org/reports/toc.asp?Report=19> (May 31, 2002).

Stellin, Susan. "Internet Companies Learn How to Personalize Service." *The New York Times*, August 28, 2000.

Further Reading

Drapkin, Michael; Lowy, Jon; and Daniel Marovitz. *Three Clicks Away: Advice from the Trenches of eCommerce.* New York: John Wiley & Sons, 2001.

Eads, Stefani. "How Personalization Keeps Online Buyers Coming Back." *BusinessWeek*, July 20, 1999. <http://www.businessweek.com/bwdaily/dnflash/july1999/nf90720a.htm> (May 31, 2002).

Farrell, Tom. "Pros and Cons of Personalisation." *Frontend Research,* February 20, 2001. <http://infocentre.frontend.com/servlet/Infocentre/Infocentre?page=article&id=83> (May 31, 2002).

Losi, Stephanie. "Personalization vs. Privacy: Rewriting the Rules." CRMDaily.com, January 22, 2001. <http://www.crmdaily.com/perl/story/6876.html> (May 31, 2002).

Related Topics

Amazon.com; Browser; Cookies; Data Mining; E-Commerce; Knowledge Management; Privacy; Security; World Wide Web

— *Kevin Featherly*

Photoshop

Photoshop is a software package from Adobe Systems, Inc., that allows users to manipulate digitized photographs; the software can be used to enhance quality, create original pieces of artwork, add text and shapes, and apply professional-quality special effects to digital images. Photoshop was one of the first programs to give users the ability to extensively manipulate graphics on a computer.

In 1987, Thomas Knoll, a Ph.D. student in computer vision at the University of Michigan, wrote a program called Display that would allow for grayscale images to be displayed on the black-and-white monitor of his Macintosh computer. Thomas' brother John was an employee at Industrial Light and Magic, and he was intrigued by the possibilities of his brother's work. He encouraged Thomas to continue working on the program, this time using a Macintosh II with a color monitor, and to enable the program to be able to save the images in varying formats. Thomas changed the name from Display to ImagePro for commercial applications, then later to Photoshop due to trademark.

By 1988, John had struck a deal with BarneyScan Corporation (later to be incorporated into PixelCraft, Inc., a division of Xerox), a leading producer of image scanners and creator of the first desktop slide scanner, to include a limited amount of bundled software with their scanners. Eventually, a demo version of Photoshop was presented to Adobe, which agreed to buy the rights to Photoshop in 1989. The first version, Photoshop 1.0, was released to the public in 1990. Photoshop was available only to Macintosh users until Adobe released Photoshop 2.5, a Windows-based version, in 1993. In 2000, Adobe released Photoshop's most updated version, 6.0, which is targeted specifically toward Web designers and publishers.

Photoshop allows adjustments to be made to a photo's hue, saturation levels, contrast, and brightness, as well as the elimination of red-eye, to name a few basic features. The software also affords its users more advanced features, such as layers, filters, and masking techniques that make complex operations easy, making it the photograph-manipulation program preferred by photographic and graphic-design professionals. Photoshop is also compatible with all other Adobe graphics programs, and allows users to export their files into varying file formats.

A signature feature of Photoshop is the concept of layers, which can best be described via a comparison to cartoon animation. Users of Photoshop start with a background image, much like a cartoon animator does. When objects or text need to be added, users can create transparent layers for each object, as when cartoon animators place a clear cellophane sheet bearing its own image onto the background to add an object or character to the picture. In Photoshop 6.0 and later versions, unlimited numbers of layers can be stacked on top of each other to create a desired effect. Users can then experiment with different colors, objects, and text without affecting the overall picture, simply by turning layers on and off, or delete a layer that is no longer necessary without deleting all of their other manipulations.

As with all software programs, there are drawbacks. One of the difficulties presented by older versions of Photoshop was the inability to undo more than one command on the current layer that a user is working on. More recent versions include a history section, which tracks user changes and allows users to undo as many functions as necessary.

Another drawback is that even though Photoshop can serve many functions and offers a wide variety of tools to cater to the imaginations of its users, the program is fundamentally a tool for professional graphic artists. It is not as user-friendly as many other programs, and the learning curve associated with mastering the software is high.

While Photoshop has made it possible to produce quality digital photographs, it has also facilitated the alteration of photographs for illegitimate purposes. Photos can easily be cut and pasted into one another, making people and objects appear to have been together when in reality they had not been. People's physical appearances can also be altered. The manipulation of photographic images has been with us since the invention of the camera, but Photoshop and programs like it have ushered in a never-before-seen level of sophistication; one cannot easily distinguish between real photos and photos that have been created or manipulated. The old adage "seeing is believing" needs to be reconsidered when viewing Web-site or printed photos, especially if the picture is "too good to be true."

Be that as it may, the benefits of Photoshop usage far outweigh the difficulties; when used properly, it can salvage old photos, fix damaged ones, enhance creativity, and add a certain artistic flair to photos that might otherwise have been thrown away.

Bibliography

Adobe Systems, Incorporated. "Adobe Photoshop 6.0: New Feature Highlights." 2000. <http://www.adobe.com/products/photoshop/pdfs/PS6NFHS.pdf> (July 12, 2002).

———. "Top 10 Ways Adobe Photoshop 6.0 Beats Macromedia Fireworks 3.0 for Web Graphics." 2000. <http://www.adobe.com/products/photoshop/pdfs/PS6_top10.pdf> (July 12, 2002).

Harris, Bill, and Jack Harris. "Adobe Photoshop 5.5." *PC Magazine*, June 5, 2000.

Further Reading

Adobe Creative Team Staff. *Adobe Photoshop 6.0 Classroom in a Book*. Berkeley, Calif.: Adobe Press, 2001.

Schewe, Jeff. "The Birth of a Killer Application: 10 Years of Photoshop." February 2000. <http://www.peimag.com/pdf/pei00/pei0200/schewepei0200.pdf> (July 12, 2002).

Related Topics

Digital Art and Animation

— *Kathy Broneck*

PLATO

PLATO (Programmed Logic for Automatic Teaching Operations) was a computer-based education system created in the early 1960s by Don Bitzer at the University of Illinois at Urbana-Champaign (UIUC). In addition to its success as a teaching tool, PLATO also spawned one of the first successful online communities. In many ways, PLATO's development foreshadowed the Internet.

Bitzer, a professor of electrical engineering at UIUC, was interested in matters of literacy. In a 1997 interview for Wired.com, Bitzer noted that he was inspired to create PLATO when he read that 50 percent of students graduating from high school in the United States were functionally illiterate. In a discussion about literacy, a colleague of Bitzer's, Chalmers Sherwin, asked him whether it might be possible to use computers for education. Bitzer believed it to be possible, and he and his colleagues at the university founded the Computer-Based Education Research Laboratory (CERL) and assembled a team of software coders ranging from professors to high-school students. Based on a timesharing computer system, PLATO users and programmers connected to a central mainframe. The programmers, faculty, and graduate (and some undergraduate) students used a programming language called TUTOR to write educational materials. The first demonstration of PLATO took place on the ILLIAC I computer.

During the 1960s, PLATO was used in a single classroom. By the early 1970s, as the processing power of mainframe computers progressed, PLATO was able to support 1,000 simultaneous users, albeit initially at a rate of only 1200bps (bits per second). Considering, however, that PLATO output only text, the rate of exchange between PLATO users seemed sufficiently fast for communication and education.

That development was an important piece of the puzzle that led to the creation of an online community. Another important piece came in the form of David Woolley's authorship of PLATO Notes, a threaded discussion application that later evolved into Group Notes, and subsequently became Lotus Notes. Woolley, a 17-year-old university student at the time, had been working at CERL, and he and his colleagues had become frustrated with the process of fixing bugs in PLATO and reporting those fixes. Woolley's solution was to create a threaded message system that incorporated user IDs and date and time stamping, allowed multiple responses to each entry, and included menus and indices.

PLATO Notes quickly came to be used for a multitude of discussions beyond the fixing of bugs. At about the same time as Woolley created Notes, Doug Brown developed a program called Talkomatic that enabled real-time chat between users. Up to five active participants could utilize a single Talkomatic channel, while any number of users could log in as observers only. Channels could be created by any user at any time. Once a channel was created, however, users could prevent others from joining or observing, thereby creating "private" chat channels.

Soon after the creation of Talkomatic and another real-time chat application, Term-talk (which was similar to America Online's Instant Messaging application), PLATO's use for online interaction and communication became predominant. Despite this multitude of communication options, PLATO did not initially have an email application with which one could send private messages; one was released in the summer of 1974.

UIUC had numerous PLATO terminals in public computer labs and public spaces. What had started as a means of creating educational materials and fostering literacy came instead to foster online communities, distance education, online classified ads, discussion groups on myriad topics, PLATO "celebrities," and even romance—features of the Internet that are still evolving. PLATO also struggled with issues that contemporary Internet users encounter, like user anonymity and identity, privacy, and security. Multi-user and single-user games were also a popular PLATO feature. Among the first games were a version of MIT's Spacewar! and a Dungeons and Dragons–like game called Avatar. Many users spent entire nights and weekends gaming in PLATO labs on the UIUC campus.

The terminals themselves consisted of two parts: a large box, which held a monochrome (amber) monitor, and a keyboard. By contemporary standards, these might seem charming at best, if not downright comical thanks to the lack of industrial design. Later iterations of the terminal came to incorporate a touch-screen interface, and both it and the keyboard were well able to withstand constant use in public places.

PLATO's development after the early 1970s came to rely on the user community. Those who worked to write applications regularly sought user feedback and input, and in many cases users who first encountered PLATO by means of a class assignment came to work in CERL.

In the mid-1970s, Control Data Corporation (CDC) licensed the PLATO system from UIUC and began to commercialize it. By the mid-1980s, there were over 100 PLATO systems around the world, most at educational institutions. Due to further software development, means were devised by which those systems could be linked to one another, and essentially "internetworks" of PLATO systems were operational by the late 1970s. Network gaming, one of the most popular PLATO pastimes, came to be banned (on and off) by university administrators.

The introduction of the personal computer (PC) in the 1980s helped bring about an end to the original version of PLATO. Networking PCs was less expensive than building out PLATO systems, and the University of Illinois campus system began using NovaNET, a PC-based education system that essentially interfaced with PLATO via PCs instead of PLATO terminals. CDC, which hewed to its mainframe history, was entirely unprepared for the PC's growth and began a retrenchment. CDC focused PLATO on delivering computer-based instruction and training for the U.S. Department of Defense and other agencies, later renaming it CYBIS and selling it in the 1990s to Vcampus Corp. In 1989, CDC sold the PLATO name to TRO, Inc., which still holds the rights to it and continues to market PLATO courseware.

PLATO's importance as a site of online community is often overlooked by those who focus on its significance as a site of development of computer applications like Notes, messaging, and the like. Although its importance as one of the first, if not the first, networked education and communication systems cannot be overstated, the social dimensions of its use are of equal importance. PLATO, like its closest analogue, The WELL (Whole Earth 'Lectronic Link)—whose founders were, it is believed, unaware of PLATO—influenced the development of software applications and structures, as well as the norms to be found in later user communities on the Internet.

Bibliography

Bitzer, D. L. "The PLATO Project at the University of Illinois." *Engineering Education*, 77–3 (December 1986), pp. 175–180.

Bitzer, D. L.; Braunfeld, P.; and W. Lichtenberger. "PLATO: An Automatic Teaching Device." CSL Report I-103, June 1961.

Silberman, Steve "'PLATO People' Reunite, Honor Founder." *Wired News*, March 17, 1997. <http://www.wired.com/news/print/0,1294,2614,00.html> (July 12, 2002).

Further Reading

Alessi, S. M., and S. R. Trollip. *Computer-Based Instruction: Methods and Development.* Englewood Cliffs, N.J.: Prentice Hall, 1985.

Badger, George, and R. F. Wilson. "The University of Illinois at Urbana-Champaign: Computing and Instructional Innovation." *Computing Across the Curriculum: Academic Perspectives.* William H.

Graves, ed. McKinney, Texas: Academic Computing, 1989.

Braunfeld, P. G. "Problems and Prospects of Teaching with a Computer." *Journal of Educational Psychology* 55 (1964), pp. 201–211.

Goshen, Charles E. "Humanizing Education Through Technology." *Engineering Education,* November 1970, pp. 133–138.

Kinzer, C. K.; Sherwood, R. D.; and J. D. Bransford, eds. *Computer Strategies for Education: Foundations and Content-Area Applications.* Columbus, Ohio: Merrill Pub. Co., 1986.

Pagliaro, L. A. "The History and Development of CAI: 1926–1981, An Overview." *The Alberta Journal of Educational Research*, vol. 29, no. 1 (1983), pp. 75–84.

Woolley, D. R. "PLATO: The Emergence of On-Line Community." *Computer-Mediated Communication Magazine*, vol. 1, no. 3 (July 1, 1994). <http://sunsite.unc.edu/cmc/mag/1994/jul/plato.html> (July 12, 2002).

Related Topics

Community Networking; Distance Learning; Virtual Community; Whole Earth 'Lectronic Link

— *Steve Jones*

Plug-Ins

Plug-ins are guest programs that set up shop in a host program, adding new functions to computer programs while keeping the user within the host program's environment. They also allow programmers to add new functions to existing programs without altering the host program itself. Programs that can accept plug-ins have a "plug-in architecture," a basic set of protocols designed to allow the program to interface with plug-ins.

Plug-ins add a great deal of flexibility to computer programs. A word processor or Web browser may be designed to do certain things, but software designers cannot anticipate all possible functions that future users may want. Without a plug-in architecture, a user has to either switch between two entirely different programs to get a job done—for instance, to display an image in a Web browser—or hope that the desired function will be included in the next software update. A plug-in circumvents such difficulties by integrating with the host program; in the case of a Web browser, plug-ins allow users to hear sounds, view images, or read specially coded files (for instance, Adobe Acrobat files).

There are several advantages to plug-in architecture for users and programmers. For users, plug-ins allow them to stay within a single program's environment and still take advantage of many different functions. In the above Web-browser example, when a plug-in runs, the user's interface is altered somewhat to show that another program is running as a plug-in within the browser, but the user doesn't actually need to switch between programs. The browser and, for instance, a document viewer work in tandem, allowing a user to move seamlessly from Web pages to specially formatted documents and back again.

Plug-in architectures also allow programs to be more open-ended. By sharing plug-in architecture with other companies, software developers create useful synergies between their own products and a variety of related products. Each plug-in enhances the value of the host program, and the success of the host program enhances the value of the plug-ins.

Plug-ins first gained popularity in the 1990s, as software and microprocessors became more powerful. One of the first programs to make extensive use of plug-ins was Adobe Photoshop, an image-processing and editing program originally written for Macintosh computers (although it was eventually brought over to PCs). Photoshop edited images, and plug-ins provided enhanced functions such as special effects, filters, and other options for manipulating images within Photoshop. One of the first popular plug-in packages for Photoshop was Kai's Power Tools, a collection that provides an array of image-enhancing special effects. Today, all major image-editing programs make use of plug-ins.

Plug-ins are also widely used in digital audio and Web browsing. In analog audio, an engineer who wanted to change a sound, filter it, or add an effect (such as an echo) to it would literally "plug in" a hardware device designed to do the desired job. In digital-audio editing, plug-ins often mimic the work formerly done by these hardware devices, allowing the user to add a wide range of effects to sounds. Sound-creation programs can also operate as plug-ins within larger sound-editing programs. In Web browsers, plug-ins allow users to experience a wide range of audiovisual effects beyond simply viewing text and still images; Shockwave and QuickTime, for example, allow users to see full-screen animations, coordinated image and sound, and online movies.

Plug-ins are becoming increasingly common, and as processor speeds and Internet bandwidth increase, it is likely that this trend will continue. Today, many plug-ins also run as stand-alone programs, and many stand-alone programs are also configured to run as plug-ins within other programs.

Bibliography

Story, Derrick. "From Darkroom to Desktop— How Photoshop Came to Light." Storyphoto.com, February 18, 2000. <http://www.storyphoto.com/multimedia/ multimedia_photoshop.html> (May 31, 2002).

Strauss, Howard. "The Answers Are Java and JavaScript. What Are the Questions?" CIT, Princeton University. <http://webware.princeton.edu/howard/cren/java.htm> (May 31, 2002).

Further Reading

Barroca, Leonor; Hall, Jon; and Patrick Hall. "An Introduction and History of Software Architectures, Components, and Reuse." Faculty of Mathematics and Computing, The Open University, 1999. <http://mcs.open.ac.uk/lmb3/introduction.pdf> (May 31, 2002).

Taylor. "Hercules and the History of Plug-ins: Battling the Incompatibility." Lycos.com—Webmonkey, October 1, 1999. <http://hotwired.lycos.com/webmonkey/99/40/ index4a.html?tw=authoring> (May 31, 2002).

Related Topics

Browser; Digital Art and Animation; Digital Audio; Interface; Photoshop; QuickTime

— *Jonathan Sterne*

Privacy

The interactive domains of new media present many challenges with respect to privacy, which is defined not only as the right to be free from intrusion and interruption, but also as the right to have control over one's personal information. Some e-commerce practices present a threat to online users' privacy, while technological developments both create and prevent privacy intrusions. Policy and legislation at domestic and international levels have been created to protect personal privacy, while privacy advocates and groups have been promoting the idea of privacy as a fundamental human right.

In their famous 1890 *Harvard Law Review* article, Samuel Warren and Louis Brandeis defined privacy as "an individual's right to be left alone." The U.S. legal concept of privacy, as it has developed over the years, maintains four prevalent concepts relating to the violation of individual privacy: 1) trespass, or unreasonable intrusion into another's seclusion while gathering information; 2) theft, or appropriation of another's name or likeness for commercial purposes; 3) libel, slander, or injury to reputation, such as being portrayed in a false light; and 4) public disclosure of embarrassing facts.

Challenges to privacy in the information age are many. Globalization, media convergence, and the malleability of multimedia have created a fascinating and often conflicted landscape, where the definition of individual privacy is simultaneously being eroded and transformed by technological means. Some critics contend that we have entered an era of surveillance, where everyday actions, from surfing the Web to registering our automobiles, have come under the eye of Big Brother. A common characteristic of the new media is their two-sided nature; while they have the ability to empower citizens, they also make citizens more vulnerable to surveillance and manipulation through tools such as cookies, the personal information gathered by search engines, and workplace email surveillance.

E-commerce practices present unique challenges to privacy, as data mining of personal information and demographics is proliferating at a rapid rate. Increasingly, the privacy of online consumers is not well protected in electronic transactions, as companies rely on cookies to monitor their visitors' online activities. Most Web browsers are configured to reveal every Web site people visit, as well as the IP (Internet protocol) addresses that may identify individual users. This information can be—and often is—collected and stored to create detailed profiles of user tastes and preferences in shopping, reading, and other habits, all of which are of great value to corporations that rely upon mass marketing. The risk of adding this information to commercial databases has become the focus of consumer activism.

Email is a particularly insecure form of communication, and ethical and legal issues concerning the privacy of email are quite complex. Email can create an electronic trail that can discourage secure communications. Although email might be considered private communication between the sender and the recipient, in reality it can easily be forwarded and exchanged to others without the consent of the original sender. Users of email can be subjected to breaches of confidentiality; for instance, employers can easily monitor email.

A variety of privacy-enhancing technologies (PETs) have been developed. Cryptography, a technique for transforming ordinary text (plaintext) into unintelligible text (ciphertext) through encryption, is a popular way of ensuring the privacy and security of electronic communications. Cryptography can improve identification and access control through password encryption; protect confidentiality and data integrity by encrypting the data; and improve non-repudiation services through encrypted electronic signatures.

Encryption systems consist of the following four fundamental parts: 1) plaintext, the message to encrypt; 2) ciphertext, the message after it is encrypted; 3) the encryption algorithm, the mathematical function used to encrypt the message; and 4) the key, the number, word, or phrase that is used by the encryption algorithm.

Digital signatures are a cryptographic method, provided by public-key cryptography, that is used by a message's recipient or any third party to verify the identity of the sender and the integrity of the message. Digital signature standards can facilitate electronic funds transfers and the signing of documents, prevent the forgery of email messages, and be used to sign official documents, rules, or regulations.

New Web-browsing software is being designed to give users more control over their personal information online. These products are based on the Platform for Privacy Preferences Project (P3P), a set of software-writing guidelines developed by the World Wide Web Consortium (W3C), the standard-setting body for the Web. In the United States, privacy legislation designed to protect individuals' right to privacy from both the private and government sectors has developed through a variety of industry-specific statutes. These include the 1970 Fair Credit Reporting Act (privacy of financial information); the Privacy Act of 1974 (privacy of government collections); the 1986 Electronic Communications Privacy Act and the Telephone Consumer Protection Act of 1991 (privacy of communications); the Video Privacy Protection Act of 1988 (privacy of other personal records); and the Health Insurance Portability and Accountability Act of 1996 (privacy of medical records). The Federal Trade Commission (FTC) has taken an active role in Internet privacy, urging commercial Web site operators, for example, to post privacy policies on their Web sites. A variety of legislation has been introduced into Congress, including the Online Privacy Protection Act, the Electronic Privacy Bill of Rights Act, and the Secure On-Line Communication Enforcement Act.

As more and more young people are going online, concerns have been raised about commercial Web sites that target kids. Children and young people are vulnerable to a number of privacy threats, including the capture of data from their Web surfing that is collected by marketers. In 2000, the Children's Online Privacy Protection Act (COPPA) was enacted to provide safeguards to protect children's privacy on the Internet by regulating the collection of personal information from children under age 13. In particular, Web sites must post their privacy policies and obtain parental consent before collecting, using, or disclosing personal information about a child.

Internationally, the creation of privacy legislation is a very active arena. The European Union (EU) has taken the lead with its 1995 Data Protection Directive, which requires the harmonization of strong EU privacy laws and compliance with the laws of other countries that the EU deals with, including the United States. The directive grants individuals a number of important privacy rights, including the right of access to personal data, the right to know where the data originated (if such information is available), the right to have inaccurate data rectified, and a right of recourse in the event of unlawful processing.

Because privacy issues present a tangle of ethical, legal, and policy conundrums, many feel it is necessary to affirm privacy as a human right and institute national guidelines. The challenge is in the negotiation between industry and citizens. Rather than having technology dictate the extent of privacy protection, many argue that consumers and targeted individuals should be able to choose when to relinquish their privacy and how much of it they wish to relinquish, with the baseline presumption always biased toward privacy. The market for goods and services that protect privacy is increasing, with a surge in privacy-related trademarks and patents. Privacy consultants and the creation of "chief privacy officers" are new trends for industry and governmental organizations. Meanwhile, privacy "seals of approval" such as TRUSTe (www.truste.org) are becoming more common.

Privacy is essential to freedom of expression, and to the maintenance of a democratic society. Many stakeholders are active in privacy debates, including privacy advocates, policymakers, and the high-tech industry. The goals of these organizations are to raise public awareness of online privacy issues, often through the promotion of legal protections for personal privacy on the Internet, and through education and awareness about constitutional privacy protections, user rights, responsible industry information practices, and technological initiatives.

It has been suggested that, much as the 1960s were concerned with civil rights, so the first decade of the twenty-first century will be concerned with privacy rights. Education and awareness of privacy rights and issues will be on the agenda for schools, organizations, governments, and non-profit groups. Already privacy activism is thriving, and governments and corporations both realize that privacy concerns are of paramount importance for both effective citizenship and good business.

Bibliography

Agre, Philip E., and Marc Rotenberg, eds. *Technology and Privacy: The New Landscape.* Cambridge, Mass.: MIT Press, 1997.

Bennett, Colin J., and Rebecca Grant, eds. *Visions of Privacy: Policy Choices for the Digital Age.* Toronto: University of Toronto Press, 1999.

Council of Europe. *Directive on the Protection of the Individual with Respect to the Processing of Personal Data and on the Free Movement of Such Data.* 95/46/EC. October 24, 1995.

Warren, Samuel, and Louis Brandeis. "The Right to Privacy." *Harvard Law Review* 4 (1890), pp. 193–220.

Whitaker, Reginald. *The End of Privacy: How Total Surveillance Is Becoming a Reality.* New York: New Press, 1999.

Further Reading

The Center for Democracy and Technology. Web site. <http://www.cdt.org/> (May 31, 2002).

Electronic Privacy Information Center. Web site. <www.epic.org> (May 31, 2002).

Federal Trade Commission (FTC). "Privacy Initiatives." <http://www.ftc.gov/privacy/> (May 31, 2002).

Levy, Steven. *Crypto: How the Code Rebels Beat the Government, Saving Privacy in the Digital Age.* New York: Viking, 2001.

World Wide Web Consortium (W3C). "Platform for Privacy Preferences (P3P) Project." <http://www.w3.org/P3P/> (May 31, 2002).

Related Topics

Anonymity; Child Online Protection Act and Child Online Privacy Protection Act; Cookies; Data Mining; Encryption and Cryptography; Security

— *Leslie Regan Shade*

Project MAC

Project MAC was a computer development endeavor in the 1960s; its pioneering exploration of the working methods of multiple-user access became a foundation for modern computer networking and online collaboration.

Founded in 1963 at the Massachusetts Institute of Technology (MIT), Project MAC was the name given to the task of developing a "control and command" system for the U.S. government. The innovation of computer scientist J.C.R. Licklider, Project MAC was funded by the Department of Defense's Advanced Research Projects Agency (ARPA), as well as by the National Science Foundation. It was first directed by Robert M. Fano. The goal established by ARPA was to enable decisions to be made swiftly and disseminated to many locations. For example, a military officer could notify dispersed troops of an important decision simultaneously.

The acronym "MAC" had several meanings, highlighting the multiple motives of the project. "Machine-Aided Cognition" stood for the broad objective of Project MAC's creators, who desired a way to make computers more useful than previous machines that were used to perform calculations. "Multiple-Access Computer" explained the mechanism for achieving the creators' aforementioned goal of allowing many users admittance and access to one computer's programs. "Project" was used, rather than "laboratory," to inspire individuals at MIT to join the effort without disaffiliating themselves from their current laboratories.

According to the National Research Council (NRC), the project's acronym also stood for "Man and Computer." The NRC credits Project MAC with changing the role and environment of computers, allowing software applications to be developed to aid in tasks and run on minicomputers instead of large mainframes.

Project MAC contributed to a concept known as the Compatible Time-Sharing System (CTSS), which permits multiple users at dispersed terminals to run programs centrally located on one machine. The focus on building the CTSS was supported by Licklider. According to *Technology Review* writer M. Mitchell Waldrop, Licklider believed that dividing computer time among users would facilitate greater efficiency of the technology. Cost reduction and time savings also fueled the development of the system; many users could share one large computer, instead of many users employing many small machines.

Within six months of Project MAC's creation, 200 users were able to access the system in ten different MIT departments. By 1967, Project MAC became its own interdepartmental laboratory, separated from its earlier Department of Electrical Engineering home. Further development of Project MAC evolved into the 1969 creation of Multics, the "Multiplexed Information and Computing Service," which advanced from computer time-sharing into an online computer system. Multics, which was developed by Project MAC through the combined efforts of Bell Labs and General Electric, incorporated features such as file sharing and management, and system security into its design. The complex system could support 300 simultaneous users on 1,000 MIT terminals.

Project MAC became the Laboratory for Computer Science (LCS) at MIT in 1976, and broadened its focus. According to a 1970s MIT brochure, lab director Michael L. Dertouzos explained the expanding goals of the LCS to include three principal areas in computer science and engineering. Dertouzos pushed for developing more intelligent programs to run on the computer systems. In addition, to promote computer use, the laboratory would study how to develop cost effective, user-friendly systems, and would also explore the theoretical foundations in computer science that sought to understand limitations on space and time. Advancing the role of the computer system, the LCS focused on creating applications that would foster online computing in several academic disciplines, including architecture, biology, medicine, and library sciences.

A few of Project MAC's team members went on to develop additional hardware and software for the computer industry. Project MAC member Dan Bricklin created the application known as VisiCalc, the first electronic spreadsheet, and another team member, Bob Metcalfe, went on to invent Ethernet and found 3Com. In addition, Bell Labs' joint development with the Multics system prompted it to employ a simpler form of the UNIX operating system.

Project MAC's development of CTSS and Multics provided two noteworthy contributions that built a foundation for concepts of networking and computer operating systems that were later employed in Internetworking. CTSS allowed users on teletypewriter terminals to communicate with a computer simultaneously through MIT's telephone system; the Multics system introduced now-standard features into computer operating systems. Modern advances in computer technology and networking have become possible thanks to the foundations laid by Project MAC nearly 30 years ago.

Bibliography
MIT Project on Mathematics and Computation. "Project MAC ('Switzerland')." November 29, 2000. <http://www.swiss.ai.mit.edu/projects/mac/> (April 12, 2002).

National Research Council. "The Organization of Federal Support: A Historical Review." *Funding a Revolution: Government Support for Computing Research.* Washington, D.C.: National Academy Press, 1999. <http://www.nap.edu/readingroom/books/far/ch4_b2.html> (April 12, 2002).

Waldrop, M. Mitchell. "Computing's Johnny Appleseed." *Technology Review, an MIT Enterprise,* January/February 2000. <http://www.technologyreview.com/articles/waldrop0100.asp> (April 12, 2002).

Further Reading
MIT Libraries. "History of the Laboratory for Computer Science (LCS)." 1995. <http://libraries.mit.edu/archives/mithistory/histories-offices/lcs.html> (April 12, 2002).

Rheingold, Howard. "Witness to History: The Mascot of Project MAC." *Tools for Thought.* Cambridge, Mass.: MIT Press, April 2000. <http://www.rheingold.com/texts/tft/8.html> (April 12, 2002).

Related Topics
ARPANET; Human-Computer Interaction; Internet; Licklider, J. C. R.

— *James Pyfer*

Qube

Qube was the first two-way cable commercial television service. It was a joint venture, developed and operated by Warner Communications and Amex Cable in Columbus, Ohio. It ran from December 1977 until 1985, when costs for the service were determined to be prohibitive and the project was scrubbed. Today, Qube is recalled as perhaps the earliest experiment in genuinely interactive television, and some even consider it as kind of a primitive predecessor to the World Wide Web.

Compared to what is possible now on the Internet, and to what is likely to come when digital television hits its stride, Qube's experimentally interactive offerings were unsophisticated, even quaint. It allowed cable TV subscribers in Columbus to select pay-per-view movies, participate in simple, selective polls, and offer audience feedback. But even those simple viewer-participation functions allowed for an early form of electronic democracy; by punching buttons in a keypad viewers could respond to issues raised during live city-council and school-board meeting broadcasts. Viewers also could win prizes during quiz shows, and occasionally select plays for local football teams during live game telecasts. Despite its archaic nature, *Media Visions Journal* writer Ken Freed has noted, Qube set the mark for all interactive television to come.

According to Freed, Warner Communications president Steve Ross first dreamed up the idea of Qube after staying in a Tokyo hotel in 1975. The facility's closed-circuit TV system was mildly interactive, and had been built by Pioneer Electronic of Japan. Ross contacted Pioneer and asked the company to develop a similar system for commercial cable TV in the United States. Warner Cable's CEO approved of the idea, and Pioneer's design for Qube was deployed two years later.

On December 1, 1977, with studios located in a remodeled Columbus appliance store, Qube launched to tremendous fanfare. Initially, it offered what then was an unprecedented 30 channels. Ten of these were standard broadcast channels running on cable, ten were either premium or pay-per-view channels, and the remaining ten consisted of original, local, interactive programming. Only one year after the launch of the Apple I personal computer in 1976, Qube's 30,000 subscribers received a set-top box with a computer chip and some computerized memory. Data traffic over the eight-bit system traveled both to and from set-top boxes at 256kbps (kilobits per second), about the effective rate of today's broadband digital subscriber line (DSL) Internet-connection technology.

The service was heavily hyped in the 1970s, and media attention helped Warner Cable land a lot of lucrative local cable franchises at the height of the early cable bidding wars of the time. Strangely, as Roger Fidler notes in his 1997 book *Mediamorphosis: Understanding New Media,* Qube failed to generate much excitement among viewers. According to Fidler, this may have been partly due to the system's limited interactive capabilities. In most cases, feedback was limited to yes or no answers, or to selecting answers from a list of numbered options; viewers felt like they were taking multiple-choice exams, Fidler writes. Indirectly, that paucity of serious interactivity may actually have contributed to the later boom of commercial Internet services. Future America Online chief Steve Case, then a young college student in Cincinnati, decided to buy a computer and check out the early online services after finding himself disappointed in Qube's interactive offerings.

The service faced other obstacles as well, not the least of which was cost. Subscribers paid $200 for the Qube terminals in their homes, more than four times the cost of a regular cable box. Equipment needed at the cable company head-end cost roughly $2 million to $3 million. It was also extremely expensive to produce the ten channels of original interactive TV content, even though the budgets and production values of each individual show were quite low, and low-budget interactive programming couldn't compete for audience attention with big-budget network programming. In the end, Fidler writes, the Warner-Amex partnership lost $30 million on the experiment. In 1985,

Warner Cable allowed Qube to revert back to a standard cable-TV system.

Yet another problem, one that also appears to have hurt viewer interest, was the system's capability of monitoring what people were watching on TV, to study their interests and viewing habits. According to Fidler, Warner-Amex pledged that they would keep any information gleaned from their observations private, but they also reserved the right to sell aggregated information to advertisers, and to use it to compile marketing databases. The only way to avoid being monitored as a Qube subscriber was to keep the TV turned off.

Despite its problems, today Qube is viewed in hindsight as a primarily successful experiment in early interactive television, if also a bit ambitious and ahead of its time. Columbia University new media professor John Carey credits the system for inventing the pay-per-view TV model that is ubiquitous today, but argues that Qube's principal legacy may be the lesson that interactive media cannot compete with traditional, one-way mass media head-on for the same audience. Instead, Carey insists, interactive media must be developed in an economic and technical context that makes sense. Further, Carey says, even with all the right elements in place, "producers must learn to create with the new medium, and audiences should not be expected to change their media habits overnight."

Bibliography

Fidler, Roger. *Mediamorphosis: Understanding New Media.* Thousand Oaks, Calif.: Pine Forge Press, 1997.

Freed, Ken. "When Cable Went Qubist." *Media Visions Journal,* 2000.
<http://www.media-visions.com/itv-qube.html> (April 12, 2002).

Rupp, Katherine. "Warner Amex QUBE Cable-Communications." ElectraBlue.com, 1999.
<http://www.electrablue.com/bluesky/qube/> (April 12, 2002).

Swerdlow, Tracy. "The First 2-Way Set-top Box." *Interactive TV Today* [itvt], 2000.
<http://www.itvt.com/etvwhitepaper-4.html> (April 12, 2002).

Further Reading

Harmon, Amy. "How Blind Alleys Led Old Media to New." *The New York Times,* January 16, 2000, pp. 3–11.

"Will It Play in Columbus?" *TV Guide,* December 24, 1977.

Related Topics

Case, Stephen M.; Desktop Video; Electronic Democracy; Gaming; Graphical User Interface; Interactivity; Interface; Multimedia

— *Kevin Featherly*

QuickTime

QuickTime is a file-compression and translation format developed by Apple Computer that facilitates the distribution of audio-visual material over networks such as the Internet, and contributes to the multimedia environment of the World Wide Web. The two key attributes of QuickTime are its abilities to operate within a variety of computer operating systems and to allow video compression.

QuickTime is an industry-standard multimedia architecture used to deliver synchronized graphics, sound, video, text, and music. Apple describes it as a suite, or a group, of files, applications, and plug-ins. It can be used as a movie player, image viewer, audio player, and virtual reality (VR) tool. It can also be downloaded as a Web browser plug-in, although many browsers already include it. QuickTime is supported by Director, HyperCard, PowerPoint, and Movieworks, and by many other standard multimedia authoring applications. One of the most significant features that it brings to the Internet is its enabling of video streaming over networks; thanks to QuickTime, live streaming and Internet TV and radio can be delivered through a Web browser.

The Web has become an increasingly visual environment, and the need to disseminate moving-picture and sound files is met in part through QuickTime. Film and video are highly versatile multimedia components, but file sizes prohibited their usage in the early stages of the Web. QuickTime, along with other standards such as MPEG for moving images and JPEG for still images, allow smaller files to be used by reducing file size while still retaining a presentable level of quality. QuickTime compresses, retrieves, and changes the format of still images, but it also allows these functions to be extended to the use of film and video in conjunction with audio. In addition to still images, sound, and streaming video, QuickTime also enables forms of virtual reality (VR); it can be used to create virtual walk-throughs of buildings or other 3-D structures.

The QuickTime player appears on the computer desktop with stop/play/pause functions and channel choices that tap into QuickTime radio and television. These QuickTime channels are supported by Fox, ABC News, Virgin Radio, Time-Warner, Disney, CNN, and BBC World. This cross-media support and application of QuickTime has in some ways revitalized Apple's share of the computing market. Although

RealNetworks is also a main competitor, the release of QuickTime 4 in 1999 placed Apple more firmly in the multimedia market. QuickTime's VR feature also contributes to this consolidated position, as it enables a relatively cutting-edge modeling process with many different industry applications. Apple looks to retain this market lead through QuickTime's ability to grow and be upgraded.

In general, multimedia authoring is an evolving field, and new approaches continually feed into the market. The presentation quality of compressed files is not yet satisfactory in comparison to other forms of uncompressed delivery. One of the aims of multimedia computing is to reproduce a cinematic level of quality in sound and image delivery on the Web; until this goal is realized, there will be continual research and development.

Bibliography

Botto, Francis. *Dictionary of Multimedia and Internet Applications: A Guide for Developers and Users.* Chichester, N.Y.: Wiley, 1999.

Gulie, Steven W. *QuickTime for the Web.* San Diego, Calif.: Academic Press, 2000.

Vince, John, and Rae Earnshaw, eds. *Digital Media: The Future.* London: Springer, 2000.

Further Reading

Apple Computer, Inc. Web-site tutorials, 2002. <http://www.apple.com/quicktime/tools_tips/tutorials> (July 12, 2002).

Towner, George. *Discovering QuickTime: An Introduction for Windows and Macintosh Programmers.* San Francisco, Calif.: Morgan Kaufmann, 1999.

Related Topics

MPEG; Multimedia; Streaming Media; Virtual Reality; World Wide Web

— *Kate O'Riordan*

Race and Ethnicity and New Media

The term digital divide refers to the gap between those who have access to the Internet and those who do not. A portion of this digital divide is drawn along racial lines, with whites being more likely to have access, and minorities being less likely to. However, access and usage are only part of the picture. Minority media on the whole tend to tell different stories than general-audience media, and many people argue that minority groups need to make it a priority to get online and tell their own stories, in their own way. What minority-oriented content is available, and what challenges do minorities face when launching an Internet venture?

RACIAL-ETHNIC MINORITIES AND INTERNET CONTENT

It has been said that minorities will be more inclined to go online when they know that they will be able to find Web sites presenting content that interests them, and when they know that they can connect with others like them via email, chat rooms, and so on. The number of ethnically focused sites on the Internet grows constantly, and includes both domestic and international portals. These range from www.bet.com (African-American) to www.uol.com.br (Universo Online, Brazil's largest portal) and www.click2asia.com (with separate sites for the United States, Korea, China, and Japan). In addition to providing news and information specific to different racial and ethnic groups, many minority-oriented sites feature job banks, email, chat rooms, shopping, and more. Specialty foods and recipes from just about every culture are available online, as are goods used (or given) during various ethnic holidays.

When targeting minority audiences, language and design issues need special attention. Some analysts argue that sites targeting Hispanics should be bilingual; sites targeting other groups might need to be multilingual. Just as with traditional media, poor translations on the Internet can result in inappropriate words being used, and American humor might backfire. Basic site designs also need careful translations because different cultures have different likes and dislikes; for example, designers of sites for Asian markets should know that Japanese Internet users tend to prefer site maps, while Chinese users tend not to like frames.

The Internet provides extensive resources—many maintained by universities—for and about various racial and ethnic groups. The University of Illinois offers Asian resources at www.gateway.library.uiuc.edu/asx; the University of Texas at Austin hosts Latin American resources at www.lanic.utexas.edu. Information and resources about African-American history and experiences are available at www.academicinfo.net/africanam.html. There are also guides to race and race relations, such as the one maintained by the University of Miami at www.library.miami.edu/netguides/socrace.html.

Some people do not use the Internet to improve race relations and increase tolerance. Quite the contrary—more than 350 hate Web sites serve as virtual hubs of vast racist networks, spreading propaganda and attempting to recruit new members. Hate sites are in turn monitored by other sites, including www.tolerance.org, which is operated by the Southern Poverty Law Center. Tolerance.org provides a virtual tour of several hate sites, but does not take visitors to the actual sites themselves. It also features discussion forums, links to groups promoting tolerance, special activities designed for children, resources for parents and teachers, and more.

USING THE WEB TO BUILD AND SUSTAIN COMMUNITY

Many people are using new technologies to engage in activities that unite them as virtual communities. People can escape barriers of geographic, physical, or social isolation and find strength and empowerment in such communities. Members of various groups who have been dispersed from their place or culture of origin can share common experiences with others like themselves, get in touch with their roots, and feel some of the comforts of home. Distance and time become irrelevant. The online environment can be used to find or reinforce a sense of identity that had previously seemed difficult, if not impossible, to acquire or maintain.

Any new technology that supports interaction can support an online community: USENET news groups, mailing lists, chat rooms, Multi-User Domains (MUDs), Multi-User Object-Oriented domains (MOOs), etc. Web sites can also serve diasporic peoples by providing a forum for sharing information, developing educational resources, and responding to social and political issues.

A variety of online newsgroups (bulletin board–like postings of messages about a specified topic of interest) target specific nationalities and discrete communities within nations, and are organized like the ethnic neighborhoods found in large cities. For example, the soc.culture USENET group has numerous subgroups, each corresponding to a specific nation, community, or tribe: soc.culture.indian, soc.culture.korean, soc.culture.hawaii, and so forth. Users participate by reading and responding to posted messages. Sometimes members of these communities share information about or search for people from "back home"; sometimes they just wish to announce their presence. Sometimes, members debate political, cultural, social, or spiritual issues of importance to both the virtual (online) and the actual (tangible, original) communities. At other times, conflicts and antagonisms are interjected as individuals who are not members of a particular discrete community "crosspost" inflammatory messages to that community (as might happen if a member of soc.culture.pakistani posted an angry message to soc.culture.indian).

BUSINESS CHALLENGES FACING RACIAL/ETHNIC MINORITIES

The Internet is sometimes viewed as a fairly level playing field for diverse people to create a substantial media presence where none had existed before. Some observers encourage a sense of urgency for minorities to participate, arguing that minorities cannot afford to be left out of the new media revolution.

A major problem facing minority entrepreneurs is a lack of access to venture capital. Entrepreneurs count on venture capitalists to fund new business ventures, and even when they get a foot in the door to make a presentation, many minority businesspeople find venture capitalists uninformed when it comes to minority-targeted business plans. Many venture capitalists simply don't believe that significant numbers of minorities are online, nor that minorities will spend money once they get there. Neither of these beliefs are true, and as the digital divide lessens, they will become even less so. However, much of the networking done by venture capitalists and entrepreneurs takes place in traditional "old boy" networks, and it can be difficult to encourage people of all races and ethnicities to look outside their own networks. Yes, the Internet is technically colorblind, but even if all else is equal, minority business owners are less likely than whites to obtain funding for their Internet ventures.

A second challenge facing many minority-owned Web sites is that they are often created based on a business model that includes advertising as a key source of revenue. Advertising income is difficult to count on, in part because the overall effectiveness of the Internet as a vehicle for advertising is being questioned. In particular, Web sites targeting African Americans find it hard to secure advertising revenue, because most such sites don't generate enough traffic to be ranked among the most popular Web sites—and only the most popular generate significant revenue. So it remains a challenge for minority sites both to attract advertisers and to maintain ad rates, despite the fact that studies have shown that minorities click to online ads nearly twice as often as whites.

Several minority Internet ventures have resolved this problem by forming strategic partnerships with other, more well-established media organizations. Afronet and Sprint have partnered, as have NetNoir and AOL, and BlackVoices has paired with the *Chicago Tribune*. Such team-ups can be very helpful, especially if the larger company's sales force encourages advertisers to buy ads on the Web site and includes the two media outlets in a single sales package. Another tactic is for individual sites to become network affiliates, with advertisements rotating among similar sites on a "channel." Ad rates are based on the combined traffic to the channel, which is significantly higher than the traffic to any of the individual sites. These and other creative approaches are bound to assist racial and ethnic minorities as they continue to build a strong presence on the Internet.

Bibliography

Abramson, Jeffrey. "Emerging Internet: The Internet and Community." The Aspen Institute, 1998. <http://www.aspeninstitute.org/publications1/ bookstore_communications_emerging_community.html> (April 12, 2002).

Barber, John T., and Alice A. Tait, eds. *The Information Society and the Black Community*. Westport, Conn.: Praeger, 2001.

Entman, Robert M. "Coming Together: Bridging the Gap Between Investors and Minority Internet Entrepreneurs." Aspen Institute, Forum on Diversity and the Media, 2000. <http://www.aspeninstitute.org/c&s/pdfs/minority.pdf> (April 12, 2002).

Mitra, Ananda. "Virtual Commonality: Looking for India on the Internet." *Virtual Culture: Identity & Communication in Cybersociety.* Steven G. Jones, ed. Thousand Oaks, Calif.: Sage Publications, 1997.

National Telecommunications and Information Administration, U.S. Department of Commerce. "Falling Through the Net: Toward Digital Inclusion." <http://www.ntia.doc.gov/ntiahome/fttn00/contents00.html> (April 12, 2002).

Further Reading

Beckles, Colin. "Black Struggles in Cyberspace: Cyber-Segregation and Cyber-Nazis." *Western Journal of Black Studies,* vol. 21, no. 1 (1997), pp. 12–19.

Brown, Carolyn M. "A Dash of Color." *Black Enterprise* 30 (November 2000), p. 34.

DePalma, Donald A. "How to Design Your Site to Take Advantage of the Growing Number of Hispanic and Asian Consumers Online." *Target Marketing* 23 (December 2000), pp. 46–49.

Ford-Livene, Marcelino. "The Digital Dilemma: Ten Challenges Facing Minority-Owned Media Ventures." *Communications Law Journal* 51 (1999), pp. 577–608.

Gardyn, Rebecca. "Cultural Factors Influence the Online Behavior of Ethnic Consumers." *American Demographics* 23 (April 2001), pp. 14–17.

Gooding, Helen. "Racial Integration." *Marketing Week* 21 (1998), pp. 41–42.

Haegele, Katie. "A Crash Course in Culturally-Sensitive Marketing." *Target Marketing* 3 (March 2000), pp. 97–99.

Lach, Jennifer. "Diversity in a Virtual World." *American Demographics* 21 (1999), pp. 17–18.

Mowbray, Rebecca. "Internet Helps Minority Companies Take on the Big Boys." *Houston Chronicle,* May 13, 2000. <http://www.chron.com/cs/CDA/c100story.hts/special/chron100/552076> (April 12, 2002).

Muhammad, Tariq. "Dot Com Fever." *Black Enterprise,* March 2000, pp. 82–89.

Ofori, Kofi Asiedu. "Reinventing Minority Media for the 21st Century." The Aspen Institute, 2001. <http://aspeninstitute.org/c&s/pdfs/diversity.pdf> (April 12, 2002).

Parrish, Deidra-Ann. "Learn How the Internet Can Benefit Your Business." *Black Enterprise* 30 (January 1999), pp. 99–102.

Race and Race Relations on the Internet. University of Miami Libraries, 2001.
<http://www.library.miami.edu/netguides/socrace.html> (April 12, 2002).

Rutledge, Keisha. "Increased Interest Speaks Well for Spanish Language Web Sites." *Retailing Today* 9 (May 8, 2000), pp. 25–27.

Related Topics
Digital Divide; MUDs and MOOs; USENET; World Wide Web

— *Rebecca Ann Lind*

Raymond, Eric
1957–
Author, Programmer

Eric Raymond is a self-styled "hacker anthropologist" and a leading advocate for open-source programming. The open-source movement challenges conventional notions of intellectual property by embracing a volunteerist, collaborative, and non-proprietary model for software development. Its origins can be traced to Richard Stallman's development, beginning in the 1980s, of the GNU operating system as a free alternative to UNIX. The greatest accomplishment of the open-source movement so far is the creation, building on GNU, of the Linux operating system.

Raymond has been involved with the development of non-proprietary software since the earliest days of GNU. Along the way, however, he has split sharply with Stallman. Stallman describes GNU as "free software," which he defines as "free as in speech, not free as in beer." Developers can still sell their products; they just don't have the right to restrict adaptations and alterations of the underlying source code. Stallman's primary impetus in the development of GNU, and of his Free Software Foundation, is the belief that programmers have an ethical and political responsibility to make software, and its underlying source code, available to all who wish to use and modify it.

Raymond, by contrast, is much more interested in the practical benefits of non-proprietary collaborative development. He has criticized Stallman for needlessly alienating potential supporters with his politicized language; Stallman counters that Raymond's vision misses the whole point of free software.

The rift between Raymond and Stallman has led to a shift in terminology; concerned that the phrase "free software" would discourage potential business investors, Raymond has convinced many in the GNU and Linux communities to use the term "open-source software" instead, with its emphasis on practical access rather than political ideals. Raymond has also been much more willing to compromise with software developers who are interested in making only some parts of their code open-source, without completely embracing the ideology of free software.

Raymond's most influential work is his essay called "The Cathedral and the Bazaar," a manifesto for open-source development first published online in 1997, then later collected in Raymond's book of the same title. The essay tries to explain the enormous success of the development of the Linux operating system, which was produced by the collaborative work of thousands of volunteers around the world, overseen by Finnish programmer Linus Torvalds. It draws on Raymond's own experience in developing one component of Linux, an email program called fetchmail.

In "The Cathedral and the Bazaar," Raymond posits two models of software development: the cathedral model and the bazaar model. The cathedral model has been the default for almost all commercial software development since the invention of the computer, and is certainly the way that Microsoft, the leading software company today, structures its operations. It presumes that projects must be carefully planned in advance and hierarchically structured. The bazaar model, by contrast, treats software development as a kind of marketplace of ideas, in which competition to contribute the most to the project will inspire programmers to greater heights of creativity and productivity, while more effectively weeding out bugs and poor design decisions. Of course, since most Linux programmers are volunteers, they're not in it for the money, but rather for the respect of colleagues, or what Raymond calls "egoboo" (short for "ego boost," a term borrowed from the world of science-fiction fandom).

"The Cathedral and the Bazaar" proved to be a tremendously influential document. Seven months after its initial appearance online, Netscape announced that it would release the source code to its flagship product, Netscape Communicator, so that all interested parties could collaborate on its further development. Netscape executives acknowledged that Raymond's arguments had played a key role in their deliberations. Since that high-water mark for the open-source movement, however, things haven't been quite as rosy; Netscape was purchased soon afterward by America Online (now AOL/Time Warner), which has shown less enthusiasm for open source. The open-source project based on the Communicator code, now called Mozilla, has moved forward slowly, while Microsoft's Internet Explorer has continued to increase its dominance of the Web-browser market.

Raymond gained further notoriety in October 1998, when a Microsoft employee leaked to him confidential Microsoft memoranda that demonstrated that the company was taking the threat of Linux and open source far more seriously than their dismissive public statements had indicated. Raymond dubbed these memos the "Halloween Documents," and released them to the press, much to Microsoft's embarrassment. Ironically, Microsoft would later embrace some parts of the memos during its anti-trust trial, when it argued that the legitimate business threat of Linux demonstrated that the company did not hold a monopoly on operating software. Microsoft continues, however, to criticize the open-source model as impractical and a danger to copyright holders.

Raymond is also known as a chronicler of the life and lore of the devoted computer programmers who call themselves hackers. Raymond has worked to rescue the term from its pejorative use to refer to criminals who illegally break into computer systems, and to recuperate its original, more benign meaning. His essay, "A Brief History of Hackerdom," traces the history of "a more or less continuous and self-conscious technical culture of enthusiast programmers, people who built and played with software for fun" from the development of the first ENIAC computer in 1945 to the present. Raymond first published his history online in 1992, and has continually updated it since.

Raymond is also the current maintainer of the JARGON file, "a comprehensive compendium of hacker slang illuminating many aspects of hackish tradition, folklore and humor." Begun at Stanford in 1975, the database contains definitions dating back to the 1960s. A version of the file, compiled and edited by Raymond, is published by MIT Press as *The New Hacker's Dictionary*, and has gone through three editions so far.

Selected Works

Raymond, Eric S. *The Cathedral and the Bazaar: Musings on Linux and Open Source by an Accidental Revolutionary*. Sebastopol, Calif. and Cambridge, Mass.: O'Reilly & Associates, 1999.

———. *The New Hacker's Dictionary*. Third edition. Cambridge, Mass.: MIT Press, 1996.

Bibliography

Moody, Glyn. *Rebel Code: Linux and the Open Source Revolution*. Cambridge, Mass.: Perseus Publishing, 2001.

Rosenberg, Donald K. *Open Source: The Unauthorized White Papers*. Foster City, Calif.: M&T Books, 2000.

Wayner, Peter. *Free for All: How LINUX and the Free Software Movement Undercut the High-Tech Titans.* New York: HarperBusiness, 2000.

Further Reading

Himanen, Pekka. *The Hacker Ethic and the Spirit of the Information Age.* New York: Random House, 2001.

Leonard, Andrew. "Salon.com Technology & Business: Free Software Project." *Salon*, 2001. <http://www.salon.com/tech/fsp> (May 10, 2002).

Related Topics

"The Cathedral and the Bazaar"; Copyleft; Hacking, Cracking, and Phreaking; Linux; Open Source; Stallman, Richard

— *Ted Friedman*

Responsive Environments

Responsive environments, which have applications in both real and virtual environments, present opportunities for novel, automated relationships between computers and the human body. They use sensory technology, coupled with computer equipment, to create a collaborative relationship between objects in an environment and movements of the human body. Similar to a computer mouse's ability to allow interaction between a computer and its user, responsive environments permit movement and gestures of the body to interact with objects within the environments.

In responsive environments, walking into a room or making physical contact with materials like walls and surfaces causes a computer to react in a certain way. Various sensors in an environment allow computers to process changes and execute a corresponding reaction. For instance, a room lined with cameras, lasers, or light receptors permits a computer to become aware of a worker's presence. The sensors then communicate with a computer that automatically controls variables in the environment. The room then becomes responsive to the individual by adjusting or changing elements like temperature levels or light intensities, or even emits sounds that fit the worker's personal preference.

The concept of a responsive environment is not entirely new. In the early 1990s, Myron Krueger developed a virtual environment called Videoplace. According to Krueger's description, Videoplace created an environment where the human body served as an interactive device. Videoplace housed a large screen; a user stood in front of the screen and, through cameras and lights, silhouettes of the body's movement were captured. The computer was able to recognize the body silhouette as an object, and to include it within the projected video environment. While the video screen projected animated images of dogs, the computer was able to process the shadowy image of the human body and share it within the environment of the dogs, causing the dogs to look at the silhouette and react with a barking sound.

The environments in which responsive technologies can be used are not limited to video screens and virtual arenas. Developments in sensors and computer technology led to the experimental testing of office buildings that could react to the behavior of employees. By installing cameras and various other pieces of equipment that notify a central processing unit of activity within a room, building management could take on a new and automated form. Through an intricate system of computer networking and sensors, the responsive office environment would intelligently know when workers entered a room via opening doors or detectors. Once activated by motion, or even by a microchip badge, overhead lights would turn on and ventilation systems would run, all without anyone flipping a switch or turning a dial. Once the workers leave the building for the day, the responsive system would then automatically react by turning off the lights and lowering the temperature, thereby conserving power and increasing efficiency.

Other responsive materials are in development. The Responsive Environments Group (REG) at the Massachusetts Institute of Technology (MIT) is researching the possible intrinsic relationships between sensors and environments. The REG examines the different types of plausible sensors, the required components of systems, and environments that are capable of becoming receptive. One novel development from the REG is a smart material called the Magic Carpet, which employs special wires underneath a carpet and Doppler radar sensors above it to react to people walking. The interactive environment uses the radar to detect movement patterns of the upper body, while piezoelectric wires embedded in the carpet identify position and pressure from the foot. Each step of the foot, coupled with movement of the upper body, causes tones and music to emit from nearby speakers. The Magic Carpet produces low tones for normal motion, while jumping triggers sharper and louder sounds.

Additional work in responsive environments seeks to blur the boundary between the user and computers. Computer-science researchers Wolfgang Krueger and Bernd Froehlich are designing a desktop computer that functions without extra input devices. Analysis of computer use by a variety of professionals has led Krueger and Froehlich to develop an alternative to virtual reality and multimedia systems known as the Responsive Workbench, a responsive-environment creation that utilizes tracking systems, microphones, and camera projectors to transform the traditional multimedia desktop computer into an impressive graphics workstation. The hand of the Responsive Workbench user can control the operation of the computer by virtually moving objects, similar to the way that the clicking of a mouse permits interaction with traditional computers.

Responsive environments are expected to revolutionize the interaction between computers, inanimate objects, and people. A couch that can adjust temperature and firmness levels to the preferences of its occupants, or a car that can automatically sense a driver's radio-listening mood, may be in the near future.

Bibliography

Elrod, Scott; Hall, Gene; Costanza, Rick; Dickson, Michael; and Jim Des Rivieres. "Responsive Office Environments." *Communications of the ACM*, vol. 36, no. 7 (July 1993), pp. 84–85.

Gold, Stuart. "Intelligent Environments (or My Friends and Other Floor Tiles)." *Digital Space*, 2000. <http://www.digitalspace.com/papers/sgoldfloortile.html> (May 31, 2002).

Krueger, Myron. "Responsive Environments." *Multimedia: From Wagner to Virtual Reality*. Randall Packer and Ken Jordan, eds. New York: W. W. Norton, 2001.

Krueger, Wolfgang, and Bernard Froehlich. "The Responsive Workbench." *IEEE Computer Graphics and Applications,* vol. 14, no. 3 (May 1994), pp. 12–15

Further Reading

Durbin, Jim, et al. "Battlefield Visualization on the Responsive Workbench." *IEEE Visualization Proceedings,* 1998, pp. 463–66.

Paradiso, Joseph; Abler, Craig; Hsiao, Kai-Yuh; and Matthew Reynolds. "The Magic Carpet: Physical Sensing for Immersive Environments." Responsive Environments Group, MIT Media Lab. Presented at the ACM 1997 SIGCHI Conference, March 25, 1997. <http://www.media.mit.edu/resenv/pubs/papers/97_03_CHI97_Floor.pdf> (May 31, 2002).

Paradiso, Joseph; Hsiao, Kai-Yuh; Strickton, Joshua; Lifton, Joshua; and Ari Adler. "Sensor Systems for Interactive Surfaces." *IBM Systems Journal,* vol. 39, nos. 3 & 4 (2000).

Responsive Environments Group, MIT Media Lab. Web site. <http://gn.www.media.mit.edu/resenv> (May 31, 2002).

Related Topics

Human-Computer Interaction; Interface; Media Lab, Massachusetts Institute of Technology; Virtual Reality

— *James Pyfer*

Rheingold, Howard

1947–

Author, Online Pioneer

Writer, editor, speaker, and online community builder, Howard Rheingold is best known as the author of *The Virtual Community: Homesteading on the Electronic Frontier* (1993), one of the first book-length attempts to treat the Internet as a social and cultural environment worthy of popular and academic attention.

Rheingold was born in 1947 in Tucson, Arizona, and was raised in Phoenix. He was a National Merit Scholar at Reed College, where he graduated in 1968. With the help of a variety of day jobs—including clerk, typist, steel worker, warehouse worker, and babysitter—he began writing in earnest in 1973. Gradually, he became a full-time writer; over the last 25 years, his work has appeared in such venues as *The New York Times, Esquire, Newsweek,* and *Omni.*

Rheingold spent much of the 1980s exploring the intersections between human consciousness, creative activity, and new technologies. His books from this period include *Talking Tech: A Conversational Guide to Science and Technology* (with Howard Levine, 1982), *Tools for Thought: The People and Ideas Behind the Next Computer Revolution* (1985), and *The Cognitive Connection: Thought and Language in Man and Machine* (1986). Although Rheingold gained considerable attention with *Virtual Reality* (1991), it was not until *The Virtual Community* that he became a leading commentator on cyberspace in general, and the notion of online communities in particular.

Focusing especially on the Whole Earth 'Lectronic Link (WELL), a pioneering Bay Area–based online community, *The Virtual Community* serves, along with Sherry Turkle's *Life on the Screen: Identity in the Age of the Internet* (1995), as one of the twin pillars of the nascent field of Internet studies. In the book, Rheingold makes the 'Net—still in its early, pre-Netscape days—more familiar, and sheds light on what users do within virtual communities, from arguing over politics in one of the WELL's conference rooms to trading recipes within a cooking forum. Along the way, Rheingold explores community formation within USENET newsgroups as well as identity representation on Multiple User Domains (MUDs), and recounts a brief, simplified history of the Internet, sprinkling his anecdotal yet experienced observations with more theoretical frameworks, including theories of social contracts, reciprocity, and gift economies.

Perhaps the most important contribution of *The Virtual Community* is its definition of online communities, one that has been worked with (and over) by subsequent scholars of computer-mediated communication. According to Rheingold, "virtual communities are social aggregations that emerge from the Net when enough people carry on . . . public discussions long enough, with sufficient human feeling, to form webs of personal relationships in cyberspace." Herein lie two crucial Rheingoldian themes. First, building off of the ideas of ARPANET grandfather J. C. R. Licklider, virtual communities are social networks based on common and shared interests rather than on geographic proximity. Second, virtual communities represent human agency at its finest; by "taking to the wires," everyday users of the Internet transformed a once-militaristic computer network into an online public sphere—or, to use Rheingold's words, "an electronic agora."

One of the lasting results of Rheingold's pivotal book is a research agenda focused on the social and cultural elements of cyberspace. For example, many of the chapters in anthologies like *Virtual Culture: Identity and Communication in Cybersociety* (1997) and *Internet Culture* (1997) build upon ideas introduced by Rheingold, and bring a more theoretically grounded framework to the terrain he travels through and the questions he asks. Further, anthologies like *Wired Women: Gender and New Realities in Cyberspace* (1996) and *Race in Cyberspace* (2000) use Rheingold as a starting point, yet quickly critique and problematize his findings. Indeed, while many readers enthusiastically embrace Rheingold's positive portrayal of cyberspace, most scholars find his utopian rhetoric to be deserving of critique and in need of more empirically based and theoretically grounded scholarship.

Since the original publication of *The Virtual Community*, Rheingold has been busy building, writing about, and sharpening his arguments on virtual communities. In 1994, he helped create *HotWired*, the first commercial Webzine with a virtual community; it doubled as the online component of the then relatively new *Wired* magazine. He served as *HotWired*'s first executive editor, but left almost immediately after it launched, assembling a team of writers, communitarians, and investors to start Electric Minds, a generously funded yet ultimately unsuccessful virtual community that, among other things, enjoyed more than 70,000 registered users and served as the online platform upon which the Kasparov versus Deep Blue II chess match took place.

Recently, he founded Brainstorms, a private, non-profit Web-conferencing community in the tradition of the WELL and Electric Minds; Brainstorms includes a few hundred people from around the world who communicate about such topics as technology, the future, life online, culture, society, health, work, and academia. Rheingold is also the founder of Rheingold Associates, a for-profit, online management-strategy business that offers guidance in creating and maintaining successful, sustainable social networks, teamwork spaces, and virtual conventions.

Rheingold also continues to write, both as a contributing writer for *Wired* magazine and, more recently, as the author of the second edition of *The Virtual Community*. While he remains optimistic about the Internet in general and online communities in particular, his writing has become more intellectually grounded and theoretically sophisticated.

Selected Works

Rheingold, Howard. *The Cognitive Connection: Thought and Language in Man and Machine.* New York: Prentice Hall, 1987.

———. *Tools for Thought: The People and Ideas Behind the Next Computer Revolution.* New York: Simon & Schuster, 1985. Reprinted as *Tools for Thought: The History and Future of Mind-Expanding Technology.* Cambridge, Mass.: MIT Press, 2000.

———. *The Virtual Community: Homesteading on the Electronic Frontier.* Reading, Mass.: Addison-Wesley, 1993.

———. *Virtual Reality.* New York: Summit Books, 1991.

Bibliography

Cherny, Lynn, and Elizabeth Reba Weise, eds. *Wired Women: Gender and New Realities in Cyberspace.* Seattle: Seal Press, 1996.

Jones, Steven G., ed. *Virtual Culture: Identity and Communication in Cybersociety.* Thousand Oaks, Calif.: Sage Publications, 1997.

Kolko, Beth; Nakamura, Lisa; and Gilbert B. Rodman, eds. *Race in Cyberspace.* New York: Routledge, 2000.

Licklider, J. C. R. "Man-Computer Symbiosis." *IRE Transactions on Human Factors in Electronics,* vol. HFE-1 (March 1960), pp. 4–11.

Porter, David, ed. *Internet Culture.* New York: Routledge, 1997.

Turkle, Sherry. *Life on the Screen: Identity in the Age of the Internet.* New York: Simon & Schuster, 1995.

Further Reading

Dibbell, Julian. *My Tiny Life: Crime and Passion in a Virtual World.* New York: Henry Holt, 1998.

Horn, Stacy. *Cyberville: Clicks, Culture, and the Creation of an Online Town.* New York: Warner Books, 1998.

Smith, Marc A., and Peter Kollock, eds. *Communities in Cyberspace*. New York: Routledge, 1999.

Related Topics

Cyberculture; Cyberspace; Licklider, J. C. R.; Turkle, Sherry; Virtual Community

— *David Silver*

Robotics

Just as the personal computer brought computing to the masses, mobile robotics have begun to find their way into the home. And just as home video-game consoles paved the way for personal computing, robotic toys and virtual pets may one day be considered the forerunners of more versatile and practical personal robots.

Robots of one form or another have existed in fiction and in fact for several millennia. The ancient Egyptians and Greeks created hydraulically driven statues; by the eighteenth century, mechanical automatons had reached new levels of complexity, allowing for a wide range of behaviors. These machines, which were created as amusing diversions for the aristocracy, are direct ancestors of the personal entertainment robots being created today. They are a world apart from the industrial robots that continue to be employed in large-scale manufacturing and other commercial applications; these robots are normally limited to particular repetitive tasks, are relatively expensive, and require ongoing maintenance. Other special-purpose robots include those that are designed to work in environments inhospitable to humans—under water or in space, for example. These robots are often controlled by a remote operator rather than being autonomous, although there are many exceptions. The robots emerging now for a consumer market are designed mainly to entertain, although over time their social consequences may be serious indeed.

Sony's Aibo has garnered a significant amount of public attention, and serves as an example of why these kinds of technologies are particularly interesting. The Aibo, a three-pound toy dog that appears to exhibit a personality, set a sales record when it was introduced, and dozens of similar products have now entered the market. It is very much like the automatons of centuries past, as well as more recent virtual pets like the Furby and Tamagotchi, in that it mimics the behavior of live animals in order to give the appearance of consciousness. However, the use of digital electronics and sensing systems allows the Aibo to interact with its environment much more than earlier devices were able to. The most recent generation of the Aibo, for example, is equipped with a small video camera, microphones, heat sensors, and pressure sensors, and can learn to understand several dozen simple spoken commands as well as navigate home environments with some success. The behaviors the robot is capable of are pre-programmed rather than learned, but are designed to mimic the development of skills in live pets, advancing gradually in stages as the robot "ages." The popularity of the $2,000 Aibo has provided an economic impetus for continued research.

While it is primarily an expensive toy at present, Sony sees a more practical role for the device in the future. Indeed, as representatives from Sony have repeatedly explained, Aibo was not designed to replace dogs as pets, but as an attempt to discover how humans can "live with robots." Like the robotic cat called Tama from Matsushita, the Aibo is seen as a potential companion robot for the elderly. These robots would eventually help to watch over the infirm, and would help maintain a stronger link to the outside world. This unification of entertainment and service has been attempted in other areas, like the robotic guides that provide tours for visitors at the Museum für Kommunikation in Berlin. In 1999, an annual publication titled *World Robotics* that reports on the development of the robotics industry introduced a new category, "service robots," which included entertainment robots. The attention garnered by this newly popular type of robot over the last few years has ensured that service robotics will remain an area of rapid advancement.

Simple, animal-like robots also play an important role in the research and development of robotics in general. While replicating either the intelligence or the functionality of a human is far beyond the current state of the art, some hope that creating simple robotic insects or other animals may provide a more fertile research platform. In researching "multi-agent systems," robotic insects are created that may have rudimentary artificial intelligence, but can complete complex projects by working in a "swarm."

Just as games drove a portion of computer development, they also challenge robotics engineers. Increasingly, robots are employed in contests and games that provide a venue for exchanging ideas and testing machines. The RoboCup Challenge, for example, allows teams from universities and manufacturers around the globe to design teams of robots that will compete in soccer tournaments. Just as programmers designed computer chess systems with the ultimate aim of winning against a human grand master, the stated aim of the RoboCup project is to design a team of humanoid robots that will by 2050 be capable of winning against a team of champion human players. In addition, television programs like *Robot Wars* and its derivatives provide interesting competitive venues, tapping into the popular fascination with robots.

Some suggest that by the end of this decade, personal robots will begin appearing in the home that can perform routine housekeeping tasks and interact with their owners. It would be incorrect to assume that these more practical robots will replace the toys and robotic pets now appearing. Rather, like the personal computer, we are likely to see a blending of entertainment and utility—multifunctional robots that can play games with the children and then clean up afterwards, for example. The question will increasingly become one not of the technology itself, but of how we interact with it. Just as a generation that grew up on video games has embraced the growing information society, will children who grow up with virtual pets guide us to a new era of acceptance of robots that appear to be both intelligent and emotional?

Bibliography

Apicella, Mario. "Robots Are Marching Toward a More Intelligent Future." *Infoworld*, November 20, 2000.

Pransky, Joanne. "AIBO—The No. 1 Selling Service Robot." *Industrial Robot: An International Journal* 28 (Jan./Feb. 2001), pp. 24–26.

RoboCup Federation. "RoboCup 2002." <http://www.robocup.org/> (May 31, 2002).

Further Reading

Arkin, Ronald C. *Behavior-Based Robotics*. Cambridge, Mass.: MIT Press, 1998.

Nehmzow, Ulrich. *Mobile Robotics: A Practical Introduction*. New York: Springer, 2000.

"The Rossum Project: Open-Source Robotics Software." <http://rossum.sourceforge.net/> (May 31, 2002).

Thomas, Douglas. "Thinking Through Technology: AIBO Project." <http://www.aiboproject.com/> (May 31, 2002).

Related Topics

Brooks, Rodney; Cyborg; Kurzweil, Raymond; Moravec, Hans; Turing, Alan; von Neumann, John

— *Alexander Halavais*

S S S S S S **S** S S S S S

Samuelson, Pamela

1948–

Legal Theorist, Professor

Pamela Samuelson is a leading authority on legal issues in new media, particularly on intellectual property rights (IPR) and the Internet. She has passionately argued for the need to strike a balance between corporate and public interests in defense of the common good.

Born in Seattle and raised in Washington state, Samuelson attended the University of Hawaii in Honolulu, where she earned a bachelor's degree in history and master's in political science. She then attended Yale Law School, where she received her law degree in 1976. She spent six years in private practice in New York, then joined the University of Pittsburgh Law School as a faculty member. While at Pittsburgh, she became interested in computer law, and in 1989 began writing a column on technology and law issues for the *Communications of the ACM* (Association for Computing Machinery). Since 1996, Samuelson has been a member of the faculty at University of California–Berkeley, where she teaches courses on the social and policy issues surrounding the information society, cyberlaw, intellectual property, and copyright theory.

Samuelson's early writings on cyberlaw, featured in the "Legally Speaking" columns of the *Communications of the ACM*, focused on First Amendment rights for information providers; copyright implications of computer software that had similar "looks and feels"; whether the "structure, sequence, and organization" of a computer program was protectable expression; and whether algorithms could be patented. With the development of the National Information Infrastructure in the 1990s, Samuelson became a key voice in debates about intellectual property in a digital environment. Using both academic and popular platforms for discussion (for example, she wrote a series of articles for *Wired* magazine), Samuelson criticized the Clinton administration's "White Paper" on intellectual property, arguing that its treatment of fair use favored industry

and corporate interests at the expense of the wider community of users.

The promotion of public-interest perspectives for the information society is at the core of Samuelson's writings. She advocates for an open information environment with a robust public domain, and warns of the dangers of too much commodification of information. She argues for a new politics of intellectual property to counteract the content industry's move toward stronger rights. Of special concern to Samuelson is how the traditional notion of fair use is being erased because of digitization. Fair use gives a user the right to make a copy of a work that they own; since digital media are so easy and cheap to copy, content providers are attempting to restrict the definition of fair use as much as possible.

Samuelson has been an ardent defender of the individual's right to engage in private, non-commercial uses of information, arguing that it is necessary to impose some limits on the corporate world's power over information. For instance, Samuelson has criticized the Digital Millennium Copyright Act (DMCA) of 1998, characterizing it as an unprecedented expansion of copyright law with myriad First Amendment problems. She has argued that the anti-circumvention and anti-trafficking provisions of the DMCA punish new categories of non-infringing, protected speech.

Samuelson believes strongly that lawyers and legal scholars must take a lead in formulating policies for a just and equitable information society. To support her sense of the importance of the public interest, Samuelson founded the Samuelson Law, Technology, and Public Policy Clinic at UC–Berkeley's School of Law (Boalt Hall). This is the first law clinic in the country to allow students to work on Internet law issues from a public-interest perspective. Samuelson and her husband, Robert Glushko, an engineer at e-commerce and software provider Commerce One, financed the clinic along with Mitchell Kapor, co-founder of the Electronic Frontier Foundation, and the Markle Foundation. The clinic focuses on anti-trust, copyright, privacy, and encryption policy. Students provide legal assistance to individuals filing lawsuits against corporations or governmental entities, draft model legislation, file amicus (friend-of-the-court) briefs, and comment on proposed legislation.

Samuelson is also co-director of the Berkeley Center for Law and Technology. In 2001, she was named a Chancellor's Professor at UC–Berkeley. Samuelson is a MacArthur Fellow, a Fellow of the Electronic Frontier Foundation, a Fellow of the Association of Computing Machinery, and a Fellow of the Cyberspace Law Institute.

Selected Works

Samuelson, Pamela. "Copyright's Fair Use Doctrine and Digital Data." *Communications of the ACM,* vol. 37, no. 1 (1994), pp. 21–27.

———. "Five Challenges for Regulating the Information Society." *Regulating the Global Information Society.* Christopher T. Marsden, ed. London: Routledge Press, 2000.

———. "Intellectual Property for an Information Age: Introduction." *Communications of the ACM,* vol. 44, no. 2 (2001), pp. 66–68.

———. "Intellectual Property Rights and the Global Information Economy." *Communications of the ACM,* vol. 39, no. 1 (1996), pp. 23–28.

———. "Is Information Property?" *Communications of the ACM,* vol. 34, no. 3 (1991), pp. 15–18.

———. "A Manifesto Concerning the Legal Protection of Computer Programs: Why Existing Laws Fail To Provide Adequate Protection." *KnowRight,* 1995, pp. 105–115.

———. "Privacy as Intellectual Property?" *Stanford Law Review* 52 (2000), p. 1,125.

———. "Toward a New Politics of Intellectual Property." *Communications of the ACM,* vol. 44, no. 3 (2001), pp. 98–99.

Bibliography

Committee on Intellectual Property Rights and the Emerging Information Infrastructure; Computer Science and Telecommunications Board; Commission on Physical Sciences, Mathematics, and Applications; National Research Council. *The Digital Dilemma: Intellectual Property in the Information Age.* Washington, D.C.: National Academy Press, 2000. <http://stills.nap.edu/html/digital_dilemma/> (April 12, 2002).

School of Information Management and Systems, University of California at Berkeley. "Pamela Samuelson." Web page. <http://www.sims.berkeley.edu/~pam/> (April 12, 2002).

Further Reading

Baird, Robert M.; Ramsower, Reagan Mays; and Stuart E. Rosenbaum, eds. *Cyberethics: Social & Moral Issues in the Computer Age.* Amherst, N.Y.: Prometheus Books, 2000.

Dratler, Jay. *Cyberlaw: Intellectual Property in the Digital Millennium.* New York: Law Journal Press, 2000.

Girasa, Rosario J. *Cyberlaw: National and International Perspectives.* Upper Saddle River, N.J.: Prentice Hall, 2002.

Related Topics

Copyleft; Copyright; Digital Millennium Copyright Act; Electronic Frontier Foundation; Lessig, Lawrence

— *Leslie Regan Shade*

Sandin, Daniel

1942–

Scientist and Artist

Daniel Sandin is a computer graphics/video artist and pioneer in the virtual-reality (VR) field who, along with Tom DeFanti, conceived the CAVE VR theater in 1991. Sandin was also responsible for the design and construction in the early 1970s of the Image Processor (IP), an analog computer for video image processing. His video work *Spiral PTL* (1980) is included in the film and video collection of the Museum of Modern Art in New York.

Sandin was born in 1942 in Rockford, Illinois, and earned a master's in physics from the University of Wisconsin in 1967. In 1969, he was hired by the faculty of the School of Art and Design at the University of Illinois at Chicago (UIC; then known as the University of Illinois Chicago Circle) with a mandate to bring computers into the art program. In 1972, Tom DeFanti, creator of the Graphics Symbiosis System (GRASS), a computer graphics programming language, joined Sandin at UIC. DeFanti had just completed the GRASS project as part of his Ph.D. thesis at Ohio State University. Sandin and DeFanti then formed the Circle Graphics Habitat, a research center at UIC that became the site of experiments in computer graphics and video art. Although there have been attempts to commercialize their early computer graphics and later VR hardware and software, Sandin and DeFanti have remained resolute in their desire to make the tools as widely available as possible to artists and others.

Inspired to some extent by the work that Robert Moog was doing with audio synthesis, Sandin sought to create similar instruments for those interested in video synthesis and processing. Informed by an early interest in radio and electronics, he went so far as to get the plans for Moog's synthesizer and teach himself electronic design. By 1973, he had designed the Image Processor (IP), which was essentially an analog video processor that allows video signals to be sent through individual processing modules, resulting in output to a color encoder and video or videotape. Much as musicians in the 1970s, thanks to Moog, were creating never-before-heard sounds with the audio synthesizer, the IP allowed video artists to create never-before-seen visual images , and to do so in real time. The IP led to later developments of special-effects technologies for film and video, and became the most widely adopted system among video artists.

Apart from the IP's value to video artists, another of Sandin's unique contributions stemmed from his desire to distribute the IP non-commercially. According to Sandin, the hope was that IP users would "learn to use High-Tech machines for personal, aesthetic, religious, intuitive, comprehensive, and exploratory growth." The IP was therefore made available to video artists and not-for-profit organizations to build themselves; Sandin even included tips for soldering and buying parts in the plans for the IP.

A significant effort was underway at UIC in the 1970s to use technology in education, and Sandin and DeFanti sought to discover ways to use computer graphics and video in undergraduate education. An early project was the development of an introductory curriculum for the Department of Chemistry with a self-paced learning environment for the diverse student population of an urban university. Sandin and DeFanti combined the IP and the GRASS to create animations for the educational materials, and developed Circle Graphics Habitat into a production facility.

Meanwhile, the two also collaborated with faculty with backgrounds in chemistry, engineering, and art, and continued their efforts in video art. In 1974, they organized the first Electronic Visualization Event (EVE), a performance of improvised, real-time video-image manipulations and music. At times during the event, audience members were invited to play the instruments. During this time, Sandin also created special effects for the 1974 feature film *UFO: Target Earth*. He also assisted with video pre-visualization for *Star Wars* (1977), which also used the GRASS for some of its animation sequences of the Death Star.

Sandin's interests migrated to scientific visualization, information display, televisualization, telepresence, and VR. The Circle Graphics Habitat became well-known for its work on video-game hardware and software, and for its innovative use of video-game technology as a basis for making art production systems. Upon the introduction of the PC, similar developments took place, as the Habitat sought to employ PCs as a foundation for creating visual art in real time. Interactive multimedia installations continued to be exhibited on a regular basis.

Sandin and DeFanti conceived of the CAVE VR theater in 1991. By that time, Circle Graphics Habitat had evolved into the Electronic Visualization Lab (EVL), a graduate research laboratory specializing in VR and real-time interactive computer graphics. The CAVE, a networked immersive virtual environment (best described in short as an early version of the Holodeck portrayed in the *Star Trek: The Next Generation* television series), along with related software and hardware technologies, have been EVL's main research effort since 1991.

Although he retired officially in 2001, Sandin has continued his art and VR activities. His most recent efforts have extended beyond computer animation in VR, and involve the use of video images in the CAVE. His work has inspired numerous other artists to work in the CAVE and other VR media, and his insights have spurred the development of software and hardware for VR applications.

Sandin has received numerous grants and fellowships from organizations such as the Rockefeller Foundation, the Guggenheim Foundation, and the National Endowment for the Arts. His work has been displayed at the Walker Art Center in Minneapolis and the Museum of Modern Art in New York, and is a regular feature at the annual Ars Electronica festival in Linz, Austria.

Selected Works

Sandin, Daniel. *Poverty Island with Video Skies*. 1997. Virtual-reality environment. <http://www.evl.uic.edu/dan/Poverty_Island.html> (September 17, 2002)
———. *Spiral PTL*. Video. New York: Museum of Modern Art, 1980.

Further Reading

Burdea, Grigore, and Philippe Coiffet. *Virtual Reality Technology*. New York: J. Wiley & Sons, 1994.
Cruz-Neira, C.; Leigh, J.; Barnes, C.; Cohen, S. M.; Das, S.; Engelmann, R.; Hudson, R.; Papka, M. E.; Roy, T.; Siegel, L.; Vasilakis, C.; DeFanti, T. A.; and D. J. Sandin. "Scientists in Wonderland: A Report on Visualization Applications in the CAVE Virtual Reality Environment." Proceedings of the IEEE 1993 Symposium on Research Frontiers in Virtual Reality, October 1993, pp. 59–66.
Cruz-Neira, C.; Sandin, D.; and T. DeFanti. "Virtual Reality: The Design and Implementation of the CAVE." Proceedings of the SIGGRAPH 93 Computer Graphics Conference, ACM SIGGRAPH, 1993, pp. 135–142.

Cruz-Neira, C.; Sandin, D.; DeFanti, T.; Kenyon, R.; and J. Hart. "The CAVE: Audio Visual Experience Automatic Virtual Environment." *Communications of the ACM,* vol. 35, no. 6 (1992), pp. 65–72.

Roussos, M.; Johnson, A.; Leigh, J.; Vasilakis, C.; and T. Moher. "Constructing Collaborative Stories Within Virtual Learning Landscapes." Proceedings of the European Conference on AI in Education, Lisbon, Portugal, 1996, pp. 129–135.

Stuart, Rory. *The Design of Virtual Environments.* New York: McGraw Hill, 1996.

Vince, John. *Virtual Reality Systems.* Reading, Mass.: Addison-Wesley, 1995.

———. *Essential Virtual Reality Fast: How to Understand the Techniques and Potential of Virtual Reality.* New York: Springer Verlag, 1998.

Related Topics

CAVE; DeFanti, Thomas; Virtual Reality

— *Steve Jones*

Satellite Networks

In an article called "Extra-Terrestrial Relays," which appeared in the October 1945 issue of the magazine *Wireless World,* journalist and science-fiction author Arthur C. Clarke theorized that three satellites orbiting the globe at equal distances from each other could provide communication between almost any two points in the world. Nearly 20 years later, in July 1962, the American Telephone and Telegraph Company (AT&T) launched Telstar, the first real-time telecommunications satellite. Most people have some knowledge of satellites—we see large satellite dishes in our neighbor's yards, or small dishes on rooftops—but few people realize the global impact that these orbiting clusters of electronics have had, or the impact that they are likely to have in the future of communications.

Satellite communication systems are made up of two parts: the satellite itself and the ground station that sends and/or receives the signal. In a simple use of a satellite system, a signal at a ground station is amplified and transmitted to a satellite. There, the signal is amplified once again and transmitted back down to other receiving ground stations. True to Clarke's prediction, it takes only three satellites spaced around the globe to cover all but the polar regions of the planet. At least, that is the case with a signal that is meant primarily as a one-way, or broadcast, transmission. Because of the altitude of the satellites in orbit, the time it takes for the signal to make a complete trip may be over half a second, which is fine for a broadcast signal, but not very useful for a telephone or Internet signal. To reduce transmission time, satellites must be put into lower orbit.

High, Geostationary Earth Orbit (GEO) and lower, Low Earth Orbit (LEO) satellites are differentiated by their positions relative to Earth's surface. GEO satellites are positioned at about 35,400 kilometers (about 22,000 miles) above Earth, and their position is constant; they revolve along with Earth, and are always over the same spot. LEO satellites are positioned much closer to the surface, orbiting at altitudes between 645 and 1,610 kilometers (400 to 1,000 miles). Because of gravitational pull, they must be in motion, and their area of signal coverage is much smaller than that of a GEO satellite. For example, a GEO can cover about one-third of the planet, but a LEO can cover an area no larger than a small country, or a state in the United States.

The advantage of LEO satellites is that signal transmission takes much less time, and can be used effectively for telephone and Internet communication. LEO satellites may also be used to cover the polar regions that GEO satellites cannot cover. The more complex problem is that, since LEO satellites do not remain in a constant position relative to ground stations, they must be "tracked" by antenna arrays as they pass overhead. Also, since they move faster relative to Earth than GEOs, there must be more of them to create an effective network. LEO satellites pass transmissions off to each other, creating wireless networks that ring the planet; these are called "constellation" systems, and they work well for global voice and data networks.

The impact of satellite networks reaches beyond the global transmission of data or wireless cellular networks. A contemporary global reality is that sophisticated communication infrastructures serve far less than half of the world's population. The International Telecommunications Union (ITU) estimates that about 500 million households worldwide have telephone service, out of a total of about 1.5 billion households worldwide. In many cases, the cost of bringing traditional, wire-based telephone service to outlying and rural areas is prohibitive. A global network or constellation of satellites can be built for a fraction of the cost of stringing telephone cable to thinly populated or developing areas.

If the history of satellite networks is any indication, the future of global networks will be one of constant adaptation to the needs of consumers, and of the development of new and existing technologies. For example, as transmission technology moved from unmodulated analog signals (such as those used with Telstar) to digital signals, the need for satellite bandwidth decreased; it takes far less bandwidth to send a high-quality digital signal than it does to send a high-quality analog signal. This has made small satellite dishes commercially viable for television reception. The future may hold the promise of interactive video-on-demand services, real-time video and voice linkups with any other person in the world, and streams of data that move faster than a computer can process, but only if the necessary bandwidth is available.

Bibliography

Cooper, P., and J. Bradley. "Communications: A Satellite Network for Internet Access in Space." *IEEE Spectrum* 35, January 1998. <http://www.spectrum.ieee.org/spectrum/jan98/features/comms1.html> (July 12, 2002).

International Telecommunications Union. Web site. 2002. <http://www.itu.int> (July 12, 2002).

Lax, Stephen. *Beyond the Horizon: Communications Technologies Past, Present and Future.* Luton, Bedfordshire, U.K.: University of Luton Press, 1997.

Parsons, Patrick R., and Robert M. Frieden. *The Cable and Satellite Television Industries.* Boston, Mass.: Allyn & Bacon, 1998.

Further Reading

Chen, Guo-Ming, and William J. Starosta, eds. *Communication and Global Society.* New York: Peter Lang, 2000.

Clarke, Arthur C. "Extra-Terrestrial Relays." *Wireless World,* October 1945, pp. 305–08.

———. *The Exploration of Space.* New York: Harper, 1951; revised edition, New York: Pocket Books, 1959.

Cozic, Charles P., ed. *The Information Highway.* San Diego, Calif.: Greenhaven Press, 1996.

Pavlik, John B. *New Media Technology: Cultural and Commercial Perspectives.* Second edition. Boston, Mass.: Allyn & Bacon, 1998.

Related Topics

Access; Cellular Telephony; Interactivity; Telephony; Wireless Networks

— *Gary W. Larson*

Search Engine

A search engine is a site on the World Wide Web that provides users with access to an index of Web pages and a program for matching page content to key words supplied by the user. Unlike a library, where books are carefully cataloged and arranged on the shelves systematically, Web pages are scattered, literally, worldwide. Web addresses, also known as URLs (Universal Resource Locators), unlike book titles and indices, provide few clues about page content. With millions and millions of pages on every imaginable topic now available on the Web, a reliable search engine is an essential tool for locating information.

Search engines vary in their goals, in the ways that they collect information about Web sites, and in the ways that users may search for information. Therefore, it is not surprising that some search engines are better suited to particular types of searches than others.

PORTALS, DIRECTORIES, AND CRAWLERS

The most specialized search engines are found on portal sites. A portal is a Web site devoted to a particular subject area, and that indexes only other Web sites devoted to that topic; it is designed to be a first stop for users seeking information on a subject. Portal sites exist devoted to government, religion, health and medicine, automobiles, college scholarships, and many other subjects. If the portal is a good one, its operators will have assembled a fairly thorough list of sites on the topic of interest, and will update the listing frequently. The portal will also allow users to search the list by sub-topics that may be more specific than the keywords understood by a more general search engine.

Directories are search engines that gather information about Web sites by asking the individual authors of Web sites to register. In a few instances, Webmasters must pay a fee for having their site listed in the directory, and in many cases the owners of a Web site can pay to have their site featured more prominently in search results for particular topics. This means that if a user is searching for information about what makes for a superior "widget," and uses the word "widget" as the search keyword, the top listings among the search results on a directory-type search engine may be those of widget dealers who have paid for the privilege in order to boost sales, rather than those sites with the most information about what makes for a quality widget.

A crawler (sometimes also described as a "bot" or a "spider") is a software program operated by the owners of a search-engine site that is designed to continuously seek unknown Web sites, determine the subjects and topics of information on the site's pages, and add the pages to the search engine's index. Crawlers have the advantage of finding sites even if the site's owners have not taken the time to register them in a

SELECTED SEARCH ENGINES

Alta Vista: http://www.altavista.digital.com

DevSearch: http://www.devsearch.com/

Excite: http://www.excite.com

Google: http://www.google.com

Hotbot: http://www.hotbot.com

Infoseek: http://www.infoseek.com

Lycos: http://www.lycos.com

Overture: http://www.overture.com

WebCrawler: http://www.webcrawler.com

SELECTED METASEARCH ENGINES

Dogpile: http://www.dogpile.com

Mamma: http://www.mamma.com

SELECTED DIRECTORIES

The Mining Company: http://www.miningco.com

Yahoo!: http://www.yahoo.com

SELECTED PORTALS

America Online: http://www.aol.com

Go Network: http://www.go.com

Microsoft Network: http://www.msn.com

SEARCH ENGINE INFORMATION

Search Engine Alliance:
    http://www.searchenginealliance.com/

Search Engine Watch:
    http://www.searchenginewatch.com

popular search engines, and including invisible (to human eyes) codes in their Web pages called meta tags (essentially, key words chosen by the designers for the crawler to index), Web designers can sometimes make their sites appear to the crawler to be more than what they really are. When used properly, meta tags help crawlers to avoid errors in sorting and classifying the topics of sites, adding to the accuracy of search engines. Crawlers typically slow down access to a Web site while they are doing their indexing work; Webmasters can prevent a crawler from indexing a site by inserting a file named "robots.txt" in a Web site's directory.

Directory sites, such as yahoo.com or dmoz.org, have the advantage of being edited by humans, rather than just by machines, so they are less prone to topic classification errors.

ORIGIN AND FUNCTIONALITY OF THE MODERN SEARCH ENGINE

What we now think of as modern search engines got their start in 1993, when six Stanford University undergraduates created the Architext system, the precursor to the Excite search site that launched in October 1995. Around the same time, two Stanford Ph.D. students named David Filo and Jerry Yang began compiling a database of interesting Web sites, which they called Yahoo! The popularity of this searchable directory grew at an astounding rate, mirroring the general growth of the Web. Other notable search engines also came out of university research. Webcrawler was developed in early 1994 at the University of Washington, where it became so popular that its traffic overwhelmed the university network. It was purchased by America Online (AOL), which later sold it to Excite. Distributed computing technologies have aided in the development of Web searching by contributing to the increasing capacity and performance of Web indexing systems.

Today, most major search engines employ a combination of directory and crawler methods for building and maintaining their indexes of Web sites. Yahoo.com, which began as a very large directory system, has been forced by competition from crawler search engines to add a crawler of its own. Crawler search engines, such as Google.com or AltaVista.com, have found it difficult to remain in business without the profit sources of advertisers who want to prominently display their sites in searches. Ethical search engines, however, display non-paying sites in the search results separately

particular directory. Further, since the crawler is a computer program, it can access, process, and record information about a Web site very rapidly and move on without being distracted. And of course, unlike a human Web surfer, the crawler never needs to stop to sleep. Therefore, the indexes of Web sites created by a crawler can become very large and relatively complete.

Crawlers can be tricked, however, by Web-page authors who want their sites to be displayed more prominently in search results. By learning the sorting characteristics of the crawlers used by the more from those who have paid for exposure, or at the very least provide an indication of which sites have paid a fee to the search-engine operator.

The Web is a very dynamic environment. Thousands of new pages appear daily, and other pages are changed or removed by their owners regularly. For this reason, even the most efficient crawlers can't possibly keep up. No single search engine can index the entire Web accurately; therefore, it is always a good idea to consult several search engines when searching for information about a particular topic. In fact, metasearch engines now exist to conduct simultaneous searches of other search engines, saving the user the trouble of visiting a number of search-engine Web sites and repeating the same search at each one. Dogpile.com is one example of such a search engine of search engines.

INNOVATIONS

The greatest innovations in search engines in recent years have not been in the ways that they assemble their indexes, but in the ways that users are able to look up listings in those indexes. The programs that compare a user's search request to the entries in the index, and prepare sets of search results to the users, are becoming far more sophisticated.

For example, AskJeeves.com is a search engine that encourages users to put their requests in the form of a question. For instance, the user in the example above, rather than being limited to simply entering the key word "widget," would Ask Jeeves "What qualities make a superior widget?" The search engine then attempts to analyze the syntax of the question and select appropriate keywords for the user. It then consults not only its own index, but also a number of other search engines online, and displays its report. While the approach is novel and often helpful, the software is far from perfect in its analysis of the questions posed to it. The question suggested in this example might return entries for Lake Superior as well as for widgets, forcing the user to further refine the search.

Other search engines allow users to enter complex search requests based on multiple keywords with Boolean logical operators. AltaVista.com, as one example, would permit a user to enter this request: "(quality AND widget) AND NOT (buy OR sell)." This search instruction would ask the search engine to provide only sites that mention both widgets and quality, but eliminate sites that mention the words "buy" or "sell." However, a user must be very familiar with how logical operators work in order to get good results from such a system. When the request

above was actually entered, the search engine reported more than 8,000 Web sites matching these criteria, even though the widget is a mythical device that does not actually exist in the real world.

Still other search engines allow users to sort, prioritize, bookmark, store, or otherwise customize search results. Search-engine sites such as iLor.com do not even maintain an index of their own, but utilize the indexes of other search engines. Their uniqueness lies in the way that search results can be refined and manipulated by the user.

As the Web continues to rapidly expand, users will need better and more efficient tools for finding the information they need. Search-engine technology will continue to try to keep up with this need by developing faster and more accurate crawlers that will build more complete indexes of Web sites. Further, better programs for matching user requests with index data will provide users with the key to utilizing the vast resources the Web now offers. And, search engines that catalog graphics, audio, and video are being deployed as a means of making all types of content easy to find on the Web.

Bibliography

Meyer, Harold A. "AllSearchEngines.com Home Page." 2002. <http://www.allsearchengines.com> (May 31, 2002).

Moschovitis, Christos J. P.; Poole, Hilary; Schuyler, Tami; and Theresa M. Senft. *History of the Internet: A Chronology, 1843 to the Present*. Santa Barbara, Calif.: ABC-CLIO, 1999.

Szuprowicz, Bohdan O. *Search Engine Technologies for the World Wide Web and Intranets*. Charleston, S.C.: Computer Technology Research Corporation, 1997.

Further Reading

Dowling Jr., Paul J.; Kuegler Jr., Thomas J.; Taylor, Brent F.; and Joshua O. Testerman. *Web Advertising and Marketing*. Rocklin, Calif.: Prima Publishing, 1998.

Related Topics

Blog; Hypertext; World Wide Web

— *Shing-Ling Sarina Chen*

Security

Computer security is a paradoxical term. The vast network of networks known as the Internet is complex, and it is open. As many have observed, without those two characteristics in place, there is no Internet. But with both present, there can be no perfect security, especially since there are many people on the Internet who have an interest in exploiting its weaknesses for simple amusement, for criminal purposes, or even for waging war.

Computer security threats take several forms. First, there are hackers, computer-savvy individuals using their skills to break into computer networks to steal or alter data, or simply to experience the thrill of virtual cat-burglary. Next, there are viruses, destructive programs designed to attach to system files or other handy files in a computer; a virus lies dormant until the file is accessed, and then executes its destructive functions. Third, there are worms, powerful programs that usually gain access to computers through the Internet—often through email, sometimes by Web browsing. Many operate autonomously, but some, like the famous Internet Relay Chat–based PrettyPark worm, are executed only on the command of a hacker. Once worms infect a terminal, they usually seek other computers on the Internet to infect. Some worms, like the email-driven Code Red, have been known to cause many millions of dollars in damage, especially to corporations experiencing expensive down time and the destruction of valuable equipment and data.

Security has been an issue almost as long as there have been networked computers. In 1980, John Shoch and Jon Hupp of Xerox Palo Alto Research Center (PARC) in California created the first malicious worm by accident. Their idea was for the worm, as they called it, to automatically install Ethernet performance-measurement tools on 100 PARC computers, so the duo wrote a program capable of sending and installing itself across Xerox's closed network. However, as Robert Lemos recounted for *CNET* in March 2001, the program contained a bug, and bad code spread to each computer. Each time a terminal would install the worm, it would start to run, then crash the computer. Before long, Shoch and Hupp had rendered 100 Xerox computers useless.

In 1987, the first worm hit a public network, the IBM-only Internet precursor known as BITNET. The "Christmas Tree virus" drew a picture of a Christmas tree on an infected computer's screen before mailing itself to other computers. It eventually clogged IBM's entire international network.

In 1988, 23-year-old Cornell University graduate student Robert Morris wrote a worm that exploited "sendmail" flaws in the UNIX operating system. Like Shoch and Hupp, however, Morris wrote inadvertent bugs in the worm's code that caused it to propagate much faster than intended, according to *Tangled Web* author Richard Power. The Cornell worm spread rapidly, overloading between 3,000

and 4,000 servers, roughly 5 percent of the servers then present on the Internet.

Malicious programmers learned much from the Christmas Tree and Cornell worms. Because of their self-perpetuating properties and destructive capabilities, worms have become the weapon of choice for those bent on creating havoc on the Internet.

Unfortunately, that is no great trick. As writer Kevin Werbach points out, "there are simply too many moving parts" on the Internet, each "dependent on too many layers of software with poorly understood interactions, managed by too many different organizations, with too many points of interconnection and access and too many actors." The Web, after all, was created to allow incompatible computer systems and operators who do not know each other to communicate. It is a recipe for poor security.

Further, the demands of users for sound security and ease of operation are often in conflict, as the World Wide Web Consortium (W3C) points out. To facilitate ease and flexibility of operation, and to take advantage of database and middleware functions, many network servers—particularly those running on UNIX and Microsoft Windows NT platforms—run massively complex software that is difficult to configure and that often contains exploitable bugs. Says the W3C: "It's a maxim in system security circles that buggy software opens up security holes. It's a maxim in software development circles that large, complex programs contain bugs. Unfortunately, Web servers are large, complex programs that can (and in some cases have been proven to) contain security holes." Indeed, news reports about new vulnerabilities in Web servers and the fixes, or "patches" to those vulnerabilities, seem to arrive weekly.

To combat the problems of computer security, many solutions have been devised. Individual PCs connected to the Internet, for instance, often have virus-scanning software installed. But these are only as effective as they are up-to-date, and many companies like Symantec, the company that produces the Norton AntiVirus software, allow customers to automatically update their virus protections weekly to ward off new, constantly proliferating viruses.

At the corporate level, firewalls have long been the first line of defense against intrusion. A firewall is basically a barrier between two networks—a secure corporate intranet and the unsecured Internet, for example. Firewalls examine incoming and outgoing data packets according to set criteria, either blocking them or passing them through. Firewalls were once considered sufficient protection against network intrusion, but hackers have learned to work around them, forcing more sophisticated responses; among these is the virtual private network (VPN), which allows encrypted, secure communications to take place through the public Internet.

Even more sophisticated is a system known as public key infrastructure (PKI), which allows users to encrypt and decrypt data over public networks like the Internet, provided that each user has the necessary key to lock down information and to unlock it upon delivery. PKIs are widely in use to verify identities and to secure transactions between businesses online. Private transactions such as consumer purchases at sites like Amazon.com rely on a Netscape innovation known as the Secure Sockets Layer (SSL), a technology that protects transactions between browsers and Web servers. This technology has done a lot to protect consumers from credit-card theft and online fraud.

The battle between hackers, virus and worm writers, and the system administrators and programmers who would ward them off, has been likened to an arms race. As more threats appear, more safeguards appear, followed by increased threats. In recent years, high-profile worms have infested the Internet under names such as Code Red, AnnaKournikova, and LoveLetter; some of these have done significant damage to private and corporate systems. But even more vexing security threats such as cyberterrorism have begun to seep into the public consciousness.

In May 2001, Senator Robert Bennett (R.-Utah) made the startling pronouncement that cyber-attacks from a hostile nation could disrupt water and power supplies, shut down airports, close banks and hospitals, and wreak untold havoc. In short, Bennett said, such an attack could have a more destructive effect than a nuclear missile detonating over a U.S. metropolis. The September 11, 2001, terrorist attacks on the United States only heightened such worries, prompting Attorney General John Ashcroft to seek and obtain special legislation aimed in part at snooping on the Internet to detect cyberattackers and other online security breaches. His moves have been applauded by many, but others have sounded the alarm about the civil liberties implications.

"We should encourage freedom-supporting governments to use the powers they already have more effectively," wrote Internet consultant Esther Dyson, "rather than pass new laws that would make it easier for such powers to be abused."

In the end, where there is an open network, there is no perfect security. And as author Richard Power

notes, it is people, not technologies, that must be regarded as the primary line of defense against cyber-intrusion. "Not firewalls, not crypto, not IDS (intrusion detection systems), not policies, not background checks, not biometrics. Power writes, "It is people who build and maintain the defenses of cyberspace to ensure that it is a commons in which the planetary population can communicate with, inform, educate, express, liberate, empower and enrich itself."

Bibliography

Koprowski, Gene. "Keeping the Pace in Net Security." *Wired News,* November 3, 1997. <http://www.wired.com/news/technology/1,1282,8204,00.html> (June 7, 2002).

Krebs, Brian. "In Wake of Attacks, Feds Review Cyber-Security." *Newsbytes,* September 12, 2001.

Lemos, Robert. "Fast-spreading Code Is Weapon of Choice for Net Vandals." *CNET News,* March 15, 2001. <http://news.cnet.com/news/0-1003-201-5125673-0.html?tag=arcv> (June 7, 2002).

McGuire, David. "In Response to Attacks ICANN Eyes Security Matters." *Newsbytes,* September 27, 2001.

Power, Richard. *Tangled Web: Tales of Digital Crime from the Shadows of Cyberspace.* Indianapolis, Ind.: Que Corporation, 2000.

Stein, Lincoln, and John N. Stewart. "The World Wide Web Security FAQ." July 28, 2001. <http://www.w3.org/Security/Faq/wwwsf1.html> (June 7, 2002).

Weisman, Robyn. "Senator Compares Cyber War to Nuclear Attack." *NewsFactor Network,* May 15, 2001. <http://www.newsfactor.com/perl/story/9739.html> (June 7, 2002).

Further Reading

Dyson, Esther. "Identity and Security." EDventure.com, October 18, 2001. <http://www.edventure.com/conversation/article.cfm?Counter=7911978> (June 7, 2002).

———. *Release 2.1: A Design for Living in the Digital Age.* New York: Broadway Books, 1998.

Garfinkel, Simson. *Database Nation: The Death of Privacy in the 21st Century.* Cambridge: O'Reilly & Associates, 2000.

Glave, James. "U.S. Computer Security Called a Critical Mess." *Wired News,* October 28, 1997. <http://www.wired.com/news/technology/0,1282,8053,00.html> (June 7, 2002).

Hafner, Katie, and John Markoff. *Cyberpunk: Outlaws and Hackers on the Computer Frontier.* New York: Simon & Schuster, 1991.

Hollinger, Richard C., ed. *Crime, Deviance and the Computer.* Brookfield, Vt.: Dartmouth, 1997.

Related Topics
Dyson, Esther; Email; Encryption and Cryptography; Hacking, Cracking, and Phreaking; Virus; Xerox Palo Alto Research Center

— *Kevin Featherly*

Shannon, Claude

1916–2001

Mathematician and Scientist

Mathematician, engineer, scientist, inventor, and juggler Claude Shannon is the founder of information theory and is widely regarded as having provided the conceptual framework for modern communications systems.

Born in Gaylord, Michigan, in 1916, Shannon received a B.S. from the University of Michigan and a M.S. and Ph.D. from the Massachusetts Institute of Technology (MIT) in 1940. Shannon's master's thesis, entitled *A Symbolic Analysis of Relay and Switching Circuits,* used George Boole's algebraic system for manipulating the numbers 0 and 1 to explain electrical switching. Shannon argued that binary values in symbolic logic and electric circuits were essentially identical, and that it would therefore be possible to build a "logic machine" that used switching circuits according to the principles of Boolean algebra.

After completing his doctorate, Shannon went to work for AT&T's Bell Laboratories, where he did some of his most famous work. He was hired to help Bell increase the efficiency of signal transmission down telephone lines. Bell wanted to be able to transmit a maximum number of signals down a single line, thereby using its system to its full capacity. By applying the principles of Boolean algebra to telephone switches, Shannon provided a major breakthrough in resolving this efficiency problem.

In 1948, Shannon published his landmark "Mathematical Theory of Communication" in two parts in the *Bell System Technical Journal.* In this work, Shannon showed that information could be quantified and therefore analyzed mathematically, providing a conceptual basis for information theory. Many commonplace analytical terms of information science and computer engineering, such as "bit," come from "Mathematical Theory."

Shannon wrote that the fundamental unit of information—a bit—is a yes/no situation, which could be represented by a switch that is either on or off. All information, even very complex information, can be built from this basis of zeroes and ones. Complex concepts can be conveyed as in a game of 20 Questions, where the number of bits is sufficient to provide fairly detailed information. As a system uses more bits, it is able to perform more complex computations at an exponential rate. A single bit system has two states: 0 and 1. A 2-bit system has 4 states: 0,0; 0,1; 1,0; and 1,1. A 4-bit system has sixteen states, and so forth.

Shannon's insight was significant for two reasons. First, it quantified information, thereby making it measurable, and therefore useful, for engineering purposes. It also separated information, which could be measured, from meaning, which to this day has not been quantified in any significant way. Scholars interested in the meaning of communicative events have had to look beyond Shannon for their inspiration; but Shannon's work allowed for a totally new way to conceptualize the process of communication in circuits of people or machines.

In Shannon's model, information is a degree of order in a system. But entropy (disorder) is also very important for information theory. If there is too much entropy, then no information is communicated; but if there is no entropy, then no information is communicated and the system remains static. Shannon used mathematical proofs to show that one could use a measure of entropy to define the capacity of a communication channel. So long as the channel stays under capacity, the transmission will be free of errors. This was useful to AT&T, because people needed to be able to hear one another at both ends of a phone line.

"Mathematical Theory" provides a "schematic diagram of a general communication system" modeled on telephony. Shannon wrote that "the fundamental problem of communication is reproducing at one point either exactly or approximately the message selected at another point."

Shannon's "schematic diagram" included six components:

1. An information source, which produces a message suitable for transmission. Shannon's examples were series of numbers or letters in telegraph systems, sonic vibrations ("a function of time") in telephone and radio systems, and "function[s] of time and other variables" such as television, color television, and combined audio and video signals.

2. A transmitter, to encode the message for transmitting along a specific channel. This could be a telephone transmitter, a radio set, a television camera, etc.

3. A channel, which is the medium through which the information travels: a series of cables, or even

the part of the electromagnetic spectrum through which broadcast signals pass.

4. A receiver, to perform the "inverse" operation of the transmitter, decoding the message back into its original form.

5. A destination, for which the message is intended.

6. Although not formally part of the circuit, noise or entropy can enter the system at any point, interfering with the transmission of the signal.

The point of communication for Shannon was therefore to effectively transmit the signal with sufficient order that it could be reproduced in exact or approximate fashion. His basic scheme was applied and developed by mathematicians throughout the world. As Shannon's colleague, R.G. Gallager, put it, he was "the person who saw that the binary digit was the fundamental element in all of communication. That was really his discovery, and from it the whole communications revolution has sprung."

Shannon's scholarship has been expanded by other authors to include most electronic media as well as circuits, and has even been applied to life systems and entire societies. Today, Shannon's principles are at work in all electronic and digital devices. It explains why computers can process complex information without errors, why elevators come when they are called, and why dirty compact discs can still play. Still, Shannon was skeptical of some of the extensions of his work. Later in life, he would write that "information theory has perhaps ballooned to an importance beyond its actual accomplishments."

Shannon was a professor of communication sciences and mathematics at MIT from 1957 until his retirement in 1978. In off hours, he could be seen juggling while riding a unicycle down the hallway to his office.

Selected Works

Shannon, Claude. *Claude Elwood Shannon: Collected Papers*. N.J.A. Sloane and Aaron D. Wyner, eds. New York: IEEE Press, 1993.

Shannon, Claude, and Warren Weaver. *The Mathematical Theory of Communication*. Urbana: University of Illinois Press, 1963.

Bibliography

Gimon, Charles A. "Heroes of Cyberspace: Claude Shannon." INFO NATION. <http://www.skypoint.com/~gimonca/shannon.html> (June 7, 2002).

Linguistics Department, New York University. "Claude Shannon." <http://www.nyu.edu/pages/linguistics/courses/v610003/shan.html> (June 7, 2002).

Lucent Technologies, Bell Labs Innovations. "Claude Shannon, Father of Information Theory, Dies at 84." <http://www.bell-labs.com/news/2001/february/26/1.html> (June 7, 2002).

Mattelart, Armand, and Michèle Mattelart. *Theories of Communication: A Short Introduction*. Thousand Oaks, Calif.: Sage, 1998.

O'Connor, John J., and Edmund F. Robinson. "Claude Elwood Shannon." School of Mathematics and Statistics, University of St. Andrews, Scotland, March 2001. <http://www-groups.dcs.st-and.ac.uk/~history/Mathematicians/Shannon.html> (June 7, 2002).

Further Reading

Pierce, J.R. *Symbols, Signals, and Noise: The Nature and Process of Communication*. New York: Harper, 1961.

Wyner, Aaron D. "The Significance of Shannon's Work." Bell Labs, June 28, 1997. <http://cm.bell-labs.com/cm/ms/what/shannonday/work.html> (June 7, 2002).

Related Topics

Internet; Telephony; von Neumann, John

— *Jonathan Sterne*

Shockwave

Shockwave is the name for interactive multimedia content created with Macromedia's Director program and delivered over the Web.

Web designers believe that people browsing the Web are drawn to rich content combining audio, video, graphics, animation, and text. One of the most popular formats for online interactive multimedia is Macromedia's Shockwave. A key reason for Shockwave's popularity is its ability to package interactive audio and video in a very small data file. Early multimedia files were very large; even though people were attracted to the idea of online audio and video, they were often frustrated by the amount of time that it took for the content to download. With the help of several compression strategies, Shockwave reduces download time to seconds instead of minutes. And since Shockwave files can be streamed, people can start using them before they've finished downloading the entire file.

Shockwave content begins its journey to a computer screen in Macromedia's Director, a powerful and popular authoring program that is used to create interactive multimedia projects. Director arrived on the scene in the late 1980s/early 1990s, and quickly became the authoring program of choice for most multimedia developers. Originally, Director was used to create guided tours, product demonstrations, and presentations, and the content was burned onto CD-ROMs. Even today, the majority of interactive CD-ROMs are created in Director. But in 1995, Macromedia added Shockwave to Director, which meant that Director files could be sent over the Web and viewed with a Shockwave Player. The Shockwave Player displays the content inside a Web browser window.

Like many other software companies producing plug-ins for the Internet, Macromedia decided to make the Shockwave Player available for free, while continuing to charge for Director, the program that creates the content. This tactic ensured that there would be a large audience for Shockwave content. By 2001, over 165 million Web users had Shockwave Player installed on their computers; it was preinstalled on all new Macintosh OS and Windows 98/2000 computers, was included on every America Online CD-ROM, and was automatically installed by both Microsoft's Internet Explorer and Netscape's Communicator.

The range of content that can be created with Shockwave is surprising. Online retailers use it for product demonstrations, such as allowing people to virtually try on clothes. It is used to deliver educational simulations in distance-education classes. Independent producers create films in Director that are made available to the general public. With the help of the music company Beatnik, Macromedia created an application called MixMaker that makes it possible for fans to re-mix the vocal, guitar, percussion, and other tracks of a song with the click of a mouse. And users can play a wide variety of games using Shockwave.

Due to its fast downloading speed, widespread adoption and availability, and range of use, Shockwave has become the de facto standard for online interactive multimedia content.

Bibliography

Luening, Erich. "Shockwave Inks Deals to Energize Web Site." CNET News.com, March 20, 2000. <http://news.cnet.com/news/0-1005-200-1576595.html> (July 12, 2002).
Macromedia. "Shockwave White Paper." November 2000. <http://www.macromedia.com/software/shockwaveplayer/ whitepaper/whitepaper_nov00.pdf> (July 12, 2002).
Schussler, Terry. The Director Intelligence Agency. Web site. <http://www.director8.com> (July 12, 2002).

Further Reading

Clarke, Cathy; Swearingen, Lee; and David K. Anderson. *Shocking the Web*. Berkeley, Calif.: Macromedia Press, 1997.
Gross, Phil, and Jason Roberts. *Director 8 Demystified*. Berkeley, Calif.: Peachpit, 2000.
Rosenzweig, Gary, and John Thompson. *Special Edition: Using Macromedia Director 8*. Indianapolis, Ind.: Que, 2000.

Related Topics

Authoring Tools; Compression; Interactivity; Multimedia; Streaming Media

— Norman Clark

Short Messaging System

The short messaging system (SMS), also known at times as "short message service," is a two-way communications technology that allows brief written messages to be sent to and from cellular phones. The system is wildly popular in countries such as the United Kingdom, Finland, and the Philippines, especially among teenagers. It allows alphanumeric email-like messages to be sent between mobile-phone handsets. Users write their messages by tapping them out on their cell phone's keypads, sending them in exactly the same way that they make phone calls. In effect, SMS users' phone numbers are their email addresses.

SMS messages can be up to 160 characters long if users write in the Latin alphabet; they are limited to 70 characters when languages such as Arabic and Chinese are being used. The system was created in the early 1990s as part of the Global System for Mobile Communications (GSM) Phase 1 standard, and is supported by the Interim Standard 41C (IS-41C) signaling protocol. According to the GSM Association, the first short message reportedly was sent from a personal computer to a mobile phone over the U.K.'s Vodafone GSM network in December 1992. The first commercial service was launched in 1994.

Incompatible cellular networks have hobbled the adoption of SMS communications in the United States, where devices like the Blackberry two-way pager and PC-based instant-messaging platforms such as ICQ and America Online's Instant Messenger (AIM) have proven much more popular. In Europe, too, the SMS service was slow to take off. It was marketed in the early 1990s as a way for business people to keep in contact when on the road or away from phones, but most people rejected SMS because it is difficult to use. It requires users to tap numbers on the phone keypad that correspond to various characters in the alphabet, which can be cumbersome. For instance, due to the way that letters on a keypad are arranged and

In October 2001, a Malaysian woman receives notice of her traffic summons via SMS. (© AFP/CORBIS)

grouped, one would have to tap the keypad 14 times to spell out the name "Fritz." Nonetheless, in 1999, SMS' fortunes began to turn around dramatically in Europe, where residents have relied on digital cellular phones for years. SMS has also achieved great success in Asia. In both cases, it has been largely a young person's phenomenon.

In a January 2001 presentation at the GSM Association's Mobile Messaging Forum in London, Mobile Lifestreams Ltd. business development director Ben Wood outlined the rapid growth of SMS services, and projected possible directions that the services might take. That presentation, which is online at the GSM Association Web site (http://www.gsmworld.com), indicated that one billion SMS messages were sent in Europe during March 1999; by August 2000, there were six billion messages a month exchanged on the continent. The GSM Association later released numbers indicating that by the end of May 2001, 13 billion messages a month were being carried worldwide using SMS, with nearly

50 billion messages sent in the first three months of the year. GSM Association estimates also indicated that, by the beginning of 2001, SMS users were sending and receiving nearly 35 messages a month on average. The IDC research firm estimated that, in Western Europe alone, 57.3 billion messages were sent by 82 million subscribers in 2001.

While SMS technology can allow users to order movie tickets, track stock quotes, and check bank account balances, 90 percent of SMS traffic has consisted of person-to-person messaging, much of it between teenagers. Teens, who began obtaining cellular phones in large numbers, were undeterred by the difficulty of tapping out messages on their phone keys. For one thing, it gave them a new high-tech way to pass notes in class. The SMS platform also allows them to send messages to groups of their friends simultaneously, thus turning Europe's GMS system into what the *Industry Standard* magazine once dubbed "a mobile chat room." Asia has witnessed a similar phenomenon.

It was a success that few in the industry expected, especially after SMS went almost unnoticed for five years. But the Mobile Streams Web site suggests that it was its very user-unfriendliness that made the platform attractive to teens. "The fact that the entry barriers to learning the service were so high (was) an advantage, because it meant that parents and teachers and other adult authority figures were unlikely and unable and unwilling to…use the service," the site says.

At first, SMS in Europe was free, but after massive use patterns were established there, carriers began charging. By September 2000, the messages cost an average of 15 cents to send, although accessing such information as stock quotes, news, and traffic reports over the system could sometimes cost double that amount. In Europe, usage dropped off about 40 percent soon after carriers began making users pay for the service, but SMS was so entrenched among the young that it quickly bounced back and surpassed pre-payment usage levels, according to the Mobile Streams Web site.

One interesting aspect of the SMS boom is the new language that has sprung up around it, as teens seek shortcuts that allow them to express themselves with compressed words that almost amount to encryption, allowing them to press a minimum number of keys while having their say. "See you tomorrow," for instance, might appear on a screen as "C U 2moro," or a different salutation, like "C U L8er" (see you later), might be used instead.

SMS' popularity has survived a concerted push by carriers to coax subscribers to adopt the mobile Internet platform known as WAP (wireless access protocol). But WAP, which is an attempt to modify Web sites so they can be viewed on small cellular-phone view screens, is just as difficult to use, and is too slow for most people. By June 2001, *Business Week* was reporting that many WAP developers were abandoning the format and turning their focus to the simpler SMS technology.

Perhaps the main reason that SMS has become almost ubiquitous in Europe and Asia is the way that mobile communications are structured in those regions. On both continents, phone carriers in the late 1990s began to adopt GSM as a uniform mobile-communication standard. The picture is different in the United States, where there are three competing standards: Time Division Multiple Access (TDMA), Code Division Multiple Access (CDMA), and a variation of GSM that is incompatible with the version used in the rest of the world. Due to these multiple standards, SMS messages cannot be exchanged between U.S.

users unless they subscribe to the same carrier's network; someone who subscribes to a TDMA-based AT&T Wireless SMS service cannot message a friend on Verizon's CDMA package. (This problem has been mitigated to an extent by the appearance on wireless networks of PC-based instant-messaging platforms like AOL's AIM service.)

In April 2001, *Business Week* magazine judged U.S. carriers' inability to get together on SMS to be a big business failure. "Since most people neither know nor care who provides service to their friends and colleagues, this restriction defeats the whole purpose," columnist Stephen H. Wildstrom wrote. "By failing to get together and make intercarrier SMS work, the U.S. industry is missing a huge opportunity."

Meanwhile, Europeans SMS services are not standing still. At the January 2001 GMS Association forum in London, Ben Wood described new variations of SMS that could take "texting" much further. The first step, Wood indicates, was unveiled at Germany's CeBIT 2001 conference, where the first Enhanced Messaging Service (EMS) handset debuted. These phones allow cellular-phone users to send and receive simple media such as images, sounds, animations, and modified text.

But according to Wood, EMS is merely an interim step to the real next stage of SMS: Multimedia Messaging Service (MMS), which would allow users to send and receive rich-media messages that include sounds, images, even video, over cell phones. Such features as business cards, telegrams, photos, and screensavers are all expected to be major parts of the format. But MMS services can't be used with existing GSM networks, though they are compatible with the General Packet Radio Service, a non-voice wireless network that can be used to supplement SMS. Wood says it will take the arrival of the forthcoming third-generation (3G) broadband wireless network for MMS to truly arrive.

Bibliography

Giussani, Bruno. "What's Up 2Nite?" *The Industry Standard*, September 11, 2000. <http://www.thestandard.com/article/0,1902,18115,00.html> (June 7, 2002).

Gold, Steve. "15 Billion Text Messages A Month—and Counting." *Newsbytes*, May 21, 2001.

Hafner, Katie. "U.S. Is Lagging Behind Europe In Short Messaging Services." *The New York Times*, December 7, 2000.

Mitram, Kushan, and Siddharth Zarabi. "Operators Cashing in on SMS." *Hindustan Times*, August 30, 2001.

Mobile Streams Ltd. "SMS History Zone." 1999–2001. <http://www.mobilesms.com/history.asp> (June 7, 2002).

Rose, Frank. "Tele-Prompter: Europe Leads the Way in Advancing Wireless." *Wired* 8.12, December 2000. <http://www.wired.com/wired/archive/8.12/wireless.html> (June 7, 2002).

Wildstrom, Stephen H. "Sanyo's Best-in-the-U.S. Cell Phone." *BusinessWeek,* April 5, 2001. <http://www.businessweek.com/bwdaily/dnflash/apr2001/nf2001045_187.htm> (June 7, 2002).

Further Reading

Batista, Elisa. "Don't Go Gently Into That SMS." *Wired News*, May 25, 2001. <http://www.wired.com/news/wireless/0,1382,43782,00.html> (June 7, 2002).

Featherly, Kevin. "Sprint PCS, AOL Take Mobile Instant-Messaging Plunge." *Newsbytes*, October 19, 2000.

Reinhardt, Andy. "After WAPlash, Europe Gets the Message." *BusinessWeek,* June 19, 2001. <http://www.businessweek.com/bwdaily/dnflash/jun2001/nf20010619_536.htm> (June 7, 2002).

Thompson, Valerie. "Cell Phones Aren't Just for Gabbing." *The Industry Standard,* October 4, 1999. <http://www.thestandard.com/article/0,1902,6530,00.html> (June 7, 2002).

Related Topics

Broadband; Cellular Telephony; Chat; Minitel; Telephony; Virtual Community; Wireless Networks

— *Kevin Featherly*

SIGGRAPH

The Association for Computing Machinery (ACM) sponsors meetings in several technical areas; in the context of new media, the most important is probably the one held annually by SIGGRAPH, the Special Interest Group for Computer Graphics and Interactive Techniques. This international conference draws the world's top graphics artists and programmers, who come to present their research innovations in graphic design. Researchers from private graphics production houses, non-profit institutions, government laboratories, academia, and industry meet to disseminate information about the theory and practice of computer graphics. SIGGRAPH provides an opportunity for researchers and artists to present ideas about how to interact with graphics in new-media environments.

Subgroups of SIGGRAPH are devoted to studying the creation of 2D and 3D imagery, environments, and special effects for display on a variety of new and old media: film, games, television, Web graphics, medical imaging, and virtual reality (VR). SIGGRAPH contributors have, over the years, focused on new technologies to synthetically create photo-realistic imagery; new hardware and software developments over the years continually enable further advancements. For example, at SIGGRAPH 2000, attention was focused on ways of improving a graphic image by rendering light reflected below the surface of an object. New algorithmic lighting models, such as reflected subsurface light, generate visual detail not evident with existing, older methods, such as light reflected from the surface.

SIGGRAPH was formed in 1969, after members of the ACM started taking special interest in computer-generated graphics. SIGGRAPH organizers were interested in exploring tools and techniques for image generation, as well as in the ways that people interact with graphics. In the early years, the organization began hosting conferences and publishing proceedings, making scientists in the growing field of computing aware of innovations in technology, application disciplines, and art forms. Within a few years, there were local U.S. chapters in Los Angeles; Syracuse, N.Y., and Washington, D.C.; and overseas chapters in Bologna and Berlin. The academics who started SIGGRAPH in 1969 also helped start SIGCHI (Special Interest Group for Computer/Human Interaction); interactive techniques have always been part of SIGGRAPH, too.

The first national SIGGRAPH conference was held in 1974, and with 600 attendees the organization had enough momentum to become the primary professional association for computer-graphics experts in the United States. Also in the mid-1970s, SIGGRAPH encouraged participation by artists, by Hollywood production companies, and by vendors of film, video, and other new media equipment; these new participants helped enliven the conferences. Future VR pioneers Tom DeFanti and Dan Sandin attended the first SIGGRAPH and brought along a VCR to show videotapes; this grew into SIGGRAPH's "academy award" Electronic Theater event. The conference started to grow in 1977 (its attendance nearly tripled from 1976), and by 1979, when DeFanti was co-chair of the conference, it grew to 5,000 people. DeFanti's colleague Maxine Brown served as exhibits co-chair that year, and doubled the companies and tripled the floor space available, making the exhibition a vital part of the conference.

By the 1980s, the SIGGRAPH conferences had grown larger than the parent ACM meetings, and recent conferences have attracted more than 50,000 participants. Moreover, firms devoted to producing special effects for movies, television, and video games came not only to present their achievements, but also to recruit talent. By 1992, when the conference was held in Chicago, Brown was chair of the conference and DeFanti headed up the Showcase event. It was the first time that SIGGRAPH was networked, and the push for VR that more than one person could experience at a time led to significant developments in VR technology, including the CAVE.

Today, SIGGRAPH members are industrial and academic experts, artists, designers, engineers, scientists, researchers, and students, all sharing common interests in the advancement of computer graphics and interactive techniques. Over the last three decades, SIGGRAPH conferences have become an important means of professional coordination: computer-graphics standards, white papers (e.g., on scientific visualization), machine and platform independent graphics, and collections of research results have all been developed through SIGGRAPH workshops. Many components of new-media technologies, including raster graphics, storage-tube displays, vector graphics, and innovations in color reproduction, were as much the result of collaboration as of competition among SIGGRAPH members.

Early SIGGRAPH conferences attracted computer scientists and artists interested both in the algorithms for creating computer-graphics imagery and in the tools and techniques for real-time interaction. SIGGRAPH conference content has always had broad appeal—to business, NASA, the military, crime-scene reconstruction, medical imaging, astronomy, and geographical information systems. SIGGRAPH's content has been likened to a "conveyor belt"—ideas sparked in panel presentations one year come back as published research and/or creatively applied artwork in the following year's technical and art venues, and ultimately as products in the commercial exhibition space in subsequent years.

Bibliography

ACM Press, ed. *SIGGRAPH 1999 Conference Proceedings: Computer Graphics Annual Conference Series.* New York: ACM, 1999.

Dodsworth, Clark, ed. *Digital Illusion: Entertaining the Future with High Technology.* New York: ACM, 1998.

Further Reading

ACM Press, ed. *OOPSLA 2000 Minneapolis: Conference on Object-Oriented Programming Systems, Languages, and Applications.* New York: ACM, 2000.

Related Topics

CAVE; Computer Graphics; DeFanti, Thomas; Digital Art and Animation; Sandin, Daniel; Virtual Reality

— *Philip E. N. Howard*

Sketchpad

Sketchpad, the first interactive computer-graphics program, originated as a graduate student's thesis project in the early 1960s. It became a foundation for graphical sciences, computer operating system (OS) interfaces, and software applications that are used in many facets of today's computer work.

At the Massachusetts Institute of Technology (MIT), Ivan Sutherland published his 1963 doctoral thesis, titled "Sketchpad: A Man-Machine Graphical Communications System," which described a program that was capable of drawing simple geometrical shapes on the screen of a computer. The software's functionality was unique, and required the use of a rather complex hardware system.

In 1961, Sutherland had developed a primitive application that would run on one of the first programmable computers. During that time period, it was difficult to find computers to work with, due to their size and cost. With the Sketchpad idea in mind, Sutherland found a computer that he could use at MIT's Lincoln Laboratory, and began to develop the program. MIT's Lincoln Laboratory computer was a TX-2 machine, a huge computer whose capacity was twice that of the largest commercial machines. Impressive for its programmable capabilities, the TX-2 possessed 320KB (kilobytes) of memory for fast storage, magnetic tape storage, and a feeding mechanism for paper-tape programs—long strips of paper with holes punched into them that communicated instructions to the computer.

The TX-2 also powered a nine-inch Cathode Ray Tube (CRT) display, an essential component that allowed the computer user to view the graphics created with Sketchpad. A light pen allowed drawings to be represented on the screen, and was used to manipulate the line objects, similar to the way that the mouse selects and moves files and windows on today's computers. When used in collaboration with the light pen, several switches located on the computer were used to control certain aspects of the graphics, such as size and ratio.

Sketchpad's process for drawing lines, shapes, and corners was quite complicated. The Research

Laboratory of Electronics (RLE) at MIT reported the system's functionality to be heavily electrical, and described Sketchpad's drawing process as electronic pulses that are shared between the photoelectric cell of the light pen and an electronic gun fired from the CRT. The timing of the pulse displayed a cursor, representing the light pen's position on the screen, thus converting the computer screen into a sketchpad upon which objects could be drawn.

Sketchpad permitted precise drawings to be fashioned, copied, and stored. In fact, the concept of graphical computing originated from the way that objects created using Sketchpad could be visualized and modeled on a screen. This inaugurated the new research field of computer-graphical sciences. In 1964, Sutherland collaborated with Dr. David Evan at the University of Utah to initiate one of the first educational computer-graphics labs. With a foundation created, computer graphics was able to evolve into its current roles in advertising, business, entertainment, architecture, and Web design, among many other fields.

Sketchpad's performance in computer-graphics representation also led to the advanced development of other imaging software. One such example is computer-aided drafting (CAD), used by engineers to create architectural designs for new products and buildings. Sketchpad demonstrated a way in which graphics can be drawn to exact scale, and models can be changed quicker than by hand.

The process of using a light pen to draw shapes on the screen changed the way the computer users interacted with the screen. Sketchpad, which is also considered one of the first graphical user interfaces (GUI), allowed users to visualize and control program functions. Scholar Brad Myers credits Sutherland's Sketchpad with being one of the first mechanisms that allowed basic interaction between the computer and the user. The OSs of later computers, created by Apple and Microsoft, use GUIs to simplify users' interactions with their machines. However, computer users of today use a mouse, rather than a light pen, to take control of GUIs.

Researcher Paul Pangaro argues that Sketchpad has dramatically influenced human-computer interaction. He describes Sketchpad as possessing all of the essential elements of present-day interaction: Sketchpad manipulated drawn objects and required user control. The only differences between Sutherland's program and the interactive systems of today are speed, size, and complexity.

Bibliography

Myers, Brad A. "A Brief History of Human Computer Interaction Technology." *ACM Interacts,* vol. 5, no. 2 (March 1998).

Pangaro, Paul. "Beyond Menus: The Rats-A-Stratz or the Bahdeens." *Harvard Computer Graphics Week,* 1982. <http://www.pangaro.com/published/Beyond-Menus.html> (May 10, 2002).

"Visualizing the Past at RLE." RLE Currents, vol. 11, no. 1 (Spring 1999). <http://webrle.mit.edu/Publications/currents/cur11-1/11-1visualize.htm> (May 10, 2002).

Further Reading

Goff, Leslie Jaye. "TX-0: The Technology." *Computerworld*, February 22, 1999. <http://www.computerworld.com/news/1999/story/0,11280,27313,00.html> (May 10, 2002).

Sutherland, Ivan. "Sketchpad: A Man-Machine Graphical Communications System." *AFIPS Spring Joint Computer Conference*, 1963.

"Theorising Computer-Generated Imagery (CGI)." Multiliteracy.com, November 2000. <http://www.multiliteracy.com/persist/comanim.html> (May 10, 2002).

Related Topics

Computer Graphics; Graphical User Interface; Human-Computer Interaction; Sutherland, Ivan

— *James Pyfer*

Software Agents

Software agents are computer programs that perform customized, automated tasks, such as searching the Internet for the lowest price for a particular product, prioritizing incoming email, or coordinating production schedules.

As the term implies, software agents allow users to delegate some of the labor of navigating the surging sea of information that flows through computer networks. They function as what computer scientist Alan Kay describes as "soft" robots, carrying out the bidding of their clients in cyberspace, and thereby taking on the work of information filtering and prioritizing. If the Internet promises to lower transaction costs by making prodigious amounts of information readily available, software agents contribute by reducing the time and energy spent in sifting through this information.

Given the scope of activities envisioned for software agents, the term is a flexible one, characterized, as writer Neil Fawcett notes, by the attributes of customization, autonomy, and the ability to "learn" and adapt to new situations. Other definitions add the attributes of longevity (that such agents endure long enough to "remember" their clients' preferences and directives), communicability (that they are able to communicate with other agents), and proactivity (that they anticipate client needs). For example, a basic online search engine exhibits some of the attributes of a software agent, but not all. Search engines allow users to delegate the task of searching the Internet based on customized preferences, whereas software agents incorporate the additional ability to learn from, and eventually anticipate, user preferences.

Learning is critical to the performance of software agents, and therefore their development is closely linked to research in artificial intelligence (AI). Fawcett traces their genesis to the notion of "roving software," developed by the AI community at the Massachusetts Institute of Technology (MIT). Kay credits MIT's John McCarthy with coming up with the idea of software agents in the mid-1950s, and Oliver G. Selfridge with coining the term a few years later. The goal was to develop software that could not only follow instructions, but also seek assistance and advice along the way.

If AI researchers envisioned the software agent and its capabilities, the development of the Internet and the World Wide Web helped to create its habitat. A networked environment provides roaming room for software agents, allowing them to interact with each other and with computer users. MIT Media Laboratory founder Nicholas Negroponte suggests, for example, that software agents—perhaps with voice-recognition capability and programmed "personalities" of their own—will increasingly mediate the interface between humans and the network, allowing clients to spend less time online.

As is the case with new technology in general, many of the current and developing applications of software agents are commercial. For example, the MIT Media Laboratory's Software Agents Group is exploring the use of software agents to facilitate real-estate purchases and airline bookings. Emerging corporate applications include the use of networked agents to decentralize and streamline industrial production. Julian Perkin, for example, describes the use of networked software agents by DaimlerChrysler to increase flexibility in the automated production of automobile engines. A system of specialized agents responsible, in turn, for monitoring the progress of a specific part, plotting its path through the production process, and updating the availability of individual machines all work together to make the manufacturing process as efficient as possible. The results of this decentralized, collaborative approach, according to Perkin, are often superior to those of top-down automated systems.

In the realm of consumption, Microsoft's Bill Gates envisions the role that software agents will play in contributing to the development of "friction-free" capitalism by reducing informational costs and bypassing the notoriously fraught process of human haggling and decision-making. Personal software agents would record their clients' preferences and seek out products and services that match their profiles. Such agents would presumably have the autonomy to make purchases that anticipate consumer needs, as in the case of automated grocery services that replenish the refrigerator when supplies are low. Emerging interactive television technologies anticipate the role that software agents will play not just in retrieving specified movies and programs, but also in anticipating viewer tastes and seeking out appropriate programming. The goal is to develop "intelligent" devices that will know what clients want to watch better than the clients themselves. At the extreme, software agents can replicate and autonomize entire market systems, standing in for individual buyers and sellers to negotiate prices and terms of service.

Software agents help bridge the gap between interactivity and autonomy: As an agent grows to "know" its client through ongoing interactions, it gains the information it needs to make decisions on his or her behalf. The anticipated autonomy of such agents raises a host of ethical and practical questions, including the extent to which clients retain responsibility for decisions made by their agents. Author Michael Schrage suggests that software agents may be used to shield their clients from the consequences of decisions that the agents are programmed to make autonomously—including, for example, screening email or telephone messages so that they don't reach their human addressee.

Since software agents serve to remove their clients from direct access to the information that they coordinate, the ability to discern whose interests they are serving is potentially compromised. Will users have the time to check to see whether the price retrieved by their agent is really the lowest available for a particular item, or whether the agent has been co-opted or deceived by the seller (or the seller's agent)?

By definition, allowing software agents a degree of autonomy means ceding control over certain decisions to a program that may not be well understood or easily evaluated by its user. In the case of agents that record consumer preferences and seek out customized products (some of which will presumably be developed in response to these preferences), the question remains as to whom the agent is really working for: the buyer or the seller. Finally, the level and detail of information available to agents about their clients raises ever-present concerns of online privacy. If, as Bradshaw suggests, agents are virtual servants, to some extent the master's dependence on them may become a form of subjection.

Bibliography

Bradshaw, Jeffrey M., ed. "An Introduction to Software Agents." *Software Agents.* Cambridge, Mass.: MIT Press, 1997.

Fawcett, Neil. "Interrogating the Software Agents." *Computer Weekly,* March 6, 1997, p. 28.

Gates, Bill, with Nathan Myhrvold and Peter Rinearson. *The Road Ahead.* New York: Viking, 1995.

Kay, Alan. "Computer Software." *Scientific American,* vol. 251, no. 3 (September 1984).

MIT Media Lab: Software Agents Group. May 2001. <http://agents.www.media.mit.edu/groups/agents/> (July 12, 2002).

Negroponte, Nicholas. "Agents: From Direct Manipulation to Delegation." Jeffrey M. Bradshaw, ed. *Software Agents.* Cambridge, Mass.: MIT Press, 1997.

Perkin, Julian. "Software Agents 'Negotiate' Production Schedules." *Financial Times* (London), November 1, 2000, p. 7.

Schrage, Michael. "New Dimension in Deception: The Computer." *Los Angeles Times,* March 4, 1993, p. D1.

Further Reading

Bradshaw, Jeffrey M., ed. *Software Agents.* Cambridge, Mass.: MIT Press, 1997.

Minsky, Marvin. *The Society of Mind.* New York: Simon and Schuster, 1986.

Minsky, Marvin, and Doug Riecken. "A Conversation with Marvin Minsky About Agents." *Communications of the ACM,* vol. 37, no. 7 (1994), pp. 22–29.

Murch, Richard, and Tony Johnson. *Intelligent Software Agents.* Upper Saddle River, N.J.: Prentice Hall PTR, 1999.

Nwana, Hyacinth S. "Software Agents: An Overview." *Knowledge Engineering Review,* vol. 11, no. 3 (1996), pp. 205–44.

Related Topics

Content Filtering; Interface; Maes, Pattie; Media Lab, Massachusetts Institute of Technology; Personalization

— *Mark Andrejevic*

The Soul of a New Machine

Tracy Kidder's 1981 Pulitzer Prize and American Book Award winner, *The Soul of a New Machine,* chronicles the development of a mainframe computer, the Eagle, at the Data General Corporation. In the book, Kidder provides a window into the high-tech culture of computer software and hardware engineering that few had previously seen, describing the culture of the fast-paced computer industry, along with the lives of the engineers who were seeking to accomplish the impossible.

Aside from earning prestigious awards, the book is considered a classic text about the culture of the computer industry, and is the benchmark against which all later books, such as Douglas Coupland's *Microserfs,* are compared. Many college courses in departments from computer science to sociology and English literature use the book as required reading. Its popularity is rooted in its vivid description of a computer-industry corporation, and in Kidder's writing style, which combined elements of storytelling common to fiction and of historical narrative common to journalism.

Kidder presents his inside look at the Data General Corporation in the form of an ethnography. Ethnographies are detailed studies of a group of individuals or a society by an author who observes and interviews participants to understand their culture. The book chronicles real events and people during the two-year development of Data General's big mainframe supercomputer, from its initial design phase to its product release. Kidder followed the lives of the engineers, staying by their side during 18-hour working days. He also observed their lives (or the lack thereof) outside of Data General with their families and friends.

Before Silicon Valley, the computer industry centered in Boston, with its prestigious universities and the technology companies surrounding them on the now-famous Route 128 highway. The computer-science graduates from these institutions provided a constant stream of new programmers and engineers to build the next greatest invention; their credo was, "The product is king, and we must beat the other companies to market." In *The Soul of a New Machine,* the organizational culture of high-tech firms is exposed, allowing the reader to understand the "soul" of a new product.

The book is more than just a chronological description of the production process. It is a rich examination of the struggles and triumphs of the human spirit that go into the creation of a new machine or invention. As Kidder wrote, "Promising to achieve a nearly impossible schedule was a way of signing up . . . Signing up required, of course, that you fervently desire the right to build your machine and that you do whatever was necessary for success . . . " The tales of the individuals at Data General offer the reader a deeper understanding of the determination, drive, and conviction of engineers who are often maligned and dismissed as nerds and geeks.

Kidder's award-winning text on computer culture is still relevant today, offering an understanding of the high-tech industry and the feverish development of the Internet and new media. While labels such as Internet appliances and Web designers have been added to those of mainframes and software engineers, the underlying computer culture remains the same. The entrepreneurial spirit and sense of a higher calling are still very much a part of the individuals working in the Internet and computer industries.

Bibliography

Kenney, Martin, ed. *Understanding Silicon Valley: The Anatomy of an Entrepreneurial Region*. Stanford, Calif.: Stanford University Press, 2000.

Kidder, Tracy. *The Soul of a New Machine*. New York: Avon Books, 1981.

Further Reading

Coupland, Douglas. *Microserfs*. New York: ReganBooks, 1995.

Saxenian, AnnaLee. *Regional Advantage: Culture and Competition in Silicon Valley and Route 128*. Cambridge, Mass.: Harvard University Press, 1994.

Related Topics

Cyberculture

— *Gates Matthew Stoner*

Spam

Spam refers to widely transmitted, inappropriate, and unsolicited online messages. Most historical references trace the original usage to the early 1990s. The term most likely originated among users of the USENET bulletin-board system. USENET allows people to post messages in topically divided newsgroups that can be read and responded to by hundreds of others on computers connected to the Internet. On USENET, spam refers to messages, usually of a commercial nature, posted to multiple newsgroups without regard to the topic of the newsgroups. The term spam is now used in a variety of different online forums, including chat forums, where it refers to large amounts of repetitious or meaningless text, and email, where it usually refers to unsolicited advertisements. In general, spam increases the "noise-to-signal" ratio of online communication, decreasing its worth and usability.

The word spam comes from two sources. First, SPAM refers to a canned pork product produced by Hormel Foods. The British comedy group Monty Python spoofed SPAM's popularity in post–World War II Britain in a comedy sketch. In the skit, the reading of a breakfast menu containing numerous mentions of SPAM is repeatedly drowned out by a chorus of Vikings singing "SPAM, SPAM, SPAM, SPAM," over and over. Thus the use of the term SPAM in the Monty Python skit represents two features that define online spam: mindless repetition and the drowning out of useful content.

Originally, the USENET use of spam referred only to commercial messages sent to multiple newsgroups. However, spammers soon became more sophisticated in their techniques, acquiring email addresses from USENET and other online postings and sending commercial messages directly through email. Such email messages are also referred to as UBE (unsolicited bulk email) or UCE (unsolicited commercial email). Some people have even referred to any unsolicited email as spam, although clearly there is a difference between "unsolicited" email from people one knows or would desire contact with, and unsolicited email from companies randomly marketing a product of no interest to the receiver of the email.

One of the most famous early cases of USENET spamming involved the attorneys Laurence Canter and Martha Siegel. In April 1994, they posted a message to 6,000 USENET newsgroups advertising their services in assisting non-U.S. citizens in entering the then-upcoming "green card lottery." The scale of their action was unprecedented, and the spamming was considered particularly egregious because the content: 1) was of little use to most readers; 2) was of questionable legality; and 3) seemed to many to be a scam, since it proposed to charge a fee for the service of helping applicants fill out a form for a lottery that was free to enter. The negative response from USENET users was also unprecedented. Even simple email requests to Canter and Siegel's service provider to terminate their account were so numerous that they crashed the service provider's computers multiple times.

Some users took more aggressive anti-spam actions. One particularly famous one came from an individual or individuals called Cancelmoose. Any USENET posting can be canceled by the sender. The cancellation message spreads throughout the Internet, canceling any appearance of the posting. It is also possible to forge a cancel message to make it look as if it has come from the original sender. Forging cancel messages is considered extremely bad form, but Cancelmoose considered it a justifiable action in the face of Canter and Siegel's massively disseminated and inappropriate messages. (Cancelmoose also developed techniques for stopping spam received in private email, and can be found today at http://www.cm.org.) Despite considerable bad press, Canter and Siegel remained unrepentant, and went on to publish a book instructing other commercial enterprises in spamming methods.

Spamming remains an appealing method to some marketers because of its very low cost, particularly when compared to physical mass-mailing marketing techniques. Advice on techniques for avoiding backlash against spammers is widely available from marketing consultants, both online and in print. However, some marketing consultants advise against spamming because of the potential for ill will, and instead provide information on other online marketing techniques such as Web-based advertising. Responding to pressure from consumer and online privacy groups, many online consumer-product companies either refrain from making email addresses of customers available, or provide information about their privacy policies on their Web sites.

A wide variety of books, Web pages, and other resources provide detailed information on avoiding or stopping spam, protesting against spammers, and using computer programs to automatically delete any spam received. Several organizations also seek to influence legislation to decrease or eliminate spam, including the Electronic Frontier Foundation and CAUCE, the Coalition Against Unsolicited Commercial Email. CAUCE, an all-volunteer lobbying organization formed in 1997, produces an online newsletter and lobbies congress regarding proposed legislation relating to spam. Anti-spam legislation has been introduced in some states, but the U.S. Congress has not enacted federal anti-spam laws. In early 2002, a California appeals court upheld a lower-court ruling that commercial emails must have valid return addresses and other means to make it possible for consumers to remove themselves from mailing lists. The Washington state supreme court upheld a similar ruling in 2001 against a spammer.

Bibliography

Campbell, K. K. "A Net.Conspiracy So Immense . . . : Chatting with Martha Siegel of the Internet's Infamous Canter & Siegel." *Computer Underground Digest*, vol. 6, no. 89 (October 12, 1994). Reprinted from *Toronto Computes*. <http://venus.soci.niu.edu/~cudigest/CUDS6/cud6.89> (June 7, 2002).
Hormel Foods. "SPAM & the Internet." <http://www.spam.com/ci/ci_in.htm> (June 7, 2002).

Further Reading

Canter, Laurence, and Martha Siegel. *How to Make a Fortune on the Information Superhighway*. New York: HarperCollins, 1994.
Electronic Frontier Foundation. "Net Abuse: Spam (Junk E-Mail, UBE)." Archive, updated February 22, 2002. <http://www.eff.org/Spam_cybersquatting_abuse/Spam> (June 7, 2002).
Schwartz, Alan; Russell, Debby; and Simson Garfinkel. *Stopping Spam*. Sebastopol, Calif.: O'Reilly, 1998.

Related Topics

Cyberculture; E-Commerce; Electronic Frontier Foundation; Email; MUDs and MOOs; Netiquette; Privacy; USENET

— *Lori Kendall*

SRI International

SRI International is an organization known for innovation, investigation, and consulting. This research-and-design (R&D) institution has developed advanced technologies for more than 55 years, contributing to the creation of many products, pharmaceuticals, and computer tools currently used in countless areas.

Originally named the Stanford Research Institute, the SRI was established in 1946 through a joint effort between Stanford University and several business executives. The idea behind the institution's formation was an interest in understanding the change of science and technology in a manner that could shape the future. The most distinctive feature of the research center is the way it operates. The institution functions as a business in a sense that it must solely support itself. Comprised of several scholars, well known for contributions to particular research areas, SRI receives negotiated fees from customers in return for consulting, research, or concept developments. SRI has a customer base that includes governments, businesses, and other establishments. Research conducted at SRI includes study in a wide range of areas and topics. Such disciplines as communication, information sciences, biotechnology, chemistry, and physics serve as a backdrop for the establishment's areas of expertise.

As early as 1946, the institution began work on and introduced a chemical called dodecyl benzene that changed household cleaning forever. While consulting for a petroleum company named Chevron, SRI found a substitute for components that were used in hand soap, and dodecyl benzene became a standard part of household detergent.

During the 1950s, Walt Disney asked SRI for help in developing Disneyland. The R&D center offered recommendations on an Anaheim, California, location, set plans for making the amusement park feasible, and even predicted attendance trends. SRI also delved into computer technology after a request from the Bank of America. With a growing increase in financial patronage, the bank requested a technology that could aid in the processes of accounting and handling checks. SRI's solution was to produce a primitive automated teller machine called ERMA (Electronic Recording Machine, Accounting). ERMA was commercially released in 1959, and was used by the Bank of America until the early 1970s. It created a foundation for the highly electronic methods of banking in use today.

During the 1960s, SRI became a birthplace for communication technologies. According to the SRI Technology Web site, the organization was only one of four remote locations to be connected to the Advanced Research Projects Agency's (ARPA) ARPANET, the first form of the Internet. On October 20, 1969, SRI received the very first data transmission from the University of California, Los Angeles. This decade also served as a time of drastic computer-technology innovation for SRI. Under the direction of Douglas Engelbart, the organization produced concepts of a software widows interface, data sharing, and devices that permitted interactivity with computers.

The efforts of Engelbart and SRI have been a major force in the creation of additional computer technology and tools. The first computer mouse, made of wood, was only one of many inventions constructed by Engelbart. His contributions include conceptions of hypermedia and hypertext similar to that employed by Web pages, easy-to-use computer interfaces, and teleconferencing.

In the 1970s, SRI split from its home at Stanford University and changed its name to SRI International; now based in Menlo Park, California, it continued developing new technologies, including ultrasound imaging. Utilizing modified pulse echoing, an ultrasound scanner employs sound waves to determine shapes that are then graphically represented. Today, ultrasound imagining is a commonplace medical tool.

In the 1980s, SRI International continued to generate ideas and products that changed traditional practices. In an effort to advance marketing tactics within business, the institution developed a market-research system known as VALS, which stood for "Values and Lifestyles." The system used surveys and other methods to determine factors that motivated purchasing among consumers. In addition, SRI International made available a television technology that dramatically boosted reception for viewers: High Definition Television (HDTV), designed by the Sarnoff Corporation, a smaller company owned and operated by SRI International, became commercialized during the beginning of the twenty-first century.

From the 1990s to the present, SRI International has continued to advance both software applications and pharmaceutical products. Discoveries in speech-recognition software have prompted SRI International to form the Speech Technology and Research (STAR) Laboratory. STAR produced a technology dubbed DECIPHER, which permits computers to understand naturally spoken words. Unique among other forms of speech-recognition software, DECIPHER understands continuous speech without training the software to specific vocal behaviors and allows the voice to be converted to text, as well as offering a way to control computer actions. The research center also introduced a new family of medicine: Tirapazamine is an anti-cancer drug that helps destroy cancer cells that are missed by traditional radiation treatments.

Bibliography

Gibson, Weldon B. *Stanford Research Institute; A Story of Scientific Service to Business, Industry, and Government*. New York: Newcomen Society in North America, 1968.

SRI International. "SRI Technology." <http://www.sri.com/technology> (June 7, 2002).

Further Reading

"SRI International Aims to 'Map' the Internet with .geo Proposal." *GIS Café*. October 23, 2000. <http://www.giscafe.com/NEWS/CorpNews2/20001023_sri.html> (June 7, 2002).

Related Topics

Engelbart, Douglas; Human-Computer Interaction; Interactivity

— *James Pyfer*

Stallman, Richard

1953–

Computer Scientist

Richard M. Stallman is the developer of the GNU operating system (OS) and the founder of the Free Software Foundation. He pioneered the concept of "copyleft," and made possible the development of the Linux operating system (or, as Stallman prefers to call it, GNU-Linux).

Stallman (who often goes by just his initials, RMS) got his start as a programmer in 1971 at the Artificial Intelligence (AI) Lab of the Massachusetts Institute of Technology (MIT), while still an undergraduate at Harvard. He quickly became known both as a brilliant programmer (he authored EMACS, a powerful text editor) and as a fierce advocate of what some call "the hacker ethic": the idea that information should be freely shared without proprietary restrictions. Upset by the growing bureaucratization of the freewheeling AI Lab, Stallman responded by organizing a boycott of the password system, advocating that everybody just enter a "null string" instead. Stallman is immortalized in Steven Levy's 1984 book *Hackers* as "The Last of the True Hackers."

Working at MIT, Stallman grew frustrated by the restrictions imposed on programmers using proprietary versions of software. The AI Lab hackers had grown accustomed to tweaking the software that they used to improve performance—modifying a printer's driver software, for example, to alert users of paper jams. Increasingly, however, software providers were refusing to release the source code to their programs, making modifications impossible. A breaking point for Stallman occurred when the lab received one of the very first laser printers from Xerox in 1979. It was great—except for the frequent paper jams. Despite Stallman's pleas, Xerox refused to give him the source code to modify the printer software.

Finally, Stallman quit the lab in 1984 to write his own OS, one that could be freely distributed, modified by any user, and portable to any hardware platform. Stallman named the system GNU (pronounced "guh-NEW"), which, in a recursive joke, stands for "GNU's not UNIX."

To make sure that his software would remain freely available and open to continued modification, Stallman organized the Free Software Foundation and developed the GNU General Public License (GPL for short). The GPL allows any user to copy, distribute, and/or modify software released under the license, as long as the user always makes all source code available, and as long as all terms of the GPL are transferred to all subsequent users. Software distributed under the GPL is copyrighted, but Stallman prefers the term copyleft, to emphasize that the purpose of the copyright is to guarantee users' continual freedom to distribute and modify the product, rather than to lock up proprietary rights.

Stallman clarified that when he talks about "free software," he means "free as in free speech, not free beer." Programmers are welcome to sell their versions of software for a price, as long they adhere to the GPL. But Stallman's system offers a fundamental critique to conventional capitalist notions of intellectual property. He insists that when a valuable commodity like software is infinitely reproducible at practically no extra cost, to refuse to share it is unjust. Stallman contrasts a computer program with a loaf of bread. If someone has a loaf of bread and someone else takes it, then the first person does not have it any more; it is a limited resource. But software is like an infinitely replicable loaf of bread. For someone not to share his program when he would still have his own is what Stallman calls "software hoarding."

When Stallman began the GNU project, most computer-industry observers considered him a hopeless idealist. Crafting a whole OS from the bottom up is an enormous task requiring the collaboration of many programmers. Who would help Stallman write "freeware" with little hope of compensation? Still, Stallman and his supporters plugged away for years; cheap living, borrowed office space from MIT, and a 1991 MacArthur "genius" grant helped keep the project alive.

By 1991, only one crucial piece of GNU was missing: the "kernel," the OS core that communicates most directly with the hardware. Finnish programmer Linus Torvalds added this piece, and brought together a tremendous collection of programmers who continue to expand the system. The result has been dubbed Linux, although Stallman's supporters argue that the system should rightly be called "GNU-Linux."

Today, Stallman remains active in developing GNU and proselytizing for free software, while rigorously criticizing what he sees as compromises to his original vision. He has attacked the transition within part of the Linux community from the original concept of "free software," with its broad ethical and political implications, to the term "open source," which suggests that all that matters is the availability of source code. He also criticizes companies that claim to support open source while continuing to keep parts of their software proprietary. Meanwhile, his Free Software Foundation continues to enforce the GPL, making sure that programs released under the license remain free. (The term *free* is used in the sense of without restriction, as in free speech, rather than in the sense of without cost, as in the popular example of free beer).

Still a free spirit, Stallman often appears at conventions in costume, dressed as "Saint IGNUcius of the Church of EMACS," complete with a halo fashioned from an old computer-disk platter. The Saint IGNUcius persona is at once a bold declaration of righteousness and a silly self-parody; while to many it epitomizes the playfulness of the hacker ethic, the more business-minded proponents of free software worry that he scares off investors.

Many in the software world continue to judge Stallman to be a hopeless idealist, a self-righteous martyr for free software. But his vision of collaborative, volunteerist software development has proven remarkably prescient, as Linux has emerged as the primary challenger to Microsoft's OS dominance. As the spread of the Internet has made it easier for volunteers across the globe to collaborate on projects while making it increasingly difficult to enforce (and justify) traditional notions of intellectual property, free software has become a model for what intellectual production in the twenty-first century might look like.

Selected Works

Stallman, Richard. "Free Software: Freedom and Cooperation." Transcript of speech delivered at New York University, May 29, 2001. <http://www.fsf.org/events/rms-nyu-2001-transcript.txt>

———. "The GNU Manifesto." 1993. <http://www.fsf.org/gnu/manifesto.html>

———. "The GNU Operating System and the Free Software Movement." *Open Sources: Voices from the Open Source Revolution.* Chris Dibona, Sam Ockman, and Mark Stone, eds. Cambridge, Mass.: O'Reilly, 1999.

———. "St. IGNUcius." 2000. <http://www.stallman.org/saint.html>

Bibliography

Benedek, Emily. "Steal This Program." *Lingua Franca,* August 1997, pp. 45-48.

Leonard, Andrew. "The Richard Stallman Saga, Redux." *Salon,* September 11, 1998. <http://archive.salon.com/21st/feature/1998/09/cov_31feature.html> (April 12, 2002).

———. "The Saint of Free Software." *Salon,* August 31, 1998. <http://archive.salon.com/21st/feature/1998/08/11feature.html> (April 12, 2002).

Levy, Steven. *Hackers: Heroes of the Computer Revolution.* New York: Dell, 1984.

Rosenberg, Donald K. *Open Source: The Unauthorized White Papers.* New York: John Wiley & Sons, 2000.

Further Reading

The Free Software Foundation. "GNU's Not UNIX!" <http://www.fsf.org> (April 12, 2002).

Hall, Michael, and Brian Proffitt. *The Joy of Linux: A Gourmet Guide to Open Source.* Roseville, Calif.: Prima Publishing, 2001.

Himanen, Pekka. *The Hacker Ethic and the Spirit of the Information Age.* New York: Random House, 2001.

Leonard, Andrew. "Salon.com Technology & Business: Free Software Project." *Salon,* 2001. <http://www.salon.com/tech/fsp> (April 12, 2002).

Moody, Glyn. *Rebel Code: Inside Linux and the Open Source Revolution.* Cambridge, Mass.: Perseus Publishing, 2001.

Wayner, Peter. *Free for All: How Linux and the Free Software Movement Undercut the High-Tech Titans.* New York: HarperBusiness, 2000.

Williams, Sam. *Free as in Freedom: Richard Stallman's Crusade for Free Software.* Cambridge, Mass./Sebastopol, Calif.: O'Reilly & Associates, 2002. <http://www.oreilly.com/openbook/freedom/> (April 12, 2002).

Related Topics

Copyleft; Hacking, Cracking, and Phreaking; Linux; Open Source; Raymond, Eric

—*Ted Friedman*

Stanford Research Institute

See SRI International.

Sterling, Bruce

1954–
Author

As a science-fiction author, journalist, and social critic, Bruce Sterling has made numerous contributions to the field of new media. He is one of the earliest and most famous writers in the science-fiction genre called cyberpunk, and is credited, along with novelist William Gibson, with coining that term. Sterling also wrote *The Hacker Crackdown: Law and Disorder on the Electronic Frontier* (1992), one of the first non-fiction books on hackers. Currently engaged in a variety of projects relating to new media, science, and society, he continues to write science fiction as well as non-fiction.

Cyberpunk began in the 1980s among a loosely affiliated group of young science-fiction writers. Influenced by and drawing on traditional science-fiction themes, but also critical of the current state of science-fiction writing, cyberpunk authors shared a particular aesthetic that became influential in various computer-related subcultures. This aesthetic includes repeated themes and symbols, such as mirrored sunglasses, black clothing, high-tech body enhancements, and protagonists who are frequently involved in gray-market or outright illegal activities. Cyberpunk works tend to emphasize the role of computer technology in future society, often depict human/computer couplings such as cyborgs or brain/computer interfaces, and are usually dark, dystopic, and graphically violent. Many computer programmers read and are influenced by cyberpunk, while developments in computer and Internet technologies also influence cyberpunk authors.

Using the pseudonym Vincent Omniaveritas, Sterling edited an early 1980s, online cyberpunk fanzine called *Cheap Truth*. With contributions from other cyberpunk writers, this periodic newsletter (which he has compared to Eastern European "samizdat" underground newspapers) included biting criticism of mainstream science fiction. It also served to promote the work of the cyberpunk authors who contributed to it.

Sterling's most important contribution to cyberpunk culture is the edited volume *Mirrorshades* (1988). Compiling short stories by William Gibson, Pat Cadigan, Rudy Rucker, and other well-known cyberpunk authors, this anthology of short fiction also included a "state of the genre" introduction by Sterling, which summarized the precursors, contributors, and aesthetic of cyberpunk fiction. For many, this collection continues to define the genre.

Sterling has written several science-fiction novels, and has three collections of short stories in print. He also collaborated with William Gibson on *The Difference Engine* (1992), an alternative-history novel that explores a nineteenth-century England in which computers already exist, powered by steam.

Sterling's fame among hackers and members of other computer subcultures stems as much from his nonfiction writing as from his fiction. In particular, *The Hacker Crackdown* cemented his reputation as one of the "digerati," the people in the know about computer technology and new media. *The Hacker Crackdown*, which chronicles a variety of law enforcement actions in 1988–90 in the then-new field of computer crime, also describes the formation of the Electronic Frontier Foundation (EFF), an organization seeking to protect civil liberties online and in relation to computers.

Sterling became interested in cyberliberties in part because of the infamous seizure of computers and equipment belonging to Steve Jackson Games, Inc., which took place in Sterling's home town of Austin, Texas. One of the items seized in that raid was a game book called *GURPS Cyberpunk*, intended for use in face-to-face role-playing games. Although deemed by law-enforcement agents to provide instructions for the commission of computer crime, this work essentially constituted a form of science fiction. As such, the Steve Jackson Games raid hit close to Sterling's home in more ways than one.

Like the founders of the EFF, Sterling felt that the general public and many members of law enforcement did not sufficiently understand hacker culture and activities. Also like the members of EFF, and like many hackers themselves, Sterling agrees, as he puts it in an online introduction to *The Hacker Crackdown*, that "information wants to be free." He therefore wanted the book to get as wide an audience as possible, particularly among members of the groups he describes in the book: hackers, computer law-enforcement personnel, and electronic civil-liberties activists. Because of this, he took the unique step of acquiring the electronic rights to *The Hacker Crackdown* in order to make it available online shortly after publication.

Sterling's other nonfiction writings include a well-respected series of science columns for *The Magazine of Fantasy and Science Fiction*. One of those columns is an oft-cited history of the Internet. He has written articles for *Wired* since its first issue, including articles on virtual warfare, the Burning Man festival, and post–Soviet Union Russia.

In addition to writing, Sterling engages in a variety of other activities related to computers, technology, and media. He is in great demand as a speaker, particularly at conferences related to computers. In 1996, he started the Dead Media Project, an online collaborative project that attempts to chronicle the history of various forms of media that no longer exist. Conceived of by Sterling and another writer, Richard Kadrey, the project was originally intended to produce a book on the topic. Currently, it exists as an exhaustive series of online notes on everything from well-known historical media such as Edison's wax cylinders to lesser-known and never fully realized projects such as the delivery of mail by guided missile.

Sterling's concerns about global warming are reflected in many of his novels, and led him in 1999 to found Viridian Design, an electronic mailing list and Web site devoted to discussion and encouragement of industrial designs that decrease people's use of fossil fuels. Viridian Design hosts periodic design contests, and provides links to environmental news and information. Sterling also recently guest-edited a special Viridian issue of *Whole Earth Magazine*.

Currently, Sterling cohosts the Mirrorshades forum on the WELL, an online bulletin-board service that allows members to log on and post typed messages. Mirrorshades, a continuation of the older Cyberpunk "conference," is one of many topical conferences on the WELL.

Selected Works

Sterling, Bruce. *Distraction: A Novel*. New York: Bantam Books, 1998.

———. *The Hacker Crackdown: Law and Disorder on the Electronic Frontier*. New York: Bantam Books, 1992. <http://www.eff.org/Publications/Bruce_Sterling/Hacker_Crackdown> (July 3, 2002).

———. *A Good Old-Fashioned Future: Stories*. New York: Bantam Books, 1999.

———. *Islands in the Net*. New York: Ace Books, 1989.

———. *Zeitgeist*. New York: Bantam Books, 2000.

Sterling, Bruce, ed. *Mirrorshades: The Cyberpunk Anthology*. New York: Arbor House, 1986.

Sterling, Bruce, and William Gibson. *The Difference Engine*. New York: Bantam Books, 1991.

Bibliography

"Bruce Sterling Online Index." <http://lonestar.texas.net/~dub/sterling.html> (June 7, 2002).

Sterling, Bruce. "A Statement of Principle." *EFF's (Extended) Guide to the Internet*. Reprinted from *Science Fiction Eye #10*. <http://www.eco.utexas.edu/help/EEGTTI/eeg_266.html> (June 7, 2002).

The WELL. "Mirrorshades Postmodern Archive." <http://www.well.com/conf/mirrorshades> (June 7, 2002).

Further Reading

Aurbach, Laurence. Viridian Design. Home page. <http://www.viridiandesign.org> (June 7, 2002).

Center for the Studies of Digital Libraries, Texas A&M University. *Cheap Truth* archives. <http://bush.cs.tamu.edu/~erich/cheaptruth> (June 7, 2002).

Sterling, Bruce. "The DEAD MEDIA Project: A Modest Proposal and a Public Appeal." <http://www.deadmedia.org/modest-proposal.html> (June 7, 2002).

Sterling, Bruce, ed. *Whole Earth Magazine* (Viridian issue), Summer 2001.

Related Topics

Cyberculture; Cyberpunk; Electronic Frontier Foundation; Gibson, William; Hacking, Cracking, and Phreaking; Whole Earth 'Lectronic Link

— *Lori Kendall*

Stone, Allucquère Rosanne

1957–

Academic

Allucquère Rosanne "Sandy" Stone is a teacher, performer, and theorist in the area of cyberculture studies. She is founder and director of the Advanced Communication Technologies Laboratory (ACT-LAB) at the University of Texas, Austin. In addition, Stone is a pioneer in the rapidly growing field of transgender studies.

Deemed a prodigy at a young age, Stone remembers being sent to private schools for a time, and then "returning to public schools ones when the money ran out." Interspersed with a formal education were "years during which I [would show] up on the doorstep of this and that scholar whose work I admired and asking if I could audit classes." During this time, Stone also began a lifelong interest in performance, creating and acting in 8mm films, composing music, and developing one of the first early multimedia experiments that would now be easily recognizable as raves.

Stone won a one-year scholarship to St. John's College in Annapolis, Maryland. To earn money, she worked in a dizzying array of jobs, all of which ultimately served to expand her knowledge of sound and light production. One year, for example, she worked in digital research at the Bell Telephone Laboratories Special Systems Exploratory Group. Another year, she studied retinal neurology at the Eye Research Foundation. Throughout, Stone assisted in film and music production companies as a cinematographer, sound engineer, or mixer.

After a brief time in New York, Stone moved to California to continue working in rock-n-roll sound engineering, collaborating with Jimi Hendrix, Jefferson Airplane, and others. It was during this time that Stone began transitioning as a transgendered woman.

With her transgendered status and her intimate knowledge of audio and visual technologies, Stone became a persuasive spokesperson for what feminist historian Donna Haraway has called the "cyborg ontology." Cyborgs are bodies that are part organic and part mechanical (or chemically enhanced). They routinely traverse the boundaries between technological and natural, male and female, animal and human.

Stone has long been interested in how cyborgs function via what she terms "communications prostheses." As she related in *Wired* magazine, one of her most influential memories came as the result of an experiment she conducted with cats and FM transmitters. She implanted electrodes in a cat's inner ear, running them to a miniature stereo FM transmitter attached to its collar. "I would let the cat wander around outside in the fields, then I would go to my receiver and put on the stereo headphones and 'become' the cat," recalls Stone. Likewise, Stone considers the computer-generated voice of physicist Stephen Hawking to be a type of communication prosthesis, writing that "When I speak, I sound different if you're in the room with me or if you hear me over the phone. But Hawking sounds exactly the same. The boundary between his human voice and communication technology has broken down."

Like Marshall McLuhan before her, Stone maintains that the social ramifications for communications prostheses extend far beyond the stories of "obvious" cyborgs like Hawking. Everyone in media culture has a relationship to communications prosthetics, Stone maintains, if only because communications technologies "interpenetrate us in ways we'd never anticipated and change us in ways we don't realize."

One of the many famous examples that Stone has provided in her ethnographic work is the case of phone-sex participants. "Sex usually involves as many of the senses as possible—taste, touch, smell, sight, hearing," Stone explains. "Phone-sex workers translate all those modalities of experience into sound, then boil that down into a series of highly compressed tokens. They squirt those tokens down a voice-grade line and someone at the other end just adds water, so to speak, to reconstitute the tokens into a fully detailed set of images and interactions in multiple sensory modes."

In the 1980s, Stone moved to Santa Cruz, California, which she describes as "my spiritual home since the 1960s." Sometime around 1984, she was offered the opportunity to be a "mercenary teaching assistant" at the University of California, where she discovered there that "academics was my calling, even though I'd avoided formal education for years." At about the same time, she met Haraway, a feminist historian of science at Santa Cruz's History of Consciousness program who was already informally known as the "mother of cyborg anthropology."

By 1987, Stone entered the History of Consciousness program herself, "though not without a fair amount of trepidation on both sides," she recalls. Stone's dissertation was later published as *The War of Desire and Technology at the Close of the Mechanical Age.* In it, she charted a series of cyborgian "border crossings" in and out of cyberspace: a woman with multiple-personality syndrome, role-players on MUDs, the young hackers who brought down an early BBS called CommuniTree, and stories from the early days of the Atari Lab.

Stone received her Ph.D. in 1993, all the while continuing to work in sound engineering (she designed a successful digital music synthesizer), running her own software consulting company, and working as a teaching assistant. Since 1992, she has taught in the Department of Radio-TV-Film at the University of Texas at Austin. Stone is a popular lecturer around the country, and remains committed to her performance work, functioning as artist in residence at Banff during periods in 1995, 1997, and 1998.

Selected Works

Stone, Allucquère Rosanne. "Cyberdammerung at Wellspring Systems." *Immersed in Technology: Art and Virtual Environments.* Mary Ann Moser and Douglas MacLeod, eds. Cambridge, Mass.: MIT Press, 1996; pp. 103–17.

———. "The Empire Strikes Back: A Posttranssexual Manifesto." *Body Guards: The Cultural Politics of Gender Ambiguity.* Julia Epstein and Kristina Straub, eds. New York: Routledge, 1991; pp. 280–304.

———. "The Empire Strikes Back: A Posttranssexual Manifesto." (Revised and updated from the 1991 version, with afterword.) *Camera Obscura* 29 (1993).

———. "Identity in Oshkosh." *Posthuman Bodies.* Judith Halberstam and Ira Livingston, eds. Bloomington, Ind.: Indiana University Press, 1995; pp. 23–37.

———. "Sex and Death Among the Disembodied: VR, Cyberspace, and the Nature of Academic Discourse." *Cultures of Computing.* Susan Leigh Star, ed. Chicago: University of Chicago Press, 1995.

———. "Split Subjects, Not Atoms, or How I Fell in Love With My Prosthesis." *Configurations.* Special Issue: Located Knowledges. Roddey Reid, ed. Baltimore, Md.: Johns Hopkins University Press, 1994.

———. "Violation and Virtuality: Two Cases of Physical and Psychological Boundary Transgression and Their Implications." *Posthuman Bodies.* Judith Halberstam and Ira Livingston, eds. Bloomington: Indiana University Press, 1995.

———. *The War of Desire and Technology at the Close of the Mechanical Age.* Cambridge, Mass.: MIT Press, 1995.

———. "Will the Real Body Please Stand Up?: Boundary Stories About Virtual Cultures." *Cyberspace: First Steps.* Michael Benedikt, ed. Cambridge, Mass.: MIT Press. 1991.

Bibliography

Lebkowsky, Jon, and Paco Xander Nathan. "Allucquère Rosanne Stone Interview for *Mondo 2000*." (Unpublished version of interview that ran in *Mondo 2000*, 1993.) <http://www.sandystone.com/Mondo-interview> (May 10, 2002).

Stone, Allucquère Rosanne. "Bait and Switch with Sandy Stone: Interview." *Mondo 2000*, 1994.

———. Personal email communication with Theresa M. Senft, November 4, 2001.

———. "Allucquère Rosanne/Sandy Stone." Home page. <http://www.sandystone.com/> (May 10, 2002).

Stryker, Susan. "Sex and Death Among the Cyborgs." *Wired* 4.05, May 1996. <http://www.wired.com/wired/archive//4.05/stone_pr.html> (May 10, 2002).

Further Reading

Goodeve, Thyrza. "How Like a Goddess." *Artforum*, September 1995, pp. 117–21.

Hershman-Leeson, Lynn. "Sandy Stone interviewed by Lynn Hershman-Leeson." *Clicking In: Hot Links to a Digital Culture.* Seattle: Bay Press, 1996; pp. 105–15.

Nideffer, Robert, et al. "Techno-Prosthetics and Exterior Presence: A Conversation with Sandy Stone." *Speed* 1.2, February 4, 1998. <http://proxy.arts.uci.edu/%7Enideffer/_SPEED_/1.2/stone.html> (May 10, 2002).

Shade, Leslie Regan. "Review Essay: The Gendered Mystique." *CMC Magazine*, Special Focus: Women and Gender Online, March 1, 1996. <http://www.december.com/cmc/mag/1996/mar/shade.html> (May 10, 2002).

Related Topics

Cyberfeminism; Cyborg; Gender and New Media; Haraway, Donna J.

— *Theresa M. Senft*

Streaming Media

Streaming is a method of transmitting online audio and video files for immediate playback, in which playback begins even before all of the file's data packets have traveled over the Internet to the user's computer. This characteristic makes streaming media distinct from downloadable media, which is slower to launch and requires that files be downloaded completely before they can be seen or heard, which in turn requires large storage capacity on the end user's computer. With streaming, the only thing that is downloaded is a small buffer file that takes about ten seconds to arrive over most Internet connections; the buffer prevents playback delays that can otherwise result from network congestion. No part of a streaming media file is stored on the user's receiving device, which again makes it different from downloadable formats such as MP3, .WAV, and .AIFF. Streaming media can be delivered from Web or intranet media servers, across broadband channels such as cable and digital subscriber (DSL) lines, or via satellite and can be received and played on everything from PCs and laptops to cellular phones and personal digital assistants (PDAs).

The term "streaming" was used in the early 1990s to refer to a method of online information delivery that allowed text to appear on Web pages quickly. Graphics were allowed to fill in more slowly afterward. This innovation was first used by Netscape in its early Web browsers, allowing Web surfers to read articles on a page while waiting for data-heavy images to show up over slow-loading dial-up modems. However, in 1994, ex-Microsoft executive Rob Glaser redefined the term to name the data-compression and delivery model for audio and video that allows rich media files to play while many of the file's packets are still traveling over the Internet to their destination. Before the launch of Progressive Networks' first RealAudio player in 1995, streaming in this sense was impossible. Audio and video files had to show up in their entirety to work, much in the same way that email attachments still function. And with the modems of the time, multimedia delivery was painfully slow. Streaming media worked almost instantly, and as a result quickly found a large audience after the July 1995 launch of RealAudio 1.0 and its Real media servers.

RealAudio heralded a new phase in the development of the Internet. Soon after its release, radio stations began popping up all over the Internet—both standard "terrestrial" stations that simply streamed their on-air signals over the Internet, and numerous online-only radio competitors. Before long, television stations, educators, and online retailers like Amazon.com and CDNow.com all began using streaming media as a genuine multimedia platform on the Internet. Musicians started giving live concerts for Web-only audiences. Movie studios began streaming their promotional trailers online. For the first time, the Internet had become, at a practical level, more than just text and still pictures.

Despite streaming media's popularity, however, the relatively high cost of producing quality video and audio, and fear among advertisers and media companies about supporting it prior to wide consumer broadband Internet adoption, have combined to stifle the development of solid streaming-media business models. At the same time, the streaming-media model is being challenged by the very format it was designed to overtake, downloadable media. So-called "fast download" services such as the peer-to-peer file-sharing systems (which include Morpheus and KaZaA), and commercial subscription services such as RealNetworks' own MusicNet and the record-label venture Pressplay (the latter two of which combine streaming and downloading services), have proven to be a big business challenge to companies hoping to ride the streaming-media wave to newfound riches.

STREAMING PROGRESSIVELY

Streaming-media pioneer Progressive Networks was the brainchild of Rob Glaser, the son of a social worker and a printer, born in Yonkers, New York. An energetic and driven man in his mid-30s who at one time served as the youngest vice president at Microsoft Corp., he reportedly resigned from Bill Gates' software giant after losing an internal struggle over control of Microsoft's multimedia operations to another company executive, Nathan Myhrvold. In 1994, he launched his own company, which has proven to be as much a challenge to crucial parts of Microsoft's Internet business strategy as Netscape and America Online have in other contexts.

According to an August 1999 article in *Wired* magazine, Glaser, fresh from his departure from Microsoft, took some of his accrued millions, hired three programmers, and set them loose to find a way to deliver audio and video over the Internet without the excruciatingly long waits that had been the norm up to then. Glaser had heard about new technology that made fast multimedia delivery possible, and his programmers set about designing the needed software. He started relatively small, concentrating on tiny, tightly compressed audio files that people could hear in real time, even using the 14.4kbps (kilobit per second) modems that were in popular use in 1994 and 1995. However, upon completing the first version of his RealAudio player, Glaser and his team reportedly did not realize the value of their innovation, initially leaning toward creating a progressive, politically conscious company that would mix the Internet with television to bring socially conscious

content to the Internet; they hoped to create what *BusinessWeek* magazine suggested would have been a kind of cross between MTV and PBS.

However, after the RealAudio software was developed, *Wired* reported in 1999, Glaser and Progressive Networks' co-founder David Halperin went to Washington, D.C., to discuss their plans with several liberal advisers. After demonstrating the technology by streaming the signal of a baseball game from a server in Seattle to Glaser's laptop in D.C., Glaser and Halperin were convinced to drop the political focus and build a streaming-media software business. Glaser was encouraged to donate a percentage of his new company's proceeds to favored charities instead, and he has done so ever since.

For many on the Internet, streaming was both a revelation and a minor disappointment. The signal of the earliest RealAudio feeds was weak and hollow, sounding a little like an AM radio signal being piped through a wind tunnel, and they often enough would break down, and the stream would halt. Still, RealAudio worked well enough to make it obvious to early users that multimedia on the Internet could indeed be more than a frustrating side application, and could propel the Internet to new heights. The differences between what had been available before and what streaming could do were immediately apparent to anyone who had ever tried to listen to a .WAV file posted to a Web site. Using a 14.4kbps modem, it took about seven minutes for a 30-second snippet of a song to arrive and play, but that same file, streamed, would play in about ten seconds.

Glaser was rewarded for his success with a company that for several years dominated the streaming-media market, along with a personal fortune that, in February 2000, was listed at about $5 billion (it later tumbled to about $385 million with the dot-com collapse of 2001). In 1999, *Wired* magazine reported that about 85 percent of the streaming media flowing across the Internet used Real technology. (By then, Progressive Networks had been renamed RealNetworks.) Even as recently as September 2001, about 50 percent of streaming media was formatted for Real software.

Among those who noticed Glaser's momentum was Microsoft's Bill Gates, who arranged in 1997 to have Microsoft license the RealPlayer version 4.0 source code for $30 million, while spending another $30 million on a 10 percent stake in the company. But the alliance was short-lived. Soon, Microsoft dropped its stake in the company and began developing its own player, Windows Media Player—which, because it was bundled with a new version of Microsoft's operating systems, instantly gained a major slice of the streaming media marketplace. The streaming war was on.

In January 2000, *The New York Times* quoted the Nielsen/NetRatings Web measurement service's numbers indicating that, as of November 1999, 8.9 million people, or 12.1 percent of Internet users, were using various versions of RealPlayer. Microsoft's Windows Media Player was far behind at the time, capturing only 2.4 million users, or 3.2 percent of the market. With that audience, the *Times* noted, it was not even in second place, but was well behind Apple's QuickTime player software, which had 5.4 million users, a 7.4 percent market share.

A year later, the situation had shifted radically. According to a January 2001 Jupiter Media Metrix report, RealPlayer software remained the market leader, representing 28 percent of all multimedia streams used, while Windows Media Player had gained significantly, with 24 percent, and QuickTime players represented 4 percent. Many people, of course, have all three players (and possibly others) on their computers, and their usage therefore depends on the media formats that Web sites offer. Many sites place streaming files online in both RealPlayer and Windows Media formats, allowing users to choose their favorite.

By now, almost every major broadcaster now streams content over the Internet. CBSNews.com frequently Webcasts news stories to accompany its text articles, and MSNBC.com, CNN.com, and ABCNews.com all do the same. Online versions of newspapers like the *Washington Post* and *The New York Times* frequently stream news features from the Associated Press. Original, online-only financial-news video can be found in streaming format on sites like Finance.Yahoo.com, while many educators use the technology to conduct live distance-learning classes. Major corporations stream presentations of their quarterly financial reports to analysts and reporters online, while other businesses use streaming media to save on travel expenses by Webcasting live business meetings to far-flung employees and clients over the Internet. For many, streaming media is a normal part of a day on the job.

THE FUTURE OF STREAMING MEDIA

Even as more operations make streaming media part of their online rituals, however, there is evidence that interest among Web users has peaked. A January 2001 Jupiter Media Metrix study indicates that streaming-media usage levels plateaued during 2000. Forty percent of PC-equipped U.S. homes reported using a streaming-media player in January 2000, a number that rose to only 47 percent in November, the research firm said. "The type of content has not changed, and there are a lot of great things to do with your computer," analyst Robert Hertzberg told *Newsbytes*. "Streaming media is competing with activities like Web surfing, sending e-mail and, for that matter, watching television."

Perhaps the most important reason for this plateau is that broadband Internet connections over copper DSL lines, cable, and satellite systems have been adopted slowly by U.S. consumers, and most still use 56.6kbps dial-up connections. The problem with dial-up connections is that streaming signals tend to fade and break up the longer they run, particularly during times of high network congestion, whereas an online radio listener with a DSL connection is likely to be able to listen in all day without losing the signal. Analysts like Hertzberg think that the wide adoption of broadband, a phenomenon still expected to be years away, might be the needed remedy to make streaming media a strong business. By 2003, Jupiter Media Metrix has predicted, about 23 percent of Internet-connected homes in the United States, about 15 million households, will have broadband access.

"This is one of those markets that other pieces have to come together to take off," Hertzberg told *Newsbytes*. "Until broadband is widely distributed, the experience of streaming media is not going to be that great, especially video. This is also a chicken-and-the-egg problem, however, because content providers need to see that broadband is widely distributed before they push out content."

Streaming media, despite its many challenges, is not likely to disappear, according to a 1999 white paper by ViewCast Corp. Demand is there, the paper notes, especially among broadband users. Once broadband reaches critical mass in the marketplace, that demand will only accelerate, ViewCast predicted, particularly because streams of video—usually regarded as the most compelling media form—will attain a clarity and quality that only broadband users can now appreciate. "And video," the white paper stresses, "gives sites a great way to attract and retain visitors."

The stakes are very high. *The New York Times* reported in January 2000 that the ongoing war between RealNetworks and Microsoft for supremacy over the streaming-media market not only presages the direction that online audio and video will take, but also may map out the future of television, films, music, and other media in the coming era of convergence. "By most accounts," *Times* reporter Matt Richtel wrote, "convergence is still many years away. But it could mean huge business for the companies that sell software to media distributors."

Bibliography

Alderman, John. *Sonic Boom: Napster, MP3, and the New Pioneers of Music.* Cambridge, Mass.: Perseus Publishing, 2001.

Bartlett, Michael. "Media Players Installed on 99% of US Home PCs." *Newsbytes*, January 22, 2001.

Greene, Jay; Hamm, Steve; and Jack Ewing. "Rob Glaser Is Racing Upstream." *BusinessWeek*, September 3, 2001. <http://www.businessweek.com/magazine/content/01_36/b3747602.htm> (June 7, 2002).

Mowrey, Mark A. "Streaming Bleeds Cash." *The Industry Standard*, September 25, 2000. <http://www.thestandard.com/article/0,1902,18745,00.html> (June 7, 2002).

Pidgeon, Billy; Hertzberg, Robert; Sinnreich, Aram; and Seamus McAteer. "Streaming Video: Effective Deployment Necessitates Contextual Integration." *Jupiter Vision Report*, October 18, 2000.

Poon, Theresa V. "What's Next for Streaming Media?" *The Industry Standard*, February 14, 2001. <http://www.thestandard.com/article/0,1902,22225,00.html> (June 7, 2002).

Richtel, Matt. "Microsoft Aims at RealNetworks in Media-Player Software Duel." *The New York Times*, January 10, 2000, p. C1.

Rothenberg, Randall. "Rob Glaser, Moving Target." *Wired* 7.08, August 1999. <http://www.wired.com/wired/archive/7.08/glaser.html> (June 7, 2002).

ViewCast Corporation. "Streaming Media Guide." 1999. <http://www.atlanticomtech.com/InfoCenter1/PDF_Files/Solutions_Video/streamingGuide.pdf> (June 7, 2002).

Further Reading

Barboza, David. "Broadcast.com Soars in an Opening-Day Frenzy." *The New York Times*, July 18, 1998, p. D1.

Harmon, Amy. "RealNetworks Goes After Bigger Piece of Media Library Pie." *The New York Times*, June 20, 2001, p. C2.

House Judiciary Committee, Subcommittee on Courts, Intellectual Property and the Internet. "Testimony of Rob Glaser, Chairman and CEO of RealNetworks, Inc." May 17, 2001. <http://www.house.gov/judiciary/glaser_051701.htm> (June 7, 2002).

Ketchum, Bob. "A Timeline of Audio/Video Technology." *Robin's Video Web Site*, c. 1997. <http://penny100.home.mindspring.com/info/timeline.htm> (June 7, 2002).

Lohr, Steve. "Ally or Foe? A Complaint on Microsoft." *The New York Times*, July 24, 1998, p. D1.

——. "Real Networks Hopes New Streaming Software Will Open Up Medium." *New York Times*, July 13, 1998, p. D3.

Mann, Charles C. "The Heavenly Jukebox." *The Atlantic*, September 2000. <http://www.theatlantic.com/issues/2000/09/mann.htm> (June 7, 2002).

Mewton, Conrad. *All You Need to Know About Music & the Internet Revolution.* London, England: Sanctuary Publishing, 2001.

Packer, Randall, and Ken Jordan, eds. *Multimedia: From Wagner to Virtual Reality.* New York: W. W. Norton, 2001.

Samuels, Edward. *The Illustrated Story of Copyright.* New York: Thomas Dunne Books/St. Martin's Press, 2000.

Sinnreich, Aram; Brooks, Dylan; and Marissa Gluck. "Online Music Radio: Luring Listeners as Worlds Collide." *Jupiter Vision Report*, December 20, 2000.

Related Topics

Broadband; Compression; Digital Music; Gates, William H., III; MP3; Multimedia; QuickTime

— Kevin Featherly

Sutherland, Ivan

1938–

Computer Graphics Pioneer

Ivan Sutherland has been credited as the father of computer graphics, and has made significant contributions to virtual reality (VR), augmented reality (AR), 3D representations and simulation, computer-aided design (CAD), graphics hardware, integrated-circuit design, and robotics. His Sketchpad program, years ahead of its time, provided a new way of interfacing with computers, and influenced engineers for years to come. He is presently a vice president and research fellow at Sun Microsystems.

Sutherland had the distinction of being one of the earliest students to enter the Carnegie Institute of Technology (now Carnegie-Mellon University) as an undergraduate having already gained some programming experience. When he was a teenager, the Sutherland family was lent a computer called SIMON by its inventor, Edmund Berkeley. SIMON was arguably the first true personal electronic computer. Programming this machine entailed creating a machine code in punched tape, which was then fed through the computer. The young Sutherland wrote a program that allowed the computer to perform division—a significant programming task at the time.

Sutherland went on to earn a bachelors degree at the Carnegie Institute of Technology in 1959, followed by a masters degree from the California Institute of Technology in 1960, and a Ph.D. in electrical engineering from the Massachusetts Institute of Technology (MIT) in 1963.

At MIT, Sutherland studied under Claude Shannon, one of the originators of information theory, and became interested in the idea of computer graphics. His dissertation described a basic drawing program that he called Sketchpad. Sketchpad was important not only in making use of computer-generated graphics, but also in changing the way that people could interact with a computer. Using a light pen, a user could touch and move points, and the computer would respond by straightening lines and curves to correct for any small mistakes, or by offering pop-up menus. This use of a pointing device and graphic feedback would open the door for the graphical user interfaces (GUIs) that we use today, and served as a strong influence on later pioneers in computer interaction like Alan Kay and Douglas Engelbart.

At a meeting on interactive graphics organized by the Advanced Research Projects Agency (ARPA), Sutherland was asked to give a talk on his research. J. C. R. Licklider, who would come to be known as one of the originators of large-scale computer networking, was so impressed by Sutherland's research that he arranged for him to work as an ARPA administrator after graduation. After a short stint at the National Security Agency, Sutherland spent two years working for ARPA, overseeing projects and distributing a sizable amount of funding.

In 1966, Sutherland joined the faculty at Harvard University. With the help of Robert Sproull, he designed the first head-mounted display (HMD), a display screen mounted inside a helmet that changed perspective as the user's head moved. Although displays had been mounted in helmets before, Sutherland was the first to use them to display computer-generated images, wire-frame models in three dimensions that were produced using computing hardware designed specifically for the project. There was a pole mounted between the helmet and the ceiling, used to track head movements, and this led to the device being nicknamed the Sword of Damocles. Although it would be nearly two decades before this work would be advanced by others, Sutherland's system is considered to be the first primitive example of VR. Since the images could be traced onto semi-transparent lenses, giving the illusion of simulated objects existing in real space, this is also seen as the first AR system.

Along with University of Utah professor David C. Evans, Sutherland founded Evans & Sutherland in 1968, a company that continues to be at the leading edge of computer-based simulation. In 1976, with Carver Mead, he helped found the computer-science department at the California Institute of Technology, where he introduced elements of circuit design to the curriculum. In 1980, Sutherland began a consulting partnership with his brother Bert and Robert Sproull, which was eventually acquired by Sun Microsystems. His current work is in computer architecture and asynchronous processors.

Sutherland's "side project" since the late 1970s has been legged robots. He has built a six-legged walking robot large enough to carry a human, among other devices. While the robot, nicknamed the Trojan Cockroach, was functional, Sutherland found that the most important outcome of the project was the conclusion that large devices would better function with four or fewer legs.

Having received the Turing award from the Association of Computing Machinery (the computer-science equivalent of a Nobel Prize) in 1988, as well as the Von Neumann Medal from the Institute of Electrical and Electronic Engineers, an award from the Smithsonian, the Pioneers award from the Electronic Frontier Foundation, and numerous other awards, Sutherland is justifiably regarded as one of the central figures in the development of computers. He says that he chooses projects that seem simple and that interest him, and many have noted that he does groundbreaking work only to leave the details to later researchers. This ability to find and solve interesting problems, including those that others have not even recognized as problems, has made Sutherland an invaluable part of computing history.

Selected Works

Raibert, Marc, and Ivan Sutherland. "Machines that Walk." *Scientific American*, January 1983, pp. 44–53.

Sutherland, Ivan. *A Walking Robot*. Pittsburgh, Pa.: The Marcian Chronicles, 1983.

———. "Computer Displays." *Scientific American*, June 1970, pp. 56–81.

Bibliography

Barfield, Woodrow, and Thomas A. Furness III. *Virtual Environments and Advanced Interface Design*. New York: Oxford University Press, 1995.

Evans & Sutherland. "About E&S: History." <http://www.es.com/about_eands/history/index.asp> (April 12, 2002).

Frenkel, Karen. "An Interview with Ivan Sutherland." *Communications of the ACM*, June 1989.

Rheingold, Howard. *Tools for Thought: The History and Future of Mind-Expanding Technology.* Cambridge, Mass.: MIT Press, 2000.

Sun Microsystems. "Profile: Ivan Sutherland, Sun Fellow and VP of Sun Microsystems." <http://www.sun.com/960710/feature3/ivan-profile.html> (April 12, 2002).

"Trailing Edge: Simple Simon." *Technology Review*, March 2001. <http://www.technologyreview.com/articles/trailing0301.asp> (April 12, 2002).

Further Reading

Pimentel, Ken, and Kevin Teixeira. *Virtual Reality: Through the New Looking Glass.* New York: Intel/Windcrest, 1993.

Related Topics

Computer Graphics; Engelbart, Douglas; Graphical User Interface; Interface; Kay, Alan; Robotics; Shannon, Claude; Sketchpad; Virtual Reality

— *Alexander Halavais*

Synchrony and Asynchrony

Synchrony is the occurrence of events at the same time, while asynchrony is the occurrence of events at different times. When used in connection with media, synchrony refers to simultaneous communication, while asynchrony refers to communication interspersed over a period of time.

When human beings first began to communicate verbally, their interaction had to take place face-to-face, or at least within shouting distance. One of the primary reasons for the invention of communications media was so that people could send messages across long distances, to people living in other cities. But communications media also extended interaction through time. Laws could be written on stone tablets in one century, and still read in the next. Plato could put his thoughts down on papyrus, and students could read them hundreds, even thousands of years later.

Many early philosophers were concerned about asynchrony, since communicating across space and time meant a marked decrease in the level of interaction. When Socrates spoke with people face-to-face, the interaction was very rich: Questions could be asked and answered, and nonverbal communication was possible. But when students read Plato's works in other towns or centuries, they could not ask Plato what he meant, nor could Plato engage them in dialogue. The lack of feedback when communicating across space and time led many to question whether new media were actually an improvement.

For centuries, communication was tied to physical transportation—sending messages across space took time. But the invention of electronic media meant that one no longer had to travel to send a message; instead, it became possible to transmit messages electronically, almost instantaneously, to anywhere in the world.

With these new media, the distinction between synchrony and asynchrony has begun to blur. Telephones, for example, are normally used for synchronous interaction, but they can be augmented by answering machines that allow messages to be recorded and delivered at a later time. Televisions can create the illusion of displacing time with the use of a video recorder. When online, we can have faster-than-synchronous communication, since information can be downloaded faster than it can be read or viewed. Chat rooms are an even more bizarre blend of synchrony and asynchrony, wherein one user's comment and another's immediate reply might be separated in the flow of text by the comments of several others. While one user is typing a message, other users are typing theirs; by the time one finishes writing a response to one person, four other people could have sent messages in reply to previous messages. With new media, time does not necessarily adhere to the seemingly "linear" constraints of either face-to-face conversation or early media.

There are advantages and disadvantages to both synchrony and asynchrony. With synchronous communication, as already noted, the amount of interaction and feedback is very high. However, because of the speed of give-and-take in synchronous communication, people often speak before they are really ready, and may not listen carefully to others; the interaction may deteriorate into an argument. With an asynchronous interface such as email, communicators don't have to reply immediately; they can think about the message for a while, and reply when they're ready. The lack of nonverbal communication can cause confusion, but the ability to think through and carefully compose an answer can be an advantage.

Some of the less obvious but extremely significant effects on communication occur when people mistakenly assume that their interaction is synchronous. For example, video conferencing over the Internet appears to be synchronous. However, there is a small delay between one user speaking and the other user hearing.

This means that turn-taking, which depends in large part on timing, is very difficult. When speaking face-to-face, we often begin our turn right after the other person has finished. But with video conferencing, by the time we hear the other person pause, they may already have started speaking again; people often end up talking at the same time.

Being slightly out of synchronization alters conversation in other significant ways. Feedback is slightly delayed, which makes it difficult to respond accurately. Studies have shown that video conferences contain less humor (since humor requires precise timing) or other complex interactions than face-to-face conversations, and typically consist of long monologues instead of rapid exchanges. Out-of-synch communication also creates two cues that we normally associate with lying: delays in responding to a question, and unfilled pauses. Finally, the human face moves very quickly; some expressions last as little as 200 milliseconds. Video cameras on a very good Internet connection might manage to send 24 pictures every second, but with increased network traffic, the transmission might drop down to one frame per second or less, causing many of those micro-expressions to be lost. When engaged in a video conference, communicators often assume that since they can see the other person, they are accurately receiving all verbal and non-verbal messages; in fact, they typically are not.

With electronic media, the boundaries of synchronous and asynchronous communication are being stretched and merged in new ways. As humans continue to invent and use new media, it is likely that we will develop and learn new understandings of communication and interaction.

Bibliography

Bruce, V. "The Role of the Face in Face-to-Face Communication: Implications for Videotelephony." *Information Superhighways: Multimedia Users and Futures.* Stephen J. Emmott, ed. London: Academic Press, 1995; pp. 227–238.

Rafaeli, S., and J. Newhagen. "Why Communication Researchers Should Study the Internet: A Dialogue." *Journal of Communication,* vol. 46 (1996), pp. 4–13.

Tang, J., and E. Isaacs. "Studies of Multimedia-Supported Collaboration." *Information Superhighways: Multimedia Users and Futures.* Stephen J. Emmott, ed. London: Academic Press, 1995; pp. 123–160.

Zuckerman, M.; DePaulo, D.; and R. Rosenthal. "Verbal and Nonverbal Communication of Deception." *Advances in Experimental Social Psychology,* vol. 2 (1981), pp. 1–59.

Further Reading

Bender, John, and David E. Wellbery, eds. *Chronotypes: The Construction of Time.* Stanford, Calif.: Stanford University Press, 1991.

Innis, Harold. *The Bias of Communication.* Toronto: University of Toronto Press, 1991.

McLuhan, Marshall, and Bruce R. Powers. *The Global Village: Transformations in World Life and Media in the 21st Century.* New York: Oxford University Press, 1989.

Negroponte, Nicholas. *Being Digital.* New York: Knopf, 1995.

Related Topics

Broadband; Email; Interactivity; *Understanding Media: The Extensions of Man*; Videoconferencing

— *Norman Clark*

Systers

Systers is an online community for technical women in computer science. Initiated in 1987 by Anita Borg, the network now comprises more than 2,300 members in 38 countries, and is a project of the Institute for Women and Technology, located at the Xerox Palo Alto Research Center (PARC).

Systers started as a small electronic mailing list for 12 women who met at an academic conference on operating systems—hence, the name Systers. The purpose of Systers is to provide a women-only space where women in the technical field of computer science—whether academics, students, or those workers in government or industry—can meet and discuss issues of concern, from technical issues to workplace concerns. The membership rules of Systers state that "those in marketing, writing, or administrative positions within a computer company, or studying or writing about women in the computer industry, or just interested in the problems of female computer professionals" are not allowed to participate.

Borg has often been asked to justify the exclusion of men from her list, particularly since Systers is not limited solely to discussions of women's issues, but deals with professional and technical concerns. Borg justifies her decision to maintain a gender-segregated site by stating that since women in the computer sciences are both geographically dispersed and a "frequently individually isolated minority," they rarely have the chance to interact professionally. An all-female forum allows for mentoring; further, Borg says that "the likelihood that an underpowered minority is keeping otherwise inaccessible information from the large empowered majority . . . seems small indeed."

Debra Winter and Chuck Huff conducted a survey on Systers, and found that the segregated nature of the list enabled women who were unwilling to involve themselves in mixed-sex forums to interact with each other in a climate that they found more congenial. L. Jean Camp characterizes the topics discussed on Systers: "How to recruit more women to science. How to deal with illegal questions on interviews. . . . What to do about childcare at conferences. . . . What effect would the selection of C rather than LISP or Scheme for a first programming language have upon women in computer science?" Systers members in particular geographic locations have met and formed groups (e.g., Bay Area Systers), and separate electronic groups that first met on Systers have subsequently formed subgroups (Systers-Students, Systers-Academia, and Systers-Out).

Because growth in Systers has been exponential and the list is unmoderated, the community has adopted two rules for usage. The first states that responses to requests for advice be sent only to the sender of the email, who will then compile replies and summarize for the list. The second states that all content must relate to women in computer science. To further accommodate Systers' growth, a redesign of the infrastructure began in 2000.

Before design changes to Systers were instituted, a survey of the membership was undertaken. Its objectives were to assess Systers' demographic composition, needs, and preferences. Survey data revealed that long-time Systers are senior in industry and email-oriented, whereas younger women—students and those new to high-tech—are Web-oriented, and that active participation is motivated by job-related needs and problems.

Based on this information, the Systers redesign aims to provide a way for members to customize the information they receive, to offer both email and Web access, to ensure that core communications are available to members with low bandwidth and limited Web access (particularly for those Systers in developing countries), and to enhance the sense of community by matching experienced Systers with new members. The software re-engineering will be modeled on open-source projects. One of the changes will allow members to indicate which conversation threads are of interest to them, and to block those that are not of interest. The redesign will also allow Systers to read messages on the Web or in email formats, to create discussion summaries, and to access archives.

Bibliography

Borg, Anita. "Why Systers?" *Computing Research News*, 1993. <http://www.systers.org/keeper/whysys.html> (April 12, 2002).

Camp, L. Jean. "We Are Geeks, and We Are Not Guys: The Systers Mailing List." *wired_women: Gender and New Realities in Cyberspace*. Lynn Cherny and Elizabeth Reba Weise, eds. Seattle: Seal Press, 1996; pp. 114–121.

Systers. Web site. <www.systers.org> (April 12, 2002).

Winter, Debra, and Chuck Huff. "Adapting the Internet: Comments from a Women-Only Electronic Forum." *The American Sociologist*, Spring 1996, pp. 30–54.

Further Reading

Borg, Anita. "Models for Innovation Bring Women to the Table." *Computing Research News Online*, March 1999.

———. "What Draws Women to and Keeps Women in Computing?" *Women in Science and Engineering: Choices for Success* (*The Annals of the New York Academy of Sciences*, Vol. 869). Cecily Cannan Shelby, ed. New York: New York Academy of Sciences, 1999.

Related Topics

Access; Borg, Anita; Digital Divide; Gender and New Media; Xerox Palo Alto Research Center

— Leslie Regan Shade

Technological Determinism

Until the mid-1980s, technological determinism was the most popular and influential theory of the relationship between technology and society. Technological determinism views the development and diffusion of technology as developing independently of society, but producing societal effects. Scholars have since criticized this assumption, and a new, more nuanced theory of technology in society has been articulated, often referred to as the social shaping, or social constructivist, approach to technology.

Historically, the dominant approaches toward technology tended to focus on the ideology of technological determinism, where technology is perceived to be an autonomous, self-determining, and omniscient process. Such determinism treats technology as both panacea and scapegoat and, for instance, can detract from questions regarding power and political prestige. Many of these dominant discourses about technology (for example, popular media treatments) treat technology as something inevitable. This uncritical perspective is apolitical and often ahistorical; technological change is seen as something somehow divorced from societal concerns, or from the history and politics surrounding the development and deployment of a technology. It perceives technological development as a passive activity, and focuses on thinking about how people and societies should adapt to technology, rather than how people and societies can actively shape technology.

Historians of technology who adhered to this deterministic agenda tended to focus on either particular technological artifacts, or on the individuals who designed the technologies (for example, through biographies of brilliant inventors). No attention was paid to the influencing factors of socio-economics, ideology, or how particular members of society were affected by, or affecting, technological change. Critics of this philosophy worry that an objectification of technology can distract people from asking crucial questions regarding the varied social actors that contribute to the design, development, and diffusion of technology.

Subscribing to technological determinism can lead to an unwitting assumption that technological change causes social change.

Technological determinism assumes that technical progress follows a unified and unilinear path, with technological "progress" as the ultimate result. It also assumes that societies, individuals, and organizations must adapt themselves to technology, and that other societal and organizational outcomes will necessarily follow. The difficulty with assigning "effects" to technology, as determinists would have us do, is that not all of the "effects" are the same for everyone and every situation. Different social actors exhibit varying levels of interpretation in how they design, conceive, or expropriate technologies.

Futuristic scenarios for communication technologies provide a good example of technologically determinist discourse. Many of the technologies were heralded as signaling a revolution in social applications, leading to widespread social change. For instance, early pronouncements on the telegraph assumed that global peace would transpire after its advent, as everyone would be "linked up." Another example of technological determinist theorizing can be found in early "information superhighway" discourse in both media and governmental policy statements, which positioned the Internet as a necessary technology for economic competitiveness, social edification, and job creation. This was also extended to proclamations that the Internet could connect and revive dispersed communities in a sympathetic global village.

An example of technological determinist theorizing on reproduction can be found in the discourse that positions medical and technical progress in reproductive technology as portending more equity for women. For example, the birth-control pill has been extolled for promoting the 1960s sexual revolution, and for allowing more women to participate in the workforce. But these simplistic assertions detract from more complex explanations, emanating from a rapidly changing socio-cultural and political-economic milieu.

The uncritical position that technological determinism assumes lends itself to the technological imperative—the stance that one cannot retreat from technological development, since so much, in terms of both financial and ideological capital, has been invested in the future of such technology. The determination to continue developing nuclear energy, rather than designing alternative energy resources, serves as an example of this trajectory.

To counteract the pervasiveness of technological determinism, recent social studies of technology have been useful in delineating the myriad social actors that shape technological change. The research imperatives of social constructivism, or the social shaping of technology, concentrate on the effects of society on technology, rather than on the effects of technology on society. An example of this can be found in the 1992 study by Claude Fischer on the development of the telephone in the United States, where he recommends that studies of emergent technologies consider the social uses that individuals make of the technology, its effect on their everyday lives, and the change in social structure resulting from the collective use and response to a technology. In Fischer's social history of the telephone, he stresses the agency of consumers, notably women and farmers, in adapting the technology of the telephone for myriad social uses, against the predisposed business imperatives of the vendors.

A social-shaping examination of technological systems places an emphasis on the social factors that shape technological change, departing from dominant approaches toward technology that typically study the effect or impact of technology on society. Constructivism focuses on the diverse social alliances that lie behind technical choices, revealing that technology and society are mutually constitutive.

Bibliography

Feenberg, Andrew. *Questioning Technology*. London/ New York: Routledge, 1999.

Fischer, Claude S. *America Calling: A Social History of the Telephone to 1940*. Berkeley, Calif.: University of California Press, 1992.

MacKenzie, Donald, and Judy Wajcman, eds. *The Social Shaping of Technology*. Second edition. Buckingham, England/Philadelphia: Open University Press, 1999.

Smith, Merritt Roe, and Leo Marx, eds. *Does Technology Drive History?: The Dilemma of Technological Determinism*. Cambridge, Mass.: MIT Press, 1994.

Further Reading

Bijker, Wiebe, and John Law, eds. *Shaping Technology/Building Society: Studies in Sociotechnical Change*. Cambridge, Mass.: MIT Press, 1992.

Bijker, Wiebe E.; Hughes, Thomas P.; and Trevor J. Pinch. *The Social Construction of Technological Systems: New Directions in the Sociology and History of Technology*. Cambridge, Mass.: MIT Press, 1987.

Winner, Langdon. "Do Artifacts Have Politics?" *Daedalus* 109 (1980), pp. 121–36.

Related Topics

Gender and New Media; Joy, Bill; Kurzweil, Raymond; McLuhan, Marshall

— *Leslie Regan Shade*

Telecommuting

Telecommuting refers to the use of information and communication technologies (ICTs) to enable significant regular work to be done at sites away from a traditional workplace. Although telecommuting often takes place in a home-based location, it also takes place in a variety of flexible arrangements, including satellite and neighborhood centers. The term telework is often used interchangeably with telecommuting, and tends to be used in Britain, Canada, Europe, and Australia. Telework is a more encompassing term, and refers to the use of telecommunications to maintain work ties outside of the traditional office—at home, or on business or vacation travel.

Jack Nilles has been described as the father of telecommuting. Nilles coined the term in the 1970s in response to developing strategies for dealing with the energy crisis that the United States was experiencing— in particular, as a way to ameliorate the traffic congestion in southern California. Telecommuting is therefore seen as a mechanism to reduce traffic congestion and air pollution, and this is a key distinction between the conception of telecommuting in the United States and telework in other countries. Although Nilles' original predictions for the massive growth of telecommuting have not come to fruition, he is still an ardent advocate of it, predicting its exponential international growth (as many as 360 million telecommuters by 2030).

According to the International Telework Association and Council, an industry group in Washington, D.C., more than 16.5 million people in the United States, or about 12 percent of the work force, worked at home one or more days a month in 2001. Slightly more than 17 percent, or 2.8 million, of these were new teleworkers. There are 9.3 million U.S. teleworkers who telework at least one full day per week. Teleworkers are employed by small and medium sized companies, as well as large corporations.

Governments have been promoting telework, and many countries have official telework policies. For instance, Canada's Telework Policy has as its objective "to allow employees to work at alternative locations, thereby achieving a better balance between their work and personal lives, while continuing to contribute to the attainment of organizational goals." The U.S. federal government is hoping to increase the number of its workers that telecommute, particularly in areas such as Washington, D.C., where traffic congestion is high. Telecommuting centers in D.C. suburbs are being created to accommodate eligible workers; however, telecommuting is not suitable for some workers who handle classified and highly sensitive materials.

While both telecommuting and telework assume a dependence on ICTs, there are many variables in the nature of the work, including the location of the telework; the proportion of time spent telecommuting; and the relationship of the teleworker to the employer (employee, contractor).

Telecommuting has been increasingly promoted as a workplace option with benefits for both the employer and the employee. To attract and retain employees in a tight labor market, many companies have been offering flexible work arrangements as a key perk that helps to both recruit new employees and retain existing staff. For the employer, telecommuting is attractive because it promotes organizational flexibility, reduces the cost of finding office space in high-cost and crowded locales, and enhances customer service. Employers can ensure that the workforce is happier and more productive, and can hire the best people for the job, regardless of their home location. For the employee, telecommuting can be attractive because it reduces commute time and other costs (such as clothing and meals), provides a better balance of work and family life, increases productivity, and benefits workers with specific disabilities.

Disadvantages of telework for employers include a loss of managerial control, decreased organizational flexibility, offsite technical problems, and reduced face-to-face contact. For employees, the disadvantages include isolation and loneliness because of a lack of face-to-face contact; increased surveillance of activities; reduced access to office equipment, services, and administrative support; a less conducive work environment; and a blurring between home and work environments that can lead to work intensification and workaholism.

Many companies have set up satellite offices, where employees share desks ("hoteling") or telework in drop-in centers. Drop-in centers provide employees with a desk, a computer workstation, a telephone, administrative support, and parking. Just as in a hotel, employees make reservations, check in, and check out.

As the Internet becomes more ubiquitous, more people will use it to increase the efficacy of telecommuting, and for occasional telework. Because many forms of work are not suited for telework, it will not become a social or economic imperative. However, a social and legal framework for telework needs to be developed that considers the best conditions for teleworkers and respects them in their role as workers. An example of such a framework is the European Union–wide agreement on guidelines for telework in the commerce sector. Twelve principles for telework have been elaborated, including those applying to health and safety issues at the home site. The principles state that telework should be voluntary; suitable to the individual, the work, and the environment; and subject to the appropriate collective rights agreements that apply to other employees. They also state that all equipment needed for the job will be provided, installed, and maintained by the employer, while additional costs accrued by teleworkers to meet their job duties will be considered by the employer. Finally, in order to decrease the isolating effects of telework, teleworkers should have appropriate access to company information, as well as opportunities to meet with other colleagues on a regular basis.

Bibliography

EuroCommerce and UNI-Europa. European Agreement on Guidelines on Telework in Commerce. <http://www.telework-mirti.org/uni.doc> (April 12, 2002).

The International Telework Association & Council (ITAC). Web site. <http://www.telecommute.org/> (April 12, 2002).

Jackson, Paul J., and Jos M. van der Wielen, eds. *Teleworking: International Perspectives—From Telecommuting to the Virtual Organisation*. London: Routledge, 1998.

JALA International. Jack Nilles home page. <http://www.jala.com/> (April 12, 2002).

Nilles, Jack M. *Managing Telework: Strategies for Managing the Virtual Workforce*. New York: John Wiley & Sons, 1998.

Further Reading

Electronic Commerce and Telework Trends (ECaTT). Benchmarking Progress on Electronic Commerce and New Methods of Work. 2001. <http://www.ecatt.com/ecatt/> (April 12, 2002).

InnoVisions Canada and the Canadian Telework Association (CTA). Web site. <http://www.ivc.ca/> (April 12, 2002).

International Workplace Studies Program, Cornell University. Web site.

<http://iwsp.human.cornell.edu/default.html>
(April 12, 2002).

Related Topics

Distance Learning; Videoconferencing

— *Leslie Regan Shade*

Telemedicine

Telemedicine refers to health care or health education that is transferred to remote locations via computer networks, using multimedia applications. Telemedicine is a component of the wider realm of telehealth, which is concerned with the delivery of health information over the Internet, and with cooperative educational ventures among health practitioners. Many predict that, with developments in telecommunications such as broadband, lowered technology costs, and the widespread diffusion of the Internet, telemedicine will continue to expand over the course of the twenty-first century, influencing the delivery of medical care throughout the world. However, evolving ethical and policy issues, such as privacy, will need to be resolved before telemedicine is widely adapted.

According to the American Telemedicine Association, telemedicine utilizes information and communications technologies (ICTs) to transfer medical information for diagnosis, therapy, and education. Telemedicine information may include medical images, live two-way audio and video, patient medical records, or output data from medical devices. Interactions between medical practitioner and patient (or between medical practitioners operating remotely) can utilize two-way live audio and video transmissions. For instance, patient-monitoring data can be transmitted from the home to a remote clinic, or a patient medical file can be transmitted from a primary-care provider to a specialist in another location.

In the United States, the most popular uses of telemedicine are teleradiology, patient monitoring, and diagnosis for residents in correctional facilities. Teleradiology is the transmission of medical images, such as X rays or MRIs, to a radiologist in another location for interpretation. Patient monitoring allows patients to remain at home while data is delivered to the remote health professional through the telephone. Currently, cardiac, fetal, and pulmonary monitoring are the most widely used telemedicine applications. Telemedicine is also widely

In December 2001, Dr. Anthony diBartolomeo examines a patient's arthritic hands via the Mountaineer Doctor Television (MDTV) telemedicine program. (AP Photo/Dale Sparks)

used for those in correctional facilities, due to safety concerns and to the costs of transporting prisoners to remote facilities.

One of the key impediments to the widespread use of telemedicine in the United States is in payment for services, as not all telemedical services are covered by Medicare or private insurance plans. State medical licenses that restrict where physicians may perform their services are also an impediment.

Telemedicine initiatives have been accelerating internationally. Scandinavia, and especially Norway, was one of the first regions to widely deploy telemedicine. Other projects have been established in Europe (France, the United Kingdom), Japan, Australia, and Canada. Increasingly, telemedicine applications have also been promoted for developing countries.

However, the public is not widely aware of telemedicine. A recent Canadian survey about knowledge of and attitudes toward telemedicine, conducted by PricewaterhouseCoopers, revealed that fewer than one-third (29.0 percent) of respondents knew that videoconferencing could be used to conduct medical tests and make diagnoses, and that only 26.1 percent of respondents were familiar with the concept of dispensing medical advice and assessments via videoconferencing.

New developments in ICTs will undoubtedly encourage a more widespread use of telemedicine. However, technological developments and new telemedicine applications also create new policy issues. The next-generation Internet, utilizing video, voice, text, and still images, will create new telemedicine applications such as online consultations, prescription purchases, and health-administrative transactions. Alongside these new applications, however, arise security concerns and jurisdictional issues concerning the right to practice medicine across state or even country borders. New developments in digitization (smart cards, digital medical libraries, compressed video and images, imbedded chips, and so on) create technical issues such as the need for standards and interoperability. Wireless or mobile computing allow for prescription writing, clinical documentation, lab-test management, and alert messaging/communication, but also heighten concerns over security, interoperability, and bandwidth needs.

Other ethical and policy issues related to telemedicine include protection of appropriate entities (medical practitioners and clinics) from undue liability arising out of the use of telemedicine, and maintenance of patient privacy and confidentiality in both the transmission of medical information and the electronic storage of personal medical information.

For telemedicine to be successful, it is imperative that clinical and technical standards and guidelines be developed. Technical standards include interoperability and interconnection. A uniform set of communication standards, DICOM (Digital Imaging and Communications in Medicine), has been established by the American College of Radiology and the National Electronic Manufacturers Association. Clinical standards include protocols such as preliminary scheduling procedures, consult procedures, and telemedicine equipment-operation procedures, and telecommunications transmission specifications. Professional associations such as the American Telemedicine Association, the American Nurses Association, and the American Psychological Association are increasingly adopting such clinical practice protocols.

Reliance on telecommunications networks and the Internet makes the privacy of personal information vulnerable to security breaches. In the United States, The Health Insurance Portability and Accountability Act of 1996 (HIPAA) was passed in order to protect personal health information, but critics contend that it does not effectively protect online health information, such as that presented on proliferating health-oriented Web sites.

With an aging U.S. population, telemedicine might become more popular in the next few decades. Equity of use remains an issue, though, as digital-divide issues could persist in who has access to telemedicine applications, because of both socio-economic and geographical (rural vs. urban) factors. The real challenge for telemedicine will not be in the development and deployment of the technology, but rather in reconciling the complex legal, jurisdictional, privacy/security, and quality issues that telemedicine raises.

Bibliography

Health Privacy Project, Institute for Health Care Research and Policy, Georgetown University. Web site. <http://www.healthprivacy.org/> (June 7, 2002).

Martin, Shelly. "Public Ignorant About Telemedicine, Survey Finds." *Canadian Medical Association Journal,* vol. 164, no. 7 (2001), p. 1,035.

Office for the Advancement of Telehealth, U.S. Department of Health and Human Services. "2001 Report to Congress of Telemedicine." <http://telehealth.hrsa.gov/pubs/report2001/main.htm> (June 7, 2002).

Turisco, Fran, and Joanna Case. "Wireless and Mobile Computing." California HealthCare Foundation, 2001.

<http://ehealth.chcf.org/view.cfm?section=Industry& itemID=4382> (June 7, 2002).

Further Reading

The American Telemedicine Association. Web site. <http://www.atmeda.org/> (June 7, 2002).

Bareiss, Walter. "Telemedicine in South Dakota: A Cultural Studies Approach." *New Media & Society,* vol. 3, no. 3 (2001), pp. 327–55.

Maheu, Marlene M.; Allen, Ace; and Pamela Whitten. *eHealth, Telehealth, and Telemedicine: A Comprehensive Guide to Start-Up and Success.* San Francisco, Calif.: Jossey-Bass, 2001.

Telemedicine Information Exchange. Web site. <http://tie.telemed.org/> (June 7, 2002).

Wootton, Richard. "Telemedicine." *British Medical Journal,* vol. 323, no. 7,312 (September 8, 2001), p. 557.

Related Topics

Videoconferencing

— *Leslie Regan Shade*

Telephony

While the term telephony usually conjures images of point-to-point communication by voice, telephony actually describes a related set of technologies: telephones, switchboards, and telecommunication networks. Widely taken for granted in modern society, telephony is actually the backbone of modern telecommunications.

A telephone has a small microphone in the mouthpiece that converts the user's voice into electricity, which is then passed through the telephone network and converted back into sound for the person at the other end. As the number of users of a telephone system increases, it becomes more complex. Switchboards, first used in the 1880s, allowed all telephone users to be connected up to a central station. There, operators would connect one phone line with another, enabling users to talk. This process was automated in the early twentieth century, first through dial telephones and later through touch-tone phones. Today, phone companies use digital switching to route calls.

For promotional and practical purposes, it made sense that any point on the telephone system ought to be able to reach any other point in the system. On this basis, American Telephone and Telegraph (AT&T) appealed for and received monopoly status from the U.S. government for the better part of the twentieth century. In exchange, it had to follow the postal system model of "universal service," where anyone who wanted to be hooked into the phone system could be. In practice, the expense of telephony prevented most Americans from having a phone in their own home until after World War II. Today, about 97 percent of American homes have active telephone service.

Some key twentieth-century ideas about communication were originally developed from the phone system. In 1909, the N.W. Ayer advertising agency ran a series of ads for long-distance telephony (then a new technology), calling telephone networks "highways of information." The "information superhighway" moniker for the Internet is clearly a play on that phrase. More abstractly, mathematical studies of telephone-system circuits eventually grew into cybernetic communication theory. AT&T was mainly interested in getting its phone system to work better. How much noise could be present on a line before people could no longer understand one another? What was the best way of routing and managing the huge volume of calls passing through the telephone network? From these basic questions, mathematicians like Claude Shannon and Norbert Wiener developed cybernetics as a "science" of information and control. Although cybernetics is no longer in wide use as an omnibus theory of communication, descriptions of communication as following a path from sender to receiver still bear the mark of the telephone system.

"Wireless telephony" was first used as a term to describe the broadcasting of voice by radio in the first decade of the twentieth century. Today, it encompasses the use of cellular telephony and other technologies that allow people to take phones with them wherever they go. Although we think of it as telephony, wireless telephony is actually more like a form of radio. Wireless companies purchase a group of frequencies in the radio spectrum; rather than assigning a phone a permanent frequency, wireless companies make use of electronic and digital routing technologies to automatically and temporarily assign frequencies when a user wishes to make a call. As users move through a wireless service area (for instance, driving across town in a car), the frequencies to which their phones are assigned may change. This happens quickly and quietly enough to escape user notice. Once a phone call is being picked up by a wireless company's radio towers, it can be routed into a regular telephone network.

Although wireless telephony has some of the disadvantages of radio, such as interference and poor reception, the mobility of the phones has been their big selling point in developed countries. In countries without an elaborate and preexisting telecommunications infrastructure, wireless telephony has the added advantage of allowing individuals to get telephone service without having to live in neighborhoods that are wired for telephone use, or even for electricity.

Throughout its history, the telephone system has provided the backbone for a whole host of communication technologies. Before the invention of satellite technology, national networking of radio was made possible by the use of leased phone lines. The networking of television also relied on technologies like microwave relay stations and coaxial cable, which were originally developed to allow more bandwidth in telephone transmission.

Today, the telephone system is struggling to cope with the massive proliferation of telecommunication technologies and practices. In addition to wireless communication, the telephone system also provides the infrastructure for fax machines to communicate with one another, for automatic teller machines (ATMs) to send and receive back-account data, and for millions of Internet users to dial into their accounts from home or work.

From its beginnings to the present day, the telephone has been an important technology for business and for sociability. It has helped to break down barriers between private and public space, and has become a staple of modern life.

Bibliography

Lubar, Steven. *Infoculture: The Smithsonian Book of Information Age Inventions.* Boston: Houghton-Mifflin, 1993.

Martin, Michèle. *Hello, Central?: Gender, Technology, and Culture in the Formation of Telephone Systems.* Montreal/Buffalo: McGill-Queen's University Press, 1991.

Schement, Jorge R. "Beyond Universal Service: Characteristics of Americans Without Telephones, 1980-1993." Communications Policy Working Paper #1, 1995. <http://www.benton.org/Library/Universal/Working1/working1.html> (April 12, 2002).

Shannon, Claude E., and Warren Weaver. *Mathematical Theory of Communication.* Urbana: University of Illinois Press, 1949.

Wiener, Norbert. *The Human Use of Human Beings: Cybernetics and Society.* Boston: Houghton Mifflin, 1954.

Further Reading

Brooks, John. *Telephone: The First Hundred Years.* New York: Harper and Row, 1976.

Douglas, Susan. *Inventing American Broadcasting, 1899–1922.* Baltimore: Johns Hopkins University Press, 1987.

Marvin, Carolyn. *When Old Technologies Were New: Thinking About Electric Communication in the Late Nineteenth Century.* New York: Oxford University Press, 1988.

Rakow, Lana F. *Gender on the Line: Women, the Telephone, and Community Life.* Urbana: University of Illinois Press, 1992.

Related Topics

Cellular Telephony; Cyberculture; Shannon, Claude; von Neumann, John; Wireless Networks

— Jonathan Sterne

TinyMUD

MUDs (multi-user dungeons or dimensions) are software programs that allow multiple users to interact with each other. Representing an important step in MUD program development, TinyMUD was developed in 1988 by James Aspnes, then a student at Carnegie-Mellon University. TinyMUD ran on the UNIX operating system (OS), and the growing use of that OS, especially in university computer-science departments, contributed to TinyMUD's rapid rise in popularity.

Inspired by the original MUD1, written in 1980 by Roy Trubshaw and Richard Bartle, Aspnes created TinyMUD as an experiment in game design. Expected to remain active only a couple of weeks, TinyMUD in fact lasted approximately nine months, but its influence on MUDs in general far outlived that short span. All of the many social MUDs and MOOs (MUDs, object-oriented) currently online trace their roots back to Aspnes' student project.

In contrast to most previous MUD programs, TinyMUD did not keep a point score, and therefore had no game-related hierarchy of players. TinyMUD did have a sort of economy based on "pennies," which could be found while exploring the text-based virtual environment. Players were required to use these pennies in order to perform certain commands that taxed the program's capabilities or expanded the database. This "economy" helped keep the program from crashing (although it did not work particularly well in many other ways). Unlike "combat" MUDs, TinyMUD also did not allow characters to kill each other. There was a "kill" command, but it sent a character back to its home base, as opposed to disconnecting it from the game. With these changes, Aspnes sought to create a game that could continue indefinitely, and that emphasized programming and exploration rather than hack-and-slash-style combat.

TinyMUD allowed all users to create extensions to the database, programming objects and rooms that other users could explore and interact with. This enabled participants to experiment with MUD programming and virtual reality creation. Many building practices, which later became famous (or infamous) on MUDs, began on TinyMUD. For instance, many mudders choose as a first building project to duplicate a familiar real-world environment, such as their dorm room or (for the ambitious or obsessive) their entire university. In subsequent years, entire MUDs have followed this pattern. Two famous examples are LambdaMOO, based on a description of the house of its founder, Pavel Curtis; and MediaMOO, a MUD intended as a virtual meeting place for media researchers, patterned after the Media Lab at the Massachusetts Institute of Technology.

The term TinyMUD refers both to Aspnes' original MUD and to the program used to run it. Aspnes made the program available to other interested college students, and many other MUDs began using the TinyMUD program. To differentiate between the original TinyMUD and later MUDs using the TinyMUD program, mudders came to refer to the original as "TinyMUD Classic," or just "Classic." Mudders refer to those who had characters on Classic as "dinos" (from dinosaur), indicating their long-term mudding status. The term dino now generally refers to anyone who has been mudding for a long time.

Aspnes announced the opening of TinyMUD to friends and acquaintances at Carnegie-Mellon in August 1989, and word spread from there through postings on USENET newsgroups, listservs, etc. By early 1990, hundreds of people had found TinyMUD. With so many people contributing new objects to the program's database, the program became unmanageable and unstable. Following a program crash at the end of April 1990, Aspnes announced that the database had grown too large, and that he would no longer continue running it. Classic participants scattered to the many other similar MUDs that were available by that time. While most of these MUDs no longer exist, DragonMUD, begun in November 1989, still runs on a heavily revised version of Aspnes' original code. Many people currently participating on DragonMUD began there in 1989 and the early 1990s, demonstrating both the continuing appeal of MUDs as a social environment and the lasting ties that some people form with their fellow mudders.

Although users continued to build rooms and puzzles for their fellow mudders to explore, hanging out and chatting almost immediately became the main activity on TinyMUD. In this regard also, TinyMUD set patterns and contributed cultural references that would live on for years in the mudding subculture. In particular, TinyMUD has left its mark on online language. "Tiny" has become a prefix to indicate the existence of something online or in virtual reality, rather than in "real life." Julian Dibbell followed this convention in titling his 1998 book about his adventures on LambdaMOO *My Tiny Life*. Probably the most prevalent example of this terminology is "tinysex," which has moved beyond MUDs to refer to sexual activities, especially text-based, on various online forums. Other terms such as "tinyjerk"—referring to a person who behaves badly online—have tended to stay within the MUD community.

Bibliography
Burka, Lauren P. "The MUDdex." 1993. <http://www.apocalypse.org/pub/u/lpb/muddex> (July 15, 2002).
Dibbell, Julian. *My Tiny Life: Crime and Passion in a Virtual World*. New York: Henry Holt, 1998.

Further Reading
Crane, John. "DragonMUD: About_Us." 2000. <http://dragonmud.org/aboutus.html> (July 15, 2002).
Reid, Elizabeth. "Cultural Formations in Text-Based Virtual Realities." Master's thesis, University of Melbourne, 1994. <http://www.aluluei.com> (July 15, 2002).

Related Topics
LambdaMOO; MUDs and MOOs; USENET; Virtual Community

— *Lori Kendall*

Trademark

A trademark is a word, image, sign, symbol, or combination of these that identifies products and services, pointing to their origin or ownership. Since the legal right to use a trademark is reserved to its registered owner, the trademark serves as a legally protected guarantee of authenticity.

Trademarks announce that products and services come from one organization rather than another. Business firms, public-sector agencies, and non-profit organizations use them, as do universities and professional associations. Along with tangible products and services, trademarks identify the information products and virtual services of the knowledge economy. As ownership marks, they protect communications and property.

Trademarks are a central feature of contemporary life. They appear in every forum and medium, on every kind of object and artifact. A walk though any kind of shop or store reveals thousands of trademarked products, multiplied by the number of items in stock for several hundred thousand trademark impressions. While trademarks are present everywhere and all the time, they are so completely integrated into daily experience that most people hardly notice them.

The general trademark concept is simple. The industrial revolution made manufactured goods a common feature of daily life, and trademarks emerged to identify them.

Different marks have long been used to indicate identity, ownership, or origin. Ownership marks have been used for more than 5,000 years to identify animals in the fields and at market. The act of branding livestock gave us the term "brand" to describe trademarked products or services. Other forms of identity mark include heraldry and monograms.

Origination marks declared the origin of goods. These included ceramic marks, stonemasons' marks, hallmarks, printers' marks, watermarks, gold- and silversmith marks, and furniture marks. The first true trademarks were stamped into the mass-manufactured oil lamps of the Roman Empire.

In legal terms, a trademark is a mark used by a legal person to identify goods offered to the public, distinguishing them from goods offered by other persons. Goods include services as well as products. A person in legal terms may be an individual, a corporation, a non-profit corporation, a government, a government agency, an unincorporated association, or any legal or commercial entity. In every case, the trademark is used to distinguish goods from those offered by another legal entity.

There are many kinds of trademarks. Most are words, names, symbols, or some combination of these in a specific form. The name Coca-Cola written in its characteristic script, the distinct word Coke, and the special bottle shape are the world's best-known trademarks. Others include the stylized IBM letters, the Nike swoosh, and the rainbow Apple with a bite missing.

Service marks identify services. McDonald's Golden Arches, the Red Cross and the Red Crescent, the Amazon.com logo, and the Merrill Lynch bull are service marks.

Certification marks guarantee geographic origin, material, quality, accuracy, or other characteristics. The controlled names of French wines, the Woolmark, guildhall marks for metals, and national manufacturing marks are certification marks. So are the TM and SM marks that protect trademarks and service marks.

The information economy has given rise to many new forms of trademark. Animated marks and domain names are common on the Web. Architectural trademarks such as the mansard roof identify Pizza Hut locations, and sound marks identify radio stations. One of the great business cases of the past half-century is the construction of the Absolut Vodka brand, a product built around the trademarked shape of the Absolut bottle.

The concept of trademark is still evolving for the digital-media environment. A central issue in any digital product is "look and feel." This is such a new area of law that the jurisdictions of trademark, patent, and copyright sometimes overlap. The Macintosh operating system, for example, affords many unique look and feel features that are protected by Apple as trademarked or patented property. Amazon.com has applied for patent rights on business-process concepts, while also seeking protection under patent law. In theory, digital-media software that produce artifacts or services with a special look and feel under a unique product name might well be protected under all three forms of intellectual property law.

The trademark concept has grown over the past three thousand years, to a point where it sometimes has a life of its own. A trademarked Wilson ball was Tom Hanks' co-star in the movie *Cast Away* (2000), and the FedEx company served as part of the supporting cast. Trademarks today have a far more complex social role than the marks of ancient Rome.

Bibliography

Arden, Thomas P. *Protection of Nontraditional Trademarks: Trademark Rights in Sounds, Scents, Colors, Motions, and Product Designs in the U.S.* New York: International Trademark Association, 2000.

Cristal, Lisa E., and Neals S. Greenfield, eds. *Trademark Law and the Internet.* New York: International Trademark Association, 1999.

Hamilton, Carl. *Absolut: Biography of a Bottle.* New York: Texere, 2000.

International Trademark Association (INTA). Web site. <http://www.inta.org/> (April 12, 2002).

Legal Information Institute, Cornell University Law School. "Trademark Law: An Overview." <http://www.law.cornell.edu/topics/trademark.html> (April 12, 2002).

Mollerup, Per. *Marks of Excellence.* London: Phaidon, 1997.

United States Patent and Trademark Office, an Agency of the United States Department of Commerce. Web site. <http://www.uspto.gov/> (April 12, 2002).

Further Reading

Aaker, David A. *Managing Brand Equity: Capitalizing on the Value of a Brand Name.* New York: Free Press, 1991.

Bryer, Lanning G., and Reese Taylor, eds. *2000 Trademark Handbook US and International,* Vol. II. New York: International Trademark Association, 2000.

Dyer, Gillian. *Early Printers' Marks.* London: Victoria and Albert Museum, 1962.

Firth, Raymond W. *Symbols, Public and Private.* London: Allen & Unwin, 1973.

Fletcher, Anthony L., and David J. Kera, eds. *2000 Trademark Handbook US and International,* Vol. I. New York: International Trademark Association, 2000.

Gagliarde, Pasquale, ed. *Symbols and Artifacts: Views of the Corporate Landscape.* Berlin/New York: W. de Gruyter, 1992.

International Trademark Association. "Model State Trademark Bill. An Act to Provide for the Registration and Protection of Trademarks." New York: International Trademark Association, 2000. <http://www.inta.org/policy/mstb.shtml> (April 12, 2002).

Legal Information Institute, Cornell University Law School. "GATT 1994 (1999–2000 ed.)" <http://www2.law.cornell.edu/cgi-bin/foliocgi.exe/GATT> (April 12, 2002).

National Conference of Commissioners on Uniform State Laws. "Revised Uniform Deceptive Trade Practices Act." 1966. <http://www.law.upenn.edu/bll/ulc/fnact99/1920_69/rudtpa66.htm> (April 12, 2002).

TrademarkTracker.com. Web site. <http://www.trademarktracker.com/> (April 12, 2002).

Related Topics

Copyleft; Copyright; Patent

— *Ken Friedman*

Tufte, Edward

1942–

Information Design Pioneer

Edward R. Tufte is professor emeritus of statistics and political science at Yale University. After studying statistics at Stanford University, he earned a doctorate in political science at Yale. He was always interested in visual phenomena; he began to paint on the day he completed his dissertation, and has been making art ever since.

Tufte's first book on graphic design was *The Visual Display of Quantitative Information,* which he published in 1983. It became a bestseller, and propelled Tufte to a level of public fame rarely achieved by statistics professors. In 1990, Tufte published *Envisioning Information*; in 1997, he published *Visual Explanations: Images and Quantities, Evidence and Narrative.*

Tufte's goals are to understand the way that information works and to develop principles for better information. He has been a seminal figure in the field of information design, which he approaches with a scientific rigor that enables the discovery and application of broad, general principles, in contrast to the cookbook approach generally used by designers.

Tufte approaches design using the analytic principles of science and computing. He is a rigorous thinker who respects the tools of design more than many designers do, bringing such tools as typography, color, vision, and layout to scientific data. He believes that the tools of graphic design are important to human knowledge and decision-making; his mission is to understand how these tools can be put to best use.

According to Tufte, *The Visual Display of Quantitative Information* is about pictures of numbers. *Envisioning Information* is about pictures of nouns, because maps, or aerial photographs, show nouns lying on the ground. *Visual Explanations: Images and Quantities, Evidence and Narrative* is about pictures of verbs; it considers graphs and models that show motion, dynamic systems, mechanics, and processes. Each book is richly illustrated with the information artifacts that Tufte describes, and each is designed as a model of the principles it presents.

Tufte's books also offer concise summaries of the principles that he has developed in studying information artifacts. For example, *Visual Display* offers nine points that summarize principles for communicating complex ideas clearly, precisely, and efficiently:

1. Excellent statistical graphs show the data.
2. They focus on substance rather than method or graphic technology.
3. They do not distort the data through content or visual presentation.
4. They present many numbers in a small space.
5. They make large data sets coherent.
6. They encourage visual comparison of different pieces of data.
7. They reveal data at several levels of detail, giving a broad overview while offering fine structure.
8. They serve a clear purpose; they describe, explore, tabulate, or decorate.
9. They are closely integrated with the statistical and verbal descriptions of the data sets they present.

Tufte's vision of excellence involves revealing relationships among data, among the factors that the data represent, and among the concepts that can be used to explore them. The concise, elegant presentation of significant relationships is at the core of Tufte's thinking. *Visual Display* demonstrates how to achieve it and what to avoid.

Using intelligent techniques to present information well is also the core issue of *Envisioning Information*. "Confusion and clutter are failures of design, not attributes of information," Tufte states. "And so the point is to find design strategies that reveal detail and complexity, rather than to fault the data for an excess of complication." Tufte's ideal designer is a thinker and a strategist.

Thinking also lies at the heart of Tufte's book, *Visual Explanations*. Thinking and explanation require us to understand and describe change. In order to explain much of what happens in the world, we must explain the dynamic relationships among the elements of any system, and we must understand the nature of causes and their effects. "To understand," Tufte writes, "is to know what cause provokes what effect, by what means, at what rate." This book is about how that knowledge should be represented.

The act of representing knowledge is the heart of Tufte's work. He explores how we should represent what we know in order to help others know and understand it. In so doing, he establishes a clear goal for design: using the science and art of representation to generate knowledge and insight. By contributing to better information artifacts, in print and on the Web, Edward Tufte's work makes the information age more informative by adapting information more effectively to the needs of information users.

Selected Works

Tufte, Edward R. *Data Analysis for Politics and Policy.* Englewood Cliffs, N.J.: Prentice-Hall, 1974.

———. *Envisioning Information.* Cheshire, Conn.: Graphics Press, 1990.

———. *Political Control of the Economy.* Princeton, N.J.: Princeton University Press, 1978.

———. *The Visual Display of Quantitative Information.* Cheshire, Conn.: Graphics Press, 1983.

———. *Visual Explanations: Images and Quantities, Evidence and Narrative.* Cheshire, Conn.: Graphics Press, 1997.

The Work of Edward Tufte and Graphics Press. Web site. <http://www.edwardtufte.com/330026927/tufte/index> (March 30, 2001).

Bibliography

Guterman, Jimmy. "Envisioning Interfaces." *Wired* 2.08, August 1994. <http://www.wired.com/wired/archive/2.08/tufte.html> (April 12, 2002).

Rosenberg, Scott. "The Data Artist: Chart-master Edward Tufte Finds Meaning in Numbers. Then He Shows How Good Graphs Can Save Lives." *Salon*, March 1997. <http://www.salon.com/march97/tufte970310.html> (April 12, 2002).

Further Reading

Henderson, Denise. *Information Design . . . For Real People.* McDonough, Ga.: Zipodee Publishing, 2001.

Tonfoni, Graziella. *Information Design: The Knowledge Architect's Toolkit.* Lanham, Md.: Scarecrow Press, 2002.

Related Topics

Computer Graphics; Graphical User Interface; Information Design; Interface

— *Ken Friedman*

Turing, Alan
1912–1954

Computer Scientist, Mathematician

Alan M. Turing's work on the hypothetical Turing machine, a programmable mechanical device for solving mathematical problems, laid the groundwork for computer science, and his Turing Test endures as a fundamental concept in artificial intelligence (AI). During World War II, Turing contributed to breaking Germany's Enigma code, aiding the Allies in defeating the Nazis.

Alan Turing was born in London on June 23, 1912. He attended public school, where he developed interests in mathematics, physics, and chemistry. Despite his keen curiosity and affinity for mathematics, Turing struggled with the classically focused curriculum.

He won a scholarship to Cambridge in 1931, and in 1935, during a lecture by the mathematician M. H. A. Newman, he was introduced to the *Entscheidungsproblem* (decision-making problem) of David Hilbert. The problem asked three questions: First, is mathematics complete, in the sense that every statement is either provable or disprovable? Second, is mathematics consistent, such that an untrue statement could not be arrived at through valid methods? Third, is mathematics decidable, such that there is a method that could be applied to any problem that will either prove or disprove it? Hilbert believed the answer to all three questions to be yes.

Kurt Gödel's Incompleteness Theorem had answered the first two questions, proving that formal arithmetic was necessarily incomplete, because there are assertions that are neither provable nor disprovable. Gödel also showed that arithmetic could not be proved consistent within its own terms. This left the third question, posed to Turing by Newman, of whether there could be a mechanical process that, when applied to any mathematical statement, could determine whether it was provable or not.

Turing took up this question, focusing specifically on the mechanical nature of computation. In 1936, he published "On Computable Numbers, with an Application to the *Entscheidungsproblem*." Recalling Babbage's Analytical Engine, Turing devised a hypothetical computer, which he called a Turing machine, that would perform a set of instructions without human aid. The machine consisted of an infinitely long tape and a scanning head that could read the contents of a frame and imprint symbols on the tape, like a typewriter. The head would follow a basic set of instructions based on what it read on each frame; these instructions included rewriting the contents of a frame and/or moving a certain number of frames in one direction or another. The head could also read the tape in different states, depending on its instructions, but given a complete set of instructions determining different states and the corresponding actions to be taken, the machine would work automatically. The specifics of the instruction sets and how the machine functioned are not so important as the implications of its functionality. Turing proved that a set of instructions could, theoretically, solve any solvable problem. Further, Turing theorized what he called a Universal Turing Machine, which encompassed all possible specific Turing machines. Its instruction sets were infinite, but its design and function were simple and proved adequate, hypothetically, to any logical problem that might be posed to it.

In essence, Turing created what would become the computer—a machine that, without human aid, can follow simple procedures to perform functions and solve problems. Using this theoretical machine, Turing answered the third part of the *Entscheidungsproblem*, proving that some problems were, in fact, undecidable; if a problem given to the machine results in an infinite computation, it cannot be proven that the machine will ever halt, therefore showing that the problem is not solvable.

During World War II, Turing worked for the British government to build code-breaking machines. The Germans employed a code system named Enigma, based on a machine that used interchangeable rotors, a keyboard, and an electric screen to generate coded messages. In 1941, through work done as part of the Ultra project headed by Turing, the British cut in half the number of ships lost to German U-boats. Throughout the following years, however, the Germans continually improved on the Enigma technology, so that incredible numbers of calculations per second were needed to effectively break the code. This led to the building of Colossus, an electronic digital computer that could calculate more than 5,000 Enigma keystrokes per second, giving the British a decisive intelligence edge over the Germans.

After the war, Turing worked for several years at the National Physical Laboratory and then at Manchester University on the construction of digital computers, which were then called Automatic Computing Engines and Automatic Digital Machines. In 1950, after making controversial comments about how computers would one day be intelligent, Turing published in 1950 an article called "Computer Machinery and Intelligence," a much anthologized piece that is often retitled, "Can Computers Think?" This piece detailed the Turing Test, a founding contribution to the field of AI.

The Turing test posits an interrogator who sits at a computer terminal and writes messages to two correspondents, A and B, who are at terminals in another room. Turing originally posed the test as a party game, in which A and B are a man and a woman, and the interrogator's job is to ask questions of A and B to determine their genders; correspondent A intentionally misleads the interrogator, while B attempts to help. Turing proposed that a computer could be programmed to answer questions as a human would. If a computer could pass itself off as human in such a blind test, Turing argued, then it should be considered intelligent. Turing's essay raised numerous questions and lines of research dealing with whether functional equivalence was sufficient to claim that a computer might actually think, and these issues are still controversial within the fields of AI and philosophy today.

In 1952, Turing was arrested and convicted of "gross indecency" due to his sexual relationship with another man. The trial caused a scandal, and resulted in Turing undergoing "organo-therapy," a medical "treatment" for homosexuality that involved taking high doses of the hormone estrogen. It is unknown exactly what effect these hormones and the trial itself had on Turing, but in 1954 he committed suicide at the age of 42 by eating a cyanide-laced apple.

Alan Turing's work has been centrally important in computer science and AI; he is considered by many to be a founder of both fields. The circumstances of his arrest and suicide, along with the secrecy surrounding his key role in breaking the Enigma code, have made his accomplishments less widely known than they might otherwise have been. Nonetheless, his work remains important for linking the theoretical worlds of mathematics and logic to the practical problems of building and programming computing machines.

Selected Works

Britton, J.L., et al. *The Collected Works of A.M. Turing.* New York: Elsevier, 1992.

Turing, Alan M. "Can a Machine Think?" *World of Mathematics.* James R. Newman, ed. Redmond, Wash.: Tempus Books, 1988.

———. "Intelligent Machinery." National Physical Laboratory Report, 1948. *Cybernetics: Key Papers.* C.R. Evans and A.D.J. Robertson, eds. Baltimore, Md.: University Park Press, 1968.

———. "On Computable Numbers, with an Application to the *Entscheidungsproblem.*" *Proceedings of the London Mathematical Society*, vol. 2, no. 42 (1936–37).

Bibliography

Gottfried, Ted. *Alan Turing: The Architect of the Computer Age.* New York: Franklin Watts, 1996.

Hodges, Andrew. "The Alan Turing Home Page." June 12, 2001. <http://www.turing.org.uk/turing/> (April 12, 2002).

———. *Alan Turing, the Enigma.* New York: Simon and Schuster, 1983.

———. *Turing: A Natural Philosopher.* London: Phoenix, 1997; New York: Routledge, 1997.

Related Topics

Human-Computer Interaction; Minsky, Marvin; Robotics

— *Shawn Miklaucic*

Turkle, Sherry

1948–
Sociologist

Sherry Turkle is a sociologist and psychologist, best known for her ethnographic studies of computer users during the 1980s and 1990s. In her own words, Turkle writes on "the evolving computer culture and on the questions that surround the relationship between technology and the self." She is currently Abby Rockefeller Mauzé Professor of the Sociology of Science at the Massachusetts Institute of Technology (MIT).

Born in New York City in 1948, Turkle attended Radcliffe College at Harvard University. She took a year off from college and studied in Paris, attending seminars led by such intellectuals as Jacques Lacan, Claude Lévi-Strauss, and Lucien Goldman. She received the Certificat d'Etudes Politiques from the Institut d'Etudes Politiques in Paris.

After 18 months in France, Turkle returned to Harvard to finish her degree. She then spent a year at the Committee on Social Thought at the University of Chicago, where she studied with anthropologist Victor Turner. In 1971, Turkle began a joint doctorate in sociology and personality psychology at Harvard University, graduating in 1976. During this time, she also became a licensed clinical psychologist, and undertook psychoanalytic training. Building on her time in France, her dissertation (published in 1978 as a book) was entitled *Psychoanalytic Politics: Jacques Lacan and Freud's French Revolution.*

With her interests in psychoanalysis and culture, Turkle's decision to teach at MIT in 1975 was not entirely clear to many. As she recently told *Scientific American*, "Some people said, 'What's a nice girl like you who knows about French poststructuralism doing in a place like this?'" However, Turkle did not see herself as a student of French culture; she saw herself as a student of popular cultures that grow up around the mind. She sensed that the world of high technology was about to become an extremely important factor.

While at the University of Chicago, Turkle had become interested in Turner's notion of liminal objects—that is, objects that stand on a threshold between one realm and another—through which individuals in society begin reevaluating their culture. Turkle believed that personal computers were going to become liminal objects for Americans. As she describes it, "Right away when I got there, I began to see ways in which ideas about the computer as a model of mind were getting into people's individual ways of thinking about themselves."

Following the lead of French child analyst Jean Piaget, Turkle began studying how both children and adults were incorporating computers into their daily lives. She noted that young children often practiced a type of animism, asking questions like, "Did the computer cheat?" Even older children and adults, socialized out of animism, nonetheless continued to treat their PCs as "psychological machines."

Turkle published her research in her 1984 book *The Second Self: Computers and the Human Spirit.* The title refers to her argument that computer users often conceptualize their relationship to their computer as a "second self," a place where they can reflect on personal identity. It is important to remember that Turkle has always maintained that every person has not one, but rather multiple "selves." In computing environments, people sometimes self-identify in traditional ways—i.e., along gender, racial, or age-based lines. For example, she observed that girls and boys use different styles to understand computing, which she called "soft learning" and "hard learning," respectively. At other times, Turkle discovered that the computer allowed its user to create an identity barely present in any other environment—one's identity as a computing hacker or a newbie, for example.

Turkle's ideas regarding computing and multiple selves became even more appropriate in the early 1990s, as yet another liminal object began saturating popular culture: the Internet. "For over a decade I studied the psychology of people interacting with computers—where the focus of my work was the relationship between person and machine," she explained. "In the late 1980s, I realized that the focus of my work had to shift. Increasingly, people were using computers to interact with other people." Turkle's 1995 book *Life on the Screen: Identity in the Age of the Internet* details her time spent researching behavior in online communities. She sketches out a psychology of Internet use in which users "cycle through" various online personae. As the phrase "life on the screen" hints, Turkle respects both the physical and virtual "real." "Life on the screen may be play," she writes, "but it is very serious play."

At the same time, however, she has warned educators that they mustn't accept simulation culture at what she terms "interface value." She criticizes schools that teach students only how to use software packages, for example, without teaching computer programming. "On one level, high school sophomores playing [the video game] SimCity for two hours may learn more about city planning than they would pick up from a textbook," Turkle argues. "But on another level they may not know how to think about what they are doing." In an essay in the *American Prospect*, Turkle recalls that for one of her subjects, the most useful rule for playing SimCity was "Raising taxes always leads to riots." Because the subject had never learned computer programming, Turkle points out, "She had no language for asking how one might write the game so that increased taxes led to increased productivity and social harmony."

In recent years, Turkle's work has shifted away from "objects to think with" toward what she terms "objects to nurture," as she considers peoples' relationships with digital and robotic pets such as Tamagotchis, Furbies, AIBOs, and the humanoid robots in the MIT Artificial Intelligence Laboratory. "What are we becoming," Turkle wonders, "if we are emotionally relating to these objects that are evoking these responses that are meant to be our responses to our children?" As a recent *Scientific American* article pointed out, "It is a question she seems destined to answer."

Selected Works

Turkle, Sherry. "Constructions and Reconstructions of Self in Virtual Reality: Playing in the MUDs." *Mind, Culture, and Activity*, vol. 1, no. 3 (Summer 1994). <http://web.mit.edu/sturkle/www/constructions.html> (July 3, 2002).

———. "Identity in the Age of the Internet" *The Media Reader: Continuity and Transformation*. Hugh Mackay and Tim O'Sullivan, eds. London/Thousand Oaks, Calif.: Sage Publications, 1999.

———. *Life on the Screen: Identity in the Age of the Internet*. New York: Simon & Schuster, 1995.

———. *Psychoanalytic Politics: Freud's French Revolution*. New York: Basic Books, 1978.

———. *The Second Self: Computers and the Human Spirit*. New York: Simon and Schuster, 1984.

———. "Seeing Through Computers: Education in a Culture of Simulation." *The American Prospect*, vol. 8, no. 31 (March 1–April 1, 1997). <http://www.prospect.org/print/V8/31/turkle-s.html> (July 3, 2002).

———. "Toys to Change Our Minds." *Predictions*. Sian Griffiths, ed. Oxford: Oxford University Press, 1999.

Bibliography

Goldsborough, Margaret. "M.I.T. Professor Reconsiders Children's Online Lives." *The New York Times*, February 14, 2001.

Holloway, Marguerite. "Profile: An Ethnologist in Cyberspace." *Scientific American*, April 1998.

HotWired. "Sherry Turkle Interview." November 30, 1995. <http://hotwired.lycos.com/talk/club/special/transcripts/turkle.html> (June 7, 2002).

McCorduck, Pamela. "Sex, Lies and Avatars." *Wired* 4.04, April 1996. <http://www.wired.com/wired/archive//4.04/turkle_pr.html> (June 7, 2002).

Raymond, Ron. "Sherry Turkle." Fall 1998. <http://www.cc.gatech.edu/fac/Gregory.Abowd/hci-resources/bios/rraymond/turkle.html> (June 7, 2002).

Further Reading

Cohen, Adam. "Margaret Mead in Cyberspace." *Time*, 2000. <http://www.time.com/time/innovators/web/profile_turkle.html> (June 7, 2002).

"Sherry Turkle on the Future of the Internet: Addiction, Stereotypes and Cyborgs." Cybergrrl, Inc., 2001.

<http://www.cybergrrl.com/fs.jhtml?/tech/ttopic/art1261/>
(June 7, 2002).

Starr, Linda. "An Education World e-Interview with
Sherry Turkle: Is Technology Just for Boys?"
Education World, May 25, 2000.
<http://www.education-world.com/a_curr/curr228.shtml>
(June 7, 2002).

Related Topics

Cyborg; Gender and New Media; MUDs and MOOs;
Robotics; TinyMUD; Virtual Community

— *Theresa M. Senft*

2600: The Hacker Quarterly

Called "the hacker's bible," *2600: The Hacker Quarterly* is both a technical journal, focusing on technological exploration and know-how, and a muckraking magazine, exposing government and corporate misdeeds. *2600* has continuously been involved in the legal, ethical, and technical debates over the hacker's craft.

2600 began in 1984 as a three-sheet newsletter with a circulation of 25. It was named for the 2600-hertz tone that used to control AT&T's switching system. Mimicking the frequency—allowing free access to long-distance lines—was one of the first modifications learned by phone phreaks, the forerunners of computer hackers.

The magazine is closely identified with its founder, publisher, and editor, "Emmanuel Goldstein" (real name Eric Corley); the pseudonym comes from the shadowy leader of the resistance in George Orwell's *1984.* He was arrested in 1983 for allegedly hacking into a system that gave him access to a number of corporations' emails. The charges were later dropped, but the experience led him to decide to channel his energies into a magazine that would give the digital underground community a printed forum.

For many, Goldstein has taken on the role of spokesperson for young hackers. Goldstein served as technical consultant on the Hollywood film *Hackers* (1995), has testified in Congress, and has been hosting *Off the Hook,* a talk-radio show on New York's WBAI station, since the early 1990s.

2600, currently an 8"x 5", 58-page glossy-covered magazine, publishes articles that address topics such as system entry and exploration, security vulnerabilities, protection from invasive software, the implications of new encryption techniques, how to remove ad banners from Web sites, and the ethics of viruses. An extensive "letters to the editors" section makes up a large portion of the magazine, and contains responses to previous articles and other letters (sometimes in precise technical detail), legal advice, anecdotes about authoritarian responses to hacking, and tales of hacking adventures. Since 1989, *2600* has regularly featured its signature photos of payphones from around the world. In addition, the magazine has continuously countered mainstream media representations of the hacker as computer terrorist. It has routinely run editorials in support of jailed hackers like "Phiber Optik" (technical consultant to the magazine), Bernie S., and especially Kevin Mitnick, on whose behalf *2600* mounted a spirited defense.

All of this is part of *2600's* mission to define the "hacker ethic." For Goldstein, this ethic begins with the notion that "all information should be free," and involves a hard-line stance against corporate and government control of information technologies, as well as an affirmation of knowledge-seeking and technological innovation on the part of hackers. This ethic maintains that hackers should not damage or profit from the systems that they crack. *2600's* stance is that hackers perform a public service by exposing the vulnerabilities of electronic systems—a kind of consumer advocacy. The political stance of the magazine can be described as anti-authoritarian and vaguely libertarian; Goldstein himself prefers the label "dissident."

The magazine is only the printed version of the activities that fall under the category "2600." The Web site (2600.com) chronicles the latest activities in the hacker world, as well as carrying an archive of hacked Web sites and an online store. The 2600 Club meets on the first Friday of every month in more than 100 cities worldwide. These gatherings are held near clusters of pay phones, so other meetings can be called. In 1994, *2600* sponsored Hackers on Planet Earth (HOPE), a conference marking the magazine's ten-year anniversary. The HOPE convention is held every three years in New York City, and attracted more than 3,000 attendees in 2000.

Recently, *2600* has found itself in the media spotlight due to legal troubles. In January 2000, the Motion Picture Association of America (MPAA) filed suit against *2600* for violating the Digital Millennium Copyright Act (DMCA). The online version of the magazine featured a story on the Norwegian teen who cracked the CSS (Content Scramble System) encryption scheme on DVDs, allowing users to run DVDs on Linux systems and distribute them over the

Internet. The story posted a link to the teen's DeCSS program. The case had implications for free-speech protections (both of the DeCSS program and of fair use in news coverage of technology) and for the constitutionality of the DMCA.

Because of the intense media attention paid to the MPAA case, as well as to hacking in general, *2600: The Hacker Quarterly* has become more prominent than ever. The magazine's increasing circulation (67,500 in 2000) and its publisher's principal role in the hacking community demonstrate that *2600* is and will continue to be an important forum for the ethical, legal, and cultural implications of new media.

Bibliography

Cha, Ariana Eunjung. "From Teen Hackers to Job Hunters: Notorious 2600 Club Motivates Young to Pursue Loftier Goals." *The Washington Post,* April 17, 2001, p. E01.

Ciolli, Rita. "A David Takes on Goliath: Hackers' Backer Fights Control of Technology." *Newsday* (Nassau and Suffolk Edition), July 16, 2000, p. A07.

Harmon, Amy. "Defining the Ethics of Hacking." *The Los Angeles Times,* August 12, 1994, p. A1.

Lappe, Anthony. "The Good. The Bad. The Geeks." *The New York Times,* June 14, 1998.

Sterling, Bruce. *The Hacker Crackdown: Law and Disorder on the Electronic Frontier.* New York: Bantam Books, 1992.

Further Reading

2600: The Hacker Quarterly. 2600 Enterprises, Inc., 1984–present.
<http://www.2600.com> (May 10, 2002).

Related Topics

DeCSS; Digital Millennium Copyright Act; Hacking, Cracking, and Phreaking

— *Jack Bratich*

Typography

Before the age of digital electronic media, typography focused on type design and its placement on the printed page. At first, many typographers worked in printing houses, where the work revolved around designing and creating printed material, from one-page documents to newspapers, magazines, and books. Later, the division of labor separated specialized type foundries from printing workshops and stationery stores. Printers were also publishers when every printing press functioned under government license. As these changes took place, typography branched into specialized functions, from the design and physical casting of type to the functions of what is now graphic design.

To market and distribute periodicals and books today requires increased focus on overall graphic design as well as on audience. Typographers and designers must address and manage design matters. The style, form, and appearance of printed material explicitly position publications in discourse fields and market sectors.

The birth of digital electronic media introduced new dimensions to typography. Typeset material was not always printed. It appeared on screen, and some type was active rather than static. While style, form, and appearance remained a central focus of typography, other factors became important.

Some changes were the result of technology. Computer-based typesetting followed photomechanical typesetting. It required the adaptation of classical typefaces, as well as significant modifications to typographic management. Desktop publishing required even greater changes. New approaches to type design and print production were a central result, along with major developments in onscreen visualization.

Technological change led to another kind of change, a reconceptualization of typography. Originally, typographical work was shaped by the physical and mechanical constraints of type. Designing type for foundry technology, cutting molds and dies, casting lead type, locking it into wooden chases, and printing on presses descended from Gutenberg's original printing process influenced all aspects of typography from type design to the make-up of the printed page. Advances in mechanical typography and printing did little to change this process. Even offset printing required an original typeset sheet from which the offset photo was made, or a lead-cast linotype lock-up for high-speed mechanical presses.

The birth of computer-based technologies transformed all this. The constraints imposed on typography by physical type media no longer existed. For example, the concept of leading, the distance between separate lines of type, originated with printing-press technology. Physical blocks of lead were used to lock in and separate lines of type. What began as a physical constraint on typography became a factor in visual ergonomics. When lead vanished, leading changed from a constraint to a development factor that many young typographers began to neglect or ignore. While negative leading became possible for showpiece typography, it was more common that type was badly leaded simply because unskilled typographers never learned to set leading properly.

Desktop publishing and computer-based typography had an even more profound impact. Where typography was once an expert art developed through apprenticeship or advanced training, the advent of the PC meant that anyone who could type letters on a keyboard and manipulate a mouse could set type. This led to exciting new experiments by thoughtful and adventurous amateurs, and resulted in the "new typography" movement of the 1980s and 1990s. Led by *Émigré* magazine's Rudy VanderLans and Zuzana Licko, and by designers like David Carson and Neville Brody, the movement sought to use typography itself as an art form. While often successful at creating visually stunning publications, it also resulted in vast streams of bad typography and shabby home-brewed design.

Electronic digital media led to equally revolutionary changes in type design. The arts of typography were no longer bound up in skills descended from cuneiform, stone-cutting, engraving, and die-casting. The first typography began with cuneiform wedges pressed into clay; today's typography involves manipulating pixels on a WYSISWYG (What You See Is What You Get) monitor, writing programs, and setting algorithms for the appropriate forms and dimensions.

Many of the great type houses now have digital-type divisions, and some firms exist only to set type for digital typography. Adobe is the best known of the latter.

The birth of new media also gave rise to special firms whose programs enabled designers to lay the new type. The past twenty years saw an explosion of specific typography and layout programs, beginning with Aldus PageMaker and QuarkXpress. Word-processing programs such as Microsoft Word now support typography and layout functions.

New challenges emerged when typography became a factor in designing sites for the World Wide Web, CD-ROM, DVD, and hypermedia. It became necessary to address the multiple experiences and meanings that type could create, beyond the possibilities inherent in typefaces and static pages; to understand how type could function by remaining the same, animating, changing, or even morphing; and to consider issues inherent in translating and transferring messages through different combinations of possibilities. The typography of the page took on a new and richer series of dimensions. As the page extended into interactive time and space, designers had to consider the way that typography and design could facilitate or hinder navigation.

The media convergence that is impacting so many issues in contemporary media also affects typography. Once again, the typographer can be a jack of many trades, and the same individual may once again fulfill many functions: designing type, setting it, printing, and publishing the content. Because today's typographers work in digital electronic media, however, their activities will also converge with distribution and communication, placing type on the Web and managing a complex series of interactive responses.

Bibliography

O'Donnell, James J. *Avatars of the Word: From Papyrus to Cyberspace.* Cambridge, Mass.: Harvard University Press, 1998.

Lee, Marshall. *Bookmaking: The Illustrated Guide to Design and Production.* New York: R.R. Bowker and Company, 1965.

McGovern, Gerry, and Rob Norton. *Content Critical: Gaining Competitive Advantage through High-Quality Web Content.* Harlow: Financial Times Prentice Hall, 2002.

McGovern, Gerry; Norton, Rob; and Catherine O'Dowd. *The Web Content Style Guide.* London: Financial Times Prentice Hall, 2002.

McLean, Ruari. *The Thames and Hudson Manual of Typography.* London: Thames and Hudson, 1980.

Tracy, Walter. *Letters of Credit: A View of Type Design.* London: G. Fraser, 1986.

Further Reading

Bernsen, Jens. *The Design Before the Design.* Copenhagen: Danish Design Council, 1996.

———. *Design Management in Practice.* Copenhagen: Danish Design Council, 1987.

Carter, Sebastian. *Twentieth Century Type Designers.* New York: Taplinger, 1987.

Drucker, Johanna. *The Alphabetic Labyrinth: The Letters in History and Imagination.* New York: Thames and Hudson, 1995.

Gill, Eric. *An Essay on Typography.* Boston: David R. Godine, 1988.

Guterman, Jimmy. "Envisioning Interfaces." *Wired* 2.08, August 1994. <http://www.wired.com/wired/archive/2.08/tufte.html> (May 17, 2002).

Hobart, Michael E., and Zachary S. Schiffman. *Information Ages: Literacy, Numeracy, and the Computer Revolution.* Baltimore: Johns Hopkins University Press, 1998.

Jackson, Donald. *The Story of Writing.* London: Studio Vista, 1981.

Mollerup, Per. *Good Enough Is Not Enough: Observations on Public Design.* Copenhagen: Danish Design Council, 1992.

Perfect, Christopher, and Gordon Rookledge. *Rookledge's International Typefinder: The Essential Handbook of Typeface Recognition and Selection.* New York: F.C. Beil, 1983.

Swanson, Gunnar. *Graphic Design and Reading: Explorations of an Uneasy Relationship.* New York: Allworth Press, 2000.

Tufte, Edward R. *Envisioning Information.* Cheshire, Conn.: Graphics Press, 1990.

———. *Visual Explanations: Images and Quantities, Evidence and Narrative.* Cheshire, Conn.: Graphics Press, 1997.

Wurman, Richard Saul. *Information Anxiety: What to Do When Information Doesn't Tell You What You Need to Know.* New York: Bantam Books, 1990.

Related Topics

Computer Graphics; Graphical User Interface; Information Design; Interface; Knowledge Management

— Ken Friedman

Understanding Media: The Extensions of Man

Understanding Media: The Extensions of Man, a timeless work by Marshall McLuhan published in 1964, is a discussion of the various media and their effects on society and the individual. The book's publication transformed McLuhan from an English professor at the University of Toronto into a media celebrity. His writing not only gained attention and scrutiny in academic circles, but many of the ideas and phrases in the book also lodged themselves in the popular discourse, and McLuhan himself became a household name.

McLuhan defined media in the subtitle of the book as "The Extensions of Man." For him, media include not only radio and TV, but also written words, clothing, money, and so on. McLuhan was interested in how media extend our auditory, visual, and tactile senses, as well as other capacities.

According to McLuhan, media not only extend but also alter and fix sense ratios. He often compared old media with new, noting how a new medium changed and fixed the senses ratios: "Each new impact shifts the ratios among all the senses." The visual order of print, for example, structures a sequentially ordered thought. Electronic media, on the other hand, invite a form of thinking that is nonlinear, repetitive, discontinuous, and intuitive, proceeding by analogy instead of sequential argument.

McLuhan's famous aphorism, "the medium is the message," expresses his belief that the effect of a medium is not carried by its content, but rather in its format; every medium transmits a powerful message of its own in its format, above and beyond its content. The idea is easier to comprehend when we compare different media experiences while holding the content constant. For example, given the same piece of music, the experience generated from listening to a high-quality stereo system is different from that of listening to a Walkman.

Recognizing the interactive relationships between a medium and the social context of its use, McLuhan wrote, "We shape our tools and afterwards our tools shape us." Humans construct new technologies, utilizing existing resources, in order to extend their various capacities. However, technologies have after-the-fact impacts on social relationships and sensory experiences.

Although *Understanding Media* was published in the 1960s, and the discussion was mainly about the electronic media, its ideas hold true for the technological developments in the 1980s and onward, and it shows relevance for understanding new media as well. Scholars, columnists, marketers, and critics continue to revisit and reflect on McLuhan's discussions to help them make sense of their environment, and to provide the vocabularies to describe it.

In his statement, "As electrically contracted, the globe is no more than a village," McLuhan contended that electronic media would create a global village in which matters would be shared by all. The idea of media as extensions of the human was useful for understanding live TV broadcasts (extending our auditory and visual senses) and the use of cellular phones (extending our auditory senses), both of which overcome spatial constraints. The phenomena of Cable News Network (CNN) and the Internet attest to the validity of McLuhan's "global village" idea. Although he died in 1979, too early to witness the development of CNN, the Internet, and wireless communications, his thoughts hold true for understanding these technological innovations, leading many to hail McLuhan as a visionary.

However, other individuals who are interested in studying media content dismiss McLuhan, and label him as technological determinist. Technological determinists are scholars who centralize information technologies and deny human agency in their writings, and who believe in the direct, uniform, and powerful effects of information technologies. Critics of McLuhan's writings generally believe that the medium is transparent or neutral, failing to recognize the impact of the technological features of a medium.

Bibliography

McLuhan, Marshall. *Understanding Media: The Extensions of Man.* New York: McGraw-Hill, 1964.

Press, Larry. "McLuhan Meets the Net." *Communications of the ACM,* vol. 38, no. 7 (July 1995), pp. 15–20.

Stearn, Gerald Emanuel. *McLuhan, Hot & Cool.* New York: Dial Press, 1967.

Further Reading

Innis, Harold A. *The Bias of Communication.* Toronto: University of Toronto Press, 1964.

McLuhan, Marshall. *The Gutenberg Galaxy: The Making of Typographic Man.* Toronto: University of Toronto Press, 1962.

Related Topics

McLuhan, Marshall; Technological Determinism; Virtual Community

— *Shing-Ling Sarina Chen*

United States vs. Thomas

United States vs. Thomas was one of the first prosecutions involving the distribution of "obscene" material in cyberspace. The case was notable because it extended the concepts of "community" and "community standards" beyond physical location and into the Internet and virtual space. It also raised the question of whether officials in one community, in this case Tennessee, had the legal right to determine the content of a computer located in another geographic location, California.

In 1991, from their residence in Milpitas, California, Robert and Carleen Thomas created, owned, and operated a small adult-oriented computer bulletin-board system (BBS), named the Amateur Action Bulletin Board Service (AABBS). The service was operated from a dedicated computer and phone line, which allowed dial-in access (using modems) to the BBS from individual's homes. Once connected, individuals could read and post messages, as well as download any materials (such as photographs) available on the BBS.

The AABBS began life with 12 photographs and a single telephone. By 1993, it had become one of the most popular BBSs in the United States, with approximately 3,500 customers and more than 20,000 images available for downloading, earning it the moniker of "the nastiest place on Earth."

In 1993, a man in Tennessee dialed into the AABBS and viewed what he believed to be images of child pornography. Upon his request, authorities from the U.S. Postal Service in Memphis launched an

investigation into the BBS. Working with an assistant United States attorney in Memphis, a Tennessee postal investigator joined the BBS, downloaded sexually explicit images, ordered a videotape from the AABBS (which was delivered by United Parcel Service), and sent the AABBS an unsolicited child-pornography videotape.

In early 1994, Robert and Carleen Thomas were arrested after a five-month investigation by federal authorities, and charged with distributing obscene materials across state lines, a violation of interstate commerce laws. Although most charges were based on the downloads of sexually explicit images, a charge of child-pornography was also included as a result of the couple's receipt of the unsolicited videotape described above.

The case against the Thomases was based on another landmark court decision, reached in 1973's *Miller vs. California,* in which the U.S. Supreme Court attempted to provide a framework for defining obscenity by arguing that it should be based on "community standards." In doing so, the Court avoided describing specifically what those standards should be, and left it to the discretion of individual communities. Chief Justice Berger argued that such an approach was needed to avoid having standards from one community dictate the standards of another.

The *Miller vs. California* decision included a three-part test to determine what may qualify as obscenity, and was applied in the *United States vs. Thomas* case. A material is considered obscene and excluded from First Amendment protection if: 1) applying contemporary standards, the average person would judge the material, on the whole, as arousing "prurient interest" (e.g., immoral or lustful desire); 2) the material describes or depicts, in a patently offensive manner, sexual conduct specifically defined by the applicable state law; and 3) the material, on the whole, lacks any serious artistic, literary, political, or scientific value. Only material that fails all three parts of this test can be deemed obscene within a community, and therefore denied protection.

In December 1994, based on this standard, the Thomases were tried, convicted of the obscenity charges, and sentenced in a federal court in Memphis. Robert Thomas was sentenced to serve 37 months and Carleen Thomas to 30 months in a federal penitentiary; they were, however, acquitted of the child pornography charge.

According to Mike Godwin, staff counsel of the Electronic Frontier Foundation, a Washington, D.C., public-interest civil-liberties organization, the use of *Miller vs. California* in the Thomas case, and its eventual outcome, raised several questions about the applicability of the almost 20-year-old ruling to virtual communities. The fact that virtual communities exist outside of geographic boundaries makes them unique, and applying the *Miller vs. California* ruling essentially means that the standards of the community in which an individual physically lives determines what a person can do in cyberspace. Consequently, this can be viewed as an attempt to regulate new communication technologies by applying outdated precedents based on old forms of communication.

Other critics of the application of the *Miller vs. California* ruling argued that materials could be downloaded from the AABBS without the knowledge of the owner/operators, calling into question the issue of intent to distribute. In other words, just because material can be accessed from certain locations, does that automatically mean that the intent was to distribute into specific geographic areas?

Appeals based on these arguments and others filed with the circuit court failed to overturn the convictions, with the court ruling that the application of the obscenity standards, per *Miller vs. California,* was appropriate. Furthermore, the court ruled against redefining "community" for materials sent by computer, and supported the ruling that the Thomases could be prosecuted in Memphis, even with its more conservative "community standards," although the BBS was based in California. The court argued that since a BBS owner/operator could control the locations from which images could be accessed, the Thomases were in violation of interstate commerce laws.

United States vs. Thomas is commonly regarded as the reason why adult-oriented sites with sexually explicit material now contain disclaimers regarding age authentication, sexual content, and legal jurisdiction of the Web sites.

Bibliography

American Library Association. "Notable First Amendment Court Cases." 2000. <http://www.ala.org/alaorg/oif/1stcases.html#43> (April 12, 2002).
Beck, Stephanie Lyn. "When Hormones and Technology Collide: Silicon Sexuality, Stale Statutes and the Supreme Court." ibiblio, The Public's Library and Digital Archive, December 6, 1995. <http://www.ibiblio.org/steph/paper.html> (April 12, 2002).
Cole, Wendy. "The Marquis de Cyberspace." *Time*, vol. 146, no. 1 (July 2, 1995), p. 43.
Godwin, Mike. "Virtual Community Standards." *Reason*, vol. 26, no. 6 (November 1994), pp. 48–51.

Further Reading

Elias, James E.; Jarvis, Will; and Vern L. Bullough, eds. *Porn 101: Eroticism, Pornography, and the First Amendment.* Amherst, N.Y.: Prometheus Books, 1999.
Lane, Fredrick S. *Obscene Profits: The Entrepreneurs of Pornography in the Cyber Age.* New York: Routledge, 2000.
United States Court of Appeals for the Sixth Circuit. "United States versus Thomas (case # 94-6648/6649)" [court briefing]. January 29, 1996. FindLaw: Case Law Server. <http://laws.lp.findlaw.com/6th/960032p.html> (April 12, 2002).

Related Topics

Bulletin-Board Systems; Communications Decency Act; Cyberethics; Electronic Frontier Foundation; Obscenity; USENET; Virtual Community

— *Art Ramirez*

Universal Design

Universal design refers to the design of products and environments that are made to be usable by all people, to the greatest extent possible, without the need for physical adaptation or specialized design. The objective of universal design is to simplify life for everyone through the creation of products, communications, and built environments that are made more usable for as many people as possible. Universal design thus benefits people of all ages and abilities.

In relation to new media, universal design refers to the design of telecommunication devices and services, including telephones, television programming, and computers, that are accessible for people with diverse disabilities, as well as ensuring Web accessibility for people with disabilities. Seven principles for universal design, as elaborated by the Center for Universal Design at North Carolina State University, are as follows:

1. *Equitable Use.* The design is useful and marketable to people with diverse abilities.
2. *Flexibility in Use.* The design accommodates a wide range of individual preferences and abilities.
3. *Simple and Intuitive.* Use of the design is easy to understand, regardless of the user's experience, knowledge, language skills, or current concentration level.
4. *Perceptible Information.* The design communicates necessary information effectively to the user,

regardless of ambient conditions or the user's sensory abilities.

5. *Tolerance for Error.* The design minimizes hazards and the adverse consequences of accidental or unintended actions.

6. *Low Physical Effort.* The design can be used efficiently and comfortably, and with a minimum of fatigue.

7. *Size and Space for Approach and Use.* The design provides appropriate size and space for approach, reach, manipulation, and use, regardless of the user's body size, posture, or mobility.

Changing demographics in North America have necessitated the movement toward universal design. People are living longer lives, and more people are also living with diverse disabilities. In the United States, universal design rights are recognized by legislation influenced by the disability rights movement and various advances in rehabilitation engineering and assistive technology. Examples of U.S. federal legislation include the Architectural Barriers Act of 1968, which requires that all buildings designed, constructed, altered, or leased with federal funds be made accessible; Section 504 of the Rehabilitation Act of 1973, which made it illegal to discriminate on the basis of disability, and which applied to institutions receiving federal funds; and the Americans with Disabilities Act of 1990 (ADA), which prohibits discrimination in employment, access to places of public accommodation, services, programs, public transportation, and telecommunications.

The Telecommunications Act of 1996 requires that telecommunication services and equipment, as well as customer-premises equipment, be "designed, developed, and fabricated to be accessible to and usable by individuals with disabilities, if readily achievable." The act applies to all types of telecommunication devices and services, including telephones, television programming, and computers.

As the Web displaces traditional sources of information (such as print media) and becomes indispensable to the dissemination of government information, news and current events, educational resources, and civic material, it is crucial that it be accessible for all citizens. Accessibility of the Web is one area of research in the universal design field that has been very active. The World Wide Web Consortium has initiated the Web Accessibility Initiative (WAI), in coordination with international organizations, in order to pursue Web accessibility through six main areas of work: technology, guidelines, tools, education, outreach, and

research and development. Many governments, including those of the United States, Canada, the U.K., Australia, and France, require Web accessibility for certain kinds of sites, most often including government sites. Often, these accessibility guidelines are referred to as a "common look and feel."

The Web presents particular challenges for people with disabilities. For those with visual disabilities, unlabeled graphics, undescribed video, poorly marked-up tables or frames, and a lack of keyboard support or screen-reader compatibility present problems. For those with hearing disabilities, a lack of captioning for audio and text without visual signposts presents problems. For those with physical disabilities, a lack of a keyboard or single-switch support for menu commands is an impediment. People with cognitive or neurological problems are faced with the Web's lack of a consistent navigation structure, its non-plain language, its absence of illustrative non-text materials, and its potentially poor visual displays (such as flickering or strobing designs).

The WAI has created three guidelines to address different issues of Web accessibility:

1. Web Content Accessibility Guidelines explain accessible use of Web technologies for page authors and site developers.

2. Authoring Tool Accessibility Guidelines support the creation of accessible Web content, particularly through the accessibility of the Web interface.

3. User Agent Accessibility Guidelines address browsers, multimedia players, and assistive technologies.

Assistive technologies facilitate access for people with diverse disabilities. For computers and the Internet, assistive technologies include: alternative keyboards, alternative mouse systems, Braille embossers, closed-circuit television (CCTV), speech synthesizers, haptic devices (which provide users with tactile feedback), optical character recognition (OCR) devices, screen magnifiers and readers, voice output communication devices, and voice recognition systems.

History has demonstrated that universal design benefits all citizens. Consider sidewalk curb cuts: initially designed for people in wheelchairs, curb cuts are also of use to bicyclists and people pushing baby strollers. Likewise, accessible Web design contributes to better Web usability for all users. As the Internet permeates our lives through e-commerce, distance education, and the dissemination of government and civic information, there is an economic and social imperative to make sure that all citizens, regardless of disability, can access the Internet. Therefore, universal design is an important element in bridging the digital divide.

Bibliography

Center for Universal Design, North Carolina State University. Web site. <www.design.ncsu.edu/cud> (April 12, 2002).

Center for Universal Design, North Carolina State University. "What Is Universal Design?" <http://www.design.ncsu.edu:8120/cud/univ_design/princ_overview.htm#princ> (April 12, 2002).

Government of Canada Internet Guide, Third Edition. "Building the Site: Universal Accessibility." July 1998. <http://www.canada.gc.ca/programs/guide/3_1_4e.html> (April 12, 2002).

HCI Bibliography. "Accessibility Resources." <http://www.hcibib.org/accessibility/> (April 12, 2002).

Telecommunications Act Accessibility Guidelines. *Federal Register*, February 3, 1998. <http://www.access-board.gov/telecomm/html/telfinal.htm> (April 12, 2002).

W3C (World Wide Web Consortium). Web Accessibility Initiative (WAI) home page. <http://www.w3.org/WAI> (April 12, 2002).

W3C (World Wide Web Consortium) Web Accessibility Initiative (WAI). "Policies Relating to Web Accessibility." <http://www.w3.org/WAI/Policy/> (April 12, 2002).

Further Reading

Adaptive Technology Resource Centre, University of Toronto. Web site. <http://www.utoronto.ca/atrc/index.html> (April 12, 2002).

Association for Computing Machinery. ACM SIGCAPH (Special Interest Group on Computers and the Physically Handicapped). Web site. <www.acm.org/sigcaph> (April 12, 2002).

TRACE Center, College of Engineering, University of Wisconsin–Madison. "Designing a More Usable World—for All." <http://trace.wisc.edu/world> (April 12, 2002).

Related Topics

Access; Digital Divide; Optical Character Recognition; Usability; World Wide Web Consortium

— *Leslie Regan Shade*

Usability

Usability is a well-established concept in the theory and practice of human-computer interaction (HCI) design. HCI is concerned with the design, evaluation, and implementation of interactive computing systems for human use. Usability is particularly concerned with ensuring optimal relationships between humans and computers. Its goal is to develop computer systems that support rapid learning, high skill retention, and low error rates. Systems with high usability support high productivity, and are consistent, controllable, predictable, pleasant, and effective to use. Contemporary usability studies focus on World Wide Web usability, usability for online communities, and the creation of universal usability.

There is no concrete definition of usability, because usability encompasses multiple components that change over time as technology develops. However, it is generally agreed that there are five usability attributes:

1. *Learnability.* Systems should be easy to learn, so that users can quickly start working.
2. *Efficiency.* Systems should be efficient to use, so that users can quickly increase their productivity.
3. *Memorability.* Systems should be easy to remember, so that users can quickly reacquaint themselves with the system if time has elapsed since they last used the system.
4. *Errors.* Systems should have low error rates; if users do make errors, they should be quickly correctable.
5. *Satisfaction.* Systems should be pleasant to use, so that users are not reluctant to work on them.

Usability supports, rather than hinders, people's creativity. Three general principles help to ensure usability:

1. *Consistency.* Software should employ the same terms and procedures for achieving the same functionality throughout the program. Design elements (typography, color, font sizes, grammar, etc.) should be consistent.
2. *Controllability.* Let the users be in control of the software.
3. *Predictability.* Software that is consistent and controllable is predictable. Cross-platform stability is important.

Usability focuses on users—their tasks and their individual attributes, including physical and mental characteristics. It considers the users' experience with computer systems, and whether they are novice or expert users. Users are extraordinarily diverse, and parameters for discussing human diversity include physical, cognitive, perceptual, cultural, experience, age, gender, and capability elements.

Usability engineering refers to a set of activities that assesses human factors in involvement with computer systems. Ideally, usability engineering takes place throughout the life cycle of a product. Stages of the usability-engineering life cycle model include:

1. Developing the product and concept.
2. Knowing the user (cognizance of diverse user attributes, the relationship between the user and the job).
3. Setting usability goals.
4. Creating iterative design and refinements.
5. Providing rollout support.

Very often, usability testing involves participatory design: consulting with the actual users of a system in the design, development, and deployment of the technology. Participatory design processes are important, because they give users a voice in the design process, thus increasing the probability of a usable design; they enable both technical and non-technical participants to participate equally; and they provide opportunities for developers to meet, work with, and understand their users.

Ensuring universal usability for Web-based and other interactive information and communication technologies is a recent movement and call to action, spearheaded by many computer scientists, sociologists, and policymakers. Universal usability for the Web can be defined as having more than 90 percent of all households be successful users of information and communication services at least once a week.

There are three main challenges in attaining universal usability. First, technological variety is important; in order to cope with the fast pace of technological change, support for a range of hardware, software, and network access is needed. Second, user diversity must be considered, in order to accommodate a wide range of user attributes, including skill and knowledge levels, cognitive abilities, physical disabilities, age, gender, literacy levels, culture, and socio-economic influences. The third challenge is presented by the frequent gaps in user knowledge: The technology must bridge gaps between what users know and what they need to know. Users approach technology with multiple intelligences, and interface design needs to support these different forms of learning.

Advocates of universal usability are encouraging Web site designers to post a Universal Usability statement on their sites, similar to the privacy policy statements that are found on commercial and non-commercial Web sites. Such a statement would describe the contents of the site, technical attributes (browser and network requirements), and other usability characteristics (for instance, is the site suitable for users with disabilities?).

The widespread use of the Web for e-commerce has created the need for usability for Web sites. Simply put, low usability translates into little Web traffic and no customers. Too often, flashy technological innovations detract from the good and steady use of a site. Usability guru Jakob Nielsen's foundation of good Web design is summarized by the acronym HOME (high quality content, often updated, minimal download time, and ease of use).

Designing for Web usability is a constantly changing process, and it is important to know the types of users that one wishes to attract. General principles of usability for the Web include: design simplicity, standardization, and legibility; concise and clear writing that encourages scannability; designing for people with cognitive and physical disabilities; reasonable and reliable response time; and designing for internationalization. Internationalization refers to a single design that can be used worldwide, and encompasses sensitivity to cultural differences and idiosyncrasies, the creation of multilingual and translated sites, and consideration for the vast array of technical platforms and network access that are available around the world.

As more online communities are created (both for commercial and non-commercial uses), usability related to this creation is especially important. The intertwined issues of usability and sociability are key elements in the creation of viable and vibrant communities. Usability focuses on human-computer interaction, whereas sociability focuses on social interaction between humans. Usability issues in online communities are centered on how software is designed for use by diverse individuals situated in many contexts (home, work, schools, community centers, etc.), and on user satisfaction and feedback. Factors that contribute to the usability of online-community software include the nature of user tasks, user diversity, and software design. Specific design features include navigation, message formats, support tools, registration forms, archives, and feedback. Sociability is concerned with community policies that support convivial communities, such as membership policies, codes of conduct, security, privacy, copyright, and free speech.

Many organizations are active in the field of usability, through annual conferences and publications. These include the Association of Computing Machinery's (ACM) Special Interest Group on Computer & Human Interaction (SIGCHI), as well as other ACM special interest groups (SIGCAPH, Computers and the Physically Handicapped; SIGGRAPH, Graphics; and SIGCAS, Computers and

Society); the Usability Professionals' Association (UPA); and Computer Professionals for Social Responsibility (CPSR). Books, journals, and conferences are burgeoning on the topic of usability; usability studies are found in many interdisciplinary academic programs, including those in computer science, engineering, psychology, communication, and library and information science.

Usability is a critical component in creating healthy and sustainable online communities, in bridging the digital divide, and in supporting economic structures. Particularly with the proliferation of the Web, the user experience is paramount, and usability professionals will be needed to implement the basics of usability, which encourage and promote ease of learning, efficiency, memorability, low error rates—and most of all, user satisfaction.

Bibliography

Conference on Universal Usability. Web site. <http://universalusability.org/> (April 12, 2002).

Hochheiser, Harry, and Ben Shneiderman. "Universal Usability Statements." *Interactions*, March-April 2001, pp. 16–18.

Nielsen, Jakob. *Designing Web Usability: The Practice of Simplicity.* Indianapolis, Ind.: New Riders Publishing, 2000.

———. *Usability Engineering.* Boston: Academic Press, 1993.

———. "Useit.com: Jakob Nielsen's Website (Usability and Web Design)." <http://www.useit.com/> (April 12, 2002).

Preece, Jennifer. *Online Communities: Designing Usability, Supporting Sociability.* New York: John Wiley, 2000. <http://www.ifsm.umbc.edu/onlinecommunities/> (April 12, 2002).

Shneiderman, Ben. "Universal Usability." *Communications of the ACM,* May 2000, pp. 85–91.

Further Reading

Association for Computing Machinery. ACM Conference on Universal Usability, 2000. <http://www.acm.org/sigchi/cuu/index.html> (April 12, 2002).

Computer Professionals for Social Responsibility. "Participatory Design." <www.cpsr.org/program/workplace/PD.html> (April 12, 2002).

HCI Bibliography—Human-Computer Interaction Resources. Web site. <http://www.hcibib.org/> (April 12, 2002).

Shneiderman, Ben. *Designing the User Interface: Strategies for Effective Human-Computer Interaction.* Third edition. Reading, Mass.: Addison-Wesley Longman, 1998.

Usability Professionals' Association (UPA). Web site. <www.upassoc.org/> (April 12, 2002).

Related Topics

Access; Digital Divide; Engelbart, Douglas; Graphical User Interface; Human-Computer Interaction; Interface; Nielsen, Jakob; Universal Design

— *Leslie Regan Shade*

USENET

USENET, an abbreviation of USEr NETwork, is a global, distributed bulletin board system (BBS)—in effect, a series of international discussion groups—that can be accessed through the Internet, or through online services. USENET comprises more than 50,000 discussion groups, or newsgroups, covering a huge range of topics. International in scope, USENET is used daily by millions of people around the world. It may well be the largest decentralized information utility in existence.

A HISTORY OF USENET

USENET was created in late 1979 by graduate students at Duke University and the University of North Carolina (UNC). Duke's Tom Truscott and UNC's Jim Ellis connected their department computers together via phone lines, using Unix version 7 and UNIX-to-UNIX Copy (UUCP), a communications protocol designed to transfer data between computers. Steve Bellovin, also at UNC, constructed the first version of the News software, and Steve Daniel further modified it for public distribution. Thereafter, a series of software developments unfolded that enabled USENET to expand.

In 1981, Mark Horton and Matt Glickman designed the "B" News version to expand the capacity of the network to accommodate an increased volume of news. In late 1986, under the direction of Rick Adams, another modification of the software allowed a new naming structure for newsgroups. Also in 1986, a software package developed out of the work of Brian Kantor and Phil Lapsley was released, enabling news transmission, posting, and reading using the Network News Transfer Protocol (NNTP). In 1987, "C" News, developed by Geoff Collyer and Henry Spencer, was released to the Internet to increase article-processing speed, decrease article-expiration processing, and improve the reliability of the system.

In 1992, Collyer implemented News Overview (NOV), a database to store the headers of news articles, which allowed for fast article presentation by sorting and threading (grouping together articles on the same topic) article headers. In addition, ANU-NEWS, a news package designed by Geoff Huston, was adopted that allowed for reading, posting, direct replies, moderated newsgroups, and so on. FNEWS was implemented to provide full-screen interface and fast response to thousands of newsgroups without overloading local machines.

Early newsreaders included Pine (Program for Internet News & Email), Hypernews, NewsWatcher, Nuntius (for Macintosh), trumpet, and WinVN (both for Microsoft and Windows).

The messages or articles on USENET newsgroups are distributed through news servers, which are operated by Internet service providers (ISPs), schools, universities, and corporations. A newsgroup article is sent from one server to another, starting from the local server where the article is first posted. Generally, all the articles in a newsgroup travel to all news servers that carry the newsgroup. Therefore, when a user posts one article, the final result is tens of thousands of copies, all over the world.

Although USENET originated in the United States, it has swiftly become international in scope. The heaviest concentrations of USENET sites outside the United States include Canada, Europe, Australia, and Japan. USENET is available on a wide variety of computer systems and networks, but the majority of USENET traffic is transported over either the Internet or UUCP.

THE STRUCTURE OF USENET

USENET is completely decentralized and is maintained by volunteers; it has no central authority or policing agency. USENET groups can be unmoderated, meaning that anyone can post and the articles are automatically posted without screening, or moderated, meaning that articles must be reviewed and approved by a moderator prior to posting. This moderation process can be performed by human moderators or by moderation software. Due to the moderation process, messages sent to moderated newsgroups are not automatically posted, as there is a delay before the messages are either posted or returned to their senders. If a message is judged to be inappropriate for posting to a newsgroup, the human moderator or the moderation software will return the message to the sender with a rejection notice, which states the reason for rejection and provides the address where the rejection may be appealed. Newsgroups are generally unmoderated, however; there are fewer than 300 moderated groups.

Newsgroup articles can be read using either Web browsers or newsreaders. Most Web browsers, such as those of Netscape or Microsoft, have USENET support. Web sites such as groups.google.com and liszt.com provide a subject-oriented directory of USENET newsgroups, as well as a search mechanism to help users locate and participate in newsgroups.

Newsgroup articles look much like email messages, but they are potentially read by millions all over the world. One should not confuse the exchanges taking place on USENET with private email correspondence; USENET is inherently a public medium.

There are several newsgroups that are constructed specifically for "new users," and that provide an orientation to USENET. News.announce.newusers is a newsgroup that regularly posts FAQs (Frequently Asked Questions) and explains netiquette (appropriate online behavior) and other common questions that potential users might have about newsgroups. Another newsgroup, news.newusers.questions, provides a forum for new users to ask questions and receive answers about USENET and other Internet services.

THE FUTURE OF USENET

Before the arrival of broadband connections, sophisticated graphics, and real-time communication, users around the world communicated via USENET's text-only message system. Nowadays, technological innovations threaten USENET. Chat rooms and other online message boards, serving the same purpose as USENET, have more advanced features. For example, chat rooms offer real-time communication; postings on USENET newsgroups, on the other hand, are more like a message in a bottle—there is generally a waiting period before a message is replied to, if at all. In addition, many users, disappointed by the spamming (massive commercial postings) that is common on USENET, have found more productive platforms for exchanging information online. Some suspect that USENET may have outlived its usefulness, and that it will be replaced by other, more user-friendly online discussion services.

Despite these predictions, USENET has reentered the popular discourse due to two events that took place in 2001. In February, Google, Inc., an Internet search service, acquired significant assets from Deja.com, an online information site, including its archive of more than 650 million messages, the largest archive of USENET newsgroups. In 1995, Deja.com (previously known as Deja News) had provided a user-friendly interface to USENET and had begun archiving and indexing messages. By making USENET more accessible, Deja.com had contributed to the growth of USENET as a vibrant online community. The archiving and indexing allowed messages to be searched and sorted, and transformed ephemeral communications and unmanageable resources into a reference tool.

However, those who did not see archiving and indexing as positive features protested. They argued that indexing provided online surveillance, and that archiving threatened individual privacy. Many believed that BBSs were never intended to be traceable or permanent.

The debates intensified when Google, Inc. purchased the USENET archive from Deja.com. A for-profit company now claims ownership of the contributions of a collaborative online community. Author Ronda Hauben has argued that the purchase of USENET posts for a fee, or the claim of ownership to these posts, is contrary to users' initial understanding with regard to their posts; users generally considered their contributions as input to construct online communities, not profit-seeking. Hauben warned that declaring USENET correspondence to be commercial entities might curtail the communication processes on USENET.

Another event that brought USENET back into public discourse was the death of Jim Ellis, in June 2001, at age 45. Ellis and Truscott were recognized for creating USENET, the precursor of the Internet, and ushering in an era of email culture. At the time when USENET was conceived, interconnected computers were open only to government researchers and contractors—members of the Advanced Research Projects Agency, or ARPANET. Ellis, Truscott, Bellovin, and Daniel set up a system to allow university and non-governmental computers to share data over phone lines, and enable individual users to log on and post

messages. USENET quickly became a popular means of sharing information internationally, before the World Wide Web came into existence. Although it is being supplanted by email, chat, and other more user-friendly forms of online communication, USENET continues to be an important virtual community.

Bibliography

Hauben, Ronda. "Culture Clash: The Google Purchase of the 1995–2001 Usenet Archive and the Online Community." *TELEPOLIS*, February 26, 2001. <http://www.heise.de/tp/english/inhalt/te/7013/1.html> (June 7, 2002).

Moraes, Mark, "Answers to Frequently Asked Questions about Usenet." January 16, 1998. <news.announce.newusers>

———. "What Is Usenet?" January 16, 1998. <news.announce.newusers>.

Moschovitis, Christos J. P.; Poole, Hilary; Schuyler, Tami; and Theresa M. Senft. *History of the Internet: A Chronology, 1843 to the Present*. Santa Barbara, Calif.: ABC-CLIO, 1999.

Usenet Info Center Launch Pad. Web site. <http://www.ibiblio.org/usenet-i/> (June 7, 2002).

Further Reading

Harrison, Mark. *The Usenet Handbook: A User's Guide to Netnews*. Sebastopol, Calif.: O'Reilly & Associates, 1995.

Hauben, Michael, and Ronda Hauben. *Netizens: On the History and Impact of Usenet and the Internet*. Los Alamitos, Calif.: IEEE Computer Society Press, 1997.

Moraes, Mark. "Usenet Software: History and Sources." February 9, 1998. <news.admin.misc>

Related Topics

Bulletin-Board Systems; Netiquette; Newsgroups; Privacy; Spam; Virtual Community

— *Shing-Ling Sarina Chen*

Varian, Hal

1947–
Economist

Hal Varian is a central theorist of the knowledge economy. He earned a B.S. in economics at the Massachusetts Institute of Technology (MIT), an M.A. in mathematics and a Ph.D. in economics at the University of California–Berkeley (UCB), and has been a professor of economics and finance at MIT and the University of Michigan. He is professor and dean of the School of Information Management and Systems (SIMS) at UCB, and is also a professor in UCB's Haas School of Business and in its department of economics.

Varian's core principle is that "technology changes . . . economic laws do not." Based on this simple foundation, Varian has developed a series of insights by applying general economic principles to the specifics of the information economy.

Together with Carl Shapiro, Varian wrote *Information Rules: A Strategic Guide to the Network Economy* (1999). This book helps working managers to understand and apply the economic theories of the past quarter-century to a world in which information touches every aspect of business. Shapiro and Varian analyze historical and contemporary cases to illuminate today's information environments.

The book sums up Varian's central concerns. An overview of the information economy demonstrates that a new economy does not require new economics; what is needed is a thorough understanding of economics in information and technology, together with a grasp of policy issues.

Information is costly to create. Once information is developed, however, the production cost of each new unit is limited to the cost of the medium itself. In a digital world, producing information is as costly as ever, but reproducing it is nearly free. This determines how information industries should price their products and services. The book shows managers how to use such competitive strategies as product differentiation, cost leadership, and first-mover advantage, as well as how to customize products and pricing.

By applying the principle of customizing products and prices to information, Varian developed a concept he calls "versioning." Offering a menu of product versions allows a company's customers to segment themselves around products without costly market information.

In the information environment, intellectual property creates new challenges, including decisions on what information to give away and how to charge for the rest. Cheap reproduction and costly production make it imperative to adopt effective strategies to recover sunk costs. The problems of lock-in and switching costs—the costs associated with installing, learning, and adapting to new technology—are also serious issues in an information-technology environment. Sellers and buyers of information products must recognize and manage lock-in and switching costs in order to succeed.

The information economy also involves network effects and positive feedback or increasing returns. Network effects arise when products or services become increasingly valuable to each user in a network as more users use them. This principle is visible in networks of all kinds. For example, railroads become more valuable and useful as rail networks expand and link more users. While this principle predates the information economy, it becomes particularly visible in the kinds of networks shaped by information technology. The telephone systems that reshaped urban society at the beginning of the twentieth century are an example. Shapiro and Varian shape a useful chapter around the strategies that companies can use to exploit network effects to best advantage.

Networks give rise to specific strategy choices involving compatibility, standards, and cooperation between and among different firms, products, and systems. This, in turn, leads to a range of public-policy issues that any information company must face. *Information Rules* covers the many issues and choices that confront managers and companies in the information economy.

Varian also works in several areas of classical economic theory. He is the author of best-selling books on microeconomics and economic methodology, and has written many research papers and articles. His ability to simplify and generalize in clear, readable prose makes him a public intellectual in the tradition of economists such as Adam Smith and John Maynard Keynes.

Selected Works

Kahin, Bryan, and Hal R. Varian, eds. *Internet Publishing and Beyond: The Economics of Digital Information and Intellectual Property.* Cambridge, Mass.: MIT Press, 2000.

Lyman, Peter, and Hal R. Varian. *How Much Information?* Berkeley: School of Information Management and Systems, University of California, 2000. <http://www.sims.berkeley.edu/research/projects/how-much-info/summary.html> (April 15, 2002)

Shapiro, Carl, and Hal R. Varian. *Information Rules: A Strategic Guide to the Network Economy.* Cambridge, Mass.: Harvard Business School Press, 1998. <http://www.inforules.com/> (April 15, 2002)

———. "How to Build an Economic Model in Your Spare Time." *American Economist,* vol. 41, no. 2 (1997), pp. 3–10.

———. "The Information Economy. The Economics of the Internet, Information Goods, Intellectual Property, and Related Issues." School of Information Management and Systems, University of California–Berkeley. <http://www.sims.berkeley.edu/resources/infoecon/> (May 4, 2000)

———. *Selected Papers of Hal R. Varian.* London: Edward Elgar, Ltd., 2000.

Bibliography

"The e.biz 25. The Most Influential People in Electronic Business." *Business Week,* May 14, 2001.

Varian, Hal R. Home page. <http://www.sims.berkeley.edu/~hal/> (November 20, 2000)

Further Reading

Economides, Nicholas. "Economics of Networks Internet Site." Leonard N. Stern School of Business, New York University. <http://www.stern.nyu.edu/networks/site.html> (April 12, 2002).

National Research Council. *Fostering Research on the Economic and Social Impacts of Information Technology.* Washington, D.C.: National Academy Press, 1998.

Related Topics

Berners-Lee, Tim; E-Commerce; Electronic Publishing; Internet; World Wide Web

— *Ken Friedman*

vBNS

The acronym vBNS stands for "very high-speed backbone network service," which is a physical connection of wires and components that make up a special network. The functions of vBNS are similar to those of the Internet; however, the vBNS network possesses very unique features that differentiate the two.

Created in 1995 through a five-year agreement between the National Science Foundation (NSF) and MCI Telecommunications Corporation, the vBNS service is used to investigate new Internet technologies and protocols. The NSF, an independent federal agency that funds research in all fields of science, took an initiative in 1985 to support development of the Internet for education and research. Through a $50 million agreement with MCI, it was decided that the telecommunications company would supply and operate the necessary hardware for vBNS network operations.

The vBNS spans a large geographical area. Called a backbone service, it acts much like the nervous system of the human body, connecting the vital components of an organism—in this case, offering a structure for electronic communications between computers. The vBNS connects Super Computer Centers (SCCs) of selected institutions with Network Access Points (NAPs), which determine how Internet traffic is routed.

This service is unique in two major ways: speed of data transmission and permission for network access. Access is available only to vBNS-authorized institutions (VAIs) that have been granted a High Performance Connection Award by the NSF. In addition, the speed of the vBNS network can achieve rates that are multiple times faster than those of the commercial Internet. As described by *Interactive Age* contributor Richard Karpinski, the commercial Internet backbone mainly functions at a rate of 45mbps (megabits per second). Using advanced-technology networking components in 1996, the vBNS was capable of transmitting data at rates of 622mbps. The vBNS was an efficient alternative for research institutions, allowing massive amounts of information to be shared among researchers; for example, it could transfer 322 copies of a 300-page book every seven seconds.

The vBNS evolved from other experimental networks funded by the NSF. Decades earlier, the NSF constructed a network named NSFnet to facilitate communication between researchers. However, in

1995, the NSFnet was removed and replaced with a commercial Internet backbone to allow for the many World Wide Web functions of today. This led to the development of vBNS, and to the experimentation with the next generation of Internet technologies.

The vBNS played a critical role in former president Bill Clinton's Next Generation Internet (NGI) project. NGI called for the creation of the Internet2, which is directed by the University Corporation for Advanced Internet Development (UCAID). Internet2 was created in October 1996 to give non-commercial institutions, a chance to use a speedy service without NSF sanctioning. According to *Library Journal* writer Michael Rogers, the Internet2 would provide institutions with the ability to transfer the complete *Encyclopedia Britannica* in nearly one second. The vBNS offers part of its infrastructure to the Internet2.

The success of vBNS lies largely in what separates it from the commercial Internet. George Strawn and Mark Luker of the NSF state that the vBNS' additional characteristics significantly improve the high-bandwidth network; it allows researchers to reserve time on the network for optimal transfer or processing, and it allows for distributed computing (multiple remote computers administrating bulks of information simultaneously). Furthermore, the service can support multicasting for highly defined video and multimedia communications.

In 2000, the NSF and MCI agreed to continue the development and operation of the vBNS until March 2003. Currently, the vBNS is able to transmit data at 2.4gbps (gigabits per second), or 2,400,000,000 bits per second, compared to 622mbps in 1996. As of 2000, the vBNS connects 101 institutions, 94 of which are universities within the United States.

While the future of the vBNS, as well as that of other advanced Internet technologies, may be dependent on funding from the NSF, its invention has already shaped the networks of tomorrow. Opportunities are becoming available to commercial businesses with the advent of vBNS+, vBNS service that is being made available to any consumer willing to pay for it.

Bibliography

Karpinski, Richard. "MCI Kicks Off vBNS." *Interactive Age,* vol. 2, no. 13 (April 24, 1995).

National Science Foundation. "vBNS—Very High Speed Backbone Network System." <http://www.nsf.gov/od/lpa/nsf50/nsfoutreach/htm/n50_z2/pages_z3/47_pg.htm> (May 10, 2002).

Rogers, Michael. "VP Gore Unveils Plans for Superfast Academic Internet2." *Library Journal,* May 15, 1998.

Further Reading

Engebreston, Joan. "A Framework for Growth." *Telephony*, October 25, 1999.

Goth, Nikki. "An Express Lane?" *Industry Week,* June 22, 1998.

"NSFnet." Webopedia, 2002. <http://www.webopedia.com/TERM/N/NSFnet.html> (May 10, 2002).

NSF News. "NSF and MCI Agree to Three-Year No-Cost Extension of vBNS." April 10, 2000. <http://www.nsf.gov/od/lpa/news/press/00/pr0020.htm> (May 10, 2002).

Related Topics

Internet; World Wide Web

— *James Pyfer*

Videoconferencing

Videoconferencing refers to the transmission of images (via video) and sounds (via audio) between two or more physically separate locations. Once the sole province of the corporate boardroom, videoconferencing is used today in telemedicine, distance education, theatrical productions, political trials, and anywhere else the ability to "be here now" is desired. Travel fears subsequent to the September 11, 2001, terrorist attacks seem to have bolstered U.S. market interest in videoconferencing even further, prompting TeleSpan publisher Elliot Gold to recently quip, "We are now a 10-year overnight success."

THE RISE AND FALL OF THE PICTUREPHONE

The story of videoconferencing began in the United States in the 1920s, when Bell Labs connected two callers between Washington, D.C., and New York City) and continued during the 1930s in Europe, where television technologies were more mature. By 1964, AT&T was ready to introduce its first public videoconferencing tool—the Picturephone—at the World's Fair. After spending $500 million on development and predicting one million users by 1980, AT&T was stunned when the Picturephone turned out to be a financial failure, garnering only 200 subscribers.

Some researchers have suggested that the Picturephone failed because people simply dislike face-to-face communication via telephone. Others maintained that it was wrongly designed for one-to-one communication, whereas "multipoint" communication (à la conference calls) is how most businesses conduct remote conferencing. As industry expert James

A video conference. (Robert Llewellyn/CORBIS)

Wilcox explains, much of the 1970s and 1980s was spent developing multipoint technologies, with British Telecom persuading telephone companies around Europe to conduct country-to-country trials of equipment. These trials paved the way for the videoconferencing interoperability standards that exist today, and allow multipoint videoconferencing like Stanford's "virtual auditorium" project.

FROM TOY TO TOOL

In its early days, videoconferencing seemed to many to be more a high-tech toy than a necessary communications tool: Videoconferences could be conducted only out of specially equipped rooms costing from $250,000 to $1,000,000 or more. It was only after the arrival of low-cost solid-state memory in the late 1980s that "set-top" systems started becoming available, with prices at a more manageable $10,000 or so. Set-tops, often configured as rolling carts, were responsible for broadening videoconferencing's uses beyond the traditional office. Director Peter Jackson recently used it to coordinate multiple film crews shooting *Lord of the Rings* (2001) in remote New Zealand locations, and President George W. Bush

conducts videoconferences with his advisers in Washington on days when he is at his Texas ranch.

Whether room-based or set-top, the mechanics of videoconferencing are the same. First, analog signals from video cameras and microphones are translated to digital information inside one's home computer. This is done by way of a codec (a truncated combination of the words "compression" and "decompression"), a compression and decompression standard that is often called the heart of a videoconferencing system. Codecs, which can be either hardware or software, compress outgoing information so it can be quickly and successfully sent via telephone connections; later, the codec decompresses incoming information for viewing. Finally, if multipoint videoconferencing is desired, an expensive multipoint processing unit, sometimes called a "bridge," must also be implemented. Although another solution, called "multicasting," does exist, it is not technically feasible for most users today.

With high bandwidth connections, it is now possible to view videoconferences at so-called "television quality" levels—that is, at 30 frames per second. Unfortunately, videoconferencing still seems to many to be a technology that promises more than it delivers. For example, because it is often more important to hear what is being said in a meeting than it is to see clearly, it is a rule of thumb that a good videoconferencing system will sacrifice video for audio clarity. Nonetheless, participants are often confused by the mechanics of half-duplex ("walkie-talkie") sound, and even have trouble figuring out turn-taking when full-duplex is used. What's more, according to technology reporter Clive Thompson, "If you have an automated camera that tracks you by the sound of your voice, it will become totally confused the instant more than one person begins to speak."

The technical term for what Thompson describes is "spatialization," perhaps best thought of as the "here" part of videoconferencing's mission to "be here now." Specialization drives much of the research of virtual-reality pioneer Jaron Lanier, who recently introduced a full-scale immersive videoconferencing system that he calls the "telecubicle." William Buxton, on the other hand, maintains that rather than building immersion rooms, videoconferencing's problems are better solved by what he calls a mobile and "ubiquitous media approach." One such example is the Hydra system, which uses head-mounted cameras in addition to stationary units, in order to designate who is looking at whom during a videoconferencing session.

IP-BASED AND DESKTOP VIDEOCONFERENCING

When discussing high-quality videoconferencing, it is important to understand that, almost without exception, transmissions are occurring via high-bandwidth phone connections (such as T1s or multiple ISDN lines) or via satellite connections. Although ISDN is the preferred videoconferencing conduit of 80 percent of businesses today, there is increased interest in "IP-based videoconferencing." Most of this interest stems from experiments like those of Buxton and Lanier, using the power of Internet 2. Internet 2, an exclusive network created by 150 universities, is rumored to have 45 times more bandwidth than the ordinary Internet. Unfortunately for businesses, Internet 2 is not available for public use, but Wire One and Sprint have recently rushed to fill that gap, launching proprietary networks designed to carry video over IP.

Today, it is common to hear people speak of "desktop videoconferencing" over the Internet. This practice began in 1994, when Intel introduced ProShare for Windows PCs, which required only a Web-camera and microphone, a sound card, a reasonably high-speed Internet connection, and videoconferencing software

such as Microsoft NetMeeting or ISPQ. Today, some four million users "videoconference on the cheap"— enough to prompt Yahoo and Windows XP to recently announce that they would offer video imaging with their instant-message services.

Videoconferencing over the Internet is not a new idea. Indeed, experiments were conducted to this end as early as the 1970s, but most were abandoned as scientists discovered what many desktop users now know all too well: Two-way videoconferencing requires a great deal of bandwidth to execute successfully. Even with a broadband connection via cable modem or DSL, the average desktop videoconferencer deals with grainy images and poor sound quality. Still, many people seem happy to experience the novelty and convenience of videoconferencing with one another at any quality level, particularly after the terrorist attacks of September 11, 2001, when fear of travel rose dramatically.

In 2002, videoconferencing operated as a $2 billion industry, with projections of $7 billion by 2006. What's more, videoconferencing is increasingly used worldwide in a variety of ways, altering what it means to "be here now" on a daily basis. Recently, the Securities and Exchange Commission debated what constituted a binding agreement arrived at during a videoconference, while the United Nations announced a plan to use videoconferencing to help remote witnesses to testify safely during Rwanda's genocide trials. These two examples alone illustrate that, even more than its financial future, videoconferencing's social present begs deeper analysis and discussion.

Bibliography

Benford, Steve, et al. "Understanding and Constructing Shared Spaces with Mixed-Reality Boundaries." *Transactions on Computer-Human Interaction* 5, no. 3 (1998), pp. 185–223.

Buxton, William. "Living in Augmented Reality: Ubiquitous Media and Reactive Environments." *Video Mediated Communication*. K. Finn, A. Sellen, and S. Wilber, eds. Mahwah, N.J.: Erlbaum Associates, 1997; pp. 363–84.

Chen, Milton. "Design of a Virtual Auditorium." Paper presented at the MM 01: International Conference on Multimedia, Ottawa, Canada, September 30–October 5, 2001.

Denison, D.C. "Videoconferencing Hot." *The Boston Globe*, September 23, 2001, p. E1.

Dixon, Robert S. "Internet Videoconferencing: Coming to Your Campus Soon!" *Educause Quarterly*, no. 4 (2000), pp. 22–27.

Earon, S. Ann. "The Economics of Deploying Videoconferencing." *Business Communications Review* 28, no. 11 (1998), pp. 43–48.

Gallagher, Leigh. "Videoconferencing—a Costly, Glitch-Ridden Dream." *The Business Times Singapore*, August 13, 2001, p. SS8.

Gertrude Stein Repertory Company. Web site. <http://www.gertstein.org/> (June 7, 2002).

Gilmer, Kelly Ryan. "High-Tech Language Lessons Go Far." *St. Petersburg Times,* January 6, 2002, p. 1B.

Heun, Christopher T. "Videoconferencing Makes the White House." *Information Week,* November 19, 2001, p. 16.

Lundsten, Apryl, and Robert Doiel. "Digital Video and Internet 2: Growing Up Together." *Syllabus Magazine,* August 2000. Center for Scholarly Technology, University of Southern California. <http://www.usc.edu/isd/locations/cst/techbytes.html> (June 7, 2002).

Lyons, Sheridan. "Jail Video Funds Likely." *The Baltimore Sun*, January 28, 2002, p. 1B.

McCracken, Harry. "Reach Out and See Someone." *PC World*, April 2001, 35-36.

Noll, A. M. "Anatomy of a Failure: Picturephone Revisited." *Telecommunications Policy* 16, no. 4 (1992), pp. 307–16.

O'Neil, John. "Improving Care, Via the Phone Line." *The New York Times*, January 22, 2001, p. F8.

Phan, Monty. "Triumph of the Teleconference; Meetings Via Phone, Video and Web Surge after Mass Travel Cancellations." *Newsday*, November 7, 2001, p. C10.

Thompson, Clive. "Never Mind Videoconferencing. 'Telepresence' Is the New Virtual Reality." *The Globe and Mail*, October 27, 2000, p. 33.

Varian, Hal R. "Economic Scene; Videoconferencing May at Last Get the Critical Mass It Needs." *The New York Times*, October 4, 2001, p. C2.

Further Reading

Buxton, William. "Space-Function Integration and Ubiquitous Media." BillBuxton.com, 2002. <http://www.billbuxton.com/ubiVid.html> (June 7, 2002).

Cadiz, J. J.; Balachandran, Anand; Sanocki, Elizabeth; Gupta, Anoop; Grudin, Jonathan; and Gavin Jancke. "Distance Learning through Distributed Collaborative Video Viewing." Paper presented at the ACM 2000 Conference on Computer Supported Cooperative Work, Philadelphia, Pennsylvania, 2000.

Finn, Kathleen E.; Sellen, Abigail J.; and Sylvia B. Wilber, eds. *Video-Mediated Communication*. Mahwah, N.J.: Erlbaum Associates, 1997.

Fister, Sarah. "Videoconferencing: Good, Fast and Cheap." *Training* 37, no. 4 (2001), pp. 30–32.

Proximity Inc. "Proximity Videoconferencing: Glossary." 2001. <http://www.proximity.com/glossary/index.html> (June 7, 2002).

Rhodes, John. *Videoconferencing for the Real World: Implementing Effective Visual Communications Systems.* Boston, Mass.: Focal Press, 2001.

Schneider, Laura. "About Internet Conferencing—Instant Messaging, Video Chat, Webcams, and More." 2002. <http://netconference.about.com/> (June 7, 2002).

Video Development Initiative. "Videoconferencing Cookbook Version 2.0." June 2000. <http://www.vide.gatech.edu/cookbook2.1/> (June 7, 2002).

Webster, Jane. "Desktop Videoconferencing: Experiences of Complete Users, Wary Users, and Non-Users." *MIS Quarterly* 22, no. 3 (1998), pp. 257–86.

Related Topics

Broadband; Chat; Codec; Distance Learning; Lanier, Jaron; Telemedicine; Webcamming

— Theresa M. Senft

Videotex

Designed in the late 1970s to mid-1980s, videotex was an information delivery system for the home, and one of the earliest incarnations of "end-user information systems." Typically, videotex systems were menu-driven systems designed for display on television sets. Videotex information included news, weather, and local information and services (such as bus schedules, entertainment event listings, etc.). Many large media firms implemented videotex systems in the United States, and several countries (notably England and Canada) invested large amounts of money in videotex. However, by the late 1990s, with the exception of the Minitel system in France, videotex was defunct.

Videotex systems comprised three major components: information retrieval and display terminals, typically television sets with an attached decoder that translated digital signals into an audio display; transmission lines for interactive communication, usually the public-switched telephone network, a cable-television coaxial-cable network, a communications-satellite system, microwave facilities, or a combination thereof; and computer hardware and software as the delivery device.

In the mid-1980s, giant media firms in the United States such as Times Mirror, Knight-Ridder, Warner, and Time invested large amounts of money into developing videotex systems, only to see them fail. For instance, Knight-Ridder's Videotron service in southern Florida was launched in 1983 with 5,000 subscribers, but three years later lost $50 million in revenue. The reasons for failure were numerous: Videotex operators found it difficult to attract customers, and advertisers were reluctant to sign up; delivery by telephone line meant that customers' lines were tied up; the decoder boxes were notoriously difficult to use; and the touted interactivity was negligible.

Unlike in the United States, where commercial interests (including many newspaper chains) developed videotex systems, in Europe several governments developed and funded them. In England, the British Post Office (now British Telecom) developed the Prestel system in 1979. Initially predicting 100,000 users by 1981, in 1989 Prestel had only 90,000 customers. Canada's Communications Research Centre, the research arm of the federal Department of Communications, developed Telidon, which was widely touted in policy circles as key to positioning Canada as a leader in technological innovation. However, as with other videotex systems, Telidon failed miserably in the market.

Minitel, developed by France Télécom in the early 1980s to provide an online telephone directory, has proven to be a resilient and popular videotex system. Minitel accesses the Teletel Network, a distributed information network for email and diverse information resources. One of the reasons that Minitel became so successful was the popularity of its *messageries*, or chat services; particularly popular are the *messageries roses*, or adult-oriented chat lines. In 1998, Minitel was more popular in France than the Internet, with 6.5 million Minitel terminals used by 14 million people, and 24,600 services provided by over 10,000 companies.

The failure of videotex systems can be attributed to their technical limitations, and to their lack of varied social uses; many customers were deterred by awkward interfaces and poor interactivity. Despite the prognostications of information-society theorists, the commercial content provided on videotex was just not compelling enough, nor was it sustainable for advertisers and content providers.

Bibliography

Case, Donald. "The Social Shaping of Videotex: How Information Services for the Public Have Evolved." *Journal of the American Society for Information Science,* vol. 45, no. 7 (1994), pp. 483–97.

Madden, John C. *Videotex in Canada.* Ottawa, Ont.: Government of Canada, Department of Communications, 1979.

Mosco, Vincent. *Pushbutton Fantasies: Critical Perspectives on Videotex and Information Technology.* Norwood, N.J.: Ablex Publishing, 1982.

Pryor, Larry. "The Videotex Debacle." *American Journalism Review,* vol. 16, no. 9 (November 1994), p. 40.

Tagliabue, John. "Online Cohabitation: Internet and Minitel: Videotex System in France Proves Unusually Resilient." *The New York Times,* June 2, 2001, p. B1.

Further Reading

"Clunk-click Every Trip. (12-year-old Minitel Service Is Part of Everyday Life in France)." *The Economist,* vol. 336, no. 7,928 (August 19, 1995), p. 62.

Godfrey, David, and Ernest Chang, eds. *The Telidon Book: Designing and Using Videotex Systems.* Reston, Va.: Reston Publishing, 1981.

Lytel, David. "Media Regimes and Political Communication: Democracy and Interactive Media in France." *Political Communication* vol. 13, no. 4 (October–December 1996), p. 483.

Tydeman, John, et al. *Telextext and Videotex in the United States: Market Potential, Technology, Public Policy Issues.* New York: McGraw-Hill, 1982.

Related Topics

Minitel

— *Leslie Regan Shade*

Virtual Community

While there is no general agreement regarding the exact definition of virtual community, at a minimum, virtual communities are groups of people connected primarily (if not solely) through online interaction. The term virtual community has been applied to groups formed through a variety of online forums, including email listservs, bulletin-board services (BBSs), USENET newsgroups, MUDs and MOOs (Multi-User Dungeons and MUDs Object-Oriented), and other forms of online chat. Virtual communities have also been an important focus of researchers studying online communication. The two key questions that such research has addressed have been whether or not online groups can be considered communities, and whether such online communities enhance or detract from offline connections. A focus on virtual community has therefore been at the very center of debates regarding the potential positive or negative effects of the increased use of computers and the Internet.

One reason for the lack of agreement on a definition of virtual community is the long history of disagreement over the definition of community itself. While heavily used in sociological research, community researchers themselves have pointed out that the term community is vague, means different things to different people, and is often used in a way that does not so much objectively describe a form of human organization as convey a moral ideal for human connection and interdependence. Similarly, the term virtual community has been applied to various types of online groups without much consistency regarding what factors qualify a group as a virtual community.

Concerns regarding community are central to discussions of new uses of computers and the Internet. In these discussions, some common themes emerge regarding the content and composition of virtual communities. One necessary component seems to be sufficient time to form relationships among members, develop shared culture and norms, and give a sense of shared history to group members. Other components discussed in definitions of virtual community include: honest and open communication among members, interdependence and mutual support, shared interests, and the ability of the community as a whole to provide something useful to its members, whether that is information and knowledge, emotional support, or economic benefits.

THE WELL AND LAMBDAMOO

A variety of online groups have been described as virtual communities. The WELL (Whole Earth 'Lectronic Link), an online BBS, is one of the oldest and most famous examples of a virtual community. Founded in 1985, the WELL allows users to log on and post typed messages for others to read. Messages are organized in topically subdivided "conferences." *The Virtual Community: Homesteading on the Electronic Frontier* (1993), Howard Rheingold's influential book on the topic of online communities, includes a description of his experiences on the WELL, as well as discussions of the definitions, origins, and importance of virtual communities.

Rheingold and other WELL participants who have written accounts of their experiences have emphasized several aspects of those experiences that lead them to term the WELL a virtual community. The most important of these aspects is the emotional connection between the people involved. Participants speak of forming close relationships with others, some of which involve contact and interaction offline as well as online. The WELL has also evolved a culture that includes particular norms and understandings, as reflected in documents intended to educate new members, and stories of sanctions against those who violated group rules.

Another famous example of virtual community is LambdaMOO. One of the oldest and most famous

still-running MUDs on the Internet, LambdaMOO, like other MOOs and MUDs, is a computer program that allows multiple users to connect from remote locations, and to interact with the program and communicate with each other. Unlike the WELL, where one person's posts may be read hours or days later by others, LambdaMOO provides a forum for chat, in which communication more closely resembles face-to-face discussions.

LambdaMOO shares several features with the WELL, related to its status as a virtual community. Like the WELL, LambdaMOO attempts to educate newcomers. The first text seen upon connection to LambdaMOO compares it to an international city, and specifically requests that journalists and researchers ask permission before quoting material from LambdaMOO. LambdaMOO's "help manners" document provides more detailed information regarding behavioral expectations and norms. Both the WELL and LambdaMOO also have traditions of offline gatherings. Participants often find these gatherings to be important to their feelings of connection to other members of the group, suggesting that some offline contact may be an important component of virtual communities.

FREENETS AND COMMUNITY NETWORKS

Virtual communities have also been started and fostered by existing offline communities. Town governments and civic organizations have sought to use the Internet to help strengthen relationships and participation in offline communities. Goals of these auxiliary virtual communities often include providing greater access to governmental documents and procedures, fostering an increase in civic participation, and providing free access to the Internet for less-affluent community members. Many community networks are oriented toward social change and improved government.

Cleveland Freenet was started by Dr. Tom Grundner in 1984 at the School of Medicine at Case Western Reserve University as a project to provide answers to medical questions, and expanded in 1986 to become a more general public network. To facilitate the proliferation of public-access freenets, Dr. Grunder also established the National Public Telecomputing Network (NPTN) in 1989. Many other communities adopted the Cleveland Freenet model. These freenets usually offer email accounts, access to local newsgroups and community information, and sometimes connection to the Internet.

Neither NPTN nor the original Cleveland Freenet still exist, but numerous other international organizations have sprung up to facilitate community networking, and several alternative freenets now offer services in Cleveland.

Most freenets are started by private individuals or non-profit groups, but some community networks are also started by governmental agencies. The first of these was Public Electronic Network (PEN) in Santa Monica, California. Started in 1989, PEN was intended to give citizens access to governmental documents and information, but as it developed, community members used it primarily to talk to each other rather than to city hall.

PEN was also formed with the specific intent to provide access to Santa Monica's less-affluent members, and was remarkably successful in connecting people from different walks of life. In particular, it fostered the formation of a homelessness activist group, which helped develop better city services for the homeless. However, PEN was also plagued by increasingly hostile invective, possibly facilitated by the anonymity provided by the system.

VIRTUAL COMMUNITIES, WORK, AND COMMERCE

The term virtual community has also been applied to a variety of work-oriented groups. Researchers engaged in computer-supported collaborative work have been interested in ways to foster a sense of community among people collaborating on projects from distant locations. Such virtual communities may be limited to a particular project or company group, or they may provide a forum for all members of a particular profession. One example of the latter was BioMOO, a MUD intended as a virtual meeting place for biologists. (BioMOO ran for many years, but was shut down in 2001 due to lack of participation.)

In addition, during the dot-com boom of the 1990s, when increasing numbers of companies were attempting to find profitable ways to use the Internet, corporations became interested in the concept of virtual community. Some companies attempted to find ways to provide and charge for community-building services, while others attempted to build "communities" around particular products. The question of whether commercially oriented groups constitute communities continues to foster debate.

Both for-profit and non-profit organizations have also sought to build virtual communities among members, employees, or groups that are tied to the organizations in some way, such as clients, contributors, or suppliers. These intranets (available solely to people within a single company) and extranets (providing access to a limited set of people outside the company) seek to strengthen relationships and provide forums for the exchange of organizational knowledge.

POSSIBILITIES AND PROBLEMS

Perhaps because of the specialized focus of virtual communities formed for work and business purposes, definitions of virtual communities provided in discussions of computer-supported collaborative work and of organizational virtual communities have emphasized many-to-many communication and the exchange of information. Much of the material available online and in print in this area consists of suggestions for building such communities. Discussions of other types of virtual community have focused more on communal feeling and interdependence of members. Descriptions of leisure-oriented virtual communities often provide tales of community reaction to the life trauma of a member, with the willingness of community members to provide support and assistance given as evidence of the strength and importance of such communities.

Beyond just psychological and moral support for virtual-community members, other forms of assistance are often provided, such as money, transportation, etc., much as in offline communities. These forms of assistance demonstrate the fact that virtual communities often do not exist solely online; the connections between people may extend to their offline lives as well. Researchers studying virtual communities have found that community members often desire to meet each other face-to-face. Many groups that last for more than a few months organize offline group meetings. Such meetings do not always include all members of the community, but face-to-face contact, even among only a few core members, appears to strengthen communal bonds.

Probably the most controversial issue regarding virtual communities concerns their relationship to non-virtual communities. Rheingold, among others, has suggested that virtual communities have arisen in response to a perceived void in modern life, implying that virtual communities increase as offline community decreases. Others have been less concerned about the effect of offline life on virtual communities and more concerned with the effect of virtual communities on cities, neighborhoods, and other offline communities. Does online participation detract from or enhance people's offline relationships? Can virtual communities be effectively used for the purpose of offline community action? Or does online participation lead people to neglect the physical communities in which they reside? Both popular opinion and the growing body of research on virtual communities provide conflicting information on these questions, providing no clear answers as yet.

Some studies suggest that virtual communities are merely quasi-communal "enclaves" of people sharing similar interests that lack the diversity and interdependence of a real community. This gives rise to fears that people will neglect the difficult work of building coalitions in physical communities, and that the relatively privileged online participants will neglect their responsibilities to offline communities that also include less-privileged others.

Some research has also suggested that people who are active online and in virtual communities become more physically isolated. Other research has directly contradicted this, suggesting that, if anything, online connections add to and even strengthen offline ties, increasing the overall level of sociability. Virtual communities may also foster continuity in the face of increasing mobility, particularly among the middle class.

While many virtual communities, such as the WELL and LambdaMOO, have existed for more than ten years, others have failed or persist only in a reduced form. It is too early in the history of the Internet to tell how important virtual communities will become or what forms they will take, and several central questions remain. Primary among these, and probably the most hotly debated, is the issue of whether virtual communities are generally only insular pseudo-communities—enclaves of people with similar backgrounds and interests who seek comfort with others like themselves rather than doing the difficult work of connecting with people from different backgrounds.

While research begins to provide answers to the question of what makes for a successful virtual community, remaining questions include: 1) whether and to what extent some face-to-face contact is necessary; 2) the effect of identity continuity on interpersonal relationships and community cohesiveness, including the question of balancing accountability and anonymity; and 3) what role various types of economic relationships play in such communities. One certainty is that people do continue to have an interest in connecting to and communicating with each other online; therefore, discussions of these issues and many others are likely to remain central to ongoing debates about the Internet and online life.

Bibliography

Cothrel, Joseph. "Virtual Communities Today." *The Journal of the Association for Global Strategic Information*, July 1999. <http://www.participate.com/research/art-virtualcommunities.asp> (June 7, 2002).

Dibbell, Julian. *My Tiny Life: Crime and Passion in a Virtual World.* New York: Henry Holt, 1998.

Hegel III, John, and Arthur G. Armstrong. *Net.Gain: Expanding Markets Through Virtual Communities.* Boston, Mass.: Harvard Business School Press, 1997.

Jones, Steven, ed. *Cybersociety: Computer-Mediated Communication and Community.* Thousand Oaks, Calif.: Sage, 1995.

Rheingold, Howard. *The Virtual Community: Homesteading on the Electronic Frontier.* Reading, Mass.: Addison-Wesley, 1993.

Salmons, Janet. "Virtual Community-Building for Nonprofit Organizations." Techsoup.org, June 19, 2001. <http://www.techsoup.org/articlepage.cfm?ArticleId=301&topicid=5> (June 7, 2002).

Further Reading

Jones, Steven. *Virtual Culture: Identity and Communication in Cybersociety.* London: Sage, 1997.

Kendall, Lori Sue. *Hanging Out in the Virtual Pub: Masculinities and Relationships Online.* Berkeley, Calif.: University of California Press, 2002.

Porter, David. *Internet Culture.* New York: Routledge, 1997.

Smith, Marc, and Peter Kollock, eds. *Communities and Cyberspace.* New York: Routledge, 1999.

Turkle, Sherry. *Life on the Screen: Identity in the Age of the Internet.* New York: Simon & Schuster, 1995.

Related Topics

Chat; Computer-Supported Collaborative Work; Freenet (Community Networks); LambdaMOO; MUDs and MOOs; Rheingold, Howard; TinyMUD; USENET; Whole Earth 'Lectronic Link

— *Lori Kendall*

Virtual Reality

Virtual reality (VR) is a computer-created and computer-mediated simulation of a real or imagined environment. It has uses in many fields, including design, entertainment, art, and education. VR is most commonly a visual environment that is experienced in three dimensions of width, height, and depth to provide an illusion of reality. This notion of illusion has led to another common use of the term virtual reality to refer to any virtual (as opposed to corporeal) environment represented by the use of the computer, be it text-based or graphic representation. This popular use of the term describes any computer-mediated environment, and has little to do with the three-dimensional simulation to be discussed here.

VR can be created with a wide variety of computer hardware and software. As a result, the quality of simulation provided by VR offers various degrees of fidelity depending on the technologies employed. The simplest form of VR with the lowest level of fidelity is desktop VR, which allows users to view environments as they move around using the keyboard or the mouse. By manipulating keys or controlling the mouse, users can move an image in different directions or zoom in and out as desired. This type of VR system lacks the three-dimensional display common to most VR technology. However, some desktop VR does offer three-dimensional images to be explored at a personal computer. Popular products for creating VR effects on personal computers include Extreme 3D, Ray Dream Studio, trueSpace, 3D Studio MAX, and Visual Reality. The Virtual Reality Modeling Language (VRML) allows the creator to specify images and the rules for their interaction using textual language statements.

A more complex form of VR involves the use of head-mounted displays, headphones, motion platforms, data suits, and other interaction devices. All of these devices feed sensory input to the user and monitor, or track, the user's actions. Head-mounted displays are stereoscopic goggles that provide three-dimensional imagery and also track the user's eye/head movement in order to supply images correlated to that movement. Headphones supply three-dimensional sound. Motion platforms can provide simulated gravitational and inertial forces. Data suits offer tactile input and provide the computer with body-movement tracking information. Data gloves allow the user to point to and manipulate computer-generated objects displayed on the monitor inside the goggles. Speech-recognition systems may also be employed. The more technologies that are used, the higher the fidelity of VR experience that is generated, and the greater the perception of reality on the part of the user. When using these various VR technologies, the user's various senses are occupied by the computer's simulations.

Even more sophisticated efforts involve the use of multi-sided rooms augmented with wearable computers and joystick devices that allow the user to feel the display images in motion. The user can walk into a room (typically 10' x 10') that has screens that completely fill the user's peripheral vision, creating an immersive experience. The CAVE virtual environment is the most common technology employed for this kind of VR. As such systems require advanced and expensive computer hardware and software, they are presently generally limited to research laboratories.

THE USES OF VR

With its capacity to create an illusion of reality, VR has many uses for training and entertainment. For example, the military and medical industries use VR environments for training pilots and surgeons. VR improves upon older training methods, such as manuals and videos, by providing an experience. Both print and video contain descriptions and visual demonstrations using static photographs or images in motion, but they do not provide the opportunity to exercise the skills. Military or medical students can acquire not only the knowledge of flying or operating, but can also experience the sensation of actually executing the skills, without putting anyone at risk.

VR also has uses in architecture and real estate. Architects use VR to design simulated homes and buildings, and clients can take virtual "walk-throughs" of buildings, not only to see what their homes will be like, but also to make changes to a plan if needed.

VR can also serve as a communication medium connecting multiple users. VR devices can be linked together like a computer or telephone network. Print, telephone, or email all generate social ties among users; however, the experience with these technologies is restricted to visual and/or aural modes. VR can enhance the experience by providing motion, tactile contact, interaction with objects, and a greater sense of collaboration due to shared space.

VR is widely used in entertainment as well. Video arcades have many VR games, such as simulated car, motorcycle, watercraft, and snowboard rides. Disney Corporation's Disney Quest attractions are an example of the use of VR technology to create virtual theme parks. Sophisticated VR games provide an enclosed environment eliminating any corporeal input, where the user becomes a self-contained entity. The user, then, instead of controlling a character with a joystick, becomes the character him/herself.

Much like offering the experience of playing a character in video games, VR systems provide the opportunity to role-play fictional characters. Users of video games generally choose from a selection of predetermined characters, and live out the sensation of being the chosen character during the game. Similarly, VR provides a simulated environment in which users construct an enhanced—stronger or more attractive—self-image.

VR also allows users to acquire experiences beyond physical or social limitations. People who are physically restricted can use VR systems to engage in activities that are impossible in the corporeal environment—for instance, experiencing the sensation of playing sports through the use of VR. In addition, individuals who do not have the financial means to travel could virtually travel around the world with the use of VR, visiting landmarks or experiencing a walk on the moon.

THE EXPERIENCE OF VR

With a capacity to create an illusion of reality, and with many uses in training and entertainment, VR generates significant impacts on users. Effects of VR are most evident in the areas of telepresence, suspension of disbelief, role playing, and the carry-over effect.

VR is able to generate a vivid experience of being present in an artificial environment by providing input to occupy the user's various senses. The illusion of presence is a form of telepresence, the experience of presence in a mediated environment, as opposed to the experience of presence in the immediate physical environment.

Although many media provide telepresence, VR may very well be the best medium for telepresence with high fidelity, as it utilizes more senses than any other medium. Additionally, VR, particularly in more immersive forms such as the CAVE, is experienced from a user-centered perspective, further enhancing the feeling of telepresence. Instead of being presented with particular views and images, as is the case with other media, the user's choices of direction, viewing angle, sightline, and the like are what determine the experience.

The high fidelity of VR experience, compared to the use of other media, requires much less effort on the part of the users to suspend their disbelief during use. It is believed that in order to enjoy the environment/content offered by the media, users must temporarily suspend their knowledge that it is a pretense, and willfully accept the environment/content as real. Readers of novels and viewers of television shows exercise suspension of disbelief to enjoy the storyline and to feel for the characters. Suspension of disbelief seems to require more effort when the medium uses only one or two senses; by occupying various senses, VR makes it easier to suspend disbelief.

Unlike the plot in a novel or a television show, which is predetermined, the storyline in a VR environment can be partially determined by the user. The VR experience is therefore less predictable and more eventful. In addition, the opportunity to role-play or express oneself in a virtual environment could have both psychological ramifications and social implications. From the outset, the sensations provided by VR activities can energize a user emotionally.

VR activities can also serve as release valves by providing the users with a safe environment in which to release their emotions without consequences. The enhanced self experienced in role-play also serves to compensate for whatever is lost or less desirable in the real-life situation. VR has been used by therapists and psychologists to transform patients' experiences and to assist in adjusting to life in the corporeal environment. Joan Hamilton and associates reported that psychologists found VR environments useful to alter the perspectives of their patients, and to treat depression; Barbara Rothbaum and associates also found that therapists successfully utilized VR environments to treat acrophobia. The successful treatment of depression and acrophobia attests to the transformative effect of VR technology.

The experience of role-playing others in VR may also enhances users' consciousness of the experience of others. According to Michael Shapiro and Daniel McDonald, a man who role-played a woman in VR could feel the sensory experience of a female character, and derive a feminine experience when others acted toward him as though he were a woman. The virtually "first-hand" experience of role-playing people of different sexual orientations or races in VR may entice the users to be more sensitive and understanding to these individuals in real-life situations because, according to Frederick, they have virtually "walked a mile in someone else's shoes."

The development of VR technology is still in its early stages. However, with its potential in education, communication, and entertainment, many researchers have recognized it as a powerful medium. Howard Rheingold has argued that VR will redefine the notion of "reality" in the twenty-first century, much as the telephone and television did in the twentieth century.

Bibliography

Biocca, Frank. "Communication Within Virtual Reality: Creating a Space for Research." *Journal of Communication* 42, no. 4 (1992), pp. 5–22.

Couch, Carl. *Social Processes and Relationships*. Dix Hills, N.Y.: General Hall, 1989.

Frederick, Douglas. *Am I Virtually Me?* M.A. thesis, Department of Communication Studies, University of Northern Iowa, 1997.

Gottschalk, Simon. "Videology: Video-Games as Postmodern Sites/Sights of Ideological Reproduction." *Symbolic Interaction* 18, no. 1 (1995): 1–18.

Hamilton, Joan; Smith, Emily; McWilliams, Gary; Schwartz, Evan; and John Carey. "Virtual Reality: How a Computer-Generated World Could Change the Real World." *BusinessWeek*, October 5, 1992, pp. 96–105.

Rheingold, Howard. *Virtual Reality.* New York: Summit Books, 1991.

Rothbaum, Barbara; Hodges, Larry; Kooper, Rob; Opdyke, Dan; Williford, James; and Max North. "Virtual Reality Graded Exposure in the Treatment of Acrophobia: A Case Report." *Behavior Therapy* 26 (1995), pp. 547–54.

Shapiro, Michael, and Daniel McDonald. "I'm Not a Real Doctor, But I Play One in Virtual Reality: Implications of Virtual Reality for Judgments about Reality." *Journal of Communication* 42, no. 4 (1992), pp. 94–114.

Steur, Jonathan. "Defining Virtual Reality: Dimensions Determining Telepresence." *Journal of Communication* 42, no. 4 (1992), pp. 73–93.

Further Reading

Biocca, Frank, and Mark R. Levy, eds. *Communication in the Age of Virtual Reality.* Hillsdale, N.J.: L. Erlbaum Associates, 1995.

Burdea, Grigore C. *Force and Touch Feedback for Virtual Reality.* New York: John Wiley & Sons, 1996.

Hayles, Katherine. *How We Became Posthuman: Virtual Bodies in Cybernetics, Literature, and Informatics.* Chicago: University of Chicago Press, 1999.

Mantovani, Giuseppe. "Virtual Reality as a Communication Environment: Consensual Hallucination, Fiction, and Possible Selves." *Human Relations* 48, no. 6 (1995), pp. 669–83.

Related Topics

CAVE; Cyberspace; DeFanti, Thomas; Lanier, Jaron; Sandin, Daniel

— *Shing-Ling Sarina Chen*

Virus

The virus, a computer program designed to replicate and spread itself without the user's knowledge, has become a stock character in popular culture. In books and movies, computer viruses are the villains of the Internet Age, wreaking unimaginable havoc on computer systems and threatening the future of civilization. However, that popular portrayal is not very accurate. The majority of viruses are relatively harmless, and very few have the destructiveness of their fictional counterparts. But when a malicious virus does strike, it can cause significant damage.

When the first viruses appeared in 1986, their ability to inflict damage was relatively limited. Early viruses were designed to spread either by attaching themselves to an executable program file, such as a game or word processor, or by infecting the boot sector of a disk. At startup, and when disks are first inserted, computers read the disk's boot sector, and a virus can thus be transmitted before a computer's operating system has a chance to load and prevent the virus' transmission. Regardless of how these early viruses are spread, they were designed to affect files on a single computer. Most viruses were harmless, perhaps popping up a message on a particular day; but others would slowly or rapidly alter or delete files, and particularly vicious ones could wipe out an entire file system.

Early viruses could cause great damage to one computer on their own, but the virus had to have human help in order to spread. For the most part, this meant transmission via floppy disks. For example, a user might be typing up a document on a computer that had a virus. When that file was saved to a floppy disk, the boot sector of that floppy might get infected. Then, when that disk was inserted into the drive of another computer, and the boot sector was read, the new computer would pick up the virus. Or someone might create a game with a built-in virus; a user might put that game on a disk to share with a friend, and unknowingly share the virus as well.

The medium of email has become the biggest carrier of computer-virus infections. Boot-sector viruses are still transmitted by floppy disks, but most other viruses are spread via email attachments. The growth of email as a medium for communication has also led to a phenomenal growth in viruses. From December 1998 to October 1999, for example, the number of known viruses more than doubled, jumping from 20,500 to 42,000. In early 2001, there were over 52,000 known viruses.

Email has also helped foster several new types of malicious programs. A Trojan horse program is an executable file that does something that the user doesn't expect, such as deleting files, but it doesn't replicate itself. For a while, only executable files (programs) could spread viruses, so users could protect themselves by simply not running programs attached to email messages that they received. But with the invention of macro viruses, text documents could also be used to spread viruses. Macros are a series of commands that can be recorded in a word processor or spreadsheet and included in the document file. Since they are in essence small programs, they can be set up to delete files or otherwise damage a system. Most macro viruses target Microsoft's suite of office programs (Word, Excel, Outlook, and so on), since they are so widely used and the programming language of their macros is relatively basic.

The worm is probably the most damaging, malicious program that email has made possible. Many people call worms viruses, but there are significant technical differences between worms and viruses. A virus is designed to spread by itself on one computer, and needs the help of humans to infect other computers. A worm, on the other hand, is designed to spread across a network of computers with little or no human aid. Worms and viruses can be combined, as was the case with the widespread Melissa macro virus/worm, which would open up Microsoft's Outlook program and email itself to 50 other people whose email addresses were listed in the program's address book. The Explore.zip worm emailed itself as an attached file named "zipped_files.exe." When the attachment was opened, the worm altered a system file to cause it to automatically run the worm every time the computer started, used the person's email program to gather up email addresses, and sent itself out again. Explore.zip also destroyed random files on the computer's hard drive. Since worms can spread themselves, they can cause much greater damage and spread much more rapidly than standard viruses.

Most worms are directed at Microsoft's Outlook program, partly because of security flaws in Microsoft's ActiveX and Visual Basic codes, and partly because of the widespread use of Outlook and other Microsoft Office products. The cross-platform compatibility of macros also makes Microsoft products a tempting target; a virus written for a computer running the Windows operating system can't infect a Macintosh computer, but a macro virus or worm written for Microsoft Outlook or Word can infect *any* computer running a Microsoft Office product.

One of the most infamous Internet "infections" occurred on November 2, 1988. Robert Morris, Jr., a graduate student at Cornell University, released a worm that actually worked much better than he expected, infecting machines all over the United States. Over 6,000 computers were infected; numerous computers were shut down, countless others disconnected from the Internet, and millions of dollars in damage was done before programmers finally came up with a fix to stop the spread of the worm. Morris was convicted of computer fraud and abuse, and was sentenced to three years' probation, community service, and a fine of $10,050 plus costs of supervision.

Email's ability to spread viruses has led to the creation of a new type of urban legend: the virus warning hoax. Warnings about bogus viruses such as the Budweiser screen-saver virus or the Good Times virus circulate throughout the Internet. Newcomers to email often receive these warnings and pass them on to all of their friends without checking the validity of the warning, wasting time and resources and making it very difficult to stop these hoaxes. Antivirus software Web sites maintain lists of virus hoaxes that can be used to verify the validity of a virus warning. However, experienced email and computer users usually can spot virus hoaxes simply by the tone of the message, which usually predicts catastrophic damage through unrealistic methods.

Computers can be protected from viruses in many ways. Most users have virus-scanning programs that check files as they are opened (and floppy disks as they are mounted). In general, all email attachments should be scanned for viruses, and most antivirus software can do this automatically. As more and more viruses are spread through the Internet, some network administrators are setting up programs to automatically scan email for viruses and/or to block certain types of attachments. Because of the rapid increase in viruses and worms that attack systems through Microsoft Outlook, Outlook 2002 is set up to refuse to open most attachments by default.

Viruses, no matter what form they take, and even if they are only hoaxes, are a drain on time and resources. New ones continue to appear; ten to 15 are created daily. While many of these new viruses never leave computer research labs, and most are harmless, the Internet has significantly increased the speed with which they spread.

Bibliography

Cohen, Fred B. *A Short Course on Computer Viruses.* Second edition. New York: John Wiley & Sons, 1994.

Ludwig, Mark A. *The Giant Black Book of Computer Viruses.* Second edition. Show Low, Ariz.: American Eagle Publications, 1998.

Wilcox, Joe. "Microsoft's Virus Antidote: Ban Attachments." *News.com*, April 6, 2001. <http://news.cnet.com/news/0-1003-200-5529034.html> (July 15, 2002).

Further Reading

Ludwig, Mark A. *The Giant Black Book of Computer Viruses.* Second edition. Show Low, Ariz.: American Eagle Publications, 1998.

Schmauder, Phil. *Virus Proof.* Roseville, Calif.: Prima Publishing, 2000

Shoch, J. F., and J. A. Hupp. "The 'Worm' Programs: Early Experience with a Distributed Computation," *Communications of the ACM*, March 1982, pp. 172–80.

Symantec AntiVirus Research Center. Hoaxes. 1995–2002. <http://www.symantec.com/avcenter/hoax.html> (July 15, 2002).

Related Topics

Cyberwarfare; Email; Hacking, Cracking, and Phreaking; Security

— *Norman Clark*

Von Neumann, John

1903–1957

Mathematician

John von Neumann made key contributions in numerous fields of research during his relatively short life. His work in mathematics, particularly in set theory, was groundbreaking, and his definition of ordinal numbers, published at age 20, still sets the standard. In addition, he contributed significantly to quantum physics, computer science and meteorology, and game theory.

Born in Hungary, von Neumann studied chemistry at the University of Berlin while simultaneously completing doctoral work in mathematics at the University of Budapest. He received a Ph.D. in mathematics after completing a dissertation on set theory in 1926. In the same year, he earned a degree in chemical engineering from the Eidgennossische Technische Hochscule in Zurich. He lectured at the University of Berlin from 1926 to 1929, then accepted a position at Princeton University in 1930. In 1933, he was one of the original faculty at Princeton's newly founded Institute for Advanced Study (IAS); he held that position until his death from pancreatic cancer in 1957. During and after World War II, he held numerous research and governmental posts, contributing to the development of the hydrogen bomb. He received many awards, including the Medal of Freedom and the Enrico Fermi Award, both given in 1956 during his battle with cancer.

With the 1944 publication of *Theory of Games and Economic Behavior*, which he co-authored with Oskar Morgenstern, von Neumann applied mathematical analysis to economics and initiated the branch of economics and mathematics known as game theory. Game theory categorizes numerous types of "games," in which interested parties compete or cooperate based on predefined rules. By analyzing such games, game theory determines the best strategies that rational, self-interested actors would take, providing economists with a rigorous, logical, mathematical framework to determine the actions of economic actors.

Von Neumann developed the minimax theorem, which applies to most two-person, zero-sum games, in which one player's losses are the other's gain. In such games, a value can be calculated that determines the best strategy, on average, for both players to follow. A simple example is the game of paper-rock-scissors: Each person must choose one of these three options without knowledge of what the other will choose. Von Neumann's minimax theorem proved mathematically that the best strategy for such a game is a mixed strategy of picking randomly. If one player follows this strategy, the best the other can do is to follow it as well, assuring 50/50 success. Von Neumann later applied the theorem to a simplified version of poker to devise a successful bidding strategy. Over the decades following the publication of *Theory of Games and Economic Behavior*, game theory grew and influenced other research in decision-making. By the 1950s, game theory was applied to military and political matters—most notably to the growing game of deterrence and brinksmanship that was the Cold War.

John von Neumann (right) poses with J. Robert Oppenheimer in front of the IAS Machine, 1952 (CORBIS).

Von Neumann's genius did not usually entail boldly developing new areas of research; instead, he had a striking ability to take the ideas of others and logically extend them in practical directions. His contributions to computer science were of this type. In 1944, while working on various military projects, including atomic-bomb research at Los Alamos, von Neumann became indirectly involved with the design and construction of ENIAC, the first electronic digital computer. Asked to write a report on improvements for ENIAC's successor, EDVAC, von Neumann circulated a first draft of the report, which others immediately copied and distributed. This report detailed proposed improvements on the logical structure of computers, including the use of central programming and memory to avoid having to reset the computer for every computation. Rethinking and extending the work of others, von Neumann envisioned the computer as a logical rather than a mechanical problem, allowing him to provide the model on which all future computers would be built. His report represents a crucial step in the history of computer science.

From 1946 to 1952, von Neumann began the construction of his own computer at Princeton's IAS. In completing the IAS Machine, von Neumann and his assistants produced numerous papers dealing with design issues, all of which were made publicly available at von Neumann's urging. This spurred enormous advances in computer science. The next generation of computers built during these years, including IBM's 701, the MANIAC at Los Alamos, and the University of Illinois' ILLIAC, all owed much to von Neumann's work. While at Princeton, von Neumann also left his mark on the field of meteorology by using weather forecasting as a complex computational problem. Today's meteorological weather models have their roots in the computer models generated on the IAS computer.

From 1952 until his death, von Neumann's advice was much sought after by the government and the military, and he held numerous advisory positions in the Truman and Eisenhower administrations. From 1950 to 1955, he served on the Armed Forces Special Weapons Project, and in 1955 he was appointed to the Atomic Energy Commission.

The far-ranging effects of von Neumann's thought are difficult to assess, as are the possibilities of what he might have contributed in other fields had he lived longer. His fame rests on his ability to move from abstract research and apply his logical acuity to practical problems in physics, engineering, and computer science. At the time of his death, he was beginning to consider combining his work on computers with research in biochemistry, and it is impossible to know what profound strides might have been made in genetic research, a field that was in its infancy at the time, had he been able to devote himself to it.

Selected Works

Von Neumann, John. *The Computer and the Brain.* New Haven: Yale University Press, 1958.

———. *Theory of Self-Reproducing Automata.* Arthur W. Burks, ed. Urbana: University of Illinois Press, 1966.

Von Neumann, John, and Oskar Morgenstern. *Theory of Games and Economic Behavior.* Princeton: Princeton University Press, 1947.

Bibliography

Heims, Steve J. *John von Neumann and Norbert Wiener: From Mathematics to the Technologies of Life and Death.* Cambridge, Mass.: MIT Press, 1980.

Macrae, Norman. *John von Neumann.* New York: Pantheon, 1992.

Poundstone, William. *Prisoner's Dilemma.* New York: Doubleday, 1992.

Further Reading

Aspray, William. *John von Neumann and the Origins of Modern Computing.* Cambridge, Mass.: MIT Press, 1990.

Related Topics

Gaming; Shannon, Claude

— *Shawn Miklaucic*

W W W W W W W W W

Webcamming

Webcamming (also known as webcasting) is the broadcast of images, sometimes with sound, over the Internet. Webcamming has exploded in popularity over the last ten years, in part because it is the most inexpensive form of broadcasting currently available to the public. In order to webcam, five things are needed: a computer, a modem, an Internet service provider (ISP), a place to send images online, and a Web camera—also known as a webcam. The cheapest webcam can be had for less than $100; far and away, the most popular one is the inexpensive "eyeball" variety that sits on or near the computer. Alternately, one may hook an ordinary video camera into a computer through a video-capture device, and webcast that way. Although most digital cameras cannot function as Web cameras at this time, this too is changing. In general, if you can hook a camera up to your computer and manage to transfer images to the Web, you can webcast.

HISTORY OF WEBCAMMING

The very first webcam has origins that predate the World Wide Web, and by its creator's own admission, it began as something of a joke. In 1991, computer scientist Quentin Stafford-Fraser found himself frustrated in his attempts to get a fresh cup of coffee from the continuously drained pot that was shared among computer scientists at Cambridge University. The Trojan Room Coffee Cam was born after Stafford-Fraser took a small camera, pointed it at the coffee machine, and wired the camera to the computing staff's network for public viewing.

As he describes it on his homepage, "The image was only updated about three times a minute, but that was fine because the pot filled rather slowly, and it was only grayscale, which was also fine, because so was the coffee." Later, the Coffee Cam was put up on the World Wide Web for public viewing, thus becoming the most watched pot on the Internet.

In 1998, Sherri Uhrick of the Earthcam Directory estimated that 60 percent of all webcams are currently indoor cameras. Of these, autobiographical "homecams" are by far the most prevalent type being used today. The homecam phenomenon began in 1996, with Jennifer Ringley of Jennicam fame. Jennifer began webcasting from her Dickinson College dorm room as a social experiment of sorts. Today, most people associate homecamming with the Jennicam and the site's attendant ideology: that of unfettered reality. This ideology was for years borne out on the splash page (opening document) of her Web site: Produced in a simple Courier font, with no images, Jennifer's "dictionary definition" of the Jennicam read, "A real-time look into the real life of a young woman." Although that tagline has now been updated to read "Life, online," the *vérité* sentiment remains.

Because her life story has now been covered in literally hundreds of media outlets, it is fair to say that Ringley now has the distinction of being the Web's first reality micro-celebrity. In essence, she is famous (although to a lesser degree than many television or film personalities) simply for being the first person to "be herself" in front of a webcam.

Webcamming now covers a wide range of activities, from private videoconferencing between individuals, to semi-public surveillance via corporate intranets, to public broadcasting over the Web. Webcams can be found in nurseries, as part of art exhibits, on street corners, in public parks, in prisons and hospitals, inside offices (with or without employee knowledge), as part of news-reporting efforts, and inside the most intimate of places in the home. In mainstream media, webcamming has served as a lightning rod of sorts, fueling debate about the proper uses of entertainment and surveillance in the digital age. And although anyone using common sense understands that the social ramifications of public prison surveillance differ from outdoor weather webcasts, which differ still from for-pay pornographic "peep cams," all of these examples use the same technology: the webcam.

ESTABLISHING TELEPRESENCE VIA WEBCAM

No matter what its intended purpose, the power of all webcamming lies in its ability to convey telepresence—

that is, its ability make things at a distance seem close and current. It is important to understand, however, that the telepresence effect of webcams is something of an illusion, because there are always significant losses between what a broadcaster's webcam sees and what a viewer ultimately sees. For instance, most popular webcams capture with a resolution of 640 x 480 pixels, which is broadcast quality for TV. From there, however, webcam images often need to be resized to as small as 160 x 120 pixels and compressed as much as 20:1 before being uploaded to the Web, eliminating 90 percent of the data in order to accommodate end-viewers with slower modems. And finally, what is presented to a homecam viewer as "here and now" cannot ever truly be so, in part because general Internet congestion will always create time-delays.

Webcams capture motion as a series of still images called frames, the same way that video cameras do. As the old technique of the flipbook demonstrates, when a series of frames is shown, an illusion of continuous motion is established in the eye of a viewer; the faster that these frames are shown, the smoother the illusion of motion appears. Likewise, the higher the number of frames per second that a webcam is set to record, the smoother the image projected through a webcam will appear. Most of the newer webcams on the market have speeds as high as 30 frames per second, which is the standard video rate. This is why current videoconferencing programs require nothing more sophisticated than a basic Web camera, a decent microphone, and a high-speed Internet connection. Indeed, one useful (if perhaps overly simplistic) way to think about how webcams work is to imagine turning a video camera on without a tape in it, hitting "record," and running the camera to the Internet.

But aside from one-on-one videoconferencing or streaming media (i.e., full-motion video online), frame rates have very little to do with how most webcam images are viewed on the Internet. The fact is, there are two main ways in which these images are generally delivered to viewers over the Internet. The less common method, used only in practices like videoconferencing and on lucrative streaming sites, is called server push. In this method, a viewer's browser is told (via HTML) to prepare itself to receive a series of images, which are then sent at the server's leisure. A technique called fast push is often used by companies that claim to support "near-real-time video" on the Web. The other, far more popular method, called client pull, works the way it sounds: Viewers are required to refresh single still images on their browsers at set intervals in order to see new motion.

BANDWIDTH AND THE FUTURE OF WEBCAMMING

Although people routinely engage in one-on-one video-conferencing at a fast-push rate of 30 frames per second, once they begin broadcasting to large numbers of people over the Web, they must make a choice. Either they switch to client pull and reduce their frame rate significantly, or they pay their ISP for additional bandwidth. Bandwidth is the rate at which a telecommunication system can transmit information to end-users, and it affects both webcamming broadcasters and viewers. From the broadcaster's perspective, not having enough bandwidth is roughly analogous to planning a performance space to accommodate a few people, and having a large group show up for the performance. From the viewer's perspective, the problem is even clearer: When a broadcast takes up too much bandwidth, any images or sounds received will seem jumpy or halting.

Bandwidth is a serious concern for streaming-media companies and high-traffic homecammers like Jennifer Ringley. However, most people using webcams today avoid bandwidth problems by choosing to broadcast their surroundings as silent still images, which refresh every few minutes on the Web. For some, this is a dissatisfying compromise, and they eagerly wait for the day when they can take advantage of the server-push opportunities that are already at the disposal of those with greater financial resources. The arrival of much-touted broadband capacity, a range of technologies that enable access to the Internet at speeds 10 to 80 times faster than today's typical dial-up connections, may help these people in the near future.

Other webcammers, however, are happy to stay where they are technologically. These users concede that while refreshed silent still images are certainly not as telepresent as full-motion video and audio, webcamming as it exists today has a charm and a usefulness of its own. Thus far, the advantages of webcams seem to be outweighing their limitations, at least in the marketplace. In 1999, Logitech, a leading manufacturer of webcams, reported selling its millionth unit; by 2000, sales had reached two million units. That number is sure to continue to rise, as webcams are bundled by manufacturers with home computers, cable modems, and DSL connections. In perhaps an ultimate vote of market confidence in the future of webcamming, the no-longer-functional, original Trojan Coffee Pot was recently purchased for just under $5,000 U.S. in an eBay auction. According to a *New York Times* report, the buyer, German media conglomerate Spiegel, reportedly did it both "for a digital joke" and to acquire a "piece of webcamming history."

Bibliography

Campanella, Thomas J. "Be There Now." *Salon*, August 7, 1997. <http://www.salon.com/aug97/21st/cam970807.html> (May 10, 2002).

Dyson, Jonathan, "Ready for Your Close-Up? A Brief History of Webcam TV." *The Independent* (London), October 31, 1998.

Friedricks, Bruce. "Now You See It: The Cam Clan and Pictures that Move." (Panel title.) Speech delivered at Shout 2000 Conference, San Francisco, California, February 3, 2000.

Mieszkowski, Katharine. "Nowhere Left to Hide." *Salon*, June 18, 2001. <http://www.salon.com/tech/feature/2001/06/18/webcam_privacy/index.html> (May 10, 2002).

Stafford-Fraser, Quentin. "The Life and Times of the First Web Cam: When Convenience Was the Mother of Invention." *Communications of the ACM*, vol. 44, no. 7 (July 2001). <http://www.cl.cam.ac.uk/coffee/qsf/cacm200107.html> (May 10, 2002).

Teschland, Leland. "Live! Exposed! And on the Web!' *Machine Design*, vol. 72 no. 16 (August 17, 2000), pp. 42–48.

Zeller, Tom. "Seen My Sock Drawer Lately?" *The New York Times*, August 19, 2001.

Further Reading

Campanella, Thomas. "Eden by Wire: Webcameras and the Telepresent Landscape." *The Robot in the Garden: Telerobotics and Telepistemology in the Age of the Internet.* Ken Goldberg, ed. Cambridge, Mass.: MIT Press, 2000.

Firth, Simon. "Live! From My Bedroom!" *Salon*, January 1998. <http://www.salon.com/21st/feature/1998/01/cov_08feature.html> (May 10, 2002).

Houston, June. "The Ghost Watcher." <http://www.ghostwatcher.com/cgi-bin/gw/home.pl> (May 10, 2002).

Lombard, Matthew, and Teresa Ditton. "At the Heart of It All: The Concept of Telepresence." JCMC 3, no. 2 (September 1997).

Lunenfeld, Peter. *The Digital Dialectic: New Essays on New Media.* Cambridge, Mass.: MIT Press, 1999.

———. *Snap to Grid: A User's Guide to Digital Arts, Media, and Cultures.* Cambridge, Mass.: MIT Press, 2000.

Parker, Elisabeth. *The Little Web Cam Book.* Berkeley, Calif.: Peachpit Press, 1999.

Ringley, Jennifer. "The Jennicam." <http://www.jennicam.org> (May 10, 2002).

Snyder, Donald. "Webcam Women: Life on Your Screen." *Web.Studies: Rewiring Media Studies for the Digital Age.* David Gauntlett, ed. London/New York: Edward Arnold, 2000.

Surveyor Corporation. "The Webcam Resource." May 2002. <http://www.webcamresource.com/> (May 10, 2002).

Voog, Ana. "The Anacam." 2002. <http://www.anavoog.com> (May 10, 2002).

Wilson, Stephen. "The Telepresent Project." 1997. <http://userwww.sfsu.edu/~swilson/> (May 10, 2002).

Related Topics

Broadband; Compression; Cyberculture; Privacy; Streaming Media; Videoconferencing

— *Theresa M. Senft*

Whitman, Margaret

1957–

Entrepreneur

Margaret C. (Meg) Whitman is the business executive who has shaped the eBay online auction site into one of the World Wide Web's most successful businesses. She has overseen the site's transition from its roots as a hobby site selling Pez dispensers into a huge, multifaceted marketplace where it is possible to bid on and buy anything from classic baseball cards to real estate.

Whitman grew up in Cold Spring Harbor on New York's Long Island in a middle-class family. She has said that her early interests were in sports, and she didn't begin to think seriously about a career until she enrolled in Princeton University at age 18. Her first exposure to business was a stint selling advertising at a student-run business magazine; the experience inspired her to change majors from pre-med to economics.

Whitman graduated from Princeton with an economics degree in 1977, and two years later received her MBA from the Harvard Business School. She joined Procter & Gamble, then went to work for Bain & Co. consulting firm. Stints at Walt Disney Co., Stride Rite Shoes, and Florists' Transworld Delivery (FTD) followed. At FTD, Whitman served for the first time as a chief executive officer (CEO), and was present when the company devised FTD.com, one of the first successful business ventures on the Web. She later went to Hasbro, where she oversaw marketing for the Playskool and Mr. Potato Head brands. She joined eBay in 1998.

In a March 2001 interview with *Business Week* editor-in-chief Stephen B. Shepard, Whitman said that when a corporate headhunter first came to her with the offer to run eBay, she immediately refused the job, not wanting to uproot her neurosurgeon husband and three children. When the company persisted, she relented and agreed to an interview. The night before the interview, she said, she looked at the site, then known as Auction Web, for the first time, and was stunned to see that, in addition to a black-and-white design, the site gave equal space to a personal home page for the company founder's girlfriend, and to an attached hobby site about the Ebola virus, which was a pet concern of founder Pierre Omidyar. During the interview, Whitman said, she began changing her mind about the job, impressed by Omidyar's description of the auction community that was forming around the site. Some site users had met their best friends through the site. At that point, Whitman said, she began to understand the concept, and to see its potential.

When Whitman signed on in May 1998, eBay had some 750,000 users. By 2001, the site was being visited by some seven million people a day. It handled 79 million transactions in the fourth quarter of 2000 alone. Whitman has set plans for eBay to reach $3 billion in annual revenue by 2005. She led eBay's metamorphosis away from what *Business Week* called its "flea-market roots" into a company that sells cars, art, electronics, and many other products. In so doing, she has created one of the few profitable businesses on the Web.

The company has had its share of problems under Whitman's guidance. In July 2000, eBay experienced a 24-hour shutdown that some thought could push users away. It has also survived several controversies involving demands from anti-racism groups and the French government that the site forbid the sale of Nazi memorabilia.

However, under Whitman's leadership, eBay has outlasted furious competition in the online auction space from companies like Amazon.com and Yahoo! while continuing to expand its own business. The site now has subsidiary sites in Germany, the United Kingdom, Canada, Australia, France, Italy, Ireland, and Switzerland; and on February 15, 2001, eBay purchased majority interest in Internet Auction Co., a South Korean site.

The dot-com collapse of 2000–01, which shut down a lot of big online companies, did not leave eBay unaffected. After peaking at more than $165 a share in November 1999, eBay stock had fallen to an all-time low of $27.93 on December 20, 2000, and

wouldn't rise much above $40 until late April 2001. Even in the midst of the stock's slump, Whitman was still striking a confident pose at the March 2001 Spring Internet World conference in Los Angeles. The Internet is not dead, she said during a keynote speech at the show; people are still experimenting with the medium, broadband access has not yet hit its stride, and many Internet companies went into the business without solid business plans. She said that she expects eBay to continue prospering, and that "the best days of the Internet are ahead." The message seemed to resonate; the company reported first-quarter 2001 earnings of $0.08 a share in April 2001, and stock prices rose to $65.60 by mid-June.

At last report, Whitman was leading the company into an online shopping-mall project called eBay Stores, aimed at allowing the site's estimated 30 million registered users to make fixed-price purchases on various goods. It also had instituted a "Buy It Now" system that made it possible to purchase auction items outright.

Bibliography

eBay Inc. "eBay Names Meg Whitman President and CEO." May 7, 1998. <http://pages.ebay.com/community/aboutebay/releases/pr98.html#20> (June 7, 2002).

Helft, Miguel. "EBay Defies Dot-Com Gravity." *The Industry Standard,* July 19, 2001. <http://www.thestandard.com/article/0,1902,28089,00.html> (June 7, 2002).

Himelstein, Linda. "Q&A with eBay's Meg Whitman." *Business Week,* May 31, 1999. <http://www.businessweek.com/1999/99_22/b3631008.htm> (June 7, 2002).

The Learning Network. "Biography: Margaret C. 'Meg' Whitman." 2000–2002. <http://www.infoplease.com/ipa/A0880020.html> (June 7, 2002).

Shepard, Stephen B. "Q&A: A Talk with Meg Whitman." *Business Week,* March 19, 2001. <http://www.businessweek.com:/print/magazine/content/01_12/b3724117.htm?popWin1> (June 7, 2002).

"Time Digital 50: Meg Whitman, The New Auctioneer." *Time,* 1999. <http://www.time.com/time/digital/digital50/05.html> (June 7, 2002).

Further Reading

Bartlett, Michael. "Ebay's Whitman: 'Net's Not Dead!'" *Newsbytes,* March 14, 2001.

Bunnell, David. *The eBay Phenomenon: Business Secrets Behind the World's Hottest Internet Company.* New York: John Wiley & Sons, 2000.

Drapkin, Michael; Lowy, Jon; and Daniel Marovitz. *Three Clicks Away: Advice from the Trenches of eCommerce.* New York: Wiley, 2001.

Fishman, Charles. "Face Time with Meg Whitman." FastCompany.com, May 2001. <http://www.fastcompany.com/online/46/facetime.html> (June 7, 2002).

Helft, Miguel. "What Makes eBay Unstoppable?" *The Industry Standard*, August 6, 2001. <http://www.thestandard.com/article/0,1902,28310,00.html> (June 7, 2002).

Related Topics

E-Commerce; Virtual Community; World Wide Web

— Kevin Featherly

Whole Earth 'Lectronic Link

The Whole Earth 'Lectronic Link (WELL) is one of the oldest and most famous examples of a virtual community. Started in 1985 as a local dial-in bulletin board service (BBS), the WELL is currently owned by Salon.com, and is accessible through the World Wide Web. As with other BBSs, the WELL allows users to log on and post typed messages for others to read. Messages may be anywhere from a few words long to several paragraphs, and are organized topically in conferences. A directory lists conferences in broader categories. (For example, the broader category "Computers and Internet Conferences" includes such conferences as "World Wide Web" and "Hacking and Cracking.") Each conference is hosted by one or more WELL members who moderate the discussion. Conferences are further subdivided into topics, allowing members to read only those discussions pertaining to a particular conference topic that they find interesting.

The WELL began as a collaboration between Laurence Brilliant and Stewart Brand. Brilliant, a physician who had previously been involved in fighting smallpox in India, ran a company called Network Technologies International (NETI). He was interested in finding a group of people who could spark interest in computer-conferencing technology, which his company sold and which he felt had the potential to become an important new communications tool. Brand was well known for editing several publications catering to the counterculture, including the *Whole Earth Catalog* (initially published in 1968). He and several of his associates had already become interested in computer conferencing. His non-profit organization, Point Foundation, became joint owner of the WELL; NETI supplied the technology, and Point Foundation supplied the participants.

The WELL used a somewhat difficult-to-use conferencing system called Picospan. Participation on the WELL thus required either technical facility or enough persistence to gain such facility. In addition, an expectation for erudite conversation developed early on, owing in part to the connection with the *Whole Earth* publications community. Therefore, WELL participation also required facility with written language.

These requirements, combined with the interpersonal connections and interests brought online by the earliest WELL users (or WELLbeings, as they sometimes call themselves), meant that particular types of people were attracted initially to the WELL. For the first few years, most WELL users were either: 1) people involved in 1960s and 1970s countercultural movements; 2) early personal-computer programmers, enthusiasts, and tinkerers; 3) journalists (many of whom were given free accounts) and other writers; or 4) fans of the Grateful Dead. The last group took to the WELL enthusiastically in 1986, and by 1987 made up nearly a third of all participants.

Brand started the WELL with the explicit aim of creating an online community. At a time when very few people had any experience with computer-mediated communication and almost no research on the topic of online community existed, Brand's ideas about how to create such a community were presciently effective. His previous experience with computer conferencing convinced him that some face-to-face contact among members was important. While by some accounts, the early face-to-face meetings were not particularly scintillating, most participants felt that they played an important part in fostering interpersonal connections. The WELL also required people to use their real names. Nicknames could be used and changed at will, but were always attached to a user's real name.

Another early WELL policy, and one of the few "rules" of discourse, is summed up in Brand's somewhat enigmatic phrase, "You Own Your Own Words." Abbreviated by WELL participants as YOYOW, this phrase has sparked lengthy online discussions, and lends itself to several interpretations. YOYOW establishes the management of the WELL as a limited facilitator, not responsible for the policing of content. In addition to limiting the WELL's liability, YOYOW highlights the importance and power of words, and sets a tone of interpersonal responsibility. YOYOW is also now explicitly interpreted as lodging copyright for WELL contributions with the author; each WELL post is in effect a published work owned by the person who wrote it.

In addition to Brand's philosophical influence, some of the WELL's success might also be attributed to his hiring decisions. Several early directors and facilitators had previous experience in the creation of intentional communities from their past participation in the Farm, one of the most famous and longest-lived back-to-the-land communes.

In 1991, Bruce Katz, who had previously built the Rockport shoe company from a small family business to a multimillion-dollar enterprise, bought half of the WELL from the failing NETI corporation. In 1994, he bought the remaining half from the Point Foundation. Katz infused much-needed capital into the WELL, enabling it to upgrade computer equipment, connect members to the Internet (thereby allowing them to receive email through their WELL accounts), and move the organization to larger offices. However, many WELL participants felt that Katz did not share the WELL's now well-developed community values and norms. After running the WELL himself for about a year, Katz hired Maria Wilhelm as director in 1996. Although Wilhelm met with greater favor from WELL participants, relations between Katz and the users remained tense, and Katz soon indicated a desire to sell. Over the next few years, Katz searched unsuccessfully for a buyer. Wilhelm left as director after considering purchasing the WELL herself. Finally in 1999, online magazine company Salon.com purchased the WELL. Gail Williams, Wilhelm's successor, remained as director.

Some early participants feel that the WELL's glory days are over. Around 1996, many WELL participants left to form their own online communities. These include the River, a member-owned virtual community, and Electric Minds, which was founded by Howard Rheingold, a writer who has written several pieces about the WELL. Members of both of these communities have had to come up with creative funding and organizational strategies to keep their communities going. Electric Minds was successively bought by several different companies, each instituting its own software; when the last buyer shut down, Electric Minds was reconstituted through member donations. This demonstrates how important such online communities can become to their members, and suggests that even if the relationship between Salon.com and the WELL should end, the WELL or something like it will persist.

Bibliography

Hafner, Katie. "The Epic Saga of The Well: The World's Most Influential Online Community (And It's Not AOL)." *Wired* 5.05, May 1997. <http://www.wired.com/wired/archive/5.05/ff_well.html> (June 7, 2002).

"Salon Buys The Well." *Wired News*, April 7, 1999. <http://www.wired.com/news/print/0,1294,18992,00.html> (June 7, 2002).

"The WELL Member Agreement." The WELL, 2002. <http://www.well.com/member_agreement.html> (June 7, 2002).

Further Reading

"About The WELL." The WELL, 2002. <http://www.well.com/aboutwell.html> (June 7, 2002).

Hafner, Katie. *The Well: A Story of Love, Death & Real Life in the Seminal Online Community*. New York: Carroll & Graf, 2001.

Rheingold, Howard. *The Virtual Community: Homesteading on the Electronic Frontier*. Reading, Mass.: Addison-Wesley, 1993.

Related Topics

Brand, Stewart; Rheingold, Howard; Virtual Community

— *Lori Kendall*

Wireless Application Protocol

Wireless Application Protocol (WAP) defines an open, universal standard for the delivery of the Internet and other value-added services to wireless networks and mobile communication devices such as mobile phones and personal digital assistants (PDAs). In general, WAP specifications encourage the creation of wireless devices that are compatible with each other, regardless of the manufacturer or service provider.

WAP is not a true protocol in the sense of the Internet Protocol (IP) or the Secure Sockets Layer (SSL); rather, it is a set of communication networking- and application-environment specifications that mirror functions similar to those performed by older, more common ones associated with the Internet, such as Hypertext Transfer Protocol (HTTP) and Transmission Control Protocol (TCP).

Compared to other specifications, WAP is a fairly recent development in information delivery. In 1997, the WAP forum (www.wapforum.org) was founded and organized with the goal of defining specifications for WAP. While original members Motorola, Nokia, and Phone.com (formerly Unwired Planet) had begun individually to define their own wireless data protocols, the WAP forum provided a cooperative opportunity to develop and share protocols for providing information to wireless communication devices. The result was a series of documents detailing the current standards that have been widely adopted by the industry. The WAP Forum has since grown from its modest size, and currently includes over 350 companies in its membership.

WAP recognizes that handheld wireless devices create a challenge not only for hardware and software designers but also for consumers. As a result, the protocols attempt to directly address constraints such as small display size, limited bandwidth and memory, and weak processing power that are typically associated with wireless devices. Two major considerations make WAP compliance attractive for potential wireless-device users. First, WAP-compliant devices allow these users to access and retrieve information from virtually anywhere, which complements many services offered by, for instance, mobile-telephone service providers. Second, WAP ensures "interoperatability" among compliant devices and network components, reducing potential software and architecture conflicts.

The foundation for WAP protocols has been and will continue to be the existing industry Internet standards, which WAP extends and leverages. As such, WAP includes familiar Internet-based tools such as browsers, URLs, and gateways. The current set of protocols defines key features, including: the WAP Programming Model, analogous to the World Wide Web Programming Model; Wireless Markup Language (WML) and WMLScript, a programming language analogous to HTML; a microbrowser, analogous to a Web browser; a complete protocol stack, designed to minimize the need for bandwidth as well as enable changes in one specification to occur independent of the others; and a Wireless Telephony Applications (WTA) framework for the development of advanced telephone features such as text messaging.

WAP is designed according to a "client server" approach, similar to that employed by the Internet. When someone requests information using a WAP microbrowser-enabled device, the request is processed by a WAP gateway, which translates it from WML to HTML and forwards it to a server. The request is then processed by the server, which returns a response; the response is sent to the WAP gateway, where the information is extracted, encoded into WML, and forwarded to the microbrowser, which decodes and shows the response.

Early WAP applications have focused on extending the capabilities of mobile telephones to allow users to do rather mundane tasks, such as checking email, stock quotes, news feeds, and weather forecasts. Recent advances have extended these capabilities into the e-commerce domain, including stock trading and limited banking services. Furthermore, recent applications allow users to request and view audiovisual information on specially enabled wireless devices such as PDAs; the current cost of these devices, however, has limited their widespread use.

WAP has been more exalted for what it can be, and less publicized for what it currently can do, and as a result, it has been the subject of backlash from critics and consumers. Common complaints include: wireless connectivity is slow and unreliable; WAP complicates rather than simplifies the marketplace, since other protocols (such as the SIM Application Toolkit) are already widely supported; and the cost of WAP services continues to be prohibitive, thereby discouraging consumers from adopting it. WAP proponents counter that the full potential of WAP has yet to be reached, as the protocol is still in its infancy; that the wireless technology of today parallels the first generations of personal computers, and should continue to improve; and that WAP protocols are designed in such a manner to allow for the development of future applications without requiring a complete redesign.

Bibliography

Batista, Elisa. "Combating WAP's Bad Rap." *Wired News,* March 19, 2001. <http://www.wired.com/news/business/0,1367,42421,00.html> (July 5, 2002).

Held, Gilbert. *Data Over Wireless Networks: Bluetooth, WAP, and Wireless LANs.* New York: McGraw-Hill, 2000.

Lee, Stephen, and Dale Bulbrook. *WAP: A Beginner's Guide.* New York: McGraw-Hill, 2001.

van der Heijden, Marcel, and Marcus Taylor, eds. *Understanding WAP: Wireless Applications, Devices, and Services.* Boston: Artech House, 2000.

WAP Forum. *Wireless Application Protocol* [White Paper]. *Wireless Internet Today,* June 2000. <http://www.wapforum.org/what/WAP_white_pages.pdf> (September 17, 2002).

Further Reading

Batista, Elisa. "A Growing Epidemic of 'Waplash.'" *Wired News,* December 26 2000. <http://www.wired.com/news/business/0,1367,40826,00.html> (July 5, 2002).

Dornan, Andy. *The Essential Guide to Wireless Communications Application: From Cellular Systems to*

WAP and M-Commerce. Upper Saddle River, N.J.: Prentice Hall, 2001

McGrath, Peter. "Plenty Wrong with WAP." *Newsweek*, December 18, 2000.

Walters, Mike, and Yasim Hamed. "The Bottom Line about WAP." *Wireless Review,* February 29, 2000.

Related Topics

Bluetooth; Cellular Telephony; Personal Digital Assistants; Wireless Networks

— *Art Ramirez*

Wireless Networks

Traditional communication and computer-data networks rely upon extensive connections of wires. The wires support the flow of information through networks as a backbone, similar to the way that nerves relay sensations in the body. However, advances in networking technology have enabled the option of building wireless networks. Wireless networks can help overcome some of the physical limitations that conventional-network users must endure.

Conventional networks differ from wireless in several ways. While regular networks require the computer attached to them to be located within designated spaces that house outlets and connections, wireless networks transmit data through the open air, freeing the user from confined places. Wireless networks are a solution of convenience. By using them, laptop computers can be mobile, users in older buildings can get Internet access, and office Intranets can become rearrangeable. Whether it allows nurses to record patient information from portable devices or students to check email from the grass in front of their next class, a wireless network boasts a novel level of computing freedom.

COMPONENTS OF A WIRELESS NETWORK

A network free of wires utilizes several different components in order to operate. Since the connection between computers does not employ wires, radio frequencies function as the method for transmitting data. In order for a computer to relay information via radio waves, a wireless modem must be connected to the computing device, and a receiver that connects the air-flowing data must be connected to an existent, traditional, local-area network (LAN). The wireless modem is often a credit card–sized electronic apparatus that fits into a slot within a laptop or desktop computer, permitting the computer to send and receive data. To provide the remote computer with Internet access, there must also be a device that connects the computer to a physically located LAN of wires. This connection is achieved through what is called an access point.

As described by Nancy Ferris, a writer for *Government Executive,* the components of a wireless network are very distinctive, yet critical to its successful operation. Ferris explains that radio frequency permits a linkage between the access point and the wireless modem within a certain distance. Since signal strength is critical to the connection between the network and the node (the remotely located wireless computer), the distance between the two becomes a critical factor. Depending on the vendor and equipment being used, computers can often communicate at distances of 125 feet and beyond. However, the distance at which a computer will be able to communicate is largely determined by the architecture of the building that contains it, as well as by the strength of the modem and access point.

The area in which the data is diffused is also a significant component; obstructions lessen the efficiency and effectiveness of a wireless network. If the interior walls of a building are constructed of dense materials like cement, data will not flow between the modem and the access point. Data-transmission rates of the modem and access point must also be sufficiently powerful. However, the design of wireless networks can remedy non-conducive environments. For instance, access points can be placed almost anywhere, and computers can still communicate with wired LANs in areas where an access point is installed; the more access points to a LAN, the more locations become operable for information passage.

The components of a wireless network allow it to function in a manner that is similar to conventional networks that employ Ethernet interface cards and strung wires. However, this functioning requires a series of communication protocols, or universally agreed-upon standards for communication formats. A protocol is basically the language that the various pieces of wireless equipment use to communicate with each other. For example, the Internet requires a protocol to allow computers to communicate with Web servers.

In 1997, the Institute of Electrical and Electronic Engineers (IEEE), an organization of scientists, engineers, and students that sets technical standards, developed an open-air protocol for interactivity called 802.11, which defines compatibility among the hardware devices constructed by various vendors. The 802.11 standard also defines three types of possible wireless-network communication protocols, each of which works differently to address interference issues.

One type of wireless protocol is Diffused Infrared, which uses infrared light waves to pass information between components. Diffused Infrared works well when machines are located close together. Direct Sequence, another type of protocol, combines the data signal of the sending station with powerful data-rate bit sequences, for the strong ordered transfer of information. Direct Sequence protocol helps to reduce interference, which can be caused by other radio frequencies emitted within a location; information is repeatedly sent in sequences, allowing any lost information to be recovered. A third wireless transmission protocol, Frequency-Hopping Spread Sequence (FHSS) alters the data signal in a manner that lets information "hop" in selected order from frequency to frequency. This hopping helps to alleviate interference by avoiding the same frequencies already occupied by other wireless devices.

The IEEE develops standards that attempt to unify the functional equipment designs of vendors. However, its standards are not the only ones offered to consumers. Another alternative language for wireless communication, called Bluetooth, is designed to occupy short-range radio frequencies. Variety in the market of wireless equipment becomes a purchasing issue when compatibility between wireless equipment is desired. The difference between Bluetooth and 802.11 protocols lies in the desired distance of data transmission and the strength. Bluetooth works best at short distances of 30 feet for handheld devices, while 802.11 utilizes more power to transfer information at distances of 150 feet.

PROBLEMS AND LIMITATIONS

Despite its convenience, wireless network technology has a few drawbacks. Primary among them is the slow rate at which information flows in wireless networks. Versions of the 802.11 protocols allow information to travel between 1mbps (megabits per second) and 2mbps, and the newer high-rate standard communicates at rates near 11mbps. This is dramatically slower than the transmission rates of traditional Ethernet networks. According to Ephraim Schwartz of InfoWorld, this lack of speed poses a huge problem for companies that implement wireless networks. Schwartz explains that companies often use large applications that require massive amounts of data to operate business activities. These applications control a lot of the available bandwidth (the amount of data that can be handled through the medium), slowing down the rest of network activity.

Network security is also a problem. The News Bytes News Network reports that wireless networks are vulnerable to manipulation attacks by outsiders. Individuals armed with a laptop, wireless modem, and special computer software can gain access to files and information on wireless networks. Using "sniffers," programs that monitor data traveling over a network, individuals can also acquire the necessary information to allow Internet access through the networks.

THE FUTURE OF WIRELESS NETWORKS

Wireless networks provide remotely located users with access to the Internet and to company information via LANs without confining them to enclosed spaces. Advanced network equipment technology allows components to communicate using protocol languages. Wireless technology, which has already changed the concepts of network design, will continue to evolve toward greater standards of speed and distance.

According to Alex Salkever of *Business Week Online*, wireless networks in Scandinavia are beginning to expand their capabilities. Broadband systems are going wireless in Denmark, similar to the way that Digital Subscriber Lines and cable modems presently supply boosted network services to individual consumers. Using a new technology called Multichannel Multipoint Distribution Systems (MMDS), companies can use antennas on top of homes to communicate with cellular towers within distances of 30 miles. In the near future, wireless broadband systems will become a reality, solving the issues of distance, speed, and security that currently limit wireless networks.

Bibliography

"Driving Away with Wireless Secrets." News Bytes News Network, August 9, 2001.

Ferris, Nancy. "Liberating the Laptop." *Government Executive,* vol. 31, no. 11 (November 1999), pp. 81–83.

Harbaugh, Logan. "Wireless Networking." *Information Week,* June 7, 1999, pp. 71–86.

Salkever, Alex. "Broadband's Next Wave: Wireless?" *Business Week Online,* May 17, 2001. <http://www.businessweek.com/print/bwdaily/dnflash/may2001/nf20010517_453.htm> (June 7, 2002).

Schwartz, Ephraim. "High-speed Wireless on a Bumpy Road." *InfoWorld,* July 27, 2001. <http://www2.infoworld.com/articles/fe/xml/01/07/30/010730feedge.xml> (June 7, 2002).

Further Reading

Cupito, Mary Carmen. "Getting Connected Without Getting Wired." *Health Management Technology*, vol. 18, no. 8 (July 1997), pp. 20–24

Garfinkel, Simson. "Wireless Gets Real." *Wired* 5.10, October 1997.
<http://www.wired.com/wired/archive/5.10/es_wired_pr.html> (June 7, 2002).

Gillooly, Caryn. "Wireless LANs Set to Take Off." *Information Week*, July 19, 1999, pp. 71–76.

Sanborn, Stephanie. "Taking Off with Wireless." *InfoWorld*, July 6, 2001.
<http://www2.infoworld.com/articles/fe/xml/01/07/09/010709fetrend.xml> (June 7, 2002).

Related Topics

Bluetooth; Broadband; Satellite Networks; Security

— James Pyfer

World Wide Web

The World Wide Web is the Internet application that most people turn to when they want to access or publish information online. Developed beginning in 1989 and released publicly in 1991, the Web allows people to retrieve and publish information through use of a single user interface (the Web browser), a simple word-processing-style publishing language (hypertext markup language, or HTML), and a less simple communication standard (hypertext transfer protocol, or HTTP) that specifies how information on the Internet is transmitted and retrieved by controlling how computers issue and respond to requests for information. Reduced to its simplest definition, the Web consists of documents and links to and from documents transmitted over the Internet.

The Web is one of the most revolutionary inventions in history, combining the word-processing abilities, data retrieval-and-storage power, and graphical-display capabilities of the personal computer with the publishing capacity of Gutenberg's printing press. Then it throws in all the possibilities of TV, radio, photography, and animation. In addition, due to the immense growth in its popularity over the course of a decade, the Web has become one of the world's foremost "places" of business, through e-commerce. While a number of researchers and even a few politicians knew such things were possible before it was created, the advent of the World Wide Web suddenly made it clear to the public that the Internet combined the characteristics of all of the media that had come before it, while adding the unique, hypertext-driven power of interactivity to the mix. The Web offered anyone with a computer and the inclination to take advantage of the innovation a chance to become a part of a linked world of information. While the Internet had existed in one form or another since 1969, it was after the introduction of the Web that the Internet became the wildly popular medium that it is today.

Although the two are often confused, the Web is not the Internet, even though the former could not exist without the latter. The Internet is much larger than the Web, and contains many other information exchange applications, including email, file transfer protocol (FTP), Gopher, chat, Telnet, and USENET, among others. None of these are the Web either, although the Web can be and often is used to display them all.

That is the key to the Web: It is a system of organizing, linking, and displaying information in a way that computers all over the world can access, regardless of the operating system they employ, the kind of software they use to render information, the kind of server the information is stored on, or the online network that information is passing through. Today, the Web can even be accessed on personal digital assistants (PDAs) and cellular phones as well as computers. Its lack of limitation is by design; the Web was created specifically to foster universal access. The Web's inventor, Tim Berners-Lee, wrote in his book *Weaving the Web* that he had believed since high school that computers could be much more powerful if they could be programmed to link otherwise unconnected information. "Inventing the World Wide Web," he wrote, "involved my growing realization that there was a power in arranging ideas in an unconstrained, web-like way."

INVENTING THE WEB

The Web wasn't worldwide at its outset. It was initially invented so that a single physics lab in Switzerland, the European Center for Nuclear Research (CERN), could organize, store, and access reams of research information generated on its many incompatible computer hardware and software systems. Although one might not expect a particle-physics lab to be the source of such a key advance in computing, in fact CERN was an unexpectedly apt proving ground. Over the course of 20 years, CERN had developed a culture based on distributed computing, in which tasks were divided up among computers and researchers, and information was swapped and shared. But there were problems. Distributed computing often involves incompatible software and computer systems that make sharing research a grueling and frustrating task, and that problem was exacerbated by the fact that CERN research teams were usually available on site only for short periods. Many were in Switzerland on two-year grants, and their complex work often disappeared in the catacombs of CERN's incompatible computer systems.

The Web was Berners-Lee's way out of this mess. He had spent six months at CERN as a programming consultant in 1980, during which time he wrote a program called Enquire that was similar to Apple's HyperCard program for the Macintosh; it allowed subjects to be indexed and stored on a computer through a hierarchy of links. Berners-Lee returned to CERN in 1989 to assist researchers in the daunting task of retrieving and organize the center's often difficult-to-locate research. In March 1989, he wrote his proposal for what would become the World Wide Web.

In many ways, Berners-Lee and his collaborators had to develop the Web furtively. Inventing a worldwide computer network interface was not what Berners-Lee had been hired to do, and he was constantly worried that a superior would at some point assess his work and ask him to stop. He had to see to it that the project addressed CERN's specific needs. What he came up with was a single user interface that could access many classes of computerized information; this was crucial at CERN, where many varieties of incompatible mainframe and personal computers were in use. His first move was to create a searchable phone book for the center that could be easily searched and kept up to date, although that task did not take advantage of the Web's true abilities.

Developing the Web required three primary innovations: a simple protocol that would allow people—as opposed to computers—to request and retrieve information regardless of the system or software they were using; a uniform protocol that both the sending computer and the receiving computer could render and interpret; and a way to legibly display the retrieved information on computer screens.

There was interesting history behind these ideas. In 1945, Vannevar Bush wrote an *Atlantic Monthly* article that described a theoretical device that he called the "Memex" (memory extension), which would create and follow links between microfiche documents. Later, in 1965, Ted Nelson coined the term "hypertext" to describe his "information docuverse," wherein all the writing ever put down by humans would be published in hypertext form, linked universally to all other information, and be made accessible to all people everywhere, equally. Nelson called this Utopian idea Xanadu, and he began working on it in 1961; it has never been finished. Also, in 1968, Doug Engelbart at Stanford University created and presented a prototype for his "oNLine System" (NLS), which could edit and browse hypertext documents, manage email, and perform other tasks. Engelbart also invented the computer mouse to accompany the NLS.

Berners-Lee's plans for the Web stemmed from all these ideas. However, his plans were more limited in scope and more practical than Nelson's grandiose scheme, which had also included a system of automatic micropayments to be given to all authors whenever their works were accessed. Berners-Lee aimed simply to link documents to other relevant documents, and to make it possible for hyperlinks displayed on a screen to make these documents accessible regardless of where the actual pages were stored. For example, source material referenced in a research report's footnote could be linked to directly, even if the referenced document was stored on some remote server on the other side of the planet. This is a fundamental idea behind the World Wide Web, one that made Berners-Lee's invention truly global in scale.

There is yet another reason why the Web is worldwide. Berners-Lee worked hard convincing his bosses at CERN that his invention should be given away to the public, that it not be patented or turned into a proprietary or for-profit system. He worried that if the Web were made commercial, then competitors would arise, standards would clash, and the whole idea of universal access to documents across computing platforms would be lost. Instead of one Web, there might be three, or 20, or 100 variations on the theme. So Berners-Lee saw to it that the Web's source code was released to the public, so that anyone could work on it, improve it, and use it for free. Had he not insisted on this, users would probably have to pay to access the various networks. It was a decision that most likely prevented Berners-Lee from becoming enormously wealthy in the way that Marc Andreessen became wealthy after creating the Mosaic browser and using the idea to establish the Netscape company. Berners-Lee's selfless choice was made in the interests of the world community as a whole.

It took Berners-Lee about a year to devise the Web from start to finish, a fact that author John

Naughton finds astonishing. "Looking back, it is not so much the elegance of Berners-Lee's creation which makes one gasp at its blinding comprehensiveness," Naughton wrote in *A Brief History of the Future: From Radio Days to Internet Years in a Lifetime* (2001). "In just over a year, he took the Web all the way—from original conception to hacking out primitive browsers and servers, to the creation and elaboration of the protocols needed to make the whole thing work. And on the seventh day he rested."

The Web went public on January 15, 1991, and a "line-mode" browser that was capable only of displaying text was distributed by CERN to a limited number of Internet users so they could view content using the new creation. Those who wished to could dial up CERN over the Internet using "anonymous FTP," download the line-mode browser, and begin viewing the first rudimentary, text-heavy Web sites. The first browser, also created by Berners-Lee, was also called WorldWideWeb; the name was later changed to Nexus. Crude as it was, Nexus made real the promise of a global hypertext network. Once the Web was out to the public, other researchers began working to improve Berners-Lee's innovation. In January 1993, University of Illinois at Urbana-Champaign undergraduate Marc Andreessen, assisted by friend and fellow National Center for Supercomputing Applications (NCSA) staffer Eric Bina and a small team laboring for $6.85 an hour, worked around the clock for three months to unleash Mosaic in the spring of 1993.

Mosaic was the first browser to make it possible for surfers to point and click their way around the Web; Berners-Lee's original browser operated with keystrokes because of the incompatibility of so many computer systems. Mosaic made it possible to view hypertext documents with embedded graphics, to launch sound files, and to open movie clips and other "rich hypermedia." Just as importantly, it ran on simple PC desktops, rather than requiring high-powered Unix machines (although it ran on those too). For a time in the early 1990s, Mosaic was the Web's most popular browser. Then Andreessen left the NCSA, formed a company with Silicon Graphics founder Jim Clark, and launched the Netscape Navigator browser. The company went public in August 1995 in one of the most lucrative and successful initial public offerings in U.S. history. Netscape's share of the browser market ballooned in four months from zero percent to 75 percent; the World Wide Web had well and truly arrived.

Not long after Netscape's introduction, Microsoft developed and began distributing a competing browser, Internet Explorer, which it gave away for free, drastically undercutting Netscape's business. In 1998, its market share badly eroded, Netscape was bought by America Online.

THE WEB TAKES OFF

In October 1993, the Clinton administration opened the Internet, which had been a U.S. military project, to commercial traffic just as Mosaic was being released. In March of that year, the Web had accounted for 0.1 percent of the traffic on the Internet; by March 1995, several months after Netscape's December 1994 release, that figure had risen to 23.9 percent. FTP traffic, which had accounted for 43.9 percent of the Internet's traffic, was reduced to 24.2 percent of traffic, as measured by the National Science Foundation.

The Web gained momentum throughout the late 1990s. By 1999, it was cruising at stratospheric heights, achieving immense popularity. Within just a few years, every major media operation in existence, from CNN to *Time* to the *St. Paul Pioneer Press* was represented on the Web. Meanwhile, millions of average citizens had learned basic HTML programming and published their own home pages detailing their interests, telling their life stories—or, in one man's case, exacting revenge on a former girlfriend by uploading her cajoling and threatening voicemail messages for all the world to hear. Universities, libraries, and museums made substantial portions of their collections available online. If pornography became rampant on the Web, so did more edifying instructional materials from high schools and community colleges.

Another reason for the Web's rise was the recognition among consumers that the Internet was a convenient way to do many kinds of shopping—and the realization among businesses that they could use the Web to extend their brands to customers and even to other businesses that they might otherwise never have had a chance to work with. Major companies like IBM, for instance, reportedly have more than one million pages on the Web. The medium has arisen as a place to transact e-commerce, to listen to and download music, to maintain personal appointment schedules, even to watch movies. By 1999, massive, precariously unprofitable businesses like Amazon.com had become household names, and CEOs like Amazon's Jeff Bezos and eBay's Meg Whitman were new corporate superstars. For a time, the Web resembled nothing so much as the Yukon in Gold Rush days; it seemed that everyone with any kind of idea for doing business on the Web was rewarded with outrageous sums of venture capital to get their businesses started. Stock prices were spiraling to the heavens, and company valuations were approaching free orbit. However, by April 2000, the dot-com bubble burst, and many Web-based companies that could not prove imminent profitability saw their investment money pulled out. Many Web sites died rapid, ignominious deaths, while their employees joined the swelling ranks of the unemployed.

However, despite the shock of that downturn, reverberations of which were still being felt in the world economy at the time of this writing, the Web remains more immensely popular than ever. In August 2001, the Nielsen/NetRatings firm estimated that the Web-Internet population—which is roughly synonymous with the number of Web users—was 459 million people worldwide. The service said that more than 30 million Web surfers had been added to that population during the first quarter of 2001.

The Web's population is not the only thing that can be expected to grow and evolve; the Web itself is destined to undergo significant change—led again, possibly, by Tim Berners-Lee. In a *Scientific American* article published in May 2001, he wrote of new innovations that he generically called the Semantic Web. "The Semantic Web will bring structure to the meaningful content of Web pages, creating an environment where software agents roaming from page to page can readily carry out sophisticated tasks for users," wrote Berners-Lee and his co-authors James Hendler and Ora Lassila. In this scheme, Web users will employ software agents to scour special tags encoded into Web sites, which will tell the agents whether the user will find anything on that site interesting or useful. "The Semantic Web is not a separate Web but an extension of the current one in which information is given well-defined meaning, better enabling computers and people to work in cooperation," Berners-Lee and his team wrote. The new Semantic Web will rely heavily on two technologies, eXtensible Markup Language (XML) and the Resource Description Framework (RDF), that already exist and are in use.

Bibliography

Berners-Lee, Tim. "Frequently Asked Questions." Last revised October 15, 2001. <http://www.w3.org/People/Berners-Lee/FAQ.html#Influences> (May 17, 2002).

Berners-Lee, Tim. "Information Management: A Proposal." *Multimedia: From Wagner to Virtual Reality.* Randall Packer and Ken Jordan, eds. New York: W.W. Norton & Company, 2001; pp. 189–205.

Berners-Lee, Tim, and Mark Fischetti. *Weaving the Web: The Original Design and Ultimate Destiny of the World Wide Web by Its Inventor.* New York: HarperCollins, 2000.

Gillies, James, and Robert Cailliau. *How the Web Was Born.* Oxford, England: Oxford University Press, 2000.

Naughton, John. *A Brief History of the Future: From Radio Days to Internet Years in a Lifetime.* Woodstock, N.Y.: Overlook Press, 2000.

Segaller, Stephen. *Nerds 2.0.1: A Brief History of the Internet.* New York: TV Books, 1998.

Further Reading

Auletta, Ken. *World War 3.0: Microsoft and Its Enemies.* New York: Random House, 2001.

Berners-Lee, Tim. "The Future of the Web." Transcript of speech delivered at the 35th anniversary celebration of the MIT Laboratory of Computer Science, Cambridge, Massachusetts, April 14, 1999. <http://www.w3.org/1999/04/13-tbl.html> (May 17, 2002).

Berners-Lee, Tim; Hendler, James; and Ora Lassila. "The Semantic Web." *Scientific American,* May 2001, pp. 35–43.

Dertouzos, Michael L. *The Unfinished Revolution: Human-Centered Computers and What They Can Do for Us.* New York: HarperCollins, 2001.

Featherly, Kevin. "Forget The Web, Make Way For 'X Internet'—Report." *WashingtonPost.com,* May 7, 2001. <http://www.newsbytes.com/news/01/165405.html> (May 17, 2002).

Fidler, Roger. *Mediamorphosis: Understanding New Media.* Thousand Oaks, Calif.: Pine Forge Press, 1997.

Gromov, Gregory R. "The Roads and Crossroads of Internet History." 1995–2000. <http://www.netvalley.com/intval.html> (May 17, 2002).

Pavlik, John V. *New Media Technology: Cultural and Commercial Perspectives.* Boston, Mass.: Allyn and Bacon, 1996.

Wolfe, Gary. "The (Second Phase of the) Revolution Has Begun." *Wired* 2.10, October 1994. <http://www.wired.com/wired/archive/2.10/mosaic.html> (May 17, 2002).

Related Topics

"As We May Think"; Berners-Lee, Tim; Browser; E-Commerce; Engelbart, Douglas; Hypermedia; Hypertext; Interactivity; Internet; Linking; Markup Languages; Multimedia; Nelson, Theodor Holm (Ted); World Wide Web Consortium

— Kevin Featherly

World Wide Web Consortium

The World Wide Web Consortium (W3C), founded by Web inventor Tim Berners-Lee in October 1994, has as its goal the development of protocols and standards to promote the evolution and interoperability of the Web. The W3C now comprises more than 500 members, including a wide range of transnational corporations in the telecommunications and media sectors, international academic institutions, and smaller multimedia companies.

Membership in W3C is open to for-profit and non-profit commercial, educational, and governmental entities. Full membership is available to all prospective members at $50,000 per year. Affiliate membership is available for $5,000 per year to non-profit or governmental organizations; or to for-profit organizations with an annual gross income of less than $50,000,000 that are not majority-owned by an entity with over $50,000,000 in revenue, or that are subsidiaries of full members of the W3C.

The operating principles of the W3C include universal access, the Semantic Web, trust, interoperability, evolvability, and decentralization. Universal access involves making the Web accessible to all users, regardless of system hardware and software, physical disability, or geographic location. The Semantic Web involves the development of languages to support Web work. Creating a climate of trust ensures that users operate the Web in an efficient and proactive manner. Interoperability, evolvability, and decentralization extend and refine the capabilities of the Web, and allow users to work across and between platforms.

THE DOMAINS OF THE W3C

The five areas of activity, or domains, that the W3C pursues are Architecture, Document Formats, Interaction, Technology and Society, and the Web Accessibility Initiative.

The goals of the Architecture domain are to enhance the infrastructure of the Web and to increase its automation. Berners-Lee has articulated some architectural principles to guide the work of W3C. In his view, the concept of interoperability encompasses both technical and social elements; these include "the principles of universality of access irrespective of hardware or software platform, network infrastructure, language, culture, geographical location, or physical or mental impairment."

Five specific architectures are the focus of work: DOM, Jigsaw, XML, XML Protocol, and URI. DOM, or Document Object Model, is an API (Application Programming Interface) for the structure of documents. Essentially, DOM allows programmers to write applications that work across a variety of browsers and servers, and on all platforms. Jigsaw, one of the W3C's open-source projects, is a Java-based, object-oriented Web server for the storage of files and the processing of incoming requests, with the goal of creating efficiency and extensibility of Web services. XML (Extensible Markup Language) is the universal format for structuring documents and data on the Web. XML Protocol allows technologies with two or more peers to communicate in a distributed environment. URI, the Universal Resource Identifier, is the fundamental specification of the Web, providing a global identifier for Web pages.

The Document Formats domain is concerned with improving the technology that allows Web users to effectively perceive and express information. This domain develops formats and languages to present information to users with higher levels of accuracy and control. Specific areas of focus include: HTML (Hypertext Markup Language); style sheets, using Cascading Style Sheets (CSSs); the creation of a Mathematical Markup Language (MathML); graphics development; and the establishment of standards toward internationalization, such as the development of Unicode, which provides a unique number for every character, regardless of platform, program, or language.

The Interaction domain develops new Web-access devices for other technologies such as cellular phones, televisions, and audiovisual presentations. Activities supporting this development include Device Independence, the creation of interoperability across platforms and multiple devices (for example, in-car computers, TVs, digital cameras, and cellular phones). Synchronized Multimedia focuses on designing a language for scheduling real-time multimedia presentations that combines audio, video, text, and graphics. The development of voice browsers will allow users to interact with Web sites through spoken commands, and to listen to pre-recorded speech, music, and synthetic speech.

The Technology and Society Domain is concerned with the social impacts of the Web, and with reaching out to affected communities. Areas of focus include designing privacy and trust for the Web through the Platform for Privacy Preferences (P3P), developing

XML signatures, and assuming a public policy role through education and awareness activities.

The Web Accessibility Initiative is concerned with increasing the accessibility of the Web through the creation of accessibility guidelines for Web site development. In particular, this domain is concerned with accessibility issues for people with disabilities, addressing them through the creation of technology, guidelines, and tools, as well as through education, outreach, and research and development.

Bibliography

Berners-Lee, Tim. "Web Architecture from 50,000 Feet." W3C, September 1998. Updated October 1999. <http://www.w3.org/DesignIssues/Architecture.html> (June 7, 2002).

World Wide Web Consortium. "About the World Wide Web Consortium." 2000. <http://www.w3.org/Consortium> (June 7, 2002).

Further Reading

Berners-Lee, Tim, and Mark Fischetti. *Weaving the Web: The Original Design and Ultimate Destiny of the World Wide Web by Its Inventor.* New York: HarperCollins, 2000.

Related Topics

Berners-Lee, Tim; Universal Design; Usability; World Wide Web

— *Leslie Regan Shade*

Xerox Palo Alto Research Center

The Palo Alto Research Center (PARC), created by the Xerox Corporation in 1970 to map out the future of document technology, has played an important role in the history of new media by fostering the development of personal computing and multimedia. PARC has become the paradigmatic "think-tank" for the information age, coupling computer programmers, hardware engineers, and physicists with anthropologists, educators, and designers in an open, creative atmosphere. The result has been a series of significant innovations, including one of the first prototypes of what we now think of as a personal computer.

In 1970, IBM introduced its first office photocopier, bringing to an end Xerox's monopoly on the market. Xerox, recognizing the potential impact of computing on the future of office machines, acquired a fledgling computer company called Scientific Data Systems (SDS). The intention was to marry Xerox's expertise and market share in document imaging with digital technologies from SDS, and design new systems for the office of the future, creating a new "architecture of information." While this vision for the company may not have been fully realized, it provided the impetus for the creation of the PARC, a new research center in northern California that would provide direction for the coming computer age.

The PARC was modeled after AT&T's successful Bell Labs and IBM's Yorktown Heights lab, and the hope was that it would generate the same kind of long-term returns that Xerox had captured by funding the development of the photocopier. By recruiting

A demonstration of the Alto computer, created at Xerox PARC. (Courtesy of Xerox)

researchers from the surrounding area—including those hired away from the Stanford Research Institute and the Berkeley Computer Corporation—the PARC became a significant concentration of research talent in the first years of the 1970s. By 1973, the developments that would form the basis of today's computerized office had been demonstrated, including a personal computer with word-processing software, a local-area network (LAN) for connecting machines within an office, and a laser printer.

THE FIRST OFFICE WORKSTATION

While the PARC was responsible for dozens of other technological breakthroughs, it is most readily associated with the strain of research that led to contemporary personal computing. The Alto, unveiled in 1973, provided a view of what Xerox correctly predicted would be the future of computing. Even though computers were getting smaller and smaller at the time, they were still designed for time-sharing—that is, hundreds of users would each be given a small slice of the computing power of a single machine. The idea that a single user might be able to make exclusive use of a computer was heretical at the time, at least in part because the expense of such computers (about $12,000 for the production model) was extraordinary. However, those working at the PARC recognized that the prices of memory and other computing components were dropping quickly, and that while the personal computer might not be a reality in 1973, in five years' time it could reach the point of being a viable business machine.

The Alto was created as a means for demonstrating a new way to work with computers. Time-sharing usually implied batch processing: giving the computer instructions and waiting for it to process those instructions and reply. In some cases, the process could be interactive, with the computer responding quickly to a request, but it was not interactive enough for the innovators at the PARC. Recognizing that the most efficient way to communicate information between the computer and the user was via visuals, they hoped to create a computer that could provide interactive graphics. While the Alto is most often recognized for its size (it could roll beneath a desk) and its orientation toward individual users, the real breakthroughs it allowed were in the graphical user interface (GUI). Building upon ideas that had been presented several years earlier by Doug Engelbart, the Alto featured a graphic display, a system for display "windows," and a mouse for controlling actions on the screen.

Before the Alto, the idea of using a computer to edit a document was unheard of, but in the two years following the advent of the first Alto, the PARC created two word-processing programs, Bravo and Gypsy. These programs, which featured WYSIWYG ("What You See Is What You Get," pronounced "wiz-ee-wig") layout and icon-driven menus, would not be unfamiliar to the user of contemporary word-processing software. By itself, the word processor proved to be the "killer application" for the Alto, showing just how valuable a personal computer could be. But two complementary technologies, Ethernet local-area networking and laser printing, made this system look uncannily like those that would be common a quarter of a century later.

The laser printer was among the earliest coups of the new research center. Gary Starkweather thrived in the open atmosphere of the PARC, and despite the contentions of the more traditional researchers at the other major Xerox lab, he showed that a laser could be made practical in office printing. By 1975, the more difficult task of processing computer output had been completed, and the printer could be hooked up to the growing LAN. Although it took several more years for Xerox to commercialize the device, the laser printer would be the greatest commercial success the company achieved based on research at the PARC.

During the early 1970s, PARC researchers Robert Metcalfe and David Boggs collaborated to design what would become the most widespread way of allowing computers to talk to one another, a system that Metcalfe called Ethernet because its wires had no carrier voltage. The system was a simple adaptation of ALOHANET, a radio network developed by University of Hawaii researcher Norm Abramson, and allowed for a resilient and easily adapted network without a central server. The Ethernet standard continues to be used widely in LANs.

Certainly, the progress in these areas may be attributed to a number of luminaries, but Bob Taylor and Alan Kay are the most easily identifiable figureheads for a particular culture associated with the PARC, which is identified as much by its atmosphere of playful creativity as it is by its many technological innovations. Photographs from the first decade of the research center invariably depict researchers sitting in circles of bean-bag chairs or playing volleyball. This playful culture was popularized, and perhaps amplified, by a 1972 article written by Stewart Brand in *Rolling Stone* casting the "Computer Bums," as he called them, as the counter-culture heroes of the new generation. The PARC environment would contribute significantly to the emerging Silicon Valley culture of entrepreneurism. When Sony decided to create a new research center in 1990, it, like so many others, explicitly used the PARC as its model. This PARC atmosphere has influenced the flexible workplaces of recent dot-com companies as well.

RESEARCH, PRODUCTS, AND THE FUTURE OF THE PARC

Given the fact that the PARC created many of the technologies that are now central to the way we use computers, one would expect Xerox to be on the cusp of the new media revolution. In fact, many of the breakthroughs from the PARC never made it to the product stage within Xerox. That is not to say that Xerox failed entirely to capitalize on the work being done at PARC—the returns on the laser printer alone justified the cost of the laboratory—but, partly because Xerox was undergoing a significant change in its corporate culture, opportunities were missed.

By fumbling the marketing and production of the Alto and its successor, the Star, Xerox missed out on the early stages of the personal-computer revolution. Other companies took advantage of these missed opportunities, most famously Apple, which modeled its Lisa (which would lead to the Macintosh) on the work done at the PARC. Many of the PARC's greatest advances, from the computer-programming language Smalltalk to new network architectures, were taken up by Silicon Valley entrepreneurs or passed quietly into the public domain.

Because the PARC made up such a small portion of Xerox's operating budget, it managed to thrive even during economic downturns. The PARC remains a vibrant research environment, producing more innovations now than ever before. Recently, however, the future of funding for the center has been questioned, as Xerox has faced more serious economic straits.

Xerox PARC's mission has always been tied up with the future: The stated aim of the research center has been to predict the future by inventing it. Among the wide range of projects that the PARC currently supports are those aimed at unseating the desktop metaphor that it helped introduce to the world. PARC researchers have recently presented new ways of navigating through large sets of documents, by zooming in and out on details; they have been leaders in developing reusable "electronic paper," and have been instrumental in presenting possible directions for "ubiquitous computing," in which computers are so enmeshed in the living environment that they become invisible. While the PARC has recently been under financial pressures that did not hinder it during its earliest days, it remains among the premier research institutions within the new-media field, and there can be little doubt that among the projects it is working on today lurk the precursors of the systems of tomorrow.

Bibliography

Brand, Stewart. "Spacewar: Fanatic Life and Symbolic Death Among the Computer Bums." *Rolling Stone,* December 7, 1972, p 58.

Hiltzik, Michael. *Dealers of Lightning: Xerox PARC and the Dawn of the Computer Age.* New York: HarperBusiness, 1999.

Johnstone, Bob. "California Dreamin' Sony Style." *Technology Review,* Jan./Feb. 2000.

Krause, Jason. "Will Xerox Shut the PARC?" *The Industry Standard,* October 20, 2000.

Smith, Douglas, and Robert Alexander. *Fumbling the Future: How XEROX Invented, Then Ignored, the First Personal Computer.* New York: William Morrow, 1988.

Further Reading

Freiberger, Paul, and Michael Swaine. *Fire in the Valley: The Making of the Personal Computer.* New York: McGraw-Hill, 2000.

Waldrop, M. Mitchell. *The Dream Machine: J.C.R. Licklider and the Revolution that Made Computing Personal.* New York: Viking, 2001.

Palo Alto Research Center (PARC). Web site. <http://www.parc.xerox.com/> (June 7, 2002).

Related Topics

Computer Graphics; Desktop Publishing; Engelbart, Douglas; Graphical User Interface; Human-Computer Interaction; Interactivity; Kay, Alan; Local Area Network; Multimedia; Object-Oriented Programming; Virtual Community

— *Alexander Halavais*

Aarseth, Espen. *Cybertext: Perspectives on Ergodic Literature.* Baltimore, Md.: Johns Hopkins University Press, 1997.

Acland, Charles R., and William J. Buxton, eds. *Harold Innis in the New Century: Reflections and Refractions.* Montreal and Kingston, Canada: McGill-Queen's University Press, 1999.

Adams, Tyrone, and Norman Clark. *The Internet: Effective Online Communication.* Fort Worth, Tex.: Harcourt College Publishers, 2001.

Albarran, Alan B., and David H. Goff, eds. *Understanding the Web: Social, Political, and Economic Dimensions of the Internet.* Ames: Iowa State University Press, 2000.

Alderman, John. *Sonic Boom: Napster, MP3, and the New Pioneers of Music.* Cambridge, Mass.: Perseus Books, 2001.

Alexander, Cynthia, and Leslie A. Pal, eds. *Digital Democracy: Policy and Politics in the Wired World.* Toronto and New York: Oxford University Press, 1998.

Allen, Moira Anderson. *Writing.com: Creative Writing Strategies to Advance Your Writing Career.* New York: Allworth Press, 1999.

Aronowitz, Stanley, Barbara Martinsons, and Michael Menser, eds. *Technoscience and Cyberculture.* New York: Routledge, 1996.

Auletta, Ken. *World War 3.0: Microsoft and Its Enemies.* New York: Random House, 2001.

Balnaves, Mark, James Donald, and Stephanie Hemelryk Donald. *The Penguin Atlas of Media and Information: Key Issues and Global Trends.* New York: Penguin Books, 2001.

Barber, John T., and Alice A. Tait, eds. *The Information Society and the Black Community.* Westport, Conn.: Praeger Publishers, 2001.

Bardini, Thierry. *Bootstrapping: Douglas Engelbart, Coevolution, and the Origins of Personal Computing.* Stanford, Calif.: Stanford University Press, 2000.

Barnes, Susan B. *Online Connections: Internet Interpersonal Relationships.* Cresskill, N.J.: Hampton Press, 2001.

Baym, Nancy. *Tune In, Log On: Soaps, Fandom, and Online Community.* Thousand Oaks, Calif.: Sage Publications, 2000.

Behar, Joseph E., ed. *Mapping Cyberspace: Social Research on the Electronic Frontier.* Oakdale, N.Y.: Dowling College Press, 1997.

Bell, David. *An Introduction to Cybercultures.* London: Routledge, 2001.

Bell, David, and Barbara M. Kennedy, eds. *The Cybercultures Reader.* London: Routledge, 2000.

Benedikt, Michael, ed. *Cyberspace: First Steps.* Cambridge, Mass.: MIT Press, 1992.

Bennahum, David S. *Extra Life: Coming of Age in Cyberspace.* New York: Basic Books, 1998.

Berman, Marshall. *All That Is Solid Melts into Thin Air: The Experience of Modernity.* New York: Simon & Schuster, 1982.

Berners-Lee, Tim, with Mark Fischetti. *Weaving the Web: The Original Design and Ultimate Destiny of the World Wide Web by Its Inventor.* San Francisco: Harper SanFrancisco, 1999.

Bolter, J. David. *Turing's Man: Western Culture in the Computer Age.* Chapel Hill: The University of North Carolina Press, 1984.

Borden, Diane L., and Kerric Harvey, eds. *The Electronic Grapevine: Rumor, Reputation, and Reporting in the New Online Environment.* Mahwah, N.J.: Lawrence Erlbaum Associates, Publishers, 1998.

Brand, Stewart. *The Last Whole Earth Catalog.* New York: Random House, 1972.

———. *The Media Lab: Inventing the Future at MIT.* New York: Viking Press, 1987.

———. *The Clock of the Long Now: Time and Responsibility—The Ideas Behind the World's Slowest Computer.* New York: Basic Books, 1999.

Branscomb, Anne Wells. *Who Owns Information? From Privacy to Public Access*. New York: Basic Books, 1994.

Brasher, Brenda E. *Give Me that Online Religion*. San Francisco: Jossey-Bass, 2001.

Bridges, Joe. *An Internet Guide for Mass Communication Students*. Madison, Wis.: Brown & Benchmark Publishers, 1997.

Brin, David. *The Transparent Society*. Reading, Mass.: Addison-Wesley Pub. Co., 1998.

Brook, James, and Ian A. Boal, eds. *Resisting the Virtual Life: The Culture and Politics of Information*. San Francisco: City Lights Books, 1995.

Brooks, John. *Telephone: The First Hundred Years*. New York: Harper & Row, 1976.

Brown, Hugh, et al., eds. *Fibreculture Reader: An Inventory of Australian Net Culture Criticism and Theory*. Melbourne, Australia: Fibreculture Publications, 2001.

Bucy, Erik P. *Living in the Information Age: A New Media Reader*. Belmont, Calif.: Wadsworth/Thomson Learning, 2002.

Burnham, David. *The Rise of the Computer State*. New York: Vintage Books, 1983.

Calvert, Sandra. *Children's Journeys Through the Information Age*. Boston: McGraw-Hill College, 1999.

Carpenter, Edmund, and Marshall McLuhan, eds. *Explorations in Communication*. Boston: Beacon Press, 1960.

Castells, Manuel. *The Rise of the Network Society*. Cambridge, Mass.: Blackwell Publishers, 1996.

———. *The Internet Galaxy: Reflections on the Internet, Business, and Society*. Oxford: Oxford University Press, 2001.

Chandler, Alfred D., Jr. *Inventing the Electronic Century: The Epic Story of the Consumer Electronics and Computer Industries*. New York: The Free Press, 2001.

Chandler, Alfred D., Jr., and James W. Cortada, eds. *A Nation Transformed by Information: How Information Has Shaped the United States from Colonial Times to the Present*. New York: Oxford University Press, 2000.

Chesterman, John, and Andy Lipman. *The Electronic Pirates: DIY Crime of the Century*. London: Routledge, 1988.

Clements, Richard Barrett. *Internet Technology Handbook*. Paramus, N.J.: Prentice Hall, 1999.

Computer Science and Telecommunications Board, National Research Council. *The Digital Dilemma: Intellectual Property in the Information Age*. Washington, D.C.: National Academy Press, 2000.

Congress of the United States, Office of Technology Assessment. *Critical Connection: Communication for the Future*. Washington, D.C.: U.S. Government Printing Office, January 1990.

Cooper, Al, ed. *Cybersex: The Dark Side of the Force*. Philadelphia: Brunner-Routledge, 2000.

Cotton, Eileen Giuffré. *The Online Classroom*. 2nd ed. Bloomington, Ind.: ERIC/EDINFO Press, 1997.

Couch, Carl J. *Information Technologies and Social Orders*. Hawthorne, N.Y.: Aldine de Gruyter, 1996.

Courtright, John A., and Elizabeth M. Perse. *Communicating Online: A Guide to the Internet*. Mountain View, Calif.: Mayfield Publishing, 1998.

Cronin, Mary J. *Doing Business on the Internet*. New York: Van Nostrand Reinhold, 1994.

Crowley, David, and Paul Heyer. *Communication in History*. 2nd ed. White Plains, N.Y.: Longman Publishers, 1995.

Czitrom, Daniel J. *Media and the American Mind*. Chapel Hill: University of North Carolina Press, 1982.

Danet, Brenda. *Cyberplay: Communicating Online*. Oxford, U.K.: Berg, 2001.

De Bra, Paul, and John Leggett, eds. *WebNet World Conference 99 on the WWW and Internet*. Volume 2. Honolulu, Hawaii: Association for the Advancement of computing in Education, October 24-30, 1999.

Dertouzos, Michael. *The Unfinished Revolution: Human-Centered Computers and What They Can Do for Us*. New York: HarperCollins, 2001.

Dery, Mark. "Flame Wars: The Discourse of Cyberculture." *The South Atlantic Quarterly* 94, 4 (Fall 1993).

Dibbell, Julian. *My Tiny Life: Crime and Passion in a Virtual World*. New York: Henry Holt, 1998.

Dodge, Martin, and Rob Kitchin. *Atlas of Cyberspace*. Harlow, U.K.: Addison-Wesley, 2001.

Doheny-Farina, Stephen. *The Wired Neighborhood.* New Haven, Conn.: Yale University Press, 1996.

Dordick, Herbert S., and Georgette Wang. *The Information Society: A Retrospective View.* Newbury Park, Calif.: Sage Publications, 1993.

Doyle, Terrence, and Doug Gotthoffer. *Quick Guide to the Internet for Speech Communication.* Boston: Allyn and Bacon, 1999.

Dreyfus, Hubert L. *On the Internet.* London: Routledge, 2001.

Druckrey, Timothy, ed. *Ars Electronica: Facing the Future.* Cambridge, Mass: The MIT Press, 1999.

Dunne, Anthony. *Hertzian Tales.* London: Royal College of Art, 1999.

Dyson, Esther. *Release 2.0: A Design for Living in the Digital Age.* New York: Broadway Books, 1997.

Ellul, Jacques. *The Technological Society.* New York: Vintage Books, 1964.

Ess, Charles, ed. *Philosophical Perspectives on Computer-Mediated Communication.* Albany: State University of New York Press, 1996.

Ess, Charles, and Fay Sudweeks, eds. *Culture, Technology and Communication: Towards an Intercultural Global Village.* Albany, N.Y.: State University of New York Press, 2001.

——. *Proceedings: Cultural Attitudes Towards Technology and Communication.* Sydney, Australia: University of Sydney, 1998.

——. *Second International Conference on Cultural Attitudes Towards Technology and Communication 2000.* Murdoch, Australia: Murdoch University, School of Information Technology, 2000.

Fidler, Roger. *Mediamorphosis: Understanding New Media.* Thousand Oaks, Calif.: Pine Forge Press, 1997.

Finkelstein, Sidney. *Sense & Nonsense of McLuhan.* New York: International Publishers, 1968.

Fortier, François. *Virtuality Check: Power Relations and Alternative Strategies in the Information Society.* London: Verso Books, 2001.

Foster, Hal, ed. *The Anti-Aesthetic: Essays on Post-Modern Culture.* Port Townsend, Wash.: Bay Press, 1983.

Free Software Foundation. "GNU's Not UNIX!" <http://www.fsf.org> (April 12, 2002).

Freedom Forum Media Studies Center. *Media at the Millennium: Report of the First Fellows Symposium on the Future of Media and Media Studies.* New York: Columbia University, November 1991.

——. *Media, Democracy, and the Information Highway: A Conference Report on the Prospects for a National Information Service.* New York: Columbia University, October 1992.

Gannett Center for Media Studies. *The Cost of Technology: Information Prosperity and Information Poverty, a Conference Report.* New York: Columbia University, November 9, 1986.

Gates, Bill, with Nathan Myhrvold and Peter Rinearson. *The Road Ahead.* New York: Viking, 1995.

Gibbs, Donna, and Kerri-Lee Krause, eds. *Cyberlines: Language and Culture of the Internet.* Albert Park, Australia: James Nicholas Publishers, 2000.

Gibson, William. *Neuromancer.* New York: Ace Books, 1984.

——. *Burning Chrome.* New York: Ace Books, 1986.

Gillies, James, and Robert Cailliau. *How the Web Was Born.* New York: Oxford University Press, 2000.

Gordo-López, Ángel, and Ian Parker, eds. *Cyberpsychology.* London: Macmillan Press, 1999.

Gray, Chris Hables, ed. *The Cyborg Handbook.* New York: Routledge, 1995.

Gunkel, David J. *Hacking Cyberspace.* Boulder, Colo.: Westview Press, 2001.

Hafner, Katie. *The Well: A Story of Love, Death & Real Life in the Seminal Online Community.* New York: Carroll & Graf, 2001.

Hafner, Katie, and Matthew Lyon. *Where Wizards Stay Up Late: The Origins of the Internet.* New York: Simon and Schuster, 1996.

Hamelink, Cees J. *The Ethics of Cyberspace.* London: Sage Publications, 2000.

Hanhardt, John, ed. *Video Culture: A Critical Investigation.* Rochester, N.Y.: Visual Studies Workshop Press, 1986.

Haraway, Donna. *Simians, Cyborgs, and Women: The Reinvention of Nature.* New York: Routledge, 1991.

——. *Modest_Witness@Second_Millennium. FemaleMan©_Meets_OncoMouse™: Feminism and Technoscience.* New York: Routledge, 1997.

Selected Bibliography

Harnack, Andrew, and Eugene Kleppinger. *Online! A Reference Guide to Using Internet Sources.* Boston: Bedford/St. Martin's, 2000.

Harper, Christopher. *The New Mass Media.* Boston: Houghton Mifflin, 2002.

Hauben, Michael, and Ronda Hauben. *Netizens: On the History and Impact of Usenet and the Internet.* Los Alamitos, Calif.: IEEE Computer Society Press, 1997.

Hayles, N. Katherine. *How We Became Posthuman: Virtual Bodies in Cybernetics, Literature, and Informatics.* Chicago: University of Chicago Press, 1999.

Helfand, Jessica. *Six(+2) Essays on Design and New Media.* New York: William Drenttel, 1997.

Herman, Andrew, and Thomas Swiss, eds. *The World Wide Web and Contemporary Cultural Theory.* New York: Routledge, 2000.

Hiltzik, Michael A. *Dealers of Lightning: Xerox PARC and the Dawn of the Computer Age.* New York: HarperBusiness, 1999.

Himanen, Pekka. *The Hacker Ethic and the Spirit of the Information Age.* New York: Random House, 2001.

Holeton, Richard. *Composing Cyberspace: Identity, Community, and Knowledge in the Electronic Age.* Boston: McGraw-Hill, 1998.

Hoorigan, John B., Thomas M. Lenard, and Stephen McGonegal. *Cities Online: Urban Development and the Internet.* Washington, D.C.: The Progress & Freedom Foundation & the Pew Internet and American Life Project, 2001.

Horn, Stacy. *Cyberville: Clicks, Culture, and the Creation of an Online Town.* New York: Warner Books, 1998.

Howard, Tharon W. *A Rhetoric of Electronic Communities.* Greenwich, Conn.: Ablex Publishing, 1997.

Illich, Ivan. *Tools for Conviviality.* New York: Harper Colophon Books, 1973.

Illich, Ivan, and Barry Sanders. *ABC: The Alphabetization of the Popular Mind.* New York: Vintage Books, 1988.

Innis, Harold A. *The Bias of Communication.* Toronto, Canada: University of Toronto Press, 1951.

———. *Staples, Markets, and Cultural Change.* Montreal and Kingston, Canada: McGill-Queen's University Press, 1995.

Jacobson, Linda, ed. *Cyberarts: Exploring Art and Technology.* San Francisco: Miller Freeman, 1992.

Jenkins, Philip. *Beyond Tolerence: Child Pornography on the Internet.* New York: New York University Press, 2001.

Johnson, Larry. *The Heritage of Time: The People and Times of GTE Southwest 1876–1988.* San Angelo, Tex.: Newsfoto Publishing Co., 1990.

Jones, Steve G., ed. *Cybersociety: Computer-mediated Communication and Community.* Thousand Oaks, Calif.: Sage Publications, 1995.

———. *Virtual Culture: Identity and Communication in Cybersociety.* Thousand Oaks, Calif.: Sage Publications, 1997.

———. *Cybersociety 2.0: Revisiting Computer-Mediated Communication and Community.* Thousand Oaks, Calif.: Sage Publications, 1998.

———. *The Internet for Educators and Homeschoolers.* Palm Springs, Calif.: ETC Publications, 2000.

Joy, Bill. "Why the Future Doesn't Need Us." *Wired* 8.04, April 2000. <http://www.wired.com/wired/archive/8.04/joy.html> (May 17, 2002).

Kahin, Brian, and Hal R. Varian, eds. *Internet Publishing and Beyond: The Economics of Digital Information and Intellectual Property.* Cambridge, Mass.: The MIT Press, 2000.

Kardas, Edward P., and Tommy M. Milford. *Using the Internet for Social Science Research and Practice.* Belmont, Calif.: Wadsworth Publishing, 1996.

Katsh, M. Ethan. *The Electronic Media and the Transformation of Law.* New York: Oxford University Press, 1989.

Katz, James E., and Mark, Aakhus, eds. *Perpetual Contact: Mobile Communication, Private Talk, Public Performance.* Cambridge, U.K.; Cambridge University Press, 2002.

Kaye, Barbara K., and Norman J. Medoff. *The World Wide Web: A Mass Communication Perspective.* Mountain View, Calif.: Mayfield Publishing, 1999.

Keating, Anne B., and Joseph Hargitai. *The Wired Professor: A Guide to Incorporating the World Wide Web in College Instruction.* New York: New York University Press, 1999.

Keeble, Leigh, and Brian D. Loader, eds. *Community Informatics: Shaping Computer-Mediated Social Relations.* London: Routledge, 2001.

Kendall, Lori. *Hanging Out in the Virtual Pub: Masculinities and Relationship Online.* Berkeley and Los Angeles: University of California Press, 2002.

Kiesler, Sara, ed. *Culture of the Internet.* Mahwah, N.J.: Lawrence Erlbaum Associates, 1997.

Kling, Rob, et al. *Information Technologies in Human Contexts: Learning from Organizational and Social Informatics.* Bloomington, Indiana: Center for Social Informatics, Indiana University, 1998, 1999.

Kolko, Beth E., Lisa Nakamura, and Gilbert B. Rodman, eds. *Race in Cyberspace.* New York: Routledge, 2000.

Kramarae, Cheris. *The Third Shift: Women Learning Online.* Washington, D.C.: American Association of University Women Educational Foundation, 2001.

Kuhn, Thomas. *The Structure of Scientific Revolutions.* 2nd ed. Chicago: University of Chicago Press, 1970.

Kuhns, William. *The Post-Industrial Prophets' Interpretation of Technology.* New York: Harper Colophon Books, 1971.

Kurzweil, Raymond. *The Age of Intelligent Machines.* Cambridge, Mass.: MIT Press, 1990.

———. *The Age of Spiritual Machines: When Computers Exceed Human Intelligence.* New York: Viking/Penguin, 1999.

Landow, George P. *Hypertext 2.0.* Baltimore, Md.: Johns Hopkins University Press, 1997.

Langer, Susanne K. *Philosophy in a New Key: A Study in the Symbolism of Reason, Rite, and Art.* Cambridge, Mass.: Harvard University Press, 1951.

Leeson, Lynn Hershman, ed. *Clicking In: Hot Links to a Digital Culture.* Seattle, Wash.: Bay Press, 1996.

Lehman, Bruce A. *Intellectual Property and the National Information Infrastructure: The Report of the Working Group on Intellectual Property Rights.* Washington, D.C.: Information Infrastructure Task Force, September 1995.

Lengel, James G., and Diane S. Kendall. *Kids, Computers, & Homework: How You and Your Kids Can Make Schoolwork a Learning Adventure.* New York: Random House, 1995.

Leonard, Andrew. *Bots: The Origin of New Species.* New York: Penguin Books, 1997.

Lessig, Lawrence. *Code and Other Laws of Cyberspace.* New York: Basic Books, 1999.

Levine, John R., Arnold Rheinhold, and Margaret Levine Young. *The Internet for Dummies.* 4th ed. Foster City, Calif.: IDG Books Worldwide, 1998.

Liberty, The National Council for Civil Liberties. *Liberating Cyberspace: Civil Liberties, Human Rights and the Internet.* Sterling, Va.: Pluto Press, 1999.

Licklider, J. C. R. "Man-Computer Symbiosis." In *Computer Media and Communication: A Reader,* edited by P.A. Mayer. New York and Oxford: Oxford University Press, 1999.

Lin, Carolyn A., and David J. Atkin, eds. *Communication Technology and Society: Audience Adoption and Uses.* Cresskill, N.J.: Hampton Press, 2002.

Lipschultz, Jeremy Harris. *Free Expression in the Age of the Internet: Social and Legal Boundaries.* Oxford: Westview Press, 2000.

Livingstone, Sonia, and Moira Bovill, eds. *Children and Their Changing Media Environment: A European Comparative Study.* Mahwah, N.J.: Lawrence Erlbaum Associates, 2001.

Lull, James, ed. *Culture in the Communication Age.* New York: Routledge, 2001.

Mann, Chris, and Fiona Stewart. *Internet Communication and Qualitative Research: A Handbook for Researching Online.* London: Sage Publications, 2000.

Mansell, Robin. *The New Telecommunications: A Political Economy of Network Evolution.* London: Sage Publications, 1993.

Marc, David. *Demographic Vistas: Television in American Culture.* Philadelphia: University of Pennsylvania Press, 1984.

Marchand, Philip. *Marshall McLuhan: The Medium and the Messenger.* New York: Ticknor & Fields, 1989.

Marcus, George E., ed. *Connected: Engagements with Media.* Chicago: The University of Chicago Press, 1996.

Marcuse, Herbert. *One-Dimensional Man: Studies in the Ideology of Advanced Industrial Society.* Boston: Beacon Press, 1964.

Selected Bibliography

Markham, Annette N. *Life Online: Researching Real Experience in Virtual Space*. Walnut Creek, Calif.: Sage Publications, 1998.

Marvin, Carolyn. *When Old Technologies Were New: Thinking about Electric Communication in the Late Nineteenth Century*. New York: Oxford University Press, 1988.

Marx, Leo. *The Machine in the Garden: Technology and the Pastoral Ideal in America*. New York: Oxford University Press, 1964.

Matzat, Uwe. *Social Networks and Cooperation in Electronic Communities: A Theoretical-Empirical Analysis of Academic Communication and Internet Discussion Groups*. Amsterdam: Thela Publishers, 2001.

Mayer, Paul A., ed. *Computer Media and Communication: A Reader*. Oxford: Oxford University Press, 1999.

McKelvey, Roy. *Hyper Graphics*. Crans-Près-Céligny, Switzerland: RotoVision, 1998.

McLuhan, Eric, and Frank Zingrone, eds. *Essential McLuhan*. New York: Basic Books, 1995.

McLuhan, Marshall. *The Gutenberg Galaxy*. Toronto, Canada: University of Toronto Press, 1962.

———. *Understanding Media: The Extensions of Man*. New York: McGraw-Hill, 1964.

———. *The Mechanical Bride: Folklore of Industrial Man*. New York: Beacon Press, 1967.

———. *Counter-Blast*. New York: Harcout, Brace & World, 1969.

———. *Culture Is Our Business*. New York: Ballantine Books, 1970.

McLuhan, Marshall, and Quentin Fiore. *The Medium Is the Massage*. New York: Bantam Books, 1967.

———. *War and Peace in the Global Village*. New York: Bantam Books, 1968.

Mcluhan, Marshall, and Eric McLuhan. *Laws of Media: The New Science*. Toronto: University of Toronto Press, 1988.

McLuhan, Marshall, and Harley Parker. *Through the Vanishing Point: Space in Poetry and Painting*. New York: Harper & Row, 1968.

McLuhan, Marshall, and Bruce R. Powers. *The Global Village: Transformations in World Life and Media in the 21st Century*. New York: Oxford University Press, 1989.

McLuhan, Marshall, and Wilfred Watson. *From Cliché to Archetype*. New York: Viking Press, 1970.

Miller, Daniel, and Don Slater. *The Internet: An Ethnographic Approach*. Oxford, U.K.: Berg, 2000.

Mitcham, Carl, and Robert Mackey, eds. *Philosophy and Technology: Readings in the Philosophic Problems of Technology*. New York: The Free Press, 1972.

Molinaro, Matie, Corinne McLuhan, and William Toye, eds. *Letters of Marshall McLuhan*. Toronto: Oxford University Press, 1987.

Moll, Marita, and Leslie Regan Shade, eds. *e-Commerce vs. e-Commons: Communications in the Public Interest*. Ottawa, Canada: The Canadian Centre for Policy Alternatives, 2001.

Moschovitis, Christos J. P., Hilary Poole, Tami Schuyler, and Theresa M. Senft. *History of the Internet: A Chronology, 1843 to the Present*. Santa Barbara, Calif.: ABC-CLIO, 1999.

Mumford, Lewis. *Technics and Civilization*. New York: Harcourt, Brace & World, 1963.

Münker, Stefan, and Alexander Roesler. *Mythos Internet*. Frankfurt, Germany: Suhrkamp, 1997.

Naughton, John. A *Brief History of the Future: From Radio Days to Internet Years in a Lifetime*. Woodstock, N.Y.: Overlook Press, 1999.

Negroponte, Nicholas. *Being Digital*. New York: Vintage Books, 1995.

Nelson, Theodor H. *Computer Lib/Dream Machines*. Redmond, Wash.: Tempus Books of Microsoft Press, 1987.

Newcomb, Horace, ed. *Television: The Critical View*. 4th ed. New York: Oxford University Press, 1987.

Noll, A. Michael. *Highway of Dreams: A Critical View along the Information Superhighway*. Mahwah, N.J.: Lawrence Erlbaum Associates, 1997.

Norman, Adrian R. D. *Computer Insecurity*. New York: Chapman and Hall, 1985.

Ong, Walter J. *Orality and Literacy: The Technologizing of the Word*. New York: Methuen, 1982.

Pacey, Arnold. *The Culture of Technology*. Cambridge, Mass.: The MIT Press, 1984.

Packer, Randall, and Ken Jordan, eds. *Multimedia: From Wagner to Virtual Reality*. New York: W. W. Norton & Co., 2001.

Pargman, Daniel. *Code Begets Community: On Social and Technical Aspects of Managing a*

Virtual Community. Linköping, Sweden: Linköpings Universitet, 2000.

Patton, Phil. *Open Road: A Celebration of the American Highway*. New York: Simon & Schuster, 1986.

Pavlik, John V. *New Media Technology: Cultural and Commercial Perspectives*. Needham Heights, Mass.: Allyn & Bacon, 1996.

Pavlik, John V., and Everette E. Dennis. *Demystifying Media Technology*. Mountain View, Calif.: Mayfield Publishing, 1993.

Pitt, Joseph C. *Thinking about Technology: Foundations of the Philosophy of Technology*. New York: Seven Bridges Press, 2000.

Porter, David, ed. *Internet Culture*. New York: Routledge, 1997.

Poster, Mark. *The Mode of Information: Poststructuralism and Social Context*. Cambridge: Polity Press, 1990.

———. *What's the Matter with the Internet*. Minneapolis: University of Minnesota Press, 2001.

Postman, Neil. *Amusing Ourselves to Death*. New York: Elizabeth Sifton Books/Viking, 1985.

Powazek, Derek M. *Design for Community: The Art of Connecting Real People in Virtual Places*. Indianapolis, Ind.: New Riders, 2002.

Power, Richard. *Tangled Web: Tales of Digital Crime from the Shadows of Cyberspace*. Indianapolis, Ind.: Que, 2000.

Preece, Jenny. *Online Communities: Designing Usability, Supporting Sociability*. Chichester, U.K.: John Wiley & Sons, 2000.

Qvortrup, Lars. *Det Hyperkomplekse Samfund*. Copenhagen, Denmark: Gyldendal, 2000.

Raymond, Eric S. *The Cathedral and the Bazaar: Musings on Linux and Open Source by an Accidental Revolutionary*. Cambridge, Mass.: O'Reilly & Associates, 1999.

Reid, T. R. *The Chip: How Two Americans Invented the Microchip and Launched a Revolution*. New York: Simon & Schuster, 1984.

Rheingold, Howard. *The Virtual Community: Homesteading on the Electronic Frontier*. Reading, Mass.: Addison-Wesley, 1993.

———. *Tools for Thought: The History and Future of Mind-Expanding Technology*. Cambridge, Mass.: MIT Press, 2000.

Rice, Ronald E. and Katz, James E., eds. *The Internet and Health Communication: Experiences and Expectations*. Thousand Oaks, Calif.: Sage Publications, 2001.

Rose, Mark. *Authors and Owners: The Invention of Copyright*. Cambridge, Mass.: Harvard University Press, 1993.

Rosenthal, Raymond, ed. *McLuhan: Pro & Con*. Baltimore, Md.: Penguin Books, 1968.

Roszak, Theodore. *The Cult of Information: The Folklore of Computers and the True Art of Thinking*. New York: Pantheon Books, 1986.

Rushkoff, Douglas. *Cyberia: Life in the Trenches of Hyperspace*. San Francisco: HarperCollins Publishers, 1994.

Samoriski, Jan. *Issues in Cyberspace: Communication, Technology, Law, and Society on the Internet Frontier*. Boston: Allyn & Bacon, 2002.

Schiller, Herbert I. *Mass Communications and American Empire*. 2nd ed. Boulder, Colo.: Westview Press, 1992.

Schuler, Douglas. *New Community Networks: Wired for Change*. New York: Addison-Wesley Publishing, 1996.

Schumacher, E. F. *Small Is Beautiful: Economics As If People Mattered*. New York: Harper & Row, 1973.

———. *A Guide for the Perplexed*. New York: Harper & Row, 1977.

Schwartz, Hillel. *The Culture of the Copy: Striking Likenesses, Unreasonable Facsimiles*. New York: Zone Books, 1996.

Schwartz, Tony. *The Responsive Chord*. Garden City, N.Y.: Anchor Books, 1973.

Segaller, Stephen. *Nerds 2.0.1: A Brief History of the Internet*. New York: TV Books, 1998.

Senft, Theresa M., and Stacy Horn, eds. *Sexuality and Cyberspace: Performing the Digital Body*. New York: Women and Performance Press, 1997. <http://www.echonyc.com/~women/Issue17/index.html> (April 26, 2002).

Shade, Leslie Regan. *Gender and Community in the Social Construction of the Internet*. New York: Peter Lang, 2002.

Shea, Virginia. *Netiquette*. San Francisco: Albion Books, 1994.

Shields, Rob, ed. *Cultures of the Internet: Virtual Spaces, Real Histories, Living Bodies*. London: Sage Publications, 1996.

Silverstone, Roger. *Why Study the Media?* London: Sage Publications, 1999.

504

Silverstone, Roger, and Eric Hirsch, eds. *Consuming Technologies: Media information in Domestic Spaces.* London: Routledge, 1992.

Slevin, James. *The Internet and Society.* Cambridge, U.K.: Polity Press, 2000.

Smedinghoff, Thomas J., ed. *Online Law: The SPA's Legal Guide to Doing Business on the Internet.* Reading, Mass.: Addison-Wesley Developers Press, 1996.

Smith, Marc A., and Peter Kollock, eds. *Communities in Cyberspace.* London: Routledge, 1999.

Stanley, Manfred. *The Technological Conscience: Survival and Dignity in an Age of Expertise.* Chicago: University of Chicago Press, 1978.

Stearn, Gerald Emanuel, ed. *McLuhan Hot and Cool: A Critical Symposium.* New York: The Dial Press, 1967.

Stefik, Mark. *Internet Dreams: Archetypes, Myths, and Metaphors.* Cambridge, Mass.: The MIT Press, 1996.

Stephenson, Neal. *Snow Crash.* New York: Bantam Books, 1992.

Sterling, Bruce. *The Hacker Crackdown: Law and Disorder on the Electronic Frontier.* New York: Bantam Books, 1992.

Stiftinger, Edeltraud, and Edward Strasser. *Binary Myths: Cyberspace—the Renaissance of Lost Emotions.* Vienna: Zukunfts und Kulturwerkstätte, 1997.

Stone, Allucquère Rosanne. *The War of Desire and Technology at the Close of the Mechanical Age.* Cambridge, Mass.: MIT Press, 1995.

Sudweeks, Fay, Margaret McLaughlin, and Sheizaf Rafaelai, eds. *Network and Netplay: Virtual Groups on the Internet.* Menlo Park, Calif.: AAAI Press/MIT Press, 1998.

Sveningsson, Malin. *Creating a Sense of Community: Experiences from a Swedish Web Chat.* Linköping, Sweden: The TEMA Institute, Department of Communication Studies, Linköping Universitet, 2001.

Swisher, Kara. *AOL.COM: How Steve Case Beat Bill Gates, Nailed the Netheads, and Made Millions in the War for the Web.* New York: Times Books, 1998.

Tannenbaum, Robert S. *Theoretical Foundations of Multimedia.* New York: Computer Science Press, 1998.

Tapscott, Don. *Growing Up Digital: The Rise of the Internet Generation.* New York: McGraw-Hill, 1998.

Taylor, Jeanie H., Cheris Kramarae, and Maureen Ebben, eds. *Women, Information Technology, and Scholarship.* Urbana: The Board of Trustees of the University of Illinois, 1993.

Terry, Jennifer, and Melodie Calvert, eds. *Processed Lives: Gender and Technology in Everyday Life.* London: Routledge, 1997.

Thornburg, David D. *Education in the Communication Age.* San Carlos, Calif.: Starsong Publications, 1994.

Tiihonen, Paula, ed. *Politics & the Internet: 2nd International Congress.* Helsinki: Parliament of Finland, 1999.

Tuomi, Ilkka. *From Periphery to Center: Emerging Research Topics on Knowledge Society.* Helsinki, Finland: Tekkes, August 2001.

Turkle, Sherry. *The Second Self: Computers and the Human Spirit.* New York: Simon & Schuster, 1984.

———. *Life on the Screen: Identity in the Age of the Internet.* New York: Simon and Schuster, 1995.

Vallee, Jacques. *The Network Revolution: Confessions of a Computer Scientist.* Berkeley, Calif.: And/Or Press, 1982.

Van Dijk, Jan. *The Network Society.* London: Sage Publications, 1999.

Vinge, Vernor. *True Names . . . and Other Dangers.* New York: Baen Books, 1987.

Virilio, Paul. *The Art of the Motor.* Minneapolis: University of Minnesota Press, 1995.

———. *Open Sky.* New York: Verso, 1997.

Waldrop, M. Mitchell. *The Dream Machine: J.C.R. Licklider and the Revolution that Made Computing Personal.* New York: Viking, 2001.

Wallace, Jonathan D., and Mark Mangan. *Sex, Laws, and Cyberspace.* New York: M&T Books, 1996.

Wartella, Ellen, Barbara O'Keefe, and Ronda Scantlin. *Children and Interactive Media: A Compendium of Current Research and Directions for the Future.* New York: The Markle Foundation, May 2000.

Werry, Chris, and Miranda Mowbray, eds. *Online Communities: Commerce, Community Action, and the Virtual University.* Upper Saddle River, N.J.: Prentice Hall PTR, 2001.

Whitaker, Reginald. *The End of Privacy: How Total Surveillance Is Becoming a Reality.* New York: The New Press, 1999.

Wienbroer, Diana Roberts. *Rules of Thumb for Online Research*. New York: McGraw-Hill, 2001.

Wiener, Norbert. *The Human Use of Human Beings: Cybernetics and Society*. New York: Avon Books, 1967.

Williams, Frederick, Ronald E. Rice, and Everett M. Rogers. *Research Methods and the New Media*. New York: The Free Press, 1988.

Williams, Raymond. *The Long Revolution: An Analysis of the Democratic, Industrial and Cultural Changes Transforming Our Society*. New York: Columbia University Press, 1961.

Winston, Brian. *Media Technology and Society, A History: From the Telegraph to the Internet*. London: Routledge, 1998.

Wise, J. Macgregor. *Exploring Technology and Social Space*. Thousand Oaks, Calif.: Sage Publications, 1997.

Wolfe, Tom. *The Electric Kool-Aid Acid Test*. New York: Farrar, Straus and Giroux, 1968.

Yates, JoAnne, and John Van Maanen, eds. *Information Technology and Organizational Transformation: History, Rhetoric, and Practice*. Thousand Oaks, Calif.: Sage Publications, 2001.

Yurick, Sol. *Behold, Metatron, the Recording Angel*. New York: Semiotext(e), 1985.

Contributors

MARK ANDREJEVIC is an assistant professor in the Department of Communication at Fairfield University. His research interests include new media, online surveillance, and digital aesthetics.

ANDREA BAKER, Ohio University–Lancaster, is an associate professor of sociology, who researches the relationships of people who met online, teaches online and offline, and hosts conferences at two online communities.

JACK BRATICH is assistant professor in the Department of Communication, University of New Hampshire.

CHARLIE BREINDAHL is a Ph.D. student in the Department of Film and Media Studies, University of Copenhagen, where he studies computer games and other rich media.

KATHY BRONECK is a Ph.D. student and research associate in the University of Arizona Department of Management Information Systems.

JUDITH R. BROWN is the president of ACM SIGGRAPH and recently retired manager of Advanced Research Computing at the University of Iowa.

HEIDI MARIE BRUSH is working towards her doctorate at the Institute of Communications Research, University of Illinois, Urbana-Champaign. Her research interests address the convergences between Internet insurgencies, cellular organizations, and the governance of the Internet.

SHING-LING SARINA CHEN is a faculty member in the Department of Communication Studies, University of Northern Iowa.

NORMAN CLARK, Department of Communication, Appalachian State University, is co-author of *The Internet: Effective Online Communication.*

MIA CONSALVO, Ohio University, studies popular culture, new media, and gender from a critical and cultural standpoint, and her current research examines video games and video game players.

NOSHIR CONTRACTOR is a professor of speech communication and psychology at the University of Illinois at Urbana-Champaign where he teaches and conducts research on the emergence of communication and knowledge networks in organizations.

NICOLE ELLISON's research focuses on telework and the ways in which individuals and organizations design, use, and reinterpret new information and communication technologies.

KEVIN FEATHERLY is Minneapolis-based managing editor at *Newsbytes*, a Washington Post–Newsweek Interactive technology-news site; and a contributing writer for numerous print publications, Web sites, and books.

IAN FOSTER is associate division director at Argonne National Laboratory, professor of computer science at the University of Chicago, and co-leader of the open source Globus Project, which forms the basis for the emerging grid computing industry.

KEN FRIEDMAN is associate professor of leadership and strategic design in the Department of Technology and Knowledge Management, Norwegian School of Management.

TED FRIEDMAN, assistant professor, Department of Communication, Georgia State University, is currently completing *Electric Dreams: Cyberculture and the Utopian Sphere.*

ALEXANDER HALAVAIS, School of Informatics, State University of New York–Buffalo, researches the role of communication technologies in the organization of large-scale collective problem-solving.

PHILIP E. N. HOWARD, assistant professor, Department of Communication, University of Washington, studies the role of new media in political communication, and has done field work with presidential campaigns, lobbyists, and grassroots activists in the United States.

JEREMY HUNSINGER, Center for Digital Discourse and Culture, Virginia Polytechnic Institute and State University (Virginia Tech), is an active member of the community of scholars studying the relationship between the Internet and information technology.

NICHOLAS JANKOWSKI is associate professor in the Department of Communication, University of Nijmegen, the Netherlands.

STEVE JONES is professor and head of communication, University of Illinois at Chicago. He is founder and president of the Association of Internet Researchers.

LORI KENDALL is on the faculty of Purchase College, State University of New York, and has written a book and several articles regarding identity and relationships online.

EDWARD LEE LAMOUREUX (Ph.D., University of Oregon, 1985) is associate professor of speech communication and multimedia at Bradley University in Peoria, Illinois. He is editor of the *Journal of Communication and Religion* (1997-2003) and is completing *Rhetoric in the Background of 21st Century Digital Communication*.

GARY W. LARSON is an assistant professor of media Studies at the Greenspun School of Communication, University of Nevada–Las Vegas, writing about mediated constructions of reality, and about the history and practice of broadcast journalism.

REBECCA ANN LIND (Ph.D. 1992, University of Minnesota) is associate professor of communication at the University of Illinois at Chicago; her research interests are race and gender in the media, journalism, audience studies, new media, and ethics.

SALLY McMILLAN is assistant professor, Department of Advertising, University of Tennessee.

SHAWN MIKLAUCIC is a doctoral student in the Institute of Communications Research at the University of Illinois.

CHRIS NELSON is a winner of the National Journalism Award whose work has appeared in *Mojo*, *Rolling Stone*, and on sonicnet.com.

KATE O'RIORDAN is a research student at the University of Brighton, United Kingdom

JAMES PYFER is a graduate student in the Department of Communication, University of Illinois at Chicago.

ART RAMIREZ is assistant professor in the Department of Communication, University of Minnesota–Duluth.

THERESA M. SENFT, doctoral candidate at New York University, Department of Performance Studies, is author of *Homecam Heroines: Autobiography, Celebrity and the Web*, forthcoming from Peter Lang Publishers.

LESLIE REGAN SHADE, assistant professor, University of Ottawa, focuses on social, policy, and ethical aspects of new media.

DAVID SILVER is an assistant professor in the Department of Communication at the University of Washington and the founder/director of the Resource Center for Cyberculture Studies.

JONATHAN STERNE, Department of Communication, University of Pittsburgh, has written widely on the history and philosophy of communication technology and is author of *The Audible Past: Cultural Origins of Sound Reproduction* (Duke University Press, 2002).

GATES MATTHEW STONER, M.A., is assistant specialist of interactive learning at the University of Arizona, College of Medicine.

YVONNE WAERN, professor of communication studies, Linköping University, Sweden, focuses on studies of ICT from a cognitive and communicative perspective.

JODI WHITE, MPA, is director of advancement, College of Urban Planning and Public Affairs, University of Illinois at Chicago.

DIANE WITMER is associate professor of communications at California State University–Fullerton.

CHRIS WOODFORD is a freelance science and technology writer based in England.

Name Index

Note: Page numbers in **bold** refer to main discussion of a topic; page numbers in *italic* refer to illustrations

Comprehensive Index

Note: Page numbers in **bold** refer to main discussion of a topic; page numbers in *italic* refer to illustrations